Vietnam, Cambodia, Laos & Northern Thailand

Vietnam
p48

Laos
p288

Northern
Thailand
p401

Cambodia
p178

Phillip Tang
Tim Bewer, Greg Bloom, Austin Bush, Nick Ray, Richard Waters,
China Williams

PLAN YOUR TRIP

RICE FIELDS, NORTHERN VIETNAM P71

NAI-EI / GETTY IMAGES ©

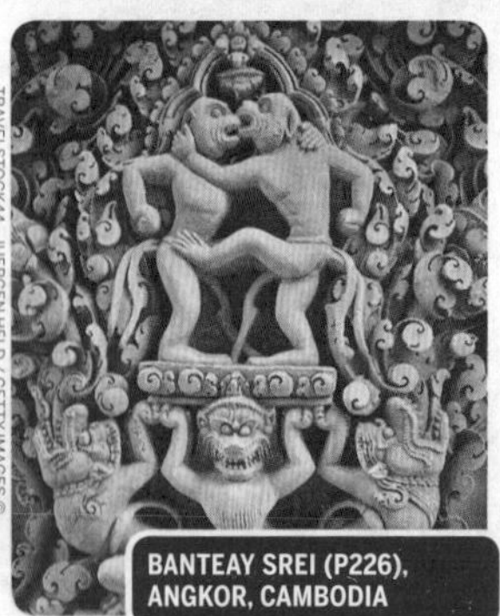

BANTEAY SREI (P226), ANGKOR, CAMBODIA

TRAVELSTOCK44 - JUERGEN HELD / GETTY IMAGES ©

ON THE ROAD

Contents

UNDERSTAND

SURVIVAL GUIDE

SPECIAL FEATURES

Welcome to the Mekong Region

The Mekong – it's an exotic name guaranteed to fire up the imagination, with such iconic sights as Angkor Wat, Halong Bay and Luang Prabang.

A River Runs Through It

One of the world's great rivers, the Mekong winds its way down from the foothills of Tibet to the South China Sea, encompassing some of the most diverse backdrops in Asia. Its dramatic journey southward takes in remote national parks and immense waterfalls in Laos, traditional towns and 21st-century cities in Thailand, freshwater dolphins and forgotten temples in Cambodia and a patchwork of emerald greens in Vietnam's Mekong Delta. Take it all in by boat, or delve in with a community homestay on one of thousands of islands formed by the mighty river.

Adrenalin Buzz

You're never far from adventure in these parts. Go motorbike touring in Vietnam's highlands, then descend to the coast to kitesurf on the South China Sea. Trek deep into the rainforest to spot gibbons and other rare wildlife in Cambodia or northern Thailand. For something mellower, take a cycle around Angkor or walk with elephants at one of several elephant sanctuaries in the region. Rock climbing in central Laos, diving off the southern rim of Cambodia and Vietnam, ziplining through virgin jungle around Chang Mai or the Bolaven Plateau – you can pick your own adventure.

Old Asia, New Asia

Experience old Asia and new Asia jostling for space. One minute it's Bangkok, where you're riding the Skytrain to a state-of-the-art shopping mall, the next it's walking with an elephant in the jungle of Cambodia. In the cities, the pace of life runs at a dizzying speed, matched only by the endless rush of motorbikes and call of commerce. In the countryside, life seems timeless – the rural rhythms the same as they have been for centuries – with traditionally clothed farmers tending the fields and monks wandering the streets in search of alms.

The Spirit of the Mekong

Travelling in the Mekong region is as much about the journey as the destination. Whether you're venturing into a distant minority village or plunging into the backstreets of a seething megalopolis, your senses will be bombarded as never before. Delve deeper to discern the mosaic of ethnicities and learn about their cultures and lifestyles. The people are irrepressible, the experiences unforgettable and the stories impossible to re-create, but sometime during your journey, the Mekong and its people will enter your soul. Go with the flow and let the Mekong's spirit course through your veins.

Why I Love Vietnam, Cambodia, Laos & Northern Thailand

By Greg Bloom, Writer

My affair with the Mekong region began in 1997. An overnight bus from Bangkok and the next morning I'm in Vientiane. It's traffic- and tourist-free, and it's surely the most relaxed place on earth. The next month is a somnolent, seemingly interminable journey north along misty mountain roads and rivers coloured caramel by the monsoon. A decade later I returned, this time to live in Cambodia, where the icons of Mekong life – exuberant temples, radiant green rice fields, glistening water buffalo – became part of daily life.

For more about our writers, see p576

Above: Novice monk at Wat Xieng Thong (p317), Luang Prabang, Laos

Vietnam, Cambodia, Laos & Northern Thailand

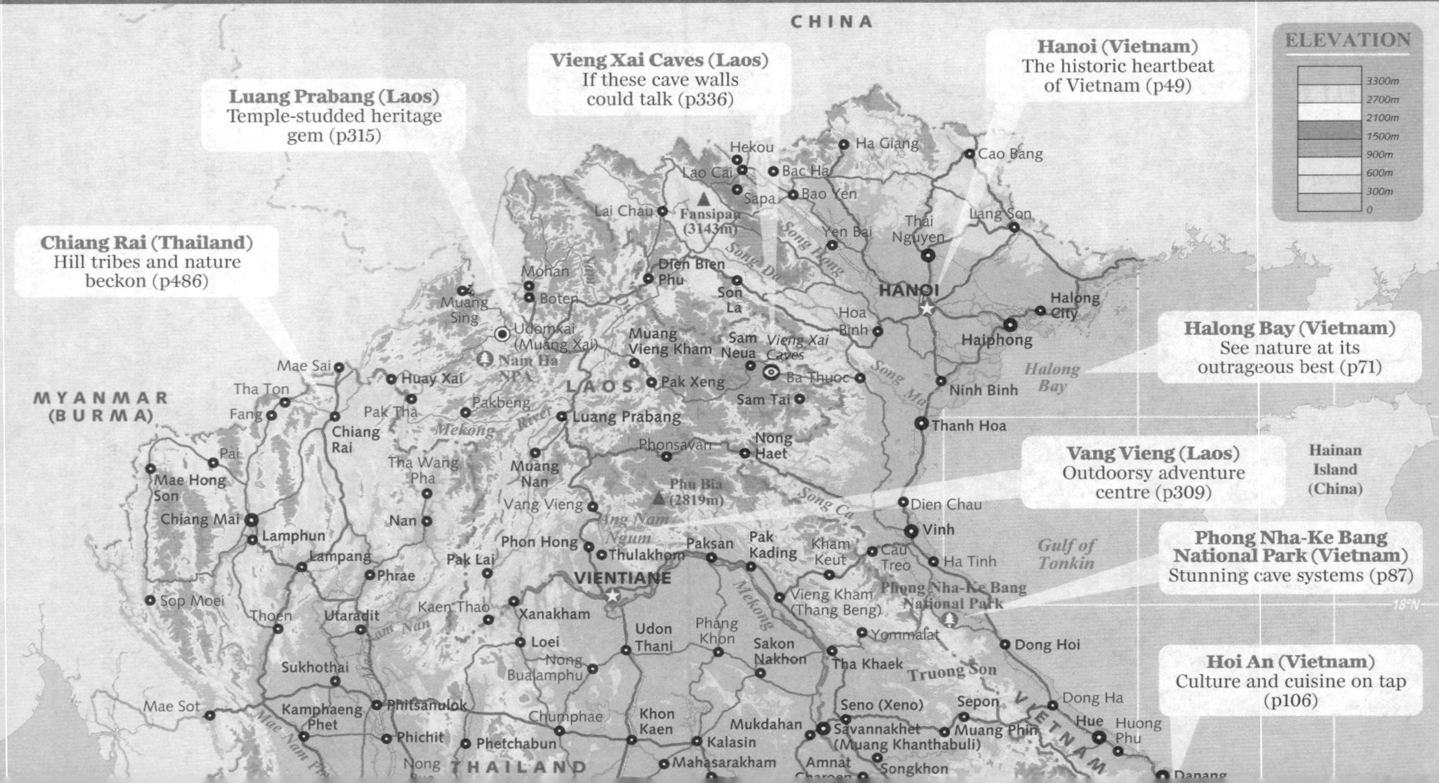

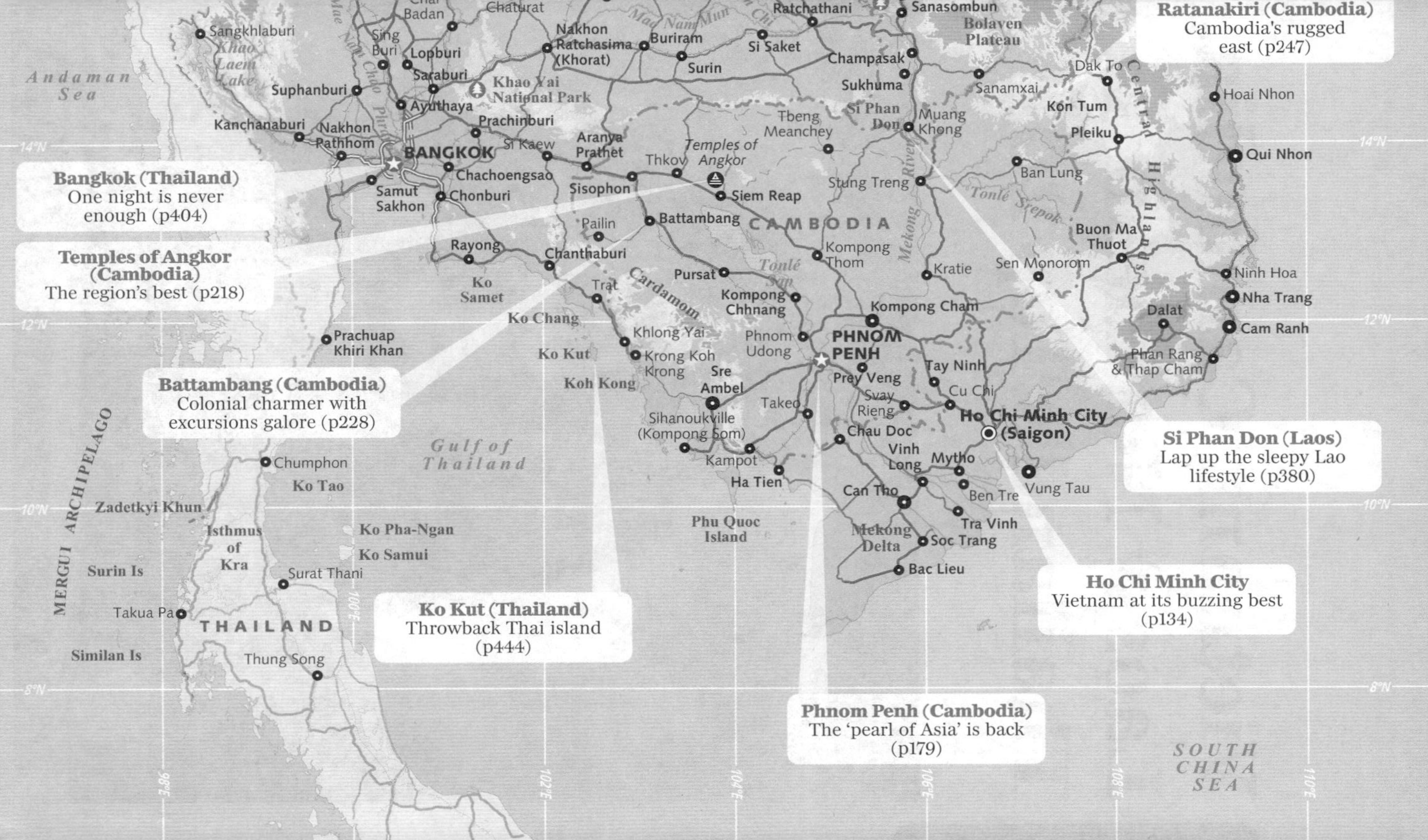
Ratanakiri (Cambodia)
Cambodia's rugged east (p247)
Bangkok (Thailand)
One night is never enough (p404)
Temples of Angkor (Cambodia)
The region's best (p218)
Battambang (Cambodia)
Colonial charmer with excursions galore (p228)
Ko Kut (Thailand)
Throwback Thai island (p444)
Phnom Penh (Cambodia)
The 'pearl of Asia' is back (p179)
Ho Chi Minh City
Vietnam at its buzzing best (p134)
Si Phan Don (Laos)
Lap up the sleepy Lao lifestyle (p380)
Andaman Sea
Gulf of Thailand
South China Sea
Mergui Archipelago
THAILAND
CAMBODIA
BANGKOK
PHNOM PENH
Ho Chi Minh City (Saigon)
Sangkhlaburi
Suphanburi
Kanchanaburi
Nakhon Pathom
Samut Sakhon
Chonburi
Chachoengsao
Ayutthaya
Saraburi
Lopburi
Sing Buri
Khao Yai National Park
Prachinburi
Nakhon Ratchasima (Khorat)
Buriram
Surin
Si Saket
Ratchathani
Sanasombun
Bolaven Plateau
Champasak
Sukhuma
Si Phan Don
Muang Khong
Sanamxai
Dak To
Kon Tum
Pleiku
Hoai Nhon
Qui Nhon
Central Highlands
Aranya Prathet
Sisophon
Thkov
Temples of Angkor
Siem Reap
Tbeng Meanchey
Stung Treng
Ban Lung
Tonlé Srepok
Buon Ma Thuot
Pailin
Battambang
Rayong
Ko Samet
Chanthaburi
Trat
Ko Chang
Ko Kut
Koh Kong
Cardamom
Khlong Yai
Krong Koh Krong
Pursat
Kompong Chhnang
Kompong Thom
Tonlé Sap
Kratie
Sen Monorom
Ninh Hoa
Nha Trang
Cam Ranh
Dalat
Phan Rang & Thap Cham
Kompong Cham
Phnom Udong
Prey Veng
Tay Ninh
Cu Chi
Svay Rieng
Sre Ambel
Takeo
Sihanoukville (Kompong Som)
Kampot
Ha Tien
Chau Doc
Vinh Long
Mytho
Ben Tre
Vung Tau
Can Tho
Tra Vinh
Mekong Delta
Soc Trang
Bac Lieu
Phu Quoc Island
Prachuap Khiri Khan
Chumphon
Ko Tao
Ko Pha-Ngan
Ko Samui
Surat Thani
Isthmus of Kra
Zadetkyi Khun
Surin Is
Takua Pa
Similan Is
Thung Song
Mekong River
14°N
12°N
10°N
8°N
98°E
100°E
102°E
104°E
106°E
108°E
110°E

Vietnam, Cambodia, Laos & Northern Thailand's Top 20

1

Temples of Angkor (Cambodia)

1 One of the world's most magnificent sights, the temples of Angkor (p218) are better even than the superlatives. Choose from Angkor Wat, the world's largest religious building; Bayon, one of the world's weirdest; or Ta Prohm, where nature runs amok. Siem Reap is the base for exploring the world's grandest collection of temples and is abuzz with a superb selection of restaurants and bars. Beyond the temples lie floating villages on Tonlé Sap lake, adrenalin-inducing activities such as quad biking and microlighting, and cultured pursuits such as cooking classes and birdwatching. Bayon (p219)

Luang Prabang (Laos)

2 Hemmed in by the Mekong River and Nam Khan (Khan River), this timeless city of temples (p315) is a travel writer's dream: rich in royal history, saffron-clad monks, stunning river views, world-class French cuisine and the best boutique accommodation in Southeast Asia. Hire a bike and explore the tropical peninsula's backstreets, take a cooking class or just ease back with a restful massage at one of the many affordable spas. Prepare to adjust your timetable and stay a little longer than planned. Wat Xieng Thong (p317)

ARTIE PHOTOGRAPHY / GETTY IMAGES ©

2

WESTUDIO / SHUTTERSTOCK ©

Halong Bay (Vietnam)

3 The stunning combination of karst limestone peaks and sheltered, shimmering seas makes Halong Bay (p71) one of Vietnam's top tourist draws, but with more than 2000 islands there's plenty of superb scenery to go around. Definitely book an overnight cruise and make time for your own special moments on this World Heritage wonder – rising early for an ethereal misty dawn, or piloting a kayak into grottoes and lagoons. If you're hankering for more karst action, move on to the less touristy but equally spectacular Lan Ha Bay.

Bangkok (Thailand)

4 The original City of Angels lives up to its hype as one of Southeast Asia's most buzzing cities. Excuses to delay your trip upcountry include the city's excellent-value accommodation, cheap and spicy eats, unparalleled shopping and a rowdy but fun nightlife scene. Bangkok (p404) also functions as the unofficial gateway to the rest of the region, with cheap flights, cosy train rides, modern buses and a variety of other convenient and comfortable transport options to your next destination – when you finally decide to leave, that is.

Vendor preparing street food

5

6

Si Phan Don (Laos)

5 Legends don't happen by accident: Laos' hammock-flopping mecca has been catering to weary travellers for years. While these tropical islands (p380) bounded by the waters of the Mekong are best known as a happy haven for catatonic sun worshippers, the more active souls who venture here will be spoilt for choice. After some river-tubing or cycling through paddy fields, grab a kayak or fish with the locals, rounding off your day with a sunset boat trip to see the rare Irrawaddy dolphin. Don Det (p381)

Hoi An (Vietnam)

6 Vietnam's most cosmopolitan town, the beautiful, ancient port of Hoi An (p106) is replete with gourmet Vietnamese restaurants, hip bars and cafes, quirky boutiques and expert tailors. Immerse yourself in history in the warren-like lanes of the Old Town, shop till you drop, tour the temples and pagodas, then dine like an emperor on a peasant's budget – and learn how to cook like the locals. Then hit glorious An Bang Beach, wander along the riverside and bike the back roads. Yes, Hoi An has it all. Paper-lantern shop

Phong Nha-Ke Bang National Park (Vietnam)

7 Picture jungle-crowned limestone hills, turquoise streams and traditional villages. Then throw in the globe's most impressive cave systems – the river-carved Phong Nha Cave and the cathedral-like chambers of Son Doong (the world's largest cave) – and you can see why Phong Nha-Ke Bang (p87) is Vietnam's most rewarding national park. Accommodation options are fast improving, and as it's a little way off the main tourist trail it's a great place to experience rural Vietnam at its most majestic.
Hang Son Doong (p87)

Sukhothai (Thailand)

8 Step back some 800 years in time at one of Thailand's most impressive historical parks (p482). Exploring the ruins of this former capital by bicycle is a leisurely way to wind through the crumbling temples, graceful Buddha statues and fish-filled ponds. Worthwhile museums and some of the country's best-value accommodation round out the package. Sukhothai rarely feels crowded, but for something off the beaten track head to nearby Si Satchanalai Historical Park, where you might be the only one scaling an ancient stairway.
Sukhothai Historical Park (p482)

7

BARTU JUAN / SHUTTERSTOCK ©

ELITE STUDIO / SHUTTERSTOCK ©

Mondulkiri & Ratanakiri Provinces (Cambodia)

9 Eventually the endless rice fields and sugar palms of the Cambodian lowlands give way to the rolling hills of the wild northeast (p245). Here you can spend days trekking amid threatened forests and ethnic minority villages where animism and ancestor worship are still practised. Elephants still roam this part of the country, and while you might not spot them in the wild, you can interact with them at several sanctuaries in the region. Add gibbon-spotting and thunderous waterfalls to the mix and you have the perfect recipe for adventure.

Phnom Penh (Cambodia)

10 Cambodia's capital (p179) is a chaotic yet charming city that has thrown off the shadows of the past to embrace a brighter future. Boasting one of the most beautiful riverfronts in the region, it is in the midst of a boom, with designer restaurants, funky bars and hip hotels ready to welcome the adventurous. Experience emotional extremes at the inspiring National Museum and the depressing Tuol Sleng Museum, between them showcasing the best and worst of Cambodian history. Once called the 'Pearl of Asia', Phnom Penh is regaining its shine. Royal Palace (p179)

Ho Chi Minh City (Vietnam)

11 Increasingly international, but still unmistakably Vietnamese, the former Saigon's visceral energy will delight big-city devotees. HCMC (p134) doesn't inspire neutrality: either you'll be drawn into its thrilling vortex and hypnotised by the perpetual whir of its orbiting motorbikes, or you'll find the whole experience just too overwhelming. Dive in to be rewarded with a wealth of history, delicious food and a vibrant nightlife that sets the standard for Vietnam. The heat is always on in HCMC – loosen your collar and enjoy.

Đ Bui Vien in Pham Ngu Lao (p141)

Cambodia's Southern Islands

12 A secret no more, the islands (p263) off Sihanoukville are reminiscent of Thailand in the 1980s, when Ko Samui and Ko Pha Nga were new frontiers. Koh Rong and Koh Rong Sanloem are those islands now, fulfilling remote Southeast Asian paradise fantasies while ensuring enough buzz to keep the party people happy. The more remote bits of these large twin islands hide secret beaches, often occupied by a solitary resort, and a score of islands stretching along Cambodia's southern coastline are similarly blissful.

Koh Rong (p264)

GUOZHONGHUA / SHUTTERSTOCK ©

RAY HEMS / GETTY IMAGES ©

Khmer Temple Trail (Thailand)

13 If you want to see Angkor Wat but don't want the crowds, consider following northeastern Thailand's informal Angkor temple trail from Phimai Historical Park (p450) to Phanom Rung. The area's Khmer-era ruins cover the spectrum from immaculate to rubble, and visiting them is a good excuse to explore Thailand on rented wheels. In addition to taking in some pretty impressive history, a visit offers a unique chance to experience the laid-back rural lifestyle and unique culture of this little-visited region.

Phimai Historical Park

Battambang (Cambodia)

14 This is the real Cambodia, far from the jet-set destinations of Phnom Penh and Siem Reap. Unfurling along the banks of the Sangker River, Battambang (p228) is one of the best-preserved colonial-era towns in the country. Streets lined with graceful old shophouses host art galleries and social enterprises ranging from fair-trade cafes to bike excursions. In a word? Charming. Beyond Battambang lies the Cambodian countryside and a cluster of ancient temples that, while not exactly Angkor Wat, mercifully lack its crowds.

Vang Vieng (Laos)

15 The riverine jewel in Laos' karst country, Vang Vieng (p309) sits under soaring cliffs beside the Nam Song (Song River) and has an easy, outdoorsy vibe. Since the party crowd was moved on a few years ago, tranquillity reigns, with more family-oriented visitors dropping in to soak up well-organised activities like ziplining, trekking, caving and climbing – and not forgetting the main draw: tubing. As budget guesthouses and fast-food joints wind down, smarter boutique hotels and delicious restaurants are blossoming in their wake. There's never been a better time to visit.

DITTY_ABOUT_SUMMER / SHUTTERSTOCK ©

Ko Kut (Thailand)

16 Still looking for that paradise island where the crowds are thin, the water aquamarine and clear, and the beaches wide and long? Try Ko Kut (p444). There are beautiful stretches of sand, fine snorkelling and hidden waterfalls to hike to. Best of all, Ko Kut retains a supremely unhurried pace of life that visitors soon find themselves imitating. There is nothing in the way of nightlife, apart from listening to the ocean. But that's why you're here.

Hanoi's Old Quarter (Vietnam)

17 Don't worry, it happens to everyone when they first get to Hanoi: getting agreeably lost in the city's centuries-old Old Quarter (p49), a frantic commercial labyrinth where echoes of the past are filtered and framed by a thoroughly 21st-century energy. Discover Vietnam's culinary flavours and aromas at street level, perched on a tiny chair eating iconic Hanoi dishes such as *pho bo* (beef noodle soup). Later, join the socialising throngs enjoying refreshingly crisp *bia hoi* at makeshift street corner bars.

Vieng Xai Caves (Laos)

18 This is history writ large in stone. An area of outstanding natural beauty, Vieng Xai (p336) was home to the Pathet Lao communist leadership during the US bombing campaign of 1964–73. Laos became the most heavily bombed country in the world at this time and the leadership burrowed into these natural caves for protection. A superb audio tour brings the experience alive. When the bombers buzz overhead to a soundtrack of Jimi Hendrix you'll be ducking for cover in the Red Prince's lush garden.

Chiang Rai Province (Thailand)

19 The days of the Golden Triangle opium trade are over, but intrigue still lingers at Chiang Rai (p486) in the form of fresh-air fun such as trekking and self-guided exploration. It's also a great destination for cultural experiences, ranging from a visit to an Akha village to a stay at the Yunnanese-Chinese hamlet of Mae Salong. From the Mekong River to the mountains, Chiang Rai is arguably Thailand's most beautiful province, and it's also a convenient gateway to Laos and China.

Akha woman, Mae Salong (p491)

Tham Kong Lor (Laos)

20 Imagine your deepest nightmare: the snaggle-toothed mouth of a river cave beneath a towering limestone mountain, the boatman in his rickety longtail taking you into the heart of darkness. Puttering beneath the cathedral-high ceiling of stalactites in this extraordinary 7.5kmlong underworld in remote Khammuan Province (p357) is an awesome experience. You'll be very glad to see the light at the other end of the tunnel. The village of Ban Kong Lor is now the most convenient base for visiting the cave.

19

20

Need to Know

For more information, see Survival Guide (p535)

Currency

Cambodia: riel (r)
Laos: kip (K)
Thailand: baht (B)
Vietnam: dong (d)

Languages

Cambodia Khmer
Laos Lao
Thailand Thai
Vietnam Vietnamese

Visas

Cambodia US$30 (on arrival).
Laos US$30 to US$42 (on arrival).
Thailand Waivers (on arrival).
Vietnam US$20 (in advance; some countries exempt).

Money

ATMs are widely available in Thailand and Vietnam, and most Cambodian and Lao provincial capitals. Credit cards are accepted at most midrange and top-end hotels.

Mobile Phones

Roaming possible in all countries, but expensive. Local SIM cards and unlocked mobile phones are available in all countries.

Time

Indochina Time (GMT/UTC plus seven hours)

When to Go

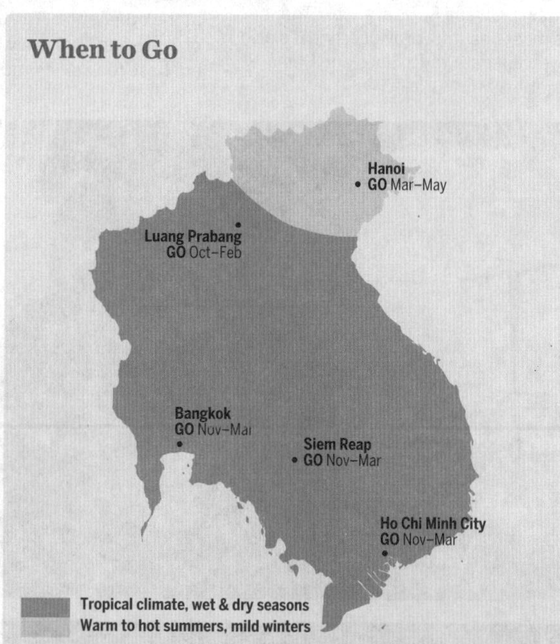

High Season (Dec–Mar)

➡ Cool and dry in the southern Mekong region.

➡ Cold in Hanoi and the mountains of Laos and Vietnam.

➡ Watch out for Chinese New Year in January/February, when everyone is on the move.

Shoulder (Apr & May, Oct & Nov)

➡ April to May is sweltering hot in the lowlands.

➡ October and November offer good trekking, lush landscapes and a pleasant climate.

➡ Songkram (April) is a blast, but Cambodia, Laos and Thailand shut down for business.

Low (Jun–Sep)

➡ Wet season means emerald-green landscapes and respite from the searing sun.

➡ Big hotel discounts at beaches and in touristy spots like Siem Reap.

➡ Thailand remains busy as Western visitors flock there for summer holidays.

Useful Websites

Lonely Planet (www.lonelyplanet.com) Destination information, hotel bookings, traveller forum and more.

Travelfish (www.travelfish.org) Opinionated articles and reviews about the region.

Mekong Tourism (www.mekongtourism.org) Updated links to latest regional travel news and trends.

Golden Triangle Rider (www.gt-rider.com) The motorbiking website for the Mekong region.

Important Numbers

Always remember to drop the initial 0 from the mobile prefix or regional (city) code when dialling into Cambodia, Laos, Thailand or Vietnam from another country.

Cambodia	☎855
Laos	☎856
Thailand	☎66
Vietnam	☎84

Exchange Rates

Cambodia	US$1	4000r
Laos	US$1	8200K
Thailand	US$1	36B
Vietnam	US$1	22,800d

For current exchange rates, see www.xe.com.

Daily Costs

Budget: Less than US$50

- Dorm bed: US$2–3
- Cheap guesthouse room: US$5–10
- Local meals and street eats: US$1–2
- Local buses and trains: US$2–3 per 100km

Midrange: US$50–150

- Air-con hotel room: US$15–50
- Decent local restaurant meal: US$5–10
- Short taxi ride: US$2–3
- Local tour guide per day: US$20

Top End: More than US$150

- Boutique hotel or resort: US$50–500
- Gastronomic meal with drinks: US$25–75
- 4WD rental per day: US$60–120
- Upmarket adventure tour: US$100-200

Getting Around

Trains, planes, automobiles and boats are equally viable options in the Mekong region.

Bus The reliable warhorse of the region; will likely be your main form of transport.

Plane Plenty of interregional and domestic routes between major cities. Domestic routes in Cambodia and Laos are more limited.

Train Alternative to buses in Thailand and Vietnam; just relaunched after decades of dormancy in Cambodia; non-existent in Laos.

Boat Losing popularity as roads improve.

Car Private vehicle hire affordable for those who prefer private transport. Self-drive rentals becoming more popular.

Motorbike Great for localised travel; rentals cheap and widely available.

Local transport Cheap tuk-tuks and motorcycle taxis are ideal for short hops.

Travelling Responsibly

- Much of the Mekong region is extremely poor, so consider how you might put a little back into the countries you visit. Stay longer, travel further and travel independently, or utilise locally based tour companies that are clearly on the side of pro-poor, ecofriendly travel in the region. Eat at local restaurants; try out a community-based tourism project or homestay (p539); use local guides. On shorter stays, consider spending money in local markets and in restaurants and shops that assist disadvantaged locals.
- Avoid giving money to begging children, as this is more likely to go directly to a begging 'pimp' or human trafficker than to the child; giving food is an option since at least it is likely to benefit the children directly.
- Child-welfare organisations would counsel against giving to children altogether to avoid creating a culture of dependency from a young age. Instead, consider making a donation to one of the many local organisations assisting in the battle against poverty.
- For more information, see www.thinkchildsafe.org.

For much more on **getting around**, see p549

If You Like...

Temples & Tombs

Cambodia is the temple heavyweight, but Laos and Thailand are dotted with elegant wats and ancient stupas. Vietnam has emperors' tombs and pagodas that are a world apart from their Mekong neighbours.

Angkor, Cambodia The one and only – the temples that put all others in the shade. (p218)

Wat Xieng Thong, Laos The jewel in Luang Prabang's crown, with its roofs sweeping majestically low to the ground. (p317)

Hue, Vietnam Vietnamese emperors constructed dazzling monuments around Hue. Don't miss Tu Duc and Minh Mang. (p90)

Sukhothai, Thailand The ancient capital of one of Thailand's first home-grown kingdoms. (p482)

Prasat Preah Vihear, Cambodia The most mountainous Khmer temple, perched imperiously on the cliff-face of the Dangkrek Mountains. (p236)

Wat Phu Champasak, Laos A bastion of the ancient Khmers, who once controlled much of the Mekong region. (p377)

Banteay Chhmar, Cambodia An explorer's delight, with minitemples lost in the jungle and crumbling ruins revealing hidden faces. (p227)

Beautiful Beaches

Vietnam, Cambodia and Thailand all boast lengthy and beautiful coastlines with hidden lagoons, coves, tropical islands and seemingly infinite stretches of sand.

Ko Kut, Thailand A paradise where the crowds are thin, the water aquamarine, the beaches wide and long. (p444)

Phu Quoc Island, Vietnam Signature Long Beach offers white sand in profusion, while Sao Beach is a quieter crescent. (p157)

Ream National Park, Cambodia Tranquillity and endless stretches of empty white sand, just 30 minutes from party mecca Sihanoukville. (p263)

Mui Ne, Vietnam Squeaky sands along the shore, towering dunes and expanses of empty beaches up the coast. (p123)

Koh Rong, Cambodia Emerging backpacker haven boasts myriad empty beaches around its substantial perimeter. (p264)

Ko Samet, Thailand An expat fave for good reason: 14 gorgeous white-sand beaches just a half-day from Bangkok. (p436)

Fabulous Food

There's no surer way to spice up your life than with a culinary odyssey through the Mekong region. Learn the tricks of the trade with a cooking class.

Bangkok, Thailand Undisputed food capital of the Mekong region. (p421)

Phnom Penh, Cambodia Enjoy the cosmopolitan food scene or dine to make a difference at a training restaurant. (p190)

Hanoi, Vietnam Hanoi's famous street-food scene features specialities like *bun cha* (barbecued pork) and crab noodle soup. (p63)

Vientiane, Laos Not just Laos' capital, but its culinary capital – think Lao home cooking with a Gallic flare. (p295)

Chiang Mai, Thailand Sample delicious northern Thai cuisine and choose from more than a dozen cooking schools. (p473)

Ho Chi Minh City, Vietnam Foodie paradise: roadside stalls, swish gourmet restaurants, to-die-for Vietnamese eateries and international cuisine. (p142)

Luang Prabang, Laos Learn to make *mok pa* (steamed fish in banana leaves) at traditional eatery Tamarind. (p318)

Spectacular Treks

Thailand is the original trekking hot spot, but these days all countries of the Mekong region offer great hikes featuring mountains,

Top: Koh Rong (p264), Cambodia
Bottom: *Pho bo* (beef noodle soup), Vietnam

minority cultures and – if you're lucky – rare wildlife.

Sapa, Vietnam Join chatty Hmong guides to explore surrounding ethnic minority villages framed by verdant rice terraces. (p81)

Khao Yai National Park, Thailand Spot elephants, monkeys, snakes and creepy-crawlies on treks in Thailand's oldest national park. (p450)

Nam Ha National Protected Area (NPA), Laos Laos' first national park offers responsibly coordinated trekking amid impressive original-growth forest. (p342)

Chiang Rai, Thailand The area boasts a diversity of ethnic groups and some of Thailand's best hikes. (p486)

Mondulkiri Province, Cambodia Take an early-morning gibbon-spotting trek or 'walk with the herd' at the Elephant Valley Project. (p542)

Cuc Phuong National Park, Vietnam Hike through wildlife-rich forests and up to tribal villages in this national park. (p70)

Phongsali Province, Laos In the country's far north you can trek to visit colourful hill tribes. (p347)

Koh Kong Conservation Corridor, Cambodia Ground-breaking ecotourism projects like Chi Phat offer treks in the wildlife-rich Cardamom Mountains. (p254)

Cultural Encounters

Luang Namtha, Laos A centre of Lao ethnic minority culture, offering community-based activities and fine minority cuisine. (p342)

Battambang, Cambodia Roll up, roll up – catch a performance of Phare, the Cambodia Circus where it all began. (p232)

Chiang Rai, Thailand A good base for exploring both hill-tribe culture and Lanna (ancient Thai-Lao kingdom) history. (p486)

Hoi An, Vietnam The Portuguese, Spanish, Japanese, Chinese and French all left their architectural mark on this stunning old port town. (p106)

Ratanakiri Province, Cambodia Hire a tribal trekking guide or homestay in minority villages around Virachey National Park. (p247)

Phonsavan, Laos Jumping-off point for homestays with Hmong families and visits to the ancient Plain of Jars. (p328)

Ba Be National Park, Vietnam Recharge from hiking in the rustic homestays and village guesthouses of the Tay minority. (p78)

Nightlife

Bangkok grabs the Hollywood storylines but several other regional hubs have plenty of buzz when it comes to getting a buzz on.

Bangkok, Thailand Bangkok is home to the original 24-hour party people and sleep is still optional. (p425)

Phnom Penh, Cambodia The Cambodian capital rocks: hit the happy hours, crawl some bar strips, then hit a nightclub. (p179)

Ho Chi Minh City, Vietnam Rooftop cocktail bars, raucous nightclubs and the latest craze – anything-goes 'beer clubs' – fuel Saigon's nightlife. (p145)

Chiang Mai, Thailand A nice mix of backpacker bars, brew pubs and beer gardens, plus an abundance of live music. (p465)

Siem Reap, Cambodia Pub St says it all – this temple town is officially a party town as well. (p204)

Nha Trang, Vietnam Plenty of R & R is available at this lively coastal city. (p116)

Vang Vieng, Laos The all-night raves of yesteryear have given way to a chilled riverside drinking scene. (p309)

Markets & Shopping

From ethnic minority meets in the highlands to floating wholesalers on the local river, the Mekong region does markets like nowhere else.

Bac Ha, Vietnam See the unique costume of the Flower Hmong at one of Asia's most colourful markets. (p80)

Luang Prabang, Laos The Handicraft Night Market is an endless ribbon of colourful textiles, paper lanterns and ethnic motifs. (p325)

Chiang Mai, Thailand Shop till you drop, with a healthy dose of culture, at the Chiang Mai Night Bazaar. (p474)

Mekong Delta's floating markets, Vietnam Get up early and experience the delta's famous floating markets. (p154)

Phnom Penh, Cambodia The Russian Market is the city's premier shopping destination – if it's available in Cambodia, it's somewhere in here. (p197)

Muang Sing, Laos The new market pulsates early in the morning as ethnic minorities hit the town to trade. (p346)

Cycling & Motorbiking

Adventure motorbiking is huge, including along the legendary Ho Chi Minh Trail in Vietnam and Laos. Cyclists can experience highs in the region's many mountain ranges, or lows along the pancake-flat trails of the Mekong River.

Northwest Loop, Vietnam Dien Bien Phu to Sapa offers glorious mountain scenery, river valleys and tribal villages galore. (p86)

Nong Khiaw, Laos The base for adventure cycling trips through beautiful scenery, organised by responsible local operators. (p336)

Sukhothai, Thailand Explore the first Thai capital's 200 temples and stupas on two wheels. (p483)

Preah Vihear Province, Cambodia Ride 'Route 66' from Beng Mealea to the lost temple of Preah Khan of Kompong Svay – not for novices. (p236)

Tha Khaek, Laos A great place to launch dirtbike trips around The Loop and to Tham Kong Lor. (p359)

Wellness & Massage

Siem Reap, Cambodia Glorious variety, with everything from multiday wellness retreats to tickly 'Dr Fish' spas possible. (p207)

Luang Prabang, Laos The spiritual home of wellness in Laos is awash with impressive spas. (p317)

Bangkok, Thailand When you consider value and ubiquity, Bangkok may well be the massage capital of the world. (p413)

Nha Trang, Vietnam The natural and thermal mud baths here are catching on for health mavens. (p117)

Champasak, Laos The eponymous Champasak Spa helps create a sustainable living for young women in this small town. (p375)

Month by Month

TOP EVENTS

Tet/Chinese New Year, January/February

Khmer/Lao/Thai New Year, April

Rocket Festival, May

Pchum Ben, September/October

Loi Krathong, November

January

This is peak tourist season as Europeans and North Americans escape the cold winter. For serious revellers, January also sees the rare occurrence of two new-year celebrations in a month.

Tet

The Big One! Vietnamese Lunar New Year is Christmas, new year and birthdays all rolled into one. Travel is difficult at this time, as transport is booked up and many businesses close. Falls in late January or early February.

Chinese New Year

Always occurring at the same time as Vietnamese New Year (Tet), these festivities are headline news in major cities in the region such as Phnom Penh and Bangkok. Expect businesses to close for a few days and dragon dances to kick off all over town.

February

Still peak season for the region, and the coastline is busy with sun-seekers. Inland, the first round of rice harvesting is over, but in parts of Vietnam and Thailand they are already onto round two.

Bun Wat Phu Champasak

The three-day Wat Phu Champasak Festival has an atmosphere somewhere between a kids' carnival and music festival. The central ceremonies performed are Buddhist, culminating with a dawn parade of monks receiving alms, followed that evening by a candlelit *wían thíen* (circumambulation) of the lower shrines.

Makha Bucha

One of three holy days marking important moments of Buddha's life, Makha Bucha falls on the full moon of the third lunar month and commemorates Buddha preaching to 1250 enlightened monks who came to hear him 'without prior summons'. Mainly a day for temple visits.

Flower Festival

Chiang Mai displays its floral beauty during this three-day event. The festival highlight is the flower-decorated floats that parade through town.

April

The hottest time of year, so book an air-con room. New year is ushered in all over the region. The accompanying water fights in Laos and Thailand are a guaranteed way to keep cool.

Songkran

Songkran, the Thai New Year, is a no-holds-barred countrywide water fight that has to be seen to be believed. Bangkok and Chiang Mai are some of the most raucous battlegrounds. Like Lao and Khmer New Year, it always falls in mid-April.

Bun Pi Mai

Lao New Year is one of the most effusive, fun-splashed

events in the calendar as houses and Buddha statuary are cleaned, and the country has a weeklong national water fight with water pistols and buckets of H_2O. Protect your camera and join in the fun.

Chaul Chnam

Khmer New Year is a more subdued event than in neighbouring Laos and Thailand, but water fights still kick off in much of the countryside. It's mainly a family holiday, when city dwellers return to the place of their ancestry to meet distant relatives.

Liberation Day

Saigon fell to the north on 30 April 1975 and was renamed Ho Chi Minh City. It's celebrated by the Communist Party; expect the reaction to be more subdued in the south.

May

The hottest time of year in many parts of the region; escape to northern Vietnam for springlike weather. This is low season, when visitor numbers drop and prices follow.

Chat Preah Nengkal

Led by the royal family, the Royal Ploughing Ceremony is a ritual agricultural festival held to mark the traditional beginning of the rice-growing season. It takes place in early May in Phnom Penh. If the royal oxen eat, the harvest will be bountiful; should they refuse, it may spell drought. Also celebrated at the Royal Palace in Bangkok.

Rocket Festival

Villagers craft bamboo rockets (*bang fai*) and fire them into the sky to provoke rainfall to bring a bountiful rice harvest. Mainly celebrated in northeastern Thailand and Laos; things can get pretty wild with music, dance and folk theatre. Dates vary from village to village.

Visaka Bucha

The holy day of Visaka Bucha falls on the 15th day of the waxing moon in the sixth lunar month and commemorates Buddha's birth, enlightenment and *parinibbana* (passing away). Activities centre on the temple.

June

The wet season begins in much of the Mekong region. Expect a daily downpour, but much of the time it should be dry. River levels begin to rise again.

Hue Festival (Biennial)

Vietnam's biggest cultural event (www.huefestival.com) is held every two years, including 2018 and 2020. Most of the art, theatre, music, circus and dance performances, including many international acts, are held inside Hue's Citadel.

Phi Ta Khon

The Buddhist holy day of Bun Phra Wet is given a Carnival makeover in Dan Sai village in northeastern Thailand. Revellers disguise themselves in garish 'spirit' costumes and parade through the village streets wielding wooden phalluses and downing rice whisky. Dates vary.

July

A mini-high in the midst of the low season, the summer months see Europeans head to the region to coincide with long summer holidays back home. The rain keeps falling.

Khao Phansaa

Early in the monsoonal rains, Buddhist monks retreat into monasteries in Cambodia, Laos and Thailand – the traditional time for young men to enter monasteries or when monks begin a retreat for study and meditation. Worshippers offer candles and donations to the temples and attend ordinations.

September

The height of the wet season: if places like Bangkok or Phnom Penh are going to flood this is when it usually happens. Occasional typhoons sweep in across Vietnam, wreaking havoc.

Pchum Ben

A sort of Cambodian All Souls' Day – respects are paid to the dead through offerings made at wat to resident monks. Often falls in October. Trung Nguyen is a similar festival celebrated in Vietnam, usually in the preceding month.

October

The rains are easing off and farmers prepare for the harvest season. A series of festivals fall around this time and the temples are packed as monks emerge from their retreat.

Bon Om Tuk

Cambodia's Water Festival, held mainly in Phnom Penh, celebrates Jayavarman VII's victory over the Chams in 1177 and the reversal of the Tonlé Sap river. After a stampede killed 347 people in 2010, it was cancelled for several years but is up and running again.

Ork Phansaa

The end of the Buddhist Lent (three lunar months after Khao Phansaa) is marked by the *gà·tĭn* ceremony, in which new robes are given to monks by merit-makers. The peculiar natural phenomenon known as the '*naga* fireballs' coincides with Ork Phansaa.

November

The cool, dry season begins and is an ideal time to visit for lush landscapes. In the far north of the region, temperatures begin to drop.

Loi Krathong

Join Thais in launching floating candles during the festival of Loi Krathong, usually held in early November. If you happen to be in Chiang Mai, the banana-leaf boats are replaced by *yêe peng* (floating paper lanterns).

Bun Pha That Luang

That Luang Festival is tied to the November full moon. Based in Vientiane and lasting a week, this celebration involves music, a lot of drinking, processions to That Luang, fireworks and a cast of many thousands who flock to the capital.

Surin Elephant Roundup

Held on the third weekend of November, Thailand's biggest elephant show celebrates this northeastern province's most famous residents. The event in Surin begins with a colourful elephant parade and culminates in a fruit buffet for the pachyderms.

December

Peak tourism season is back and the weather is fine, so the chances of a white Christmas are very slim unless you happen to be climbing Vietnam's highest peak, Fansipan.

Christmas

Most of the region has adopted Christmas in some shape or form, and while not a national holiday, it is celebrated throughout Vietnam particularly, by the sizeable Catholic population. It's a special time to be in places like Phat Diem and HCMC, where thousands attend midnight Mass.

Ramadan

Observed in southern Thailand and the Cham areas of Cambodia and Vietnam during October, November or December, the Muslim fasting month requires that Muslims abstain from food, drink, cigarettes and sex between sunrise and sunset.

Lao National Day

This 2 December holiday celebrates the 1975 victory over the monarchy with parades and speeches. Lao national and communist hammer-and-sickle flags are flown all over the country. Celebration is mandatory.

Angkor Wat International Half Marathon

Held the first weekend in December amid the incredible backdrop of the temples of Angkor, with 3km and 10km events complementing the 21km main event, which draws big crowds to cheer on participants from all over the world.

LENA SERDITOVA / SHUTTERSTOCK ©

Plan Your Trip
Itineraries

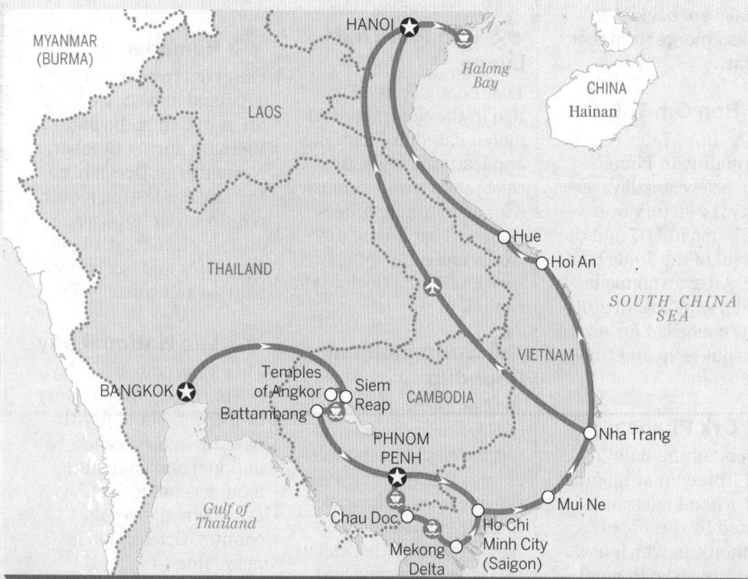

The Classic

Traverse the fertile belly of the region, taking in the Mekong's metropolises and its most iconic sight, Angkor Wat.

Like many Southeast Asian journeys, yours begins in **Bangkok**. Acclimatise with the sights, sounds, smells and divine culinary flavours of the City of Angels before flying or taking a bus to **Siem Reap**, gateway to the incredible temples of Angkor.

See the mother of all temples, **Angkor Wat**, the world's largest religious building; the Bayon, with its enigmatic faces; and jungle-clad Ta Prohm. In the wet season, the boat trip from Siem Reap to colonial-flavoured **Battambang** is not to be missed. From Battambang continue south by bus to experience the contrasts of **Phnom Penh**, then make your way to **Ho Chi Minh City** by bus or boat via **Chau Doc** and the **Mekong Delta**.

Now you're ready for some beach time. Take a bus to **Mui Ne** or **Nha Trang** on the South China Sea, then fly north to **Hanoi** – or meander overland via the historical hubs of **Hoi An** and **Hue** if you have time. Wind up with some sea-kayaking or a boat cruise among the karsts in **Halong Bay**.

Halong Bay (p71), Vietnam

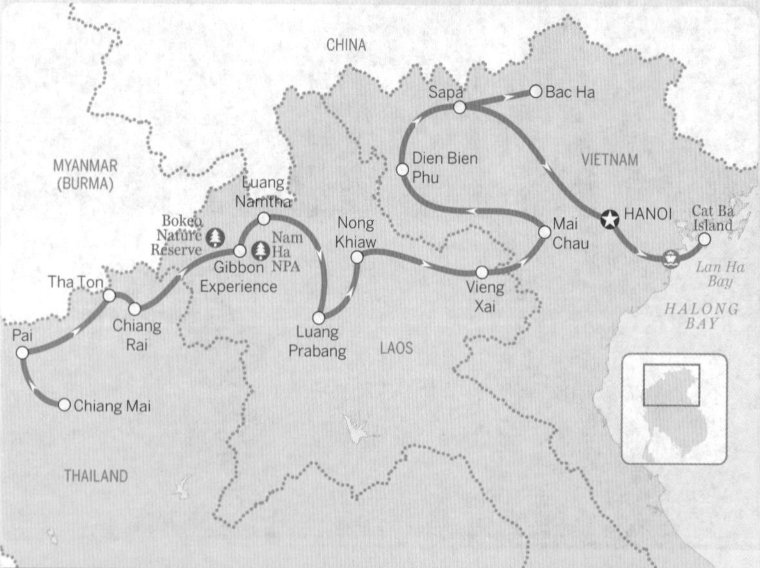

CHINA
MYANMAR (BURMA)
VIETNAM
LAOS
THAILAND
Sapa
Bac Ha
Dien Bien Phu
HANOI
Cat Ba Island
Mai Chau
Lan Ha Bay
HALONG BAY
Luang Namtha
Bokeo Nature Reserve
Nam Ha NPA
Gibbon Experience
Nong Khiaw
Vieng Xai
Luang Prabang
Tha Ton
Chiang Rai
Pai
Chiang Mai

TPM13THX / SHUTTERSTOCK ©

GIL.K / SHUTTERSTOCK ©

Top: Rafting, Chiang Mai (p465), Thailand
tom: Hmong woman and child, Bac Ha (p80), Vietnam

Highland Adventure

This itinerary takes you from northern Thailand to Halong Bay, Vietnam, via the rugged and thrilling northern route. Traversing the Mekong's highest mountains, you'll get up close and personal with colourful hill tribes and have a range of outdoor adventures at your disposal.

Start in **Chiang Mai**, where every activity known to athletes – mountain biking, kayaking, abseiling, trekking, ziplining – has a following. Take the winding road to **Pai**, a mountain retreat that proves the hippie trail is alive and well. Then head on to **Tha Ton**, the entry point for boat trips down to **Chiang Rai**, itself a good base for responsible trekking. Cross into Laos and check out the **Gibbon Experience** at Bokeo Nature Reserve before continuing east to **Luang Namtha** for trekking, cycling, or rafting in and around the Nam Ha National Protected Area (NPA).

Head south to beautiful **Luang Prabang** on the banks of the Mekong to soak up the culture, before boomeranging north once more to explore the karst-laden wonderland of the Nam Ou (Ou River) on a boat ride or kayak trip out of **Nong Khiaw**. From here an adventurous overland trail runs east to Vietnam via **Vieng Xai** and the Pathet Lao caves, a sort of Cu Chi Tunnels cast in stone. Once over the border in **Mai Chau**, try the northwest loop through **Dien Bien Phu** to experience incredible scenery and some of the country's most dramatic mountain passes.

Sapa, an old French hill station, is the gateway to the minority communities of this region. Consider a side trip to **Bac Ha**, home to the colourful Flower Hmong folk and great walking country. Head south to **Hanoi**, where you'll appreciate that you bought your ethnic souvenirs directly from the minority people and not in the designer boutiques of the Old Quarter.

Still haven't had your fill of adventure? Set off for **Halong Bay**. Take to the waters of Lan Ha Bay by local boat to see the 'new' Halong Bay without the tourists. Boating, kayaking and Robinson Crusoe–style camping are possible here, and there are some beautiful hidden coves. Then leave the water behind and head to the spectacular limestone outcrops of **Cat Ba Island**. Experienced craggers will find challenging routes here, and there's instruction available for novice climbers as well.

6 WEEKS Mekong River Meander

This trip follows the famous river downstream from northern Laos all the way to its terminus in Vietnam's Mekong Delta. En route you'll encounter a wide range of landscapes, cultures and adventures as you slice through all four countries of the Mekong region.

Leave behind the bustle of **Bangkok** and make a beeline for **Chiang Rai** near the Golden Triangle, where the borders of Laos, Myanmar (Burma) and Thailand converge. Crossing the Mekong into Laos at **Huay Xai** is like stepping back in time. Take a slowboat down the Mekong to **Luang Prabang**, stopping overnight in **Pak Beng**. Soak up the magic before leaving the river for some relaxation in **Vang Vieng**.

Continue to **Vientiane** and reunite with the mighty waterway. The Lao capital is a sleepy place with some great cafes, restaurants and bars – which you won't be encountering for a while after here. Board a bus and follow the river southeast, stopping off in **Tha Khaek** and **Savannakhet** before arriving in **Pakse**. Visit the imposing Khmer sanctuary of **Wat Phu Champasak**, in the shadow of Lingaparvata Mountain; explore the waterfalls and villages of the **Bolaven Plateau**; or enjoy the laid-back islands of **Si Phan Don**.

Cross into Cambodia. If you missed the Irrawaddy dolphins near Don Khon in Si Phan Don, you can see them near the border at **Preah Rumkel**, or a few hours further south in the laid-back Mekong riverside town of **Kratie**. From Kratie, consider peeling off to visit the mountains of **Mondulkiri Province**, home to elephants, hill tribes and pristine nature.

Weeks in rural provinces will have you happy to see **Phnom Penh**, where the Mekong merges with another vital regional waterway, the Tonlé Sap. Take a sunset boat cruise or participate in an aerobics session on the riverfront promenade. When you're recharged, board a fast boat downstream to **Chau Doc**, Vietnam, gateway to the Mekong Delta. Check out **Can Tho**, the delta's commercial heart. Hotfoot it to **Ho Chi Minh City** for some fun; delve deeper into the delta with a homestay around **Vinh Long**, or make for the tropical retreat of **Phu Quoc Island**, a well-earned reward for following the mother river.

Top: Si Phan Don (p380), Laos
Bottom: Floating market, Can Tho (p154), Vietnam

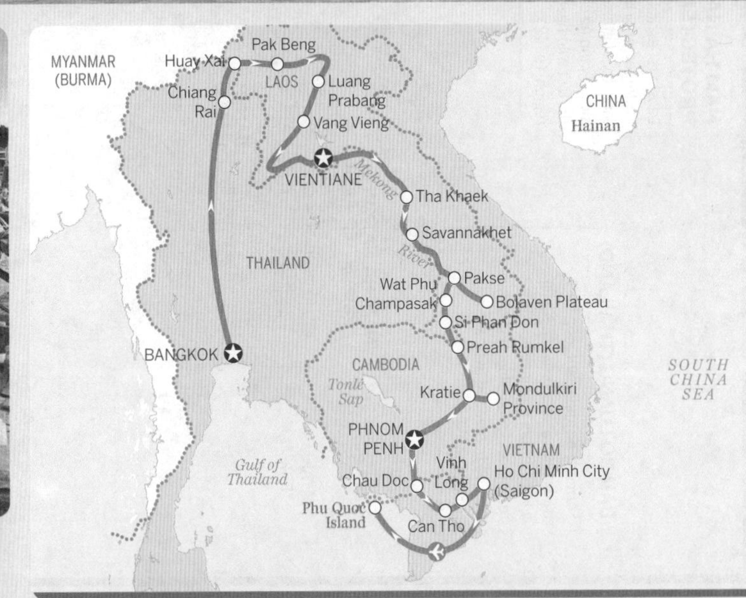

MYANMAR (BURMA)
Huay Xai
Pak Beng
LAOS
Luang Prabang
Chiang Rai
Vang Vieng
CHINA
Hainan
VIENTIANE
Mekong River
Tha Khaek
Savannakhet
THAILAND
Pakse
Wat Phu Champasak
Bolaven Plateau
Si Phan Don
Preah Rumkel
BANGKOK
CAMBODIA
SOUTH CHINA SEA
Tonlé Sap
Kratie
Mondulkiri Province
PHNOM PENH
VIETNAM
Vinh Long
Ho Chi Minh City (Saigon)
Gulf of Thailand
Chau Doc
Phu Quoc Island
Can Tho

Off the Beaten Track: Vietnam, Cambodia, Laos & Northern Thailand

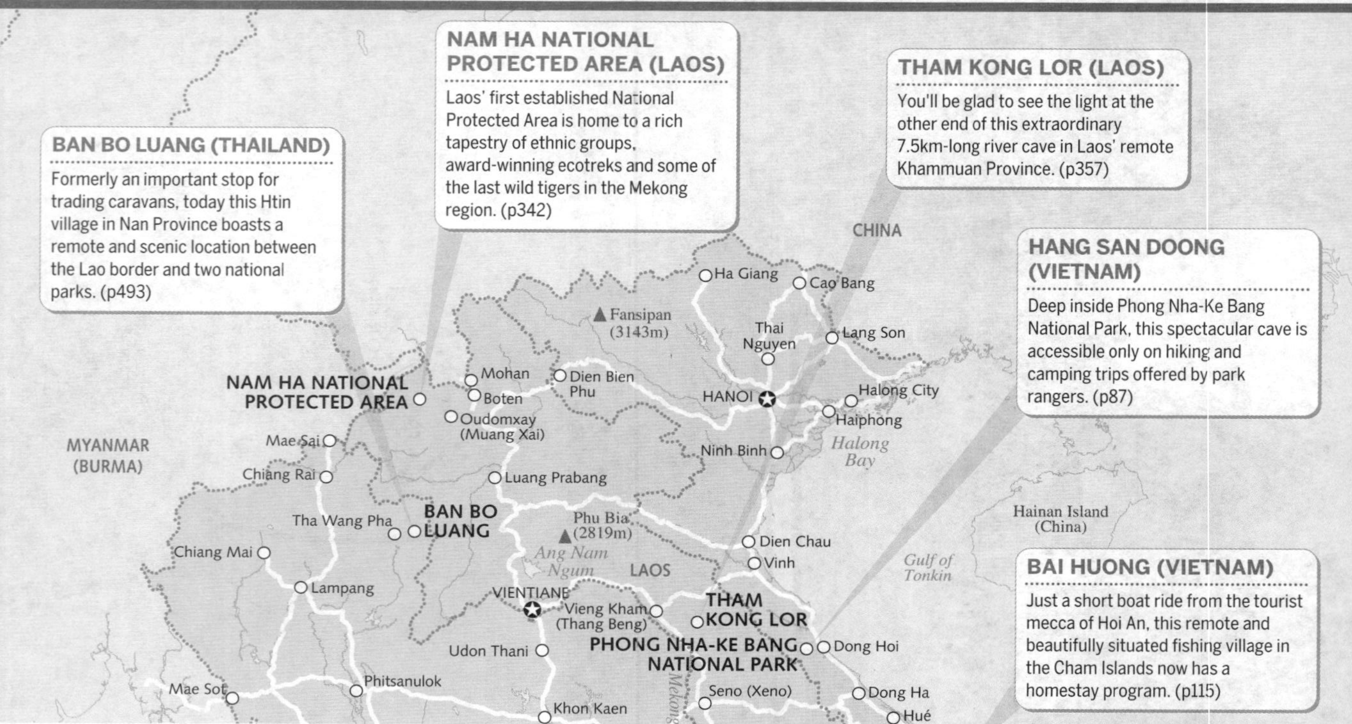

BAN BO LUANG (THAILAND)

Formerly an important stop for trading caravans, today this Htin village in Nan Province boasts a remote and scenic location between the Lao border and two national parks. (p493)

NAM HA NATIONAL PROTECTED AREA (LAOS)

Laos' first established National Protected Area is home to a rich tapestry of ethnic groups, award-winning ecotreks and some of the last wild tigers in the Mekong region. (p342)

THAM KONG LOR (LAOS)

You'll be glad to see the light at the other end of this extraordinary 7.5km-long river cave in Laos' remote Khammuan Province. (p357)

HANG SAN DOONG (VIETNAM)

Deep inside Phong Nha-Ke Bang National Park, this spectacular cave is accessible only on hiking and camping trips offered by park rangers. (p87)

BAI HUONG (VIETNAM)

Just a short boat ride from the tourist mecca of Hoi An, this remote and beautifully situated fishing village in the Cham Islands now has a homestay program. (p115)

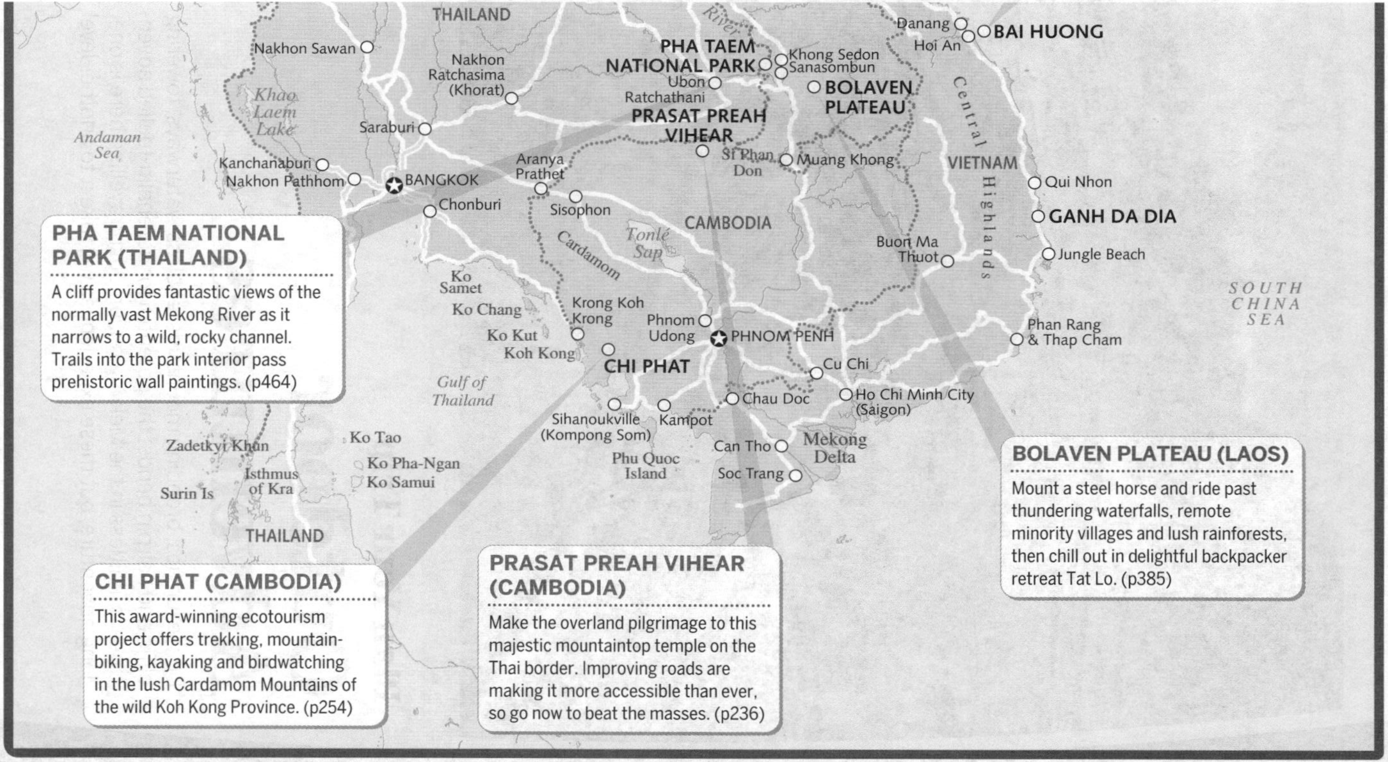

PHA TAEM NATIONAL PARK (THAILAND)

A cliff provides fantastic views of the normally vast Mekong River as it narrows to a wild, rocky channel. Trails into the park interior pass prehistoric wall paintings. (p464)

CHI PHAT (CAMBODIA)

This award-winning ecotourism project offers trekking, mountain-biking, kayaking and birdwatching in the lush Cardamom Mountains of the wild Koh Kong Province. (p254)

PRASAT PREAH VIHEAR (CAMBODIA)

Make the overland pilgrimage to this majestic mountaintop temple on the Thai border. Improving roads are making it more accessible than ever, so go now to beat the masses. (p236)

BOLAVEN PLATEAU (LAOS)

Mount a steel horse and ride past thundering waterfalls, remote minority villages and lush rainforests, then chill out in delightful backpacker retreat Tat Lo. (p385)

Rice terraces, Sapa (p81), Vietn

Outdoor Adventures

Dense jungles, brooding mountains, endless waterways, towering cliffs and hairpin bends: the potential for adrenalin-fuelled adventures is limitless in the Mekong region. Just travelling here is one long adventure, but these experiences will take it to another level.

Best Outdoors

Best Trekking

Sapa Superlative views but very popular.

Nam Ha National Protected Area (NPA) Responsible treks in old-growth forest.

Chiang Rai Explore hill-tribe terrain.

Ratanakiri Province Disappear for days in Virachey National Park.

Best Cycling

Mekong Delta Ride the back roads through Vietnam's rice bowl.

Sukhothai Pedal into Thai history.

Vientiane Tailor-made for bicycles.

Angkor Free-wheel past ancient wonders.

Best Motorbiking

Mondulkiri Province Mountains and jungle.

Luang Namtha Dramatic scenery, fecund forests and minority villages.

Nan Plenty of jungles and parks to explore.

Dien Bien Phu Mountain roads with views.

Best Diving & Snorkelling

Con Dao Islands Remote water adventures.

Nha Trang Vietnam's most popular diving.

Sihanoukville Head well offshore to dive Cambodia.

Ko Rang Thai marine park that's best in the western gulf.

Trekking

Trekking is a huge draw in all four countries. Hike one to several days to minority hill-tribe villages, walk a half-day through the jungle to pristine waterfalls, or launch an assault on Fansipan (3143m), the region's highest mountain. The scenery – think plunging highland valleys, tiers of rice paddies and soaring limestone mountains in much of Laos, Thailand and Vietnam – is often remarkable.

Prices for organised treks usually include all food, guides, transportation, accommodation and park fees, and start at around per day per person US$25 for larger groups. For more specialised long treks into remote areas, prices can run into several hundred US dollars. It may be necessary to arrange special permits for some treks, especially if you plan to spend the night in remote mountain villages in parts of Laos and Vietnam.

Cambodia

Trekking in northeast Cambodia is beginning to take off in the provinces of Mondulkiri and Ratanakiri thanks to their wild natural scenery, abundant waterfalls and ethnic minority populations. Remote Virachey National Park in Ratanakiri offers the possibility of multiday trips. Some of the most accessible trekking is in the Cardamom Mountains near Koh Kong.

Laos

Trekking through the mountains and forests of Laos is almost a mandatory part of any visit to the country. And thanks to projects aimed at getting money into poor communities, there are now a dozen or

SAFETY GUIDELINES FOR HIKERS

- Don't stray from established paths, as there are landmines and unexploded ordnance (UXO) in parts of Cambodia, Laos and Vietnam.
- Guides are worth hiring; they're inexpensive, speak the language and understand indigenous culture.
- Dogs can be aggressive; a stout stick may come in handy.
- Boots with ankle support are a great investment.
- Carry a mosquito net if trekking in malarial zones of the region.
- Consider quality socks and repellent to reduce the likelihood of leeches.
- Carry water-purification tablets if you have a weak constitution.
- Invest in some snack bars or energy snacks to avoid getting 'riced out' on longer treks.

more areas you can choose from. Luang Namtha has developed an award-winning ecotourism project for visits to local ethnic minority villages in Nam Ha National Protected Area (NPA). In southern Laos, Se Pian NPA, close to Pakse, is a great option for multiday treks combined with traditional canoe rides or birdwatching. Dong Natad has treks through beautiful landscapes, organised by Savannakhet's Eco-Guide Unit (p366).

Thailand

The northern Thai cities of Chiang Mai and Chiang Rai are very popular for treks, often in combination with white-water rafting and elephant experiences. Pai has also emerged as an alternative place to trek. Many of these treks are run by ethical operators with sustainable trips to help disadvantaged minority peoples, but there are also a lot of cowboys out there. Doi Phu Kha National Park, centred on a 2000m peak of the same name, presents endless opportunities for day and longer treks in the northern province of Nan, passing waterfalls, caves and ethnic minority villages along the way.

Motorbiking in Sapa (p81), Vietnam

Vietnam

Vietnam's trekking mecca is Sapa. The scenery is remarkable, with majestic mountains, impossibly green rice paddies and some fascinating tribal villages. But the main trails are incredibly popular and some villagers see hiking groups on a hourly basis. Bac Ha, at a lower elevation, is less rainy and the trails here are not as heavily tramped. Phong Nha-Ke Bang National Park is an up-and-coming destination for guided treks. Adventure-tour operators in Hoi An also offer some intriguing treks in the tribal areas west of town.

Cycling

For hard-core cyclists, the mountains of northern Vietnam and northern Laos are the ultimate destination. The trails of Doi Suthep-Pui National Park in northern Thailand offer adrenalin-charged descents, with mountain-bike gear and guides available for hire in Chiang Mai. In Cambodia, mountain-bike rental and guided tours are available out of Chi Phat in the Southern Cardamom Mountains, or out of Kratie and Stung Treng on the Mekong River. Dalat in Vietnam's southwest highlands is another good base for mountain-bike tours.

For those who like a more gentle workout, meandering along Mekong villages is memorable, particularly around Luang Prabang and Vientiane in Laos, and in the Mekong Delta in Vietnam. Hoi An's Old Town is closed to motorised traffic during the daytime these days, allowing cyclists to take over. Biking around Angkor is a great way to get around. And Thailand's northeast can be rewarding thanks to good roads and light traffic.

Throughout the region, basic bicycles can be rented for US$1 to US$3 per day and good-quality mountain bikes for US$10 to US$25. When it comes to cycling tours, Bangkok-based Spice Roads (www.spiceroads.com) is the acknowledged expert for the Mekong region and Asia beyond, but there are good local operators in each country.

Hiking in Chiang Dao (p477), Thailand

Motorbiking

For those with a thirst for adventure, motorbike trips into remote areas of the region are unforgettable. The mobility of two wheels is unrivalled. Motorbikes can traverse trails that even the hardiest 4WD cannot follow, and put you closer to the countryside – its smells, people and scenery – compared with getting around by car or bus. Just remember to watch the road, even when the passing scenery is sublime.

All four countries offer prime off-road territory for motorcyclists: 'the Loop' in central Laos; the highlands of north Vietnam and northern Thailand; and forgotten temple trails in Cambodia. And it hardly stops there. The old Ho Chi Minh Trail, a symbol of war's futility to some, is a holy grail of sorts to trail bikers: a network of rugged dirt paths that criss-cross the border of Laos and Vietnam. Cambodia's mazelike Cardamom Mountains are legendary, just don't get lost or you may end up spending a cold night in the jungle (a fate met by at least one Lonely Planet writer). Want something a bit easier (ie paved) but still plenty adventurous? The Southern Swing around Laos' Bolaven Plateau is one of many options.

Specialist motorcycle-touring companies can organise multiday trips into remote areas using the roads less travelled. Costs for these trips start from US$50 per day, going up to US$150 or more for the premium tours, depending on accommodation. Most tours are confined to a single country. Hanoi-based Explore Indochina (www.exploreindochina.com) is one company that does cross-border trips into Laos and sometimes Cambodia.

Based in Vientiane, the Midnight Mapper (www.laosgpsmap.com) is a GPS service that hires out satellite-navigation machines with your route especially programmed in. Golden Triangle Rider (www.gt-rider.com) is an excellent source for exploring the more remote bits of the Mekong region, including the Golden Triangle area and the Ho Chi Minh Trail.

Motorbikes are widely available for rent throughout the region; hiring usually requires a licence in Thailand but you rarely

OLESYA KUZNETSOVA / SHUTTERSTOCK ©

Cycling in Laos

need to show one in Laos, Cambodia and Vietnam. See p550 in our Transport chapter for more information.

Boat Trips

With the Mekong cutting a swath through the heart of the country, it is hardly surprising to find that boat trips are a major drawcard here. There are also opportunities to explore small jungled tributaries leading to remote minority villages.

Kayaking & Rafting

Though white-water rafting and kayaking is in its infancy in the Mekong region and the rivers are fairly tame most of the year, things can get a little more vigorous in the wet season. White water can be found in Vietnam on the Langbian River near Dalat, with class II, III or IV rapids. Companies based in Nha Trang also offer trips.

In northern Thailand, the rivers around Chiang Mai have white water from July to March (class II to class V). If you're up for an adventurous trip from Chiang Mai or Bangkok, up near the Myanmar border is where you'll find several companies offering trips in class III to class IV rapids from August to October. Note that rivers are prone to flash-flooding after heavy monsoon rain and can be dangerous at this time. When choosing a white-water operator take a careful look at their safety equipment and procedures.

Mellower river-rafting and kayaking trips are a hit throughout the region. In Thailand you can try a two- to three-day rafting trip out of Nan or Pai . In Laos you'll find similar trips offered around Luang Namtha in the north. In the south, paddling around Si Phan Don is a must. The Nam Song (Song River) in Vang Vieng is a hot spot for kayaking and of course tubing, while the extraordinary Tham Kong Lor cave in Khammuan Province is navigable by kayak. In Vietnam you can explore the rivers and cave systems around Phong Nha by kayak, and the Hoi An region also has delightful rivers for kayaking. In Cambodia, use Stung Treng as a base to paddle from the dolphin pools on the Lao border downstream through bird-infested flooded forests, where the Mekong River is at its most brilliant. Mellow river paddling trips are also offered in the Cambodian towns of Kratie, Battambang and Kampot.

There has been an explosion in popularity in sea kayaking in the past few years. In Vietnam, many standard Halong Bay tours now include kayaking through the karsts, or you can choose a kayaking specialist and paddle around majestic limestone pinnacles, before overnighting at a remote bay. Nearby in less touristed Lan Ha Bay you can kayak to hidden coves and sandy beaches. Sea-kayaking opportunities abound on Cambodia's Otres Beach, Koh Rong and Koh Rong Sanloem, and over the border on Ko Chang, Thailand.

Diving & Snorkeling

Compared with destinations like Indonesia and the Philippines, diving and snorkel-

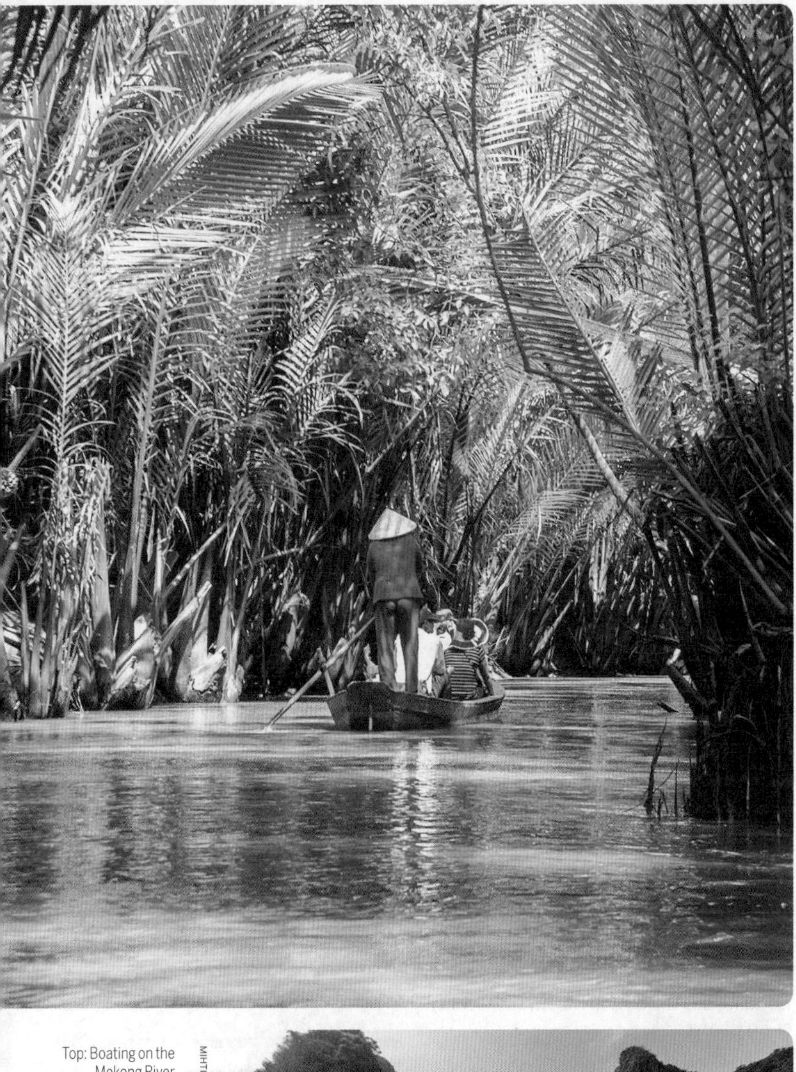

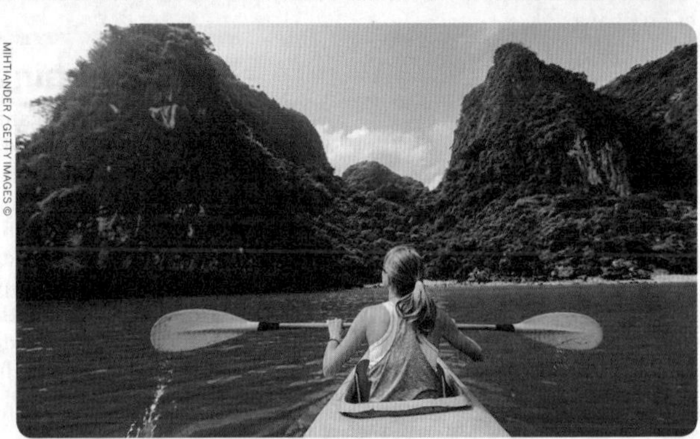

Top: Boating on the Mekong River

Bottom: Kayaking in Halong Bay (p71), Vietnam

MIHTIANDER / GETTY IMAGES ©

DIVING & SNORKELLING COSTS

Discover Scuba US$70–95

Two fun dives US$70–85 (US$160 in Con Dao Islands)

PADI Open Water US$325–500

Snorkelling day trip US$20–40

ling opportunities in the Mekong region are limited, although Vietnam and to a lesser extent Cambodia, have growing dive industries.

The Con Dao Islands offer unquestionably the best diving and snorkelling in Vietnam, with bountiful marine life, fine reefs and even a wreck dive, though it's much more costly than the rest of Vietnam. The most popular place to dive in Vietnam is Nha Trang, which has plenty of reputable dive operators – as well as several dodgy dive shops, some of which have fake Professional Association of Diving Instructors (PADI) credentials, so stick to reputable, recommended dive schools with qualified instructors and well-maintained equipment. Phu Quoc Island has some beautiful coral gardens full of marine life, although visibility can be a challenge. Dive trips out of Hoi An head to the lovely Cham Islands, where the focus is on macro life.

In Cambodia, the best diving is on the islands off the south coast. Sihanoukville has several dive operators, but you're better off basing yourself on Koh Rong or Koh Rong Sanloem to be closer to the action. Overnights on a boat are possible further offshore near Koh Tang or Koh Prins. Just over the border in Thailand, uninhabited Ko Rang has the best diving in the vicinity of Ko Chang.

Kitesurfing & Windsurfing

In Vietnam, Mui Ne Beach is the undisputed top spot for Asian wind chasers. You can kitesurf in Mui Ne year-round (rare for Southeast Asia), although it's best in the dry season (November to April); Nha Trang and Vung Tau (just outside HCMC) are other possibilities. In Cambodia, Otres Beach and Kampot have nascent kitesurfing scenes.

If you've never kitesurfed before, go for a taster lesson (US$80 to US$100) before you enrol in a lengthy course – a three-day course costs around US$400 to US$500.

Surfing

Unfortunately, that wave scene in *Apocalypse Now* was shot in the Philippines. The Mekong region is hardly known for surfing, but if you need your fix you can find some swell at certain times of the year – finding a board can be decidedly more problematic, however.

With a 3000km coastline, Vietnam is the obvious top candidate. Your best bet is Danang, where there's a small scene and some surf shops with boards for hire. Board hire costs US$5 to US$20 per day, while a two-hour surfing lesson will set you back about US$25. Mui Ne and Vung Tau also have occasional waves and board rental available. The peak season is December to March, when the waves are small but steady. July to November is fickle, but occasional typhoons passing offshore can produce clean peaks over 2m (though watch out for pollution after heavy rains).

In Cambodia, we have heard of waves happening on Sihanoukville's Otres Beach during the June-to-October wet season, when the southwest monsoon winds are raging, but it's a choppy onshore break. There are a few surboards and stand-up paddleboards available for rent.

Rock Climbing

When it comes to organised climbing, Chiang Mai in Thailand has the most on offer, but the region is liberally peppered with karsts and climbing in Laos and Vietnam has really taken off. In Vietnam, the pioneers and acknowledged specialists are Asia Outdoors (p75), a highly professional outfit based on Cat Ba that offers instruction for beginners and dedicated trips for rock hounds. In Dalat there are a couple

Kitesurfing in Mui Ne (p123), Vietnam

of good adventure tour operators offering climbing and canyoning. Over the border in southern Cambodia Climbodia (p270) runs courses and guides climbs in karst-laden hills around Kampot.

In Laos, Vang Vieng has some of the best climbing in Southeast Asia, with 200 routes – many of them bolted – up the limestone cliffs (most are rated between 4a and 8b). Adam's Rock Climbing School (p311) has excellent instructors and safe equipment. Nong Khiaw has attracted the adventure specialist Green Discovery (p337), with climbs up the limestone karsts under close and experienced instruction. Tha Khaek is home to the Green Climbers

ZIPLINING IN THE MEKONG REGION

Ziplining has, well, taken off in the region. Laos was the pioneer and is still the undisputed king. The Gibbon Experience (p351) in Bokeo Nature Reserve in Laos pioneered the use of ziplines to explore the jungle canopy. Visitors hang from a zipline and glide through the forest where the gibbons roam, then overnight in tree-houses.

In nearby Udomxai, Nam Kat Yorla Pa Adventure Park (p340) offers similarly thrilling ziplines and tree-house lodging, as does Green Discovery (p369) down south in Pakse. Adventure hotbed Vang Vieng has several options, including the pulsating Vang Vieng Challenge (p312). Green Jungle Flight (p317) near Luang Prabang features monkey bridges and rope courses in addition to ziplines, while Flight of the Gibbon (p469) spans the borders of Thailand and Cambodia, and offers thrilling treetop zipline adventures in Siem Reap, Chiang Mai, Koh Pha Ngan and around Bangkok. These family-friendly day trips have a forest-conservation component and are run in tandem with programs to reintroduce gibbons to the surrounding forest.

Home (p361), a climbing school in range of some 250 routes ranging from beginner to expert level.

Climbing costs in the region start from about US$25 to US$30 and rise for more specialised climbs in the Halong Bay area or for instruction.

Wildlife-Watching

While wildlife-spotting may not be quite as straightforward as in the Serengeti, it is still possible to have some world-class encounters in the Mekong region.

Gibbons are the big draw. You'll need to arrive at a gibbon colony superearly – before dawn in most cases – to have a chance at seeing them, so sleep on-site the night before if it's an option. Good spots for seeing gibbons include Cat Tien National Park in Vietnam, and Cambodian Gibbon Ecotours and the Jahoo Gibbon Camp, both in eastern Cambodia. In addition, several canopy zipline experiences (p41) around the region assist with protecting gibbon habitat, and some offer the chance to briefly spot wild or reintroduced gibbons.

At Thailand's remote Khao Yai National Park, the massive jungle is home to one of the world's largest monsoon forests. Here you can track shy wildlife, including more than 200 elephants. Laos has plenty of wildlife, including the region's largest population of wild elephants and a few tigers, but spotting them is difficult to impossible.

WHEN TO GO

For most activities, the dry season (November to May in most of the region) is the best time to visit. Trekking during the wet season can be particularly difficult, and leeches are all but guaranteed. On the other hand, swollen rivers make for great kayaking and scenic boat trips during this time. Cycling is doable year-round, but can be challenging in September and early October when the rains really pick up.

Great hornbill, Khao Yai National Park (p450), Thailand

Birdwatching is also popular throughout the region. Cambodia is the best place in the world to spot six critically endangered species: the giant ibis, white-shouldered ibis, Bengal florican and three species of vulture. The Prek Toal Bird Sanctuary is a premier wetland birdwatching spot. The award-winning Sam Veasna Center runs trips to all the best sites. In Thailand, Khao Yai National Park is also a top site for twitchers.

Off land, the freshwater Irrawaddy dolphin is one of the rarest mammals on earth, with fewer than 100 inhabiting stretches of the Mekong. Kayak with a small pod on the Laos–Cambodia border, or further south near Kratie in eastern Cambodia.

Lastly, interacting in a natural environment with retired domesticated elephants is possible here, with a few dozen sanctuaries set up for this purpose across the region, including Laos' Elephant Conservation Center and Cambodia's Elephant Valley Project. See p542 for more information on elephant encounters.

Plan Your Trip

Travel with Children

Children can live it up in the Mekong region, as they are always the centre of attention and almost everybody wants to play with them. This goes double for exotic-looking foreign children from faraway lands, who become instant celebrities wherever they go.

Mekong Region for Kids

Locals in the Mekong region can overcome their natural conservatism to immediately interact with the young ones. This works in a diverse range of environments from the market and street stall through to international restaurants, as long as they are not too pretentious or packed with customers.

As the toddler moves into childhood, a certain wariness towards strangers may develop and this can create some conflicts along the way. People in the Mekong are not backwards in coming forwards with children and this extends to pinching cheeks and patting bums. While this might be tolerable from the great aunt they get to see once in a blue moon, it's not so fun when it is happening a dozen times a day with random people in the street. Soon enough you'll find your child wants to be carried on your shoulders whenever the opportunity arises.

For the full picture on surviving and thriving on the road, check out Lonely Planet's *Travel with Children*, which contains useful advice on how to cope on the road. There is also a rundown on health precautions for kids and advice on travel during pregnancy.

Amenities specially geared towards young children – such as child-safety seats for cars, high chairs in restaurants or nappy-changing facilities – are virtually nonexistent in the Mekong region. It is sometimes possible to arrange a child seat

Best Regions for Kids

Bangkok

The City of Angels does a surprising cameo as the City of Little Angels, although you have to seek out the experiences. Boat rides on the *klorng* (canals), and shopping centres are fun.

Temples of Angkor

If the children are *Tomb Raider* fans, look no further than the temples of Angkor. Ta Prohm has the jungle, Bayon has the weirdness and Angkor Wat has the proportions. Leave time for floating villages and bicycle rides.

Vietnamese Coastline

If they want beaches, they'll get them in Vietnam. Hoi An combines culture with cavorting on the sand, Nha Trang has fun boat trips, and the older kids can windsurf or sandboard in Mui Ne.

Luang Prabang

While its cultural credentials draw mature visitors in their thousands, Luang Prabang has plenty to offer younger visitors, including kayaking, cycling and wildlife encounters. The waterfalls are also a hit thanks to jungle bathing opportunities.

if booking a regional tour through a high-end travel agent, but otherwise parents have to seek out substitutes. Or just follow the example of local families, which means holding smaller children on their laps. Cot beds (cribs) are available in international-standard midrange and top-end hotels, but not elsewhere. However, many hotels are happy to add an extra bed or a mattress for a nominal charge.

Baby formula and nappies (diapers) are available at minimarts and supermarkets in the larger towns and cities, but sizes are usually smallish, small and smaller. For larger sizes, you will need to hit a major supermarket in one of the big cities of the region. Nappy-rash cream is sold at pharmacies. Breastfeeding in public is quite common, so there is no need to worry about crossing a cultural boundary.

Some restaurants will only have chopsticks, especially in Vietnam. You might want to pack a plastic fork and spoon for such situations.

Health & Safety

For the most part, parents needn't worry too much, although it pays to lay down a few ground rules (such as hand-washing) to head off potential medical problems.

The main worry throughout the region is keeping an eye on what strange things infants are putting in their mouths. Their natural curiosity can be a lot more costly in countries where dysentery, typhoid and hepatitis are commonplace. Keeping hydration levels up and using sunscreen are also important.

Children should be warned not to play with animals as rabies is relatively common in Thailand. 'Cute' monkeys are some of the biggest offenders when it comes to bites, so be extravigilant when they are around. Mosquito and sandfly bites often leave big welts on children. Use child-friendly repellents around dusk and arrange for them to sleep under a mosquito net in remote areas, especially in the wet season. One of the nastier bites in the region comes from innocuous-looking sandflies. These are present on some beaches in Cambodia and Vietnam. The main problem is the itchiness of the bites, which if infected can cause complications. Use sticking plasters and encourage children to itch with fingers not nails.

Parts of rural Cambodia, Laos and Vietnam are not such good travel destinations for children, as there are landmines and unexploded ordnance (UXO) littering the countryside. No matter how many warnings a child is given, you can't be certain they won't stray from the path.

Getting Around

Many children are really into their transport and the Mekong region can deliver in style. For kids who have never been on a sleeper train, both Thailand and Vietnam offer a great chance to experience this. Unlike buses, trains allow children to walk around and children are usually assigned the lower sleeping berths with views of the stations.

Boats provide a lot of fun, provided you do a sweep for life jackets before committing to a trip and stay vigilant on the way. River trips are generally less likely to churn the stomach and the scenery can be more dramatic. From our experience, Halong Bay will stun children of any age, including youngsters, as the scenery is simply out of this world. Overnights are an adventure for many and it is also possible to cruise the Mekong from Huay Xai to Luang Prabang, and from Phnom Penh to Ho Chi Minh City.

Local transport can be a blast, providing you throw away the parental health-and-safety manual for a while. *Cyclo* (bicycle rickshaw) rides in Cambodia, Laos and Vietnam are a timeless way to explore. Tuk-tuks, or their local equivalent, are a buzz, but sometimes the drivers need to be reminded to use the brakes.

Hauling around little ones can be a challenge. Pavements and footpaths are often too crowded to push a stroller, especially today's full-sized SUV versions. Instead opt for a compact umbrella pushchair that can squeeze past the fire hydrant and the mango cart and that can be folded up and thrown in a tuk-tuk. A baby backpack is also useful but make sure that the child's head doesn't sit higher than yours: there are lots of hanging obstacles poised at that level.

Children familiar with urban environments will do well in the region's cities, where traffic is chaotic and pedestrian paths are congested. Mekong cities are very loud and can be sensory overloads for young children. Be sure that your child cooperates with your safety guidelines before heading out as it will be difficult for them to focus on your instructions amid all the street noise.

Countries at a Glance

Many a Mekong adventure begins or ends in Bangkok. It works as a convenient launch pad into hilly northern Thailand, Thailand's eastern seaboard, or Laos and Cambodia to the east.

Laos is the remote backwater of Indochina, but diverse minorities and national parks have made it the ecotourism darling of the region. Cambodia is best known for the Angkorian temples around Siem Reap, but also features outstanding beaches on the south coast, fine food in Phnom Penh and wildlife-watching opportunities in the mountainous east. A range of excellent community-based ecotourism initiatives bring much-needed income to more remote areas.

Vietnam is catching up with Thailand fast. Spiralling cities, designer dining and ultraluxury beach resorts point to the future, while war relics and traditional minority lifestyles are reminders of the past.

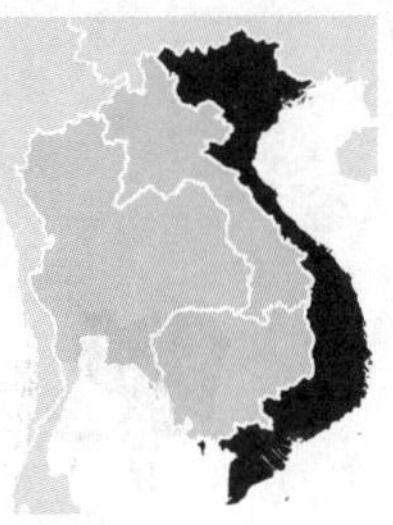

Vietnam

Beaches
Food
History

Coastal Delights

Vietnam has a voluptuous coastline. Hoi An, Mui Ne and Nha Trang are the big hitters, but there are hundreds of kilometres of empty beaches to discover, including islands such as Phu Quoc and Con Dao.

Culinary Delights

You don't have to be a gastronome to experience the culinary delights of Vietnam. Surf the streets for sumptuous local snacks, discover the bounty of the sea along the lengthy coastline or learn the secrets of the kitchen with a cooking class.

Old Cities

Explore the bustling Old Quarter of 1000-year-old Hanoi, discover the tombs and royal relics of imperial Hue, and browse the backstreet galleries, cafes and bars of delightful Hoi An – in Vietnam you are literally spoilt for choice when it comes to cities with a story to tell.

p48

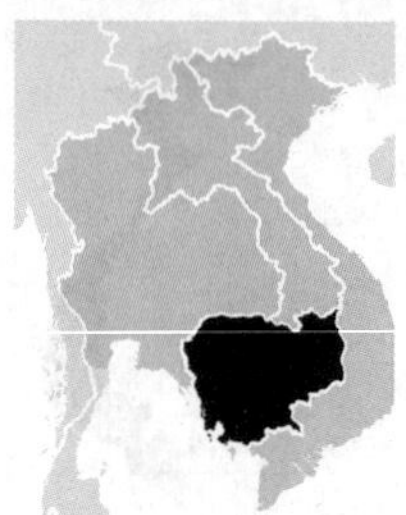

Cambodia

Architecture
Giving Back
Nature

Ancient Temples

Heard enough about Angkor Wat? Well, don't forget the pre-Angkorian capital of Sambor Prei Kuk, the region's first temple city, or the jungle temples of Preah Vihear Province.

Good Causes

There are many ways to give something back to the communities you visit in Cambodia. Dine at sumptuous training restaurants that lend a helping hand to ex–street kids, buy designer dresses stitched by disabled seamstresses or try a community homestay deep in the countryside.

Ecotourism

While it's best known for temples, Cambodia offers a surprisingly rich array of pursuits for nature addicts, including jungle trekking, rare-primate-spotting and world-class birdwatching. Just around Siem Reap you can zipline through the jungle, boat into remarkable Prek Toal Bird Sanctuary or waterfall-hop at Phnom Kulen National Park.

p178

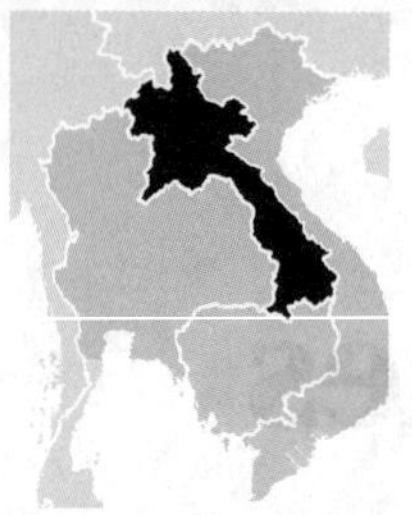

Laos

Nature
Hill Tribes
Activities

Protected Forests

With around 20 National Protected Areas, Laos has more dense forest per square kilometre than anywhere else in Southeast Asia and is begging to be explored. Award-winning ecotreks take you deep into the jungle realm of the clouded leopard, wild elephant and Asiatic tiger.

Minority Cultures

More than 65 tribes compose Laos' colourful ethnic quilt. In the rugged north, rural homestay programs allow you to encounter animism and observe cultures that have changed little in the last century.

Ziplines

Glide like gibbons on one of a number of tree-canopy ziplines that take you up close to nature and offer jaw-dropping jungle views. By night, sleep in a treehouse and listen for the predawn call of gibbons.

p288

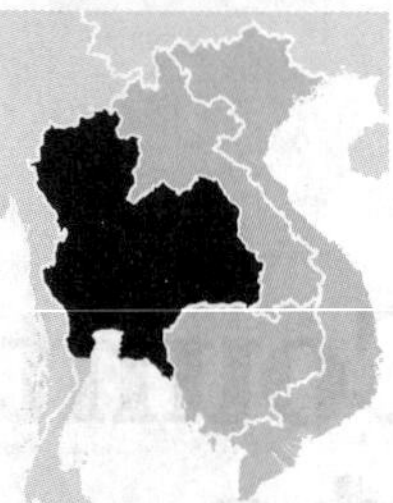

Northern Thailand

Food
Shopping
Communities

Taste Sensations

Start getting your taste buds in shape – everything you've heard about Thai food is true. From spicy stir-fries to sadistic salads, chillies form their own food group for Thais.

Retail Therapy

Believe us, you've never encountered commerce the way they do it in Thailand. From the megamalls of Bangkok to Chiang Mai's more sedate Saturday and Sunday Walking Streets, you'll inevitably leave Thailand with a souvenir or five.

Local Experiences

Provincial Thailand invites you to see the countryside from the saddle of a motorcycle, live in a homestay in rice-growing country or trek to a remote hill-tribe village; prerequisites include a Thai phrasebook and a willingness to live like a local. You'll leave with unforgettable memories.

p401

On the Road

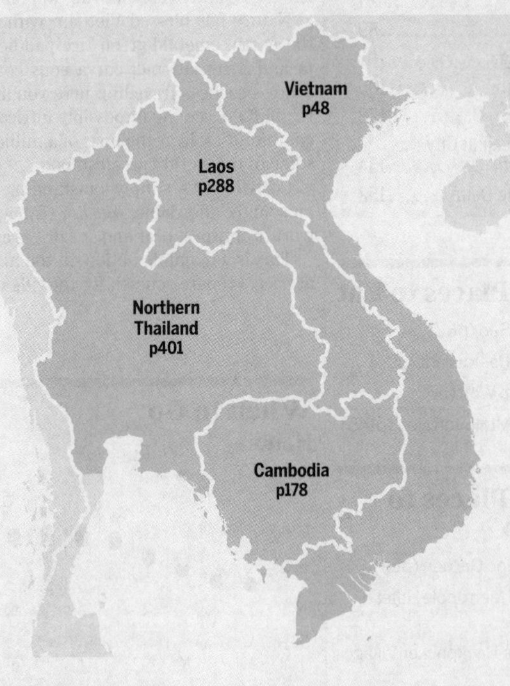
Vietnam
p48
Laos
p288
Northern
Thailand
p401
Cambodia
p178

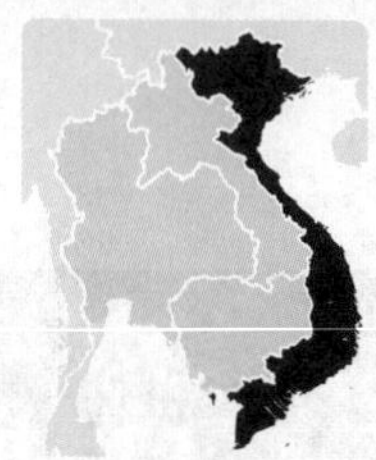

Vietnam

POP 95.3 MILLION / ☎84

Includes ➡

Best Places to Eat

- ➡ Chim Sao (p62)
- ➡ Hanh Restaurant (p95)
- ➡ Tim Ho Wan (p62)
- ➡ Banh Mi Huynh Hoa (p145)

Best Places to Sleep

- ➡ Tam Coc Garden (p69)
- ➡ Sofitel Metropole Hotel (p58)
- ➡ Mui Ne Backpacker Village (p123)
- ➡ Mia Resort Nha Trang (p120)

Why Go?

Astonishingly exotic and utterly compelling, Vietnam is a kaleidoscope of vivid colours and subtle shades, grand architecture and deeply moving war sites.

Nature has blessed Vietnam with soaring mountains in the north, emerald-green rice paddies in the Mekong Delta and a sensational, curvaceous coastline with ravishing sandy beaches. Travelling here you'll witness children riding buffalo, see the impossibly intricate textiles of hill-tribe communities, hear the buzz of a million motorbikes and eat some of the world's greatest food.

Costwise, it's simply outstanding value: dining out is amazingly affordable, *bia hoi* (draught beer) must be the world's cheapest beer and spa prices are a complete bargain.

This is a dynamic nation on the move, where life is lived at pace. Prepare yourself for the ride of your life.

When to Go

Hanoi

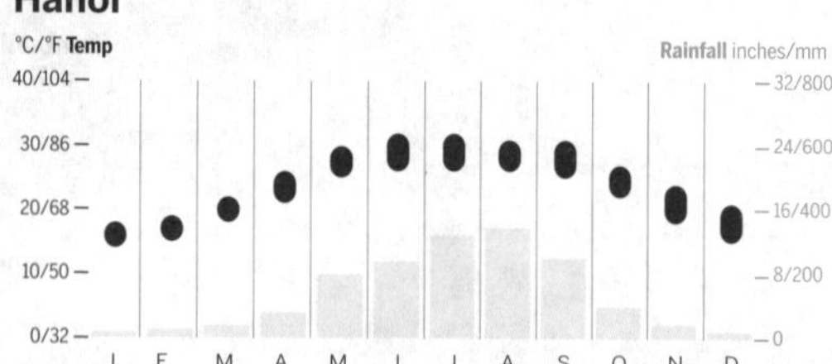

Dec–Mar Cool weather north of Hue; the winter monsoon brings cloud and drizzle.

Apr–May On balance perhaps the best time to tour the nation as a whole.

Jul–Aug High season on the central coast, with balmy temperatures.

HANOI

Sights

Vietnam's capital races to make up for time lost to the ravages of war and a government that as recently as the 1990s kept the outside world at bay. Its streets surge with scooters vying for right of way amid the din of constantly blaring horns, and all around layers of history reveal periods of French and Chinese occupation – offering a glimpse into the resilience of ambitious, proud Hanoians.

Negotiate a passage past the ubiquitous knock-off merchants and you'll find the original streets of the Old Quarter. Defiant real-deal farmers hawk their wares, while city folk breakfast on noodles, practise t'ai chi at dawn on the shores of Hoan Kiem Lake, or play chess with goateed grandfathers.

Dine on the wild and wonderful at every corner, sample market wares, uncover an evolving arts scene, then sleep soundly in a little luxury for very little cost. Meet the people, delve into the past and witness the awakening of a Hanoi on the move.

Old Quarter

Hanoi's historic heart, 'The Old Quarter', is home to more than 1000 years of trade, commerce and activity, with no signs of slowing down. Although its name tends to evoke images of ancient lamp-lit streets lined with the wooden storefronts of traditional artisans, merchants and craftspeople, you'll find the reality of the Old Quarter more gritty than romantic. In spite of this, the Old Quarter is what Hanoi is all about and adjusting your expectations will help you make the most of your time here.

★Bach Ma Temple BUDDHIST TEMPLE

(Den Bach Ma; Map p60; cnr P Hang Buom & P Hang Giay; ⏲8-11am & 2-5pm Tue-Sun) FREE In the heart of the Old Quarter, the small Bach Ma Temple is said to be the oldest temple in the city, though much of the current structure dates from the 18th century and a shrine to Confucius was added in 1839. It was originally built by Emperor Ly Thai To in the 11th century to honour a white horse that guided him to this site, where he chose to construct his city walls.

Pass through the wonderful old wooden doors of the pagoda to see a statue of the legendary white horse, as well as a beautiful red-lacquered funeral palanquin.

Memorial House HISTORIC BUILDING

(Ngoi Nha; Map p60; 87 P Ma May; 5000d; ⏲9am-noon & 1-5pm) One of the Old Quarter's best-restored properties, this traditional merchants' house is sparsely but beautifully decorated, with rooms set around two courtyards and filled with fine furniture. Note the high steps between rooms, a traditional design incorporated to stop the flow of bad energy around the property.

There are crafts and trinkets for sale here, including silver jewellery, basketwork and Vietnamese teasets, and there's usually a calligrapher or other craftsperson at work too.

Dong Xuan Market MARKET

(Cho Dong Xuan; Map p60; cnr P Hang Khoai & P Dong Xuan; ⏲7am-9pm) The largest covered market in Hanoi was originally built by the French in 1889 and almost completely destroyed by fire in 1994. Almost everything you can think of from fresh (and live) produce to cheap clothing, souvenirs, consumer goods and traditional arts and crafts can be found inside.

Long Bien Bridge BRIDGE

(Cau Long Bien; Map p52) FREE A symbol of the tenacity and resilience of the Hanoian people, the Long Bien Bridge (built between 1899 and 1902) was bombed on several occasions during the American War, and on each, quickly repaired by the Vietnamese. Designed by Gustave Eiffel (of Eiffel Tower fame) the bridge, used by trains, mopeds and pedestrians, is undergoing reconstruction to restore its original appearance. It's colourfully illuminated at night.

Around Hoam Kiem Lake

★Hoa Lo Prison Museum HISTORIC BUILDING

(Map p56; ☎04-3824 6358; cnr P Hoa Lo & P Hai Ba Trung; adult/child 30,000d/free; ⏲8am-5pm) This thought-provoking site is all that remains of the former Hoa Lo Prison, ironically nicknamed the 'Hanoi Hilton' by US prisoners of war (POWs) during the American War. Most exhibits relate to the prison's use up to the mid-1950s, focusing on the Vietnamese struggle for independence from France. A gruesome relic is the ominous French guillotine, used to behead Vietnamese revolutionaries. There are also displays focusing on the American pilots who were incarcerated at Hoa Lo during the American War.

These pilots include Pete Peterson (the first US ambassador to a unified Vietnam

Vietnam Highlights

❶ **Hoi An** (p106) Taking a trip back in time in a maze of cobbled lanes.

❷ **Hanoi** (p49) Getting seduced by a blend of Parisian-style grace and Asian pace.

❸ **Halong Bay** (p71) Being spellbound by the natural wonder.

❹ **Phong Nha-Ke Bang National Park** (p87) Discovering limestone highlands riddled with extraordinary cave systems.

❺ **Ho Chi Minh City** (p134) Delighting in the visceral energy and vibrant nightlife.

❻ **Northwest Highlands** (p79) Exploring the dramatic landscape, which is dotted with tribal villages.

❼ **Cat Ba Island** (p73) Climbing and sailing karst peaks.

❽ **Mui Ne** (p123) Laying back on the pristine beach or kitesurfing sick waves.

❾ **Con Dao Islands** (p126) Visiting idyllic, remote beaches and dive sites.

❿ **Hue** (p89) Following in the footsteps of emperors in this majestic city.

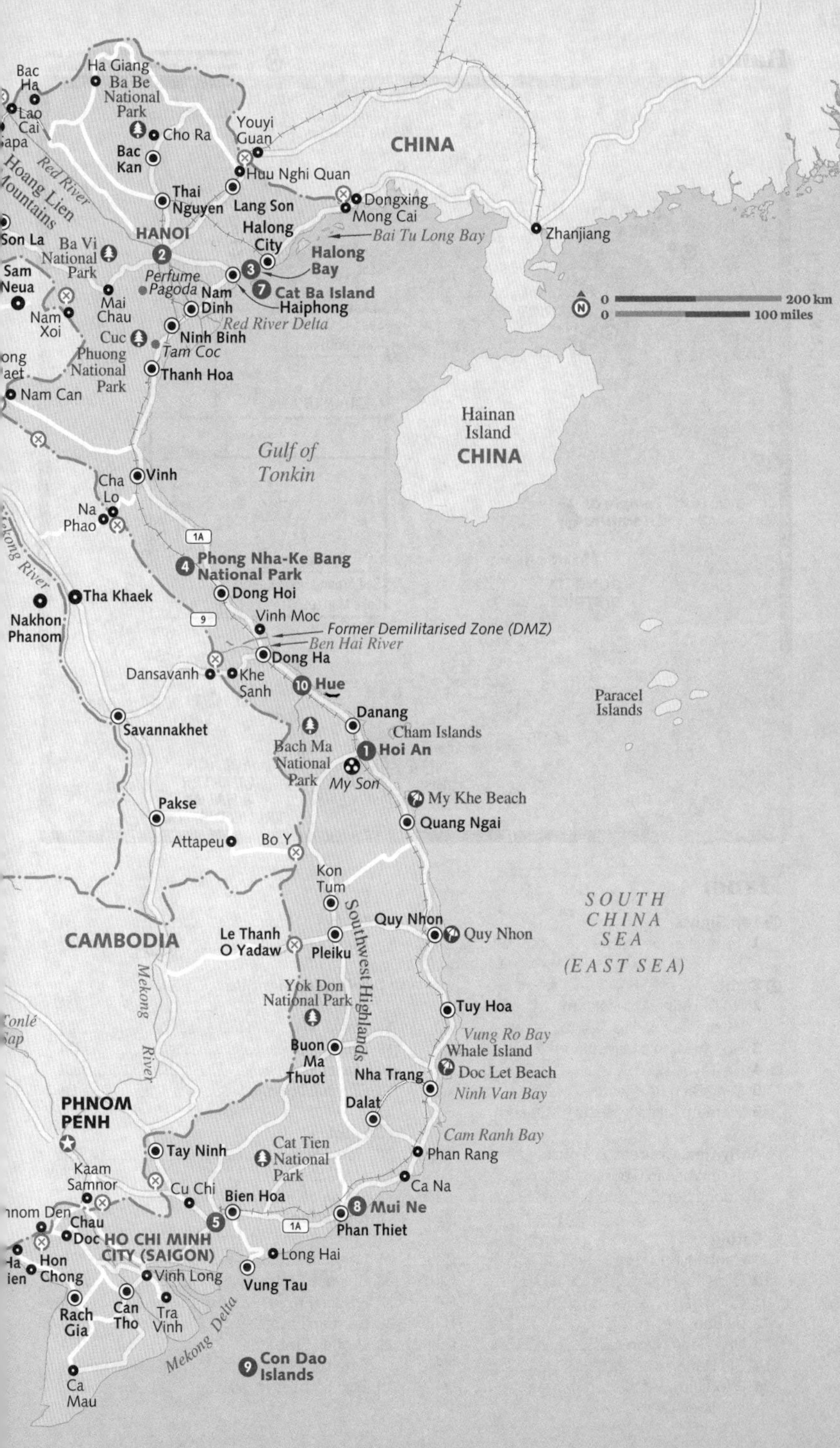

Bac Ha
Ha Giang
Ba Be National Park
Lao Cai
Sapa
Cho Ra
Bac Kan
Red River
Hoang Lien Mountains
Thai Nguyen
Youyi Guan
Huu Nghi Quan
Lang Son
CHINA
Dongxing
Mong Cai
Bai Tu Long Bay
Zhanjiang
Son La
HANOI
Ba Vi National Park
Halong City
Halong Bay
Sam Neua
Perfume Pagoda
Cat Ba Island
Haiphong
Mai Chau
Nam Dinh
Nam Xoi
Red River Delta
Ninh Binh
Cuc Phuong National Park
Tam Coc
Thanh Hoa
Nam Can
0 200 km
0 100 miles
Hainan Island
CHINA
Gulf of Tonkin
Vinh
Cha Lo
Na Phao
1A
Phong Nha-Ke Bang National Park
Mekong River
Tha Khaek
Dong Hoi
Nakhon Phanom
9
Vinh Moc
Former Demilitarised Zone (DMZ)
Ben Hai River
Dong Ha
Dansavanh
Khe Sanh
Hue
Paracel Islands
Danang
Savannakhet
Cham Islands
Hoi An
Bach Ma National Park
My Son
My Khe Beach
Pakse
Quang Ngai
Attapeu
Bo Y
Kon Tum
SOUTH CHINA SEA
(EAST SEA)
Quy Nhon
Quy Nhon
Le Thanh
O Yadaw
Pleiku
CAMBODIA
Southwest Highlands
Mekong River
Yok Don National Park
Tuy Hoa
Tonlé Sap
Vung Ro Bay
Buon Ma Thuot
Whale Island
Doc Let Beach
Nha Trang
Ninh Van Bay
PHNOM PENH
Dalat
Cam Ranh Bay
Tay Ninh
Cat Tien National Park
Phan Rang
Kaam Samnor
Ca Na
Cu Chi
Bien Hoa
Mui Ne
Chau Doc
1A
Phan Thiet
HO CHI MINH CITY (SAIGON)
Long Hai
Hon Chong
Vinh Long
Vung Tau
Rach Gia
Can Tho
Tra Vinh
Mekong Delta
Con Dao Islands
Ca Mau

Hanoi

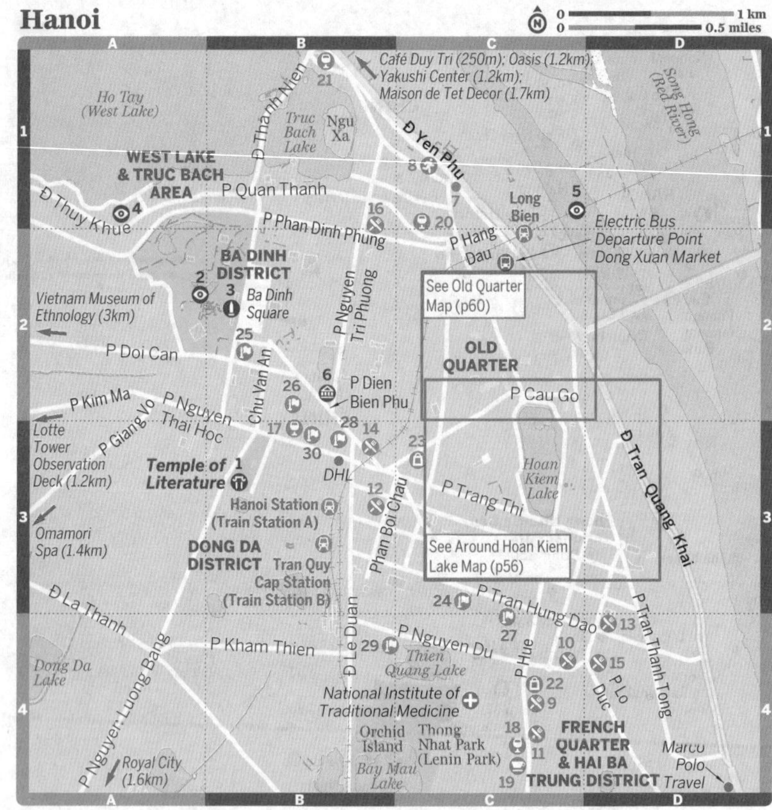

Hanoi

Top Sights
1 Temple of Literature B3

Sights
2 Ho Chi Minh Mausoleum Complex A2
3 Ho Chi Minh's Mausoleum B2
4 Ho Tay A1
5 Long Bien Bridge C1
6 Vietnam Military History Museum B2

Activities, Courses & Tours
7 Free Wheelin' Tours C1
8 Huong Sen C1

Eating
9 Banh Mi Pho Hue C4
10 Bun Cha Huong Lien C4
11 Chim Sao C4
12 La Badiane B3
13 Nha Hang Ngon D4
14 Old Hanoi B3
15 Pho Thin D4
16 Quan An Ngon B1
Quan An Ngon .... (see 12)

Drinking & Nightlife
17 Bar Betta B3
18 Cama ATK C4
19 Cong Caphe C4
20 Manzi Art Space C1
21 Summit Lounge B1

Shopping
22 Hom Market C4
23 Mai Gallery C3

Information
24 Cambodian Embassy C3
25 Canadian Embassy B2
26 Chinese Embassy B2
27 French Embassy C4
28 German Embassy B3
29 Laotian Embassy B4
Singaporean Embassy .... (see 26)
30 Thai Embassy B3

in 1995), and Senator John McCain (the Republican nominee for the US presidency in 2008). McCain's flight suit is displayed, along with a photograph of Hanoi locals rescuing him from Truc Bach Lake after being shot down in 1967.

The vast prison complex was built by the French in 1896. Originally intended to house around 450 inmates, records indicate that by the 1930s there were close to 2000 prisoners. Hoa Lo was never a very successful prison, and hundreds escaped its walls over the years – many squeezing out through sewer grates.

Polyglots might notice that the French signs are watered down compared with the English equivalents.

★Hoan Kiem Lake — LAKE

(Map p56) Legend claims in the mid-15th century Heaven sent Emperor Ly Thai To a magical sword, which he used to drive the Chinese from Vietnam. After the war a giant golden turtle grabbed the sword and disappeared into the depths of this lake to restore the sword to its divine owners, inspiring the name Ho Hoan Kiem (Lake of the Restored Sword).

The area is best Fridays to Sundays when nearby traffic is banned 7pm–midnight and a public-square, funfair vibe takes over.

Every morning at around 6am local residents practise traditional t'ai chi on the shore.

The ramshackle **Thap Rua** (Turtle Tower; Map p56), on an islet near the southern end, is topped with a red star and is often used as an emblem of Hanoi.

★Vietnamese Women's Museum — MUSEUM

(Map p56; ☎04-3825 9936; www.baotangphunu.org.vn; 36 P Ly Thuong Kiet; 30,000d; ⏲8am-5pm) This excellent, modern museum showcases women's role in Vietnamese society. Labelled in English and French, it's the memories of the wartime contribution by individual heroic women that are most poignant. If the glut of information sometimes feels repetitive, for visual stimulation there is a stunning collection of propaganda posters, as well as costumes, tribal basketware and fabric motifs from Vietnam's ethnic minority groups. Check the website for special exhibitions.

★National Museum of Vietnamese History — MUSEUM

(Bao Tang Lich Su Quoc Gia; Map p56; ☎04-3824 2433; http://baotanglichsu.vn; 1 P Trang Tien; adult/student 40,000/15,000d; ⏲8am-noon & 1.30-5pm, closed 1st Mon of the month) Built between 1925 and 1932, this architecturally impressive museum was formerly home to the École Française d'Extrême Orient. Its architect, Ernest Hebrard, was among the first in Vietnam to incorporate a blend of Chinese and French design elements. Exhibit highlights include bronzes from the Dong Son culture (3rd century BC to 3rd century AD), Hindu statuary from the Khmer and Champa kingdoms, jewellery from imperial Vietnam, and displays relating to the French occupation and the Communist Party.

Ngoc Son Temple — BUDDHIST TEMPLE

(Den Ngoc Son; Map p56; Hoan Kiem Lake; adult/student 20,000/10,000d; ⏲7.30am-5.30pm) Meaning 'Temple of the Jade Mountain', Hanoi's most visited temple sits on a small island in the northern part of Hoan Kiem Lake, connected to the lakeshore by an elegant scarlet bridge, constructed in classical Vietnamese style. The temple is dedicated to General Tran Hung Dao (who defeated the Mongols in the 13th century), La To (patron saint of physicians) and the scholar Van Xuong.

Martyrs' Monument — MONUMENT

(Map p56) This photogenic monument depicting a woman with a sword and two men holding guns and a torch was erected as a memorial to those who died fighting for Vietnam's independence.

Museum of Vietnamese Revolution — MUSEUM

(Bao Tang Cach Mang Viet Nam; Map p56; ☎04-3825 4151; 216 Đ Tran Quang Khai; adult/student 40,000/20,000d; ⏲8am-noon & 1.30-5pm, closed 1st Mon of the month) Inaugurated in 1959 and housing more than 40,000 exhibits, this museum enthusiastically presents the histories of conflict and revolution within Vietnam, from the liberation movements against the French occupation to the establishment of the Communist Party and the Socialist Republic of Vietnam.

St Joseph Cathedral — CHURCH

(Nha To Lon Ha Noi; Map p56; P Nha Tho; ⏲8am-noon & 2-6pm) Hanoi's neo-Gothic St Joseph Cathedral was inaugurated in 1886, and boasts a soaring facade that faces a little plaza. Its most noteworthy features are its twin bell towers, elaborate altar and fine stained-glass windows. Entrance via the main gate is only permitted during Mass: times are listed on a sign on the gates to the left of the cathedral.

At other times, enter via the Diocese of Hanoi compound, a block away at 40 P Nha

Chung. When you reach the side door to the cathedral, to your right, ring the small bell high up on the right-hand side of the door.

Other Areas

★ Temple of Literature CONFUCIAN TEMPLE

(Van Mieu Quoc Tu Giam; Map p52; ☎04-3845 2917; P Quoc Tu Giam; adult/student 30,000/15,000d; ⏰8am-5pm) Founded in 1070 by Emperor Ly Thanh Tong, the Temple of Literature is dedicated to Confucius (Khong Tu). Inside you'll find a pond known as the 'Well of Heavenly Clarity', a low-slung pagoda and statues of Confucius and his disciples. A rare example of well-preserved traditional Vietnamese architecture, the complex honours Vietnam's finest scholars and men of literary accomplishment. It is the site of Vietnam's first university, established here in 1076, when entrance was only granted to those of noble birth.

★ Vietnam Museum of Ethnology MUSEUM

(☎04-3756 2193; www.vme.org.vn; Đ Nguyen Van Huyen; adult/concession 40,000/15,000d, guide 100,000d; ⏰8.30am-5.30pm Tue-Sun) This fabulous collection relating to Vietnam's ethnic minorities features well-presented tribal art, artefacts and everyday objects gathered from across the nation, and examples of traditional village houses. Displays are well labelled in Vietnamese, French and English. If you're into anthropology, it's well worth the approximately 200,000d each-way taxi fares to the Cau Giay district, about 7km from the city centre, where the museum is located.

Local bus 14 (4000d) departs from P Dinh Tien Hoang on the east side of Hoan Kiem Lake and passes within a couple of blocks (around 600m) of the museum; get off at the Nghia Tan bus stop and head to Đ Nguyen Van Huyen.

★ Lotte Tower Observation Deck VIEWPOINT

(☎04-3333 6016; www.lottecenter.com.vn/eng/observation/visit_information.asp; 54 P Lieu Giai, Ba Dinh; adult/student day 230,000/170,000d, night 130,000/110,000d; ⏰9am-10pm) The city's best views can be found on the 65th floor of the landmark Lotte building, opened in 2014, in the western corner of Hanoi's Ba Dinh district. From this uninterrupted vantage point, high above Hanoi's hustle and bustle, one can consider the size of the Old Quarter relative to the sheer scale of Hanoi's voracious growth. The tower also houses a hotel, all manner of restaurants, a rooftop bar and a department store on its lower floors.

Lotte Tower is around 20 minutes by taxi from the Old Quarter.

Ho Tay LAKE

(West Lake; Map p52) The city's largest lake, known as both Ho Tay and West Lake, is 15km in circumference and ringed by upmarket suburbs, including the predominantly expat Tay Ho district. On the south side, along Đ Thuy Khue, are seafood restaurants, and to the east, the Xuan Dieu strip is lined with restaurants, cafes, boutiques and luxury hotels. The atmosphere makes a calm change from the chaos of the Old Quarter. A pathway circles the lake, making for a great bicycle ride.

Ho Chi Minh Mausoleum Complex HISTORIC SITE

(Map p52; ☎04-3845 5128; www.bqllang.gov.vn; entrance cnr P Ngoc Ha & P Doi Can) The Ho Chi Minh Mausoleum Complex is an important place of pilgrimage for many Vietnamese. A traffic-free area of botanical gardens, monuments, memorials and pagodas, it's usually crowded with groups of Vietnamese who come from far and wide to pay their respects to 'Uncle Ho'. Within the complex are Ho Chi Minh's Mausoleum, Ho Chi Minh's Stilt House and the Presidential Palace, Ho Chi Minh Museum and the One Pillar Pagoda.

Ho Chi Minh's Mausoleum MONUMENT

(Lang Chu Tich Ho Chi Minh; Map p52; ☎04-3845 5128; www.bqllang.gov.vn; ⏰8-11am Tue-Thu, Sat & Sun Dec-Sep, last entry 10.15am) FREE In the tradition of Lenin, Stalin and Mao, Ho Chi Minh's Mausoleum is a monumental marble edifice. Contrary to his desire for a simple cremation, the mausoleum was constructed from materials gathered from all over Vietnam between 1973 and 1975. Set deep in the bowels of the building in a glass sarcophagus is the frail, pale body of Ho Chi Minh. The mausoleum is usually closed from 4 Sep to 4 Nov while his embalmed body goes to Russia for maintenance.

Dress modestly: wearing shorts, tank tops or hats is not permitted. You may be requested to store day packs, cameras and phones before you enter. Talking, putting your hand in your pockets and photography is strictly prohibited in the mausoleum. The queue usually snakes for several hundred metres to the mausoleum entrance and inside, filing past Ho's body at a slow but steady pace.

If you're lucky, you'll catch the changing of the guard outside Ho's mausoleum – the pomp and ceremony displayed here rivals the British equivalent at Buckingham Palace.

Vietnam Military History Museum MUSEUM

(Bao Tang Lich Su Quan Su Viet Nam; Map p52; ☎04-733 6453; www.btlsqsvn.org.vn; 28a P Dien Bien Phu; admission 30,000d, camera fee 20,000d; ⏲8-11.30am daily & 2-4pm Tue-Thu, Sat & Sun) Easy to spot thanks to a large collection of weaponry at the front, the Military Museum displays Soviet and Chinese equipment alongside French- and US-made weapons captured during years of warfare. The centrepiece is a Soviet-built MiG-21 jet fighter, triumphant amid the wreckage of French aircraft downed at Dien Bien Phu, and a US F-111.

Activities

★Omamori Spa MASSAGE

(☎04-3773 9919; www.blindlink.org.vn/spa; 102 B1, Alley 5, P Huỳnh Thúc Kháng, Dong Da; massage 60min from 190,000d) You'll need a taxi to get to this wonderful little spa, operated by a not-for-profit organisation that provides training and employment opportunities for the blind. Masseuses here are vision impaired and speak excellent English. If you haven't received a massage by a trained blind therapist before, it's quite an experience: there's a level of gentleness and body awareness that differs from traditional practitioners. Tips are not accepted, and the pricing and quality of services is excellent.

Yakushi Center MASSAGE

(☎04-3719 1971; www.yakushicenter.com; 20 P Xuan Dieu, Quang An, Tay Ho; treatments from 210,000d; ⏲9am-7.30pm) In the fashionable expat-centric suburb of Tay Ho, you'll find this fabulous clinic that specialises in a range of traditional Vietnamese and Chinese medicine practices, as well as therapeutic and relaxing massages. Bookings are essential: your English-speaking practitioner will conduct a brief consultation with you prior to commencing your treatment.

Huong Sen MASSAGE

(Map p52; ☎04-3825 4911; http://huongsen healthcare.com; 78 Đ Yen Phu; massage from 250,000d; ⏲9.30am-10.30pm) A wide range of beauty treatments and services, including Jacuzzi and steam baths, are available at this professional outfit with good facilities and English-speaking staff. A full menu is available on the website.

Annam Foot Spa & Massage MASSAGE

(Map p56; ☎0913 211 558; 71 P Hang Bong; massage from 250,000d; ⏲10am-10pm) In the heart of the Old Quarter, this multilevel establishment is well priced and easy to find.

Royal City SWIMMING, SKATING

(☎04-3974 3550; http://royalcity.com.vn; 72a P Nguyen Trai, Thanh Xuan; water park & skating under 130cm/over 130cm 100,000/170,000d; ⏲11am-9pm) Opened in 2013 as part of the Royal City Mega Mall complex (Vietnam's largest shopping and entertainment complex), the Vinpearl Water Park and Vinpearl Ice Rink are among a bunch of attractions appealing to travelling families. There's also a bowling alley, cinema complex, games area and shopping for mum and dad. Royal City is about 7km southwest of the Old Quarter.

Ho Tay Water Park SWIMMING

(Cong Vien Ho Tay; ☎04-3718 4222; www.congvienhotay.vn; under 130cm/over 130cm 80,000/150,000d; ⏲9am-9pm Wed-Mon Apr-Nov) If you're desperate for a swim, this water park 5km north of the Old Quarter on the northern edge of Ho Tay has pools, slides and a lazy river. It gets extremely busy here on hot summer afternoons and might not satisfy everyone's standards for safety and hygiene.

NGO Resource Centre VOLUNTEERING

(☎04-3832 8570; www.ngocentre.org.vn; Room 201, Bldg E3, 6 Dang Van Ngu, Trung Tu Diplomatic Compound, Dong Da, Hanoi) For information on volunteer work opportunities, chase up the full list of nongovernment organisations (NGOs) at the NGO Resource Centre, which keeps a database of all of the NGOs assisting Vietnam. For more on volunteering see p547.

Tours

Sophie's Art Tour CULTURAL

(☎0168 796 2575; www.sophiesarttour.com; tours from $55) These fascinating tours are based on the lives of artists who studied, fought, witnessed and documented major changes in 20th- and 21st-century Vietnam, and will be appreciated not only by art lovers, but those who want to gain a deeper understanding of the complexities of Vietnam's unique history and culture.

Gay Hanoi Tours WALKING

(☎0947 600 602; www.facebook.com/gayhanoi tour; half-day tours from US$75) The inimitable Tuan offers personal and small group walking tours exploring lesser-known, real-life corners of the ancient city. While tours aren't gay themed, Tuan, a gay Hanoian man, offers a unique perspective on his beloved home town, regardless of your sexuality.

Around Hoan Kiem Lake

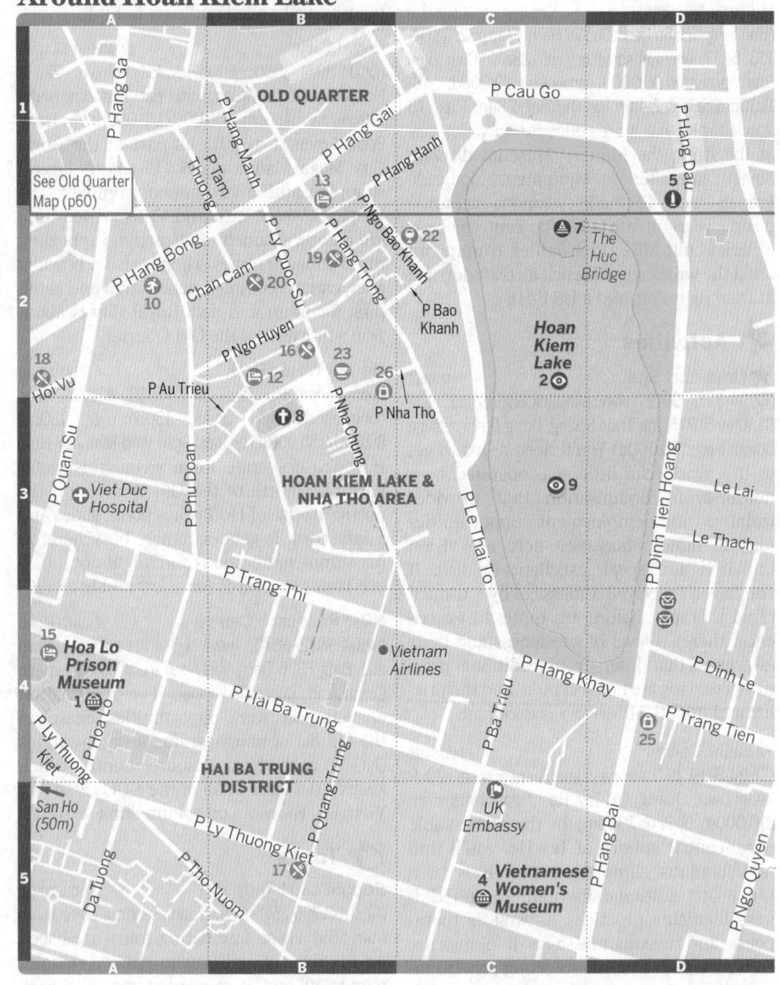

Hanoi Kids WALKING

(☎0976 217 886; www.hanoikids.org; by donation) This volunteer organisation partners visitors with Hanoi teens and young adults wishing to improve their English-language skills. Tours are customised to the needs of visitors and can include Hanoi sights like the Temple of Literature and Hoa Lo Prison Museum, or street-food and market visits. It's best to arrange tours online a couple of weeks before you arrive in Hanoi.

Free Wheelin' Tours TOUR

(Map p52; ☎04-3926 2743; www.freewheelin-tours.com; 62 Đ Yen Phu, Ba Dinh; ⏰10am-7pm) Offers motorbike and 4WD tours around the north, including an eight-day trip to the northeast on Minsk bikes.

Festivals & Events

Tet CULTURAL

(Tet Nguyen Dan, Vietnamese Lunar New Year; ⏰late Jan or early Feb) During the week preceding Tet, there is a flower market on P Hang Luoc. There's also a colourful, two-week flower exhibition and competition, beginning on the first day of the new year, that takes place in Thong Nhat Park (Lenin Park) near Bay Mau Lake.

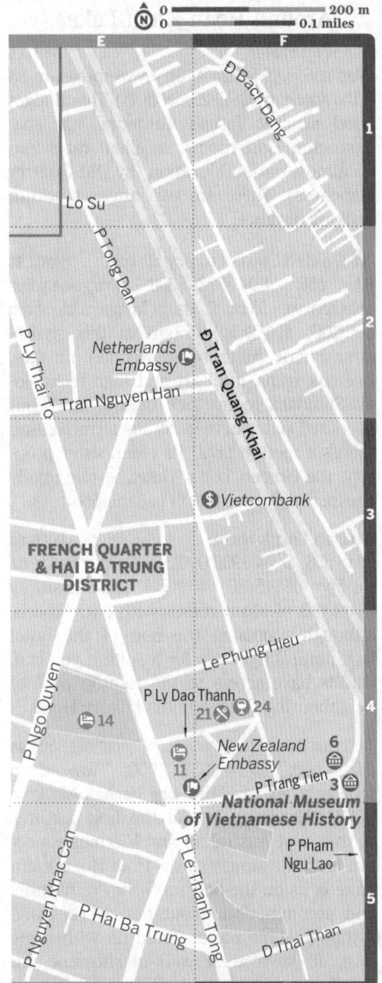

Around Hoan Kiem Lake

Top Sights

Sights

Activities, Courses & Tours

Sleeping

Eating

Drinking & Nightlife

Shopping

Vietnam's National Day CULTURAL

(2 Sep) Celebrated with a rally and fireworks at Ba Dinh Sq, in front of Ho Chi Minh's Mausoleum. There are also boat races on Hoan Kiem Lake.

Sleeping

Most budget and midrange visitors make for the busy Old Quarter and neighbouring Hoan Kiem Lake area for a glut of options. For luxury stays in calmer surrounds, continue south to the French Quarter or venture further afield.

Old Quarter

May De Ville Backpackers HOSTEL $

(Map p60; 04-3935 2468; www.maydevillebackpackershostelvietnam.com; 1 Hai Tuong, P Ta Hien; dm/d from US$6/25;) A short walk from Ta Hien's bars, May De Ville is one of Hanoi's best hostels. Dorms have firm beds but are spotless and there's also a movie room. Doubles are also good value.

Hanoi Hostel HOSTEL $

(Map p60; 0972 844 804; www.vietnam-hostel.com; 91c P Hang Ma; dm/d/tr US$6/25/30;

) This small, quiet, privately owned hostel is nicely located away from Hanoi's conglomeration of hostels. It's well run and clean, with tours on tap and plenty of information about onward travel to China or Laos.

Hanoi Rendezvous Hotel HOTEL $
(Map p60; 04-3828 5777; www.hanoirendezvoushotel.com; 31 P Hang Dieu; dm/s/d/tr US$10/27/30/40;) Deliciously close to several brilliant street-food places, Hanoi Rendezvous features spacious rooms and friendly staff, and organises well-run tours to Halong Bay, Cat Ba Island and Sapa.

★**Art Trendy Hotel** HOTEL $$
(Map p60; 04-3923 4294; www.hanoitrendyhotel.com; 6 Hang But; d/tw US$30/65;) Art Trendy enjoys a quiet location on the western edge of the Old Quarter. Rooms are stylish and relatively spacious, and there's a real can-do attitude from the exceptional and friendly staff. Each room has a laptop, and breakfast (included in the price) includes warm baguettes, omelettes, *pho* (noodle soup) and fresh fruit.

★**La Beaute de Hanoi** HOTEL $$
(Map p60; 04-3935 1626; www.la-beautehanoihotel.com; 15 Ngo Trung Yen; d/ste from US$41/62;) Opened in 2014, this 18-room hotel has a fresh white and cream palette with red accents, cable TV, fast wi-fi, and the larger suites and family rooms have small private balconies. It's in an excellent location on a quiet lane just a hop, skip and a jump from all the action on P Ma May.

Art Hotel HOTEL $$
(Map p60; 04-3923 3868; www.hanoiartboutiquehotel.com; 65 P Hang Dieu; s/d from US$25/35;) The young, friendly and welcoming crew at the Art Hotel make this well-located spot really stand out. Rooms are spacious with spotless bathrooms and wooden floors, and within a 30m radius you'll find some of Hanoi's best opportunities for partaking in the city's great street food.

★**La Siesta Hotel & Spa** BOUTIQUE HOTEL $$$
(Map p60; 04-3926 3641; www.hanoilasiestahotel.com; 94 P Ma May; d/ste from US$85/125;) La Siesta scores points not only for excellence in service and the quality of its rooms, which come in a variety of sizes (including some snazzy bilevel duplex configurations), but for its cracker location on P Ma May with scores of restaurants, bars and things to do on your very doorstep. If that's all a bit too hectic for you, chill out in the day spa.

Around Hoan Kiem Lake

Especen Hotel HOTEL $
(Map p56; 04-3824 4401; www.especen.vn; 28 P Tho Xuong; d US$13-25;) This budget hotel near St Joseph Cathedral has spacious and light rooms, excellent rates and an almost-tranquil location (by Old Quarter standards). There are two annexes within walking distance.

★**Golden Lotus Luxury Hotel** HOTEL $$
(Map p56; 04-3828 5888; www.goldenlotushotel.com.vn; 53-55 P Hang Trong; d/ste from $65/100;) Rooms at this stylish, atmospheric hotel boast wooden finishes, fine silk trims, local art and high technology. Standard rooms lack natural light, but oversized suites have generous terraces. And there's a rooftop pool! Its older, sister property, the Golden Lotus Hotel, is marginally cheaper, and you can still use the pool.

Golden Lotus Hotel HOTEL $$
(Map p56; 04-3938 0901; 32 P Hang Trong; d/ste from US$45/80;) This 12-storey hotel has pleasant rooms with dark woods, although rooms at the rear of the hotel lack natural light. Go for a suite if you can. Guests have access to the rooftop pool of neighbouring Golden Lotus Luxury Hotel.

Artisan Boutique Hotel BOUTIQUE HOTEL $$
(Map p60; 04-3938 1900; www.artisanboutiquehotel.com; 24 P Hang Hanh; d/ste from US$28/110;) One of the best features of this joint Australian and Vietnamese co-production a stone's throw from Hoan Kiem Lake is its on-the-ball staff: they're friendly and accommodating but not overbearing. Although some rooms could do with some love, all have great walk-in showers and tasteful design elements. The penthouse, if available, is a steal. A winner for location, service and price.

B&B Hanoi Hotel HOSTEL $$
(Map p60; 04-3935 2266; www.bbhanoihotel.com; 16 Hang Trung; d from US$30;) This clean, refurbished hotel has friendly, hard-working staff and is located a short walk to the northeastern shore of Hoan Kiem Lake. Fresh flowers, fruit and Vietnamese coffee give the place a homey feel.

★**Sofitel Metropole Hotel** HOTEL $$$
(Map p56; 04-3826 6919; www.sofitel.com; 15 P Ngo Quyen; r from US$220;) Hanoi's finest hotel is a slice of colonial history, with its restored French-colonial facade,

SCAMS

While there's no need to be paranoid, Hanoi is riddled with scams, many of them inextricably linked. Most problems involve budget hotels and tours, and occasionally things can get nasty. We've received reports of verbal aggression and threats of physical violence towards tourists who've decided against a hotel room or a tour. Stay calm and back away slowly or things could quickly flare up.

The taxi and minibus mafia at the airport shuttle unwitting tourists to the wrong hotel. Invariably, the hotel has copied the name of another popular property and will then attempt to appropriate as much of your money as possible. Taxi swindles are also becoming increasingly common. Try to avoid the taxis loitering at Hanoi's bus stations; many have superfast meters.

Some shoeshine boys and *cyclo* (pedicab or bicycle rickshaw) drivers attempt to add a zero or two to an agreed price for their services; stick to your guns and give them the amount you originally agreed.

Watch out for friendly, smooth-talking strangers approaching you around Hoan Kiem Lake. There are many variations, but sometimes these con artists pose as students and suggest a drink or a meal. Gay men are also targeted in this way. Your new friend may then suggest a visit to a karaoke bar, snake-meat restaurant or some other venue and before you know it you're presented with a bill for hundreds of dollars. Be careful and follow your instincts, as these crooks can seem quite charming.

We've also heard reports of male travellers being approached by women late at night in the Old Quarter, and then being forced at gunpoint by the women's male accomplices to visit multiple ATMs and empty their accounts. Keep your wits about you, and try to stay in a group if you're returning from a bar late at night.

mahogany-panelled reception rooms and haute cuisine. Rooms in the Heritage Wing offer unmatched colonial style, while the modern Opera Wing has sumptuous levels of comfort but not quite the same heritage character. Even if you're not staying here, pop in for a drink at the Bamboo Bar.

Other Areas

★Somerset Grand Hanoi APARTMENT $$
(Map p56; ☎04-3934 2342; www.somerset.com; 49 P Hai Ba Trung; apt from US$107; ❄📶🏊) Rates vary dramatically due to the nature and location of this sprawling apartment-hotel tower, but if you book ahead, bargains can be found. For the location and amenities alone, the selection of studio to three-bedroom apartments with full kitchen and laundry facilities can't be beat; perfect for traveling families.

★Conifer Boutique Hotel HOTEL $$
(Map p56; ☎04-3266 9999; www.coniferhotel.com.vn; 9 P Ly Dao Thanh; d from US$70; ❄📶) This is a fantastic little hotel tucked away on a pleasant side street in the French Quarter, opposite a wonderfully dilapidated French-colonial mansion. Rooms are on the smaller side, but functional and well thought out. Be sure to pay the extra for a street-facing room with a generous, enclosed balcony: perfect for watching afternoon storms.

★Fraser Suites Hanoi APARTMENT $$$
(☎04-3719 8877; http://hanoi.frasershospitality.com; 51 Xuan Dieu, Tay Ho; apt from US$187; 🏊) These sumptuous, fully equipped serviced apartments in buzzing lakeside Tay Ho are the perfect choice for the discerning traveller staying a few days or more. The gorgeous, landscaped outdoor pool is the city's most alluring.

Eating

Old Quarter

Quan An Ngon VIETNAMESE $
(Map p52; ☎04-3734 9777; www.ngonhanoi.com.vn; 34 P Phan Đinh Phung; meals 70,000-150,000d; ⏰11am-11pm) This small kitchen elevates Vietnamese street food in a beautiful indoor setting while keeping prices reasonable.

Highway 4 VIETNAMESE $$
(Map p60; ☎04-3926 0639; www.highway4.com; 3 P Hang Tre; meals 120,000-275,000d; ⏰noon-late) This is the original location of a restaurant family famed for adapting Vietnamese cuisine for Western palates, although with increasing popularity it becomes harder to please everybody. There are now four other branches in Hanoi: check the website for locations. Come for small plates to share, cold beer and funky decor.

Old Quarter

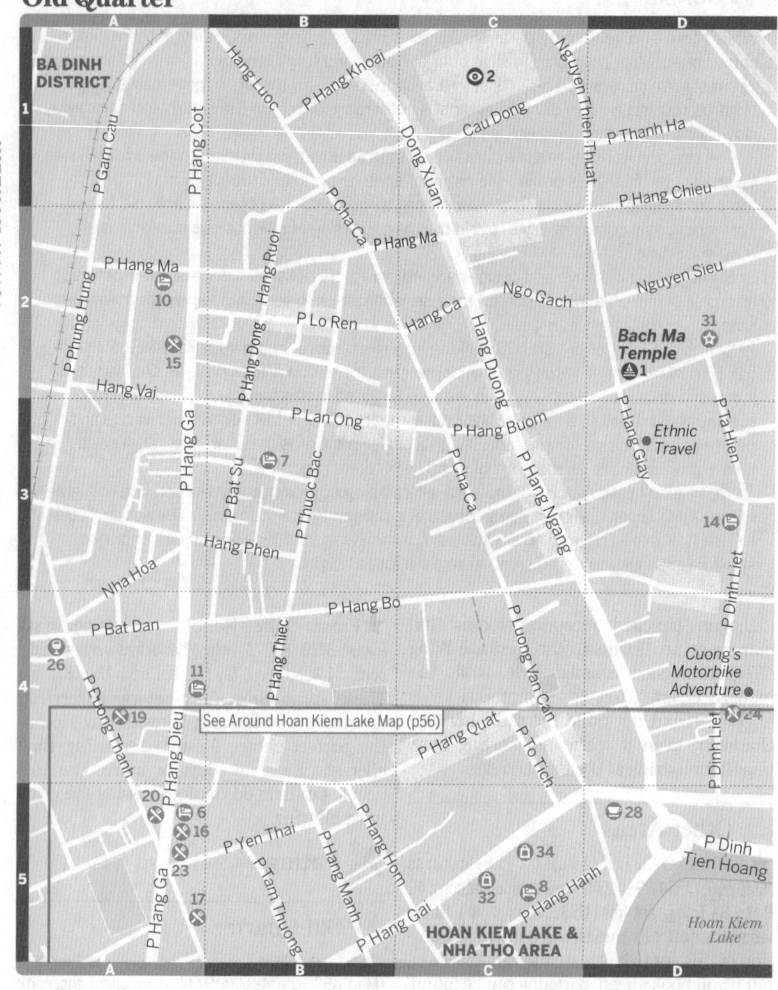

Cha Ca Thang Long VIETNAMESE **$$**
(Map p60; ☎04-3824 5115; www.chacathanglong.com; 19-31 P Duong Thanh; cha ca fish meal 180,000d; ⏲10am-3pm & 5-10pm) Bring along your DIY cooking skills and grill your own succulent fish with a little shrimp paste and plenty of herbs. *Cha ca* is an iconic Hanoi dish heavy on turmeric and dill, and while another nearby more-famous *cha ca* eatery gets all the tour-bus traffic, the food here is actually better.

Quan Bia Minh VIETNAMESE **$$**
(Map p60; 7a P Dinh Liet; meals 90,000-130,000d; ⏲8am-late) This *bia hoi* joint has evolved into an Old Quarter favourite with well-priced Vietnamese food and excellent service led by the eponymous Mrs Minh. Grab an outdoor table and a cold beer and watch the beautiful chaos unfold below.

Green Tangerine FUSION **$$**
(Map p60; ☎04-3825 1286; www.greentangerinehanoi.com; 48 P Hang Be; meals US$12-20; ⏲noon-late) Experience the mood and flavour of 1950s Indochina at this elegant restaurant located in a beautifully restored French-colonial house with a cobbled courtyard. The fusion French-Vietnamese cuisine is not always entirely successful, but it's still

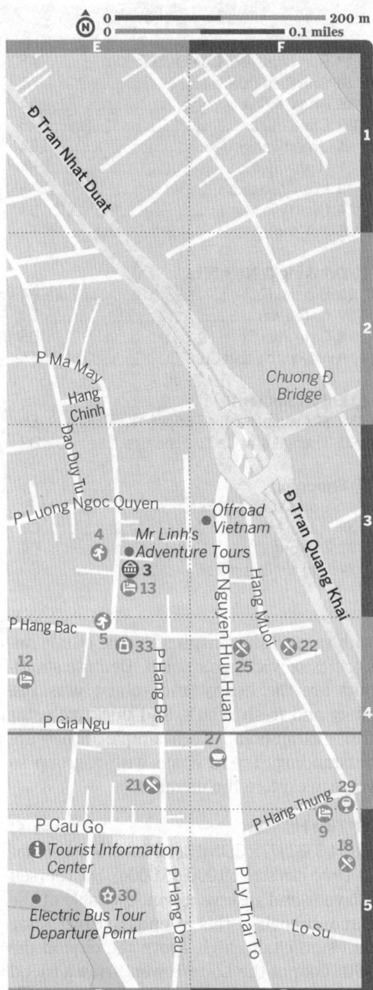

worth popping in for coffee or a drink. Two-course lunches (218,000d) are good value.

Around Hoan Kiem Lake

Jalus Vegan Kitchen VEGAN $
(Map p56; ☎04-3266 9730; 2nd fl, 46 Hang Trong; meals 30,000-60,000d; ⏱8am-10pm Tue-Sun; ❄📶✍) Pull up a pine table at this modern, hidden restaurant and try some delicious coconut and chia smoothies and meat-free takes on burgers, or pizza, quiche and ravioli that use vegan cheese. There are definite Vietnamese twists with lemongrass and spice, and sometimes special all-Vietnamese menus.

★**Hanoi Social Club** CAFE $$
(Map p56; ☎04-3938 2117; www.facebook.com/TheHanoiSocialClub; 6 Hoi Vu; meals 95,000-175,000d; ⏱8am-11pm) On three funky levels with retro furniture, the Hanoi Social Club is the city's most cosmopolitan cafe and an artist hub. Dishes include potato fritters with chorizo for breakfast, and pasta, burgers and wraps for lunch or dinner. Vegetarian options feature a tasty mango curry, and the quiet laneway location is a good spot for an end-of-day coffee, beer or wine. It also hosts regular gigs and events. Check its Facebook page for what's on.

Madame Hien VIETNAMESE $$$
(Map p56; ☎04-3938 1588; www.facebook.com/madamehienrestaurant; 15 Chan Cam; meals 95,000-350,000d, set menus from 365,000d; ⏱11am-10pm) Housed in a restored 19th-century villa, Madame Hien is a tribute to French chef Didier Corlu's Vietnamese grandmother. Look forward to elegant versions of traditional Hanoi street food, with the '36 Streets' fixed menu (535,000d) an easygoing place to kick off your culinary knowledge of the city.

Other Areas

★**Moto-san Uber Noodle** NOODLES $
(Map p56; ☎04-6680 9124; 4 P Ly Dao Thanh; meals 45,000-70,000d) Brainchild of Hanoi artist, journalist and designer Nguyen Qui Duc (of Tadioto fame, p64), this wonderful noodle stall seats eight eager eaters. The menu is simple: miso, shōyu (soy) or *shio* (salty) ramen, and spicy *banh my thit ko* (stewed pork) sandwiches with killer hot sauce (optional) à la central Vietnam. Sake and beer are, of course, readily available.

Quan An Ngon VIETNAMESE $
(Map p52; ☎04-3942 8162; www.ngonhanoi.com.vn; 18 Phan Boi Chau; meals 70,000-150,000d; ⏱7am-11pm) This branch of a number of small same-named kitchens turns out street-food specialities from across Vietnam. Try and visit just outside the busy lunch and dinner periods, or consider Quan An Ngon's newest branch in a lovely French villa just north of the Old Quarter (p59).

Oasis DELI $
(☎04-3719 1196; www.oasishanoi.net; 24 P Xuan Dieu; ⏱8am-6pm) Italian-owned deli with excellent bread, cheese and salami, as well

Old Quarter

Top Sights
1 Bach Ma Temple ... D2

Sights
2 Dong Xuan Market ... C1
3 Memorial House ... E3

Activities, Courses & Tours
4 Handspan Adventure Travel ... E3
5 Vega Travel ... E4

Sleeping
6 Art Hotel ... A5
7 Art Trendy Hotel ... B3
8 Artisan Boutique Hotel ... C5
9 B&B Hanoi Hotel ... F5
10 Hanoi Hostel ... A2
11 Hanoi Rendezvous Hotel ... A4
12 La Beaute de Hanoi ... E4
13 La Siesta Hotel & Spa ... E3
14 May De Ville Backpackers ... D3

Eating
15 Banh Cuon ... A2
16 Bun Bo Nam Bo ... A5
17 Bun Cha Nem Cua Be Dac Kim ... A5
18 Bun Rieu Cua ... F5
19 Cha Ca Thang Long ... A4
20 Che ... A5
21 Green Tangerine ... E4
22 Highway 4 ... F4
23 Mien Xao Luon ... A5
24 Quan Bia Minh ... D4
25 Xoi Yen ... F4

Drinking & Nightlife
26 Bia Hoi Ha Noi ... A4
27 Cafe Lam ... F4
28 Cafe Pho Co ... D5
29 Nha Hang Lan Chin ... F4

Entertainment
30 Municipal Water Puppet Theatre ... E5
31 Thang Long Ca Tru Theatre ... D2

Shopping
Dong Xuan Market ... (see 2)
32 Hanoi Moment ... C5
33 Mekong+ ... E4
34 Tan My Design ... C5

as homemade pasta and sauces. It's north of central Hanoi in the Tay Ho restaurant strip on P Xuan Dieu.

Fanny Ice Cream ICE CREAM $
(Map p56; www.fanny.com.vn; 51 P Ly Thuong Kiet; ice creams from 49,000d; 8am-9pm) The place for French-style ice creams and sorbets in Hanoi. During the right season try the *com,* a delightful local flavour extracted from young sticky rice; other innovative flavours include ginger and green tea.

Bun Cha Huong Lien VIETNAMESE $
(Map p52; 24 P Le Van Hu; meals to 90,000d; 10am-8pm) Bun Cha Huong Lien was launched into stardom thanks to Barack Obama, who dined here with celebrity chef Anthony Bourdain in May 2016. Customers line up to sample the grilled-pork-and-noodle delicacy while staff call out 'Obama *bun cha*!' to passers-by. The 'Combo Obama' gets you a bowl of *bun cha,* fried seafood roll and Hanoi beer for US$3.80. While this isn't the best *bun cha* in the city, it's worth a visit for the experience.

★**Chim Sao** VIETNAMESE $$
(Map p52; 04-3976 0633; www.chimsao.com; 63-65 Ngo Hue; meals 45,000-120,000d; 11am-11pm;) Sit at tables downstairs or grab a more traditional spot on the floor upstairs and discover excellent Vietnamese food, with some dishes inspired by the ethnic minorities of Vietnam's north. Definite standouts are the hearty and robust sausages, zingy and fresh salads, and duck with star fruit (carambola). Even simple dishes are outstanding. Try to come with a group so you can explore the menu fully.

★**Tim Ho Wan** DIM SUM $$
(04-3333 1725; 36th fl, Lotte Tower, 54 P Lieu Giai, Ba Dinh; dim sum 69,000-95,000d) Do yourself a favour and reserve a window table at the Hanoi branch of this legendary Hong Kong dim sum chain, high above the city on the 36th floor of the Lotte Tower. Bring a friend or six and an empty stomach, and we guarantee you won't regret it.

★**Maison de Tet Decor** CAFE $$
(0966 611 383; http://tet-lifestyle-collection.com; 156 Tua Hoa, Nghi Tam, Tay Ho; meals from 180,000d; 7am-10pm) Sumptuous, healthy and organic (wherever possible) wholefoods are presented with aplomb in this, one of Hanoi's loveliest settings, an expansive, airy villa overlooking lake Ho Tay.

Nha Hang Ngon VIETNAMESE $$
(Map p52; 04-3933 6133; 26a P Tran Hung Dao; meals 80,000-130,000d; 7am-9.30pm) With a focus on authentic flavours from around Vietnam, this joint gets popular with locals and

visitors alike. It's street food taken off the street and presented in a delightful restored French villa and courtyard.

★**La Badiane** INTERNATIONAL $$$
(Map p52; ☎04-3942 4509; www.labadiane-hanoi.com; 10 Nam Ngu; meals from 280,000d; ⏰11.30am-9.45pm) This stylish bistro is set in a restored whitewashed French villa arrayed around a breezy central courtyard. French cuisine underpins the menu – La Badiane translates as 'star anise' – but Asian and Mediterranean flavours also feature. Menu highlights include sea-bass tagliatelle with smoked paprika, and prawn bisque with

HANOI STREET EATS: OUR TOP 10

Deciphering Hanoi's street-food scene can be bewildering, but it's worth persevering and diving in. The city's best food definitely comes from the scores of vendors crowding the city's pavements with smoking charcoal burners, tiny blue plastic stools and expectant queues of canny locals. Many of the stalls have been operating for decades, and often they offer just one dish. After that long perfecting their recipes, it's little wonder the food can be sensational. Note that opening hours may change and prices vary. Expect to pay 25,000d to 70,000d, depending on what you devour.

Old Quarter

Bun Cha Nem Cua Be Dac Kim (Map p60; 67 P Duong Thanh; ⏰11am-7pm) Visiting Hanoi and not eating *bun cha* (barbecued pork with rice vermicelli) with a side of *nem cua be* (sea-crab spring rolls) should be classed as a capital offence. This is an excellent spot to try this street-food classic.

Banh Cuon (Map p60; 14 P Hang Ga; ⏰8am-3pm) Don't even bother ordering here; just squeeze in and a plate of gossamer-light *banh cuon* (steamed rice crêpes filled with minced pork, mushrooms and shrimp) will be placed in front of you.

Bun Bo Nam Bo (Map p60; 67 P Hang Dieu; ⏰11am-10pm) *Bun bo nam bo* (dry noodles with beef) is a dish from southern Vietnam, but it's certainly travelled north well. Mix in bean sprouts, garlic, lemongrass and green mango for a filling treat.

Xoi Yen (Map p60; cnr P Nguyen Huu Huan & P Hang Mam; ⏰7am-11pm) Equally good for breakfast or as a hangover cure, Xoi Yen specialises in sticky rice topped with goodies, including sweet Asian sausage, gooey fried egg and slow-cooked pork.

Mien Xao Luon (Map p60; 87 P Hang Dieu; ⏰7am-2pm) Head to this humble stall trimmed with minimountains of fried eels for three different ways of eating the crisp little morsels. Try them stir-fried in vermicelli with egg, bean sprouts and shallots.

Che (Map p60; 76 P Hang Dieu; ⏰7am-3pm) In winter try *che banh troi tau*, sweet mung beans with sesame and ginger, or in summer *che thap nam* with coconut milk, crushed peanuts, lotus seeds and dried apples.

Around Hoan Kiem Lake

Bun Rieu Cua (Map p60; 40 P Hang Tre; ⏰7-10:30am) Get to this incredibly popular spot early, as its sole dish of *bun rieu cua* (noodle soup with beef in a spicy crab broth) is only served for a couple of hours from 7am. A Hanoi classic.

Banh Goi (Map p56; 52 P Ly Quoc Su; ⏰10am-7pm) Nestled under a banyan tree near St Joseph Cathedral, this humble stall turns out *banh goi*, moreish deep-fried pastries crammed with pork, vermicelli and mushrooms.

Other Areas

Banh Mi Pho Hue (Map p52; 118 P Hue; ⏰8am-9pm) *Banh mi* (sandwich) vendors abound in Hanoi, although the phenomenon is less popular than in Ho Chi Minh City. This place is usually packed with locals, which is always a good sign.

Pho Thin (Map p52; 13 P Lo Duc; ⏰5am-9pm) Negotiate your way to the rear of this narrow, rustic establishment and sit down to some excellent *pho bo* (beef noodle soup). A classic Hanoi experience that hasn't changed in decades.

wasabi tomato bruschetta. Three-course lunches from 375,000d are excellent value.

★Old Hanoi VIETNAMESE $$$

(Map p52; ☎04-3747 8337; www.oldhanoi.com; 4 Ton That Thiep; meals 90,000-179,000d; ⊙11am-2pm & 5-10pm) This sophisticated eatery in a restored French-colonial villa with a pleasant casual courtyard outside and starched white tablecloths inside was once host to celebrity chef Gordon Ramsay. It serves traditional Hanoian and Vietnamese specialities with aplomb; you'll enjoy the selection and find the best value for money if you dine in a group.

Drinking & Nightlife

Hanoi's eclectic drinking scene features grungy dive bars, Western-style pubs, sleek lounge bars, cafes and hundreds of *bia hoi* joints. Travellers flock to noisy P Ta Hien in the Old Quarter, and Ngo Bao Khanh near the northwest edge of Hoan Kiem Lake. Expect more activity Friday to Sunday, when the Old Quarter is allowed to stay open beyond midnight, until 2am.

Tadioto BAR

(Map p56; ☎04-6680 9124; www.tadioto.com; 24b P Tong Dan; ⊙7am-midnight) Nguyen Qui Duc's unofficial clubhouse for the underground arts scene's latest incarnation is this dark and quirky colonial bar in the French Quarter. Obligatory red accents (seat covers, wrought-iron grill on the doors), reworkings of art deco furniture and plenty of recycled ironwork feature heavily. The highlight of the cool cocktail list is the sweet mojito.

Manzi Art Space BAR

(Map p52; ☎04-3716 3397; www.facebook.com/manzihanoi; 14 Phan Huy Ich; ⊙cafe 9am-midnight, shop 10am-6pm) Part cool art gallery, part chic cafe and bar, Manzi is worth seeking out north of the Old Quarter. A restored French villa hosts diverse exhibitions of painting, sculpture and photography, and the compact courtyard garden is perfect for a coffee or glass of wine. There's also a small shop selling works by contemporary Vietnamese artists.

Cama ATK BAR

(Map p52; www.cama-atk.com; 73 P Mai Hac De; ⊙6pm-midnight Wed-Sat) Make the trek south of Hoan Kiem Lake to this bohemian bar run by Hanoi's Club for Art and Music Appreciation (CAMA). Check the website for what's on, which includes everything from Japanese funk and dancehall DJs through to experimental short films and reggae sound systems.

GC Pub GAY & LESBIAN

(Map p56; ☎04-3825 0499; 7 P Ngo Bao Khanh; ⊙noon-midnight) Hanoi's long-standing, only established gay bar, and unofficial LGBT HQ, might seem small and vanilla midweek, but it gets pumped on weekend nights. The reasonably priced drinks and chatty bar staff make it popular with a mixed local crowd and it's easy for gay visitors to drop by, especially those fond of playing pool.

Café Duy Tri CAFE

(☎04-3829 1386; 43a P Yen Phu) In the same location since 1936, this caffeine-infused labyrinth is a Hanoi classic. You'll feel like Gulliver as you negotiate the tiny ladders and stairways to reach the 3rd-floor balcony. Order the delicious *caphe sua chua* (iced coffee with yoghurt), and you may have discovered your new favourite summertime drink. You'll find P Yen Phu a couple of blocks east of Truc Bach Lake north of the Old Quarter.

Cong Caphe CAFE

(Map p52; http://congcaphe.com; 152 P Trieu Viet Vuong) Settle in to the eclectic beats and kitsch Communist memorabilia at Cong Caphe with a *caphe sua da* (iced coffee with condensed milk). There's a bunch of branches around the city; a full list appears on its website.

Cafe Pho Co CAFE

(Map p60; 4th fl, 11 P Hang Gai) One of Hanoi's best-kept secrets, this place has plum views over Hoan Kiem Lake. Enter through the silk shop, and continue through the antique-bedecked courtyard up to the top floor for the mother of all vistas. You'll need to order coffee and snacks before tackling the final winding staircase. For something deliciously different, try the *caphe trung da,* coffee topped with a silky-smooth beaten egg yolk.

Bar Betta BAR

(Map p52; ☎0165 897 9073; www.facebook.com/barbetta34; 34 Cao Ba Quat; ⊙9am-midnight) Retro decor and a jazz-age vibe combine with good cocktails, coffee and cool music in this breezy French-colonial villa. Two-for-one beers are available from 3pm to 7pm, and the rooftop terrace (from 8pm) is essential on a sultry Hanoi night.

Summit Lounge BAR

(Map p52; 20th fl, Sofitel Plaza, 1 Đ Thanh Nien; ⊙4.30pm-late) Enjoy fabulous views from this 20th-floor lounge bar. Order a (pricey) cocktail or beer, grab a spot on the outside deck, and take in Truc Bach Lake and the city beyond.

Bia Hoi Ha Noi
BIA HOI

(Map p60; 2 P Duong Thanh) A *bia hoi* junction that is local in flavour is where P Nha Hoa meets P Duong Thanh on the western edge of the Old Quarter. Bia Hoi Ha Noi does the best spare ribs in town for a little something to go with the beer.

Nha Hang Lan Chin
BIA HOI

(Map p60; cnr P Hang Tre & P Hang Thung) A good spot to sample the brew is Nha Hang Lan Chin, one of the most popular local lunch spots in town.

Cafe Lam
CAFE

(Map p60; ☎04-3824 5940; www.cafelam.com; 60 P Nguyen Huu Huan) A classic cafe that's been around for years – long enough to build up a compact gallery of paintings left behind by talented patrons who couldn't afford to pay their tabs during the American War. These days you're just as likely to spy Converse-wearing and Vespa-riding bright young things refuelling on wickedly strong *caphe den* (black coffee).

Hanoi House
CAFE

(Map p56; ☎04-2348 9789; 2nd fl, 47a P Ly Quoc Su; ⏰8.30am-11pm; 📶) A chic and bohemian cafe with superb upstairs views of St Joseph Cathedral. Chill out on the impossibly slim balcony with excellent juices and Hanoi's best ginger tea.

☆ Entertainment

Municipal Water Puppet Theatre
THEATRE

(Map p60; ☎04-3824 9494; www.thanglongwaterpuppet.org; 57b P Dinh Tien Hoang; adult/child 100,000/60,000d; ⏰four afternoon performances daily, also 9.30am Sun) Water-puppetry shows are a real treat for children. Multilingual programs allow the audience to read up on each vignette as it's performed. Although there are multiple performances daily, book well ahead, especially from October to April.

Thang Long Ca Tru Theatre
LIVE MUSIC

(Map p60; ☎0122 326 6897; www.catruthanglong.com; 28 P Hang Buom; 210,000d; ⏰8pm Tue, Thu & Sat) Concerts of traditional Vietnamese music are held in this intimate restored house in the Old Quarter. *Ca tru* is indigenous to the north of Vietnam, and concerts feature a selection of the 100 or so *ca tru* melodies. The art form has also been recognised as an endangered 'intangible cultural heritage' by Unesco.

Shopping

In the historic Old Quarter, you'll find clothes, cosmetics, sunglasses, musical instruments, plumbing supplies, herbal medicines, jewellery, religious offerings, spices, coffee and much more. Assume that almost all brand-label merchandise you see here is fake.

Art & Handicrafts

Hanoi has a burgeoning art scene and you can pick up an original work on canvas by a local artist from as little as US$40 in any one of the private galleries concentrated on P Trang Tien, between Hoan Kiem Lake and the Opera House. For Vietnamese handicrafts, including textiles and lacquerware, head to the stores along P Hang Gai, P To Tich, P Hang Khai and P Cau Go. P Hang Gai and its continuation, P Hang Bong, are good places to look for embroidered tablecloths, T-shirts and wall hangings.

Mai Gallery
ART

(Map p52; ☎04-3828 5854; www.maigallery-vietnam.com; 113 P Hang Bong; ⏰9am-7pm) Run by resident artist Mai, this is a good place to learn more about Vietnamese art before making a purchase.

Mekong+
ARTS & CRAFTS

(Map p60; ☎04-3926 4831; https://mekong-plus.com; 13 P Hang Bac; ⏰8am-8pm) Beautiful quilts handcrafted by rural women working in a not-for-profit community-development program.

Hanoi Moment
ARTS & CRAFTS

(Map p60; ☎04-3926 3630; www.hanoimoment.vn; 101 P Hang Gai; ⏰8am-9pm) An oasis of classier Vietnamese souvenirs, including lacquerware and jewellery, amid the T-shirt overkill of nearby stores. Bamboo, stone and porcelain are also used to great effect.

Books

Thang Long
BOOKS

(Map p56; 53-55 P Trang Tien; ⏰9am-6pm) One of the biggest bookshops in town, with English and French titles, international newspapers and magazines, and a good selection of titles on the history of Hanoi.

Clothing & Silk Products

P Hang Gai is a fine place to buy silk and have clothes custom-made.

Tan My Design
CLOTHING

(Map p60; ☎04-3938 1154; www.tanmydesign.com; 61 P Hang Gai; ⏰8am-8pm) Stylish clothing, jewellery and accessories, with the added bonus of a funky cafe when you need a break from shopping. The homewares and bed linen are definitely worth a look.

Three Trees FASHION & ACCESSORIES
(Map p56; ☎04-3928 8725; 15 P Nha Tho; ⊙9am-7pm) Stunning, very unusual designer jewellery, including many delicate necklaces, which make special gifts.

Markets

Dong Xuan Market MARKET
(Map p60; Dong Xuan; ⊙6am-7pm) A large, non-touristy market located in the Old Quarter of Hanoi, 900m north of Hoan Kiem Lake. There are hundreds of stalls here, and it's a fascinating place to explore if you want to catch a flavour of Hanoian street life. The area around it also has loads of bustling shops.

Hom Market MARKET
(Map p52; cnr P Hué & P Tran Xuan Soan; ⊙6am-5pm) On the northeast corner of P Hué and P Tran Xuan Soan, this is a good general-purpose market and excellent for local fabric, if you plan to have clothes made.

Information

EMERGENCY

The emergency services should be able to transfer you to an English-speaker.

AMBULANCE	☎115
FIRE	☎114
POLICE	☎113

INTERNET ACCESS

Most budget and midrange hotels offer free access to a computer and the internet: at fancier places in the rooms, at cheaper places in the lobby. Free wi-fi access is virtually ubiquitous in the city's cafes and bars, but dedicated internet cafes are largely a thing of the past, so pack a tablet or smartphone. Phone SIM cards with unlimited data are available from many travel agencies for under US$10.

MEDICAL SERVICES

National Institute of Traditional Medicine (Map p52; ☎04-3826 3616; 29 P Nguyen Binh Khiem; ⊙7.30-11.30am & 1.30-4pm) For Vietnamese-style medical solutions.

SOS International Clinic (☎04-3826 4545; www.internationalsos.com/locations/asia-pacific/vietnam; 51 Xuan Dieu; ⊙24hr) English, French, German and Japanese are spoken and there is a dental clinic. It's 5km north of central Hanoi near Ho Tay lake.

Viet Duc Hospital (Benh Vien Viet Duc; Map p56; ☎04-3825 3531; 40 P Trang Thi; ⊙24hr) Old Quarter unit for emergency surgery; the doctors here speak English, French and German.

MONEY

Hanoi has many ATMs, and on the main roads around Hoan Kiem Lake are international banks where you can change money. Some ATMs limit the amount you can withdraw to only 3,000,000d. ANZ, Citibank and HSBC ATMs are usually more generous.

Vietcombank (Map p56; ☎04-3826 8045; 198 Đ Tran Quang Khai) This towering headquarters is located a few blocks east of Hoan Kiem Lake. It has an ATM and offers most currency services.

POST

DHL (Map p52; ☎04-3733 2086; www.dhl.com.vn; 49 P Nguyen Thai Hoc)

Domestic Post Office (Buu Dien Trung Vong; Map p56; ☎04-3825 7036; 75 P Dinh Tien Hoang; ⊙7am-9pm) For internal postal services in Vietnam; also sells philatelic items.

International Postal Office (Map p56; ☎04-3825 2030; cnr P Dinh Tien Hoang & P Dinh Le; ⊙7am-8pm) The entrance is to the right of the domestic post office.

TOURIST INFORMATION

In the cafes and bars of the Old Quarter, look for the excellent local magazine *The Word*.

Tourist Information Center (Map p60; ☎04-3926 3366; P Dinh Tien Hoang; ⊙9am-7pm) City maps and brochures, but privately run with an emphasis on selling tours. In the cafes and bars of the Old Quarter, look for the excellent local magazine *The Word*.

TRAVEL AGENCIES

Hanoi has hundreds of travel agencies and plenty are of ill repute. When you book accommodation at properties, check there are no strings attached and that it's not mandatory to book tours at the same business also.

Trips or tickets booked through guesthouses and hotels are usually of a very basic standard. Dealing directly with tour operators will give you a better idea of what you'll get for your money. It's worth seeking out an outifit that sticks to small groups, offers trips away from the main tourist trail and uses its own vehicles.

Beware of clones of popular agencies; check addresses and websites carefully.

Cuong's Motorbike Adventure (Map p60; ☎0913 518 772; www.cuongs-motorbike-adventure.com; 46 P Gia Ngu; ⊙8am-6pm) This highly recommended operator conducts motorbike tours all around the north. Look out for the bright-pink Minsk motorbike.

Ethnic Travel (Map p60; ☎04-3926 1951; www.ethnictravel.com.vn; 35 P Hang Giay; ⊙9am-6pm Mon-Sat, 10am-5pm Sun) Off-the-beaten-track trips across the north in small groups. Some trips are low-impact using public transport and homestays, others are activity based (including hiking, cycling and cooking). Offers Bai Tu Long Bay tours and also has an office in Sapa.

Handspan Adventure Travel (Map p60; ☎04-3926 2828; www.handspan.com; 78 P Ma May; ⊙9am-8pm) Sea-kayaking trips in Halong Bay and around Cat Ba Island, and 4WD, mountain-biking and trekking tours. Other options include remote areas such as Moc Chau and Ba Be National Park, community-based tourism projects in northern Vietnam, and the *Treasure Junk*, the only true sailing craft cruising Halong Bay. Handspan also has offices in Sapa and Ho Chi Minh City.

Marco Polo Travel (Map p52; ☎04-3997 5136; www.marcopoloasia.com; Room 107b, N14-49 Nguyen Khoai, Hanoi; ⊙9am-5pm) Runs kayaking trips around Halong Bay and Ba Be Lakes. Also good mountain-biking trips and hiking expeditions around the north of Vietnam.

Mr Linh's Adventure Tours (Map p60; ☎04-642 5420; www.mrlinhadventure.com; 83 P Ma May) A professional, well-meaning outfit specialising in off-the-beaten-track and adventure travel in Vietnam's remote north. Ba Be Lakes homestay trips are recommended.

Vega Travel (Map p60; ☎04-3926 2092; www.vegatravel.vn; cnr P Ma May & 24a P Hang Bac; ⊙8am-8pm) Family-owned-and-operated company offering well-run tours around the north and throughout Vietnam. Excellent guides and drivers, and it also financially supports ethnic minority kindergartens and schools around Sapa and Bac Ha. Halong Bay tours on a private boat are excellent value and bespoke touring is available.

Getting There & Away

AIR

Hanoi has fewer direct international flights than Ho Chi Minh City, but with excellent connections through Singapore, Hong Kong or Bangkok you can get almost anywhere easily.

Jetstar Airways (☎1900 1550; www.jetstar.com) This Australian budget airline has very affordable fares, and serves 16 airports in Vietnam.

Vietjet Air (☎1900 1886; www.vietjetair.com) A privately owned airline with an expanding number of internal and international flights.

Vietnam Airlines (Map p56; ☎1900 545 486; www.vietnamair.com.vn; 25 P Trang Thi; ⊙8am-5pm Mon-Fri) Links Hanoi to destinations throughout Vietnam. Popular routes include Hanoi to Dalat, Danang, Dien Bien Phu, Ho Chi Minh City, Hue and Nha Trang, all served daily.

BUS

Hanoi has four main long-distance bus stations of interest to travellers. They are fairly well organised, with ticket offices, fixed prices and schedules, though can be crowded and at times chaotic. Consider buying tickets the day before you plan to travel on the longer distance routes to ensure a seat. It's often easier to book through a travel agent, but you'll obviously be charged a commission. Tourist-style minibuses can be booked through most hotels and travel agents. Popular destinations include Halong Bay and Sapa. Prices are usually about 30% to 40% higher than the regular public bus, but include a hotel pick-up.

Many open-ticket tours through Vietnam start or finish in Hanoi.

Gia Lam Bus Station (☎04-3827 1569; 132 Ngo Gia Kham) Has buses to the northeast of Hanoi. It's located 3km northeast of the city centre, across the Song Hong (Red River).

Giap Bat Bus Station (☎04-3864 1467; Đ Giai Phong) Serves points south of Hanoi, and offers more comfortable sleeper buses. It is 7km south of Hanoi train station.

My Dinh Bus Station (☎04-3768 5549; Đ Pham Hung) This station 7km west of the city provides services to the west and the north, including sleeper buses to Dien Bien Phu for onward travel to Laos. It's also the best option for buses to Ha Giang and Mai Chau.

Nuoc Nam Bus Station Services Cat Ba Island. Đ Ngoc Hoi in Hoang Mai District, about 2km south of Giap Bat.

CAR & MOTORCYCLE

Car rental is best arranged via a travel agency or hotel. Rates almost always include a driver, a necessity as many roads and turnings are not signposted. The roads in the north are in OK shape, but narrow lanes, potholes and blind corners equate to an average speed of 35km/h to 40km/h. During the rainy season, expect serious delays as landslides are cleared and bridges repaired. You'll definitely need a 4WD.

Rates start at about US$110 a day (including a driver and petrol). Make sure the driver's expenses are covered in the rate you're quoted.

Offroad Vietnam (Map p60; ☎0913 047 509; www.offroadvietnam.com; 36 P Nguyen Huu Huan; ⊙8am-6pm Mon-Sat) For reliable Honda trail bikes (from US$20 daily) and road bikes (US$17). The number of rental bikes is limited, so booking ahead is recommended. Offroad's main business is running excellent tours, mainly dealing with travellers from English-speaking countries. Tours are either semiguided, excluding meals and accommodation, or all-inclusive fully guided tours.

TRAIN

Tickets can be purchased from most travel agencies, and their commission for booking usually offsets the language hassle of buying tickets directly from the train station. They also often have preferential access to tickets to popular destinations like Hue, Ho Chi Minh City and Lao Cai (for Sapa).

If you've already booked for one of the private carriages to Sapa, you'll need to exchange your voucher for a ticket at the appropriate tour desk at Tran Quy Cap Station.

The main **Hanoi Train Station** (Ga Hang Co, Train Station A; ☎ 04-3825 3949; 120 Đ Le Duan; ⏱ ticket office 7.30am-12.30pm & 1.30-7.30pm) is at the western end of P Tran Hung Dao; trains from here go to southern destinations. Foreigners can buy tickets for southbound trains at counter 2, where the staff speak English. We recommend buying your tickets at least one day before departure to ensure a seat or sleeper.

Eastbound (Haiphong) trains depart from Gia Lam Train Station on the eastern side of the Song Hong (Red River), or Long Bien on the western (city) side of the river. Be sure to check which station. Trains to Nanning, China, also depart from here. Note that you cannot board international Nanning-bound trains in Lang Son or Dong Dang.

To the right of the main entrance of the Hanoi train station is a separate ticket office for northbound trains to Lao Cai (for Sapa) and China. Tickets to China must be bought from counter 13. Note that all northbound trains leave from a separate station (just behind) called **Tran Quy Cap Station** (Train Station B; ☎ 04-3825 2628; P Tran Quy Cap; ⏱ ticket office 4-6am & 4-10pm).

Getting Around

TO/FROM THE AIRPORT

Express bus 86 (30,000d, one hour, every 20 to 30 minutes, 5.10am to 10.30pm) is a new comfortable service that runs from Hanoi train station, and the north side of Hoan Kiem Lake

BUSES FROM HANOI

Gia Lam Bus station

DESTINATION	DURATION (HR)	COST (D)	FREQUENCY
Ba Be	5	150,000	Noon
Bai Chay (Halong City)	3½	130,000	Every 30min
Haiphong	2	70,000	Frequent
Lang Son	5	90,000	Every 45min
Lao Cai	9	320,000	6.30pm, 7pm (sleeper)
Mong Cai	9	230,000	Hourly (approx)
Sapa	10	250,000	6.30pm, 7pm (sleeper)

Giap Bat Bus Station

DESTINATION	DURATION (HR)	COST (D)	FREQUENCY
Dalat	35	470,000	9am, 11am
Danang	12	380,000	Frequent sleepers noon-6.30pm
Dong Ha	8	380,000	Frequent sleepers noon-6.30pm
Dong Hoi	8	380,000	Frequent sleepers noon-6.30pm
Hue	10	380,000	Frequent sleepers noon-6.30pm
Nha Trang	32	710,000	10am, 3pm, 6pm
Ninh Binh	2	70,000	Frequent 7am-6pm

My Dinh Bus Station

DESTINATION	DURATION (HR)	COST (D)	FREQUENCY
Cao Bang	10	120,000	Every 45min
Dien Bien Phu	8	365,000	11am, 6pm
Ha Giang	8	200,000	Frequent
Hoa Binh	2	40,000	Frequent
Son La	7	190,000	Frequent

TRAINS FROM HANOI

DESTINATION	HARD SEAT	SOFT SEAT	HARD SLEEPER	SOFT SLEEPER
Danang	From 430,000d	From 630,000d	From 782,000d	From 954,000d
HCMC	From 790,000d	From 1,160,000d	From 1,340,000d	From 1,692,000d
Hue	From 374,000d	From 545,000d	From 675,000d	From 894,000d
Nha Trang	From 692,000d	From 998,000d	From 1,240,000d	From 1,647,000d

outside the tourist information centre, to the international airport.

Airport Taxi (☎04-3873 3333) charges US$20 for a taxi ride door-to-door to or from Noi Bai International Airport. They do *not* require that you pay the toll for the bridge you cross en route. Some other taxi drivers require that you pay the toll, so ask first.

BICYCLE

Many Old Quarter guesthouses and cafes rent bikes for about US$3 per day. Good luck with that traffic – be safe!

BUS

Hanoi has an extensive public bus system, though few tourists take advantage of the rock-bottom fares (3000d).

CYCLO

A few cyclo drivers still frequent the Old Quarter, and if you're only going a short distance, it's a great way to experience the city (despite the fumes). Settle on a price first and make sure it is not just per person. Aim to pay around 50,000d for a shortish journey; night rides are more.

ELECTRIC BUS

Hanoi's golf-buggy-esque ecofriendly **Electric Bus** (Dong Xuan; per buggy/6 passengers per hour 300,000d; ⏲8.30am-10pm) tour is actually a pretty good way to get your bearings in the city. It traverses a network of 14 stops in the Old Quarter and around Hoan Kiem Lake, parting the flow of motorbikes and pedestrians like a slow-moving white dragon.

MOTORBIKE TAXI

You won't have any trouble finding a *xe om* (motorbike taxi) in Hanoi. An average journey in the city centre costs around 15,000d to 20,000d, while a trip further to Ho Chi Minh's Mausoleum is around 35,000d to 40,000d. For two or more people, a metered taxi is usually cheaper than a convoy of *xe om*.

TAXI

Flag fall is around 20,000d, which takes you 1km to 2km, then every kilometre after costs around 15,000d. Some operators have high-speed meters, so use one of the more reliable companies: **Hanoi Taxi** (☎04-3853 5353), **Mai Linh** (☎04-3822 2666), **Thanh Nga Taxi** (☎04-3821 5215) or **Van Xuan** (☎04-3822 2888).

AROUND HANOI

Ninh Binh

Ninh Binh is a good base for exploring quintessentially Vietnamese limestone scenery including Tam Coc, and for hiking Cuc Phuong National Park to geek out at its 1000-year-old tree. Few Western tourists head here, but many Vietnamese flock to the region, which has made many of its attractions heavily commercialised.

Sleeping & Eating

Xuan Hoa Hotel 1 HOTEL $

(☎030-388 0970; www.xuanhoahotel.com; 31d P Minh Khai; r US$15-30; ❄@🛜) A friendly operation with rooms across two buildings. The original Xuan Hoa Hotel 1 has a room where guests can leave luggage or have a free shower after checkout. Before dining here, have a beer on the edge of the compact lake. Free transport to the bus or train station is available too. Nearby Xuan Hoa Hotel 2 has balconies overlooking a quiet neighbourhood.

Xuan Hoa Hotel 2 HOTEL $

(☎030-388 0970; www.xuanhoahotel.com; 3d P Minh Khai; r US$6-15; ⊖❄@🛜) A friendly option with quiet, comfortable and clean rooms. Meals are served in the nearby Xuan Hoa Hotel 1.

★**Nguyen Shack** BUNGALOW $$

(☎030-361 8678; www.nguyenshack.com; near Mua Cave, Hoa Lu district; bungalows US$22-55; 🛜) With a riverside setting around 5km from Tam Coc, Nguyen Shack's easygoing lazy-days thatched bungalows are the perfect antidote to the bustle of Hanoi. Lie in a hammock, drop a fishing rod off your rustic terrace, or grab a bicycle and go exploring. There's an on-site restaurant and bar too.

★**Tam Coc Garden** BOUTIQUE HOTEL $$$

(☎096-603 2555; www.tamcocgarden.com; Hai Nham village, Hoa Lu district; d US$145-175; P❄🛜≋) The most Zen place to stay around Ninh Binh is this lovely boutique hotel. In a private location and with a sea of rice paddies at your balcony, Tam Coc Garden has eight stone and timber bungalows set in a luxuriant garden, and other hotel rooms. Following a day of cycling or exploring nearby attractions, there's the compact pool to look forward to.

Trung Tuyet VIETNAMESE $
(14 Đ Hoang Hoa Tham; meals 40,000-75,000d; 7am-10pm;) Expect filling portions, options for vegetarians, and a warm welcome from the host family at this busy little place that's popular with travellers. The owners will even drop you off at the nearby train station if you're kicking on after your meal.

Information

Hospital (Benh Vien Da Khoa Tinh; 030-387 1030; Đ Hai Thuong Lan Ong; 24hr) Main city hospital.

Main Post Office (Đ Tran Hung Dao; 7am-6pm Mon-Fri, 8am-1pm Sat)

Vietin Bank & ATM (Đ Tran Hung Dao; 7am-2.30pm Mon-Fri, 7.30am-noon Sat) One of two branches on this street.

Getting There & Away

Public buses leave every 15 minutes until 7pm for the Giap Bat bus station in Hanoi (from 65,000d, 2½ hours), and there are regular buses to Haiphong (85,000d, three hours, every 1½ hours) and twice-daily connections to Halong City (120,000d, 3½ hours).

Ninh Binh is also a stop for open-tour buses between Hanoi (US$6, two hours) and Hue (US$14, 10 hours). Hotel pick-ups and drop-offs are available.

The train station is a scheduled stop on the main north–south line between Hanoi and Ho Chi Minh City (HCMC) but travelling by road is faster.

Bus Station (Đ Le Dai Hanh) Ninh Binh's bus station is located near the Lim Bridge, just below the overpass to Phat Diem.

Train Station (Ga Ninh Binh; 1 Đ Hoang Hoa Tham) The recently built, green-roofed train station is a scheduled stop for Reunification Express trains, with destinations including Hanoi, Vinh and Hue.

Tam Coc

With breathtaking limestone outcrops amid serene rice paddies along the Ngo Dong River, Tam Coc (Three Caves) is best appreciated on a languorous rowing **boat ride** (boat base fare 150,000d plus adult/child 120,000/60,000d; 7am-3.30pm), with the soundtrack of the river lapping against the oars. In fact a rowboat is the only way to see 'Halong Bay on the Rice Paddies'; be prepare for no shade on board.

Consider visiting early morning or late afternoon when things are quieter. Rowers use their feet to propel the oars, as the route (around two hours) negotiates Tam Coc's three caves. There's a maximum of two people per boat.

It's 9km southwest of Ninh Binh. Ninh Binh hotels run tours, or make your own way by bicycle or motorbike. Hotels can advise on beautiful back roads. Hanoi tour operators offer day trips from around US$25.

Cuc Phuong National Park

One of Vietnam's most important protected areas, Cuc Phuong spans two limestone mountain ranges and three provinces. In 1962 Ho Chi Minh declared this Vietnam's first national park, saying: 'Forest is gold'. Wildlife is notoriously elusive, so manage your expectations accordingly.

The park is home to the minority Muong people, whom the government relocated from the park's central valley to its western edge in the late 1980s

Sights

Cuc Phuong National Park NATIONAL PARK
(030-384 8006; www.cucphuongtourism.com; adult/child 40,000/20,000d) Established in 1962, this national park is one of Vietnam's most important protected areas. Though wildlife has suffered a precipitous decline in Vietnam in recent decades, the park's 222 sq km of primary tropical forest remains home to an amazing variety of animal and plant life: 307 species of bird, 133 species of mammal, 122 species of reptile, 2000 plant species and counting.

Endangered Primate Rescue Center WILDLIFE RESERVE
(030-384 8002; www.eprc.asia; 30,000d; 9-11.30am & 1.30-4pm) The Endangered Primate Rescue Center is supervised by the Frankfurt Zoological Society, and is home to around 150 monkeys: 12 kinds of langur, three species of gibbon and two loris. All the centre's animals were either bred here or rescued from illegal traders. Tours with a nature-conservation focus are on offer. Your entry ticket also allows access to the Turtle Conservation Center.

The centre has bred more than 100 offspring in all, from nine different species, including the world's first captive-born Cat

Ba langur and grey-shanked douc langur. Because it's difficult to rehabilitate primates once they've lived in cages, only 30 or so gibbons and langurs have been released into semiwild areas (one site is adjacent) since the centre opened in 1993. Your entry ticket also allows access to the Turtle Conservation Center.

Turtle Conservation Center WILDLIFE RESERVE
(☎030-384 8090; www.asianturtleprogram.org; 30,000d; ⏲9-11am & 2-4.45pm) The Turtle Conservation Center houses more than 1000 terrestrial, semiaquatic and aquatic turtles representing 20 of Vietnam's 25 native species. Many have been confiscated from smugglers who have been driven by demand from the domestic and Chinese markets – eating turtle is thought to aid longevity. Visitors can see turtles in tanks and incubators, as well as in ponds in near-wild settings. Signs in English about the endangered turtles are informative. Your entry ticket also allows access to the Endangered Primate Rescue Center.

The centre successfully breeds and releases turtles from 11 different species, including six native turtles. Around 60 turtles are released back into the wild each year.

Sleeping & Eating

There is accommodation in the park, and one luxury resort nearby. It's advisable to book for weekends and public holidays. Camping (per person US$4) is also available at the visitor centre or Mac Lake. There are simple restaurants and snack shops at the park headquarters and Mac Lake.

Getting There & Away

Cuc Phuong National Park is 45km west of Ninh Binh. A direct bus from Hanoi's Giap Bat southern bus station departs at 3pm, with a return bus to Hanoi at 9am. From Ninh Binh, catch a *xe om* or taxi to the park.

Hanoi tour companies offer trips to Cuc Phuong, usually combined with other sights in the Ninh Binh area.

WORTH A TRIP

BAI TU LONG BAY

The spectacular islands of Bai Tu Long Bay, immediately northeast of Halong Bay, form Bai Tu Long National Park (100,000d) and are every bit as beautiful as its famous neighbour. In some ways it's actually more stunning, since it's only in its initial stages as a destination for travellers. The bay and its islands are still unpolluted and relatively undeveloped. As with Halong Bay, the best way to experience the full limestone-pinnacle-scattered seascape is by cruise.

Hanoi travel agencies, including Ethnic Travel (p66), run boat trips into the Bai Tu Long from US$115 for one night. Charter boats can also be arranged to Bai Tu Long Bay from Halong City's Bai Chay Tourist Wharf; rates start at around 300,000d per hour and the trip there takes about five hours.

NORTHERN VIETNAM

Vistas. This is Vietnam's big-sky country; a place of rippling mountains, cascading rice terraces and the winnowed-out karst topography for which the region is famed.

Halong Bay's seascape of limestone towers is the view everyone's here to see, but the karst connection continues inland, to Ba Be National Park, until it segues into the evergreen hills of the northwest highlands.

Not to be outdone by the scenery, northern Vietnam's cultural kaleidoscope is just as diverse. In this heartland of hill-tribe culture, villages snuggle between paddy-field patchworks outside of Sapa, and the scarlet headdresses of the Dzao and the indigo fabrics of the Black Hmong add dizzying colour to chaotic highland markets.

Halong Bay

Majestic and mysterious, inspiring and imperious, Halong Bay's 3000 or more incredible islands rise from the emerald waters of the Gulf of Tonkin. This mystical seascape of limestone islets is a vision of breathtaking beauty.

Sights

★**Halong Bay** NATIONAL PARK
(150,000d) Towering limestone pillars and tiny islets topped by forest rise from the emerald waters of the Gulf of Tonkin. Designated a World Heritage Site in 1994, Halong Bay's spectacular scatter of islands, dotted with wind- and wave-eroded grottoes, is a vision of ethereal beauty and, unsurprisingly, northern Vietnam's number-one tourism hub.

The most popular way to experience the bay's astounding vistas is by taking an overnight cruise.

DON'T MISS

CRUISING THE KARSTS

The most popular way to experience Halong Bay's karst scenery is on a cruise. It can be a false economy to sign up for an ultracheap tour. Spend a little more and enjoy the experience a whole lot more. At the very least, check basic on-board safety standards. Life jackets should be provided.

Most cruise-tours include return transport from Hanoi, Halong Bay entrance fees and meals. A decent overnight tour usually includes kayaking with a guide. Drinks and even water are extra, payable in cash only.

Tours sold out of Hanoi start from a rock-bottom US$60 per person for a dodgy day trip, and can rise to around US$220 for two nights. For around US$110 to US$130, you should get a worthwhile overnight cruise, though you need more time to stray far from Halong City. Many cruises are marketed as 'two-day' trips but are actually overnight tours.

Cruising the karsts aboard a luxury Chinese-style junk is hard to beat. But be aware that paying top dollar doesn't necessarily compute into heading away from the crowds. If you want to experience less-crowded karst views, consider cruises focussed on Lan Ha Bay, near Cat Ba Island, which is more untouched and has sublimely sandy beaches.

Halong translates as 'Where the Dragon Descends into the Sea' and legend tells that this mystical seascape was created when a great mountain dragon charged towards the coast, its flailing tail gouging out valleys and crevasses. As the creature plunged into the sea, the area filled with water, leaving only the pinnacles visible. The geological explanation of karst erosion may be more prosaic, but doesn't make this seascape any less poetic.

Halong Bay attracts visitors year-round with peak season between late May and early August. January to March is often cool and drizzly, and the ensuing fog can make visibility low, but adds bags of eerie atmosphere. From May to September tropical storms are frequent, and year-round tourist boats sometimes need to alter their itineraries, depending on the weather.

Activities & Tours

Vega Travel BOATING
(Map p60; ☎04-3926 2092; www.vegatravel.vn; cnr P Ma May & 24a P Hang Bac, Hanoi; overnight tour s/d cabin from US$130/240; ⏲8am-8pm) Good-value overnight tours of Halong Bay, with comfortably fitted-out cabins and two-night tours that also explore Lan Ha Bay and Cat Ba Island, including kayaking, cycling and hiking.

Handspan Adventure Travel BOATING
(Map p60; ☎04-3926 2828; www.handspan.com; 78 P Ma May, Hanoi; overnight cruise d cabin from US$354; ⏲9am-8pm) Handspan's Treasure Junk is the only true sailing ship operating on the bay. That means you get to meander peacefully through the karsts without the constant hum of a diesel engine. Crack open a cold Bia Hanoi and you'll be in heaven.

Indochina Sails BOATING
(☎04-3984 2362; www.indochinasails.com; overnight tour d cabin from US$478) Cruise Halong on a traditional junk kitted out to a three-star standard. Indochina operates two 42m junks and one smaller craft; all have attractive wooden cabins and great viewing decks. Tours include transfer from Hanoi.

Information

Halong Bay Tourist Information Centre
(☎033-384 7481; www.halong.org.vn; Bai Chay Tourist Wharf, Đ Halong; ⏲7am-4pm) The official Halong Bay Tourist Information Centre is at Bai Chay Tourist Wharf in Halong City. Here you'll find English-speaking staff and excellent maps (20,000d) of the Halong Bay area.

Halong City

Development has not been kind to Halong City (Bai Chay). Despite enjoying a stunning position on the cusp of Halong Bay, this is a gritty town with pockets of bland high-rise hotel development dotting the shoreline.

Many travellers opt to skip Halong City completely, preferring to spend a night in Halong Bay itself. Increased competition for a dwindling clientele means budget hotel rates are some of the cheapest in Vietnam. Chinese and Korean visitors are now prevalent, preferring to enjoy terra firma attractions like casinos and karaoke after a day exploring the bay.

Activities

Boat Day Trips BOATING

(Đ Halong; ⏲7am-6pm) From Tuan Chau Ferry Pier there are two main boat day trips of Halong Bay. Route One (100,000d, four hours) potters around the waters of nearby islands visiting the caves of Hang Dau Go and Hang Thien Cung. Route Two (150,000d, six hours) heads further into the bay to Hang Sung Sot and Dao Titop.

Sleeping

Light Hotel HOTEL $

(☎033-384 8518; www.thelighthalong.vn; 108a Đ Vuon Dao; r 350,000-450,000d; ❄📶) The good-sized, modern and superclean rooms here are excellent value. Chuck in the fact that some of the helpful staff speak English and you've got Halong City's best budget find.

Halong Backpacker Hostel HOSTEL $

(☎033-361 9333; www.halongbackpackerhostel.com; 41 Đ Anh Dao; dm/tw US$5/17; ❄📶) This hostel (don't confuse it with the 'Halong Backpacker's Hostel' on Đ Vuon Dao) has small, light-filled six-bed dorms and a lively downstairs bar.

Novotel HOTEL $$$

(☎033-384 8108; www.novotelhalongbay.com; 160 Đ Halong; r from US$110; ⊖❄@📶≋) The Novotel fuses Asian and Japanese influences with contemporary details. The rooms are simply stunning, with teak floors, marble bathrooms and sliding screens to divide living areas. Facilities include an oval infinity pool and a great restaurant.

Getting There & Away

All buses leave from Bai Chay bus station, 6km south of central Bai Chay. For Tam Coc, hop on the Ninh Binh–bound bus. Note that many buses to Halong City will be marked 'Bai Chay' rather than 'Halong City'.

Cat Ba Island

Rugged, craggy and jungle-clad Cat Ba, the largest island in Halong Bay, has experienced a tourism surge in recent years. The central hub of Cat Ba Town is now framed by a chain of low-rise concrete hotels along its once-lovely bay, but the rest of the island is largely untouched and as wild as ever. With idyllic Lan Ha Bay just offshore you'll soon overlook Cat Ba Town's overdevelopment.

Almost half of Cat Ba Island (total area of 354 sq km) and 90 sq km of the adjacent waters were declared a national park in 1986 to protect the island's diverse ecosystems. Most of the coastline consists of rocky cliffs, but there are some sandy beaches and tiny fishing villages hidden away in small coves.

Lakes, waterfalls and grottoes dot the spectacular limestone hills, the highest rising 331m above sea level. The island's largest body of water is Ech Lake (3 hectares).

Sights

★Lan Ha Bay BAY

(30,000d) Lying south and east of Cat Ba Town, the 300 or so karst islands and limestone outcrops of Lan Ha are just as beautiful as those of Halong Bay and have the additional attraction of numerous white-sand beaches.

Due to being a fair way from Halong City, not so many tourist boats venture here, meaning Lan Ha Bay has a more isolated appeal. Sailing and kayak trips here are best organised in Cat Ba Town.

Cannon Fort HISTORIC SITE

(40,000d; ⏲sunrise-sunset) For one of the best views in Vietnam – no, we're not

BUSES FROM HALONG CITY

DESTINATION	COST (D)	DURATION (HR)	FREQUENCY
Cai Rong (Van Don Island)	35,000	1½	every 30 minutes 8am-6pm
Haiphong	60,000	2	frequent 6.20am-5pm
Hanoi	100,000	4	frequent 5.45am-6pm
Lang Son	110,000	5½	6am, 11.45am, 12.15pm
Mong Cai	80,000	4	every 40 minutes 6.20am-3pm
Ninh Binh	100,000	4	5.30am, 11.30am
Sapa	400,000	12	7am, 6pm

kidding – head to Cannon Fort where there are astounding panoramas of Cat Ba Island's jungle hills rolling down to colourful tangles of fishing boats in the harbour and out to the karst-punctuated sea beyond.

The entrance gate is a steep 10-minute walk from Cat Ba Town and from the gate it's another stiff 20-minute walk to the fort, or take a *xe om* from Cat Ba Town (15,000d).

Cat Ba National Park NATIONAL PARK
(☎031-216 350; 30,000d; ⏰sunrise-sunset) Cat Ba's beautiful national park is home to 32 types of mammal, including most of the world's 65 remaining golden-headed langur, the world's most endangered primate. There are some good hiking trails here, including a hard-core 18km route up to a mountain summit. To reach the park headquarters at Trung Trang, hop on the green QH public bus from the docks at Cat Ba Town, hire a *xe om* (around 80,000d one way) or rent a motorbike for the day.

A guide is not mandatory but is definitely recommended to help you make sense of the verdant canopy of trees. Most visitors opt to visit the park on an organised tour – Cat Ba Ventures (p75) runs good day-trips here – but you can also arrange guides with the rangers at the park headquarters. Within the park the multichambered Hang Trung Trang (Trung Trang Cave) is easily accessible, but you will need to contact a ranger to make sure it's open. Bring a torch (flashlight).

The challenging 18km hiking trail in the park takes six hours and is best done with a guide. Boat or bus transport to the trailhead and a boat to get back to town also need to be arranged. Again, rangers at the headquarters can help with this or speak to Cat Ba Ventures or Asia Outdoors (p75) in Cat Ba Town. Take proper hiking shoes, a raincoat and a generous supply of water for this hike. Independent hikers can buy basic snacks at the kiosks in Viet Hai (a remote minority village just outside the park boundary), which is where many hiking groups stop for lunch. This is not an easy walk, and is much harder and more slippery after rain. There are shorter hiking options that are less strenuous.

Many hikes end at Viet Hai from where taxi boats shuttle back to Ben Beo Pier (about 200,000d per boat). A shared public boat (50,000d per person) departs from Ben Beo at 6am on weekdays and 7am on weekends.

Of the mammals present in the park, the more commonly seen include macaques, deer, civets and several species of squirrel, including the giant black squirrel. Seventy bird species have been spotted here, including hawks, hornbills and cuckoos. Cat Ba also lies on a major migration route for waterfowl that feed and roost on the beaches in the mangrove forests. Over a thousand species of plant have been recorded in the park, including 118 trees and 160 plants with medicinal value.

Cat Ba Island Market MARKET
(⏰7am-7pm) The market at the northern end of Cat Ba Town's harbour is a great local affair with twitching crabs, jumbo shrimp and pyramids of fresh fruit.

Ho Chi Minh Monument MONUMENT
(off Đ Nui Ngoc) This monument stands up on imaginatively named Mountain No 1; the hillock opposite the pier in Cat Ba Town.

Activities

Cat Ba is a superb base for adventure sports – on the island, and in, on and over the water.

Mountain Biking

Hotels can arrange Chinese mountain bikes (around US$6 per day). Blue Swimmer rents better-quality mountain bikes for US$15 per day.

One possible route traverses the heart of the island, past Hospital Cave down to the west coast's mangroves and crab farms, and then in a loop back to Cat Ba Town past tidal mu flats and deserted beaches.

Rock Climbing

If you've ever been tempted to climb, Cat Ba Island and Lan Ha Bay are superb places to go for it – the karst cliffs here offer exceptional climbing amid stunning scenery. The limestone is not too sharp and quite friendly

KAYAKING

A kayak among the karsts is an option on most Halong Bay tours. Count on about an hour's paddling, often including negotiating your way through karst grottoes and around lagoons, or to a floating village in the bay.

If you're really keen on kayaking, contact Handspan Adventure Travel (p67) in Hanoi or Blue Swimmer on Cat Ba Island, both of which run professionally organised trips and have qualified guides. Trips are operated in less touristed Lan Ha Bay.

on the hands, and climbing is almost always possible, rain or shine.

A few inexperienced locals may offer climbing excursions to new arrivals on Cat Ba, but beginners should sign up with the experienced crew at Asia Outdoors, who pioneered climbing here.

Most climbers in Cat Ba are complete novices, but as the instruction is excellent, many leave Cat Ba completely bitten by the bug.

Sailing & Kayaking

Plenty of hotels in Cat Ba Town and travel companies rent kayaks (half-day around US$8) ideal for exploring the Cat Ba coast independently. Due to shifting, strong currents, exploring the karst formations of Lan Ha Bay by kayak is best done with a guide, particularly if you're not an experienced kayaker.

Trekking

Most of Cat Ba Island consists of protected tropical forest. Cat Ba National Park has the most hiking opportunities.

Tours

Boat trips around Lan Ha Bay are offered by nearly every hotel on Cat Ba Island. Typical prices start at around US$80 for overnight tours, but it is usually worth spending a bit more as we receive unfavourable feedback – cramped conditions and dodgy food – about some of these trips.

★Asia Outdoors CLIMBING

(☎031-368 8450; www.asiaoutdoors.com.vn; Noble House, Đ 1-4, Cat Ba Town; half-/full-day climbing US$67/86; ⏲8am-7.30pm) The pioneers of climbing in Vietnam, Asia Outdoors is a one-stop shop for adventurous travellers. Climbing is its real expertise, with fully licensed and certified instructors leading trips, but it also offers climbing and kayaking packages with an overnight on its boat (US$132). It has also launched stand-up paddle-boarding (SUP) trips (US$37).

Advanced climbers can hire gear here, talk shop and pick up a copy of *Vietnam: A Climber's Guide* (US$20) by Asia Outdoors' Erik Ferjentsik, which describes climbs and has some great tips about Cat Ba too.

Cat Ba Ventures BOATING

(☎031-388 8755, 0912 467 016; www.catbaventures.com; 223 Đ 1-4, Cat Ba Town; overnight boat tour per person from US$130; ⏲8am-7pm) Locally owned and operated company offering boat trips around Lan Ha and Halong Bays, one-day kayaking trips (US$30) and guided hikes in Cat Ba National Park. Excellent service from Mr Tung is reinforced by multiple reader recommendations. These guys are a font of knowledge on everything Cat Ba and a great source of information on onward transport options.

Blue Swimmer ADVENTURE

(☎031-368 8237, 0915 063 737; www.blueswimmersailing.com; Ben Beo Harbour; overnight sailing trip per person from US$182; ⏲8am-6pm) This environmentally conscious outfit was established by Vinh, one of the founders of respected tour operator Handspan Adventure Travel. Superb sailing and kayaking trips, trekking and mountain-biking excursions (some with overnight homestay accommodation) are offered. Check it out at Ben Beo Harbour or at its booking office in Cat Ba Town at the Green Bamboo Forest restaurant.

Sleeping

Most basic hotels are clustered on (or just off) the waterfront in Cat Ba Town. There are also some interesting options on other parts of Cat Ba Island and offshore on isolated islands in Lan Ha Bay. Room rates fluctuate wildly; from June to July they can double. In August some hotels continue to hike prices while others just raise rates on Friday and Saturday nights.

Cat Ba Town

Cat Ba Sea View HOTEL $

(☎031 388 8201; www.catbaseaviewhotel.com; 220 Đ 1-4; r US$15, with sea view US$25; ❄📶) Neat-as-a-pin, light-coloured rooms are further spruced up by snazzy fake-flower decor. All are a good size, though the seafront ones are by far the most spacious. Each floor has a teensy communal balcony so you can take in the harbour vistas without shelling out extra for your room.

Cat Ba Central Hostel HOSTEL $

(☎0913-311 006; http://fb.me/CatbaCentralHostel; 240 Đ 1-4; dm/tw US$6/13; 🚭❄📶) Owner Kong is your English-speaking host at this friendly hostel that's fast becoming the heart of Cat Ba's backpacker action. Beds in the clean dorms (one with 28 beds and one with 14 beds and two with six beds, including a female-only room) come with lockers built into beds, and power points.

Cat Ba Dream HOTEL $

(☎031-388 8274; www.catbadream.com; 226 Đ 1-4; r US$13, with sea view US$15; ❄📶) Service may be a bit lacklustre, but Cat Ba Dream has smart, small rooms at the back, and larger sea-facing ones with killer views of the bay (room 606 is the best). Ignore the rack rates, which are five times those listed here.

Thu Ha HOTEL $

(031-388 8343; Đ 1-4; r US$12-17;) This small family-run place has basically furnished, clean rooms. Negotiate hard for a front room and wake up to sea views.

Sea Pearl Hotel HOTEL $$

(031-368 8567; www.seapearlcatbahotel.com.vn; 219 Đ 1-4; r US$36-54;) Although we'd like to see the bathrooms be refurbished at this price, the Sea Pearl is a solid choice. Classically styled rooms are comfortable and a decent size, and staff are professional and helpful.

Hung Long Harbour Hotel HOTEL $$

(031-626 9269; www.hunglonghotel.vn; 268 Đ 1-4; r US$45-65; P) At the quieter southeastern end of Cat Ba Town, the Hung Long Harbour has very spacious rooms, many with excellent views. Don't bother upgrading to a superior room, the standards are the ones with balconies.

Cat Ba Beach Resort RESORT $$$

(031-388 8686; www.catbabeachresort.com; Cat Co 2; bungalows from around US$105;) Rimming the furthest sandy edge of Cat Co 2 beach, the dinky stone-and-thatch bungalows of this resort sit within a manicured lawn dotted with palm trees. Windsurfing and a sauna are all on tap, and there's a breezy open-sided bar-restaurant with water views.

Around Cat Ba Island

Ancient House Homestay HOMESTAY $

(0915 063 737, 0916 645 858; www.catba-homestay.com; Ang Soi village; shared house per person US$15, private house per 2 people US$60;) Located around 3km from Cat Ba Town, down an unmarked alley in the village of Ang Soi, this heritage house was carefully moved here from the outskirts of Hanoi. Antiques fill the high-ceilinged interior and outside are well-tended gardens. It's not set up to receive independent travellers and is best booked through Blue Swimmer (p75). Lunch and dinner set menus (US$9 per person) are available on request.

Whisper of Nature BUNGALOW $$

(031-265 7678; www.vietbungalow.com; Viet Hai village; dm/d incl breakfast US$15/30;) Whisper of Nature is a simple place for nature lovers to kick back and enjoy some downtime. Little concrete-and-thatch bungalows are set on the edge of the forest, surrounded by trees and vegetable gardens. Getting here is an adventure in itself, with the final stage a bicycle ride through lush scenery. Ask about transport when you book.

Eating

You can't beat the ambience-factor for feasting on seafood at a floating restaurant. For a cheap feed, head to the food stalls in front of the market, or one block back from the waterfront on the cross street that links the loop of Đ Nui Ngoc.

Green Bamboo Forest VIETNAMESE $

(Đ 1-4; meals 50,000-150,000d; 7am-11pm;) Friendly and well-run waterfront eatery that also acts as a booking office for Blue Swimmer (p75). There's some good seafood on offer and myriad rice and noodle dishes. The quieter location is also a bonus.

Buddha Belly VEGETARIAN $

(Đ 1-4; meals 30,000-80,000d; 10am-9pm;) Right next to Cat Ba market, this bamboo-clad place serves up lots of vegetable and tofu goodness, and doesn't use any dairy or eggs (or much seasoning) so is a top choice for vegans as well. Its 30,000d daily-changing set menu is excellent value.

Green Mango INTERNATIONAL $$

(031-388 7151; www.greenmango.vn; Đ 1-4; meals 110,000-220,000d; 8am-10pm;) With a menu traipsing from steaks, to seafood, and over to Italy for pasta and pizza (with a small selection of Asian dishes as well), Green Mango is a great dinner choice, with friendly staff. It's also a chilled-out spot for a glass of wine or cocktail.

Quang Anh SEAFOOD $$

(031-388 8485; Ben Beo Pier; meals from 200,000d) At this 'floating' fish-farm-meets-restaurant at Ben Beo Pier, select your seafood from the pen and it will be grilled, fried or steamed in no time. Prices go by weight and type of seafood; you can eat your fill of a selection of fish for around 200,000d per person.

Vien Duong VIETNAMESE $$

(12 Đ Nui Ngoc; meals from 120,000d; 11am-11pm) One of the most popular of the seafood spots lining Đ Nui Ngoc, and often heaving with Vietnamese tourists diving into local crab, squid and steaming seafood hotpots. Definitely not the place to come if you're looking for a quiet night.

Drinking & Nightlife

Oasis Bar BAR

(Đ 1-4; noon-11pm;) A free-use pool table, smiley staff and a location slap in the centre of the seafront strip make Oasis a popular spot to plonk yourself down for a beer or two. The menu is pretty decent if you're feeling peckish.

Rose Bar BAR

(15 Đ Nui Ngoc; noon-3am;) With cheap (US$2) cocktails, loads of happy-hour specials and *shisha* (water pipes), Rose Bar ticks all the boxes for backpacker fun a long way from home.

Bia Hoi Stalls BIA HOI

(Đ 1-4) For a cheap and cheerful night out, head to the *bia hoi* stalls near the entrance to Cat Ba Town's fishing harbour.

Information

For tourist information, the best impartial advice is at Asia Outdoors (p75). Cat Ba Ventures (p75) is also very helpful. Both companies have websites with local information.

Getting There & Away

Cat Ba's public **QH Green Bus** (20,000d) trundles between Cat Ba Harbour and Gia Luan Harbour in the north of the island, passing the national park headquarters en route.

The easiest way to/from Hanoi is on transport operated by **Hoang Long Bus Company** (031-268 8008; http://hoanglongasia.com; Đ 1-4; ticket 250,000d). A bus takes you to Haiphong, followed by a minibus to nearby Dinh Vu port, then a 40-minute ferry to Cai Vieng Harbour (also known as Phu Long) on Cat Ba Island. From there, another minibus whisks passengers to Cat Ba Town.

Between May and September buses depart Hanoi's Nuoc Nam bus station (in the city's south) at 5.20am, 7.20am, 11.20am and 1.20pm, and return from Cat Ba Town at 7.15am, 9.15am, 1.15pm and 3.15pm. From October to April buses leave Hanoi at 7.20am and 11.20am; and depart Cat Ba Town at 9.15am and 1.15pm.

Haiphong-bound hydrofoils depart Cat Ba Town Pier at 8am, 10am, 2pm and 4pm (250,000d, one hour).

Getting Around

In summer a tourist train (basically oversized golf carts) whizzes between Cat Ba Town to Cat Co 1 and 2 (10,000d per person).

A good way to explore is on two wheels, and bicycle and motorbike rentals are available from most Cat Ba hotels (both around US$5 per day). If you're heading out to the beaches or national park, pay the parking fee for security.

Haiphong

Northern Vietnam's most approachable city centre has a distinctly laid-back air with its tree-lined boulevards host to a bundle of graceful colonial-era buildings. The central area buzzes with dinky cafes where tables spill out onto the pavements – perfect for people-watching. Most travellers only use Haiphong as a transport hop between the bus from Hanoi and the ferry to Cat Ba Island.

Sleeping & Eating

Bao Anh Hotel HOTEL $

(031-382 3406; www.hotelbaoanh.com; 20 P Minh Khai; d/tw incl breakfast 400,000/600,000d;) Refurbished with lots of white paint and new white linen, the Bao Anh has a great location in a leafy street framed by plane trees and buzzy cafes. It's a short walk to good beer places if you're after something stronger. The friendly English-speaking reception is definitely open to negotiation.

Com Vietnam VIETNAMESE $

(031-384 1698; 4a P Hoang Van Thu; meals 40,000-60,000d; 11am-9pm) This restaurant hits the spot for its affordable local seafood and Vietnamese specialities. Diminutive, unpretentious and with a small patio.

★**Nam Giao** VIETNAMESE $$

(22 P Le Dai Hanh; meals 90,000-300,000d; 7am-11.30pm) Haiphong's most atmospheric dining choice is hidden within this dilapidated colonial building. Rooms are an artful clutter of Asian art, old carved cabinets and antiques, while the small but well-executed menu includes an aromatic herby sea bass wrapped in banana leaf and a succulent caramelised pork belly cooked in a clay pot.

Phono Box CAFE $$

(79 P Dien Bien Phu; meals 100,000-250,000d; 9am-11pm;) With its brick-wall interior displaying old music paraphernalia and a jazzy soundtrack, Phono Box is a hip hang-out for coffee and beer lovers that also serves up a European-style menu of steaks and other meaty offerings.

Information

Cafes on P Minh Khai have free wi-fi. ATMs dot the city centre.

Getting There & Away

Cat Bi airport is 6km southeast of central Haiphong. Daily flights to Ho Chi Minh City and

Danang are offered by **Jetstar Pacific Airways** (☎1900 1550; www.jetstar.com), **Vietnam Airlines** (☎031-3810 890; www.vietnamair.com.vn; 30 P Hoang Van Thu) and the largest carrier at Cat Bi, **VietJet** (☎1900 1886; www.vietjetair.com). A new runway now handles occasional domestic flights to Phu Quoc, Dalat and Nha Trang; and soon international destinations China, Japan, Thailand and South Korea.

A fast hydrofoil departs Haiphong's Ben Binh Harbour at 7am, 9am, 1pm and 3pm, and goes straight to Cat Ba Town Pier (250,000d, one hour).

Haiphong has three long-distance bus stations:

Lac Long Bus Station (P Cu Chinh Lan) The closest bus station to Haiphong city centre and very convenient for those connecting with the Cat Ba boats at nearby Ben Binh Harbour. Operates services heading north from Haiphong and to Hanoi.

Niem Nghia Bus Station (Đ Tran Nguyen Han) Serves destinations south of Haiphong, such as to Ninh Binh (120,000d, 3½ hours, every 30 minutes). Also serves Hanoi (70,000d, two hours, frequent).

Thuong Ly Bus Station (☎031-352 9558; http://benxethuongly.net) This newer station northwest of the centre has buses to Hanoi (70,000d, two hours, frequent).

Note that the Tam Bac Bus Station has closed down and its Hanoi routes pushed to other stations, including Thuong Ly station, a 10-minute ride away.

A slow spur-line service travels daily from Haiphong Train Station to Hanoi's Long Bien station (48,000d, 2½ hours, 6.05am, 8.55am, 2.55pm and 6.40pm).

Ba Be National Park

Boasting mountains high, rivers deep, and waterfalls, lakes and caves, **Ba Be National Park** (☎0281-389 4721; per person 25,000d; ⏲5am-9pm) is an incredibly scenic spot. The region is surrounded by steep peaks (up to 1554m), while the park contains tropical rainforest with hundreds of plant species. Wildlife in the forest includes bears, monkeys, bats and lots of butterflies. The region is home to 13 tribal villages, most belonging to the Tay minority, who live in stilt homes, plus smaller numbers of Dzao and Hmong.

Often referred to as the Ba Be Lakes, Ba Be National Park was established in 1992 as Vietnam's eighth national park. The scenery here swoops from towering limestone mountains peaking at 1554m down into plunging valleys wrapped in dense evergreen forests, speckled with waterfalls and caves, with the lakes themselves dominating the very heart of the park.

The park entrance fee is payable at a checkpoint about 15km before the park headquarters, just beyond the town of Cho Ra.

Ba Be (meaning Three Bays) is in fact three linked lakes, which have a total length of 8km and a width of about 400m. More than a hundred species of freshwater fish inhabit the lake. Two of the lakes are separated by a 100m-wide strip of water called Be Kam, sandwiched between high walls of chalk rock.

The park is a rainforest area with more than 550 named plant species, and the government subsidises the villagers not to cut down the trees. The hundreds of wildlife species here include 65 (mostly rarely seen) mammals, 353 butterflies, 106 species of fish, four kinds of turtle, the highly endangered Vietnamese salamander and even the Burmese python. Ba Be bird life is equally prolific, with 233 species recorded, including the spectacular crested serpent eagle and the oriental honey buzzard. Hunting is forbidden, but villagers are permitted to fish.

The enthusiastic local **tourist office** (☎0281-389 4721; www.babenationalpark.com.vn; Bo Lu village), dealing in everything Ba Be, can arrange kayaking, boating, hiking and cycling trips (or a combo of all four) that work out at around US$50 per day. Hires kayaks for US$5 per hour. It specialises in multiday treks (from $159 for three days) and camping trips in the further reaches of the national park.

Ba Be also has a well-established homestay program allowing travellers to experience lakeside village life in typical stilted houses. Most of the homestays are in Pac Ngoi village. All have hot water and can provide meals (50,000d to 80,000d) as long as they are ordered in advance. The even-quieter lake villages of Bo Lu and Coc Toc also have a couple of options.

The Ba Be National Park office can organise homestays for independent travellers but you can also just show up and check in.

Another option is to use the nearby town of Cho Ra as a base.

ℹ Getting There & Away

Ba Be National Park is 240km from Hanoi, 61km from Bac Kan and 18km from Cho Ra.

Most people visit Ba Be as part of a tour, or by chartered vehicle from Hanoi (a 4WD is not necessary).

Mai Chau

Set in an idyllic valley, hemmed in by hills, the Mai Chau area is a world away from Hanoi's hustle. The small town of Mai Chau itself is unappealing, but just outside the patchwork of rice fields rolls out, speckled by tiny Thai villages where visitors doss down for the night in traditional stilt houses and wake up to a rural soundtrack defined by gurgling irrigation streams and birdsong.

The villagers are mostly White Thai, distantly related to tribes in Thailand, Laos and China. Most no longer wear traditional dress, but the Thai women are masterful weavers producing plenty of traditional-style textiles. Locals do not employ strong-arm sales tactics here: polite bargaining is the norm.

Due to its popularity, some find the Mai Chau tour group experience too sanitised. If you're looking for hard-core exploration, this is not the place, but for biking, hiking and relaxation, calm Mai Chau fits the bill nicely.

Sights & Activities

Most visitors come simply to sleep in a stilt house and to stroll (or cycle) the paths through the rice fields to the separate minority villages. Most stilt-house homestays rent bikes to explore the valley at your own pace and can organise a local guide for about US$10.

A popular 18km trek is from Lac village (Ban Lac) in Mai Chau to Xa Linh village, near a mountain pass (elevation 1000m) on Hwy 6. Lac village is home to White Thai, while the inhabitants of Xa Linh are Hmong. The trek is strenuous in one day, so most people spend a night in a village. Arrange a guide, and a car to meet you at the mountain pass for the journey back to Mai Chau. Note there's a 600m climb in altitude, and the trail is slippery after rain.

Ask around in Mai Chau about longer treks of three to seven days. Other options include kayaking and mountain-biking excursions; enquire at Mai Chau Lodge.

Many travel agencies in Hanoi run inexpensive trips to Mai Chau.

Sleeping

Mai Chau is a successful grassroots tourism project and stilt-house homestays in the villages of Lac or Pom Coong are firmly stamped on the tour-group agenda, as well as being an extremely popular weekend getaway for locals from Hanoi – try to come midweek if possible.

Thai Stilt Houses HOMESTAY $
(per person 80,000-200,000d) Virtually every visitor to Mai Chau stays in one of the numerous Thai stilt-house homestays in the villages of Lac or Pom Coong, a five-minute stroll apart. Overnighting in these minority villages comes with electricity, Western-style toilets, hot showers, and roll-up mattresses with mosquito nets provided. Plan on one night plus dinner and breakfast costing around 250,000d.

★ **Mai Chau Nature Lodge** BUNGALOW $$
(☎0946-888 804; www.maichaunatureplace.com; Lac village; dm US$5, d with fan US$36; wi-fi) For a little more privacy than the neighbourhood homestays, this friendly operation in Lac village offers nine bungalows with rickety bamboo furniture. Dorms are also available. Grab a bungalow at the back to wake up to verdant rice-field views. There are free bikes to explore the surrounding countryside.

Mai Chau Lodge HOTEL $$
(☎0218-386 8959; www.maichaulodge.com; r US$86-145; air-con, internet, wi-fi, pool) This tour-group favourite has contemporary rooms with wooden floors, designer lighting and local textiles. The thatched-roof restaurant overlooks a small lake and the pool. Activities on offer include visits to caves, cookery classes, and guided walking, kayaking and mountain-biking excursions.

Getting There & Around

Direct buses to Mai Chau (100,000d, 3¾ hours) leave Hanoi's My Dinh Bus Station at 6am, 8.30am and 11am. If you want to stay in Lac or Pom Coong villages, just ask the bus driver to drop you off there. You'll be dropped off at the crossroads, just a short stroll from both villages. You may have to pay a 7000d entry fee to Mai Chau, but the toll booth is often unattended.

Heading back to Hanoi, buses leave at 9am, 11am and 1pm. Homestay owners can book these buses for you and arrange for you to be picked up from the village.

Lao Cai

For travellers, Lao Cai is the jumping-off point when journeying between Hanoi and Sapa by train, and a stopover when heading further north to Kunming in China. The bustling town is squeezed right next to the Vietnam–China border, and with Sapa just a half-hour hop away, it's no place to linger, yet it offers everything China-bound travellers will need for an overnight stay.

GETTING TO CHINA: LAO CAI TO KUNMING

Getting to the border The Chinese border at the **Lao Cai/Hekou border crossing** is about 3km from Lao Cai train station, a journey done by *xe om* (motorbike taxi; around 25,000d) or taxi (around 50,000d).

At the border The border is open daily between 7am and 10pm Vietnam time. Note that China is one hour ahead of Vietnam. You'll need to have a prearranged visa for China, and border-crossing formalities usually take around one hour. China is separated from Vietnam by a road bridge and a separate rail bridge over the Song Hong (Red River). Note that travellers have reported Chinese officials confiscating Lonely Planet *China* guides at this border, so you may want to try masking the cover.

Moving on The new Hekou bus station is around 6km from the border post. There are regular departures to Kunming, including sleeper buses which leave at 7.20pm and 7.30pm, getting into Kunming at around 7am. There are also four daily trains.

Around the train station there are ATMs, hotels, and restaurants with free wifi that run as one-stop traveller shops selling train tickets, cheap beds and drinks while you wait for your next ride.

Getting There & Around

Virtually everyone travelling to and from Hanoi uses the train, the safest and most comfortable option.

There are four daily services to Hanoi from Lao Cai train station. Cheapest is the LC4 train (hard/soft seat 130,000/215,000d, 10 hours), which leaves at 9.50am. The other three services are all sleepers (425,000d, eight hours); the SP8 leaves at 1.15pm, the SP2 at 8.20pm and SP4 at 9.10pm.

Hotels and travel agencies in both Hanoi and Sapa can book tickets, or you can book at the station yourself.

Several companies operate special private rail carriages that hitch a ride on the main trains, including **ET Pumpkin** (☎0438-295 571; www.et-pumpkin.com; sleeper berth US$42), **Livitrans** (☎0437-350 069; www.livitrantrain.com; sleeper berth US$34) and the exclusive **Victoria Express** (www.victoriahotels-asia.com), which is only available to guests at Sapa's Victoria Sapa Resort.

The new speedway toll road connecting Lao Cai and Hanoi can shave hours off bus journey times, but at the moment is only used by sleeper buses. The bus station, at the end of Đ Pha Dinh Phung, is two blocks west of the train station.

If you're heading to Sapa yellow-and-red minibuses and larger buses (30,000d, 30 minutes) leave at least hourly between 5.20am and 6pm from the car park in front of Lao Cai train station. Touts will try to push you to their private minibuses for an inflated 100,000d.

Minibuses to Bac Ha (70,000d, 2½ hours) leave from the minibus terminal next to the Song Hong (Red River) bridge; there are seven daily services at 6.30am, 8.15am, 9am, 11.30am, noon, 2pm and 3pm.

Bac Ha

Sleepy Bac Ha wakes up for the riot of colour and commerce that is its Sunday market, when the lanes fill to choking point and villagers flock in from the hills and valleys. Once the barter, buy and sell is done and the day-tripper tourist buses from Sapa have left, the town rolls over and goes back to bed for the rest of the week.

Despite being surrounded by countryside just as lush and interesting as Sapa, Bac Ha has somehow flown under the radar as a trekking base so far. In town, woodsmoke fills the morning air, the main street is completely bereft of hawkers, and chickens and pigs snuffle for scraps in the back lanes where a small clutch of traditional adobe houses valiantly clings on in the age of concrete.

Sights

★Bac Ha Market MARKET

(off Đ Tran Bac; ⏲sunrise-2pm Sun) This Sunday market is Bac Ha's big draw. There's an increasing range of handicrafts for sale, but it's still pretty much a local affair. Bac Ha market is a magnet for the local hill-tribe people, above all the exotically attired Flower Hmong. If you can, stay overnight in Bac Ha on Saturday, and get here early before hundreds of day trippers from Sapa start arriving.

Sin Cheng Market MARKET

(⏲5am-2pm Wed) This market, in the remote border area of Si Ma Cai, 40km from Bac Ha, is a vibrant and chaotic weekly hub for the local Nung and Thulao ethnic minorities who live in the surrounding villages.

Coc Ly Market MARKET

(⌚8.30am-1.30pm Tue) The impressive Coc Ly market attracts Dzao, Flower Hmong, Tay and Nung people from the surrounding hills. It's about 35km southwest of Bac Ha along reasonably good roads. Tour operators in Bac Ha can arrange day trips here.

Lung Phin Market MARKET

(⌚6am-1pm Sun) Lung Phin market is between Can Cau market and Bac Ha, about 12km from town. It's less busy than other markets, with a really local feel, and is a good place to move on to once the tour buses arrive in Bac Ha from Sapa.

Sleeping & Eating

Room rates tend to increase by about 20% on weekends due to the Sunday market.

★**Ngan Nga Bac Ha Hotel** HOTEL $$

(☎0203-880 286; www.nganngabachahotel.com; 117 P Ngoc Uyen; r incl breakfast US$30-37; ❄📶) This friendly place is above a popular restaurant that does a roaring trade in tasty *lau*. Rooms here are the best budget deal in town; they are a decent size and are decked out with a few homey touches that give them some character. Bag a front room for a balcony.

Congfu Hotel HOTEL $$

(☎0203-880 254; 152 P Ngoc Uyen; s US$27, d US$29-32, tr US$34-38; ❄@📶) This place has freshly painted rooms with white linen, though the bathrooms could do with a spruce up. Book room 105, 108, 205 or 208 for their floor-to-ceiling windows overlooking Bac Ha Market. There's a restaurant (meals from 60,000d) downstairs and hiking can be arranged.

Hoang Yen Restaurant VIETNAMESE $

(Đ Tran Bac; meals 60,000-120,000d; ⌚7am-10pm; 📶) Hoang Yen's menu includes decent breakfast options and a set menu for 200,000d. Cheap beer is also available.

BEST DRESSED?

Flower Hmong women wear several layers of dazzling clothing. These include an elaborate collar-meets-shawl that's pinned at the neck and an apron-style garment; both are made of tightly woven strips of multicoloured fabric, often with a frilly edge. Highly ornate cuffs and ankle fabrics are also part of their costume, as is a checked headscarf (often electric pink or lime green).

Information

There's an **Agribank** (P Ngoc Uyen; ⌚8am-3pm Mon-Fri, to 11am Sat, ATM 24hr) with ATM

Getting There & Away

Tours to Bac Ha from Sapa cost from around US$20 per person; on the way back you can bail out in Lao Cai and catch the night train to Hanoi.

Bac Ha's bus station is out of the town centre, across the Na Co River. To Hanoi there's a 4.30am service (11 hours), and two sleeper buses at noon and 8.30pm (300,000d, seven hours). Buses run hourly between 6am and 4pm to Lao Cai (70,000d, 2½ hours). Coming into town from Lao Cai buses usually drop you in the town centre.

Sapa

Established as a hill station by the French in 1922, Sapa today is the tourism centre of the northwest.

Sapa is oriented to make the most of the spectacular views emerging on clear days; it overlooks a plunging valley, with mountains towering above on all sides. Views of this epic scenery are often subdued by thick mist rolling across the peaks, but even when it's cloudy, local hill-tribe people fill the town with colour.

If you were expecting a quaint alpine town, recalibrate your expectations. Modern tourism development has mushroomed haphazardly. Thanks to rarely enforced building-height restrictions, Sapa's skyline is continually thrusting upwards.

But you're not here to hang out in town. This is northern Vietnam's premier trekking base, from where hikers launch themselves into a surrounding countryside of cascading rice terraces and tiny hill-tribe villages that seem a world apart. Once you've stepped out into the lush fields, you'll understand the Sapa area's real charm.

Sights

★**Sapa Museum** MUSEUM

(103 P Cau May; ⌚7.30-11.30am & 1.30-5pm) FREE Excellent showcase of the history and ethnology of the Sapa area, including the colonial times of the French. Dusty exhibitions demonstrate the differences between the various ethnic minority people of the area, so it's definitely worth a quick visit when you first arrive in town, even if some

descriptions are too faded to read. Behind Sapa Tourism.

Tram Ton Pass VIEWPOINT

The road between Sapa and Lai Chau crosses the Tram Ton Pass on the northern side of Fansipan, 15km from Sapa. At 1900m this is Vietnam's highest mountain pass, and acts as a dividing line between two weather fronts. The lookout points here have fantastic views. Most people also stop at 100m-high Thac Bac (Silver Waterfall), 12km from Sapa.

On the Sapa side it's often cold and foggy, but drop a few hundred metres onto the Lai Chau side and it can be sunny and warm. Surprisingly, Sapa is the coldest place in Vietnam, but Lai Chau can be one of the warmest.

Sapa Church CHURCH

(⏲Mass from 6am Sun) Sapa's small stone church was built by the French. It's only open for Mass on Sunday and on certain evenings for prayers. It also functions as a landmark in the centre of town.

Sapa Market MARKET

(Đ Ngu Chi Son; ⏲6am-2pm) Unfortunately turfed out of central Sapa, and now in a purpose-built modern building near the bus station, Sapa Market is still a hive of colourful activity outside with fresh produce, a butcher's section not for the squeamish and hill-tribe people from surrounding villages heading here most days to sell handicrafts. Saturday is the busiest day.

Activities

For longer treks with overnight stays in villages, it's important to hook up with someone who knows the terrain and culture and speaks the language. We recommend using minority guides, as this offers them a means of making a living. Note it's illegal to stay overnight in villages that are not officially recognised as homestays. Ignoring this could cause significant problems for your hosts and yourself. Always go through a reputable tour agency and be sure to ask how legitimate they are.

★ Sapa O'Chau HIKING

(☎020-377 1166; www.sapaochau.com; 8 Đ Thac Bac; ⏲6.30am-6.30pm) Excellent local company offering day walks, longer homestay treks, Bac Ha market trips and Fanispan hikes. It also runs culturally immersive tours that focus on handicrafts and farmstays. Profits provide training to Hmong children in a learning centre.

Fansipan HIKING

Surrounding Sapa are the Hoang Lien Mountains, dubbed the Tonkinese Alps by the French. These mountains include the often-cloud-obscured Fansipan (3143m), Vietnam's highest peak. Fansipan is accessible year-round to sensibly equipped trekkers in good shape with a guide, but don't underestimate the challenge. It is very wet, and can be perilously slippery and generally cold.

Fansipan's wild, lonesome beauty has been somewhat shattered with the opening of a 6282m-long cable car (return adult/child 600,000/400,000d), taking people across the Muong Hoa Valley and up to the summit in 15 minutes where a new complex of shops awaits. A taxi here is a little over 100,000d.

For the full satisfaction of earning that view, the summit of Fansipan is 19km by foot from Sapa. The terrain is rough and adverse weather is frequent. The round trip usually takes three days; some experienced hikers do it in two days, but you'll need to be fit. After walking through hill-tribe villages on the first morning, it's just forest, mountain vistas and occasional wildlife, including monkeys, mountain goats and birds. Weather-wise the best time is from mid-October to mid-December, and in March, when wildflowers are in bloom. Don't attempt an ascent if Sapa's weather is poor, as limited visibility on Fansipan can be treacherous.

No ropes or technical climbing skills are needed, just endurance. There are a few rudimentary shelters at a couple of base camps en route, but it's better to be self-sufficient with sleeping bag, waterproof tent, food, stove, raincoat, compass and other miscellaneous survival gear. It's important to carry out all your garbage, as some of the camps are now impacted by rubbish. Hiring a reputable guide is vital (and a legal requirement, some claim) and porters are also recommended.

Through local operators, count on an all-inclusive rate of around US$150 per person for a couple, US$125 per person for a group of four, and US$100 per person for the sensible maximum group size of six.

Cat Cat HIKING

(40,000d) The nearest village within walking distance is Cat Cat, 3km south of Sapa. It's beautiful and the consistent souvenir soft sell doesn't spoil it for most visitors. It's a steep and beautiful hike down, and there are plenty of *xe om* for the return uphill journey.

Sapa

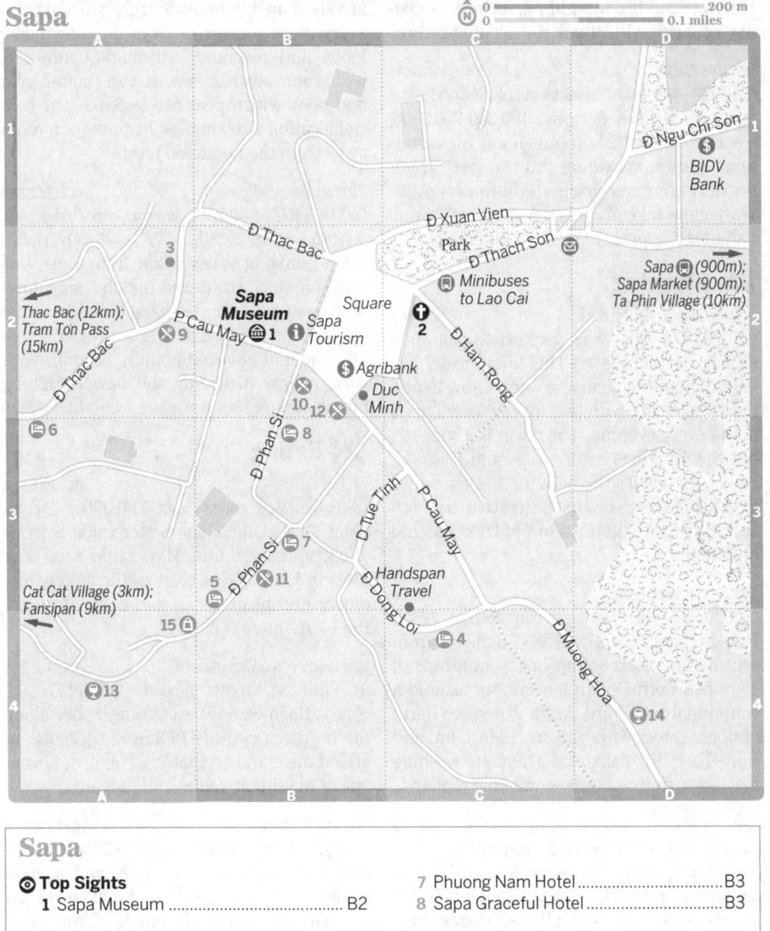

Sapa

Top Sights
1 Sapa Museum B2

Sights
2 Sapa Church C2

Activities, Courses & Tours
Hill Station Signature Restaurant .... (see 11)
Indigo Cat .... (see 5)
3 Sapa O'Chau A2
Sapa Sisters .... (see 8)

Sleeping
4 Amazing Hotel C4
5 Cat Cat View Hotel B3
6 Go Sapa Hostel A3
7 Phuong Nam Hotel B3
8 Sapa Graceful Hotel B3

Eating
9 Baguette & Chocolat A2
10 Barbecue Restaurants B2
11 Hill Station Signature Restaurant B3
12 Little Sapa B2

Drinking & Nightlife
13 Cafe in the Clouds A4
14 Hmong Sisters D4

Shopping
15 Hemp & Embroidery A4
Indigo Cat .... (see 5)

Hill Station Signature Restaurant COOKING
(☎0203-887 112; 37 Đ Phan Si; per person US$29; ⊙from 9am) Excellent three-hour cooking classes with an English-speaking Hmong chef starting with a 30-minute market tour and featuring five local dishes, including homemade tofu, smoked buffalo and

Hmong-style black pudding, as well as tasting local rice wine. Book the evening before.

Indigo Cat CRAFTS
(☎0982 403 647; www.facebook.com/indigocatsapa; 46 Đ Phan Si; class 100,000-200,000d; ⊙9am-7pm) Craft shop Indigo Cat runs afternoon workshops where you can learn traditional Hmong weaving and embroidery skills. Workshops take place in the village of Ta Ven. Call into the lovely Sapa shop for details.

Sleeping

Sapa Graceful Hotel HOSTEL $
(☎0203-773 388; www.gracefulhotel.com; 9 Đ Phan Si; dm US$5-6;) This bijou hostel has bags of homey charm and knows how to pull backpackers in, with two-for-one beer happy hours every evening. The dorm is a squeeze, but the foyer has comfy sofas and stacks of books, and as it's the base for **Sapa Sisters** (☎0203-773 388; www.sapasisters.com; 9 Đ Phan Si; ⊙8am-5pm), there's a ton of trekking info on offer.

Go Sapa Hostel HOSTEL $
(☎0203-871 198; www.gosapahostel.com; 25 Đ Thac Bac; dm/d US$5/20; @) Up the hill from central Sapa, this set-up has a multitude of eight-bed dorms (with lockers) set around a communal courtyard. More expensive dorm options come with private bathroom and some have tiny balconies. There are washing machines, free computers and bike rentals.

Phuong Nam Hotel HOTEL $
(☎0203-871 286; www.phuongnamhotelsapa.com; 33 Đ Phan Si; dm/r incl breakfast US$8/20;) Inside this nondescript concrete hotel there's a decent budget deal to be had, with two four-bed dorms with large beds. Private rooms are basic but spick and span, though don't bother on weekends when the room price is hiked to a ridiculous US$35.

Cat Cat View Hotel HOTEL $$
(☎0203-871 946; www.catcathotel.com; 46 Đ Phan Si; r incl breakfast US$35-60, f apt US$100-180; @) There's plenty of choice at this rambling, family-run spot with comfortable pine-trimmed rooms over nine floors, many opening onto communal terraces with views. The spacious apartments are a great option for travelling families or groups of friends.

Amazing Hotel HOTEL $$$
(☎020-386 5888; http://amazinghotel.com.vn; Đ Dong Loi; r/ste from US$161/209; P@) It's not just the name, the misty valley vista at this four-star hotel is truly amazing. It's everywhere you turn - from the all-window lobby and restaurant, through handsome, plain rooms with a view, up to a rooftop gym and pool, which peer across Sapa. The central location also amazes. Just ask for a room away from the nightclub level.

Topas Ecolodge ECOLODGE $$$
(☎0203-872 404; www.topasecolodge.com; bungalows US$115-180; @) Overlooking a plunging valley 18km from Sapa, this ecolodge has stone-and-thatch bungalows with front balconies to make the most of the magnificent views. The whole project is sustainable and environmentally friendly, with solar energy providing the power. Hiking, biking and market tours are available.

Eating

Little Sapa VIETNAMESE $
(18 P Cau May; meals 50,000-80,000d; ⊙8am-10pm;) One of the better-value eateries along touristy P Cau May, Little Sapa also lures in locals. Steer clear of the largely mediocre European dishes and concentrate on the Vietnamese menu.

Barbecue Restaurants VIETNAMESE $
(Đ Phan Si; meals around 70,000-120,000d; ⊙noon-11pm) Several easygoing spots along the northern end of Đ Phan Si specialise in grilled meat and vegetables. Pull up a pew at one of the simple tables and tuck in.

Sapa Market VIETNAMESE $
(Đ Ngu Chi Son; dishes around 30,000d; ⊙6am-1pm) Lots of local food stalls and a good alternative to another hotel breakfast or for a cheap and authentic lunch, if you don't mind a walk by a lake to get there.

★**Hill Station Signature Restaurant** VIETNAMESE $$
(www.thehillstation.com; 37 Đ Phan Si; meals 60,000-180,000d; ⊙7am-11pm;) A showcase of Hmong cuisine with cool Zen decor and superb views. Dishes include flash-cooked pork with lime, ash-baked trout in banana leaves, and traditional Hmong-style black pudding. Tasting sets of local rice and corn wine are also of interest to curious travelling foodies. Don't miss trying the delicate rainbow-trout rice-paper rolls; think of them as 'Sapa sushi'.

Baguette & Chocolat CAFE $$
(☎020-387 1766; Đ Thac Bac; cakes from 30,000d, snacks & meals 70,000-160,000d; ⊙7am-10pm;

) Head to this converted villa for a decent breakfast, baguette or slab of lemon tart. Many of the staff are students at the Hoa Sua School for disadvantaged youth and are being trained in the cooking and hospitality industry.

Drinking & Nightlife

Cafe in the Clouds BEER GARDEN

(020-377 1011; 60 Đ Phan Si; 6am-11pm;) The large terrace of this bar is a great corner of Sapa (and the planet) to pause and ponder the valley or, often, the wandering mist at eye level. The crisp air must come with lofty prices? Actually drinks are priced very reasonably, plus wi-fi is zippy for logging in to electronic clouds. The food isn't bad either.

Hmong Sisters BAR

(0915 042 366; 31 Đ Muong Hoa; 4pm-late;) This spacious bar with pool tables and an open fire has pretty decent music, but can feel a bit sparse if it's a quiet night. Bar prices are reasonable, though, so it's always worth checking out.

Shopping

Hemp & Embroidery ARTS & CRAFTS

(www.facebook.com/hempandembroidery; 50 Đ Phan Si; 9am-8pm) A superfriendly shop owned by a charming Hmong lady, selling gorgeous textiles all made in the Sapa area. There are some divine bedspreads and cushion covers to browse through and the sales pitch is distinctly low-key, which many travellers will heartily appreciate.

Indigo Cat ARTS & CRAFTS

(www.facebook.com/indigocatsapa; 46 Đ Phan Si; 9am-7pm) This Hmong-owned handicrafts shop offers a wonderful selection of interesting local crafts, including bags, clothing, pillows and belts. Many items have hip design touches unique to the store and the set-price labels are a relief if you have haggling fatigue. Co-owner Pang speaks good English and her kids are real charmers.

Information

Agribank (P Cau May; 8am-3pm Mon-Fri, ATM 24hr)

BIDV Bank (020-387 2569; Đ Ngu Chi Son; 8am-3pm Mon-Fri, to 11am Sat, ATM 24hr)

Main Post Office (Đ Ham Rong; 8am-6pm Mon-Fri) International phone calls can also be made here.

Sapa Tourism (020-387 3239; www.sapa-tourism.com; 103 Đ Xuan Vien; 7.30-11.30am & 1.30-5pm) Helpful English-speaking staff offering details about transport, trekking and weather. Internet access is free for 15 minutes, and the website is also a mine of useful information.

TRAVEL AGENCIES

Duc Minh (020-387 1881; www.ducminhtravel.com; 10 P Cau May) Friendly English-speaking operator organising transport, treks to hill-tribe villages and assaults of Fansipan.

Handspan Travel (020-387 2110; www.handspan.com; Chau Long Hotel, 24 Dong Loi) Offers trekking and mountain-biking tours to villages and markets.

Getting There & Away

Minibuses to Lao Cai Minibuses and buses to Lao Cai (30,000d, 30 minutes) leave every half-hour between 6am and 6pm, from a bus stop near Sapa Church. Look for yellow and red buses with price lists in the window.

Sapa Bus Station (Đ Luong Dinh Cua) Sapa's bus station is in the northeast of town. Buses to Hanoi (250,000d, 10 hours) leave at 7.30am, 8.30am, 4pm and 5pm, and there are two sleeper services (300,000d, six hours), that take the new speedway toll road direct to Hanoi, at 9pm and 10pm. Heading to Lai Chau there are 10 buses between 6.30am and 5.15pm.

Dien Bien Phu

It was in the surrounding countryside here, on 7 May 1954, that the French-colonial forces were defeated by the Viet Minh in a decisive battle, and the days of their Indochina empire became numbered.

The town sits in the heart-shaped Muong Thanh Valley, surrounded by heavily forested hills. The scenery along the way here is stunning, with approach roads scything through thick forests and steep terrain. The city itself lies more prosaically on a broad dry plain, and boasts expansive boulevards and civic buildings.

Sights

★**A1 Hill** MONUMENT

(Đ 7-5; 3000d; 7-11am & 1.30-5pm) This vantage point was crucial in the battle of Dien Bien Phu. There are tanks and a monument to Viet Minh casualties on this former French position, known to the French as Eliane and to the Vietnamese as A1 Hill. The elaborate trenches at the heart of the French defences have also been re-created. Little background information is given on-site.

★**Dien Bien Phu Museum** MUSEUM
(☎0230-382 4971; Đ 7-5; 15,000d; ⏲7-11am & 1.30-4.30pm) This well-laid-out museum, contained in a space-agey modern structure, features an eclectic collection that commemorates the 1954 battle. Alongside weaponry and guns, there's a bath-tub that belonged to the French commander Colonel de Castries, a bicycle capable of carrying 330kg of ordnance, and photographs and documents, some with English translations.

Sleeping & Eating

There are basic guesthouses around the bus station, some with creepy crawlies. Better midrange options can be found a few blocks away on Tran Dang Ninh. There are good-value, simple restaurants along P Nguyen Chi Tranh, all with pick-and-choose counters where you can tuck into everything from chicken to fried locusts. Opposite the bus station are cheap and cheerful **pho stalls** (dishes around 30,000d; ⏲8am-10pm) and simple restaurants; some serve delicious fresh sugar-cane juice.

★**Ruby Hotel** HOTEL $
(☎0913 655 793; www.rubyhoteldienbien.com; off Đ Nguyen Chi Thanh; s/d/tr 415,000/515,000/615,000) The best deal in Dien Bien Phu is this friendly hotel, down a signposted alleyway. Rooms are comfortably fitted out with good beds, flat-screen TVs and bathrooms featuring rain shower heads. If you're travelling solo, treat yourself to a double room as the singles are quite small.

Yen Ninh VIETNAMESE $
(P Be Van Dan; meals 35,000-70,000d; ⏲8am-10pm; ✎) This modest fully vegetarian diner dishes up tasty noodle and rice plates with plenty of tofu and mock-meat Vietnamese dishes.

Information

There's an **Agribank** (☎0230-382 5786; Đ 7-5; ⏲8am-3pm Mon-Fri, to 11.30am Sat, ATM 24hr) in town, with a 24-hour ATM.

Getting There & Away

The 480km drive from Hanoi to Dien Bien Phu on Hwys 6 and 279 takes around 11 hours.

DBP's bus station (Hwy 12) is at the corner of Đ Tran Dang Ninh. There are plentiful services heading south to Hanoi and there are early morning services to destinations across the border into Laos.

Vietnam Airlines (☎0230-382 4948; www.vietnamairlines.com; Đ Nguyen Huu Tho; ⏲7.30-11.30am & 1.30-4.30pm) operates two flights daily between Dien Bien Phu and Hanoi. The office is near the airport, about 1.5km from the town centre, along the road to Muong Lay.

CENTRAL VIETNAM

The geographic heart of the nation, central Vietnam is packed with historic sights and cultural interest, and blessed with ravishing beaches and outstanding national parks.

Marvel at Hue and its imperial citadel, royal tombs and excellent street food. Savour the unique heritage grace of riverside jewel Hoi An, and tour the military sites of the Demilitarised Zone (DMZ). Check out Danang, fast emerging as one of the nation's most dynamic cities. Also emerging as a must-visit destination is the extraordinary Phong Nha region, home to three gargantuan cave systems (including the world's largest cave), and a fascinating war history concealed amid stunning scenery. Enjoy well-earned downtime on the golden sands of An Bang Beach or learn to cook central Vietnamese cuisine, the nation's most complex.

With improving highways, and upgraded international airports at Hue and Danang, access to this compelling and diverse part of Vietnam has never been easier.

BUSES FROM DIEN BIEN PHU

CONNECTION	COST (D)	DURATION (HR)	FREQUENCY
Hanoi	290,000-310,000	11½	frequent 4.30am-9pm
Lai Chau	130,000	6-7	6.15am, 7am, 8am, 9am, 10am, 12.30pm, 1.15pm
Muang Khua (Laos)	110,000	7-8	5.30am
Muong Lay	62,000	3-4	2.30pm, 3pm, 4pm
Son La	105,000	4	4.30am, 8am, noon, 2pm

THE HIGH ROADS ON TWO WHEELS

With spectacular scenery and relatively minimal traffic, more travellers are choosing to motorcycle around the northwest loop from Hanoi up to Lao Cai, over to Dien Bien Phu and back to the capital. For the more intrepid, the roads venturing north towards China into the spectacular provinces of Ha Giang and Cao Bang are the newest frontier for travel in Vietnam.

Hanoi is the place to start making arrangements. Consider joining a tour company, such as Offroad Vietnam (p67), or hiring a guide who knows the roads and can help with mechanical and linguistic difficulties. Be sure to get acquainted with your bike first and check current road conditions and routes.

Rental agencies will provide checklists, but essentials include a good helmet, a local SIM card in your mobile phone for emergencies, rain gear, a spare parts and repair kit (including spark plugs, spanners, inner tube and tyre levers), air pump and decent maps. Knee and elbow pads and gloves are also a good idea.

Highways can be hell in Vietnam, so let the train take the strain on the long route north to Lao Cai. Load your bike into a goods carriage while you sleep in a berth. You'll have to (almost) drain your bike of petrol.

Take it slowly, particularly in the rain: smooth paved roads can turn into muddy tracks in no time. Do not ride during or immediately after heavy rainstorms as this is when landslides might occur; many mountain roads are quite new and the cliff embankments can be unstable. Expect to average about 35km/h. Only use safe hotel parking. Fill up from petrol stations where the petrol is less likely to have been watered down.

If running short on time or energy, remember that many bus companies will let you put your bike on the roof of a bus, but get permission first from your bike-rental company.

Phong Nha-Ke Bang National Park

Designated a Unesco World Heritage Site in 2003, the remarkable **Phong Nha-Ke Bang National Park** (052-367 7021; http://phongnhakebang.vn/en) FREE contains the oldest karst mountains in Asia, formed approximately 400 million years ago. Riddled with hundreds of cave systems – many of extraordinary scale and length – and spectacular underground rivers, Phong Nha is a speleologists' heaven on earth.

Serious exploration only began in the 1990s, led by the British Cave Research Association and Hanoi University. Cavers first penetrated deep into Phong Nha Cave, one of the world's longest systems. In 2005 Paradise Cave was discovered, and in 2009 a team found the world's largest cave – Son Doong. In 2015 public access to two more cave systems was approved.

The caves are the region's absolute highlights, but the above-ground attractions of forest trekking, the area's war history, and rural mountain biking means it deserves a stay of around three days.

Most of the mountainous 885 sq km of Phong Nha-Ke Bang National Park is near-pristine tropical evergreen jungle, more than 90% of which is primary forest. It borders the biodiverse Hin Namno reserve in Laos to form an impressive, continuous slab of protected habitat. More than 100 types of mammal (including 10 species of primate, tigers, elephants and the saola, a rare Asian antelope), 81 types of reptile and amphibian, and more than 300 varieties of bird have been logged in Phong Nha.

In the past, access to the national park was limited and strictly controlled by the Vietnamese military. Access is still quite tightly controlled, for good reason (the park is still riddled with unexploded ordnance). Officially you are not allowed to hike here without a licensed tour operator. You can, however, travel independently (on a motorbike or car) on the Ho Chi Minh Hwy or Hwy 20, which cut through the park.

The Phong Nha region is changing fast. Son Trach village (population 3000) is the main centre, with an ATM, a growing range of accommodation and eating options, and improving transport links with other parts of central Vietnam.

Sights

★ **Hang Son Doong** CAVE

Hang Son Doong (Mountain River Cave) is known as the world's largest cave, and is one of the most spectacular sights in Southeast Asia. The government only approved (very restricted) access to the cave system in June 2013. The only specialist operator permitted (by the Vietnamese president no less) to lead tours here is Son Trach–based Oxalis.

Son Doong is no day-trip destination, it's in an extremely remote area and the only way to visit is by booking a seven-day expedition with around 16 porters. It costs US$3000 per person, with a maximum of 10 trekkers on each trip.

★ Hang Toi CAVE

(Dark Cave; per person 350,000d) Incorporating an above-water zip line, followed by a swim into the cave and then exploration of a pitch-black passageway of oozing mud, it's little wonder Hang Toi is the cave experience you've probably already heard about from other travellers. Upon exiting the cave, a leisurely kayak paddle heads to a jetty where there's more into-the-water zip-line thrills to be had.

★ Tu Lan Cave CAVE

(www.oxalis.com.vn; 2-day tours 5,500,000d) The Tu Lan cave trip begins with a countryside hike then a swim (with headlamps and life jackets) through two spectacular river caves before emerging in an idyllic valley. Then there's more hiking through dense forest to a 'beach' where rivers merge that's an ideal campsite. There's more wonderful swimming here in vast caverns. Moderate fitness levels are necessary. Tu Lan is 65km north of Son Trach and can only be visited on a guided tour.

Phong Nha Cave & Boat Trip CAVE

(adult/child under 1.3m 150,000/25,000d, boat up to 14 people 320,000d; 7am-4pm) The spectacular boat trip through Phong Nha Cave is an enjoyable, though touristy, experience beginning in Son Trach village. Boats cruise along past buffalo, limestone peaks and church steeples to the cave's gaping mouth. The engine is then cut and the boats are negotiated silently through cavern after garishly illuminated cavern. On the return leg there's the option to climb (via 330 steps) up to the mountainside Tien Son Cave (80,000d) with the remains of 9th-century Cham altars.

The ticket office and departure jetty are in Son Trach village. Allow two hours.

Hang Va CAVE

(www.oxalis.com.vn; per person 8,000,000d) Discovered in 2012, and opened to visitors in 2015, Hang Va is explored on a two-day/one-night excursion that travels firstly along an underground river in Hang Nuoc Nut. Tours overnight in a jungle camp at the entrance to Hang Va, where the cave's highlight is a spectacular stalagmite field partly submerged in crystalline waters. Ropes and harnesses are used extensively.

Tours

★ Oxalis Adventure Tours TOURS

(0919 900 423; www.oxalis.com.vn; Son Trach) Oxalis are unquestionably *the* experts in caving and trekking expeditions, and are the only outfit licensed to conduct tours to Hang Son Doong. Staff are all fluent English-speakers, and trained by world-renowned British cavers Howard and Deb Limbert.

Jungle Boss Trekking HIKING

(094-374 8041; www.junglebosshomestay.com; Phong Nha village, Son Trach; per person US$75) Originally from the DMZ, Dzung – aka 'Jungle Boss' – has been in Phong Nha for eight years, and is an experienced guide to the area. He speaks excellent English and runs an exciting one-day tour around the Ho Chi Minh Trail and the remote Abandoned Valley area of the national park. You'll need moderate to high fitness levels.

Phong Nha Farmstay Tours ADVENTURE

(052-367 5135; www.phong-nha-cave.com; Cu Nam) The Farmstay can book cave tours – in conjunction with Oxalis – but equally interesting is bouncing in a US jeep or Russian Ural motorbike and sidecar exploring the area's scenery and war history. The Farmstay's popular National Park Tour (per person 1,450,000d) travels by minibus to incorporate the Ho Chi Minh Trail with Paradise Cave and Hang Toi.

Hai's Eco Conservation Tour HIKING

(096 260 6844; www.phong-nha-bamboo-cafe.com; per person 1,300,000d) Interesting day tours combining hiking in the jungle – you'll need to be relatively fit – with a visit to Phong Nha's Wildlife Rescue and Rehabilitation Centre, which rehabilitates rescued animals (mainly macaques from nearby regions, but also snakes and birds). Prices include a barbecue lunch, and there's an opportunity to cool off at the end of the

day in a natural swimming hole. Hai is usually at his Bamboo Cafe in the evenings.

Sleeping

Easy Tiger HOSTEL $
(052-367 7844; www.easytigerphongnha.com; Son Trach; dm 160,000d;) In Son Trach town, this hostel has four-bed dorms, the great Jungle Bar (p89), a pool table and excellent travel information. A swimming pool and beer garden make it ideal for relaxation after trekking and caving. And yes, the bedspreads are actually (faux) *leopard* skin. Don't ask. Do ask about free bicycles and a map to explore the interesting Bong Lai valley. Email reservations preferred.

★ **Phong Nha Farmstay** GUESTHOUSE $$
(052-367 5135; www.phong-nha-cave.com; Cu Nam; r 800,000-1,200,000d, f 1,000,000-2,000,000d;) The place that really put Phong Nha on the map, the Farmstay has peaceful views overlooking an ocean of rice paddies. Rooms are smallish but neat, with high ceilings and shared balconies. The bar-restaurant serves up Asian and Western meals, and there's a social vibe and occasional movies and live music. Local tours are excellent and there's free bicycle hire.

The Farmstay is in Cu Nam village, 9km east of Son Trach.

Phong Nha Lake House Resort HOTEL $$
(052-367 5999; www.phongnhalakehouse.com; Khuong Ha; dm/f US$10/70, d US$42-60;) Owned by an Australian-Viietnamese couple, mpressive lakeside resort has an excellent dorm (quality beds, mosquito nets, en suite bathroom and high ceilings), and spacious and stylish villas. A pool and newer lake-view bungalows are more proof this is the area's most comfortable place to stay. The wooden restaurant is a traditional structure from Ha Giang province in northern Vietnam.

The Lake House is 7km east of Son Trach.

Oxalis Home HOTEL $$
(052-367 7678; www.oxalis.com.vn; Son Trach; d mountain/river view 1,200,000/1,500,000d;) This riverside hotel is used by travellers booking cave tours with Oxalis (p88), but is also open to others. Accommodation is in spacious rooms, with views either over the river, or to equally spectacular karst mountain peaks. Bikes and kayaks – Oxalis Home has its own compact beach – are free for guests, and the on-site Expedition Cafe has elevated river views.

Pepper House GUESTHOUSE $$
(0167 873 1560; www.facebook.com/PepperHouseHomestay; Khuong Ha; dm/villas 200,000/1,400,000d;) Run by long-term Aussie expat Dave (aka 'Multi') and his local wife Diem, this welcoming place combines a rural setting and new double rooms in villas arrayed around a compact swimming pool. There are also simpler dorms inside the main house. Look forward to good food and cold beer as well.

Located 6km east of Son Trach.

Eating & Drinking

Bamboo Cafe CAFE $
(www.phong-nha-bamboo-cafe.com; Son Trach; meals 35,000-80,000d; 7am-10.30pm;) This laid-back haven on Son Trach's main drag has colourful decor, a cool outside deck, and well-priced food and drink, including excellent fresh fruit smoothies and varied vegetarian options. It's also where you'll usually find the friendly Hai who runs eco-conservation tours.

Mountain Goat Restaurant VIETNAMESE $$
(Son Trach; goat from 150,000d; 11am-9pm) Dine on grilled and steamed *de* (goat) – try the goat with lemongrass – at this riverside spot in Son Trach. Other options include spicy chicken and ice-cold beer. From the Phong Nha Cave boat station, walk 150m along the river, just past the church.

Jungle Bar BAR
(Son Trach; 7am-midnight;) The in-house bar/cafe at Easy Tiger (p89) is the most happening place in Son Trach, with cheap beer, pool tables, and live music four nights a week. Add to the growing display of national flags if you're feeling patriotic. There's loads of local information on hand, even if you're not staying at Easy Tiger.

Hue

Hue is the intellectual, cultural and spiritual heart of Vietnam. Palaces and pagodas, tombs and temples, culture and cuisine, history and heartbreak – there's no shortage of poetic pairings to describe Hue. A World Heritage Site, the capital of the Nguyen emperors is where tourists come to see the decaying, opulent royal tombs and the grand, crumbling Citadel.

Hue owes its charm partly to its location on the Perfume River – picturesque on a clear day, atmospheric even in less flattering weather. Today the city blends new and old as sleek modern hotels tower over crumbling century-old Citadel walls.

A few touts are a minor hassle, but Hue remains a tranquil, conservative city with just the right concentration of nightlife.

Sights

Most of Hue's principal sights lie within the moats of its Citadel and Imperial Enclosure. Other museums and pagodas are dotted around the city. The royal tombs (p91) are south of Hue. A good-value 'package tour ticket' (adult/child 360,000/70,000d) is available that includes admission to the Citadel and the tombs of Gia Long, Khai Dinh and Minh Mang.

Inside the Citadel

Built between 1804 and 1833, the Citadel (Kinh Thanh) is still the heart of Hue. Heavily fortified, it consists of 2m-thick, 10km-long walls, a moat (30m across and 4m deep) and 10 gateways.

The Citadel has distinct sections. The Imperial Enclosure and Forbidden Purple City formed the epicentre of Vietnamese royal life. On the southwestern side were temple compounds. There were residences in the northwest, gardens in the northeast, and the Mang Ca Fortress (still a military base) in the north.

★ Imperial Enclosure HISTORIC SITE
(adult/child 150,000/30,000d; ⌚7am-5.30pm) The Imperial Enclosure is a citadel-within-a-citadel, housing the emperor's residence, temples and palaces, and the main buildings of state, within 6m-high, 2.5km-long walls. What's left is only a fraction of the original – the enclosure was badly bombed during the French and American Wars, and only 20 of its 148 buildings survived. This is a fascinating site easily worth half a day, but poor signage can make navigation a bit difficult. Restoration and reconstruction is ongoing.

Expect a lot of broken masonry, rubble, cracked tiling and weeds as you work your way around. Nevertheless it's enjoyable as a leisurely stroll and some of the less-visited areas are highly atmospheric. There are little cafes and souvenir stands dotted around.

It's best to approach the sights starting from Ngo Mon Gate and moving anticlockwise around the enclosure.

Ngo Mon Gate GATE
The principal entrance to the Imperial Enclosure is Ngo Mon Gate, which faces the Flag Tower. The central passageway with its yellow doors was reserved for the use of the emperor, as was the bridge across the lotus pond. Others had to use the gates to either side and the paths around the pond. On top of the gate is Ngu Phung (Belvedere of the Five Phoenixes); on its upper level is a huge drum and bell.

Thai Hoa Palace PALACE
(Palace of Supreme Harmony) This 1803 palace is a spacious hall with an ornate timber roof supported by 80 carved and lacquered columns. It was used for the emperor's official receptions and important ceremonies. On state occasions the emperor sat on his elevated throne, facing visitors entering via the Ngo Mon Gate. No photos are permitted, but be sure to see the impressive audiovisual display, which gives an excellent overview of the entire Citadel, its architecture and the historical context.

Halls of the Mandarins HISTORIC BUILDING
Located immediately behind Thai Hoa Palace, on either side of a courtyard, these halls were used by mandarins as offices and to prepare for court ceremonies. The hall on the right showcases fascinating old photographs (including boy-king Vua Duya Tan's coronation), gilded Buddha statues and assorted imperial curios. Behind the courtyard are the ruins of the Can Chanh Palace, where two wonderful long galleries, painted in gleaming scarlet lacquer, have been reconstructed.

Emperor's Reading Room HISTORIC BUILDING
(Royal Library; Thai Binh Lau) The exquisite (though crumbling) little two-storey Emperor's Reading Room was the only part of the Forbidden Purple City to escape damage during the French reoccupation of Hue in 1947. The Gaudí-esque, yin-yang roof mosaics outside are in stark contrast to the sombre, recently renovated interior, the circular hallway of which you can now walk around on the small ground level. The exterior features poems by Emperor Khai Dinh on either side, and three Chinese characters that translate as 'Emperor's Reading Room'.

Royal Theatre HISTORIC BUILDING
(Duyen Thi Duong; ☎054-351 4989; www.nhanhac.com.vn; performances 50,000d-100,000d; ⌚performances 9am, 10am, 2.30pm & 3.30pm) The Royal Theatre, begun in 1826 and later

home to the National Conservatory of Music, has been rebuilt on its former foundations. Even when performances aren't on, it's free to sit in the plush chairs or examine the fascinating display of masks and musical instruments from Vietnamese theatre, with English descriptions. Cultural performances here last 45 minutes.

Co Ha Gardens GARDENS

(Royal Gardens) Occupying the northeast corner of the Imperial Enclosure, these delightful gardens were developed by the first four emperors of the Nguyen dynasty but fell into disrepair. They've been beautifully re-created in the last few years, and are dotted with little gazebo-style pavilions and ponds. This is one of the most peaceful spots in the entire Citadel. The latest section to be discovered, excavated and restored was completed in early 2017.

Forbidden Purple City RUINS

(Tu Cam Thanh) In the very centre of the Imperial Enclosure, there's almost nothing left of the once-magnificent Forbidden Purple City. This was a citadel-within-a-citadel-within-a-citadel and was reserved solely for the personal use of the emperor – the only servants allowed into this compound were eunuchs who would pose no threat to the royal concubines. The Forbidden Purple City was almost entirely destroyed in the wars, and its crumbling remains are now overgrown with weeds.

Dien Tho Residence HISTORIC BUILDING

The stunning, partially ruined Dien Tho Residence (1804) once comprised the apartments and audience hall of the queen mothers of the Nguyen dynasty. The audience hall houses an exhibition of photos illustrating its former use, and there is a display of embroidered royal garments. Just outside, a pleasure pavilion above a lily pond has been transformed into a cafe worthy of a refreshment stop.

★**To Mieu Temple Complex** BUDDHIST TEMPLE

Taking up the southwest corner of the Imperial Enclosure, this highly impressive walled complex has been beautifully restored. The imposing three-tiered Hien Lam Pavilion sits on the south side of the complex; it dates from 1824. On the other side of a courtyard is the solemn To Mieu Temple, housing shrines to each of the emperors, topped by their photos. Between these two temples are Nine Dynastic Urns *(dinh)* cast between 1835 and 1836, each dedicated to one Nguyen sovereign.

Nine Holy Cannons HISTORIC SITE

Located just inside the Citadel ramparts, near the gates to either side of the Flag Tower, are the Nine Holy Cannons (1804), symbolic protectors of the palace and kingdom. Commissioned by Emperor Gia Long, they were never intended to be fired. The four cannons near Ngan Gate represent the four seasons, while the five cannons next to Quang Duc Gate represent the five elements: metal, wood, water, fire and earth.

Outside the Citadel

South of Hue are the extravagant mausoleums of the rulers of the Nguyen dynasty (1802–1945), spread out along the banks of the Perfume River between 2km and 16km south of the city. The three listed are the most impressive, but there are many others.

Tomb of Tu Duc TOMB

(adult/child 100,000/20,000d) This tomb, constructed between 1864 and 1867, is the most popular and impressive of the royal mausoleums. Emperor Tu Duc designed it himself to use before and after his death. The enormous expense of the tomb and the forced labour used in its construction spawned a coup plot that was discovered and suppressed. Tu Duc's tomb is 5km south of Hue on Van Nien Hill in Duong Xuan Thuong village.

Tomb of Minh Mang TOMB

(adult/child 100,000/20,000d) This majestic tomb is renowned for its architecture and sublime forest setting. The tomb was planned during Minh Mang's reign (1820–40) but built by his successor, Thieu Tri.

Minh Mang's tomb is in An Bang village, on the west bank of the Perfume River, 12km from Hue.

Tomb of Khai Dinh TOMB

(adult/child 100,000/20,000d) This hillside monument is a synthesis of Vietnamese and European elements. Most of the tomb's grandiose exterior is covered in blackened concrete, creating an unexpectedly Gothic air, while the interiors resemble an explosion of colourful mosaic. Khai Dinh was the penultimate emperor of Vietnam, from 1916 to 1925, and widely seen as a puppet of the French. The construction of his flamboyant tomb took 11 years. The tomb of Khai Dinh is 10km from Hue in Chau Chu village.

Hue's Imperial Enclosure

EXPLORING THE SITE

An incongruous combination of meticulously restored palaces and pagodas, ruins and rubble, the Imperial Enclosure is approached from the south through the outer walls of the Citadel. It's best to tackle the site as a walking tour, winding your way around the structures in an anticlockwise direction.

You'll pass directly through the monumental ❶ **Ngo Mon Gateway** where the ticket office is located. This dramatic approach quickens the pulse and adds to the sense of occasion as you enter this citadel-within-a-citadel. Directly ahead is the ❷ **Thai Hoa Palace** where the emperor would greet offical visitors from his elevated throne. Continuing north you'll step across a small courtyard to the twin ❸ **Halls of the Mandarins**, where mandarins once had their offices and prepared for ceremonial occasions.

To the northeast is the Royal Theatre, where traditional dance performances are held several times daily. Next you'll be able to get a glimpse of the Emperor's Reading Room built by Thieu Tri and used as a place of retreat. Just east of here are the lovely Co Ha Gardens. Wander their pathways, dotted with hundreds of bonsai trees and potted plants, which have been recently restored.

Guarding the far north of the complex is the Tu Vo Phuong Pavilion, from where you can follow a moat to the Truong San residence and then loop back south via the ❹ **Dien Tho Residence** and finally view the beautifully restored temple compound of To Mieu, perhaps the most rewarding part of the entire enclosure to visit, including its fabulous ❺ **Nine Dynastic Urns**.

TOP TIPS

➡ Allow half a day to explore the Citadel.

➡ Drink vendors are dotted around the site, but the best places to take a break are the delightful Co Ha Gardens, the Tu Vo Phuong Pavilion and the Dien Tho Residence (the latter two also serve food).

PETER STUCKINGS / SHUTTERSTOCK ©

Dien Tho Residence
This pretty corner of the complex, with its low structures and pond, was the residence of many Queen Mothers. The earliest structures here date from 1804.

Nine Dynastic Urns
These colossal bronze urns were commissioned by Emperor Minh Mang and cast between 1835 and 1836. They're embellished with decorative elements including landscapes, rivers, flowers and animals.

LULU AND ISABELLE / SHUTTERSTOCK ©

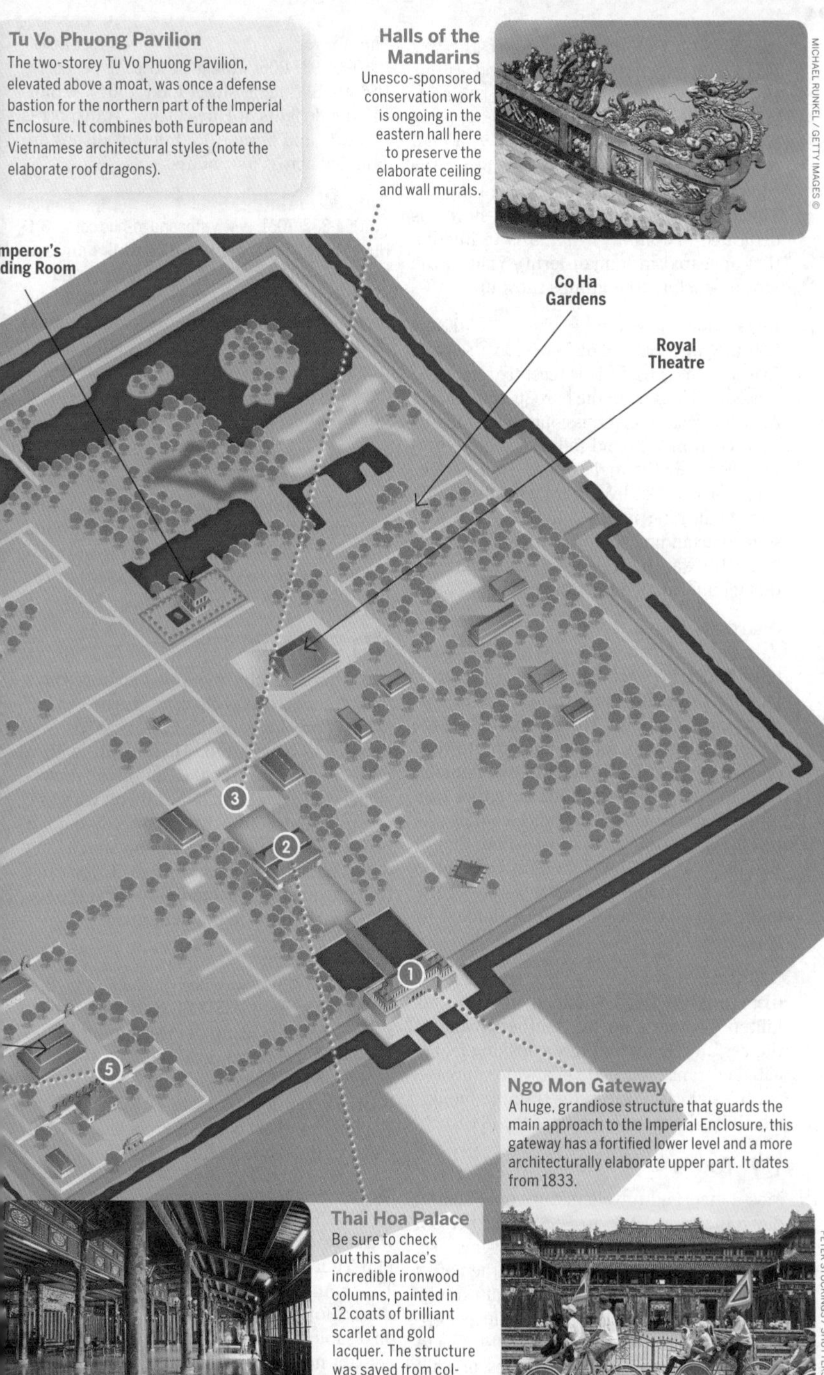

Tu Vo Phuong Pavilion
The two-storey Tu Vo Phuong Pavilion, elevated above a moat, was once a defense bastion for the northern part of the Imperial Enclosure. It combines both European and Vietnamese architectural styles (note the elaborate roof dragons).

Halls of the Mandarins
Unesco-sponsored conservation work is ongoing in the eastern hall here to preserve the elaborate ceiling and wall murals.

MICHAEL RUNKEL / GETTY IMAGES ©

Ngo Mon Gateway
A huge, grandiose structure that guards the main approach to the Imperial Enclosure, this gateway has a fortified lower level and a more architecturally elaborate upper part. It dates from 1833.

Thai Hoa Palace
Be sure to check out this palace's incredible ironwood columns, painted in 12 coats of brilliant scarlet and gold lacquer. The structure was saved from collapse by restoration work in the 1990s.

PETER STUCKINGS / SHUTTERSTOCK ©

★Thien Mu Pagoda BUDDHIST TEMPLE
FREE Built on a hill overlooking the Perfume River, 4km southwest of the Citadel, this pagoda is an icon of Vietnam and as potent a symbol of Hue as the Citadel. The 21m-high octagonal tower, Thap Phuoc Duyen, was constructed under the reign of Emperor Thieu Tri in 1844. Each of its seven storeys is dedicated to a *manushi-buddha* (a Buddha that appeared in human form). Visit in the morning before tour groups show up.

Royal Fine Arts Museum MUSEUM
(150 Đ Nguyen Hue; ⏲6.30am-5.30pm summer, 7am-5pm winter) FREE This recently renovated museum is located in the baroque-influenced An Dinh Palace, commissioned by Emperor Khai Dinh in 1918 and full of elaborate murals, floral motifs and trompe l'œil details. Emperor Bao Dai lived here with his family after abdicating in 1945. Inside, you'll find some outstanding ceramics, paintings, furniture, silverware, porcelain and royal clothing, though information is a little lacking.

Dieu De National Pagoda BUDDHIST TEMPLE
(Quoc Tu Dieu De; 102 Đ Bach Dang) FREE Overlooking Dong Ba Canal, this pagoda was built under Emperor Thieu Tri's rule (1841–47) and is famous for its four low towers, one either side of the gate and two flanking the sanctuary. The pavilions on either side of the main sanctuary entrance contain the 18 La Ha, whose rank is just below that of Bodhisattva, and the eight Kim Cang, protectors of Buddha. In the back row of the main dais is Thich Ca Buddha, flanked by two assistants.

Bao Quoc Pagoda BUDDHIST TEMPLE
(Ham Long Hill) FREE Founded in 1670, this hilltop pagoda is on the southern bank of the Perfume River and has a striking triple-gated entrance reached via a wide staircase. On the right is a centre for training monks, which has been functioning since 1940.

Tours

Most hotels and travellers cafes offer shared day tours from US$5 to US$20 per person. Better ones start with a morning river cruise, stopping at pagodas and temples, then after lunch a minibus travels to the main tombs before returning to Hue. On the cheaper options you'll often have to hire a motorbike to get from the moorings to the tombs, or walk in tropical heat.

Hue Flavor FOOD & DRINK
(☎0905 937 006; www.hueflavor.com; per person US$49) Excellent street-food tours exploring the delights of Hue cuisine. Transport is by *cyclo* and around 15 different dishes are sampled across four hours.

Stop & Go Café DRIVING
(☎054-382 7051; www.stopandgo-hue.com; 3 Đ Hung Vuong) Personalised motorbike and car tours. A full-day DMZ car tour guided by a Vietnamese vet costs around US$30 per person for four people, representing a good deal. Guided trips to Hoi An stopping at beaches are also recommended. Note, there are similarly named, unrelated businesses at other addresses.

Cafe on Thu Wheels TOURS
(☎054-383 2241; minhthuhue@yahoo.com; 10/2 Đ Nguyen Tri Phuong) Inexpensive cycle hire, and motorbike, minibus and car tours around Hue and the DMZ. Can also arrange transfers to Hoi An by motorbike (US$45) or car (US$55).

Sleeping

★Canary Boutique Hotel BOUTIQUE HOTEL $
(http://canaryboutiquehotel.com; Lane 8, 43 Đ Nguyen Cong Tru; r US$18-28; ⊖❄@📶) You don't *need* a bath-tub. Then again, with a budget price for such cleanliness, professional staff, a great breakfast menu with free seconds, and competitively priced tours, a bath-tub is just the cherry on top after a long day at the Citadel or nearby bars. If you can't find the hotel's small lane, enquire at the sister Canary Hotel on the main road.

★Home Hotel HOTEL $
(☎054-383 0014; www.huehomehotel.com; 8 Đ Nguyen Cong Tru; r US$17-24; ❄@📶) Run by a really friendly team, the welcoming Home Hotel has a younger, hip vibe, and spacious rooms arrayed across several levels. Ask to book a room looking over Đ Nguyen Cong Tru for a compact balcony, French doors and views of the river. No lift.

★Beach Bar Hue HOTEL $
(☎0908 993 584; www.beachbarhue.com; Phu Thuan beach; dm US$10; ⊖📶) At glorious Phu Thuan beach (about 7km southeast of Thuan An), the Beach Bar Hue has excellent shared four-bed bungalows and sits pretty on a sublime stretch of sand (with no hawkers…for now). There's a funky bamboo-and-thatch bar for drinks and snacks.

Jade Hotel GUESTHOUSE **$**
(☎054-393 8849; http://jadehotelhue.com; 17 Đ Nguyen Thai Hoc; r incl breakfast US$17-33;) You'll find simply excellent service standards at this fine place; staff are very sweet and welcoming indeed. Rooms enjoy soft comfy mattresses and there's a nice lobby-lounge for hanging out.

Hue Backpackers HOSTEL **$**
(☎054-382 6567; www.vietnambackpackerhostels.com; 10 Đ Pham Ngu Lao; dm US$8-12, r US$18, all incl breakfast;) Backpackers mecca thanks to its central location, eager-to-please staff, good info and sociable bar-restaurant which hosts happy hour and big sporting events. Dorms are well designed and have air-con and lockers.

HueNino GUESTHOUSE **$**
(☎054-625 2171; www.hueninohotel.com; 14 Đ Nguyen Cong Tru; r incl breakfast US$18-25;) Family-owned, this warm, welcoming guesthouse has an artistic flavour with stylish furniture, artwork and smallish rooms with minibar, cable TV and good-quality beds. Generous breakfast.

Star City Hotel HOTEL **$**
(☎054-383 1358; http://starcityhotelhue.com; 2/36 Đ Vo Thi Sau; r US$18-26;) Good value, five-storey hotel with a lift and clean, spacious rooms, all with TV and air-con. It's set off the street so traffic noise isn't an issue.

Orchid Hotel HOTEL **$$**
(☎054-383 1177; www.orchidhotel.com.vn; 30a Đ Chu Van An; r incl breakfast US$33-47;) This is a modern hotel rightly renowned for its warm service – staff really make an effort here. The accommodation is excellent: all options have laminate flooring, bright scatter cushions and a DVD player, while some pricier rooms even have a Jacuzzi with city views. Your complimentary breakfast is good (eggs are cooked to order) and children are well looked after.

Moonlight Hotel Hue HOTEL **$$**
(☎054-397 9797; www.moonlighthue.com; 20 Đ Pham Ngu Lao; r US$50-75, ste US$80-135;) This 'new generation' Hue hotel charges modest bucks for rooms that boast a very high spec that have polished wooden floors, marble-clad bathrooms (with tubs) and lavish furnishings. Pay a bit more for a balcony with a Perfume River view. The pool area is small and covered, and there are good rooftop drinks in the Sirius bar (p98).

Villa Louise BOUTIQUE HOTEL **$$$**
(☎0917 673 656; www.villalouisehue.com; Phu Thuan beach; d US$75-135, villas US$120-244;) Villa Louise has wonderful villas, private rooms and two swimming pools. The villas are lovingly decorated in heritage Vietnamese style.

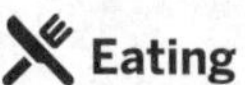

Eating

Vegetarian food has a long tradition in Hue. Stalls in Dong Ba Market serve it on the first and 15th days of the lunar month.

Hue also has great street food.

★**Hanh Restaurant** VIETNAMESE **$**
(☎0905 520 512; 11 Pho Duc Chinh; meals 30,000-100,000d; 10am-9pm) Newbies to Hue specialities, start at this busy restaurant. Order the five-dish set menu (100,000d) for a speedy lesson of *banh khoai* (savoury prawn pancakes), *banh beo* (steamed rice cakes topped with shrimp and spring onions), and divine *nem lui* (grilled pork on lemongrass skewers) wrapped in rice paper and herbs. Ask the patient staff how to devour everything.

★**Hang Me Me** VIETNAMESE **$**
(16 Đ Vo Thi Sau; meals from 40,000d; 8am-11pm;) A top, unfussy spot to try Hue's dizzying menu of royal rice cakes. Serving portions are pretty big, so rustle up a few friends to try the different variations. Our favourite is the *banh beo*, perfect little mouthfuls topped with spring onions and dried shrimp.

Quan Bun Bo Hue VIETNAMESE **$**
(17 Đ Ly Thuong Kiet; meals 35,000d; 6am-2pm) Excellent spot for a hearty bowl of *bun bo Hue*, the city's signature noodle dish combining tender beef, vermicelli and lemongrass. Next door at number 19, Ly Thuong Kiet is equally good. Both sell out by early afternoon.

Lien Hoa VEGETARIAN **$**
(☎054-381 2456; 3 Đ Le Quy Don; meals 50,000-75,000d; 6.30am-9pm;) No-nonsense Viet vegetarian restaurant renowned for filling food at bargain prices. Fresh *banh beo*, noodle dishes, crispy fried jackfruit and aubergine with ginger all deliver. The menu has very rough English translations to help you order (staff speak little or no English).

Stop & Go Café INTERNATIONAL **$**
(www.stopandgo-hue.com; 3 Đ Hung Vuong; meals 35,000-90,000d; 7am-10pm;) Atmospheric little place with decent Vietnamese and backpacker fare: *banh beo* (steamed rice cakes), beef noodle soup, tacos, pizza and pasta, and

Hue

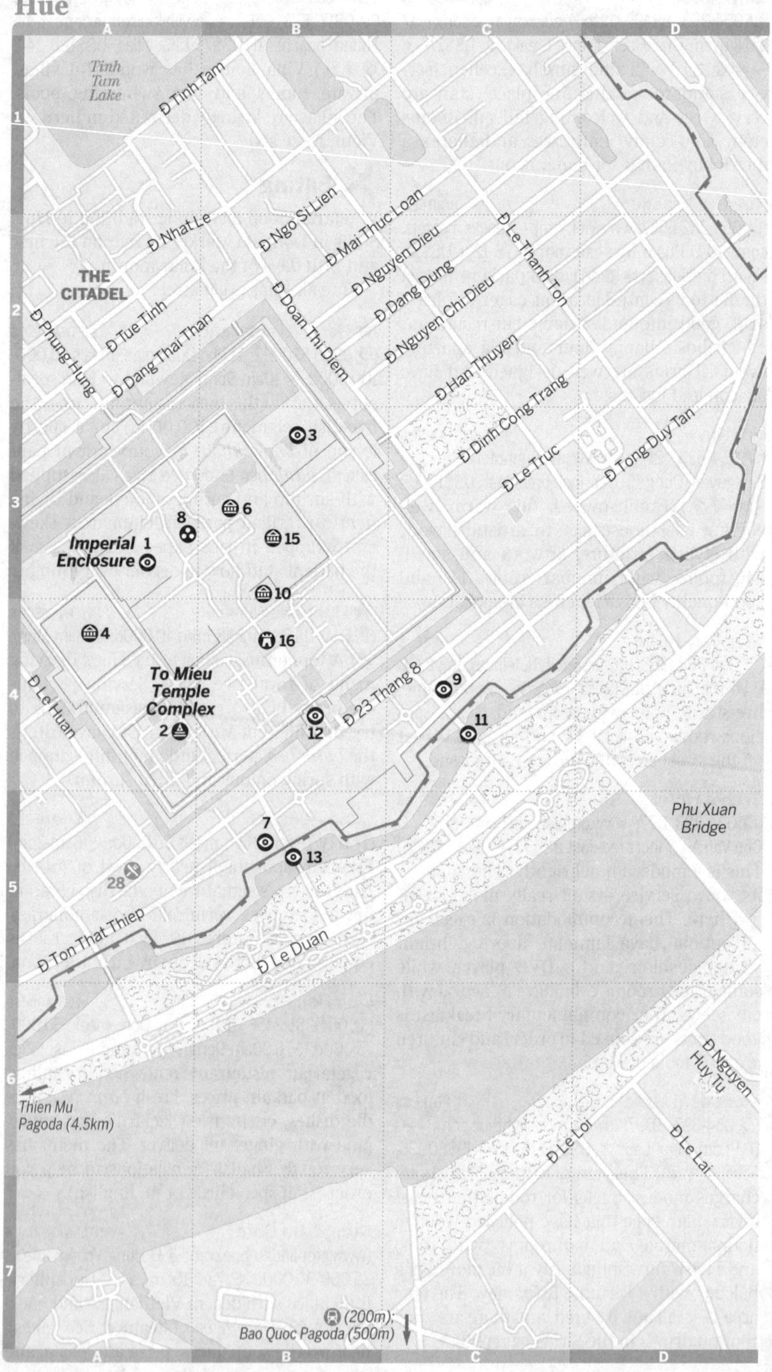

A
B
C
D
1
2
3
4
5
6
7
Tinh Tam Lake
Đ Tinh Tam
Đ Nhat Le
Đ Ngo Si Lien
Đ Mai Thuc Loan
Đ Nguyen Dieu
Đ Le Thanh Ton
THE CITADEL
Đ Doan Thi Diem
Đ Dang Dung
Đ Nguyen Chi Dieu
Đ Phung Hung
Đ Tue Tinh
Đ Dang Thai Than
Đ Han Thuyen
Đ Dinh Cong Trang
Đ Tong Duy Tan
Đ Le Truc
3
6
8
Imperial Enclosure 1
15
10
4
16
To Mieu Temple Complex
2
Đ Le Huan
12
Đ 23 Thang 8
9
11
Phu Xuan Bridge
7
13
28
Đ Ton That Thiep
Đ Le Duan
Thien Mu Pagoda (4.5km)
Đ Nguyen Huy Tu
Đ Le Loi
Đ Le Lai
(200m); Bao Quoc Pagoda (500m)

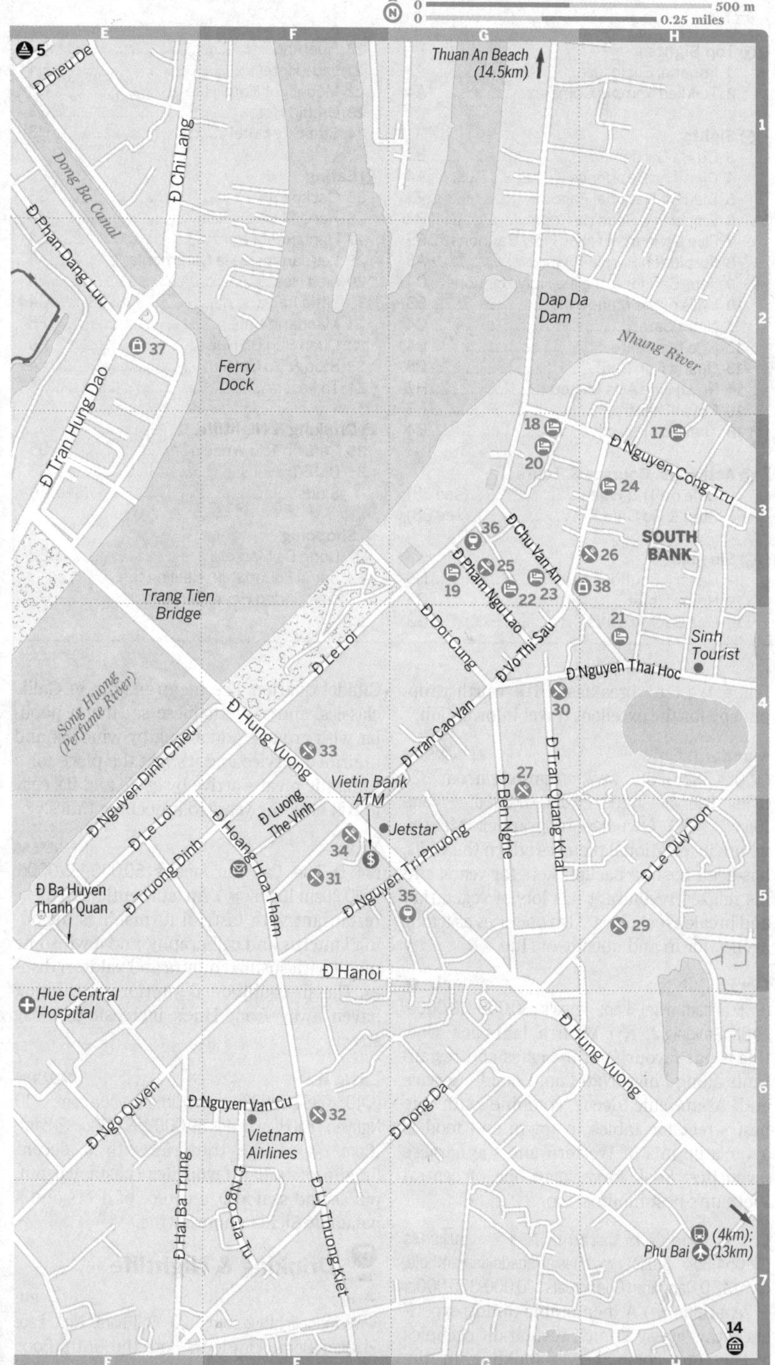
0 500 m
0 0.25 miles
E
F
G
H
5
Đ Dieu De
Thuan An Beach (14.5km)
Đ Chi Lang
Dong Ba Canal
Đ Phan Dang Luu
Dap Da Dam
Nhung River
37
Ferry Dock
Đ Tran Hung Dao
18
17
20
Đ Nguyen Cong Tru
24
36
Đ Chu Van An
SOUTH BANK
26
Đ Pham Ngu Lao
25
19
22
23
38
Trang Tien Bridge
21
Đ Doi Cung
Đ Le Loi
Đ Vo Thi Sau
Sinh Tourist
Đ Nguyen Thai Hoc
30
Song Huong (Perfume River)
Đ Hung Vuong
Đ Tran Cao Van
Đ Nguyen Dinh Chieu
33
27
Vietin Bank ATM
Đ Ben Nghe
Đ Tran Quang Khai
Đ Luong The Vinh
Jetstar
Đ Le Loi
Đ Hoang Hoa Tham
34
Đ Nguyen Tri Phuong
Đ Le Quy Don
Đ Truong Dinh
31
Đ Ba Huyen Thanh Quan
35
29
Đ Hanoi
Hue Central Hospital
Đ Hung Vuong
Đ Ngo Quyen
Đ Nguyen Van Cu
32
Đ Dong Da
Vietnam Airlines
Đ Hai Ba Trung
Đ Ngo Gia Tu
Đ Ly Thuong Kiet
(4km);
Phu Bai (13km)
14
1
2
3
4
5
6
7

Hue

Top Sights
1 Imperial Enclosure ... A3
2 To Mieu Temple Complex ... A4

Sights
3 Co Ha Gardens ... B3
4 Dien Tho Residence ... A4
5 Dieu De National Pagoda ... E1
6 Emperor's Reading Room ... B3
7 Five Cannons of Nine Holy Cannons ... B5
8 Forbidden Purple City ... A3
9 Four Cannons of Nine Holy Cannons ... C4
10 Halls of the Mandarins ... B3
11 Ngan Gate ... C4
12 Ngo Mon Gate ... B4
13 Quang Duc Gate ... B5
14 Royal Fine Arts Museum ... H7
15 Royal Theatre ... B3
16 Thai Hoa Palace ... B4

Activities, Courses & Tours
Cafe on Thu Wheels ... (see 35)
Stop & Go Café ... (see 33)

Sleeping
17 Canary Boutique Hotel ... H3
18 Home Hotel ... G3
19 Hue Backpackers ... G3
20 HueNino ... G3
21 Jade Hotel ... H4
22 Moonlight Hotel Hue ... G3
23 Orchid Hotel ... G3
24 Star City Hotel ... H3

Eating
25 Gecko Pub ... G3
26 Hang Me Me ... H3
27 Hanh Restaurant ... G4
28 Les Jardins de la Carambole ... A5
29 Lien Hoa ... H5
30 Little Italy ... G4
31 Mandarin Café ... F5
32 Quan Bun Bo Hue ... F6
33 Stop & Go Café ... F4
34 Ta.ke ... F5

Drinking & Nightlife
35 Café on Thu Wheels ... G5
36 DMZ Travel ... G3
Sirius ... (see 19)

Shopping
37 Dong Ba Market ... E2
38 Spiral Foundation Healing the Wounded Heart Center ... H3

filling Western breakfasts. It's worth dropping by for the excellent travel information.

Mandarin Café VIETNAMESE $

(054-382 1281; www.mrcumandarin.com; 24 Đ Tran Cao Van; meals 25,000-69,000d; 6am-10pm;) Owner-photographer Mr Cu, whose inspirational pictures adorn the walls, has been hosting backpackers for years, and his relaxed restaurant has lots of vegetarian and breakfast choices. Also operates as a tour agency for in and outside of Hue.

Gecko Pub CAFE $$

(9 Đ Pham Ngu Lao; meals 30,000-110,000d; 8am-midnight;) With a laid-back vibe, this is our favourite of the cafes and restaurants along Pham Ngu Lao. Friendly service and Asian chic decor combine with the best streetside tables in town, and food is a versatile mix of Western and Vietnamese favourites. Look forward to one of central Vietnam's best mojitos, too.

Les Jardins de la Carambole FUSION $$

(054-354 8815; www.lesjardinsdelacarambole.com; 32 Đ Dang Tran Con; meals 120,000-300,000d; 7am-11pm;) A memorable dining experience, this classy French restaurant occupies a gorgeous colonial-style building in the Citadel quarter. The menu majors in Gallic classics, and a Vietnamese set menu popular with groups. Add a lengthy wine list and informed service and it's just the place for a romantic meal – arrive by *cyclo* and it's easy to roll back the years to Indochine times.

Ta.ke JAPANESE $$

(34 Đ Tran Cao Van; meals 50,000-135,000d; 10.30am-10pm;) An authentic Japanese restaurant with tasteful furnishings including lanterns and calligraphy, and a winsome menu with sushi, tempura and yakitori dishes. The air-conditioned interior is a calming haven away from Hue's increasingly busy streets.

Little Italy ITALIAN $$

(054-382 6928; www.littleitalyhue.com; 10 Nguyen Thai H□c; mains 59,000-139,000d; 8am-10pm;) Large trattoria with a decent line-up of Italian favourites (pasta, calzoni, pizzas and seafood), a choice of beers and a palatable Sicilian house wine.

Drinking & Nightlife

Sirius BAR

(www.moonlighthue.com; 20 Đ Pham Ngu Lao; 10am-10pm) Outdoors, on the 15th floor of the Moonlight Hotel (p95), Sirius is the best place in town for sunset drinks. Combine BBQ snacks (beef, squid, prawns; from 55,000d) and a few beers or a cocktail and view the arrival of dusk on the Perfume River.

DMZ Travel BAR

(www.dmz.com.vn; 60 Đ Le Loi; ⌚7am-1am; 📶) Ever-popular bar near the river with a free pool table, cold Huda beer, cocktails (try a watermelon mojito) and antics most nights. Also serves Western and local food till midnight, smoothies and juices. Happy hour is 3pm to 8pm. Check out the upside-down map of the DMZ – complete with a US chopper – on the ceiling of the bar.

Café on Thu Wheels BAR

(☎054-383 2241; lnhin60@yahoo.com; 3/34 Đ Nguyen Tri Phuong; ⌚7am-11pm; 📶) Graffiti-splattered walls, a sociable vibe, excellent food and smoothies all combine at this welcoming spot owned by a friendly family. They also offer good tours (p94), and have books and mags to browse.

Shopping

Spiral Foundation Healing the Wounded Heart Center ARTS & CRAFTS

(☎054-383 3694; www.spiralfoundation.org; 23 Đ Vo Thi Sau; ⌚8am-6pm) Generating cash from trash, this shop stocks lovely handicrafts – such as quirky bags from plastic, and picture frames from recycled beer cans – made by artists with disabilities. Profits aid heart surgery for children in need.

Dong Ba Market MARKET

(Đ Tran Hung Dao; ⌚6.30am-8pm) Just north of Trang Tien Bridge, this is Hue's largest market, selling anything and everything.

Information

Hue Central Hospital (Benh Vien Trung Uong Hue; ☎054-382 2325; 16 Đ Le Loi; ⌚6am-10pm) Well-regarded local hospital.

Post Office (8 Đ Hoang Hoa Tham; ⌚7am-5.30pm Mon-Sat)

Sinh Tourist (☎054-384 5022; www.thesinhtourist.vn; 37 Đ Nguyen Thai Hoc; ⌚6.30am-10pm) Books open-tour buses, and buses to Laos and many other destinations in Vietnam.

Vietin Bank ATM (12 Đ Hung Vuong) Centrally located ATM.

Getting There & Away

Jetstar (☎1900 1550; Đ Hung Vuong; ⌚Mon-Sat) and **VietJet** (☎1900 1886; www.vietjetair.com) fly to/from Ho Chi Minh City (HCMC); while **Vietnam Airlines** (☎054-382 4709; 23 Đ Nguyen Van Cu; ⌚Mon-Sat) can fly you to/from Hanoi and HCMC.

The main bus station, 4km southeast of the centre, has connections to Danang and south to HCMC.

An Hoa Bus Station (Hwy 1), northwest of the Citadel, serves northern destinations, including Dong Ha (44,000d, two hours, every half hour).

One daily bus (look for 'Phuc Vu' in the windscreen) heads for Phong Nha Farmstay and Son Trach at 11.15am (150,000d, four hours) from An Hoa bus station.

For Phong Nha (around 135,000d, five hours), the Hung Thanh open-tour bus leaves 49 Đ Chu Van An at 4.30pm, and the Tan Nha bus leaves from the Why Not? bar on Đ Vo Thi Sau around 6.30am.

Hue is a regular stop on open-tour bus routes. Most drop off and pick-up passengers at central hotels. Expect some hassle from persistent hotel touts when you arrive.

Hue Train Station (☎054-382 2175; 2 Đ Phan Chu Trinh) is a regular stop on the Reunification Express.

Getting Around

Hue's Phu Bai Airport is 14km south of the city. Metered **taxis** (☎054-389 8989) cost about 220,000d to the centre, or take the Vietnam Airlines minibus service (50,000d) from outside the airport to its offices a 15-minute walk from the hotel area of Hue – taxis and *xe om* will be waiting here.

Pedal power is a fun way to tour Hue and the royal tombs. Hotels rent bicycles for around US$3 per day.

ROYAL RICE CAKES

These savoury Hue specialities come in different shapes and sizes, but are all made with rice flour. The most common is the crispy fried, filled pancake *banh khoai* (smaller and denser than southern Vietnam's *banh xeo* pancakes). The other variations are steamed and sticky-rice-like, and are usually topped with shrimp and dipped in sweet fish sauce. Look for *banh beo*, which come in tiny dishes; banana-leaf-wrapped *banh nam*; transparent dumplings *banh loc*; and the leaf-steamed pyramids *banh it*, which can come in sweet mung-bean or savoury varieties.

TRANSPORT FROM HUE

DESTINATION	AIR	BUS	CAR & MOTORBIKE	TRAIN
Danang	N/A	60,000d, 3hr, frequent	2½-4hr	US$4-8, 2½-4hr, 7 daily
Dong Hoi	N/A	85,000d, 4hr, frequent	3½hr	US$5-11, 3-5½hr, 7 daily
Hanoi	from 1,000,000d, 1hr, 3 daily	260,000d, 13-16hr, 9 daily	16hr	US$25-42, 12-15½hr, 6 daily
HCMC	from 480,000d, 1¼hr, 4 daily	490,000d,19-24hr, 9 daily	22hr	US$33-55, 19½-23hr, 5 daily
Ninh Binh	N/A	250,000d, 10½-12hr, 8 daily	11hr	US$19-35, 10-13hr, 5 daily
Vinh	N/A	150,000d, 7½-9hr, frequent to 1pm	7hr	US$23-38, 6½-10hr, 5 daily

Around Hue

Demilitarised Zone (DMZ)

From 1954 to 1975 the Ben Hai River acted as a buffer between North and South Vietnam. The area just south of the DMZ was the scene of some of the bloodiest battles in America's first TV war, turning Quang Tri, the Rockpile, Khe Sanh, Lang Vay and Hamburger Hill into household names.

Most sites have now been cleared, the land reforested or planted with rubber and coffee. Only Ben Hai, Vinh Moc and Khe Sanh have small museums. Unless you're a veteran, or military buff, you might find it a little hard to appreciate the place – which is all the more reason to hire a knowledgeable guide.

Sights

Vinh Moc Tunnels HISTORIC SITE

(20,000d; 7am-4.30pm) A highly impressive complex of tunnels, Vinh Moc is the remains of a coastal North Vietnamese village that literally went underground in response to unremitting American bombing. More than 90 families disappeared into three levels of tunnels running for almost 2km, and continued to live and work while bombs rained down around them. Most of the tunnels are open to visitors and are kept in their original form (except for electric lights, a recent addition).

An English-speaking guide will accompany you around the complex, pointing out the 12 entrances until you emerge at a glorious beach, facing the South China Sea. The museum has photos and relics of tunnel life, including a map of the tunnel network. The Vinh Moc tunnels are often compared to the Cu Chi tunnels, which are more cramped and humid and were intended for soldiers, not civilians.

The turn-off to Vinh Moc from Hwy 1 is 6.5km north of the Ben Hai River in the village of Ho Xa. Follow this road east for 13km.

Hamburger Hill HISTORIC SITE

FREE Hamburger Hill (Ap Bia) was the site of a tumultuous battle in May 1969 between US forces and the North Vietnamese Army (NVA) over a 900m-high mountain – resulting in over 600 North Vietnamese and 72 American deaths. Today you need a special permit (US$25 and only obtained in the town of Aluoi) and a guide to see the remaining trenches and bunkers. Hamburger Hill is 8km northwest of Aluoi, about 6km off Hwy 14, and less than 2km from Laos.

There's a rudimentary visitor centre (with a map and information in English) at the base of the hill, from where a 6km trail leads up the mountain. Bring water and be sure to stick to the main trail. Security is tight around here and you're sure to get your permits inspected by border guards.

Rockpile HISTORIC SITE

Visible from Hwy 9, this 230m-high karst outcrop once had a US Marine Corps lookout on top and a base for American long-range artillery nearby. The Rockpile is 29km west of Dong Ha on Hwy 9.

Bach Ma National Park

A French-era hill station, this **national park** (Vuon Quoc Gia Bach Ma; ☎054-387 1330; www.bachmapark.com.vn; adult/child 40,000/20,000d) reaches a peak of 1450m at Bach Ma mountain, only 18km from the coast. The French were attracted by the cool climate, and started building villas here in 1930; by 1937 the number of holiday homes had reached 139 and it became known as the 'Dalat of central Vietnam'.

Today there are walking trails, birdwatching, zip lines and a pagoda to explore in the relative cool.

The park is home to more than 1400 plant species, including rare ferns and orchids, representing a fifth of the flora of Vietnam. There are 132 kinds of mammals, three of which were only discovered in the 1990s: the antelope-like saola, the Truong Son muntjac and the giant muntjac. Nine primate species are also present, including small numbers of the rare red-shanked Douc langur. It's hoped wild elephants will return from the Lao side of the border.

Activities

The Rhododendron Trail (from Km 10 on the road) leads to the upper reaches of a spectacular waterfall; it's 689 steps down for a dip. The Five Lakes Trail passes pools for swimming before reaching a much smaller waterfall. The short Summit Hike leads to a viewpoint with magnificent views (on a clear day) over the forest, Cau Hai lagoon and the coast. Unexploded ordnance is still around, so stick to the trails.

As most of the park's resident mammals are nocturnal, sightings demand a great deal of effort and patience. Birdwatching is fantastic, but you need to be up at dawn for the best chance of glimpsing some of the 358 species logged, including the fabulous crested argus pheasant.

At the **visitor centre** (www.bachmapark.com.vn) by the park entrance there's an exhibition on the park's flora and fauna, and hiking booklets are available. You can book village and birdwatching tours and English- or French-speaking guides (300,000d to 500,000d per day). Ask if Mr Cam is available.

WORTH A TRIP

TOMBS & DUNES

From the centre of Hue it's only 15km north to the coast, the road shadowing the Perfume River before you hit the sands of Thuan An Beach. Southeast from here there's a beautiful, quiet coastal road to follow with very light traffic (so it's ideal for bikers). The route traverses a narrow coastal island, with views of the Tam Giang-Cau Hai lagoon on the inland side and stunning sandy beaches and dunes on the other. This coastal strip is virtually undeveloped, but between September and March, the water's often too rough for swimming.

From Thuan An the road winds past villages alternating with shrimp lagoons and vegetable gardens. Thousands of garishly colourful and opulent graves and family temples line the beach, most the final resting places of Viet Kieu (overseas Vietnamese) who wanted to be buried in their homeland. Tracks cut through the tombs and sand dunes to the beach. Pick a spot and you'll probably have a beach to yourself.

At glorious Phu Thuan Beach (about 7km southeast of Thuan An), are the funky Beach Bar Hue (p94) and charming Villa Louise (p95). The villa's pools, restaurant and beach can all be used by outside guests – there's an entrance fee of 100,000d which can be offset against food and beverage purchases in the beachfront bar. A taxi from Hue to Phu Thuan is around 250,000d and a xe om (motorbike taxi) around 125,000d.

Around 8km past Beach Bar Hue, the remains of Phu Dien, a small Cham temple, lie protected by a glass pavilion in the dunes just off the beach. There are seafood shacks here too.

Continuing southeast, a narrow paved road weaves past fishing villages, shrimp farms, giant sand dunes and the settlement of Vinh Hung until it reaches the mouth of another river estuary at Thuon Phu An, where there's a row of seafood restaurants. This spot is 40km from Thuan An. Cross the Tu Hien bridge here and you can continue around the eastern lip of the huge Cau Hai lagoon and link up with Hwy 1.

Another recommended Hue-based tour company offering regular overnight explorations of Bach Ma National Park from Hue with a car and driver is **Oriental Sky Travel** (☎0985 555 827; www.orientalskytravel.com).

Sleeping & Eating

There is are guesthouses and limited camping near the entrance, and villas near the summit. Arrange accommodation and eating (they might need time to send up ingredients) with the visitor centre before you ascend.

Getting There & Around

Bach Ma is 28km west of Lang Co and 40km southeast of Hue. The turn-off is signposted in the town of Cau Hai on Hwy 1. You can also enter from the town of Phu Loc.

Buses from Danang (80,000d, two hours) and Hue (60,000d, one hour) stop at Cau Hai, where *xe om* drivers can ferry you around 3km (25,000d) to the entrance.

From the visitor centre at the park entrance, it's a steep, serpentine 15km ascent, and the road almost reaches the summit. Walking down from the summit takes about three to four hours; you'll need water and sunscreen. Private transport to the summit is available from the visitor centre, and a return same-day journey is 900,000d for a six-person minibus. At busy times, travellers can usually share the cost with other passengers. For an overnight stay, transport to the summit is 1,300,000d for six people. Note that cars are allowed in the park, so it's worth considering a tour here from Hue, or arranging a car and driver for around US$50 return. Motorbikes are not allowed in the park, but there is a secure parking area near the visitor centre.

Danang

Nowhere in Vietnam is changing as fast as Danang. For decades it had a reputation as a provincial backwater, but big changes are ongoing. Stroll along the Han riverfront and you'll find gleaming new modernist hotels, and apartments and restaurants are emerging. Spectacular new bridges now span the river, and in the north of the city, the landmark new D-City is rising from the flatl ands. Venture south and the entire China Beach strip is booming with hotel and resort developments.

That said, the city itself still has few conventional sightseeing spots, except for a very decent museum and a stunningly quirky bridge (or three). So for most travellers, a few days enjoying the city's beaches, restaurants and nightlife is probably enough. Book an after-dark tour to see Danang at its shimmering neon-lit best. The city's street-food scene also deserves close investigation.

Sights

★**Dragon Bridge** BRIDGE
(Cau Rong; ⏲24hr) FREE Welcome to the biggest show in town every Saturday and Sunday night. At 9pm, this impressive dragon sculpture spouts fire and water from its head, near the Han River's eastern bank. The best observation spots are the cafes lining the eastern bank to the north of the bridge; boat trips also depart from Đ Bach Dang on the river's western bank to make the most of Danang's neon-lit splendour. The colour-changing dragon sees selfie-takers every night.

★**Museum of Cham Sculpture** MUSEUM
(Bao Tang; 1 Đ Trung Nu Vuong; 40,000d; ⏲7am-5pm) This fine, small museum has the world's largest collection of Cham artefacts, housed in buildings marrying French-colonial architecture with Cham elements. Founded in 1915 by the École Française d'Extrême Orient, it displays more than 300 pieces including altars, *lingas*, garudas, apsaras, Ganeshes and images of Shiva, Brahma and Vishnu, all dating from the 5th to 15th centuries. Explanations are slim. To hire an MP3 audio guide (20,000d), you'll need to show ID – passport or driving licence – or leave a refundable US$50 bond.

Tours

Funtastic Tours TOURS
(☎0903 561 777; www.funtasticdanang.com; per person US$45) Run by the funky young team behind Danang's Funtastic hostels, with tours including street food and sightseeing. Transport is by car. Check out www.danang cuisine.com for Danang tips by operator Summer Le, a local food blogger who's been featured in the *New York Times*.

Danang Food Tour FOOD & DRINK
(www.danangfoodtour.com; per person US$45) Excellent morning and evening explorations of the local food scene by a passionate expat foodie. Check the website for his great blog on the best of Danang.

Sleeping

Staying near the river west of the Dragon Bridge is the sweet spot for eating and nightlife options; staying east across the Han River near My Khe Beach saves you short taxi trips back and forth, and you can get some off-season accommodation bargains, but things are definitely less exciting.

Danang has a fast-expanding selection of modern hotels along the riverside, and a few much-needed new hostels.

★Memory Hostel HOSTEL **$**
(0511-374 7797; http://memoryhostel.com; 3 Đ Tran Quoc Toan; dm US$8;) Sweet memories are made of casual strolls to the Dragon Bridge, good restaurants and nightlife, all nearby to this hostel. If you just want to stay in, the decor is arty, eclectic and clean, and beds have privacy curtains. An excellent budget option.

Funtastic Danang Hostel HOSTEL **$**
(0511-389 2024; www.funtasticdanang.com; 115 Đ Hai Phong; dm US$6.50, d & tw US$19;) Danang's original specialist hostel is a goodie, with young and energetic owners, colourful rooms and dorms, and a comfortable lounge area for when all you want to do is chill and watch a movie. Ask about the street-food tours (p102).

Dai A Hotel BUSINESS HOTEL **$$**
(0511-382 7532; 51 Đ Yen Bai; d incl breakfast US$21-35;) Near the river, Dai A offers good breakfast and comfortable beds. It lacks personality and the rooms are small, but the tall building gets an A for being clean, private and a good escape from street noise. Staff speak good English and can arrange transport to Hoi An.

Sun River Hotel HOTEL **$$**
(0511-384 9188; www.sunriverhoteldn.com.vn; 132-134 Đ Bach Dang; r 900,000-1,800,000d;) A tempting option, this riverfront hotel offers immaculate rooms with really fancy bathrooms (some with space-age showers). Note the standard-class options do not have windows and only the VIPs have a river view.

New Moon Hotel HOTEL **$$**
(0511-382 8488; www.newmoonhotel.vn; 126 Đ Bach Dang; r 550,000-1,000,000d;) Modern minihotel with a selection of inviting rooms in different price categories, all with flat-screen TV, minibar, wi-fi and en-suite marble bathrooms. The river-view options enjoy incredible vistas.

Eating

Danang's restaurant scene is growing more cosmopolitan by the day. Street food is also great here, with copious *bun cha* (barbecued pork), *com* (rice and buffet) and *mi quang* (noodle soup) stalls. Dedicated foodies should strongly consider booking a food tour to really explore the Danang scene.

★Fatfish FUSION **$$**
(www.fatfishdanang.com; 439 Đ Tran Hung Dao; meals 80,000-290,000d; 9am-11.30pm Tue-Sun;) This stylish restaurant and lounge bar is leading the eating and drinking charge across the river on the Han's eastern shore. Innovative Asian fusion dishes, pizza and wood-fired barbecue all partner with flavour-packed craft beers from Ho Chi Minh City's Pasteur Street Brewing (p146). Fatfish is good for a few snacks or a more leisurely full meal.

Book in for before 9pm on a Saturday or Sunday night for front-row seats to see the nearby Dragon Bridge (p102) do its fiery party trick. A new boating marina and boardwalk is being completed around Fatfish, and the area will no doubt develop into Danang's hottest restaurant precinct.

Waterfront INTERNATIONAL **$$**
(0511-384 3373; www.waterfrontdanang.com; 150-152 Đ Bach Dang; meals 150,000-350,000d; 9am-11pm;) A riverfront lounge and restaurant that gets everything right on every level. It works as a stylish bar for a chilled glass of New Zealand sauvignon blanc or an imported beer, and also as a destination restaurant for a memorable meal (book the terrace deck for a stunning river vista). The menu features imported meats, Asian seafood, good vegie options and also terrific 'gourmet' sandwiches.

Le Bambino FRENCH **$$**
(0511-389 6386; www.lebambino.com; 122/11 Đ Quang Trung; meals 140,000-430,000d; 11.30am-1.30pm Mon-Sat, 4.30-10pm daily;) Atmospheric place run by a couple (French husband, Vietnamese wife) who have crafted a great menu that takes in French classics, pub food, barbecued meat (try the ribs) and a few Vietnamese favourites. Eat inside or around the pool, and don't neglect the wine list or the cheese selections, both of which are superb.

Danang

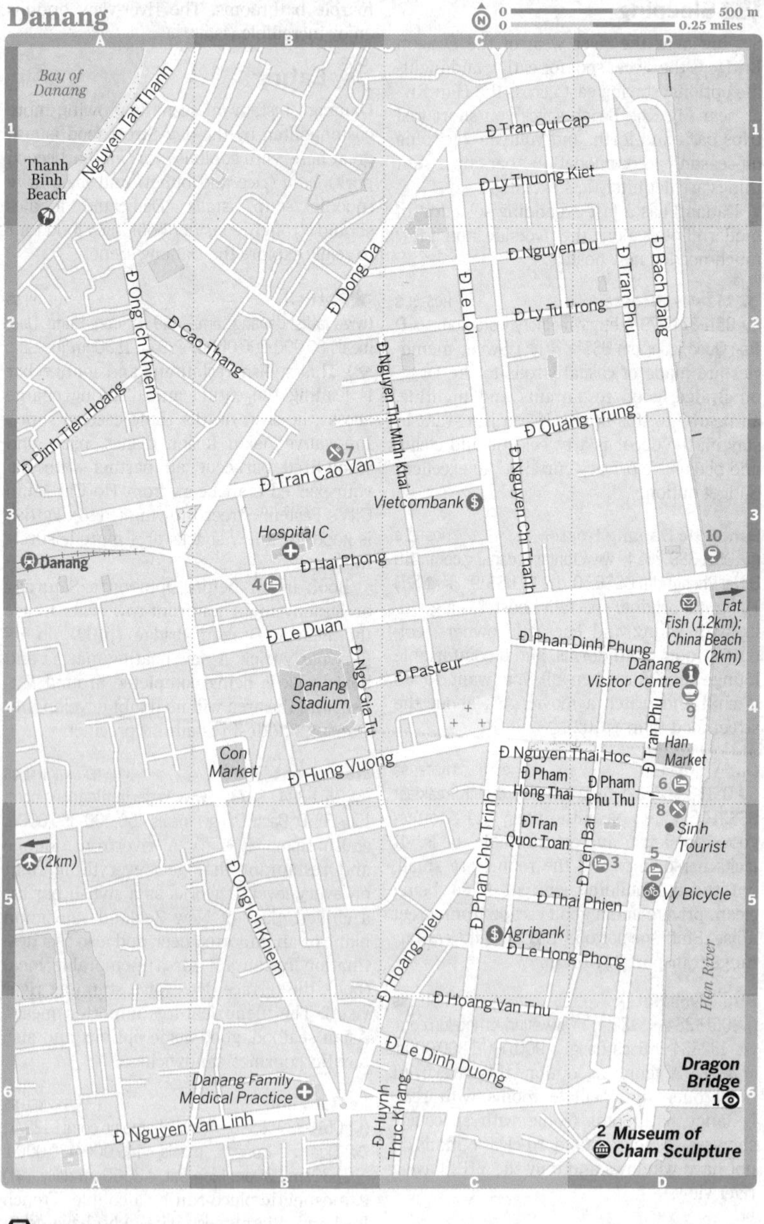

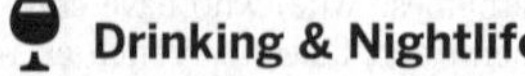

Drinking & Nightlife

Cong Caphe CAFE

(1 Đ Bach Dang; drinks from 40,000d; ⏲7am-11pm; 📶) The Danang offshoot of Hanoi's quirky Communist-themed cafes is a top spot for a riverside caffeine fix – try the superb coffee with yoghurt – or a well-priced beer or cocktail later in the day. It can get busy and smoky, so try and grab a seat near the windows.

Danang

Top Sights
1 Dragon Bridge D6
2 Museum of Cham Sculpture D6

Sleeping
3 Dai A Hotel D5
4 Funtastic Danang Hostel B3
5 Memory Hostel D5
6 New Moon Hotel D4
Sun River Hotel .... (see 6)

Eating
7 Le Bambino B3
8 Waterfront D5

Drinking & Nightlife
9 Cong Caphe D4
10 Memory Lounge D3

Memory Lounge LOUNGE
(www.loungememory.com; 7 Đ Bach Dang; drinks from US$5; ⌚8am-10pm; 📶) This landmark bar-restaurant juts over the river near the Song Han bridge. It works better as a bar, as the restaurant prices are stratospheric and the cooking rarely hits the expected heights. It's fine for a coffee, but its strength is a beer with a night view. Note that Vietnamese bands and crooners are often part of the evening entertainment.

Information

Agribank (202 Đ Nguyen Chi Thanh; ⌚7.30am-3.30pm Mon-Sat) With ATM.

Danang Visitor Centre (☎0511-3863 595; www.tourism.danang.vn; 32A Đ Phan Dinh Phung; ⌚7.30am-9pm) Really helpful, with English spoken, and good maps and brochures. Danang's official tourism website is one of Vietnam's best.

Danang Family Medical Practice (☎0511-358 2700; www.vietnammedicalpractice.com; 50-52 Đ Nguyen Van Linh; ⌚7am-6pm) With in-patient facilities; run by an Australian doctor.

Hospital C (Benh Vien C; ☎0511-382 1483; 122 Đ Hai Phong; ⌚24hr) The most advanced of the four hospitals in town.

Main Post Office (64 Đ Bach Dang; ⌚7am-5.30pm) Near the Song Han Bridge.

Vietcombank (☎0511-381 7441; 140 Đ Le Loi) The only bank that changes travellers cheques.

Getting There & Around

Danang is the main gateway to Hoi An and one of the entry points to the Cham Islands, so it is well connected with trains and an international airport. Staff at all hotels and hostels can help arrange transport to and from Hoi An, other sights and the airport. It's possible to arrange onward transport from the airport or train station direct to Hoi An.

AIR

Danang's **airport** (☎0511-383 0339) is 2km west of the city centre. There is no airport bus and a taxi is around 60,000d.

Jetstar Pacific (☎0511-358 3538; www.jetstar.com) To/from HCMC and Hanoi, and flights to/from Singapore on Jetstar Asia.

BICYCLE

Vy Bicycle (☎0914 575 450; www.facebook.com/vy.bicycle; 202 Đ Bach Dang; ⌚8am-8pm) Handy cityside spot for those who wish to hire two wheels and explore the beach area east across the river.

BUS

Sinh Tourist (☎0511-384 3258; www.thesinhtourist.vn; 154 Đ Bach Dang; ⌚7am-10pm) open-tour buses pick-up from the company office on Đ Bach Dang (near the Dragon Bridge) twice daily to both Hue (90,000d, 2½ hours)

TRANSPORT FROM DANANG

DESTINATION	AIR	BUS	CAR & MOTORCYCLE	TRAIN
Dong Hoi	N/A	120,000d, 6½hr, 7 daily	6-7hr	US$12-20, 5½-8½hr, 6 daily
Hanoi	from US$42, 1hr 10min, 9 daily	365,000d, 16-19hr, 7 daily	19hr	US$35-50, 14½-18hr, 6 daily
Ho Chi Minh City	from US$47, 1hr 15min, 18 daily	380,000d, 19-25hr, 9 daily	18hr	US$35-55, 17-22hr, 5 daily
Hue	N/A	55,000d, 3hr, every 20min	2½-4hr	US$4-7, 2½-4hr, 6 daily
Nha Trang	from US$45, 30min, 2 daily	230,000d, 10-13hr, 8 daily	13hr	US$20-35, 9-12hr, 5 daily

and Hoi An (80,000d, one hour), and Sinh Tourist can also advise on travel to Laos.

The large **Intercity Bus Station** (☎0511-382 1265; Đ Dien Bien Phu) is 3km west of the city centre. A metered **taxi** (☎0511-356 5656) to the riverside will cost 70,000d.

TRAIN

The train ride to Hue is one of the best in the country – it's worth taking as an excursion in itself for the stunning coastline.

Services from the **train station** (202 Đ Hai Phong) go to all destinations on the north–south main line.

Hoi An

Graceful, historic Hoi An is Vietnam's most atmospheric and delightful town. Once a major port, it boasts the grand architecture and beguiling riverside setting that befits its heritage, and the 21st-century curses of traffic and pollution are almost entirely absent.

The face of the Old Town has preserved its incredible legacy of tottering Japanese merchant houses, Chinese temples and ancient tea warehouses – though, of course, residents and rice fields have been gradually replaced by tourist businesses. Lounge bars, boutique hotels, travel agents and a glut of tailor shops are very much part of the scene here. And yet, down by the market and over on Cam Nam Island, you'll find life has changed little. Travel a few kilometres further – you'll find some superb bicycle, motorbike and boat trips – and some of central Vietnam's most enticingly laid-back scenery and beaches are within easy reach.

Sights

Hoi An Old Town AREA

(www.hoianworldheritage.org.vn; Old Town five-attractions tickets 120,000d) By Unesco decree, more than 800 historic buildings in Hoi An have been preserved, so much of the Old Town looks as it did several centuries ago. Eighteen of these buildings are open to visitors and require an Old Town ticket for admission; the fee goes towards funding conservation work.

Each ticket allows you to visit five different heritage attractions: museums, assembly halls, ancient houses and a traditional music show at the **Handicraft Workshop** (9 Đ Nguyen Thai Hoc; admission by Old Town ticket). Tickets are valid for 10 days.

★ **Japanese Covered Bridge** BRIDGE

(Cau Nhat Ban; 24hr) FREE This beautiful little bridge is emblematic of Hoi An. A bridge was first constructed here in the 1590s by the Japanese community to link them with the Chinese quarters. Over the centuries the ornamentation has remained relatively faithful to the original Japanese design. The French flattened out the roadway for cars, but the original arched shape was restored in 1986. The bridge is due for a complete removal for repair, so check it's open before you travel, if making a special trip.

Phung Hung Old House HISTORIC BUILDING

(4 Đ Nguyen Thi Minh Khai; admission by Old Town ticket; 8am-7pm) Just a few steps down from the Japanese Covered Bridge, this old house has a wide, welcoming entrance hall decorated with exquisite lanterns, wall hangings and embroidery. You can walk out on to a balcony and there's also an impressive suspended altar.

Assembly Hall of the Cantonese Chinese Congregation HISTORIC BUILDING

(Quang Trieu Hoi Quan; 176 Đ Tran Phu; admission by Old Town ticket; 8am-5pm) Founded in 1786, this assembly hall has a tall, airy entrance, which opens on to a splendidly over-the-top mosaic statue of a dragon and a carp. The main altar is dedicated to Quan Cong. The garden behind has an even more incredible dragon statue. The goat statue at the rear is a symbol of Canton (Guǎngzhōu), China.

★ **Assembly Hall of the Fujian Chinese Congregation** TEMPLE

(Phuc Kien Hoi Quan; opposite 35 Đ Tran Phu; admission by Old Town ticket; 7am-5.30pm) Originally a traditional assembly hall, this structure was later transformed into a temple for the worship of Thien Hau, a deity from Fujian province. The green-tiled triple gateway dates from 1975. The mural on the right-hand wall depicts Thien Hau, her way lit by lantern light as she crosses a stormy sea to rescue a foundering ship. Opposite is a mural of the heads of the six Fujian families who fled from China to Hoi An in the 17th century.

★ **Tan Ky House** HISTORIC BUILDING

(101 Đ Nguyen Thai Hoc; admission by Old Town ticket; 8am-noon & 2-4.30pm) Built two centuries ago by an ethnically Vietnamese family, this gem of a house has been lovingly preserved through seven generations. Look out for

signs of Japanese and Chinese influences on the architecture. Japanese elements include the ceiling (in the sitting area), which is supported by three progressively shorter beams, one on top of the other. Under the crab-shell ceiling are carvings of crossed sabres wrapped in silk ribbon. The sabres symbolise force, the silk represents flexibility.

Tran Family Chapel HISTORIC BUILDING
(21 Đ Le Loi; admission by Old Town ticket; ⏲7.30am-noon & 2-5.30pm) Built for worshipping family ancestors, this chapel dates back to 1802. It was commissioned by Tran Tu, one of the clan who ascended to the rank of mandarin and served as an ambassador to China. His picture is to the right of the chapel. The architecture of the building reflects the influence of Chinese (the 'turtle' style roof), Japanese (triple beam) and vernacular (look out for the bow-and-arrow detailing) styles.

Quan Cong Temple CONFUCIAN TEMPLE
(Chua Ong; 24 Đ Tran Phu; admission by Old Town ticket; ⏲8am-5pm) Founded in 1653, this small temple is dedicated to Quan Cong, an esteemed Chinese general who is worshipped as a symbol of loyalty, sincerity, integrity and justice. His partially gilded statue, made of papier mâché on a wooden frame, is on the central altar at the back of the sanctuary. When someone makes an offering to the portly looking Quan Cong, the caretaker solemnly strikes a bronze bowl that makes a bell-like sound.

Chinese All-Community Assembly Hall HISTORIC BUILDING
(Chua Ba; ☎0510-861 935; 64 Đ Tran Phu; ⏲8am-5pm) FREE Founded in 1773, this assembly hall was used by Fujian, Cantonese, Hainanese, Chaozhou and Hakka congregations in Hoi An. To the right of the entrance are portraits of Chinese resistance heroes in Vietnam who died during WWII. The well-restored main temple is a total assault on the senses, with great smoking incense spirals, demonic-looking deities, dragons and lashings of red lacquer – it's dedicated to Thien Hau.

Museum of Trading Ceramics MUSEUM
(80 Đ Tran Phu; admission by Old Town ticket; ⏲7am-5.30pm) Occupies a restored wooden house and contains a small collection of artefacts from all over Asia, with oddities from as far afield as Egypt. While this reveals that Hoi An had some rather impressive trading links, it takes an expert's eye to appreciate the display. The exhibition on the restoration of Hoi An's old houses provides a useful crash course in Old Town architecture.

Quan Thang House HISTORIC BUILDING
(77 Đ Tran Phu; admission by Old Town ticket; ⏲7am-5pm) This house is three centuries old and was built by a Chinese captain. As usual, the architecture includes Japanese and Chinese elements. There are some especially fine carvings of peacocks and flowers on the teak walls of the rooms around the courtyard, on the roof beams and under the crab-shell roof (in the salon beside the courtyard).

Cam Kim Island ISLAND
The master woodcarvers who crafted the intricate detail adorning Hoi An's public buildings and the historic homes of the town's merchants came from Kim Bong village on Cam Kim Island. Most of the woodcarvings on sale in Hoi An are produced here.

Boats to the island leave from the boat landing (Map p108) at Đ Bach Dang in Hoi An (30,000d, 30 minutes). The village and island, quite rural in character, are fun to explore by bicycle for a day.

Activities

Diving, Snorkelling & Kayaking

Cham Island Diving Center DIVING
(☎0510-391 0782; www.vietnamscubadiving.com; 88 Đ Nguyen Thai Hoc; snorkelling day trips US$44, overnight snorkelling/diving trips US$82/112) Run by a friendly, experienced team, this dive shop's mantra is 'no troubles, make bubbles'. It has a large boat and also a speedboat for zippy transfers. Also runs one-day and overnight trips to the Cham Islands.

Blue Coral Diving DIVING
(☎0510-627 9297; www.divehoian.com; 77 Đ Nguyen Thai Hoc) A friendly, professional outfit with an 18m dive boat and additional speedboat. Snorkelling trips are US$40 and there are Professional Association of Diving Instructors (PADI) courses too.

Hoi An Kayak Center KAYAKING
(☎0905 056 640; www.hoiankayak.com; 125 Đ Ngo Quyen) Self-paddle rentals for US$10 per hour, or two-hour guided leisure paddles for US$25 per person.

Massage & Spa

Countryside Charm SPA
(Duyen Que; ☎0510-350 1584; http://spahoian.vn; 512 Đ Cua Dai; 1hr massages from US$20; ⏲8am-10pm) On the beach road, this treatment

Hoi An

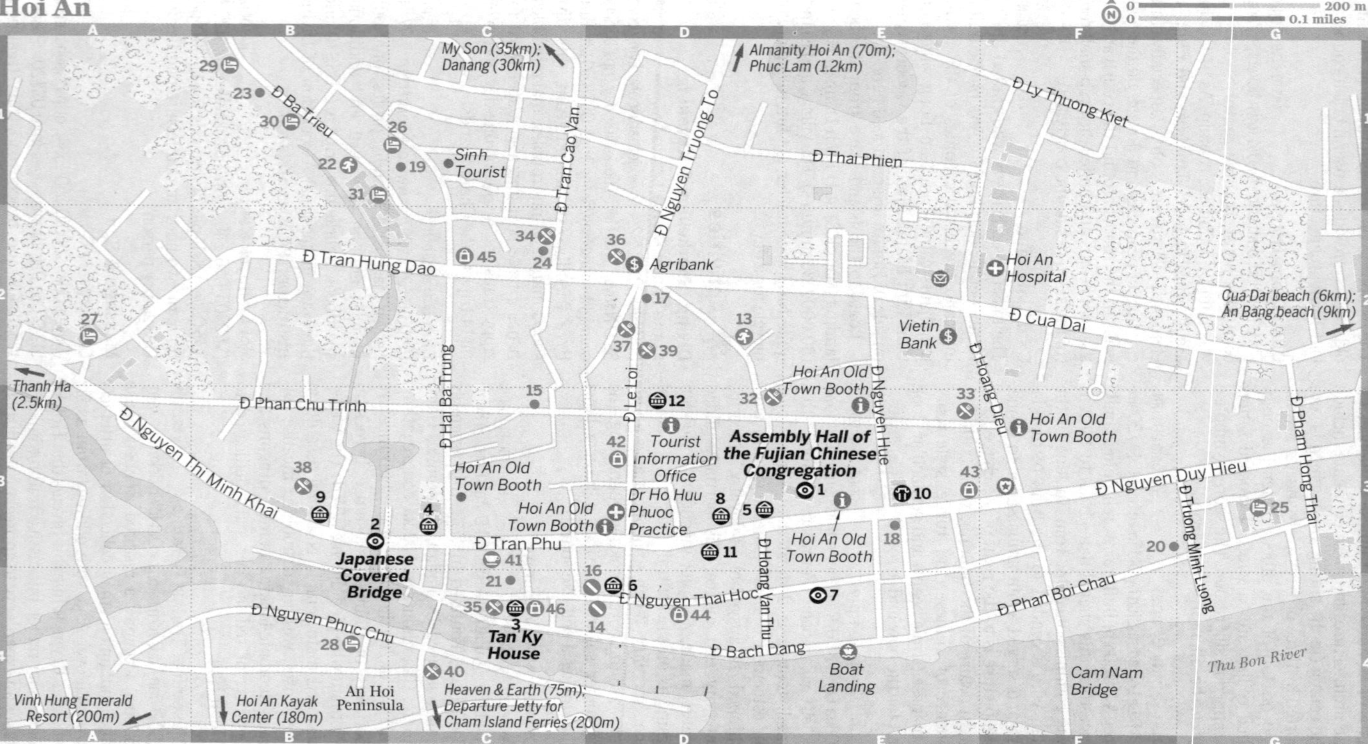
0 200 m
0 0.1 miles
My Son (35km); Danang (30km)
Almanity Hoi An (70m); Phuc Lam (1.2km)
Cua Dai beach (6km); An Bang beach (9km)
Thanh Ha (2.5km)
Vinh Hung Emerald Resort (200m)
Hoi An Kayak Center (180m)
Heaven & Earth (75m); Departure Jetty for Cham Island Ferries (200m)
Đ Ba Trieu
Đ Ly Thuong Kiet
Đ Thai Phien
Đ Tran Cao Van
Đ Nguyen Truong To
Đ Tran Hung Dao
Đ Cua Dai
Đ Phan Chu Trinh
Đ Hai Ba Trung
Đ Le Loi
Đ Nguyen Hue
Đ Hoang Dieu
Đ Pham Hong Thai
Đ Nguyen Thi Minh Khai
Đ Tran Phu
Đ Nguyen Duy Hieu
Đ Truong Minh Luong
Đ Nguyen Thai Hoc
Đ Hoang Van Thu
Đ Phan Boi Chau
Đ Nguyen Phuc Chu
Đ Bach Dang
Sinh Tourist
Agribank
Hoi An Hospital
Vietin Bank
Hoi An Old Town Booth
Tourist Information Office
Dr Ho Huu Phuoc Practice
Assembly Hall of the Fujian Chinese Congregation
Japanese Covered Bridge
Tan Ky House
An Hoi Peninsula
Boat Landing
Cam Nam Bridge
Thu Bon River
1
2
3
4
5
6
7
8
9
10
11
12
13
14
15
16
17
18
19
20
21
22
23
24
25
26
27
28
29
30
31
32
33
34
35
36
37
38
39
40
41
42
43
44
45
46
A
B
C
D
E
F
G

Hoi An

Top Sights
1 Assembly Hall of the Fujian Chinese Congregation E3
2 Japanese Covered Bridge B3
3 Tan Ky House C4

Sights
4 Assembly Hall of the Cantonese Chinese Congregation C3
5 Chinese All-Community Assembly Hall D3
6 Diep Dong Nguyen House D4
7 Handicraft Workshop E4
8 Museum of Trading Ceramics D3
9 Phung Hung Old House B3
10 Quan Cong Temple E3
11 Quan Thang House D3
12 Tran Family Chapel D3

Activities, Courses & Tours
13 Ba Le Beauty Salon D2
14 Blue Coral Diving D4
15 Cactus Tours C3
16 Cham Island Diving Center D4
17 Herbs and Spices D2
18 Hoi An Love of Life E3
19 Hoi An Motorbike Adventures C1
20 Hoi An Photo Tour F3
21 Morning Glory Cooking School C4
22 Palmarosa B1
23 Phat Tire Ventures B1
24 Vespa Adventures C2

Sleeping
25 Ha An Hotel G3
26 Hoa Binh Hotel C1
27 Hoang Trinh Hotel A2
28 Little Hoi An B4
29 Phuong Dong Hotel B1
30 Thien Nga Hotel B1
31 Vinh Hung Library Hotel B1

Eating
32 Bale Well D3
33 Banh Mi Phuong E3
34 Cafe Zoom C2
35 Cargo Club C4
Cocobox .... (see 6)
36 Ganesh Indian Restaurant D2
37 Little Menu D2
38 Nu Eatery B3
39 Streets D2
40 Vy's Market C4

Drinking & Nightlife
Dive Bar .... (see 16)
41 Hoi An Roastery C3
Q Bar .... (see 16)

Shopping
42 A Dong Silk D3
43 Friendly Shop E3
44 Hoang Kim D4
45 Kimmy C2
46 Yaly C4

centre has functional premises, but staff are well trained. It also arranges complimentary pick-up from Hoi An.

Ba Le Beauty Salon SPA
(☎0905 226 974; www.balewellbeautysalon.com; 45-11 Đ Tran Hung Dao; ⏰9am-7pm) Ba Le is run by a fluent English-speaker, who has trained in the UK, and offers inexpensive threading, waxing, facials, manicures and pedicures.

Palmarosa SPA
(☎0510-393 3999; www.palmarosaspa.vn; 90 Đ Ba Trieu; massages & treatments from 220,000d; ⏰10am-9pm) This highly professional spa offers massages (including Thai and Swedish), scrubs and facials, as well as hand and foot care.

Courses

Green Bamboo Cooking School COOKING
(☎0905 815 600; www.greenbamboo-hoian.com; 21 Đ Truong Minh Hung, Cam An; per person US$45) Directed by Van, a charming local chef and English-speaker, these courses are more personalised than most. Groups are limited to a maximum of 10, and classes take place in Van's spacious kitchen. Choose what to cook from a diverse menu including vegetarian choices. It's 5km east of the centre, near Cu Dai beach; transport from Hoi An is included.

Herbs and Spices COOKING
(☎0510-393 6868; www.herbsandspicesvn.com; 2/6 Đ Le Loi; per person US$35-59; ⏰10.30am, 4.30pm & 8pm) Excellent classes with three different menu options, and smaller, more hands-on groups than some other cookery classes.

Morning Glory Cooking School COOKING
(☎0510-224 1555; www.msvy-tastevietnam.com; 106 Đ Nguyen Thai Hoc; half-day courses US$25-32) This is the cooking course that launched Hoi An cooking courses. Classes are directed by Trinh Diem Vy, owner of several restaurants in town, or by one of her protégés. Classes concentrate on local recipes including *cao lau* and 'white rose' (*banh vac*; a delicate, subtly flavoured shrimp dumpling topped with crispy onions). Classes can have up to 30

people and some feel the whole experience is a little too organised.

Festivals & Events

Full Moon Festival CULTURAL

(5-11pm) Hoi An is a delightful place to be on the 14th day of each lunar month, when the town celebrates a Full Moon Festival. Motorised vehicles are banned from the Old Town, street markets selling handicrafts, souvenirs and food open up, and all the lanterns come out! Traditional plays and musical events are also performed

Sleeping

Hoi An has good-value accommodation in all price categories. There are only a couple of hotels in the Old Town, but nightlife finishes early here so there is little need to be right in the middle of things when there are plenty of good sleeping options close by. The best places book up fast, so plan as far ahead as you can.

TOURS AROUND HOI AN

Vespa Adventures (0938 500 997; www.vespaadventures.com; 134 Đ Tran Cao Van; per person $US65-76) Quite possibly the most fun and most stylish way to explore around Hoi An, Vespa Adventures offers the opportunity to ride pillion on classic retro two-wheelers with an Italian accent. There are morning and afternoon departures, and a popular after-dark 'Streets & Eats' option with lots of good food and cold beer. Tours kick off from Cafe Zoom (p112).

Hoi An Free Tour (0905 164 397; www.hoianfreetour.com) Ride on a bike around the fringes of Hoi An with students. You get to meet the locals and see village life, they get to practise their English. Although tours are free, you will need a reasonable additional 100,000d for bike rental, ferries and local community support.

Phat Tire Ventures (0510-653 9839; www.ptv-vietnam.com; 62 Đ Ba Trieu) Offers a terrific mountain-bike trip to My Son ruins that takes in country lanes and temple visits. Pick-up from hotels included. Also offers adventure thrills via rappelling and rock climbing.

Hoi An Photo Tour (0905 671 898; www.hoianphototour.com; 42 Đ Phan Boi Chau; per person US$45) Excellent tours with experienced photographer Etienne Bossot. Sunrise and sunset tours are most popular, harnessing Hoi An's delicate light for images of fishers and rice paddies. Experienced and newbie photographers are both catered for, and specialist private and night-time workshops are also available. Check the website for details of occasional three-day photography trips uncovering more remote areas around Hoi An.

Hoi An Love of Life (www.hoian-bicycle.com; 12 Đ Tran Quy Cap; tours US$29; 7am-8pm) Runs interesting themed bicycle tours in and around Hoi An that focus on either farms, beaches and rivers, or pottery and lantern artisans. Confusingly, there is more than one business running 'Love of Life' bicycle tours in Hoi An, so look out for this one's distinctive heart logo.

Cactus Tours (235 350 5017; www.hoian-bicycle.com.vn; 66 Đ Phan Chu Trinh; tours US$29; 9am-8.30pm) Has good bicycle tours along quiet country lanes, past vegetable gardens and fishing villages, as well as walking tours of Hoi An. Also uses the name 'Love of Life'.

Heaven & Earth (0510-386 4362; www.vietnam-bicycle.com; 57 Đ Ngo Quyen, An Hoi; tours US$12-49) Cycling tours are well thought out and not too strenuous; they explore the Song Thu river delta area. Recently launched mountain-bike tours take in local dirt trails and rickety bamboo bridges.

Taste of Hoi An (0905 382 783; www.tasteofhoian.com) Walk the streets to meet the vendors, then munch your lunch at an ancient (air-conditioned!) Hoi An town house.

Hoi An Motorbike Adventures (0905 101 930; www.motorbiketours-hoian.com; 111 Đ Ba Trieu) Specialises in tours on cult Minsk motorbikes. The guides really know the terrain and the trips make use of beautiful back roads and riverside tracks.

Hoi An Backpackers Hostel HOSTEL $
(☎0510-391 4400; www.vietnambackpackerhostels.com; 252 Đ Cua Dai; dm/s/tw/d incl breakfast US$7/18/36/36; ❄@☏) Offering loads of backpacker-friendly attractions, this is the new Hoi An location for a hostel empire spanning Vietnam. Bikes, breakfast and the occasional beer are all free, and accommodation ranges from dorms through to private rooms with en suite bathrooms. Regular tours take in Hoi An's street-food scene, and there's an exceedingly social bar with regular happy-hour deals.

Hoang Trinh Hotel HOTEL $
(☎0510-391 6579; www.hoianhoangtrinhhotel.com; 45 Đ Le Quy Don; r incl breakfast US$22-35; ❄@☏) Well-run hotel with helpful, friendly staff where travellers are made to feel welcome. Rooms are quite 'old school' Vietnamese but spacious and clean. Generous breakfast. Pick-up from bus stations is included.

Hoa Binh Hotel HOTEL $
(☎0510-391 6838; www.hoabinhhotelhoian.com; 696 Đ Hai Ba Trung; dm US$8, r US$16-20, all incl breakfast; ❄@☏≋) A good selection of modern rooms, all with minibar, cable TV and air-con, and a reasonable dorm. The inclusive breakfast is good, but the pool is covered by a roof.

Phuong Dong Hotel HOTEL $
(☎0510-391 6477; www.phuongdonghoian.com; 42 Đ Ba Trieu; s/d/tr US$13/16/20; ❄@☏) It's nothing fancy, but a safe budget bet: plain, good-value rooms with comfortable mattresses, reading lights, fridge and air-con. The owners rent motorbikes at fair rates too.

★ **Vinh Hung Emerald Resort** HOTEL $$
(☎0510-393 4999; www.vinhhungemeraldresort.com; Minh An, An Hoi; r US$51-77, ste US$80; ⊖❄☏≋) A beautifully designed new hotel with a riverside location in An Hoi, and modernist rooms that represent exceptional value for money. All rooms face the lovely central pool, or have a terrace facing the river. There's a fitness centre and small spa.

Ha An Hotel HISTORIC HOTEL $$
(☎0510-386 3126; www.haanhotel.com; 6-8 Đ Phan Boi Chau; r 1,320,000-2,398,000d; ❄@☏) Elegant and refined, the Ha An feels more like a colonial mansion than a hotel. All rooms have nice individual touches – a textile wall hanging or painting – and views over a gorgeous central garden. The helpful, well-trained staff make staying here a very special experience. It's about a 10-minute walk from the centre in the French Quarter.

Thien Nga Hotel HOTEL $$
(☎0510-391 6330; www.thienngahotel.com; 52 Đ Ba Trieu; r US$23-35; ❄@☏≋) This place has a fine selection of rooms – most are spacious, light and airy and have a balcony and a minimalist feel (though the bathrooms are more prosaic). Book one at the rear if you can for garden views. Staff are smiley and accommodating, and breakfast is generous. The pool is covered by a roof though.

★ **Hoi An Beach Rentals** RENTAL HOUSE $$$
(www.hoi-an-beach-rentals.com; An Bang; houses US$180-230; ❄☏) Asian-chic decor is the common theme of these three lovely self-contained rental homes in An Bang village. The white-sand expanse of An Bang Beach is close by, along with good bars and restaurants. Temple House (sleeps five; US$230) is the most spacious and stunning of all three, and has a lush garden leading to a private pavilion overlooking the beach.

Annam House (sleeps six; US$200) is a converted village home with three bedrooms and a beautiful garden. Nearby, CoChin House (sleeps four; US$180) is constructed in wood in heritage Vietnamese style and has an expansive garden and a private lookout.

Almanity Hoi An BOUTIQUE HOTEL $$$
(☎0510-366 6888; www.almanityhoian.com; 326 Đ Ly Thuong Kiet; d from US$152; ❄☏≋) Heritage style and modern rooms combine at the Almanity, just maybe the most relaxing hotel in town. Gardens and swimming pools create a laid-back haven despite the central location, happy hour in the bar often runs for three hours, and there's a full menu of spa and massage services on tap. Check online for good-value Spa Journey packages.

Little Hoi An HOTEL $$$
(☎0510-386 9999; www.littlehoian.com; 2 Đ Thoai Ngoc Hau; r/ste from US$65/81; ❄☏≋) Boasting a superb position opposite the Old Town in tranquil An Hoi, this new hotel has real polish and class. Rooms are very comfortable indeed, with furnishings that are very high grade, and sleek en suite bathrooms. Staff are welcoming and there's a good restaurant and small spa. The pool is tiny and covered.

Vinh Hung Library Hotel HOTEL $$$
(☎0510-391 6277; www.vinhhunglibraryhotel.com; 96 Đ Ba Trieu; r incl breakfast 1,554,000-2,664,000; ❄@☏≋) A fine minihotel with modish

rooms that have huge beds, dark-wood furniture, writing desks and satellite TV; some rooms also have balconies. All bathrooms are sleek and inviting. The rooftop pool area is perfect for catching some rays or cooling off.

Eating

★Streets VIETNAMESE $
(☎0510-391 1949; www.streetsinternational.org; 17 Đ Le Loi; mains 75,000-145,000d; ⏰8am-10pm) Do the meals taste exceptional here because Streets is for a good cause? Perhaps it helps to know that the staff are disadvantaged youths trained up in hospitality, but the textbook-good *cao lau* and white-rose dumplings deserve an A+ regardless. Although endlessly busy, it's a comfortable, if warm, spot to linger with a cocktail too.

Banh Mi Phuong VIETNAMESE $
(2b Đ Phan Chu Trinh; banh mi 20,000-30,000d) What makes the *banh mi* at this cramped joint draw the crowds? It's the dense, chewy bread, the freshness of the greens and the generous serves of *thit nuong* (chargrilled pork), beef or other meat that seals the deal. A celebrity-chef endorsement helps too.

Cafe Zoom CAFE $
(www.facebook.com/cafezoomhoian; 134 Đ Tran Cao Van; meals 70,000-120,000d; ⏰7am-11pm; 📶) Look for the cool retro Vespas outside this hip cafe and bar, which also doubles as the Hoi An location for the friendly Vespa Adventures (p110) crew. Cold beer is well-priced, comfort eats include burgers and tacos, and there's a good mix of classic songs you can hum along to while you're deciding which Vespa trip to sign up for.

Cocobox CAFE $
(http://fb.me/cocoboxvietnam; 94 Đ Le Loi; juices & smoothies 60,000-75,000d; ⏰7am-10pm) Refreshing cold-press juices are the standout at this compact combo of cafe and deli. Our favourite is the Watermelon Man juice combining watermelon, passionfruit, lime and mint. Coffee, salads and snacks are also good – try the chicken pesto sandwich.

The attached 'farm shop' sells Vietnamese artisan produce including local honey and cider from Ho Chi Minh City.

Vy's Market VIETNAMESE $
(www.msvy-tastevietnam.com/the-market/; Nguyen Hoang, An Hoi; meals 80,000-120,000d; ⏰8am-11pm; 📶) Offering a (sanitised) street-food-style experience for those slightly wary, this huge place has food stations cranking out Vietnamese favourites from all around the country. You sit on benches in a courtyard-like space and the menu is available on electronic tablets. Drinks include beer, lassis, smoothies and juices, and don't leave without trying the cinnamon or lemongrass ice cream.

★Cargo Club INTERNATIONAL $$
(☎0510-391 1227; www.msvy-tastevietnam.com/cargo-club; 107 Đ Nguyen Thai Hoc; meals 70,000-160,000d; ⏰8am-11pm; 📶) Remarkable cafe-restaurant, serving Vietnamese and Western food, with a terrific riverside location (the upper terrace has stunning views). A relaxing day here munching your way around the menu would be a day well spent. The breakfasts are legendary (try the eggs Benedict), the patisserie and cakes are superb, and fine-dining dishes and good cocktails also deliver.

★Nu Eatery FUSION $$
(www.facebook.com/NuEateryHoiAn; 10A Đ Nguyen Th[illegible] Minh Khai; mains 80,000d; ⏰noon-9pm Mon-Sat) Don't be deceived by the humble decor at this compact eatery tucked away near the Japanese Bridge. There's a real wow factor to the seasonal small plates at this newish Hoi An favourite. Combine the pork belly steamed buns with a salad of grilled pineapple, coconut and pomelo, and don't miss the homemade lemongrass, ginger or chilli ice cream.

Bale Well VIETNAMESE $$
(45-51 Đ Tran Cao Van; meals 150,000d; ⏰11.30am-10pm) Down a little alley near the famous well, this local place is renowned for one dish: barbecued pork, served up satay-style, which you then combine with fresh greens and herbs to create your own fresh spring roll. A global reputation means it can get busy.

Ganesh Indian Restaurant INDIAN $$
(☎0510-386 4538; www.ganesh.vn; 24 Đ Tran Hung Dao; meals 70,000-155,000d; ⏰11am-10pm; 📶🌿) A highly authentic, fine-value North Indian restaurant, where the tandoor oven pumps out perfect naan bread and the chefs' fiery curries don't pull any punches. Unlike many curry houses, this one has atmosphere, and also plenty of vegetarian choices. Slurp a lassi or slug a beer and you're set.

Little Menu VIETNAMESE $$
(www.thelittlemenu.com; 12 Đ Le Loi; meals 115,000-225,000d; ⏰9.30am-11pm; 📶) English-speaking owner Son is a fantastic host at this popular little restaurant with an open

A HOI AN TASTER

Hoi An is a culinary hotbed and there are some unique dishes you should be sure to sample.

'White rose' *(banh vac)* is an incredibly delicate, subtly flavoured shrimp dumpling topped with crispy onions. *Banh bao* is another steamed dumpling, this time with minced pork or chicken, onions, eggs and mushrooms, that's said to be derived from Chinese dim sum. *Cao lau* is an amazing dish: Japanese-style noodles seasoned with herbs, salad greens and bean sprouts and served with slices of roast pork. Other local specialities are fried *hoanh thanh* (wonton) and *banh xeo* (crispy savoury pancakes rolled with herbs in fresh rice paper). Most restaurants serve these items, but quality varies widely.

kitchen and short menu – try the fish in banana leaf or duck spring rolls, which feature on the set menu (225,000d). Flavours are made easy for most to like.

Drinking & Nightlife

Hoi An is not a huge party town as the local authorities keep a fairly strict lid on late-night revelry; backstreets can be very dark after 10pm.

Dive Bar BAR
(88 Đ Nguyen Thai Hoc; ⏲8am-midnight; 📶) A top bar option in Hoi An with a great vibe thanks to the welcoming service, contemporary electronic tunes and sofas for lounging. There's also a cocktail garden and bar at the rear, a pool table and pub grub.

Hoi An Roastery CAFE
(www.hoianroastery.com; 135 Đ Tran Phu; ⏲8am-10pm) With single-origin brews, excellent cakes, juices and smoothies, this cool little spot wouldn't be out of place in the hipster precincts of Portland or Melbourne, and neither would its prices. Recharge with one of 200 different caffeine-fuelled variations, and watch the passing promenade on busy Tran Phu.

Q Bar LOUNGE
(94 Đ Nguyen Thai Hoc; ⏲noon-midnight; 📶) Q Bar offers stunning lighting, lounge music and electronica, and the best (if pricey, at around 120,000d) cocktails and mocktails in town. Draws a cool crowd.

Shopping

Hoi An has long been known for fabric production, and tourist demand has swiftly shoehorned many tailor shops into the tiny Old Town. Shoes, also copied from Western designs, and supposed 'leather' goods are also popular but quality is variable. Get something made to order at **Yaly** (☎0510-391 0474; www.yalycouture.com; 47 Đ Nguyen Thai Hoc; ⏲8am-9pm) or **A Dong Silk** (☎0510-391 0579; www.adongsilk.com; 40 Đ Le Loi; ⏲8am-9.30pm).

Hoi An also has more than a dozen art galleries; check out the streets near the Japanese Covered Bridge, along Đ Nguyen Thi Minh Khai.

Friendly Shop SHOES
(www.friendlyshophoian.com; 18 Đ Tran Phu; ⏲9am-9pm)' One of a number of Hoi An's (better) tailors that has now diversified into making shoes and bags also.

Hoang Kim CLOTHING
(☎0510-386 2794; 57 Đ Nguyen Thai Hoc; ⏲8am-9pm) A well-established Hoi An tailor that receives excellent feedback from customers.

Kimmy CLOTHING
(☎0510-386 2063; www.kimmytailor.com; 70 Đ Tran Hung Dao; ⏲7.30am-9.30pm) Owned by Vietnamese-Canadians, with an excellent website for online orders.

Information

Hoi An is one of Vietnam's safer towns, but there are infrequent stories of late-night bag-snatching, pickpockets and (very occasionally) assaults on women. Many street lights are turned off from 9.30pm and it may not be advisable to walk home alone. There have also been reports of drinks being spiked in some bars.

Agribank (12 Tran Hung Dao; ⏲8am-4.30pm Mon-Fri, 8.30am-1pm Sat) Changes cash and has ATMs.

Dr Ho Huu Phuoc Practice (☎0510-386 1419; 74 Đ Le Loi; ⏲11am-12.30pm & 5-9.30pm) English-speaking doctor.

Hoi An Police Station (☎0510-386 1204; 84 Đ Hoang Dieu)

Main Post Office (6 Đ Tran Hung Dao; ⏲7am-5pm) On the edge of the Old Town.

Tourist Information Office (☎0510-366 633; www.quangnamtourism.com.vn; 47 Đ Phan Chau Trinh; ⊙8am-5pm) Helpful office with good English spoken.

Vietin Bank (☎0510-386 1340; 4 Đ Hoang Dieu; ⊙8am-5pm Mon-Fri, 8.30am-1.30pm Sat) Changes cash and has an ATM.

Getting There & Away

Convenient open-tour buses offer regular connections for Hue (US$12, four hours) and Nha Trang (regular/sleeper US$14/19, 11 to 12 hours). Most accommodation owners can book tickets.

For Danang (one hour), it is much more convenient to organise a bus (110,000d) to pick you up at your accommodation, or at **Sinh Tourist** (☎0510-386 3948; www.thesinhtourist.vn; 587 Đ Hai Ba Trung; ⊙6am-10pm; 80,000d). Yellow buses to Danang (20,000d) leave from the northern bus station just off Đ Le Hong Phong, a 15-minute walk or 15,000d *xe om* from central Hoi An. The last bus back from Danang leaves around 6pm.

The closest airport is 45 to 60 minutes away in Danang.

Getting Around

Hoi An is best explored on foot; cars and motorbikes (but not bicycles) are banned from the central Old Town streets from 8am to 11am and 3pm to 9pm. To go further afield, rent a bicycle (25,000d per day). The route east to Cua Dai Beach is quite scenic. A motorbike without/with a driver will cost around US$6/12 per day. Reckon on about 70,000d for a taxi to An Bang Beach. A *xe om* will always be more expensive than a metered taxi.

Hoi An Taxi (☎0510-391 9919) Good local taxi operators.

Mai Linh (☎0510-392 5925) Local partners to a reliable Vietnam-wide taxi company.

Around Hoi An

An Bang Beach

Cua Dai Beach might be nearest to Hoi An, but the sandy beach has largely disappeared due to development. Just 3km further north, An Bang is one of Vietnam's most happening and enjoyable beaches. At present there's a wonderful stretch of fine sand and an enormous horizon, with little sign of the serious erosion evident at Cua Dai, and with only the distant Cham Islands interrupting the seaside symmetry. Staying at the beach and visiting Hoi An on day trips is a good strategy for a relaxing visit to the area.

Access to Hoi An is easy – it's just a 20-minute bike ride or a five-minute (70,000d) taxi journey.

My Son

The effusive have described this as Vietnam's Angkor Wat, but that's hardly fair: **My Son** (100,000d; ⊙6.30am-4pm) contains fewer ruins (and they are very much ruined) within a small area of about 200 sq metres. Still, it's the most extensive of Vietnam's Cham remains, and enchanting in its own way – if appreciated on its own merits.

Hotels in Hoi An can arrange day trips to My Son (US$5 to US$10). Most minibuses depart at 8am and return between 1pm and 2pm. For the boat-ride option on the return leg, add an extra hour.

'Sunrise' trips do not mean you'll see the first ray of morning light, but they do beat the crowds.

Cham Islands

A breathtaking cluster of granite islands, set in aquamarine seas, around 15km directly offshore from Hoi An, the Cham Islands make a wonderful excursion. The islands were once closed to visitors and under close military supervision, but now day trips, diving or snorkelling the reefs, and overnight stays are possible.

A rich underwater environment features 135 species of soft and hard coral and varied macrolife. The islands are officially protected as a marine park. Fishing and the collection of birds' nests (for soup) are the two key industries here.

There are plans afoot to develop the islands into something of a central Vietnam version of Phu Quoc, and coastal land has been confirmed for resort development.

Sleeping & Eating

The Chams have only simple guesthouses (in Bai Lang). If possible, we recommend a few nights at the Bai Huong homestay program to experience the best of the islands. Dive operators in Hoi An can also arrange overnight camping stays. Currently holders of passports from China or Hong Kong are not permitted to stay overnight on the Cham Islands.

There are a few restaurants in the main village of Bai Lang. While tiny Bai Huong has only a couple of coffee shops, you are most likely to eat with your homestay here.

★Bai Huong homestays HOMESTAY $
(www.homestaybaihuong.com; per person 120,000d, meals 30,000-70,000d) Live with the locals in Bai Huong village. Visitors are given a bed with a mozzie net, and bathrooms have sit-down toilets and cold-water showers. Delicious home-cooked meals are available. The program works with nine families, generating income from community tourism. Note that little or no English is spoken by locals and there's usually electricity from 6pm to 10pm only.

Luu Ly GUESTHOUSE $
(☎0510-393 0240; Bai Lang village; r with shared bathroom 300,000d) An excellent place with neat little rooms that have mosquito nets, TVs and fans (and a generator to power them during blackouts). Three meals a day cost around 200,000d.

Thu Trang GUESTHOUSE $
(☎0510-393 0007; Bai Lang village; r with shared bathroom 300,000d) Right by the whale temple in the main village of Bai Lang, Thu Trang is tidy, clean and simple. Meals are available (around 200,000d for breakfast, lunch and dinner).

Cham Restaurant VIETNAMESE $
(☎0510-224 1108; meals 50,000-120,000d; ⏲10am-5pm) About 2km southwest of Bai Lang village, Cham Restaurant sits pretty on a stunning sandy beach and serves wonderful Vietnamese dishes, including lots of seafood. Most of the day-trip boats from Hoi An also stop along this beach.

Ngan Ha SEAFOOD $
(☎0510-3862 178; Bai Lang village; mains 70,000-150,000d) Well-priced seafood – including squid dishes and occasionally lobster – feature at this newish Bai Lang eatery with harbour views from the balconies. There are also rooms for rent (300,000d) if the other guesthouses in the village are full.

ℹ Getting There & Away

Public boats to Cham Island dock at Bai Lang village. There's a scheduled daily connection from a jetty on Đ Nguyen Hoang in Hoi An (two hours, 7am daily). Foreigners are routinely charged up to 150,000d. Bring a copy of your passport and visa as the boat captain needs to prepare a permit. From Bai Lang, a return ferry back to Hoi An leaves around 11am.

Tour agencies charge US$25 to US$40 for island tours, but most day trips are very rushed and give you little time to enjoy the Chams. For the best one-day experience, book with one of the specialised dive operators in Hoi An. They can also arrange overnight camping stays.

SOUTHEAST COAST

Once the heartland of the Cham civilisation, today this sparkling coastline of ravishing white sands is Vietnam's premier destination for beach holidays.

If your idea of paradise is reclining in front of turquoise waters, weighing up the merits of a massage or a mojito, then you have come to the right place. On hand to complement the sedentary delights are activities to set the pulse racing, including scuba-diving, snorkelling, surfing, windsurfing and kitesurfing.

Nha Trang and Mui Ne attract the headlines, but the beach breaks come thick and fast in this part of the country. Set aside a few days to explore more and you'll find that hidden coves, lonely lighthouses and a barefoot vibe are all in reach. And for the definitive castaway experience, the fabled Con Dao Islands are the ultimate off-grid destination.

Quy Nhon

A large, prosperous coastal city, Quy Nhon (hwee ngon) boasts a terrific beach-blessed shoreline and grand boulevards. Its seaside appeal and tidy, litter-free streets make it worth a stop to sample some fresh seafood.

Sights & Activities

★Municipal Beach BEACH
The long sweep of Quy Nhon's beachfront extends from the port in the northeast to the hills in the south. It's a beautiful stretch of sand and has been given a major facelift in recent years, making it almost as nice as Nha Trang, but with a fraction of the visitors.

Bai Bau BEACH
(10,000d) Just 2km south of Bai Xep (16km from Quy Nhon), Bai Bau is a beautiful white-sand crescent no more than 150m wide, sheltered by rocky headlands, with mountains for a backdrop. It can get busy on the weekend and during Vietnamese holidays, but midweek you'll likely have the place to yourself.

Quynhonkids English Club TOURS
(☎0122 820 3228; www.facebook.com/quynhonkids) This friendly bunch of locals loves to meet up with foreigners to chat in English. You're welcome to join them on countryside

TRANSPORT FROM QUY NHON

DESTINATION	AIR	BUS	CAR/ MOTORBIKE	TRAIN (SOFT SEAT)
Danang	N/A	105,000-160,000d, 6½hr,14-17 daily	7hr	5½hr, from 203,000d, 5 daily
HCMC	from 620,000d, 1hr, 3 daily	220,000-380,000d, 16hr, 10 daily	18hr	from 393,000d, 11hr, 4 daily
Hanoi	from 700,000d, 1½hr, daily	from 480,000d, 23hr, 7 daily	around 26hr	from 665,000d, 20hr, 4 daily

tours by motorbike, hillside hikes or for football games and just contribute to fuel costs.

Sleeping & Eating

★Life's a Beach GUESTHOUSE $
(☎0162 993 3117, 0963 289 096; http://lifesabeachvietnam.com; To 2, Khu Vuc 1, Bai Xep; dm US$7, r US$42-57, all incl breakfast; ❄🛜) A mecca for travellers, this sociable Western-run place has a hostel vibe and is the perfect spot to share a few tales, meet others and kick back on a lovely sandy bay. There's a choice of digs including dorms, bungalows and a tree house, plus family-style dinners (US$7), barbecues and bonfires (or board games and beers during the rainy season).

★C.ine SEAFOOD $$
(☎056-651 2675; 94 Đ Xuan Dieu; dishes 50,000-150,000d; ⏲11am-10pm) A very popular seafood restaurant with gingham tablecloths and views over the bay. Feast on delectable dishes including sweet soft-shell crab, hot and sour fish soup and green-mango prawn salad.

Drinking & Nightlife

Cafe Xua & Nay CAFE
(5 Đ An Duong Vuong; drinks from 25,000d; ⏲6.30am-9.30pm; 🛜) Beachfront cafe based in a traditional Vietnamese wooden house (built in 1832) that serves authentic coffee, teas, snacks and juices. It's a great place to catch the sea breeze and take in atmospheric night views across the water.

Barbara's: the Kiwi Connection CAFE
(☎056-389 2921; www.barbaraquynhon.weebly.com; 12 Đ An Duong Vuong; ⏲7am-10pm; 🛜) This was a Quy Nhon institution for years but times have changed and the owner has moved on. The Western food is forgettable but it's still an option for an evening beer (15,000d), juice or cup of Earl Grey tea.

ℹ Information

Binh Dinh Tourist (☎056-389 2524; 10 Đ Nguyen Hue; ⏲7.30am-4pm) Government-run tourist office. Don't expect much practical help.

Main Post Office (197 Đ Phan Boi Chau; ⏲6.30am-10pm).

Vietcombank (148 Đ Le Loi; ⏲7.30am-3pm Mon-Sat) With ATM.

ℹ Getting There & Away

Flights link Quy Nhon with Hanoi and Ho Chi Minh City. **Vietnam Airlines** (☎056-382 5313; www.vietnamairlines.com; 1 Đ Nguyen Tat Thanh) offers a minibus transfer (50,000d) for airline passengers between the office and Phu Cat airport, 32km north of the city.

Quy Nhon Bus Station (☎056-384 6246; Đ Tay Son), on the south side of town, has frequent buses to Quang Ngai (78,000d, four hours, hourly), Nha Trang and towns in the central highlands including Pleiku (85,000d, four hours, six daily). It's also possible to get a bus all the way to Pakse (from 400,000d, 20 hours, three per week) in Laos, crossing the border at Bo Y.

Quy Nhon Train Station (☎056-382 2036; Đ Le Hong Phong) is at the end of a 10km spur off the main north–south track. Only very slow local trains stop here and they are not worth bothering with.

Nha Trang

Loud and proud (say it!), the high-rise, high-energy beach resort of Nha Trang enjoys a stunning setting: ringed by a necklace of hills, with a sweeping crescent beach, the city's turquoise bay is dotted with tropical islands.

Nha Trang is a party town at heart, most of it is aimed directly at the many Russian and Chinese tourists. There are more sedate activities on offer too. Try an old-school spa treatment with a visit to a mudbath or explore centuries-old Cham towers still standing in the town centre.

Sights

★Nha Trang Beach BEACH

Forming a magnificent sweeping arc, Nha Trang's 6km-long golden-sand beach is the city's trump card. Various sections are roped off and designated for swimmers (where you won't be bothered by jet skis or boats). The turquoise water is fabulously inviting, and the promenade a delight to stroll.

Two popular lounging spots are the Sailing Club (p122) and Louisiane Brewhouse (p121). If you head south of here, the beach gets quieter and it's possible to find a stretch of sand to yourself.

★Po Nagar Cham Towers BUDDHIST TEMPLE

(Thap Ba, Lady of the City; admission 22,000d, guide 50,000d; ⌚6am-6pm) Built between the 7th and 12th centuries, these four Cham Towers are still actively used for worship by Cham, Chinese and Vietnamese Buddhists. Originally the complex had seven or eight towers, but only four remain, of which the 28m-high North Tower (Thap Chinh), which dates from AD 817, with its terraced pyramidal roof, vaulted interior masonry and vestibule, is the most magnificent.

The towers stand on a granite knoll 2km north of central Nha Trang, on the banks of the Cai River.

Long Son Pagoda BUDDHIST TEMPLE

(⌚7.30-11.30am & 1.30-5.30pm) FREE Climb steep steps for this striking pagoda, founded in the late 19th century. The entrance and roofs are decorated with mosaic dragons constructed of glass and ceramic tile while the main sanctuary is a hall adorned with modern interpretations of traditional motifs.

Behind the pagoda is a huge white **Buddha** (Kim Than Phat To) seated on a lotus blossom. Around the statue's base are fire-ringed relief busts of Thich Quang Duc and six other Buddhist monks who died in self-immolations in 1963.

Alexandre Yersin Museum MUSEUM

(☎058-382 2355; 10 Đ Tran Phu; 26,000d; ⌚7.30-11am & 2-4.30pm Mon-Fri, 8-11am Sat) Highly popular in Vietnam, Dr Alexandre Yersin (1863–1943) founded Nha Trang's Pasteur Institute in 1895. Swiss-born Yersin learned to speak Vietnamese fluently, introduced rubber and quinine-producing trees to Vietnam, and discovered (in Hong Kong) the rat-borne microbe that causes bubonic plague.

See Yersin's library and office at this small, interesting museum; displays include laboratory equipment (such as astronomical instruments) and a fascinating 3D photo viewer. Tours are conducted in French, English and Vietnamese, with a short film on Yersin's life.

Long Thanh Gallery GALLERY

(☎058-382 4875; www.longthanhart.com; 126 Đ Hoang Van Thu; ⌚8am-5.30pm Mon-Sat) FREE Paradise for monochrome afficionados, this gallery showcases the work of Vietnam's most prominent photographer. Long Thanh developed his first photo in 1964 and continues to shoot extraordinary black-and-white images of everyday Vietnamese moments and compelling portraits. The powerful images capture the heart and soul of Vietnam.

Do Dien Khanh Gallery GALLERY

(DDK Gallery; ☎058-351 2202; www.ddk-gallery.com; 126B Đ Hong Bat; ⌚8am-9pm) FREE Do Dien Khanh is a welcoming host and very talented photographer of Vietnamese landscapes and life – his portraits of surrounding Cham communities are hauntingly beautiful. Prints can be purchased.

National Oceanographic Museum MUSEUM

(☎058-359 0037; 1 Cau Da; adult/child 30,000/12,000d; ⌚6am-6pm) Housed in a grand French-colonial building in the port district of Cau Da at the far south end of Nha Trang, this drab museum has 60,000 or so jars of pickled marine specimens, stuffed birds and sea mammals, and displays of local boats and fishing artefacts. There are tanks with fascinating reef fish (and sharks), three rescued seals kept here (not for entertainment) and a whale skeleton. Refreshingly nonglitzy, the displays focus on environmental education, with good English descriptions, rather than tourism.

Activities

The Nha Trang area is a key diving, surfing, wakeboarding, parasailing, white-water rafting and mountain-biking centre. Boat trips around the bay and up the Cai River are also a great day out.

★Vietnam Active ADVENTURE SPORTS

(☎058-351 5821; www.vietnamactive.com; 115 Đ Hung Vuong) Offers a diverse range of excellent activities including rafting, kayaking, mountain-biking trips and scuba-diving (Scuba School International – SSI – and

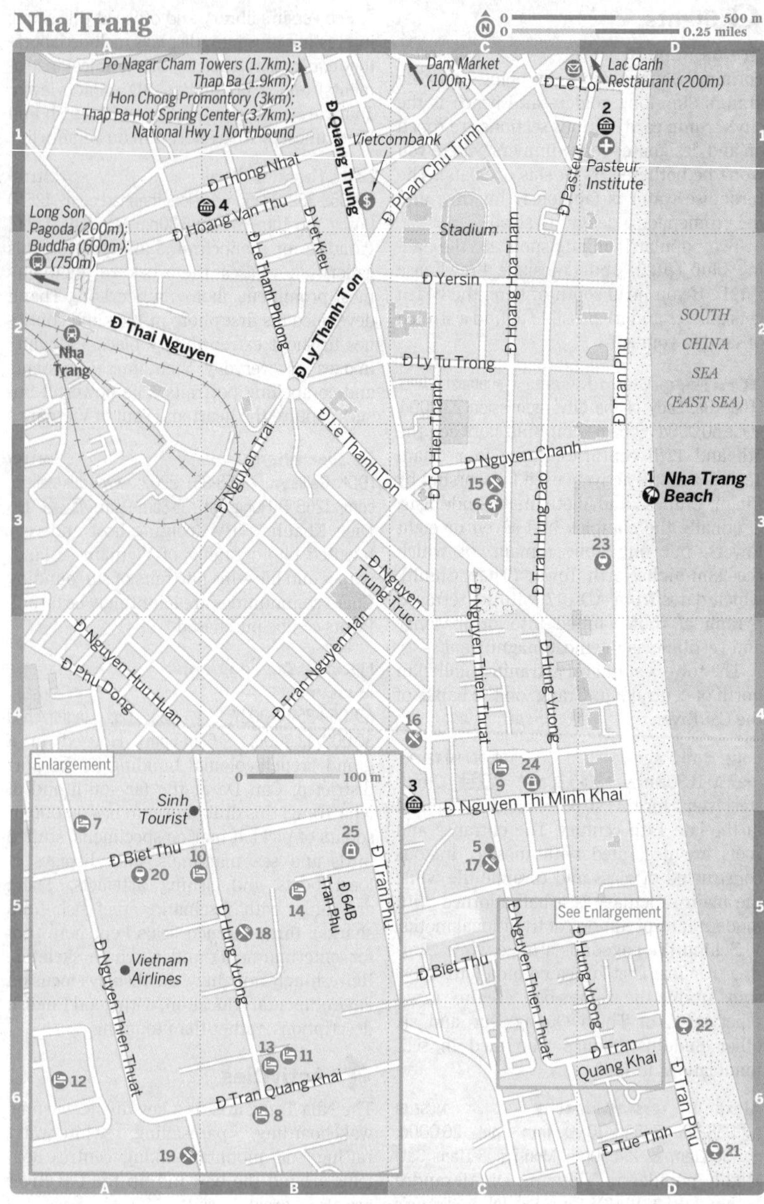

PADI accredited). Exact prices depend upon numbers. Stretch those aching limbs afterwards at one of the hatha or ashtanga yoga classes. It also rents quality bikes (from US$5 per day).

★I Resort THERMAL BATHS

(☎058-383 8838; www.i-resort.vn; 19 Xuan Ngoc, Vinh Ngoc; packages from 250,000d; ⊙8am-6pm) Just the place to really indulge, this upmarket thermal spa is the most attractive of the mud-fests around Nha Trang, with hot-

Nha Trang

Top Sights
1 Nha Trang Beach ... D3

Sights
2 Alexandre Yersin Museum ... D1
3 Do Dien Khanh Gallery ... C4
4 Long Thanh Gallery ... B1

Activities, Courses & Tours
5 Lanterns Tours ... C5
Vietnam Active ... (see 13)
6 Vietnam Bike Tours ... C3

Sleeping
7 Galliot Hotel ... A5
8 Golden Summer Hotel ... B6
9 Happy Angel Hotel ... C4
10 King Town Hotel ... A5
11 Le Duong ... B6
12 Mojzo Inn ... A6
13 Ngoc Thach ... B6
14 Sunny Sea ... B5

Eating
15 Au Lac ... C3
16 Kiwami ... C4
17 Lanterns ... C5
18 Mix ... B5
19 Yen's Restaurant ... A6

Drinking & Nightlife
20 Crazy Kim Bar ... A5
21 Louisiane Brewhouse ... D6
22 Sailing Club ... D6
23 Skylight Bar ... D3

Shopping
24 Lemongrass House ... C4
25 XQ ... B5

mineral mudbaths, lovely bathing pools and even waterfalls. The rural setting is gorgeous, with distant mountain views, and there's a decent restaurant and spa/massage centre. It's worth spending at least half a day here. All kinds of mud/spa packages are available.

It's 7km northwest of the centre. Call for a shuttle (20,000d one way) from your hotel.

Hon Mot SNORKELLING

Sandwiched neatly between Ebony Island and Hon Tam, or Silkworm Island, is tiny Hon Mot, a popular place for snorkelling.

Hon Yen BOATING

(Bird's-Nest Island) Also known as Salangane Island, this is the lump-shaped land mass visible from Nha Trang Beach. These and other islands off Khanh Hoa province are the source of Vietnam's finest *salangane* (swiftlet) nests; locals climb up tottering bamboo ladders to fetch them. There is a small, secluded beach here. The 17km trip here takes three hours or so by small boat from Nha Trang.

100 Egg Mud Bath THERMAL BATHS

(Tam Bun Tram Trung; 058-371 1733; www.tambuntramtrung.vn; Nguyen Tat Thanh, Phuoc Trung; 8am-7pm) This place is named for its egg-shaped private pods where you can indulge in a little mud play. All kinds of mud plastering, wraps and scrubs are offered. You'll also find pools and tubs (that can be filled with herbs and essential oils) scattered around this huge complex, which also has a restaurant and (human-made) waterfall. Full packages including all facilities cost 500,000d.

It's 6km southwest of Nha Trang. From the Cau Binh Tan bridge on the southwest side of town, head along Đ Nguyen Tat Thanh until you reach the highway at Phuoc Trung, it's just over the road from here and clearly signposted.

Tours

★ Lanterns Tours CULTURAL

(058-247 1674; www.lanternsvietnam.com; 34/6 Đ Nguyen Thien Thuat; tour US$25) This nonprofit restaurant offers an interesting tour (US$25) of the nontouristy town of Ninh Hoa, taking in a local market and lunch with a local family. Its walking street-food tours (200,000d) of Nha Trang are also highly recommended, featuring seven dishes including *banh tai vac* (shrimp dumplings) and *che chuoi nuong* (banana and sticky rice).

Vietnam Bike Tours CYCLING

(0905 779 311; www.vietnambiketours.com; 17/14 Đ Hoang Hoa Tham) Organises excellent local tours of the countryside and coastline, taking in mudbaths and fishing villages with patient, experienced guides. All levels are catered for.

Sleeping

Mojzo Inn HOSTEL $

(0988 879 069; www.facebook.com/mojzoInn; 120/36 Đ Nguyen Thien Thuat; dm US$7, r US$19-23;) OK, the name is more cocktail list than hotel bed, but this funky hostel gets most things right, with well-designed dorms and a lovely cushion-scattered lounge area. Staff really go the extra mile to help here.

Sunny Sea HOTEL $

(☎058-352 2286; sunnyseahotel@gmail.com; 64b/9 Đ Tran Phu; r 250,000-300,000d; ❄@📶) A bit above the others on 'budget alley' just off the beach, this good-value place is owned by a welcoming local couple (a doctor and nurse) and their superhelpful staff. The rooms are kept clean, with springy mattresses, minibar and modern bathrooms; some have a balcony.

Ngoc Thach HOTEL $

(☎058-352 5988; http://ngocthachhotel.com; 6l Quan Tran, Đ Hung Vuong; r 400,000-600,000d; ❄📶) A pleasant minihotel in the thick of things with spacious, modern rooms (some with balcony) that represent decent value. There's a lift.

Golden Summer Hotel HOTEL $$

(Ha Vang; ☎058-352 6662; www.goldensummerhotel.com.vn; 22-23 Đ Tran Quang Khai; r US$28-40; ❄@📶) This modish hotel has a superstylish lobby and inviting, modern rooms all with nice artistic touches such as statement photography on the walls. The location is excellent with myriad restaurants and the beach a short stroll away.

Le Duong HOTEL $$

(www.nhatrangleduonghotel.com; 5 & 6 Quan Tran, Đ Hung Vuong; r US$20-38; ❄📶) Close to restaurants and nightlife, this modern hotel has 50 light, spacious rooms with pale furniture and white linen, cable TV and fridges. Prices are flexible to a degree, depending on demand.

King Town Hotel HOTEL $$

(☎058-352 5818; www.kingtownhotel.com.vn; 92 Đ Hung Vuong; r US$23-40; ❄@📶🏊) This place discounts heavily during slow periods, making it fine value considering the rooftop swimming pool with city views and spacious rooms. At other times of year it's still worth considering.

Galliot Hotel HOTEL $$

(☎058-352 8555; http://galliothotel.com; 61a Đ Nguyen Thien Thuat; r US$38-54; ❄@📶🏊) This recent addition is convenient to the heart of the city with a bevy of bars and restaurants just steps away. There's a wide choice of well-presented rooms; avoid the very cheapest which don't have a window. The rooftop pool is perfect for cooling off.

★ Mia Resort Nha Trang HOTEL $$$

(☎058-398 9666; www.mianhatrang.com; Bai Dong, Cam Hai Dong; condos/villas from 450,000/605,000d; 🚭❄@📶🏊) This exceptional hotel enjoys a privileged position, occupying a private cove beach and the hillside behind.

Accommodation units are modern, spacious and commodious – freshen up in a vast bath-tub or take an alfresco shower. Ocean villas have private pools, garden villas are closer to the shore. Great service, a top spa and a stunning waveside restaurant complete the Mia experience.

Fusion Resort Nha Trang RESORT $$$

(☎058-398 9777; http://fusionresortnhatrang.com; Nguyen Tat Thanh; ste/villas incl breakfast & spa from US$215/373; ❄@📶🏊) For sybaritic living look no further. New in 2015, this resort's selling point is its complimentary spa treatments (two daily per guest guaranteed). It's a huge complex where the suites and villas all have sea views, and many have private plunge pools. It's located on the ocean road 30km south of Nha Trang; there's a free shuttle-bus service from the airport.

Happy Angel Hotel BOUTIQUE HOTEL

(☎058-3525 006; 11 Nguyen Thien Thuat; dm/d US$7/24; ❄📶) The designer touches found in the sleek furniture, bright bathrooms and cute balconies will make you happy at these prices. It's quietly tucked back off the main drag, yet walking distance to the beach.

Eating

Dam Market VIETNAMESE $

(Đ Trang Nu Vuong; meals 15,000-50,000d; ⏰6am-4pm) For a traditional local experience, try Dam Market, which has a colourful collection of stalls, including *com chay* (vegetarian) options, in the 'food court'.

Yen's Restaurant VIETNAMESE $

(☎0933 766 205; http://yensrestaurantnhatrang.com; 3/2a Đ Tran Quang Khai; dishes 55,000-120,000d; ⏰8am-11pm; 📶) Stylish restaurant with a hospitable atmosphere and a winning line-up of flavoursome clay-pot, curry, noodle, rice and stir-fry dishes. Lilting traditional music and waitresses in *ao dai* (the national dress of Vietnam) add to the vibe.

Au Lac VEGETARIAN $

(28c Đ Hoang Hoa Tham; meals 15,000-30,000d; ⏰10am-7pm; 🌿) Long-running, no-frills vegan/vegetarian with more mock meat than greens, near the corner of Đ Nguyen Chanh.

A mixed plate (15,000d) is just about the best-value meal you can find in Nha Trang.

★**Mix** GREEK $$

(☎0165 967 9197; 77 Đ Hung Vuong; meals 90,000-180,000d; ⊙11am-10pm Thu-Tue;) Somehow Christos, the affable, kind-hearted Greek owner, manages to keep the quality high and prices moderate at his ever-busy, noisy restaurant – a Herculean effort. Everything is freshly prepared and beautifully presented, highlights include the seafood and meat platters, salads and souvlaki. Book ahead.

★**Lac Canh Restaurant** VIETNAMESE $$

(44 Đ Nguyen Binh Khiem; dishes 30,000-150,000d; ⊙11am-8.45pm) This bustling, smoky, scruffy and highly enjoyable place is crammed most nights with groups firing up the tabletop barbecues (beef, richly marinated with spices, is the speciality, but there are other meats and seafood, too). It closes quite early.

Nha Trang Xua VIETNAMESE $$

(☎058-389 6700; Thai Thong, Vinh Thai; dishes 40,000-210,000d; ⊙8am-9pm;) A classic Vietnamese restaurant set in a beautiful old house in the countryside surrounded by rice paddies and a lotus pond, around 7km west of town (100,000d in a taxi). Think a refined (handwritten) menu, chunky wooden tables and a rustic ambience. Highlights include the hotpots, Vietnamese salads, five-spice beef and fish (try the snakehead grilled in banana leaf).

Thap Ba SEAFOOD $$

(Thap Ba; meals 40,000-200,000d; ⊙6-10pm) This street is famous for its evening-only seafood places, which produce fine steamed or barbecued clams, crab and prawns.

Lanterns VIETNAMESE $$

(www.lanternsvietnam.com; 34/6 Đ Nguyen Thien Thuat; dishes 48,000-117,000d; ⊙7.30am-9.30pm;) This restaurant supports local orphanages and provides scholarships programs. Flavours are predominantly Vietnamese, with specials including curries, clay pots and steaming hotpots (210,000d for two). The 'street-food' items are not bad and international offerings include pasta. Cooking classes and tours get good feedback. Eat between 2pm and 4pm and 20% is knocked off your bill.

★**Kiwami** JAPANESE $$$

(☎058-351 6613, 0956 130 933; www.kiwamirestaurantsushi.info.vn; 136 Bach Dang; meals 250,000-600,000d; ⊙noon-10pm Thu-Tue;) An intimate, highly authentic neighbourhood Japanese place that gets everything right. There's a specialist sushi chef: perch on a bar stool and watch him at work or sit in one of the side alcoves. All your favourite dishes are present and correct, from sashimi to teriyaki. Visit at lunchtime for special sushi sets and bentos (145,000d to 210,000d).

Drinking & Nightlife

Pay serious attention to your drink and possessions if you're in the party bars of Nha Trang.

★**Louisiane Brewhouse** BREWERY

(☎058-352 1948; 29 Đ Tran Phu; per glass 40,000d; ⊙7am-midnight;) Microbreweries don't get

VEGETARIANS & VEGANS

The good news is that there is now more choice than ever before when it comes to vegetarian dining. The bad news is that you have not landed in Veg Heaven, for the Vietnamese are voracious omnivores. While they dearly love vegies, they also adore much of what crawls on the ground, swims in the sea or flies in the air.

However, if you are willing to seek out small eateries where no English is spoken, it is actually quite possible to travel in Vietnam eating just meat-free Vietnamese dishes. There are vegetarian *(com chay)* establishments in most towns, usually near Buddhist temples, or in city centres. Often these are local, simple places popular with observant Buddhists. Many use 'mock meat', tofu and gluten, to create meat-like vegan dishes that can be quite delicious. More places put on lunch buffets then close after that.

In keeping with Buddhist precepts, many vendors and eateries go vegetarian on the 1st and 15th days of each lunar month; this is a great time to scour the markets and sample dishes that would otherwise be offlimits. Otherwise, be wary. Any dish of vegetables may well have been cooked with fish sauce or shrimp paste, so it can be easier to say that you are a vegetarian Buddhist to a potential cook, even if you aren't, as Vietnamese people understand what this means.

much more sophisticated than this. Louisiane's copper vats have a helluva view, gazing over an inviting swimming pool down to a private strip of sand. There are six brews to try, including a red ale and superb *witbier* (a dark lager brewed Belgian-style).

Skylight Bar BAR
(http://skylightnhatrang.com; Best Western Premier Havana Nha Trang, 38 Đ Tran Phu; admission incl drink 100,000d; ⏲4.30-11pm; 📶) Soaring above the city on the 43rd floor, this bombastic shiny place set up by a team from LA boasts mile-high vistas from its rooftop perch, a killer cocktail list (120,000d to 150,000d), *shishas*, cigars, DJs and pool parties. It is the Saturday place to be, for now.

Sailing Club BAR, CLUB
(www.sailingclubnhatrang.com; 72-74 Đ Tran Phu; ⏲7am-2am; 📶) This Nha Trang beach club is a city institution with DJs and bands, and draws a beautiful, up-for-it crowd of foreigners. On Thursdays, Fridays and Saturdays a bonfire is lit and the action moves to the sand (weather permitting). 'Ladies night' starts the week.

Crazy Kim Bar BAR
(http://crazykimvietnam.wordpress.com; 19 Đ Biet Thu; ⏲9am-late; 📶) This place is home to the commendable 'Hands off the Kids!' campaign, working to prevent paedophilia – part of the profits go towards the cause. Crazy Kim's has regular themed party nights, devilish cocktail buckets (60,000d), shooters, cheap beer and tasty grub. La Rue beer is two-for-one during happy hour (noon to 8.30pm).

Shopping

★Lemongrass House COSMETICS
(http://fb.com/lemongrasshouse.vn; 38 Đ Nguyen Thi Minh Khai; ⏲10am-10pm) A terrific little branch of a brand selling wonderful face creams (270,000d), masks, hair products, essential oils and some teas. The products are sourced from natural ingredients and made in small batches in Thailand.

XQ ARTS & CRAFTS
(☎058-352 6579; www.xqvietnam.com; 64 Đ Tran Phu; ⏲8am-8pm) At this place, designed to look like a traditional rural village, you can watch the artisans at work in the embroidery workshop and gallery.

Information

Main Post Office (4 Đ Le Loi; ⏲6.30am-8pm Mon-Fri, to 1pm Sat).

Pasteur Institute (☎058-382 2355; www.pasteur-nhatrang.org.vn; 8-10 Đ Tran Phu; ⏲7-11am & 1-4.30pm) Offers medical consultations and vaccinations. Located inside the Alexandre Yersin Museum (p117).

Sinh Tourist (☎058-352 2982; www.thesinhtourist.vn; 90C Đ Hung Vuong; ⏲6am-10pm) A reliable, professional company for inexpensive local trips, including a city tour for 259,000d (excluding entrance fees) and island boat cruises, as well as open-tour buses.

Vietcombank (17 Đ Quang Trung; ⏲7.30am-4pm Mon-Fri) Has an ATM.

Getting There & Around

The **Cam Ranh International Airport** (☎058-398 9913) is located 30km south of Nha Trang and has international connections to Moscow with **Vietnam Airlines** (☎058-352 6768; www.vietnamairlines.com; 91 Đ Nguyen Thien Thuat) and Seoul with Asiana. Vietnam Airlines also

TRANSPORT FROM NHA TRANG

DESTINATION	AIR	BUS	CAR/ MOTORCYCLE	TRAIN
Dalat	N/A	US$7, 5hr, 15 daily	4hr	N/A
Danang	from US$31, 1hr, 1 daily	US$11-15, 12hr, 13-15 daily	11hr	US$15-21, 9-11hr, 6 daily
Ho Chi Minh City	from US$21, 1hr, 8 daily	US$10-15, 11hr, 13 daily	10hr	US$11-16, 7-9hr, 7 daily
Mui Ne	N/A	US$7, 5hr 30min, open-tour buses only	5hr	N/A
Quy Nhon	N/A	US$6.50, 6hr, every 2hr	6hr	US$5.50-8, 4hr, 6 daily

connects Nha Trang with Ho Chi Minh City, Hanoi and Danang domestically.

Nha Trang Taxi (☎ 058-382 6000), the official maroon-coloured cabs, cost 380,000d from the airport to downtown. It's cheaper in the other direction (around 300,000d) if you fix a price ahead rather than using taxi meters, which work out to be more expensive. **Mai Linh** (☎ 058-382 2266) is another reliable taxi company.

Nha Trang's main intercity bus terminal, **Phia Nam Nha Trang Bus Station** (Đ 23 Thang 10), is 500m west of the **train station** (☎ 058-382 2113; Đ Thai Nguyen; ⏱ ticket office 7-11.30am, 1.30-6pm & 7-9pm). It has regular daily buses heading north to Danang. Heading south, there are frequent connections to Phan Rang and HCMC.

Mui Ne

Once upon a time, Mui Ne was an isolated stretch of beach where pioneering travellers camped on the sand. It's now a string of (mercifully low-rise) beach resorts set amid pretty gardens by the sea. The original fishing village is still here, but tourists outnumber locals these days. Mui Ne is definitely moving upmarket, with swish restaurants and swanky shops, but there is still a (kite) surfer vibe to the town.

Sights

Sand Dunes BEACH

Mui Ne is famous for its enormous red and white sand dunes. The 'white dunes' (*doi cat trang*), 24km northeast of Mui Ne are the more impressive – the near-constant oceanic winds sculpt the pale yellow sands into wonderful Saharaesque formations – while the 'red dunes' (*doi hong*) are convenient to Hai Long. But as this is Vietnam (not deepest Mali) there's little chance of experiencing the silence of the desert.

Prepare yourself for the hard sell as children press you to hire a plastic sledge to ride the dunes. Unless you're supermodel-light, it can be tricky to travel for more than a few metres this way.

Po Shanu Cham Towers HINDU SITE

(Km 5; 5000d; ⏱ 7.30-11.30am & 1-4.30pm) West of Mui Ne, the Po Shanu Cham towers occupy a hill near Phan Thiet, with sweeping views of the town and a cemetery filled with candy-like tombstones. Dating from the 9th century, this complex consists of the ruins of three towers, none of which are in very good shape. There's a small pagoda on the site, as well as a gallery and shop.

Activities

Mui Ne is the adrenalin capital of southern Vietnam. There's no scuba-diving or snorkelling to speak of, but when Nha Trang and Hoi An get the rains, Mui Ne gets the waves. Surf's up from August to December.

★ **Forester Beach Spa** SPA

(☎ 062-374 1899; 82 Nguyen Dinh Chieu; 1hr massage 320,000d) A class above the cheap joints, this well-designed spa has lovely little bamboo massage cabins right by the shore, so you can tune into rolling waves while you're being pampered. Staff are very well trained and discounts are often available.

Manta Sail Training Centre BOATING

(☎ 0908 400 108; http://mantasailing.org; 108 Đ Huynh Thuc Khang; sailing instruction per hour US$66) Excellent new sailing school offering International Sailing Federation training (from beginner to advanced racing), wakeboarding (US$110 per hour including boat) and stand-up paddleboard rentals. Staff are very professional and they also have budget rooms available.

Surfpoint Kiteboarding School KITESURFING, SURFING

(☎ 0167 342 2136; www.surfpoint-vietnam.com; 52a Đ Nguyen Dinh Chieu; 3hr course incl all gear US$150; ⏱ 7am-6pm) With well-trained instructors and a friendly vibe, it's no surprise Surfpoint is one of the best-regarded kite schools in town. A five-hour course costs US$250. Surfing lessons on soft boards are also offered (from US$50) when waves permit and there are short boards for rent.

Courses

Taste of Vietnam COOKING

(☎ 0916 655 241; www.muinecookingschool.com; Sunshine Beach Resort, 82 Đ Nguyen Dinh Chieu; 2½hr class US$30; ⏱ classes 8.45am-12.30pm) Well-regarded Vietnamese cooking classes by the beach. Pay US$35 and a market visit is included (3½ hours total). Make sure you have a light breakfast first as there's lots of grub to try!

Sleeping

★ **Mui Ne Backpacker Village** HOSTEL $

(☎ 062-374 1047; www.muinebackpackervillage.com; 137 Đ Nguyen Dinh Chieu; dm/r from US$5/25; ⊖❄☎≋) Cornering the backpacker

Mui Ne Beach

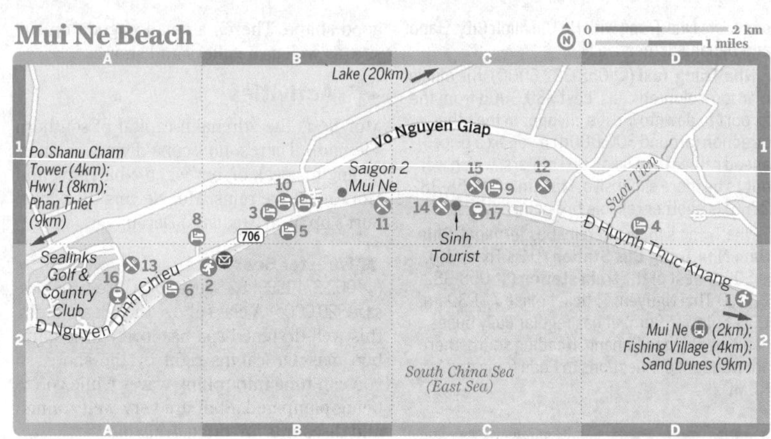

Mui Ne Beach

Activities, Courses & Tours

Forester Beach Spa .... (see 5)
1 Manta Sail Training Centre D2
2 Surfpoint Kiteboarding School B2
Taste of Vietnam .... (see 5)

Sleeping

3 Coco Sand Hotel B1
4 Duy An Guesthouse D1
5 Full Moon Beach Hotel B1
6 Mia Resort A2
7 Mui Ne Backpacker Village B1
Mui Ne Hills Budget Hotel .... (see 8)
8 Mui Ne Hills Villa Hotel A1
9 Song Huong Hotel C1
10 Xin Chao B1

Eating

11 Bo Ke B1
12 Com Chay Vi Dieu C1
13 Ganesh A2
14 Nhu Bao C1
Sandals .... (see 6)
15 Sindbad C1

Drinking & Nightlife

16 Deja Vu A2
Dragon Beach .... (see 11)
Joe's Café .... (see 5)
17 PoGo C1

market, this ambitious, well-designed modern construction proves wildly popular thanks to its inviting pool, bar-restaurant and social vibe. All dorms have air-con, individual beds (no bunks!) and lockers while the 18 private rooms all have a balcony or patio.

Mui Ne Hills Budget Hotel HOTEL $
(☎062-374 1707; www.muinehills.com; 69 Đ Nguyen Dinh Chieu; dm/r from US$5/19; ❄📶🏊) This place offers a good bed for your buck, with several air-con dorms that have en suites while the rooms have quality furnishings and contemporary design touches. It's around 300m north of the main strip, via an incredibly steep access road.

Coco Sand Hotel GUESTHOUSE $
(☎0127 364 3446; http://cocosandhotel.com; 119 Đ Nguyen Dinh Chieu; r US$13-21; ❄📶) Excellent-value rooms are grouped around a shady courtyard garden (with hammocks) at this very hospitable place. It's just off the main drag, down a little lane so it's quiet. The owners rent out motorbikes at fair rates.

Song Huong Hotel HOTEL $
(☎062-384 7450; www.songhuonghotel.com; 241 Đ Nguyen Dinh Chieu; s/d US$12/15 incl breakfast; ❄📶) Run by welcoming family owners, this hotel is set well back from the road and boasts spacious, light airy rooms in a modern house.

Duy An Guesthouse GUESTHOUSE $
(☎062-384 7799; 87a Đ Huynh Thuc Khang; s/d US$10/15; ❄@📶) This traditional guesthouse is run by a friendly soul who looks after guests well (try his wild-honey wine). It's close to the eastern end of the strip in a shady compound, and has a good restaurant.

Mui Ne Hills Villa Hotel BOUTIQUE HOTEL $$
(☎062-374 1707; www.muinehills.com; 69 Đ Nguyen Dinh Chieu; r US$35-50; ❄@📶🏊) Formerly Mui Ne Hills 1, this fine villa-style hotel has wonderful vistas from its pool. Rooms are

superb value, all with contemporary design touches and full facilities, but it's the personal touch from staff and owners that makes a real difference. It's located up a dusty, very steep lane (but is close to the best section of beach).

Xin Chao BOUTIQUE HOTEL **$$**
(062-374 3086; www.xinchaohotel.com; 129 Đ Nguyen Dinh Chieu; r US$30-45;) Impressive modern hotel (owned by kitesurfers) set well back from the busy coastal road. A lot of thought has gone into the design, with rooms grouped around a pool at the rear. A small lounge area (with pool table) and roadside bar-restaurant add to its appeal.

Full Moon Beach Hotel HOTEL **$$**
(062-384 7008; www.fullmoonbeach.com.vn; 84 Đ Nguyen Dinh Chieu; r incl breakfast US$56-70;) An artistically designed place where the committed owners have consistently upgraded the facilities to keep up with the competition. Features a bamboo-shaded pool, rooms with four-poster beds and terracotta tiling, and an oceanfront bar.

★ **Mia Resort** BOUTIQUE HOTEL **$$$**
(062-384 7440; www.miamuine.com; 24 Đ Nguyen Dinh Chieu; r US$135, bungalows US$158-266, all incl breakfast;) This seriously stylish beachfront hotel is top dog in Mui Ne. A calm ambience pervades and the friendly, efficient staff really give the hotel a little extra polish; it's wonderfully relaxing here. The pool is small but it's a great place to chill, facing the ocean. You'll love Sandals, the in-house restaurant, where a magnificent breakfast spread is served.

Eating

Mui Ne is one of the most expensive places to dine in Vietnam. The incredible selection of restaurants is mostly geared to the cosmopolitan tastes of its visitors.

Com Chay Vi Dieu VEGETARIAN **$**
(15B Đ Huynh Thuc Khang; meals 25,000d; 7am-9pm;) This simple roadside place scores strongly for inexpensive Vietnamese vegetarian dishes, and serves great smoothies (20,000d). It's opposite the Eiffel Tower of the Little Paris resort. No English is spoken but you can point and choose.

Sindbad MIDDLE EASTERN **$**
(www.sindbad.vn; 233 Đ Nguyen Dinh Chieu; mains 50,000-70,000d; 11am-1am;) A kind of kebab shack par excellence. Come here for *shawarma* (doner kebabs) and shish kebabs and other Med favourites such as Greek salad. Very inexpensive and portions are generous; opens late.

Nhu Bao SEAFOOD **$**
(0914 531 767; 146 Đ Nguyen Dinh Chieu; mains 50,000-180,000d; 9am-9.30pm) A classic, no-nonsense Vietnamese seafood place: step past the bubbling tanks and there's a huge covered terrace which stretches down to the ocean. It's renowned for its crab.

★ **Sandals** INTERNATIONAL **$$**
(062-384 7440; www.miamuine.com/dine; Mia Resort, 24 Đ Nguyen Dinh Chieu; meals 120,000-370,000d; 7am-10pm;) This outstanding hotel restaurant is the most atmospheric place in town. It's particularly romantic at night, with tables set around the shoreside pool or in the elegant dining rooms. Wait staff are knowledgeable, attentive and welcoming. The menu is superb with everything from pasta dishes to Vietnamese clay pots executed and presented beautifully. Consider visiting for the wonderful breakfast buffet.

Ganesh INDIAN **$$**
(www.ganesh.vn; 57 Đ Nguyen Dinh Chieu; mains 60,000-160,000d; 11am-10pm;) Excellent, authentic Indian restaurant with a wide selection of dishes from the subcontinent, including plenty of choice for vegetarians (including a generous thali). The garlic naan really is to savour.

Bo Ke SEAFOOD **$$**
(Đ Nguyen Dinh Chieu; mains 40,000-120,000d; 5-10pm) A group of seafood shacks on the beach.

Drinking & Nightlife

★ **PoGo** BAR
(0912 000 751; www.thepogobar.com; 138 Đ Nguyen Dinh Chieu; 8.30am-2am) A mighty fine bar with a prime beach location, day beds for lounging, DJs on weekends and regular movie nights. Staff are very friendly and there's a full menu too.

Joe's Café BAR
(http://joescafemuine.com; 86 Đ Nguyen Dinh Chieu; 7am-1am;) If bangin' techno is not your bag, Joe's is worth a try with live music (every night at 7.30pm) and a pub-like vibe. During the day it's a good place to hang too, with a sociable bar area, lots of drinks specials and an extensive food menu.

Deja Vu BAR
(21 Đ Nguyen Dinh Chieu; noon-1am;) A kind of hip bar-restaurant at the Phan Thiet end of the strip, offering *shishas*, cocktails and an international menu. There's a set lunch for 80,000d.

Dragon Beach BAR, CLUB
(120-121 Đ Nguyen Dinh Chieu; 1pm-4am) Western and local DJs play electronic dance music (EDM), bass, house and techno at this shoreside bar-club. There's a chill-out deck with cushions to one side and *shishas* for puffing. Happy hour is 8pm to 10pm.

Information

Post Office Branch (44 Đ Nguyen Dinh Chieu; 9am-4.30pm Mon-Fri) A convenient location at Swiss Village.

Getting There & Around

Open-tour buses are the most convenient option for Mui Ne, as most public buses only serve Phan Thiet. Several companies have daily services to/from Ho Chi Minh City (109,000d to 119,000d, six hours), Nha Trang (from 109,000d, 5½ hours) and Dalat (119,000d, four hours). Sleeper open-tour night buses usually cost more; HCMC with **Sinh Tourist** (www.thesinhtourist.vn; 144 Đ Nguyen Dinh Chieu; 7am-10pm) is 109,000d.

Phuong Trang has four comfortable buses a day running between Mui Ne and HCMC (120,000d).

Mai Linh (062-389 8989) Mai Linh operates reliable metered taxis, although call ahead to book later in the evening or ask the restaurant or bar to assist.

Saigon 2 Mui Ne (0126 552 0065; www.saigon2muine.com; 165/1 Đ Nguyen Dinh Chieu) It costs around US$100/125 to rent a car/minivan for the run to HCMC (five to six hours). Saigon 2 Mui Ne gets good reports for reliability.

Con Dao Islands

Isolated from the mainland, the Con Dao Islands are one of Vietnam's star attractions. Con Son, the largest of this chain of 15 islands and islets, is ringed with lovely beaches, coral reefs and scenic bays, and remains partially covered in thick forests. In addition to hiking, diving and exploring deserted coastal roads and beaches, there are excellent opportunities to watch wildlife, such as the black giant squirrel and endemic bow-fingered gecko.

Long the preserve of thousands of political prisoners in no less than a dozen jails during French rule and the American-backed regime, Con Son now turns heads thanks to its striking natural beauty.

Sights

To get a feel of Con Son's ghosts, visit Phu Hai Prison, the largest of the 11 jails on the island.

★Bai Dat Doc BEACH
The best beach on Con Son Island, Bai Dat Doc is a simply beautiful cove, consisting of a kilometre-long crescent of pale sand, backed by green hills. It has a gently shelving profile and no pollution, so it's ideal for swimming. Though it's backed by the luxury bungalows of the Six Senses hotel, it's not a private beach and there are access points close to the road.

Very rarely dugongs have been seen frolicking in the water off the nearby cape.

★Bay Canh ISLAND
Perhaps the best all-round island to visit is Bay Canh, to the east of Con Son Island, which has lovely beaches, old-growth forest, mangroves, coral reefs and sea turtles (seasonal). There is a fantastic two-hour walk to a functioning French-era lighthouse on Bay Canh's eastern tip, although it involves a steep climb of 325m. Once at the summit, the panoramic views are breathtaking.

Bai Dram Trau BEACH
Reached via a dirt track 1km before the airport on Con Son Island, Bai Dram Trau is a sublime but remote 700m half-moon crescent of soft sand, fringed by casuarina trees and bookended by forest-topped rocky promontories. It's best visited at low tide.

There's some snorkelling on reefs offshore and three very simple seafood shacks (all open noon till dusk only).

Bai Loi Voi BEACH
On the north side of Con Son Town, Bai Loi Voi is a broad sand-and-shingle beach with lots of seashells and shade-providing casuarinas. There's a good stretch of sandy beach right in the centre of Con Son, around the Con Dao Resort.

Bai An Hai BEACH
Bai An Hai, on the south side of town, is an appealing beach with a green mountain backdrop, but there are a good number of fishing boats moored nearby.

Tre Lon ISLAND
Some of the more pristine beaches are on the smaller islands, such as the beautiful

white-sand beach on Tre Lon, to the west of Con Son Island.

Activities

Con Dao offers the most pristine marine environment in the country. Diving is possible year-round, but for ideal conditions and good visibility, January to June is considered the best time.

There are lots of treks around Con Son Island, as much of the interior remains heavily forested. It's necessary to take a national-park guide (180,000d to 300,000d) when venturing into the forest.

★Dive! Dive! Dive! DIVING
(☎064-383 0701; www.dive-condao.com; Đ Nguyen Hue; ⊙8am-9pm) Instructor Larry has been in Con Dao since 2011 and has vast experience diving the island reefs. This is an experienced, conservation-minded operation. It offers Rebreather Association of International Divers (RAID) courses and the dive shop is a great source of general information on the Con Daos. The company constantly monitors reefs to remove fishing nets and rubbish from corals.

Bamboo Lagoon HIKING
(Dam Tre) One of the more beautiful walks leads through thick forest and mangroves, past a hilltop stream to Bamboo Lagoon. There's good snorkelling in the bay here. This leisurely two-hour trek starts from near the airport runway, but you'll definitely need a local guide to do this.

Ong Dung Bay HIKING
A hike that you can do yourself is a 1km walk (about 30 minutes each way) through rainforest to Ong Dung Bay. The trail begins a few kilometres north of town passing Ma Thien Lanh Bridge. The bay has only a rocky beach, although there is a good coral reef about 300m offshore.

Ma Thien Lanh Bridge HIKING
Near the trailhead for Ong Dung Bay, you'll find the ruins of the Ma Thien Lanh Bridge, which was built by prisoners under the French occupation.

Sleeping & Eating

Expect to pay about double the rate for the equivalent sleeping option on the mainland.

★Red Hotel HOTEL $
(☎064-363 0079; 17B Đ Nguyen An Ninh; r 350,000-650,000d; ❄📶) A good budget option, this minihotel has spotless, spacious rooms and is in the thick of things, close to the night market and plenty of eating options. It's run by a helpful team who are very welcoming, though they speak little English.

Nha Nghi Thanh Xuan GUESTHOUSE $
(☎064-383 0261; 44 Đ Ton Duc Thang; r 350,000-500,000d; 📶) Painted in marine blue, this guesthouse has rooms with good mattresses and duvets; the upstairs rooms are light and airy. The owners speak little or no English.

Thien Tan Star Hotel HOTEL $$
(☎064-363 0123; http://thientanstarhotel.com; 4 Đ Nguyen Duc Thuan; r 800,000-1,500,000d; ❄📶) This hotel occupies a prime beachfront plot close to everything in Con Son. Rooms are simple with whitewashed walls, minibar, flat-screen TV and good bed linen; you can save some dong if you forgo a sea view.

★Six Senses Con Dao BOUTIQUE HOTEL $$$
(☎064-383 1222; www.sixsenses.com; Dat Doc Beach; villas from US$651; ❄@📶🏊) In a class of its own, the astonishing Six Senses is located on the island's best beach, 4km northeast of Con Son town. One of Vietnam's most exclusive resorts, it has 50 or so ocean-facing timber-clad beach units that fuse contemporary style with rustic chic, each with its own pool, giant bath tub (and a couple of bikes). Staff are very well trained.

Eating options include a casual cafe where you can grab a panini, and the magnificent restaurant by the shore. Diving, sailing trips and trekking can all be arranged and the spa has indoor and outdoor rooms for Ayurvedic treatments.

Bar200 Con Dao CAFE $
(http://divecondao.com; Đ Pham Van Dong; meals from 35,000d; ⊙8am-10.30pm; 📶) Popular place to hang for travellers in town, with a relaxed, sociable vibe; the owners are cluedup when it comes to island info. There's great coffee (including espresso and cappuccino) and Western comfort grub including burgers, pizza, sandwiches and breakfast cereals. After dark the beers and cocktails start flowing.

Night Market MARKET $
(cnr Đ Tran Huy Lieu & Đ Nguyen An Ninh; snacks 20,000-90,000d) If you're on a tight budget,

THE TEENAGE MARTYR

If breeze is blowing from the north, you can probably smell the incense from a specific grave in Con Son's cemetery: the tomb of Vo Thi Sau, a national icon.

Vo Thi Sau, a teenage resistance fighter executed in Con Dao during the French occupation, was politically active from a very early age. She killed a French captain in a grenade attack at the age of 14, and was only captured years later following a second assassination attempt. Vo Thi Sau was taken to Con Dao and executed here, aged 19.

Visit the cemetery at midnight and you'll find crowds of people packed around her grave, saying prayers and making offerings. The Vietnamese believe that this is the most auspicious time to pay respects and venerate the spirit of this national heroine, who was killed in the early hours of 23 January 1952.

check out the small night market around the intersection of Đ Tran Huy Lieu and Đ Nguyen An Ninh for cheap eats.

Information

Larry of Dive! Dive! Dive! (p127) is a great contact and very knowledgeable about the islands.

BQL Cang Ben Dam Huyen Con Dao (064-383 0619; Đ Quy Hoach, Ben Dam pier; 8-11.30am & 1-5pm) Sells tickets for ferries connecting Con Son Island with Vung Tau.

National Park Headquarters (064-383 0669; www.condaopark.com.vn; 29 Đ Vo Thi Sau; 7-11.30am & 1.30-5pm) Since the military controls access to parts of the national park, stop here first to learn more about possible island excursions and hikes, plus pick up a useful free handout on island walks – some hiking trails have interpretive signage in English and Vietnamese. It also has an exhibition hall with displays on local forest- and marine-life diversity, local environmental threats and conservation activities.

Vietin Bank (Đ Le Duan; 8am-2pm Mon-Fri, to noon Sat) With ATM; does not change foreign currency.

Getting There & Around

Con Dao Airport is a tiny airport is about 15km from the town centre. There are three to five daily flights between Con Son and Ho Chi Minh City jointly operated by **Vasco** (038-330 330; www.vasco.com.vn; 44 Đ Nguyen Hue) and Vietnam Airlines.

It's nearly always possible to show up and grab a seat on one of the hotel shuttle vans that meet the planes; drivers charge 50,000d and will usually drop you off at your hotel or in the town centre.

Con Son Island has several taxis. However, as metered rates are astronomically high (around 20,000d per km!) negotiate hard for a fixed-price rate to destinations outside Con Son town.

SOUTHWEST HIGHLANDS

There's a rugged charm to this distinctly rural region, with pine-studded hilltops soaring over intensively farmed fields and remote, bumpy roads meandering through coffee plantations. Looking for big nature? Check out Cat Tien National Park, where there are gibbons, crocodiles and elusive tigers.

Dalat, a former French hill station that still boasts plenty of colonial charm, makes a great base. An adventure-sports mecca, its cool climate offers myriad biking and hiking trips for daytime thrills and atmospheric restaurants and bars for after-dark chills.

Dalat

Dalat is Vietnam's alter ego: the weather is springlike cool (daily temperatures hover between 15°C and 24°C) instead of tropical hot, the town is dotted with elegant French-colonial villas rather than stark socialist architecture, and the farms around are thick with strawberries and flowers, not rice.

The French left behind holiday homes and the vibe of a European town. Dalat is a big draw for domestic tourists – it's Le Petit Paris, the honeymoon capital. For travellers, the moderate climate makes it a superb place for adrenalin-fuelled activities or less demanding natural wonders.

Sights

Xuan Huong Lake LAKE

Created by a dam in 1919, this banana-shaped lake was named after an antiauthoritarian 17th-century Vietnamese poet. It has become a popular icon of Dalat and a magnet for joggers and those in love. The lake can be circumnavigated along a scenic 7km sealed path that passes the flower gardens, golf club, night market and Dalat Palace hotel.

★**Hang Nga Crazy House** ARCHITECTURE
(☎063-382 2070; 3 Đ Huynh Thuc Khang; 40,000d; ⊙8.30am-7pm Mon-Fri) A free-wheeling architectural exploration of surrealism, Hang Nga Crazy House is a joyously designed, outrageously artistic private home. Imagine sculptured rooms connected by superslim bridges rising out of a tangle of greenery, an excess of cascading lava-flow-like shapes, wild colours, spiderweb windows and an almost-organic quality to it all, with the swooping hand rails resembling jungle vines. Think of Gaudí and Tolkien dropping acid together.

A note of caution for those with young kids: the Crazy House's maze of precarious tunnels, high walkways with low guard rails and steep ladders are certainly not child-safe.

Dalat Cathedral CATHEDRAL
(Đ Tran Phu) The gingerbread-style Dalat Cathedral was built between 1931 and 1942 for use by French residents and holidaymakers. The cross on the spire is topped by a weathercock, 47m above the ground. The church itself is rarely open outside Mass times.

Datanla Falls WATERFALL
(adult/child 20,000/10,000d, bobsled ride one-way/return 40,000/50,000d) This is the closest waterfall to Dalat, so expect lots of tour groups. You can reach the cascade (which is pretty but quite modest) either by walking down or taking the exhilarating bobsled on rails instead. Datanla is 7km south of Dalat. Take Hwy 20 and turn right about 200m past the turn-off to Tuyen Lam Lake.

Linh Son Pagoda ARCHITECTURE
(Chua Linh Son; 120 Đ Nguyen Van Troi) Built in 1938, the Linh Son Pagoda is a lovely ochre-coloured building that fuses French and Chinese architecture. The giant bell is said to be made of bronze mixed with gold, its great weight making it too heavy for thieves to carry off.

Tours

★**Phat Tire Ventures** ADVENTURE
(☎063-382 9422; www.ptv-vietnam.com; 109 Đ Nguyen Van Troi; ⊙8am-7pm) A highly professional and experienced operator with mountain-biking trips from US$49, trekking from US$39, kayaking from US$39, canyoning (US$75) and rapelling (US$57), and white-water rafting (US$67) in the rainy season. Multiday cycling trips are available and it also ventures into Cat Tien National Park.

Dalat Happy Tours FOOD & DRINK
(☎0912 893 091; www.dalathappytours.com; street-food tour US$4) After all the active exertions around Dalat, replenish your calories by going on an entertaining nightly street-food tour with friendly Lao. Start from the central Hoa Binh cinema at 6.30pm and proceed to sample *bahn xeo* (filled pancakes), buffalo-tail hotpot, delectable grilled skewers, 'Dalat pizza', rabbit curry, hot rice wine and more. Food costs are not included.

Groovy Gecko Adventure Tours ADVENTURE
(☎063-383 6521; www.groovygeckotours.net; 65 Đ Truong Cong Dinh; ⊙8am-7pm) Experienced agency operated by a lively young team with prices starting at US$38 for rock climbing, canyoning or mountain biking, day treks from US$25 and two-day treks from US$65.

Pine Track Adventures ADVENTURE
(☎063-383 1916; www.pinetrackadventures.com; 72b Đ Truong Cong Dinh; ⊙8am-7pm) Run by an enthusiastic local team, this operator offers canyoning (from US$50), white-water rafting (US$68), trekking, biking and some excellent multisport packages. A six-day exploration of the area around Dalat and bike ride down to Mui Ne is US$635.

Sleeping

★**Dalat Central Hostel** HOSTEL $
(Hotel Phuong Hanh; ☎0989 878 879; 80 Đ Ba Thang Hai; dm US$5, r US$15-25; ❄📶) More budget hotel than hostel, though it's a popular traveller hub. The vast eight- and 12-bed dorms come with comfy bunks and privacy curtains, a women-only dorm is available, and the private rooms are huge and equipped with triangular bath-tubs.

★**Ken's House** HOSTEL $
(☎063-383 7119; http://kenhousedalat.com; D59 Hoang Van Thu; r US$12-22; ⊖❄📶) With walls covered with creeping vines, Parisian scenes and jungle imagery, and patterned quilts on beds, this is by far Dalat's most colourful hostel. Join an impromptu hotpot party/communal dinner with the friendly staff.

Sleep In Dalat Hostel HOSTEL $
(☎0913 923 379; 83/5b Đ Nguyen Van Troi; dm US$5, d US$18-30; 📶) Haunted by Ben the sausage dog, this welcoming hostel is tucked away down a narrow alleyway, insulating you from main-street noise. Owner Linh

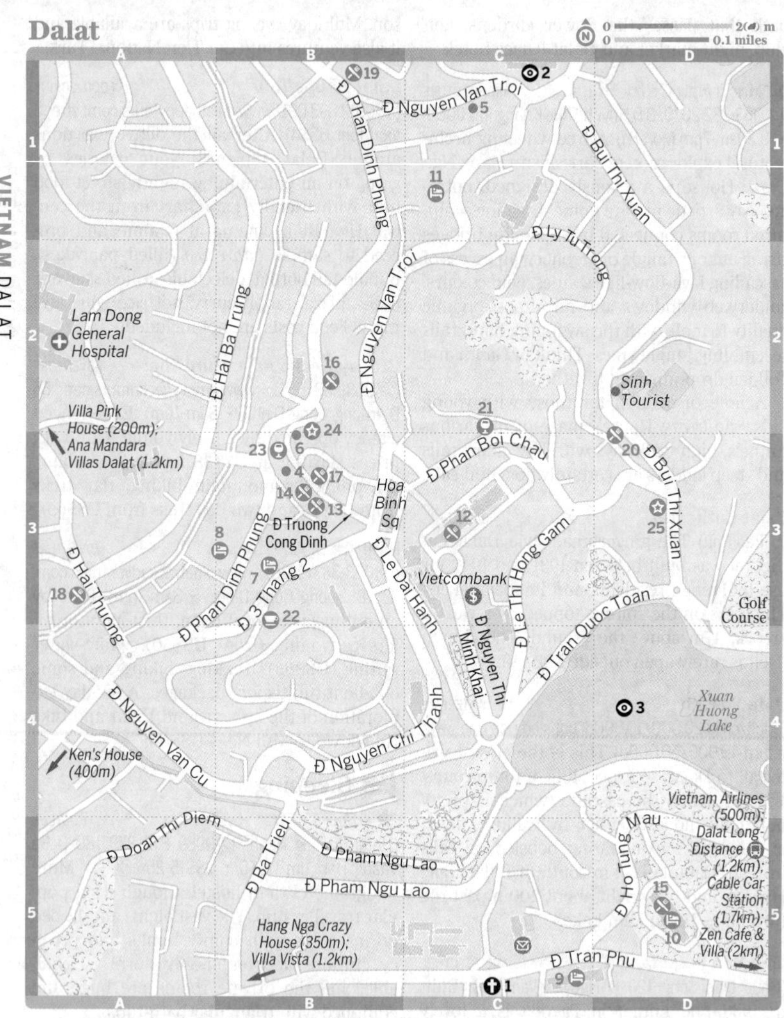

cooks communal dinners so that you can get to know your fellow travellers, and the canyoning tours get rave reviews. Private rooms have bathrooms; dorms share (clean) facilities.

Dalat Cozy Nook Hostel HOSTEL $
(☎0949 691 553; 45/5a Đ Phan Dinh Phung; dm incl breakfast US$6; ❄📶) Two spotless mixed dorms with the most comfortable bunks in Dalat attract a constant crowd of international backpackers. The lively group dinners, organised by helpful owners, offer the perfect opportunity to swap traveller tales.

Villa Pink House HOTEL $
(☎063-381 5667; ahomeawayfromhome_dalat@yahoo.com; 7 Đ Hai Thuong; s/d/tr US$16/20/30; @📶) A well-run family-owned place, where many rooms have great views. It's managed by the affable Mr Rot, who can arrange motorbike tours in the countryside around Dalat.

★ **Villa Vista** BOUTIQUE HOTEL $$
(☎063-351 2468; http://villavistadalat.com; 93 Ngo Thi Sy, Phuong 4; r from US$91; 🚭📶) Look down from this mansion on the hill and the whole of Dalat opens up in the valley below

Dalat

Sights
1 Dalat Cathedral ... C5
2 Linh Son Pagoda ... C1
3 Xuan Huong Lake ... D4

Activities, Courses & Tours
4 Groovy Gecko Adventure Tours ... B3
5 Phat Tire Ventures ... C1
6 Pine Track Adventures ... B3

Sleeping
7 Dalat Central Hostel ... B3
8 Dalat Cozy Nook Hostel ... B3
9 Dalat Hotel du Parc ... C5
10 Dalat Palace ... D5
11 Sleep In Dalat Hostel ... C1

Eating
12 Central Market ... C3
13 Da Quy ... B3
14 Goc Ha Thanh ... B3
15 Le Rabelais ... D5
16 Nhat Ly ... B2
17 Quan Trang ... B3
18 Restaurant Ichi ... A3
19 Trong Dong ... B1
20 V Cafe ... D3

Drinking & Nightlife
21 100 Roofs Café ... C2
22 An Cafe ... B3
23 Hangout ... B3

Entertainment
24 Beepub ... B2
25 Escape Bar ... D3

you. There are only four exquisite rooms here, decorated in 19th-century French fashion (albeit with flat-screen TVs and rain showers). Delightful owners Tim and Huong prepare remarkable breakfasts and will share their Dalat knowledge.

Dalat Hotel du Parc HOTEL $$
(☎063-382 5777; www.dalathotelduparc.com; 7 Đ Tran Phu; r 1,000,000-2,350,000d, ste 2,200,000-3,150,000d; ❄📶) A respectfully refurbished 1932 building that offers colonial-era style at enticing prices. The grand lobby lift sets the tone and the spacious rooms include classy furnishings and polished wooden floors. It's bristling with facilities, from a spa and fitness centre to an excellent restaurant.

Zen Cafe & Villa GUESTHOUSE $$
(☎0994 799 518; www.zencafedalat.com; 27c Pham Hong Thai; r US$25-48; 📶) Lodge in spacious, characterful rooms in a century-old French villa, surrounded by tranquil gardens, sufficiently high up to give you mountain views. Owners Axel and Mai Dung regale you with local anecdotes and the coffee served at their cafe is wonderful.

★**Ana Mandara Villas Dalat** BOUTIQUE HOTEL $$$
(☎063-355 5888; www.anamandara-resort.com; Đ Le Lai; r US$139-165; 🚭❄📶) Elegant property spread across seven lovingly restored French-colonial villas. Finished in period furnishings, the villas have the option of private dining; most come with a fireplace in the lounge and all have wonderful panoramic views. The spa is glorious. It's located in the suburbs.

Dalat Palace HISTORIC HOTEL $$$
(☎063-382 5444; www.dalatpalacehotel.com; 12 Đ Tran Phu; d/ste from US$189/413; 🚭❄📶) With unimpeded views of Xuan Huong Lake, this grande dame of hotels has vintage Citroën cars in its sweeping driveway, and lashings of wood panelling and period class. The opulence of French-colonial life has been splendidly preserved: claw-foot tubs, fireplaces, chandeliers and paintings. However, it can be empty at times, and consequently lack ambience. Look for online deals.

Eating

Toasted rice-paper *banh trang nuong* (Dalat pizza) is a street food growing in popularity, and tastier than it sounds, just opt for it without the (cream) cheese.

★**Trong Dong** VIETNAMESE $
(☎063-382 1889; 220 Đ Phan Dinh Phung; meals 80,000-120,000d; ⏲11.30am-3pm & 5.30-9.30pm; 📶) Intimate restaurant run by a very hospitable team where the creative menu includes spins on Vietnamese delights such as shrimp paste on a sugar-cane stick, beef wrapped in *la lut* leaf, and fiery lemongrass and chilli squid.

Quan Trang VIETNAMESE $
(☎063-382 5043; 15 Tang Bat Ho; dishes 40,000d; ⏲1.30-7pm) Love it or hate it, the local speciality *banh uot long ga* here is among the best, so you can decide for yourself. The rice

WORTH A TRIP

DAMBRI FALLS

En route to Bao Loc and Ho Chi Minh City, 130km south of Dalat, Dambri Falls are one of the highest (90m), most magnificent and easily accessible waterfalls in Vietnam – they are worth visiting even in dry season. For some incredible views, ride the vertical cable car (5000d) or trudge up the steep path to the top of the falls.

The road to the falls branches off Hwy 20, 18km north of Bao Loc.

A second path leads down some steep stairs to the front of the falls for more great views, and carries on down to the smaller Dasara Falls.

noodles are saucy not soupy, the liver easy to avoid in the bowl (if you hate it) and the fresh shredded chicken, herbs and chilli lift the dish. Delicious – people certainly aren't here for the plastic decor.

Da Quy VIETNAMESE $
(Wild Sunflower; 49 Đ Truong Cong Dinh; meals from 50,000d; ⏲8am-10pm) Run by Loc, a friendly English speaker, this place has a sophisticated ambience, yet accessible prices. The traditional clay-pot dishes and hotpots are more exciting than the Western menu.

Central Market VIETNAMESE $
(Cho Da Lat; meals from 20,000d; ⏲7am-3pm) For cheap eats during the day, head to the upper level of the Central Market. In the evening, food stalls pop up around the market along Nguyen Thi Minh Khai.

★**Restaurant Ichi** JAPANESE $$
(☎063-355 5098; 1 Đ Hoang Dieu; meals 120,000-300,000d; ⏲5.30-10pm Tue-Sun) Dalat's only truly genuine Japanese restaurant is compact, with subdued lighting and jazz in the background. Spicy tuna rolls, chicken yakitori and tempura are all fantastic, the bento boxes are a bargain and there's even *natto* (fermented soybeans) for aficionados. Perch in front of the bar (with extensive whisky offerings from around the world) to watch sushi-master Tommo at work.

Goc Ha Thanh VIETNAMESE $$
(53 Đ Truong Cong Dinh; meals 100,000-150,000d; ⏲7am-10pm; 📶📝) Casual place with attractive bamboo furnishings owned by a welcoming Hanoi couple. Strong on dishes such as coconut curry, hotpots, clay pots, tofu stir-fries and noodles.

V Cafe INTERNATIONAL $$
(☎063-352 0215; www.vcafedalatvietnam.com; 1/1 Đ Bui Thi Xuan; meals 99,000-145,000d; ⏲7am-10.30pm; 📶📝) Atmospheric bistro-style place that serves international cuisine, such as chicken curry Calcutta, vegie lasagne, Grandma's Hungarian goulash and Mexican-style quesadillas. The interior is decorated with atmospheric photography and there's live music every night from 7.30pm to 8.45pm.

Nhat Ly VIETNAMESE $$
(☎063-382 1651; 88 Đ Phan Dinh Phung; meals 55,000-160,000d; ⏲11am-9pm) This place serves hearty highland meals on tartan tablecloths; including sumptuous hotpots, grilled meats and seafood, try the steamed crab in beer (1kg costs 320,000d). Draws plenty of locals – always a good sign.

★**Le Rabelais** FRENCH $$$
(☎063-382 5444; www.dalatpalacehotel.com; 12 Đ Tran Phu; meals 600,000-1,700,000d; ⏲7am-10pm) The signature restaurant at the Dalat Palace is *the* colonial-style destination with the grandest of dining rooms and a spectacular terrace that looks down to the lake shore. Set dinner menus (1,700,000d) offer the full treatment; otherwise, treat yourself to flawless à la carte dishes, such as seared duck breast with orange or roast rack of lamb.

Drinking & Nightlife

★**100 Roofs Café** BAR
(Duong Len Trang; ☎063-837 518; 57 Đ Phan Boi Chau; ⏲8.30am-midnight) Designed by a student of the Crazy House school of architecture, this is a surreal drinking experience. They claim Gandalf and his hobbit friends have drunk here, and this dim labyrinth of rooms and sculptures does resemble a Middle Earth location. A cheap happy hour and Wonderland-like rooftop garden add to the fun.

An Cafe CAFE
(☎0975 735 521; www.ancafe.vn; 63bis Ba Thang Hai; ⏲6am-10pm; 📶) Perched high above an intersection, this cafe feels like a hip tree house. Sip good lattes, juices or ice-blended matcha at the wood-chic booths inside or on garden bench-swings outside. If you tire of people-watching Dalat's cool crowd, there are crayons and paper for doodling, and an atrium filled with coffee beans for sniffing.

Hangout BAR
(71 Đ Truong Cong Dinh; ⏲11am-midnight; 📶) This late-night watering hole is a popular spot for locals as well as visiting backpackers. It has a relaxed vibe, a pool table and inexpensive beers. The owner, a fluent English-speaker, is an excellent source of local information.

☆ Entertainment

★ Escape Bar LIVE MUSIC
(www.escapebardalat.com; Basement, Muong Thanh Hotel, 4 Đ Phan Boi Chau; ⏲4pm-midnight; 📶) Outstanding live-music bar, owned by blues guitarist Curtis King who performs here nightly with a rotating band (from 9.15pm). Expect covers of Hendrix, the Eagles, the Doors and other classics, but the improvisation is such that each tune takes on a life of its own; travelling musicians are welcome to jam. The bar's decor, all 1970s chic, suits the sonics perfectly.

Beepub LIVE MUSIC
(74 Đ Truong Cong Dinh; ⏲5.30pm-midnight) Every night draws a good mix of locals and foreigners for the live music. The pool table and cheap drinks help too. On good nights the owner leads the place in a hot jam session, but there are occasional DJs cranking the volume up blisteringly loud.

ℹ Information

Lam Dong General Hospital (☎063-382 1369; 4 Đ Pham Ngoc Thach; ⏲24hr) Emergency medical care.

Main Post Office (14 Đ Tran Phu; ⏲7am-6pm) Post office in Dalat.

Sinh Tourist (☎063-382 2663; www.thesinhtourist.vn; 22 Đ Bui Thi Xuan; ⏲8am-7pm) Reliable tours, including city sightseeing trips and open-tour bus bookings.

Vietcombank (6 Đ Nguyen Thi Minh Khai; ⏲7.30am-3pm Mon-Fri, to 1pm Sat) Changes travellers cheques and foreign currencies.

ℹ Getting There & Around

AIR

The Vietnam Airlines bus between **Lien Khuong Airport** (30km south of Dalat) and Dalat (40,000d, 40 minutes) is timed around flights. It leaves from in front of the Ngoc Phat Hotel at 10 Đ Ho Tung Mau two hours before each departure; your lodgings can organise to have it pick you up (though most rarely advertise this service), so include an extra 30-minute buffer to pick everybody else up too!

Vietnam Airlines (☎063-383 3499; www.vietnamairlines.com; 2 Đ Ho Tung Mau) Has daily services to HCMC and Hanoi.

BUS

Dalat's long-distance bus station (Ben Xe Lien Tinh Da Lat; Đ 3 Thang 4) is 1.5km south of Xuan Huong Lake. It's dominated by smart **Phuong Trang** (☎063-358 5858; https://futabus.vn) buses that offer free hotel pick-ups and dropoffs and cover all main regional destinations.

TAXI

A transfer company offers taxi services to Dalat from the airport for a fixed 180,000d; fixed-fee taxis from Dalat are 200,000d. Metered taxis cost around 430,000d - Try the ubiquitous and reliable green **Mai Linh** (☎063-352 1111; www.mailinh.vn) taxis..

Cat Tien National Park

Wildlife lovers, this is the place to do your spotting. Fauna in the spectacular Cat Tien National Park includes 100 types of mammal (including the bison-like guar), 79 types of reptile, 41 amphibian species, plus an incredible array of insects, including 400 or so butterfly species. Of the 350-plus birds, rare species include the orange-necked partridge and Siamese fireback.

◉ Sights

Cat Tien National Park NATURE RESERVE
(☎061-366 9228; www.namcattien.org; adult/child 50,000/20,000d; ⏲7am-10pm) One of the outstanding natural treasures of the region, the 72,000-hectare Cat Tien National Park comprises an amazingly biodiverse region of lowland tropical rainforest. The hiking, mountain biking and birdwatching are the best in southern Vietnam. Always call ahead for reservations as the park can accommodate only a limited number of visitors. However, a word of caution, visitors rarely see any of the larger mammals resident in the park, so don't come expecting to encounter rhinos and tigers.

★ Dao Tien Endangered Primate Species Centre NATURE RESERVE
(www.go-east.org; adult/child incl boat ride 300,000/150,000d; ⏲tours 8.30am & 2pm) This centre, on an island in the Dong Nai River, is a rehabilitation centre hosting golden-cheeked gibbons, pygmy loris (both endemic to Vietnam and Cambodia), black-shanked douc and silvered langur that have been illegally trafficked. The eventual goal is

to release the primates back into the forest. You can view gibbons in a semiwild environment and hear their incredible calls.

Sleeping

★ **Ta Lai Long House** GUESTHOUSE $

(0935 160 730; www.talai-adventure.vn; dm 450,000d;) Excellent, traditional-style lodge managed by Westerners and locals from the S'Tieng and Ma minorities. Accommodation is in a well-constructed timber longhouse, with good, screened bedding, modern facilities and plenty of activities on offer. It's a 12km bicycle ride from the park HQ in the indigenous village of Ta Lai.

River Lodge LODGE $

(0973 346 345; r US$13;) A 250m walk from the ferry crossing, River Lodge (aka Green Bamboo Lodge) consists of a cluster of thatched bamboo-and-brick bungalows (with plug-in air-con and fan) overlooking the rolling river. It's run by a friendly family and their restaurant serves decent standards.

Cat Tien National Park GUESTHOUSE $

(061-366 9228; cattienvietnam@gmail.com; dm/d/tr from 80,000/200,000/680,000d, 2-person tents 200,000d;) Rooms at the national park's HQ are fairly basic and overpriced but include a bathroom. There are also canvas tents for couples, and large tents (sleeping up to 12) that operate on a communal basis. There are two simple places to eat near the park HQ: a canteen and a slightly fancier restaurant.

★ **Forest Floor Lodge** LODGE $$$

(061-366 9890; www.forestfloorlodge.com; luxury tent or house US$125;) This ecolodge – inside the national park – sets the standard for atmospheric accommodation in Vietnam's protected areas. There are three lovely safari tents overlooking the river rapids, and larger, stylish rooms set in traditional wooden houses. The lodge is located across from the Dao Tien primate centre, so it's often possible to see and hear gibbons on the island.

Getting There & Away

One approach to Cat Tien National Park is to take a boat across Langa Lake and then go by foot from there. Phat Tire Ventures (p129) is a reputable ecotour operator in Dalat that can offer this option.

All buses between Dalat and Ho Chi Minh City (every 30 minutes) pass the junction Vuon Quoc Gia Cat Tien on Hwy 20 for the park. The junction is around four hours' travel (190,000d to 200,000d) from both cities. From this junction, you can hire a *xe om* (around 170,000d, but negotiate very hard) to cover the remaining 24km to the park. Lodges can also arrange a transfer to/from the main road.

Sinhbalo Adventures (p149) runs recommended tours to Cat Tien from HCMC.

HO CHI MINH CITY (SAIGON)

Ho Chi Minh City (HCMC) is Vietnam at its most dizzying: a high-octane city of commerce and culture that has driven the country forward with its pulsating energy. A chaotic whirl, the city breathes life and vitality into all who settle here, and visitors cannot help but be hauled along for the ride.

From the finest of hotels to the cheapest of guesthouses, the classiest of restaurants to the tastiest of street stalls, the choicest of boutiques to the scrum of the markets, HCMC is a city of energy and discovery.

Wander through timeless alleys to incense-infused temples before negotiating chic designer malls beneath sleek 21st-century skyscrapers. The ghosts of the past live on in buildings that one generation ago witnessed a city in turmoil, but now the real beauty of the former Saigon's urban collage is the seamless blending of these two worlds into one exciting mass.

Sights

Reunification Palace & Around

★ **War Remnants Museum** MUSEUM

(Bao Tang Chung Tich Chien Tranh; Map p135; 08-3930 5587; http://warremnantsmuseum.com; 28 Đ Vo Van Tan, cnr Đ Le Quy Don; 15,000d; 7.30am-noon & 1.30-5pm) Formerly the Museum of Chinese and American War Crimes, the War Remnants Museum is consistently popular with Western tourists. Few museums anywhere convey the brutal effects of war on its civilian victims so powerfully. Many of the atrocities documented here were well-publicised but rarely do Westerners hear the victims of US military action tell their own stories. While some displays are one-sided, many of the most disturbing photographs illustrating US atrocities are

Ho Chi Minh City

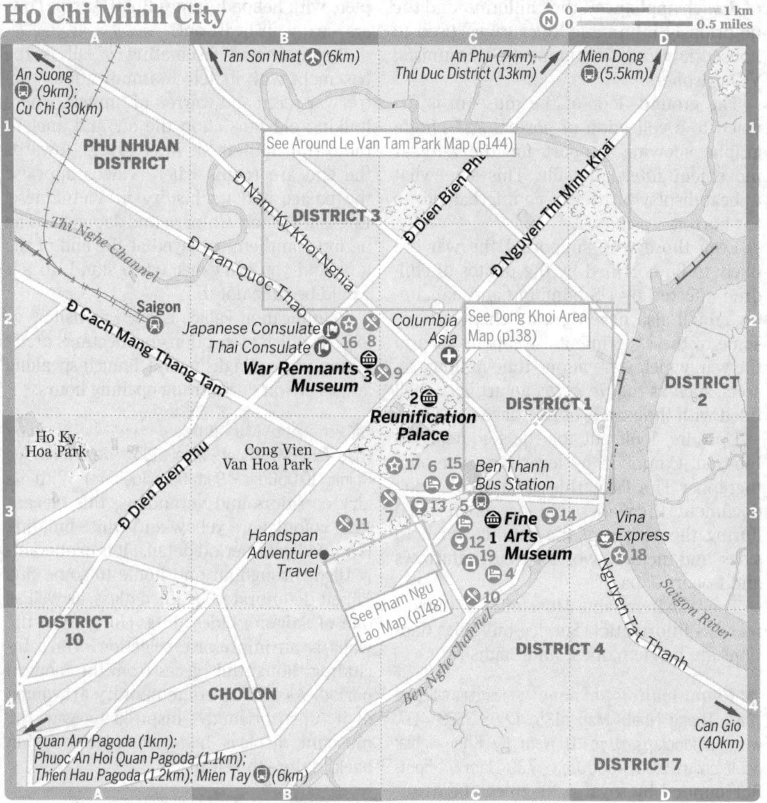

Ho Chi Minh City

Top Sights
1 Fine Arts Museum C3
2 Reunification Palace C2
3 War Remnants Museum B2

Sleeping
4 Blue River Hotel 2 .... C3
Saigon Central Hostel .... (see 4)
5 Town House 23 .... C3
6 Zoolut Stay 278 .... C3

Eating
7 Banh Mi Huynh Hoa C3
8 Beefsteak Nam Son B2
9 Hum Vegetarian Cafe & Restaurant C2
10 Quan Ut Ut C3
11 Vegetarian Lien Huong B3

Drinking & Nightlife
12 Air 360 .... C3
13 Chill Skybar C3
14 Heritage Republic C3
15 OMG C3

Entertainment
16 Acoustic B2
17 Galaxy C3
18 Observatory D3

Shopping
19 Dan Sinh Market C3

from US sources, including those of the infamous My Lai Massacre.

US armoured vehicles, artillery pieces, bombs and infantry weapons are on display outside. One corner of the grounds is devoted to the notorious French and South Vietnamese prisons on Phu Quoc and Con Son Islands. Artefacts include that most iconic of French appliances, the guillotine, and the notoriously inhumane 'tiger cages' used to house Viet Cong (Vietnamese Communists; VC) prisoners.

The ground floor of the museum is devoted to a collection of posters and photographs showing support for the antiwar movement internationally. This somewhat upbeat display provides a counterbalance to the horrors upstairs.

Even those who supported the war are likely to be horrified by the photos of children affected by US bombing and napalming. You'll also have the rare chance to see some of the experimental weapons used in the war, which were at one time military secrets, such as the *flechette,* an artillery shell filled with thousands of tiny darts.

Upstairs, look out for the Requiem Exhibition. Compiled by legendary war photographer Tim Page, this striking collection documents the work of photographers killed during the course of the conflict, on both sides, and includes works by Larry Burrows and Robert Capa.

The War Remnants Museum is in the former US Information Service building. Captions are in Vietnamese and English.

★Reunification Palace HISTORIC BUILDING
(Dinh Thong Nhat; Map p135; ☎08-3829 4117; www.dinhdoclap.gov.vn; Đ Nam Ky Khoi Nghia; adult/child 30,000/5000d; ⏲7.30-11am & 1-5pm) Surrounded by royal palm trees, the dissonant 1960s architecture of this government building and the eerie mood that accompanies a walk through its deserted halls make it an intriguing spectacle. The first Communist tanks to arrive in Saigon rumbled here on 30 April 1975 and it's as if time has stood still since then. The building is deeply associated with the fall of the city in 1975, yet it's the kitsch detailing and period motifs that steal the show.

The ground floor is arranged with meeting rooms, while upstairs is a grand set of reception rooms, used for welcoming foreign and national dignitaries. In the back of the structure are the president's living quarters; check out the model boats, horse tails and severed elephants' feet. The 2nd floor contributes a shagadelic card-playing room, complete with a cheesy round leather banquette, a barrel-shaped bar, hubcap light fixtures and groovy three-legged chairs set around a flared-legged card table. There's also a cinema and a rooftop nightclub, complete with helipad: James Bond/Austin Powers – eat your heart out.

Perhaps most fascinating of all is the basement with its telecommunications centre, war room and warren of tunnels, where hulking old fans chop the air and ancient radio transmitters sit impassively. Towards the end are rooms where videos appraise the palace and its history in Vietnamese, English, French, Chinese and Japanese. The national anthem is played at the end of the tape and you are expected to stand up – it would be rude not to.

Reunification Palace is open to visitors as long as official receptions or meetings aren't taking place. English- and French-speaking guides are on duty during opening hours.

★Fine Arts Museum GALLERY
(Bao Tang My Thuat; Map p135; 97a Đ Pho Duc Chinh; 10,000d; ⏲9am-5pm Tue-Sun) With its airy corridors and verandahs, this elegant 1929 colonial-era yellow-and-white building is stuffed with period details; it is exuberantly tiled throughout and home to some fine (albeit deteriorated) stained glass, as well as one of Saigon's oldest lifts. Hung from the walls is an impressive selection of art, including thoughtful pieces from the modern period. As well as contemporary art, much of it (unsurprisingly) inspired by war, the museum displays historical pieces dating back to the 4th century.

Dong Khoi Area

★Notre Dame Cathedral CHURCH
(Map p138; Đ Han Thuyen) Built between 1877 and 1883, Notre Dame Cathedral enlivens the heart of Ho Chi Minh City's government quarter, facing Đ Dong Khoi. A brick, neo-Romanesque church with 40m-high square towers tipped with iron spires, the Catholic cathedral is named after the Virgin Mary. Interior walls are inlaid with devotional tablets and some stained glass survives. English-speaking staff dispense tourist information from 9am to 11am Monday to Saturday. Mass is 9.30am Sunday. If the front gates are locked, try the door on the side facing the Reunification Palace.

★Central Post Office HISTORIC BUILDING
(Map p138; 2 Cong Xa Paris; ⏲7am-9.30pm) Right across the way from Notre Dame Cathedral, Ho Chi Minh City's striking French post office is a period classic, designed by Gustave Eiffel and built between 1886 and 1891.

Painted on the walls of its grand concourse are fascinating historic maps of South Vietnam, Saigon and Cholon, while a mosaic of Ho Chi Minh takes pride of place at the end of its barrel-vaulted hall. Note the magnificent tiled floor of the interior and the copious green-painted wrought iron.

HCMC Museum MUSEUM

(Bao Tang Thanh Pho Ho Chi Minh; Map p138; www.hcmc-museum.edu.vn; 65 Đ Ly Tu Trong; 15,000d; ⏲8am-5pm) A grand, neoclassical structure built in 1885 and once known as Gia Long Palace (and later the Revolutionary Museum), HCMC's city museum is a singularly beautiful and impressive building, telling the story of the city through archaeological artefacts, ceramics, old city maps and displays on the marriage traditions of its various ethnicities. The struggle for independence is extensively covered, with most of the upper floor devoted to it.

★ **Bitexco Financial Tower** VIEWPOINT

(Map p138; www.saigonskydeck.com; 2 Đ Hai Trieu; adult/child 200,000/130,000d; ⏲9.30am-9.30pm) The 68-storey, 262m-high, Carlos Zapata–designed skyscraper dwarfs all around it. It's reportedly shaped like a lotus bulb, but also resembles a CD rack with a tambourine shoved into it. That tambourine is the 48th-floor Saigon Skydeck, with a helipad on its roof. Choose a clear day and aim for sunset – or down a drink in the EON Heli Bar (p146) instead.

People's Committee Building NOTABLE BUILDING

(Hôtel de Ville; Map p138; ĐL Nguyen Hue) Ho Chi Minh City's glorious People's Committee Building, one of the city's most prominent landmarks, is home to the Ho Chi Minh City People's Committee. Built between 1901 and 1908, the former Hôtel de Ville decorates the northwestern end of ĐL Nguyen Hue, but unfortunately the ornate interior is not open to the public. In 2015 the centre of ĐL Nguyen Hue was turned into a vibrant pedestrian-only mall bookended by a new statue of Ho Chi Minh to commemorate his 125th birthday.

Around Le Van Tam Park

★ **Jade Emperor Pagoda** TAOIST TEMPLE

(Phuoc Hai Tu, Chua Ngoc Hoang; Map p144; 73 Đ Mai Thi Luu; ⏲7am-6pm, on 1st & 15th of lunar month 5am-7pm) FREE Built in 1909 in honour of the supreme Taoist god (the Jade Emperor or King of Heaven, Ngoc Hoang), this is one of the most spectacularly atmospheric temples in Ho Chi Minh City, stuffed with statues of phantasmal divinities and grotesque heroes. The pungent smoke of incense *(huong)* fills the air, obscuring the exquisite woodcarvings. Its roof is encrusted with elaborate tile work, and the temple's statues, depicting characters from both Buddhist and Taoist lore, are made from reinforced papier mâché.

Inside the main building are two especially fierce and menacing Taoist figures. On the right (as you face the altar) is a 4m-high statue of the general who defeated the Green Dragon (depicted underfoot). On the left is the general who defeated the White Tiger, which is also being stepped on.

Worshippers mass before the ineffable Jade Emperor, who presides – draped in luxurious robes and shrouded in a dense fug of incense smoke – over the main sanctuary. He is flanked by his guardians, the Four Big Diamonds (Tu Dai Kim Cuong), so named because they are said to be as hard as diamonds.

★ **History Museum** MUSEUM

(Bao Tang Lich Su; Map p144; Đ Nguyen Binh Khiem; 15,000d; ⏲8-11.30am & 1.30-5pm Tue-Sun) Built in 1929 by the Société des Études Indochinoises, this notable Sino-French museum houses a rewarding collection of artefacts illustrating the evolution of the cultures of Vietnam, from the Bronze Age Dong Son civilisation (which emerged in 2000 BC) and the Funan civilisation (1st to 6th centuries AD), to the Cham, Khmer and Vietnamese. The museum is just inside the main gate to the city's botanic gardens and zoo.

Highlights include valuable relics taken from Cambodia's Angkor Wat; a fine collection of Buddha statues; the perfectly preserved mummy of a local woman who died in 1869, excavated from Xom Cai in District 5; and some exquisite stylised mother-of-pearl Chinese characters inlaid into panels.

Cholon

★ **Binh Tay Market** MARKET

(Cho Binh Tay; www.chobinhtay.gov.vn; 57a ĐL Thap Muoi; ⏲6am-7.30pm) Cholon's main market has a great clock tower and a central courtyard with gardens. Much of the business here is wholesale but it's popular with tour groups. The market was originally built by the French in the 1880s; Guangdong-born philanthropist Quach Dam paid for its rebuilding and was commemorated by a statue that is now in the Fine Arts Museum

Dong Khoi Area

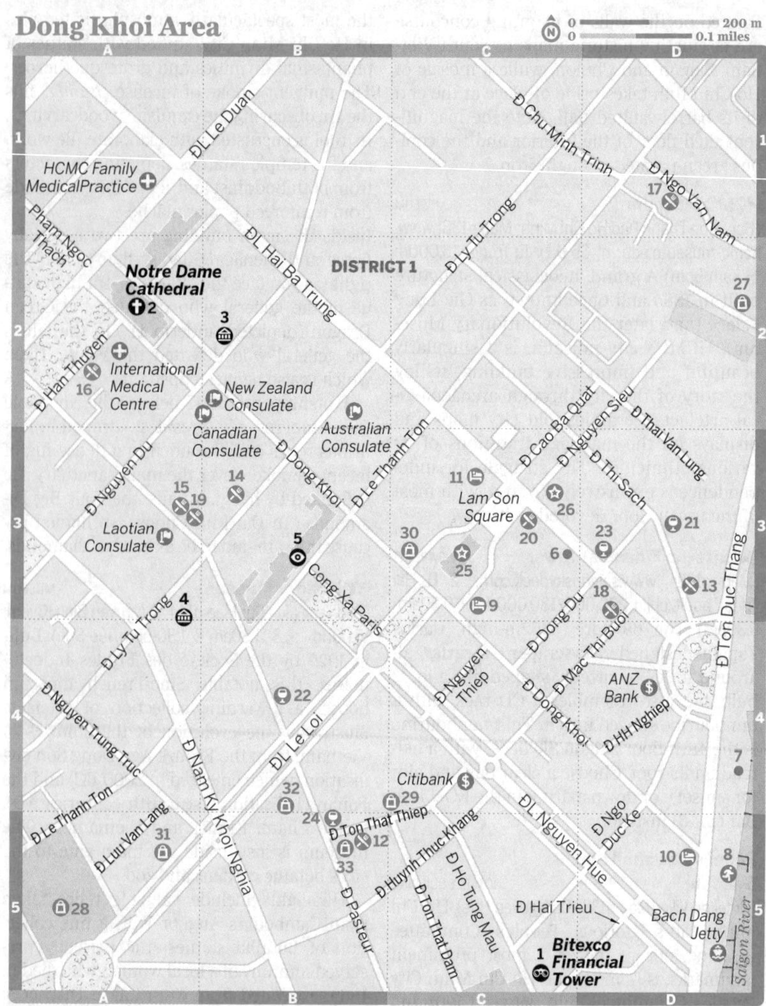

(p136). Expect a friendly welcome when you sit down for breakfast or coffee with the market's street-food vendors.

Thien Hau Pagoda TAOIST TEMPLE

(Ba Mieu, Pho Mieu, Chua Ba Thien Hau; 710 Đ Nguyen Trai) FREE This gorgeous 19th-century temple is dedicated to the goddess Thien Hau, and always attracts a mix of worshippers and visitors who mingle beneath the large coils of incense suspended overhead. It is believed that Thien Hau can travel over the oceans on a mat and ride the clouds to save people in trouble on the high seas.

★ Phuoc An Hoi Quan Pagoda TAOIST TEMPLE

(Quan De Mieu; 184 Đ Hong Bang) FREE Delightfully fronted by greenery and opening to an interior blaze of red, gold, green and yellow, this is one of the most beautifully ornamented temples in town, dating from 1902. Of special interest are the elaborate brass ritual ornaments and weapons, and the fine woodcarvings on the altars, walls, columns, hanging lanterns and incense coils. From the exterior, look out for the ceramic scenes, each containing innumerable small figurines, that decorate the roof.

Dong Khoi Area

Top Sights
1 Bitexco Financial Tower C5
2 Notre Dame Cathedral A2

Sights
3 Central Post Office B2
4 HCMC Museum A3
5 People's Committee Building B3

Activities, Courses & Tours
6 GRAIN Cooking Classes C3
7 Indochina Junk D4
8 Les Rives D5

Sleeping
9 Caravelle Hotel C3
10 Majestic Hotel D5
11 Park Hyatt Saigon C3

Eating
12 3T Quan Nuong B5
Fanny .... (see 12)
13 Hum Lounge & Restaurant D3
14 Huong Lai B3
15 Nha Hang Ngon A3
16 Propaganda A2
17 Quan Bui D1
18 Racha Room D3
19 Secret Garden A3
Square One .... (see 11)
20 Xu C3

Drinking & Nightlife
21 Apocalypse Now D3
EON Heli Bar .... (see 1)
M Bar .... (see 10)
22 Pasteur Street Brewing Company B4
23 Republic Lounge D3
Saigon Saigon Bar .... (see 9)
24 Shrine B5

Entertainment
25 Municipal Theatre C3
26 Saigon Ranger C3

Shopping
27 3A Alternative Art Area D2
28 Ben Thanh Market A5
29 Chung Cu 42 Ton That Thiep C4
30 Mai Lam C3
31 Mekong Quilts A5
32 Saigon Centre B4
33 Saigon Kitsch B5

Quan Am Pagoda BUDDHIST TEMPLE
(Chua Quan Am; 12 Đ Lao Tu) FREE One of Cholon's most active and colourful temples, this shrine was founded in the early 19th century. It's named after the Goddess of Mercy, whose full name is Quan The Am Bo Tat, literally 'the Bodhisattva Who Listens to the Cries of the World' (觀世音菩萨 in Chinese characters), in reflection of her compassionate mission.

Traditional Herb Shops AREA
(Đ Hai Thuong Lan Ong) While you're roaming, you can stroll over to the strip of traditional herb shops between Đ Luong Nhu Hoc and Đ Trieu Quang Phuc for an olfactory experience you won't soon forget. The streets here are filled with amazing sights, sounds and rich herbal aromas.

Greater Ho Chi Minh City

Giac Lam Pagoda BUDDHIST TEMPLE
(Chua Giac Lam; 118 Đ Lac Long Quan, Tan Binh District; 6am-noon & 2-8.30pm) FREE Believed to be the oldest temple in HCMC (1744), Giac Lam is a fantastically atmospheric place set in peaceful, gardenlike grounds. The Chinese characters that constitute the temple's name (覚林寺) mean 'Feel the Woods Temple' and the looming Bodhi tree (a native fig tree, sacred to Buddhists) in the front garden was the gift of a Sri Lankan monk in 1953. Prayers are held daily from 4am to 5am, 11am to noon, 4pm to 5pm and 7pm to 9pm.

About 3km from Cholon, Giac Lam Pagoda is best reached by taxi or *xe om* (motorbike taxi).

Activities

Aveda SPA
(08-3519 4679; www.facebook.com/avedaherbal; Villa 21/1 Đ Xuan Thuy; 9am-8pm) Across in District 2, but worth the journey for its intensely soothing Indian-influenced Ayurvedic spa and massage treatments.

Dam Sen Water Park WATER PARK
(www.damsenwaterpark.com.vn; 3 Đ Hoa Binh, District 11; adult/child before 4pm 150,000/100,000d, after 4pm 130,000/90,000d; 9am-6pm Mon-Sat, 8.30am-6pm Sun) Water slides, rivers with rapids (or slow currents) and rope swings.

Indochina Junk BOATING
(Map p138; 08-3895 7438; www.indochinajunk.com.vn; 159/21 Đ Bach Dang) A lunch and dinner cruise with set menus (US$15 to US$35) in an atmospheric wooden junk on the

Saigon River, departing from the Vuon Kieng pier (opposite the Renaissance Hotel).

Les Rives BOATING
(Map p138; ☎0128 592 0018; www.lesrivesexperience.com; Bach Dang jetty; sunset cruises adult/child 1,399,00/980,000d, Mekong Delta cruises adult/child 2,499,000/1,799,000d) Runs sunset boat tours (minimum two people) at 4pm along canals beyond the city edges, and a Mekong Delta cruise which departs at 7.30am and takes seven to nine hours.

It can also convey you to the Cu Chi Tunnels (adult/child 1,899,000/1,299,000d) by boat. Other options include incorporating *cyclo* excursions or cooking classes.

Oasis Saigon SWIMMING
(Map p148; 40/15 Đ Bui Vien; US$8; ⊗6.30am-10pm) Cunningly squeezed into a side alley in Pham Ngu Lao, this compact pool is a welcome haven from the city's heat. Drinks and food (40,000d to 90,000d) are also available. If you're staying at any of the hotels belonging to the Beautiful group, you can use the pool for free.

Courses

GRAIN Cooking Classes COOKING
(Map p138; ☎08-3827 4929; www.grainbyluke.com; Level 3, 71-75 ĐL Hai Ba Trung; per person from US$48; ⊗9am-noon & 2-5pm Mon-Sat) These cooking classes are designed and coordinated by Vietnamese-Australian celebrity chef Luke Nguyen. Four-course menus change regularly to reflect seasonal produce, and Luke himself is on hand for some classes throughout the year. Check the website for timings.

Tours

Vespa Adventures TOURS
(Map p148; ☎0122 299 3585; www.vespaadventures.com; 169a Đ De Tham; per person from US$69) Zooming out of Café Zoom (p145), Vespa Adventures offers entertaining, guided city tours on vintage scooters, as well as multiday trips around southern Vietnam. Embracing food, drink and music, the Saigon After Dark tour is brilliant fun.

Back of the Bike Tours TOURS
(☎08-2221 5591; www.backofthebiketours.com; from US$48) Hop on the back of a motorbike and dine like a local on the wildly popular four-hour Street Food tours, or lasso in the sights of HCMC. Excellent guides.

Saigon Riders TOURS
(☎0919 767 118; www.saigonriders.vn; from US$29) Runs a variety of motorbike tours in and around HCMC, including full-day two-wheeled excursions to Cu Chi. Also longer overnight trips to the Mekong Delta.

Festivals & Events

Saigon Cyclo Challenge CHARITY RACE
(www.saigonchildren.com; ⊗mid-Mar) Professional and amateur *cyclo* drivers find out who's fastest; money raised is donated to local charities supporting disadvantaged children.

Sleeping

Within District 1 (the most convenient district) head east towards Đ Dong Khoi for smarter options close to the best restaurants and bars; west towards Pham Ngu Lao for budget accommodation, or somewhere in between – geographically and price-wise, such as around Ben Thanh Market.

Dong Khoi Area

Home to Ho Chi Minh City's top-notch hotels, the Dong Khoi area is also sprinkled with attractive midrange options.

Zoolut Stay 278 BOUTIQUE HOTEL $$
(Map p135; ☎08-3825 6039; www.zoolutstay.com; 271 Đ Le Thanh Ton; d incl breakfast US$28-70; ⊛❄📶) Boutique stylings on a budget come to this well-located pocket of HCMC. The modern yellow hues make spaces feel fresh and clean. Regular rooms are large but the tiniest 'fun' rooms barely fit a double bed and are only a good fit for solo travellers...or a svelte couple. Nice touches include free water coolers and safes and modern bathrooms.

Park Hyatt Saigon HOTEL $$$
(Map p138; ☎08-3824 1234; www.saigon.park.hyatt.com; 2 Lam Son Sq; r from US$310; ❄@📶🏊) Following extensive renovations in 2015, this is one of the jewels in HCMC's hotel crown. A prime location opposite the Opera House combines with exemplary service, fastidiously attired staff and lavishly appointed rooms. Relaxation opportunities include an inviting pool and the acclaimed Xuan Spa. Highly regarded (yet affordable) restaurants include Opera, for Italian, and **Square One** (www.saigon.park.hyattrestaurants.com/squareOne; meals from 240,000d; ⊗noon-2.30pm & 5.30-10.30pm; 📶), serving Vietnamese and international fare.

Caravelle Hotel HOTEL $$$
(Map p138; ☎08-3823 4999; www.caravellehotel.com; 19 Lam Son Sq; r from US$185;) One of the first luxury hotels to reopen its doors in postwar Saigon, the five-star Caravelle remains a classic operation. Rooms in the modern 24-floor block are quietly elegant, with two rooms bigger than the others on each floor (ask); the priciest rooms and suites are in the historic 'signature' wing. The rooftop Saigon Saigon Bar (p146) is a spectacular spot for a cocktail.

Majestic Hotel HOTEL $$$
(Map p138; ☎08-3829 5517; www.majesticsaigon.com; 1 Đ Dong Khoi; s/d incl breakfast from US$135/150;) Dollar for dollar it may not have the best rooms in town, but the colonial atmosphere of this venerable 1925 riverside hotel makes it a romantic option. Take a dip in the courtyard pool on a hot afternoon or sip a cocktail at the rooftop bar on a breezy evening. Breakfast and fruit basket included.

Pham Ngu Lao

HCMC's budget zone with more than 100 accommodation choices. The main backpacker arterial is Đ Bui Vien but even midrange travellers can find excellent deals here, often at budget prices. Options include countless family-run guesthouses (US$15 to US$35) and minihotels (US$30 to US$55), and even a few dorms (from US$7).

★**Lily's Hostel** HOSTEL $
(Map p148; ☎0948 213 181; lilyhostel.hcm@gmail.com; 35/5 Đ Bui Vien; dm/d US$8/26;) One of the new breed of modern hostels popping up in Pham Ngu Lao, Lily's has a warm and welcoming ambience courtesy of the elegant and soothing decor. Located in a quiet lane just off bustling Đ Bui Vien, Lily's easily bridges the gap between hostel and boutique guesthouse. Some private rooms have a flat-screen TV and minibar.

Hideout Hostel HOSTEL $
(Map p148; ☎08-3838 9147; www.vietnamhideouthostels.com; 281 Đ Pham Ngu Lao; dm US$8;) A modern PNL hostel with an emphasis on good times and meeting other travellers. Dorms are spick and span with bright colours; two free beers per day are on offer at the Hideout Bar next door; and the hostel also runs pub crawls three times a week that are free for guests (US$2 for nonguests).

Long Hostel HOSTEL $
(Map p148; ☎08-3836 0184; longhomestay@yahoo.com; 373/10 Đ Pham Ngu Lao; dm/d US$7/19;) This popular, simple and clean 12-room guesthouse, tucked away down an alley near Thai Binh Market, is run by a pleasant and helpful family. Five- and six-bed dorms available.

MyHotel HOTEL $
(Map p148; ☎08-3837 2016; 100/2a3 Đ Tran Hung Dao; d US$20-30;) This hotel is mixed up. It's tucked quietly back from the backpacker area, yet most of the refurbished rooms, while comfortable, have the old problem of letting in noise from adjacent rooms. If you don't mind chatter, MyHotel is a modern, clean place to stay with helpful English-speaking staff.

Town House 23 GUESTHOUSE $
(Map p135; ☎08-3915 1491; www.townhousesaigon.com; 23 Đ Dang Thi Nhu; dm US$11, r US$32-37;) Located in a quiet cafe-lined street a short walk from the bustle of Pham Ngu Lao, Town House 23 is a modern and well-designed combination of hostel and guesthouse. Decor is particularly stylish and the team at reception is very helpful. Note that not all rooms have windows.

Giang Son GUESTHOUSE $
(Map p148; ☎08-3837 7547; www.guesthouse.com.vn; 283/14 Đ Pham Ngu Lao; r US$20-30;) Tall and thin, Giang Son has three rooms on each floor, a roof terrace and charming service; the sole downer is that there's no lift. Consider upgrading to a room with window.

Hong Han Hotel GUESTHOUSE $
(Map p148; ☎08-3836 1927; http://honghanhotelhcm.com; 238 Đ Bui Vien; r incl breakfast US$18-30;) A corker guesthouse (seven floors, no lift), Hong Han has front rooms with ace views and smaller, quieter and cheaper rear rooms. Breakfast is served on the 1st-floor terrace.

Bich Duyen Hotel GUESTHOUSE $
(Map p148; ☎08-3837 4588; bichduyenhotel@yahoo.com; 283/4 Đ Pham Ngu Lao; r US$22-25;) This spruce 15-room guesthouse offers a welcoming stay. The US$25 rooms are worth the extra money for a window. No lift.

Diep Anh GUESTHOUSE $
(Map p148; ☎08-3836 7920; dieptheanh@hcm.vnn.vn; 241/31 Đ Pham Ngu Lao; r US$21-26;) A step above most PNL guesthouses,

Diep Anh's tall and narrow shape makes for light and airy upper rooms. The gracious staff ensure they're kept in good nick.

Madame Cuc 127 GUESTHOUSE $$
(Map p148; ☎08-3836 8761; www.madamcuchotels.com; 127 Đ Cong Quynh; d incl breakfast US$25-39; ❄@🛜) The original and by far the best of the three hotels run by the welcoming Madame Cuc and her friendly and fantastic staff. Rooms are clean and spacious.

Green Suites HOTEL $$
(Map p148; ☎08-3836 5400; www.greensuiteshotel.com; 102/1 Đ Cong Quynh; s US$22-29, d $US26-33, all incl breakfast; ❄@🛜) Slung down a quiet alley off Đ Cong Quynh, immediately south of Đ Bui Vien, this trim, comfy and spacious hotel exudes a pea-green theme, although the tiled rooms are clean and actually not very green at all.

Other Neighbourhoods

Saigon Central Hostel HOSTEL $
(Map p135; ☎08-3914 1107; saigoncentralhostel@gmail.com; 54/6 Đ Ky Con; dm/d US$6/26; ❄@🛜) Friendly, family-owned guesthouse located in a quiet lane in a more local area of town – still just a short walk to Pham Ngu Lao, Dong Khoi and Ben Thanh Market, though.

Blue River Hotel 2 GUESTHOUSE $
(Map p135; ☎08-3915 2852; 54/13 Đ Ky Con; r US$12-20; ❄@🛜) Fronted by bamboo fronds, and within reach of both Dong Khoi and Pham Ngu Lao but far enough away to escape the tourist buzz, this friendly and quiet guesthouse is excellent. It's down a quiet cul-de-sac, offering a window into local urban life. Cheaper rooms have no window.

★**Ma Maison Boutique Hotel** HOTEL $$
(☎08-3846 0263; www.mamaison.vn; 656/52 Cach Mang Thang Tam, District 3; s US$60-70, d US$70-110; ❄@🛜) Down a peaceful lane off a busy arterial route, friendly Ma Maison is halfway between the airport and the city centre, and partly in the French countryside, decor-wise. Wooden shutters soften the exterior of the modern, medium-rise block, while in the rooms, painted French-provincial-style furniture and first-rate bathrooms add a touch of panache.

★**Villa Song** BOUTIQUE HOTEL $$$
(☎08-3744 6090; www.villasong.com; 187/2 Đ Nguyen Van Huong, District 2; r US$159-220, ste US$350-460; ⊖❄🛜≋) In a District 2 garden location with river views, this French-inspired boutique hotel is one of HCMC's most relaxing places to stay. Very romantic rooms and suites are filled with heritage Indochinese style and contemporary Vietnamese art, and the property's Song Vie bar has an absolute riverside location. The spa is also well regarded and luxury speedboat trips are available.

A free minibus shuttle – around 30 minutes – to central HCMC is available.

Eating

Hanoi may consider itself more cultured, but HCMC is Vietnam's culinary capital. Delicious regional fare is complemented by a well-developed choice of international restaurants, with Indian, Japanese, Thai, Italian and East–West fusions well represented. Unsurprisingly, given its heritage, HCMC has a fine selection of French restaurants, from the casual bistro to haute cuisine.

Good foodie neighbourhoods include the Dong Khoi area, with a high concentration of top-quality restaurants, as well as the bordering sections of District 3. Some of Pham Ngu Lao's eateries, attempting to satisfy every possible culinary whim, are good value but generally less impressive, although others stand out. There are also a few escapes further afield for those willing to explore.

Markets have a good selection of stalls whipping up tasty treats. Ben Thanh's night market is particularly good.

The largest concentration of vegetarian restaurants is around the Pham Ngu Lao area, and you'll usually find one within a chopstick's throw of Buddhist temples.

Reunification Palace & Around

Beefsteak Nam Son VIETNAMESE $
(Map p135; 157 Đ Nam Ky Khoi Nghia; meals from 60,000d; ⏰6am-10pm; 🛜) For first-rate, affordable steak in a simple setting, this is a superb choice. Local steak, other beef dishes (such as the spicy beef soup *bun bo Hue*), imported Canadian fillets and even cholesterol-friendly ostrich are on the well-priced menu.

★ Propaganda VIETNAMESE $$

(Map p138; ☎08-3822 9048; www.propagandasaigon.com; Đ 21 Han Thuyen; meals 105,000-185,000đ; ⊙7.30am-10.30pm) Colourful murals and retro socialist posters brighten up this popular bistro with park views. The menu focuses on street-food classics from around Vietnam, all enjoyed with a bustling and energetic ambience. Salads are particularly good: try the wild pepper and green-mango salad with BBQ chicken. Retreat to the 1st floor if downstairs is too crowded.

Hum Vegetarian Cafe & Restaurant VEGETARIAN $$

(Map p135; ☎08-3930 3819; www.hum-vegetarian.vn; 32 Đ Vo Van Tan; meals 80,000-190,000đ; ⊙10am-10pm; ☑) Even if you're not a vegetarian, this serene and elegant restaurant requires your attention. Everything – from the charming service to the delightful Vietnamese dishes and peaceful outside tables – makes dining here an occasion to savour. There's also a new, equally laid-back and more central location (p143).

Dong Khoi Area

Huong Lai VIETNAMESE $

(Map p138; ☎08-3822 6814; www.huonglai2001saigon.com; 38 Đ Ly Tu Trong; meals 70,000-180,000đ; ⊙noon-3pm & 6-10pm) A must for finely presented, traditional Vietnamese food, the airy and high-ceilinged loft of an old French-era shophouse is the setting for dining with a difference. Staff are from disadvantaged families or are former street children and receive on-the-job training, education and a place to stay.

Secret Garden VIETNAMESE $

(Map p138; 8th fl, 158 Đ Pasteur; meals 55,000-80,000đ; ⊙8am-10pm; ☑) Negotiate the stairs in this faded HCMC apartment building to arrive at Secret Garden's wonderful rooftop restaurant. Rogue chickens peck away in the herb garden, Buddhist statues add Asian ambience, and delicious homestyle dishes are served up with city views. Service can sometimes be a little *too* casual, but it's worth persevering for the great flavours.

Fanny ICE CREAM $

(Map p138; www.fanny.com.vn; 29-31 Đ Ton That Thiep; scoops from 40,000đ; ⊙8am-11pm; ☜) On the ground floor of a lavish French villa, Fanny concocts excellent Franco-Vietnamese ice cream in a healthy range of home-grown flavours. Refreshing favourites include coconut, star anise and green tea.

★ Nha Hang Ngon VIETNAMESE $$

(Map p138; ☎08-3827 7131; 160 Đ Pasteur; meals 60,000-260,000đ; ⊙7am-10pm; ☜) Thronging with locals and foreigners, this is one of HCMC's most popular spots, with a large range of the very best street food in stylish surroundings across three levels. Set in a leafy garden ringed by food stalls, each cook serves up a specialised traditional dish, ensuring an authentic taste of Vietnamese, Thai, Japanese or Chinese cuisine.

★ Racha Room THAI $$

(Map p138; ☎0908 791 412; www.facebook.com/theracharoom; 12-14 Đ Mac Thi Buoi; shared plates 195,000-320,000đ; ⊙11.30am-midnight) The Racha Room is one of the city's most hip eateries. Thai street food underpins the diverse menu of bar snacks (40,000đ to 150,000đ) and shared plates, but it effortlessly stretches to include neighbouring countries as well. Asian-inspired cocktails ensure the Racha Room is also one of the city's best bars. Pop in for happy hour from 5pm to 7.30pm.

Hum Lounge & Restaurant VEGETARIAN $$

(Map p138; ☎08-3823 8920; www.humvietnam.vn; 2 Đ Thi Sach; meals 80,000-190,000đ; ⊙10am-10pm; ☜☑) This new opening brings the excellent Vietnamese-inspired vegetarian cuisine of the city's long-established Hum Vegetarian Cafe & Restaurant to a central garden location. Settle into the elegant and verdant space and enjoy dishes including papaya and banana flower salads, mushrooms steamed in coconut, and the subtle combination of braised tofu with star anise and cinnamon.

Quan Bui VIETNAMESE $$

(Map p138; ☎08-3829 1545; http://quan-bui.com; 17a Đ Ngo Van Nam; mains 69,000-169,000đ; ⊙8am-11pm; ❄) Stylish Indochinese decor features at this recent opening in up-and-coming Đ Ngo Van Nam. Nearby restaurants offer Japanese flavours, but Quan Bui's focus is on authentic Vietnamese dishes served by hip young waitstaff. Cocktails – delivered from the associated bar across the lane – are among HCMC's best, and upstairs there's an air-conditioned and smoke-free dining room.

3T Quan Nuong BARBECUE $$

(Map p138; ☎08-3821 1631; 29 Đ Ton That Thiep; meals 85,000-280,000đ; ⊙5-11pm) This breezy alfresco Vietnamese barbecue restaurant on the rooftop of the Temple Club is in many a

Around Le Van Tam Park

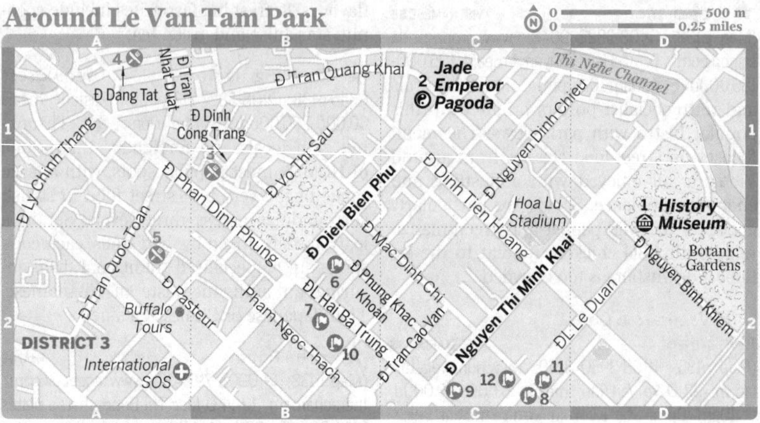

Around Le Van Tam Park

Top Sights
1 History Museum D1
2 Jade Emperor Pagoda C1

Eating
3 Banh Xeo 46A B1
4 Cuc Gach Quan A1
5 Pho Hoa A2

Entertainment
Saigon Water Puppet Theatre ..... (see 1)

Information
6 Cambodian Consulate B2
7 Chinese Consulate B2
8 Dutch Consulate C2
9 French Consulate C2
10 German Consulate B2
11 UK Consulate C2
12 US Consulate C2

HCMC diner's diary: choose your meat, fish, seafood and vegies and flame them up right there on the table.

Xu VIETNAMESE $$
(Map p138; ☎08-3824 8468; www.xusaigon.com; 1st fl, 75 ĐL Hai Ba Trung; 3-course set lunches Mon-Fri 295,000d, meals 115,000-320,000d, 8-course tasting menus 850,000d; ⏲11.30am-midnight) This superstylish restaurant-lounge serves up a menu of Vietnamese-inspired fusion dishes. It's pricey, but well worth the flutter for top service and a classy wine list. Innovative bar snacks (70,000d to 150,000d) and top-notch cocktails reinforce Xu's status as one of the city's most elegant lounge bars.

Around Le Van Tam Park

Pho Hoa VIETNAMESE $
(Map p144; 260c Đ Pasteur; meals 60,000-75,000d; ⏲6am-midnight) This long-running establishment is more upmarket than most but is definitely the real deal – as evidenced by its popularity with regular local patrons. Tables come laden with herbs, chilli and lime, as well as *gio chao quay* (fried Chinese bread), *banh xu xe* (glutinous coconut cakes with mung-bean paste) and *cha lua* (pork-paste sausages wrapped in banana leaves).

Banh Xeo 46A VIETNAMESE $
(Map p144; ☎08-3824 1110; 46a Đ Dinh Cong Trang; regular/extra large 70,000/110,000d; ⏲10am-9pm; 🌱) Locals will always hit the restaurants that specialise in a single dish and this renowned spot serves some of the best *banh xeo* in town. These Vietnamese rice-flour pancakes stuffed with bean sprouts, prawns and pork (vegetarian versions available) are legendary. Other dishes available include excellent *goi cuon* (fresh summer rolls with pork and prawn).

Cuc Gach Quan VIETNAMESE $$
(Map p144; ☎08-3848 0144; www.cucgachquan.com.vn/en; 10 Đ Dang Tat; meals 75,000-200,000d; ⏲9am-midnight) It comes as little surprise that the owner is an architect when you step into this cleverly renovated old villa. The decor is rustic and elegant at the same time, which is also true of the food. Despite its tucked-away location in the northernmost reaches of District 1, this is no secret hideaway: book ahead.

Pham Ngu Lao Area

★Banh Mi Huynh Hoa VIETNAMESE $
(Map p135; 26 Le Thi Rieng; banh mi 33,000d; ⏲2.30-11pm) This hole-in-the-wall *banh mi* joint is busy day and night with locals zipping up on motorbikes for stacks of excellent baguettes stuffed with pork, pork and more pork in tasty ways you may not have known existed. Street standing room only.

Vegetarian Lien Huong VEGETARIAN $
(Com Chay Lien Huong; Map p135; ☎08-3925 0547; 149/31a Le Thi Rieng; meals 40,000-110,000d; ⏲8am-10pm; ❄✎) You might hardly notice this corner vegetarian restaurant but the creative flavours are worth getting off the main road for. The standouts are its own creations such as green-banana and mushroom hotpot with lemongrass and rice noodles. The English menu has excellent descriptions of the health benefits of each dish. Great value.

Coriander THAI $
(Map p148; 16 Đ Bui Vien; meals 75,000-180,000d; ⏲11am-2pm & 5-11pm) The blonde-wood furniture and cheap bamboo wallpaper do Coriander few favours, but the menu is stuffed with authentic Siamese delights. The lovely fried *doufu* (tofu) is almost a meal in itself, the green curry is zesty, and the clay-pot seafood fried rice is excellent.

Five Oysters VIETNAMESE $
(Map p148; www.fiveoysters.com; 234 Đ Bui Vien; meals from 35,000d; ⏲9am-11pm) With a strong seafood slant and friendly service, light and bright Five Oysters in backpackerland is frequently packed with travellers feasting on oysters (30,000d), grilled octopus, seafood soup, snail pie, *pho,* fried noodles, grilled mackerel with chilli oil and more. Bargain-priced beer also makes it a popular spot along the PNL strip.

Café Zoom BURGERS $
(Map p148; www.facebook.com/cafezoomsaigon; 169a Đ De Tham; meals 55,000-90,000d; ⏲7am-2am) Paying homage to the classic Vespa, this buzzing place has a perfect location for watching the world go by. The menu includes great burgers with original toppings, plus tacos and a mix of Italian and Vietnamese favourites. It's also where Vespa Adventures (p140) launches its excellent tours from.

Margherita INTERNATIONAL $
(Map p148; 175/1 Đ Pham Ngu Lao; meals 35,000-100,000d; ⏲8am-10pm) A golden oldie, Margherita cooks up Vietnamese, Italian and Mexican food at a steal. Secure an outdoor table, order a freshly squeezed juice and watch the world go by on one of PNL's busier side streets.

Mon Hue VIETNAMESE $
(Map p148; www.nhahangmonhue.vn; 201 Đ De Tham; meals 45,000-120,000d; ⏲6am-11pm; ❄📶✎) Hue's famous cuisine comes to HCMC's hungry hordes through this chain of eight restaurants. This handy branch offers a good, air-conditioned introduction for travellers who don't make it to the old capital.

★Quan Ut Ut BARBECUE $$
(Map p135; ☎08-3914 4500; www.quanutut.com; 168 Đ Vo Van Kiet; meals 180,000-300,000d; ⏲4-11.30pm) With a name roughly translating to the 'Oink Oink Eatery', this casual place with river views celebrates everything porcine with an American-style BBQ spin. Huge streetside grills prepare great ribs, spicy sausages and pork belly, and tasty sides include charred sweetcorn and grilled pineapple. Huge burgers are also good, and the owners even make their own flavour-packed craft beers.

Baba's Kitchen INDIAN $$
(Map p148; ☎08-3838 6661; www.babaskitchen.in; 164 Đ Bui Vien; meals 80,000-210,000d; ⏲11am-11pm; ✎) Baba's sets Bui Vien alight with the fine flavours, aromas and spices of India. There's ample vegetarian choice and the atmosphere is as inviting as the cuisine is delectable. If you like your food eye-poppingly spicy, the vindaloo dishes can assist, although the waiter may politely caution you that they are 'rather hot'. Rather-excellent service too.

Drinking & Nightlife

Reunification Palace & Around

Chill Skybar COCKTAIL BAR
(Map p135; www.chillsaigon.com; 26 & 27th fl, AB Tower, 76a Đ Le Lai; ⏲5.30pm-late) The most upmarket of HCMC's sky bars – it's very popular with local high rollers working their way through a bottle of Hennessy cognac or Johnnie Walker Blue Label – and the only one to enforce a pretty strict dress code. Dig out your cleanest long trousers and maybe leave the Beer Lao or Vang Vieng rafting T-shirt in your backpack.

Air 360 BAR

(Map p135; www.air360skybar.com; 21st fl, Ben Thanh Tower, 136-138 Đ Le Thi Hong Gam; ⏲5.30pm-2am) Happy hour runs from 5pm to 8pm at this modern sky bar – perfect to make the most of sunset and secure a good discount on the pricey drinks menu. Pâtés, terrines and charcuterie selections underpin the food menu. It's just a short walk from the heaving backpacker bars on Pham Ngu Lao.

Dong Khoi Area

★Pasteur Street Brewing Company CRAFT BEER

(Map p138; www.pasteurstreet.com; 144 Đ Pasteur; small/large beers from 45,000/95,000d; ⏲11am-10pm; 📶) Proving there's hoppy life beyond 333 lager, Pasteur Street Brewing turns out a fine selection of excellent craft beer. Brews utilise local ingredients including lemongrass, rambutan and jasmine, and up to six different beers are always available. Great bar snacks – try the spicy Nashville fried chicken – are also served in Pasteur Street's hip upstairs tasting room.

★Heritage Republic LOUNGE

(Map p135; ☎0906 227 576; http://fb.me/heritagerepublic; 10 Đ Pasteur; ⏲24hr; 📶) It's easy to lose track of time in tiny Heritage. By day, relax on a vintage sofa with a smoothie, snuggling up to the resident bulldogs. Suddenly it's evening and this 24-hour lounge transforms into one of HCMC's most chilled bars, with a hip crowd spilling on to the streets for beer and cocktails. Discount days for patrons dressed in black.

Shrine COCKTAIL BAR

(Map p138; ☎0916 806 093; www.shrinebarsaigon.com; 64 Đ Ton That Thiep; ⏲11am-1am Mon-Sat, 4pm-midnight Sun) Decked out with replica Khmer sculptures, Shrine is a chic and sophisticated alternative to more rowdy sports and hostess bars nearby. There's a proud focus on creating interesting – and very potent – cocktails (100,000d to 200,000d) from the team behind the bar, and pan-Asian flavours infuse a versatile food menu stretching from bar snacks (85,000d to 230,000d) to larger shared plates (220,000d to 460,000d).

Apocalypse Now CLUB

(Map p138; ☎08-3824 1463; www.facebook.com/apocalypsenowsaigon; 2c Đ Thi Sach; ⏲7pm-4am) 'Apo' has been around since 1991 and remains one of the must-visit clubs. A sprawling place with a big dance floor and an outdoor courtyard, the bar's eclectic cast combines travellers, expats, Vietnamese movers and shakers, plus the odd working girl. The music is thumping and it's apocalyptically rowdy. The 150,000d weekend charge gets you a free drink.

M Bar BAR

(Map p138; www.majesticsaigon.com/mb.php; 1 Đ Dong Khoi; ⏲4pm-1am) On the 8th floor of the Majestic Hotel (p141), this is a great spot for a sundowner, with panoramic views of the river and a certain colonial-era cachet.

Republic Lounge BAR

(Map p138; 63/201 Đ Dong Du; ⏲10am-2am) This gay bar is quiet, mild-mannered and often empty during the week. Come late Friday and Saturday night and Republic throngs with a crowd of proud locals. Jugs of cocktails get the young, trendy (and mostly Vietnamese) crowd dancing and cheering on the occasional drag show.

EON Heli Bar BAR

(Map p138; 52nd fl, Bitexco Financial Tower, 2 Đ Hai Trieu; ⏲11.30am-2am) Secure a window seat and catch the sun going down from this snappy 52nd-floor vantage point over town.

Bliss Pub BAR

(Map p148; 24-26 Đ Bui Vien; ⏲6pm-4am) A modern, casual bar in the backpacker district that attracts locals and visitors, gay and straight, with *shisha* pipes and cocktails.

Saigon Saigon Bar BAR

(Map p138; www.caravellehotel.com; 19 Lam Son Sq; ⏲11am-2am; 📶) For excellent views in the city centre, stop by Saigon Saigon for a drink around dusk. This fancy bar has live music, cool breezes and a casually upscale feel.

OMG BAR

(Map p135; www.facebook.com/omgsaigon; Tan Hai Long Hotel, 15-19 Đ Nguyen An Ninh; beers/cocktails from 90,000/160,000d; ⏲11am-1am) Get past the silly name, and OMG is a decent rooftop bar near Ben Thanh Market that's less pretentious than some other sky bars around town. Food-wise, there's an adventurous spirit evident with offerings including crocodile tartare with wasabi and mango.

Pham Ngu Lao Area

View BAR

(Map p148; www.ducvuonghotel.com; 8th fl, Duc Vuong Hotel, 195 Đ Bui Vien; ⏲10am-midnight Mon-Fri, to 2am Sat & Sun) Not as elevated as other rooftop bars around town, but less pretentious and a whole lot easier on the wallet. It's still a good escape to look down on the heaving backpacker bustle of Pham Ngu Lao, and the food menu is also good value.

Other Neighbourhoods

★Saigon Outcast BAR
(www.saigonoutcast.com; 188 Đ Nguyen Van Huong; ⌚10am-11.45pm) Head across to District 2 for this venue's diverse combo of live music, DJs, cinema nights and good times amid funky street art. Cocktails, craft beer and local ciders are available in the raffish garden bar, and there's a cool outdoor market occasionally on Sunday mornings. Check the website for what's on. From District 1, it's around 150,000d in a taxi.

☆ Entertainment

For up-to-date information on what's happening in town, check out the excellent monthly magazine the *Word HCMC* (www.wordhcmc.com), or countrywide *AsiaLIFE Magazine* (www.asialifemagazine.com).

Acoustic LIVE MUSIC
(Map p135; ☎08-3930 2239; www.facebook.com/acousticbarpage; 6e1 Đ Ngo Thoi Nhiem; ⌚7pm-midnight; 📶) Don't be misled by the name: most of the musicians are fully plugged in and dangerous when they take to the intimate stage of the city's leading live-music venue. And judging by the numbers that pack in, the local crowd just can't get enough. It's at the end of the alley by the upended VW Beetle, and the cocktails are deceptively strong.

Saigon Ranger LIVE MUSIC
(Map p138; www.facebook.com/saigonranger; 5/7 Đ Nguyen Sieu; ⌚3pm-late Tue-Sun) Centrally located just a short stroll from Lam Son Park, Saigon Ranger is a raffish live-music and performance venue with different acts from Tuesday to Sunday. Look forward to an eclectic roster of performers – including rock, blues and Latin sounds – with most gigs kicking off around 9pm.

Observatory LIVE MUSIC
(Map p135; www.facebook.com/theobservatoryhcm; 5 Đ Nguyen Tat Thanh; ⌚6pm-6am Wed-Sun) Happening venue with everything from live bands to DJs from around the globe. Now relocated to just across the river in District 4.

Saigon Water Puppet Theatre PUPPET THEATRE
(Map p144; History Museum, Đ Nguyen Binh Khiem; 100,000d) Within the History Museum (p137), this small theatre has performances at 9am, 10am, 11am, 2pm, 3pm and 4pm, lasting about 20 minutes.

Municipal Theatre CONCERT VENUE
(Opera House; Map p138; ☎08-3829 9976; Lam Son Sq) The French-era Opera House is home to the HCMC Ballet and the Ballet & Symphony Orchestra (www.hbso.org.vn), and hosts performances by visiting artists.

Galaxy CINEMA
(Map p135; www.galaxycine.vn; 116 Đ Nguyen Du; tickets 90,000-150,000d) One of the best cinemas in town, with Hollywood blockbusters and local hits.

🛍 Shopping

Dong Khoi Area

Mekong Quilts ARTS & CRAFTS
(Map p138; ☎08-2210 3110; www.mekong-quilts.org; 1st fl, 68 ĐL Le Loi; ⌚9am-7pm) 🍃 Beautiful handmade silk quilts, sewn by the rural poor in support of a sustainable income.

Chung Cu 42 Ton That Thiep CLOTHING
(Map p138; 42 Đ Ton That Thiep; ⌚most shops 9am-9pm) Come for the apartment building partially converted into cool boutique shops, and linger for the young, social-media savvy fashion labels that produce stylish (but affordable) clothing. There is a sense that HCMC's hipster boom starts here. Head upstairs, and also through to the back to the second building.

Saigon Kitsch GIFTS & SOUVENIRS
(Map p138; 33 Đ Ton That Thiep; ⌚9am-10pm) This colourful French-run shop specialises in reproduction propaganda items, emblazoning its revolutionary motifs on coffee mugs, coasters, jigsaws and T-shirts. Also cool laptop and tablet covers fashioned from recycled Vietnamese packaging.

Ben Thanh Market MARKET
(Cho Ben Thanh; Map p138; ĐL Le Loi, ĐL Ham Nghi, ĐL Tran Hung Dao & Đ Le Lai; ⌚5am-6pm) Centrally located, Ben Thanh and its surrounding streets comprise one of HCMC's liveliest areas. Everything that's commonly eaten, worn or used by the Saigonese is piled high, and souvenir items can be found in equal abundance. Vendors are determined

Pham Ngu Lao

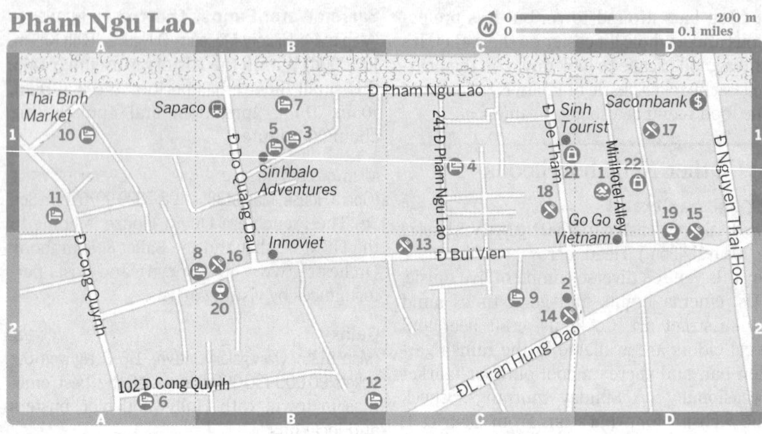

Pham Ngu Lao

Activities, Courses & Tours
1 Oasis Saigon D1
2 Vespa Adventures C2

Sleeping
3 Bich Duyen Hotel B1
4 Diep Anh C1
5 Giang Son B1
6 Green Suites A2
7 Hideout Hostel B1
8 Hong Han Hotel B2
9 Lily's Hostel C2
10 Long Hostel A1
11 Madame Cuc 127 .... A1
12 MyHotel B2

Eating
13 Baba's Kitchen C2
14 Café Zoom C2
15 Coriander D1
16 Five Oysters B2
17 Margherita D1
18 Mon Hue C1

Drinking & Nightlife
19 Bliss Pub D1
20 View B2

Shopping
21 Ginkgo C1
22 SahaBook D1

and prices usually higher than elsewhere (restaurant stalls are reasonable), so bargain vigorously and ignore any 'Fixed Price' signs.

Good restaurant stalls are usually open until midafternoon. It's an area where it pays to be extravigilant about looking after personal items and electronics.

Once the indoors market closes, a small night market just outside takes over until midnight.

Mai Lam CLOTHING
(Map p138; www.mailam.com.vn; 132-134 Đ Dong Khoi; ⏲9am-9pm) Vibrant, colourful, creative and highly inspiring, Mai Lam carries beautiful (but pricey) hand-stitched men's and women's clothing and accessories.

Saigon Centre SHOPPING CENTRE
(Map p138; http://saigoncentre.com.vn; 65 ĐL Le Loi; ⏲9.30am-9.30pm) A sleek tower block with flashy international shops, cafes and a Japanese-style food court in its basement level.

Pham Ngu Lao Area

SahaBook BOOKS
(Map p148; www.sahabook.com; 175/24 Đ Pham Ngu Lao; ⏲9am-5.30pm Mon-Fri) Specialises in guidebooks and travel literature, including authentic Lonely Planet guidebooks with readable maps – unlike the knock-offs you'll see on the street.

Ginkgo CLOTHING
(Map p148; www.ginkgo-vietnam.com; 254 Đ De Tham; ⏲8am-10pm) With three branches in the PNL area, this fun upmarket shop sells exuberant, brightly coloured T-shirts and hoodies, some decorated with Chinese characters and ironic English logos.

Other Neighbourhoods

Dan Sinh Market MARKET
(Map p135; 104 Đ Yersin; ⏰7am-6pm) Also known as the War Surplus Market, this is the place to find authentic combat boots or rusty (and perhaps less authentic) dog tags among the hardware stalls. There are also handy gas masks, field stretchers, rain gear, mosquito nets, canteens, duffel bags, ponchos, boots and flak jackets.

3A Alternative Art Area ART
(Map p138; 3a Đ Ton Duc Thang) Street art, galleries, interesting homeware shops and a growing range of hip cafes and bars make this an essential destination if you're keen to understand how Saigon is evolving. At weekends it's a popular location for edgy fashion shoots and wedding photos.

Information

MEDICAL SERVICES

Columbia Asia (Map p135; ☎08-3823 8888; www.columbiaasia.com/saigon; 8 Alexandre de Rhodes; ⏰emergency 8am-9pm) Centrally located near Notre Dame.

HCMC Family Medical Practice (Map p138; ☎24hr emergency 08-3822 7848; www.vietnammedicalpractice.com; rear, Diamond Department Store, 34 ĐL Le Duan; ⏰24hr) Well-run practice with branches in Hanoi and Danang.

International Medical Centre (Map p138; ☎08-3827 2366; www.cmi-vietnam.com; 1 Đ Han Thuyen; ⏰8.30am-7pm Mon-Fri, 9am-1pm Sat) A nonprofit organisation with English-speaking French doctors.

International SOS (Map p144; ☎08-3829 8520; www.internationalsos.com; 167a Đ Nam Ky Khoi Nghia; ⏰24hr)

MONEY

ANZ Bank (Map p138; ☎08-3829 9319; 11 Me Linh Sq) With ATM.

Citibank (Map p138; 115 ĐL Nguyen Hue) Citibank in the foyer of the Sun Wah Tower dispenses 8,000,000d, but only for Citibank cards (2,000,000d for other cards).

Sacombank (Map p148; ☎08-3836 4231; www.sacombank.com; 211 Đ Nguyen Thai Hoc) Conveniently located in the backpacker zone, with a 24-hour ATM.

POST

FedEx (☎08-3948 0370; www.fedex.com; 6 Đ Thang Long, Tan Binh District; ⏰7.30am-6pm Mon-Fri, to 4.30pm Sat) Private freight carrier.

Post Office (Buu Dien Quan 5; ☎08-3855 1763; 3 Đ Mac Cuu, District 5) Look for the light-yellow building with a clock.

TRAVEL AGENCIES

Buffalo Tours (Map p144; ☎08-3827 9170; www.buffalotours.com; 157 Đ Pasteur; ⏰8.30am-5pm Mon-Fri, to 2.30pm Sat) Top-end travel agency.

EXO Travel (☎08-3519 4111; www.exotissimo.com; 261-263 Đ Phan Xich Long, District 2; ⏰9am-6pm Mon-Sat) Excellent Indochina specialists.

Go Go Vietnam (Map p148; ☎08-3920 9297; www.gogo-vietnam.com; 40/7 Đ Bui Vien) Well-run tour company and travel agency with excellent credentials in visa extensions and renewals, and good-value day trips.

Handspan Adventure Travel (Map p135; ☎08-3925 7605; www.handspan.com; 10th fl, Central Park Bldg, 208 Đ Nguyen Trai) Excellent, high-quality tours are available from this HCMC branch of the Hanoi-based travel agency.

Innoviet (Map p148; ☎08-6291 5407; www.innoviet.com; 1st fl, 161 Đ Bui Vien; ⏰8am-9pm) Budget travel agency.

Sinh Tourist (Map p148; ☎08-3838 9593; www.thesinhtourist.vn; 246 Đ De Tham; ⏰6.30am-10.30pm) Popular budget travel agency.

Sinhbalo Adventures (Map p148; ☎08-3837 6766; www.sinhbalo.com; 283/20 Đ Pham Ngu Lao; ⏰7.30am-noon & 1.30-6pm Mon-Sat) For customised tours this is a great choice. Sinhbalo specialises in cycling trips, but also arranges innovative special-interest journeys to the Mekong Delta, central highlands and further afield. Its most popular package trips include a two-day Mekong tour and three-day Mekong cycling tour.

Getting There & Away

AIR

HCMC is served by Tan Son Nhat Airport. A number of airlines serve domestic routes from HCMC.

Jetstar Pacific Airlines (☎1900 1550; www.jetstar.com/vn/en/home) Flies to/from Hanoi, Haiphong, Vinh, Hue, Phu Quoc, Nha Trang, Buon Ma Thuot, Dong Hoi and Danang.

Vietnam Air Service Company (Vasco; ☎08-3845 8017; www.vasco.com.vn) Flies to/from Rach Gia, Con Dao Islands and Ca Mau.

Vietnam Airlines (☎08-3832 0320; www.vietnamairlines.com) Flies to/from Hanoi, Haiphong, Vinh, Dong Hoi, Hue, Danang, Quy Nhon, Nha Trang, Dalat, Buon Ma Thuot, Pleiku, Rach Gia and Phu Quoc Island.

BOAT

Bach Dang Jetty (Map p138; Đ Ton Duc Thang) Centrally located pier at the bottom end of town.

Vina Express (Map p135; ☎08-3825 3333; www.vinaexpress.com.vn; 5 Đ Nguyen Tat Thanh, District 4; adult/child Mon-Fri 200,000/100,000d, weekends & public holidays 250,000/120,000d) Hydrofoils depart for Vung Tau (around 1¼ hours) from Saigon port near the Ho Chi Minh Museum in District 4. Departures at 8am, 10am, noon, 2pm, 4pm and 6pm daily, plus 9am Saturday.

BUS

Plenty of international bus services connect HCMC and Cambodia, most with departures from the Pham Ngu Lao area. **Sapaco** (Map p148; ☎08-3920 3623; www.sapacotourist.vn; 325 Đ Pham Ngu Lao) has nine direct daily services to Phnom Penh (230,000d, six hours, departures 6am to 3pm), as well as one to Siem Reap (450,000d, 12 hours, 6am).

An Suong Bus Station (Ben Xe An Suong; District 12) Buses to Tay Ninh, Cu Chi and other points northwest of HCMC depart from the newer An Suong bus station, way to the west of the city centre. Note that it's not really worth using local buses to visit Tay Ninh and Cu Chi, as many of the smaller tunnel sites are off the main highways, making it a nightmare to navigate. To get here, head all the way out on Đ Cach Mang Thang Tam and Đ Truong Chinh. The station is close to the flyover for Quoc Lo 1 (Hwy 1).

Cholon Bus Station (District 5) Bus 1 links Ben Thanh bus station and Ben Thanh market with Cholon bus station and Cholon's Binh Tay Market. Local bus 152 takes you to Tan Son Nhat International Airport.

Mien Dong Bus Station (Ben Xe Mien Dong; ☎08-3829 4056) Buses to locations north of HCMC leave from the immensely huge and busy Mien Dong bus station, in Binh Thanh district, about 5km from central HCMC on Hwy 13 (Quoc Lo 13; the continuation of Đ Xo Viet Nghe Tinh). The station is just under 2km north of the intersection of Đ Xo Viet Nghe Tinh and Đ Dien Bien Phu. Note that express buses depart from the east side, and local buses connect with the west side of the complex.

Mien Tay Bus Station (Ben Xe Mien Tay; ☎08-3825 5955; Đ Kinh Duong Vuong) This bus station serves all areas south of HCMC, which basically means the Mekong Delta, using air-conditioned express buses and premium minibuses. This huge station is about 10km west of HCMC in An Lac, a part of Binh Chanh district (Huyen Binh Chanh).

CAR & MOTORCYCLE

Enquire at almost any hotel or tourist cafe to arrange car hire. The travel agencies in the Pham Ngu Lao area generally offer the lowest prices. Motorbikes are available in this area for around US$10 to US$12 per day, although this is one city where it definitely helps to have experience. Check the quality of the helmet provided.

Saigon Scooter Centre (☎08-6681 2362; www.saigonscootercentre.com; 20 Cong Hoa, Tan Binh District; ⏲noon-5pm Tue-Fri, 10am-4pm Sat) This scooter centre is a reliable source for restored classic Vespa and Lambretta scooters, which are also rented out by the day. Daily rates start from US$10 and discounts are offered for long-term rentals. For an extra fee it is possible to arrange a one-way service, with a pick-up of the bikes anywhere between HCMC and Hanoi.

TRAIN

Saigon Train Station (Ga Sai Gon; ☎08-3823 0105; 1 Đ Nguyen Thong, District 3; ⏲ticket office 7.15-11am & 1-3pm) Trains from Saigon train station serve coastal cities to the north of HCMC.

GETTING TO CAMBODIA: HO CHI MINH CITY TO PHNOM PENH

Getting to the border The busy **Moc Bai/Bavet border crossing** is the fastest land route between Ho Chi Minh City and Phnom Penh. Pham Ngu Lao traveller cafes sell through bus tickets (US$10 to US$15) to Phnom Penh; buses leave from Pham Ngu Lao between 6am and 3pm. Reliable bus companies include Mekong Express (www.catmekongexpress.com) and Sapaco (www.sapacotourist.vn). Allow six hours for the entire trip, including time spent on border formalities.

At the border Cambodian visas (US$30) are issued at the border (you'll need a passport-sized photo). Moc Bai is two hours from HCMC by bus and is a major duty-free shopping zone. It's a short walk from Moc Bai to Bavet (the Cambodian border) and its enclave of casinos.

Moving on Most travellers have a through bus ticket from HCMC to Phnom Penh, a further four-hour bus ride away.

TRANSPORT FROM HO CHI MINH CITY

DESTINATION	AIR	BUS	TRAIN
Dalat	50min; from US$41	7hr; US$11-15	N/A
Hanoi	2hr; from US$62	41hr; US$39-49	30hr; US$47-69
Hue	80min; from US$48	29hr; US$26-37	18hr; US$17-44
Nha Trang	55min; from US$22	12hr; US$10-20	6½hr; US$14-32

Getting Around

TO/FROM THE AIRPORT

Tan Son Nhat Airport is 7km northwest of central HCMC.

Bus

There are two new dedicated airport buses:

Route 109 (20,000d, 50 minutes, 5.30am to 1.30am, every 15 to 20 minutes) Goes to the 'backpacker district' of Pham Ngu Lao via Ben Thanh Bus Station.

Route 49 (40,000d, 40 minutes, 5.30am to 1.30am, every 15 to 30 minutes) Stops at the Pham Ngu Lao area, via Ben Thanh Market.

Both are air-conditioned, modern yellow buses that allow you to take luggage at no extra cost. Exit the international airport, cross to the centre platform and turn right to the marked stop with English-speaking staff selling tickets.

There is also an economical air-con bus (route 152; 6000d, plus a variable fee for luggage, 6am to 6pm, every 15 minutes) to/from the international airport terminal. Buses make regular stops along Đ De Tham (Pham Ngu Lao area) and at international hotels along Đ Dong Khoi to *Cholon Bus Station* (p150).

Taxi

Choose metered Mai Linh or Vinasun taxis and especially avoid similar-sounding and coloured imitations; Mai Linh Taxi has a counter in arrivals. Sasco Taxi has the concession for the domestic terminal. From the arrivals taxi rank, a taxi should cost around 170,000d to Dong Khoi, plus a 15,000d vehicle access ticket to the airport. You can pay in US dollars if you want. To get to the airport from town, ask your hotel to call a trustworthy taxi for you. Most hotels will pick you up at the airport for US$5 to US$20.

BICYCLE

Bicycles are available for hire (US$2) from many budget hotels and cafes. Use parking lots to safeguard against theft.

CYCLO

Cyclos are an interesting way to get around town, but overcharging tourists is the norm. Short hops should be 30,000d to 40,000d.

MOTORCYCLE

HCMC is not the place to learn to ride a motorbike. They are nevertheless available for hire around Pham Ngu Lao for US$10 to US$12 per day.

TAXI

Metered taxis cruise the streets, but it is worth calling ahead if you are off the beaten path. The flagfall is around 12,000d for the first kilometre; expect to pay around 25,000d (US$1) from Dong Khoi to Pham Ngu Lao. Some companies have dodgy taxi meters, rigged to jump quickly, but both **Mai Linh Taxi** (☎08-3838 3838) and **Vinasun Taxi** (☎08-3827 2727) can be trusted. Uber is also becoming more popular in the city.

XE OM

If catching a *xe om*, agree on a price in advance. A trip from Pham Ngu Lao to Dong Khoi shouldn't cost more than 30,000d.

AROUND HO CHI MINH CITY

Dai Nam Theme Park

Equal parts Disneyland, Buddhist fantasia, historical homage and national propaganda piece, **Dai Nam Theme Park** (Lac Canh Dai Nam Van Hien; ☎0650 351 2660; www.laccanhdainamvanhien.vn; adult/child 100,000/50,000d; ⏲8am-6pm) is a fantastically cheesy experience. About 30km from HCMC on Hwy 13, it's split into four constituent parts sheltered behind giant walls (guarded by life-size model soldiers).

It has a serious roller coaster with corkscrews and loops, a log flume, an indoor snow world and plenty of rides for smaller kids. The 12.5-hectare zoo is the only one in the greater HCMC area we'd recommend visiting. The menagerie include tigers, lions, white rhinos and bears. The neighbouring beach (adult/child 100,000/60,000d) has large fresh and saltwater pools and is a good place for cooling off the kids.

Local bus 18 runs from Ben Thanh bus station to Dai Nam daily. There's plenty of car parking on-site.

Beaches

There are several beach resorts within striking distance of downtown HCMC, although most travellers make for Mui Ne. If time is short and you want a quick fix, consider Vung Tau, which you can reach by hydrofoil.

Cu Chi

If the tenacious spirit of the Vietnamese can be symbolised by a place, few sites could make a stronger case for it than Cu Chi. The **tunnel network** (adult/child 110,000/30,000d) became legendary during the 1960s for its role in facilitating VC control of a large rural area only 30km to 40km from HCMC. At its peak the tunnel system stretched from the South Vietnamese capital to the Cambodian border; in the district of Cu Chi alone more than 250km of tunnels honeycomb the ground.

Two sections of the remarkable tunnel network (which are enlarged and upgraded versions of the real thing) are open to the public. One is near the village of Ben Dinh and the other is 15km beyond at Ben Duoc (admission slightly cheaper). Most tourists visiting the tunnels end up at Ben Dinh, as it's easier for tour buses to reach. Even if you stay above ground, it's still an interesting experience learning about the region's ingenious and brave resistance activities.

Both sites have gun ranges attached where you can shell out a small fortune to fire genuine AK-47s and machine guns. You pay per bullet so be warned: if you're firing an automatic weapon, they do come out pretty fast.

Getting There & Away

By far the easiest way to get to the tunnels is by guided tour and, as the competition is stiff, prices are exceptionally reasonable, varying depending on group size and choice of tunnels. For something different, hop on a boat to the Cu Chi tunnels with Les Rives (p140); boats depart twice daily, and include hotel pick-up, meals, refreshments, guide and admission fees. The entire trip takes five hours. Another option is a motorbike tour with Saigon Riders (p140), which costs US$79 per person (minimum two people).

MEKONG DELTA

The 'rice bowl' of Vietnam, the delta is carpeted in a dizzying variety of greens. It's a water world that moves to the rhythms of the mighty Mekong, where boats, houses and markets float upon the innumerable rivers, canals and streams that criss-cross the landscape like arteries.

The bustling commerce of its towns contrasts sharply with the languid, almost-soporific pace of life in the countryside. Here buffalo wallow in rice paddies, coconut- and fruit-laden boats float slowly along the mud-brown waters, and two-wheeled exploration of the narrow lanes is amply rewarded with a true taste of rural hospitality (and delicious river fish).

Elsewhere, mangrove forests teem with a wealth of bird life and bristle with the remains of Viet Cong bunkers, ornate Khmer pagodas and Buddhist temples reaching for the sky, while off-coast islands offer white-sand beaches and tropical hideaways to some, and pirate havens to others.

Bac Lieu

The **Bac Lieu Bird Sanctuary** (Vuon Chim Bac Lieu; ☎0781-383 5991; 20,000d; ⏰7.30am-5pm), 6km southwest of the little-visited town of Bac Lieu, is notable for its 50-odd species of bird, including a large population of graceful white herons. Bird populations peak in the rainy season – approximately May to October – and the birds nest until about January.

Guides should be hired at the sanctuary entrance; little English is spoken. **Bac Lieu Tourist Office** (☎0781-382 4272; www.baclieutourist.com; 2 Đ Hoang Van Thu; ⏰7-11am & 1-5pm) also arranges transport and guides.

Bac Lieu is on the bus route between Soc Trang and Ca Mau.

My Tho

Gateway to the Mekong Delta, My Tho is the capital of Tien Giang province and an important market town – although for the famous floating markets, you'll need to continue on to Can Tho.

My Tho's proximity to Ho Chi Minh City means it's a popular day-trip destination for a taste of river life – a flotilla of boats tour the local islands and their cottage industries daily, though many bypass the town itself. The riverfront makes for a pleasant stroll and the town, including the lively market (Đ Trung Trac), is easily explored on foot.

Tours

My Tho Tourist Boat Station BOATING
(8 Đ 30 Thang 4) In a prominent building on the riverfront, the My Tho Tourist Boat Station is home to several tour companies offering cruises to the neighbouring islands and through the maze of small canals. Depending on what you book, destinations usually include a coconut-candy workshop, a honey farm (try the banana wine) and an orchid garden.

Sleeping

Song Tien Annex HOTEL $
(073-387 7883; www.tiengiangtourist.com; 33 Đ Thien Ho Duong; r US$27-30;) First, the good news: there are river views from the balconies, the location is handy and central, bathrooms come with freestanding claw-footed bathtubs (rare as unicorn eggs in Vietnam) and the staff are sweet (even though you have to be good at expressing yourself through mime). Now the bad: fittings are tired and six-legged scuttling friends sometimes show up.

★**Island Lodge** BOUTIQUE HOTEL $$$
(073-651 9000; www.theislandlodge.com.vn; 390 Ap Thoi Binh, Xa Thoi Son; r US$175;) It's hard to imagine a more tranquil place than this island hideaway. At this intimate luxury hotel, the occupants of its 12 rooms are cheerfully attended to by professional staff. You can watch the goings-on on the river from the riverside pool, indulge in gourmet cuisine, or retreat to your light, bright room, complete with contemporary art and bamboo-framed beds.

After crossing the bridge from My Tho in the Ben Tre direction, take the turn towards Thoi Son and travel for another 3km or so.

Eating

My Tho is known for its vermicelli soup, *hu tieu My Tho*, garnished with fresh and dried seafood, pork, chicken, offal and fresh herbs. It's served either with broth or dry and can be made vegetarian.

Chi Thanh CHINESE, VIETNAMESE $
(073-387 3756; 279 Đ Tet Mau Than; meals 50,000-100,000d; 10am-9pm) This small but extremely popular restaurant does a steady trade in tasty Chinese and Vietnamese fare (beef, chicken, pork, squid, crab, noodles, hotpots). There's an English menu.

Hu Tieu Chay 24 VIETNAMESE $
(24 Đ Nam Ky Khoi Nghia; mains 15,000-24,000d; 8am-9pm;) Vegetarian-friendly local noodle specialities.

Hu Tieu 44 VIETNAMESE $
(44 Đ Nam Ky Khoi Nghia; soup 25,000d; 8am-9pm) Carnivore-friendly noodle dishes.

Getting There & Around

If heading to Ben Tre, a taxi (around 260,000d) or *xe om* (around 120,000d) will be considerably faster than a bus. Buses head to Ben Tre (10,000d, 25 minutes, frequent), Can Tho (70,000d, 2½ hours, several daily) and HCMC (80,000d, 1½ hours, hourly).

Tien Giang Bus Station (Ben Xe Tien Giang; 42 Đ Ap Bac) The bus station is 2.3km northwest of town, on the main Hwy 1A towards Ho Chi Minh City. A *xe om* into town should cost around 40,000d.

Ben Tre

The picturesque little province of Ben Tre has a sleepy waterfront, lined with ageing villas, and is easy to explore on foot, as is the rustic settlement across the bridge to the south of the centre. This is also a good place to arrange boat trips in the area, particularly for those wanting to escape the tour-bus bustle. Plus, the riverside promenade and the narrow lanes on both sides of the river are ideal for two-wheeled exploration.

Tours

★**Mango Cruises** TOURS
(0902 880 120; www.mangocruises.com) Unlike cookie-cutter tours from HCMC, Mango Cruises focuses on the less-visited back roads and canals around Ben Tre and beyond. Day tours comprise a nice mix of cycling, dining on local specialities and observing how rice paper and other local staples are made. Longer tours include outings on its day cruisers and multiday boat trips in the delta.

Sleeping & Eating

★**Mango Home Riverside** BOUTIQUE HOTEL $$
(075-351 1958; www.mangohomeriverside.com; d/ste US$45/57;) Set amid coconut and mango trees along the bank of a Mekong tributary, this delightful mango-coloured B&B, run by a Canadian-Vietnamese couple,

provides a welcome place to unwind. Spacious rooms have air-con, some have outdoor bathrooms, and there are hammocks for lounging. The food is excellent and at night there's complete silence. It's 10km out of town; call for pick-up.

Oasis Hotel HOTEL $$
(075-383 8800; http://bentrehoteloasis.com; 151c My An C, My Thanh An; d 720,000-855,000d, f 1,080,000d;) There's always a warm welcome at this popular, small, bright-yellow hotel with bar and pool, run by a very helpful Kiwi-Vietnamese couple. It's in the village south of the river and best reached by taxi. Free bicycles facilitate countryside exploration.

Food Stalls VIETNAMESE $
(dishes around 15,000d; 7-10pm) Sizzling meat and seafood skewers and bowls of noodles await at the market food stalls.

Getting There & Away

Buses to Vinh Long drop you at Pha Dinh Kao, the ferry port across the river from town; take the ferry across.

Bus Station (Ben Xe Thanh Pho Ben Tre; Đ Dong Khoi) Buses stop at the bus station 2.5km northwest of the town centre. The last buses to HCMC depart between 4pm and 5pm; Thinh Phat are among the most comfortable.

Vinh Long

The capital of Vinh Long province, plonked about midway between My Tho and Can Tho, Vinh Long is a major transit hub. It's a gateway to island life, Cai Be floating market, abundant orchards and rural homestays.

The river **market** (5am-noon) is still the principal attraction on a boat tour from Vinh Long, though it has shrunk considerably due to the building of bridges in the delta and the subsequent transportation of goods by road rather than river. The market is at its best around 6am. Wholesalers on big boats moor here, each specialising in different types of fruit or vegetable, hanging samples of their goods from tall wooden poles. It's an hour by boat from Vinh Long.

A notable sight is the huge and photogenic Catholic cathedral on the riverside.

Most people make detours on the way there or back to see the canals or visit orchards. For those travelling on an organised tour of the delta, it is customary to board a boat here, explore the islands and moor in Vinh Long before continuing to Can Tho.

Sleeping & Eating

Ngoc Sang HOMESTAY $
(070-385 8694; 95/8 Binh Luong, Dao Trinh Nhat, An Binh; per person 250,000d;) Most travellers love this friendly, canal-facing rustic homestay. The grandmother cooks up some wonderful local dishes, free bikes are available, the owner runs decent early-morning boat tours and there's a languid atmosphere about the place. The family seems shy when it comes to hanging out with the guests, though.

Vinh Long Market VIETNAMESE $
(Cho Vinh Long; Đ 3 Thang 2; meals 10,000d) Great spot for local fruit and inexpensive street snacks, such as *nem* (fresh spring rolls).

Getting There & Around

Buses leave the **Provincial Bus Station** (Ben Xe Khach Vinh Long; Hwy 1A) hourly for Can Tho (50,000d, one hour) and Ho Chi Minh City (105,000, three hours). It's 2.5km south of town on the way to Can Tho. A taxi costs around 130,000d and a xe om half that. Coming from HCMC, the larger bus companies Phuong Trang and Mai Linh provide a free shuttle bus to town.

Can Tho

The epicentre of the Mekong Delta, Can Tho is the largest city in the region and feels like a metropolis after a few days exploring the backwaters.

As the political, economic, cultural and transportation centre of the Mekong Delta, it's a buzzing town with a lively waterfront lined with sculpted gardens, an appealing blend of narrow backstreets and wide boulevards, and perhaps the greatest concentration of foreigners in the Delta.

Can Tho is also the perfect base for nearby floating markets, the major draw for tourists who come here to boat along the many canals and rivers leading out of town.

Sights

★**Cai Rang Floating Market** MARKET
(5am-noon) Just 6km from Can Tho in the direction of Soc Trang is Cai Rang, the biggest floating market in the Mekong Delta. There is a bridge here that serves as a great vantage point for photography. The market is best around 6am to 7am, and it's well

worth getting here early to beat boatloads of tourists. This is a wholesale market, so look at what's tied to the long pole above the boat to figure out what they're selling to smaller traders.

Cai Rang can be seen from the road, but getting here is far more interesting by boat (US$10 to US$15). From the market area in Can Tho it takes about 45 minutes by river, or you can drive to the Cau Dau Sau boat landing (by the Dau Sau Bridge), from where it takes only about 10 minutes to reach the market.

★**Phong Dien Floating Market** MARKET
(5am-noon) The Mekong Delta's most intimate and best floating market, Phong Dien has fewer motorised craft and more stand-up rowing boats, with local vendors shopping and exchanging gossip. Less crowded than Cai Rang, there are also far fewer tourists. It's at its bustling best between 5am and 7am with little to see later. The market is 20km southwest of Can Tho; you can get there by road but many operators offer a six-hour combined Cai Rang–Phong Dien tour, returning to Can Tho through quieter backwaters.

Tours

★**Hieu's Tour** CULTURAL
(0939 666 156; www.hieutour.com; 27a Đ Le Thanh Ton) Young, enthusiastic, English-speaking guide Hieu offers excellent tours around Can Tho, from early-morning jaunts to the floating markets (US$23 to Cai Rang, US$30 to both markets) to cycling tours, food tours and even visits to **Pirate Island** (Quan Dao Ha Tien; Hai Tac) further afield. Hieu is keen to show visitors true delta culture and a floating homestay is in the works.

Sleeping & Eating

★**Nguyen Shack Can Tho** GUESTHOUSE $$
(0966 550 016; www.nguyenshack.com; Ong Tim Bridge, Thanh My, Thuong Thanh; dm/d with shared bathroom US$9/25, bungalows US$49-69;) Not a shack, but rather a clutch of rustic thatched bungalows with fans, this great place overlooks the Ong Tim River, 6km from Can Tho. It's the kind of place where backpackers are inspired to linger longer, thanks to the camaraderie between staff and guests. The engaging boat and bicycle tours and the proximity to Cai Rang floating market are bonuses.

★**Kim Tho Hotel** HOTEL $$
(071-381 7517; www.kimtho.com; 1a Đ Ngo Gia Tu; r 935,000-1,670,000d;) A smart hotel, verging on the boutique, Kim Tho is decked out with attractive fabric furnishings in the foyer. Rooms are stylish throughout and include designer bathrooms. Cheaper rooms are on lower floors, but superior rooms have hardwood flooring and the pricier river-view rooms are still a great deal. There is also a rooftop coffee bar on the 12th floor.

★**Nem Nuong Thanh Van** VIETNAMESE $
(071-0382 7255; cnr Nam Ky Khoi Nghia & 30 Thang 4; meals 45,000d; 8am-9pm) The only dish this locally acclaimed little spot does is the best *nem nuong* in town. Roll your own rice rolls using the ingredients provided: pork sausage, rice paper, green banana, star fruit (carambola), cucumber and a riot of fresh herbs, then dip into the peanut-and-something-else sauce, its secret jealously guarded. Simple and fantastic!

★**L'Escale** VIETNAMESE, INTERNATIONAL $$
(071-381 9139; http://nambocantho.com; 1 Đ Ngo Quyen, Nam Bo Boutique Hotel; meals 200,000-500,000d; 6am-10.30pm;) With tantalising river views from the top of the Nam Bo hotel and subdued romantic lighting, this is the place to canoodle with your sweetie over glasses of wine from the strong wine list and beautifully executed dishes such as clay-pot fish with pineapple, sautéed garlic shrimp with spinach and smoked-duck salad.

★**Spices Restaurant** VIETNAMESE, INTERNATIONAL $$$
(071-0381 0111; Cai Khe, Ninh Kieu, Victoria Can Tho Resort; meals 200,000-680,000; 6am-10pm;) Go for a table overlooking the river at this fine restaurant, refined without being stuffy, and opt for the beautifully presented trio of salads (green papaya, banana flower, green mango) or the assortment starter for two, and follow up with deep-fried elephant fish or pork-stuffed squid. Lamb shanks and seared duck cater to homesick palates and the desserts are magnificent.

Information

Can Tho Tourist (071-382 1852; www.canthotourist.com.vn; 50 Đ Hai Ba Trung; 8am-7pm) Helpful staff speak both English and French here and decent city maps are available, as well as general information on attractions in the area.

Hospital (Benh Vien; 071-382 0071; 4 Đ Chau Van Liem) Emergency medical care.

Getting There & Around

AIR

Can Tho International Airport (www.canthoairport.com; Đ Le Hong Phong) is served by **Vietnam Airlines** (071-384 4320; 64 Đ Nguyen An Ninh), Vietjet Air and Vasco, with flights to Dalat (one hour, twice weekly), Danang (1½ hours, daily), Hanoi (2¼ hours, three daily) and Phu Quoc (one hour, daily).

The airport is 10km northwest of the city centre. A taxi into town will cost around 220,000d.

BOAT

There are several boat services to other cities in the Mekong Delta, including hydrofoils to Ca Mau (300,000d, three to four hours), passing through Phung Hiep.

BUS

All buses now depart from the main **bus station** (Ben Xe 91B; Đ Nguyen Van Linh), 2.5km northwest of the centre. A *xe om* into town costs around 50,000d or up to 100,000d in a taxi.

Chau Doc

Draped along the banks of the Hau Giang River (Bassac River), Chau Doc sees plenty of travellers washing through on the river route between Cambodia and Vietnam.

A likeable little town with significant Chinese, Cham and Khmer communities, Chau Doc's cultural diversity – apparent in the mosques, temples, churches and nearby pilgrimage sites – makes it fascinating to explore even if you're not Cambodia-bound. Taking a boat trip to the Cham communities across the river is another highlight, while the bustling market and intriguing waterfront provide fine backdrops to a few days of relaxation.

Sleeping & Eating

Trung Nguyen Hotel HOTEL $

(076-356 1561; 86 Đ Bach Dang; s/d US$12/17;) One of the better budget places, with more midrange trim. Rooms are more decorative than the competition, with balconies overlooking the market. It's a busy corner site, so pack earplugs or ask for a room facing the rear.

★ **Murray Guesthouse** GUESTHOUSE $$

(076-356 2108; www.themurrayguesthouse.com; 11 Truong Dinh; s/d US$26/45;) Its walls decorated with indigenous art, collected from around the world by the Kiwi-Vietnamese owners, this wonderful guesthouse raises the standard of Chau Doc accommodation dramatically. Boons include a guest lounge with snooker table and honour bar, a rooftop terrace drowning in greenery, wonderfully comfortable beds and some of Vietnam's best *pho* for breakfast. Owners are happy to advise and lend bicycles.

★ **Victoria Chau Doc Hotel** HOTEL $$$

(076-386 5010; www.victoriahotels.asia; 32 Đ Le Loi; r/ste from US$150/205;) Chau Doc's most luxurious option, the Victoria delivers classic colonial charm, overseen by staff clad in *ao dai* (national dress of Vietnam). With a striking location on the riverfront, the grand rooms have dark-wood floors and furniture, and inviting bath-tubs. The swimming pool overlooks the busy river and there's a small spa upstairs. A range of tours is available to guests.

★ **Memory Delicatessen** INTERNATIONAL $$

(57 Đ Nguyen Huu Canh; meals 60,000-200,000d; 7am-10pm;) This sophisticated cafe-restaurant that attracts local trendies is memorable for its wonderful melange of international dishes, from the excellent pizzas topped with imported ingredients, to the fragrant vegetable curry with coconut milk and lemongrass, accompanied by an array of fresh juices and imaginative shakes. Skip dessert, though, unless it's the homemade ice cream.

Getting There & Away

Chau Doc Bus Station (Ben Xe Chau Doc; Đ Le Loi) The bus station is on the eastern edge of town, around 2km out of the centre, where Đ Le Loi becomes Hwy 91. All buses depart from here, with the exception of the Hung Cuong buses to Ho Chi Minh City.

Hang Chau (Chau Doc 076-356 2771, Phnom Penh 855-12-883 542; www.hangchautourist.com.vn; per person US$25) Hang Chau departs Chau Doc at 7.30am and Phnom Penh at noon; the journey takes about five hours and the price includes lunch.

Tourist Boats (Đ Le Loi) Hire a boat for a river jaunt.

Ha Tien

Ha Tien may be part of the Mekong Delta but lying on the Gulf of Thailand it feels a world away from the rice fields and rivers that typify the region. There are dramatic limestone formations peppering the area, which are home to a network of caves, and the town has a languid charm, with crumbling colonial villas and a colourful riverside market.

Its sleepy charm is set for a shake-up with the recent increase to four car ferries to Phu Quoc, attracting an influx of Phu Quoc– and Cambodia-bound travellers.

The **Thach Dong Cave Pagoda** (Chua Thanh Van; ⌚6.30am-5.30pm) is a Buddhist cave temple is 4km northeast of town. Scramble through the cave chambers to see the funerary tablets and altars to Ngoc Hoang, Quan The Am Bo Tat and the two Buddhist monks who founded the temples of this pagoda. To the left of the entrance is the Stele of Hatred (Bia Cam Thu), shaped like a raised fist, which commemorates the Khmer Rouge massacre of 130 people here on 14 March 1978.

A great spot for a cold beer, plunger coffee, impartial travel information and for leafing through copies of the *Evening Standard*, the *Observer* and the *Daily Mail* is **Oasis Bar** (☎077-370 1553; www.oasisbarhatien.com; 30 Đ Tran Hau; meals 60,000-150,000d; ⌚9am-9pm; 📶). The menu runs to all-day, full-English breakfasts, filled baguettes, Greek salad, mango shakes and more.

For transport bookings, including boats to Phu Quoc and buses to Cambodia, and Cambodian visas (US$35), try **Ha Tien Tourism** (☎077-395 9598; Đ Tran Hau; ⌚8am-5pm). Look for the neon 'food & drink' sign.

Getting There & Away

Ferries to Phu Quoc stop across the river from the town.

The **bus station** (Ben Xe Ha Tien; Hwy 80) has recently relocated to large, purpose-built facilties 1.5km south of the bridge next to a hospital. Buses for Ho Chi Minh City depart either between 7am and 10am or 6pm and 10pm.

Trang Ngoc Phat (www.taxihatien.vn) runs the most comfortable buses to Rach Gia.

Rach Gia

Rach Gia is something of a boom town, flush with funds from its thriving port and an injection of Viet Kieu (Overseas Vietnamese) money. The population here includes significant numbers of ethnic Chinese and ethnic Khmers. If you're in town for longer than it takes to catch a boat to Phu Quoc Island, explore the lively waterfront and bustling backstreets, where you'll discover some inexpensive seafood restaurants. There is a French-colonial museum and a temple if you want to linger.

Sleeping & Eating

An An Hotel HOTEL $

(☎0917 888 957; 13-14 Đ Lo G Huynh Thuc Khang; r 300,000-350,000d; ❄📶) Particularly handy for the central bus station, this place is friendly, cheap and comes with somewhat dark but spacious rooms.

Palace Hotel HOTEL $$

(☎0913 864 730; 16a Đ Hoa Bien; d/tr from US$28/34; ❄📶) A 10-minute walk from the ferry jetty for Phu Quoc you'll find large rooms with sea views (if you opt for pricier doubles) or more modest but nonetheless comfortable ones. A decent overnighter.

Quan F28 VIETNAMESE, SEAFOOD $

(28 Đ Le Thanh Thon; meals from 40,000d; ⌚11am-10pm) Convenient for the bus-station hotels, this is lively by night and does inexpensive molluscs: shrimp, snails, blood cockles and the like.

Information

Kien Giang Tourist (Du Lich Lu Hanh Kien Giang; ☎077-386 2081; ctycpdulichkg@vnn.vn; 5 Đ Le Loi; ⌚7am-5pm) Provincial tourism authority.

Getting There & Around

AIR

Vietnam Airlines has daily flights to and from Ho Chi Minh City and Phu Quoc Island (in high season). The **Rach Gia Airport** is around 10km southeast of the centre, along Hwy 80; a taxi into town costs around 150,000d and takes about 20 minutes.

BOAT

Ferry Terminal (Ban Tau Rach Gia Phu Quoc) Fast ferries to Phu Quoc Island.

Rach Meo Ferry Terminal (Ben Tau Rach Meo; ☎077-381 1306; Đ Ngo Quyen) Three speedboats daily leave for Ca Mau (300,000d, three to five hours) from the Rach Meo ferry terminal, about 2km south of town.

BUS

Just north of the city centre, the **Rach Gia Central Bus Station** (Ben Xe Khach Rach Gia) primarily serves Ha Tien. Trang Ngoc Phat buses are the most comfortable way to go, followed by Mai Linh.

Phu Quoc Island

Fringed with white-sand beaches and with large tracts still cloaked in dense trop-

GETTING TO CAMBODIA FROM THE MEKONG

Visas at the border Cambodian visas officially cost US$30 at the time of writing but be prepared to overpay by around US$5 at the border to join the 'express line', or be made to wait indefinitely.

It's a really good idea to have US dollars on you when crossing into Cambodia; you can pay for the Cambodian visa in dong but they'll get you with a really unfavourable exchange rate. On the Cambodian side, you can withdraw dollars from ATMs.

Ha Tien to Kiep

Getting to the border The **Xa Xia/Prek Chak border crossing** connects Ha Tien with Kep and Kampot on Cambodia's south coast, making a trip to Cambodia from Phu Quoc via Ha Tien, or vice versa, that much easier. Several minibus companies leave Ha Tien for Cambodia at around 1pm, heading to Kep (US$9, one hour, 47km), Kampot (US$12, 1½ hours, 75km), Sihanoukville (US$15, four hours, 150km) and Phnom Penh (US$15, four hours, 180km). Bookings can be made through Ha Tien Tourism (p157), which can arrange the Cambodian visa too.

In peak season, when minibuses get booked up way in advance, if you're travelling light you can go all the way to Kep or Kampot on the back of a *xe om* (motorbike taxi) – Oasis

ical jungle, Phu Quoc rapidly morphed from a sleepy island backwater to a must-visit beach escape for Western expats and sun-seeking tourists. Beyond the resorts lining Long Beach and development beginning on the east coast, there's still ample room for exploration and escaping. Dive the reefs, kayak in the bays, eat up the back-road kilometres on a motorbike, or just lounge on the beach, indulge in a massage and dine on fresh seafood.

Phu Quoc is not really part of the Mekong Delta and doesn't share the delta's extraordinary ability to produce rice. The most valuable crop is black pepper, but the islanders here have traditionally earned their living from the sea. Phu Quoc is also famed across Vietnam for its production of high-quality fish sauce *(nuoc mam).*

Sights

Duong Dong — VILLAGE

The island's main town and chief fishing port on the central west coast is a tangle of budget hotels catering to domestic tourists, streetside stalls, bars and shops. The old bridge in town is a great vantage point to photograph the island's scruffy fishing fleet crammed into the narrow channel, and the filthy, bustling produce market makes for an interesting stroll.

Long Beach — BEACH

(Bai Truong) Long Beach is draped invitingly along the west coast from Duong Dong almost to An Thoi port. Development concentrates in the north near Duong Dong, where the recliners and rattan umbrellas of the various resorts rule; these are the only stretches that are kept garbage-free. With its west-facing aspect, sunsets can be stupendous.

A motorbike or bicycle is necessary to reach some of the remote stretches flung out towards the southern end of the island.

Sao Beach — BEACH

(Bai Sao) With picture-perfect white sand, the delightful curve of beautiful Sao Beach bends out alongside a sea of mineral-water clarity just a few kilometres from An Thoi, the main shipping port at the southern tip of the island. There are a couple of beachfront restaurants, where you can settle into a deckchair or partake in water sports. If heading down to Sao Beach by motorbike, fill up with petrol before the trip.

Phu Quoc National Park — NATURE RESERVE

About 90% of Phu Quoc is forested and the trees and adjoining marine environment enjoy official protection. This is the last large stand of forest in the south, and in 2010 the park was declared a Unesco Biosphere Reserve. The forest is densest in northern Phu Quoc, in the Khu Rung Nguyen Sinh forest reserve; you'll need a motorbike or mountain bike to tackle the bumpy dirt roads that cut through it. There are no real hiking trails.

Bar (p157) can recommend reputable motorbike drivers. If you make an independent arrangement with a *xe om* driver, do not hand over the money until you reach your destination, or else you risk being abandoned at the border.

Moving on It's possible to take a local bus to the border and then wait for a local bus on the Cambodian side, but since tourist minibuses cost only slightly more and are far comfier, most travellers opt for a through minibus ticket.

Chau Doc to Phnom Penh

Getting to the border Eclipsed by the newer Xa Xia crossing, the **Tinh Bien/Phnom Den border crossing** is less convenient for Phnom Penh–bound travellers, but may be of interest for those who savour the challenge of obscure border crossings. A bus to Phnom Penh (US$25, five to six hours) passes through Chau Doc en route from Can Tho at around 7.30am and can be booked through **My Way Travel** (84 90 201 1200; www.mekongvietnam.com; 14 Đ Nguyen Huu Canh; 8am-8pm) in Chau Doc; double-check the pick-up point. The roads leading to the border have improved but are still bumpy.

Moving on Most travellers opt for a through bus ticket from Chau Doc.

Dai Beach BEACH
(Bai Dai) A relatively isolated northern beach that retains its remote tropical charm.

Thom Beach BEACH
(Bai Thom) The road from Dai Beach to Thom Beach via Ganh Dau is very beautiful, passing through dense forest with tantalising glimpses of the coast below.

Fish Sauce Factory FACTORY
(www.hungthanhfishsauce.com.vn; Duong Dong; 8-11am & 1-5pm) FREE The distillery of Nuoc Mam Hung Thanh is the largest of Phu Quoc's fish-sauce makers, a short walk from the market in Duong Dong. At first glance, the giant wooden vats may make you think you've arrived for a wine tasting, but one sniff of the festering *nuoc mam* essence jolts you back to reality. Take a guide along unless you speak Vietnamese.

Activities

There's plenty of underwater action around Phu Quoc, but only during the dry months (from November to May). Two fun dives cost from US$70 to US$90 depending on the location and operator; four-day PADI Open Water courses hover between US$340 and US$380; snorkelling trips are US$30 to US$35.

Flipper Diving Club DIVING
(077-399 4924; www.flipperdiving.com; 60 Đ Tran Hung Dao; 7am-7pm) Centrally located, multilingual PADI dive centre for everything from novice dive trips to full instructor courses. Very professional, with plenty of diving experience worldwide, and with instructors who put you at ease if you're a newbie.

Rainbow Divers DIVING, SNORKELLING
(0913 400 964; www.divevietnam.com; 11 Đ Tran Hung Dao; 9am-6pm) This reputable PADI outfit was the first to set up shop on the island and offers a wide range of diving and snorkelling trips. As well as the walk-in office, it's well represented at resorts on Long Beach. Some of the equipment is worn and could use replacing.

Tours

Jerry's Jungle Tours BOAT TOUR, HIKING
(0938 226 021; www.jerrystours.wixsite.com/jerrystours; 112 Đ Tran Hung Dao; day trips from US$30) Archipelago explorations by boat, snorkelling, fishing, one-day and multiday trips to islands, motorbike tours, bouldering, birdwatching, hiking and cultural tours around Phu Quoc.

John's Tours BOATING
(0918 939 111; www.johnsislandtours.com; 4 Đ Tran Hung Dao; tour per person US$12-40) Well represented at hotels and resorts; cruises include snorkelling, island-hopping, sunrise fishing and squid-fishing trips.

Anh Tu's Tours BOATING
(0913 820 714; anhtupq@yahoo.com) Snorkelling, squid fishing, island tours, plus motorbike rental.

Sleeping

Accommodation prices on Phu Quoc yo-yo depending on the season and visitor numbers. You'll get less for your money than you'd expect for the price. Bookings are crucial for the December-to-January peak season.

Duong Dong

Sea Breeze HOTEL $
(Gio Bien; 077-399 4920; www.seabreezephuquoc.com; 62a Đ Tran Hung Dao; r fan from US$15, air-con US$25-40;) This curvaceous hotel has clean, modern and attractive rooms; accommodation roadside is noisier. Rooms can get very bright in the morning – fine for early risers, not for late sleepers.

Long Beach

★**Langchia Hostel** HOSTEL $
(0939 132 613; www.langchia-village.com; 84 Đ Tran Hung Dao; dm/d US$7/30;) A favourite with solo travellers, this hostel gets plenty of praise for the friendliness and helpfulness of its staff, the lively bar with pool table and the swimming pool to cool down in. Dorm beds come with mozzie nets and individual fans and it's worth paying extra for the decent breakfast.

Son Vinh Guesthouse GUESTHOUSE $
(0967 000 525; 113 Đ Tran Hung Dao, Duong Dong; r US$22-25) It's the combination of a garden, free airport transfer, being a short stroll to Long Beach and friendly staff that make Son Vinh Guesthouse a good budget option. Pity about its hard beds and shabby decor.

Sunshine Bungalow HOTEL $$
(www.sunshinephuquoc.com; Đ Tran Hung Dao; bungalows US$48-60;) Friendly place run by a Vietnamese family, just 80m from the sea and sand. Light, bright, large rooms nestle amid lush vegetation and the owners do their best to help. Some English and German spoken.

Lan Anh Garden Resort RESORT $$
(077-398 5985; www.lananhphuquoc.com.vn; KP7 Tran Hung Dao; d US$45-64, f US$96;) Enticing little resort hotel with friendly, professional staff, a clutch of rooms arranged around a small pool and motorbikes for rent. Nab an upstairs room if you can for the breezy verandahs. Book on its website for discounted rates.

Lien Hiep Thanh Hotel HOTEL $$
(0934 995 882; www.lienhiepthanhresort.com; 118/12 Đ Tran Hung Dao; r US$42-73;) This friendly place has well-maintained rooms and bungalows amid trees, right on the beach. Splurge on a beachfront bungalow if you can. The downside? The beach is not the cleanest and the restaurant is only so so.

★**La Veranda** RESORT $$$
(077-398 2988; www.laverandaresort.com; 118/9 Đ Tran Hung Dao; r US$250-434, villas US$422-595;) Shaded by palms, this is the most elegant place to stay on the island, designed in colonial style and small enough to remain intimate. There's an appealing pool with a kiddies' area, a stylish spa and all rooms feature designer bathrooms. The beach is pristine and dining options include a cafe on the lawn and the **Pepper Tree Restaurant** (meals 250,000-700,000d; 6am-11pm;) upstairs.

Around the Island

★**Bamboo Cottages & Restaurant** RESORT $$
(077-281 0345; www.bamboophuquoc.com; r US$95-130;) Run by a friendly family with a coterie of cheeky dogs, Bamboo Cottages has Vung Bau Beach largely to itself. The focal point is an open-sided restaurant and bar, right by the beach. Set around the lawns, the attractive, lemon-coloured villas have private, open-roofed bathrooms with solar-powered hot water. The family supports an education scholarship for local kids in need.

Guests get timed, free use of kayaks, snorkels and bicycles.

Freedomland HOMESTAY $$
(077-399 4891; www.freedomlandphuquoc.com; 2 Ap Ong Lang, Xa Cua Duong; bungalows US$50-120; Oct-Jun;) With an emphasis on switching off (no TV) and socialising – fun, communal dinners are a mainstay – Freedomland has 11 basic bungalows (mosquito nets, fans, solar-heated showers) scattered around a shady plot. The beach is a five-minute walk away, or you can slump in the hammocks strung between the trees. Popular with solo travellers; call ahead. Shut in the rainy season.

★**Chen Sea Resort & Spa** RESORT $$$
(077-399 5895; www.centarahotelsresorts.com; villas US$224-497;) Tranquil and chilled-out Chen Sea has lovely villas with sunken baths, some with hot tubs, and deep

verandahs, designed to resemble ancient terracotta-roofed houses. The large azure rectangle of the infinity pool faces the resort's beautiful sandy beach. The isolation is mitigated by plenty of activities on hand: cycling, kayaking, catamaran outings, in-spa pampering and dining in the open-sided restaurant.

Eating

Duong Dong

Dinh Cau Night Market VIETNAMESE $
(Đ Vo Thi Sau; meals from 70,000d; 5pm-midnight;) The most atmospheric place to dine on the island, Duong Dong's night market has around a dozen stalls serving a delicious range of Vietnamese seafood, grills and vegetarian options. It's geared towards tourists and quality can be a mixed bag, so look for a local crowd, as they are a discerning bunch.

Buddy Ice Cream INTERNATIONAL $$
(6 Đ Bach Dang; meals 80,000-180,000d; 8am-10pm;) With the coolest music in town, this cafe is excellent for sides of tourist info with its New Zealand ice-cream combos, toasted sandwiches, fish 'n' chips, thirst-busting fruit juices, shakes, smoothies, all-day breakfasts, comfy sofas and book exchange.

Long Beach

Heaven Restaurant VIETNAMESE $
(0975 542 769; 135 Đ Tran Hung Dao; meals 30,000-130,000d; 8am-11pm;) You may not expect heaven to have plastic chairs but it does at this good-value family joint. Fresh, generous servings of Vietnamese dishes such as lemongrass chicken, and a very long list of vegetarian options, is paradise for every taste.

Winston's Burgers & Beer BURGERS $
(0126 390 1093; 121 Đ Tran Hung Dao; burgers from 70,000d; 1-10pm) The name says it all: this bar is all about (really good) burgers, beer and a large selection of cocktails, mixed by the eponymous Winston. Linger for a chat or challenge your drinking companions to a game of Connect 4. It has few vegetarian options.

Alanis Deli CAFE $
(077-399 4931; 98 Đ Tran Hung Dao; pancakes from 80,000d; 8am-10.30pm;) Fab caramel pancakes, American breakfast combos, plus good (if pricey) coffees and wonderfully friendly service.

★ **Mango Bay Restaurant** INTERNATIONAL $$
(077-398 1693; Mango Bay Resort, Ong Lang Beach; meals 210,000-330,000d; 7am-9pm;) One of the best eating experiences around is to sit on the deck at Mango Bay, dining on tamarind blue-swimmer crab and peering out to sea. There are Australian beef steaks, honey duck breast and lots of Thai flavours too. The calm atmosphere and bar with a good drinks list add to the pleasure.

★ **Nha Ghe Phu Quoc Crab House** SEAFOOD $$
(077-384 5067; 21 Đ Tran Hung Dao; meals 200,000-780,000d; 11am-10pm;) At this crustacean sensation you won't be crabby once you get your claws into the likes of soft-shell crab with green-peppercorn salsa, *com ghe* (jasmine rice with crab meat and fish sauce) or Cajun-style blue crab. Extra-hungry? Don't be shellfish and share the mega squid-crab-shrimp-sausage combo with your nearest and dearest.

★ **Spice House at Cassia Cottage** VIETNAMESE $$
(www.cassiacottage.com; 100c Đ Tran Hung Dao; meals 190,000-300,000d; 7-10am & 11am-10pm) Nab a beachside high table, order a papaya salad, grilled garlic prawns, cinnamon-infused okra, a delectable fish curry or grilled beef skewers wrapped in betel leaves and time dinner to catch the sunset at this excellent restaurant.

Drinking & Nightlife

★ **Le Bar** BAR
(118/9 Đ Tran Hung Dao; 6am-11pm;) With its gorgeous tiled floor, art deco furniture and colonial charms, this highly elegant and well-poised upstairs lounge-bar at La Veranda is a superb spot for a terrace sundowner.

Coco Bar BAR
(118 Đ Tran Hung Dao; 10am-late) With chairs and music spilling on to the pavement, Coco is a great place for a roadside bevvy and chat with the mix of travelling folk, Gallic wayfarers, local drinkers and passing pool sharks.

Information

There are ATMs in Duong Dong and in many resorts on Long Beach.

Getting There & Away

AIR

Phu Quoc International Airport (www.phuquocairport.com) The airport is 10km southeast of Duong Dong.

Vietnam Airlines (☎077-399 6677; www.vietnamairlines.com; 122 Đ Nguyen Trung Truc) Flies to/from Rach Gia (from 500,000d, daily), Can Tho (from 500,000d, daily) and Ho Chi Minh City (from 450,000d, 10 daily).

BOAT

Fast boats connect Phu Quoc to both Ha Tien (1½ hours) and Rach Gia (2½ hours). Phu Quoc travel agents have the most up-to-date schedules and can book tickets. Five virtually identical operators, including Duong Dong Express and Superdong, run fast boats from Rach Gia to Phu Quoc's Bai Vong on the east coast, most departing at 8am and making the return journey at 1pm (350,000d).

From Ha Tien, two car ferries run to Phu Quoc's Da Chong port, in the northeast part of the island. They depart daily at 8am and 8.20am from Ha Tien and 1pm from Phu Quoc (185,000/80,000/700,000d per passenger/motorbike/car). Two more car ferries are due to be added to meet demand.

Bai Vong Ferry Terminal (Pha Bai Vong) Ferries to Rach Gia and Ha Tien.

Duong Dong Express (☎Phu Quoc 077-399 0747, Rach Gia 077-387 9765) A hydrofoil company, it has an office by the dock in Rach Gia and in Duong Dong. Most travel agents can book your passage for the same fare.

Superdong (Ha Tien) (☎077-395 5933; www.superdong.com.vn; 10 Đ 30/4; per passenger 230,000d) Fast ferry from Ha Tien departs at 7.30am, 8am and 1.15pm (1½ hours), returning from Phu Quoc at 8.30am, 9.45am and 1pm.

Getting Around

Agree on a price for a *xe om* before setting off. For short rides, 20,000d should be sufficient. Otherwise, figure on around 60,000d for about 5km. From Duong Dong to Bai Vong costs about 70,000d.

Motorbikes can be hired from most hotels and bungalows for around 120,000d (semiautomatic) to 150,000d (automatic) per day. Inspect cheaper bikes thoroughly before setting out.

A good paved road now runs south from Duong Dong to An Thoi, the southern tip of the island, and north as far as Cape Ganh Dau, the northwest tip of Phu Quoc. A two-lane highway connects Duong Dong with the car-ferry port, but other roads tend to be dirt and gravel, potholed and bumpy – a bicycle nightmare. **Mai Linh** (☎077-397 9797) is a reliable taxi company.

UNDERSTAND VIETNAM

Vietnam Today

A period of rising, sustained growth has transformed Vietnam. Change is most apparent in the big cities, where steel-and glass high-rises define skylines and a burgeoning middle class now has the spending power to enjoy air-conditioned living and overseas travel. Yet, in rural areas the nation's newfound prosperity is less evident, and up the highlands, life remains a day-to-day struggle for millions of minority people.

The Big Picture

In the forty-odd years since the end of the American War, Vietnam has made giant strides. A victorious, though bankrupt, nation has worked around the clock, grafting its way forward, overcoming a series of formidable hurdles (including a 19-year US trade embargo). Per-capita income has grown from US$98 in 1993 to more than US$2000 by 2015, and today Vietnam is one of the 10 fastest-growing economies in the world, boosted by strong manufacturing. Start-up business numbers are booming. And yet this rapid development is disjointed. The state sector remains huge, controlling around two-fifths of the economy – 100 of the 200 biggest Vietnamese companies are state-owned (including oil production, shipbuilding, cement and coal).

The spectre of corruption casts a shadow over development every step of the way. Transparency International ranked Vietnam the lowest of all the Asia-Pacific countries it measured in 2014. Corruption scandals emerge on a daily basis, such as the nine Vinashin shipbuilding execs jailed following the company's near collapse under US$4.5 billion of debt. For most Vietnamese people corruption is simply a part of day-to-day life, as they have to pay backhanders for everything from securing a civil-service job to an internet connection.

Tourism Woes: a Blip or a Trend?

Recently the Vietnamese government did what its tourism industry had been urging it to do for years – it (partially) relaxed visa regulations, allowing easier access to the country for several European nationalities. E-visas are being implemented, making things less daunting for more nationalities. After years of exponential growth, tourist arrivals were on the slide, with a knock-on effect for the nation's important service sector. Further visa reforms may or may not boost tourism. The reasons for the downturn, and whether it's a blip or a long-term trend, are complex. Falling visitor numbers from Russia (due to the collapse of the rouble) and China (due to political tensions) were particularly evident.

As tourism chiefs pondered the stats, an EU-funded study found that just 6% of tourists surveyed said they would want to return to Vietnam, provoking a barrage of newspaper headlines. The clearly alarmed Vietnam Tourism authority quickly ordered a countersurvey (which suggested higher approval ratings). But an underlying message was clear: overseas visitors considered road transport dangerous and the nation's infrastructure poor, felt hassled by street vendors and overcharged by shopkeepers, and were frustrated by the lack of reliable travel information. There's clearly work to be done, not least by Vietnam Tourism, which critics allege is far too concerned with pedalling tours for profit than dispensing independent advice to travellers.

Uneasy Neighbours

On the surface, Vietnam and its northern neighbour China have much in common, with a shared heritage, common frontier and all-powerful ruling Communist parties. But for the Vietnamese, China represents something of an overbearing big brother (and 1000 years of subordination). The nations fought a recent on-off border war that rumbled on for years, only ending in 1990, and there are concerns that another conflict could erupt over offshore islands in the South China Sea (always the 'East Sea' in Vietnam). China claims virtually the whole area, and is busy constructing port facilities and airstrips. In May 2014, anti-Chinese riots erupted in several provinces, resulting in at least 21 deaths, in response to China deploying an oil rig in the Paracel Islands. Thousands of Chinese nationals fled the country. By November 2015 tensions remained, but the situation had calmed enough for China's President Xi Jinping to visit Hanoi as the countries sought to repair ties.

The two nations have plenty of mutual ground. Trade has continued to boom, (though more one-way than the Vietnamese would like), reaching US$58 billion in 2014 and Chinese is the second-most popular foreign language studied in Vietnam. Ultimately, Presidents Trong and Xi signed various cooperation agreements concerning investment and infrastructure but little progress was evident over territorial disputes.

History

The Vietnamese trace their roots back to the Red River Delta where farmers first cultivated rice. Millenniums of struggle against the Chinese then followed. Vietnam only became a united state in the 19th century, but quickly faced the ignominy of French colonialism and then the devastation of the American intervention. The Vietnamese nation has survived tempestuous, troubled times, but its strength of character has served it well. Today, the signs are it's continuing to grow with some promise.

Early Vietnam

From the 1st to 6th centuries AD, southern Vietnam was part of the Indianised Cambodian kingdom of Funan, famous for its refined art and architecture. Based around the walled city of Angkor Borei, it was probably a grouping of feudal states rather than a unified empire. The people of Funan constructed an elaborate system of canals both for transportation and the irrigation of rice. Funan's principal port city was Oc-Eo in the Mekong Delta, and archaeological excavations here suggest there was contact with China, Indonesia, Persia and even the Mediterranean. Later on, the Chenla empire replaced the Funan kingdom, spreading along the Mekong River.

The Hindu kingdom of Champa emerged around present-day Danang in the late 2nd century AD. Like Funan, it adopted Sanskrit as a sacred language and borrowed heavily from Indian art and culture. By the 8th century, Champa had expanded southward to include what is now Nha Trang and Phan Rang. The Cham were a feisty bunch who conducted raids along the entire coast of Indochina, and thus found themselves in a perpetual state of war with the Vietnamese to the north and the Khmers to the south. Ultimately this cost them their kingdom, as they found themselves squeezed between these two great powers.

Chinese Occupation

The Chinese conquered the Red River Delta in the 2nd century BC. Over the following centuries, large numbers of Chinese settlers, officials and scholars moved south, seeking to impress a centralised state system on the Vietnamese.

In the most famous act of resistance, in AD 40, the Trung Sisters (Hai Ba Trung) rallied the people, raised an army and led a revolt against the Chinese. The Chinese counterattacked, but, rather than surrender, the Trung Sisters threw themselves into the Hat Giang River. There were numerous small-scale rebellions against Chinese rule – which was characterised by tyranny, forced labour and insatiable demands for tribute – from the 3rd to 6th centuries, but all were defeated.

However, the early Vietnamese learned much from the Chinese, including the advancement of dykes and irrigation works for rice cultivation, Confucianism, Taoism and Mahayana Buddhism. Monks carried with them the scientific and medical knowledge of these two great civilisations and Vietnam was soon producing its own doctors, botanists and scholars.

In 1418, wealthy philanthropist Le Loi sparked the Lam Son Uprising by refusing to serve as an official for the Chinese Ming dynasty. By 1425, local rebellions had erupted in several regions and Le Loi travelled the countryside to rally the people, and eventually defeat the Chinese, ending their one-thousand-year occupation.

Portuguese Catholics

The first Portuguese sailors came ashore at Danang in 1516 and were soon followed by a party of Dominican missionaries. For decades the Portuguese traded with Vietnam, setting up a commercial colony alongside those of the Japanese and Chinese at Faifo (present-day Hoi An). With the exception of the Philippines, the Catholic Church has had a greater impact on Vietnam than on any country in Asia.

French Occupation

France's military activity in Vietnam began in 1847, when the French Navy attacked Danang harbour in response to Emperor Thieu Tri's imprisonment of Catholic missionaries. Saigon was seized in early 1859 and, in 1862, Emperor Tu Duc signed a treaty that gave the French the three eastern provinces of Cochinchina (the southern part of Vietnam during the French-colonial era).

By 1883 the French had imposed a Treaty of Protectorate on Vietnam. French rule often proved cruel and arbitrary. Ultimately, the most successful resistance came from the Communists, first organised by Ho Chi Minh in 1925.

The French-colonial authorities carried out ambitious public works, such as the construction of the Saigon–Hanoi railway and draining of the Mekong Delta swamps. These projects were funded by heavy government taxes and workers on abysmal wages under appalling treatment.

During WWII, the only group that significantly resisted the Japanese occupation was the Communist-dominated Viet Minh. When WWII ended, Ho Chi Minh – whose Viet Minh forces already controlled large parts of the country – declared Vietnam independent. French efforts to reassert control soon led to violent confrontations and full-scale war. In May 1954, Viet Minh forces overran the French garrison at Dien Bien Phu. The Geneva Accords of mid-1954 provided for a temporary division of Vietnam at the Ben Hai River. When Ngo Dinh Diem, the anti-Communist Catholic leader of the southern zone, refused to hold the 1956 elections, the Ben Hai line became the border between North and South Vietnam.

The American War

Around 1960, the Hanoi government changed its policy of opposition to the Diem regime from one of 'political struggle' to one of 'armed struggle'. The National Liberation Front (NLF), a Communist guerrilla group better known as the Viet Cong (VC), was founded to fight against Diem.

An unpopular ruler, Diem was assassinated in 1963 by his own troops. When the Hanoi government ordered North Vietnamese Army (NVA) units to infiltrate the South in 1964, the situation for the Saigon regime became desperate. In 1965 the USA committed its first combat troops, soon joined by soldiers from South Korea, Australia, Thailand and New Zealand in an effort to bring global legitimacy to the conflict. The USA had been waiting, and as early as 1954, US military aid to the French topped US$2 billion.

As Vietnam celebrated the Lunar New Year in 1968, the VC launched a surprise attack, known as the Tet Offensive, marking a crucial turning point in the war. Many Americans, who had for years believed their government's insistence that the USA was winning, started demanding a negotiated end to the war. The Paris Agreements, signed in 1973, provided for a ceasefire, the total withdrawal of US combat forces and the release of American prisoners of war.

Reunification

Saigon surrendered to the NVA on 30 April 1975; the same day, the Communists changed Saigon's name to Ho Chi Minh City (HCMC). Vietnam's reunification by the Communists meant liberation from more than a century of colonial oppression, but it was soon followed by large-scale internal repression. Hundreds of thousands of southerners fled Vietnam, creating a flood of refugees for the next 15 years. Vietnam's campaign of repression against the ethnic Chinese, plus its invasion of Cambodia at the end of 1978, prompted China to attack Vietnam in 1979. The war lasted only 17 days, but Chinese-Vietnamese mistrust lasted for well over a decade.

Post–Cold War

After the collapse of the Soviet Union in 1991, Vietnam and Western nations sought rapprochement. The 1990s brought foreign investment and Association of Southeast Asian Nations (Asean) membership. The US established diplomatic relations with Vietnam in 1995, and in 2000 Bill Clinton became the first US president to visit north Vietnam. George W Bush followed suit in 2006, as Vietnam was welcomed into the World Trade Organization (WTO) in 2007; and then Barack Obama in 2016. Relations have also greatly improved with the historic enemy, China, barring tensions over the South China Sea. China may still secretly think of Vietnam as 'the one that got away', but Vietnam's economic boom has caught Beijing's attention and trade and tourism are booming across mutual borders.

People & Culture

People

The Vietnamese are battle-hardened, proud and nationalist, as they have earned their stripes in successive skirmishes with the world's mightiest powers. But that's the older generation, which remembers every centimetre of the territory for which it fought. For the new generation, Vietnam is a place to succeed, a place to ignore the staid structures set in stone by the Communists, and a place to go out and have some fun.

As in other parts of Asia, life revolves around the family; there are often several generations living under one roof. Poverty, and the transition from a largely agricultural society to that of a more industrialised nation, is changing the structure of the modern family unit as more people head to the bigger cities to seek their fortune. Today more women are delaying marriage to get an education: around 50% of university students are female and women make up 52% of the nation's workforce, but are not well represented in positions of power.

Vietnam's population is 84% ethnic Vietnamese (Kinh) and 2% ethnic Chinese; the rest is made up of Khmers, Chams and members of more than 50 minority peoples, who mainly live in highland areas. Prejudices against hill-tribe people endure. Attitudes are changing slowly but the Vietnamese media can still present them as primitive and exotic.

Religion

Over the centuries, Confucianism, Taoism and Buddhism have fused with popular Chinese beliefs and ancient Vietnamese animism to form what's collectively known as the Triple Religion (Tam Giao). Most Vietnamese people identify with this belief system but, if asked, they'll usually say they're Buddhist. Vietnam also has a significant percentage of Catholics (8% to 10% of the total population).

The unique and colourful Vietnamese sect Cao Daism was founded in the 1920s. It combines secular and religious philosophies of the East and West, and is based on seance messages revealed to the group's founder, Ngo Minh Chieu.

There are also small numbers of Muslims (around 60,000) and Hindus (50,000).

Arts

CONTEMPORARY ART

It is possible to catch modern dance, classical ballet and stage plays in Hanoi and Ho Chi Minh City.

The work of contemporary painters and photographers covers a wide swath of styles and gives a glimpse into the modern Vietnamese psyche.

Youth culture is most vibrant in Ho Chi Minh City, where there is more freedom for musicians and artists. There are small hip-hop, rock, punk, reggae and DJ scenes. Hot bands include rock band Microwave, metal merchants Black Infinity, the punk band Giao Chi and alt-roots band 6789. Skank The Tank and Sub Elements are two leading reggae sound systems based in Hanoi.

ARCHITECTURE

The Vietnamese were not great builders like their neighbours the Khmer. Most early Vietnamese buildings were made of wood and other materials that proved highly vulnerable in the tropical climate. The grand exceptions are the stunning towers built by Vietnam's ancient Cham culture. These are most numerous in central Vietnam. The Cham ruins at My Son are a major draw.

LITERATURE

Contemporary writers include Nguyen Huy Thiep, who articulates the experiences of Vietnamese people in *The General Retires and Other Stories*, while Duong Van Mai Elliot's memoir, *The Sacred Willow: Four Generations in the Life of a Vietnamese Family*, was nominated for a Pulitzer Prize.

Other books include Graham Greene's classic account of Vietnam in the 1950s as the French empire is collapsing, *The Quiet American*; *The Sorrow of War* by Bao Ninh – a poignant tale told from the North Vietnamese perspective; *Shadows and Wind* by Robert Templer; a biographical tale of a Vietnamese-American by Andrew X Pham in *Catfish & Mandala* and *Vietnam: Rising Dragon* by Bill Hayton for a candid assessment of the nation today.

SCULPTURE

Vietnamese sculpture has traditionally centred on religious themes and has functioned as an adjunct to architecture, especially that of pagodas, temples and tombs. The Cham civilisation produced exquisite carved sandstone figures for its Hindu and Buddhist sanctuaries. The largest single collection of Cham sculpture is at the Museum of Cham Sculpture in Danang.

WATER PUPPETRY

Vietnam's ancient art of *roi nuoc* (water puppetry) originated in northern Vietnam at least a thousand years ago. Developed by rice farmers, the wooden puppets were manipulated by puppeteers using water-flooded rice paddies as their stage. Hanoi is the best place to see water-puppetry performances, which are accompanied by music played on traditional instruments.

Food & Drink

Fruit

Aside from the usual delightful Southeast Asian fruits, Vietnam has its own unique *trai thang long* (green dragon fruit), a bright fuchsia-coloured fruit with green scales. Grown mainly along the coastal region near Nha Trang, it has white flesh flecked with edible black seeds, and tastes something like a mild kiwi fruit.

Meals

Pho is the noodle soup that built a nation and is eaten at all hours of the day, but especially for breakfast. *Com* are rice dishes. You'll see signs saying *pho* and *com* everywhere. Other noodle soups to try are *bun bo Hue* (combining beef vermicelli and lemongrass) and *hu tieu* (vermicelli soup garnished with fresh and dried seafood, pork chicken, offal and fresh herbs).

Spring rolls (*nem* in the north, *cha gio* in the south) are a speciality. These are normally dipped in *nuoc mam* (fish sauce), though many foreigners prefer soy sauce (*xi dau* in the north, *nuoc tuong* in the south).

Because Buddhist monks of the Mahayana tradition are strict vegetarians, *an chay* (vegetarian cooking) is an integral part of Vietnamese cuisine.

Snacks

Street stalls or roaming vendors are everywhere, selling steamed sweet potatoes, rice porridge and ice-cream bars even in the wee hours.

There are also many other Vietnamese nibbles to try:

Bap xao Made from fresh, stir-fried corn, chillies and tiny shrimp.

Bo bia Nearly microscopic shrimp, fresh lettuce and thin slices of Vietnamese sausage rolled up in rice paper and dipped in a spicy-sweet peanut sauce.

Sinh to Shakes made with milk and sugar or yoghurt, and fresh tropical fruit.

Sweets

Many sticky confections are made from sticky rice, like *banh it nhan dau*, made with sugar and bean paste and sold wrapped in banana leaf.

Most foreigners prefer *kem* (ice cream) or *yaourt* (yoghurt), which is generally of good quality.

Try *che*, a cold, refreshing sweet soup made with sweetened beans (black or green) or corn. It's served in a glass with ice and sweet coconut cream on top.

Drink

ALCOHOLIC DRINKS

Memorise the words *bia hoi*, which mean 'draught beer' – it's probably the cheapest beer in the world. Starting at around 5000d a glass, anyone can afford a round. Places that serve *bia hoi* usually also serve cheap food.

Several foreign labels brewed in Vietnam under licence include Tiger, Carlsberg and Heineken. National and regional brands include Halida and Hanoi in the north, Huda and Larue in the centre, and BGI and 333 (*ba ba ba*) in the south of the country.

Wine and spirits are available but at higher prices. Local brews are cheaper but not always drinkable.

NONALCOHOLIC DRINKS

Whatever you drink, make sure that it's been boiled or bottled. Ice is generally safe on the tourist trail, but not guaranteed elsewhere.

Vietnamese *ca phe* (coffee) is fine stuff and there is no shortage of cafes in which to sample it.

Foreign soft drinks are widely available in Vietnam. An excellent local treat is *soda chanh* (carbonated mineral water with lemon and sugar) or *nuoc chanh nong* (hot, sweetened lemon juice).

Environment

Environmental consciousness is low in Vietnam. Rapid industrialisation, deforestation and pollution are major problems facing the country.

Unsustainable logging and farming practices, as well as the extensive spraying of defoliants by the US during the American War, have contributed to deforestation. This has resulted not only in significant loss of biological diversity, but also in a harder existence for many minority people.

The country's rapid economic and population growth duirng the past decade – demonstrated by the dramatic increase in industrial production, motorbike numbers and construction – has put additional pressure on the already stressed environment.

The Land

Vietnam stretches more than 1600km along the east coast of the Indochinese peninsula. The country's land area is 329,566 sq km, making it slightly larger than Italy and a bit smaller than Japan.

As the Vietnamese are quick to point out, it resembles a *don ganh* – the ubiquitous bamboo pole with a basket of rice slung from each end. The baskets represent the main rice-growing regions of the Red River Delta in the north and the Mekong Delta in the south.

Of several interesting geological features found in Vietnam, the most striking are its spectacular karst formations (limestone peaks with caves and underground streams). The northern half of Vietnam has a spectacular array of karst areas, particularly around Halong Bay, Tam Coc and Phong Nha.

Wildlife

We'll start with the good news. Despite some disastrous bouts of deforestation, Vietnam's flora and fauna is still incredibly exotic and varied. Intensive surveys by the World Wildlife Fund along the Mekong River (including the Vietnamese section) found a total of 1068 new species from 1997 to 2007, placing this area on Conservation International's list of the top five biodiversity hot spots in the world. Numerous areas inside Vietnam remain unsurveyed or poorly known, and many more species are likely to be found.

The other side of the story is that despite this outstanding diversity, the threat to Vietnam's remaining wildlife has never been greater due to poaching, hunting and habitat loss. Three of the nation's iconic animals

– the elephant, saola and tiger – are on the brink. It's virtually certain that the last wild Vietnamese rhino was killed inside Cat Tien National Park in 2010.

And for every trophy animal there are hundreds of other less 'headline' species that are being cleared from forests and reserves for the sake of profit (or hunger). Many of the hunters responsible are from poor minority groups who have traditionally relied on the jungle for their survival.

National Parks

There are 31 national parks, covering about 3% of Vietnam's total territory. In the north, the most interesting and accessible include Cat Ba, Bai Tu Long, Ba Be and Cuc Phuong.

Heading south, Phong Nha-Ke Bang, Bach Ma, Yok Don and Cat Tien are well worth investigating.

SURVIVAL GUIDE

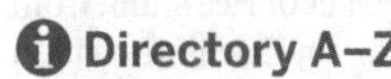

Directory A–Z

ACCOMMODATION

Accommodation in Vietnam is superb value for money. Big cities and the main tourism centres have everything from hostel dorm beds to luxe hotels. In the countryside and provincial towns, there's less choice; you'll usually be deciding between guesthouses and midrange hotels.

Cleanliness standards are generally good and there are very few real dumps – even remote rural areas have some excellent budget places. Communication can often be an issue (particularly off the beaten path where few staff speak English), but it's usually possible to reach an understanding. Perhaps because of this, service standards in Vietnam can be a little haphazard.

Prices are quoted in dong or US dollars based on the preferred currency of the particular property; some charge a percentage fee for paying by card rather than cash. Most rooms fall into a budget price category and dorm-bed prices are given individually. Discounts are often available at quiet times of year. Some hotels (particularly those on the coast) raise their prices in the main tourist season (July and August) and for public holidays.

Passports are almost always requested on arrival at a hotel. It is not absolutely essential to hand over your passport, but at the very least you need to provide a photocopy of the passport details and visa.

Homestays

Homestays are a popular option in parts of Vietnam. As the government imposes strict rules about registering foreigners who stay overnight, all places have to be officially licensed.

Areas that are well set up include the Mekong Delta, the White Thai villages of Mai Chau, Ba Be and the Cham Islands.

Some specialist tour companies and motorbike touring companies have developed excellent relations with remote villages and offer homestays as part of their trips.

Sleeping Price Ranges

The following price ranges refer to a double room with bathroom in high season. Unless otherwise stated, tax is included, but breakfast excluded, from the price.

$ less than US$25 (560,000d)

$$ US$25 (560,000d) to US$75 (1,680,000d)

$$$ more than US$75 (1,680,000d)

CHILDREN

Children get to have a good time in Vietnam, mainly because of the overwhelming amount of attention they attract and the fact that almost everybody wants to play with them. However, this attention can sometimes be overwhelming, particularly for blonde-haired, blue-eyed babes.

Big cities have plenty to keep kids interested, though in most smaller towns and rural areas boredom may set in from time to time. There are some great beaches, but pay close attention to any playtime in the sea, as there are some big rip tides along the main coastline. Some popular beaches have warning flags and lifeguards, but at quieter beaches parents should test the current first. There are sheltered seas around Phu Quoc Island, but also beaches with choppy waters.

Kids generally enjoy local cuisine, which is rarely too spicy: the range of fruit is staggering and spring rolls usually go down very well. Comfort food from home (pizzas, pasta, burgers and ice cream) is available in most places too.

Pack plenty of high-factor sunscreen before you go as it's not that widely available in Vietnam (and costs more than in many Western countries).

ELECTRICITY

The usual voltage is 220V, 50 cycles, but you'll (very rarely) encounter 110V, also at 50 cycles, just to confuse things. Electrical sockets usually accommodate plugs with two round pins.

EMBASSIES & CONSULATES

Generally speaking, embassies won't be that sympathetic if you end up in jail after committing a crime. In genuine emergencies you might get some assistance, but only if other channels have been exhausted.

If you have your passport stolen, it can take some time to replace it as some embassies in Vietnam do not issue new passports, which have to be sent from a regional embassy.

Australian Embassy (☎04-3774 0100; www.vietnam.embassy.gov.au; 8 Đ Dao Tan, Ba Dinh District, Hanoi)

Australian Consulate (Map p138; ☎08-3521 8100; www.hcmc.vietnam.embassy.gov.au; 20th fl, Đ 47 Ly Tu Truong, Vincom Center, HCMC)

Cambodian Embassy (Map p52; camemb.vnm@mfa.gov.kh; 71a P Tran Hung Dao, Hanoi)

Cambodian Consulate (Map p144; ☎08-3829 2751; camcg.hcm@mfa.gov.kh; 41 Đ Phung Khac Khoan, HCMC)

Canadian Embassy (Map p52; www.canadainternational.gc.ca/vietnam; 31 Đ Hung Vuong, Hanoi)

Canadian Consulate (Map p138; ☎08-3827 9899; hochi@international.gc.ca; 10th fl, 235 Đ Dong Khoi, HCMC)

Chinese Embassy (Map p52; ☎04-8845 3736; http://vn.china-embassy.org/chn; 46 P Hoang Dieu, Hanoi)

Chinese Consulate (Map p144; ☎08-3829 2457; http://hcmc.chineseconsulate.org; 175 Đ Hai Ba Trung, HCMC)

French Embassy (Map p52; ☎04-3944 5700; www.ambafrance-vn.org; P Tran Hung Dao, Hanoi)

French Consulate (Map p144; www.consulfrance-hcm.org; 27 Đ Nguyen Thi Minh Khai, HCMC)

German Embassy (Map p52; ☎04-3845 3836; www.hanoi.diplo.de; 29 Đ Tran Phu, Hanoi)

German Consulate (Map p144; ☎08-3829 1967; www.ho-chi-minh-stadt.diplo.de; 126 Đ Nguyen Dinh Chieu, HCMC)

Japanese Embassy (☎04-3846 3000; www.vn.emb-japan.go.jp; 27 P Lieu Giai, Ba Dinh District, Hanoi)

Japanese Consulate (Map p135; ☎08-3933 3510; www.hcmcgj.vn.emb-japan.go.jp; 261 Đ Dien Bien Phu, HCMC)

Laotian Embassy (Map p52; ☎04-3942 4576; www.embalaohanoi.gov.la; 22 P Tran Binh Trong, Hanoi)

Laotian Consulate (Map p138; ☎08-3829 7667; 93 Đ Pasteur, HCMC)

Netherlands Embassy (Map p56; ☎04-3831-5650; www.hollandinvietnam.org; 7th fl, BIDV Tower, 194 Đ Tran Quang Khai, Hanoi)

Netherlands Consulate (Map p144; ☎08-3823 5932; www.hollandinvietnam.org; Saigon Tower, 29 ĐL Le Duan, HCMC)

New Zealand Embassy (Map p56; ☎04-3824 1481; www.mfat.govt.nz; Level 5, 63 P Ly Thai To, Hanoi)

New Zealand Consulate (Map p138; ☎08-3822 6907; www.mfat.govt.nz/en/countries-and-regions/south-east-asia/viet-nam/new-zealand-embassy/; 8th fl, The Metropolitan, 235 Đ Dong Khoi, HCMC)

Singaporean Embassy (Map p52; ☎04-3848 9168; www.mfa.gov.sg/hanoi; 41-43 Đ Tran Phu, Hanoi)

Thai Embassy (Map p52; ☎04-3823 5092; www.thaiembassy.org; 3-65 P Hoang Dieu, Hanoi)

Thai Consulate (Map p135; ☎08-3932 7637; www.thaiembassy.org/hochiminh; 77 Đ Tran Quoc Thao, HCMC)

UK Embassy (Map p56; ☎04-3936 0500; http://ukinvietnam.fco.gov.uk; 4th fl, Central Bldg, 31 P Hai Ba Trung, Hanoi)

UK Consulate (Map p144; ☎08-3829 8433; consularenquiries.vietnam@fco.gov.uk; 25 ĐL Le Duan, HCMC)

US Embassy (☎04-3850 5000; http://vietnam.usembassy.gov; 7 P Lang Ha, Ba Dinh District, Hanoi)

US Consulate (Map p144; ☎08-3822 9433; http://hochiminh.usconsulate.gov; 4 ĐL Le Duan, HCMC)

FOOD

The following price ranges refer to a typical meal (excluding drinks). Unless otherwise stated, taxes are included in the price.

$ less than US$5 (107,000d)

$$ US$5 (107,000d) to US$15 (323,000d)

$$$ more than US$15 (323,000d)

INSURANCE

Insurance is a must for Vietnam, as the cost of major medical treatment is prohibitive. A travel-insurance policy to cover theft, loss and medical problems is the best bet.

Some insurance policies specifically exclude such 'dangerous activities' as riding motorbikes, diving and even trekking. Check that your policy covers an emergency evacuation in the event of serious injury.

If you're driving a vehicle, you need a Vietnamese insurance policy (p176).

Worldwide travel insurance is available at www.lonelyplanet.com/bookings. You can buy, extend or claim anytime – even if you're already on the road.

LEGAL MATTERS

If you lose something really valuable such as your passport or visa, you'll need to contact the police. Few foreigners experience much hassle from police and demands for bribes are rare – it's a different story for the Vietnamese though...

The Vietnamese government is seriously cracking down on the burgeoning drug trade. You may face imprisonment and/or large fines for drug offences, and drug trafficking can be punishable by death.

LGBTIQ TRAVELLERS

Vietnam is a relatively hassle-free place for gay, lesbian and trans travellers. There are no official laws prohibiting same-sex relationships or same-sex sexual acts in Vietnam, nor is there much in the way of individual harassment.

Hanoi and especially Ho Chi Minh City both have (small) gay nightlife scenes, but there is still plenty of social stigma.

Checking into hotels as a same-sex couple is perfectly acceptable, though be aware that Vietnamese people don't react well to passionate public displays of affection, by heterosexual or nonheterosexual couples.

VietPride (www.vietpride.com) marches have been held in Hanoi and HCMC since 2012. The Hanoi event now takes place over several days in late July/early August and includes film screenings, talks, parties and a bike rally.

In January 2015, a Law on Marriage and Family was passed which officially removes a ban on same-sex marriages. Vietnam now has more progressive governmental policies than many of its Asian neighbours.

Interestingly, the outgoing US ambassador to Vietnam, Ted Osius, is openly gay and often attended official events with his husband and their children. Vietnamese-speaking Osius is seen as an icon by many gay Vietnamese.

Utopia (www.utopia-asia.com) has useful gay travel information and contacts in Vietnam. The gay dating app Grindr is popular in Vietnam.

MAPS

The road atlas *Tap Ban Do Giao Thong Duong Bo Viet Nam* is the best available, but the latest roads are not included. It's available in bookstores including Fahasa (which has shops in HCMC, Hanoi and Danang) and costs 220,000d.

Vietnamese street names are preceded by the words Pho, Duong and Dai Lo; on maps they appear respectively as P, Đ and ĐL.

MONEY

The Vietnamese currency is the dong (abbreviated to 'd'). US dollars are also widely used, though less so in rural areas.

For the last few years the dong has been fairly stable at around 22,000d to the dollar.

Tipping isn't expected, but it's appreciated, especially for tour guides.

ATMs

ATMs are widespread in Vietnam and present in virtually every town in the country. You shouldn't have any problems getting cash with a regular Maestro/Cirrus debit card, or with a Visa or MasterCard debit or credit card. Watch for stiff withdrawal charges (typically 25,000d to 50,000d; Citibank charges no fees to its customers using Citibank ATMs) and limits: most are around 2,000,000d; Agribank allows up to 6,000,000d and Commonwealth Bank up to 10,000,000d.

Bargaining

For *xe om* (motorbike taxi) and *cyclo* (pedicab or bicycle rickshaw) trips, as well as anywhere that prices aren't posted, bargaining is possible. In tourist hot spots, you may be quoted as much as five times the going price, but not everyone is trying to rip you off. In less travelled areas, foreigners are often quoted the Vietnamese price, but you can still bargain a little bit.

Credit & Debit Cards

Visa and MasterCard are accepted in major cities and many tourist centres, but don't expect budget guesthouses or noodle bars to take plastic. Commission charges (around 3%) sometimes apply.

If you wish to obtain a cash advance, this is possible at Vietcombank branches in most cities. Banks generally charge at least a 3% commission for this service.

OPENING HOURS

Lunch is taken very seriously and virtually everything (bar lunch spots) shut down between noon and 1.30pm.

Hours vary very little throughout the year.

Banks 8am to 3pm weekdays, to 11.30am Saturday

Offices and museums 7am or 8am to 5pm or 6pm; museums generally close on Monday and some take a lunch break

Restaurants 11.30am to 9pm

Shops 8am to 6pm

Temples and pagodas 5am to 9pm

PHOTOGRAPHY

Memory cards are pretty cheap in Vietnam, which is fortunate given the visual feast awaiting even the amateur photographer. Slide and monochrome film can be bought in Hanoi and HCMC, but don't count on it elsewhere.

Cameras are reasonably priced in Vietnam and all other camera supplies are readily available in major cities.

Avoid snapping airports, military bases and border checkpoints. Don't even think of trying to get a snapshot of Ho Chi Minh in his glass sarcophagus!

Photographing anyone, particularly hill-tribe people, demands patience and the utmost respect for local customs. Photograph with discretion and manners. It's always polite to ask first and if the person says no, don't take the photo. If you promise to send a copy of the photo, make sure you do.

PUBLIC HOLIDAYS

If a public holiday falls on a weekend, it is observed on the Monday.

New Year's Day (Tet Duong Lich) 1 January

Vietnamese New Year (Tet) January or February; a three-day national holiday

Founding of the Vietnamese Communist Party (Thanh Lap Dang CSVN) 3 February; the date the party was founded in 1930

Hung Kings Commemorations (Hung Vuong) 10th day of the 3rd lunar month (March or April)

Liberation Day (Saigon Giai Phong) 30 April; the date of Saigon's 1975 surrender is commemorated nationwide

International Workers' Day (Quoc Te Lao Dong) 1 May

Ho Chi Minh's Birthday (Sinh Nhat Bac Ho) 19 May

Buddha's Birthday (Phat Dan) Eighth day of the fourth moon (usually June)

National Day (Quoc Khanh) 2 September; commemorates the Declaration of Independence by Ho Chi Minh in 1945

SAFE TRAVEL

All in all, Vietnam is an extremely safe country to travel in. The police keep a pretty tight grip on social order and we rarely receive reports about muggings, robberies or sexual assaults. Sure there are scams and hassles in some cities, particularly in Hanoi, HCMC and Nha Trang (and to a lesser degree in Hoi An). But perhaps the most important thing you can do is to be extracareful if you're travelling on two wheels on Vietnam's anarchic roads – traffic accident rates are woeful and driving standards are pretty appalling.

Since 1975 many thousands of Vietnamese have been maimed or killed by rockets, artillery shells, mortars, mines and other ordnance leftover from wars. Stick to defined paths and never touch any suspicious war relic you might come across.

TELEPHONE

International Calls

It's usually cheapest to use a mobile phone to make international phone calls; rates can be as little as US$0.15 a minute.

Otherwise, you can call abroad from any phone in the country. Just dial ☎171 or ☎178, the country code and your number – most countries cost a flat rate of just US$0.60 per minute. Many budget hotels now operate even cheaper webcall services.

You'll also find many hotels have Skype and webcams set up for their guests.

Local Calls

Phone numbers in Hanoi, HCMC and Haiphong have eight digits. Elsewhere around the country phone numbers have seven digits. Telephone area codes are assigned according to the province.

Local calls can usually be made from any hotel or restaurant phone and are often free. Domestic long-distance calls are also quite reasonably priced.

Mobile Phones

To avoid roaming charges, local SIM cards can be used in most European, Asian and Australian (and many North American) phones.

Phone Codes

In January 2015 the Vietnamese government announced that phone codes across the country (affecting 59 of Vietnam's 63 provinces) were to change. Businesses resisted, but this may change by force as this book goes to press, switching all numbers at the exchange. If your number does not work, check for a new area code (before the hyphen).

To call Vietnam from outside the country, drop the initial 0 from the area code. Mobile numbers begin with 09 or 01.

COUNTRY CODE	☎84
INTERNATIONAL ACCESS CODE	☎00
DIRECTORY ASSISTANCE	☎116
POLICE	☎113
GENERAL INFORMATION SERVICE	☎1080

TIME

Vietnam is seven hours ahead of Greenwich Mean Time/Universal Time Coordinated (GMT/UTC). Because of its proximity to the equator, Vietnam does not have daylight saving or summer time.

TOILETS

Western-style sit-down toilets are the norm but the odd squat bog still survives in some cheap hotels and bus stations. Hotels usually supply a roll of toilet paper, but it's wise to bring your own while on the road.

TOURIST INFORMATION

Tourist offices in Vietnam have a different philosophy from the majority of tourist offices worldwide. These government-owned enterprises are really travel agencies whose primary interests are booking tours and turning a profit. Don't come here hoping for independent travel information.

Vietnam Tourism (www.vietnamtourism.com), the main state organisation, and Saigon Tourist (www.saigon-tourist.com) are examples of this genre, but nowadays most provinces have at least one such organisation. Travel agents, backpacker cafes and your fellow travellers are a much better source of information than these so-called 'tourist offices'.

There are fairly helpful tourist offices in Hanoi and Ho Chi Minh City.

VISAS

The (very complicated) visa situation has recently changed for many nationalities, and is fluid – always check the latest regulations. The government has relaxed visa-exemption rules to include more countries and reduced visa fees in a bid to stimulate tourism.

Firstly, if you are staying more than 15 days and from a Western country, you'll still need a visa (or approval letter from an agent) in advance. If your visit is less than 15 days, some nationalities are now visa-exempt.

Tourist visas are valid for either 30 days or 90 days. A single-entry 30-day visa costs US$20, a three-month multiple-entry visa is US$70.

Until recently there have been two methods of applying for a visa: via online visa agents, or via a Vietnamese embassy or consulate. That is changing as e-visas are rolled out for many visitors.

Visa Extensions

If you have the dollars, they have the rubber stamp. Tourist visa extensions officially cost as little as US$10, and have to be organised via agents. The procedure can take seven days and you can only extend the visa for 30 or 90 days, depending on the visa you hold.

You can extend your visa in big cities, but if it's done in a different city from the one you arrived in (oh the joys of Vietnamese bureaucracy!), it'll cost you around US$30. In practice, extensions work most smoothly in HCMC, Hanoi, Danang and Hue.

Multiple-Entry Visas

It's possible to enter Cambodia or Laos from Vietnam and then reenter Vietnam without having to apply for another visa. However, you must hold a multiple-entry visa before you leave Vietnam.

If you arrived in Vietnam on a single-entry visa, multiple-entry visas are easiest to arrange in Hanoi or HCMC, but you will have to ask a visa or travel agent to do the paperwork for you. Agents charge about US$50 for the service and visa fees are charged on top of this; the procedure takes up to seven days.

Visa On Arrival

This is now the preferred method for most travellers arriving by air, since it's cheaper, faster and you don't have to part with your passport by posting it to an embassy. It can only be used if you are flying into any of Vietnam's five international airports, not at land crossings. The process is straightforward: you fill out an online application form and pay the agency fee (around US$20). You'll then receive by email a Visa on Arrival approval letter signed by Vietnamese immigration which you print out and show on arrival in a separate queue at customs, where you pay your visa stamping fee in US dollars, cash only. The single-entry stamping fee is US$25, a multiple-entry stamping fee is US$50. There is no additional visa fee. There are many visa agents, but we recommend you stick to well-established companies;the following two are professional and efficient:

Vietnam Visa Choice (www.vietnamvisachoice.com) Online support from native English-speakers and they guarantee your visa will be issued within the time specified.

Vietnam Visa Center (www.vietnamvisacenter.org) Competent all-rounder which offers a two-hour express service for last-minute trips.

E-Visas

A pilot e-visa program introduced in early 2017 allows visitors to apply for visas online through the Vietnam Immigration Department. Citizens of 40 countries are eligible, including those from the UK and the USA. E-visas are single-entry only, valid for 30 days (nonextendable), and cost US$25. Processing takes three to five days. As this is a pilot program, conditions may change and some website glitches have been reported; check the latest and apply at www.immigration.gov.vn.

VOLUNTEERING

Opportunities for voluntary work are quite limited in Vietnam as there are so many professional development staff based here.

For information, chase up the full list of non-government organisations (NGOs) at the NGO Resource Centre (p55), which keeps a database of all of the NGOs assisting Vietnam. Service Civil International (www.sciint.org) has links to options in Vietnam, including the Friendship Village (www.vietnamfriendship.org), established by veterans from both sides to help victims of Agent Orange. The Center for Sustainable Development Studies (http://csds.vn) addresses development issues through international exchange and nonformal education.

Or try contacting the following organisations if you want to help in some way.

KOTO (www.koto.com.au) helps give street children career opportunities in its restaurants in Hanoi or HCMC; a three-month minimum commitment is required.

International organisations offering placements in Vietnam include Voluntary Service Overseas (www.vsointernational.org) in the UK, Australian Volunteers International (www.australianvolunteers.com), Volunteer Service Abroad (www.vsa.org.nz) in New Zealand and US-based International Volunteer HQ (www.volunteerhq.org), which has a wide range of volunteer projects in Hanoi. The UN's volunteer program details are available at www.unv.org.

WOMEN TRAVELLERS

Vietnam is relatively free of serious hassles for Western women. There are issues to consider of course, but thousands of women travel alone through the country each year and love the experience. Most Vietnamese women enjoy relatively free, fulfilled lives and a career; the sexes mix freely and society does not expect women to behave in a subordinate manner.

Many Vietnamese women dress modestly and expose as little body flesh as possible (partly to avoid the sun). Be aware that exposing your upper arms (by wearing a sleeveless top) or short shorts can attract plenty of attention away from the beach.

WORK

There's some casual work available in Western-owned bars and restaurants throughout the country. This is of the cash-in-hand variety; that is, working without paperwork. Dive schools and adventure-sports specialists will always need instructors, but for most travellers the main work opportunities are teaching a foreign language.

Looking for employment is a matter of asking around – jobs are rarely advertised.

English is by far the most popular foreign language with Vietnamese students. There's some demand for Mandarin and French too.

Private language centres (US$10 to US$18 per hour) and home tutoring (US$15 to US$25 per hour) are your best bet for teaching work. You'll get paid more in HCMC or Hanoi than in the provinces.

Government-run universities in Vietnam also hire some foreign teachers.

Getting There & Away

Most travellers enter Vietnam by plane or bus, but there are also train links from China and boat connections from Cambodia via the Mekong River. Flights, tours and rail tickets can be booked online at lonelyplanet.com/bookings.

ENTERING VIETNAM

Formalities at Vietnam's international airports are generally smoother than at land borders. Crossing overland from Cambodia and China is now also relatively stress-free. Crossing the border between Vietnam and Laos can be slow.

AIR

Airports

There are five international airports in Vietnam. Others, including Hue, are officially classified as 'international' but have no overseas connections (apart from the odd charter).

Cam Ranh International Airport (☎058-398 9913) Located 36km south of Nha Trang, with flights to Hong Kong, Chengdu and Seoul.

Danang Airport (☎0511-383 0339) International flights to Lao airports including Pakse, Savannakhet and Vientiane; also Kuala Lumpur, Siem Reap, Singapore, Tokyo and airports in China including Hong Kong, Guangzhou and Nanning.

Noi Bai Airport (HAN; ☎04-3827 1513; www.hanoiairportonline.com) Serves the capital Hanoi.

Phu Quoc International Airport (www.phuquocairport.com) International flights including Hanoi, HCMC and Singapore.

Tan Son Nhat International Airport (☎08-3848 5383; www.tsnairport.hochiminhcity.gov.vn/vn; Tan Binh District) For Ho Chi Minh City.

Cat Bi International Airport In Haiphong, 60km west of Halong City, with flights to China, Thailand, South Korea and Phu Quoc.

Airlines

The state-owned carrier Vietnam Airlines (www.vietnamairlines.com.vn) has flights to 17 countries, mainly in East Asia, but also to the UK, Germany, France and Australia.

The airline has a modern fleet of Airbuses and Boeings, and has a good recent safety record.

Airlines that service Vietnam include Jetstar Airways (p67), Vasco (p174) and Vietjet Air (p67)

LAND & RIVER

Vietnam shares land borders with Cambodia, China and Laos and there are plenty of border crossings open to foreigners with each neighbour – a big improvement on a decade ago.

Cambodia

Cambodia and Vietnam share a long frontier with seven border crossings. One-month Cambodian visas are issued on arrival at all border crossings for US$30, but overcharging is common at all borders except Bavet.

Cambodian border crossings are officially open daily between 8am and 8pm.

CROSSING	VIETNAMESE TOWN	CONNECTING TOWN
Le Thanh–O' Yadaw (p250)	Pleiku	Ban Lung

Moc Bai–Bavet (p173)	Ho Chi Minh City	Phnom Penh
Tinh Bien–Phnom Den (p159)	Ha Tien, Chao Doc	Takeo, Phnom Penh
Vinh Xuong–Kaam Samnor (p202)	Chau Doc	Phnom Penh
Xa Xia–Prek Chak (p274)	Ha Tien	Kep, Kampot

China

There are currently three borders where foreigners are permitted to cross between Vietnam and China: Huu Nghi Quan (the Friendship Pass), Lao Cai and Mong Cai. It is necessary to arrange a Chinese visa in advance.

China time is one hour ahead.

CROSSING	VIETNAMESE TOWN	CONNECTING TOWN
Dong Dang–Pingxiang	Lang Son	Nanning
Lao Cai–Hekou (p174)	Lao Cai	Kunming
Mong Cai–Dongxing	Mong Cai	Dongxing

Laos

There are seven overland crossings between Vietnam and Laos. Thirty-day Lao visas are available at all borders.

The golden rule is to try to use direct city-to-city bus connections between the countries, as potential hassle will be greatly reduced. If you travel step by step using local buses expect transport scams (eg serious overcharging) on the Vietnamese side. Devious drivers have even stopped in the middle of nowhere to renegotiate the price.

Transport links on both sides of the border can be hit-and-miss, so don't use the more remote borders unless you have plenty of time, and patience, to spare.

CROSSING	VIETNAMESE TOWN	CONNECTING TOWN
Bo Y–Phou Keau	Kon Tum, Pleiku	Attapeu
Cau Treo–Nam Phao (p359)	Vinh	Lak Sao
Lao Bao–Dansavanh (p363)	Dong Ha, Hue	Sepon, Savannakhet
Nam Can–Nong Haet	Vinh	Phonsavan
Tay Trang–Sop Hun (p348)	Dien Bien Phu	Muang Khua

Getting Around

AIR

Vietnam has good domestic flight connections, with new routes opening up all the time, and very affordable prices (if you book early). Airlines, including Jetstar Airways (p67), Vasco (☎038 422 790; www.vasco.com.vn), Vietjet Air (p67) and Vietnam Airlines (www.vietnamairlines.com.vn), accept bookings on international credit or debit cards. Note, however, that cancellations are quite common. It's safest not to rely on a flight from a regional airport to make an international connection the same day – travel a day early if you can. Vietnam Airlines are the least likely to cancel flights, but their fares are usually higher than rival airlines. Deals can be booked directly from their site that won't show up on other flight search engines.

Tan Son Nhat International Airport (HCMC) Taxis to central districts (around 190,000d) take about 30 minutes. There's also an air-conditioned Route 152 bus (6000d, every 15 minutes, 6am to 6pm, around 40 minutes).

Noi Bai Airport (Hanoi) Taxis to the centre cost 400,000d and take around 50 minutes. Jetstar shuttles (35,000d) and Vietnam Airlines minibuses (50,000d) run hourly. The Route 17 public bus to Long Bien bus station is 5000d.

BICYCLE

Hotels and some travel agencies rent bicycles for US$1 to US$3 per day, better-quality models cost from US$6. Cycling is the perfect way to explore smaller cities such as Hoi An, Hue or Nha Trang (unless it's the rainy season!). There are innumerable bicycle repair stands along the side of the road to get punctures and the like fixed.

BOAT

Vietnam has an enormous number of rivers that are at least partly navigable, but the most important by far is the Mekong and its tributaries. Scenic day trips by boat are possible on rivers in Hoi An, Danang, Hue, Tam Coc and even HCMC.

Boat trips are also possible on the sea. Cruising the islands of Halong Bay is a must for all visitors to northern Vietnam. In central Vietnam the lovely Cham Islands (accessed from Hoi An) are a good excursion, while in the south, trips to the islands off Nha Trang and around Con Dao are also popular.

BUS

Vietnam has an extensive network of buses that reach the far-flung corners of the country. Modern buses, operated by myriad companies, run on all the main highways. Out in the sticks expect seriously uncomfortable local services.

Most travellers never visit a Vietnamese bus station at all, preferring to stick to the convenient, tourist-friendly open-tour bus network.

Whichever class of bus you're on, bus travel in Vietnam is never speedy – reckon on just 50km/h on major routes (including Hwy 1) due to the sheer number of motorbikes, trucks and pedestrians competing for space.

Bus Stations

Cities can have several bus stations, and responsibilities can be divided according to the location of the destination (whether it is north or south of the city) and the type of service (local or long distance, express or nonexpress).

Bus stations can look chaotic but many now have ticket offices with official prices and departure times clearly displayed.

Reservations & Costs

Reservations aren't required for most of the frequent, popular services between towns and cities, but it doesn't hurt to purchase the ticket the day before. Always buy a ticket from the office, as bus drivers are notorious for overcharging.

On many rural runs foreigners are typically overcharged anywhere from twice to 10 times the going rate. As a benchmark, a typical 100km ride *should be* between US$2 and US$3.

Deluxe Buses

Modern air-con buses operate between the main cities. This is the deluxe class and you can be certain of an allocated seat and enough space.

Some offer comfortable reclining seats, others have padded flat beds for really long trips. These sleeper buses can be a good alternative to trains, and costs are comparable.

Deluxe buses are nonsmoking and some even have wi-fi (don't count on fast connections though). On the flipside, most of them are equipped with TVs (expect crazy kung fu videos) and some with dreaded karaoke machines. Ear plugs and eye masks are recommended.

Deluxe buses stop at most major cities en route, and for meal breaks.

Mai Linh Express (☎0985 292 929; www.mailinhexpress.vn) This reliable, punctual company operates clean, comfortable deluxe buses across Vietnam. Destinations covered include all main cities along Hwy1 between Hanoi and HCMC, Hanoi to Haiphong, HCMC to Dalat, and cities in the central highlands.

The Sinh Tourist (☎08-3838 9597; www.thesinhtourist.vn) An efficient company that has nationwide bus services, including sleepers. You can book ahead online. Look out for special promotional prices.

Open Tours

In backpacker haunts throughout Vietnam, you'll see signs advertising 'Open Tour' or 'Open Ticket' bus services catering mostly to foreign budget travellers. The air-con buses run between HCMC and Hanoi (and other routes such as HCMC–Mui Ne–Dalat–Nha Trang) and passengers can hop on and hop off the bus at any major city along the route.

Prices are reasonable. A through ticket from HCMC to Hanoi costs between US$30 and US$75, depending on the operator and exact route. The more stops you add, the higher the price.

Buses usually depart from central places (like popular hostels), avoiding an extra journey to the bus station. Some open-tour buses also stop at sights along the way. The downside is that you're herded together with other backpackers and there's little contact with locals.

The Sinh Tourist has a good reputation, with computerised seat reservations and comfortable buses.

Local Buses

Few travellers deal with city buses due to communication issues and the cheapness of taxis, *cyclos* and *xe om*. That said, the bus systems in Hanoi and HCMC are not impossible to negotiate – get your hands on a bus map.

CAR & MOTORCYCLE

Having your own set of wheels gives you maximum flexibility to visit remote regions and stop when and where you please. Car hire always includes a driver. Motorbike hire is good value and this can be self-drive or with a driver.

Driving Licence

Foreigners are now permitted to drive in Vietnam with an International Drivers' Permit (IDP). This must be combined with local insurance for it to be valid.

In reality on the ground virtually no car-rental agency will rent a car to a foreign visitor without including a driver. If you do manage to acquire a car without a driver an IDP is tecnically required.

Fuel

Fuel costs around 20,500d per litre of unleaded gasoline.

Even the most isolated communities usually have someone selling petrol by the roadside. Some sellers dilute fuel to make a quick profit – try to fill up from a proper petrol station.

Hire

The major considerations are safety, the mechanical condition of the vehicle, the reliability of the rental agency, and your budget.

Car & Minibus

Self-drive rental cars are unavailable in Vietnam, which is a blessing given traffic conditions, but cars with drivers are popular and plentiful. Renting a vehicle with a driver-cum-guide is a realistic option even for budget travellers, provided there are enough people to share the cost.

Hanoi, HCMC and the main tourist centres have a wide selection of travel agencies that rent vehicles with drivers for sightseeing trips. For the rough roads of northwestern Vietnam you'll definitely need a 4WD.

Approximate costs per day are between US$80 and US$120 for a standard car, or between US$120 and US$135 for a 4WD.

Motorbike

Motorbikes can be rented from virtually anywhere, including cafes, hotels and travel agencies. Some places will ask to keep your passport until you return the bike. Try to sign some sort of agreement, clearly stating what you are renting, how much it costs, the extent of compensation and so on.

To tackle the mountains of the north, it is best to get a slightly more powerful model such as a road or trail bike. Plenty of local drivers are willing to act as chauffeur and guide for around US$20 per day.

The approximate costs per day without a driver are between US$5 and US$7 for a semiauto moped, between US$6 and US$10 for a fully automatic moped, or US$20 and up for trail and road bikes.

Insurance

If you're travelling in a tourist vehicle with a driver, the rental company organises insurance. If you're using a rental bike, the owners should have some insurance. If you're considering buying a vehicle, Baoviet (www.baoviet.com.vn) has a third-party fire and theft coverage policy which includes liability for 87,000d.

Many rental places will make you sign a contract agreeing to a valuation for the bike if it is stolen. Make sure you always leave it in guarded parking where available.

Do not even consider renting a motorbike if you are daft enough to be travelling in Vietnam without travel insurance. The cost of treating serious injuries can be bankrupting for budget travellers.

Road Conditions & Hazards

Road safety is definitely not one of Vietnam's strong points. The intercity road network of two-lane highways is becoming more and more dangerous. High-speed, head-on collisions are a sickeningly familiar sight on main roads.

In general, the major highways are paved and reasonably well maintained, but seasonal flooding can be a problem. A big typhoon can create potholes the size of bomb craters. In some remote areas, roads are not surfaced and transform themselves into a sea of mud when the weather turns bad – such roads are best tackled with a 4WD vehicle or motorbike. Mountain roads are particularly dangerous: landslides, falling rocks and runaway vehicles can add an unwelcome edge to your journey.

LOCAL TRANSPORT

Cyclos

Thease are bicycle rickshaws. Drivers hang out in touristy areas and some speak broken English. Bargaining is imperative; settle on a fare before going anywhere. A short ride costs 10,000d to 30,000d in most towns.

Taxis

Taxis with meters are found in all cities and are very, very cheap by international standards and a safe way to travel around at night. Average tariffs are about 10,000d to 15,000d per kilometre. Only travel with reputable or recommended companies. Mai Linh (www.mailinh.vn) and Vinasun (www.vinasuntaxi.com) are excellent nationwide firms.

Xe Om

These motorbike taxis are everywhere. Fares are comparable with those for a cyclo. Drivers hang out around street corners, markets, hotels and bus stations. They will find you before you find them.

TRAIN

Operated by national carrier, **Vietnam Railways** (Duong Sat Viet Nam; ☎04-3747 0308; www.vr.com.vn), the Vietnamese railway system is an ageing but pretty dependable service, and offers a relaxing way to get around the nation. Travelling in an air-con sleeping berth sure beats a hairy overnight bus journey along Hwy 1. And of course, there's some spectacular scenery to lap up too.

Routes

Aside from the main HCMC–Hanoi run, three rail-spur lines link Hanoi with the other parts of northern Vietnam. One runs east to the port city of Haiphong. A second heads northeast to Lang Son and continues across the border to Nanning, China. A third runs northwest to Lao Cai (for trains on to Kunming, China).

'Fast' trains between Hanoi and HCMC take between 32 and 36 hours.

Classes & Costs

Trains classified as SE are the smartest and fastest, while those referred to as TN are slower and older.

There are four main ticket classes: hard seat, soft seat, hard sleeper and soft sleeper. These are also split into air-con and non-air-con options. Presently, air-con is only available on the faster express trains. Some SE trains now have wi-fi (though connection speeds, like Vietnamese trains, are not the quickest). Hard-seat class is usually packed and tolerable for day travel, but expect plenty of cigarette smoke.

Reservations

You can can buy tickets in advance from the Vietnam Railways bookings site (http://dsvn.vn; however, at the time of writing only Vietnamese credit cards were accepted. You can also book online using the travel agency Bao Lau (www.baolau.vn), which has an efficient website, details seat and sleeper-berth availability, and accepts international cards. E-tickets are emailed to you; there's a 40,000d commission per ticket.

You can reserve seats/berths on long trips 60 to 90 days in advance (less on shorter trips). Most of the time you can book train tickets a day or two ahead without a problem, except during peak holiday times. But for sleeping berths, it's wise to book a week or more before the date of departure.

Schedules, fares, information and advance bookings are available on Bao Lau's website. Vietnam Impressive (www.vietnamimpressive.com) is another dependable private booking agent and will deliver tickets to your hotel in Vietnam, free of charge (or can send them abroad for a fee).

Many travel agencies, hotels and cafes will also buy you train tickets for a small commission.

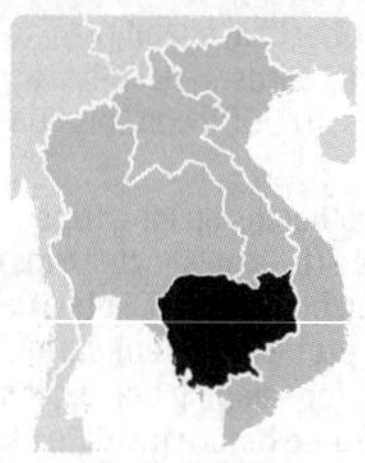

Cambodia

POP 16 MILLION / ☎855

Includes ➡

Best Places to Eat

- ➡ Jaan Bai (p233)
- ➡ Cuisine Wat Damnak (p212)
- ➡ Romdeng (p190)
- ➡ Sailing Club (p274)
- ➡ Fishmarket (p269)

Best Places to Sleep

- ➡ Raffles Hotel Le Royal (p188)
- ➡ Grand Hotel d'Angkor (p211)
- ➡ Suns of Beaches (p264)
- ➡ Oasis Bungalow Resort (p252)
- ➡ Rikitikitavi (p267)

Why Go?

Ascend to the realm of the gods at Angkor Wat, a spectacular fusion of spirituality, symbolism and symmetry. Descend into the darkness of Tuol Sleng to witness the crimes of the Khmer Rouge. This is Cambodia, a country with a history both inspiring and depressing, a captivating destination that casts a spell on all those who visit.

Fringed by beautiful beaches and tropical islands, sustained by the mother waters of the Mekong River and cloaked in some of the region's few remaining emerald wildernesses, Cambodia is an adventure as much as a holiday. This is the warm heart of Southeast Asia, with everything the region has to offer packed into one bite-size chunk.

Despite the headline attractions, Cambodia's greatest treasure is its people. The Khmers have been to hell and back, but thanks to an unbreakable spirit and infectious optimism, they have prevailed with their smiles and spirits largely intact.

When to Go

Phnom Penh

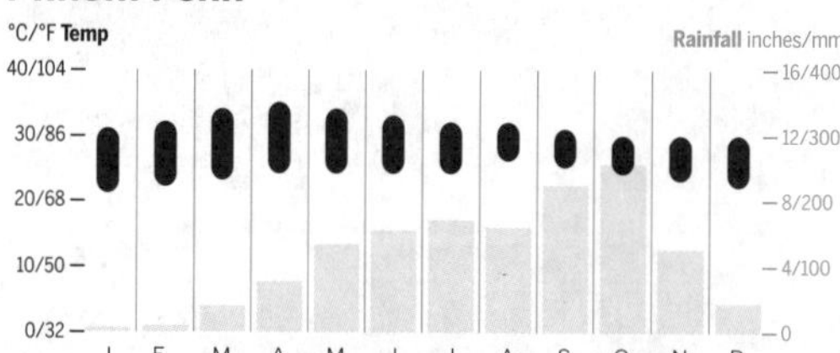

Nov–Feb The windy season brings relatively cool climes and is the best all-round time to visit.

Apr–May Khmer New Year falls in mid-April and the mercury regularly hits 40°C.

Jul–Sep Green season: rice paddies shimmer, and prices plummet.

PHNOM PENH

Phnom Penh (ភ្នំពេញ): the name can't help but conjure up an image of the exotic. The glimmering spires of the Royal Palace, the fluttering saffron of the monks' robes and the luscious location on the banks of the mighty Mekong – this is the Asia many daydream about from afar.

Cambodia's capital can be an assault on the senses. Motorbikes whiz through laneways without a thought for pedestrians; markets exude pungent scents; and all the while the sounds of life – of commerce, of survival – reverberate through the streets. But this is all part of the attraction.

Once the 'Pearl of Asia', Phnom Penh's shine was tarnished by the impact of war and revolution. But the city has since risen from the ashes to take its place among the hip capitals of the region, with an alluring cafe culture, bustling bars and a world-class food scene.

Sights

★Royal Palace PALACE

(ព្រះបរមរាជវាំង; Map p192; Sothearos Blvd; admission incl camera 25,000r, guide per hour US$10; 7.30-11am & 2-5pm) With its classic Khmer roofs and ornate gilding, the Royal Palace dominates the diminutive skyline of Phnom Penh. It's a striking structure near the riverfront, bearing a remarkable likeness to its counterpart in Bangkok. Being the official residence of King Sihamoni, parts of the massive palace compound are closed to the public. The adjacent Silver Pagoda is open to visitors.

Visitors are only allowed to visit the throne hall and a clutch of buildings surrounding it. They need to wear shorts that reach the knee, and T-shirts or blouses that reach to the elbow; otherwise they will have to rent appropriate covering. The palace gets very busy on Sundays, when countryside Khmers come to pay their respects, but being among crowds of locals can be a fun experience.

★Silver Pagoda BUDDHIST TEMPLE

(Map p192; Samdech Sothearos Blvd; incl in admission to Royal Palace; 7.30-11am & 2-5pm) Within the Royal Palace compound is the extravagant Silver Pagoda, also known as Wat Preah Keo or Temple of the Emerald Buddha. It is so named for its floor, which is covered with five tons of gleaming silver. You can sneak a peek at some of the 5000 tiles near the entrance, but most are covered to protect them.

The pagoda was originally constructed of wood in 1892 during the rule of King Norodom, who was apparently inspired by Bangkok's Wat Phra Kaew, and was rebuilt in 1962. It was preserved by the Khmer Rouge to demonstrate to the outside world its concern for the conservation of Cambodia's cultural riches. Although more than half of the pagoda's contents were lost, stolen or destroyed in the turmoil that followed the Vietnamese invasion, what remains is spectacular. This is one of the few places in Cambodia where bejewelled objects embodying some of the brilliance and richness of Khmer civilisation can still be seen.

★National Museum of Cambodia MUSEUM

(សារមន្ទីរជាតិ; Map p184; www.cambodiamuseum.info; cnr Sts 13 & 178; US$5; 8am-5pm) Located just north of the Royal Palace, the National Museum of Cambodia is housed in a graceful terracotta structure of traditional design (built from 1917 to 1920), with an inviting courtyard garden. The museum is home to the world's finest collection of Khmer sculpture: a millennium's worth and more of masterful Khmer design.

Highlights include an imposing, eight-armed Vishnu statue from the 6th century found at Phnom Da, and a staring Harihara, combining the attributes of Shiva and Vishnu, from Prasat Andet in Kompong Thom Province. The Angkor collection includes several striking statues of Shiva from the 9th, 10th and 11th centuries; a giant pair of wrestling monkeys (Koh Ker, 10th century); a beautiful 12th-century stele (stone) from Oddar Meanchey Province inscribed with scenes from the life of Shiva; and the sublime statue of a seated Jayavarman VII (r 1181–1219), his head bowed slightly in a meditative pose (Angkor Thom, late 12th century).

Note that visitors are not allowed to photograph the collection, only the central courtyard. English-, French- and Japanese-speaking guides are available for tours (US$6). A booklet, *The New Guide to the National Museum* (US$10), is available at the front desk, while the smaller Khmer Art in Stone (US$2) covers some signature pieces.

★Tuol Sleng Museum of Genocidal Crimes MUSEUM

(សារមន្ទីរប្រល័យពូជសាសន៍; Map p192; cnr Sts 113 & 350; US$3, guide US$6, audio tour US$3; 7am-5.30pm) In 1975, Tuol Svay Prey High School was taken over by Pol Pot's security forces and turned into a prison known as Security Prison 21 (S-21); it soon became the largest centre of detention and torture in the

Cambodia Highlights

1 Angkor Wat (p218) Discovering the eighth wonder of the world.

2 Phnom Penh (p179) Enjoying the 'Pearl of Asia', with its striking museums, sublime riverside setting and happening nightlife.

3 Sihanoukville (p255) Island-hopping and soaking up the city's hedonistic vibe.

4 Battambang (p228) Wandering around the lush countryside, climbing hilltop temples and exploring caves.

5 Mondulkiri (p245) Exploring this wild land of rolling hills, thundering waterfalls and indigenous minorities

6 Kampot (p266) Slipping into the soporific pace of riverside life.

7 Prasat Preah Vihear (p236) Making the pilgrimage to the awe-inspiring hilltop temple.

8 Kratie (p241) Exploring the bucolic Mekong islands and dolphin pools by bicycle and boat.

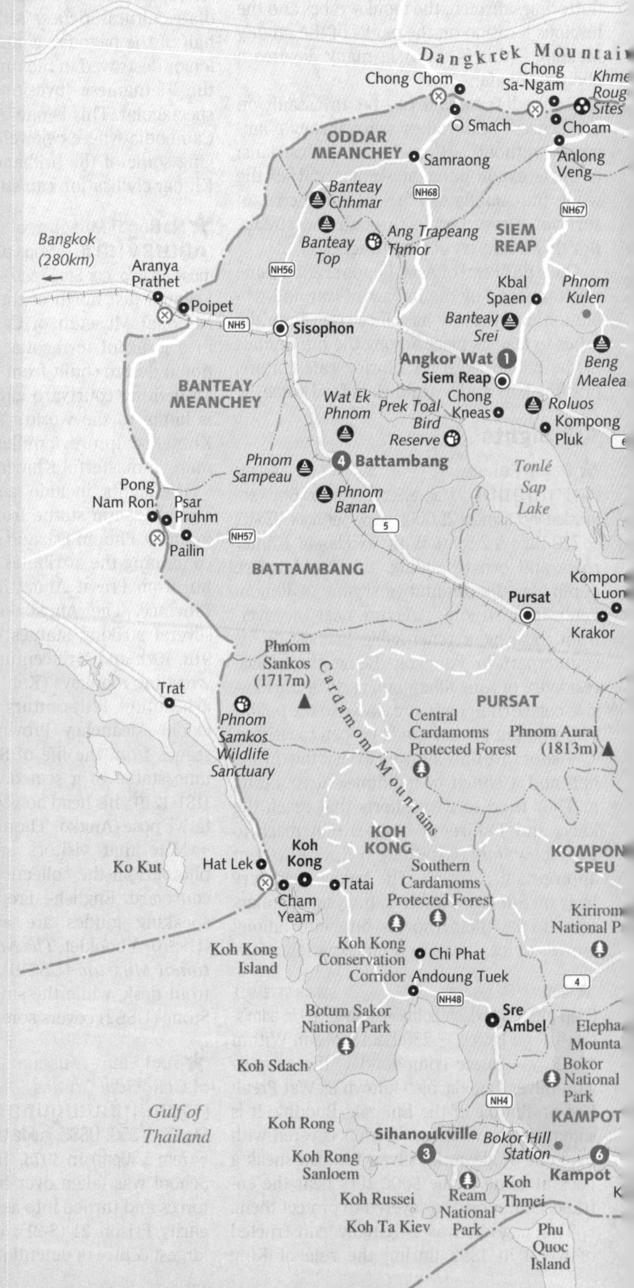

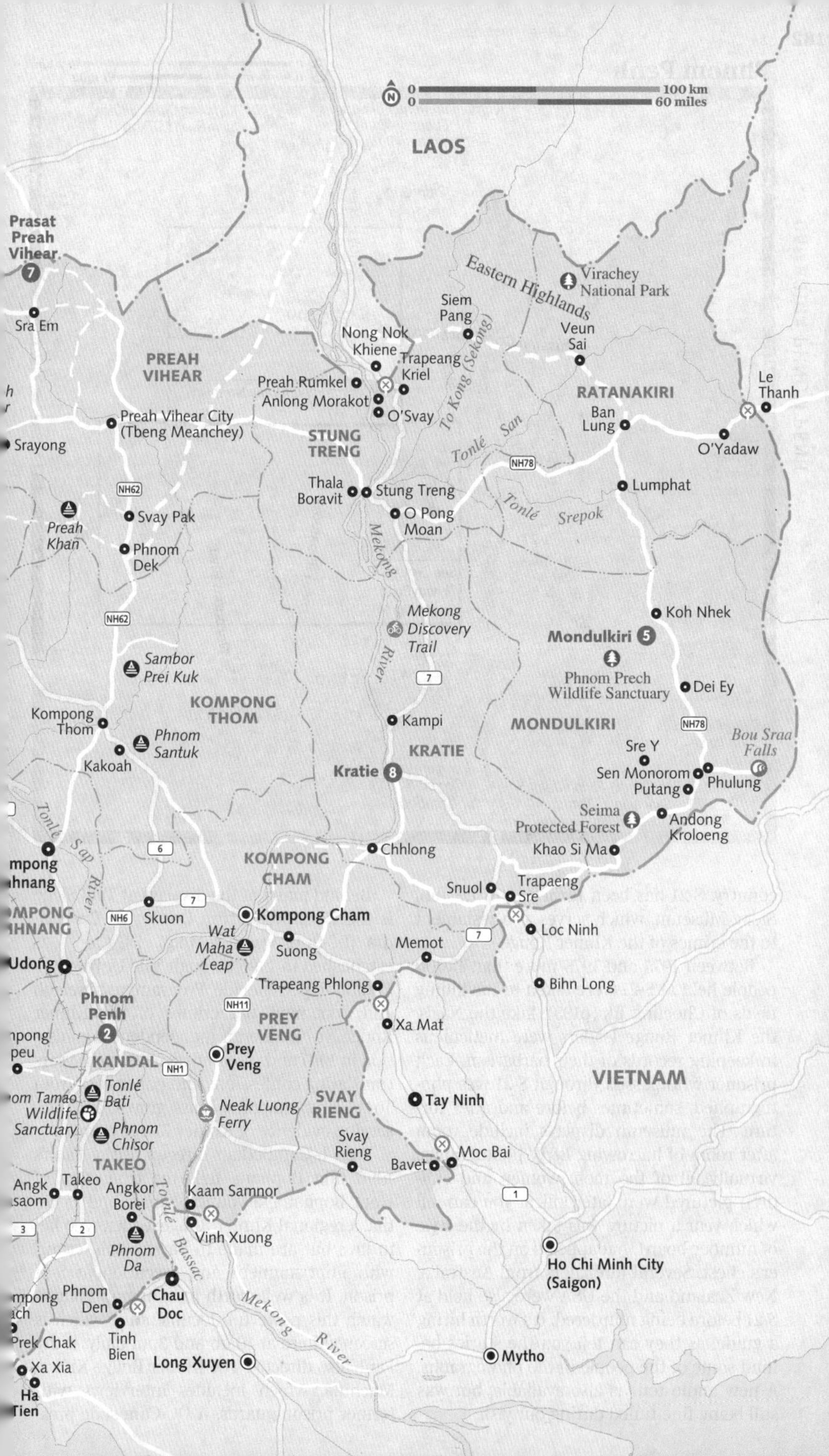

0 100 km
0 60 miles
LAOS
Prasat Preah Vihear
7
Sra Em
PREAH VIHEAR
Preah Vihear City (Tbeng Meanchey)
Srayong
NH62
Svay Pak
Preah Khan
Phnom Dek
NH62
Sambor Prei Kuk
Kompong Thom
Phnom Santuk
Kakoah
KOMPONG THOM
Tonlé Sap River
Kompong Chhnang
KOMPONG CHHNANG
6
7
NH6
Skuon
Udong
Phnom Penh
2
KANDAL
NH1
Tonlé Bati
Phnom Tamao Wildlife Sanctuary
Phnom Chisor
TAKEO
Angkor Borei
Takeo
Phnom Da
3
2
Phnom Den
Tinh Bien
Prek Chak
Xa Xia
Ha Tien
Chau Doc
Long Xuyen
Eastern Highlands
Virachey National Park
Siem Pang
Nong Nok Khiene
Trapeang Kriel
Veun Sai
Preah Rumkel
Anlong Morakot
O'Svay
To Kong (Sekong)
Tonlé San
RATANAKIRI
Le Thanh
Ban Lung
O'Yadaw
STUNG TRENG
NH78
Thala Boravit
Stung Treng
O Pong Moan
Lumphat
Tonlé Srepok
Mekong
Mekong Discovery Trail
River
7
Koh Nhek
Mondulkiri 5
Phnom Prech Wildlife Sanctuary
Dei Ey
Kampi
MONDULKIRI
NH78
KRATIE
Kratie 8
Bou Sraa Falls
Sre Y
Sen Monorom
Phulung
Putang
Seima Protected Forest
Andong Kroloeng
Khao Si Ma
Chhlong
KOMPONG CHAM
Kompong Cham
Snuol
Trapaeng Sre
Loc Ninh
7
Wat Maha Leap
Suong
Memot
Trapeang Phlong
Bihn Long
NH11
PREY VENG
Xa Mat
Prey Veng
VIETNAM
Neak Luong Ferry
SVAY RIENG
Tay Ninh
Svay Rieng
Moc Bai
Bavet
1
Kaam Samnor
Vinh Xuong
Tonlé Bassac
Ho Chi Minh City (Saigon)
Mekong River
Mytho

Phnom Penh

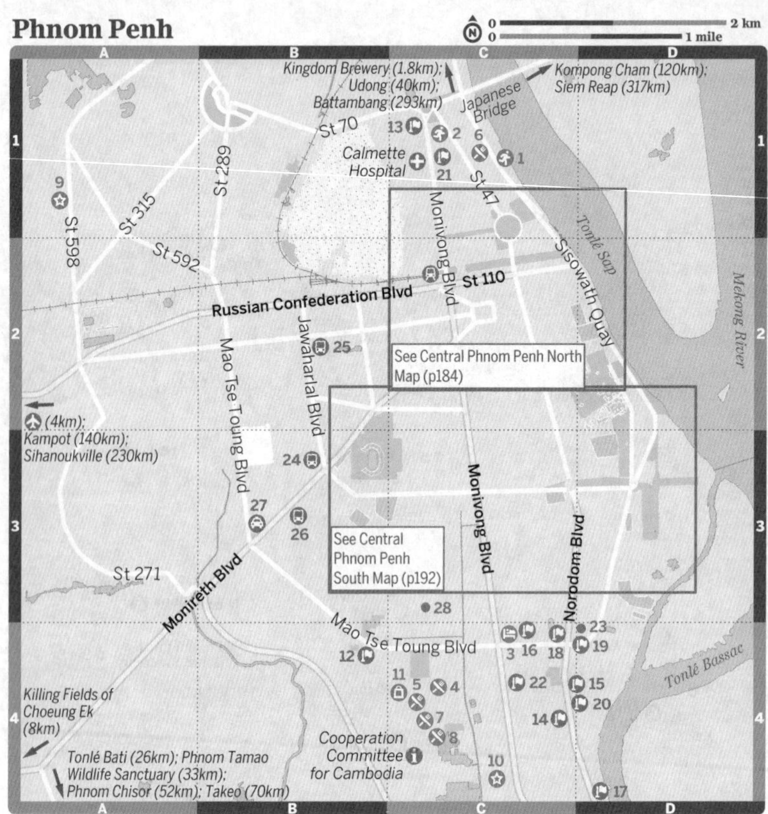

country. S-21 has been turned into the Tuol Sleng Museum, which serves as a testament to the crimes of the Khmer Rouge.

Between 1975 and 1978 more than 17,000 people held at S-21 were taken to the killing fields of Choeung Ek (p183). Like the Nazis, the Khmer Rouge leaders were meticulous in keeping records of their barbarism. Each prisoner who passed through S-21 was photographed, sometimes before and after torture. The museum displays include room after room of harrowing B&W photographs; virtually all of the men, women and children pictured were later killed. You can tell which year a picture was taken by the style of number-board that appears on the prisoner's chest. Several foreigners from Australia, New Zealand and the USA were also held at S-21 before being murdered. It's worth hiring a guide, as they can tell you the stories behind some of the people in the photographs. A new audio tour is also available, but was still being fine-tuned during our visit.

Behind many of the displays at Tuol Sleng is the **Documentation Center of Cambodia** (DC-Cam; www.dccam.org). DC-Cam was established in 1995 through Yale University's Cambodian Genocide Program to research and document the crimes of the Khmer Rouge. It became an independent organisation in 1997 and researchers have spent years translating confessions and paperwork from Tuol Sleng, mapping mass graves, and preserving evidence of Khmer Rouge crimes.

French-Cambodian director Rithy Panh's 1996 film Bophana tells the true story of Hout Bophana, a young woman, and Ly Sitha, a regional Khmer Rouge leader, who fall in love but are made to pay for this 'crime' with imprisonment and execution at S-21 prison. It is well worth investing an hour to watch this powerful documentary, which is screened here at 10am and 3pm daily. Rithy Panh also directed The Khmer Rouge Killing Machine, which includes interviews with former prison guards. A DC-Cam slide pres-

Phnom Penh

Activities, Courses & Tours
1 Cruising Boats C1
2 O Spa C1

Sleeping
3 Rambutan Resort C4

Eating
4 Brooklyn Bistro C4
5 Café Yejj C4
6 Chinese House C1
7 Sesame Noodle Bar C4
8 Sumatra C4

Entertainment
9 Apsara Arts Association A1
10 Sovanna Phum Arts Association C4

Shopping
11 Russian Market C4

Information
12 Chinese Embassy B4
13 French Embassy C1
14 Indian Embassy C4
Indonesian Embassy .... (see 14)
15 Japanese Embassy D4
16 Lao Embassy C4
17 Malaysian Embassy D4
18 Myanmar Embassy C4
19 Philippine Embassy D4
20 Thai Embassy D4
21 UK Embassy C1
22 Vietnamese Embassy C4

Transport
23 Cambodia Angkor Air D4
24 Kampot Express B3
25 Kim Seng Express B2
26 Olympic Express B3
27 Psar Dang Kor Taxi Park B3
28 Two Wheels Only C3

entation takes place Monday and Friday at 2pm and Wednesday at 9am.

Wat Phnom BUDDHIST TEMPLE
(វត្តភ្នំ; Map p184; Norodom Blvd at St 94; temple US$1, museum US$2; 7am-6.30pm, museum 7am-6pm) Set on top of a 27m-high tree-covered knoll, Wat Phnom is on the only 'hill' in town. According to legend, the first pagoda on this site was erected in 1373 to house four statues of Buddha deposited here by the waters of the Mekong River and discovered by Lady Penh. Hence the city name Phnom Penh or 'hill of Penh'.

Be aware that Wat Phnom can be a bit of a circus, with beggars, street urchins, women selling drinks and children selling birds in cages. You pay to set the bird free, but the birds are trained to return to their cage afterwards.

Wat Ounalom BUDDHIST TEMPLE
(វត្តឧណ្ណាលោម; Map p184; Samdech Sothearos Blvd; 6am-6pm) FREE This wat is the headquarters of Cambodian Buddhism. It was founded in 1443 and comprises 44 structures. It received a battering during the Pol Pot era, but today the wat has come back to life. The head of the country's Buddhist brotherhood lives here, along with a large number of monks.

Killing Fields of Choeung Ek MUSEUM
(វាលពិឃាតជើងឯក; admission incl audio tour US$6; 7.30am-5.30pm) Between 1975 and 1978 about 17,000 men, women, children and infants who had been detained and tortured at S-21 were transported to the extermination camp of Choeung Ek. It is a peaceful place today, where visitors can learn of the horrors that unfolded here decades ago.

The remains of 8985 people, many of whom were bound and blindfolded, were exhumed in 1980 from mass graves in this one-time longan orchard; 43 of the 129 communal graves here have been left untouched. Fragments of human bone and bits of cloth are scattered around the disinterred pits. More than 8000 skulls, arranged by sex and age, are visible behind the clear glass panels of the Memorial Stupa, which was erected in 1988.

The audio tour includes stories by those who survived the Khmer Rouge, plus a chilling account by Him Huy, a Choeung Ek guard and executioner, about some of the techniques they used to kill innocent and defenceless prisoners, including women and children. There's also a museum here with some interesting information on the Khmer Rouge leadership and the ongoing trial. A memorial ceremony is held annually at Choeung Ek on 9 May.

The site is well signposted in English about 7.5km south of the city limits. Figure on about US$10 for a *remork-moto* (*tuk-tuk*; drivers may ask for more). A shuttle-bus tour is available with **Phnom Penh Hop On Hop Off** (016 745880; www.phnompenhhoponhopoff.com; 1/2 passengers US$15/25, excl entry fees), which includes hotel pick-up from 8am in the morning or 1.30pm in the afternoon.

Central Phnom Penh North

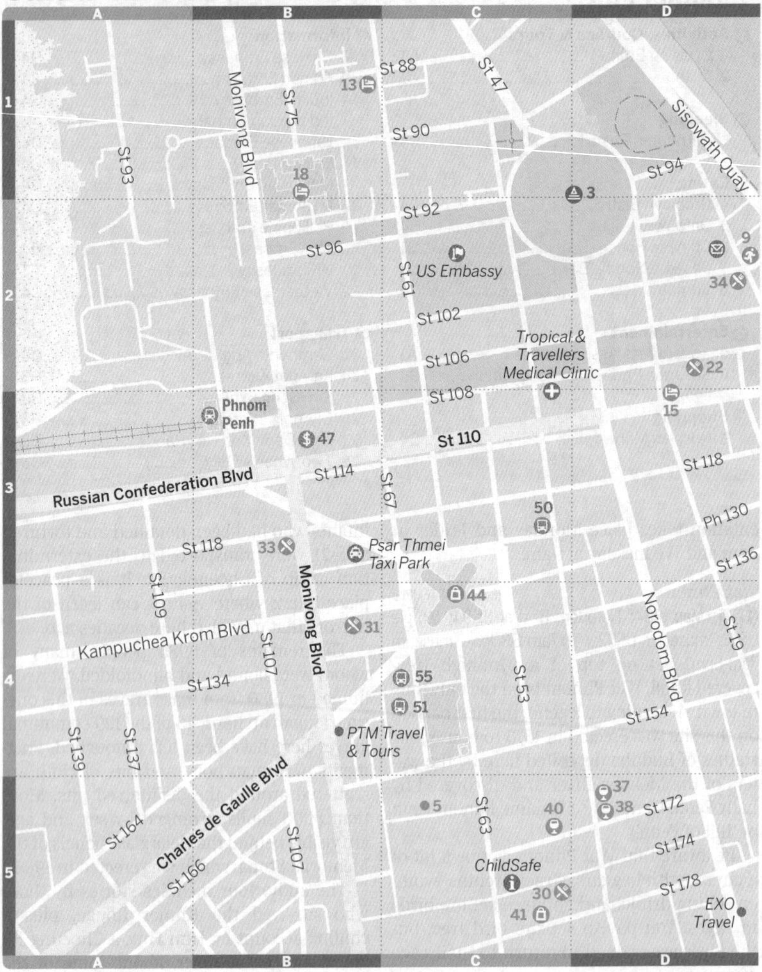

Activities

Every morning at the crack of dawn, and again at dusk, Cambodians gather in several pockets throughout the city to participate in quirky and colourful aerobics sessions. Join or watch at parks and the riverfront.

Boat Cruises

Koh Dach Boat Trips BOATING

(Map p184; Sisowath Quay; per person US$10) Daily boat tours to Koh Dach depart at 8.30am, 9.30am and 1pm from the tourist-boat dock (minimum four people).

Cruising Boats BOATING

(Map p182) Boat trips on the Tonlé Sap and Mekong Rivers are very popular with visitors. Sunset cruises are ideal, the burning sun sinking slowly behind the glistening spires of the Royal Palace. A slew of cruising boats are available for hire on the riverfront about 500m north of the tourist-boat dock. Just rock up and arrange one on the spot for around US$20 an hour, depending on negotiations and numbers. You can bring your own drinks or buy beer and soft drinks on the boat.

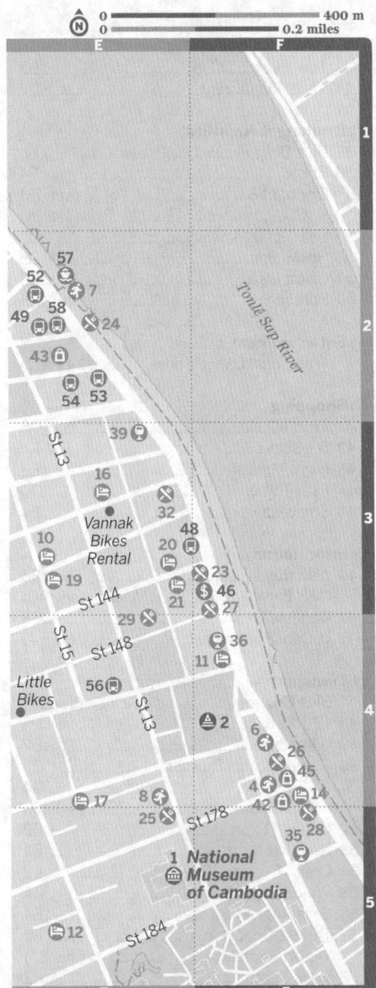

for US$3. Vicious represents well-respected Grasshopper Adventures in Phnom Penh.

Cooking Classes

Cambodia Cooking Class COOKING

(Map p192; ☎023-220953; www.frizz-restaurant.com; booking office 67 St 240; half/full day US$15/23) Learn the art of Khmer cuisine through Frizz Restaurant on St 240. Classes are held on a breezy rooftop near the Russian embassy. Reserve one day ahead.

Cycling

Vicious Cycle CYCLING

(Map p184; ☎012 430622; www.grasshopperadventures.com; 23 St 144; road/mountain bike per day US$4/8; 👪) Plenty of excellent mountain and other bikes are available here. Kiddie seats can be attached to your mountain bike

Massage & Meditation

Bodia Spa SPA

(Map p184; ☎023-226199; www.bodia-spa.com; cnr Samdech Sothearos Blvd & St 178; massages from US$32; ⏰10am-11pm) Arguably the best massages and spa treatments in town, and in a Zen-like setting just off the riverfront. All products are locally sourced and produced by the Bodia Nature team.

Seeing Hands Massage MASSAGE

(Map p184; ☎016-856188; 12 St 13; massages US$7; ⏰7am-10pm) 🍃 The original Seeing Hands establishment, this place helps you ease those aches and pains and helps blind masseurs stay self-sufficient. One of the best-value massages in the capital.

Nail Bar MASSAGE

(Map p184; www.mithsamlanh.org; Friends n' Stuff store, 215 St 13; 30/60min massages US$4/7; ⏰11am-9pm) 🍃 Provides cheap manicures, pedicures, foot massages, hand massages and nail painting, all to help Mith Samlanh train street children in a new vocation.

Spa Bliss SPA

(Map p192; ☎023-215754; www.blissspacambodia.com; 29 St 240; massages from US$23) One of the most established spas in town, set in a lovely old French house on popular St 240.

Daughters SPA

(Map p184; ☎077-657678; www.daughtersofcambodia.org; 321 Sisowath Quay; 1hr foot spa US$10; ⏰9am-5.30pm Mon-Sat) 🍃 Hand and foot massages are administered by participants in this NGO's vocational training program for at-risk women. Shorter (15- to 30-minute) treatments also available.

O Spa SPA

(Map p182; ☎023-992405; www.ospacambodia.com; 4B St 75; massages from US$20; ⏰11am-10pm) An oasis of calm, O Spa offers rejuvenating hot-stone massage, plus Balinese and Thai treatments.

Music

Cambodian Living Arts CULTURAL

(CLA; Map p192; ☎017 998570; www.cambodianlivingarts.org; 128 Samdech Sothearos Blvd) Cambodian Living Arts supports elder Cambodian musicians who train young and mostly at-risk Cambodians in traditional music, dance and other forms. You can visit many of these classes through its 'Living Arts Tours'. Among the most interesting is the **Pinpeat ensemble**

Central Phnom Penh North

Top Sights
1 National Museum of Cambodia E5

Sights
2 Wat Ounalom............F4
3 Wat Phnom............D1

Activities, Courses & Tours
4 Bodia Spa............F4
5 Cyclo Centre............C5
6 Daughters............F4
7 Koh Dach Boat Trips............E2
8 Nail Bar............E4
9 Seeing Hands Massage............D2
Vicious Cycle............(see 20)

Sleeping
10 11 Happy Backpacker............E3
11 Amanjaya Pancam Hotel............F4
12 Blue Lime............E5
13 Eighty8 Backpackers............B1
14 Foreign Correspondents' Club............F4
15 La Maison D'Ambre............D3
16 Monsoon Boutique Hotel............E3
17 Natural House Boutique Hotel............E4
18 Raffles Hotel Le Royal............B1
19 Sun & Moon Urban Hotel............E3
20 Velkommen Backpackers............E3
21 Velkommen Guesthouse............E3

Eating
22 Armand's The Bistro............D2
23 Blue Pumpkin............F3
24 Bopha Phnom Penh Restaurant............E2
Daughters Cafe............(see 6)
25 Friends............E5
26 Happy Herb Pizza............F4
27 Metro............F3
28 Pop Café............F5
29 Psar Kandal............E4
30 Romdeng............C5
31 Sam Doo Restaurant............B4
32 Sher-e-Punjab............E3
33 Thai Huot............B3
34 Van's Restaurant............D2

Drinking & Nightlife
35 Blue Dragon............F5
36 Chow............F4
Elephant Bar............(see 18)
FCC............(see 14)
37 Heart of Darkness............D5
38 Howie Bar............D5
39 Oskar Bistro............E3
40 Pontoon............C5

Entertainment
Traditional Dance Show............(see 1)

Shopping
41 Ambre............C5
42 D's Books............F4
43 Night Market............E2
44 Psar Thmei............C4
45 Smateria............F4

Information
46 ANZ Royal Bank............F3
CAB Bank............(see 46)
47 Canadia Bank............B3
U-Care Pharmacy............(see 4)

Transport
Blue Cruiser............(see 57)
48 CTT Net............E3
49 Giant Ibis............F2
50 Golden Bayon Express............C3
51 GST............C4
Hang Chau............(see 57)
52 Mekong Express............E2
53 Neak Krorhorm............E2
54 Orient Express 1907............E2
55 Phnom Penh Sorya............C4
56 Seila Angkor............E4
57 Tourist-Boat Dock............E2
Victoria Hotels............(see 57)
58 Virak Buntham............E2

class (10.45am-12.15pm Mon-Fri) in the decrepit modernist 'White Building', where students learn to play melodies that were used in the royal courts of Angkor to accompany ceremonies, dances and masked plays.

Swimming

Himawari Hotel SWIMMING
(Map p192; 023-214555; 313 Sisowath Quay; weekday/weekend US$7/8) The Himawari has one of the best hotel pools in town. It's located near the banks of the Mekong. Admission includes use of the gym.

Kingdom Resort SWIMMING
(023-721514; www.thekingdomresort.net; off NH1; adult/child US$5/3) Kingdom Resort is a great option for those willing to make a short excursion (6km) out of town; it has a huge pool and some slides.

Tours

Cyclo Centre TOURS
(Map p184; 097-700 9762; www.cyclo.org.kh; 95 St 158; per hour/day from US$3/12) Dedicated to supporting *cyclo* (bicycle rickshaw) drivers in Phnom Penh, these tours are a great way to see the sights. Themed trips such as pub crawls or cultural tours are also available.

Cambodia Expeditions TOURS
(www.cambodiaexpeditions.com) This team has been running motorbike tours and rallies in

Cambodia since 1998. Very professional with some great routes in the north of the country.

Kingdom Brewery TOURS
(023-430180; 1748 NH5; tours US$6; 1-5pm Mon-Fri) It costs just US$6 to tour the facilities of Kingdom Brewery. Tours include two drinks, and you don't even have to book ahead: just show up. It's exactly 1km north of the Japanese Bridge on NH5.

Sleeping

Accommodation in Phnom Penh, as in the rest of the country, is great value no matter your budget, with quite literally hundreds of guesthouses and hotels to choose from.

The traditional backpacker area around Boeng Kak ('The Lake') all but died when the lake was filled in with sand in 2011. Four miniature backpacker colonies have emerged in its wake: St 172, between St 19 and St 13 (the most popular area); St 258 near the riverfront; Psar O Russei area west of busy Monivong Blvd; and St 278 (aka 'Golden St') in the trendy Boeng Keng Kang (BKK) district south of Independence Monument.

Central Phnom Penh North

★**Eighty8 Backpackers** HOSTEL $
(Map p184; 023-500 2440; www.88backpackers.com; 98 St 88; dm US$6.40-8, r US$10-34;) A hostel with a swimming pool means party time, and this place hosts a big one on the first Friday of every month. The pool and the extensive villa are home to a variety of dorms and private rooms. The courtyard has a central bar, with a pool table and plenty of spots to lounge around the pool. The dorms come in air-con and fan varieties, plus a female dorm.

11 Happy Backpacker HOSTEL $
(Map p184; 088-777 7421; www.11happybackpackers.com; 87-89 St 136; dm US$5, r US$8-18;) This is one of the original backpacker pads in Phnom Penh, with a sprawling rooftop bar-restaurant offering chairs for chilling out and a pool table. It's mellow by day, fun by night. The white-tiled rooms are clean and functional. The Flicks 2 cinema is conveniently located downstairs.

Velkommen Backpackers HOSTEL $
(Map p184; 077-757701; www.velkommenbackpackers.com; 17 St 144; dm US$6, r US$10-30;) The popular Velkommen has been looking after travellers for the better part of a decade now. Dorms are air-conditioned and rooms come in a pick 'n' mix of shapes and sizes. There is a bar-restaurant downstairs and lots of useful travel info. Directly across the road is the **Velkommen Guesthouse** (077-757701; www.velkommenguesthouse.com; 18 St 144; r US$20-45;), with spiffier rooms.

★**Blue Lime** BOUTIQUE HOTEL $$
(Map p184; 023-222260; www.bluelime.asia; 42 St 19z; r incl breakfast US$55-95;) The Blue Lime offers smart, minimalist rooms and a leafy pool area that invites relaxation. The pricier rooms have private plunge pools, four-poster beds and concrete love seats. The cheaper rooms upstairs in the main building are similarly appealing. No children.

★**Foreign Correspondents' Club** BOUTIQUE HOTEL $$
(FCC; Map p184; 023-210142; www.fcccambodia.com; 363 Sisowath Quay; r incl breakfast US$75-95;) This landmark location is a fine place to recapture the heady days of the war correspondents. The rooms are exquisitely finished in polished wood and include fine art, top-of-the-line furniture and vintage *Phnom Penh Post* covers on the wall. The deluxe rooms have breezy balconies with prime river views.

Sun & Moon Urban Hotel DESIGN HOTEL $$
(Map p184; 023-961888; www.sunandmoonhotel.com.kh; 68 St 136; r US$69-129;) This is one of the most stylish high-rises in the Cambodian capital, offering designer rooms with geometric patterns on the walls and splashes of saffron in the furnishings. One of the most impressive features is the rooftop infinity pool with expansive views across the city and the attached Cloud 9 Sky Bar.

Natural House Boutique Hotel HOTEL $$
(Map p184; 097-263 4160; 52-54 St 172; r incl breakfast US$20-35;) Arguably the best-looking $20 rooms in the St 172 area are here. Plush bedding and kitchenettes in all rooms are the highlights. Breakfast is opposite at the Bistro Corner, owned by the same Japanese expat.

Monsoon Boutique Hotel BOUTIQUE HOTEL $$
(Map p184; 023-989856; www.monsoonhotel.com; 53-55 St 130; r incl breakfast US$30-45;) Blink and you'll miss this little oasis on chaotic St 130. Hidden inside are attractive rooms with polished concrete walls and pleasing murals. It's a real deal considering the sophistication of the design and a location close to the river.

★**Raffles Hotel Le Royal** HOTEL $$$
(Map p184; ☎023-981888; www.raffles.com/phnompenh; cnr Monivong Blvd & St 92; r from US$200; ❄@🛜🏊) From the golden age of travel, this is one of Asia's grand old dames, in the illustrious company of the Oriental in Bangkok and Raffles in Singapore. This classic colonial-era property is Phnom Penh's leading address, with a heritage to match its service and style. Between 1970 and 1975 many famous journalists working in Phnom Penh stayed here. More recent celebrated guests have included Barack Obama and Angelina Jolie. Indulgent diversions include two swimming pools, a gym, a spa and lavish bars and restaurants.

★**La Maison D'Ambre** BOUTIQUE HOTEL $$$
(Map p184; ☎023-222780; www.lamaisondambre.com; 123 St 110; ste incl breakfast US$100-190; ❄@🛜) A designer hotel linked to Ambre, a leading house of couture, this place is fit for a fashion shoot. The ample themed suites feature stunning contemporary art, space-age lamps and designer kitchens. The psychedelic rooftop bar, the Fifth Element, has funky furniture and prime views of Wat Phnom, making it a great place for breakfast or a sundowner.

Amanjaya Pancam Hotel BOUTIQUE HOTEL $$$
(Map p184; ☎023-214747; www.amanjaya-suites-phnom-penh.com; 1 St 154; r incl breakfast US$130-180; ❄@🛜) Amanjaya boasts a superb riverfront location and spacious rooms finished with luxuriant dark-wood floors, elegant Khmer drapes and tropical furnishings. Luscious Le Moon bar is on the roof, trendy K West cafe at ground level.

Central Phnom Penh South

★**Mad Monkey** HOSTEL $
(Map p192; ☎023-987091; www.madmonkeyhostels.com; 26 St 302; dm US$6-8, r from US$16-30; ❄@🛜) This colourful and vibrant hostel is justifiably popular. The spacious dorms have air-con and sleep six to 20; the smaller ones have double-width bunk beds that can sleep two. The private rooms are swish for the price but lack TVs and, often, windows. The rooftop bar above quiet St 302 serves free beer on Mondays from 6pm to 8pm.

Top Banana Guesthouse HOSTEL $
(Map p192; ☎012-885572; www.topbananahostels.weebly.com; 9 St 278; dm from US$4, r US$12-18; ❄@🛜) A facelift, 15 years after first opening, has greatly improved the rooms, and there are some dorms available, including a four-bed female dorm. The main draw is the strategic location overlooking Wat Langka and St 278, plus the open-air chill-out area. Book way ahead. **One Up Banana Hotel** (Map p192; ☎023-211344; www.1uphotelcambodia.com; Z9-132 St 51; r US$29-49; ❄@🛜) is its nearby flashpacker upgrade.

St 63 Hostel HOSTEL $
(Map p192; ☎015-647062; 179 St 63; dm US$8-10; ❄@🛜) This is a smart little hostel in the usually upscale BKK 1 area of town. Dorm beds are wider than average and include a reading light and charging point. Female-only dorms are available, plus four-bed dorms for US$10. Added bonus: free laundry.

★**Rambutan Resort** BOUTIQUE HOTEL $$
(Map p182; ☎017-992240; www.rambutanresort.com; 29 St 71; r incl breakfast US$55-150; ❄🛜🏊) Sixties-groovy, gay-friendly and extremely well run, this striking villa once belonged to the US Embassy. The soaring original structure and a newer wing shade a boot-shaped swimming pool. Concrete floors set an industrial tone in the smart rooms, which are outfitted with top-quality furnishings.

★**Pavilion** BOUTIQUE HOTEL $$
(Map p192; ☎023-222280; www.thepavilion.asia; 227 St 19; r incl breakfast US$60-110, apt US$120-150; ❄@🛜🏊) Housed in an elegant French villa, this immensely popular and atmospheric place kick-started Phnom Penh's boutique-hotel obsession. All rooms have inviting four-poster beds, stunning furniture, personal computers and iPod docks. Some of the newer rooms include a private plunge pool. Guests can use bamboo bikes for free. No children allowed.

★**Villa Langka** BOUTIQUE HOTEL $$
(Map p192; ☎023-726771; www.villalangka.com; 14 St 282; r incl breakfast US$55-125; ❄@🛜🏊) One of the first players in the poolside-boutique game, Villa Langka has long been a Phnom Penh favourite, even as the competition heats up. The 48 rooms ooze post-modern panache, although there are big differences in size and style. The leafy pool area is perfect.

Khmer Surin Boutique Guesthouse BOUTIQUE HOTEL $$
(Map p192; ☎012-731909; www.khmersurin.com.kh; 11A St 57; r incl breakfast US$40-65; ❄🛜) This guesthouse is attached to the long-running restaurant of the same name, set in a sumptuous villa. The 19 rooms come with flat-screen TVs, leafy balconies and antique furnishings,

not to mention bathrooms that would put most four-star properties to shame.

Circa 51 BOUTIQUE HOTEL $$

(012-585714; www.circa51.com; 155 St 222; r incl breakfast US$40-120;) In a classic '60s villa, Circa 51 has just 10 rooms and they are all attractive. The ground level is layered in original chequerboard tiles, and the spacious rooms have ambient lighting, cool furniture, minimalist art, flat-screen TVs and silk robes. At the time of research there's a rumour that Circa will be closing down.

Anise HOTEL $$

(Map p192; 023-222522; www.anisehotel.com.kh; 2C St 278; r incl breakfast US$42-69;) If a leafy boutique hotel with a pool isn't the thing for you, Anise is one of the better midrange high-rises in town. Indigenous textiles and handsome wood trim add character to rooms that already boast extras like DVD players. Pricier rooms are gargantuan; all rooms include free laundry.

Kabiki BOUTIQUE HOTEL $$

(Map p192; 023-222290; www.thekabiki.com; 22 St 264; r incl breakfast US$55-120;) The most family-friendly place in town, the Kabiki offers a large, lush garden and an inviting swimming pool with a kiddie pool. Family rooms include bunks and most rooms have a private garden terrace.

Plantation BOUTIQUE HOTEL $$$

(Map p192; 023-215151; www.theplantation.asia; 28 St 184; r incl breakfast US$80-350;) This is the largest and most ambitious hotel among the MAADS group of properties. It ticks all the boxes with high ceilings, stylish fixtures and fittings, open-plan bathrooms and balconies. There are two swimming pools here and a beautiful courtyard reception that hosts regular art exhibitions.

La Rose Suites BOUTIQUE HOTEL $$$

(Map p192; 023-222254; www.larose.com.kh; 4B St 21; ste US$180-400;) A stylish contemporary all-suite boutique hotel in lively little St 21, it offers smart and spacious rooms, including some two-bedroom apartments for families. The elegant bathrooms include ample terrazzo bathtubs and rain showers.

Psar O Russei Area

Narin Guesthouse GUESTHOUSE $

(Map p192; 023-991955; 50 St 125; r with fan/air-con US$12/17;) One of the stalwarts of the Phnom Penh guesthouse scene (we first stayed here back in 1995). Rooms are smart, bathrooms smarter still and the price is right. There is a super-relaxed, open-air restaurant-terrace where you can take some time out.

Terrace on 95 BOUTIQUE HOTEL $$

(Map p192; 023-996143; 43 St 95; r US$35-45;) This hotel has the intimate feel of a B&B. The six attractively furnished rooms share an impeccably restored traditional house, with vegan-friendly K'nyay (p191) restaurant upstairs. Downstairs rooms share an outdoor patio.

Eating

Central Phnom Penh North

Blue Pumpkin CAFE $

(Map p184; 023-998153; www.bluepumpkin.asia; 245 Sisowath Quay; mains US$3-8; 6am-11pm;) Healthy breakfast, pastas, sandwiches and some of the capital's best ice cream lead the menu, and you can watch the nightly aerobics spectacle on the riverfront as you eat. There are plenty of other branches around town, including one at **Kids City** (Map p192; www.kidscityasia.com; Sihanouk Blvd; 8am-9.30pm;).

Thai Huot SUPERMARKET $

(Map p184; 103 Monivong Blvd; 7.30am-8.30pm) This is the place for French travellers who are missing home, as it stocks many French products, including Bonne Maman jam and the city's best cheese selection. There's an additional **branch** in BKK (Map p192; cnr Sts 63 & 352; 7.30am-8.30pm).

★**Sam Doo Restaurant** CHINESE $$

(Map p184; 017-427688; 56-58 Kampuchea Krom Blvd; mains US$2.50-15; 7am-2am;) Many Chinese Khmers swear that this upstairs eatery near Central Market has the best Middle Kingdom food in town. Choose from the signature Sam Doo fried rice, *trey chamhoy* (steamed fish with soy sauce and ginger), fresh seafood, hotpots and dim sum.

Metro FUSION $$

(Map p184; 023-222275; 271 Sisowath Quay; small plates US$4-10, large plates US$8-26; 9.30am-1am;) Metro is one of the hottest spots on the riverfront strip thanks to a striking design and an adventurous menu. Small plates are for sampling and include beef with red ants and tequila black-pepper prawns; large plates include steaks and honey-soy roasted chicken. It also does a mean eggs Benedict.

GOOD-CAUSE DINING IN PHNOM PENH

There are several restaurants around town that are run by aid organisations to help fund their social programs in Cambodia. The proceeds of a hearty meal go towards helping Cambodia's recovery and allow restaurant staff to gain valuable work experience.

Friends (Map p184; ☎012-802072; www.tree-alliance.org; 215 St 13; tapas US$4-7, mains US$6-10; ⏰11am-10.30pm; 📶) One of Phnom Penh's best-loved restaurants, this place is a must, with tasty tapas bites, heavenly smoothies and creative cocktails. Take two tapas or one main for a filling meal. It offers former street children a head start in the hospitality industry. Book ahead.

Romdeng (Map p184; ☎092 219565; www.tree-alliance.org; 74 St 174; mains US$5-8; ⏰11am-9pm; 📶) Set in a gorgeous colonial villa with a small pool, Romdeng specialises in Cambodian country fare, including a famous baked-fish *amok*, two-toned pomelo salad and tiger-prawn curry. Sample deep-fried tarantulas or stir-fried tree ants with beef and holy basil if you dare. It is staffed by former street youths and their teachers.

Daughters Cafe (Map p184; www.daughtersofcambodia.org; 321 Sisowath Quay; sandwiches US$4-5.50; ⏰9am-6pm Mon-Sat; ❄📶) This fantastic cafe on the top floor of the Daughters visitors centre features soups, smoothies, original coffee drinks, cupcakes and fusionish mains served by former victims of trafficking, who are being trained by Daughters to reintegrate into society.

Hagar (Map p192; ☎023-221501; www.hagarcatering.com; 44 St 310; lunch buffet US$7.50; ⏰7am-2pm; ❄📶) Proceeds from the all-you-can-eat buffets here go towards assisting destitute or abused women. The spread is usually Asian fusion or barbecue, except for Tuesday lunchtime when Hagar lays out its legendary Italian buffet.

Sher-e-Punjab INDIAN $$
(Map p184; ☎023-216360; 16 St 130; mains US$3-8; ⏰11am-11pm; 🖉) This is the top spot for a curry fix according to many members of Phnom Penh's Indian community. The tandoori dishes here are particularly good, as are the excellent-value prawn curries.

Bopha Phnom Penh Restaurant CAMBODIAN $$
(Map p184; ☎023-427209; www.bopha-phnom-penh.com; Sisowath Quay; mains US$5-15; ⏰6am-10.30pm; 📶) Also known as Titanic, it's on the river and designed to impress, with Angkorian-style carvings and elegant wicker furniture. The menu is punctuated with exotic flavours – especially water buffalo – but there's a European menu for the less adventurous.

Pop Café ITALIAN $$
(Map p184; ☎012-562892; 371 Sisowath Quay; mains US$6-12; ⏰11am-2pm & 6-10pm; ❄) Owner Giorgio welcomes diners as if they are coming to his own home for dinner, making this a popular spot for authentic Italian cooking. Thin-crust pizzas, homemade pastas and tasty gnocchi – it could be Roma.

Happy Herb Pizza PIZZA $$
(Map p184; ☎012-921915; 345 Sisowath Quay; medium pizzas US$6-9; ⏰8am-11pm; 📶) Another Phnom Penh institution. No, happy doesn't mean it comes with free toppings, it means pizza à la ganja. The non-marijuana pizzas are also pretty good, but don't involve the free trip. It's a good place to sip a cheap beer and watch the riverfront action unfold.

★**Van's Restaurant** FRENCH $$$
(Map p184; ☎023-722067; www.vans-restaurant.com; 5 St 13; mains US$15-45; ⏰11.30am-2.30pm & 5-10.30pm; ❄) Located in one of the city's grandest buildings, the former Banque Indochine, Van's features old vault doors en route to the refined dining room upstairs. Dishes are presented with a decorative flourish; menu highlights include langoustine ravioli, tender veal and boneless quail. Business lunches (US$15) include a glass of wine and a coffee.

★**Chinese House** FUSION $$$
(Map p182; ☎023-991514; 45 Sisowath Quay, cnr St 84; mains US$6-60; ⏰11am-1am Mon-Thu, to 2am Fri & Sat, to midnight Sun; 📶) Housed in one of the city's true colonial-era masterpieces, Chinese House is worth a visit for the ambience alone. The relaunched menu promises contemporary Asian flavours like beef cheek and steamed swordfish, plus East-meets-West fusion tapas and lunch specials. Doubles as a chic cocktail bar downstairs, with regular music events.

Armand's The Bistro FRENCH $$$
(Map p184; ☎092-305401; 33 St 108; meals US$12-25; ⏲from 6pm Tue-Sun; ❄) The best steaks in town are served flambé style by the eponymous owner of this French bistro. The meat is simply superb, but every item on the chalkboard menu shines. Space is tight, so this is one place to book ahead.

Central Phnom Penh South

★The Shop CAFE $
(Map p192; ☎023-986964; 39 St 240; mains US$3.50-6; ⏲7am-7pm, to 3pm Sun; 📶🖉) If you are craving the local deli back home, make for this haven, which has a changing selection of sandwiches and salads with healthy and creative ingredients like wild lentils, forest mushrooms and lamb. The pastries, cakes and chocolates are delectable and well worth the indulgence.

★Boat Noodle Restaurant THAI $
(Map p192; ☎012-774287; 57 Samdech Sothearos Blvd; mains US$3-7; ⏲7am-9pm; 📶) This long-running Thai-Khmer restaurant has some of the best-value regional dishes in town. Choose from the contemporary but traditionally decorated space at the front or a traditional wooden house behind. There are delicious noodle soups and lots of local specialities ranging from fish cakes to spicy curries.

Asian Spice ASIAN $
(Map p192; ☎012-237113; 79 St 111; mains US$2-4; ⏲6am-9pm; 📶) The house speciality is the zesty Singapore laksa, but you'll also find a host of appropriately spicy Indonesian and Malaysian specialities on the menu, along with some European fare. One of Phnom Penh's bargain eateries.

Ramen & Gyoza Bar Masamune JAPANESE $
(Map p192; ☎012-734163; Bassac Lane, M47 St 308; mains US$2.50-10; ⏲11.30am-3pm & 5.30pm-midnight) At this hip new Japanese ramen bar in the hipster Bassac Lane area of town, the ramen is lip-slurpingly good and comes in both dry and wet (soup) varieties. There are some great-value set lunches from US$7 to US$8. By night, it doubles as a bar and serves sake to a backdrop of live music.

The Vegetarian CAMBODIAN, VEGETARIAN $
(Map p192; 158 St 19; mains US$2-4; ⏲10.30am-8.30pm Mon-Sat; 🖉) This is one of the best-value spots in Phnom Penh, as it doesn't skimp on portions. Noodles and fried rice are the specialities. The leafy setting in a quiet nook off central Sihanouk Blvd is yet another plus.

★Malis CAMBODIAN $$
(Map p192; ☎023-221022; www.malis-restaurant.com; 136 Norodom Blvd; mains US$6-20; ⏲7am-11pm; ❄📶) The leading Khmer restaurant in the capital, Malis is a chic place to dine alfresco. The original menu includes beef in bamboo, goby with Kampot peppercorns, and traditional soups and salads. It's popular for a boutique breakfast: the breakfast sets are a good deal at US$3 to US$4. Book ahead for dinner.

★K'nyay CAMBODIAN, VEGAN $$
(Map p192; ☎011 454282; 43 St 95; mains US$4-7; ⏲noon-10pm Tue-Fri, 8am-10pm Sat & Sun; 📶🖉) A handsome restaurant upstairs at the Terrace on 95 (p189) boutique hotel, K'nyay complements meat-infused traditional Cambodian fare with a vegan menu and prepares vegan lunch boxes for day-trippers. Try the tasty banana or pumpkin curry or drop by for an original health shake after visiting sweltering Tuol Sleng nearby.

★Yi Sang Riverside CHINESE $$
(Map p192; Sisowath Quay; mains US$3-20; ⏲6am-11pm; ❄📶) The riverfront location is one of the only places in the city where you can dine right on the riverside, perfect for a relaxing sunset cocktail. The menu here includes a mix of well-presented Cambodian street flavours like *nam ben choc* (rice noodles with curry), plus plenty of dim sum and some international flavours.

Java Café CAFE $$
(Map p192; ☎023-987420; www.javaarts.org; 56 Sihanouk Blvd; mains US$4-8; ⏲7am-10pm; ❄📶) Consistently popular thanks to a breezy balcony and a creative menu that includes crisp salads, delicious homemade sandwiches, burgers and excellent coffee from several continents. The upstairs doubles as an art gallery, the downstairs as a bakery.

Backyard Cafe VEGAN $$
(Map p192; ☎078-751715; www.backyardeats.com; 11B St 246; dishes US$4-7; ⏲7.30am-4.30pm Mon, 7.30am-8pm Tue-Sun; ❄📶🖉) A cool and contemporary superfoods cafe, this is the place to check the pulse(s) of the vegetarian dining scene in the capital. Raw foods include stuffed avocado and a vegan abundance bowl. The mouth-watering desserts are also vegan.

Central Phnom Penh South

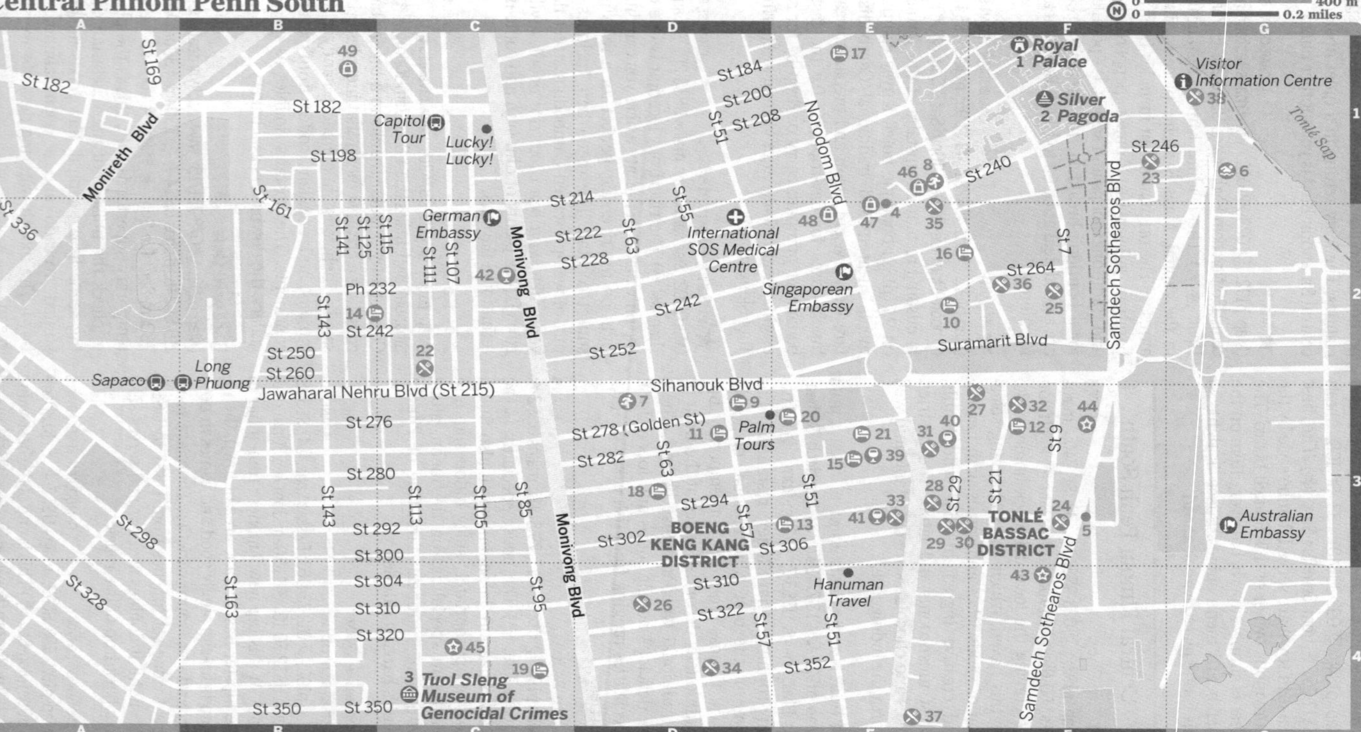

Central Phnom Penh South

Top Sights
1 Royal Palace F1
2 Silver Pagoda F1
3 Tuol Sleng Museum of Genocidal Crimes C4

Activities, Courses & Tours
4 Cambodia Cooking Class E2
5 Cambodian Living Arts F3
6 Himawari Hotel G1
7 Kids City D3
8 Spa Bliss E1

Sleeping
9 Anise D3
10 Kabiki E2
11 Khmer Surin Boutique Guesthouse D3
12 La Rose Suites F3
13 Mad Monkey E3
14 Narin Guesthouse B2
15 One Up Banana Hotel E3
16 Pavilion E2
17 Plantation E1
18 St 63 Hostel D3
19 Terrace on 95 .... C4
20 Top Banana Guesthouse E3
21 Villa Langka E3

Eating
22 Asian Spice C2
23 Backyard Cafe F1
24 Boat Noodle Restaurant F3
25 Curry Noodle Stalls F2
26 Hagar D4
27 Java Café F3
K'nyay .... (see 19)
28 Malis E3
29 Meat & Drink E3
Piccola Italia Da Luigi .... (see 29)
30 Ramen & Gyoza Bar Masamune E3
31 Red Cow E3
32 Sovanna F3
33 Sushi Bar E3
34 Thai Huot D4
35 The Shop E2
36 The Vegetarian F2
37 Topaz E4
38 Yi Sang Riverside G1

Drinking & Nightlife
39 Battbong E3
40 Botanico Wine & Beer Garden E3
41 Che Culo E3
Cicada Bar .... (see 30)
D-22 .... (see 42)
42 Eclipse C2
Hangar 44 .... (see 29)
Harry's Bar .... (see 29)
Library .... (see 30)
Seibur .... (see 30)

Entertainment
43 Cambodia Living Arts Yike Class F4
Flicks .... (see 19)
44 Meta House F3
45 Showbox C4

Shopping
46 Couleurs d'Asie E1
47 D's Books E2
48 Monument Books E2
49 Psar O Russei B1

Piccola Italia Da Luigi PIZZA $$
(Map p192; ☎017-323273; 36 St 308; pizzas US$5-10; ⏰11am-2pm & 6-10pm; 📶) This is the place that kick-started the St 308 scene. A bustling kerbside eatery, Luigi's certainly has a claim to making some of the best pizza in Phnom Penh. It has a small deli attached if you're in the mood for some zingy antipasti. After dark, reservations recommended.

Sushi Bar JAPANESE $$
(Map p192; ☎023-726438; 2D St 302; sushi sets from US$6; ⏰11am-10pm; ❄📶) Purists will scoff at the low sushi prices, but it's always packed for a reason. Definitely one of the better places in town for quick-and-easy raw fish. Sit downstairs at the bar, outside on the patio or in private rooms upstairs.

Topaz FRENCH $$$
(Map p192; ☎023-221622; www.topaz-restaurant.com; 162 Norodom Blvd; dishes US$8-50; ⏰11am-2pm & 5.30-10.30pm; ❄📶) One of Phnom Penh's original designer restaurants, Topaz is housed in an elegant villa with reflective pools and a walk-in wine cellar. The menu is classic Paris, including delicate Bourgogne snails drizzled in garlic, and steak tartare for those with rare tastes.

Russian Market Area

Café Yejj CAFE $
(Map p182; ☎092-600750; 170 St 450; mains US$3.50-6; ⏰8am-9pm; ❄📶✍) 🍃 An air-con escape from Russian Market (walk upstairs), this bistro-style cafe uses organic ingredients to prepare pasta, salads and wraps, as well as a few more ambitious dishes like Moroccan lamb stew and chilli con carne. Promotes fair trade and responsible employment.

Sesame Noodle Bar NOODLES $
(Map p182; ☎089-750212; www.sesamenoodlebar.com; 9 St 460; mains US$2.50-5; ⏰11.30am-2.30pm & 5-9.30pm Tue-Sun; 📶) A Japanese-American

LOCAL FLAVOURS

Markets

Street fare is not quite as familiar or user-friendly here as in, say, Bangkok. But if you're a little adventurous and want to save boatloads of money, look no further. Breakfast is when the streetside eateries really get hopping, as many Cambodians eat out for breakfast. Look for filled seats and you can't go wrong.

Phnom Penh's many markets all have large central eating areas, where stalls serve up local faves like noodle soup and fried noodles. Most dishes cost a reasonable US$1 to US$2. The best market for eating is Russian Market (p197), with an interior food zone that's easy to find and a nice variety of Cambodian specialities; the large car park on the west side converts to seafood barbecues and more from around 4pm. Psar Thmei (p197) and Psar O Russei (p197) are other great choices.

Just off the riverfront **Psar Kandal** (Map p184; btwn Sts 144 & 154) is an early-evening option where Cambodian's come for takeaway.

If the markets are just too hot or claustrophobic for your taste, look out for the mobile street sellers carrying their wares on their shoulders or wheeling them around in small carts. Another popular all-day option is the row of **curry noodle stalls** (Map p192; St 7) opposite Wat Botum Park.

Khmer Barbecues

After dark, Khmer eateries scattered across town illuminate their neon signs, hailing locals in for fine fare and generous jugs of draught beer. The speciality at most of these places is grilled strips of meat or seafood, but they also serve fried noodles and rice, curries and other pan-fried faves, along with some vegie options.

Many of these places also offer *phnom pleung* (hill of fire), which amounts to cook-your-own meat over a personal barbecue. Another speciality is *soup chhnang dei* (cook-your-own soup in a clay pot), which is great fun if you go in a group.

Sovanna (Map p192; 2C St 21; mains US$2-8; ⏲6-11am & 3-11pm) Sovanna is always jumping with locals and a smattering of expats who have made this their barbecue of choice thanks to the huge menu. It's also as good a place as any to sample the national breakfast, *bei sait chrouk* (pork and rice).

Red Cow (Map p192; 126 Norodom Blvd; mains US$2.50-7; ⏲4-11pm) Grills up everything imaginable – eel, eggplant, frog, pig intestine, quail – along with curries and other traditional Khmer dishes.

duo is behind Russian Market's trendiest little diners. Cold noodles arrive in vegetarian or egg varieties and come heaped with an egg and carmelised pork or grilled tofu. Simply delicious.

Sumatra INDONESIAN $
(Map p182; 67 St 123; mains US$2.50-5; ⏲11am-8pm; 📶🌱) The vegetarian dishes, which average around US$3, are fantastic value, although hearty eaters may want to order two. The spicy *balado* (tomato and chilli sauce) dishes are good. The restaurant recently relocated and dining is in a garden patio under a tin roof or an air-con interior.

★**Brooklyn Bistro** INTERNATIONAL $$
(Map p182; ☎089-925926; 20 St 123; dishes US$3-17; ⏲11am-10pm; ❄📶) A stylish American diner, this is incredibly popular with Phnom Penh expats in the know. The 16in pizzas are the largest in town, plus there's a dedicated menu of wings, as well as great deli sandwiches and the best New York cheesecake we've tasted in this part of the world.

Drinking & Nightlife

Phnom Penh has some great bars and clubs, so it's definitely worth planning at least one big night on the town. There are some good pub-crawl strips around town, with lots of late-night spots clustered around the intersection of Sts 51 and 172, where seemingly everybody ends up for a late night. 'Golden St' (St 278) is also popular, and the riverfront has its share of bars as well. Another up-and-coming area is St 308 and the adjacent Bassac Lane. Further north off the riverfront, the bar strips take on a sleazier complexion, while many of the drinking spots clustered on Sts 104 and 136 are hostess bars (aka 'girlie bars'), where female staff are employed mainly to flirt with and entertain customers.

★FCC BAR
(Foreign Correspondents' Club; Map p184; 363 Sisowath Quay; ⏲6am-midnight; 📶) A Phnom Penh institution, the 'F' is housed in a colonial gem with great views and cool breezes. It's one of those must-see places in Cambodia. Happy hours are 5pm to 7pm and 10pm to midnight. If the main bar is too crowded, head up to the rooftop, which often sees live music at weekends. It also offers an excellent menu both day and night.

★Pontoon CLUB
(Map p184; www.pontoonclub.com; 80 St 172; weekends US$3-5, weekdays free; ⏲9.30pm-late) After floating around from pier to pier for a few years (hence the name), the city's premier nightclub has finally found a permanent home on terra firma. It draws top local DJs and occasional big foreign acts. Thursday is gay-friendly night, with a 1am lady-boy show. Adjacent Pontoon Pulse is more of a lounge-club, with electronica and ambient music.

Botanico Wine & Beer Garden CRAFT BEER
(Map p192; ☎077 943135; www.craftbrewhouse.org; 9B St 29; ⏲9am-9pm Mon-Sat; 📶) Bringing US-style craft-brewing to Phnom Penh, this great little hideaway stocks Irish Red, IPA and other homebrewed beers. It is set in a verdant garden tucked down a winding alley. Monthly specials include yoga and beer, plus pork-knuckle nights.

Oskar Bistro BAR
(Map p184; www.oskar-bistro.com; 159 Sisowath Quay; ⏲5pm-2am; 📶) This new gastro-pub blends the bar and restaurant to perfection. Choose from creative cocktails and a huge wine list of 55 tipples, set to subtle DJ beats. A top spot for a late-night feed, as the kitchen stays open until 11pm.

Elephant Bar BAR
(Map p184; Raffles Hotel Le Royal, St 92; ⏲noon-midnight; 📶) Few places are more atmospheric than this sophisticated bar at the Raffles. It has been drawing journalists, politicos, and the rich and famous for more than 80 years. Singapore slings and many more drinks are half-price during the generous happy hour (4pm to 9pm).

Heart of Darkness CLUB
(Map p184; www.heartofdarknessclub.com.kh; 26 St 51; ⏲8pm-late) This Phnom Penh institution with an alluring Angkor theme has evolved more into a nightclub than a bar over the years. It goes off every night of the week, attracting all – and we mean *all* – sorts. Everybody should stop in at least once just to bask in the aura and atmosphere of the place.

Howie Bar BAR
(Map p184; 32 St 51; ⏲7pm-6am) Friendly, fun and unpredictable, 'way-cool' Howie is the perfect spillover when neighbouring places are packed. It draws a convivial crowd of expats, travellers and locals into the wee hours.

Battbong BAR
(Map p192; ☎069-291643; St 288 Alley East; ⏲6pm-late; 📶) A new speakeasy, Battbong is tricky to locate. Look out for the Coca-Cola machine at the end of the alley and locate the hidden button. Inside is a decadent beatnik-style bar with bottled beers, wine by the glass and some stiff drinks. Smoking is allowed, so the air can get hazy.

Seibur BAR
(Map p192; St 308; ⏲5pm-1am) The smallest of the many small Bassac Lane bars, this is an intimate spot for a drink.

Blue Dragon BAR
(Map p184; 391 St 184; ⏲5.30pm-1am) The location doesn't get better than this, with a front-row view of the Royal Palace and the chance for some river breezes on a balmy evening. Beers, wines and spirits flow.

Eclipse BAR
(Map p192; Phnom Penh Tower, 445 Monivong Blvd; ⏲5pm-2am) Located on the 24th floor, this open-air venue is the dry-season venue of choice for big breezes and bigger views. When the wet season kicks in, venture two floors down to **D-22** (⏲7am-midnight), a stylish, enclosed bar-restaurant offering the same views without the elements.

Che Culo BAR
(Map p192; www.checulocambodia.com; 6B St 302; ⏲11am-late Mon-Sat; 📶) A likeable little spot in popular BKK district, this bar is all retro tiles and seated alcoves, making for an intimate atmosphere. Great cocktails are even greater during happy hours from 5pm to 7pm. A tapas-style menu is available day and night.

Chow BAR
(Map p184; 277 Sisowath Quay; ⏲7am-11pm) The Quay hotel's swanky rooftop has river views, cooling breezes, a plunge pool and happy hours (half-price off US$6 drinks) from 4pm

LOCAL KNOWLEDGE

BASSAC LANE BARS

Bassac Lane is the moniker given to an alley that leads south off St 308. The brainchild of Kiwi brothers the Norbert-Munns, who have a flair for drinks and design, there are half a dozen or more hole-in-the-wall boozers in this eclectic spot. Choose from fusion wraps and burgers at the original Meat & Drink, tiny and intimate Seibur, the refined Library newcomer Harry's Bar or custom-bike tribute bar, Hangar 44. There's even a gin palace, the tiny Cicada Bar. From out of nowhere, Bassac Lane has become the new Bohemian district of Phnom Penh and is well worth a visit.

to 8.30pm. The creative cocktail list includes zesty infusions like ginger and lemongrass, plus a passionfruit caipirinha.

Rainbow Bar BAR
(134 St 136; 5pm-late) Phnom Penh's friendliest, most laid-back gay bar, with a 10pm drag show every night. At the time of research there's a rumour that it will be closing down.

☆ Entertainment

For news on what's happening in town, *AsiaLife* is a free monthly with entertainment features and regular listings. The Friday edition of the *Phnom Penh Post* includes the '7 Days' supplement with listings information.

★Traditional Dance Show PERFORMING ARTS
(Fruitful; Map p184; 023-986032; www.cambodianlivingarts.org; National Museum, St 178; adult/child from US$15/6; 7pm Mon-Sat Oct-Mar, Fri & Sat May-Sep) Plae Pakaa is a series of must-see performances put on by Cambodian Living Arts (p185). There are three rotating shows, each lasting about an hour: *Children of Bassac* showcases traditional dance styles; *Passage of Life* depicts the various celebrations and rituals that Khmers go through in their lifetimes (weddings, funerals etc); *Mak Therng* is a traditional *yike* opera.

★Meta House CINEMA
(Map p192; www.meta-house.com; 37 Samdech Sothearos Blvd; 4pm-midnight Tue-Sun;) This German-run cinema screens art-house films, documentaries and shorts from Cambodia and around the world most evenings at 4pm (admission free) and 7pm (admission varies). Films are sometimes followed by Q&As with those involved. Order German sausages, pizza-like 'flamecakes' and beer to supplement your viewing experience.

Showbox LIVE MUSIC
(Map p192; 11 St 330; 11am-1am;) This grungy music bar supports regular live acts and open-mic nights, as well as doubling up as a popular clubbing venue and occasional comedy club. Look out for cheap deals, including a rather generous free beer from 6.30pm to 7pm daily.

Cambodia Living Arts Yike Class OPERA
(Map p192; 65 Samdech Sothearos Blvd) These daily traditional-opera classes for at-risk youth are run by master theatre performer Ieng Sithul from Cambodia Living Arts, and are open to tourists.

Flicks CINEMA
(Map p192; www.theflicks-cambodia.com; 39B St 95; tickets US$3.50;) It shows at least two movies a day in an uber-comfortable air-conditioned screening room. You can watch both films on one ticket.

Apsara Arts Association DANCE
(Map p182; 012-979335; www.apsara-art.org; 71 St 598; tickets US$6-7) Alternate performances of classical dance and folk dance are held most Saturdays at 7pm (call to confirm). Visitors are also welcome from 7.30am to 10.30am and from 2pm to 5pm Monday to Saturday to watch the students in training (suggested donation: US$3). Please remember that this is a training school – noise and flash photography should be kept to a minimum. It's in Tuol Kork district, in the far north of the city.

Sovanna Phum Arts Association PERFORMING ARTS
(Map p182; 023-987564; www.shadow-puppets.org; 166 St 99, btwn Sts 484 & 498; adult/child US$5/3) Regular traditional shadow-puppet performances and occasional classical dance and traditional drum shows are held here at 7.30pm every Friday and Saturday night. Audience members are invited to try their hand at the shadow puppets after the 50-minute performance. Classes are available in the art of shadow puppetry, puppet making, classical and folk dance, and traditional Khmer musical instruments.

Shopping

Monument Books BOOKS
(Map p192; 111 Norodom Blvd; 7am-8.30pm) The best-stocked bookshop in town, with al-

most every Cambodia-related book available and a superb maps and travel section.

D's Books BOOKS
(Map p184; 7 St 178; ⏲9am-9pm) The largest chain of secondhand bookshops in the capital, with a good range of titles. There's a second **branch** (Map p192; 79 St 240; ⏲9am-9pm) just east of Norodom Blvd.

Ambre CLOTHING
(Map p184; ☎023-217935; www.romydaketh.net; 37 St 178; ⏲10am-6pm) Leading Cambodian fashion designer Romyda Keth has turned this striking French-era mansion into the perfect showcase for her stunning silk collection.

Couleurs d'Asie FASHION & ACCESSORIES
(Map p192; www.couleursdasie.net; 33 St 240; ⏲8am-7pm) Great place for gift shopping, with lots of kids' clothes, silks, chunky jewellery, beautiful bags, knick-knacks and fragrant soaps, lotions, incense and oils.

Smateria ACCESSORIES, CHILDREN
(Map p184; 7 St 178; ⏲9am-9.30pm) It does some clothing but Smateria's speciality is bags, including a line of quirky kids' backpacks, made from fishing net and other recycled materials. There's another branch in BKK on St 57.

★ **Psar Thmei** MARKET
(ផ្សារធំថ្មី, Central Market; Map p184; St 130; ⏲6.30am-5.30pm) A landmark building in the capital, the art-deco Psar Thmei (literally 'New Market') is often called the Central Market, a reference to its location and size. The huge domed hall resembles a Babylonian ziggurat and some claim it ranks as one of the 10 largest domes in the world. The design allows for maximum ventilation, and even on a sweltering day the central hall is cool and airy.

Psar Thmei is undoubtedly the best market for browsing. However, it has a reputation among Cambodians for overcharging on most products.

Russian Market MARKET
(Psar Tuol Tom Pong; Map p182; St 155; ⏲6am-5pm) This sweltering bazaar is the one market all visitors should come to at least once during a trip to Phnom Penh. It is *the* place to shop for souvenirs and discounted name-brand clothing. We can't vouch for the authenticity of everything, but along with plenty of knock-offs you'll find genuine articles stitched in local factories.

You'll pay less than one-third of the price back home for brands like Banana Republic, Billabong, Calvin Klein, Colombia, Gap and Next. The Russian Market, so-called by foreigners because the predominantly Russian expat population shopped here in the 1980s, also has a large range of handicrafts and antiquities (many fake), including miniature Buddhas, woodcarvings, betel-nut boxes, silks, silver jewellery, musical instruments and so on. Bargain hard, as hundreds of tourists pass through here every day. There are some good food stalls in the Russian Market if you are feeling peckish.

Night Market MARKET
(Psar Reatrey; Map p184; cnr St 108 & Sisowath Quay; ⏲5-11pm Fri-Sun) A cooler, alfresco version of Russian Market, this night market takes place every Friday, Saturday and Sunday evening if it's not raining. Bargain vigorously, as prices can be on the high side. Interestingly, it's probably more popular with Khmers than foreigners.

Psar O Russei MARKET
(Map p192; St 182; ⏲6.30am-5.30pm) Much bigger than other noted markets in town, Psar O Russei sells foodstuffs, costume jewellery, imported toiletries, secondhand clothes and everything else you can imagine from hundreds of stalls. The market is housed in a huge labyrinth of a building that looks like a shopping mall from the outside.

ℹ Information

DANGERS & ANNOYANCES

Phnom Penh is not as dangerous as people imagine, but it is important to take care. Armed robberies do sometimes occur, but statistically you would be very unlucky to be a victim. However, bag and smartphone snatching (p199) is a huge problem, and victims are often hurt when they are dragged off their bicycles or motorbikes.

Do not carry a bag at night, because it is more likely to make you a target. If you ride your own motorbike during the day, some police may try to fine you for the most trivial of offences, such as turning left in violation of a no-left-turn sign. The trick is not to stop in the first place by not catching their eye.

The riverfront area of Phnom Penh, particularly places with outdoor seating, attracts many beggars, as do Psar Thmei and Russian Market. Generally, however, there is little in the way of push and shove.

EMERGENCY

In the event of a medical emergency it may be necessary to be evacuated to Bangkok.

AMBULANCE	☎ 119 in emergency; ☎ 023-723840 in English
FIRE	☎ 118 in emergency
POLICE	☎ 117 in emergency; ☎ 097 778 0002 in English

INTERNET ACCESS

Internet cafes are less common since the wi-fi explosion, but the main backpacker strips – St 258, St 278 and St 172 – have a few places. Most internet cafes are set up for Skype or similar services.

MEDICAL SERVICES

Calmette Hospital (Map p182; ☎ 023-426948; www.calmette.gov.kh; 3 Monivong Blvd; ⌚ 24hr) The best of the local hospitals, with the most comprehensive services and an intensive-care unit, but it really helps to go with a Khmer speaker.

International SOS Medical Centre (Map p192; ☎ 012 816911, 023-216911; www.internationalsos.com; 161 St 51; ⌚ 8am-5.30pm Mon-Fri, to noon Sat, emergency 24hr) Top clinic with a host of international doctors and dentists, and prices to match.

Tropical & Travellers Medical Clinic (Map p184; ☎ 023-306802; www.travellersmedicalclinic.com; 88 St 108; ⌚ 9.30-11.30am & 2.30-5pm Mon-Fri, to 11.30am Sat) Well-regarded clinic, run by a British general practitioner for nearly two decades.

U-Care Pharmacy (Map p184; 26 Samdech Sothearos Blvd; ⌚ 8am-10pm) International-style pharmacy with a convenient location near the river.

MONEY

There's little need to turn US dollars into riel, as greenbacks are universally accepted in the capital. You can change a wide variety of other currencies into dollars or riel in the jewellery stalls around Psar Thmei and Russian Market. Many upmarket hotels offer 24-hour money-changing services, although this is usually reserved for their guests. Banks with ATMs and money-changing facilities are ubiquitous. Malls and supermarkets are good bets, and there are dozens of ATMs along the riverfront.

ANZ Royal Bank (Map p184; 265 Sisowath Quay; ⌚ 8.30am-4pm Mon-Fri, to noon Sat) ANZ has ATMs galore all over town, including at supermarkets and petrol stations, but there is a US$5 charge per transaction.

CAB Bank (Map p184; 263 Sisowath Quay; ⌚ 8am-9pm) Convenient hours and location; cashes travellers cheques in a range of currencies (3% commission). There's also a Western Union office here (one of several in the city).

Canadia Bank (Map p184; cnr St 110 & Monivong Blvd; ⌚ 8am-3.30pm Mon-Fri, to 11.30am Sat) Has ATMs around town, with a US$4 charge. At its flagship branch you can also change travellers cheques of several currencies for a 2% commission, plus get free cash advances on MasterCard and Visa. Also represents MoneyGram.

POST

Central Post Office (Map p184; St 13 at St 100; ⌚ 8am-6pm) A landmark, it is housed in a French colonial classic just east of Wat Phnom.

TOURIST INFORMATION

Visitor Information Centre (Map p192; Sisowath Quay; ⌚ 8am-5pm Mon-Sat; 📶) Located on the riverfront near the Chatomuk Theatre in the Yi Sang Riverside, it doesn't carry a whole lot of information. On the other hand, it does offer free internet access, free wi-fi, air-con and clean public toilets.

ChildSafe (Map p184; ☎ 023-986601, hotline 012 311112; www.childsafe-cambodia.org; 71 St 174; ⌚ 8am-5pm Mon-Fri) There's a centre here for tourists to learn about best behaviour relating to child begging, the dangers of orphanage tours, exploitation and other risks to children (see www.thinkchildsafe.org for tips). You can also look out for the ChildSafe logo on *remorks* and hotels: this network of people are trained to protect children in Cambodia.

TRAVEL AGENCIES

There are plenty of travel agents around town. The following are good bets for air tickets and all manner of domestic excursions, and can also arrange local transport and tour guides in multiple languages.

EXO Travel (Map p184; ☎ 023-218948; www.exotravel.com; 66 Norodom Blvd) Runs tours all over Cambodia and the Mekong region.

Hanuman Travel (Map p192; ☎ 023-218396; www.hanuman.travel; 12 St 310) Guides in several languages, tours and more, all over the country.

Palm Tours (Map p192; ☎ 023-726291; www.palmtours.biz; 1B St 278; ⌚ 8am-9pm) Efficient Volak and her team are a great option for bus tickets (no commission) and the like.

PTM Travel & Tours (Map p184; ☎ 023-219268; www.ptmcambodia.com; 200 Monivong Blvd; ⌚ 8am-5.30pm Mon-Sat) Good place for outbound air tickets.

ℹ Getting There & Away

AIR

Many international air services run to/from **Phnom Penh International Airport** (PNH; ☎ 023-862800; www.cambodia-airports.com). Domestically, there are now three airlines connecting Phnom Penh and Siem Reap. **Cambodia**

BAG SNATCHING

Bag snatching has become a real problem in Phnom Penh, with foreigners often targeted. Hot spots include the riverfront and busy areas around popular markets, but there is no real pattern; the speeding motorbike thieves, usually operating in pairs, can strike any time, any place. Countless expats and tourists have been injured falling off their bikes in the process of being robbed, and in 2007 a young French woman was killed after being dragged from a speeding *moto* (motorcycle taxi) into the path of a vehicle. Wear close-fitting bags (such as backpacks) that don't dangle from the body temptingly. Don't hang expensive cameras around the neck and keep things close to the body and out of sight, particularly when walking along the road, crossing the road or travelling by *remork-moto (tuk-tuk)* or especially by *moto*. These people are real pros and only need one chance.

Angkor Air (Map p182; ☎023-666 6786; www.cambodiaangkorair.com; 206A Norodom Blvd) flies four to six times daily to Siem Reap (from US$60 one way, 30 minutes), while newcomers **Bassaka Air** (☎023-217613; www.bassakaair.com) and **Cambodia Bayon Airlines** (☎023-231555; www.bayonairlines.com) have at least one flight a day, from US$40 one way.

BOAT

Fast boats up the Tonlé Sap to Siem Reap and down the Mekong to Chau Doc in Vietnam operate from the **tourist-boat dock** (Map p184; 93 Sisowath Quay) at the eastern end of St 104. There are no public boat services up the Mekong to Kompong Cham and Kratie.

The fast boats to Siem Reap (US$35, five to six hours) run from roughly August through March but aren't as popular as the cheaper, more comfortable bus.

BUS

All major towns in Cambodia are accessible by air-conditioned bus from Phnom Penh. Most buses leave from company offices, which are generally clustered around Psar Thmei or located near the corner of St 106 and Sisowath Quay. Buying tickets in advance is a good idea for peace of mind, although it's not always necessary.

Not all buses are created equal, or priced the same. Buses run by Capitol Tour and Phnom Penh Sorya are usually among the cheapest, while Giant Ibis, Mekong Express and Orient Express 1907 buses are better and pricier.

Most of the long-distance buses drop off and pick up in major towns along the way, such as Kompong Thom en route to Siem Reap, Pursat on the way to Battambang, or Kompong Cham en route to Kratie. However, full fare is usually charged anyway.

Another popular bus route is to Ho Chi Minh City.

Capitol Tour (Map p192; ☎023-724104; 14 St 182) Offers trips all the way through to Chau Doc using a combination of bus and boat. Services depart at 8am; the trip is about six to seven hours.

Giant Ibis (Map p184; ☎023-999333; www.giantibis.com; 3 St 106; wi-fi) 'VIP' bus and express-van specialist. Big bus to Siem Reap has plenty of legroom and wi-fi. A portion of profits go toward Giant Ibis conservation.

GST (Map p184; ☎023-218114; 13 St 142) Buses nationwide.

Long Phuong (Map p192; ☎097 311 0999; www.longphuongcambodia.com; 274 Sihanouk Blvd) Buses to Ho Chi Minh City.

Mekong Express (☎023-427518; www.catmekongexpress.com; Sisowath Quay) VIP buses to Ho Chi Minh City, plus Siem Reap and Sihanoukville.

Olympic Express (Map p182; ☎092 868782; 70 Monireth Blvd) Express vans to the south coast and beyond.

Orient Express 1907 (Map p184; ☎090-896666; 18 St 108) VIP buses to Siem Reap.

Phnom Penh Sorya (Map p184; ☎023-210359; cnr Sts 217 & 67, Psar Thmei area) Bus services all over the country.

Sapaco (Map p192; ☎023-210300; www.sapacotourist.com; 309 Sihanouk Blvd) Buses to Ho Chi Minh City.

Virak Buntham (Kampuchea Angkor Express; Map p184; ☎016-786270; 1 St 106) Night-bus specialist with services to Siem Reap, Sihanoukville and Koh Kong.

EXPRESS VAN

Speedy express vans (minibuses) with 12 to 14 seats serve popular destinations like Siem Reap and Sihanoukville. These cut travel times significantly, but they tend to be cramped and often travel at very high speeds, so are not for the faint of heart. Several of the big bus companies also run vans, most famously Mekong Express. It's a good idea to book express vans in advance.

CTT Net (Map p184; ☎023-217217; 223 Sisowath Quay)

Golden Bayon Express (Map p184; ☎023-966968; 3 St 126)

TRANSPORT FROM PHNOM PENH

Bus

DESTINATION	DURATION (HR)	COST (US$)	COMPANIES	FREQUENCY
Ban Lung	11	12	PP Sorya	morning only
Bangkok	12	18-23	Mekong Express, PP Sorya, Virak Buntham	1 daily
Battambang (day)	5-6	5-6	GST, PP Sorya	several daily
Battambang (night)	6	8-10	Virak Buntham	4 per night
Ho Chi Minh City	7	8-13	Capitol Tour, Long Phuong, Mekong Express, PP Sorya, Sapaco, Virak Buntham (night bus)	several daily to about 3pm
Kampot (direct)	3	5-6	Capitol Tour	2 daily
Kampot (via Kep)	4	6	PP Sorya	7.30am, 9.30am, 2.45pm
Kep	3	5	PP Sorya	7.30am, 9.30am, 2.45pm
Koh Kong	5½	7	Olympic Express, PP Sorya, Virak Buntham	2-3 daily (before noon)
Kompong Cham	3	5	PP Sorya	hourly to 4pm
Kratie	6-8	8	PP Sorya	6.45am, 7.15am, 7.30am, 9.30am, 10.30am
Poipet (day)	8	9-11	Capitol Tour, Gold VIP, PP Sorya	frequent to noon
Poipet (night)	7	10-11	Gold VIP, Virak Buntham	at least 1 daily
Preah Vihear City	7	10	GST, PP Sorya	morning only
Sen Monorom	8	9	PP Sorya	7.30am
Siem Reap (day)	6	6-8	most companies	frequent
Siem Reap (VIP)	6	13-15	Giant Ibis, Mekong Express, Orient Express 1907	7.45am, 8.45am, 12.30pm
Siem Reap (night)	6	10	Virak Buntham	6pm, 8pm, 11pm, 12.30am
Sihanoukville	5½	5-6	Capitol Tour, GST, Mekong Express, PP Sorya, Virak Buntham	frequent
Stung Treng	9	10	PP Sorya	6.45am, 7.30am

Express Van

DESTINATION	DURATION (HR)	PRICE (US$)	COMPANIES	FREQUENCY
Battambang	4½	10-12	Mekong Express, Golden Bayon	several daily
Kampot	2	8-9	Giant Ibis, Kampot Express, Olympic Express	3 daily
Kep	2½	8	Olympic Express	7.15am, 1.30pm
Sen Monorom	5½	11	Kim Seng Express	7am, 7.30am, 11am, 1.30pm
Siem Reap	5	10-12	Golden Bayon, Mekong Express, Mey Hong, Neak Krohorm, Olympic Express, Seila Angkor	3-5 daily
Sihanoukville	4	10-12	CTT Net, Giant Ibis, Golden Bayon, Mekong Express, Mey Hong	2-4 daily

Kampot Express (Map p182; ☎077 55123; 2 St 215)

Kim Seng Express (Map p182; ☎012 786000; 506 Kampuchea Krom Blvd) To Sen Monorom in Mondulkiri.

Mey Hong Transport (☎023-637 2722) Call for pick-up.

Neak Krorhorm (Map p184; ☎092 966669; 4 St 108)

Seila Angkor (Map p184; ☎077 888080; 43 St 154)

SHARE TAXI, PICK-UP & MINIBUS

Share taxis and local minibuses leave Phnom Penh for destinations all over the country. Taxis to Kampot, Kep and Takeo leave from **Psar Dang Kor** (Map p182; Mao Tse Toung Blvd), while packed local minibuses and taxis for most other places leave from the northwest corner of Psar Thmei (Map p184). Vehicles for the Vietnam border leave from Chbah Ampeau taxi park, on the eastern side of Monivong Bridge in the south of town. You may have to wait awhile (possibly until the next day if you arrive in the afternoon) before your vehicle fills up, or pay for the vacant seats yourself.

Local minibuses and pick-ups aren't much fun and are best avoided when there are larger aircon buses or faster share taxis available, which is pretty much everywhere. However, they will save you a buck or two if you're pinching pennies.

Getting Around

BICYCLE

It's possible to hire bicycles at some of the guesthouses around town for about US$1 to US$2 a day, but take a look at the chaotic traffic conditions before venturing forth. Once you get used to the anarchy, it can be a fun way to get around. There are also shops (p185) that rent out road bicycles and mountain bikes.

CAR & MOTORCYCLE

Exploring Phnom Penh and the surrounding areas on a motorbike is a very liberating experience if you are used to chaotic traffic conditions.

There are numerous motorbike hire places around town. A 100cc Honda costs US$4 to US$7 per day and 250cc dirt bikes run from US$12 to US$30 per day. You'll have to leave your passport – a driver's licence or other form of ID isn't enough. Remember you usually get what you pay for when choosing a bike.

Car hire is available through travel agencies, guesthouses and hotels in Phnom Penh. Everything from cars (from US$25) to 4WDs (from US$60) are available for travelling around the city, but prices rise fast once you venture beyond.

Little Bikes (Map p184; ☎017 329338; 97 St 154) High-quality trail bikes from US$18, and 125cc bikes for US$7/30 per day/week.

Lucky! Lucky! (Map p192; ☎023-212788; 413 Monivong Blvd) Motorbikes are US$4 to US$7 per day, less for multiday rentals. Trail bikes from US$12.

Two Wheels Only (Map p182; ☎012-200513; www.twocambodia.com; 34L St 368) Has well-maintained bikes available to rent (motorbike/trail bike per day US$5/25).

Vannak Bikes Rental (Map p184; ☎012 220970; 46 St 130) Has high-performance trail bikes up to 600cc for US$15 to US$30 per day, and smaller motorbikes for US$5 to US$7.

CYCLO, MOTO & REMORK

Travelling by *cyclo* (pedicab) is a relaxing way to see the sights in the centre of town, although they don't work well for long distances. For a day of sightseeing, expect to pay around US$10. Short jaunts cost similar to *moto* fares.

Only in areas frequented by foreigners do *moto* (motorcycle taxi) drivers generally speak English (and sometimes a little French). Most short trips are about 2000r to 3000r, although if you want to get from one end of the city to the other, you have to pay US$1 or more.

Better known as *tuk-tuks*, *remork-motos* are motorbikes with carriages and are the main way of getting around Phnom Penh for tourists. Average fares are about double those of *moto*.

TAXI

At 3000r per kilometre, taxis are cheap, but don't expect to flag one down on the street. Call **Global Meter Taxi** (☎011 311888), **Choice Taxi** (☎023-888023, 010 888010) or **Taxi Vantha** (☎012 855000) for a pick-up.

AROUND PHNOM PENH

Kirirom National Park

You can really get away from it all at this lush, elevated **national park** (US$5) a two-hour drive southwest of Phnom Penh. Winding trails lead through pine forests to cascading wet-season waterfalls and cliffs with amazing views of the Cardamom Mountains, and there's some great mountain-biking to be done if you're feeling adventurous.

Up in the actual national park, you'll find myriad walking trails and dirt roads that lead to small wet-season waterfalls, lakes, wats and abandoned buildings, but

GETTING TO VIETNAM: SOUTHEASTERN BORDERS

Phnom Penh to Chau Doc

The most scenic way to end your travels in Cambodia is to sail the Mekong to Kaam Samnor (about 100km south-southeast of Phnom Penh), cross the border to Vinh Xuong in Vietnam, and proceed to Chau Doc overloand or on the Tonlé Bassac River via a small channel. Chau Doc has onward land and river connections to points in the Mekong Delta and elsewhere in Vietnam.

Various companies do trips all the way through to Chau Doc using a single boat or some combination of bus and boat; prices vary according to speed and level of service. Capitol Tour (p199) departs Phnom Penh at 8am and involves a bus transfer; the trip is about six to seven hours. **Hang Chau** (☎088 878 7871; US$25) departs from the tourist-boat dock at noon and the entire journey is by boat; the more upmarket and slightly faster **Blue Cruiser** (☎023-633 3666; www.bluecruiser.com; US$35) departs at 1.30pm; **Victoria Hotels** (www.victoriahotels.asia; US$95) also has a boat making several runs a week between Phnom Penh and its Victoria Chau Doc Hotel. These companies take about four hours, including a slow border check, and use a single boat to Chau Doc. Backpacker guesthouses and tour companies offer cheaper bus/boat combo trips. All boats depart from Phnom Penh's **tourist-boat dock** (Map p184; 93 Sisowath Quay).

Some nationalities require a Vietnam visa in advance and some do not require a visa. Check with the Vietnamese Embassy in Phnom Penh to see if you need a visa or not, as visas are not available on arrival. If arriving from Vietnam, Cambodia visas are available on arrival.

Phnom Penh to Ho Chi Minh City

Getting to the border The original **Bavet/Moc Bai land crossing** between Vietnam and Cambodia has seen steady traffic for two decades. The easiest way to get to Ho Chi Minh City (Saigon) is to catch an international bus (US$8 to US$13, seven hours) from Phnom Penh. There are several companies making this trip.

At the border Long lines entering either country are not uncommon, but otherwise it's straightforward provided you purchase a Vietnamese visa in advance (should you require one).

Moving on If you are not on the international bus, it's not hard to find onward transport to HCMC or elsewhere.

Takeo to Chau Doc

Getting to the border The remote and seldom-used **Phnom Den/Tinh Bien border crossing** (⏰7am to 5pm) between Cambodia and Vietnam lies about 50km southeast of Takeo town in Cambodia and offers connections to Chau Doc. Most travellers prefer the Mekong crossing at Kaam Samnor or the newer Prek Chak crossing near Ha Tien to the south. Take a share taxi (10,000r), a chartered taxi (US$25) or a *moto* (US$10) from Takeo to the border (48km).

At the border Several nationalities can get 15-day Vietnam visas on arrival; everyone else needs to arrange one in advance. Coming into Cambodia from Vietnam, note that e-visas are not accepted for entry here.

Moving on Travellers are at the mercy of Vietnamese *xe om* (*moto*) drivers and taxis for the 30km journey from the border to Chau Doc. Prepare for some tough negotiations. Expect to pay somewhere between US$5 and US$10 by bike, more like US$20 for a taxi.

you'll need a map or a guide to navigate them. There's a great map of the park trails and roads made by a Phnom Penh–based mountain-bike enthusiast if you can track down a copy.

Mr Mik is a park ranger and guide who can usually be found at the barbecue shacks near the busy main parking area, about 500m northeast of the information centre.

For US$10 he can take you on a two-hour hike up to Phnom Dat Chivit (End of Life Mountain), where an abrupt cliff face offers an unbroken view of the Elephant Mountains and Cardamom Mountains to the west.

The easiest way to get to Kirirom National Park is via a rental motorbike from Phnom Penh or by chartering a share taxi for a day trip, which will cost in the region of US$80 round trip.

Phnom Chisor

A temple from the Angkorian era, **Phnom Chisor** (ភ្នំជីសូរ; US$2) is set upon a solitary hill in Takeo Province, offering superb views of the countryside. Try to get to Phnom Chisor early in the morning or late in the afternoon, as it is an uncomfortable climb in the heat of the midday sun. Phnom Chisor lies about 55km south of Phnom Penh.

The main temple stands on the eastern side of the hilltop. Constructed of laterite and brick with carved sandstone lintels, the complex is surrounded by the partially ruined walls of a 2.5m-wide gallery with windows. Inscriptions found here date from the 11th century, when this site was known as Suryagiri.

On the plain to the west of Phnom Chisor are the sanctuaries of Sen Thmol (just below Phnom Chisor), Sen Ravang and the former sacred pond of Tonlé Om. All three of these features form a straight line from Phnom Chisor in the direction of Angkor. During rituals held here 900 years ago, the king, his Brahmans and their entourage would climb a monumental 400 steps to Suryagiri from this direction.

If you haven't got the stamina for an overland adventure to Preah Vihear or Phnom Bayong (near Takeo), this is the next best thing for a temple with a view. Near the main temple is a modern Buddhist *vihara* (temple sanctuary), which is used by resident monks.

Renting a motorbike in Phnom Penh is one of the most enjoyable ways to get here in combination with Tonlé Bati or Phnom Tamao Wildlife Rescue Centre. Booking a share taxi is a comfortable option in the wet or hot seasons or you can take a Takeo-bound bus to the access road about 49km south of Phnom Penh and arrange a *moto* from there.

Phnom Tamao Wildlife Rescue Centre

This wonderful **wildlife sanctuary** (adult/child US$5/2; 8am-5pm;) for rescued animals is home to gibbons, sun bears, elephants, tigers, lions, deer, ginormous pythons and a massive bird enclosure. They were all taken from poachers or abusive owners and receive care and shelter here as part of a sustainable breeding program. Wherever possible animals are released back into the wild once they have recovered.

The sanctuary occupies a vast site south of the capital and its animals are kept in excellent conditions by Southeast Asian standards, with plenty of room to roam in enclosures that have been improved and expanded over the years with help from Wildlife Alliance (www.wildlifealliance.org), Free the Bears (www.freethebears.org) and other international wildlife NGOs. Spread out as it is, it feels like a zoo crossed with a safari park.

The centre operates breeding programs for a number of globally threatened species and is home to the world's largest captive collections of pileated gibbons and Malayan sun bears, as well as other rarities such as Siamese crocodiles and greater adjutant storks. Other popular enclosures include huge areas for the large tiger population, and there are elephants that sometimes take part in activities, such as painting. You'll also find a walk-through area with macaques and deer, and a huge aviary.

Cambodia's wildlife is usually very difficult to spot, as larger mammals inhabit remote areas of the country, so Phnom Tamao is the perfect place to discover more about the incredible variety of animals in Cambodia. If you don't like zoos, you might not like this wildlife sanctuary, but remember that these animals have been rescued from traffickers and poachers and need a home. Visitors who come here will be doing their own small bit to help in the protection and survival of Cambodia's varied wildlife.

Both Wildlife Alliance and Free the Bears offer more exclusive experiences at Phnom Tamao for fixed donations. Wildlife Alliance offers a behind-the-scenes tour, which includes access to feeding areas and the nursery area. Free the Bear has a 'Bear Care Tour', which allows guests to help out the on-site team for the day. These tours include transport from Phnom Penh. Otherwise, the easiest option is a rental motorbike or car from

Phnom Penh in combination with Tonlé Bati or Phnom Chisor.

Tonlé Bati

Tonlé Bati (US$3) is the collective name for a pair of old Angkorian-era temples, known as **Ta Prohm** (តាព្រហ្ម) and **Yeay Peau** (យាយពៅ), and a popular lakeside picnic area. It's worth a detour if you are on the way to Phnom Tamao and Phnom Chisor.

You can eat at one of many picnic restaurants here set on stilts over the water and hire an innertube to float around the lake for 2000r. Just avoid Tonlé Bati at weekends, when it's mobbed with locals.

The access road heading to Tonlé Bati is signposted on the right on NH2, 33km south of Independence Monument in Phnom Penh. The entrance to the complex is 1.8km from the highway.

Most people hire private transport to get here. Figure on US$12/25 return for a *moto/remork* from Phnom Penh. Add US$5 to combine with Phnom Tamao, and more still to throw Phnom Chisor into the mix.

Another option is to take a Takeo-bound PP Sorya bus (four daily – aim for the 7am or the 10.30am) and jump off at the access road. Returning to Phnom Penh can be problematic, however. The best advice is to buy a ticket in advance on the Takeo–Phnom Penh bus. Otherwise, hire a *moto*.

Udong

Another popular offering among Phnom Penh touts is a visit to Udong, which served as Cambodian capital under several sovereigns, although many people visit here for the retreats, including the **Cambodia Vipassana Dhura Buddhist Meditation Center** (☎ contact Mr Um Sovann 016-883090; www.cambodiavipassanacenter.com; donation US$25).

Foreigners are welcome to practise meditation here with experienced monks or nuns for one or several days. Free meditation sessions are daily from 7am to 9am and from 2pm to 5pm. In between you can hang out in the library, which contains scores of books on Buddhism, not to mention an impressive collection of pirated Lonely Planet books.

The en suite guestrooms are fairly comfortable by monastic standards, albeit sans mattresses (wicker mats are as good as it gets). You'll be fed breakfast and lunch, but no dinner. There is no fixed price for a meditative retreat here, so donate according to your means; US$25 per day would be considered about average.

The centre is near the base of the western staircase up Phnom Preah Reach Throap.

SIEM REAP

The life-support system and gateway for the temples of Angkor, Siem Reap (*see*-em ree-*ep;* សៀមរាប) was always destined for great things. Visitors come here to see the temples, of course, but there is plenty to do in and around the city when you're templed out. Siem Reap has reinvented itself as the epicentre of chic Cambodia, with everything from backpacker party pads to hip hotels, world-class wining and dining across a range of cuisines, sumptuous spas, great shopping, local tours to suit both foodies and adventurers, and a creative cultural scene that includes Cambodia's leading circus.

Angkor is a place to be savoured, not rushed, and this is the base from which to plan your adventures. Still think three days at the temples is enough? Think again with Siem Reap on the doorstep.

Sights

★ **Angkor National Museum** MUSEUM
(សារមន្ទីរអង្គរ; ☎ 063-966601; www.angkornationalmuseum.com; 968 Charles de Gaulle Blvd; adult/child under 1.2m US$12/6; ⏲ 8.30am-6pm, to 6.30pm Oct-Apr) Looming large on the road to Angkor is the Angkor National Museum, a state-of-the-art showpiece on the Khmer civilisation and the majesty of Angkor. Displays are themed by era, religion and royalty as visitors move through the impressive galleries. After a short presentation, visitors enter the Zen-like 'Gallery of a Thousand Buddhas', which has a fine collection of images. Other exhibits include the pre-Angkorian periods of Funan and Chenla; the great Khmer kings; Angkor Wat; and the inscriptions.

Exhibits include touch-screen video, epic commentary and the chance to experience a panoramic sunrise at Angkor Wat, though there seems to be less sculpture on display here than in the National Museum in Phnom Penh. The US$12 admission fee is a little high, given that US$20 buys admission to all the temples at Angkor. That said, it remains a very useful experience for first-time visitors, putting the story of Angkor and the Khmer empire in context before exploring the temples. An audio tour is available for US$3.

SIEM REAP IN THREE DAYS

You'll want to focus on the temples of Angkor, of course, but allow some downtime for relaxing in Siem Reap and spend at least a half-day exploring more out-of-the-way temples and observing local life in the countryside around Siem Reap. Start with the highlights of the so-called 'big circuit', including the massive Buddhist-Hindu fusion temple of Preah Khan (p225), the ornate water temple of Preah Neak Poan (p225), Ta Som (**Map p222; 7.30am-5.30pm**), the Eastern Mebon (**Map p222; 7.30am-5.30pm**) and Pre Rup (**Map p222; 5am-7pm**). Then join the masses for sunset views of Angkor Wat from Phnom Bakheng (p225). At night go see Phar the Cambodian Circus (p213).

Head out of town on day two to bucolic Banteay Srei District. Stretch your legs amid natural and human-made splendour at Kbal Spean (p226), and visit petite Banteay Srei (p226) temple with its intricate carvings. Tack on the remote jungle temple of Beng Mealea (p226), or head back to town early for a massage and some pool time at your guesthouse.

Save the best for last: sunrise at Angkor Wat (p218), then the other heavy hitters of the so-called 'small circuit' – Angkor Thom (p219), including the fabulous Bayon (p219), and romantically overgrown Ta Prohm (p224). Wrap things up with a night out on the town on Pub St or elsewhere.

Artisans Angkor – Les Chantiers Écoles ARTS CENTRE
(អាទីសង់អង្គរ; www.artisansdangkor.com; 7.30am-6.30pm) FREE Siem Reap is the epicentre of the drive to revitalise Cambodian traditional culture, which was dealt a harsh blow by the Khmer Rouge and the years of instability that followed its rule. Les Chantiers Écoles teaches wood- and stone-carving techniques, traditional silk painting, lacquerware and other artisan skills to impoverished young Cambodians. Free guided tours explaining traditional techniques are available daily from 7.30am to 6.30pm. Tucked down a side road, the school is well signposted from Sivatha St.

Les Chantiers Écoles Silk Farm FARM
(7.30am-5.30pm) Les Chantiers Écoles maintains a silk farm, which produces some of the best work in the country, including clothing, interior-design products and accessories. All stages of the production process can be seen here, from the cultivation of mulberry trees through the nurturing of silk worms to the dyeing and weaving of silk. Free tours are available daily and there is a free shuttle bus departing from Les Chantiers Écoles in Siem Reap at 9.30am and 1.30pm. The farm is about 16km west of Siem Reap, just off the road to Sisophon in the village of Puok.

★**Cambodia Landmine Museum** MUSEUM
សារមន្ទីរគ្រាប់មីនកម្ពុជា និងមូលនិធិសង្គ្រោះ; www.cambodialandminemuseum.org; US$5; 7.30am-5pm) Established by DIY de-miner Aki Ra, this museum has eye-opening displays on the curse of land mines in Cambodia. The collection includes mines, mortars, guns and weaponry, and there is a mock minefield where visitors can attempt to locate the deactivated mines. Proceeds from the museum are ploughed into mine-awareness campaigns. The museum is about 25km from Siem Reap, near Banteay Srei.

Banteay Srei Butterfly Centre WILDLIFE RESERVE
(សួនមេអំបៅបន្ទាយស្រី; www.angkorbutterfly.com; adult/child US$5/2; 9am-5pm) The Banteay Srei Butterfly Centre is the largest fully enclosed butterfly centre in Southeast Asia, with more than 30 species of Cambodian butterflies fluttering about. It is a good experience for children, as they can see the whole life cycle from egg to caterpillar to cocoon to butterfly. The centre aims to provide a sustainable living for the rural poor and most of the butterflies are farmed around Phnom Kulen. It's about 7km before Banteay Srei temple on the left side of the road.

Senteurs d'Angkor Botanic Garden GARDENS
(Map p222; Airport Rd; 7.30am-5.30pm) Senteurs d'Angkor's botanic garden is a sort of Willy Wonka's for the senses, where you can sample infused teas and speciality coffees.

Activities

Golf

Angkor Wat Putt GOLF
(Map p222; 012 302330; www.angkorwatputt.com; adult/child US$5/4; 7.30am-10pm) Crazy

Siem Reap

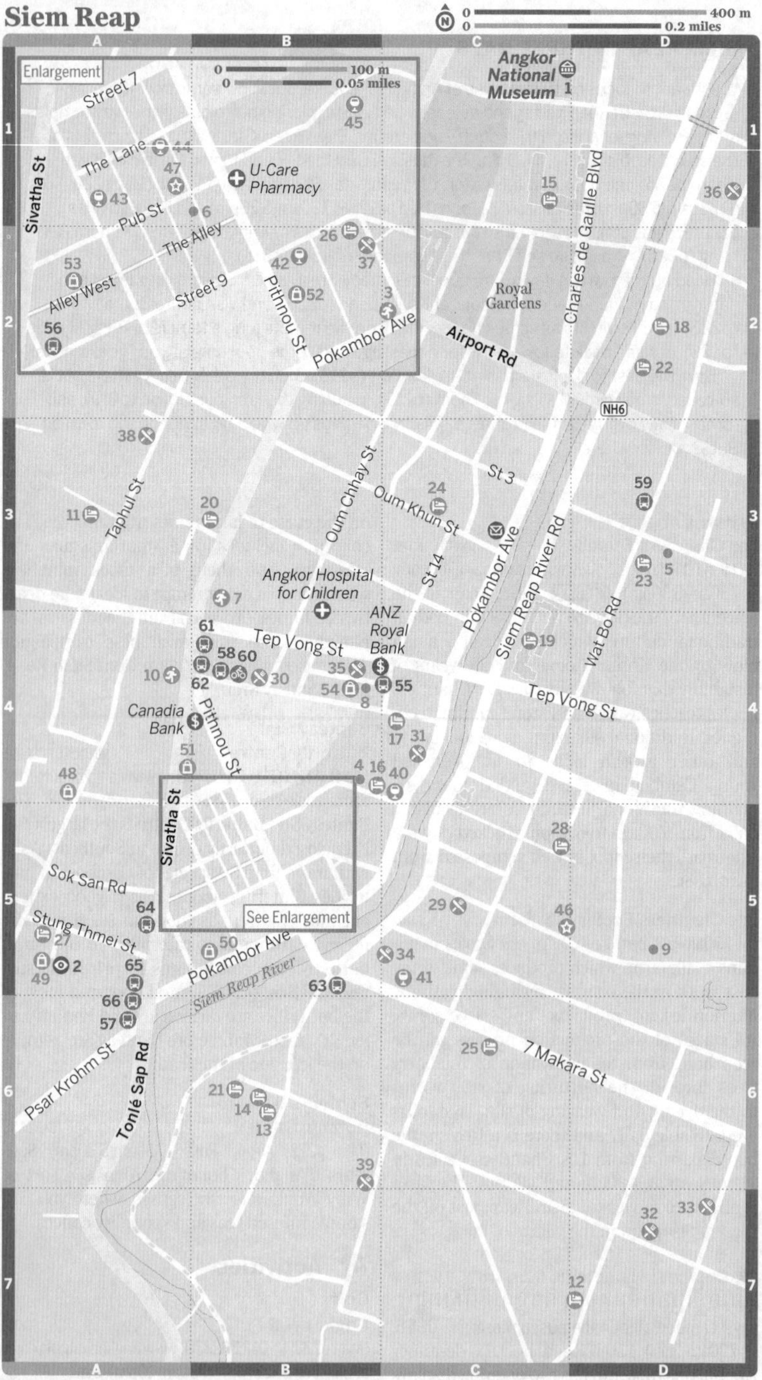

0 400 m
0 0.2 miles
Enlargement
0 100 m
0 0.05 miles
Street 7
The Lane
Sivatha St
Pub St
The Alley
Alley West
Street 9
Pithnou St
Pokambor Ave
U-Care Pharmacy
Angkor National Museum
Royal Gardens
Charles de Gaulle Blvd
Airport Rd
NH6
St 3
Oum Chhay St
Oum Khun St
Taphul St
St 14
Pokambor Ave
Siem Reap River Rd
Wat Bo Rd
Angkor Hospital for Children
ANZ Royal Bank
Tep Vong St
Canadia Bank
Pithnou St
Sivatha St
See Enlargement
Sok San Rd
Stung Thmei St
Pokambor Ave
Siem Reap River
7 Makara St
Psar Krohm St
Tonlé Sap Rd

Siem Reap

Top Sights
1 Angkor National Museum C1

Sights
2 Artisans Angkor – Les Chantiers Écoles A5

Activities, Courses & Tours
3 Bodytune C2
4 Cambodian Cooking Cottage B4
5 KKO (Khmer for Khmer Organisation) Bike Tours D3
6 Le Tigre de Papier B1
7 Lemongrass Garden B3
8 PURE! Countryside Bicycle Tour B4
9 Sam Veasna Center D5
10 Seeing Hands Massage 4 ..... A4

Sleeping
11 Auberge Mont Royal A3
12 Blue Lizard D7
13 Downtown Siem Reap Hostel B6
14 Golden Banana B&B B6
15 Grand Hotel d'Angkor C1
16 Happy Zone Inn B4
17 Ivy Guesthouse 2 ..... C4
18 La Noria Guesthouse D2
19 La Résidence d'Angkor C4
20 Mad Monkey B3
21 Rambutan Resort B6
22 Rosy Guesthouse D2
23 Seven Candles Guesthouse D3
24 Shinta Mani C3
25 Siem Reap Hostel C6
26 Steung Siem Reap Hotel B2
27 Tareach Angkor Villa A5
28 Viroth's Hotel C5

Eating
29 Banllé Vegetarian Restaurant C5
30 Blossom Cafe B4
31 Chanrey Tree C4
32 Cuisine Wat Damnak D7
33 Haven D7
34 King's Road C5
35 Little Red Fox B4
36 Marum D1
37 New Leaf Book Cafe B2
38 Sugar Palm A3
39 Tangram Garden B6

Drinking & Nightlife
40 Barcode C4
41 Full Frontal C5
42 Laundry Bar B2
43 Mezze Bar A1
44 Miss Wong A1
45 YOLO Bar B1

Entertainment
46 Apsara Theatre C5
47 Temple Club A1

Shopping
48 Angkor Night Market A4
49 Artisans Angkor A5
50 Monument Books B5
51 Rajana A4
52 Senteurs d'Angkor B2
53 Spicy Green Mango A2
54 trunkh B4

Transport
55 Asia Van Transfer C4
56 Capitol Tour A2
57 Giant Ibis A6
58 Gold VIP B4
59 Golden Bayon Express D3
60 Green e-bikes B4
61 Liang US Express B4
62 Mekong Express B4
63 Neak Krohorm B5
64 Phnom Penh Sorya A5
65 Rith Mony A5
66 Virak Buntham A6

golf to the Brits among us, this home-grown minigolf course contrasts with the big golf courses out of town. Navigate mini-temples and creative obstacles for 14 holes. Win a beer for a hole-in-one.

Phokheetra Country Club GOLF
(☎063-964600; www.sofitel.com; green fees US$100) This club hosts a tournament on the Asian tour annually and includes an ancient Angkor bridge amid its manicured fairways and greens.

Massage & Yoga

Foot massages are a big hit in Siem Reap – not surprising given all those steep stairways at the temples. There are half a dozen or more places offering a massage for about US$6 to US$8 an hour on the strip running northwest of Psar Chaa. Some are more authentic than others, so dip your toe in first before selling your sole.

For an alternative foot massage, brave the waters of Dr Fish: you dip your feet into a paddling pool full of cleaner fish, which nibble away at your dead skin. It's heaven for some, tickly as hell for others. The original is housed in the Angkor Night Market, but copycats have sprung up all over town, including a dozen or so tanks around Pub St and Psar Chaa.

Krousar Thmey MASSAGE

(Map p222; www.krousar-thmey.org; Charles de Gaulle Blvd; 1hr massage US$7; 9am-9pm) Massages here are performed by blind masseurs. In the same location is the free Tonlé Sap Exhibition, which includes a 'Seeing in the Dark' interactive exhibition exploring what it is like to be blind, guided by a sight-impaired student.

Bodytune SPA

(063-764141; www.bodytune.co.th; 293 Pokambor Ave; 1hr massage US$12-20; 10am-10pm) A lavish outpost of a popular Thai spa, this is a fine place to relax and unwind on the riverfront.

Lemongrass Garden SPA

(012 387385; www.lemongrassgarden.com; 105B Sivatha St; 1hr massage US$12-20; 11am-10pm) Smart spa in a central location, offering a range of affordable treatments, including a 45-minute kiddie massage (US$7).

Peace Cafe Yoga YOGA

(Map p222; 063-965210; www.peacecafeangkor.org; Siem Reap River Rd; per session US$6) This popular community centre/cafe has daily morning and evening yoga sessions, including ashtanga and hatha sessions.

Seeing Hands Massage 4 MASSAGE

(012 836487; 324 Sivatha St; per hour fan/air-con US$5/7) Seeing Hands trains blind people in the art of massage. Watch out for copycats, as some of these are just exploiting the blind for profit.

Courses

Cooks in Tuk Tuks COOKING

(Map p222; 063-963400; www.therivergarden.info; Siem Reap River Rd East; per person US$25) Starts at 10am daily with a visit to Psar Leu market, then returns to the River Garden for a professional class.

Cambodian Cooking Cottage COOKING

(077 566455; reservation@angkorw.com; Wat Preah Prohm Roth St; per person US$25) This sophisticated cooking class in a cottage near Wat Preah Prohm Roth includes tips on decorative presentation, a recipe book, a DVD and some take-away spices.

Le Tigre de Papier COOKING

(012 265811; www.angkor-cooking-class-cambodia.com; Pub St; per person US$15) Daily classes are held at 10am, 1pm and 5pm. Classes include a visit to the market.

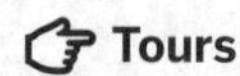

Tours

Sam Veasna Center BIRDWATCHING

(SVC; 063-963710; www.samveasna.org; per person from US$100) Sam Veasna Center, in the Wat Bo area of Siem Reap, is the authority on birdwatching in Cambodia, with professionally trained English-speaking guides, powerful spotting scopes and a network of camps and bird hides scattered throughout north Cambodia. It uses ecotourism to provide an income for local communities in return for a ban on hunting and cutting down the forest.

Locally, SVC's most popular trip is to the spectacular Prek Toal Bird Sanctuary (p217) in the Tonlé Sap wetland area. It also runs trips to Ang Trapeng Thmor Reserve (p216), about 100km from Siem Reap, one of only a handful of places in the world where it's possible to see the extremely rare sarus crane. All tours include transport, entrance fees, guides, breakfast, lunch and water.

Some proceeds from the Prek Toal tours go towards educating children and villagers about the importance of the birds and the unique flooded-forest environment, and the trip includes a visit to one of the local communities. Day trips include a hotel pick-up at around 6am and a return by nightfall.

Osmose BIRDWATCHING

(063-765506; www.osmosetonlesap.net; per person in group of 5/2 US$95/165) Runs organised day trips to Prek Toal (p217) including transport, entrance fees, guides, breakfast, lunch and water. Binoculars are available on request. Can also arrange overnight trips for serious enthusiasts.

Some proceeds from the tours go towards educating children and villagers about the importance of the birds and the unique flooded-forest environment, and the trip includes a visit to one of the local communities. Day trips include a hotel pick-up around 6am and a return by nightfall.

Prek Toal Tours & Travel TOURS

(077 797112; www.prektoal-tours.com; birdwatching per person in group of 5/2 US$65/128) Run by local villagers, this outfit offers day or overnight trips with homestay accommodation to the fascinating floating village of Prek Toal. There's an option to visit the Prek Toal Bird Sanctuary (p217) on these trips.

KKO (Khmer for Khmer Organisation) Bike Tours CYCLING

(093 903024; www.kko-cambodia.org; cnr St 20 & Wat Bo Rd; tours US$35-50) Good-

cause cycling tours around the paths of Angkor or into the countryside beyond the Western Baray. Proceeds go towards the Khmer for Khmer Organisation, which supports education and vocational training.

PURE! Countryside Bicycle Tour CYCLING
(☎097 2356862; Hup Guan St; per person US$25-35) Based out of the Srey Ma gift shop, this outfit organises long half-day tours that take in local life around Siem Reap, including lunch with a local family. All proceeds go towards supporting Pure's educational and vocational-training projects. Book a few days ahead so they can notify the families.

Siem Reap Food Tours FOOD & DRINK
(☎012 505542; www.siemreapfoodtours.com; per person US$75) Operated by an American food writer and an experienced Scottish chef with a penchant for stand-up comedy, these tours are a recipe for engaging food encounters. Choose from a morning tour that takes in local markets and the *naom banchok* noodle stalls of Preah Dak or an evening tour that takes in street stalls and local barbecue restaurants.

Sleeping

Siem Reap has the best range of accommodation in Cambodia. A vast number of family-run guesthouses charging US$5 to US$20 a room cater for budget travellers, while those looking for midrange accommodation can choose from a dizzying array of boutique accommodation in the US$30 to US$70 range. At the high end you can pay as much as you're willing to spend, but given the plethora of good-value, midrange, pool-equipped boutiques, there's little need to.

Psar Chaa Area

Psar Chaa is the liveliest part of town, brimming with restaurants, bars and boutiques. Staying here can be a lot of fun, but it's not the quietest area.

Garden Village Guesthouse GUESTHOUSE $
(Map p222; ☎012 217373; www.gardenvillageguesthouse.com; 434 Sok San Rd; dm US$4, r US$8-25;) This traditional backpacker hang-out on up-and-coming Sok San Rd offers friendly service and some of the cheapest beds in town. The delightful pool and pool bar are a good place to meet other travellers, and it has two additional properties in the centre for spillover.

Downtown Siem Reap Hostel HOSTEL $
(☎012 675881; www.downtownsiemreaphostel.hostel.com; Wat Dam Nak area; dm US$6-8, r US$12-18;) The rates here are particularly inviting when you factor in the small pool in the garden. Chill out with air-con in the more expensive dorms or rooms. Outside visitors can use the pool with a US$6 spend on food and drink.

Happy Zone Inn GUESTHOUSE $
(☎012 993484; www.happyzonevilla.com; Wat Preah Prohm Roth St; r with fan/air-con from US$10/13;) Central, yet tucked away down a side street that runs parallel to Wat Preah Prohm Roth, this is a friendly place with a wide range of rooms, including triples and quads. Free pick-up from airport, port or bus station.

★**Golden Banana B&B** GUESTHOUSE $$
(☎063-761259; www.golden-banana.com; Wat Dam Nak area; s/d incl breakfast US$33/40;) The original Golden Banana, this place has a boutique feel, set in attractive temple-like pavilions with Sino-Khmer furnishings. Breakfast is beside the charming pool, and nearby annexes are available for spillovers.

Rambutan Resort RESORT $$
(☎063-766655; www.rambutans.info; Wat Dam Nak area; r incl breakfast US$69-79;) Long a part of the iconic Golden Banana B&B empire, the (Golden) Banana Republic has now split and the outcome is this atmospheric, gay-friendly resort spread over two stunning villas, each with spacious and stylish rooms and an inviting courtyard swimming pool.

Steung Siem Reap Hotel HOTEL $$
(☎063-965167; www.steungsiemreaphotel.com; near Psar Chaa; r incl breakfast from US$65;) In keeping with the French colonial-era legacy around Psar Chaa, this hotel has high ceilings, louvre shutters and wrought-iron balconies. Three-star rooms feature smart wooden trim. The location is hard to beat.

Sivatha St Area

The area to the west of Sivatha St includes a good selection of budget guesthouses and midrange boutique hotels. Off the southern end of Sivatha St is Sok San Rd, fast becoming Siem Reap's top traveller's mecca as high rents force many budget and midrange properties out of the centre.

★**Mad Monkey** HOSTEL $
(www.madmonkeyhostels.com; Sivatha St; dm US$7-9, r US$16-26;) The Siem Reap outpost

of an expanding Monkey business, this classic backpacker has deluxe dorms with air-con and extra-wide bunk beds, good-value rooms for those wanting privacy and the obligatory rooftop bar, only this one's a beach bar!

Ivy Guesthouse 2 GUESTHOUSE $
(☎012 800860; www.ivy-guesthouse.com; Psar Kandal St; r with fan US$6-8, with air-con US$15; ❄@📶) An inviting guesthouse with a chill-out area and bar, the Ivy is a lively place to stay. The restaurant is as good as it gets among the guesthouses in town, with a huge vegetarian selection and US$1 'Tapas Fridays'.

Funky Flashpacker HOSTEL $
(Map p222; ☎070 221524; www.funkyflashpacker.com; Funky Lane; dm US$7, r US$16-35; ❄@📶🏊) Siem Reap's number-one party address among backpackers. The entire downstairs courtyard is taken up with a swimming pool where regular bouts of water polo take place, while the rooftop bar sizzles with inebriated youth hopped up on cheap shooters. Great hostel, but it's no place for quiet time.

Auberge Mont Royal HOTEL $$
(☎063-964044; www.auberge-mont-royal.com; s/d incl breakfast from US$42/54; ❄@📶🏊) Set in a classic colonial-style villa, the Auberge has smart rooms at a smart price, with the swimming pool and spa making it a cut above other offerings in this price bracket.

East Bank

This up-and-coming area on the east bank of the Siem Reap River features socially responsible guesthouses as well as some hip boutique hotels. There is a great guesthouse ghetto in a backstreet running parallel to the north end of Wat Bo Rd, which is a good option for browsers without a booking.

★ **Rosy Guesthouse** GUESTHOUSE $
(☎063-965059; www.rosyguesthouse.com; Siem Reap River Rd; d without bathroom US$9, with bathroom US$16-35; ❄📶) 🌿 A Brit-run establishment whose 13 rooms come with TV and DVD. The lively pub downstairs has great grub and hosts regular events to support community causes, including a popular quiz night.

Siem Reap Hostel HOSTEL $
(☎063-964660; www.thesiemreaphostel.com; 10 Makara St; dm US$9-11, r incl breakfast US$34-45; ❄@📶🏊) Angkor's original backpacker hostel is pretty slick. The dorms are well tended, while the rooms are definitely flashpacker and include breakfast. There is a lively bar-restaurant and a covered pool, plus a well-organised travel desk.

Seven Candles Guesthouse GUESTHOUSE $
(☎063-963380; www.sevencandlesguesthouse.com; 307 Wat Bo Rd; r US$20-38; ❄@📶) 🌿 A good-cause guesthouse,Seven Candles uses profits to help a local foundation that seeks to promote education in rural communities. Rooms include hot water, TV and fridge, plus some decorative flourishes.

Blue Lizard HOSTEL $
(☎096 7710052; www.bluelizardhostel.com; Wat Dam Nak area; dm with fan/air-con US$4/6, d US$5; ❄📶) With a side-street location and most communication done via whiteboard (the American owner is deaf), this is one of Siem Reap's quietest hostels. It's also one of the cheapest, as some dorm beds can sleep two for US$4. Has stepped up its game of late with a new hang-out area and bar.

★ **La Noria Guesthouse** GUESTHOUSE $$
(☎063-964242; www.lanoriaangkor.com; Siem Reap River Rd; r US$49-69; ❄@📶🏊) Long-running and lovely La Noria is set in a lush tropical garden with a pretty swimming pool. Rooms have a traditional trim and include a verandah but no TV or fridge. Sister hotel Borann is almost identical. Rates vary seasonally.

The restaurant is superb and every Wednesday it hosts traditional performances (US$7) put on by disadvantaged children trained at NGO Krousar Thmey (p208).

Tareach Angkor Villa HOTEL $$
(☎063-963986; www.tareachangkorvilla.com; r incl breakfast US$25-40; ❄@📶🏊) A newish hotel in the Sok San Rd area, this is a great-value flashpacker place, offering bright, modern rooms with flat-screen TV and stylish bathrooms. It's Khmer-run and owned, with a small indoor pool.

★ **Viroth's Hotel** BOUTIQUE HOTEL $$$
(☎063-766107; www.viroth-hotel.com; St 24; r incl breakfast US$86-118; ❄@📶🏊) The new Viroth's is an ultra-stylish, retro-chic property with 30 rooms fitted out with classy contemporary furnishings. Behind the impressive facade lies a 20m swimming pool, a gym and a spa. The original seven-bedroom hotel is still operating as Viroth's Villa.

La Résidence d'Angkor RESORT $$$
(☎063-963390; www.residencedangkor.com; Siem Reap River Rd; r incl breakfast from US$220; ❄@📶🏊) The 54 wood-appointed rooms, among the most tasteful and inviting in town,

come with verandahs and huge Jacuzzi-sized tubs. The gorgeous swimming pool is perfect for laps. The newer wing is ultra-contemporary, as is the sumptuous Kong Kea Spa.

Riverfront & Royal Gardens

The smart end of town, this is where the royal residence is to be found, along with many of the luxury hotels and boutique resorts.

★Grand Hotel d'Angkor HOTEL **$$$**
(063-963888; www.raffles.com; 1 Charles de Gaulle Blvd; r incl breakfast from US$220;) This historic hotel has been welcoming guests such as Charlie Chaplin, Charles de Gaulle, Jackie Kennedy and Bill Clinton since 1932. Ensconced in opulent surroundings, you can imagine what it was like to be a tourist in colonial days. Rooms include classic touches and a dizzying array of bathroom gifts.

Shinta Mani RESORT **$$$**
(063-761998; www.shintamani.com; Oum Khun St; r incl breakfast US$170-284;) With a contemporary chic design by renowned architect Bill Bensley, Shinta Mani Resort features an inviting central pool, while Shinta Mani Club offers more exclusive rooms. Shinta Mani has won several international awards for responsible tourism practices.

Further Afield

Don't shy away from venturing further afield, as some of the most memorable boutique hotels lie hidden beyond and are usually only a short *remork* ride from the centre.

Sala Bai Hotel & Restaurant School HOTEL **$$**
(Map p222; 063-963329; www.salabai.com; Tonle Sap Road, Wat Svay; r incl breakfast US$30-50; closed mid-Jul–mid-Oct;) Relocated in 2016 to a rambling villa 1.5km south of Wat Dam Nak on the east side of the river, this training-school hotel for disadvantaged youth features six spacious, minimalist rooms with brushed-concrete floors and boutique bathrooms. The deluxe rooms sleep three comfortably.

There's a fine training restaurant on-site. Some 1300 Sala Bai graduates are working in the hospitality industry across Siem Reap and other locales.

★Templation Angkor RESORT **$$$**
(Map p222; 063-969345; www.templation.asia; Rok Rak St; US$98-298;) Long a dominant force in Phnom Penh, the Plantation group of hotels comes to Siem Reap with yet another masterpiece of service and style. This edition is spread over several acres on the west bank of the river, north of the centre, with a lake-sized pool and 33 sleek concrete-and-stone villas – some with private swimming pools.

HanumanAlaya Villa BOUTIQUE HOTEL **$$$**
(Map p222; 063-760582; www.hanumanalaya.com; Siem Reap River Rd West; r US$60-150;) The most traditionally Cambodian of the boutique hotels in town, HanumanAlaya Villa is set around a lush garden and pretty swimming pool. Rooms are decorated with antiques and handicrafts but include modern touches such as flat-screen TV, minibar and safe. Equally tasteful sister hotel HanumanAlaya Boutique is nearby, but was undergoing an extensive renovation during our latest visit.

Eating

The dining scene in Siem Reap is something to savour, offering a superb selection of street food, Asian eateries and sumptuous restaurants. The range encompasses something from every continent, with new temptations regularly opening up. Sample the subtleties of Khmer cuisine in town, or indulge in home comforts prior to – or after – hitting the remote provinces. Some of the very best restaurants also put something back into community projects or offer vocational training.

Little Red Fox CAFE **$**
(Hup Guan St; dishes US$2-8; 6am-5pm Thu-Tue;) This foxy little cafe is incredibly popular with long-term residents in Siem Reap who swear that the regionally sourced Feel Good coffee is the best in town. Add to that designer breakfasts, creative juices and air-con and it's easy to pass some time here. The slick new upstairs wing is popular with the laptop crowd.

Banllé Vegetarian Restaurant VEGETARIAN **$**
(www.banlle-vegetarian.com; St 26; dishes US$2-4; 11am-9.30pm Wed-Mon;) In a traditional wooden house with its own organic vegetable garden, this is a great place for a healthy bite. The menu offers a blend of international and Cambodian dishes, including a vegetable *amok*, and zesty fruit and vegetable shakes.

★Mie Cafe CAMBODIAN, INTERNATIONAL **$$**
(Map p222; 069 999096; www.miecafe-siemreap.com; near Angkor Conservation; mains US$4-8; 11am-2pm & 5.30-10pm Wed-Mon) An impressive Cambodian eatery offering a fusion take on traditional flavours. It is set in a wooden house just off the road to Angkor and offers a

gourmet set menu for US$24. Dishes include everything from succulent marinated pork ribs to squid-ink ravioli.

★ **Sugar Palm** CAMBODIAN $$
(www.thesugarpalm.com; Taphul St; mains US$5-9; 11.30am-3pm & 5.30-10.30pm Mon-Sat;) Set in a beautiful wooden house, the Sugar Palm is the place to sample traditional flavours infused with herbs and spices, including delicious *char kreung* (curried lemongrass) dishes. Owner Kethana showed celebrity chef Gordon Ramsay how to prepare *amok*.

King's Road INTERNATIONAL $$
(www.kingsroadangkor.com; Siem Reap River Rd East; 7am-midnight) King's Road is an upmarket dining destination on the east bank of the Siem Reap River. You can browse the daily 'Made in Cambodia' community market of craft stalls, then choose from about 15 restaurants set in beautiful traditional Cambodian wooden buildings. Choose from Cambodian (Embassy), Chinese (Emperors of China), Italian (Terrazza) and more. There is also a Hard Rock Cafe attached with live music.

Chanrey Tree CAMBODIAN $$
(www.chanreytree.com; Pokambor Ave; mains US$5-12; 11am-2pm & 5.30-10pm;) Cool and contemporary, Chantrey Tree is the new face of Khmer cuisine, combining a stylish setting with expressive presentation, while retaining the essentials of traditional Cambodian cooking. Try the eggplant with pork ribs or grilled stuffed frog.

Tangram Garden INTERNATIONAL $$
(www.tangramgarden.com; Wat Dam Nak Village; mains US$6-9; 6-9.30pm Mon-Sat;) This alfresco garden restaurant near Wat Dam Nak specialises in barbecue grills, creative vegetarian dishes and Khmer staples. Friday nights usually see a set dinner served with a Cambodia-relevant movie or show related to the arts in Cambodia (US$25 for the dinner/show combo).

★ **Cuisine Wat Damnak** CAMBODIAN $$$
(077 347762; www.cuisinewatdamnak.com; Wat Dam Nak area; 5-/6-course menu US$24/28; 6.30-10.30pm Tue-Sat, last orders 9.30pm) Set in a traditional wooden house is this highly regarded restaurant from Siem Reap celeb chef Joannes Riviere. The menu delivers the ultimate contemporary Khmer dining experience. Seasonal set menus focus on market-fresh ingredients and change weekly; vegetarian options are available with advance notice.

GOOD-CAUSE DINING IN SIEM REAP

There are some good restaurants in Siem Reap that support worthy causes or assist in the training of Cambodia's future hospitality staff with a subsidised ticket into the tourism industry. When you dine at the training places, it provides the trainees with a good opportunity to hone their skills with real customers.

Marum (www.marum-restaurant.org; Wat Polanka area; mains US$3.25-6.75; 11am-10.30pm;) Set in a delightful wooden house with a spacious garden, Marum serves up lots of vegetarian and seafood dishes, plus some mouth-watering desserts. Menu highlights include red-tree, beef and chilli stir-fry and mini crocodile burgers. Marum is part of the Tree Alliance group of training restaurants; the experience is a must.

There's a great shop here too, and the whole place is extremely kid-friendly.

Haven (078-342404; www.haven-cambodia.com; Chocolate Rd, Wat Dam Nak area; mains US$3-7; 11.30am-2.30pm & 5.30-9.30pm Mon-Sat, closed Aug;) A culinary haven indeed, dine here for the best of East meets West; the fish fillet with green mango is particularly zesty. Proceeds go towards helping young adult orphans make the step from institution to employment.

Blossom Cafe (www.blossomcakes.org; St 6; cupcakes US$1.50; 10am-5pm Mon-Sat;) Cupcakes are elevated to an art form at this elegant cafe, with beautifully presented creations available in a rotating array of 48 flavours. Creative coffees, teas and juices are also on offer and profits assist Cambodian women in vocational training.

New Leaf Book Cafe (near Psar Chaa; mains US$3-6; 7.30am-10pm) The profits from this new cafe and secondhand bookshop go towards supporting NGOs working in Siem Reap Province. The menu includes some home favourites, an Italian twist and some local Cambodian specials.

Drinking & Nightlife

The transformation from sleepy overgrown village to an international destination for the jet set has been dramatic and Siem Reap is now firmly on the nightlife map of Southeast Asia.

Most bars have happy hours, as do some of the fancier hotels. The FCC Angkor (Pokambor Ave) and Grand Hotel d'Angkor (p211) hotels both have legendary bars.

Full Frontal COCKTAIL BAR
(King's Rd; 10am-10.30pm) Doubling as a gallery, this is where the creative set comes to talk art and poetry and sip strong cocktails. It looks the part, with a suitably creative interior punctuated by gorgeous tilework, and an air-conditioned loft up the stairs. Owner Jess is a force behind the Angkor Photo Festival (www.angkor-photo.com).

Laundry Bar BAR
(St 9; 4pm-late;) One of the most chilled bars in town thanks to low lighting and discerning decor, this is the place to come for electronica and ambient sounds. It heaves on weekends or when guest DJs crank up the volume. Happy hour until 9pm.

YOLO Bar BAR
(Wat Preah Prohm Roth St; 5pm-late;) A popular backpacker bar down a side street, YOLO specialises in cheap cocktails by the bucketload (quite literally) and DIY tunes played through their open table laptop. Give it a try... after all, you only live once.

Barcode BAR
(www.barcodesiemreap.com; Wat Preah Prohm Roth St; 6pm-late;) A super-stylin' gay bar that is metrosexual friendly; the cocktails here are worth the stop, as is the regular drag show at 9.30pm. There is a happy hour from 5pm to 7pm daily.

Mezze Bar BAR
(www.mezzesiemreap.com; St 11; 6pm-late;) One of the hippest bars in Siem Reap, Mezze is located above the circus that surrounds Pub St. Ascend the stairs to a contemporary lounge bar complete with original art, regular DJs and Sunday salsa nights.

Miss Wong BAR
(www.misswong.net; The Lane; 6pm-1am;) Miss Wong carries you back to chic 1920s Shanghai. The cocktails are a draw here, making it a cool place to while away an evening, with a new menu offering dim sum. Gay-friendly and extremely popular with the well-heeled expat crowd.

Entertainment

Evening Cambodian cultural performances offered by several restaurants and hotels may not be as sophisticated as a performance of the Royal Ballet in Phnom Penh, but to the untrained eye they are nonetheless graceful and alluring. Prices usually include a buffet meal.

★ **Phare the Cambodian Circus** CIRCUS
(Map p222; 015 499480; www.pharecircus.org; west end of Sok San Rd; adult/child US$18/10, premium seats US$35/18; 8pm daily) Cambodia's answer to Cirque du Soleil, Phare the Cambodian Circus is so much more than a conventional circus, with an emphasis on performance art and a subtle yet striking social message behind each production. Cambodia's leading circus, theatre and performing arts organisation Phare Ponleu Selpak opened its big top for shows in 2013 and the results are a unique form of entertainment that should be considered unmissable when staying in Siem Reap.

Apsara Theatre DANCE
(063-963561; www.angkorvillageresort.asia/apsara-theatre; St 26; show US$27; 7.30pm) The setting for this Cambodian classical dance show is a striking wooden pavilion finished in the style of a wat. The price includes dinner. It tends to be packed to the rafters with tour groups.

Rosana Broadway CABARET
(Map p222; 063-769991; www.rosanabroadway.com; NH6; show US$25-45; 7.30pm daily) Bringing a bit of Bangkok-style Broadway to Siem Reap, this show includes cultural dances from the region and a not-so-cultural ladyboy cabaret; ticket prices are on the high side.

Temple Club DANCE
(Pub St;) Temple Club stages a free traditional dance show upstairs from 7.30pm, providing punters order some food and drink from the very reasonably priced menu.

Shopping

Be sure to bargain at the markets, as overcharging is pretty common. King's Road (p212) hosts the 'Made in Cambodia' community market daily from noon to 10pm, bringing together many of the best local craftsfolk and creators in Siem Reap, many promoting good causes.

★ Artisans Angkor ARTS & CRAFTS

(www.artisansdangkor.com; ⏲7.30am-6.30pm) On the premises of Les Chantiers Écoles (p205) is this beautiful shop, which sells everything from stone and wood reproductions of Angkorian-era statues to household furnishings. There's also a second shop opposite Angkor Wat in the Angkor Cafe building, and outlets at Phnom Penh and Siem Reap international airports.

All profits from sales go back into funding the school and bringing more young Cambodians into the training program, which is 20% owned by the artisans themselves.

★ trunkh. GIFTS & SOUVENIRS

(Hup Guan St; ⏲10am-6pm) The owner here has a great eye for the quirky, stylish and original, including beautiful shirts, throw pillows, jewellery, poster art, and T's, plus some off-beat items such as genuine Cambodian water buffalo bells.

AHA Fair Trade Village ARTS & CRAFTS

(Map p222; ☎078 341454; www.aha-kh.com; Rd 60, Trang Village; ⏲10am-7pm) For locally produced souvenirs (unlike much of the imported stuff that turns up in Psar Chaa) drop in on this handicraft market. It's a little out of the way, but there are more than 20 stalls selling a wide range of traditional items.

There's a Khmer cultural show every second and fourth Saturday of the month, with extra stalls, traditional music and dancing. Two-hour pottery classes are offered here through Mordock Ceramics, one of the stalls.

Spicy Green Mango FASHION & ACCESSORIES

(www.spicygreenmango.com; Alley West; ⏲10am-10pm) Small designer boutique with fun and funky fashion and accessories, in an old house that looks like it's straight out of Provence.

Angkor Night Market MARKET

(www.angkornightmarket.com; ⏲4pm-midnight) Near Sivatha St, Siem Reap's original night market has sprung countless copycats, but it remains the best, packed with stalls selling a variety of handicrafts, souvenirs and silks and is well worth a browse. In 'Night Market A' (to the south), you can catch live music at Island Bar, while adjacent 'Night Market B' has the Brick House bar.

You can also indulge in a Dr Fish massage or watch a 3D event movie (US$3) about the Khmer Rouge or the scourge of land mines.

Senteurs d'Angkor ARTS & CRAFTS

(☎063-964801; Pithnou St; ⏲7.30am-10.30pm) Opposite Psar Chaa, this shop has an eclectic collection of silk and carvings, as well as a superb range of traditional beauty products and spices, all made locally. The Kaya Spa is on-site. It targets rural poor and disadvantaged Cambodians for jobs and training, and sources local products from farmers. Visit its Botanic Garden (p205) on Airport Rd.

Rajana ARTS & CRAFTS

(☎063-964744; www.rajanacrafts.org; Sivatha St; ⏲8am-11pm Mon-Sat) Sells quirky wooden and metalwork objects, well-designed silver and brass-bullet jewellery, and handmade cards. Rajana promotes fair-trade employment opportunities for Cambodians.

Monument Books BOOKS

(Pokambor Ave; ⏲9am-9pm) Well-stocked new book store near Psar Chaa, with an additional branch at the airport.

Information

Internet shops are fast disappearing as most restaurants, bars and hotels offer reliable free wi-fi. A few remain and prices are around US$0.50 per hour; cheap internet-based telephone calls are also offered.

TRANSPORT FROM SIEM REAP

DESTINATION	CAR & MOTORCYCLE	BUS	BOAT	AIR
Bangkok, Thailand	8hr	US$15-28, 10hr, frequent	N/A	from US$90, 1hr, 8 daily
Battambang	3hr	US$5-8, 4hr, frequent	US$20, 6-8hr, 7am	N/A
Kompong Thom	2hr	US$5, 3hr, frequent	N/A	N/A
Phnom Penh	4-5hr	US$6-15, 6hr, frequent	US$35, 5hr, 7am	from US$40, 30min, 9 daily
Poipet	3hr	US$5-8, 3hr, frequent	N/A	N/A

For cash exchanges, markets (usually at jewellery stalls or dedicated money-changing stalls) are faster and less bureaucratic than the banks.

Angkor Hospital for Children (AHC; ☎063-963409; www.angkorhospital.org; cnr Oum Chhay & Tep Vong Sts; ⏲24hr) This international-standard paediatric hospital is the place to take your children if they fall sick. They will also assist adults in an emergency for up to 24 hours. Donations accepted.

ANZ Royal Bank (Achar Mean St) Credit-card advances and can change travellers cheques in most major currencies. Several branches and many ATMs (US$5 per withdrawal) around town.

Canadia Bank (Sivatha St) Offers credit-card cash advances (US$4) and changes travellers cheques in most major currencies at a 2% commission.

Main Post Office (Pokambor Ave; ⏲7am-5.30pm) Services are more reliable these days, but it doesn't hurt to see your stamps franked. Includes a branch of EMS express mail.

Royal Angkor International Hospital (Map p222; ☎063-761888; www.royalangkorhospital.com; Airport Rd) This international facility affiliated with the Bangkok Hospital is on the expensive side as it's used to dealing with insurance companies.

U-Care Pharmacy (☎063-965396; Pithnou St; ⏲8am-10pm) Smart pharmacy and shop similar to Boots in Thailand (and the UK). English spoken.

Getting There & Away

AIR

All international flights arrive at the **Siem Reap International Airport** (Map p222; ☎063-962400; www.cambodia-airports.com), gateway to the temples of Angkor. There are no direct flights between Cambodia and the West, so all visitors will end up transiting through an Asian hub such as Bangkok, Hong Kong or Singapore. **Cambodia Bayon Airlines** (p262) generally offers the cheapest fares to Phnom Penh (US$50) and Sihanoukville (from US$93) from Siem Reap, or try **Sky Angkor Airlines** (p262).

BOAT

There are daily express boat services between Siem Reap and Phnom Penh (US$35, five to six hours) or Battambang (US$20, four to eight hours or more, depending on the season). The boat to Phnom Penh is rather overpriced these days, given it is just as fast by road and so much cheaper. The Battambang trip is seriously scenic, but breakdowns are very common.

BUS

All buses depart from the **bus station/taxi park** (Map p222), which is 3km east of town and nearly 1km south of NH6. Tickets are available at guesthouses, hotels, bus offices, travel agencies and ticket kiosks. Some bus companies send a minibus around to pick-up passengers at their place of lodging. Upon arrival in Siem Reap, be prepared for a rugby scrum of eager *moto* drivers when getting off the bus.

Bus companies in Siem Reap:

Asia Van Transfer (AVT; ☎063-963853; www.asiavantransfer.com; Hup Guan St)

Capitol Tour (☎012 830170; www.capitoltourscambodia.com)

Giant Ibis (☎095 777809; www.giantibis.com)

Gold VIP (☎070 988888; off Sivatha St)

Golden Bayon Express (☎063-966968)

Larryta Express (Map p222; ☎066 202020)

Liang US Express (☎092 881183; Sivatha St)

Mekong Express (☎063-963662; https://catmekongexpress.com; 14 Sivatha St)

Nattakan (Map p222; ☎078 795333; nattakan.sr@gmail.com)

Neak Krohorm (Siem Reap River Rd East)

Phnom Penh Sorya (☎096 766 6577; Sivatha St)

Rith Mony (☎063-677 0333)

Virak Buntham (☎017 790440)

SHARE TAXI

Share taxis and other vehicles operate along some of the main routes and these can be a little quicker than buses. Destinations include Phnom Penh (US$10, five hours), Kompong Thom (US$5, two hours), Sisophon (US$5, two hours) and Poipet (US$7, three hours). To get to the temple of Banteay Chhmar, head to Sisophon and arrange onward transport there (leave very early).

Getting Around

Many hotels and guesthouses in Siem Reap offer a free airport pick-up service with advance bookings. Official taxis are available next to the terminal for US$9. A trip to the city centre on the back of a *moto* is US$3; it costs US$7 by *remork*.

Buying boat tickets from a guesthouse usually includes a *moto* or minibus ride between the port and city centre. Otherwise, a *moto/remork*/taxi costs about US$3/7/15 costs about US$3, a *remork-moto* about US$7 and a taxi about US$15.

The average *moto* cost for a short trip within town is 2000r or so, and around US$1 or more to places strung out along the roads to Angkor or the airport.

Some of the guesthouses around town hire out bicycles, as do a few shops around Psar Chaa, usually for US$1 to US$2 a day. Try **Green e-bikes** (p226) or **White Bicycles** (www.thewhitebicycles.org; per day US$2). If you are after a motorcycle, **Angkor e-Tuk Hostel** (Map p222; ☎088 824 1919; Siem Reap River Rd East) hires out powerful, oversized electric remorks (US$24 per day).

GETTING TO THAILAND: SIEM REAP TO BANGKOK

Getting to the border The original land **Poipet/Aranya Prathet border crossing** (⏲7am to 8pm) between Cambodia and Thailand is by far the busiest and the one most people take when travelling between Bangkok and Siem Reap. It has earned itself a bad reputation over the years, with scams galore to help tourists part with their money, especially coming in from Thailand.

Frequent buses and share taxis run from Siem Reap and Battambang to Poipet. Don't get off the bus until you reach the big roundabout adjacent to the border post. Buying a ticket all the way to Bangkok can expedite things and save you the hassle of finding onward transport on the Thai side. There are now several bus companies that offer through-buses from Siem Reap to Mo Chit (p217) bus station in Bangkok.

At the border Be prepared to wait in sweltering immigration lines on both sides – waits of two or more hours are not uncommon, especially in the high season. Show up early in the morning to avoid the crowds. You can pay a special 'VIP fee' (aka a bribe) of 200B on either side to skip the lines. There is no departure tax to leave Cambodia despite what Cambodian border officials might tell you. Entering Thailand, most nationalities are issued 15-day visa waivers free of charge.

Coming in from Thailand, under no circumstances should you deal with any 'Cambodian' immigration officials who might approach you on the Thai side – this a pure scam. Entering Cambodia, the official tourist visa fee is US$30, but it's common to be charged $35. If you don't mind waiting around, you can usually get the official rate if you politely hold firm. Procuring an e-visa (US$37) before travel won't save you any money but will lower your stress levels.

Moving On Minibuses wait just over the border on the Thai side to whisk you to Bangkok's Victory Monument (230B, four hours, every 30 minutes from 6.30am to 4.30pm). Or make your way 7km to Aranya Prathet by *tuk-tuk* (100B) or *sŏrngtăaou* (15B; pick-up truck), from where there are regular buses to Bangkok's Mo Chit and Eastern station between 5am and 3pm (229B, five to six hours). Make sure your *tuk-tuk* driver takes you to the main bus station in Aranya Prathet for your 100B, not to the smaller station about 1km from the border (a common scam). The 6.40am and the 1.55pm trains (six hours) are other options to Bangkok.

AROUND SIEM REAP

Ang Trapeng Thmor Reserve

This **bird sanctuary** (អាងត្រពាំងថ្ម; admission US$10) is one of only a handful of places in the world where it's possible to see the extremely rare sarus crane, as depicted on bas-reliefs at Bayon. These grey-feathered birds have immensely long legs and striking red heads.

The reserve is based around a reservoir created by forced labour during the Khmer Rouge regime, and facilities are very basic, but it is an incredibly beautiful place. Bring your own binoculars, as none are available.

The bird sanctuary is just across the border in the Phnom Srok region of Banteay Meanchey Province, about 100km from Siem Reap. To reach here, follow the road to Sisophon for about 72km before turning north at Prey Mon. It's 22km to the site, passing through some famous silk-weaving villages. Alternatively, the Sam Veasna Center (p208) arranges birdwatching excursions (US$100 per person with a group of four) out here, which is probably the easiest way to undertake the trip.

Floating Village of Chong Kneas

The famous floating village of Chong Kneas has become somewhat of a zoo in recent years. Tour groups have taken over and locals have invented countless scams to separate tourists from their money. Boat prices are fixed at an absurd US$20 per person, plus a US$3 entrance fee (although in practice it may be possible to pay just US$20 for the boat shared between several people).

In-the-know travellers steer well clear of Chong Kneas, opting for harder-to-reach but more memorable spots such as Prek Toal or

Kompong Pluk (ព្រៃលិចទឹកកំពង់ភ្លុក; per person US$20), an other-worldly place built on soaring stilts about an hour's boat ride from Chong Kneas.

Prek Toal Bird Sanctuary

Prek Toal (ជម្រកសត្វស្លាបទឹកព្រែកទាល់; admission US$20) is one of three biospheres on the Tonlé Sap lake, and this stunning bird sanctuary makes it the most worthwhile and straightforward of the three to visit. It is an ornithologist's fantasy, with a significant number of rare breeds gathered in one small area, including the huge lesser and greater adjutant storks, the milky stork and the spot-billed pelican. Even the uninitiated will be impressed, as these birds have a huge wing-span and build enormous nests.

Visitors during the peak season (December to early February) will find the concentration of birds like something out of a Hitchcock film. As water starts to dry up elsewhere, the birds congregate here. The birds remain beyond February but the sanctuary becomes virtually inaccessible due to low water levels. It is also possible to visit from September, but the numbers may be lower. Serious twitchers know that the best time to see birds is early morning or late afternoon and this means an early start or an overnight at Prek Toal's environment office, where there are basic single beds for US$15 (doubles US$20).

Several ecotourism companies in Siem Reap arrange trips out to Prek Toal including the Sam Veasna Center (p208), Osmose (p208) and Prek Toal Tours & Travel (p208), which is run by Prek Toal villagers. Tours include transport, entrance fees, guides, breakfast, lunch and water. Binoculars are available on request, plus the Sam Veasna Center has spotting scopes that they set up at observation towers within the park. All three outfits can arrange overnight trips for serious enthusiasts. Day trips include a hotel pick-up at around 6am and a return by nightfall.

Getting to the sanctuary under your own steam requires a 20-minute moto (US$3 or so) or taxi (US$15 one way) ride to the floating village of Chong Kneas (depending on the time of day additional fees may have to be paid at the new port), and then a boat to the environment office (around US$55 return, one hour each way). From here, a small boat (US$30 including a park guide) will take you into the sanctuary, which is about one hour beyond. The park guides are equipped with booklets with the bird names in English, but they speak little English themselves, hence the advantage of visiting with a tour company that provides English-speaking guides.

Trips to the sanctuary also bring you up close with the fascinating **floating village of Prek Toal** – a much more rewarding destination than over-touristed Chong Kneas. Part of your entrance to the sanctuary goes towards educating children and villagers about the importance of the birds and the unique flooded-forest environment.

Always bring sunscreen and head protection to Prek Toal, as it's a long day in boats and the sun can be relentless.

INTERNATIONAL BUSES

Internationally, there are a few direct buses to Bangkok that do not involve a change of bus at the border, but most require a change. There are some 'night' buses to Bangkok advertised, but these are pretty pointless given the Poipet border does not open until 7am!

Nattakan (p215), the original and still one of the most reliable operators servicing Bangkok, has direct buses to Bangkok (US$28, 7½ hours, 8am and 9am), which include fast-track immigration at the border – potentially a big advantage during peak periods to bypass long lines.

From Bangkok to Siem Reap, direct buses depart in the morning from various locations and cost 550B to 1000B.

Any advertised services to Ho Chi Minh City or Pakse or the Four Thousand Islands in southern Laos invariably involve a time-consuming transfer or two. For Pakse, you're best off taking a minivan to Stung Treng and changing there – Asia Van Transfer (p215) can sort you out with this. Note that any advertised *bus* trip to Laos will invariably take a six-hour detour through Kompong Cham, with a possible overnight in Kratie. There, you've been warned.

TEMPLES OF ANGKOR

Welcome to heaven on earth. Angkor (ប្រាសាទអង្គរ) is the earthly representation of Mt Meru, the Mt Olympus of the Hindu faith and the abode of ancient gods. The temples are the perfect fusion of creative ambition and spiritual devotion. The Cambodian 'god-kings' of old each strove to better their ancestors in size, scale and symmetry, culminating in the world's largest religious building, Angkor Wat.

The temples of Angkor are a source of inspiration and national pride to all Khmers as they struggle to rebuild their lives after the years of terror and trauma. Today, the temples are a point of pilgrimage for all Cambodians, and no traveller to the region will want to miss their extravagant beauty. Angkor is one of the world's foremost ancient sites, with the epic proportions of the Great Wall of China, the detail and intricacy of the Taj Mahal, and the symbolism and symmetry of the pyramids, all rolled into one.

Admission Fees

Visitors have the choice of a one-day pass (US$37 – up from US$20 previously), a three-day pass (US$62) or a one-week pass (US$72). The three-day passes can be used over three non-consecutive days in a one-week period while one-week passes can be used on seven days over a month.

The Angkor **ticket booth & main entrance** (Map p222; Rt 60) relocated in 2016 to a new spot out by the Siem Reap Convention Centre, about 2km east of the old checkpoint in the north part of the city. It's part of a gleaming new complex that also includes the ambitious (and expensive at US$20 a head) Angkor Panorama Museum and the headquarters of the **Apsara Authority** (Authority for Protection & Management of Angkor & the Region of Siem Reap; www.apsaraauthority.gov.kh).

Passes include a digital photo snapped at the entrance booth, so queues can be slow at peak times. Visitors entering after 5pm get a free sunset, as the ticket starts from the following day. The fee includes access to all the monuments in the Siem Reap area but not the sacred mountain of Phnom Kulen (US$20) or the remote complexes of Beng Mealea (US$5) and Koh Ker (US$10).

Most of the major temples now have uniformed staff to check the tickets, which has reduced the opportunity for scams. These days all roads into the central temples (including Angkor Wat, Angkor Thom and Ta Prohm) are manned as well; foreigners who can't produce a pass will be turned away and asked to detour around the temples between 7am and 5pm.

The **Khmer Angkor Tour Guide Association** (☎063-964347; www.khmerangkortourguide.com) represents all of Angkor's authorised guides. English- or French-speaking guides can be booked from US$20 to US$40 a day; guides speaking other languages, such as Italian, German, Spanish, Japanese and Chinese, are available at a higher rate as there are fewer of them.

Angkor Wat

★ Angkor Wat HINDU TEMPLE

(អង្គរវត្ត; Map p222; incl in Angkor admission 1/3/7 days US$37/62/72; ⏲5am-5.30pm) The traveller's first glimpse of Angkor Wat, the ultimate expression of Khmer genius, is matched by only a few select spots on earth. Built by Suryavarman II (r 1112–52) and surrounded by a vast moat, Angkor Wat is one of the most inspired monuments ever conceived by the human mind. Stretching around the central temple complex is an 800m-long series of bas-reliefs, and rising 55m above the ground is the central tower, which gives the whole ensemble its sublime unity.

The temple is the heart and soul of Cambodia. It is the national symbol, the epicentre of Khmer civilisation and a source of fierce national pride. Soaring skyward and surrounded by a moat that would make its European castle counterparts blush, Angkor Wat was never abandoned to the elements and has been in virtually continuous use since it was built.

Simply unique, it is a stunning blend of spirituality and symmetry, an enduring example of humanity's devotion to its gods. Relish the very first approach, as that spine-tickling moment when you emerge on the inner causeway will rarely be felt again. It is the best-preserved temple at Angkor, and repeat visits are rewarded with previously unnoticed details.

There is much about Angkor Wat that is unique among the temples of Angkor. The most significant fact is that the temple is oriented towards the west. Symbolically, west is the direction of death, which once led a large number of scholars to conclude that Angkor Wat must have existed primarily as a tomb. This idea was supported by the fact that the magnificent bas-reliefs of the temple were designed to be viewed in an anticlockwise direction, a practice that has precedents in ancient Hindu funerary rites. Vishnu, however, is also frequently associated with the west, and it is now commonly accepted that Angkor Wat most likely served both as a temple and as a mausoleum for Suryavarman II.

Angkor Wat is famous for its beguiling *apsaras* (heavenly nymphs). More than 3000 *apsaras* are carved into the walls of Angkor Wat, each of them unique, and there are 37 different hairstyles for budding stylists to check out. Many of these exquisite *apsaras* have been damaged by centuries of bat droppings and urine, but they are now being restored by the **German Apsara Conservation Project** (GACP; www.gacp-angkor.de). The organisation operates a small information booth in the northwest corner of Angkor Wat, near the modern wat, where beautiful black-and-white postcards and images of Angkor are available.

Allow at least two hours for a visit to Angkor Wat and plan a half-day if you want to decipher the bas-reliefs with a tour guide and ascend to Bakan, the upper level, which is open to visitors on a timed ticketing system.

Eating

Khmer Angkor Restaurant CAMBODIAN $

(Map p222; mains US$3-6; ⌚6am-6pm) Popular restaurant opposite the one and only Angkor Wat.

Blue Pumpkin CAFE $$

(Map p222; Angkor Cafe; dishes US$2-8; ⌚7am-7pm; ❄) There is a handy branch of Blue Pumpkin just outside Angkor Wat turning out sandwiches, salads and ice creams, as well as divine fruit shakes, all to take away if required.

Angkor Thom

It is hard to imagine any building bigger or more beautiful than Angkor Wat, but in Angkor Thom (Great City; អង្គរធំ) the sum of the parts add up to a greater whole. Set over 10 sq km, the aptly named last great capital of the Khmer empire took monumental to a whole new level.

Centred on Bayon, the surreal state temple of Jayavarman VII, Angkor Thom is enclosed by a formidable *jayagiri* (square wall) 8m high and 12km in length and encircled by a 100m-wide *jayasindhu* (moat) that would have stopped all but the hardiest invaders in their tracks. This architectural layout is an expression of Mt Meru surrounded by the oceans.

In the centre of the walled enclosure are the city's most important monuments, including Bayon, Baphuon, the Royal Enclosure, Phimeanakas and the Terrace of Elephants. Visitors should set aside a half-day to explore Angkor Thom in depth.

Sights

★ **Bayon** BUDDHIST TEMPLE

(បាយ័ន; Map p222; ⌚7.30am-5.30pm) At the heart of Angkor Thom is the 12th-century Bayon, the mesmerising if slightly mind-bending state temple of Jayavarman VII. It epitomises the creative genius and inflated ego of Cambodia's most celebrated king. Its 54 Gothic towers are decorated with 216 gargantuan smiling faces of Avalokiteshvara, and it is adorned with 1.2km of extraordinary bas-reliefs incorporating more than 11,000 figures.

The temple's eastward orientation leads most people to visit early in the morning. However, Bayon looks equally good in the late afternoon.

Baphuon HINDU TEMPLE

(បាពួន; Map p222; ⌚7.30am-5.30pm) Some have called Baphuon the 'world's largest jigsaw puzzle'. Before the civil war the Baphuon was painstakingly taken apart piece-by-piece by a team of archaeologists, but their meticulous records were destroyed during the Khmer Rouge regime, leaving experts with 300,000 stones to put back into place. After years of excruciating research, this temple has been partially restored. On the western side, the retaining wall of the second level was fashioned, in the 16th century, into a reclining Buddha 60m in length.

Terrace of Elephants ARCHAEOLOGICAL SITE

(ទីលានជល់ដំរី; Map p222) The 350m-long Terrace of Elephants was used as a giant viewing stand for public ceremonies and served as a base for the king's grand audience hall. Try to imagine the pomp and grandeur of the Khmer empire at its height, with infantry, cavalry, horse-drawn chariots and elephants parading across Central Square in a colourful procession, pennants and standards aloft. Looking on is the god-king, shaded by multi-tiered parasols and attended by mandarins and handmaidens bearing gold and silver utensils.

Terrace of the Leper King ARCHAEOLOGICAL SITE

(ទីលានព្រះគម្លង់; Map p222) The Terrace of the Leper King is just north of the Terrace of Elephants. Dating from the late 12th century, it is a 7m-high platform, on top of which stands a nude, though sexless, statue. The front retaining walls of the terrace are decorated with at least five tiers of meticulously executed carvings. On the southern side of the Terrace of the Leper King, there is access to a hidden terrace with exquisitely preserved carvings.

Temples of Angkor

THREE-DAY EXPLORATION

The temple complex at Angkor is simply enormous and the superlatives don't do it justice. This is the site of the world's largest religious building, a multitude of temples and a vast, long-abandoned walled city that was arguably Southeast Asia's first metropolis, long before Bangkok and Singapore got in on the action.

Starting at the Roluos group of temples, one of the earliest capitals of Angkor, move on to the big circuit, which includes the Buddhist-Hindu fusion temple of ❶ **Preah Khan** and the ornate water temple of ❷ **Preah Neak Poan**.

On the second day downsize to the small circuit, starting with an early visit to ❸ **Ta Prohm**, before continuing to the temple pyramid of Ta Keo, the Buddhist monastery of Banteay Kdei and the immense royal bathing pond of ❹ **Sra Srang**.

Next venture further afield to Banteay Srei temple, the jewel in the crown of Angkorian art, and Beng Mealea, a remote jungle temple.

Saving the biggest and best until last, experience sunrise at ❺ **Angkor Wat** and stick around for breakfast in the temple to discover its amazing architecture without the crowds. In the afternoon, explore ❻ **Angkor Thom**, an immense complex that is home to the enigmatic ❼ **Bayon**.

Three days around Angkor? That's just for starters.

TOP TIPS

➡ To avoid the crowds, try dawn at Sra Srang, post sunrise at Angkor Wat and lunchtime at Banteay Srei.

➡ Three-day passes can be used on non-consecutive days over the period of a week, but be sure to request this.

Bayon
The surreal state temple of legendary king Jayavarman V where 216 faces bear down on pilgrims, asserting religiou and regal authority.

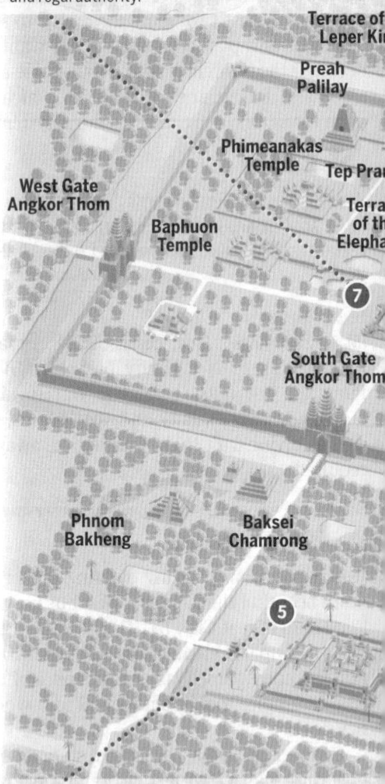

Angkor Wat
The world's largest religious building. Experience sunrise at the holiest of holies, then explore the beautiful bas-reliefs – devotion etched in stone.

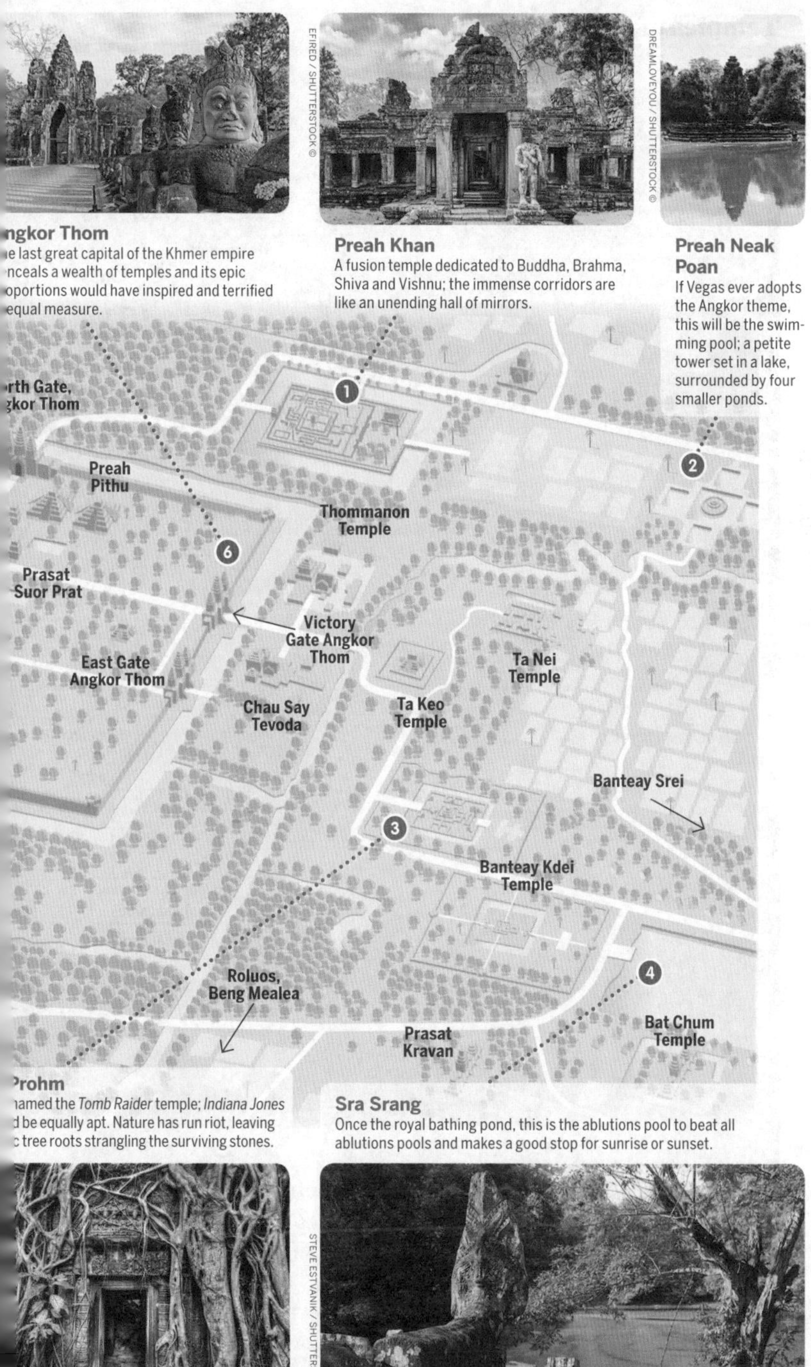

ngkor Thom

e last great capital of the Khmer empire nceals a wealth of temples and its epic oportions would have inspired and terrified equal measure.

Preah Khan

A fusion temple dedicated to Buddha, Brahma, Shiva and Vishnu; the immense corridors are like an unending hall of mirrors.

Preah Neak Poan

If Vegas ever adopts the Angkor theme, this will be the swimming pool; a petite tower set in a lake, surrounded by four smaller ponds.

rohm

amed the *Tomb Raider* temple; *Indiana Jones* d be equally apt. Nature has run riot, leaving c tree roots strangling the surviving stones.

Sra Srang

Once the royal bathing pond, this is the ablutions pool to beat all ablutions pools and makes a good stop for sunrise or sunset.

Temples of Angkor

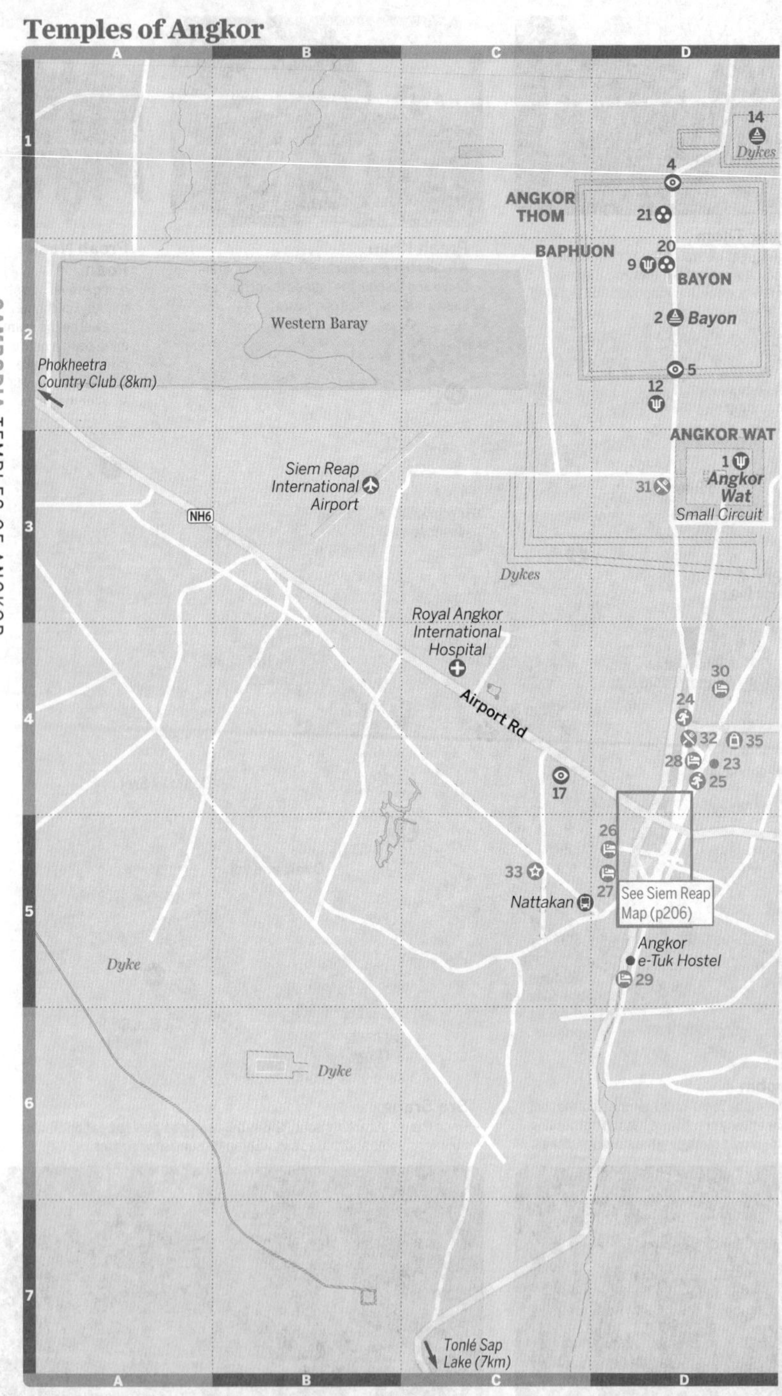

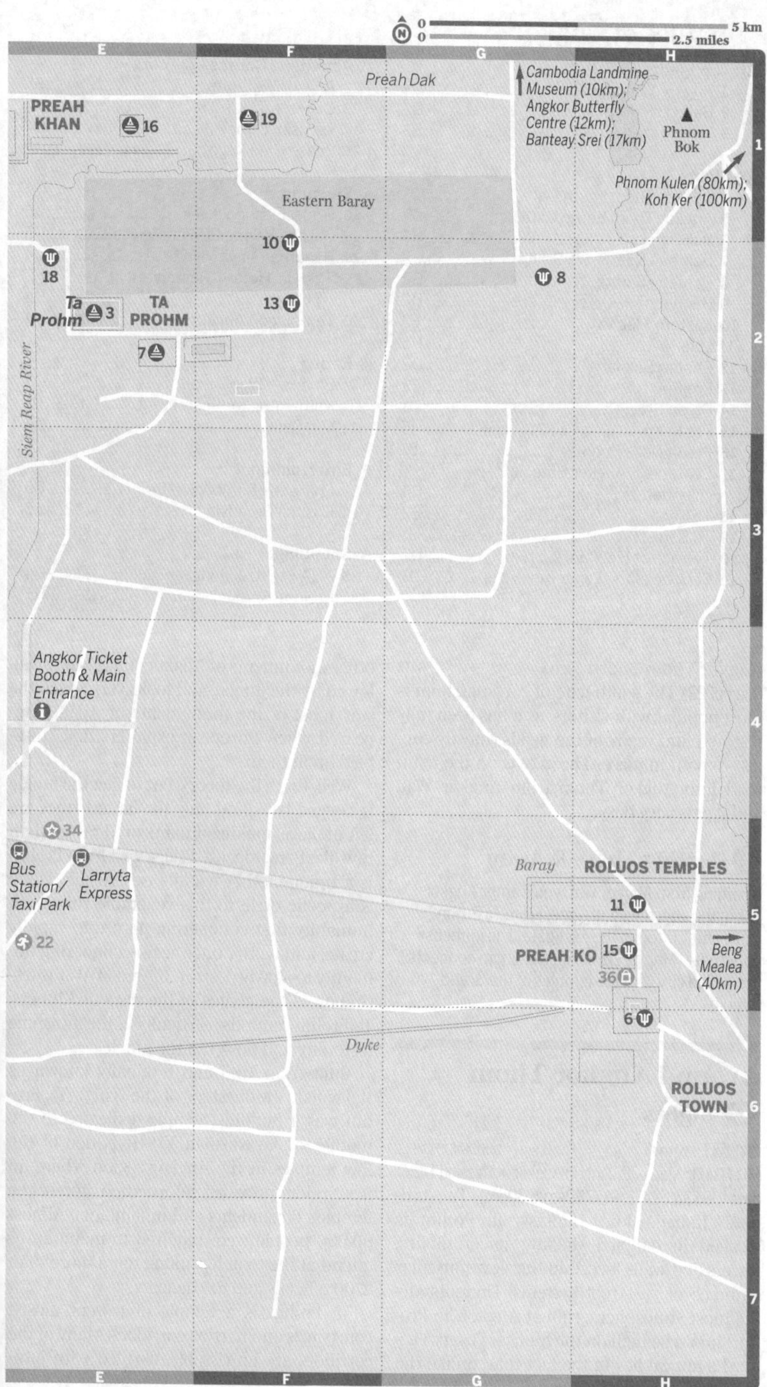
0 5 km
0 2.5 miles
Preah Dak
Cambodia Landmine Museum (10km); Angkor Butterfly Centre (12km); Banteay Srei (17km)
Phnom Bok
Phnom Kulen (80km); Koh Ker (100km)
PREAH KHAN
16
19
Eastern Baray
10
18
8
Ta Prohm
3
TA PROHM
13
7
Siem Reap River
Angkor Ticket Booth & Main Entrance
34
Bus Station/ Taxi Park
Larryta Express
22
Baray
ROLUOS TEMPLES
11
PREAH KO
15
36
Beng Mealea (40km)
6
Dyke
ROLUOS TOWN

Temples of Angkor

Top Sights
1 Angkor Wat D3
2 Bayon D2
3 Ta Prohm E2

Sights
4 Angkor Thom North Gate D1
5 Angkor Thom South Gate D2
6 Bakong H6
7 Banteay Kdei & Sra Srang E2
8 Banteay Samré G2
9 Baphuon D2
10 Eastern Mebon F2
11 Lolei H5
12 Phnom Bakheng D2
13 Pre Rup F2
14 Preah Khan D1
15 Preah Ko H5
16 Preah Neak Poan E1
17 Senteurs d'Angkor Botanic Garden C4
18 Ta Keo E2
19 Ta Som F1
20 Terrace of Elephants D2
21 Terrace of the Leper King D1

Activities, Courses & Tours
22 Angkor Wat Putt E5
23 Cooks in Tuk Tuks D4
24 Krousar Thmey D4
25 Peace Cafe Yoga D4

Sleeping
26 Funky Flashpacker D5
27 Garden Village Guesthouse D5
28 HanumanAlaya Villa D4
29 Sala Bai Hotel & Restaurant School D5
30 Templation Angkor D4

Eating
31 Blue Pumpkin D3
Khmer Angkor Restaurant .... (see 31)
32 Mie Cafe D4

Entertainment
33 Phare the Cambodian Circus C5
34 Rosana Broadway E5

Shopping
35 AHA Fair Trade Village D4
36 Prolung Khmer H5

Angkor Thom South Gate GATE

(Map p222) The south gate of Angkor Thom is most popular with visitors, as it has been fully restored and many of the heads (mostly copies) remain in place. The gate is on the main road into Angkor Thom from Angkor Wat, and it gets very busy.

Getting There & Away

If coming from Angkor Wat, you'll enter Angkor Thom through the south gate. From Ta Prohm, you'll enter through the east gate. The immense north gate (Map p222) of Angkor Thom connects the walled city with the temples of the Grand Circuit.

Around Angkor Thom

Sights

★Ta Prohm BUDDHIST TEMPLE

(តាព្រហ្ម; Map p222; incl in Angkor admission 1/3/7 days US$37/62/72; 7.30am-5.30pm) The ultimate Indiana Jones fantasy, Ta Prohm is cloaked in dappled shadow, its crumbling towers and walls locked in the slow muscular embrace of vast root systems. Undoubtedly the most atmospheric ruin at Angkor, Ta Prohm should be high on the hit list of every visitor. Its appeal lies in the fact that, unlike the other monuments of Angkor, it has been swallowed by the jungle, and looks very much the way most of the monuments of Angkor appeared when European explorers first stumbled upon them.

Well, that's the theory, but in fact the jungle is pegged back and only the largest trees are left in place, making it manicured rather than raw like Beng Mealea. Still, a visit to Ta Prohm is a unique, other-worldly experience. There is a poetic cycle to this venerable ruin, with humanity first conquering nature to rapidly create, and nature once again conquering humanity to slowly destroy. If Angkor Wat is testimony to the genius of the ancient Khmers, Ta Prohm reminds us equally of the awesome fecundity and power of the jungle.

Built from 1186 and originally known as Rajavihara (Monastery of the King), Ta Prohm was a Buddhist temple dedicated to the mother of Jayavarman VII. It is one of the few temples in the Angkor region where an inscription provides information about the temple's dependents and inhabitants. Almost 80,000 people were required to maintain or attend at the temple, among them more than 2700 officials and 615 dancers.

Ta Prohm is a temple of towers, closed courtyards and narrow corridors. Many of the corridors are impassable, clogged with jumbled piles of delicately carved stone blocks dislodged by the roots of long-decayed trees. Bas-reliefs on bulging walls are carpeted with lichen, moss and creeping plants, and shrubs sprout from the roofs of monumental porches. Trees, hundreds of years old, tower overhead, their leaves filtering the sunlight and casting a greenish pall over the whole scene.

The most popular of the many strangulating root formations is that on the inside of the easternmost *gopura* (entrance pavilion) of the central enclosure, nicknamed the Crocodile Tree. One of the most famous spots in Ta Prohm is the so-called 'Tomb Raider tree', where Angelina Jolie's Lara Croft picked a jasmine flower before falling through the earth into…Pinewood Studios.

It used to be possible to climb onto the damaged galleries, but this is now prohibited, to protect both temple and visitor. Many of these precariously balanced stones weigh a tonne or more and would do some serious damage if they came down. Ta Prohm is currently under stabilisation and restoration by an Indian team of archaeologists working with their Cambodian counterparts.

Ta Prohm is at its most impressive early in the day. Allow as much as two hours to visit, especially if you want to explore the maze-like corridors and iconic tree roots.

Phnom Bakheng HINDU TEMPLE

(ភ្នំបាក់ខែង; Map p222; incl in Angkor admission 1/3/7 days US$37/62/72; ⏲5am-7pm) Located around 400m south of Angkor Thom, the main attraction at Phnom Bakheng is the sunset view over Angkor Wat. For many years, the whole affair turned into a circus, with crowds of tourists ascending the slopes of the hill and jockeying for space. Numbers are restricted to just 300 visitors at any one time, so get here early (4pm) to guarantee a sunset spot. The temple, built by Yasovarman I (r 889–910), has five tiers, with seven levels.

Preah Khan BUDDHIST TEMPLE

(ព្រះខ័ន; Sacred Sword; Map p222; incl in Angkor admission 1/3/7 days US$37/62/72; ⏲7.30am-5.30pm) The temple of Preah Khan is one of the largest complexes at Angkor, a maze of vaulted corridors, fine carvings and lichen-clad stonework. It is a good counterpoint to Ta Prohm and generally sees slightly fewer visitors. Like Ta Prohm it is a place of towered enclosures and shoulder-hugging corridors. Unlike Ta Prohm, however, the temple of Preah Khan is in a reasonable state of preservation thanks to the ongoing restoration efforts of the World Monuments Fund (WMF; www.wmf.org).

Preah Neak Poan BUDDHIST TEMPLE

(ព្រះនាគព័ន្ធ, Temple of the Intertwined Nagas; Map p222; incl in Angkor admission 1/3/7 days US$37/62/72; ⏲7.30am-5.30pm) The Buddhist temple of Preah Neak Poan is a petite yet perfect temple constructed by Jayavarman VII in the late 12th century. It has a large square pool surrounded by four smaller square pools. In the middle of the central pool is a circular 'island' encircled by the two *nagas* whose intertwined tails give the temple its name.

Bakong HINDU TEMPLE

(បាគង; Map p222; ⏲7.30am-5.30pm) Bakong is the largest and most interesting of the Roluos Group of temples. Built and dedicated to Shiva by Indravarman I, it's a representation of Mt Meru, and it served as the city's central temple. The east-facing complex consists of a five-tier central pyramid of sandstone, 60m square at the base, flanked by eight towers of brick and sandstone, and by other minor sanctuaries. A number of the lower towers are still partly covered by their original plasterwork.

Preah Ko HINDU TEMPLE

(ព្រះគោ; Map p222; ⏲7.30am-5.30pm) Preah Ko was erected by Indravarman I in the late 9th century, and was dedicated to Shiva. Preah Ko was also dedicated to his deified ancestors in AD 880. The front towers relate to male ancestors or gods, the rear towers to female ancestors or goddesses. Lions guard the steps up to the temple.The towers of Preah Ko (Sacred Ox) feature three *nandis* (sacred oxen), all of whom look like a few steaks have been sliced off over the years.

Lolei HINDU TEMPLE

(លលៃ; Map p222; ⏲7.30am-5.30pm) The four brick towers of Lolei, an almost exact replica of the towers of Preah Ko (although in much worse shape), were built on an islet in the centre of a large reservoir – now rice fields – by Yasovarman I, the founder of the first city at Angkor. The sandstone carvings in the niches of the temples are worth a look and there are Sanskrit inscriptions on the doorposts.

According to one of the inscriptions, the four towers were dedicated by Yasovarman I to his mother, his father and his maternal grandparents on 12 July 893.

Shopping

Prolung Khmer ARTS & CRAFTS

(Map p222; www.prolungkhmer.blogspot.com; ⏲8am-5pm) Look out for Prolung Khmer on the road between Preah Ko and Bakong. It's a pottery and weaving centre producing stylish cotton *kramas* (checked scarves) and ceramics, set up as a training collaboration between Cambodia and Japan.

Further Afield

Sights

★Banteay Srei HINDU TEMPLE

(បន្ទាយស្រី; incl in Angkor admission 1/3/7 days US$37/62/72; ⏲7.30am-5.30pm) Considered by many to be the jewel in the crown of Angkorian art, Banteay Srei is cut from stone of a pinkish hue and includes some of the finest stone carving anywhere on earth. Begun in AD 967, it is one of the smallest sites at Angkor, but what it lacks in size it makes up for in stature.The art gallery of Angkor, Banteay Srei, a Hindu temple dedicated to Shiva, is wonderfully well preserved and many of its carvings are three-dimensional.

Kbal Spean HINDU SHRINE

(ក្បាលស្ពាន; incl in Angkor admission 1/3/7 days US$37/62/72; ⏲7.30am-5.30pm) A spectacularly carved riverbed, Kbal Spean is set deep in the jungle to the northeast of Angkor. More commonly referred to in English as the 'River of a Thousand Lingas', the name actually means 'bridgehead', a reference to the natural rock bridge at the site. *Lingas* (phallic symbols) have been elaborately carved into the riverbed, and images of Hindu deities are dotted about the area. Kbal Spean was 'discovered' in 1969, when ethnologist Jean Boulbet was shown the area by a hermit.

Phnom Kulen MOUNTAIN

(ភ្នំគូលែន; US$20) Considered by Khmers to be the most sacred mountain in Cambodia, Phnom Kulen is a popular place of pilgrimage on weekends and during festivals. It played a significant role in the history of the Khmer empire, as it was from here in AD 802 that Jayavarman II proclaimed himself a *devaraja* (god-king), giving birth to the Cambodian kingdom. Attractions include a giant reclining Buddha, hundreds of *lingas* carved in the riverbed, an impressive waterfall and some remote temples.

Beng Mealea BUDDHIST TEMPLE

(បឹងមាលា; admission US$5; ⏲7.30am-5.30pm) A spectacular sight, Beng Mealea, located about 68km northeast of Siem Reap, is one of the most mysterious temples at Angkor, as nature has well and truly run riot. Exploring this titanic of temples, built to the same floorplan as Angkor Wat, is the ultimate Indiana Jones experience. Built in the 12th century under Suryavarman II, Beng Mealea is enclosed by a massive moat measuring 1.2km by 900m.

Koh Ker HINDU TEMPLE

(កោះកេរ; admission US$10; ⏲7.30am-5.30pm) Abandoned to the forests of the north, Koh Ker, capital of the Angkorian empire from AD 928 to AD 944, is now within day-trip distance of Siem Reap. Most visitors start at Prasat Krahom where impressive stone carvings grace lintels, doorposts and slender window columns. The principal monument is Mayan-looking Prasat Thom, a 55m-wide, 40m-high sandstone-faced pyramid whose seven tiers offer spectacular views across the forest. Koh Ker is 127km northeast of Siem Reap.

Getting There & Around

The central temple area is just 8km from Siem Reap, and can be visited using anything from a car or motorcycle to a sturdy pair of walking boots. For the ultimate Angkor experience, try a pick-and-mix approach, with a *moto*, *remork-moto* or car for one day to cover the remote sites, a bicycle to experience the central temples, and an exploration on foot for a spot of peace and serenity.

BICYCLE

Cycling is a great way to get around the temples, as there are few hills and the roads are good, so there's no need for much experience. You take in more than from out of a car window or on the back of a speeding *moto*.

White Bicycles (www.thewhitebicycles.org; per day US$2) is supported by some guesthouses around Siem Reap, with proceeds from the hire fee going towards community projects. Many guesthouses and hotels in town rent bikes for around US$1 to US$2 per day. Electric bicycles hired out by **Green e-bikes** (☎095 700130; www.greene-bike.com; Central Market; per 24hr US$10; ⏲7.30am-7pm) and others are also a very popular way to tour the temples.

CAR

A car for the day around the central temples is US$25 to US$35 and can be arranged with hotels, guesthouses and agencies in Siem Reap.

MOTO

Many independent travellers end up visiting the temples by *moto* (unmarked motorcycle taxi). *Moto* drivers accost visitors from the moment they set foot in Siem Reap, but they often end up being knowledgeable and friendly, and good companions for a tour around the temples, starting at around US$10 per day.

REMORK-MOTO

Remork-motos, motorcycles with hooded carriages towed behind, are more commonly known around town as *tuk-tuks*. They are a popular way to get around Angkor as fellow travellers can still talk to each other as they explore. Some *remork* drivers are very good companions for a tour of the temples. Prices run from US$15 to US$25 for the day.

WALKING

Why not simply explore on foot? It's easy enough to walk to Angkor Wat and the temples of Angkor Thom, and this is a great way to meet up with villagers in the area. Those who want to get away from the roads should try the peaceful walk along the walls of Angkor Thom. It is about 13km in total, and offers access to several small, remote temples and some bird life. Another rewarding walk is from Ta Nei to Ta Keo through the forest.

NORTHWESTERN CAMBODIA

Looking for temples without the tourist hordes? The remote temples of northwestern Cambodia are a world apart. While hilltop Prasat Preah Vihear is the big-hitter, the other temple complexes – wrapped in vines and half-swallowed by jungle – are all fabulous to explore. When forays into the region's far-flung corners are complete, the northwest has one more surprise up its sleeve. Laid-back Battambang, with its colonial architecture and burgeoning arts scene, is the main city here. There's a wealth of brilliant sights all within day-tripping distance of town – making it a worthy pit stop after all the hard travelling is done.

Banteay Chhmar

Banteay Chhmar (បន្ទាយឆ្មារ; US$5; ⊙8am-6pm) and its nine satellite temples were constructed by Cambodia's most prolific builder, Jayavarman VII (r 1181–1219), on the site of a 9th-century temple. The main temple housed one of the largest and most impressive Buddhist monasteries of the Angkorian period, and was originally enclosed by a 9km-long wall. Now atmospherically encroached upon by forest, it features several towers bearing enigmatic, Bayon-style four-faced Avalokiteshvara (Buddhist deities) with their mysterious and iconic smiles, and is also renowned for its 2000 sq metres of intricate bas-relief carvings that depict war victories and scenes from daily life on the exterior of the southern section of the temple's western ramparts.

Unfortunately several of these were dismantled and trucked into Thailand in a brazen act of looting in 1998; only two figures – one with 22 arms, the other with 32 – remain in situ out of an original eight, but the dazzling, intricate artistry involved in creating these carvings is still easily evoked. The segments of the looted bas-reliefs that were intercepted by the Thais are now on display in Phnom Penh's National Museum..

The easiest temple to find is **Prasat Ta Prohm** (ប្រាសាទតាព្រហ្ម) FREE, hidden in the bush just 200m south of the main temple's southern wall, its single crumbling tower bearing a well-preserved Avalokiteshvara.

About a two-hour drive from Siem Reap, these remote ruins are also the site of a superb community-based homestay and tourism program. If you're looking for an opportunity to delve into Cambodian rural life and spend some quality time amid a temple complex far away from the crowds, you could hardly find a more perfect spot.

The Global Heritage Fund (www.globalheritagefund.org) is assisting with conservation efforts here, and a wonderful community-based tourism (CBT) scheme gives visitors incentive to stay another day. The scheme includes fantastic homestays (room US$7), activities and guides for temple tours to assist with community development in the area, all booked through the CBT Office.

Banteay Chhmar can easily be done as a day trip with private transport out of Siem Reap. Shared taxis from Sisophon, 61km south of the temple along sealed NH56, usually only go as far as Thmor Puok, although a few continue on to Banteay Chhmar (15,000r, one hour) and Samraong. A *moto* from Sisophon to Banteay Chhmar will cost US$15 to US$20 return, a taxi US$50 to US$60 return.

Sleeping & Eating

CBT Homestay Program HOMESTAY $
(☎012 435660, 097 516 5533; www.visitbanteaychhmar.org; r US$7) Thanks to the homestay

project run by the CBT Office, it's possible to stay in Banteay Chhmar and three nearby hamlets. Rooms are inside private homes and come with mosquito nets, fans that run when there's electricity (6pm to 10pm) and downstairs bathrooms. Part of the income goes into a community development fund.

Banteay Chhmar Restaurant CAMBODIAN $
(NH56; mains US$1.50-4) Near the temple's eastern entrance, this rustic restaurant is the only place to dine without pre-ordering. It serves really tasty Khmer food.

Information

CBT Office (Community-Based Tourism Office; ☎097 516 5533, 012 435660; www.visitbanteaychhmar.org; NH56) Besides arranging homestays and guides, this pioneering office also arranges activities that allow travellers a small insight into village life (such as ox-cart rides and traditional music shows) and can arrange trips to outlying temples by local transport. The office is opposite and a bit south of the Banteay Chhmar main (eastern) entrance.

Battambang

There's something about Battambang that visitors just love – colonial architecture in genteel disrepair, the riverside setting and laid-back cafes. Meanwhile, outside the friendly city, timeless hilltop temples and bucolic villages await.

Sights

Much of Battambang's charm lies in its early 20th-century architecture, a mix of vernacular shophouses and French colonial construction that makes up the historic core of the city. Some of the finest colonial buildings are dotted along the waterfront (St 1), especially just south of Psar Nath (St 1), itself an architectural monument, albeit a modernist one.

Make Maek Art Space GALLERY
(☎017 946108; 66 St 2½; suggested donation US$2) This gallery and workshop, run by respected local painter Mao Soviet, displays many of his works mixed with rotating exhibits of the paintings and photographs of other top city talents. In a beautifully renovated space above the Battambang Traveller Shop, it reopened in late 2016 after a two-year hiatus.

Tep Kao Sol GALLERY
(☎017 982992; St 2; ⊙hours vary) This is the gallery space of local artist Loeum Lorn, who's known for creating works out of melting coloured ice and then photographing it. It's open sporadically, so just stop by and hope for the best.

Romcheik 5 Artspace GALLERY
(☎092 304 210; St 201A; US$2; ⊙2-7pm) Expanded from a workshop into a bona fide gallery in 2015, this impressive space has a permanent collection upstairs displaying the contemporary works of its four Phare-graduate founders, while downstairs are rotating exhibits highlighting some of Battambang's best local talent.

It's on the east bank of Sangker River, on a little side street just north of Bambu Hotel.

Wat Somrong Knong MEMORIAL
About 4km north of Battambang, Wat Somrong Knong was built in the 19th century on the site of a pre-Angkorian temple complex. The Khmer Rouge used the temple grounds as a prison and it's believed that around 10,000 people were executed here. The complex today houses the gorgeous main pagoda and a mishmash of ancient ruins, glittery modern structures and memorials to those who perished here.

Just outside the complex's southwest wall is a memorial shrine festooned with grisly bas-reliefs of Khmer Rouge atrocities. A glass case contains victims' skulls.

To get here, cross the bridge over the Sangker River 1.7km north of the ferry pier, then continue north on the other side for another 1.7km and take a right on a small dirt road. Continue 500m down this road to the site. If coming from the north, it's about 2.5km south of the bridge near the *prahoc* factory.

Pheam Ek VILLAGE
The speciality industry of the village of Pheam Ek is making rice paper for spring rolls. All along the road, in family workshops, you'll see rice paste being steamed and then placed on a bamboo frame for drying in the sun. Plus the coconuts grown in this area are said to be especially sweet. The village is about 6km north of Battambang on the main road to Wat Ek Phnom.

Prasat Banan TEMPLE
(ប្រាសាទភ្នំបាណន់; combined ticket US$3) It's a 358-stone-step climb up Phnom Banan to reach Prasat Banan, but the incredible views across surrounding countryside from the top are worth it. Udayadityavarman II, son of Suryavarman I, built Prasat Banan in the 11th century; some locals claim the five-tower layout here was the inspiration for Angkor

Wat, although this seems optimistic. There are impressive carved lintels above the doorways to each of the towers and bas-reliefs on the upper parts of the central tower. From the temple, a narrow stone staircase leads south down the hill to three caves, which can be visited with a local guide.

It's 23km south of Battambang.

Activities

Heritage Walking Trail WALKING

FREE Phnom Penh–based Khmer Architecture Tours (www.ka-tours.org) is highly regarded for its specialist tours in and around the capital and has collaborated with Battambang Municipality to create two heritage walks in the historic centre of Battambang. The walks concentrate both on the French period and on the modernist architecture of the '60s. KA-Tours' website has two downloadable PDFs including a colour map and numbered highlights.

The maps are also available in the free *faceguide* pamphlet handed out at Bric-à-Brac (p233) and a few other places around town. This is a great way to spend half a day exploring the city. Those with less time can rent a bicycle and run the combined routes in just an hour or so.

Green Orange Kayaks KAYAKING

(855 12 718857; www.fedacambodia.org; Ksach Poy; half-day US$12) Kayaks can be rented from Green Orange Kayaks, part of FEDA, a local NGO which runs a community centre in the village of Ksach Poy, 8km south of Battambang. Half-day, self-guided kayaking trips begin at Ksach Poy's Green Orange Cafe. From there you paddle back to the city along the Sangker River. A FEDA student guide (US$5) is optional. Booking ahead is highly recommended. FEDA also runs a guesthouse, the **Green Orange Village Bungalow** (012 207957; tr per person US$5), in Ksach Poy. Ask for Ngarm.

Soksabike CYCLING

(012 542019; www.soksabike.com; St 1½; half-day US$23-27, full-day US$34-40; departs 7.30am) Soksabike is a social enterprise aiming to connect visitors with the Cambodian countryside and its people. Half-day/full-day trips cover 25km/40km and include stops at family-run industries such as rice-paper making and the *prahoc* (fermented fish paste) factory, and a visit to a local home. Tour prices depend on group size.

It's associated with **Kinyei** (www.kinyei.org; 1 St 1½; mains US$2.75-5.25; 7am-7pm;) cafe a few doors north on the same street.

Bamboo Train RAIL

(return ride for 2 or more passengers each US$5, for 1 passenger US$10; 7am-dusk) Battambang's bamboo train is one of the world's all-time unique rail journeys. From O Dambong, 3.7km east of Battambang's old French bridge (Wat Kor Bridge), the train bumps 7km southeast to O Sra Lav along warped, misaligned rails and vertiginous bridges left by the French. The journey takes 20 minutes each way, with a 20-minute stop at O Sra Lav in between.

Note that at the time of writing the train was set to be dismantled and rebuilt elsewhere in the Province. Check with the tourist office (p234) for the latest developments.

Coconut Lyly COOKING

(016 399339; www.coconutlyly.com; St 111; US$10 per person) Classes are run by Chef Lyly, a graduate from Siem Reap's Paul Dubrule Cooking School. Half-day classes (start times 9am and 3.30pm) include a visit to Psar Nath, preparing four typically Khmer dishes (recipe book included) and then eating your handiwork afterwards. The excellent restaurant here is open from 8am to 10pm.

Gecko Moto BOATING

(089 924260; St 1; 8am-10pm) Does private boat cruises on the Sangker River (per person US$6 to US$8 including a beer or two).

Also rents out motorbikes for US$6 to US$8 per day.

Aerobics Classes HEALTH & FITNESS

(St 159D; per person 1000r) Head to Battambang's east bank to see the locals burning off the rice carbs doing aerobics, from about 6am to 7am and 5pm to 7pm daily. Just five minutes of working out should be enough to teach you some numbers in Khmer.

Daitep Seeing Hand Massage MASSAGE

(078 337499; St 121; per hour US$7; 7am-10pm) Trained blind masseurs offer soothing work-overs in an air-conditioned space.

Sleeping

Most of Battambang's budget options are clustered close to Psar Nath, while midrange and luxury accommodation tends to be either on the east bank or out of the centre, and requires a short *remork* or *moto* ride to get to the tourist belt in the old quarter.

Battambang

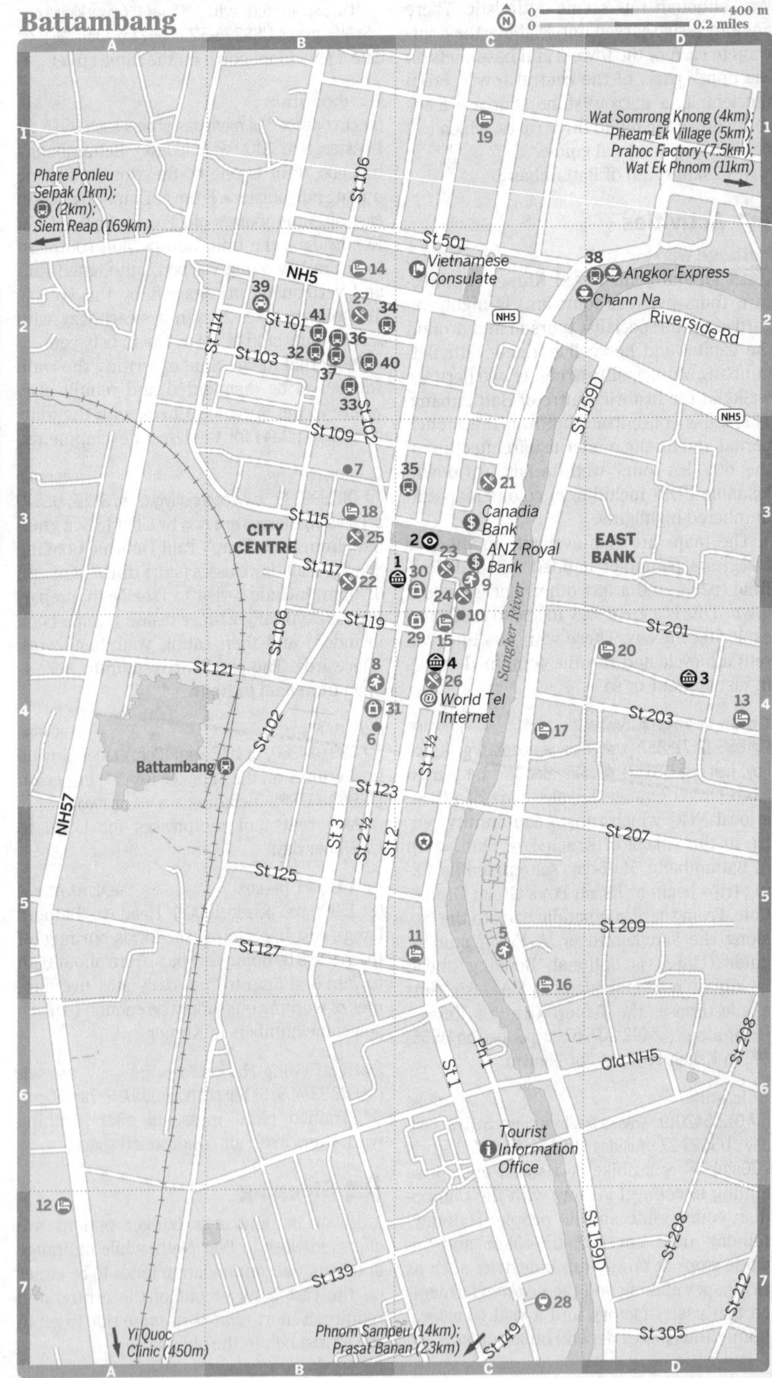

0 400 m
0 0.2 miles
Wat Somrong Knong (4km); Pheam Ek Village (5km); Prahoc Factory (7.5km); Wat Ek Phnom (11km)
Phare Ponleu Selpak (1km); (2km); Siem Reap (169km)
St 106
St 501
NH5
Vietnamese Consulate
Angkor Express
Chann Na
Riverside Rd
St 114
St 101
St 103
St 102
St 109
St 159D
St 115
CITY CENTRE
Canadia Bank
ANZ Royal Bank
EAST BANK
St 117
St 119
Sangker River
St 201
St 121
World Tel Internet
St 203
St 1½
Battambang
NH57
St 123
St 3
St 2½
St 2
St 207
St 125
St 209
St 127
Ph1
St 1
Old NH5
St 208
Tourist Information Office
St 139
St 212
Yi Quoc Clinic (450m)
Phnom Sampeu (14km); Prasat Banan (23km)
St 149
St 305

Battambang

City Centre

★**Angkor Comfort Hotel** HOTEL $
(077 306410; www.angkorcomforthotel.com; St 1; r with air-con US$15-25;) Serious bang for your buck. The Angkor's huge rooms are sparkling clean and come with white linens on the bed, flat-screen TVs, enough powerpoints to charge up all your devices at once, and modern bathrooms with walk-in showers – these are midrange amenities on a backpacker budget.

Ganesha Family Guesthouse GUESTHOUSE $
(092 135570; www.ganeshaguesthouse.com; St 1½; dm US$4.50, r US$11-14;) The best of Battambang's cheapies, Ganesha has a light-filled dorm with double-wide beds, and small private rooms with bamboo furniture and tiled bathrooms (cold water only). Downstairs is a funky cafe with a pool table.

Royal Hotel HOTEL $
(016 912034; www.royalhotelbattambang.com; St 115; s/d with fan US$7/10, r with air-con from US$15;) An old-timer on the Battambang scene, the Royal is deservedly popular. Some rooms may be faded but the air-con rooms are decently sized and come with fridge and TV. Staff here are some of the most clued-up in town.

Banan Hotel HOTEL $$
(012 739572; phaysodavy@yahoo.com; NH5; standard/deluxe incl breakfast US$25/50;) With wood-panelling in abundance, this hotel punches above its weight with friendly service, large clean rooms stuffed with mod-cons, and a huge pool between the main building and the annexe. Deluxe rooms come with balconies.

Sanctuary Villa BOUTIQUE HOTEL $$$
(053-952323; www.thesanctuaryvillabattambang.com; Tea Cham Rath St; r incl breakfast US$140-265;) This intimate luxury boutique has seven attractive villas furnished with traditional woods, tasteful silks and throw rugs – but the out-of-the-way location won't be for everybody. From the White Horse roundabout on NH5 go 500m north and take a right.

DON'T MISS

PHARE PONLEU SELPAK

Battambang's signature attraction is the internationally acclaimed circus (*cirque nouveau*) of **Phare Ponleu Selpak** (☎053-952424; www.phareps.org; US$14), a multi-arts centre for Cambodian children. Although it also runs shows in Siem Reap, it's worth timing your visit to Battambang to watch this amazing spectacle where it began. Shows are held two to four nights per week, depending on the season (check the website), and kick off at 7pm.

Phare, as it's known to locals, does a ton of stuff – contrary to popular belief it is not just a circus. It trains musicians, visual artists and performing artists as well. Many of the artists you'll bump into around town, such as Ke of **Choco l'art Cafe** (p233) fame, lived and studied at Phare. Guests are welcome to take a guided **tour** (US$5; 8-11am & 2-5pm Mon-Fri) of the Phare complex during the day and observe circus, dance, music, drawing and graphic-arts classes.

Tickets are sold at the door from 6pm or at many retailers around town. To get here from the Vishnu Roundabout on NH5, head west for 900m, then turn right and continue another 600m.

East Bank

★**Here Be Dragons** HOSTEL $
(☎089 264895; www.herebedragonsbattambang.com; St 159D; fan/air-con dm US$3/5, r from US$10/15;) A funky fun bar, leafy front garden for relaxing and free beer on arrival make Here Be Dragons a top backpacker base. Six-bed dorms come with lock-boxes, while sunny private rooms are cheerfully decked out with brightly coloured bedding. The quiet location next to the riverside park on the east bank is a bonus.

La Villa BOUTIQUE HOTEL $$
(☎053-730151; www.lavilla-battambang.net; St 159D; s/d incl breakfast from US$70/75;) For a taste of colonial life, try this French-era villa renovated in vintage 1930s style. It's one of the most romantic boutique hotels in Cambodia. Gauzy mosquito nets drape over four-poster beds, original tilework graces the floors and art deco features decorate every corner, creating an old-world ambience that can't be beaten.

Sangker Villa Hotel BOUTIQUE HOTEL $$
(☎097 764 0017; www.sangkervilla.com; off St 203; r incl breakfast US$45-55;) Sangker Villa may lack the pizazz of Battambang's fancier poolside boutiques, but it beats them hands-down on price. Out back the small pool and bar provide tranquil retreats, while the bright, simply decorated rooms come with contemporary bathrooms.

★**Bambu Hotel** HOTEL $$$
(☎053-953900; www.bambuhotel.com; St 203; r incl breakfast from US$90;) Bambu's spacious rooms are designed in a Franco-Khmer motif with gorgeous tiling, stone-inlaid bathrooms and exquisite furniture. The fusion restaurant is one of the best in town and the poolside bar invites lingering. Above all else, though, it's Bambu's gracious staff that set it in a category above Battambang's other boutique offerings. Book ahead – it's extremely popular.

Further Afield

Au Cabaret Vert BOUTIQUE HOTEL $$
(☎053-656 2000; www.aucabaretvert.com; NH57; r incl breakfast from US$75;) Contemporary meets colonial at this pretty resort, a short *remork* ride southwest of the centre. Rooms are stylish and include flat-screen TV and rain shower. The swimming pool is a natural, self-cleaning pond surrounded by lush gardens, and the French-influenced food is top-notch.

Eating

★**Lonely Tree Cafe** CAFE $
(www.thelonelytreecafe.com; St 121; mains US$4-5.50; 10am-10pm;) Upstairs from the shop of the same name, this uber-cosy cafe serves Spanish tapas-style dishes and a few Khmer options under a soaring, bamboo-inlaid ceiling. Its mascot is an actual tree on the road to Siem Reap. Proceeds support cultural preservation and people with disabilities, among other causes.

Vegetarian Foods Restaurant VEGETARIAN $
(St 102; mains 1500-3000r; 6.30am-5pm;) This hole-in-the-wall eatery serves some

of the most delicious vegetarian dishes in Cambodia, including rice soup, homemade soy milk and dumplings for just 1000r. Tremendous value.

Buffalo Alley FUSION $

(St 1½; small plates US$1.50-3, mains US$3-4; 9am-11pm Mon-Fri, 6pm-late Sat & Sun;) A friendly place run by local students, it serves up burgers and a bevvy of delicious tapas, including strong vegetarian options. The chatty owners are happy to teach you some Khmer, and the spontaneous karaoke sessions upstairs are a riot.

Lan Chov Khorko Miteanh NOODLES $

(145 St 2; mains 4000-6000r; 9am-9pm) The Chinese chef here does bargain dumplings and serves fresh noodles at least a dozen ways, including with pork or duck soup. A Battambang institution more conveniently known as Chinese Noodle by resident foreigners.

Jewel in the Lotus CAFE $

(St 2½; mains US$3.50-6; 8am-6pm;) In a beautifully renovated shophouse, this funky street-level cafe serves a few Middle Eastern–inspired vegetarian and vegan snacks plus some specials – usually including vego pizzas – on a chalkboard. It doubles as a shop and gallery, and it shows interesting films in the high season.

The owner couple, Darren Swallow and Khchao Touch, know the Battambang art scene well, and Touch, a Phare graduate, is a top artist in her own right.

Choco l'art Café CAFE $

(St 117; breakfasts & mains US$1.50-6; 9am-midnight Wed-Mon;) Run with gusto by local painter Ke and his French partner, Soline, this inviting gallery-cafe sees foreigners and locals alike gather to drink and eat Soline's wonderful bread, pastries and (for breakfast) crêpes. Occasional live music.

★ **Jaan Bai** FUSION $$

(078 263144; jaanbai@cambodianchildrenstrust.org; cnr Sts 1½ & 2; small plates US$3, mains US$4-10; 11am-10.30pm Tue-Sun;) Jaan Bai ('rice bowl' in Khmer) is Battambang's foodie treat, with a sleekly minimalist interior offset by beautiful French-Khmer tilework lining the wall. The menu likewise is successfully bold. Order a few of the small plates to savour the range of flavours, or go all-out with the tasting menu: seven plates plus wine for US$15 per person (minimum two people).

You're eating for a good cause. Jaan Bai trains and employs vulnerable youth through the Cambodia Children's Trust (www.cambodianchildrenstrust.org).

Cafe Eden CAFE $$

(www.cafeedencambodia.com; St 1; mains US$4-7; 7.30am-9pm Wed-Mon;) This American-run social enterprise offers a relaxed space for a hearty breakfast or an afternoon coffee. The compact lunch-and-dinner menu is Asian-fusion style, with burgers, Mexi flaves, the best chips in town and superior jam-jar shakes, all amid blissful air-con.

At the back, its boutique sells a small range of clothing and crafts.

La Casa ITALIAN $$

(St 115; mains US$5-10; 11am-2pm & 5-10pm) La Casa serves the best thin-crust pizza in Battambang, and excellent pasta dishes and salads, out of an attractive space near the bus offices.

Drinking & Nightlife

Here Be Dragons BAR

(St 159D; 11am-late;) Before there was the popular hostel, there was the popular bar Dragons. It hasn't forgotten its roots. The bar frequently rumbles till late with a mix of backpackers and expats. There's a Wednesday pub quiz, Friday ping-pong tourneys and wine pairings the first Thursday of every month.

Riverside Balcony Bar BAR

(010 337862; cnr Sts 1 & 149; 4-11pm Tue-Sun;) Set in a gorgeous wooden house high above the riverfront, expat-run Riverside is Battambang's original bar and a mellow place for a sundowner. It changes owner and menu from time to time. At present it serves just pizza (US$4 to US$9 – arguably some of Battambang's finest) and a few special appetisers.Reserve on weekends if you have a crew, as it fills up from 5.30pm or so.

Libations Bar BAR

(112 St 2; 5-9pm;) Downstairs in the Bric-à-Brac hotel, this classy streetside bar caters to a more refined crowd with creative cocktails, craft beer, and wine and champagne by the glass. The chatty owners are a great source of information on the area. Upstairs are three arty, designed rooms.

Shopping

Bric-à-Brac HOMEWARES

(077 531562; www.bric-a-brac.asia; 112 St 2; 11am-8pm) This swish store downstairs in the bijou hotel of the same name sells handmade *passementrie* (trimmings) items,

BUSES FROM BATTAMBANG

DESTINATION	DURATION (HR)	COST (US$)	COMPANIES	FREQUENCY
Bangkok, Thailand	9	15-16	Mekong Express, PP Sorya, Virak Buntham	8.30am, 10.30am, 11.30am, noon
Kompong Cham	8	9-10	PP Sorya, Rith Mony	9.30am, 9am
Phnom Penh (day)	6-7	5-12	All companies	Frequent
Phnom Penh (night)	5-6	6-15	Capitol, Mekong Express, TSS, Virak Buntham	Many departures, 10pm to midnight
Poipet	2¼	4-4.50	Capitol, PP Sorya, Rith Mony, TSS	Regular to 4.30pm
Siem Reap	3-4	4-6	Capitol, Golden Bayon Express, Mekong Express, Ponleu Angkor, PP Sorya, Rith Mony	Regular to 3pm

textiles, antiques and accessories. It also produces some of the world's finest tassels here for export.

Lonely Tree Shop TEXTILES
(St 121; ⏲10am-10pm) Fine silk bags, chunky jewellery, fashionable shirts and skirts. Definitely not your run-of-the-mill charity gift shop.

Jewel in the Lotus VINTAGE
(St 2½; ⏲11am-10pm) A wonderful trinket shop selling all kinds of ephemera and kitsch, plus old photos and prints by local artists. Worth stopping in even if you're not buying.

Information

A decent city map distributed by the otherwise moribund tourist office details scenic routes to the bamboo train and other attractions outside town.

ANZ Royal Bank (St 1; ⏲8.30am-4pm Mon-Fri, ATM 24hr)

Canadia Bank (Psar Nath; ⏲7.30am-3.30pm Mon-Fri, to 11.30am Sat, ATM 24hr)

Tourist Information Office (☎012 534177; www.battambang-town.gov.kh; St 1; ⏲8-11am & 2-5pm Mon-Fri) Battambang's tourist office is of little use even when it's open, but it does sometimes stock a great free map.

World Tel Internet (St 2; per hour 2000r; ⏲8am-5pm)

Yi Quoc Clinic (☎053-953163, 012 530171; off NH57; ⏲24hr) The best clinic in town.

Getting There & Away

BOAT

The riverboat to Siem Reap (US$20, daily 7am) squeezes through narrow waterways and passes by protected wetlands, taking from five hours in the wet season to nine or more hours in the height of the dry season. Cambodia's most memorable boat trip, it's operated on alternate days by **Angkor Express** (☎012 601287) and **Chann Na** (☎012 354344).

In the dry season, passengers are driven to a navigable section of the river. The best seats are away from the noisy motor. It may be possible to alight at the **Prek Toal Bird Sanctuary** (p217) and then be picked up there the next day for US$5 extra. Be aware that these boats, while scenic, are not always popular with local communities along the way, as the wake has caused small boats to capsize and fishing nets are regularly snagged. Copious travellers also complain of overcrowding and safety issues – there are rarely enough life jackets to go around.

BUS

Some buses now arrive and depart from Battambang's new **bus station** (NH5), 2km west of the centre. Companies offer free shuttles for departing passengers, but arriving passengers will have to pay for a *remork* (US$3) into town. However, most companies still use their company offices, which are clustered in the centre just south of the intersection of NH5 and St 4.

To Phnom Penh, if you're pinching pennies, Capitol Tour generally has the lowest prices, followed by Phnom Penh Sorya. For a quicker journey to the capital, many companies run express minivan services (US$8 to US$12, 4½ hours), including Cambotra Express, Capitol Tour, Golden Bayon Express, Mekong Express and Virak Buntham.

Virak Buntham runs full-recline-sleeper night buses to Phnom Penh, but be aware that these, like all night buses to Phnom Penh, arrive at an ungodly hour in the morning.

The Mekong Express minibus is the most comfortable way to Siem Reap (US$6, 3½ hours, 8am and 2pm), while Golden Bayon Express runs a speedy minivan service (US$10, three hours, four daily).

Most buses to Bangkok involve a change at the border – usually to a minibus on the Thai side.

Cambotra Express (☎017 866286; St 106)
Capitol Tour (☎012 810055; St 102)
Golden Bayon Express (☎070 968966; St 101)
Mekong Express (☎088 576 7668; St 3)
Rith Mony (☎092 288 8847; St 1)
Phnom Penh Sorya (☎092 181804; St 106)
Ponleu Angkor Khmer (☎096 4628671; St 106)
TSS Transport (☎011 892121; St 102)
Virak Buntham (St 106)

TAXI

At the **taxi station** (cnr Sts 101 & 110), share taxis to Phnom Penh (50,000r per person, 4½ hours) and Pursat (20,000r, two hours) leave from the southeast corner. Also here you'll find taxis to Pailin (20,000r, 1¼ hours) and the Psar Pruhm–Pong Nam Ron border, Poipet (20,000r, 1¾ hours), Sisophon (20,000r, 1¼ hours) and Siem Reap (26,000r, three hours).

Prices are based on six-passenger occupancy; for the price of a whole taxi, multiply the per-passenger fare by six.

Getting Around

English- and French-speaking *remork* drivers are commonplace in Battambang, and all are eager to whisk you around on day trips. A half-day trip out of town to a single sight like Phnom Sampeau might cost US$12, while a full-day trip taking in three sights – Phnom Sampeau, Phnom Banan and the bamboo train, for instance – costs US$16 to US$20, depending on your haggling skills. A *moto* costs about half that.

A *moto* ride in town costs around 2000r, while a *remork* ride starts from US$1.50.

Gecko Moto (p229) and **Royal Hotel** (p231) rent out motorbikes for US$6 to US$8 per day. Bicycles can be rented at the Royal Hotel, **Soksabike** (p229), **Battambang Bike** (☎095 578878; www.battambangbike.com; St 2½; tours US$25; ◷7.30am-7pm) and several guesthouses for about US$2 per day.

Around Battambang

Phnom Sampeau

This fabled limestone **outcrop** (ភ្នំសំពៅ; combined ticket US$3) 12km southwest of Battambang along NH57 (towards Pailin) is known for gorgeous views and a mesmerising evening display of bats. Access up to the summit is via a cement road or – if you're in need of a workout – a steep staircase. The road is too steep for *remorks*. English-speaking *moto* drivers hang out near the base of the hill, at a line of restaurants around the ticket office, and can whisk you up the hill for US$4 return.

About halfway up to the summit, a road leads under a gate and 250m up to the Killing Caves of Phnom Sampeau, now a place of pilgrimage. A staircase, flanked by greenery, leads into a cavern where a golden reclining Buddha lies peacefully next to a glass-walled memorial filled with bones and skulls – the remains of some of the people bludgeoned to death by Khmer Rouge cadres and then thrown through the skylight above. Next to the base of the stairway is the old memorial, a rusty cage made of chicken wire and cyclone fencing and partly filled with human bones.

On the summit, several viewpoints can be discovered amid a complex of temples. As you descend from the summit's golden stupa, dating from 1964, turn left under the gate decorated with a bas-relief of Eiy Sei (an elderly Buddha). A deep canyon, its vertical sides cloaked in greenery, descends 144 steps through a natural arch to a 'lost world' of stalactites, creeping vines and bats; two Angkorian warriors stand guard.

Near the westernmost of the two antennas at the summit, two government artillery pieces, one with markings in Russian, the other in German, are still deployed. Near the base of the western antenna, jockey for position with other tourists on the sunset lookout pavilion. Looking west you'll spy Phnom Krapeu (Crocodile Mountain), a one-time Khmer Rouge stronghold.

Back down at the hill base, people gather at dusk (around 5.30pm) to witness the spectacle of a thick column of bats pouring out of cave high up on the north side of the cliff face. The display lasts a good 30 minutes as millions of bats head out in a looping line to their feeding grounds near Tonlé Sap.

Wat Ek Phnom

Hidden behind a colourful modern pagoda and a gargantuan Buddha statue is this atmospheric, partly collapsed 11th-century **temple** (វត្តឯកភ្នំ; US$2) 11km north of the Battambang's river ferry pier. Wat Ek Phnom measures 52m by 49m and is surrounded by the remains of a laterite wall and an ancient baray (reservoir). A lintel showing the Churning of the Ocean of Milk can be seen above the east entrance to the central temple, whose upper flanks hold some fine bas-reliefs.

This is a very popular picnic destination for Khmers, especially at festival times, and a pilgrimage destination for women hoping to conceive.

Prasat Preah Vihear Province

Sights

★**Prasat Preah Vihear** BUDDHIST TEMPLE
(ប្រាសាទព្រះវិហារ; adult/child US$10/free; ⏲tickets 7.30am-4pm, temple 7.30am-5.30pm)
The most dramatically situated of all Angkorian monuments, Prasat Preah Vihear sprawls along a clifftop near the Thai border, with breathtaking views of lowland Cambodia 550m below. An important place of pilgrimage for millennia, the temple was built by a succession of seven Khmer monarchs, beginning with Yasovarman I (r 889–910) and ending with Suryavarman II (r 1112–52). Like other temple-mountains from this period, it was designed to represent Mt Meru and dedicated to the Hindu deity Shiva.

For generations, Prasat Preah Vihear (called Khao Phra Wiharn by the Thais) has been a source of tension between Cambodia and Thailand. This area was ruled by Thailand for several centuries, but returned to Cambodia during the French protectorate, under the treaty of 1907. But sovereignty over the temple has been an issue ever since, with tensions between Cambodia and Thailand flaring up from time to time – most recently during 2008 to 2011, when armed confrontations around the temple claimed the lives of several dozen soldiers and some civilians on both sides.

The temple is laid out along a north–south processional axis with five cruciform *gopura* (pavilions), decorated with exquisite carvings, separated by esplanades up to 275m long. From the parking area, walk up the hill to toppled and crumbling Gopura V at the north end of the temple complex. From here, the grey-sandstone Monumental Stairway leads down to the Thai border.

Walking south up the slope from Gopura V, the next pavilion you get to is Gopura IV. On the pediment above the southern door, look for an early rendition of the Churning of the Ocean of Milk, a theme later depicted awesomely at Angkor Wat. Keep climbing through Gopura III and II until finally you reach Gopura I. Here the galleries, with their inward-looking windows, are in a remarkably good state of repair, but the Central Sanctuary is just a pile of rubble. Outside, the cliff affords a stupendous viewpoint to Cambodia's northern plains, with the holy mountain of Phnom Kulen (487m) looming in the distance. This is a fantastic spot for a picnic.

Prasat Preah Vihear sits atop an escarpment in the Dangrek Mountains (elevation 625m), 30km north of the town of Sra Em and about 2½ hours by car from Siem Reap. Your first stop upon arriving should be the information centre (p237).

★**Preah Khan of Kompong Svay** BUDDHIST TEMPLE
(ប្រាសាទព្រះខាន់; US$5) For tantalising lost-world ambience, this remote temple complex about 90km south of Preah Vihear City can't be beaten. It's wrapped by vines and trees, and thanks to its back-of-beyond location, the site is astonishingly peaceful. You'll very likely be the only visitor, although you'll need private transport to get here. Preah Khan of Kompong Svay is the largest temple enclosure constructed during the Angkorian period – quite a feat when you consider the competition.

Preah Khan's history is shrouded in mystery, but it was long an important religious site, and some structures here date back to the 9th century. Both Suryavarman II, builder of Angkor Wat, and Jayavarman VII lived here at various times during their lives, suggesting Preah Khan was something of a second city in the Angkorian empire.

Don't confuse Preah Khan of Kompong Svay with the similarly gargantuan Preah Khan temple at Angkor. This Preah Khan covers almost 5 sq km, and includes the main temple as well several satellite temples, including **Prasat Damrei** (ប្រាសាទដំរី), **Prasat Preah Thkol** (ប្រាសាទព្រះថ្កោល) and **Prasat Preah Stung** (ប្រាសាទព្រះស្ទឹង, Prasat Muk Buon), distinguished by four immaculately preserved Avalokiteshvara (Bayon-style) faces.

The main temple is surrounded by a (now dry) moat similar to the one around Angkor Thom. It consists of half-toppled *prangs* (temple towers), entangled with trees and overgrown by forest. As recently as the mid-1990s, the central structure was thought to be in reasonable shape, but at some point in the second half of the decade, looters arrived seeking buried statues under each *prang*. Assaulted with pneumatic drills and mechanical diggers, the ancient temple never stood a chance – many of the towers simply collapsed, leaving the mess we see today.

One entry fee gains you admission to all of the temples in the enclosure. Locals say there are no land mines in the vicinity of Preah Khan, but stick to the marked paths just to be on the safe side.

Upgraded roads mean that you can now visit Preah Khan year-round, although it's still easiest in the dry season. It's an extra-long day trip from Siem Reap, or to do it more cheaply you can hire a *moto* or a taxi in Preah Vihear City or Kompong Thom.

To get here on your own, turn west off smooth NH62 in Svay Pak, about 60km south of Preah Vihear City and 75km north of Kompong Thom. From here an all-season dirt road (substantially pitted with potholes) takes you to Ta Seng, about 30km from the highway and just 4km from the temple. These last 4km are in good shape.

Sleeping

Preah Vihear Boutique Hotel BOUTIQUE HOTEL $$$
(088 346 0501; www.preahvihearhotels.com; Oknha Franna St, Sra Em; d incl breakfast US$35-100;) A slick boutique hotel in the unlikeliest of places, the PVBH is looking to coax higher-end temple goers from Siem Reap to stay a night. With lush bedding and a shimmering 20m pool to cool off in outside, it has a pretty good case. It's about 1km out of town on the road to Prasat Preah Vihear.

The simple but air-conditioned US$35 rooms off the parking lot are ostensibly for drivers and tour guides, but work just fine for flashpackers who don't want to pay full whack for their boutique experience.

Information

Prasat Preah Vihear Information Centre (Kor Muy; 7am-4.30pm) Your first stop when heading to Prasat Preah Vihear is the information centre in the village of Kor Muy (23km north of Sra Em). This is where you pay for entry, secure an English-speaking guide if you want one (US$15), and arrange transport via *moto* (US$5 return) or 4WD (US$25 return, maximum six passengers) up the 6.5km temple access road.

Bring your passport as you'll need it to buy a ticket. The first 5km of the access road are gradual enough, but the final 1.5km is extremely steep; nervous passengers might consider walking this last bit, especially if it's wet.

Getting There & Away

Liang US Express Has a morning bus from Sra Em to Phnom Penh (US$10, 10 hours) via Preah Vihear City and Kompong Thom.

Rith Mony (097 865 6018) Has a morning bus to Phnom Penh (US$10, 10 hours) via Siem Reap (20,000r, 3½ hours).

Kompong Thom

This friendly, bustling commercial town rims the NH6 with the lazy curves of the Stung Sen River winding through the centre. The town itself may be sparse on attractions, but it's a prime launching pad for exploring nearby sights. Both the serene, tree-entwined temples of Sambor Prei Kuk (p238) and the colourful wats of Phnom Santuk (p238) are easy half-day trips, while boutique accommodation and decent eating options make Kompong Thom an excellent base from which to head out on a long day trip to Preah Khan of Kompong Svay.

Sights & Activities

Bats WILDLIFE
(Stung Sen St) Hundreds of large bats (in Khmer, *chreoun*), with 40cm wingspans, live in three old mahogany trees next to Kompong Thom's old French Governor's Residence. They spend their days suspended upside down like winged fruit, fanning themselves with their wings to keep cool. Head here around dusk (from about 5.30pm or 6pm) to see them fly off in search of food.

Im Sokhom Travel Agency TOUR
(012 691527; St 3) Runs guided tours, including cycling trips to Sambor Prei Kuk, and can arrange transport by *moto* to Sambor Prei Kuk (US$10) or Phnom Santuk and Santuk Silk Farm (US$8).

Sleeping & Eating

Arunras Hotel HOTEL $
(062-961294; NH6; s/d with fan US$5/8, d with air-con US$15;) Dominating Kompong Thom's accommodation scene, this central establishment has 58 good-value rooms with Chinese-style decoration and on-the-ball staff. The popular restaurant downstairs dishes up tasty Khmer fare. Operates the slightly cheaper, 53-room Arunras Guesthouse next door. Extra bonus for the lazy traveller: buses through town stop literally right outside the door.

★ **Sambor Village Hotel** BOUTIQUE HOTEL $$
(062-961391; www.samborvillage.asia; Prachea Thepatay St; r/ste incl breakfast US$60/90; @) This French-owned place brings boutique to Kompong Thom. Spacious, bungalow-style rooms with four-poster beds and chic bathrooms are set amid a tranquil verdant garden with an inviting pool under the shade of a mango tree. The upstairs terrace

restaurant has international cuisine and impressive hard-wood flooring. Free use of mountain bikes. Located riverside, about 700m east of NH6.

Love Cafe INTERNATIONAL $$
(Prachea Thepatay St; mains US$2.50-8.75; ⏲3-9pm Mon-Sat; 📶) If you're in the mood for comfort food, this bamboo-walled place is a real gem. The big menu of pizzas and burgers is a winner, as is its fantastic selection of ice cream.

Kompong Thom Restaurant CAMBODIAN $$
(NH6; mains US$3-8; ⏲6.30am-9pm; 📶📝) With delightful bow-tied waiters and a pocket-sized terrace overlooking the river, this restaurant is easily Kompong Thom's fanciest, even if the food doesn't quite match the ambience. Unique concoctions featuring water buffalo and stir-fried eel feature on the menu of Khmer classics, which come in generous portions.

Information

Tourist Information Office (Stung Sen St; ⏲8-11am & 2-5pm Mon-Fri) Hands out a pamphlet on Kompong Thom sights.

Canadia Bank (NH6; ⏲8am-3.30pm Mon-Fri, 8-11.30am Sat, ATM 24hr)

Getting There & Away

Taxi Park Share taxis are the fastest way to Phnom Penh (US$5) and Siem Reap (US$5) from Kompong Thom. Heading north to Preah Vihear City, share taxis (US$5) depart in the morning only. Most taxi services depart from this taxi park, one block east of the Tela Gas Station on NH6.

Around Kompong Thom

Phnom Santuk

Its forest-surrounded summit adorned with Buddha images and a series of pagodas, this holy temple **mountain** (ភ្នំសន្ទុក; US$2) (207m) 15km south of Kompong Thom is a popular site of Buddhist pilgrimage. To reach the top, huff up 809 stairs – with the upper staircase home to troupes of animated macaques – or wimp out and take the paved 2.5km road. Santuk hosts an extraordinary ensemble of colourful wats and stupas, a kaleidoscopic mishmash of old and new Buddhist statuary and monuments.

Sambor Prei Kuk

Cambodia's most impressive group of pre-Angkorian monuments, **Sambor Prei Kuk** (សំបូរព្រៃគុក; www.samborpreikuk.com; US$5) encompasses more than 100 mainly brick temples huddled in the forest. The area has a serene and soothing atmosphere, and some of the oldest structures in the country. An easy 40-minute drive from Kompong Thom, the area has a serene and soothing atmosphere, with the sandy trails between temples looping through the shady forest. A community-based tourism initiative employs local guides, organises activities and sets up homestays for those looking to experience an authentic slice of rural Cambodia.

Sights

Prasat Yeai Poeun HINDU TEMPLE
(ប្រាសាទយាយព័ន្ធ, Prasat Yeay Peau) Prasat Yeai Poeun is arguably the most atmospheric ensemble, as it feels lost in the forest. The eastern gateway is being both held up and torn asunder by an ancient tree, the bricks interwoven with the tree's extensive, probing roots. A massive tree shades the western gate.

Prasat Sambor HINDU TEMPLE
(ប្រាសាទសំបូរ) The principal temple group, Prasat Sambor (7th and 10th centuries) is dedicated to Gambhireshvara, one of Shiva's many incarnations (the other groups are dedicated to Shiva himself). Several of Prasat Sambor's towers retain brick carvings in fairly good condition, and there is a series of large *yoni* (female fertility symbols) around the central tower.

Prasat Tao HINDU TEMPLE
(ប្រាសាទតោ, Lion Temple) The largest of the Sambor Prei Kuk complexes, Prasat Tao boasts excellent examples of Chenla carving in the form of two large, elaborately coiffed stone lions. It also has a fine, rectangular pond, Srah Neang Pov.

Sleeping

Isanborei HOMESTAY $
(☎017 936112; www.samborpreikuk.com; dm/d US$4/6) 🍃 This organisation works hard to encourage visitors to Sambor Prei Kuk to stay another day. Besides running a community-based homestay program, Isanborei offers cooking courses, rents bicycles (US$2 per day) and organises ox-cart rides.

Getting There & Away

Isanborei operates a stable of *remorks* to whisk you safely to/from Kompong Thom (US$15 one way). Call for a pick-up if you're in Kompong Thom. Otherwise, a round-trip *moto* ride out here from Kompong Thom (under an hour) should cost US$10.

EASTERN CAMBODIA

If it's a walk on the wild side that fires your imagination, then the northeast is calling. It's home to rare forest elephants and freshwater dolphins, and peppering the area are thundering waterfalls, crater lakes and meandering rivers. Trekking, biking, kayaking and elephant adventures are all beginning to take off. The rolling hills and lush forests provide a home to many ethnic minority groups. Do the maths: it all adds up to an amazing experience.

Kompong Cham & Around

This quiet Mekong city, an important trading post during the French period, serves as the gateway to Cambodia's northeast. Most action is on the riverfront. The surrounding province of Kompong Cham is a land of picturesque villages and quiet Mekong meanders. Some of Cambodia's finest silk is woven here.

Sights

Wat Nokor Bachey BUDDHIST TEMPLE
(វត្តនគរបាជ័យ; admission US$2) The original fusion temple, Wat Nokor is a modern Theravada Buddhist pagoda squeezed into the walls of a 12th-century Mahayana Buddhist shrine of sandstone and laterite. It's located down a pretty dirt road just off the highway to Phnom Penh, about 2.5km west of the centre.

Wat Hanchey TEMPLE
Wat Hanchey is a hilltop pagoda 20km north of Kompong Cham that was an important centre of worship during the Chenla period when, as today, it offered some of the best Mekong views in Cambodia. The foundations of several 8th-century structures, some of them destroyed by American bombs, are scattered around the compound, along with a clutch of bizarre fruit and animal statues. The highlight is a remarkable Chenla-era brick sanctuary with well-preserved inscriptions in ancient Sanskrit on the lintel.

Wat Maha Leap TEMPLE
Sacred Wat Maha Leap southeast of town is one of the last remaining wooden pagodas left in the country. More than a century old, this beautiful pagoda was only spared devastation by the Khmer Rouge because they converted it into a hospital. The wide black columns supporting the structure are complete tree trunks, resplendent in gilded patterns. The Khmer Rouge painted over the designs to match their austere philosophies, but monks later stripped it back to its original glory.

Koh Paen ISLAND
(កោះប៉ែន) For a supremely relaxing bicycle ride, it's hard to beat Koh Paen, a rural island in the Mekong River, connected to the southern reaches of Kompong Cham town by an elaborate **bamboo bridge** (toll 500r to 1000r) in the dry season or a local ferry (with/without bicycle 1500/1000r) in the wet season. The bamboo bridge is an attraction in itself, built entirely by hand each year and looking like it is made of matchsticks from afar.

Sleeping

★**Moon River Guesthouse** GUESTHOUSE $
(☎016 788973; moonrivermekong@gmail.com; Sihanouk St; r with fan US$7-11, with air-con US$13-19; ❄📶) One of the newer riverfront guesthouses, Moon River is a great all-rounder with smart, spacious rooms, including some triples. Downstairs is a popular restaurant-bar (mains US$2 to US$4) that serves hearty breakfasts and draws a crowd by night.

Daly Hotel HOTEL $
(☎042-666 6631; www.dalyhotel.net; d/tw US$18/20, VIP US$40; ❄📶) A swish hotel one block from the river, the Daly is the best of the many Khmer-style high-rise hotels in town. Rooms are large and bright with wall-mounted flat-screen TVs, spick-and-span bathrooms and luscious linens.

Eating

There's little reason to stray beyond the atmospheric restaurants on the river.

★**Smile Restaurant** CAMBODIAN $
(www.bsda-cambodia.org; Sihanouk St; mains US$3-5; ⌚6.30am-10pm; 📶) 🌿 Run by the Buddhism and Society Development Association (BSDA), this handsome nonprofit restaurant is a huge hit with the NGO crowd for its big breakfasts and authentic Khmer cuisine, such as *char k'dau* (stir-fry with lemongrass, hot basil and peanuts) and black-pepper squid. Western dishes are on the menu as well, and it sells BSDA-made *kramas* and trinkets.

BUSES FROM KOMPONG CHAM

DESTINATION	PRICE (US$)	DURATION (HR)	COMPANIES	FREQUENCY
Ban Lung	10	7	PP Sorya	10am
Battambang	7.50	7½	Liang US Express, PP Sorya, Rith Mony	7.30am & 8.30am
Kratie via Snuol	4.50	4	PP Sorya	10.30am & 12.30pm
Phnom Penh	4-5	3	Liang US Express, PP Sorya, Rith Mony	hourly till 6pm
Sen Monorom	9	6	Minivans only	A few in morning
Siem Reap	6.50	6	Liang US Express	7.30am & 8.30am
Stung Treng via Snuol	6.50	6	PP Sorya	10am

Mekong Crossing INTERNATIONAL $
(2 Pasteur St; mains US$2-5; ⏰6am-10pm; 📶) Occupying a prime corner on the riverfront, this old favourite has recently had a successful facelift and serves an enticing mix of Khmer curries and Western favourites, such as big burgers and tasty sandwiches. Doubles as a popular bar by night and recently added a dozen rooms upstairs (fan/air-con room US$7/12).

Lazy Mekong Daze INTERNATIONAL $
(Sihanouk St; mains US$3-5.50; ⏰7.30am-last customer; 📶) One of the go-to places to gather after dark thanks to a mellow atmosphere, a pool table and a big screen for sports and movies. The menu includes a range of Khmer, Thai and French food, plus the best pizzas in town, chilli con carne and tempting ice creams.

ℹ Information

Canadia Bank (Preah Monivong Blvd; ⏰8am-3.30pm Mon-Fri, 8-11.30am Sat, ATM 24hr) ATM plus cash advances on credit cards.

Mekong Internet (Vithei Pasteur St; per hour 1500r; ⏰6.30am-10pm) Among a cluster of internet cafes on Vithei Pasteur St.

ℹ Getting There & Away

Phnom Penh is 120km southwest of Kompong Cham. If you are heading north to Kratie or beyond, arrange transport via the sealed road to Chhlong rather than taking a huge detour east to Snuol on NH7.

Besides buses, share taxis (15,000r) and overcrowded local minibuses (10,000r) do the dash to Phnom Penh from the **taxi park** near the New Market (Psar Thmei). The trip takes two hours or more depending on traffic in the capital. Express minivans are another option to the capital (US$6, two hours); arrange these through your guesthouse.

Morning share taxis and minibuses to Kratie (US$5, two hours) and Stung Treng (US$10, four hours) depart when full from the **Caltex station** at the main roundabout, and there are morning minibuses from the taxi park as well.

There are no longer any passenger boats to other towns running on the Mekong from here.

ℹ Getting Around

Figure on US$10 to US$15 per day for a *moto* and US$15 to US$20 for a *remork* (slightly more if including Wat Maha Leap in your plans). Drivers speak great English and can guide you around the sites. Round-trip *remork* journeys to Wat Hanchey or Phnom Pros and Phnom Srei are a negotiable US$10. Most guesthouses and restaurants on the

GETTING TO VIETNAM

Getting to the border The **Trapeang Phlong/Xa Mat border crossing** (⏰7am to 5pm) has become increasingly popular for those travelling between northeast Cambodia and Ho Chi Minh City. From Kompong Cham take anything heading east on NH7 toward Snuol, and get off at the roundabout in Krek (Kraek), on NH7, 55km east-southeast of Kompong Cham. From there, it's 13km south by *moto* (US$3) along NH72 to snoozy Trapeang Phlong, marked by a candy-striped road barrier and a few tin shacks.

At the border This border is a breeze: just have your Vietnamese visa ready.

Moving on On the Vietnamese side, motorbikes and taxis go to Tay Ninh, 45km to the south – but be prepared to negotiate a bit harder than in Cambodia.

riverfront rent motorbikes (US$3 to US$5 per day) and bicycles (US$1 per day).

Kratie

A supremely mellow riverside town, Kratie (pronounced *kra-cheh*) is the most popular place in the country to see Irrawaddy dolphins, which live in the Mekong River in ever-diminishing numbers. There is a rich legacy of French-era architecture, and as a travel hub Kratie is the natural place to break the journey when travelling overland between Phnom Penh and the Four Thousand Islands area in southern Laos.

Sights & Activities

The best place to see the Irrawaddy dolphin is at Kampi, about 15km north of Kratie, on the road to Sambor. A *moto/remork* should be around US$7/10 return, depending on how long the driver has to wait.

Mekong Turtle Conservation Centre WILDLIFE RESERVE
(012 712071; www.mekongturtle.com; Sambor; adult/child US$4/2; 8.30am-4.30pm) This wildlife conservation centre is located within the temple grounds of Wat Sorsor Moi Roi (Hundred Columns Temple) in Sambor, about 35km north of Kratie. Established by Conservation International (www.conservation.org), it is home to several species of turtle, including the rare Cantor's giant softshell, which was only rediscovered along this stretch of the Mekong in 2007. One of the largest freshwater turtles, it can grow to nearly 2m in length. Hatchlings are nurtured here for 10 months before being released in the wild. Tourists can participate in the release on select weeks, usually in September and May/June. Check the website for the exact dates.

CRDTours TOURS
(Cambodia Rural Discovery Tours; 099 834353; www.crdtours.org; St 3; 8am-noon & 2-5.30pm) Run by the Cambodian Rural Development Team, this company focuses on sustainable tours along the Mekong Discovery Trail (p243). Homestays, volunteer opportunities and various excursions are available on the Mekong island of Koh Pdao, 20km north of Kampi. The typical price is US$38 to US$60 per day, including all meals and tours.

Sorya Kayaking Adventures KAYAKING
(090 241148; www.soryakayaking.com; Rue Preah Suramarit; 7am-9pm) Sorya has a fleet of seven tandem and three single kayaks and runs half-day trips on the Mekong north of Kratie (November to June only), or on the Te River to the south (August to October). The Mekong trips get you close to the dolphins, while the Te River trips are more scenic.

Sleeping

For something even more relaxed than Kratie, consider staying directly on the island of Koh Trong, where homestays and boutique accommodation await.

Le Tonlé Tourism Training Center GUESTHOUSE $
(072-210505; www.letonle.org; St 3; r without bathroom US$10-20;) CRDT runs this fantastic budget guesthouse in a beautiful wooden house in the centre. With silk pillows and bed runners, agreeable art and photos, wood floors and a great hang-out area, they put plenty of care into the design. Rooms are somewhat dark but share boutique-quality bathrooms. It doubles as a training centre for at-risk locals.

Koh Trong Community Homestay I HOMESTAY $
(Koh Trong; mattress per person US$4, room US$8) Set in an old wooden house, offering two proper bedrooms and fancy-pants bathrooms (that is, thrones not squats). It's located about 2km north of the ferry dock near Rajabori Villas. Ride your bike, take a *moto* (US$1) or ride an ox-cart.

Rajabori Villas BOUTIQUE HOTEL $$
(012 770150; www.rajabori-kratie.com; Koh Trong; r incl breakfast US$65-150;) A boutique lodge with a swimming pool and large dark-wood bungalows done up in inspired French-Khmer style? Sign us up. This is the best accommodation in the Kratie region by some margin. It's located at the northern tip of Koh Trong. They will pick you up for free from the ferry pier, or a private boat from Kratie costs US$4/5 per day/night.

Arun Mekong LODGE $$
(017 663014; www.arunmekong.wordpress.com; Koh Trong; r with/without bathroom from US$27/22) A nice mix of tastefully furnished rooms and bungalows in a lovely setting at the north tip of idyllic Koh Trong. Electricity runs only from 6pm to 11pm, however, which means hot nights at certain times of the year.

Le Bungalow BOUTIQUE HOTEL $$
(012 660902; www.rajabori-kratie.com; Rue Preah Suramarit; r with/without bathroom US$65/31;

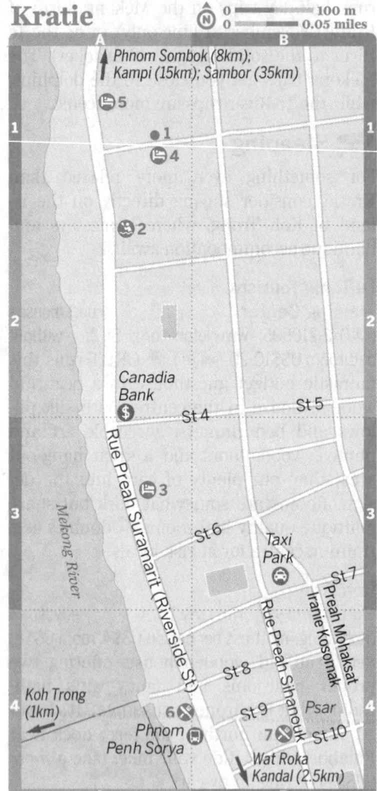

Kratie

Activities, Courses & Tours
1 CRDTours ... A1
2 Sorya Kayaking Adventures ... A2

Sleeping
3 Le Bungalow ... A3
4 Le Tonlé Tourism Training Center ... A1
5 Mekong Dolphin Hotel ... A1

Eating
6 Jasmine Boat Restaurant ... A4
7 Tokae Restaurant ... B4

) Akin to a boutique homestay, here you'll find three rooms in a traditional wooden house decorated with Sino-Khmer furnishings from the colonial period. Two spacious rooms have modern bathrooms, while the third is more suited to children travelling with their parents and has an outside bathroom.

Mekong Dolphin Hotel HOTEL $$
(072-666 6666; www.mekongdolphinhotel.com; Rue Preah Sumamarit; r US$15-50;) Looming large on the riverfront, this concrete high-rise is the fanciest in town, offering slick river-view rooms for US$35 and suites for your inner VIP at US$50. There's even a small gym and sauna (if Kratie isn't hot enough for you already). The cheaper rooms at the back are a huge step down in quality.

Eating & Drinking

Tokae Restaurant CAMBODIAN $
(St 10; mains US$2-4; 6am-11pm;) Look out for Cambodia's largest *tokae* (gecko) on the wall and you've found this excellent little eatery. The menu offers a good mix of cheap Cambodian food such as curries and *amok* (a baked fish dish), plus equally affordable Western breakfasts and comfort food.

Jasmine Boat Restaurant INTERNATIONAL $$
(Rue Preah Sumamarit; mains US$4-12; 7am-10pm;) Occupying a prime location overlooking Kratie's busy ferry dock, this is the only place on the riverbank in town. The boat-shaped restaurant has a mixed menu of affordable Khmer specials and pricey international cuts of meat. It really shines at sunset but is a good perch any time of day.

Information

Canadia Bank (Rue Preah Suramarit; 8.30am-3.30pm Mon-Fri, ATM 24hr) ATM offering cash withdrawals, plus currency exchange.

Getting There & Around

Kratie is 250km northeast of Phnom Penh (via the Chhlong road) and 141km south of Stung Treng. **Phnom Penh Sorya** (081 908005) operates three buses per day to Phnom Penh (US$8, seven hours) along the slow route (via Snuol). Rith Mony also has a bus but you must flag it down on the highway. Express minivans get to Phnom Penh in four hours via Chhlong (US$9, about six daily), and usually offer transfers onward to Sihanoukville.

Sorya's daily bus to Siem Reap (US$11, nine hours) involves a change in Suong. There's also an express minivan to Siem Reap (US$11, six hours, 7am). Share taxis (US$10) head to Phnom Penh between 6am and 8am, with possible additional departures after lunch.

For Ban Lung, Sorya (US$8, five hours, around 12.30pm) and Rith Mony (11.30am) buses transit through from Phnom Penh. A few local minibuses also serve Ban Lung from the **taxi park**. Sorya has a 2.30pm bus to Stung Treng (US$5, 2½ hours), and there's also a 7am minibus. There's a 7.30am minibus to Preah Vihear City (US$15, five hours). To get to Laos, you must transfer in Stung Treng; Kratie guesthouses can arrange this.

For Sen Monorom, take a local minibus from the taxi park (30,000r, four hours, two or three early-morning departures) or head to Snoul and change.

Stung Treng

Located on the Tonlé San near its confluence with the Mekong, Stung Treng is a quiet town with limited appeal, but sees a lot of transit traffic heading north to Laos, south to Kratie, east to Ratanakiri and west to Siem Reap. Some locals call the Tonlé San the 'Tonlé Kong', as it merges with the Tonlé Kong (well-known as the Sekong in Laos) 10km east of town. Just north of the town centre, a major bridge across the San leads north to the Lao border, while an important new bridge traverses the Mekong south of town.

Sights & Activities

Mekong Blue ARTS CENTRE

(មេគង្គប៊្លូ; ☎012 622096; www.mekongblue.com; ⏲7.30-11.30am & 2-5pm Mon-Sat) Part of the Stung Treng Women's Development Centre, Mekong Blue is a silk-weaving centre on the outskirts of Stung Treng. Mekong Blue specialises in exquisite silk products for sale and export. At this centre it is possible to observe the dyers and weavers, most of whom come from vulnerable or impoverished backgrounds. The centre is located about 4km east of the centre on the riverside road that continues under the bridge.

Xplore-Asia ADVENTURE

(☎011 433836, 074-973456; www.xplore-cambodia.com) Doles out brochures, booklets and advice, and tailors one- to several-day cycling-and-kayak combo tours along the Mekong Discovery Trail, including kayaking with the dolphins. Rents out kayaks (US$10 per day), motorbikes (US$10 per day) and sturdy Trek mountain bikes (US$5 per day).

Sleeping & Eating

Mekong Bird Lodge BUNGALOW $

(☎098 522203; ankgorlu@gmail.com; s/d/tw US$13/15/18) This self-styled ecolodge sits on a bluff overlooking a peaceful Mekong eddy north of town. It has a lush tropical garden, but remains exceedingly rustic. Sturdy wood bungalows are spacious and have balconies with sunset views, but lack furniture (beyond beds). Request a mosquito net. To get here, turn left at the sign 4km north of the Tonlé San bridge and continue 1.5km.

Golden River Hotel HOTEL $$

(☎074-690 0029; www.goldenriverhotel.com; r US$15-35; ❄@☎) The best all-rounder in town, the Golden River has 50 well-appointed rooms complete with hot-water bathrooms, fridges and TVs. Rooms at the front with a view are a few dollars more.

Ponika's Palace INTERNATIONAL $

(mains US$2-5; ⏲6.30am-10pm) Need a break from *laab* (a spicy salad with chicken, pork or fish) after Laos? Burgers, pizza and English breakfasts grace the menu, along with Indian food and wonderful Khmer curries. Affable owner Ponika speaks English and cold beer is available to slake a thirst. Also rents bicycles (US$1–2).

DON'T MISS

MEKONG DISCOVERY TRAIL

It's well worth spending a couple of days exploring the various bike rides and activities on offer along the Mekong Discovery Trail, an initiative to open up stretches of the Mekong River around Stung Treng and Kratie to community-based tourism. Once managed by the government with foreign development assistance, its trails and routes are now being kept alive by private tour companies, such as Xplore-Asia (p243) in Stung Treng and CRDTours (p241) in Kratie.

It's a worthy project, as it intends to provide fishing communities an alternative income in order to protect the Irrawaddy dolphin and other rare species on this stretch of river.

There's a great booklet with routes and maps outlining excursions around Kratie and Stung Treng, but you'll be hard-pressed to secure your own copy; ask tour operators if you can photograph theirs. The routes can be tackled by bicycle or motorbike. They range in length from a few hours to several days, with optional overnights in village homestays. Routes criss-cross the Mekong frequently by ferry and traverse several Mekong islands, including Koh Trong.

GETTING TO LAOS: TRAPAENG KRIEL TO NONG NOK KHIENE

Getting to the border The remote **Trapeang Kriel/Nong Nok Khiene border** (⏲6am to 6pm), 60km north of Stung Treng, is a popular crossing point on the Indochina overland circuit. For many years, there was a separate river crossing here, but that's no longer open. There are also no longer any through buses between Phnom Penh and Pakse. You'll need to get yourself to Stung Treng, from where there are at least two minivans per day (at noon and 2pm) that run across the border and onward to the 10,000 Islands and Pakse. The only other option to the border is a private taxi (around US$35 to US$40) or *moto* (around US$15) from Stung Treng.

At the border Both Lao and Cambodian visas are available on arrival. Entering Laos, it costs US$35 to US$42 for a visa, depending on nationality, plus a US$2 fee (dubbed either an 'overtime' or a 'processing' fee, depending on when you cross) upon both entry and exit.

Entering Cambodia, they jack up the price of a visa to US$25 from the normal US$20. The extra US$5 is called 'tea money', as the border guards have been stationed at such a remote crossing. In addition, the Cambodians charge US$1 for a cursory medical inspection upon arrival in the country, and levy a US$2 processing fee upon exit. These fees might be waived if you protest, but don't protest for too long or your vehicle may leave without you.

Moving on There's virtually zero traffic on either side of the border. If you're dropped at the border, expect to pay 150,000/50,000 kip (US$12/4) for a taxi/*săhm-lór* heading north to Ban Nakasang (for Don Det).

ℹ Information

Canadia Bank (⏲8.30am-3.30pm Mon-Fri, ATM 24hr) Has an international ATM.

Riverside Guesthouse (☎012 257207; kimtysou@gmail.com) Specialises in getting people to/from Laos, Siem Reap or just about anywhere else. Also runs boat tours to the Lao border, with a trip to see the resident dolphin pod (US$100/120 for two/four people). English-speaking guides offer motorbike tours around the province, and it rents motorbikes (from US$5) or bicycles (US$1-2).

Tourist Information Centre (☎074-210001; ⏲8-11am & 2-5pm) Inconveniently located near the Tonlé San bridge; it's rare to find it open.

ℹ Getting There & Around

NH7 north to the Lao border and south to Kratie is in good shape these days.

Express minivans with guesthouse pick-ups as early as 4am are the quickest way to Phnom Penh (US$10 to US$13, seven hours). Book through **Riverside Guesthouse** or **Ponika's Palace** (p243).

Phnom Penh Sorya (☎092 181805) has a 6.30am bus to Phnom Penh (US$12, 10 hours) via Kratie (US$5, 2½ hours) and Kompong Cham (US$8, seven hours). Additionally, local minibuses to Kratie depart regularly until 2pm from the market area.

There is a comfortable tourist van to Ban Lung (US$6, two hours, 8am and 1pm), with additional morning trips in cramped local minibuses from the market (US$5, three hours).

The new highway west from Thala Boravit to Preah Vihear via Chhep is in great shape. **Asia Van Transfer** (☎in Siem Reap 063-963853; www.asiavantransfer.com) has an express minibus to Siem Reap at 2pm daily (US$23, five hours), with a stop in Preah Vihear City (US$12, three hours).

For Laos, minivans head over the border at noon and 2pm, serving Don Det and Pakse.

Aroung Stung Treng

Preah Rumkel

This small village is emerging as a hotbed of ecotourism thanks to a splendid homestay program and its proximity to the Anlong Cheuteal Irrawaddy dolphin pool near the Lao border. With wetlands recognised by the Ramsar List of Wetlands of International Importance (www.ramsar.org), dozens of islands, a rich array of bird life, and various rapids and waterfalls cascading down from Laos, this is one of the Mekong River's wildest and most beautiful stretches.

The half-dozen frolicking dolphins in the Anlong Cheuteal pool (known as Boong Pa Gooang in Laos) can easily be sighted from shore in Preah Rumkel. There's a US$2 per person charge to see the dolphins.

Excursions out of Preah Rumkel include a hike up a nearby mountain and a boat/hiking trip to view the rampaging Mekong rapids cascading down from Laos. The rapids are an awesome display of nature's force, especially in the wet season.

Hire a longtail boat in O'Svay or, closer to the Laos border, Anlong Morakot, to explore the area and view the dolphins at Anlong Cheuteal. Boats cost a negotiable US$25 round-trip to Preah Rumkel and the dolphin pool. Add US$10 if you want to continue upstream to the rapids. Anlong Morakot is only 4km from the border so travellers coming in from Laos could get there in about 10 minutes on the back of a *moto* (about US$2). Be sure to arrange onward transport to Stung Treng – either at the border or in advance through Xplore-Asia (p243) or Riverside Guesthouse (p244) in Stung Treng. These companies can also prearrange your *moto* and boat ride from the border to Preah Rumkel. A taxi to Stung Treng from this area costs about US$45.

Better yet, through Xplore-Asia you can kayak with the dolphins and then paddle downstream to O'Svay, or through bird-rich flooded forests all the way to Stung Treng. A full-day kayak excursion south of O'Svay costs US$65 per person; add US$20 per person to include the boat trip upstream to the dolphin pool and the Mekong rapids.

If you want to stay overnight, **Mlup Baitong** (ម្លប់បៃតង; in Phnom Penh 012 413857; www.mlup-baitong.org) runs Preah Rumkel's community-based homestay program. The cost for basic accommodation is US$3 per head, with meals costing an additional US$3 to US$4 per meal.

Mondulkiri Province

Mondulkiri Province (ខេត្តមណ្ឌលគិរី), the original Wild East and most sparsely populated province in the country, is a world apart from the lowlands with not a rice paddy or palm tree in sight.

Home to the hardy Bunong people and their noble elephants, this upland area is a seductive mix of grassy hills, pine groves and rainforests of jade green. Conservationists have established several superb ecotourism projects in the province, but are facing off against loggers, poachers, pepper farmers and well-connected speculators.

Sen Monorom

A charming community where the hills meet, the area around Sen Monorom is peppered with minority villages and picturesque waterfalls, making it the ideal place to spend some time. Set at more than 800m,the town can get quite chilly so bring warm clothing.

Sights & Activities

Bou Sraa Waterfall WATERFALL

(ទឹកជ្រោះប៊ូស្រា; admission US$2.50) Plunging into the dense jungle below, this is one of Cambodia's most impressive falls. Famous throughout the country, this double-drop waterfall has an upper tier of some 10m and a spectacular lower tier with a thundering 25m drop. Getting here is a 33km, one-hour journey east of Sen Monorom on a mostly sealed road.

Elephant Valley Project WILDLIFE RESERVE

(EVP; 099 696041; www.elephantvalleyproject.org; Mon-Fri) For an original elephant experience, visit the Elephant Valley Project. The project entices local mahouts to bring their overworked or injured elephants to this 1600-hectare sanctuary. It's very popular, so make sure you book well ahead. You can visit it for a whole (US$85) or half day (US$55). It does not take overnight visitors on Friday and Saturday nights and is not open to day visitors on Saturday and Sunday.

Sam Veasna Center WILDLIFE

(012 520828, 071-553 9779; www.samveasna.org; Hefalump Cafe, Sen Monorom) Works with the international NGO Wildlife Conservation Society (WCS; www.wcscambodia.org) in promoting wildlife and birdwatching tours in the Seima Protected Forest, including rare primate spotting at its wonderful Jahoo Gibbon Camp (p247), 25km west of Sen Monrorom. In Sen Monorom, ask for Pech.

Sleeping

★ **Nature Lodge** GUESTHOUSE $

(012 230272; www.naturelodgecambodia.com; r US$10-30;) Sprawling across a windswept hilltop near town are 30 solid wood bungalows with private porches, hot showers and mosquito nets. Among them are Swiss Family Robinson–style chalets with sunken beds and ante-rooms. The magnificent restaurant has comfy nooks, a pool table and an enviable bar where guests chill out and swap travel tales.

Indigenous Peoples Lodge BUNGALOW $

(012 725375; indigenouspeopleslodge@gmail.com; d US$5-15, q US$20;) Run by a Bunong family, this is a great place to stay with a whole range of accommodation set in minority houses, including a traditional thatched Bunong house with an upgrade

WORTH A TRIP

BUNONG VILLAGES

Several Bunong villages around Sen Monorom make for popular excursions, although the frequently visited villages that appear on tourist maps have assimilated into modern society. In general, the further out you go, the less exposed the village.

Trips to Bunong villages can often be combined with waterfalls or elephant interaction tours. Each guesthouse has a preferred village to send travellers to, which is a great way to spread the wealth.

For more on Bunong culture check out the website of the **Mondulkiri Resource and Documentation Centre** (MRDC; ☎097 4087806; www.mondulkiri-centre.org), run by local NGO Mondulkiri Indigenous People Association for Development (MIPAD). MIPAD also runs the **WEHH** (☎097 273 9566) tour program, which offers an intimate look at Bunong culture in the Dak Dam community. Itineraries include 'Life on a Bunong Farm', 'The Handicrafts of the Bunong' and a trek into old-growth Bunong forest. Prices start from US$55 per person, subject to the size of the group.

or two. The cheapest rooms involve a share bathroom, but are good value. Perks include free internet and free drop-offs in town.

Tree Lodge BUNGALOW $
(☎097 723 4177; www.treelodgecambodia.com; d US$7-10, q US$12-15;) Sixteen bungalows of various shapes and sizes slink down a hill at the back. Rooms have balconies and attractive open-air bathrooms, but lack any shelf space or furniture besides a bed. Hang out at the restaurant, where hammocks and tasty Khmer food await. The young family in charge are very welcoming and can help with tour arrangements, including to their own **Mondulkiri Project** (www.mondulkiriproject.org; 1-/2-day tour per person US$50/80) elephant interaction program.

Happy Elephant GUESTHOUSE $
(☎097 616 4011; dm US$2, r US$5-8;) French-Khmer couple Vivi and Mot are your hosts with the most at this backpacker pad, which features sturdy cold-water bungalows on a hill behind the Phat Gecko bar-restaurant. They also offer tours and treks for those without a game plan.

Green House Guesthouse GUESTHOUSE $
(☎017 905 659; www.greenhouse-tour.blogspot.com; NH76; dm US$5, r US$15-25;) Partnered with the tour company of the same name (elephant encounters US$35 per person), here you'll find a wide range of rooms from singles with cold water right through to a two-bedroom family suite with air-con. It's also confusingly known as the Boran Southa Guesthouse.

★ **Mayura Hill Hotel & Resort** HOTEL $$$
(☎077 980980; www.mayurahillresort.com; r incl breakfast US$100-120, ste incl breakfast US$150;) Setting a new standard for lodgings in Mondulkiri, Mayura Hill is a lovely place to stay for those with the budget. The 14 villa rooms are tastefully appointed with woods and silks and the family villa includes a bunk for the children. Facilities include a swimming pool and a five-a-side football pitch! The restaurant is the most sophisticated in town.

Eating & Drinking

Hefalump Cafe CAFE $
(cakes US$1-3; ⏰7am-6pm Mon-Fri, 9am-4pm Sun;) A collaboration of various NGOs and conservation groups in town, this cafe doubles as a training centre for Bunong people in hospitality. Local coffee or Lavazza, teas, cakes, and healthy breakfasts make this a great spot to plan your adventures over a cuppa.

The Hangout BAR
(☎088 721 9991) The rooftop bar at this guesthouse is the most happening spot in town. There are bar sports like table football, occasional jam sessions and some of Sen Monorom's best Western food to complement a Khmer menu. It's run by an affable Tasmanian-Khmer couple and has dorms and private rooms downstairs.

Information

Acleda Bank (NH76; ⏰8.30am-3.30pm, ATM 24hr) Changes major currencies and has a Visa-only ATM.

Getting There & Away

The stretch of NH76 connecting Sen Monorom to Snuol and Phnom Penh (370km) is in fantastic shape and passes through large tracts of protected forest. Hardcore dirt bikers may still prefer the old French road, known as the 'King's Highway', that heads east from Kao Seima, which runs roughly parallel to NH76 and pops out near Andong Kroloeng, about 25km from Sen Monorom.

There are no longer any buses to Phnom Penh, so take a minivan (US$12, five hours, frequent) run by Kim Seng Express (☎011 229199; NH76), Ritya Mondulkiri Express (☎092 963243; NH76), Virak-Buntham and others.

Advertised trips to Siem Reap (US$20, 11 hours) usually involve a change of vehicle in Soung. Express minivans to Ban Lung (US$7, two hours, 8am and 1pm) and Kratie (US$9, three hours) can be booked through your guesthouse.

Local minibuses (departing from the taxi park) are another way to Kratie (30,000r, four hours). Count on at least one early morning departure and two or three departures around 12.30pm. Reserve the morning van in advance.

Ratanakiri Province

Popular Ratanakiri Province (ខេត្តរតនគិរី) is a diverse region of outstanding natural beauty that provides a remote home for a mosaic of peoples – Jarai, Tompuon, Brau and Kreung minorities, plus Lao.

Ban Lung

Affectionately known as *dey krahorm* ('red earth') after its rust-coloured affliction, Ban Lung provides a popular base for a range of Ratanakiri romps. The town itself is busy and lacks the backwater charm of Sen Monorom in Mondulkiri, but with attractions such as Boeng Yeak Lom just a short hop away, there is little room for complaint. Many of the minorities from the surrounding villages come to Ban Lung to buy and sell at the market.

Sights

Boeng Yeak Lom LAKE

(បឹងយក្សឡោម; admission US$2) At the heart of the protected area of Yeak Lom is a beautiful, emerald-hued crater lake set amid the vivid greens of the towering jungle. It is one of the most peaceful, beautiful locations Cambodia has to offer and the water is extremely clear. Several wooden piers are dotted around the perimeter, making it perfect for swimming. A small Cultural and Environmental Centre has a modest display on ethnic minorities in the province and hires out life jackets for children.

Chaa Ong WATERFALL

(admission 2000r) The tallest and most spectacular of the three waterfalls west of Ban Lung is 25m-high Chaa Ong – it's set in a jungle gorge and you can clamber behind the waterfall or venture underneath for a power shower. However, it dries up from about January to May. The Chaa Ong turn-off is on the right (north) side of NH19 about 200m west of the new bus station. The waterfall is 5.5km from the highway along a dirt road. The drive to the waterfalls can be very slippery in the wet season so think twice about driving yourself on a motorbike.

Ka Tieng WATERFALL

(admission 3000r) Ka Tieng is the most enjoyable of the three waterfalls west of Ban Lung, as it drops over a rock shelf, allowing

MONKEY BUSINESS IN MONDULKIRI

A recent Wildlife Conservation Society (WCS) study estimated populations of 20,600 black-shanked doucs and more than 1000 yellow-cheeked crested gibbons in Seima Protected Forest – the world's largest known populations of both species. Jahoo Gibbon Camp offers the chance to wind through mixed evergreen forest and waterfalls, with an excellent chance of spotting doucs and macaques along the way. It also provides local villagers with an incentive to conserve the endangered primates and their habitat through providing a sustainable income.

Gibbons are very shy and harder to see, but thanks to recent field research by WCS and the community the local gibbon families are more used to people than gibbons elsewhere. You'll need to be up before dawn to spot them, however, so sleeping at the camp is highly recommended.

Registered guides, together with local Bunong guides, accompany visitors along the trails. Prices are around US$80 per person for a day tour, or US$150 for an overnight visit, sleeping in upscale tents. Prices include transport to the camp by 4WD, guides and all meals.

For information and booking contact the Sam Veasna Center (p245) team at the Hefalump Cafe in Sen Monorom.

you to clamber all the way behind. There are some vines on the far side that are strong enough to swing on for some Tarzan action. Turn left off NH19 about 200m west of the new bus station, then proceed 5.5km to a fork in the road. Take the right fork and continue 2.5km to the falls.

Virachey National Park PARK
(admission US$5) This park is one of the largest protected areas in Cambodia, stretching for 3325 sq km east to Vietnam, north to Laos and west to Stung Treng Province. Virachey has one of the most organised ecotourism programs in Cambodia, focusing on small-scale culture, nature and adventure trekking. The program aims to involve and benefit local minority communities. All treks into the park must be arranged through the Virachey National Park Eco-Tourism Information Centre (p250) in Ban Lung.

Tours

Cambodian Gibbon Ecotours WILDLIFE
(097 752 9960; www.cambodiangibbons.wordpress.com; tours from US$100) Spend the night in the jungle, then rise well before dawn to spend time with semi-habituated northern buff-cheeked gibbons at this community-based ecotourism project (CBET) set up by Conservation International (CI; www.conservation.org) just outside the border of Virachey National Park, north of Veun Sai. The high-season-only tours cost US$100 to US$200 per person for a one-night/two-day tour, depending on group size and which tour company you choose. Most companies in Ban Lung can arrange these trips on behalf of CI.

Highland Tours TOURS
(097 658 3841; highland.tour@yahoo.com) Kimi and Horng are husband-and-wife graduates of Le Tonlé Tourism Training Center in Stung Treng, who have moved to the highlands to run a range of tours, including fun day trips and a multiday tour between Veun Sai and Ta Veng that combines trekking with floating down the Tonlé San on a bamboo raft.

DutchCo Trekking Cambodia TOURS
(097 679 2714; www.trekkingcambodia.com) One of the most experienced trekking operators in the province, run by – wait for it – a friendly Dutchman. Runs four- to five-day treks north of Veun Sai through Kavet villages and community forests, and one- to two-day trips around Kalai (south of Veun Sai), among many other tours.

Parrot Tours TOURS
(0947 4035884; www.jungletrek.blogspot.com) Parrot runs a range of overnight treks in the forests north of Itub, home to throngs of gibbons. Sitha Nan is a national-park-trained guide with expert local knowledge.

Sleeping

★**Tree Top Ecolodge** BUNGALOW $
(012 490333; www.treetop-ecolodge.com; d US$7, cottage with cold/hot water US$12/15;) This is one of the best places to stay in Cambodia's 'wild east', with oodles of atmosphere. 'Mr T's' place boasts rough-hewn walkways leading to huge bungalows featuring mosquito nets, thatch roofs and hammock-strewn verandahs with verdant valley vistas. Like the bungalows, the restaurant is fashioned from hardwood and dangles over a lush ravine.

Bamboo Backpacker GUESTHOUSE $
(015 406290; s/d from US$3/5;) The nine rooms at the back of the vegetarian restaurant of the same name are a steal. They share four bathrooms and feature high ceilings, mosquito nets, a sitting table and tasteful design. The mural-lined restaurant (mains US$2 to US$4.50) scores with its vegie burgers.

Banlung Balcony GUESTHOUSE $
(097 8097036; www.balconyguesthouse.net; Boeng Kansaign; dm US$2, r US$5-20; @) Under new management, this long-standing backpackers has upped its game with a smashing renovation of both the atmospheric main house and the enviably placed bar and restaurant, which features sunset views over the lake. The upstairs rooms, all polished wood and high ceilings, are borderline boutique, only at budget prices.

Flashpacker Pad HOTEL $
(093 785259; flashpackerpad@gmail.com; Boeng Kansaign; r US$8-15;) Quite literally a flashpacker pad run by Backpacker Pad. The rooms have a touch of class, with flat-screen TVs and indigenous-made runners on white bedspreads. Go for a room with a view for misty mornings on the lake. A good source of tour and transport information. Great value.

★**Terres Rouges Lodge** BOUTIQUE HOTEL $$
(012 660902; www.ratanakiri-lodge.com; Boeng Kansaign; r/ste incl breakfast from US$55/80; @) Even as the competition hots up, Terres Rouges remains one of the most atmospheric places to stay in provincial Cambodia. The fan-cooled standard rooms are done up in classy colonial style, with beautiful Cam-

Ban Lung

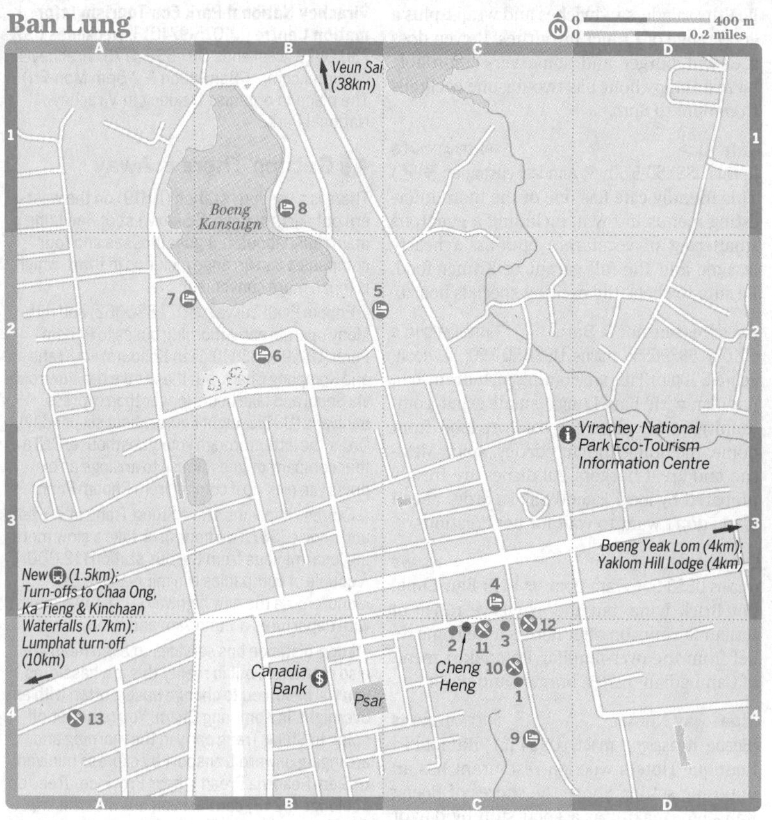

Ban Lung

Activities, Courses & Tours
1 DutchCo Trekking Cambodia C4
2 Highland Tours C4
3 Parrot Tours C4

Sleeping
4 Bamboo Backpacker C3
5 Banlung Balcony B2
6 Flashpacker Pad B2
7 Ratanakiri Boutique Hotel A2
8 Terres Rouges Lodge B1
9 Tree Top Ecolodge C4

Eating
10 Cafe Alee C4
11 Everest C4
12 Green Carrot C4
Pteas Bay Khmer .... (see 7)
13 Sal's Restaurant & Bar A4

bodian furniture, tribal artefacts and a long common verandah. The suites consist of spacious Balinese-style bungalows with open-plan bathrooms, set in the gorgeous garden.

Ratanakiri Boutique Hotel HOTEL $$
(☎070 565750; www.ratanakiri-boutiquehotel.com; standard/lakeview r incl breakfast US$29/39, ste US$69; P) This new hotel with trophy lake views is a tightly run ship. With inlaid-stone bathroom walls and indigenous bed runners, the Khmer-inspired design is OK, but you're mainly staying here for the combination of lake-view balconies and copious mod-cons.

Eating

★**Green Carrot** INTERNATIONAL $
(mains US$2-6; ⏰7am-10pm;) A great little hole-in-the-wall restaurant that turns out surprisingly sophisticated food, including

healthy salads, sandwiches and wraps, plus a good range of Khmer favourites. It even does a decent burger and some very affordable pizzas. Happy hour has two-for-one cocktails from 6pm to 8pm.

Cafe Aiee INTERNATIONAL $
(mains US$1.50-5.50; ⏲7am-last customer;) This friendly cafe has one of the more interesting menus in town, including a generous smattering of vegetarian options, a hearty lasagne and the full gamut of Khmer food. Be sure to check the exciting specials board.

Sal's Restaurant & Bar INTERNATIONAL $
(☎097 5889655; mains US$2.50-7.50; ⏲noon-2pm & 5-10pm) This welcoming restaurant-bar, popular with Ban Lung's small expat community, is the place for comfort food from home, including Indian curries, spicy Mexican and great burgers. All dishes are freshly prepared by local legend Sal, so order ahead if you don't want to wait for her creations.

Everest INDIAN $
(mains US$3-5; ⏲7am-11pm;) It's Ban Lung, not Brick Lane, but the extensive range of Indian flavours on offer here is a welcome relief from the over-familiar Ratanakiri menu of Cambodian dishes, burgers and pasta.

Pteas Bay Khmer INTERNATIONAL $$
(Boeng Kansaign; mains US$4-15) Ratanakiri Boutique Hotel's wooden restaurant has an imposing setting above the shores of Boeng Kansaign, making it a good stop by day or night. The menu includes some classic Cambodian dishes, homemade pasta and select cuts of meat.

Information

Canadia Bank (⏲8.30am-3.30pm Mon-Fri, ATM 24hr) Full-service bank with an international ATM.

Virachey National Park Eco-Tourism Information Centre (☎075-974013, weekends 097 730 0979, weekends 097 333 4775; virachey@camintel.com; ⏲8am-noon & 2-5pm Mon-Fri) The place to organise trekking in Virachey National Park.

Getting There & Away

There is a vast bus station (NH19) on the western outskirts of town, 2.5km west of Ban Lung's main roundabout, but guesthouses and tour companies can arrange pick-ups in town, which is much more convenient.

Phnom Penh Sorya (☎077 880062) and Rith Mony operate early-morning buses to Phnom Penh (US$9 to US$10, 11 to 12 hours) via Kratie and Kompong Cham, but these take the slow route via Snuol and take hours longer than express minivans (US$15, eight hours, about six per day). Order the latter through your guesthouse. Call a tour company or guesthouse to arrange an express van pick-up if coming from Phnom Penh.

Express minivans serve Stung Treng at 7.30am and noon (US$7, two hours), or take a slow morning local minibus from the bus station (12,000r). A couple of companies run minivans to Sen Monorom via the new highway (US$7, two hours), with departures around 7am and noon.

Long-distance bus services to Siem Reap are also promoted, but in reality this is a hassle, as you will be forced to change buses, often with an overnight, in Kompong Cham. You're better off going to Stung Treng early in the morning and arranging onward transport by express minivan to Siem Reap via Preah Vihear Province. Tree Top Ecolodge (p248) can sort you out with this trip (US$13, eight hours, 7am).

Advertised trips to Laos (Don Det and Pakse) by express minivan depart at 7.30am and involve a van change and a few hours' wait in Stung Treng (to Don Det US$17, seven hours).

Local minibuses and pick-up trucks use the bus station to service Lumphat (10,000r, one hour), O'Yadaw (12,000r, 1½ hours) and more

GETTING TO VIETNAM: BAN LUNG TO PLEIKU

Getting to the border Opened to tourists in 2008, the **O'Yadaw/Le Thanh border crossing** (⏲7am to 5pm) is 70km east of Ban Lung along smooth NH19. From Ban Lung, guesthouses advertise a 7.30am bus to Pleiku in Vietnam (US$11, 4½ hours). The van picks you up at your guesthouse for a surcharge, which is easier than trying to arrange a ticket independently. Alternatively, take a local minibus to O'Yadaw from Ban Lung's new bus station, and continue 25km to the border by *moto* (motorcycle taxi).

At the border Formalities are straightforward and lines nonexistent – just make sure you have a Vietnamese visa if required, as visas are not issued at the border.

Moving on Once on the Vietnamese side of the frontier, the road is nicely paved and *motos* await to take you to Duc Co (20km), where there are buses to Pleiku, Quy Nhon and Hoi An.

remote Ratanakiri villages. Local minibuses also offer cheap transport to Kratie (25,000r) and even Phnom Penh (50,000r) for the adventurous and/or masochistic. Share taxis out of Ban Lung are rare.

Getting Around

Bicycles (US$1 to US$3), motorbikes (US$5 to US$7), cars (from US$30) and 4WDs (from US$50) are available for hire from most guesthouses in town.

Cheng Heng (☎ 088 8516104; ⏲ 6am-8pm) has some 250cc trail bikes for rent (US$25) in addition to a stable of well-maintained smaller motorbikes (US$6 to US$8).

Motodups hang out around the market and some double as guides. Figure on US$15 to US$20 per day for a good English-speaking driver-guide. A *moto* to Yeak Lom costs about US$4 to US$5 return; to Veun Sai it's US$15 return; to any waterfall is about US$6 or so return.

Remorks have finally made it to Ban Lung, but there are only a handful in town and they are expensive by Cambodian standards – about double what a *moto* costs.

SOUTH COAST

Cambodia's south coast is an alluring mix of clear blue water, castaway island beaches, pristine mangrove forests, time-worn colonial towns and jungle-clad mountains, where bears and elephants lurk. Adventurers will find this region of Cambodia just as rewarding as sunseekers.

Koh Kong City

Sleepy Koh Kong was once Cambodia's Wild West with its isolated frontier economy dominated by smuggling, gambling and prostitution. Today this town is striding towards respectability as ecotourists, aiming to explore the Cardamoms, shoo away the sleaze. The dusty sprawl of streets sits on the banks of the Koh Poi River which spills into the Gulf of Thailand a few kilometres south of the centre.

Sights & Activities

Koh Kong's main appeal is as a launching pad for adventures in and around the Cardamom Mountains and the Koh Kong Conservation Corridor, but there are a few diversions around town as well. If you want a dip, the pool at Oasis Bungalow Resort (p252) is open to non-guests (adults US$4, children US$2).

Sun-worshippers will discover additional beaches further north on the Gulf of Thailand near the Thai border.

Wat Neang Kok BUDDHIST TEMPLE
(វត្តនាងកុក) This rocky promontory on the right (western) bank of the Koh Poi River is decorated with life-size statues demonstrating the violent punishments that await sinners in the Buddhist hell. This graphic tableau belongs to Wat Neang Kok, a Buddhist temple. To get there, cross the bridge, turn right 600m past the tollbooth (*motos* cost 1400r), and proceed 150m beyond the temple to the statues.

Peam Krasaop Mangrove Sanctuary NATURE RESERVE
(ជម្រកសត្វព្រៃបឹងក្រយ៉ាក នៅពាមក្រសោប; admission 5000r; ⏲ 6.30am-6pm) Anchored to alluvial islands – some no larger than a house – this 260-sq-km sanctuary's magnificent mangroves protect the coast from erosion, serve as a vital breeding and feeding ground for fish, shrimp and shellfish, and are home to myriad birds.

To get a feel for the delicate mangrove ecosystem, explore the 600m-long concrete mangrove walk, which wends its way above the briny waters to a 15m observation tower. The entrance is 5.5km southeast of Koh Kong. A *moto/remork* costs US$5/10 return.

Ritthy Koh Kong Eco Adventure Tours ADVENTURE
(☎ 012 707719; www.kohkongecoadventure.com; St 1; ⏲ 8am-9pm) A one-stop shop for all your tour needs in Koh Kong, this is the longest-running ecotourism operator in town. Ritthy's excursions include excellent Koh Kong Island boat tours, birdwatching, and three-day/two-night jungle trekking and camping in the Areng Valley within the Koh Kong Conservation Corridor (US$110 per person).

Sleeping

Koh Kong is a popular holiday destination for Khmer families; hotels fill up and raise their rates during Cambodian holidays. If staying in town doesn't appeal, check out Tatai River (18km east), with its handful of fabulous eco-accommodation options.

Koh Kong City Hotel HOTEL $
(☎ 035-936777; http://kkcthotel.netkhmer.com; St 1; r US$15-20; ❄ @ ☜) Ludicrous value for what you get: squeaky-clean rooms include a huge bathroom, two double beds, 50 TV channels, full complement of toiletries, free

Koh Kong City

Activities, Courses & Tours
Ritthy Koh Kong Eco Adventure Tours .... (see 4)

Sleeping
1 99 Guesthouse B2
2 Asian Hotel A2
3 Koh Kong City Hotel A2
4 Ritthy's Retreat A2

Eating
Baan Peakmai .... (see 2)
5 Café Laurent A2
6 Fat Sam's B3
7 Psar Leu A3
8 Seta Ice Cream A2

Drinking & Nightlife
9 Paddy's Bamboo Pub B3

water and – in the US$20 rooms – river views. Friendly staff top off the experience.

Ritthy's Retreat GUESTHOUSE $
(☎097 555 2789; ritthy.info@gmail.com; St 1; dm US$4, r US$6-15;) Long-time tour operator Ritthy has opened a welcoming guesthouse and restaurant on the riverfront. It features spacious en-suite dorms with double-wide beds and a nice variety of roomy doubles. The fancier air-con rooms upstairs have semi-private balconies with river views, while the downstairs bar-restaurant, with a pool table, is a top hang-out.

99 Guesthouse HOTEL $
(☎035-936799; 99guesthouse@gmail.com; St 6; s/d with fan US$8/10, with air-con US$13/15;) Managed by friendly Piseth, 99 is a solid budget choice with a range of bright, neat-as-a-pin, decent-sized rooms in a quiet location a few blocks off the river.

Asian Hotel HOTEL $
(☎015-936667; www.asiankohkong.com; St 1; r US$15-20;) While it may lack the river views of rival hotels across the road, the Asian makes up for it with spacious, clean and comfortable rooms with a touch of old-timer class. Bag a front (roadside) room for a balcony.

★ **Oasis Bungalow Resort** BUNGALOW $$
(☎092 228342; http://oasisresort.netkhmer.com; d/tr US$35/40;) Surrounded by lush forest, 2km north of Koh Kong centre, Oasis really lives up to its name. Five large, airy bungalows set around a gorgeous infinity pool with views of the Cardamoms provide a tranquil base in which to chill out and reset your travel batteries. To get here, follow the blue signs from Acleda Bank.

During the December to January high season bungalows are US$5 extra. The no-sex-tourist policy here is a refreshing approach for Koh Kong.

Thmorda Garden Riverside Resort RESORT $$
(☎035-6900324; www.thmordagarden.com; Neang Kok; r US$35, deluxe US$60;) This small resort over the bridge is a peaceful choice for travellers looking to fully unwind, although it may feel a bit lifeless for some. The standard rooms are only slightly bigger than a postage stamp but you are paying for the waterfront location on a peninsula overlooking the Koh Poi River.

Eating & Drinking

The best cheap food stalls are in the southeast corner of the market, **Psar Leu** (St 3; 8am-11pm); fruit stalls can be found near the southwest corner. Riverfront food carts sell noodles and cans of beer for a few thousand riel, doubling up as sunset drinking spots.

Baan Peakmai ASIAN $
(St 1; mains 7000-15,000r; 11am-2pm & 5-10pm;) Sure, you'd find more ambience in a paper bag but don't be put off by the plain-Jane

decor. Baan Peakmai does a fine line in pan-Asian dishes with large portions and on-the-ball service. The menu romps through Thai, Chinese and Khmer favourites and there are plenty of vegetarian options.

Fat Sam's INTERNATIONAL $
(off St 3; mains US$3.50-7; 9am-9.30pm Mon-Sat, 4-9.30pm Sun;) The menu at this informal, Welsh-run bar-restaurant runs the gamut from fish-and-chips and chilli con carne to authentic Khmer and Thai favourites. Also a decent beer selection and a small wine list.

Motorbike hire available.

★ **Café Laurent** INTERNATIONAL $$
(St 1; mains US$4-15; 10.30am-11pm Wed-Mon;) This chic waterfront cafe and restaurant offers atmospheric dining in over-water pavilions where you can sit back and watch the sunset while feasting on refined Western and Khmer cuisine. As well as French-accented steaks and a decent pasta menu, there's a huge range of fresh seafood and Asian classics, all served with fine-dining panache.

Seta Ice Cream INTERNATIONAL $$
(St 1; mains US$3.50-7.50; 6am-9pm) Much more than just ice cream, Seta features scrumptious French-influenced seafood dishes such as bouillabaisse, pizza, baguettes and a full range of Asian specials, with breakfast (US$1.50 to $4.50) thrown in for good measure. The friendly and knowledgeable owner speaks excellent English.

Paddy's Bamboo Pub BAR
The US$1 beers and pool table at this sociable hostel pub occasionally draw a crowd, though don't waste your time coming out here in the low season. There's a menu of home-grown comfort flavours (mains US$2 to US$4).

Information

Guesthouses, hotels and pubs are the best places to get the local low-down.Thai baht are widely used so there's no urgent need to change baht into dollars or riel. To do so, use one of the many mobile-phone shops around Psar Leu.

Canadia Bank (St 1; 8am-3.30pm Mon-Fri, to 11.30am Sat, ATM 24hr)

Sen Sok Clinic (012 555060; kkpao@camintel.com; St 3; 24hr) Has doctors who speak English and French.

Getting There & Away

The three main bus companies in town are **Olympic Transport** (011 363678; St 3), **Rith Mony** (012 640344; St 3) and **Virak Buntham** (089 998760; St 3). Most buses drop passengers at Koh Kong's unpaved **bus station** (St 12), on the northeast edge of town, where *motos* (motorbike with driver; moto-taxi) and *remork-motos* (*tuk-tuk*) await, eager to overcharge tourists. Don't pay more than US$1/2 for the three-minute *moto/remork* ride into the centre. Departures are from the company offices in town.

Destinations include the following:

Bangkok Virak Buntham and Rith Mony serve Bangkok (US$20 to US$22, eight hours) via Ko Chang (US$15 to US$18, including ferry to the island), with a change to a minivan at the border.

Phnom Penh Served by all three companies via both bus (US$7 to US$8, six hours) and minivan (US$10 to US$12, five hours); the last trip is around 1.30pm.

Sihanoukville Virak Buntham runs a direct bus (US$8, five hours, 8am) and Olympic Transport

GETTING TO THAILAND: KOH KONG TO TRAT

Getting to the border The **Cham Yeam/Hat Lek border crossing** (8am to 10pm), between Cambodia's Koh Kong and Trat in Thailand, links the beaches of Cambodia and Thailand. Leaving Cambodia, take a taxi (US$10 plus toll), *remork-moto* (*tuk-tuk*; US$8) or *moto* (motorbike taxis; US$3) from Koh Kong across the toll bridge to the border. Once in Thailand, catch a minibus to Trat, from where there are regular buses to Bangkok.

At the border Departing Cambodia via the Hat Lek border is pretty straightforward. Coming in the other direction and arriving in Cambodia, be aware that the Cham Yeam border is notorious for visa overcharging; these days you'll usually pay 1300B.

Moving on From the Hat Lek border, take a minibus straight to Trat (120B). From here there are regular buses to Bangkok (254B, six hours) heading to the Thai capital's Eastern or North and Northeastern bus stations. Buses depart hourly from 6am until 11.30pm. Anyone heading to the nearby island of Koh Chang can arrange onward transport in Trat.

Coming into Cambodia, note that you'll get a better deal on all transport from the border to Koh Kong if you pay in dollars not baht.

WORTH A TRIP

CHI PHAT

Once notorious for land-grabbing, illegal logging and poaching, the river village of Chi Phat is now home to a world-class community-based ecotourism project (CBET) launched by Wildlife Alliance (www.wildlifealliance.org). It offers travellers a rare opportunity to explore the Cardamoms ecosystems while providing an alternative livelihood to the former poachers who now act as its protectors and guides. There's a huge menu of activities on offer, from birdwatching kayak trips to combo hike-and-mountain-bike expeditions.

Note that the village only has electricity in the morning between 5am and 9am, and in the evening from 6pm to 9pm, so bring a torch (flashlight).

Many of Chi Phat's 13 **homestays** (r US$5) are in wooden, stilted Khmer houses that offer a glimpse into rural life. Rooms are all cosy and simple, and bathrooms are shared with the family. Some homestays have squat toilets and traditional shower facilities (a rainwater cistern with a plastic bucket). Dinner (US$2.50) can be provided.

has a direct minibus (US$10, 4½ hours, 1.15pm); other trips to Sihanoukville, as well as to Kampot and Kep, involve a bus transfer.

Note that Virak Buntham and Rith Mony claim to offer night buses between Siem Reap and Koh Kong, but these require a long detour and bus change in Sihanoukville, leaving many a backpacker justifiably annoyed.

From Koh Kong's **taxi lot** (St 12) next to the bus station, yu can get shared taxis head to Phnom Penh (US$11, five hours) and occasionally to Sihanoukville (US$10, four hours) and Andoung Tuek (US$5, two hours). As with anywhere the best chance for a ride is in the morning.

Getting Around

Ritthy Koh Kong Eco Adventure Tours (p251) rents out bicycles for half (US$1) and full days (US$2).

Short *moto* rides within the centre are 2000r; *remorks* are double that, but overcharging is common.

Motorbike hire is available from most guesthouses, as well as Ritthy Koh Kong Eco Adventure Tours (p251) and **Jungle Cross** (015 601633; www.junglecross.com; dirt-bike rental per day US$25; 9am-6pm).

Koh Kong Conservation Corridor

Stretching along both sides of NH48 from Koh Kong to the Gulf of Kompong Som (the bay northwest of Sihanoukville), the Koh Kong Conservation Corridor encompasses many of Cambodia's most outstanding natural sites, including the southern reaches of the fabled Cardamom Mountains, an area of breathtaking beauty and astonishing biodiversity.

Sights & Activities

Tatai Waterfall — WATERFALL

Tatai Waterfall is a thundering set of rapids during the wet season, plunging over a 4m rock shelf. Water levels drop in the dry season, but you can swim year-round in the surrounding refreshing pools. The water is fairly pure as it comes down from the isolated high Cardamoms. Access to the waterfall is by car or motorbike. The clearly marked turn-off is on NH48 about 15km southeast of Koh Kong, or 2.8km northwest of the Tatai Bridge.

From the highway it's about 2km to the falls along a rough access road. There's a stream crossing about halfway – at the height of the wet season you may have to cross it on foot and walk the last kilometre. From Koh Kong, a half-day *moto* excursion to Tatai Waterfall costs US$10 return (*remork* US$15), or less to go one way to the bridge.

Koh Kong Island — ISLAND

Cambodia's largest island towers over seas so crystal clear you can make out individual grains of sand in a couple of metres of water. A strong military presence on the island means access is tightly controlled. You must visit on a guided boat tour out of Koh Kong or Tatai. These cost US$20 per person, including lunch and snorkelling equipment, or US$55 for overnight trips with beach camping or homestay accommodation. The island is only accessible from October to May.

Neptune Adventure — ECOTOUR

(088 777 0576; www.neptuneadventure-cambodia.com) This well-established ecotourism operator is based at **Neptune River Bungalows** (bungalow incl breakfast US$35-50) on the Tatai River and offers highly recommended jungle

treks as well as multi-activity adventures combining trekking, kayaking and boating. Day tours range from US$10 to US$25 per person.

Sleeping

★Rainbow Lodge ECOLODGE $$
(012 160 2585; www.rainbowlodgecambodia.com; Tatai River; s/d/f incl all meals US$75/100/140;) A slice of jungle-chic, Rainbow Lodge proves being sustainable doesn't mean you have to sacrifice creature comforts. Powered by solar panels and biofuel, the bungalows here are set back from the river. They are reached by elevated walkways hugged by foliage and centred on a sleek open-air lounge with an impressive bar.

Four Rivers Floating Lodge RESORT $$$
(097 758 9676; www.ecolodges.asia; Tatai River; d incl breakfast US$259;) Glamping with extra wow-factor, the 12 canvas tent-villas here float on a pontoon situated on a branch of the Tatai River estuary 6km downriver from Tatai Bridge. Inside, the lavish use of wicker and rich dark wood provides a colonial-cool ambience, topped off by the most sumptuous bathrooms you'll see under canvas anywhere. Boat transfers to/from Tatai Bridge are included (20 minutes). The boat landing is on the northwest side of the bridge.

Sihanoukville

Sure, Sihanoukville would never win first prize in a pretty-town competition but thanks to a surrounding coastline of white-sand beaches and sun-drenched islands, this is Cambodia's most happening sun-sloth destination.

Sights

★Otres Beach BEACH
(ឆ្នេរអូរត្រេះ) Past the southern end of Ocheuteal Beach, beyond the Phnom Som Nak Sdach (Hill of the King's Palace) headland, lies stunning Otres Beach, a seemingly infinite strip of casuarinas that gives southern Thailand a run for its money. Although no longer the empty stretch of beach it once was, Otres has cleaner water and is more relaxed than anything in Sihanoukville proper, and is lengthy enough that finding your own patch of sand is not a challenge...just walk south.

Long eyed-up by large-scale developers, Otres has so far managed to shun major construction work, and DIY development is blossoming with dozens of small-scale independent resorts and beach bungalow places in the area, including a handful of upmarket boutique hotels. Otres is split into three distinct sections: Otres 1 is the first and busiest stretch, while about 2km south is quieter Otres 2, separated by a slated resort development currently known as 'Long Beach'. Inland lies laid-back Otres Village, an up-and-coming estuary area.

Otres Beach is about 5km south of the Serendipity area. It's a US$2 *moto* ride (*remork* US$5) to get here (more at night). If going it alone, follow the road southeast along the beach and skirt the hill by heading inland on the inviting tarmac. From the city centre, you can take Omui St from Psar Leu east out of town for 5km.

Sokha Beach BEACH
(ឆ្នេរសុខា; Map p260) Midway between Independence and Serendipity beaches lies Sihanoukville's prettiest beach, 1.5km-long Sokha Beach. Its fine, silicon-like sand squeaks loudly underfoot. The tiny eastern end of Sokha Beach is open to the public and is rarely crowded. The rest is part of the exclusive **Sokha Beach Resort** (Map p260; 034-935999; www.sokhahotels.com; Thnou St; r/ste from US$171/210;). Tourists are welcome to enjoy the sand near Sokha but are expected to buy something to drink or eat. You might even duck into the resort to use the pool (US$5).

Activities

Blue Lagoon Kitesurf Centre WATER SPORTS
(085 511145; Otres 1; 1hr lesson incl equipment US$50, 3-day course US$295; 9am-7pm) This kitesurfing centre rents equipment as well as running kitesurfing lessons and multiday courses. Now located on the main road, with a sausage truck out front manned by the same German owner.

Dive Shop DIVING
(Map p260; 034-933664; www.diveshopcambodia.com; Serendipity Beach Rd; PADI Discover Scuba US$95, 1-/2-dive package US$65/80; 9am-7pm) PADI five-star dive centre offering full gamut of PADI courses, as well as fun dives and liveaboards out of their base at Sunset Beach on Koh Rong Sanloem.

EcoSea Dive DIVING
(Map p260; 012 654104; www.ecoseadive.com; Serendipity Beach Rd; 2-dive day package US$80-85; 9am-7pm) Offers both PADI and SSI courses and has competitively priced fundive rates. Has an island base at their resort near M'Pai Bay on Koh Rong Sanloem.

Sihanoukville

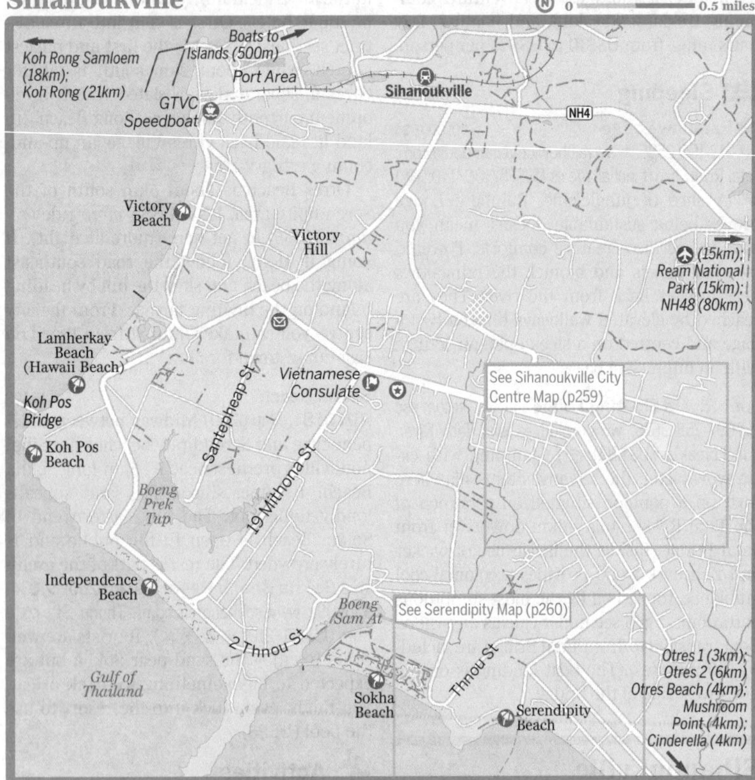

Hurricane Watersports WATER SPORTS
(☎017 471604; sydney.victor@yahoo.fr; Queenco Palm Beach Resort, Otres 1; ⏰9am-6.30pm) Rents stand-up paddleboards (US$8 per hour), windsurfers (basic/high-performance per hour US$12/25, sea kayaks (single/tandem per hour US$6/8) and skimboards (try bungee skimboarding). Otres Beach sometimes gets surf from May to October; you can rent surfboards and bodyboards here too.

Relax SPA
(Map p260; ☎085 352213; Serendipity Beach Rd; per hour from US$10; ⏰10am-9pm) This place's Khmer, lavender, jasmine-oil and foot massages get great reviews. It also offers facials, pedicures and waxing.

Sala Santepheap MASSAGE
(Map p259; Starfish Bakery, off 7 Makara St; per hour US$6-10; ⏰7am-6pm) Visually or physically disabled therapists trained by the Starfish Project perform Khmer, Thai, oil, foot and Indian head massages in the Starfish Bakery garden. Profits go towards social projects.

Sleeping

Location, location, location; each Sihanoukville district has its own distinct character and attracts a different type of clientele. We quote prices for the high season (approximately November to March). Rates drop between June and October, especially on Serendipity and Otres Beaches, but can skyrocket on Khmer holidays at some establishments.

Serendipity Area

The main backpacker hang-out is Serendipity Beach Rd which runs up the hill from Serendipity Beach, connecting to Ekareach St at the Golden Lions Roundabout. Late-night noise from the nearby clubs affects most of the accommodation here, diminishing further east but light sleepers may want to bunk elsewhere.

★Chochi Garden GUESTHOUSE $
(Map p260; ☎015 560545; www.chochigarden.com; Serendipity Beach Rd; r with fan/air-con US$15/25;) Finally! Serendipity gets its first boutique backpacker pad. Italian-Japanese couple Francesca and Taka have created the nearest Serendipity gets to a tranquil oasis right in the heart of the action. Out front is a cool bar-restaurant while simple rooms, some with palm-thatch roofs and pretty painted window-grills, are in a plant-filled garden strewn with comfy seating areas.

One Stop Hostel HOSTEL $
(Map p260; ☎096 339 0005; www.onederz.com; Golden Lions Roundabout; dm incl breakfast US$8;) The six- and eight-bed dorms here are decked out in lashings of white-on-white and centred on a wall-to-ceiling glassed courtyard with a small pool, proving slick styling doesn't have to cost the earth. The 68 beds have individual reading lamps and luggage lock-boxes, and all dorms are air-conditioned.

One fuss is that the bottom bunks are basically on the floor.

Big Easy HOSTEL $
(Map p260; ☎081 943930; Serendipity Beach Rd; dm US$4, r US$6-10;) This classic backpacker joint is accommodation, comfort food and a lively rock bar all rolled into one. Rooms are basic but you'll most likely spend your time in the bar, which has a great vibe with occasional live music and live EPL games.

Happy hour is 5pm to 8pm and it also hosts a famous pub crawl.

Cloud 9 BUNGALOW $$
(Map p260; ☎098 215166; www.cloud9bungalows.com; Serendipity Beach; d/tr from US$40/50;) The last place on Serendipity Beach is a fine choice, and not just because it's furthest removed from the club noise. It has a cosy tropical bar perched over the shore, and we really like its range of rustic, Khmer-style wooden bungalows with fans and ocean-view balconies.

Tamarind BOUTIQUE HOTEL $$
(Map p260; ☎097 5002429; www.the-tamarind.com; 23 Tola St; d/tr incl breakfast US$60/80;) Finally Sihanoukville has a poolside boutique hotel to rival those in Siem Reap and Phnom Penh. The amply sized rooms push all the right buttons, with private balconies, clean white walls, large flat-screen TVs and just the right mix of smart furniture. A lush garden and small pool lend the place an intimate vibe.

Holiday Villa Nataya HOTEL $$
(Map p260; ☎034-935061; www.holidayvillahotels.com; Serendipity Beach Rd; r incl breakfast from $50;) Set around a somewhat bizarre interior courtyard pool, the rooms here are tranquil cocoons above the din of Serendipity Beach Rd, with luscious beds, huge flat-screen TVs, attractive art and an appealing slate-grey colour scheme. Pay up for ocean view rooms with balconies.

Promo deals often bring prices down to the US$30 range, making this the steal of Sihanoukville.

Coolabah Resort HOTEL $$
(Map p260; ☎017 678218; www.coolabah-hotel.com; 14 Mithona St; r US$42-80;) Kudos to Coolabah for having the most on-the-ball staff in the Serendipity area. Rooms are classically styled in soothing neutrals with smart art and contemporary bathrooms, and come in a variety of sizes including family options.

The bar here is one of Serendipity's more relaxed places to sit down with a beer.

Serendipity Beach Resort HOTEL $$
(Map p260; ☎034-938888; www.serendipitybeachresort.com; Serendipity Beach Rd; r US$37-75;) Ignore the ugly ducking exterior, for inside a Serendipity swan awaits. Prices here remain steadfastly good value given the impressive size and style of the rooms. The huge pool is often partially in the shade of the building.

Above Us Only Sky BUNGALOW $$$
(Map p260; ☎089 822318; www.aboveusonlysky.net; Serendipity Beach; bungalows $80-100;) The five bungalows here are attractively minimalist inside with tiled floors and glass-fronted doors to make the most of the sea panoramas. Chances are you'll spend most of your time parked on the cosy balcony in a comfy cane chair, taking in the view. The bar-restaurant, perched over the rocks by the seashore, is a real gem.

Otres Beach & Otres Village

Groovy little Otres is Sihanoukville's laid-back beach colony. The beach is split into two sections, separated by a 2.5km section of empty beach. Otres 1 has most of the bungalows and guesthouses while quieter Otres 2, further south, is home to the boutique resorts.

Just inland is Otres Village with a scattering of relaxed places nestled on a river estuary.

★ **Wish You Were Here** HOSTEL $
(☎097 241 5884; Otres 1; dm US$6, r without bathroom US$12-16;) This rickety wooden building is one of the hippest hang-outs in Otres. Rooms are simple but the balcony upstairs encourages serious sloth-time and the bar-restaurant downstairs has a great vibe thanks to chilled-out tunes and friendly staff.

Even if you're not staying, stop in for a drink or to sample the Aussie meat pies ($4.50 to $7) or quesadillas ($3 to $4.50).

Otres Orchid BUNGALOW $
(☎034-6338484; www.otresorchid.com; Otres 1; bungalows with fan/air-con US$20/35;) Cracking value, the Orchid offers simple bungalows at sensible prices in a garden setting a hop, skip and jump to the beach. The fan-only bungalows have more character than the air-con options and come with hammock-strung balconies.

★ **Mushroom Point** BUNGALOW $$
(☎097-712 4635; mushroompoint.otres@gmail.com; Otres 1; dm US$8, bungalows US$25-30;) The open-air dorm in the shape of a mushroom wins the award for most creative in Cambodia. Even those averse to communal living will be content in their mosquito-net-draped pods, good for two. Quirky 'shroom-shaped bungalows are beautifully conceived with hammocks outside for lounging. The beach annexe has more bungalows and a bar.

Papa Pippo BUNGALOW $$
(☎010 359725; www.papapippo.com; Otres 1; bungalows US$30-35) Sandy-toed bliss is at hand with these cosy, and rather classy, beachfront bungalows. Glass doors make the most of the sea views while the interiors, with painted-wood walls and tiled floors, add a touch of individual style.

Sunset Lounge RESORT $$
(☎097 734 0486; www.sunsetlounge-guesthouse.com; South Ochheuteal; r/bungalows US$32/48;) Way down at the windswept far south end of Ochheuteal Beach, this secluded boutique-quality resort suits those for whom Otres Beach is too busy. With thick mattresses, dreamy shaded balconies, appealing bathrooms and a well-reputed restaurant, this is one of the top values in town. The bungalows are worth the small splurge. It's much quicker to walk to Otres Beach from here (10 minutes) than to central Ochheuteal (30 minutes).

Sok Sabay BOUTIQUE HOTEL $$
(☎016 406080; www.soksabayresort.com; Otres Village; r US$50;) Escape from the world in style at this new poolside boutique, which ups the ante for accommodation in Otres Village. The rooms have inlaid bamboo walls and balconies strewn with well-cushioned furniture. The restaurant overlooks the village lake and is the sister of top Otres Beach eatery Chez Paou (p260) (same owner).

Tamu BOUTIQUE HOTEL $$$
(☎088-901 7451; www.tamucambodia.com; Otres 2; r incl breakfast US$110-170;) This ultra-contemporary boutique hotel offers a range of simple, yet chic rooms set around a courtyard pool. Bag a poolfront room for a Balinese-style alfresco bathroom. There's also a hip beachside restaurant open to all.

Secret Garden RESORT $$$
(☎097-649 5131; www.secretgardenotres.com; Otres 2; bungalow incl breakfast from US$109;) Otres' first upmarket boutique resort is still one of its best. Cute bungalows, set amid a manicured garden with swimming pool, have bright and breezy decor, while sun-lounging heaven is available at the beachside bar-restaurant across the road.

Eating

The Serendipity area has the most international dining choice, but the gritty commercial centre also holds a few culinary surprises, as well as cheap eats around the main market, Psar Leu. Otres is your best bet for atmospheric meals on the beach.

Serendipity Area

For ambience, check out the over-the-water resort restaurants at Serendipity Beach. Two blocks inland, Tola St is developing into a restaurant zone, with a plethora of barbecue places in the evening.

Dao of Life VEGAN $
(Map p260; Serendipity Beach Rd; mains US$3.50-6; 9am-9pm;) Draped with Chinese lanterns and awash with recycled furniture, Dao dishes up creative and tasty vegan meals. Its vegie burger (made from sweet potato and kidney beans) is particularly good, or tuck into healthy options such as crispy cumin and coriander falafel.

It has movie nights every Wednesday and regularly hosts social projects with local community involvement.

★ **Sandan** CAMBODIAN $$
(Map p260; 2 Thnou St; mains US$4-10; 7am-9pm Mon-Sat;) Loosely modelled on the beloved Phnom Penh restaurant Rom-

Sihanoukville City Centre

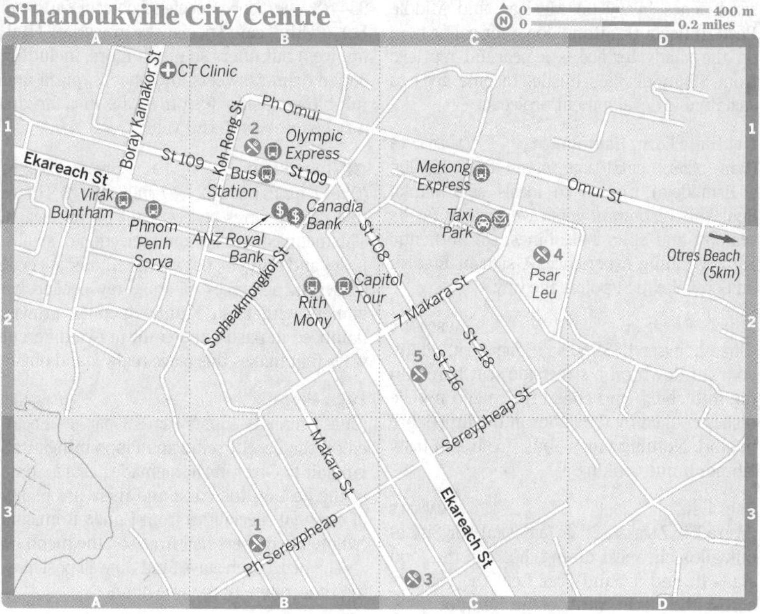

Sihanoukville City Centre

Activities, Courses & Tours

Sala Santepheap .... (see 5)

Eating

1 Cabbage Farm Restaurant B3
2 Gelato Italiano B1
3 Ku-kai C3
4 Psar Leu C2
5 Starfish Bakery & Café C2

Shopping

Starfish .... (see 5)

deng (p190), this superb restaurant is an extension of the vocational-training programs for at-risk Cambodians run by local NGO M'lop Tapang. The menu features creative Cambodian cuisine targeted at a slightly upmarket clientele. There's a kids' play area and occasional cultural shows.

Ku-kai JAPANESE **$$**

(Map p259; 144 7 Makara St; mains US$4-6; 5-9pm Tue-Sun Oct-Jul;) On a side street midway between Serendipity and the city centre, this is a haven for in-the-know expats, with a delightful dim-lit ambience and light Japanese fare including sashimi platters and rice bowls, lightly seasoned beef or braised pork belly.

Sushi Bar Shin JAPANESE **$$**

(Map p260; Serendipity Beach Rd; sushi platters from US$9.50; 11.30am-10pm) Recently relocated from Otres to the main drag in Serendipity, Shin is all about freshly prepared sushi, with just tempura and a few other alternatives on the menu. A contemporary Japanese interior rounds out the experience.

Mick & Craig's INTERNATIONAL **$$**

(Map p260; www.mickandcraigs.com; Serendipity Beach Rd; mains US$4-7; 7am-10pm;) This long-running guesthouse and restaurant serves up classic comfort food from around the globe. Indian meals are just US$6, while Thursday and Friday barbecue nights include a rack of ribs.

There's an excellent library here if you are feeling the need to read.

Around the City

Starfish Bakery & Café CAFE **$**

(Map p259; www.starfishcambodia.org; off 7 Makara St; sandwiches US$2.50-4.50; 7am-6pm;) This relaxing, NGO-run garden cafe specialises in filling Western breakfasts, baked cakes and tarts, and healthy, innovative sandwiches heavy on Mexican and Middle Eastern flavours. Sitting down for coffee here on the shady terrace is a peaceful reprieve from Sihanoukville's hustle. Income goes to sustainable development projects.

Cabbage Farm Restaurant CAMBODIAN $
(Map p259; small/large mains 8000/15,000r; ⏲11am-10pm) Known to locals as Chamka Spai, this restaurant gets rave reviews for its seafood and spicy seasonings. An authentic Khmer dining experience. A sign in English on Sereypheap St points the way.

Mom's Kitchen CAMBODIAN $
(Otres 1; mains US$2.50-5; ⏲7am-9pm) Plonk yourself down on a streetside seat here and dig into cheap and cheerful rice and noodle dishes cooked by the ladies in the little store behind. Nothing fancy – just fresh and tasty Khmer home cooking.

Psar Leu MARKET $
(Map p259; 7 Makara St; ⏲7am-9pm) For Sihanoukville's cheapest dining, head to the food stalls in and around Psar Leu; the vendors across the street, next to the Kampot taxis, are open 24 hours.

Gelato Italiano ICE CREAM $
(Map p259; St 109; mains US$2-5, gelato US$1; ⏲7.30am-9.30pm; ❄📶) Run by students from **Don Bosco Hotel School** (☎034-934478; www.donboscohotelschool.com; Ou Phram St;), this cafe specialises in *gelatos* (Italian ices) but offers so much more, including coffee drinks, sweets and snacks, pizza and full-blown Asian fusion meals in a bright, airy space. Wonderful value.

★**Chez Paou** INTERNATIONAL $$
(Otres 1; mains US$5-22; ⏲7am-10pm; 📶) This is fine dining Otres style – right on the beach. The menu contains a good selection of steaks, pasta and burgers, but it's the Khmer specials (order in advance) of sting ray cooked on embers with fresh Kampot pepper, prawns flambéed in pastis, and crabs in two different ways that makes this place really stand out.

Papa Pippo ITALIAN $$
(Otres 1; mains US$5-7; ⏲9am-9.30pm; 📶) Located on the beachfront, Papa Pippo brings Italian flair to Otres. Its homemade pasta is some of the best on the coast and there are plenty of regional specialities from Emilia-Romagna (where the owners hail from) on the menu.

The pizza oven stays fired up well past closing time, often 'til the wee hours.

Drinking & Nightlife

There's no shortage of venues in which to quaff locally brewed Angkor Beer, available on draught for as little as US$0.50.

Serendipity

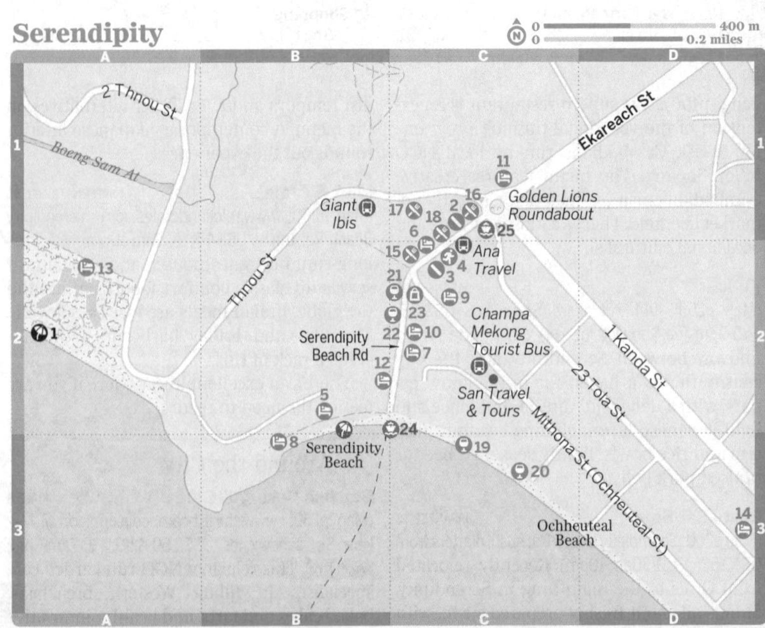

Many of the hostels on Serendipity Beach Rd have lively bars; the Big Easy (p257) was the most rocking on our visit. Heading down the hill to the beach, turn right and you'll find a series of laid-back resort bars perched over the rocks on Serendipity Beach; Above Us Only Sky (p257) is a good choice.

For relaxed sunset drinks with plenty of sand-between-the-toes appeal, Otres Beach can't be beaten, and many of the bars here now rumble on into the night.

Maybe Later BAR

(Map p260; Serendipity Beach Rd; ⌚5pm-2am) This popular little Mexican *taquería* that doubles as a late-night bar serves top margaritas and some refined tequilas for those who prefer sips to shots. It's a civilised escape from the beachside party scene.

Last Hippie Standing BAR

(Otres 1; ⌚24hr) The first place you'll see when you enter the Otres area and, often, the last place you'll been seen on particularly rowdy nights. DJs play dance and trance music 'til the wee hours and the owners offer free basic accommodation to guests who decide they never want to leave. The Friday night parties are particularly debauched.

La Rhumerie BAR

(Map p260; Serendipity Beach Rd; ⌚6pm-2am) Pull up a bar stool at La Rhumerie for salsa music and yummy rum infused with ingredients such as Kampot pepper and ginger. We're not big fans of their weird blue back-lighting, but we're more than a tad partial to the coffee-infused rum. Not a rum fan? They whip up mean cocktails as well.

JJ's Playground BAR

(Map p260; Ochheuteal Beach; ⌚6pm-6am) For a while now JJ's has been the go-to spot for those seeking late-night debauchery. The scene here is pretty much summed up by their tag line 'let's get wasted'. Expect shots, loud techno, a fire show or two, and a lot of chaos. And don't say we didn't warn you about the toilets.

Dolphin Shack BAR

(Map p260; Ochheuteal Beach; ⌚4pm-late) Dolphin Shack boasts a host of drink specials designed to get you drunk fast, and bevies of beautiful backpackers pouring drinks and passing out flyers.

Shopping

Tapang ARTS & CRAFTS

(Map p260; www.mloptapang.org; Serendipity Beach Rd; ⌚10am-8pm) Run by a local NGO that works with at-risk children, this shop sells good-quality bags, scarves and T-shirts made by street kids (and their families) so that they can attend school instead of peddling on the beach.

Has another outlet at Sandan (p258) restaurant.

Starfish ARTS & CRAFTS

(Map p259; off 7 Makara St; ⌚7am-6pm) Above the bakery of the same name; it sells silks and other gifts produced by good-cause NGO Rajana.

Serendipity

Sights

1 Sokha Beach A2

Activities, Courses & Tours

2 Dive Shop C1
3 EcoSea Dive C2
4 Relax C2

Sleeping

5 Above Us Only Sky B2
6 Big Easy C2
7 Chochi Garden C2
8 Cloud 9 .... B3
9 Coolabah Resort C2
10 Holiday Villa Nataya C2
11 One Stop Hostel C1
12 Serendipity Beach Resort B2
13 Sokha Beach Resort A2
14 Tamarind D3

Eating

15 Dao of Life C2
16 Mick & Craig's C1
17 Sandan C1
18 Sushi Bar Shin C1

Drinking & Nightlife

19 Dolphin Shack C3
20 JJ's Playground C3
21 La Rhumerie C2
22 Maybe Later C2

Shopping

23 Tapang C2

Transport

Buva Sea .... (see 24)
Island Speed Ferry Cambodia .... (see 24)
24 Serendipity Pier C2
25 Speed Ferry Cambodia C1

Information

Theft is a problem on the beaches (especially Ochheuteal Beach) so leave valuables in your room. It's often children who do the deed, sometimes in conjunction with adults. Arriving in a team, one or more will distract you while another lifts whatever valuables are lying on your towel. Or they'll strike when you're out swimming.

As in Phnom Penh, drive-by bag snatchings occasionally happen and are especially dangerous when you're riding a *moto*. Hold your shoulder bags tightly in front of you, especially at night.

The road between Otres and Sihanoukville is considered especially risky after dark, so arrange a *remork* or *moto* via your guesthouse if staying in this area, and not just a random stranger in town.

At night, travellers (especially women) should avoid walking alone along dark, isolated beaches and roads.

ANZ Royal Bank (Map p259; 215 Ekareach St; 8am-3.30pm Mon-Fri, to 11.30am Sat, ATM 24hr)

Canadia Bank (Map p259; 197 Ekareach St; 8am-3.30pm Mon-Fri, to 11.30am Sat, ATM 24hr)

CT Clinic (Map p259; 034-936666, 081 886666; 47 Boray Kamakor St; emergencies 24hr) The best medical clinic in town. Can administer rabies shots, and antivenin in the event of a snake bite.

Post Office (Map p259; 19 7 Makara St; 7am-5pm)

San Travel & Tours (Map p260; 081 555646; santravelandtours@ymail.com; Mithona St; 9am-10pm) A step ahead of the rest in terms of both friendliness and usefulness. San is an authority on regional transport schedules and can handle bookings for land, boat or air travel. Also the best internet and copying services in town.

Getting There & Away

AIR

Sihanoukville International Airport (012-333524; www.cambodia-airports.com) is 15km east of town, just off NH4. **Cambodia Bayon Airlines** (www.bayonairlines.com), **Cambodia Angkor Airlines** (in Phnom Penh 023 6660330; www.cambodiaangkorair.com), **Sky Angkor Airlines** (www.skyangkorair.com) and **Bassaka Air** all fly to Siem Reap several times per week. Flights to Phnom Penh tend to be on-again, off-again – check at your time of travel whether they are operating.

Internationally, Cambodia Angkor Air's daily flights to Ho Chi Minh City (one hour, 1.25pm) can be had for as little as US$20 one-way.

BOAT

Two companies do the hopping route between Sihanoukville, Koh Rong and Koh Rong Sanloem with large fast ferries: **Island Speed Ferry Cambodia** (Map p260; 015 811711; www.islandspeedboatcambodia.com; Serendipity Pier; return ticket US$20), the 'blue boat', stops at Saracen Bay and M'Pai Bay (both on Koh Rong Sanloem) before continuing to Koh Tuch village on Koh Rong and returning to Sihanoukville, and **Speed Ferry Cambodia** (Map p260; www.speedferrycambodia.com; Koh Rong Dive Centre, Serendipity Beach Rd; return ticket US$20), aka the 'yellow boat', goes to Koh Rong, then continues to M'pai Bay and Saracen Bay before returning to Sihanoukville.

Two new companies now service both islands with smaller speedboats that can carry 25 to 50 passengers: **Buva Sea** (Map p260; 098 888950; www.buvasea.com; Serendipity Pier) and **GTVC Speedboat** (Map p256; 016 944441; http://gtvcspeedboat.com; Old Port).

All services except for GTVC's leave from Serendipity Pier (Map p260) although adverse sea conditions often move departures and arrivals to Sihanoukville Port Ferry Dock (7km north of the Serendipity area).

BUS

All of the major bus companies have frequent connections to Phnom Penh from early morning until at least 2pm. Capitol Tour and Rith Mony are the cheapest. Giant Ibis runs a more expensive 'deluxe' minibus, complete with hostess and wi-fi, at 7.30am, 9.30am and 1.30pm.

Bookings made through hotels and travel agencies incur a commission. Most travel agents only work with two or three bus companies, so ask around if you need to leave at a different time than what's being offered.

Companies include the following:

Ana Travel (Map p260; 034-933929; Serendipity Beach Rd; 8am-10pm)

Capitol Tour (Map p259; 034-934042; 169 Ekareach St)

Champa Mekong Tourist Bus (Map p260; 034-6938282; Mithona St)

Giant Ibis (Map p260; 089 999818; www.giantibis.com; Thnou St)

Kampot Tours & Travel (in Kampot 092 125556)

Mekong Express (Map p259; 012 257599; Omui St)

Olympic Express (Map p259; 015 540240; St 109)

Phnom Penh Sorya (Map p259; 034-933888; 236 Ekareach St)

Rith Mony (Map p259; 093 465858; Ekareach St)

Virak Buntham (Map p259; ☎016 754358; Ekareach St)

SHARE TAXI

Cramped share taxis (US$6 per person or US$45 per car) and minibuses (15,000r) to Phnom Penh, depart from the **bus station** (Map p259; St 109) until about 8pm. Avoid the minibuses if you value things like comfort and your life. Hotels can arrange taxis to Phnom Penh for US$50 to US$60 (about four hours). Share taxis to Kampot (US$5, 1½ hours) leave mornings only from a taxi park (Map p259; 7 Makara St) opposite Psar Leu. This taxi park and the bus station are good places to look for share taxis to Koh Kong or the Thai border. If nobody's sharing, expect to pay US$45 to US$60 to the Thai border.

Getting Around

Arriving in Sihanoukville, most buses terminate in the newly relocated bus station in the city centre and leave from the company terminals on Ekareach St. Most bus companies will include free pick-up from the Serendipity area or Victory Hill. Otherwise figure on about US$3/1.50 for *remork*/*moto* from the bus station to the Serendipity area.

A taxi to/from the airport into town costs about US$20. Figure on US$5 one way for a *moto*, US$10 for a *remork*.

From the train station a *remork* will cost US$5.

Bicycles can be hired from many guesthouses for about US$2 a day.

Motorbikes can be rented from many guesthouses for US$5 to US$7 a day, or US$20 with a driver. The police sometimes 'crack down' on foreign drivers. Common violations: no driver's licence, no helmet, no wing mirrors, and driving with the lights on during the day.

Around Sihanoukville

Ream National Park

Just 15km east of Sihanoukville, Ream National Park (ឧទ្យានជាតិរាម) offers trekking opportunities in primary forest, invigorating boat trips through coastal mangroves and long stretches of unspoilt beach. This is an easy escape for those looking to flee the crowds of Sihanoukville.

The park is home to breeding populations of several regionally and globally endangered birds of prey, including the Brahminy kite, grey-headed fish eagle and white-bellied sea eagle: look for them soaring over Prek Toeuk Sap Estuary. Endangered birds that feed on the mudflats include the lesser adjutant, milky stork and painted stork. Despite its protected status, Ream is gravely endangered by planned tourism development, especially along its coastline.

By visiting, you can demonstrate that the park, in its natural state, is not only priceless to humanity but also a valuable economic resource.

Hiking and boating trips through the park can be arranged at the **Ream National Park Headquarters** (☎016 767686, 012 875096; NH4; ⊙7am-5pm), opposite Sihanoukville Airport entrance. When booking directly with the park headquarters, it's best (but not obligatory) to phone ahead. The income generated goes to help protect the park.

If you want to stay here, one of the pioneers on Koh Rong, the Monkey Republic group is once again a few steps ahead of the pack with **Monkey Maya** (☎078 760853; www.monkeymayaream.com; dm/bungalow US$8/45; 📶), a secluded gem of a place on the fringes of Ream National Park. Choose from solid, en-suite ocean-view bungalows or a stilted all-wood 16-bed dorm further up the hill. Also has a great bar – a Monkey Republic trademark.

To get here, follow dirt roads east from Ream Beach proper (near the Naval Base) for 5km or so. The resort has a 12.30pm boat shuttle from SeaGarden on Otres 1 (US$6 per person), or take a *remork* from Sihanoukville (US$20) or the airport (US$7).

The Southern Islands

For many a traveller Cambodia's southern islands are the tropical Shangri-La they've been seeking – as yet, untouched by the mega-resorts that have sprouted across southern Thailand. Many of the islands have been tagged for major development by well-connected foreign investors, but the big boys have been slow to press go, paving the way for DIY development to move in with rustic bungalow resorts.

That's not to say that all small-scale development is fine. Koh Rong, in particular, has changed dramatically in the past couple of years due to unchecked construction in the Koh Tuch area. But for the most part, Cambodia's islands are still paradise the way you imagined it: endless crescents of powdered-sugary soft sand, hammocks swaying in the breeze, photogenic fishing villages on stilts, technicolour sunsets and the patter of raindrops on thatch as you slumber. It seems too good to last, so enjoy it while it does.

Getting There & Away

The logical jumping-off point for any of the main habitable islands is Sihanoukville.

Scheduled boat services link Sihanoukville with Koh Rong, Koh Rong Sanloem and Koh Ta Kiev, while other islands can be reached by private boats, usually owned by the resort you're visiting.

Koh Kong is the base for visiting Cambodia's largest island, Koh Kong Island.

Koh Rong

The Koh Tuch village street-strip that leads out from the pier on Koh Rong is a bottleneck of back-to-back backpacker crash pads, restaurants, and hole-in-the-wall bars blasting competing music. Look, you'll either love it or hate it, but for young travellers who descend off the ferry in droves, Koh Rong (particularly Koh Tuch beach) is a vital stop on any Southeast Asia party itinerary.

It's still possible to escape the mayhem though. The further you walk away from the village, the more sedate it gets. The evening frog chorus overpowers the drifting bass from the late-night raves, phosphorescence shimmers in the sea and the island's natural charms of head-turning beaches backed by lush forest interior, are clear to see.

On the back (west) side of the island is Koh Rong's finest beach, a 7km stretch of drop-dead gorgeous white sand, dubbed **Long Beach** (also called Sok San Beach after the fishing village at its northern end). Longtail boats head here from Koh Tuch pier, depositing sun-seekers on the sand for a day of sunbathing and swimming. You can also walk here via a fairly rough trail through the jungle from Koh Tuch Beach (about 1½ hours).

Developers, not surprisingly, have their eye on this sensational sunset-facing strip, and have broken ground on a huge resort at the south end.

Sleeping & Eating

★ Suns of Beaches GUESTHOUSE $
(010 550355; Vietnamese Beach; dm US$3.50) On a glorious private beach a little north of Long Set (4km) Beach, this new Scottish/English-owned hostel is for shoestringers who are into serious chilling. The huge and airy fan-cooled dorms are things of beauty, while a well-stocked bar means you won't go thirsty. Hammocks are everywhere and the beach is just wow. This is backpacker bliss.

There's an excellent restaurant with some ingredients sourced from their garden. It's a loooong (about 5km) beach walk from Koh Tuch, or you can take the thrice-daily shuttle boat from Bong's Guesthouse.

Dreamcatch Inn GUESTHOUSE $
(081 796002; kohrongdreamcatch@gmail.com; Koh Tuch; r with shared bathroom US$15; wi-fi) A more mellow alternative to most of the budget offerings in Koh Tuch village, Dreamcatch Inn has clean, colourful, all-wood rooms strung with dreamcatchers and leading onto a hammock-strung terrace. Shared bathrooms have squat toilets. Guests get a 10% discount on food and drink at its Loops Bar, and a free T-shirt in the rainy season.

Paradise Bungalows BUNGALOW $$
(092 548883; www.paradise-bungalows.com; Koh Tuch Beach; bungalows US$35-100; wi-fi) Delightfully rustic bungalows here (in all shapes and sizes) climb up the hill amid rambling jungle foliage. The US$35 rooms are way up on the hill while more expensive options are practically lapped by waves at high tide. The loungey restaurant, with soaring palm-leaf panel roof and shoreline panorama, is a real highlight.

Koh Lanta INTERNATIONAL $
(Koh Tuch; mains US$3-6; 7am-10pm) Named after the famous French *Survivor* show, which is filmed on Koh Rong, this place offers some of the best pizzas on the island.

Rising Sun VEGETARIAN $
(Koh Tuch Beach; mains US$3-4; wi-fi) Occupying a central position on Koh Tuch Beach, Rising Sun attracts herbivores by serving vegan and vegetarian meals with a Middle Eastern flair, such as couscous salads and falafel wraps. Has a nice earthy vibe and also rents out kayaks and SUPs for US$5 per hour.

Information

Emergency Services Center (Koh Tuch Beach; walk-in 9.30am-4pm, emergency 24hr) First medical facility on Koh Rong, it's staffed by volunteer medics and can help with cuts and scratches and a few more serious matters like snake bites, anaphylaxis and drug overdoses. If nobody is there, ask any bartender and they can get in touch with clinic personnel via emergency radios.

Getting There & Away

From Koh Tuch, **Island Speed Ferry Cambodia** (069 811711; www.islandspeedboatcambodia.com), the 'blue boat', and **Speed Ferry Cambodia** (www.speedferrycambodia.com), the 'yellow boat', each head to Sihanoukville (return

US$20, one hour, last trip 4.45pm) and Saracen Bay on Koh Rong Sanloem (US$5, 15 minutes) three or four times daily, with stops at M'Pai Bay on request. If you have a return ticket, go to the relevant ferry office at the pier the day before you want to travel to make sure of a seat, and be ready for sudden schedule changes and trip cancellations. The daily slow cargo boat is a cheaper option to Sihanoukville from Koh Tuch.

The more isolated resorts on the west and north sides of the island offer their own private transport.

Koh Rong Sanloem

This horseshoe-shaped, 10km-long island is many peoples' ideal vision of island bliss. Koh Rong Sanloem's most popular destination is Saracen Bay on the east coast – white sand lined with small beach-bungalow resorts backed by lush jungle. The western side of the island (reached by walking trail or private boat) is home to just a couple of secluded resorts. The village of M'Pai Bay at the island's northern tip has grainy yellow (not photogenic white) sands, but the clutch of budget guesthouses provide serious chill factor with a proper local vibe that will suit the more intrepid.

Sleeping & Eating

The Drift GUESTHOUSE **$**

(015 865388; www.thedriftcambodia.com; M'Pai Bay; dm/r US$8/15) A new player on the M'Pai Bay scene, the Drift has spick-and-span dorms and a couple of private rooms in a cute wooden house on the sand. There's a good social vibe with home-cooked meals (US$3) often eaten communally.

Lazy Beach RESORT **$$**

(017 456536; www.lazybeachcambodia.com; bungalows US$60) Alone on the southwest coast of Koh Rong Sanloem, the 16 bungalows at this idyllic getaway front one of the most stunning beaches you'll find anywhere. They have balconies and hammocks outside, and spiffy stone-floor bathrooms and duelling queen-size beds inside. The combined restaurant and common area is stocked with books and board games, making it a good fit for families.

It now shuttles you overland from the Saracen Bay ferry piers in a truck.

Paradise Villas BUNGALOW **$$**

(096 954 8599; www.paradise-bungalows.com; Saracen Bay; small/big bungalows US$45/80) The sister resort of long-running favourite Paradise Bungalows on Koh Rong, this version follows a similar script: smart, solid-wood bungalows with thick mattresses, sea-facing balconies and rain showers, and a beautifully designed restaurant mixing Asian fusion with hearty European dishes (mashed potatoes and gravy, anyone?). Electricity is from 6pm to 6am. The big bungalows are closer to the sea. It's handy to the 'blue boat' ferry pier. Its Sihanoukville office is at Mick & Craig's guesthouse (p259).

Drinking & Nightlife

Good Vibz BAR

(Dec-Apr) Veering off the walking trail from Saracen Bay to Sunset Beach, 436 steps lead up the hill to this secluded jungle-bar that throws weekly raves and an epic full-moon party. Daily events include movie nights with films projected on a large screen amid the jungle backdrop.

For those who can't bear to leave there's also accommodation in hammocks (US$1) and tents (from US$3).

Getting There & Away

Competing **Island Speed Ferry Cambodia** (p262), the 'blue boat', and **Speed Ferry Cambodia** (p262), the 'yellow boat', each connect Saracen Bay with Sihanoukville three or four times daily, with stops at M'Pai Bay on request. The former usually, but not always, goes via Koh Rong; the latter usually, but not always, arrives from Koh Rong and continues to Sihanoukville. Tickets cost US$20 return from Sihanoukville. To hop from Koh Rong Sanloem to Koh Rong (15 minutes) costs US$5.

The blue boat uses a pier toward the south end of Saracen Bay, while the yellow boat's pier is toward the north end. Plan accordingly to reduce walk time to your resort, as Saracen Bay Beach is long. The last trip back to Sihanoukville is the yellow boat's 4pm trip. Validate the ticket for your return journey at the relevant pier one day before travel to make sure you get a seat. Schedules change and cancellations are common.

Another option to Sihanoukville is the 4pm 'slow boat' (US$10, 2½ hours).

Koh Sdach Archipelago

This is a modest archipelago of 12 small islands, most of them uninhabited. Basing yourself at one of the two islands with accommodation – Koh Sdach (King Island) and Koh Totang – you can spend a day or two exploring the other islands, some of which have utterly isolated beaches and good snorkelling.

In fact, it's hard to imagine a more relaxed place than **Nomads Land** (☎011 916171; www.nomadslandcambodia.com; Koh Totang; bungalows s/d incl meals from US$60/90; ⊙Nov-May). Owner Karim has made this the greenest resort in the islands with five funky bungalows powered by solar panels and rain water collected for drinking. It sits on a white beach on Koh Totang, an island speck, which is 15 minutes from the mainland's Poi Yopon village by the resort's boat.

A huge Chinese 'resort city' has taken over the mainland, but had yet to open at the time of our last visit. Existing resorts are far enough from the mainland that the commotion is out of earshot, thankfully.

Koh Ta Kiev

If your beach break perfection is about logging off and slothing out, this little island off Ream National Park ticks all the right boxes. Now is the moment to zip to a handful of budget-friendly, basic digs with serious chill-out factor in Koh Ta Kiev – major development may not be far off.

Most of the beach bungalow accommodation is along Long Beach, a white-sand beach on the west side. Various tracks branch off from here through the forest for those who want to explore, including one to an even more secluded beach on the south coast. Unfortunately rubbish regularly washes up on the island, so don't expect pristine swaths of sand.

Ten103 Treehouse Bay BUNGALOW $
(☎097 9437587; www.ten103-cambodia.com; Koh; hammock/dm US$5/7, hut without bathroom US$20-25, with bathroom US$35) Un-plug, unwind, de-stress – Ten103 is a beachfront backpacker bolt-hole that dishes up simple beach living the way it used to be. Stilted open-air 'treehouse' huts have sea views, while the open-air dorm and palm-thatch hammock shelters provide even more basic back-to-nature options.

Last Point BUNGALOW $
(☎088 5026930; www.lastpointisland.com; hammock/dm US$2/6, bungalows US$15-30) The Last Point sits in splendid isolation on a sandy stretch of Koh Ta Kiev's south coast; a 40-minute walk from the island's other accommodation options. There's a variety of small, sweet palm-thatch bungalows to play out Robinson Crusoe dreams, as well as a breezy open-air dorm just steps from the sand. There's a direct boat here from SeaGarden on Otres 1 daily at 11.30am.

Koh Thmei

The large island of Koh Thmei is part of Ream National Park. It's slated for a major development, including a bridge to the mainland, but that has progressed slowly and the large, bird-laden island remains miraculously pristine

There's only one resort here and it's a gem with super-simple bungalows that use solar panels and biofuel for electricity. The **Koh Thmei Resort** (☎097 7370400; www.koh-thmei-resort.com; bungalows US$45, f US$70) sits on a great beach, and you can easily walk to several more, plus go sea-kayaking or snorkelling (visibility varies). Management can arrange transport from Sihanoukville.

Kampot

It's not hard to see why travellers become entranced with Kampot. This riverside town, with streets rimmed by dilapidated shophouse architecture, has a dreamy quality. The Kompong Bay River serves as both attractive backdrop and water-sports playground for those staying in the boutique resorts and backpacker retreats that line its banks upstream from the town proper.

Eclipsed as a port when Sihanoukville was founded in 1959, Kampot also makes an excellent base for exploring Bokor National Park, the neighbouring seaside town of Kep, and the superb cave-temples and verdant countryside of the surrounding area.

Sights

Kampot is more about ambience than actual sights and the most enjoyable activity is strolling or cycling through the central old town district where lanes are lined with crumbling shophouses, many built in the mid-20th century by the town's then vibrant Chinese merchant population. The best streets, a couple of which have been well-restored in recent years, are between the triangle delineated by the central Durian Roundabout, the post office and the old French bridge.

Tours

Everybody and their grandmother wants to sell you a tour in Kampot. The main day trips are to Bokor hill station (US$13 to $15), and a countryside tour that usually includes Phnom Chhnork Cave, the nearby salt fields, a pepper farm and Kep (US$12 to US$14), with an option to visit Koh Tonsay (US$18 to $20).

Alternatively, you can hire a *remork* driver and cobble together your own tour of the caves, Kep and surrounding countryside. Depending on locations, a half-/full-day tour costs about US$15/25.

Sunset cruises and evening firefly-watching boat trips are also extremely popular. Firefly tours are best on a new moon, although spotting fireflies is not guaranteed due to their unpredictable nature.

Bart the Boatman BOATING
(☎092 174280; 2 people US$40) Known simply as Bart the Boatman, this Belgian expat runs original private boat tours along the small tributaries of the Kampong Bay River. His backwater tour is highly recommended by travellers.

Sok Lim Tours TOURS
(☎012 796919; St 730; ⏲8am-7pm) Kampot's longest-running outfit is well-regarded and organises all the usual day tours and river cruises. For private countryside tours they have good English-speaking *remork* driver-guides that understand the process and history behind Kampot pepper. If there's no one in the actual office, they'll be in the neighbouring Jack's Place restaurant.

Sleeping

When it comes to accommodation, Kampot is a tale of two cities. In the centre, most hotels and guesthouses are in, or near, the old town, a stone's throw from all the cafes and restaurants. Out of town, a series of places are strung out along the riverbank offering a complete chill-out (or complete party, depending on which one you pick) experience.

Old Town

Pepper Guesthouse GUESTHOUSE $
(☎017 822626; guesthousepepper@yahoo.com; St 730; dm US$3, r with fan US$10, bungalows US$25;) We're big fans of this homely, locally run guesthouse in a slightly creaky mid-century villa. Fan-only rooms have bags of character with beautiful old wood floors (room 101 is the best), while out in the front garden are two rather upmarket bungalows with rain showers and tasteful decor.

Bicycle (US$1) and motorbike (US$4) hire available.

Baraca GUESTHOUSE $
(☎011 290434; www.baraca.org; St 726; d US$12-16, f US$20;) Just off the river, Baraca has bags of old-world charm, with high ceilings and original tilework floors in the four airy rooms. There's no hot water, but it's popular nonetheless, so book ahead. Great tapas restaurant too.

Magic Sponge GUESTHOUSE $
(☎017 946428; www.magicspongekampot.com; St 730; dm US$6, d with fan US$15-23, with air-con US$23-28;) This popular backpacker place has a rooftop dorm with impressive through-breezes, personalised fans and reading lights. Good-value private rooms are exceptionally well cared for and bright. Downstairs is a movie lounge and a lively bar-restaurant with happy hours from noon to 8pm and well-regarded Indian food.

There's even minigolf in the garden.

★**Rikitikitavi** BOUTIQUE HOTEL $$
(☎012 235102; www.rikitikitavi-kampot.com; River Rd; r incl breakfast US$48-53, f US$58;) One of Cambodia's best-run boutique hotels, Rikitikitavi has rooms that are a lesson in subtle luxury, fusing Asian-inspired decor with modern creature comforts. Ceilings are graced with stunning beams, and palm panels and beautiful artwork adorn the walls. Plus you get swish contemporary bathrooms and mod-con amenities such as flat-screen TVs, DVD player, fridge and kettle. Service is sublime. Highly recommended.

On the River

Naga House HOSTEL $
(☎012 289916; nagahousekampot@gmail.com; Tuk Chhou Rd; dm US$3, bungalow US$7-12;) This classic backpacker hang-out offers basic ground-level and stilted thatched bungalows (all with shared bathroom) amid lush foliage, and a coveted four-bed dorm in the main house on the river. There's an attractive and extremely social bar-restaurant that often rocks into the night, especially on Saturdays when it hosts DJ sets.

Sunset boat cruises set out daily (US$5). Walk-in rates (listed here) are substantially cheaper than booking online.

Monkey Republic Kampot HOSTEL $
(☎012 848390; monkeyrepublickampot@gmail.com; St 730; dm with air-con US$5-7, r with fan US$8-10;) This 50-bed backpacker mecca in a restored villa features Kampot's

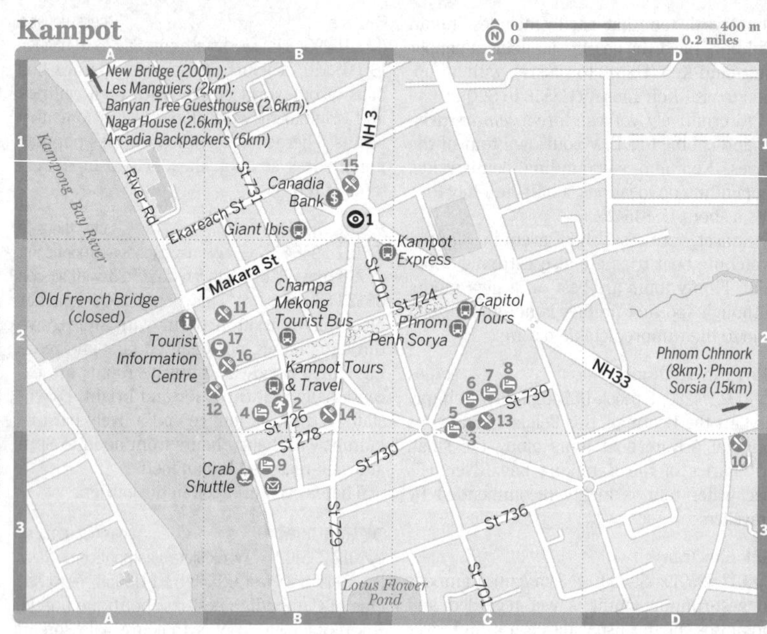

nicest dorm rooms. Choose from large dorms in the main building, or brand-new, six-bed 'pods' in the neighbouring house. Think individual lockers, privacy curtains and charging stations. There's an upstairs hammock lounge, while French tiles and big booths add character to the lively bar downstairs.

Blue Buddha Hotel HOTEL $
(☎017 843550; www.bluebuddhahotel.com; 1 St 730; d/tr/f US$22/27/38;) Raising the bar for budget digs in Kampot, Blue Buddha has exceptionally helpful owners and spacious, minimalist-style rooms with comfortable beds, cable TV, minibar and big modern bathrooms. Guests also benefit from a swag of discounts at businesses around town, and free bike hire.

Banyan Tree Guesthouse HOSTEL $
(☎078 665094; www.banyantreekampot.com; Tuk Chhou Rd; dm US$3, r US$6-12;) The erstwhile Boddhi Villa backpacker mecca is now the Banyan Tree backpacker mecca. The tried-and-true formula here involves boat sports by day, booze by night, and plenty of downtime on the sublime riverside chill-out deck in between it all. Choose from a 20-bed dorm, simple rooms above the bar or pleasing rattan bungalows at the back.

Friday is the big party night, when live music is produced by top local band Kampot Playboys or imported talent from Phnom Penh. Outsiders welcome. This is not a place for light sleepers.

Les Manguiers RESORT $$
(☎092 330050; www.mangokampot.com; Kompong Bay River east bank; r with shared bathroom US$11-24, bungalows US$32-80; @) This rambling garden complex has swags of extras with free canoes and bikes, badminton, table tennis and a children's playground. You can jump into the river from one of four over-water gazebos. There's a variety of accommodation from large, bright simple rooms to stilted wooden bungalows, all with fan and cold water. Meals are served table d'hôte style.

Eating & Drinking

Local street-food eateries line St 722 just off the riverfront and are a great place to browse for cheap eats such as fried noodles, soups and Khmer desserts such as sticky rice with coconut sauce. The bustling **night market** (NH3; 4pm-midnight) is also full of food stalls.

★Ciao ITALIAN $
(St 722; mains US$2.75-4; from 6pm) Kampot's only Western street-food vendor is an Italian who cooks delicious pizzas one at a time in a modified dustbin out of this ramshackle

Kampot

Sights

Activities, Courses & Tours

Sleeping

Eating

Drinking & Nightlife

space on Kampot's street-food row. They take awhile but are *sooo* worth it. Also serves homemade gnocchi and pasta.

KAMA Cafe CAFE $
(St 726; mains US$3.50-4; 8am-7.30pm; wi-fi) Run out of the art space of the same name, KAMA is delightfully situated in an elegant old town house – perfect for an atmospheric breakfast or happy hour. The food – especially the breakfasts – is absolutely scrumptious, featuring light bites, curries and exciting daily specials prepared by Soon, who co-runs the place with her partner, Julien of Cambodian Space Project.

Cafe Espresso CAFE $
(NH33; mains US$4-6; 8.30am-4pm Tue-Fri, 9am-4.30pm Sat & Sun; wi-fi, vegetarian) We advise making the trip to this cafe newly located to the outskirts of town. The Aussie owners are real foodies and offer a global menu that traipses from vegetarian quesadillas to Brazilian-style pork sandwiches with some especially tempting breakfast options. But it is caffeine-cravers who will be really buzzing, thanks to their regionally grown coffee blends, roasted daily in this factory.

Jack's Place CAMBODIAN $
(St 730; mains US$2.50-6; 6.30am-10.30pm; wi-fi, vegetarian) A friendly, local family-run place, this relaxed open-air restaurant dishes up *yao hon* (Khmer hotpots), *char kroeung* (vegetable and peanut stir-fry) and a whole host of Cambodian staples. The soups here are delicious and there's also sandwiches and burgers.

Jack just opened Kampot Dorm on the premises, with basic dorm beds for US$2.50.

★ **Fishmarket** FUSION $$
(012 728884; River Rd; mains US$6-15; 7.30am-10.30pm) Kampot's up-and-coming dining scene finally has its signature eatery in the form of this restored art-deco masterpiece on the banks of the Kompong Bay River. Plop down in the breezy open-air dining area and dig into Australian lamb cutlets, fish and chips, or local favourites such as peppercorn crab and fish *amok*.

Rusty Keyhole INTERNATIONAL $$
(River Rd; small/large/extra-large ribs US$5/7.50/10; 8am-11pm Nov-May, 11am-11pm Jun-Oct; wi-fi) This popular riverfront bar-restaurant turns out a global menu of comfort food and Khmer home cooking. Most people are here for its famous ribs; order in advance, but beware of the enormous, extra-large portions.

Nelly's Bar BAR
(River Rd; 3pm-late) Occupying a street corner under a bougainvillea tree outside a beautiful colonial building, Nelly's is a fine place to throw back a few drinks. Plays groovy tunes and draws a nice mix of travellers and colourful Kampot expats. The high season occasionally sees acoustic acts set up on the sidewalk.

It's named after the house dog.

Information

The free and often hilarious *Kampot Survival Guide* (www.kampotsurvivalguide.com) takes a tongue-in-cheek look at local expat life. There's also the free *Coastal* guide to Kampot and Kep, with heaps of info on local businesses.

Canadia Bank (Durian Roundabout; 8am-3.30pm Mon-Fri, to 11.30am Sat, ATM 24hr)

Sonja Kill Memorial Hospital (emergency 078 265782, outpatient clinic 077 666752; www.skmh.org; NH3) The best hospital in the area with state-of-the-art medical facilities and highly trained local and expat doctors. It's 7km west of Kampot.

Tourist Information Centre (033-6555541; lonelyguide@gmail.com; River Rd; 7am-7pm) Led by the knowledgeable Mr Pov, Kampot's tourist office doles out free advice, sells tours and

LOCAL KNOWLEDGE

ROCK CLIMBING AROUND KAMPOT

Cambodia's first outdoor rock-climbing outfit **Climbodia** (☎095 581951; www.climbodia.com; St 710; half-day US$35-40, full day US$80) offers highly recommended half-day and full-day programs of climbing, abseiling and caving amid the limestone formations of Phnom Kbal Romeas, 5km south of Kampot. Via ferratas (cabled routes) have been established across some of the cliffs and the variety of programs cater for both complete novices and the more experienced.

can arrange transport to area attractions such as caves, falls and Kompong Trach.

Getting There & Away

Kampot, on NH3, is 148km southwest of Phnom Penh, 105km east of Sihanoukville and 25km northwest of Kep.

If heading to Phnom Penh, be aware that a couple of the bus companies, including **Phnom Penh Sorya** (NH33), go via Kep, which adds at least an hour to the trip. You're better off with the direct buses (3¼ hours) run by **Capitol Tours** (☎092 665001; NH33), two daily, US$4.50, or 'luxury' bus company **Giant Ibis** (☎095 666809; www.giantibis.com; 7 Makara St), US$9, 8.30am and 2.45pm. Even quicker are the direct minivan services to Phnom Penh (US$8, 2¾ hours) run by **Kampot Express** (☎077 555123; www.kampotexpress.com; NH33) and **Kampot Tours & Travel** (☎092 125556; St 710), each with several departures daily.

To Sihanoukville, Kampot Tours & Travel and **Champa Mekong Tourist Bus** (☎033-6300036; St 724) each have three minivan departures daily (US$5, two hours). Both companies also have twice-daily departures to Ha Tien in Vietnam (US$8, 1½ hours).

Several bus companies stop in Kep (US$3, 30 minutes) en route to Ha Tien or Phnom Penh, or you can take a *remork* (US$10, 45 minutes) or *moto* (US$6). A more atmospheric way to Kep is with the **Crab Shuttle** (☎088 829 6644; crabshuttle@gmail.com; ⏲closed Jun-Sep) boat (one-way/return US$10/13.50, 2½ hours), which departs at 9am and returns at 3pm for sunset views. Rabbit Island drop-offs and pick-ups are possible for an extra few dollars, with a boat transfer at Kep's Rabbit Island Pier.

Lastly, the rehabilitated train is a (slow) option to Phnom Penh (US$6, five hours) and Sihanoukville (US$5, four hours). Departures around 11.30am in either direction are weekends-only for now.

Guesthouses and tour agencies can arrange tickets and pick-ups, although they'll usually take a commission.

Getting Around

A *moto* ride in town costs around 2000r (*remork* US$1). To get to the riverside guesthouses on the edge of town it should cost between US$2 to US$4, depending on where they're located.

Bicycles (US$2 per day) and motorbikes (about US$5 per day) can be rented from many guesthouses around town.

Bokor Hill Station

The once abandoned French retreat of Bokor hill station (កស្ថានីយភ្នំបូកគោ), inside the 1581-sq-km Bokor National Park, is famed for its refreshingly cool climate and creepy derelict buildings that had their heyday during the 1920s and 1930s.

These days the hill station is becoming more famous for the Thansur Bokor Highland Resort, the ugly modern casino that blights the summit and has sadly all but destroyed the pleasingly eerie atmosphere of bygone Bokor, although the awe-inspiring views remain.

Sights

Bokor National Park NATIONAL PARK

(ឧទ្យានជាតិបូកគោ, Preah Monivong National Park; admission motorbike/car 2000/4000r) Bokor's moist evergreen forests – with dry dipterocarp and mixed deciduous forests in the north – shelter a wide variety of rare and threatened animals, including the Indian elephant, leopard, Asiatic black bear, Malayan sun bear, pileated gibbon, pig-tailed macaque, slow loris, red muntjac deer, pangolin, yellow-throated martin, small Asian mongoose and various species of civet, porcupine, squirrel and bat.

Trekking trips here used to be very popular, but recent development within the park has scuppered trekking opportunities.

Bokor Palace Hotel HISTORIC BUILDING

(ដំណាក់បូកគោ) FREE Opened in 1925, this once grand hotel was a chief playground for hobnobbing French officials. As you wander through the building, you'll need your imagination to envisage the lavish interiors that adorned the opulent ballroom and guestrooms as today the hotel is a vast, empty shell with just scraps of original floor tilework still hanging on.

Catholic Church CHURCH

FREE The squat belfry of the Romanesque-style Catholic church still holds aloft its cross, and fragments of glass brick cling to the corners of the nave windows; one side window holds the barest outline of a rusty crucifix. It's easy to imagine a small crowd of French colonials in formal dress assembled here for Sunday Mass. The subdividing walls inside were built by the Khmer Rouge. A bit up the hill, a sheer drop overlooks rainforest.

Popokvil Falls WATERFALL

(ទឹកធ្លាក់ពពកវិល; admission 2000r) From the Thansur Bokor Highland Resort, the road heads north for several kilometres to two-tiered Popokvil Falls, which are impressive from July to October, but dry up in the dry season.

Wat Sampov Pram BUDDHIST TEMPLE

(វត្តសំពៅប្រាំ) Lichen-caked Wat Sampov Pram (Five Boats Wat) offers tremendous views over the jungle to the coastline below, including Vietnam's Phu Quoc Island. Wild monkeys like to hang out around the wat.

Getting There & Away

You can either visit the hill station on one of the numerous day trips organised in Kampot or rent a motorbike and travel under your own steam. The road up here is brand-spanking new – built by the Thansur Bokor Highland Resort – so it's in excellent condition.

Kep

Founded as a seaside retreat for the French elite in 1908 and a favoured haunt of Cambodian high-rollers during the 1960s, today tourists are being drawn back to sleepy Kep (Krong Kep, also spelled Kaeb). Seafood, sunsets and hikes in butterfly-filled Kep National Park are the main draws, with an impressive range of boutique hotels on offer that squarely target a more cultured beach crowd than the party-happy guesthouses of Sihanoukville and Kampot.

Some find Kep a bit soulless because it lacks a centre, not to mention a long sandy shoreline. Others revel in its torpid pace, content to relax at their resort, nibble on crab at the famed crab market and poke around the mildewed shells of modernist villas, which still give the town a sort of post-apocalyptic feel.

Sights & Activities

★ **Kep National Park** NATIONAL PARK

(ឧទ្យានជាតិកែប; admission 4000r) The interior of Kep peninsula is occupied by Kep National Park, where an 8km circuit, navigable by foot and mountain bike, winds through thick forest passing by wats and viewpoints. Quirky yellow signs point the way and show trailheads to off-shooting walking paths that lead into the park's interior. The 'Stairway to Heaven' trail is particularly worthwhile, leading up the hill to a pagoda, a nunnery and the Sunset Rock viewpoint.

The main park entrance is behind Veranda Natural Resort.

Fuel up or chill out after your hike at Led Zep Cafe (p274), which is on the trail 300m into the walk from the main entrance. The owner, Christian, was the driving force in creating, mapping and signposting the trails and continues to look after the park environment.

Sothy's Pepper Farm FARM

(☎088 9513505; www.mykampotpepper.asia; Phnom Vour, Kep district, off NH33; ⊙9am-5pm) FREE By far the friendliest pepper farm to visit, Sothy's has a shop and offers short tours that explain the history and process behind the Kampot pepper industry. It's about 17km northeast of central Kep.

Kep Beach BEACH

This handkerchief-sized strip of sand is Kep's only proper beach. In the pre-war period, powder-white sand was trucked in from other beaches and this practice began again in 2013, ensuring the beach is now in better shape than it has been for years. It's still somewhat pebbly and can get packed on weekends. The eastern end of the shaded promenade along the beach is marked by Sela Cham P'dey, a statue depicting a nude fisher's wife waiting for her husband to return.

Koh Tonsay ISLAND

(កោះទន្សាយ, Rabbit Island) If you like the rustic beachcomber lifestyle, Koh Tonsay's 250m-long main beach is for you, but come now as the island is tagged for development. The beach is one of the nicest of any of the Kep-area islands but don't expect sparkling white sand. This one has shorefront flotsam, chickens and wandering cows. Restaurant-shacks and rudimentary bungalows (from

US$7 per night) rim the sand. Boats to Rabbit Island (30 minutes) leave from Rabbit Island pier at 9am and 1pm.

Return trips are at 11am and 3pm. Same-day return tickets cost US$7; if you return the next day, it's US$10 return. Kep guesthouses can arrange boat tickets or you can head to the Koh Tonsay Boat Ticket Office at the pier. Private boats to the island can be arranged at the pier and cost US$25 return for up to six people. Rabbit Island is so named because locals say it resembles a rabbit – an example of what too much local brew can do to your imagination.

Other Kep-area islands include **Koh Pos** (Snake Island; about 30 minutes beyond Rabbit Island), which has a deserted beach and fine snorkelling but no overnight accommodation. Getting out there costs about US$50 for an all-day trip by 10-person boat. There's also small, beachless **Koh Svay** (Mango Island), whose summit offers nice views.

Wat Kiri Sela BUDDHIST TEMPLE
(វត្តគិរីសិលា; 7am-6pm) This Buddhist temple sits at the foot of Phnom Kompong Trach, a dramatic karst formation riddled with more than 100 caverns and passageways. From the wat, an underground passage leads to a fishbowl-like formation, surrounded by vine-draped cliffs and open to the sky. Various stalactite-laden caves shelter reclining Buddhas and miniature Buddhist shrines. The closest town is Kompong Trach. From here, take the dirt road opposite the Acleda Bank, on NH33 in the town centre, for 2km.

Kompong Trach is 28km northeast of Kep on NH33, making it an easy day trip from both Kep and Kampot. At the wat, note that friendly local kids with torches (flashlights), keen to put their evening-school English to use, are eager to serve as guides. Make sure you tip them if you use them.

Sailing Club WATER SPORTS
(078 333685; www.knaibangchatt.com/the-sailing-club; 8am-5pm) Open to all, the newly expanded sailing club and activity centre of Knai Bang Chat hires out sea kayaks (US$5 per hour), Hobie Cats (from US$15 per hour) and windsurfers (US$12 per hour). Decent mountain bikes are also available at US$10 per day.

Sleeping

Kep meanders along the shoreline for a good 5km, with resorts and guesthouses speckled along the length of the main road and snuggled along the dirt tracks that wander up the hills leading to Kep National Park.

★ **Botanica Guesthouse** BUNGALOW $
(097 899 8614; www.kep-botanica.com; NH33A; r with fan/air-con US$20/29;) A little way from the action (if Kep can be said to have any action), Botanica offers exceptional value for money with attractive bungalows boasting contemporary bathrooms. There's a well-shaded pool and guests can use free bicycles to pedal into town. Recent renovations have only improved what was already a good thing.

Bird of Paradise BUNGALOW $
(090 880413; www.birdofparadisebungalows.com; bungalows with fan/air-con incl breakfast from US$14/20;) Set in a relaxed, peaceful garden, Bird of Paradise is stupendous value, well located just up the hill from the main road within walking distance of the crab market. Simple but sweet wooden bungalows, with hammocks strung from the porch, are delightfully rustic, while the air-con concrete cottages are more spacious. Lovely little breakfast area too.

Kep Guest House HOSTEL $
(097 374 8080; www.kepguesthouse.com; NH33A; dm US$5 r with fan US$9-13, with air-con US$17;) This modest hostel is Kep's nicest backpacker pad with bright, airy and clean rooms, and a single dorm with just three double beds. There's great sea views from the rooftop restaurant.

Bacoma BUNGALOW $
(088 411 2424; www.bacoma.weebly.com; NH33A; r US$15-30;) Cheap and cheerful rondavels in the garden all have mosquito nets and fan, with a generous helping of sparkling clean shared bathrooms. There are also roomy bungalows and traditional Khmer houses with private bathroom.

★ **Tara Lodge** GUESTHOUSE $$
(097 623 6167; www.taralodge-kep.com; d incl breakfast US$50-60, f US$70;) The hugely friendly Tara Lodge gets a big tick from us for its split-level bungalows with wide verandahs and all the mod-cons, secreted within a verdant garden of palms and flowers, and set around a glistening pool. This is a secluded spot for some serious downtime. The upstairs terrace-restaurant serves excellent Khmer and French food and has views to Bokor.

The massage pavilion is sublime.

WORTH A TRIP

PHNOM CHHNORK

Phnom Chhnork (ភ្នំឈ្នុងក្រោក; admission US$1; ⊙7am-6pm) is a short walk through a quilt of rice paddies from Wat Ang Sdok, where a monk collects the entry fee and a gaggle of friendly local kids offer their services as guides. From the bottom, a 203-step staircase leads up the hillside and down into a cavern as graceful as a Gothic cathedral. The view from up top, and the walk to and from the wat, is especially magical in the late afternoon.

Inside the cave you'll be greeted by a stalactite elephant, with a second elephant outlined on the flat cliff face to the right. Tiny chirping bats live up near two natural chimneys that soar towards the blue sky, partly blocked by foliage of an impossibly green hue.

Within the main chamber stands a remarkable 7th-century (Funan-era) brick temple, dedicated to Shiva. The temple's brickwork is in superb condition thanks to the protection afforded by the cave. Poke your head inside and check out the ancient stalactite that serves as a *linga*. A slippery passage, flooded in the rainy season, leads through the hill.

To get to Phnom Chhnork turn left off NH33 about 5.5km east of Kampot. Look for the sign to 'Climbodia'. From the turn-off it's 6km to the cave on a bumpy road. A return *moto* ride from Kampot costs about US$6 (*remork* US$10).

Saravoan Hotel BOUTIQUE HOTEL $$

(036-639 3909; www.saravoanhotel-kep.com; r US$45-55;) Classic Kep contemporary minimalist design is the hallmark of Saravoan. Spacious rooms come with polished concrete floors, stone-wall detailing and floor-to-ceiling glass doors that open out onto arguably the best sea-view balconies in town, although they are susceptible to street noise. The terrace pool is just the place to cool off after exploring Kep National Park.

Le Flamboyant Resort RESORT $$

(017 491010; www.flamboyant-hotel.com; NH33A; d incl breakfast from US$70;) Although less flamboyant than the name would suggest, this attractive, large garden property (complete with lawn-mowing horse) has a boutique resort feel. Cottage-style bungalows have blue accents and wood detailing, and open out onto dinky verandahs. There are two swimming pools, a small spa hut and a good restaurant on-site.

Expect some street noise on busy weekends.

Atmaland Resort RESORT $$

(086 509021; www.atmaland.com; d/q bungalow incl breakfast from US$40/55;) This family-friendly bungalow resort sprawls along the hillside amid a rambling mature garden with pool and on-site vegetarian restaurant. It's far enough away to feel secluded, but still central enough to easily walk to Kep's crab market. Both spacious family suites and standard bungalows are comfortable and kept spick-and-span, though the decor is a bit dull.

Veranda Natural Resort RESORT $$$

(012 888619; www.veranda-resort.asia; Kep Hillside Rd; r incl breakfast from US$115;) The hillside bungalows are built of wood, bamboo and stone, and are connected by a maze of stilted walkways, making this a memorable spot for a romantic getaway. Check out several rooms because the size and shape vary wildly. The food is excellent and views from the restaurant pavilion are stunning, although price inflation here seems to have no bounds.

Eating & Drinking

Most restaurants in town offer crab in some way, shape or form. Some of Kep's hotels offer fine dining. The seafront Strand dining pavilion at **Knai Bang Chatt** (078 888556; www.knaibangchatt.com; s/d incl breakfast from US$188/319;) and Veranda Natural Resort (p273) are a couple of the top tables, and have great views to boot.

Sailing Club has the liveliest happy hour. After dark just head to the Crab Market area and see what place is happening; the best bet is La Baraka.

Crab Market MARKET $

Eating at the crab market – a row of wooden waterfront restaurants by a wet fish market – is a quintessential Kep experience. Fresh crabs fried with Kampot pepper are a taste sensation. Crabs are kept alive in pens tethered just off the pebbly beach. You can dine at one of the restaurants or buy crab and have your guesthouse prepare it.

There are lots of great places to choose from at the crab market, so keep an eye on where the Khmer crowd are eating. Crab costs around 35,000r a kilo at the wet market.

★ Sailing Club FUSION $$
(mains US$7-12.50; ⌚10am-10pm; 📶) With a small beach, breezy wooden bar and a wooden jetty poking out into the sea, this is one of Cambodia's top sundowner spots. The Asian fusion food is excellent and you can get your crab fix here too. Was undergoing a major expansion during our last visit, with an outdoor cocktail lounge and vastly expanded seafront terrace expected.

La Baraka INTERNATIONAL $$
(Crab Market; mains US$6-10; ⌚11am-10pm; 📶) A breath of fresh air from the crab market's other identikit menus, La Baraka serves up a mix of European and Asian flavours with bags of seafood dishes such as swordfish carpaccio. For non-fish lovers there's also great pizza and pasta. The terrace, over the waves, is sunset cocktail perfection.

Democrat FUSION $$
(Crab Market; mains US$5-10; ⌚11am-10.30pm; 📶) The Democrat is part of a wave of slightly more upscale eateries that are gradually moving in on the crab market scene. The crab cakes and crab *amok* are winners, and epitomise the more refined cuisine. Great drinks (two-for-one at happy hour), and you gotta love the randomness of the US-president theme (though no photos of Trump quite yet).

Led Zep Cafe CAFE
(Kep National Park; ⌚9.30am-6pm) A lovely, secluded cafe on the Kep National Park trail. Knocking back a chilled lime juice on the wide terrace with knock-out views overlooking the coast is the perfect pick-me-up after a hike. It is prone to closing at random times, however, especially in the low season.

ℹ Information

There's no bank in Kep but there is an ABA Bank ATM (⌚24 hr) at Kep Beach.

ℹ Getting There & Around

Kep is 25km from Kampot and 41km from the Prek Chak–Xa Xia border crossing to Vietnam.

Buses stop at Kep Beach in front of a line of travel agencies and minivan offices. You can purchase tickets here or from most guesthouses.

Phnom Penh Sorya (☎023-210359) buses head to Phnom Penh at 7.45am, 9.30am and 1.30pm (US$5, four hours), while **Vibol Transport** (Kep Beach Rd) buses to the capital depart at

GETTING TO VIETNAM: KEP TO HA TIEN

Getting to the border The Prek Chak/Xa Xia border crossing has become a popular option for linking Kampot and Kep with Ha Tien, and then onwards to either the popular Vietnamese island of Phu Quoc, or to Ho Chi Minh City.

The easiest way to get to Prek Chak (⌚6am to 5.30pm) and on to Ha Tien, Vietnam, is to catch a minivan from Sihanoukville (US$12, 3½ hours), Kampot (US$8, 1½ hours), or Kep (US$7, 45 minutes). Kampot Tours & Travel (p270), Anny Tours (p275) and Champa Mekong Tourist Bus (p275) run this service with no change of vehicles at the border.

A more flexible alternative from Phnom Penh or Kampot is to take any bus to Kompong Trach, then a *moto* (about US$3) for 15km, on a good road, to the border.

In Kep, guesthouses can arrange a direct *remork* (US$13, one hour) or taxi (US$20, 30 minutes). Rates and times are almost double from Kampot. Private vehicles take a new road that cuts south to the border 10km west of Kompong Trach.

At the border Vietnam grants 15-day visas on arrival for nationals of several European and Asian countries. Other nationalities, and anyone staying longer than 15 days, must purchase a visa in advance.

At Prek Chak, *motos* ask US$5 to take you to the Vietnamese border post 300m past the Cambodian one, and then all the way to Ha Tien (15 minutes, 7km). You'll save money walking across no-man's land and picking up a *moto* on the other side for US$2 to US$3.

Moving on Travellers bound for Phu Quoc should arrive in Ha Tien no later than 12.30pm to secure a ticket on the 1pm ferry (230,000d or about US$11, 1½ hours). Extreme early risers may be able to make it to Ha Tien in time to catch the 8am ferry. The morning minivans from Cambodia to Ha Tien arrive before the 1pm boat departs.

8am and 1pm. **Anny Tours** (036-652 3999; Kep Beach Rd; 6am-9pm) runs minivans to Phnom Penh (US$8, three hours, 8am and 3pm). A private taxi to Phnom Penh costs US$40 to US$45.

Anny Tours and **Champa Mekong Tourist Bus** (088 727 7277; Kep Beach Rd; 6.30am-8pm) each send minivans over the border to Ha Tien in Vietnam twice daily (US$7, 45 minutes). Ha Tien–bound minivans run by Kampot Tours & Travel (p270) out of Kampot also stop through Kep. Going the other way, the same three companies serve Sihanoukville two or three times daily, with a van change in Kampot (US$7, 3½ hours), and also serve Koh Kong with several van transfers.

For Kampot, take a remork (US$10, 45 minutes), the sunset Crab Shuttle (088 829 6644; crab-shuttle@gmail.com; closed Jun-Sep) boat trip (US$10, two hours, 4pm) or any eastbound bus or minivan. There are very few *moto* drivers in town.

Motorbike rental is US$5 to US$7 per day; ask your guesthouse or any travel agency.

UNDERSTAND CAMBODIA

Cambodia Today

The political landscape shifted dramatically in the 2013 election, with major opposition gains adding up to some interesting times for Cambodia as it heads towards the next general election in 2018. The economy continues to grow at a dramatic pace, albeit from what was 'Year Zero' just a few decades ago, but many observers are beginning to question at what cost to the delicate environment.

The Cambodian People's Party (CPP) has dominated the politics of Cambodia since 1979 when it was installed in power by the Vietnamese. Party and state are intertwined and the CPP leadership has been making plans for the future with dynastic alliances between its offspring.

However, this control was shaken in the last election when long-standing opposition leader Sam Rainsy joined with Human Rights Party leader Kem Sokha to launch the Cambodia National Rescue Party (CNRP). While official results from the National Election Commission confirmed a CPP victory, official opposition counts suggested the CNRP may have actually won the popular vote by a slight majority.

With opposition support officially hovering around the 50% mark, some of the official media may need to change its tune to remain in touch with the popular mood. Opposition demonstrations or antigovernment activities are rarely reported via CPP-dominated official channels. However, social media is plugging the gap and a new generation of young Cambodians are avid Facebook and YouTube users.

Cambodia's economy was long a gecko amid the neighbouring dragons. This has slowly started to change, as the economy has been liberalised and investors are circling to take advantage of the new opportunities. Yet Cambodia remains one of Asia's poorest countries and income is desperately low for many families. Other heated topics include the shared border with Vietnam and land reform. When it comes to land issues, it is ironic that the former communist, Hun Sen, is backing the elite tycoons, and the ex-banker, Sam Rainsy, is backing the masses with a land-redistribution scheme. Such is Cambodia, an enigmatic land of confusion and contradictions.

History

'The good, the bad and the ugly' is a simple way to sum up Cambodian history. Things were good in the early years, culminating in the vast Angkor empire, unrivalled in the region during four centuries of dominance. Then the bad set in, from the 13th century, as ascendant neighbours steadily chipped away at Cambodian territory. In the 20th century it turned downright ugly, as a brutal civil war culminated in the genocidal rule of the Khmer Rouge (1975–79), from which Cambodia is still recovering today.

Funan & Chenla

The Indianisation of Cambodia began in the 1st century AD as traders plying the sea route from the Bay of Bengal to southern China brought Indian ideas and technologies to what is now southern Vietnam.The largest of the era's nascent kingdoms, known to the Chinese as Funan, embraced the worship of the Hindu deities Shiva and Vishnu and, at the same time, Buddhism. From the 6th to 8th centuries Cambodia seems to have been ruled by a collection of competing kingdoms. Chinese annals refer to 'Water Chenla', apparently the area around the modern-day town of Takeo, and 'Land Chenla', further north along the Mekong and around Sambor Prei Kuk.

Rise & Fall of Angkor

The Angkorian era lasted from AD 802 to 1432, encompassing periods of conquest, turmoil and retreat, revival and decline, and fits of remarkable productivity. In 802, Jayavarman II (reigned c 802–50) proclaimed himself a *devaraja* (god-king). He instigated an uprising against Javanese domination of southern Cambodia and, through alliances and conquests, brought the country under his control, becoming the first monarch to rule most of what we now call Cambodia.

In the 9th century, Yasovarman I (r 889–910) moved the capital to Angkor, creating a new centre for worship, scholarship and the arts. After a period of turmoil and conflict, Suryavarman II (r 1113–52) unified the kingdom and embarked on another phase of territorial expansion, waging successful but costly wars against both Vietnam and Champa (an Indianised kingdom that occupied what is now southern and central Vietnam). His devotion to the Hindu deity Vishnu inspired him to commission Angkor Wat. The tables soon turned. Champa struck back in 1177 with a naval expedition up the Mekong, taking Angkor by surprise and putting the king to death. But the following year a cousin of Suryavarman II – soon crowned Jayavarman VII (r 1181–1219) – rallied the Khmers and defeated the Chams in another epic naval battle. A devout follower of Mahayana Buddhism, it was he who built the city of Angkor Thom. During the twilight years of the empire, religious conflict and internecine rivalries were rife. The Thais made repeated incursions into Angkor, sacking the city in 1351 and again in 1431, and from the royal court making off with thousands of intellectuals, artisans and dancers, whose profound impact on Thai culture can be seen to this day. From 1600 until the arrival of the French, Cambodia was ruled by a series of weak kings whose intrigues often involved seeking the protection of either Thailand or Vietnam – granted, of course, at a price.

French Colonisation

The era of yo-yoing between Thai and Vietnamese masters came to a close in 1864, when French gunboats intimidated King Norodom I (r 1860–1904) into signing a treaty of protectorate. An exception in the annals of colonialism, the French presence really did protect the country at a time when it was in danger of being swallowed by its more powerful neighbours.

In 1907 the French pressured Thailand into returning the northwest provinces of Battambang, Siem Reap and Sisophon, bringing Angkor under Cambodian control for the first time in more than a century.

Led by King Norodom Sihanouk (r 1941–55 and 1993–2004), Cambodia declared independence on 9 November 1953.

Independence & Civil War

The period after 1953 was one of peace and prosperity, and a time of creativity and optimism. Dark clouds were circling, however, as the war in Vietnam began sucking in neighbouring countries. As the 1960s drew to a close, the North Vietnamese and the Viet Cong were using Cambodian territory in their battle against South Vietnam and US forces, prompting devastating American bombing and a land invasion into eastern Cambodia.

In March 1970 Sihanouk, now serving as prime minister, was overthrown by General Lon Nol, and took up residence in Beijing. Here he set up a government in exile that allied itself with an indigenous Cambodian revolutionary movement that Sihanouk had dubbed the Khmer Rouge. This was a defining moment in contemporary Cambodian history: talk to many former Khmer Rouge fighters and they all say that they 'went to the hills' to fight for their monarch and knew nothing of Marxism or Mao.

Khmer Rouge Rule

Upon taking Phnom Penh on 17 April 1975 – two weeks before the fall of Saigon – the Khmer Rouge implemented one of the most radical and brutal restructurings of a society ever attempted. Its goal was to transform Cambodia – renamed Democratic Kampuchea – into a giant peasant-dominated agrarian cooperative, untainted by anything that had come before. Within days, the entire populations of Phnom Penh and provincial towns, including the sick, elderly and infirm, were forced to march into the countryside and work as slaves for 12 to 15 hours a day. Intellectuals were systematically wiped out – having glasses or speaking a foreign language was reason enough to be killed. The advent of Khmer Rouge rule was proclaimed Year Zero.

Leading the Khmer Rouge was Saloth Sar, better known as Pol Pot. As a young man, he won a scholarship to study in Paris, where he began developing the radical Marxist ideas that later metamorphosed into extreme Maoism. Under his rule, Cambodia became a vast slave-labour camp. Meals consisted of little more than watery rice porridge twice a day, meant to sustain men, women and children through a back-breaking day in the fields. Disease stalked the work camps, malaria and dysentery striking down whole families.

Khmer Rouge rule was brought to an end by the Vietnamese, who liberated the almost empty city of Phnom Penh on 7 January 1979. It is estimated that at least 1.7 million people perished at the hands of Pol Pot and his followers. The Documentation Center of Cambodia (p182) records the horrific events of the period.

A Sort of Peace

The Vietnamese installed a new government led by several former Khmer Rouge officers, including current prime minister Hun Sen, who had defected to Vietnam in 1977. In the dislocation that followed liberation, little rice was planted or harvested, leading to a massive famine. The Khmer Rouge continued to wage civil war from remote mountain bases near the Thai border throughout the 1980s. In September 1989 Vietnam, its economy in tatters and eager to end its international isolation, announced the withdrawal of all its forces from Cambodia.

In February 1991 all parties – including the Khmer Rouge – signed the Paris Peace Accords, according to which the UN Transitional Authority in Cambodia (Untac) would rule the country for two years. Although Untac is still heralded as one of the UN's success stories (elections with a 90% turnout were held in 1993), to many Cambodians who had survived the 1970s it was unthinkable that the Khmer Rouge was allowed to play a part in the process. The Khmer Rouge ultimately pulled out before polling began, but the smokescreen of the elections allowed them to re-establish a guerrilla network throughout Cambodia. Untac is also remembered for causing a significant increase in prostitution and HIV/AIDS.

The last Khmer Rouge hold-outs, including Ta Mok, were not defeated until the capture of Anlong Veng and Prasat Preah Vihear by government forces in the spring of 1998. Pol Pot cheated justice by dying a sorry death near Anlong Veng during that year, and was cremated on a pile of old tyres.

People & Culture

Population

About 16 million people live in Cambodia. According to official statistics, more than 90% of the people who live in Cambodia are ethnic Khmers, making the country the most ethnically homogeneous in Southeast Asia. However, unofficially, the figure is probably smaller due to a large influx of Chinese and Vietnamese in the past century. Other ethnic minorities include Cham, Lao and the indigenous peoples of the rural highlands. Cambodia's diverse Khmer Leu (Upper Khmer) or *chunchiet* (ethnic minorities), who live in the country's mountainous regions, probably number around 100,000.

The official language is Khmer, spoken by 95% of the population. English has taken over from French as the second language of choice, although Chinese is also growing in popularity. Life expectancy is currently 62 years.

Lifestyle

For many older Cambodians, life is centred on family, faith and food, an existence that has stayed the same for centuries. Families stick together, solve problems collectively, listen to the wisdom of the elders and pool resources. The extended family comes together during times of trouble and times of joy, celebrating festivals and successes, mourning deaths and disappointments. Whether the Cambodian house is big or small, there will be a lot of people living inside.

For the majority of the population still living in the countryside, these constants carry on as they always have: several generations sharing the same roof, the same rice and the same religion. But during the dark decades of the 1970s and 1980s, this routine was ripped apart by war and ideology, as the peasants were dragged into a bloody civil war and later forced into slavery. The Khmer Rouge organisation Angkar took over as the moral and social beacon in the lives of the people. Families were forced apart, children turned against parents, brothers against sisters. The bond of trust was broken and is only slowly being rebuilt today.

For the younger generation, brought up in a postconflict, postcommunist period of relative freedom, it's a different story – arguably thanks to their steady diet of MTV and steamy soaps. Cambodia is experiencing its very own '60s swing, as the younger generation stands ready for a different lifestyle to the one their parents had to swallow. This creates plenty of friction in the cities, as rebellious teens dress as they like, date whoever they wish and hit the town until all hours. More recently this generational conflict spilled over into politics as the Facebook generation helped deliver a shock result that saw the governing Cambodian People's Party (CPP) majority slashed in half.

Cambodia is set for major demographic shifts in the next couple of decades. Currently, just 20% of the population lives in urban areas, which contrasts starkly with the country's more developed neighbours, such as Malaysia and Thailand. Increasing numbers of young people are likely to migrate to the cities in search of opportunity, forever changing the face of contemporary Cambodian society. However, for now at least, Cambodian society remains much more traditional than that of Thailand and Vietnam, and visitors need to keep this in mind.

Religion

The majority of Khmers (95%) follow the Theravada branch of Buddhism. Buddhism in Cambodia draws heavily on its predecessors, incorporating many cultural traditions from Hinduism for ceremonies such as birth, marriage and death, as well as genies and spirits, such as Neak Ta, which link back to a pre-Indian animist past.

Under the Khmer Rouge, the majority of Cambodia's Buddhist monks were murdered and nearly all of the country's wats (more than 3000) were damaged or destroyed. In the late 1980s, Buddhism once again became the state religion.

Other religions found in Cambodia are Islam, practised by the Cham community; animism, among the hill tribes; and Christianity, which is making inroads via missionaries and Christian NGOs.

Arts

The Khmer Rouge regime not only killed the living bearers of Khmer culture, it also destroyed cultural artefacts, statues, musical instruments, books and anything else that served as a reminder of a past it was trying to efface. The temples of Angkor were spared as a symbol of Khmer glory and empire, but little else survived. Despite this, Cambodia is witnessing a resurgence of traditional arts and a growing interest in cross-cultural fusion.

Cambodia's royal ballet is a tangible link with the glory of Angkor and includes a unique *apsara* (heavenly nymphs) dance. Cambodian music, too, goes back at least as far as Angkor. To get some sense of the music that Jayavarman VII used to like, check out the bas-reliefs at Angkor Wat.

In the mid-20th century a vibrant Cambodian pop music scene developed, but it was killed off (literally) by the Khmer Rouge. After the war, overseas Khmers established a pop industry in the USA and some Cambodian Americans, raised on a diet of rap, are now returning to their homeland. The Los Angeles–based sextet Dengue Fever, inspired by 1960s Cambodian pop and psychedelic rock, is the ultimate fusion band.

The people of Cambodia were producing masterfully sensuous sculptures – much more than mere copies of Indian forms – in the age of Funan and Chenla. The Banteay Srei style of the late 10th century is regarded as a high point in the evolution of Southeast Asian art.

Food & Drink

Some traditional Cambodian dishes are similar to those of neighbouring Laos and Thailand (though not as spicy), others closer to Chinese and Vietnamese cooking. The French left their mark, too.

Thanks to the Tonlé Sap, freshwater fish – often *ahng* (grilled) – are a huge part of the Cambodian diet. The great national dish, *amok*, is fish baked with coconut and lemon grass in banana leaves. *Prahoc* (fermented fish paste) is used to flavour foods, with coconut and lemon grass making regular cameos.

A proper Cambodian meal almost always includes *samlor* (soup), served at the same time as other courses. *Kyteow* is a rice-noodle soup that will keep you going all day. *Bobor* (rice porridge), eaten for breakfast, lunch or dinner, is best sampled with some fresh fish and a dash of ginger.

Beer is immensely popular in the cities, while rural folk drink palm wine, tapped from the sugar palms that dot the landscape.

Tukaloks (fruit shakes) are mixed with milk, sugar and sometimes a raw egg.

Tap water *must* be avoided, especially in rural areas. Bottled water is widely available but coconut milk, sold by machete-wielding street vendors, is more ecological and may be more sterile.

Environment

The Land

Cambodia's two dominant geographical features are the mighty Mekong River and a vast lake, the Tonlé Sap. The rich sediment deposited during the Mekong's annual wet-season flooding has made central Cambodia incredibly fertile. This low-lying alluvial plain is where the vast majority of Cambodians live – fishing and farming in harmony with the rhythms of the monsoon.

In Cambodia's southwest quadrant, much of the land mass is covered by the Cardamom Mountains and, near Kampot, the Elephant Mountains. Along Cambodia's northern border with Thailand, the plains collide with the Dangkrek Mountains, a striking sandstone escarpment more than 300km long and up to 550m high. One of the best places to get a sense of this area is Prasat Preah Vihear.

In the northeastern corner of the country, in the provinces of Ratanakiri and Mondulkiri, the plains give way to the Eastern Highlands, a remote region of densely forested mountains and high plateaus.

Wildlife

Cambodia's forest ecosystems were in excellent shape until the 1990s and, compared with its neighbours, its habitats are still relatively healthy. The years of war took their toll on some species, but others thrived in the remote jungles of the southwest and northeast. Ironically, peace brought increased threats as loggers felled huge areas of primary forest and the illicit trade in wildlife targeted endangered species. Due to years of inaccessibility, scientists have only relatively recently managed to research and catalogue the country's plant and animal life.

Still, with more than 200 species of mammal, Cambodia has some of Southeast Asia's best wildlife-watching opportunities. Highlights include spotting gibbons and black-shanked doucs in Ratanakiri and Mondulkiri provinces, and viewing some of the last remaining freshwater Irrawaddy dolphins in Kratie and Stung Treng provinces.

Globally threatened species that you stand a slight chance of seeing include the Asian elephant, banteng (a wild ox), gaur, clouded leopard, fishing cat, marbled cat, sun bear, Siamese crocodile and pangolin. Asian tigers were once commonplace but are now exceedingly rare – the last sighting was in about 2007.

The country is a birdwatcher's paradise – feathered friends found almost exclusively in Cambodia include the giant ibis, white-shouldered ibis, Bengal florican, sarus crane and three species of vulture. The Siem Reap–based Sam Veasna Center (p208) runs birding trips.

Environmental Issues

Cambodia's pristine environment is a big draw for adventurous ecotourists, but much of it is currently under threat. Ancient forests are being razed to make way for plantations, rivers are being sized up for major hydroelectric power plants and the south coast is being explored by leading oil companies. Places like the Cardamom Mountains are in the front line and it remains to be seen whether the environmentalists or the economists will win the debate.

The greatest threat is illegal logging, carried out to provide charcoal and timber, and to clear land for cash-crop plantations. The environmental watchdog Global Witness (www.globalwitness.org) publishes meticulously documented exposés on corrupt military and civilian officials and their well-connected business partners.

In the short term, deforestation is contributing to worsening floods along the Mekong, but the long-term implications of deforestation are mind-boggling. Siltation, combined with overfishing and pollution, may lead to the eventual death of Tonlé Sap lake, a catastrophe for future generations of Cambodians.

Throughout Cambodia pollution is a problem, and detritus of all sorts, especially plastic bags and bottles, can be seen in distressing quantities all over the country.

The latest environmental threat to emerge are dams on the Mekong River. Environmentalists fear that damming the mainstream Mekong may disrupt the flow patterns of the river and the migratory patterns of fish (including the critically endangered freshwater Irrawaddy dolphin). Work on the Don

Sahong (Siphandone) Dam just north of the Cambodia–Laos border has begun, and plans under consideration include the Sambor Dam, a massive 3300MW project 35km north of Kratie.

SURVIVAL GUIDE

Directory A–Z

ACCOMMODATION

Accommodation is great value in Cambodia, just like the rest of the Mekong region. In popular tourist destinations, budget guesthouses generally charge US$5 to US$8 for a room with a cold-water bathroom. Double rooms go as low as US$3 for a room with shared facilities. Dorm beds usually cost US$2 to US$3. Rooms with air-con start at US$10. Spend US$15 or US$20 and you'll be living in style. Spend US$30 and up and we're talking boutique quality with a swimming pool. At the top end you can spend several hundred dollars a night on international-standard luxury digs in Siem Reap and Phnom Penh.

Accommodation is busiest from mid-November to March. There are substantial low-season (May to October) rates available at major hotels in Phnom Penh, Siem Reap and Sihanoukville (although you can only discount a US$5 room so much).

Homestays, often part of a community-based ecotourism project, are a good way to meet the local people and learn about Cambodian life. The Cambodia Community Based Ecotourism Network (CCBEN) has information on various ecotourism opportunities in Cambodia.

Price Ranges

The following price ranges refer to a double room in high season. Prices in Phnom Penh and Siem Reap tend to be higher.

$ less than US$25

$$ US$25–80

$$$ more than US$80

ACTIVITIES

Cambodia is steadily emerging as an ecotourism destination. Activities on offer include the following:

- Rainforest trekking in Ratanakiri, Mondulkiri and the Cardamom Mountains of the south coast;
- Elephant treks or walking with elephants in Mondulkiri;
- Scuba diving and snorkelling near Sihanoukville;
- Cycling around Phnom Penh, in Mondulkiri, along the Mekong Discovery Trail between Kratie and Stung Treng, and around the temples of Angkor; and,
- Adventurous dirt biking all over the country (for those with some experience).

BOOKS

A whole bookcase-worth of volumes examines Cambodia's recent history, including the French colonial period, the spillover of the war in Vietnam into Cambodia, the Khmer Rouge years and the wild 1990s. The best include the following:

Hun Sen's Cambodia (Sebastian Strangio; 2014) A no-holds-barred look at contemporary Cambodia and the rule of Prime Minister Hun Sen.

The Gate (François Bizot; 2003) Bizot was kidnapped by the Khmer Rouge, and later held by them in the French embassy.

Voices from S-21 (David Chandler; 2000) A study of the Khmer Rouge's interrogation and torture centre.

Cambodia's Curse (Joel Brinkley; 2011) Pulitzer Prize–winning journalist pulls no punches in his criticism of the government and donors alike.

CUSTOMS REGULATIONS

- A 'reasonable amount' of duty-free items is allowed into the country.
- Alcohol and cigarettes are on sale at well-below duty-free prices on the streets of Phnom Penh.
- It is illegal to take antiquities out of the country.

ELECTRICITY

The usual voltage is 220V, 50 cycles, but power surges and power cuts are common, particularly in the provinces. Electrical sockets are usually two-prong, mostly flat but sometimes round pin.

EMBASSIES & CONSULATES

Many countries now have embassies in Phnom Penh, though some travellers will find that their nearest embassy is in Bangkok.

In genuine emergencies assistance may be available, but only if all other channels have been exhausted. If you have all your money and documents stolen, the embassy can assist with getting a new passport, but a loan for onward travel is out of the question.

Australian Embassy (Map p192; ☎ 023-213470; 16 National Assembly St, Phnom Penh)

Chinese Embassy (Map p182; ☎ 023-720920; 256 Mao Tse Toung Blvd, Phnom Penh)

French Embassy (Map p182; ☎ 023-430020; 1 Monivong Blvd, Phnom Penh)

German Embassy (Map p192; ☎023-216381; 76-78 St 214, Phnom Penh)

Indian Embassy (Map p182; ☎023-210912; 5 St 466, Phnom Penh)

Indonesian Embassy (Map p182; ☎023-217934; 1 St 466, Phnom Penh)

Japanese Embassy (Map p182; ☎023-217161; 194 Norodom Blvd, Phnom Penh)

Lao Embassy (Map p182; ☎023-997931; 15-17 Mao Tse Toung Blvd, Phnom Penh)

Malaysian Embassy (Map p182; ☎023-216177; 220 Norodom Blvd, Phnom Penh)

Myanmar Embassy (Map p182; ☎023-223761; 181 Norodom Blvd, Phnom Penh)

Philippine Embassy (Map p182; ☎023-222303; 128 Norodom Blvd, Phnom Penh)

Singaporean Embassy (Map p192; ☎023-221875; 92 Norodom Blvd, Phnom Penh)

Thai Embassy (Map p182; ☎023-726306; 196 Norodom Blvd, Phnom Penh)

UK Embassy (Map p182; ☎023-427124; 27-29 St 75, Phnom Penh)

US Embassy (Map p184; ☎023-728000; 1 St 96, Phnom Penh)

Vietnamese Embassy (Map p182; ☎023-726274; 436 Monivong Blvd, Phnom Penh) Also has consulates in **Battambang** (☎053-952894; St 3, Battambang; ⏲8.30am-5.30pm Mon-Fri), issuing visas in a day; and **Sihanoukville** (Map p256; ☎034-934039; 310 Ekareach St, Sihanoukville; ⏲8am-noon & 2-4pm Mon-Sat), also with speedy visa processing.

FOOD

The following price ranges refer to a standard main course. Unless otherwise stated, tax is included in the price.

$ less than US$5

$$ US$5–15

$$$ more than US$15

INSURANCE

Health insurance is essential. Make sure your policy covers emergency evacuation: limited medical facilities mean that you may have to be airlifted to Bangkok in the event of serious injury or illness.

Worldwide travel insurance is available at www.lonelyplanet.com/travel-insurance. You can buy, extend and claim online anytime – even if you're already on the road.

INTERNET ACCESS

Internet access is widespread, but there are not as many internet shops as there used to be now that wi-fi is more prevalent. Charges range from 1500r to US$2 per hour. Many hotels, guesthouses, restaurants and cafes now offer free wi-fi, even in the most out-of-the-way provincial capitals.

LEGAL MATTERS

All narcotics, including marijuana, are illegal in Cambodia. However, marijuana is traditionally used in food preparation so you may find it sprinkled across some pizzas.

Many Western countries have laws that make sex offences committed overseas punishable at home.

LGBTIQ TRAVELLERS

While Cambodian culture is tolerant of homosexuality, the gay and lesbian scene here is certainly nothing like that in Thailand. Former king Norodom Sihanouk was a keen supporter of equal rights for same-sex partners and this seems to have encouraged a more open attitude among younger Cambodians. Both Phnom Penh and Siem Reap have a few gay-friendly bars, but it's a low-key scene compared with some parts of Asia.

With the vast number of same-sex travel partners – gay or otherwise – checking into hotels across Cambodia, there is little consideration over how travelling foreigners are related. As with heterosexual couples, passionate public displays of affection are considered a basic no-no.

Recommended websites when planning a trip:

Cambodia Gay (www.cambodia-gay.com) Promoting the GLBT community in Cambodia.

Siem Reap Gay Guide (www.thesiemreapgayguide.com) Also produces a free printed guide.

Sticky Rice (www.stickyrice.ws) Gay travel guide covering Cambodia and Asia.

Utopia (www.utopia-asia.com) Gay travel information and contacts, including some local gay terminology.

MAPS

The best all-round map is Gecko's *Cambodia Road Map* at a 1:750,000 scale.

MONEY

Cambodia's currency is the riel, abbreviated in our listings to a lower-case 'r' written after the sum. The US dollar is accepted everywhere and by everyone, though change may arrive in riel (handy when paying for things such as *moto* rides and drinks). When calculating change, the US dollar is usually rounded off to 4000r. Near the Thai border, many transactions are in Thai baht. Avoid ripped banknotes, which Cambodians often refuse.

ATMs

There are credit-card-compatible ATMs (Visa, MasterCard, JCB, Cirrus) in most major cities.

There are also ATMs at the Cham Yeam, Poipet and Bavet borders if arriving by land from Thailand or Vietnam. Machines usually give you the option of withdrawing in US dollars or riel. Single withdrawals of up to US$500 at a time are usually possible, providing your account can handle it. Stay alert when using ATMs late at night.

ANZ Royal Bank has the most extensive network, including ATMs at petrol stations, and popular hotels, restaurants and shops, closely followed by Canadia Bank. Acleda Bank has the widest network of branches in the country, including all provincial capitals, but their ATMs are less reliable and generally only take Visa-affiliated cards. Most ATM withdrawals incur a charge of US$5, but ABA Bank offers free withdrawals.

Bargaining

Bargaining is expected in local markets, when travelling by share taxi or *moto* and, sometimes, when taking a cheap room. The Khmers are not ruthless hagglers, so a persuasive smile and a little friendly quibbling is usually enough to get a good price.

Credit Cards

Top-end hotels, airline offices and upmarket boutiques and restaurants generally accept most major credit cards (Visa, MasterCard, JCB, sometimes American Express), but they usually pass the charges on to the customer, meaning an extra 3% or more on the bill.

Cash advances on credit cards are relatively easy to secure.

Tipping

Tipping is not traditionally expected here, but in a country as poor as Cambodia, a dollar tip (or 5% to 10% on bigger bills) can go a long way.

OPENING HOURS

Everything shuts down during the major holidays: Chaul Chnam Khmer (Khmer New Year), P'chum Ben (Festival of the Dead) and Chaul Chnam Chen (Chinese New Year).

Banks 8am to 3.30pm Monday to Friday, Saturday mornings

Bars 5pm to late

Government offices 7.30 to 11.30am and 2 to 5pm Monday to Friday

Museums Hours vary, but usually open seven days a week

Restaurants (international) 7am to 10pm or meal times

Restaurants (local) 6.30am to 9pm

Shops 8am to 6pm daily

Local markets 6.30am to 5.30pm daily

POST

The postal service is hit and miss from Cambodia; send anything valuable by courier or from another country. Ensure postcards and letters are franked before they vanish from your sight.

Letters and parcels sent further afield than Asia can take up to two or three weeks to reach their destination. Use a courier to speed things up; **EMS** (☎ 023-723511; www.ems.com.kh; Main Post Office, St 13, Phnom Penh) has branches at every major post office in the country. DHL and Fed Ex are present in major cities like Phnom Penh, Siem Reap and Sihanoukville.

PUBLIC HOLIDAYS

Banks, ministries and embassies close down during public holidays and festivals, so plan ahead if visiting Cambodia during these times. Cambodians also roll over holidays if they fall on a weekend and take a day or two extra during major festivals. Add to this the fact that they take a holiday for international days here and there, and it soon becomes apparent that Cambodia has more public holidays than any other nation on earth!

International New Year's Day 1 January

Victory over the Genocide 7 January

International Women's Day 8 March

International Workers' Day 1 May

International Children's Day 8 May

King's Birthday 13–15 May

King Mother's Birthday 18 June

Constitution Day 24 September

Commemoration Day 15 October

Independence Day 9 November

International Human Rights Day 10 December

SAFE TRAVEL

Crime

Given the number of guns in Cambodia, there is less armed theft than one might expect. Still, hold-ups and drive-by theft by motorcycle-riding tandems are a potential danger in Phnom Penh and Sihanoukville. There is no need to be paranoid, just cautious. Walking or riding alone late at night is not ideal, certainly not in rural areas.

There have been incidents of bag snatching in Phnom Penh in the last few years and the motorbike thieves don't let go, dragging passengers off *motos* (motorcycle taxis) and endangering lives. Smartphones are a particular target, so avoid using your smartphone in public, especially at night, as you'll be susceptible to drive-by thieves.

Should anyone be unlucky enough to be robbed, it is important to note that the Cambodian police are the best that money can buy! Any help, such as a police report, is going to cost you. The going rate depends on the size of the claim, but anywhere from US$5 to US$50 is a common charge.

Violence against foreigners is extremely rare, but it pays to take care in crowded bars or nightclubs in Phnom Penh. If you get into a stand-off with rich young Khmers in a bar or club, swallow your pride and back down. Many carry guns and have an entourage of bodyguards.

Drugs

Watch out for *yaba*, the 'crazy' drug from Thailand, known rather ominously in Cambodia as *yama* (the Hindu god of death). Known as ice or crystal meth elsewhere, it's not just any old diet pill from the pharmacist but homemade meta-amphetamines produced in labs in Cambodia and the region beyond. The pills are often laced with toxic substances, such as mercury, lithium or whatever else the maker can find. *Yama* is a dirty drug and more addictive than users would like to admit, provoking powerful hallucinations, sleep deprivation and psychosis. Steer clear of the stuff unless you plan on an indefinite extension to your trip.

Also be very careful about buying 'cocaine' in Cambodia. Most of what is sold as coke, particularly in Phnom Penh, is actually pure heroin and far stronger than what may be found elsewhere.

Mines, Mortars & Bombs

Never touch any rockets, artillery shells, mortars, mines, bombs or other war material you may come across. The most heavily mined part of the country is along the Thai border area, but mines are a problem in much of Cambodia. In short: *do not stray from well-marked paths under any circumstances*. If you are planning any walks, even in safer areas such as the remote northeast, it is imperative you take a guide as there may still be unexploded ordnance (UXO) from the American bombing campaign of the early 1970s.

Scams

Most scams are fairly harmless, involving a bit of commission here and there for taxi or *moto* (unmarked motorcycle taxi) drivers, particularly in Siem Reap.

There have been one or two reports of police set-ups in Phnom Penh, involving planted drugs. This seems to be very rare, but if you fall victim to the ploy, it may be best to pay them off before more police get involved at the local station, as the price will only rise when there are more mouths to feed.

There is quite a lot of fake medication floating about the region. Safeguard yourself by only buying prescription drugs from reliable pharmacies or clinics.

Beware the Filipino blackjack scam: don't get involved in any gambling with seemingly friendly Filipinos unless you want to part with plenty of cash.

Beggars in places such as Phnom Penh and Siem Reap may ask for milk powder for an infant in arms. Some foreigners succumb to the urge to help, but the beggars usually request the most expensive milk formula available and return it to the shop to split the proceeds after the handover.

Traffic Accidents

Traffic in Cambodia is chaotic, with vehicles moving in both directions on both sides of the road. Get in a serious accident in a remote area and somehow you'll have to make it to Phnom Penh, Siem Reap or Battambang for treatment. The horn is used to alert other drivers to a vehicle's presence – when walking, cycling or on a motorbike, get out of the way if you hear one honking behind you.

TELEPHONE

To place a long-distance domestic call from a landline, or to dial a mobile (cell) number, dial zero, the area code (or mobile prefix) and the number. Leave out the zero and the area code if you are making a local call. Drop the zero from the mobile prefix or regional (city) code when dialling into Cambodia from another country.

For telephone listings of businesses and government offices, check out www.yp.com.kh.

Country code ☎855
International Access Code ☎001

Mobile phones, whose numbers start with 01, 06, 07, 08 or 09, are hugely popular with both individuals and commercial enterprises.

When travelling with a mobile phone on international roaming, just select a network upon arrival, dial away and await a hefty phone bill once you return home. Note to self: Cambodian roaming charges are extraordinarily high.

Those who plan on spending longer in Cambodia should arrange a SIM card for one of the local service providers. Foreigners need to present a valid passport to get a local SIM card, but they are available free on arrival at Phnom Penh and Siem Reap international airports.

Most mobile companies now offer cheap internet-based phone calls accessed through a gateway number. Look up the cheap prefix and calls will be just US10¢ or less per minute.

TIME

Cambodia is in the Indochina time zone, which means GMT/UTC plus seven hours. Thus, noon in Phnom Penh is midnight the previous day in New York, 5am in London, 1pm in Hong Kong and 3pm in Sydney. There is no daylight saving time.

TRAVELLERS WITH DISABILITIES

Broken pavements, potholed roads and stairs as steep as ladders at Angkor ensure that for most people with mobility impairments, Cambodia is not going to be an easy country in which to travel. Few buildings have been designed with people with a disability in mind, although new projects, such as the international airports at Phnom Penh and Siem Reap, and top-end hotels, include ramps for wheelchair access. Transport in the provinces is usually very overcrowded, but taxi hire from point to point is an affordable option.

There is a growing network of information sources that can put you in touch with others who have wheeled through Cambodia before. Try contacting the following organisations:

Disability Rights UK (www.disabilityrightsuk.org)

Mobility International USA (www.miusa.org)

Society for Accessible Travel & Hospitality (SATH; www.sath.org)

Download Lonely Planet's free Accessible Travel guide from http://lptravel.to/AccessibleTravel.

VISAS

Visas on Arrival

➡ A one-month tourist visa costs US$30 on arrival and requires one passport-sized photo. Easily extendable business visas are available for US$35.

➡ Most visitors to Cambodia require a one-month tourist visa (US$30). Most nationalities receive this on arrival at Phnom Penh and Siem Reap airports, and at land borders. If you are carrying an African, South Asian or Middle Eastern passport, there are some exceptions.

➡ One passport-sized photo is required and you'll be 'fined' US$2 if you don't have one. It is also possible to arrange a visa through Cambodian embassies overseas or an online e-visa (US$30, plus a US$7 processing fee) through the Ministry of Foreign Affairs (www.mfaic.gov.kh).

➡ Passport holders from Asean member countries do not require a visa to visit Cambodia.

➡ Travellers are sometimes overcharged when crossing at land borders with Thailand, as immigration officials demand payment in baht and round up the figure considerably. Overcharging is also an issue at the Laos border, but not usually at Vietnam borders. Arranging a visa in advance can help avoid overcharging.

➡ Overstaying a visa currently costs US$5 a day.

E-Visas

However, e-visas are only accepted at Phnom Penh and Siem Reap airports (they are not accepted in Sihanoukville), and at the two main land borders: Bavet/Moc Bai (Vietnam) and Poipet/Aranya Prathet (Thailand).

Visa Extensions

➡ Visa extensions are issued by the large immigration office located directly across the road from Phnom Penh International Airport.

➡ Extensions are easy to arrange, taking just a couple of days. It costs US$45 for one month (for both tourist and business visas), US$75 for three months, US$155 for six months and US$285 for one year (the latter three prices relate to business visas only). It's pretty straightforward to extend business visas ad infinitum. Travel agencies and some motorbike-rental shops in Phnom Penh can help with arrangements, sometimes at a discounted price.

➡ Those seeking work in Cambodia should opt for the business visa (US$35) as it is easily extended for longer periods, including multiple entries and exits. A tourist visa can be extended only once and only for one month, and does not allow for re-entry.

Securing Visas for Neighbouring Countries

Vietnam For visitors continuing to Vietnam, one-month single-entry visas cost US$55 and take two days in Phnom Penh, or just one day via the Vietnamese consulate in Sihanoukville.

Laos Most visitors can obtain a visa on arrival (US$30 to US$42).

Thailand Most visitors do not need a visa.

VOLUNTEERING

Cambodia hosts a huge number of NGOs, some of which do require volunteers from time to time. The best way to find out who is represented in the country is to drop in on the **Cooperation Committee for Cambodia** (CCC; Map p182; ☎023-214152; www.ccc-cambodia.org; 9-11 St 476) in Phnom Penh.

Professional Siem Reap–based organisations helping to place volunteers include **ConCERT** (☎063-963511; www.concertcambodia.org; 560 Phum Stoueng Thmey; ⏰9am-5pm Mon-Fri) and **Globalteer** (☎063-761802; www.globalteer.org); the latter program involves a weekly charge.

WOMEN TRAVELLERS

Foreign women are unlikely to be targeted by local men, and will probably find Khmer men to be courteous and polite. As is the case in many places, walking or riding a bike alone late at night is risky, and if you're planning a trip off the beaten track it would be best to find a travel companion.

Khmer women dress fairly conservatively. It's best to follow suit, particularly when visiting wats. In general, long-sleeved shirts and long trousers or skirts are preferred. It is also worth having trousers for heading out at night on *motos*, as short skirts aren't very practical.

Tampons and sanitary napkins are widely available in the major cities and provincial capitals, but if you are heading into very remote areas for a few days, it is worth having your own supply.

 Getting There & Away

ENTERING CAMBODIA

Most travellers enter Cambodia by plane or bus, but there are also boat connections from Vietnam via the Mekong River. Formalities at Cambodia's two international airports are extremely straightforward. For details on land and river crossings see the chapter on Border Crossings (p536).

AIR

Phnom Penh International Airport (p198) is the gateway to the Cambodian capital, while **Siem Reap International Airport** (p215) serves visitors to the temples of Angkor. Both airports have a good range of services, including restaurants, bars, shops and ATMs. **Sihanoukville International Airport** (p262) currently offers just one international flight, daily to Ho Chi Minh City (Saigon) with the largest domestic carrier, **Cambodia Angkor Air** (www.cambodiaangkorair.com). Note that e-visas are not accepted at Sihanoukville's airport.

Flights to Cambodia are expanding, but most connect only as far as regional capitals. **Thai Airways** (www.thaiair.com) and **Bangkok Airways** (www.bangkokair.com) offer the most daily international flights, all connecting through Bangkok. Cambodia Angkor Air also has connections from Phnom Penh and Siem Reap to Bangkok, Ho Chi Minh City and Guangzhou; and from Phnom Penh to Vientiane and Hanoi. **Vietnam Airlines** (www.vietnamair.com.vn) has several useful connections, including from both Phnom Penh and Siem Reap to both Hanoi and Ho Chi Minh City, as well from Phnom Penh to Vientiane and Siem Reap to Luang Prabang, Danang and Phu Quoc.

Budget airlines have taken off in recent years and are steadily driving down prices. Useful budget airlines include **Air Asia** (www.airasia.com), with daily flights connecting Phnom Penh and Siem Reap to Kuala Lumpur and Bangkok; **Jetstar** (www.jetstar.com), with daily flights from both Phnom Penh and Siem Reap to Singapore; and **Cebu Pacific** (www.cebupacificair.com), with three or four weekly flights from Siem Reap to Manila.

Other regional centres with direct flights to Cambodia include Pakse, Seoul, Taipei, Hong Kong and Shanghai.

 Getting Around

AIR

Domestic flights offer a quick way to travel around the country. The problem is that the airlines themselves seem to come and go pretty quickly as well. There are currently three domestic airlines in Cambodia, operating flights between Phnom Penh and Siem Reap and Siem Reap and Sihanoukville. There are around seven flights a day between Phnom Penh and Siem Reap and it is usually possible to get on a flight at short notice. Book ahead in peak season. There are currently about three flights per day between Siem Reap and Sihanoukville in peak season.

Bassaka Air (☎023-217613; www.bassakaair.com) Offers at least one flight daily between Phnom Penh and Siem Reap and Siem Reap and Sihanoukville.

Cambodia Angkor Air (☎023-212564; www.cambodiaangkorair.com) Offers four flights a day between Phnom Penh and Siem Reap and up to two flights a day between Siem Reap and Sihanoukville. Prices are higher than the competition.

Cambodia Bayon Airlines (☎023-231555; www.bayonairlines.com) Has at least one flight daily between Phnom Penh and Siem Reap and one or two daily flights between Siem Reap and Sihanoukville.

Sky Angkor (www.skyangkorair.com) Has several weekly flights between Siem Reap and Sihanoukville.

BICYCLE

Cambodia is a great country for experienced cyclists to explore. A mountain bike is the recommended set of wheels thanks to the notorious state of the roads. Most roads have a flat unpaved trail along the side, which is useful for cyclists.

Much of Cambodia is pancake flat or only moderately hilly. Safety, however, is a considerable concern on the newer surfaced roads, as local traffic travels at high speed. Bicycles can be transported around the country in the back of pick-ups or on the roof of minibuses.

Guesthouses and hotels in Cambodia rent out bicycles for US$1 to US$2 per day, or US$7 to US$15 for an imported brand such as Giant or Trek.

Top bikes, safety equipment and authentic spare parts are now readily available in Phnom Penh at very reasonable prices.

PEPY Tours (☎023-222804; www.pepytours.com) is a bicycle and volunteer tour company offering adventures throughout Cambodia. PEPY promotes 'adventurous living, responsible giving' and puts funds put back into community education and other projects.

BOAT

Cambodia's 1900km of navigable waterways are not as important as they once were for the average tourist, given major road improvements. North of Phnom Penh, the Mekong is easily navigable as far as Kratie, but there are no longer regular passenger services on these routes, as buses have taken all the business. There are scenic boat services between Siem Reap and Battambang, and the Tonlé Sap lake is also navigable year-round, although only by smaller boats between March and July.

Traditionally the most popular boat services with foreigners are those that run between Phnom Penh and Siem Reap. The express services do the trip in as little as five hours. The first couple hours out of Phnom Penh along the Tonlé Sap River are scenic, but it becomes less interesting when the river morphs into the Tonlé Sap Lake, which is like a vast sea, offering little scenery. It's more popular (and much cheaper) to take a bus on the paved road instead.

The small boat between Siem Reap and Battambang is more rewarding, as the river scenery is truly memorable, but it can take as long as a whole day with delays.

BUS

About a dozen bus companies serve all populated parts of the country. Comfort levels and prices vary wildly, so shop around. Booking bus tickets through guesthouses and travel agents is convenient, but often incurs a commission. Also note that travel agents tend to work with only a handful of preferred companies, thus won't always offer your preferred company and/or departure time, so it pays to shop around.

While it doesn't cover all bus companies, **bookmebus** (www.bookmebus.com) is a reliable bus-ticket booking site, including for more obscure routes (Ban Lung to Siem Reap, anyone?) and cross-border trips.

CAR & MOTORCYCLE

In theory, to drive a car you need a Cambodian licence. Local travel agents and some motorbike renters can arrange these in less than a week for around US$35.

When it comes to renting motorcycles, it's a case of no licence required. If you can drive the bike out of the shop, you can drive it anywhere, or so the logic goes.

Car hire is generally only available with a driver and is most useful for sightseeing around Phnom Penh and Angkor, and for conveniently travelling between cities. Some tourists with a healthy budget also arrange cars or 4WDs with drivers for touring the provinces. Hiring a car with a driver is about US$30 to US$35 for a day in and around Cambodia's towns. Heading into the provinces it rises to US$50 or more, plus petrol, depending on the destination. Hiring 4WDs will cost around US$60 to US$120 a day, depending on the model and the distance travelled. Self-drive car rentals are available in Phnom Penh, but think twice about driving yourself due to chaotic road conditions and personal liability in the case of an accident.

It is possible to explore Cambodia by motorbike. Anyone planning a longer ride should try out the bike around town for a day or so first to make sure it is in good health.

Motorcycles are available for hire in Phnom Penh and other provincial capitals. In Siem Reap motorcycle rental is still technically forbidden, but of late authorities are taking a laxer view and a growing number of places now hire out motorbikes to tourists. It is usually possible to rent a 100cc motorbike for between US$4 and US$10 per day; costs are around US$15 to US$25 for a 250cc dirt bike.

LOCAL TRANSPORT

Taxi hire in towns and cities is getting easier, but there are still very few metered taxis, with just a handful of operators in Phnom Penh. Guesthouses, hotels and travel agents can arrange cars for sightseeing in and around towns.

Cyclo

As in Vietnam and Laos, the *cyclo* (pedicab) is a cheap way to get around urban areas. In Phnom Penh *cyclo* drivers can either be flagged down on main roads or found waiting around markets and major hotels. It is necessary to bargain the fare if taking a *cyclo* from outside an expensive hotel or popular restaurant or bar. Fares range from US$1 to US$3. There are few *cyclos* in the provinces, and in Phnom Penh the *cyclo* has almost been driven to extinction by the *moto*.

Moto

Motos, also known as *motodups* (meaning *moto* driver), are small motorcycle taxis. They are a quick way of making short hops around towns and cities. Prices range from 2000r to US$1.50 or more, depending on the distance and the town; expect to pay more at night. In the past it was rare for prices to be agreed in advance, but with the increase in visitor numbers, a lot of drivers have got into the habit of overcharging. It's probably best to negotiate up front, particularly in the major tourist centres, outside fancy hotels or at night.

Remork

The *remork-moto (tuk-tuk)* is a large trailer hitched to a motorcycle and pretty much operates as a low-tech local bus with oh-so-natural air-conditioning. They are used throughout rural Cambodia to transport people and goods, and are often seen on the edge of towns ready to ferry farmers back to the countryside.

Most popular tourist destinations, including Phnom Penh, Siem Reap and the south coast, have their very own tourist versions of the *remork*, with a canopied trailer hitched to the back of the motorbike for two people in comfort or as many as you can pile on at night. Often referred to as *tuk-tuks* by foreigners travelling in Cambodia, they're a great way to explore temples, as you get the breeze of the bike but some protection from the elements.

Taxi

Taxi hire in towns and cities is getting easier, but there are still very few metered taxis, with just a handful of operators in Phnom Penh. Guesthouses, hotels and travel agents can arrange cars for sightseeing in and around towns.

SHARE TAXI & PICK-UP TRUCKS

In these days of improving roads, share taxis are losing ground to express minivans. When using share taxis, it is an advantage to travel in numbers, as you can buy spare seats to make the journey more comfortable. Double the price for the front seat and quadruple it for the entire back row. It is important to remember that there aren't necessarily fixed prices on every route, so you have to negotiate. For major destinations they can be hired individually, or you can pay for a seat and wait for other passengers to turn up. Guesthouses are also very helpful when it comes to arranging share taxis – at a price, of course.

Once popular, old-school pick-up trucks – which work the same as share taxis – have become much less common as Cambodia's roads have improved. They can still be found on some of the more obscure and rugged routes in the provinces.

TOURS

In the early days of tourism in Cambodia, organised tours were a near necessity. The situation has changed dramatically and it is now much easier to organise your own trip. Budget and midrange travellers in particular can go it alone, as arrangements are cheap and easy on the ground. Get to Angkor, for instance, and you'll have no problem finding your own guides and transport.

If you do decide to go with a tour, shop around before booking, as there is lots of competition and some companies offer more interesting itineraries than others and/or do more to support responsible travel. Tours as well as flights can be booked online at lonelyplanet.com/bookings.

The following are reliable tour companies based in Cambodia:

About Asia (☎ 063-760190; www.aboutasiatravel.com) Small bespoke travel company specialising in Siem Reap. Profits help build schools in Cambodia.

Hanuman (☎ 023-218396; www.hanuman.travel) Long-running, locally owned and operated company with innovative tours like Temple Safari. Big supporter of responsible tourism initiatives.

Journeys Within (☎ 063-964748; www.journeys-within.com) A boutique tourism company based in Siem Reap that offers various cross-border trips in addition to appealing tours within Cambodia. Operates a charitable arm helping schools and communities.

Sam Veasna Center (p208) Genuine ecotourism operator offering one- to several-day birdwatching and wildlife watching tours that contribute directly to forest and species preservation. It has several other offices, including one at Sen Monoram (p245).

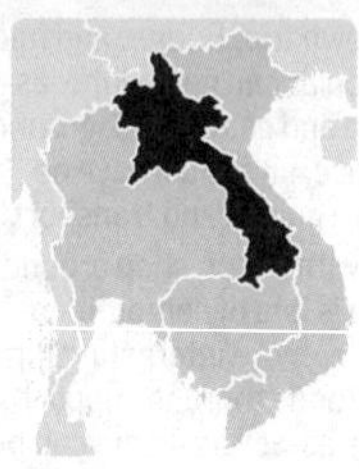

Laos

POP 6.9 MILLION / ☎856

Includes ➡

Best Places to Eat

- Coconut Garden (p323)
- Four Thousand Sunsets (p383)
- Le Silapa (p298)
- Tamarind (p324)
- Kung's Cafe Lao (p298)

Best Places to Sleep

- Hotel Khamvongsa (p294)
- Kingfisher Ecolodge (p378)
- Mandala Ou Resort (p337)
- Riverside Boutique Resort (p313)
- Satri House (p323)

Why Go?

The 'Land of a Million Elephants' oozes magic the moment you spot a Hmong tribeswoman looming from the mist, trek through a glimmering rice paddy, or hear the sonorous call of one of the country's endangered gibbons. It's a place where it's easy to make a quick detour and find yourself well and truly off the traveller circuit: the snaking Mekong River runs through it all, alongside jagged limestone cliffs and brooding jungle. But it's also a place to luxuriate, pampering yourself like a French colonial in a spa, or chilling under a wood-blade fan in a top-notch Gallic restaurant. Old-world refinement is found in pockets right across the country, especially in languid Vientiane and legendary Luang Prabang.

Laos has also adapted itself well to green tourism, harnessing forests with excellent treks and tribal homestays. Be it flying along mountain ziplines, tubing, exploring subterranean caves or traversing the jungle via dirt-bike, Laos will indelibly burn itself into your memory.

When to Go

Vientiane

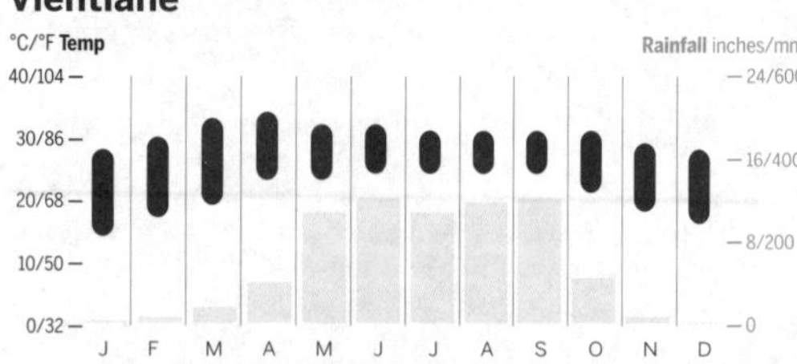

Jan Cool-season breezes: even the normally sweltering south is pleasantly bearable.

Oct Mercifully cool weather. Bun Awk Phansa sees candle-bearing boats floated down rivers.

Nov–Dec Cool weather; best time to visit. Book accommodation in advance.

VIENTIANE

From its sleepy tuk-tuk drivers to its cafe society and affordable spas, this former French trading post is languid to say the least. Eminently walkable, the historic old quarter of Vientiane (ວຽງຈັນ) beguiles with glittering temples, lunging *naga* (river serpent) statues, wandering Buddhist monks, and boulevards lined with frangipani and tamarind.

Meanwhile, with most of its old French villas now stylishly reincarnated into restaurants and small hotels, Vientiane is achieving an unprecedented level of panache with a distinctly Gallic flavour. For the well-heeled traveller and backpacker the city acquits itself equally well, be it with low-cost digs and street markets, or upscale boutique accommodation and gastronomic eateries.

Whether you spend your time in Vientiane lounging over a novel in an old-fashioned bakery, shopping in silk shops or swigging Beerlao while drinking up the fiery sunset over the Mekong, once you leave you'll miss this place more than you expected.

Sights

The bulk of sights are concentrated in a small area in the centre of the city. With the exception of Xieng Khuan (Buddha Park), all sights are easily reached by bicycle and, in most cases, on foot. Most wats welcome visitors after the monks have collected alms in the morning until about 6pm.

Wat Si Saket BUDDHIST TEMPLE
(ວັດສີສະເກດ; Map p296; cnr Th Lan Xang & Th Setthathirath; 5000K; ⏲8am-noon & 1-4pm, closed public holidays) Built between 1819 and 1824 by Chao Anou, Wat Si Saket is believed to be Vientiane's oldest surviving wat. And it is starting to show, as this beautiful temple is in need of a facelift. Along the western side of the cloister is a pile of Buddhas that were damaged during the 1828 Siamese-Lao war.

★COPE Visitor Centre CULTURAL CENTRE
(ສູນຟື້ນຟູຄົນພິການແຫ່ງຊາດ; Map p292; ☎021-218427; www.copelaos.org; Th Khu Vieng; donations welcome; ⏲9am-6pm) FREE COPE (Cooperative Orthotic & Prosthetic Enterprise) is the main source of artificial limbs, walking aids and wheelchairs in Laos. Its excellent Visitor Centre, part of the organisation's National Rehabilitation Centre, offers myriad interesting and informative multimedia exhibits about prosthetics and the unexploded ordnance (UXO) that make them necessary.

★Patuxai MONUMENT
(ປະຕູໄຊ, Victory Monument; Map p292; Th Lan Xang; 3000K; ⏲8am-5pm) Vientiane's Arc de Triomphe replica is a slightly incongruous sight, dominating the commercial district around Th Lan Xang. Officially called 'Victory Monument' *and* commemorating the Lao who died in prerevolutionary wars, it was built in 1969 with cement donated by the USA intended for the construction of a new airport. Climb to the summit for panoramic views over Vientiane.

★Pha That Luang BUDDHIST STUPA
(ພະທາດຫລວງ, Great Sacred Reliquary, Great Stupa; Map p292; Th That Luang; 5000K, rental of long skirt to enter temple 5000K; ⏲8am-noon & 1-4pm Tue-Sun) Svelte and golden Pha That Luang is the most important national monument in Laos; a symbol of Buddhist religion and Lao sovereignty. Legend has it that Ashokan missionaries from India erected a *tâht* (stupa) here to enclose a piece of Buddha's breastbone as early as the 3rd century BC. Pha That Luang is about 4km northeast of the city centre.

Xieng Khuan MUSEUM
(ຊຽງຂວັນ, Suan Phut, Buddha Park; 5000K, camera 3000K; ⏲8am-4.30pm) Located 25km southeast of central Vientiane, eccentric Xieng Khuan, aka Buddha Park, thrills with otherworldly Buddhist and Hindu sculptures, and was designed and built in 1958 by Luang Pu, a yogi-priest-shaman who merged Hindu and Buddhist philosophy, mythology and iconography into a cryptic whole. Bus 14 (8000K, one hour, 24km) leaves Talat Sao Bus Station every 15 minutes for Xieng Khuan. Alternatively, charter a tuk-tuk (200,000K return).

Wat Chanthabuli BUDDHIST TEMPLE
(Map p296; Th Fa Ngoum) This beautiful riverside wat was built in the 16th century, destroyed during the Siamese invasion of 1828 and later fully restored to its present glory. It's notable for its enormous bronze seated Buddha.

Activities & Courses

Coffee

Sinouk Coffee Pavilion COFFEE
(☎030-2000654; www.sinouk-cafe.com; Km 9, Th Tha Deua; ⏲8am-5pm) Located at the headquarters of Sinouk Coffee, one of Laos' best-known coffee producers, this is an education in the bean. Learn more about the art of coffee production at the coffee gallery and

Laos Highlights

❶ **Luang Prabang** (p315) Exploring the fabled city to find French cuisine, Buddhist temples, colonial villas, stunning river views and some of the best boutique accommodation in Southeast Asia.

❷ **Tham Kong Lor** (p357) Taking a boat ride through the exhilarating yet spooky 7.5km-long tunnel, home to fist-sized spiders and stalactite woods, while tackling the three-day dirt-bike 'Loop'.

❸ **Vientiane** (p289) Meandering along the banks of the Mekong, Vientiane is surely Southeast Asia's most languid capital. The wide streets are bordered by tamarind trees and the narrow alleys conceal French villas, Chinese shophouses, and glittering wats.

❹ **Nam Ha National Protected Area** (p342) Taking an eco-responsible trek through some of the wildest, densest jungle in the country, home to tigers and a rich variety of ethnic tribes.

❺ **Si Phan Don** (p380) Lowering your pulse in the travellers' mecca of Four Thousand Islands, where the Mekong River turns turquoise and the night air is flecked with fireflies.

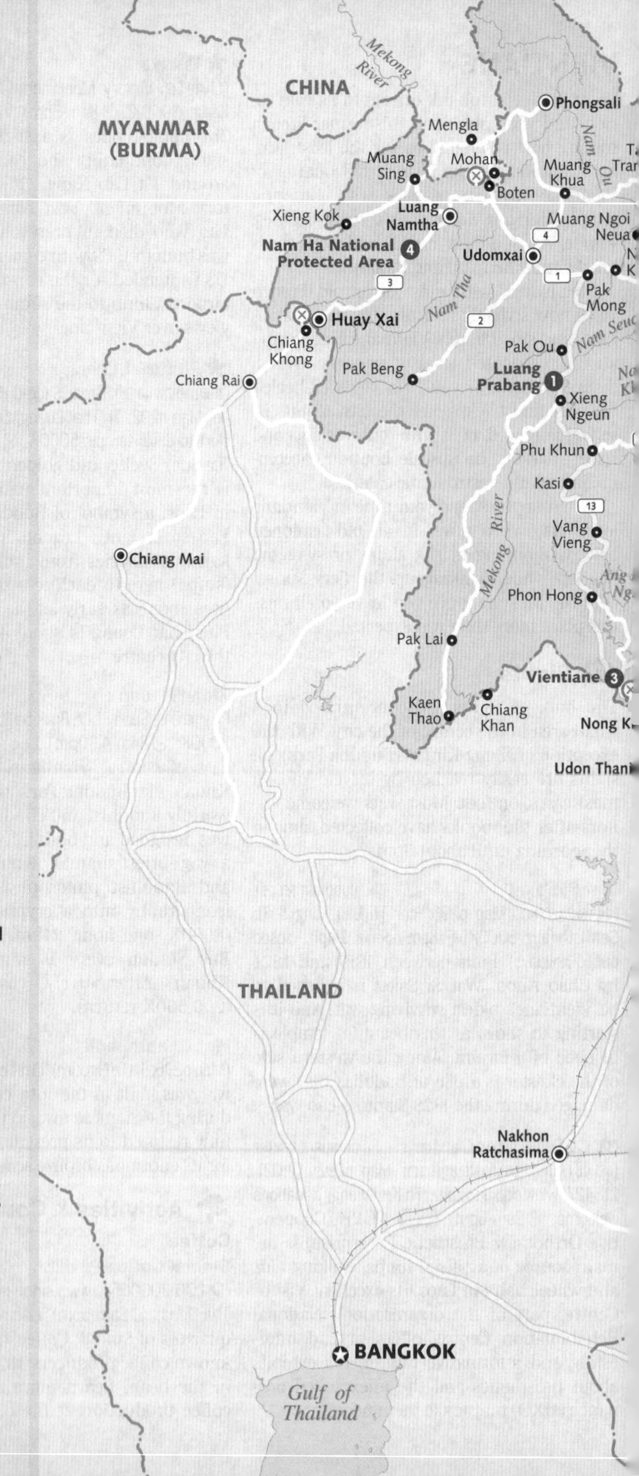

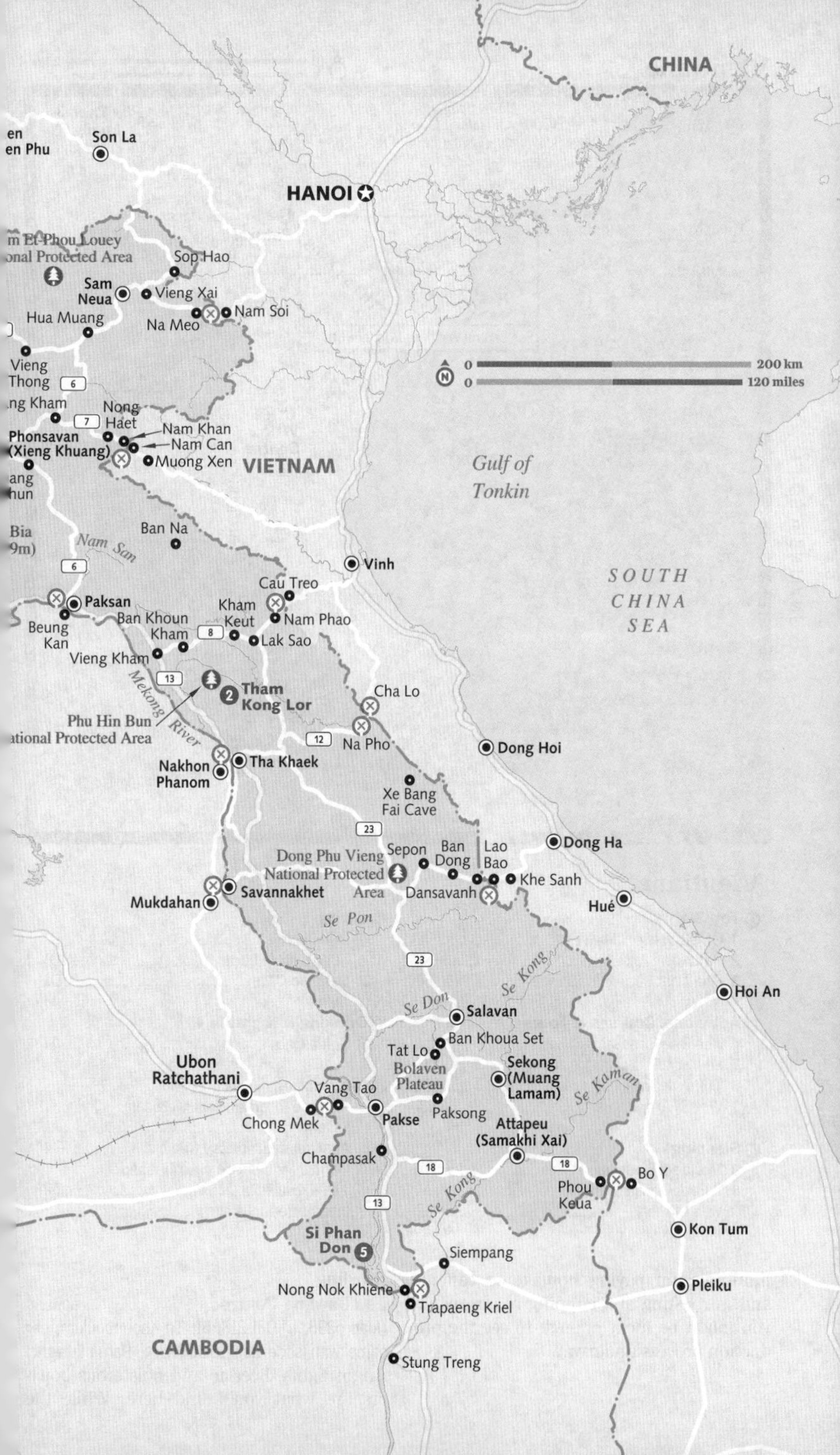

CHINA
Son La
HANOI
Sop Hao
Sam Neua
Vieng Xai
Nam Soi
Na Meo
Hua Muang
Vieng Thong
Nong Haet
Nam Khan
Nam Can
Muong Xen
Phonsavan (Xieng Khuang)
VIETNAM
Gulf of Tonkin
Ban Na
Nam San
Vinh
SOUTH CHINA SEA
Cau Treo
Paksan
Beung Kan
Kham Keut
Nam Phao
Ban Khoun Kham
Lak Sao
Vieng Kham
Tham Kong Lor
Phu Hin Bun National Protected Area
Mekong River
Cha Lo
Na Pho
Dong Hoi
Nakhon Phanom
Tha Khaek
Xe Bang Fai Cave
Dong Ha
Dong Phu Vieng National Protected Area
Sepon
Ban Dong
Lao Bao
Khe Sanh
Dansavanh
Savannakhet
Mukdahan
Hué
Se Pon
Se Kong
Se Don
Salavan
Hoi An
Ban Khoua Set
Tat Lo
Bolaven Plateau
Sekong (Muang Lamam)
Ubon Ratchathani
Vang Tao
Chong Mek
Pakse
Paksong
Attapeu (Samakhi Xai)
Se Kaman
Champasak
Bo Y
Phou Keua
Kon Tum
Si Phan Don
Siempang
Nong Nok Khiene
Trapaeng Kriel
Pleiku
CAMBODIA
Stung Treng
0 200 km
0 120 miles

Vientiane

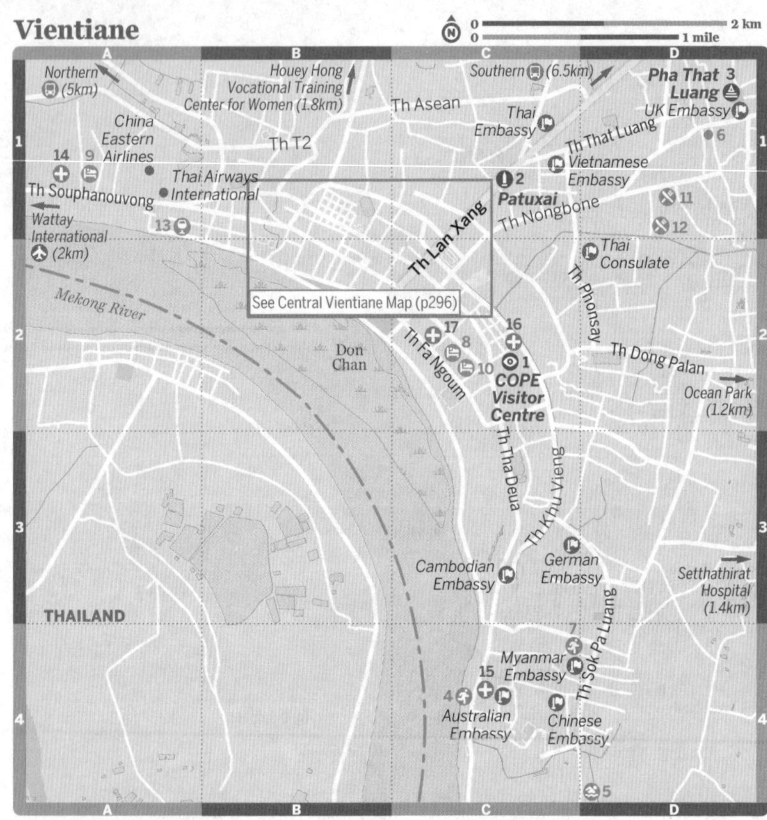

Vientiane

Top Sights
1 COPE Visitor Centre C2
2 Patuxai C1
3 Pha That Luang D1

Activities, Courses & Tours
4 Bee Bee Fitness C4
5 Le Patitoh D4
6 Tuk Tuk Safari D1
7 Wat Si Amphon C4

Sleeping
8 Mandala Boutique Hotel C2
9 S Park Design Hotel A1
10 Villa Manoly C2

Eating
11 Doi Ka Noi D1
Kung's Cafe Lao .... (see 10)
12 Senglao Cafe D1

Drinking & Nightlife
13 Spirit House A1

Information
14 Alliance International Medical Center A1
15 Australian Embassy Clinic C4
16 Centre Médical de L'Ambassade de France C2
17 International Clinic C2

mini-museum paying homage to caffeine, and in roasting and cupping rooms, where you might be lucky enough to see the production process underway.

Bowling

Lao Bowling Centre BOWLING

(Map p296; 021-218661; Th Khounboulom; per game with shoe hire 16,000K; 9am-midnight) Bright lights, Beerlao and boisterous bowlers are what you'll find here. While the equipment is in bad shape, it's still a fun place to come later in the evening for a Lao-style night out. It sometimes stays open into the wee hours.

Craft

Houey Hong Vocational Training Center for Women WEAVING
(☎021-560006; www.houeyhongcentre.com; Ban Houey Hong; ⏰8.30am-4.30pm Mon-Sat) You can learn how to dye textiles using natural pigments and then weave them on a traditional loom at this NGO centre, run by a Lao-Japanese woman. It was established north of Vientiane to train disadvantaged rural women in the dying art of natural dyeing and traditional silk-weaving practices.

Fitness

Vientiane Hash House Harriers RUNNING
(www.hashlaos.com) 'The drinkers with a running problem' is how this global expat running club is affectionately known. The Vientiane Hash House Harriers welcome runners to their two weekly hashes. The Saturday hash is the more challenging run and starts at 3.45pm from Nam Phu. It's followed by food and no shortage of Beerlao. Monday's easier run starts at 5pm.

Bee Bee Fitness HEALTH & FITNESS
(Map p292; ☎021-315877; 1-day membership 45,000K; ⏰6am-9pm Mon-Fri, 7am-9pm Sat & Sun) This terrific gym overlooks the Mekong so you can run on a treadmill and watch passing boats. There's loads of room to enjoy its decent equipment: rowing machines, spinning bikes and weightlifting apparatus. Regular Zumba and Pilates classes are available. It's located opposite the Australian embassy.

Massage & Spa

★**Oasis** MASSAGE
(Map p296; Th François Ngin; ⏰9am-9pm) Cool, clean and professional, Oasis is an excellent central place to enjoy a foot massage (50,000K), a Lao-style body massage (60,000K) or a peppermint body scrub (200,000K), to name a few. Probably the best-value spa in the city.

Tangerine Garden Spa SPA
(Map p296; ☎021-251452; off Th Fa Ngoum; ⏰9am-9pm) Arguably the most upscale spa in Vientiane, Tangerine Garden is located opposite the beautiful Ansara Hôtel and complements its colonial-era look. The Sino-Lao lobby sets the tone for a relaxing journey that includes foot massage (80,000K), aroma massage (180,000K) and the 'office syndrome' massage (100,000K) that focuses on the neck, shoulders and back.

Wat Si Amphon SPA
(Map p292; Th Si Amphon; ⏰7am-5pm) Wat Si Amphon does herbal saunas and is one of the only temples to offer this experience after the demise of the Wat Sok Pa Luang herbal sauna in a 2013 fire.

Swimming

Settha Palace Hotel SWIMMING
(Map p296; ☎021-217581; 6 Th Pangkham; 160,000K; ⏰7am-7pm) With its lovely kidney-shaped pool shaded by mature trees, the venerable old Settha Palace is less about laps and more about relaxing. Buy a cocktail and live like Liz Taylor.

Ocean Park WATER PARK
(☎030-2819014; ITECC Vientiane; adult/child 50,000/25,000K; ⏰11am-7pm) Shiver me timbers me hearties! This new water park has a pirate theme and includes a good range of slides, tubes, lazy river riding and more. A good option for families on a hot day.

Le Patitoh SWIMMING
(Map p292; ☎030-5082428; 20 Th Sithoong; swimming 30,000K; ⏰7am-9pm) Set in the suburbs, Le Patitoh is a swimming pool and cafe that is popular with expats and Laotians in the know. Its cafe menu (items 15,000K to 40,000K) includes wraps, salads and more, plus ice cream by the scoop.

Tours

★**Tuk Tuk Safari** CULTURAL
(Map p292; ☎020-54333089; www.tuktuksafari.com; adult/child under 12 US$70/40; ⏰8am-5pm) This community-conscious tour company gets under the skin of Vientiane in a tuk-tuk. Tour guide Ere spirits you to a Lao market; a silversmith's workshop; behind the scenes at a restaurant helping street kids learn to become chefs (before sampling their delicious food!); and finally, the inspiring COPE Visitor Centre for UXO victims.

Backstreet Academy TOURS
(☎020-58199216; www.backstreetacademy.com) For some original local encounters, contact Backstreet Academy, a peer-to-peer travel website that specialises in connecting travellers to cultural experiences with local hosts. Choose from a *muay Lao* (kickboxing) class, a traditional dance lesson, a Lao cooking

class in a private home, a painting class, Zen meditation and a whole lot more.

Festivals & Events

Bun Nam SPORTS

(Bun Suang Héua; Oct) A huge annual event at the end of *pansăh* (the Buddhist rains retreat) in October, during which boat races are held on the Mekong River. Rowing teams from all over the country, as well as from Thailand, China and Myanmar (Burma), compete; the river bank is lined with food stalls, temporary discos, carnival games and beer gardens for three days and nights.

Sleeping

Vientiane is bursting with a wide range of accommodation, from cheap backpacker digs to beautiful boutique hotels and huge monolithic corporate hotels. Budget-wise, for shoestringers it's easy to stretch your cash and hole up in a dorm for a few dollars, while you can pay hundreds of dollars a night in a top-end hotel. In the middle of these two extremes are some clean, intimate guesthouses for around $US20 per night (for a double room).

Central Vientiane

★ **Mixay Paradise Guesthouse** GUESTHOUSE $

(Map p296; 021-254223; laomixayparadise@yahoo.com; Th François Ngin; s/d with fan & shared bathroom 90,000/100,000K, r with air-con & bathroom 130,000-150,000K;) Mixay Paradise has 50 rooms with pastel-coloured walls, some of which have balconies, bathrooms and air-con; spotless floors; a lovely lobby cafe with lime-green walls; and a lift. One of the best, most hygienic budget options in the city. Safety deposit lockers cost 50,000K.

Niny Backpacker HOSTEL $

(Map p296; 020-96663333; ninybackpack@hotmail.com; Th Nokèokoummane; dm 50,000-60,000K;) A new hostel with cheerful orange walls, and fresh dorms accommodating four or 20 berths. Safety deposit lockers, free breakfast (toast and eggs) and clean facilities. There's no self-catering.

Lucky Backpacker HOSTEL $

(Map p296; 021-255636; Th Manthatourath; dm/d 40,000/140,000K;) A clean new joint, with spacious dorms, decent showers and a private double room with air-con but no window. Beds have lockers underneath but no locks. Friendly management.

Syri 1 Guest House GUESTHOUSE $

(Map p296; 021-212682; Th Saigon; r 50,000-150,000K;) Syri sits on a quiet street and has been a traveller fave for many years, and with good reason: generously sized rooms (with air-con or fan, en suite or shared bathroom), recesses to chill, a DVD lounge, bikes for rent, and tailored bike tours of the city. And 100% friendly.

Dream Home Hostel 2 HOSTEL $

(Map p296; 020-95591102; dreamhomehostel2@gmail.com; Th Sihom; dm 50,000K, r US$25;) A classic backpacker crash pad, this is one of the most popular hostels in the city. Reception introduces the party atmosphere with some cranked-up tunes and a pool table, and murals deck the upper walls. The rooms are actually pretty good value given the size and features like flat-screen TV – almost flashpacker territory.

★ **Hotel Khamvongsa** HOTEL $$

(Map p296; 021-218415; www.hotelkhamvongsa.com; Th Khounboulom; s/d/tr incl breakfast US$40/60/80;) Lovely French-era building lovingly reincarnated as a welcoming boutique hotel; think belle époque touches like glass tear lightshades, chequerboard-tiled floors, and softly lit simple rooms with two-poster beds, wood floors and Indo-chic decor. Rooms on the 3rd and 4th floors have masterful views. There's also a restful courtyard and restaurant. Breakfast is a treat.

★ **LV City Riverine Hotel** HOTEL $$

(Map p296; 021-214643; www.lvcitylaos.com; 48 Th Fa Ngoum; r incl breakfast 220,000-390,000K;) Not to be confused with various other 'city' hotels in the capital, the LV has a great location near the riverfront. Rooms are spacious and well appointed, although it is worth the ego-massage of VIP just for the four-poster bed and extra space. Rooms include laundry, so will be even better value if you are returning from a jungle trek.

Auberge Sala Inpeng GUESTHOUSE $$

(Map p296; 021-242021; www.salalao.com; Th In Paeng; r incl breakfast US$25-50;) Unlike anything else in the city, this vernal oasis of wood cabanas and a handsome traditional Laotian house is set in gardens spilling with tamarind and *champa* flowers. The grander rooms display rustic chic with bathrooms and air-con. And although the cheaper cabanas are small, they don't lack atmosphere. Staff are as welcoming as a slice of home.

Vayakorn Inn HOTEL $$
(Map p296; ☎021-215348; www.vayakorn.biz; 19 Th Hèngbounnoy; r US$35;) On a quiet street just off increasingly hectic Th Setthathirath, this tasteful, peaceful hotel is great value given its chandeliered lobby festooned in handicrafts and hardwood floors. Generously sized rooms are impeccably clean, with crisp linen, choice art, flat-screen TVs, desks and modern bathrooms. The rooms on the upper floors have excellent city views.

★**Ansara Hôtel** BOUTIQUE HOTEL $$$
(Map p296; ☎021-213514; www.ansarahotel.com; off Th Fa Ngoum; r US$125-160, ste US$190-330, all incl breakfast;) Achingly beautiful Ansara is housed in a pair of colonial-chic French villas with a heavy whiff of old Indochina. There are 28 rooms set across the property, including four suites, and all are lovely, offering wooden floor, balcony, flat-screen TV, bath and refined decorations. Its alfresco dining terrace is as refined as its Gallic cuisine.

Out of the Centre

Villa Manoly GUESTHOUSE $$
(Map p292; ☎021-218907; www.villa-manoly.com; off Th Fa Ngoum; r incl breakfast US$35-45;) This beautifully antiquated house, in a garden swimming in mature plants and frangipani flowers, feels like the sort of place John le Carré might ensconce himself in to write a novel, especially given its collection of vintage telephones and typewriters. Nicely furnished rooms with wood floors, air-con, en suites and bedside lamps look on to a delightful pool. It's like a boutique homestay.

★**Mandala Boutique Hotel** BOUTIQUE HOTEL $$$
(Map p292; ☎021-214493; www.mandalahotel.asia; off Th Fa Ngoum; r incl breakfast US$75-100;) This super-chic boutique hotel offers the city's brightest, coolest accommodation (we're talking *Wallpaper* rather than the Fonz). An old French villa built in the 1960s is its setting, and flashes of vivid colour and chichi flourishes such as lacquered granite floors, flat-screen TVs and dark-wood furniture blend perfectly with the aesthetic of its art-deco lines.

The four-poster beds are possibly the most comfortable in Laos. There's also a very natty Asian fusion restaurant called Blu.

★**S Park Design Hotel** BOUTIQUE HOTEL $$$
(Map p292; ☎021-256339; www.sparkdesignhotel.com; 40 Th Dongnasok; r US$70-120;) This place has some serious style on the inside. The reception will get you hooked, with a chopped-up classic Mercedes for a front desk and a vintage Vespa. It wouldn't be out of place in *Hip Hotels* with its contemporary look. It features 64 rooms, all with separate toilet.

Eating

Old-school restaurants on the streets that radiate off Th Setthathirath serve up fine Italian and French fare in the choicest of surroundings. Lao food has in recent years enjoyed a real contemporary makeover with well-executed traditional dishes given a modern twist. Bakeries left by the French footprint produce crispy croissants and full-bodied coffee. Vientiane is equally informal; cheap grilled chicken and Mekong fish on skewers can be grabbed from street vendors dotted around the old quarter. And don't miss Chinatown on Th Hengboun.

Th Samsènethai & Around

iPho VIETNAMESE $
(Map p296; ☎030-9581163; off Th Setthathirath; mains 20,000-40,000K; 7am-9pm;) This hole-in-the-wall Vietnamese eatery specialises in the eponymous *pho* (noodle soup), with various meat offerings. Other dishes include regional Vietnamese specialities like *bo bun Hue* (spicy beef noodle soup from the city of Hue) and broken-rice dishes.

Baguette & Pâté Vendor STREET FOOD $
(Map p296; Th Samsènethai; half/whole baguette 11,000/22,000K; 6am-8pm) Serves great *khào jį pá-tê* (baguettes with liver pâté, veg and cream cheese, dripping with sweet chilli sauce). There's no English-language sign here, but the stall is directly on the corner of Th Pangkham and Th Samsènethai.

That Dam Noodle LAOTIAN $
(Map p296; ☎021-214441; mains 15,000-30,000K; 8.30am-2pm) Hidden away down a side street near That Dam, this place is run by an affable Lao chef who is clearly proud of his noodle-soup creations. Duck is a speciality, but chicken, pork and fish variations are also available. Look out for the larger-than-life sign of the owner with a steaming bowl of soup.

★**Lao Kitchen** LAOTIAN $$
(Map p296; ☎021-254332; www.lao-kitchen.com; Th Hengboun; mains 40,000-70,000K; 11am-10pm;) This superb contemporary Lao

Central Vientiane

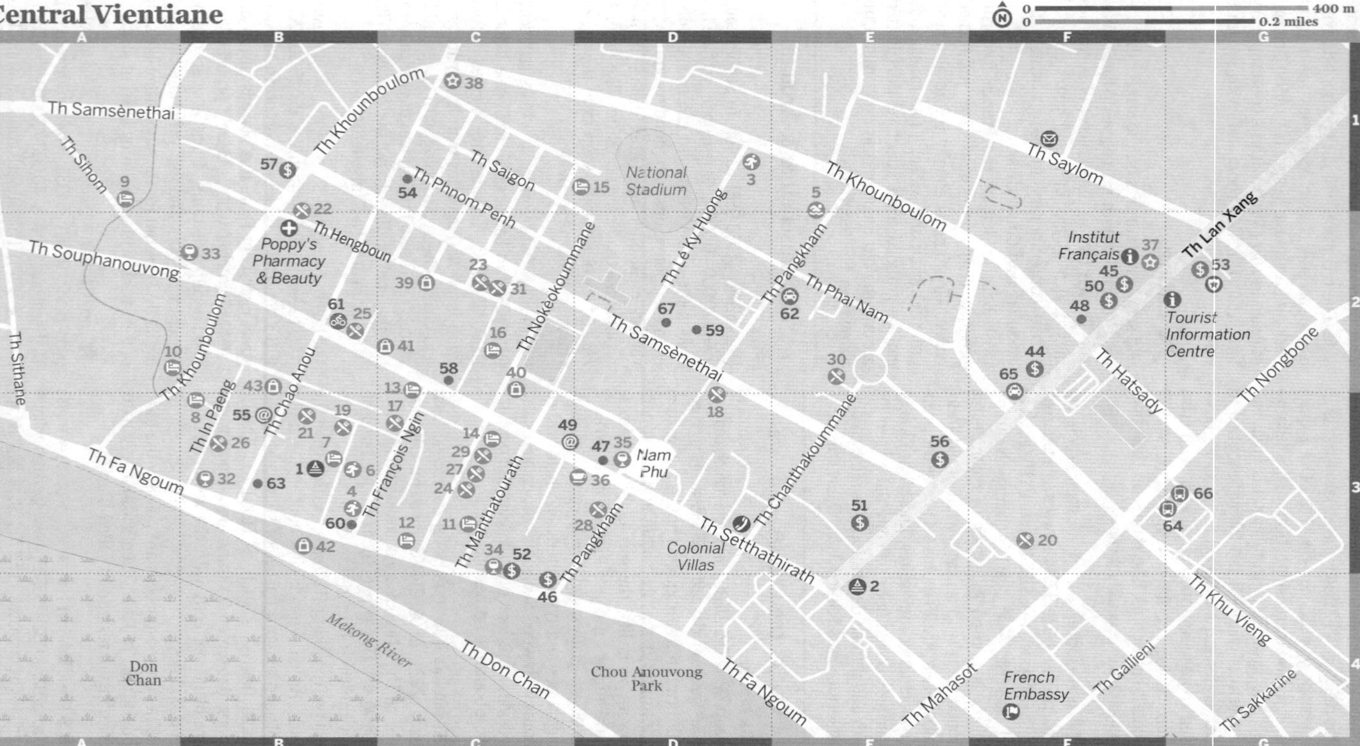

Central Vientiane

Sights
1 Wat Chanthabuli B3
2 Wat Si Saket E4

Activities, Courses & Tours
3 Lao Bowling Centre D1
4 Oasis B3
5 Settha Palace Hotel E1
6 Tangerine Garden Spa B3

Sleeping
7 Ansara Hôtel B3
8 Auberge Sala Inpeng B3
9 Dream Home Hostel 2 .... A1
10 Hotel Khamvongsa A2
11 Lucky Backpacker C3
12 LV City Riverine Hotel C3
13 Mixay Paradise Guesthouse C2
14 Niny Backpacker C3
15 Syri 1 Guest House D1
16 Vayakorn Inn C2

Eating
17 Acqua C3
18 Baguette & Pâté Vendor D3
19 Ban Vilaylac Restaurant B3
20 Bistrot 22 .... F3
21 iPho B3
22 Korean Restaurant B1
23 Lao Kitchen C2
24 Le Banneton C3
25 Le Silapa B2
26 Makphet Restaurant B3
27 Osaka C3
28 Phimphone Market D3
29 Pimentón C3
30 That Dam Noodle E2
31 Xayoh C2

Drinking & Nightlife
32 Bor Pen Yang B3
33 CCC Bar B2
34 Chokdee Cafe C3
35 Khop Chai Deu D3
36 Le Trio D3

Entertainment
37 Centre Culturel et de Coopération Linguistique F2
38 Lao National Opera Theatre C1

Shopping
39 Book Café C2
40 Carol Cassidy Lao Textiles C2
41 Indochina Handicrafts C2
42 Night Market B3
43 T'Shop Lai Gallery B2

Information
44 ANZ F2
45 Bank of Ayudhya F2
46 Banque pour le Commerce Extérieur Lao C4
47 Green Discovery D3
48 Immigration Office F2
49 Internet Cafe C3
50 Joint Development Bank F2
51 Krung Thai Bank E3
52 Krung Thai Exchange Booth C3
53 Lao-Viet Bank G2
54 Lin Travel Service C1
55 Oriental Bookshop Internet B3
56 Siam Commercial Bank E3
57 Thai Military Bank B1

Transport
58 Avis C2
59 Bangkok Airways D2
60 First-One Motorbike Rental B3
61 Lao Bike B2
62 Meter Taxi Service E2
63 Mixay Bike 2 .... B3
64 Talat Sao Bus Station G3
65 Talat Sao Taxi Stand F2
66 Thai-Lao International Bus G3
67 Vietnam Airlines D2

restaurant is unfailingly creative in its execution of trad-Lao dishes. Colourful walls, alt tunes and decent service complement a menu spanning stews, Luang Prabang sausage, *láhp* variations, stir-fried morning glory (water spinach), spring rolls, Mekong fish soup and palate-friendly sorbets. Choose the level of spice with chilli gradings of one to three.

Korean Restaurant KOREAN **$$**

(Map p296; 020-22087080; Th Hengboun; mains 30,000-180,000K; 9am-11pm;) Lacklustre name aside, this Korean-run place is great for sampling what is currently the most popular foreign cuisine in Southeast Asia. Most locals go directly for the Korean barbecue (80,000K), but we liked the kimchi stew (30,000K), served Korean-style with heaps of side dishes.

Xayoh STEAK **$$$**

(Map p296; 021-261777; www.inthira.com; mains 40,000-800,000K; 7am-10pm;) One of the more popular steakhouses thanks to its hugely tasty Japanese Kobe steak: soaked in beer it's massaged daily for 30 days before it arrives impossibly tenderised on your plate. At US$100 it's not cheap but for a special occasion, it may be the best steak you ever taste (or share!).

There's also a carnivore's delight of cutlets, sirloin, Luang Prabang sausage, slow-cooked lamb, plus the challenge to eat a burger as big as your head. Seriously! Eat inside or out.

Bistrot 22 FRENCH $$$
(Map p296; 020-55527286; Th Samsènethai; mains 65,000-250,000K; 11.30am-2pm & 6-10pm;) Moved a little further out of the centre to a less bubbly locale, Bistrot 22 is nonetheless enjoying great reviews for Chef Philippe's lustrous cuisine, with dishes like pear salad, deep-fried apple and Camembert salad, tender steaks and cauliflower soup. This intimate little restaurant is one of the gastronomic highlights of Vientiane.

Riverfront, Th Setthathirath & Around

★ **Kung's Cafe Lao** LAOTIAN $
(Map p292; 021-219101; near Ministry of Health, Phiawat Village; mains 12,000-20,000K; 7am-4pm) Approaching cult status with Vientiane residents in the know, Kung's Cafe is hard to find, but well worth the effort. Affable Kung has decorated the local diner with hanging gourds and has a simple and effective menu that is superb value. Try the sticky rice pancake or *phat Lao* and wash it down with a signature coffee and coconut.

Phimphone Market MARKET $
(Map p296; 94/6 Th Setthathirath; 7am-9pm Mon-Sat;) This self-catering oasis stocks everything from gleaming fresh veg to ice cream, imported salami, bread, biscuits and chocolate, as well as Western toiletries and magazines. It also stocks Hobo maps of the city. It's located in the same building as Benoni Café.

★ **Le Banneton** BAKERY $$
(Map p296; Th Nokèokoummane; breakfast 45,000K; 7am-9pm;) Get here early before the country's best croissants run out. The simple interior makes for a nice place to read a paper over a tart, salad, panini or omelette, or you can sit outside on the small terrace. Tasty breakfasts and homemade marmalade and jam.

Acqua ITALIAN $$
(Map p296; 021-255466; www.acqua.la; 78 Th François Ngin; mains 40,000-200,000K; 11am-10pm;) Considered by many residents to be the finest Italian restaurant in the city. The 98,000K lunch buffet is justifiably popular and includes a choice of entrées. Indulgent mains include sockeye-salmon ravioli and some sumptuous imported cuts from land and sea. The owner also runs Vinoteca, a leading wine importer, so the Italian wine list is top-notch.

Ban Vilaylac Restaurant LAOTIAN $$
(Map p296; 021-222049; Ban Wat Chan; mains 20,000-70,000K; 7am-10pm;) A long-running Lao restaurant in Ban Wat Chan, it can be easily missed amid the stellar culinary openings of recent years, but the traditional Lao food here is authentic and home-cooked by a friendly family.

Osaka JAPANESE $$
(Map p296; 021-213352; Th Nokèokoummane; mains 30,000-80,000K; 8am-10pm;) A lively hole-in-the-wall, with slatted chairs on a plant-filled verandah, cosy Osaka tempts you inside with its lipstick-red booths. Oodles of noodle variations, sashimi, vegie dishes, sushi and tempura.

★ **Pimentón** SPANISH $$$
(Map p296; 021-215506; www.pimentonrestaurant-vte.com; Th Nokèokoummane; mains 60,000-200,000K, set lunch 75,000K; 11am-2.30pm & 5-10pm Mon-Sat;) Pimentón, with its high ceilings and sleek bar, is widely considered to be the best steak restaurant in the capital. Only the choicest cuts of sirloin, chateaubriand and rib-eye make it to its fiery open grill. At lunch there's tapas: think imported *jamón ibérico* (a type of cured ham), *calamares* (squid) and charcuterie of cured meats. Run by a lovely husband-and-wife team.

★ **Le Silapa** FRENCH $$$
(Map p296; 021-219689; 88 Th Setthathirath; mains 80,000-250,000K, set lunches 65,000-120,000K; 11am-11pm;) Recently relocated Le Silapa is beautiful in its chichi whiteness complemented by the wood floors, raftered ceiling and birdcage lights. A contender for Vientiane's finest Gallic restaurant, it features favourites from foie gras to salads, and steaks to veal brains casserole. It's upstairs at the excellent iBeam bar. *Magnifique*, especially the excellent-value set lunches.

Pha That Luang

★ **Doi Ka Noi** LAOTIAN $
(Map p292; 020-55898959; 242 Sapang Mor; mains 25,000-50,000K; 10am-2.30pm Tue-Thu, 10am-9pm Fri-Sun;) An authentic Lao restaurant near That Luang, this is the place to spice up your life. The menu changes almost daily and focuses on home recipes and seasonal ingredients. Sample dishes include fish

OODLES OF NOODLES

Noodles of all kinds are popular in Laos, and Vientiane has the country's greatest variety. The most popular noodle of all is undoubtedly *fěr*, the local version of Vietnamese *pho*, served with beef or pork and accompanied, Lao-style, by a huge plate of fresh herbs and vegetables and a ridiculous amount of condiments. Also popular are *kòw þûn*, the thin rice noodles known as *kànŏm jeen* in Thailand, taken in Laos with a spicy curry-like broth or sometimes in a clear pork broth *(kòw þûn nâm jąaou)*. There's also *kòw þęeak sèn*, thick rice- and tapioca-flour noodles served in a slightly viscous broth with crispy deep-fried pork belly or chicken.

Other popular noodles include *mii* (traditional Chinese egg noodle), particularly prevalent in the unofficial Chinatown area bounded by Th Hengboun, Th Chao Anou, Th Khounboulom and the western end of Th Samsènethai, and *băn kŭan* (Lao for *bánh cuôn*), a freshly steamed rice noodle filled with minced pork, mushrooms and carrots, a Vietnamese speciality that is popular in Laos. Look for it in the mornings near the intersection of Th Chao Anou and Th Hengboun.

curry with hummingbird-tree flowers and bamboo curry with mushrooms. Co-owned by a photographer, there are some stunning food shots adorning the walls.

★**Senglao Cafe** FUSION **$$**
(Map p292; ☎030-5880588; mains 30,000-300,000K; ⏲11am-10pm Mon-Sat; ❄📶) Named after a now-defunct cinema in the centre of town, this contemporary restaurant has a cinematic theme and restored leather chairs from the old movie hall. The fusion menu is ambitious but executed with some panache and includes everything from fusion squid-ink pasta with scallops to stone-baked pizzas. Films are shown in the garden at weekends.

Drinking & Nightlife

Vientiane is no longer the illicit pleasure palace it once was. Nowadays, brothels are strictly prohibited and Beerlao has replaced opium as the nightly drug of choice. Most of the bars, restaurants and discos close by 11.30pm or midnight, apart from a few late-night stragglers.

DJs have only recently caught on in Vientiane. Karaoke is popular, as are live-music performances of international songs or Thai classics.

★**Bor Pen Yang** BAR
(Map p296; ☎020-27873965; Th Fa Ngoum; ⏲10am-midnight; 📶) Overlooking mother Mekong, a cast of locals, expats, bar girls and travellers assembles at this tin-roofed, wood-raftered watering hole to gaze at the sunset over nearby Thailand. Western tunes, pool tables and a huge bar to drape yourself over, as well as international football and rugby on large flat-screen TVs.

★**Spirit House** COCKTAIL BAR
(Map p292; ☎021-262530; Th Fa Ngoum; cocktails 40,000-60,000K; ⏲7am-11pm; 📶) This traditional Lao house facing the Mekong has a well-stocked bar with enough cocktails on the menu to keep a roué rolling along. A chilled soundtrack complements the dark woods and comfy couches of its stylish interior. Hit the exceptionally happy hours from 5pm to 7pm.

Chokdee Cafe BAR
(Map p296; ☎021-263847; www.chokdeecafe.com; Th Fa Ngoum; ⏲7am-11pm; 📶) A Belgian bar and restaurant on the riverfront, Chokdee offers one of the best selections of Belgian brews in Asia with around 70 varieties to sample. Keep the flag flying with a bucket of *moules* (mussels) and *frites* (French fries), with 20 original sauces available to douse them in.

Khop Chai Deu BAR
(Map p296; ☎021-223022; www.inthira.com; Th Setthathirath; ⏲7am-midnight) KCD boasts low-lit interiors and a sophisticated drinks list, plus activities like speed dating and women's arm wrestling. On the 3rd floor there's a super-slick bar with great views. A popular place for draught Beerlao, and there's plenty of good food to go with it.

CCC Bar BAR
(Map p296; ☎020-55448686; Th Souphanouvong; ⏲7pm-late) The most popular gay bar in town, this place draws a convivial crowd to its small bar. It pushes it up a gear at weekends with a cabaret show and draws a mixed

crowd from 1am as one of the only late, late places in the capital.

Le Trio CAFE

(Map p296; ☎020-22553552; Th Setthathirath; ⊙8am-4pm; 📶) Le Trio roasts its own coffee and is one of the top hang-outs for caffeine cravers in Vientiane. As well as original coffees, it also offers fragrant herbal teas, juices and blends, plus some creative cocktails and desserts.

☆ Entertainment

Like everything else, Vientiane's entertainment scene is picking up as money and politics allows, though the range remains fairly limited. By law, entertainment venues must close by 11.30pm, though most push it to about midnight.

Lao National Opera Theatre THEATRE

(Map p296; ☎021-26000; Th Khounboulom; ⊙7-8.30pm Tue, Thu & Sat) This state-sponsored performance venue features a smorgasbord of Lao entertainment ranging from self-proclaimed 'Lao oldies' to Lao boxing and traditional performances of *Pha Lak Pha Lam,* the Lao version of the Indian epic the Ramayana.

Centre Culturel et de Coopération Linguistique CINEMA

(French Cultural Centre; Map p296; ☎021-215764; www.ambafrance-laos.org; Th Lan Xang; entry free, cinema 10,000K; ⊙9.30am-6.30pm Mon-Fri, to noon Sat) Dance, art exhibitions, literary discussions and live music all take place in this Gallic hive of cultural activity. As well as cult French films – shown weekends at 3pm (kids) and 6.30pm (adults) – the centre also offers French and Lao language lessons.

Shopping

Just about anything made in Laos is available for purchase in Vientiane, including hill-tribe crafts, jewellery, traditional textiles and carvings. The main shopping area in town is along Th Setthathirath and the streets radiating from it.

★T'Shop Lai Gallery COSMETICS, HOMEWARES

(Map p296; ☎021-223178; www.laococo.com/tshoplai.htm; off Th In Paeng; ⊙8am-8pm Mon-Sat, 10am-6pm Sun) Vientiane's finest shop. Imagine a melange of aromas: coconut, aloe vera, honey, frangipani and magnolia, all of them emanating from body oils, soaps, sprays, perfumes and lip balms, plus bangles, prints, fountain pens and more. These wonderful products are made with sustainable, locally sourced products by disadvantaged women who make up the Les Artisans Lao cooperative.

There's also a fine gallery upstairs rotating Lao and international artists' work. Check out the old apothecary units beguilingly stocked with illumined antique bottles. Inspired.

Carol Cassidy Lao Textiles ARTS & CRAFTS

(Map p296; ☎021-212123; www.laotextiles.com; 84-86 Th Nokèokoummane; ⊙8am-noon & 2-5pm Mon-Fri, 8am-noon Sat, or by appointment) Lao Textiles sells high-end contemporary, original-design fabrics inspired by generations-old Lao weaving patterns, motifs and techniques. The American designer, Carol Cassidy, employs Lao weavers who work out the back of the attractive old French-Lao house. Internationally known, with prices to match.

Indochina Handicrafts ARTS & CRAFTS

(Map p296; ☎021-223528; Th Setthathirath; ⊙10am-7pm) Vientiane's version of the Old Curiosity Shop, this enchanting den of Buddha statuary sells antique Ho Chi Minh and Mao busts, Russian wristwatches, communist memorabilia, Matchbox cars, medals, snuff boxes and vintage serving trays. It's a visit that shouldn't be missed.

Night Market MARKET

(Map p296; Th Fa Ngoum; ⊙6-10.30pm) Vientiane's night market lights up the riverfront with a selection of stalls hawking handicrafts and T-shirts. It's not quite the atmosphere of Luang Prabang's, but nonetheless a good place to browse and hone your haggling skills.

Book Café BOOKS

(Map p296; Th Hengboun; ⊙8am-8pm Mon-Fri) Vientiane's best-stocked secondhand bookshop sells travel guides, thrillers and informative books on Laos' culture and history.

Information

DANGERS & ANNOYANCES

By international standards Vientiane has a very low crime rate, but there's a small risk of getting mugged. Be especially careful around the BCEL Bank on the riverfront, where bag snatchers, usually a two-man team with a motorbike, have been known to strike; common sense should be an adequate defence. Violent crime against visitors is extremely rare, but watch out for commando ladyboys on Th Setthathirath close to midnight, as locals suggest they are very experienced at helping drunks part with their wallets.

Also stay off the city's roads during festivals, particularly April's Pi Mai, when drunk-driving-related accidents skyrocket. Pickpocketing also occurs more frequently then.

Call the **Tourist Police** (Map p296; ☎021-251128; Th Lan Xang) if you need to talk to an English-speaking police officer.

EMERGENCY

Ambulance	☎1195
Fire	☎1190
Police	☎1191
Tourist Police	☎021-251128

INTERNET ACCESS

Wi-fi is available at most of Vientiane's guesthouses, hotels, cafes and restaurants.

There's a row of **internet cafes** (Map p296; per hour 6000K; ⏲9am-11pm) on the north side of Th Setthathirath between Nam Phu (the fountain) and Th Manthatourath. The **Oriental Bookshop** (Map p296; ☎021-215352; 121 Th Chao Anou; per hour 5000K; ⏲10am-8pm) offers several computers with internet access.

MEDIA

Laos' only English-language newspaper is the government-run *Vientiane Times*. It feature stories on Laos' commercial relations with China and other foreign countries, detailing mining and hydroelectric-power developments. French-speakers should look for *Le Rénovateur*.

MEDICAL SERVICES

Vientiane's medical facilities can leave a lot to be desired, so for anything serious make a break for the border and the much more sophisticated hospitals in Thailand. **Aek Udon International Hospital** (☎42 342555; Th Phosri) in Thailand can dispatch an ambulance to take you to Udon Thani. Less serious ailments can be dealt with in Vientiane.

Alliance International Medical Center (Map p292; ☎021-513095; www.aimclao.com; Th Luang Prabang) This hospital is fresh and clean, and treats basic ailments like broken bones and dispenses antibiotics.

Australian Embassy Clinic (Map p292; ☎021-353840; Th Tha Deua; ⏲8.30am-5pm Mon-Fri) For nationals of Australia, Britain, Canada, Papua New Guinea and New Zealand only. This clinic's Australian doctor treats minor problems by appointment; it doesn't have emergency facilities. Accepts cash or credit cards.

Centre Médical de L'Ambassade de France (French Embassy Medical Center; Map p292; ☎021-214150; cnr Th Khu Vieng & Th Simeuang; ⏲8.30am-noon & 4.30-7pm Mon, Tue, Thu & Fri, 1.30-5pm Wed, 9am-noon Sat) Open to all, but visits outside regular hours by appointment only.

International Clinic (Map p292; ☎021-214021; Th Fa Ngoum; ⏲24hr) Part of the Mahasot Hospital; probably the best place for not-too-complex emergencies. Some English-speaking doctors. Take ID and cash.

Poppy's Pharmacy & Beauty (Map p296; ☎030-9810108; Th Hengboun; ⏲8am-10pm) Bright and clean, this modern, well-stocked pharmacy is great for toiletries, cosmetics, sun cream, malaria pills (not Larium), and sleeping tablets for long bus journeys.

Setthathirat Hospital (☎021-351156) Thanks to a recent overhaul by the Japanese, this hospital northeast of the city is another option for minor ailments.

MONEY

There are plenty of banks and licensed moneychangers in the capital.

Banks listed here change cash and travellers cheques and issue cash advances (mostly in kip, but occasionally in US dollars and Thai baht) against Visa and/or MasterCard. Many now have ATMs that work with foreign cards, but it's often cheaper to get a cash advance manually.

ANZ (Map p296; ☎021-222700; 33 Th Lan Xang; ⏲8.30am-3.30pm Mon-Fri) Main branch has two ATMs and can provide cash advances on Visa or MasterCard for a flat fee of 45,000K. Additional ATMs can be found on Th Setthathirath and Th Fa Ngoum.

Bank of Ayudhya (Map p296; ☎021-214575; 79/6 Th Lan Xang; ⏲8.30am-3.30pm Mon-Fri) Cash advances on Visa cards here carry a 1.5% commission.

Banque pour le Commerce Extérieur Lao (BCEL; Map p296; cnr Th Pangkham & Th Fa Ngoum; ⏲8.30am-7pm Mon-Fri, to 3pm Sat & Sun) Best rates; longest hours. Exchange booth on Th Fa Ngoum and three ATMs attached to the main building.

Joint Development Bank (Map p296; 75/1-5 Th Lan Xang; ⏲8.30am-3.30pm Mon-Fri) Usually charges the lowest commission on cash advances. Also has an ATM.

Krung Thai Bank (Map p296; ☎021-213480; Th Lan Xang; ⏲8.30am-3.30pm Mon-Fri) Also has an **exchange booth** (Map p296) on Th Fa Ngoum.

Lao-Viet Bank (Map p296; ☎021-214377; Th Lan Xang; ⏲8.30am-3.30pm Mon-Fri) Has an ATM and money exchange.

Siam Commercial Bank (Map p296; 117 Th Lan Xang; ⏲8.30am-3.30pm Mon-Fri) ATM and cash advances on Visa.

Thai Military Bank (Map p296; ☎021-216486; cnr Th Samsènethai & Th Khounboulom; ⏲8.30am-3.30pm Mon-Fri) Cash advance on Visa only for 200B.

POST

Main Post Office (Map p296; ☎020-22206362; Th Saylom; ⊙8am-5pm Mon-Fri, to noon Sat & Sun) Come here for post restante, stamps, wiring money and courier service.

TELEPHONE

Lao Telecom Namphu Centre (Map p296; Th Setthathirath; ⊙9am-7pm) International fax, and domestic and international calls.

TOURIST INFORMATION

Midnight Mapper (☎020-58656994; espritdemer@hotmail.com) It might sound like an old Stones song but the Midnight Mapper, aka Don Duvall, has tirelessly mapped Laos over the last 10 years to produce the most in-depth, accurate GPS map available. This is a blessing for motorcyclists and cyclists alike who might otherwise get lost if heading off the beaten track. Hire one of his handheld Garmin GPS devices for US$7 per day or buy his Laos GPS map to load on your own gadget for US$50.

Tourist Information Centre (NTAL; Map p296; ☎021-212248; www.ecotourismlaos.com; Th Lan Xang; ⊙8.30am-noon & 1.30-4pm) A worthwhile tourist information centre with easy-to-use descriptions of each province, helpful staff who speak decent English, as well as brochures and regional maps.

TRAVEL AGENCIES

Central Vientiane has plenty of agencies that can book air and Thai train tickets and organise visas for Myanmar and Vietnam.

Green Discovery (Map p296; ☎021-264528; www.greendiscoverylaos.com; Th Setthathirath; ⊙9am-9pm)

Lin Travel Service (Map p296; ☎021-218707; 239 Th Hanoi/Phnom Penh; ⊙8.30am-9pm)

VISAS

Immigration Office (Map p296; ☎021-212250; Th Hatsady; ⊙8am-4.30pm Mon-Fri) Getting an extension on a tourist visa is easy. Go to the Immigration Office, in the Ministry of Public Security building opposite Talat Sao, fill out a form, supply your passport and a photo, and pay US$2 per day for the extra time you want. The whole process can be completed in one hour.

ℹ Getting There & Away

AIR

Departures from Vientiane's **Wattay International Airport** (☎021-512165; www.vientianeairport.com) are very straightforward. The domestic terminal is in the older, white building east of the more impressive international terminal. There is an (often unstaffed) information counter in the arrivals hall, and food can be found upstairs in the international terminal.

Air Asia (www.airasia.com; Wattay Airport International Terminal) Vientiane to Bangkok and Kuala Lumpur daily.

Bangkok Airways (Map p296; www.bangkokair.com; Lao Plaza Hotel, 63 Th Samsènethai; ⊙8am-5pm Mon-Fri, to noon Sat) Daily flights between Bangkok and both Vientiane and Luang Prabang, plus Chiang Mai to Luang Prabang.

China Eastern Airlines (Map p292; www.ce-air.com; Th Luang Prabang; ⊙8am-5pm Mon-Fri, to noon Sat) Flies daily to Kunming and Nanning.

Korean Air (www.koreanair.com) Daily connections between Vientiane and Seoul.

Lao Airlines (☎021-512028; Wattay Airport International Terminal; ⊙6am-6pm) Domestic flights to Savannakhet, Pakse, Luang Prabang, Phonsavan (Xieng Khuang) and Luang Namtha; plus international flights to Siem Reap, Phnom Penh, Seoul, Singapore, Bangkok, Chiang Mai, Hanoi, Ho Chi Minh, Kunming and Guangzhou.

Lao Skyway (☎021-513022; www.laoskyway.com; Domestic Terminal, Wattay International Airport; ⊙8am-8pm) Local airline with flights from Vientiane to Luang Prabang, Luang Namtha, Udomxai and Huay Xai.

Thai Airways International (Map p292; www.thaiairways.com; Th Luang Prabang, Vientiane; ⊙8.30am-5pm Mon-Fri, to noon Sat) Vientiane to Bangkok twice daily.

Vietnam Airlines (Map p296; www.vietnamairlines.com; Lao Plaza Hotel, 63 Th Samsènethai, Vientiane; ⊙9am-5pm Mon-Fri, to noon Sat) Connects Vientiane with Hanoi, Ho Chi Minh City and Phnom Penh, plus Luang Prabang with Hanoi and Siem Reap.

BOAT

Passenger-boat services between Vientiane and Luang Prabang are almost extinct as most people now take the bus, which is both faster and cheaper.

BUS

In Laos roads are poor and buses break down, so times can take longer than advertised. Buses use three different stations in Vientiane, all with some English-speaking staff, and food and drink stands.

The **Northern Bus Station** (Th Asiane), about 2km northwest of the airport, serves all points north of Vang Vieng, including China. Destinations and the latest ticket prices are listed in English.

The **Southern Bus Station** (Rte 13 South), commonly known as Dong Dok Bus Station or just *khíw lot lák káo* (Km 9 Bus Station), is 9km out of town and serves everywhere to the south. Buses to Vietnam depart from here.

The final departure point is the **Talat Sao Bus Station** (Map p296; ☎021-216507; Th Khu Vieng), from where desperately slow local buses run to destinations within Vientiane Province,

BUSES FROM VIENTIANE

DESTINATION	STATION	COST (K)	DISTANCE (KM)	DURATION (HR)	DEPARTURES
Attapeu (fan)	Southern	140,000	812	22-24	9.30am, 5pm
Attapeu (VIP)	Southern	200,000	812	14-16	8.30pm
Don Khong (fan)	Southern	150,000	788	16-19	10.30am
Huay Xai	Northern	230,000-250,000	869	24	10am, 5.30pm
Khon Kaen (a/c)	Talat Sao	50,000	197	4	8.15am, 2.45pm
Lak Sao (fan)	Southern	85,000	334	6-8	5am, 6am, 7am, 8.30pm
Luang Namtha	Northern	200,000	676	24	8.30am, 5pm
Luang Prabang	Northern	110,000	384	10-11	6.30am, 7.30am, 8.30am, 11am, 1.30pm, 4pm, 6pm, 7.30pm (a/c)
Luang Prabang (VIP)	Northern	130,000-150,000	384	9-12	8am, 9am, 7.30pm, 8pm
Nakhon Ratchasima (a/c)	Talat Sao	149,000	387	7	5pm
Nong Khai (a/c)	Talat Sao	17,000	25	1½	7.30am, 9.30am, 12.40pm, 2.30pm, 3.30pm, 6pm
Nong Khiang (fan)	Southern	130,000	818	16-20	11am
Paksan	Southern	40,000-50,000	143	3-4	7am-3pm (tuk-tuk); take any bus going south
Pakse (fan)	Southern	140,000	677	16-18	regular from 7am to 8pm
Pakse (VIP)	Southern	170,000	677	8-10	8.30pm
Phongsali	Northern	210,000-230,000	811	25-28	7.15am (fan), 6pm (sleeper)
Phonsavan	Northern	110,000	374	10-11	6.30am, 7.30am, 9.30am, 4pm, 6.40pm
Phonsavan (sleeper)	Northern	150,000	374	10-11	8pm
Sainyabuli	Northern	110,000-130,000	485	14-16	9am, 4pm, 6.30pm
Salavan (a/c)	Southern	160,000	774	16	7.30pm
Salavan (fan)	Southern	130,000	774	15-20	4.30pm, 7.30pm
Salavan (VIP)	Southern	190,000	774	13	8.30pm
Sam Neua	Northern	170,000-190,000	612	22-24	7am, 9.30am, noon (fan), 5pm
Sam Neua (sleeper)	Northern	210,000	612	22-24	2pm
Savannakhet	Southern	75,000	457	8-11	half-hourly 5.30-9am, or any bus to Pakse
Savannakhet (VIP)	Southern	120,000	457	8-10	8.30pm
Tha Khaek	Southern	60,000	332	6	4am, 5am, 6am, noon, or any bus to Savannakhet or Pakse
Tha Khaek (VIP)	Southern	80,000	332	5	noon, 1pm
Udomxai	Northern	150,000-170,000	578	16-19	6.45am, 1.45pm, 5pm
Udomxai (VIP)	Northern	190,000	578	15-17	4pm
Udon Thani (a/c)	Talat Sao	22,000	82	2½	8am, 10.30am, 11.30am, 2pm, 4pm, 6pm
Vang Vieng (fan)	Talat Sao	30,000	157	3-4	7am, 9.30am, 1pm, 3pm

including Vang Vieng, and some more distant destinations, though for the latter you're better going to the Northern or Southern Bus Stations. The **Thai-Lao International Bus** (Map p296) also uses this station for its trips to Khon Kaen, Nakhon Ratchasima, Nong Khai and Udon Thani.

For sleeper buses to Kunming, China (US$95, 38 hours, departing 2pm), contact the **Tong Li Bus Company** (☎021-242657) at the Northern Bus Station. For Vietnam, buses leave the Southern Bus Station daily at 7pm for Hanoi (220,000K, 24 hours) via Vinh (180,000K, 16 hours), and also for Danang (230,000K, 22 hours) via Hue (200,000K, 19 hours), except for Monday, Thursday and Sunday when they leave at 6pm. For Ho Chi Minh City change at Danang; contact **SDT** (☎021-720175) for details.

Getting Around

TO/FROM THE AIRPORT

Taxis to the centre cost US$7 and minivans are available for US$8. Only official taxis can pick up at the airport.

If you're on a budget and don't have a lot of luggage, simply walk 500m to the airport gate and cross Th Souphanouvong and hail a shared jumbo (20,000K per person). Prices on shared transport will rise if you're going further than the centre.

Bus 49 (Nong Taeng) from Talat Sao Bus Station makes the journey out to the airport for 6000K.

BICYCLE

Cycling is a cheap, easy and recommended way of getting around mostly flat Vientiane. Loads of guesthouses and several shops hire out bikes for 10,000K to 20,000K per day. Mountain bikes are available but are more expensive at 30,000K to 40,000K; try **Lao Bike** (Map p296; ☎020-55090471; Th Setthathirath; ⊙9am-6pm).

CAR & MOTORCYCLE

There are several international car-hire companies with representation in Vientiane, including **Avis** (Map p296; ☎021-223867; www.avis.la; Th Setthathirath; ⊙8.30am-6.30pm Mon-Fri, to 1pm Sat & Sun) and **Sixt** (☎021-513228; www.sixtlao.com; Wattay International Airport; ⊙7am-7pm).

Scooters are a popular means of getting around Vientiane and can be hired throughout the centre of town. Recommended hire places include the following:

First-One Motorbike Rental (Map p296; ☎020-55528299; Th François Ngin; scooters per day 70,000K; ⊙8.30am-6pm)

Mixay Bike 2 (Map p296; ☎020-77882510; Th Chau Anou; scooter per 24hr 60,000-80,000K; ⊙8am-8pm)

For dirt bikes try the following:

Drivenbyadventure (☎020-58656994; www.hochiminhtrail.org; rental per day US$38-95, tours per day US$160-200) Offers the most professionally maintained dirt bikes in Laos, including Honda CRF250s (US$38 per day), Honda XR400s (US$50) and KTM XCW450s (US$95). Owner Don Duvall is a GPS mapping expert who's explored every inch of the Ho Chi Minh Trail and is a great guide to the history of this legendary road: you won't get lost!

Fuark Motorcycle Hire (☎021-261970; fuarkmotorcross@yahoo.com) A leading locally owned and operated motorbike-hire place that offers a range of well-maintained dirt bikes (from US$30 per day), with drop-offs at key cities around the country. Delivers the bikes to you.

TAXIS

Meter Taxi Service (Map p296; ☎021-454168) Drivers from this company often wait for fares on Th Pangkham, just across from the Day Inn Hotel.

Talat Sao Taxi Stand (Map p296; cnr Th Lan Xang & Th Khu Vieng; ⊙7am-6pm) At the Talat Sao taxi stand, across from Talat Sao, you'll find taxis to the Thai-Lao Friendship Bridge (300B).

Taxi Vientiane Capital Lao Group (☎021-454168; ⊙24hr) A metered-taxi company that operates in Vientiane.

Tourist Taxi (☎1420; to airport around 50,000K; ⊙24hr) This new metered service just for tourists gives you a chance to keep an eye on your fare.

TUK-TUK

Drivers of jumbos and tuk-tuks will take passengers on journeys as short as 500m or as far as 20km. Understanding the various types of tuk-tuk is important if you don't want to be overcharged (and can save you arguments in addition to money). Tourist tuk-tuks are the most expensive, while share jumbos that run regular routes around town (eg Th Luang Prabang to Th Setthathirath or Th Lan Xang to That Luang) are much cheaper, usually less than 5000K per person.

AROUND VIENTIANE

Phu Khao Khuay National Protected Area (NPA)

Covering more than 2000 sq km of mountains and rivers to the east of Vientiane, the underrated Phu Khao Ķhuay Natioṇal Protected Area (NPA; ປາສະຫງວນແຫ່ງຊາດພູເຂົາຄວາຍ) is the most

GETTING TO THAILAND: VIENTIANE TO NONG KHAI

Getting to the border At the **Tha Na Leng (Laos)/Nong Khai (Thailand) border crossing** (6am to 10pm), the Thai-Lao Friendship Bridge (Saphan Mittaphap Thai-Lao) spans the Mekong River. The Laos border is approximately 20km from Vientiane, and the easiest and cheapest way to the bridge is to cross on the Thai-Lao International Bus. It conducts daily departures for the Thai cities of Khon Kaen, Nakhon Ratchasima, Nong Khai and Udon Thani. Alternative means of transport between Vientiane and the bridge include taxi (300B), tuk-tuk (shared/charter 5000K/250B), jumbo (250B to 300B) or the number 14 Tha Deua bus from Talat Sao Bus Station (15,000K) between 6am and 5.30pm.

To cross from Thailand, tuk-tuks are available from Nong Khai's train station (20B) and bus station (55B) to the Thai border post at the bridge. You can also hop on the Thai-Lao International Bus from Nong Khai bus station (55B, 1½ hours) or Udon Thani bus station (80B, two hours), both of which terminate at Vientiane's Talat Sao Bus Station. If flying into Udon Thani, a tuk-tuk from the airport to the city's bus station should cost about 120B.

It's also possible to cross the brige by train, as tracks have been extended from Nong Khai's train station 3.5km into Laos, terminating at Dongphasy Station, about 13km from central Vientiane. From Nong Khai there are two daily departures (9.30am and 4pm, fan/air-con 20/50B, 15 minutes) and border formalities are taken care of at the respective train stations. But in reality, unless you are a trainspotter, it is much more convenient to use the international bus or other road transport.

At the border Travellers from most countries enjoy 30-day, visa-free access to Thailand. Lao visas (30 days) are available for US$20 to US$42, depending on your nationality. If you don't have a photo you'll be charged an extra US$1, and be aware that an additional US$1 'overtime fee' is charged from 6am to 8am and 6pm to 10pm on weekdays, as well as on weekends and holidays. Don't be tempted to use a tuk-tuk driver to get your Lao visa, no matter what they tell you, as it will take far longer than doing it yourself, and you'll have to pay for the 'service'. Insist they take you straight to the bridge.

Moving on Sleeper trains from Nong Khai to Bangkok leave at 6.20pm and 7.10pm and cost 1217/778B for a 1st/2nd-class sleeper ticket. Tickets on the 7am day train cost 498/388B for air-con/fan seating.

accessible protected area in Laos. Treks ranging in duration from a couple of hours to three days have been developed in partnership with Ban Na (ບ້ານນາ) and Ban Hat Khai (ບ້ານຫາດໄຂ), villages on the edge of the NPA.

Phu Khao Khuay (ພູເຂົາຄວາຍ; *poo cow kwai*) means 'Buffalo Horn Mountain', a name derived from local legend, and is home to three major rivers that flow off a sandstone mountain range. It boasts an extraordinary array of endangered wildlife, including wild elephant, gibbon, Asiatic black bear, clouded leopard, Siamese fireback pheasant and green peafowl. Depending on elevation, visitors may encounter dry evergreen dipterocarp (a Southeast Asian tree with two-winged fruit), mixed deciduous forest, conifer forest or grassy uplands. Several impressive waterfalls are accessible as day trips from Vientiane.

Sights

Tat Leuk WATERFALL

Tat Leuk is a small waterfall, but is a beautiful place to camp for the night. You can swim above the falls if the water isn't flowing too fast, and the visitor centre has some information about the area, including a detailed guide to the 1.5km-long Huay Bon Nature Trail.

The guy who looks after the visitor centre can arrange local treks for 160,000K, and rents quality four-person tents for 30,000K, plus hammocks, mattresses, mosquito nets and sleeping bags for 10,000K each. There's a very basic restaurant (best supplemented with food you bring from outside), a small library of wildlife books and a pair of binoculars.

From the junction to Ban Hat Khai village, turn left and continue another 6km until you

PINNEE / GETTY IMAGES ©

1. Lao Cuisine (p392)
Rice-noodle soup is the standard Lao breakfast. The one pictured here is a spicy coconut version.

2. Si Phan Don (p380)
The picture-perfect islands of this archipelago are lovely places to unwind.

3. Buddhist Monks
Laos' saffron-clad monks are one of the country's most easy-to-spot highlights.

4. Tham Phu Kham (p309)
After a stiff climb, this beautiful lagoon near Vang Vieng is the perfect spot for a relaxing dip.

EELIZA13 / BUDGET TRAVEL ©

see a rough 4km road on the left, which leads to Tat Leuk.

Wat Pha Baht Phonsan BUDDHIST TEMPLE

(6am-6pm) En route to Ban Na it's worth stopping briefly at Wat Pha Baht Phonsan, which sits on a rocky outcrop at Tha Pha Bat, beside Rte 13 about 1.5km south of Ban Na. The wat is revered for its large *pa bàht* (Buddha footprint) shrine, monastery and substantial reclining Buddha figure. You'll recognise it by the large and well-ornamented 1933-vintage stupa.

Tat Xai & Pha Xai WATERFALL

(ຕາດໄຊ ຜາໄຊ) Tat Xai cascades down seven steps, and 800m downstream Pha Xai plunges over a 40m-high cataract. There's a pool that's good for swimming, though it can get dangerous during the wet season. Both waterfalls are accessed from Rte 13, just before Ban Tha Bok. From the junction to Ban Hat Khai, it's 9km to Tat Xai and Pha Xai.

Getting There & Away

Buses from Vientiane's **Southern Bus Station** (p302) leave regularly for Ban Tha Bok and Paksan. For Wat Pha Baht Phonsan and Ban Na get off at Tha Pha Bat (25,000K) near the Km 81 stone; the shrine is right on Rte 13 and Ban Na is about 1.5km north and well signposted.

For Ban Hat Khai, keep on the bus until a turn-off left (north) at Km 92, just before Ban Tha Bok (30,000K). If you have your own transport, continue 8km along the smooth laterite road until you cross the new bridge. Turn right at the Y-intersection and it's 1km to Ban Hat Khai. Alternatively, villagers in Ban Hat Khai can arrange motorcyle pick-up from Ban Tha Bok for 25,000K one way if you call ahead.

Note that as you come from Vientiane there are three signed entrances to Phu Khao Khuay – the second leads to Ban Na and the third to Ban Hat Khai and the waterfalls.

Ang Nam Ngum

Located midway between Vientiane and Vang Vieng, Ang Nam Ngum is a vast artificial lake created when the Nam Ngum (Ngum River) was dammed in 1971. The highest peaks of the former river valley became forested islands after the inundation and, following the 1975 Pathet Lao conquest of Vientiane, an estimated 3000 prostitutes, petty criminals and drug addicts were rounded up from the capital and banished to two of these islands; one each for men and women. Today, the Nam Ngum hydroelectric plant generates most of the electricity used in the Vientiane area. Potential stops around the lake include Nam Tok Tat Khu Khana, the Vang Sang Buddhas and Nam Lik Eco-Village.

Sights

Vang Sang Buddhas BUDDHIST SITE

FREE At Vang Sang, 65km north of Vientiane via Rte 13, sits a cluster of 10 high-relief Buddha sculptures on cliffs thought to date from the 16th century. Two of the Buddhas are more than 3m tall. The name means 'Elephant Palace', a reference to an elephant graveyard once found nearby.

Nam Tok Tat Khu Khana WATERFALL

FREE It's a bit of a mouthful, but Nam Tok Tat Khu Khana (Tat Khu Khana Waterfall, also called Hin Khana) is one of the easier waterfalls to reach from Vientiane. Follow a 10km dirt road, which leads west from Rte 13 near the village of Ban Naxaithong, near Km 17.

Sleeping & Eating

★ **Sanctuary Resort** BOUTIQUE HOTEL $$

(020-55320612; www.sanctuaryhotelsandresorts.com; Ban Tha Heua; r US$38-50;) Sanctuary Resort has impressive new bungalow villas on the shores of Ang Nam Ngum. They're lovingly appointed with contemporary fixtures; there are also larger deluxe villas with outdoor Jacuzzi that can double up as a two-bedroom family villa. There is also a floating swimming pool in the lake, quite a novelty.

Water sports are available, including jet-skis, paddleboards and boats. It's a good place to stop for lunch for those with their own transport thanks to a mixed menu of Laotian and international dishes combined with a commanding view over the resort.

Nam Lik Eco-Village BUNGALOW $$

(020-55508719; www.namlik.org; s/d US$30/40) Nam Lik Eco-Village, a riverside resort on the west bank of the Nam Lik (Lik River), makes a good base for outdoor activities such as orchid walks, kayaking in the river or mountain biking on fixed trails. It's located 7km east of the Ban Senhxoum, itself just past the Km 80 marker.

Nam Ngeum LAOTIAN $

(020-55513521; Ban Na Khuen; mains 20,000-60,000K; 9am-9pm) One of a handful of restaurants at Ban Na Khuen, Nam Ngeum gets good reviews for its tasty *gôy bạh* (tart and spicy fish salad), *gạang bạh* (fish soup) and *neung bạh* (steamed fish with fresh herbs).

Getting There & Around

It's easier to access most places around Ang Nam Ngum with your own transport. Public transport is convenient for the resorts near Ban Tha Heua, but not so straightforward for other destinations.

Getting to Ban Tha Heua is easy as it's on the main road between Vientiane and Vang Vieng. Heading north you'll probably have to pay the full fare to Vang Vieng. Heading south from Vang Vieng, you may be able to get away with a lower *sŏrngtăaou* (passenger truck) fare of around 10,000K.

For Ban Na Kheun, buses depart Vientiane's Talat Sao Bus Station for Thalat (15,000K, 2½ hours, 87km), the nearest town, every hour from 6.30am to 5.30pm; you'll then need to arrange a sŏrngtăaou to Ban Na Kheun (costing about 15,000K). Salapa Fisherman's Haven can arrange pick-ups from Thalat if you're staying there.

Nam Lik Eco-Village can provide transport with advance bookings. Otherwise, take a bus to Vang Vieng and get off at Ban Senhxoum (25,000K, three hours) and seek local transport for the remaining 7km.

Vang Vieng

Like a rural scene from an old Asian silk painting, Vang Vieng (ວັງວຽງ) crouches low over the Nam Song (Song River) with a backdrop of serene cliffs and a tapestry of vivid green paddy fields. Thanks to the Lao government closing the river rave bars in 2012, the increasingly toxic party scene has been driven to the fringes and the community is rebooting itself as an adrenalin-fuelled adventure destination with some impressive accommodation options on tap. While the town itself is no gem, as concrete hotels build ever higher in search of the quintessential view, across the Nam Song lies a rural idyll.

Spend a few days here – rent a scooter, take a motorcycle tour, go tubing or trekking – and soak up one of Laos' most stunningly picturesque spots. But explore with care and enjoy it sober, as the river and mountains around Vang Vieng have claimed too many travellers' lives already.

Sights & Activities

Caves

Of the most accessible *tàm* (caves), most are signed in English as well as Lao, and an admission fee is collected at the entrance to each cave. The caves around Vang Vieng are spectacular, but caves come with certain hazards: they're dark, slippery and disorienting. A guide (often a young village boy) will lead you through a cave for a small fee; bring water and a torch (flashlight), and be *sure* your batteries aren't about to die. In fact, bearing in mind some of the 'lost in the darkness' horror stories that circulate, it's vital to have a spare torch. For more extensive multicave tours, most guesthouses can arrange a guide. Trips including river tubing and cave tours cost around US$15/25 for a half-/full day.

Tham Jang CAVE

(ຖ້ຳຈັງ; entry incl footbridge fee 17,000K) The most famous of the caves around Vang Vieng, Tham Jang was used as a bunker to defend against marauding *jęen hór* (Yunnanese Chinese) in the early 19th century (*jąng* means 'steadfast'). Stairs lead up to the main cavern entrance.

Tham Phu Kham CAVE

(ຖ້ຳພູຄຳ, Blue Lagoon; 10,000K) The vast Tham Phu Kham is considered sacred by Lao and is popular largely due to the lagoon in the cave. The beautiful green-blue waters are perfect for a dip after the stiff climb. The main cave chamber contains a Thai bronze reclining Buddha, and from here deeper galleries branch off into the mountain. Get here via a scenic but unpaved road to the village of Ban Na Thong. From there follow the signs towards the cliff and climb 200m through scrub forest.

Tham Sang CAVE

(Elephant Cave; 5000K) Tham Sang is a small cavern containing a few Buddha images and a Buddha 'footprint', plus the (vaguely) elephant-shaped stalactite that gives the cave its name. It's best visited in the morning when light enters the cave.

Tham Loup CAVE

(combined entry 10,000K) Tham Loup is a large and delightfully untouched cavern with some impressive stalactites. The combined entry fee covers all the caves in the Tham Sang area. The entrances to the cave are reached from Tham Sang via a signed path that takes you 1km northwest through rice fields.

Tham Hoi CAVE

(combined entry 10,000K) The entrance to Tham Ho is guarded by a large Buddha figure; reportedly the cave continues about 3km into the limestone and an underground lake. The combined entry fee covers all the caves in the Tham Sang area.

Vang Vieng

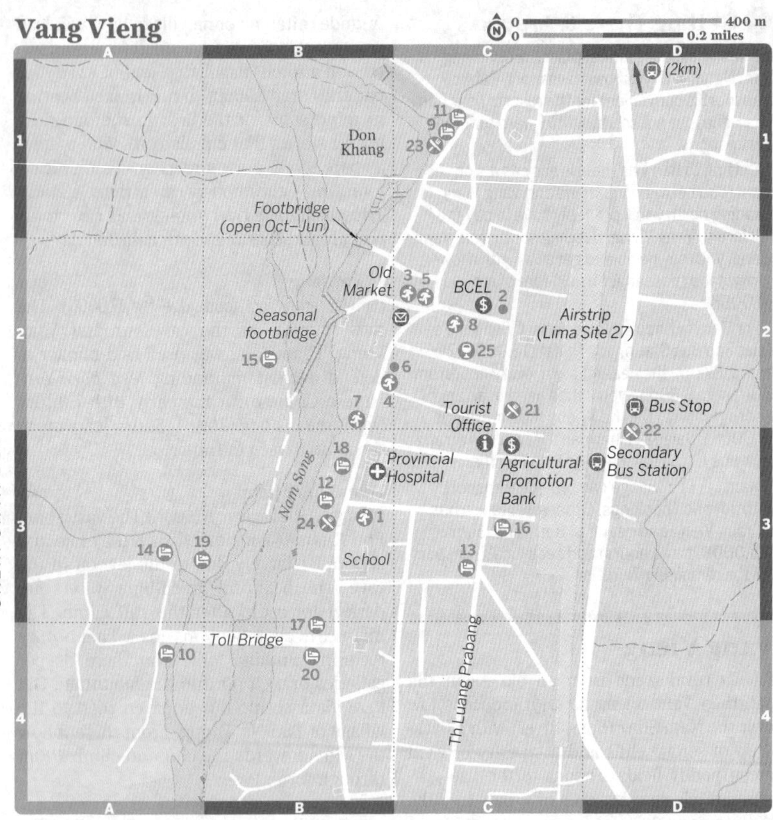

Vang Vieng

Activities, Courses & Tours
1 Adam's Rock Climbing School B3
2 Green Discovery C2
3 Nam Thip Tours C2
4 TCK B2
5 Tubing Operators C2
6 Vang Vieng Adventure Tours C2
Vang Vieng Challenge .... (see 2)
Vang Vieng Jeep Tour .... (see 10)
7 VLT B2
8 Wonderful Tours C2

Sleeping
9 Champa Lao C1
10 Chez Mango A4
11 Easy Go Hostel C1
12 Elephant Crossing B3
13 Laos Haven C3
14 Maylyn Guest House A3
15 Other Side B2
16 Pan's Place C3
17 Riverside Boutique Resort B4
18 Silver Naga B3
19 Vieng Tara Villa A3
20 Villa Vang Vieng Riverside B4

Eating
21 Breakfast Vendors C2
22 Il Tavolo D3
23 Living Room C1
Restaurant du Crabe d'Or .... (see 17)
24 Sababa Organic Restaurant B3

Drinking & Nightlife
Earth .... (see 11)
25 Gary's Irish Bar C2

It's reached via a signed path from Tham Sang that takes you 1km northwest through rice fields.

Tham Nam CAVE
(5000K) Tham Nam is the highlight of the cluster of caves near Vang Vieng. The cave is

about 500m long and a tributary of the Nam Song flows out of its low entrance. It's about 400m south of Tham Hoi, along a well-used path.

In the dry season you can wade into the cave, but when the water is higher you need to take a tube from the friendly woman near the entrance; the tube and headlamp are included in the entrance fee. Dragging yourself through the tunnel on the fixed rope is fun.

Hot-Air Ballooning

A hot-air balloon is a lovely way to see the cliffs, tapestry of paddy fields and snaking river below. The flights are at 6.30am, 4pm and 4.30pm every day, and last 40 minutes. To book contact Mr Vone at **VLT** (023-511369; www.vangviengtour.com; flights US$95).

Tubing

Virtually every younger traveller who comes to Vang Vieng goes tubing down the Nam Song in an inflated tractor-tyre tube. The tubing drop-off point is 3.5km north of town, and depending on the speed and level of the river it can be a soporific crawl beneath the jungle-vined karsts, or a speedy glide downstream back to Vang Vieng. Since the river bars shut in 2012 there's less chance of getting plastered and losing your balance in dangerous currents, but always wear a life jacket when the river runs fast (even if you're not floating in an alternative universe). The many stories of travellers who have drowned in this seemingly peaceful river don't make for pleasant reading.

Whether tubing or kayaking down the Nam Song, rivers can be dangerous, and in times of high water, rapids along the Nam Song can be quite daunting. When tubing, it's worth asking how long the trip should take (durations vary depending on the time of year) so you can allow plenty of time to get back to Vang Vieng before dark, as it's pitch black by about 6pm in winter. Finally, don't forget that while tubing the Nam Song might be more fun when you're stoned, it's also more dangerous.

The **tubing operators** (8.30am-7pm) have formed a cartel so all tubing is organised from a small building across from where the old market once was. It costs 55,000K to rent a tube and there's a 60,000K refundable deposit. Life jackets are available and you can rent a dry bag for 20,000K. The fee includes transport to the tubing drop-off point, but keep in mind that you must return the tube before 6pm, otherwise you'll have to pay a 20,000K late fee. If you lose your tube, you will forfeit the 60,000K deposit.

The other thing you should remember is to take something – a sarong, perhaps – to put on when you finish the trip and have to walk through town. The locals don't appreciate people walking around in bikinis or Speedos.

Kayaking

Kayaking is almost as popular as tubing, and trips are typically combined with other activities such as visits to caves and villages, optional climbing, cycling, and the traverse of a few rapids (the danger of which depends on the speed of the water). There are loads of operators and prices are about US$15 per person per day. Kayaking trips to Vientiane along the Nam Lik (Lik River) are conducted by the excellent **Green Discovery** (023-511230; www.greendiscoverylaos.com; Th Luang Prabang), which also runs kayaking adventures on the Nam Song, and involve a lot of paddling. These are only possible post-monsoon, when the water is sufficiently high.

Another useful tour operator for kayaking is the well-established VLT.

Rock Climbing

In just a few years the limestone walls around Vang Vieng have gained a reputation for some of the best climbing in Southeast Asia. More than 200 routes have been identified and most have been bolted. The routes are rated between 4a and 8b, with the majority being in or near a cave. The most popular climbing spots are at Tham Non (Sleeping Cave), with more than 20 routes, and the tougher Sleeping Wall nearby, where some routes have difficult overhangs.

The climbing season usually runs between October and May, with most routes too wet at other times. However, there are some rock-shaded overhangs on Phadeng Mountain that have recently been bolted down (23 routes), and can still be used in the wet season.

Adam's Rock Climbing School (020-56564499; www.laos-climbing.com; opposite the hospital; half-/full-day climbing 180,000/260,000K, 2-day course US$100, private climbing guide 320,000K) offers fully outfitted courses ranging in skill from beginner to advanced. Adam himself is one of the most experienced climbers in the area, his multilingual guides get good reports and equipment rental is also available (350,000K).

Green Discovery (p311) conducts climbing courses (half-/full day around US$27/36), and when available, can provide a handy climbing guide to the area.

Ziplining

It's all about air and cable these days, with the jungles around Vang Vieng criss-crossed with adrenalin-inducing ziplines. The following tour outfits combine a trek, kayak, abseil or tubing session with zipping:

Nam Thip Tours (020-23333616, 023-511318; 9am-7pm), **TCK** (023-511691; tckamazingtour@gmail.com; 9am-8pm), **Vang Vieng Adventure Tours** (AK Home Ziplining; 020-55033665; http://vangviengadventure.wixsite.com/home; opposite Vansana Hotel; half-/full day US$25/35), **Vang Vieng Challenge** (023-511230; www.greendiscoverylaos.com; Th Luang Prabang) and **Wonderful Tours** (023-511566; www.wonderfultourslaos.la; Th Khann Muang).

Tours

Uncle Tom's Trail Bike Tours ADVENTURE
(020-29958903; uncletomslaos@gmail.com; Rte 13, Kasi; 2 lessons & overnight stay for 1/2 people US$120/208) Operated by a British Enduro gold medallist and Tom Jones lookalike, this popular outfit is safety conscious, thorough and has decent 125cc hybrid motocross bikes on which to learn to ride off-road, which is essential if you plan to explore Laos by motorcycle. The rate includes two half-day lessons and an overnight stay in Kasi. It gets great reviews.

Vang Vieng Jeep Tour SCENIC DRIVE
(020-54435747; noedouine@yahoo.fr; minimum group of 4, per person 180,000K) Based at Chez Mango guesthouse, VV Jeep Tour takes in the best of the countryside in friendly Noé's jeep; first he'll take you to a nearby mountain that you'll gently ascend for an amazing view, then for a walk in the paddy fields followed by a swim in the Blue Lagoon at Tham Phu Kham, before taking a closer look at the cave.

FROM PARTIES TO PARADISE

In 1999, Vang Vieng was a little-known, bucolic affair. Then the word got out – Vang Vieng was Southeast Asia's next hedonistic mecca. By 2009 makeshift rave platforms replaced outdoor activities; gap-year kids were here to get wasted on reefer, Red Bull and shots, methamphetamine and opium cocktails.

By 2011 at least 25 Western kids (mainly Aussies and Brits) had variously died from heart attacks, drownings and broken necks. In 2012, under pressure from the Australian government, the Laos government closed down the rave bars and the town has since repositioned itself as the rural paradise it once was. With an influx of South Korean tourists and family visitors, locals are glad that Vang Vieng is now untroubled by thumping music, disrespectful teens and the misconception that anything goes.

Sleeping

Since the 24-hour party was officially extinguished in 2012, there's now too many guesthouses (100-plus) for the reduced footfall. And while many of the midrange and top-end hotels are enjoying good business with the wealthier demographic, it's the backpacker joints that are languishing. Increasingly boutique hotels are moving in as Vang Vieng ditches its dreads in favour of stylish threads.

In Town

★**Champa Lao** GUESTHOUSE $
(020-58234612; www.facebook.com/champalaobungalows; r without bathroom 70,000K, tr with bathroom 150,000K, cabanas with/without bathroom 120,000/60,000K; P) With new Thai owners, this stilted Lao house has basic fan rooms with mozzie nets. The garden, choked with plants, is a delight and you can swing on a hammock while taking in the sunset and karst from its aerial balcony. There are also bungalows down by the river bank.

Opposite is the beautiful Champa Lao Villa that can sleep four to eight people (US$70 to US$100).

★**Pan's Place** GUESTHOUSE $
(023-511484; Th Luang Prabang; dm 30,000K, s/d with bathroom 70,000/88,000K, without bathroom 50,000/64,000K;) Radiating a welcoming vibe, Pan's is a VV backpacking institution, with its basic but cosy fan rooms with tiled floors and en suites. Out back are cabanas in a leafy garden, plus a communal chilling area. There's also a little cafe and a cinema room upstairs with hundreds of DVDs to choose from.

Easy Go Hostel HOSTEL $
(☎020-55366679; www.easygohostel.com; dm 25,000K, r with/without air-con 90,000/60,000K, tr with air-con 120,000K;) Crafted from bamboo and rattan, and run by a lively team, Easy Go offers eight-berth and four-berth dorms and eight private rooms. The ace card is its laid-back lounge with comfy cushions, pool table and flat-screen TV, with even wider-screen views of the cliffs.

Silver Naga HOTEL $$
(☎023-511822; www.silvernaga.com; r US$65-180;) A major new hotel on the east-bank riverfront, from the owners of Elephant Crossing. The new rooms here feature contemporary decoration and lots of nice touches like private balcony, flat-screen TV and rain shower. There is a 2nd-floor pool with a killer karst view that is open to nonguests for 50,000K.

Elephant Crossing HOTEL $$
(☎023-511232; www.theelephantcrossinghotel.com; r US$40-60; @) Set in leafy gardens peppered with swing chairs and with an attractive verandah to take breakfast by the river, Elephant Crossing has 36 tasteful rooms with glass-panel walls and spotless en suites. Hmong bed runners, wood floors, air-con, TV and fridge complete the picture. It's often booked out by Contiki Travel though, so reservations are hard to score.

Laos Haven HOTEL $$
(☎020-59043944; www.laoshaven.com; r US$22-29;) While 'haven' might suggest a jungle-clad riverside hideaway, this is actually a smart contemporary hotel on the main drag. The rooms are spacious and come with air-con and hot showers.

Villa Vang Vieng Riverside BOUTIQUE HOTEL $$
(☎023-511460; www.villavangvieng.com; r US$60-76;) A smart new boutique hotel near the toll bridge. The rooms are relatively small but well appointed with tasteful furnishings and contemporary bathrooms. The swimming pool is located on the banks of the Nam Song and is open to nonguests for 30,000K per day.

★**Riverside Boutique Resort** BOUTIQUE HOTEL $$$
(☎021-511726; www.riversidevangvieng.com; r US$123-150; @) Sugar-white and uberstylish, this beautiful boutique belle offers generously spaced rooms wrapped around a citrus-green pool and a verdant garden looking out onto the karsts. Rooms themselves are gorgeous with balconies, crisp white sheets, and chic decor straight from the pages of *Wallpaper*. It's located by the toll bridge.

Over the River & Out of Town

★**Maylyn Guest House** GUESTHOUSE $
(☎020-55604095; www.facebook.com/maylynguesthouse; bungalows 80,000K, r 100,000-120,000K;) Over the bridge and run by gregarious Jo, Maylyn's cosy, well-spaced cabanas afford dramatic views of the karsts. There's also a number of immaculate rooms including a newer wing of en suite doubles with tasteful decor and private balcony overlooking the river and cliffs. The lush garden is a wonderland for kids and there is a pair of family rooms for 200,000K.

Chez Mango GUESTHOUSE $
(☎020-54435747; www.chezmango.com; r with/without bathroom 80,000/60,000K;) Located over the bridge, Mango is friendly, scrupulously clean and has seven basic but colourful cabanas (some with bathrooms) with private balconies in its flowery gardens. Shaded by trees, there's also a *sala* (open-sided shelter) to read in. Run by Noé, who also runs the excellent Vang Vieng Jeep Tour (p312) from here, this is a soporific and restful spot.

Other Side BUNGALOW $
(☎020-55126288; bungalows 70,000K; @) These stilted, mint-green bungalows on the west bank come with balconies, en suites and fan. They may be barebones basic but enjoy exquisite, uninterrupted views of the cliffs. Thanks to changes in nocturnal wildlife it's more peaceful too. Flop in that hammock and relax.

Vang Vieng Organic Farm GUESTHOUSE $
(☎023-511220; www.laofarm.org; dm 35,000-50,000K, r 150,000-250,000K; @) Located by the Nam Song in an idyllically quiet spot a few kilometres out of town, this organic farm has sparklingly clean bungalows with mosquito nets, bedside lamps, en suites and verandahs looking out onto the soaring cliffs. Up the hill are three fan-cooled, eight-bed dorms. There's also a great restaurant: try the mulberry pancakes or mulberry mojitos!

And if you have time, ask about volunteering for the permaculture program or teaching English to kids. Minimum two weeks. Cooking classes here cost US$30.

Vieng Tara Villa BOUTIQUE HOTEL $$
(☎030-5023102; www.viengtara.com; r US$50-90;) This new boutique resort really takes advantage of its location on the west-bank riverside to deliver some incredible views of the looming karst. Choose one of the villa paddy-view rooms, which are set on stilts in the middle of lush rice fields and accessible via a wooden walkway. River-view rooms are cheaper in this instance, as they look towards town. In a word: stylish.

Eating

Vang Vieng isn't exactly Luang Prabang, but there are a few decent restaurants dotted around town. You'll also find quality restaurants at the top-end hotels.

★**Living Room** ASIAN $
(☎020-54919169; mains 30,000-50,000K; 3-11pm;) Classy custard-coloured cafe with unbroken views of the cliffs from its hilltop eyrie, and a romantic place to eat with its low-lit and exposed-brick and bamboo interior. Gazpacho, homemade bread, NZ lamb, spicy beef goulash – this Lao-Austrian affair is in every sense a fusion cafe. And the best spot in town for a sunset Bloody Mary.

Sababa Organic Restaurant JEWISH $
(mains 15,000-40,000K; 7am-10pm;) Sababa ('Cool' in Hebrew), allegedly run by a Lao Jew, boasts a Hebrew-language menu and, not surprisingly, is the best place in town to find your inner falafel. The chicken schnitzel also gets good reviews, as do the tofu, salads and steak.

Breakfast Vendors LAOTIAN $
(Th Luang Prabang; mains 10,000-15,000K; 6-9am) A string of breakfast vendors sets up shop every morning, serving basic but tasty Lao dishes.

★**Il Tavolo** ITALIAN $$
(☎023-511768; Rte 13; mains 38,000-80,000K; 5-11pm Thu-Tue;) The most authentic Italian restaurant in town, 'The Table' is run by a father-and-son team. The menu includes 19 varieties of oven-baked Neapolitan pizzas and a wide selection of pasta, gnocchi and risotto dishes, plus some generous entrées. Wash down your meal with a botttle of Prosecco.

★**Restaurant du Crabe d'Or** INTERNATIONAL $$
(☎023-511726; www.riversidevangvieng.com; mains 50,000-150,000K; 7-10am & noon-10pm;) Set on the tasteful grounds of the Riverside Boutique Resort, this fine restaurant exudes high-end decor with a Lao flavour, and affords amazing views of the cliffs. The menu will please most palates with grilled salmon steak, pork cutlet with honey and lime sauce, as well as a raft of trad-Asian dishes, all delivered with panache.

The best spot in town to enjoy the sunset over a glass of chilled Taittinger.

Drinking & Nightlife

The new and improved Vang Vieng has ditched all-night parties in favour of a more chilled scene. However, there are still some late-night shenanigans at places like Sakura Bar and the twice-weekly 'Jungle' parties.

★**Gary's Irish Bar** IRISH PUB
(☎020-58255774; www.irishbar.weebly.com; 9am-11.30pm;) Still the best bar in town thanks to its friendly, unpretentious atmosphere, indie tunes, free pool and great grub like homemade pies, burgers and Lao fare (mains 40,000K to 60,000K). When there's live rugby or footy you'll find it on the flat-screen TV. It's also a good spot for breakfast (full Irish). And watch out for live music. If only all bars were like this!

Heartbeat CLUB
(☎020-55113366; Nathom Village; 6pm-late;) For something completely different with more of a Lao flavour, head to this big beer garden and nightclub about 2km north of town. This is where the visiting weekenders from Vientiane end up for fun and frolics and it often hosts live bands from the capital.

Earth BAR
(5-11.30pm;) Made from driftwood and clay, this hip hillside bar-restaurant pipes out fine tunes to match the ambience. Check out the sumptuous view of the cliffs from the candlelit garden, between snacking on toasties, waffles, sandwiches and curries (mains 20,000K to 40,000K). Look for the glowing green sign to find it.

Information

Visitors die every year from river accidents and while caving. Theft can also be a problem, with fellow travellers often the culprits. Take the usual precautions and don't leave valuables outside caves.

Despite the 2012 clean-up, magic mushrooms are on offer as happy shakes or happy pancakes and dope is still around – local police are particu-

BUSES FROM VANG VIENG

DESTINATION	COST (K)	DISTANCE (KM)	DURATION (HR)	DEPARTURES
Luang Prabang (minibus)	110,000	168	7-8	9am, 2pm, 3pm
Luang Prabang (VIP)	130,000	N/A	6-7	10am, 11am, noon, 8pm, 9pm
Vientiane (fan)	40,000	156	3-4	5.30am, 6.30am, 7am, 12.30pm, 2pm
Vientiane (minibus)	60,000	N/A	N/A	9am, 10.30am, 1.30pm
Vientiane (VIP)	80,000	N/A	N/A	1.30pm, 2pm, 3pm

larly adept at sniffing out spliffs. If you're caught with a stash of marijuana (or anything else) it can be expensive. The normal practice is for police to take your passport and fine you 5 million kip or more than US$600.

Agricultural Promotion Bank (Th Luang Prabang; ⏲8.30am-3.30pm) Exchanges cash, plus has an ATM.

BCEL (⏲8.30am-3.30pm) BCEL branch with an ATM, by the old market.

Post Office (☎023-511009; ⏲8am-5pm Mon-Sat, to noon Sun) Beside the old market.

Provincial Hospital (☎023-511604) This modest hospital has X-ray facilities and is fine for broken bones, cuts and malaria. When we visited, the doctor spoke reasonable English.

Tourist Office (☎023-511707; Th Luang Prabang; ⏲8am-noon & 2-4pm) The staff's English might be lamentable, but this is a useful port of call to pick up various leaflets on things to do in the area.

ℹ Getting There & Away

Buses, minibuses and *sŏrngtăaou* depart from the main bus station (Rte 13) about 2km north of town, although if you're coming in from Vientiane you'll most likely be dropped off at or near the bus stop (Rte 13) near the former runway, a short walk from the centre of town. When leaving Vang Vieng, be aware that, even if you purchased your tickets at the bus station, the more expensive minibuses and air-con buses often cater predominately to falang (foreigners) and will circle town, picking up people at their guesthouses, adding as much as an additional hour to the departure time. They then stop at the **secondary bus station** (☎023-511657; Rte 13) to ensure they are full before departure.

Heading north, buses for Luang Prabang stop at the bus stop for about five minutes en route from Vientiane about every hour between 11am and 8pm. These services also stop at Kasi and Phu Khoun (for Phonsavan). However, do be aware that there have been occasional attacks on night buses heading north through the edge of Saisomboun Province in the district of Kasi.

Heading south, there are several bus options to Vientiane. Alternatively, *sŏrngtăaou* (30,000K, three to four hours) leave about every 20 minutes from 5.30am until 4.30pm and, as they're often not full, the ride can be quite enjoyable.

ℹ Getting Around

Vang Vieng is easily negotiated on foot. Renting a bicycle (10,000K per day) or mountain bike (30,000K per day) is also popular; they're available almost everywhere. Most of the same places also rent motorcycles from about 50,000K per day (automatics cost 80,000K). For cave sites out of town you can charter *sŏrngtăaou* near the old market site: expect to pay around US$10 per trip up to 20km north or south of town.

LUANG PRABANG

Luang Prabang (ຫລວງພະບາງ) slows your pulse and awakens your imagination with its combination of world-class comfort and spiritual nourishment. Sitting at the sacred confluence of the Mekong River and the Nam Khan (Khan River), nowhere else can lay claim to this Unesco-protected gem's romance of 33 gilded wats, saffron-clad monks, faded Indochinese villas and exquisite Gallic cuisine.

Over the last 20 years Luang Prabang has seen a flood of investment, with once-leprous French villas being revived as fabulous – though affordable – boutique hotels, and some of the best chefs in Southeast Asia moving in. The population has swollen, and yet still the peninsula remains as sleepy and friendly as a village, as if time has stood still here. Beyond the evident history and heritage of the old French town are aquamarine waterfalls, top trekking opportunities,

TAK BAT: THE MONKS' CALL TO ALMS

Daily at dawn, saffron-clad monks pad barefoot through the streets while pious townsfolk place tiny balls of sticky rice in their begging bowls. It's a quiet, meditative ceremony through which monks demonstrate their vows of poverty and humility while lay Buddhists gain spiritual merit by the act of respectful giving.

Although such processions occur all over Laos, old Luang Prabang's peaceful atmosphere and extraordinary concentration of mist-shrouded temples mean that the morning's perambulations along Th Sakkarin and Th Kamal create an especially romantic scene. Sadly, as a result, tourists are progressively coming to outnumber participants. Despite constant campaigns begging visitors not to poke cameras in the monks' faces, the amateur paparazzi seem incapable of keeping a decent distance. Sensitive, non-participating observers should follow these guidelines:

- Stand across the road from the procession or better still watch inconspicuously from the window of your hotel (where possible).
- Refrain from taking photos or at best do so from a considerable distance with a long zoom. Never use flash.
- Maintain the silence (arrive by bicycle or on foot; don't chatter).
- Do not take part unless it's genuinely meaningful to you – meaningful in this case implies not wanting to be photographed in the process and knowing how to not cause offence.

meandering mountain-bike trails, kayaking trips, river cruises and outstanding natural beauty, the whole ensemble encircled by hazy green mountains.

Sights

★Phu Si HILL

(ພູສີ; Map p320; 20,000K; ⏲8am-6pm) Dominating the old city centre and a favourite with sunset junkies, the 100m-tall Phu Si (prepare your legs for a steep 329-step ascent) is crowned by a 24m gilded stupa called **That Chomsi** (ທາດຈອມສີ; admission incl with Phu Si). Viewed from a distance, especially when floodlit at night, the structure seems to float in the hazy air like a chandelier. From the summit, however, the main attraction is the city views.

Beside a flagpole on the same summit there's a small remnant anti-aircraft cannon left from the war years.

Ascending Phu Si from the northern side, stop at **Wat Pa Huak** (ວັດປ່າຮວກ; admission by donation). The gilded, carved front doors are usually locked but an attendant will open them for a tip. Inside, the original 19th-century murals show historic scenes along the Mekong River, including visits by Chinese diplomats and warriors arriving by river and horse caravans.

Reaching That Chomsi is also possible from the southern and eastern sides. Two such paths climb through large **Wat Siphoutthabat Thippharam** (ວັດສີພຸດທະບາດ) FREE to a curious miniature shrine that protects a **Buddha Footprint** (Map p320) FREE. If this really is his rocky imprint, then the Buddha must have been the size of a brontosaurus. Directly southwest of here a series of new gilded Buddhas are nestled into rocky clefts and niches around **Wat Thammothayalan** (Map p320); this monastery is free to visit if you don't climb beyond to That Chomsi.

★Royal Palace MUSEUM

(ພະຣາຊະວັງຊຽງແກ້ວ, Ho Kham; Map p320; ☎071-212470; Th Sisavangvong; admission 30,000K; ⏲8-11.30am & 1.30-4pm Wed-Mon, last entry 3.30pm) Evoking traditional Lao and French beaux-arts styles, the former Royal Palace was built in 1904 and was home to King Sisavang Vong (r 1905–59), whose statue stands outside. Within are tasteful, decidedly sober residential quarters, with some rooms preserved much as they were when the king was captured by the Pathet Lao in 1975. Separate outbuildings display the **Floating Buddha photography exhibition** (⏲8-11.30am & 1.30-4pm Wed-Mon, last entry 3.30pm) of meditating monks and the five-piece **Royal Palace Car Collection** (⏲8-11.30am & 1.30-4pm Wed-Mon, last entry 3.30pm).

No single treasure in Laos is more historically resonant than the **Pha Bang** (ພະບາງ; ⏲8-11.30am & 1.30-4pm Wed-Mon, last entry 3.30pm), an 83cm-tall gold-alloy Buddha. To find it, walk east along the palace's exterior southern terrace and peep in between the bars at the eastern end. In the southeast corner of the palace gardens, **Wat Ho Pha Bang** (ວັດຫໍພະບາງ; ⌚8-11.30am & 1.30-4pm Wed-Mon, last entry 3.30pm) was built to house the Pha Bang Buddha.

Inside the museum, footwear and photography are not permitted and you must leave bags in a locker room to the left side of the main entrance.

Wat Mai Suwannaphumaham BUDDHIST TEMPLE
(ວັດໃໝສຸວັນນະພູມອາຣາມ; Map p320; Th Sisavangvong; 10,000K; ⌚8am-5pm) Wat Mai is one of the city's most sumptuous monasteries, its wooden *sǐm* (ordination hall) sporting a five-tiered roof in archetypal Luang Prabang style, while the unusually roofed front verandah features detailed golden reliefs depicting scenes from village life, the Ramayana and Buddha's penultimate birth. It was spared destruction in 1887 by the Haw gangs who reportedly found it too beautiful to harm. Since 1894 it has been home to the Sangharat, the head of Lao Buddhism.

TAEC MUSEUM
(Traditional Arts & Ethnology Centre; Map p320; ☎071-253364; www.taeclaos.org; off Th Kitsarat; 25,000K; ⌚9am-6pm Tue-Sun) Visiting this professionally presented three-room museum is a must to learn about northern Laos' various hill-tribe cultures, especially if planning a trek. There's just enough to inform without overloading a beginner, including a range of ethnic costumes and a brilliant new exhibition, *Seeds of Culture: From Living Plants to Handicrafts*. TAEC sits within a former French judge's mansion that was among the city's most opulent buildings of the 1920s. There's a cafe and a shop selling handicrafts and pictorials.

★**Wat Xieng Thong** BUDDHIST TEMPLE
(ວັດຊຽງທອງ; Map p320; off Th Sakkarin; 20,000K; ⌚8am-5pm) Luang Prabang's best-known monastery is centred on a 1560 *sǐm* (ordination hall). Its roofs sweep low to the ground and there's a stunning 'tree of life' mosaic set on its western exterior wall. Close by are several stupas and three compact little chapel halls called *hǒr*. **Hǒr Đại**, shaped like a tall tomb, now houses a standing Buddha. The **Hǒr Đại Pha Sai-nyàat**, dubbed La Chapelle Rouge – Red Chapel – by the French, contains a rare reclining Buddha.

Wat Xieng Mouane BUDDHIST TEMPLE
(ວັດຊຽງມວນ; Map p320; Th Xotikhoumman; ⌚8am-5pm) FREE In the old quarter, Wat Xieng Mouane's ceiling is painted with gold *naga* (river serpents) and the elaborate *háang thíen* (candle rail) has *naga* at either end. With backing from Unesco and New Zealand, the monks' quarters have been restored as a classroom for training young novices and monks in the artistic skills needed to maintain and preserve Luang Prabang's temples. Among these skills are woodcarving, painting and Buddha-casting, all of which came to a virtual halt after 1975.

You can view their wares in the **showroom** (⌚8.30-10.30am & 1.30-4pm).

★**UXO Laos Information Centre** MUSEUM
(Map p318; ☎071-252073, 020-22575123; www.uxolao.gov.la; off Th Naviengkham; admission by donation; ⌚8-11.45am & 2-4pm Mon-Fri) The sobering UXO Laos Information Centre helps you get a grip on the devastation Laos suffered in the Second Indochina War and how nearly 40 years later death or injury from unexploded ordnance (UXO) remains an everyday reality in several provinces. If you miss it here, there's a similar centre in Phonsavan. In September 2016 the then president Barack Obama announced that the US would provide an additional US$90 million to address the problem of UXO in Laos over the next three years.

Green Jungle Flight PARK
(☎071-253899, 020-58677616; Ban Paklueang; park entrance US$3, ziplining & ropes course US$28-45, trekking US$35, return boat transfer from Luang Prabang 10,000K;) Thirty-two kilometres south of the city, this slice of natural paradise reclaimed from a rubbish dump uses the forest and a stunning cascade as its backdrop for a spectacular cat's cradle of ziplines (900m), monkey bridges and rope courses. Also here is a cafe, a restaurant and flower gardens, with plans for an organic produce market, a swimming pool, and an elephant-viewing area where ex-logging jumbos can bathe and socialise.

Activities & Courses

Some of the most popular activities in Luang Prabang are based in the countryside beyond, including trekking, cycling, motocross, kayaking and rafting tours. A popular destination is the new forest attraction Green Jungle Flight, almost nearing completion when we passed, with its botanical

Luang Prabang

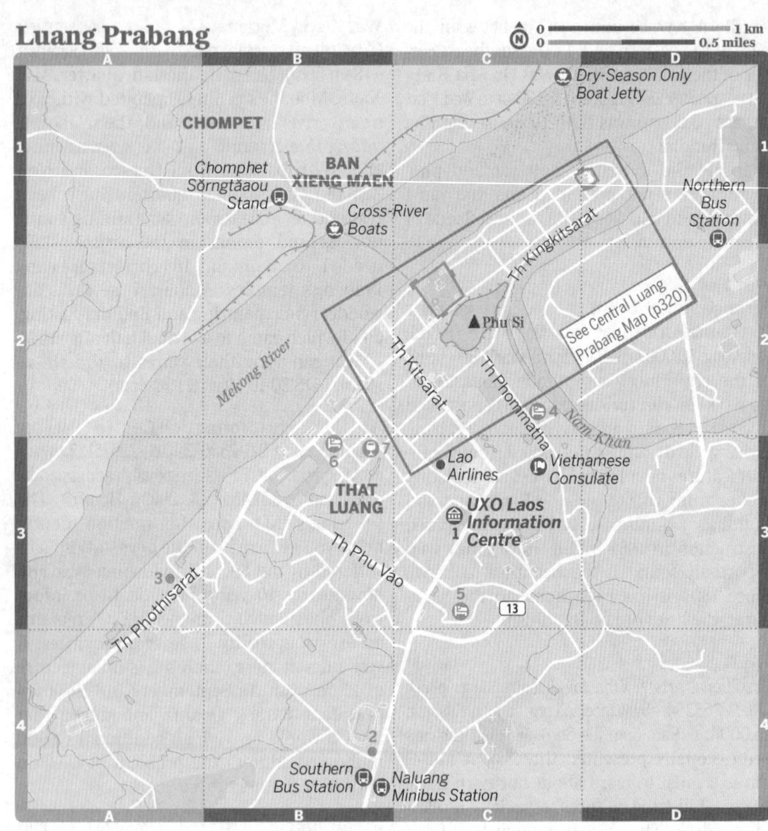

gardens, swimming pool, cafe and ziplines. In Luang Prabang itself, it's all about temple-hopping, cookery classes and cycling.

★Tamarind COOKING

(Map p320; ☎020-77770484; www.tamarindlaos.com; Ban Wat Nong; full-day/evening course 285,000/215,000K) Join Tamarind at its lakeside pavilion for a day's tuition in the art of Lao cuisine, meeting in the morning at its restaurant before heading to the market for ingredients for classic dishes such as *mok phaa* (steamed fish in banana leaves). Evening classes don't include a market visit.

Lao Red Cross MASSAGE, SPA

(Map p320; ☎071-253448; Th Wisunarat; sauna 15,000K, traditional/aromatherapy massage 50,000/80,000K per hour; ⏲7am-10.30pm) Recently renovated, this traditional blue Lao house was the original place to come for a sauna and massage before all the fancy ones arrived. It might be no frills, but well-trained staff give first-rate massages and there's a terrific sauna infused with medicinal plants that will clear your respiratory system like mentholated Drano! Now with air-con. Donations go directly to improving the lives of the poorest villages in Laos.

Dhammada MASSAGE

(Map p320; ☎071-212642; www.dhammada.com; Namneua Lane; per hour foot/aromatherapy massage 100,000/160,000K; ⏲11am-11pm) One of the best in town. A stylish rustic place beside a meditative lotus pond. As ever with massage it depends on who you get and how enlivened they are, so Dhammada gets both strong and weak reviews. We personally enjoyed it. Run by Kranchit, it's chilled, clean and restful.

Big Brother Mouse VOLUNTEERING

(BBM; Map p320; ☎071-254937; www.bigbrothermouse.com; Th Phayaluangmeungchan; ⏲9-11am & 5-7pm) Homegrown initiative dedicated

Luang Prabang

to improving literacy among kids in Laos, from cities to remote villages. Hang out at the BBM office and read to, or with, the kids who attend. If you're travelling in Laos, buy some books to take with you when you go to remote villages. It's an inspiring place.

Children's Cultural Centre VOLUNTEERING
(Map p320; ☎071-253732; www.cccluangprabang.weebly.com; Th Sisavangvong; ⊙4-5pm Tue-Fri, 8-11.30am & 2-4pm Sat) Providing after-school and weekend activities for Lao children to learn about Lao culture and traditions and develop skills that encourage healthy lifestyles and cultural preservation. Traditional music, drama, storytelling, singing and a variety of arts and crafts activities are on offer. Drop in to the centre to find out about leading a class.

Luang Prabang Yoga YOGA
(Map p320; www.luangprabangyoga.org; classes 60/90min 40,000/60,000K; ⊙classes usually at 7.30am & 5pm) Slow down, unwind and sync your spirit to the city's relaxed vibe with yoga classes taught at serene locations, from lush riverside garden decks at Utopia (p325) to rooftop sunset views. The city's yoga co-operative keeps up-to-date information on classes and venues on its website. In our experience this is a well-run network of qualified teachers. All levels welcome.

Luang Prabang Yoga also runs relaxing three-day yoga retreats at the delicious Mandala Ou Resort (p337) in Nong Khiaw. See www.laosyogaretreats.com

Tours

Luang Prabang has an abundance of travel agents vying for your patronage for half- to multiday tours. Tours to waterfalls and the Pak Ou Caves are particularly popular and prices are generally competitive, but it still pays to shop around. The **Pak Ou Caves** (ຖ້ຳປາກອູ, Tham Ting; cave admission 80,000K, return boat tickets per person/boat 65,000/300,000K; ⊙boats depart 8.30-11am) and Tat Kuang Si (p327) are an odd combination, given that the sites are in opposite directions, but the advantage is that the vehicle to the Kuang Si waterfalls should be waiting when you return to the agency office from your boat trip. Note that tour prices don't include entry fees.

★**Living Land** CULTURAL
(☎020-77778335, 020-55199208; www.livinglandlao.com; Ban Phong Van; tours per person 344,000K; ⊙8.30am-noon) About 5km out of Luang Prabang, on the road to Tat Kuang Si, is this brilliant rice farm co-operative, where you can spend half a day learning how to plant and grow sticky rice, the ubiquitous dish of Laos. This includes prepping the paddy with gregarious water buffalo Rudolph – expect to be knee deep in glorious mud! You'll never taste rice in the same way. Kids love it.

Living Land helps educate children in disadvantaged families in the local community.

★**Motolao** ADVENTURE
(Map p320; ☎020-54548449; www.motolao.com; Ban Phone Peang Rd; ⊙9am-6pm) This excellent outfit is one of the country's best motocross tour operators and has terrific two-wheel odysseys exploring authentic Lao life in the boonies that you'd usually be hard-pressed to visit. Top kit and with well-maintained bikes, this outfit is owned by dependable **Tiger Trail** (Map p320; ☎071-252655; www.laos-adventures.com; Th Sisavangvong; tours from US$50; ⊙8.30am-9pm). It also rents mountain bikes (50,000K per day) and Honda 250cc motorbikes (US$50 per day).

Green Discovery OUTDOORS
(Map p320; ☎071-212093; www.greendiscoverylaos.com; 44/3 Th Sisavangvong; ⊙8am-9pm) The daddy of ecotourism in Laos offers safety-conscious kayaking, trekking, mountain biking and multiday trips north. Staff speak good English, kit is safety conscious and the company is owned by a Lao who recycles some of the profit back into conservation.

Festivals & Events

Pi Mai CULTURAL
(Lao New Year; ⊙Apr) Large numbers of visitors converge on Luang Prabang for this 'water throwing' festival. Be careful of your

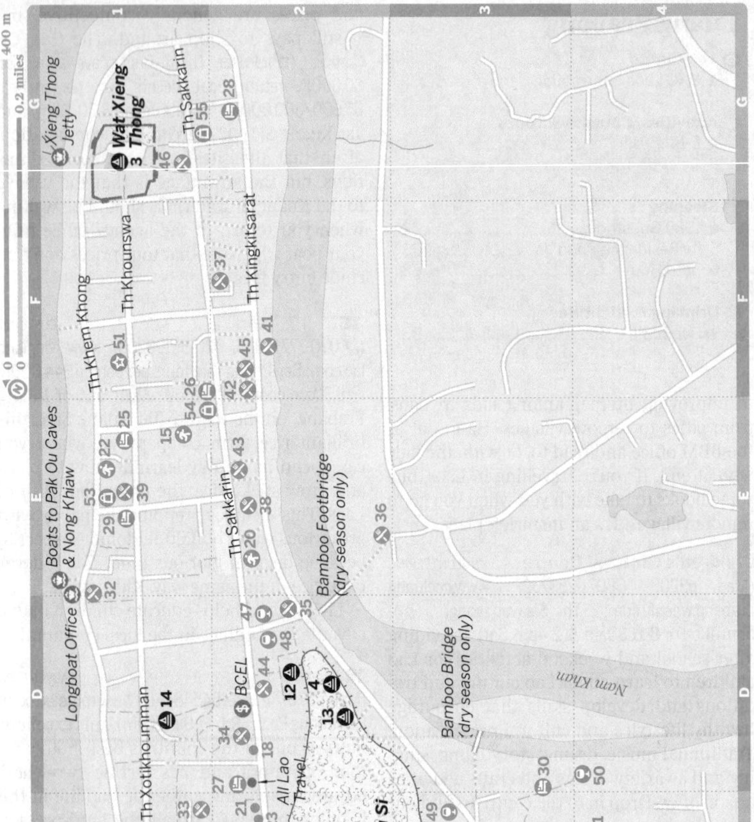

Central Luang Prabang

0 400 m
0 0.2 miles

Mekong River
Slowboat Landing
Navigation Office
Cross-River Boats
Longboat Office
Boats to Pak Ou Caves & Nong Khiaw
Xieng Thong Jetty
Th Khem Khong
Th Khounswa
Wat Xieng Thong
3
Th Sakkarin
Th Kingkitsarat
Th Xotikhoumman
Royal Palace
1
Phu Si
2
4
5
6
7
8
9
10
11
12
13
14
15
16
17
18
19
20
21
22
23
24
25
26
27
28
29
30
31
32
33
34
35
36
37
38
39
40
41
42
43
44
45
46
47
48
49
50
51
52
53
54
55
BCEL
All Lao Travel
Fresh Produce Market
Th Chao Phanya Kang
Provincial Tourism Department
ATM
Th Sisavangvong
ATM
Th Chao Fa Ngum
Minipost Booth
Bamboo Footbridge (dry season only)
Bamboo Bridge (dry season only)
Nam Khan
DSCom
KPTD
Dara Market
Th Chao Sisuphon
Th Phommatha
Provincial Hospital
Th Kitsarat
Th Bunkhong
Th Wisunarat
Immigration Office
Th Pha Mahapatsaman

Central Luang Prabang

Top Sights
1 Phu Si ... C2
2 Royal Palace ... C1
3 Wat Xieng Thong ... G1

Sights
4 Buddha Footprint ... D2
5 Floating Buddha Photographs ... C1
6 Pha Bang ... C1
7 Royal Palace Car Collection ... C1
8 TAEC ... B3
That Chomsi ... (see 1)
9 Wat Ho Pha Bang ... C2
10 Wat Mai Suwannaphumaham ... B2
11 Wat Pa Huak ... C2
12 Wat Siphoutthabat Thippharam ... D2
13 Wat Thammothayalan ... D2
14 Wat Xieng Mouane ... D1

Activities, Courses & Tours
15 Big Brother Mouse ... E1
16 Children's Cultural Centre ... B2
17 Dhammada ... B4
18 Green Discovery ... D2
19 Lao Red Cross ... C4
Luang Prabang Yoga ... (see 50)
20 Luang Say Cruise ... E2
21 Motolao ... C2
22 Shompoo Cruise ... E1
Tamarind ... (see 42)
23 Tiger Trail ... C2

Sleeping
24 Amantaka ... B3
25 Ammata Guest House ... E1
26 Chang Inn ... F1
27 Khong Kham Villa ... D2
28 Oui Guesthouse ... G2
29 Pack Luck Villa ... E1
30 Phongphilack Guesthouse ... D3
31 Villa Sayada ... C4

Eating
32 Big Tree Cafe ... E1
33 Blue Lagoon ... C1
34 Coconut Garden ... D2
35 Couleur Cafe ... D2
36 Dyen Sabai ... E2
37 Le Banneton ... F2
38 Le Café Ban Vat Sene ... E2
39 L'Elephant Restaurant ... E1
40 Morning Market ... B1
41 Rosella Fusion ... F2
42 Tamarind ... F2
43 Tamnak Lao ... E2
44 Tangor ... D2
45 The Apsara ... F2
46 Xieng Thong Noodle-Shop ... G1

Drinking & Nightlife
47 Chez Matt ... D2
48 Icon Klub ... D2
49 Lao Lao Garden ... C3
50 Utopia ... D4

Entertainment
51 Garavek Storytelling ... F1

Shopping
Big Tree Gallery ... (see 32)
52 Handicraft Night Market ... B2
53 Monument Books ... E1
54 Ock Pop Tok ... E1
55 Queen Design Lao ... G1
Wat Xieng Mouane Showroom ... (see 14)

camera getting soaked and prepare to be drenched! Advanced bookings around this time are recommended.

Bun Awk Phansa CULTURAL
(End of the Rains Retreat; Sep/Oct) Bun Awk Phansa sees boat races on the Nam Khan. Buddhists send little boats made of banana leaves with lit candles inside downriver by night, chiefly to send the bad luck of last year away, and to also make thanks to Mother Mekong and the sentinel *naga* (river serpents) who dwell within her watery arms. Pure magic.

Sleeping

For sybarites looking to recapture the comforts of old Indochine, there are more world-class hotels and stunning boutique belles here than you can shake a copy of *Hip Hotels* at! For the traveller who is vigilant with their dollars there are mid-scale bargains to be had in clean simple guesthouses, while for those on a strict budget, there are loads of hostels and super simple digs. In high season, prices rocket and it's hard to get a room anywhere. Old town peninsular accommodation generally comes at a premium but is more peaceful.

Some impressive ecolodges and resorts can be found in the lush countryside beyond Luang Prabang.

1989 Guesthouse GUESTHOUSE $
(Map p318; 020-91701061; joannethinking@yahoo.com; off Th Phommatha; dm/r US$19/25;) This delightful boho joint is run by a lovely Chinese lady. There's a patio terrace to chill in, and the reception is scattered with Tibetan photos and travel memorabil-

ia. Choose from two twin rooms or a double, and three well-spaced dorms.

Phongphilack Guesthouse GUESTHOUSE **$**
(Map p320; ☎071-252189; phongphilack@hotmail.com; Ban Aphay; r 100,000-120,000K; ❄📶) Hidden away in the alleys of Ban Aphay close to Utopia (p325) bar, this guesthouse was recently renovated to a decent level. Scrupulously clean rooms include hot water, air-con and ceiling fans. The friendly family speak English and it's walking distance to the main bar strip.

Villa Sayada HOTEL **$**
(Map p320; ☎071-254872; www.villa-shayada-laos.com; Th Phommatha; r 120,000-200,000K; ❄📶) Opposite Wat Visoun, this welcoming nine-room mini-hotel run by lovely Mr Takashi, a gentle Japanese man who welcomes you with a glass of rum, has generously sized cream and cloud-white rooms, with hung fabrics, handmade lamps and decent hot showers. There are small private balconies with pleasant views.

★**Chang Inn** BOUTIQUE HOTEL **$$**
(Map p320; ☎071-255031; www.burasariheritage.com; Th Sakkarin; r from US$150; ❄📶) This romantic bijou belle is stunningly tasteful with Indochinese style; think pendulums ticking away on walls covered with vintage Lao B&W photography, slatted wood mother-of-pearl-inlay furniture, rosewood floors, fragrant linen and chandeliers. The air-con units have been boxed in, preserving the conceit that you have travelled back 100 years. A leafy brick-floored garden lies behind.

Oui Guesthouse GUESTHOUSE **$$**
(Map p320; ☎020-54349589, 071-252374; r with/without balcony US$35/45; 📶) In a peaceful setting at the end of the peninsula facing the Nam Khan, it's so quiet here you can almost hear the breeze. Downstairs rooms are simple wood-ceiling affairs with tile floors, ethnic curtains and swish bathrooms. For an extra 10 bucks you can get an upstairs room with verandah and riverine views.

Khong Kham Villa HOTEL **$$**
(Map p320; ☎071-212800; off Th Sisavangvong; r US$45; ❄📶) Head down a side street off Th Sisavangvong and into a courtyard choking on palms to find small but stylish rooms with chequerboard-tiled bathrooms (weak showers), dough-soft beds, reading lamps, flat-screens TVs with cable, safety deposit boxes and communal balconies. In low season you can easily talk the price down.

Pack Luck Villa GUESTHOUSE **$$**
(Map p320; ☎071-253373; www.packluck.in; Th Thugnaithao; r US$55; ❄📶) This stunning boutique hotel has an eclectic feel of dark woods, paper lanterns, chrome fans and Persian rugs; by night, subtle lighting picks out flecks of gold leaf on its wine-red walls. Rooms are a little tight, but the three with upper balconies overlook the monks' morning meander. Downstairs is the popular Pack Luck Liquor wine bar.

Ammata Guest House GUESTHOUSE **$$**
(Map p320; ☎071-212175; pphilasouk@yahoo.com; Ban Wat Nong; r US$30-40; ❄📶) A friendly, family-run place, this attractively timbered guesthouse has a low-key ambience, spotless and spacious rooms with polished wood interiors, and renovated bathrooms. Most rooms are upstairs, running off a shared and shaded balcony. Management is friendly and you're perfectly located to watch the morning alms procession pass by without all the snapping cameras.

★**La Résidence Phou Vao** LUXURY HOTEL **$$$**
(Map p318; ☎071-212530; www.belmond.com/la-residence-phou-vao-luang-prabang; r incl breakfast from US$492; ❄@📶🏊) With its stunning hilltop grounds, seamless service and stylish wood rooms, Luang Prabang's first luxury hotel minted revivalist Indo-chic. The infinity pool reflects distant Phu Si and is flanked by a top-notch Franco-Lao restaurant. The Mekong Spa is spectacular and has won several global awards. No other hotel has such a spectacular view of the city and mountains. Bliss! Free use of bikes and free limo shuttle to the city five minutes away.

★**Amantaka** LUXURY HOTEL **$$$**
(Map p320; ☎071-860333; www.amanresorts.com; Th Kitsarat; ste from US$1000; ❄📶🏊) You can imagine Graham Greene writing under a wood-blade fan in the wicker-accented restaurant of this beautifully renovated French colonial-era building. Flanked by manicured lawns, a centrepiece jade swimming pool and dreamy spa and gym, suites here are capacious, with living room, four-poster beds and most featuring a private pool in their back garden. Surely Luang Prabang's finest hotel?

Substantial discounts are available in the low season.

★**Satri House** HISTORIC HOTEL $$$
(Map p318; ☎071-253491; www.satrihouse.com; off Th Phothisarath; r US$192-384; ❄📶🏊) This beautiful villa, once the former house of the Lao Red Prince, has stunning rooms with huge beds, fine furniture and a decorative flair unmatched by any other boutique in the city. Imagine pathways through lush gardens lit by statues of Indian gods, ornamental lily pools, a stunning jade swimming pool and a maze of Indo-chic corridors. The spa is terrific.

Eating

After the privations of the more remote areas in Laos your stomach will be turning cartwheels at the sheer choice and fine execution of what's on offer here. Aside from some very fine Lao restaurants, the gastro scene is largely French. Luang Prabang also has a terrific cafe scene, with bakeries at every turn.

Archetypal dishes include ubiquitous local sausages and a soup-stew called *orlam (áw lám)* made with meat, mushrooms and eggplant with special bitter-spicy wood chips added for flavouring (don't swallow them!). A great local snack is *kai pâan* (Mekong riverweed).

Food markets are great for fresh fruit, while self-caterers should check out the **morning market** (Map p320; ⏲5.30am-4pm Sat-Mon).

Peninsula Inland

★**Le Banneton** BAKERY $
(Map p320; Th Sakkarin; meals 20,000-40,000K; ⏲6.30am-6pm; ❄📶) It's the softness of the melt-in-your-mouth pastry that keeps us coming back to our favourite bakery in Luang Prabang, which serves *pain au chocolat* (chocolate croissants), pizza, terrine, baguette sandwiches, salads, crêpes and more. The ceiling is a maze of arabesques, there's a cool fan at every turn, and the white walls are offset by a passing blur of orange outside – monks from the monastery opposite.

Located on the peaceful end of the peninsula; you'll need to get here early before the croissants run out!

Le Café Ban Vat Sene FRENCH $
(Map p320; www.elephant-restau.com/cafebanvatsene; Th Sakkarin; mains 50,000-75,000K; ⏲7.30am-10pm; ❄📶) Luang Prabang's most stylish stop for afternoon tea and scones. Fans whirr above a serenely lit bar, while the dessert cabinet purrs at you like a calorific temptress – think éclairs, lemon tart and raspberry mousse. Beef steak, salads, pizza, and grilled chicken and perch are also on the menu. Eat outside or within the cool interior.

Xieng Thong Noodle-Shop LAOTIAN $
(Map p320; Th Sakkarin; noodle soup 20,000K; ⏲7am-2pm) The best *kòw pęeak sèn* (round rice noodles served in a broth with pieces of chicken or deep-fried crispy pork belly) in town is served from an entirely unexotic shopfront well up the peninsula. It usually runs out by 2pm.

★**Coconut Garden** LAOTIAN, INTERNATIONAL $$
(Map p320; ☎071-252482; www.elephant-restau.com/coconutgarden; Th Sisavangvong; meals 35,000-150,000K, set menu 100,000K; ⏲8am-11pm; 📶🌱) An excellent vegetarian set menu includes five top-quality Lao dishes, allowing a single diner to create the subtle palate of flavours that you'd normally only get from a feast with many people. Coconut Garden has front and rear yards, and is a great spot for lunch or dinner. International favourites are also available.

Blue Lagoon INTERNATIONAL $$
(Map p320; www.blue-lagoon-restaurant.com; Th Ounheun; mains 75,000-140,000K; ⏲10am-10pm; 📶) A favourite with expats for its lantern-festooned walls, leafy patio and jazz-infused atmosphere. The menu features Luang Prabang sausage, pasta, boeuf bourguignon, salads and very tasty *láhp*.

Tamnak Lao LAOTIAN $$
(Map p320; ☎071-252525; www.tamnaklao.net; Th Sakkarin; mains 40,000-75,000K; ⏲9am-4pm & 6-10pm; 🌱) Plenty of Lao and Luang Prabang options served in an archetypal half-timbered house with sturdy arched balconies overlooking the street. Service is obliging but it often fills out with international tour groups. Try the freshwater fish.

Tangor FUSION $$
(Map p320; ☎071-260761; www.letangor.com; Th Sisavangvong; mains 40,000-80,000K; ⏲11am-10pm; 📶) Atmospheric with its low-lit interior of dark woods and tangerine-coloured walls peppered with old travel posters, Tangor boasts a menu of beautifully crafted fusion food, blending the best of seasonal Lao produce with French cuisine. Dishes include beef tenderloin, pork filet mignon and tapas and there's a decent wine selection. Finish it off with a Cuban cigar.

L'Elephant Restaurant FRENCH $$$
(Map p320; www.elephant-restau.com; Ban Wat Nong; mains 80,000-250,000K; ⏲11.30am-10pm;

(❄) L'Elephant serves arguably the most sophisticated cuisine in the city in a renovated villa with wooden floors, stucco pillars, stencilled ochre walls and bags of atmosphere. The Menu du Chasseur (240,000K) includes terrines, soups, duck breast and other Gallic specialities. The buffalo steak tartare is amazing.

Peninsula Riverfronts

★Dyen Sabai LAOTIAN, INTERNATIONAL **$**
(Map p320; ☎020-55104817; www.dyensabairestaurant.wordpress.com; Ban Phan Luang; mains 20,000-35,000K; ⏲8am-11pm; 📶) One of Luang Prabang's top destinations for fabulous Lao food. The eggplant dip and fried Mekong riverweed are as good as anywhere. Most seating is on recliner cushions in rustic open-sided pavilions. It's a short stroll across the Nam Khan bamboo bridge in the dry season or a free boat ride at other times. Two-for-one cocktails between noon and 7pm.

Rosella Fusion FUSION **$**
(Map p320; www.facebook.com/rosellafusion; Th Kingkitsarat; mains 35,000K; ⏲9am-10.30pm) Established by a former Amantaka bartender, this riverside restaurant offers an innovative selection of affordable fusion flavours. The owner is particularly proud of his bargain cocktails, so consider dropping by for a sundowner before dinner. Try the steak and pepper sauce.

★The Apsara FUSION **$$**
(Map p320; ☎071-254670; www.theapsara.com; Apsara Hotel, Th Kingkitsarat; mains 60,000-110,000K; ⏲7am-10pm; 📶) This chic eatery fronting the Nam Khan offers fusion cuisine blending East and West. Choose from buffalo steak, stuffed *panin* fish to share, or braised pork belly for a main. Save some space for the divine desserts such as poached nashi pear in lime and ginger syrup served with coconut ice cream and a Lao poppadom.

★Tamarind LAOTIAN **$$**
(Map p320; ☎071-213128; www.tamarindlaos.com; Th Kingkitsarat; mains 40,000K, set dinner 100,000-150,000K; ⏲11am-10pm; 📶) On the banks of the Nam Khan, mint-green Tamarind has created its very own strain of 'Mod Lao' cuisine. The à la carte menu boasts delicious sampling platters with bamboo dip, stuffed lemongrass and *meuang* (DIY parcels of noodles, herbs, fish and chilli pastes, and vegetables). There's also buffalo *láhp* and Luang Prabang sausage. Deservedly popular.

Big Tree Cafe KOREAN, INTERNATIONAL **$$**
(Map p320; www.bigtreecafe.com; Th Khem Khong; mains 35,000-50,000K; ⏲9am-9pm; 📶🌿) Located in a stunning wooden house, Big Tree Cafe's Korean food is the best in the city and it's always packed with Koreans, as well as aesthetes who come to see photographer Adri Berger's work in the gallery (p325) upstairs. Eat inside or out on the terrace in the leafy, restful garden. There's also a choice of Western and Japanese dishes.

Couleur Cafe INTERNATIONAL **$$**
(Map p320; ☎071-254694; Th Kingkitsarat; mains 40,000-100,000K; ⏲11am-10pm; ❄📶) Well regarded by long-term residents, Couleur Cafe has relocated to the Nam Khan side of the peninsula but continues to serve French-accented and creatively presented Laotian cuisine. Menu highlights include chicken casserole with ginger and lemongrass, and duck breast with honey and mango chutney. Stylish and relaxing.

Drinking & Nightlife

The main stretch of Th Sisavangvong northeast of the palace has plenty of drinking places, including some appealing wine bars. Two of the city's best bars, Chez Matt and the delectable Icon Klub, are yards from one another on a nameless road connecting the two river banks (but much closer to the Nam Khan). The main hub for drinkers is just south of Phu Si on Th Kingkitsarat around **Lao Lao Garden** (Map p320; Th Kingkitsarat; mains 30,000K; ⏲5pm-late; 📶). Legal closing time is 11.30pm and this is fairly strictly enforced.

★Icon Klub BAR
(Map p320; www.iconklub.com; Th Sisavang Vatthana; ⏲5pm-late; 📶) Imagine a place in the afterlife where writers meet and conversation is as free-flowing as the fabulous mixology cocktails. You pull up a pew next to Jack Kerouac, and Anaïs Nin is reading in a cosy chair nearby... Icon may just be this place. A sculpted angel rises out of the wall and there are poetry slams, jam sessions and kick-ass tunes.

A night here can lead you somewhere magical and may well be the highlight of your visit to the city. Run by a charming Hungarian poet this is Laos' most atmospheric bar, bar none.

Utopia BAR
(Map p320; www.utopialuangprabang.com; ⏲8am-11pm; 📶) Lush riverside bar with peaceful views of the Nam Khan; think recliner cushions, low-slung tables and hookah pipes. Chill over a fruit shake, burger, breakfast or omelette (mains 30,000K), play a board game or volleyball, or just lose yourself in a sea of candles come sunset. Brilliantly designed with faux Khmer ruins and creeper vines, surely the city's liveliest outdoor bar.

Luang Prabang Yoga (p319) runs regular morning classes here; check the website for the schedule.

Bar 525 BAR
(Map p318; ☎071-212424; www.525.rocks; ⏲5-11.30pm; 📶) Parked down a quiet street, there's nothing retiring about this chic, urban bar. Sit outside stargazing on the terrace, inside at the long bar in low-lit style, or chill in the comfy lounge. Cocktails galore, glad rags, stunning photography on the walls and a sophisticated crowd. Snacks like buffalo sliders and quesadillas are also available.

Chez Matt BAR
(Map p320; Th Sisavang Vatthana; ⏲7pm-late; 📶) Ox-blood walls, low lights and a handsome bar glittering with polished crystal, this candlelit haunt is central and peaceful, adding a dash of upscale sophistication to the city's nocturnal landscape. With its cocktails, French and Italian wine cellar and chilled music, this makes for a good spot to dress up in your finest before going somewhere swish for dinner.

☆ Entertainment

Garavek Storytelling THEATRE
(Map p320; ☎020-96777300; www.garavek.com; Th Khounswa; tickets 50,000K; ⏲6.30pm) Garavek means 'magical bird', and this enchanting hour-long show – comprising an old man dressed in tribalwear playing a haunting *khene* (Lao-style lyre) alongside an animated storyteller (in English) recalling local Lao folk tales and legends – takes your imagination on a flight of fancy. Held in an intimate 30-seat theatre. Book ahead.

Shopping

★ **Queen Design Lao** CLOTHING
(Map p320; queendesignlao@gmail.com; Th Sakkarin, 1/17 Ban Khili; ⏲10am-6pm Mon-Sat; 📶) This stylish Aussie-run boutique has a choice selection of hand-woven linen, silk and cotton dresses, chemises, skirts, and beach shawls made by Chris Boyle, a renowned designer in Oz. Most are one-off pieces. As well as pashminas and scarves, it also sells organic face scrubs and wood designer glasses, and is the sole distributor for Article 22 Bomb Jewellery.

★ **Big Tree Gallery** ART
(Map p320; ☎071-212262; www.adriberger.com/general/luang-prabang; Th Khem Khong; ⏲9am-9pm; 📶) Photographer and film-maker Adri Berger's compositions of rural Laos capture that honeyed afternoon light like no one else. His ochre-walled gallery-cum-restaurant is in a breezy wooden house with a delightful palm-shaded terrace to read in. Upstairs you'll find the bulk of his work. His prints can be safely sent home in protective containers. Exquisite souvenirs.

★ **Handicraft Night Market** MARKET
(Map p320; Th Sisavangvong; ⏲5.30-10pm) Every evening this tourist-oriented but highly appealing market assembles along Th Sisavangvong and is deservedly one of Luang Prabang's biggest tourist lures. Low-lit, quiet and devoid of hard selling, it has myriad traders hawking silk scarves and wall hangings, plus Hmong appliqué blankets, T-shirts, clothing, shoes, paper, silver, bags, ceramics, bamboo lamps and more.

Ock Pop Tok CLOTHING, HANDICRAFTS
(Map p320; ☎071-254406; www.ockpoptok.com; Th Sakkarin; ⏲8am-9pm) Ock Pop Tok works with a wide range of different tribes to preserve their handicraft traditions. Fine silk and cotton scarves, chemises, dresses, wall hangings and cushion covers make perfect presents. **Weaving courses** (Map p318; ☎071-212597; www.ockpoptok.com; half-/full-day bamboo-weaving course 240,000/284,000K, Hmong Batik class 480,000/640,000K, 3-day natural dyeing & weaving course 1,584,000K; ⏲8.45am-4pm Mon-Sat) are also available.

Monument Books BOOKS
(Map p320; www.monument-books.com; Th Khem Khong, Ban Wat Nong; ⏲9am-9pm Mon-Fri, to 6pm Sat & Sun) Part of a regional chain, this shop stocks guidebooks, maps, novels, magazines and books on Lao history.

Information

BCEL (Map p320; Th Sisavangvong; ⏲8.30am-3.30pm Mon-Sat) Changes major currencies in cash or travellers cheques, has a 24-hour ATM and offers cash advances against Visa and MasterCard.

DSCom (Map p320; ☎071-253905; Th Kitsarat; ⏰9.30am-noon & 1-6pm Mon-Sat) We like these guys for their honesty and unflappable help in dealing with a laptop crisis.

Immigration Office (Map p320; ☎071-212435; Th Wisunarat; ⏰8.30am-4.30pm Mon-Fri) It's usually possible to extend a Lao visa for up to 30 extra days (US$2 per day) if you apply before it has expired.

Minipost Booth (Map p320; Th Sisavangvong; ⏰7.45am-8.30pm, cash advances 9am-3pm) Changes most major currencies at fair rates and is open daily.

Post Office (Map p320; Th Chao Fa Ngum; ⏰8.30am-3.30pm Mon-Fri, to noon Sat) Phone calls and Western Union facilities.

Provincial Hospital (Map p320; ☎071-254023; Ban Naxang; doctor's consultation 100,000K) OK for minor problems but for any serious illnesses consider flying to Bangkok or returning to Vientiane and neighbouring hospitals across the Thai border. Note that the hospital in Luang Prabang charges double for consultations at weekends or anytime after 4pm.

Provincial Tourism Department (Map p320; ☎071-212173; www.tourismlaos.org; Th Sisavangvong; ⏰8am-4pm Mon-Fri; 📶) General information on festivals and ethnic groups. Also offers some maps and leaflets, plus information on buses and boats. Great office run by helpful staff.

ℹ Getting There & Away

AIR

Around 4km from the city centre, **Luang Prabang International Airport** (☎071-212173; 📶) has a smart new building as of 2013 and an expanded runway. For Bangkok, **Bangkok Airways** (www.bangkokair.com) and **Lao Airlines** (Map p318; ☎071-212172; www.laoairlines.com; Th Pha Mahapatsaman) both fly twice daily. Lao Airlines also serves Vientiane several times daily and Pakse, Chiang Mai, Hanoi and Siem Reap once daily. **Vietnam Airlines** (☎071-213049; www.vietnamairlines.com) flies to both Siem Reap (codeshare with Lao Airlines) and Hanoi daily.

BOAT

For slowboats to Pak Beng (130,000K, nine hours, 8am), buy tickets from the **navigation office** (Map p320; ⏰8-11am & 2-4pm) behind the Royal Palace. Through-tickets to Huay Xai (220,000K, two days) are also available, but you'll have to sleep in Pak Beng. This also allows you to stay a little longer in Pak Beng should you like the place. The main **slowboat landing** (Map p320) is directly behind the navigation office, but departure points can vary according to river levels.

The more upscale **Luang Say Cruise** (Mekong Cruises; Map p320; ☎071-254768; www.luangsay.com; 50/4 Th Sakkarin; cruise US$362-490; ⏰9.30am-9.30pm) departs on two-day rides to Huay Xai from the Xieng Thong jetty opposite Wat Xieng Thong. Rates include an overnight stay at the Luang Say Lodge in Pak Beng. A cheaper alternative is **Shompoo Cruise** (Map p320; ☎071-213190; www.shompoocruise.com; Th Khem Khong; cruise incl breakfast & 2 lunches US$110), a two-day cruise aboard a smart boutique boat; accommodation in Pak Beng is not included.

Fast, uncomfortable and seriously hazardous six-person speedboats can shoot you up the Mekong to Pak Beng (190,000K, three hours) and Huay Xai (320,000K, seven hours). However, there are no fixed departure times and prices assume a full boat, so unless you organise things through an agency, it's worth heading up to the speedboat station the day before to make enquiries. It's around 5km north of town: turn west off Rte 13 beside the Km 390 post then head 300m down an unpaved road that becomes an unlikely dirt track once you cross the only crossroads en route.

BUS

Predictably enough, the **Northern Bus Station** (Map p318; ☎071-252729; Rte 13) and **Southern Bus Station** (Bannaluang Bus Station; Map p318; ☎071-252066; Rte 13, Km 383) are at opposite ends of town. Several popular bus routes are duplicated by minibuses/minivans from the **Naluang minibus station** (Map p318; ☎071-212979; souknasing@hotmail.com; Rte 13), diagonally opposite the latter. Typical fares include Vientiane (170,000K, seven hours) with departures at 7.30am, 8.30am and 5pm; Vang Vieng (110,000K, five hours) at 8am, 9am, 10am, 2pm and 3pm; Luang Namtha (120,000K, eight hours) at 8.30am; and Nong Khiaw (70,000K, three hours) at 9.30am.

For less than double the bus fare, another option is to gather your own group and rent a comfortable six-seater minivan. Prices include photo stops and you'll get there quicker. Directly booked through the minibus station, prices are about 1,000,000K to Phonsavan or Vang Vieng and 500,000K to Nong Khiaw, including pick-up from the guesthouse.

Sainyabuli & Hongsa

Buses to Sainyabuli (60,000K, three hours) depart from the southern bus station at 9am and 2pm. The new Tha Deua bridge over the Mekong River is now open and has reduced the journey time to Sainyabuli to two hours or so by private vehicle. There is also a new minibus service to the Elephant Conservation Center in Sainyabuli, operated by **Sakura Tour** (☎074-212112) which picks you up outside the post office. For Hongsa, the new bridge means it is easiest to travel to Sainyabuli and connect from there.

Vientiane & Vang Vieng

From the southern bus station, there are up to 10 daily Vientiane services (115,000K, nine hours) via Vang Vieng between 6.30am and 7.30pm. Sleeper buses (150,000K, nine hours) leave at 8pm and 9.30pm.

Nong Khiaw & Sam Neua

For Nong Khiaw (55,000K, four hours), 9am minibuses start from Naluang minibus station. Alternatively, from the northern bus station take the *sŏrngtăaou* (pick-up trucks fitted with benches in the back for passengers; 55,000K) at 9am, 11am and 1pm or the 8.30am bus that continues to Sam Neua (140,000K, 17 hours) via Vieng Thong (120,000K, 10 hours). Another Sam Neua–bound bus (from Vientiane) should pull in sometime around 5.30pm.

Phonsavan & Vietnam

For Phonsavan (10 hours) there's a 9am minibus (120,000K) from Naluang minibus station and a 8.30am bus (ordinary/express 90,000/105,000K, 10 hours) from the southern bus station. You can get to Dien Bien Phu (220,000K, 10 hours, leaves 6.30am) and Hanoi (380,000K, 24 hours, leaves 6pm) in Vietnam.

Northwestern Laos & China

The sleeper bus to Kunming (450,000K, 24 hours) in China departs from the southern bus station at 7am, sometimes earlier. Pre-booking, and checking the departure location, is wise. From the northern bus station, buses run to Udomxai (60,000K, five hours) at 9am, noon and 4pm; Luang Namtha (105,000K, nine hours) at 9am; and Huay Xai (Borkeo; 130,000K, 15 hours) at 5.30pm with a VIP service at 7pm (150,000K).

ℹ Getting Around

Numerous shops and some guesthouses have hire bikes for 15,000K to 30,000K per day. Luang Prabang has no motorbike taxis, only tuk-tuks, plus the odd taxi-van from the airport charging a standardised 50,000K into town. These will cost more if more than three people share the ride.

New to Luang Prabang is Lao Green Travel's **E-Bus** (www.laogreengroup.com; trips from 5000K), an electric zero-emission tuk-tuk (green and yellow), which circulates around the old town. You can buy tickets in shops and guesthouses. It also offers an **E-Bus Tour** (Map p318; ☎071-253899; www.laogreengroup.com; tour US$40, child under 10 free; ⊙tours morning 8.30am-12.30pm, afternoon 1-5.30pm), which takes passengers around the city on a guided tour.

Chomphet Sŏrngtăaou Stand (Map p318) Located on the opposite side of the Mekong to Luang Prabang, about 400m up from the river, the Chomphet *sŏrngtăaou* stand serves local villages only.

Cross-River Boats (Map p320; one-way 10,000K) Two ferries regularly ply back and forth between Luang Prabang and Ban Xieng Maen, on the other side of the Mekong. It takes about five minutes.

KPTD (Map p320; ☎071-253447, 020-97100771; Th Kitsarat; semi-automatic 100,000K, automatic 120,000K, 250cc dirt bikes per day US$70; ⊙8am-5pm) Highly recommended for its well-maintained Honda CRF 250cc dirt bikes. You can also drop off in Vientiane.

Xieng Thong Jetty (Map p320; TH Khem Khong) Located opposite Wat Xieng Thong. Luang Say Cruise and Shompoo Cruise both leave from here.

AROUND LUANG PRABANG

Pak Ou Caves

Where the Nam Ou (Ou River) and Mekong River meet at Ban Pak Ou, two famous caves in the limestone cliff are crammed with myriad Buddha images. In the lower cave a photogenic group of Buddhas are silhouetted against the stunning riverine backdrop. The upper cave is a five-minute climb up steps (you'll need a torch), 50m into the rock face. Buy boat tickets from the **longboat office** (Map p320; Th Khem Khong; ⊙9am-5pm Mon-Sat) in Luang Prabang.

Most visitors en route to Pak Ou stop at the 'Lao Lao Village' Ban Xang Hay, famous for its whisky. The narrow footpath-streets behind the very attractive (if mostly new) wat are also full of weavers' looms, colourful fabric stalls and a few stills producing the wide range of liquors sold.

An alternative is to go by road to Ban Pak Ou (30km, around 150,000K return for a tuk-tuk) then take a motor-canoe across the river (20,000K return). Ban Pak Ou is 10km down a decent unpaved road that turns off Rte 13 near Km 405.

Tat Kuang Si

Thirty kilometres southwest of Luang Prabang, **Tat Kuang Si** (ຕາດກວາງຊີ; admission 20,000K; ⊙7.30am-5.30pm) is a many-tiered waterfall tumbling over limestone formations into a series of cool, swimmable turquoise pools; the term 'Edenic' doesn't do it justice. When you're not swinging off ropes into the water, there's a public park with shelters and picnic tables where you can eat lunch. Don't miss the **Kuang Si Rescue Centre** (www.freethebears.org.au; Kuang Si Waterfall; admission incl with Tat Kuang Si ticket; ⌚8.30am-4.30pm) FREE near the park entrance, where Asiatic Wild Moon bears, confiscated from poachers who sell them for their precious bile, are given a new lease of life.

Many cheap eateries line the entrance car park at the top end of the Khamu village of Ban Thapene.

Visiting Kuang Si by hired motorcycle is very pleasant now that the road here is decently paved and allows stops in villages along the way. By bicycle, be prepared for two long, steady hills to climb. A tuk-tuk from Luang Prabang cost 250,000K for one person, and 85,000K per person in group of three, so it's best to get a group together.

Tat Sae

The wide, multi-level cascade pools of this menthol-hued **waterfall** (ຕາດແຊ; 20,000K, child under 8 free; ⌚8am-5.30pm) 15km southeast of Luang Prabang are a memorable sight from August to November. Unlike Tat Kuang Si, there's no single long-drop centrepiece and they dry up almost completely by February. But several year-round gimmicks keep visitors coming, notably a loop of 14 **ziplines** (☎020-54290848; www.flightofthenature.com; per person 300,000K) that allow you to 'fly' around and across the falls.

Part of the attraction of a visit is getting here on a very pleasant seven-minute boat ride (20,000K per person return, 40,000K minimum) that starts from Ban Aen, a peaceful Lao village that's just 1km east of Rte 13 (turn east at Km 371.5). A 30-minute tuk-tuk from Luang Prabang costs up to 150,000K return, including a couple of hours' wait.

NORTHERN LAOS

Whether it's for trekking, cycling, kayaking, ziplining or a family homestay, a visit to northern Laos is for many the highlight of their trip. Dotted about are unfettered, dense forests home to tigers, gibbons and a cornucopia of animals, with a well-established ecotourism infrastructure to take you into their very heart.

In the north you will also find a tapestry of vividly attired ethnic tribes unlike anywhere else in Laos.

Here the Land of a Million Elephants morphs into the land of a million hellish bends and travel is not for the faint-hearted, as roads endlessly twist and turn through towering mountain ranges and serpentine river valleys. By contrast, most northern towns are functional places, rebuilt after wholesale bombing during the 20th-century Indochina wars.

But visitors aren't in northern Laos for the towns. It's all about the rural life. River trips are a wonderful way to discover the bucolic scenery at a more languid pace.

Xieng Khuang & Hua Phan Provinces

Long and winding roads run in seemingly endless ribbons across these green, sparsely populated northeastern provinces towards the mysterious Plain of Jars and the fascinating Vieng Xai Caves. Both are truly intriguing places to visit if you're en route to or from Vietnam. Those with the time can add stops in Nong Khiaw and Vieng Thong. The latter is a gateway to the Nam Et/Phou Louey National Protected Area (NPA) and its 'tiger treks'. Almost anywhere else in either province is completely off the tourist radar.

Phonsavan

Phonsavan (ໂພນສະຫວັນ) is a popular base from which to explore the Plain of Jars. The town itself has an unfinished feel and is very spread out, with its two parallel main boulevards stretching for about 3km east–west. Fortunately a very handy concentration of hotels, restaurants and tour agents is crammed into a short if architecturally uninspired central 'strip'. More shops, markets and facilities straggle along Rte 7. But the town is best appreciated from the surrounding hills, several of which are pine-clad and topped with small resorts. Keep an eye out too for wooden powder-blue Hmong cottages on the mountain roads with firewood neatly stacked outside.

The region has long been a centre of Phuan language and culture (part of the Tai-Kadai family). There's also a strong Vietnamese presence.

Sights

UXO Information Centre (MAG) CULTURAL CENTRE
(☎061-211010; www.maginternational.org/laos; donations encouraged; ⏰10am-8pm) FREE Decades after America's Secret War on Laos, unexploded bombs and mines remain a devastating problem throughout this region. Visit the thought-provoking UXO Information Centre, run by British organisation MAG (Mines Advisory Group) that's been helping to clear Laos' unexploded ordnance since 1994. The centre's information displays underline the enormity of the bomb drops, and there are also examples of (defused) UXO to ponder. Donations are encouraged: US$12 pays for the clearing of around 10 sq metres and a commemorative T-shirt.

Late-afternoon screenings show the powerful documentaries *Bomb Harvest* (4.30pm; www.bombharvest.com), *Surviving the Peace* (5.50pm) and *Bombies* (6.30pm; www.itvs.org/bombies/film.html). They are distressing but important, as they show the full scale of the trauma, from footage of US bombers in action to the ongoing casualties of their horrific legacy.

★ **Xieng Khouang UXO-Survivors' Information Centre** CULTURAL CENTRE
(www.laos.worlded.org; donations encouraged; ⏰8am-8pm) FREE This unexploded ordnance (UXO) information centre and colourful, upbeat shop sells silk laptop bags, purses and handicrafts made by UXO survivors. Aside from displays including prosthetic limbs, wheelchairs and bomb parts, there's also a reading room with a wealth of information on the Secret War and the different kinds of UXO that still present a danger to Laos today. Ask to see the video *Surviving Cluster Bombs*. Note that 90% of your donations go towards the treatment of UXO survivors.

Mulberries FARM
(ປໍສາ; ☎061-561271; www.mulberries.org; ⏰8am-4pm Mon-Sat) This is a fair-trade silk farm that offers interesting free visits including a complete introduction to the silk-weaving process from cocoon to colourful scarves. It's off Rte 7 just west of the main bus station.

Tours

Lao Falang Travel Service ADVENTURE
(☎020-23305614, 020-55406868; Rte 7; one-day trip US$108) Run by a dependable Italian guy, this outfit operates multiday and one-day motorbike tours, of which 70% to 85% are spent off-road (depending on your confidence). A one-day tour typically includes Jar Site 1, the Russian tank and Muang Khoun. Dinner is included at the excellent Lao Falang Italian restaurant. Solid, experienced guides ensure you don't go beyond your comfort zone.

Sousath Travel TOURS
(☎020-23305614, 020-55406868; rasapet_lao@yahoo.com; Rte 7; ⏰8am-8pm) Sousath offers very reliable tours to the Plain of Jars and the Ho Chi Minh Trail, as well as homestays in Hmong villages. For war obsessives he can organise trips to Long Tien, the clandestine runway in the Saisombun jungle created by the CIA during the Secret War. He also rents bikes (20,000K) and scooters (manual/automatic 70,000/90,000K).

Sleeping

Kong Keo Guesthouse GUESTHOUSE $
(☎061-211354, 020-285858; www.kongkeojar.com; dm 40,000K, r in outside block 80,000K, chalets 120,000K; wi-fi) Run by Veomany; at the time of writing he was doing a great job of replacing the shoddy wood huts with six balconied brick chalets. While the seven-berth dorm is cramped, the outdoor block has large clean rooms with mint-green walls and private bathroom. The UXO-decorated restaurant-bar has nightly barbecues, and Veomany runs excellent tours to the Plain of Jars.

White Orchid Guesthouse GUESTHOUSE $
(☎061-312403; r incl breakfast with fan/air-con 60,000/150,000K, tr 180,000K; air-con wi-fi) The menthol-green rooms enjoy en suite bathrooms, double beds, cable TV and welcome blankets. The price includes a pick-up from the airport or bus station and there's also a little tour office that can arrange trips to see the Plain of Jars. Basic and clean.

Anoulack Khen Lao Hotel HOTEL $$
(☎061-213599; www.anoulackkhenlaohotel.com; Main St; r incl breakfast 200,000K; air-con wi-fi) This glass Lego tower has easily the best rooms in town, with wood floors, thick mattresses, white linen, cable TV, fridges, kettles and swish hot-water en suites. There's a great restaurant on the 5th floor where you can take breakfast and use the wi-fi. Conveniently the hotel also has a lift. Worth the extra spend.

Hillside Residence HOTEL $$
(☎061-213300; www.thehillsideresidence.com; Ban Tai; r incl breakfast US$30; wi-fi) Set in a lush little

Phonsavan

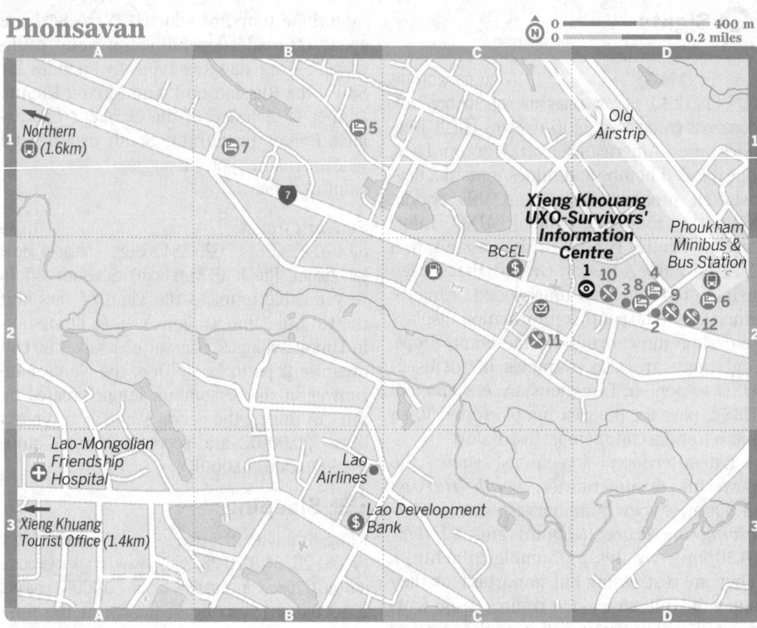

Phonsavan

Top Sights
1 Xieng Khouang UXO-Survivors' Information Centre D2

Sights
UXO Information Centre (MAG) ..... (see 1)

Activities, Courses & Tours
2 Lao Falang Travel Service D2
3 Sousath Travel D2

Sleeping
4 Anoulack Khen Lao Hotel D2
5 Hillside Residence B1
6 Kong Keo Guesthouse D2
7 Vansana Plain of Jars Hotel B1
8 White Orchid Guesthouse D2

Eating
9 Bamboozle Restaurant & Bar D2
10 Cranky-T Café & Bar D2
11 Fresh Food Market C2
Lao Falang Restaurant ..... (see 4)
12 Nisha Restaurant D2

garden, this replica half-timbered mansion looks like it belongs in a colonial-era hill town. Rooms are petite but attractive with all the trimmings, including blankets for the cool season. However, the beds are pretty hard. There's a shared upper sitting terrace and some upstairs rooms have their own balconies. Free wi-fi, and a lovely owner.

Vansana Plain of Jars Hotel HOTEL $$
(☎061-213170; www.vansanahotel-group.com; r 400,000-500,000K) Opulent by Phonsavan standards, this grand hotel built in 2004 occupies its own small summit above town. Large, comfortable rooms have plush carpeting, aged TVs, minibars, tasteful decor and big tubs in the bathrooms. Each also has a small balcony with great views over town. The place is a little tired and in need of a shot in the arm, however.

Eating & Drinking

Wild matsutake mushrooms (*hét wâi*) and fermented swallows (*nok ąen dąwng*) are local specialities; try the **fresh food market** (6am-5pm). In case you want to avoid an unpleasant surprise, note that several Vietnamese restaurants serve dog (*thit chó*).

Nisha Restaurant INDIAN $
(Rte 7; meals 20,000-30,000K; 7am-10pm;) Cream-interiored Nisha is tidy and simple but the real colour is found in its excellent cuisine. The menu includes all the usual suspects like tikka masala and rogan josh, curries and a wide range of vegetarian

options. However, it's the perfect application of spice and the freshness of the food that'll keep you coming back.

★ Lao Falang Restaurant ITALIAN $$
(☎020-5546868; mains 50,000-70,000K; ⊙7am-4pm & 5-10.30pm; ❄📶📝) Sister of Lao Falang Travel Service (p329), this spacious, stylish and impeccably clean Italian restaurant is run by a friendly Genoese man who speaks four languages. Highly recommended for alchemising sirloin steak, lamb and giant prawns into various delicious incarnations, plus its handmade pasta (carbonara and bolognese), thin-based pizza and homemade ice cream. Great wine choices, too. It can also make takeaway ham, chicken, tuna or vegie sandwiches for long bus journeys.

Bamboozle Restaurant & Bar INTERNATIONAL $$
(☎030-9523913; Rte 7; meals 25,000-52,000K; ⊙7-10.30am & 3.30-10.30pm, kitchen closes 9pm; 📶) 🍃 True to its name, with bamboo walls plus pretty lanterns strung from its ceiling, Bamboozle dishes up thin-crust pizza, salads, pasta dishes, good-sized cheeseburgers and terrific Lao cuisine. Add to this chilled beers and a rock-and-roll soundtrack and it's a winner. A percentage of the profits goes towards the Lone Buffalo Foundation (www.facebook.com/lonebuffalo), which supports the town's youth.

Cranky-T Café & Bar FUSION $$$
(☎020-55504677, 061-213263; www.facebook.com/CrankyTLaos; Main St; mains 35,000-130,000K; ⊙7am-11pm, food served 5-9pm, happy hour 4-7pm; ❄📶) Cranky-Ts has a stylish red-wine-coloured and exposed-brick interior, with the eponymous owner creating mouth-watering salads, sashimi, smoked-salmon crêpes and hearty fare like NZ sirloin with mash to fill you up after trekking the jar sites. Add to this cinnamon muffins, brownie cheesecake and a good selection of cocktails (35,000K), and you may spend all day here.

ℹ Information

BCEL (☎061-213291; Rte 7; ⊙8.30am-3.30pm Mon-Fri) Located next to Xieng Khouang Hotel. Has a 24-hour ATM and offers currency exchange.

Lao Development Bank (☎061-312188; ⊙8.30am-3.30pm Mon-Fri) Currency exchange.

Lao-Mongolian Friendship Hospital (☎061-312166) May be able to assist with minor health concerns.

Post Office (⊙8am-4pm Mon-Fri, to noon Sat) Also has a domestic phone service.

Xieng Khuang Tourist Office (☎020-22340201, 061-312217; www.xiengkhouangtourism.com; Hwy 1E; ⊙8am-4pm) Impractically located in the middle of nowhere (on the road to the airport), this otherwise helpful office has English-speaking staff, brochures and souvenirs recycled from war junk. Has free maps for Phonsavan and Xieng Khuang district, plus the photocopied sheet entitled 'What Do I Do Around Phonesavanh Town', for alternative ideas on things to do aside from the jar sites.

ℹ Getting There & Away

Airline and bus timetables usually call Phonsavan 'Xieng Khuang', even though that was originally the name for Muang Khoun.

AIR

Lao Airlines (☎061-212027; www.laoairlines.com) has daily flights to/from Vientiane (US$63). Sometimes a weekly flight to/from Luang Prabang operates in peak season.

BUS

Longer-distance bus tickets presold by travel agencies typically cost around 40,000K more than standard fares but include a transfer to the confusingly named **Northern Bus Station** (☎030-5170148), located 4km west of the centre, also sometimes known as the Provincial Bus Station. From here Vietnam-bound buses depart to Vinh (150,000K, 11 hours) at 6.30am on Tuesday, Thursday, Friday and Sunday, continuing seasonally on Mondays to Hanoi (320,000K).

For Vientiane (110,000K, 11 hours) there are air-con buses at 7.30am, 8.30am, 10.30am, 4.30pm, 6.30pm and a VIP bus (130,000K) at 8.30pm. These all pass through Vang Vieng, to where there's an additional 7.30am departure (95,000K). The sleeper here (150,000K) leaves at 8pm.

The **Southern (Bounmixay) Bus Station** (Hwy 1D), 4km south of town, has a 6am bus (four days a week) to Savannakhet (150,000K) that

BOMB VILLAGE

The Hmong double-village of Ban Tha Jok/Na Kam Peng has recycled old war junk into practical objects, hence the nickname 'Bomb Village', with cluster-bomb casings used to make the legs of rice barns, planting pots for herbs, barbecue braziers and, in one case, a whole over-engineered fence. The main concentration lies in minor lanes about 700m south of Rte 7, turning at Km 165 (27km east of Phonsavan).

continues on to Pakse (180,000K). Buses to Paksan (100,000K, eight hours) via the newly completed road depart daily at 6.30am and 8am.

Phoukham Minibus and Bus Station (☎020-99947072; Th Xaysana; ⏰7am-8pm) in the east-central side of town has minibuses leaving at 8.30am for Luang Prabang (110,000K) and Vang Vieng (100,000K), with 6.30am, 8am and 5pm minibuses for Vientiane (110,000K). There's also a VIP bus for Vientiane (130,000K) leaving from here at 7.30pm.

Getting Around

Tuk-tuks, if and when you can find them, cost from 15,000K for a short hop to about 30,000K to the airport. **Lao Falang Restaurant** (p331) rents bicycles (40,000K per day) and 100cc motorbikes (100,000K), ideal for reaching a selection of jar sites. It also has some Chinese quad bikes (160,000K) if you're feeling brave. Fill up at the **petrol station** in town.

Chauffeured six-seater vans or 4WDs can be chartered through most guesthouses and hotels; you're looking at US$150 to Sam Neua or US$120 to Luang Prabang.

Plain of Jars

Mysterious giant stone jars of unknown ancient origin are scattered over hundreds of hilly square kilometres around Phonsavan, giving the area the misleading name of Plain of Jars (ທົ່ງໄຫຫີນ). Remarkably, nobody knows which civilisation created them, although archaeologists estimate they date from the Southeast Asian iron age (500 BC to AD 200).

Smaller jars have long since been carted off by collectors but around 2500 larger jars, jar fragments and 'lids' remain. As the region was carpet-bombed throughout the Indochina wars, it's miraculous that so many artefacts survived. Only a handful of the 90 recorded jar sites have so far been cleared of unexploded ordnance (UXO), and then only within relatively limited areas. These sites, and their access paths, are delineated by easily missed red-and-white marker stones: remain vigilant. Sites 1, 2 and 3 form the bases of most tour loops.

Plain of Jars

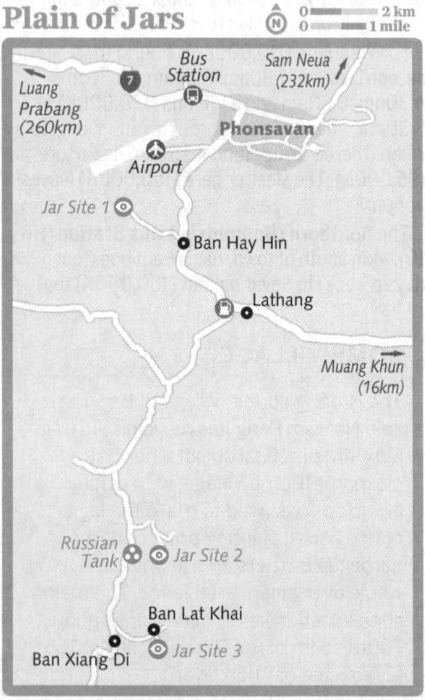

Sights

Jar Site 1 ARCHAEOLOGICAL SITE

(Thong Hai Hin; 15,000K) The biggest and most easily accessible, Site 1 of the Plain of Jars features over 300 jars relatively close-packed on a pair of hilly slopes pocked with bomb craters. The biggest, Hai Jeuam, weighs around 6 tonnes, stands more than 2.5m high and is said to have been the mythical victory cup of Khun Jeuam. The bare, hilly landscape is appealing, although in one direction the views of Phonsavan airport seem discordant. There is a small cafe, a gift shop and toilets near the entrance.

Jar Site 2 ARCHAEOLOGICAL SITE

(Hai Hin Phu Salato; 10,000K) Site 2 of the Plain of Jars is a pair of hillocks divided by a shallow gully that forms the access lane. This rises 700m from the ticket desk in what becomes a muddy slither in wet conditions. To the left in thin woodlands, look for a cracked stone urn through which a tree has managed to grow. To the right another set of jars sits on a grassy knoll with panoramas of layered hills, paddies and cow fields. It's very atmospheric.

Basic cold drinks are available at the ticket booth.

Jar Site 3 ARCHAEOLOGICAL SITE

(Hai Hin Lat Khai; 10,000K) The 150-jar Site 3 of the Plain of Jars sits on a scenic hillside in pretty woodland near Ban Lat Khai village. The access road to Lat Khai leads east beside a tiny motorbike repair hut just before Ban Xiang Di (Ban Siang Dii). The ticket booth is beside a simple local restaurant that offers somewhat overpriced *fĕr* (rice noodles; 30,000K). The jars are accessed by a little wooden footbridge and an attractive 10-minute walk across rice fields.

Getting There & Away

All three main jar sites can be visited by rented motorbike from Phonsavan in around five hours, while Site 1 is within bicycle range. Site 1 is just 8km southwest of central Phonsavan, 2.3km west of the Muang Khoun road: turn at the signed junction in Ban Hay Hin. For Sites 2 and 3, turn west off the Muang Khoun road just past Km 8. Follow the unpaved road for 10km/14km to find the turnings for Sites 2/3, then follow muddy tracks for 1.5/1.8km respectively.

Alternatively, sign up the night before to join one of several regular guided minibus tours. Most throw in a noodle-soup lunch at Site 3 and a quick stop to see the lumpy rusting remnant of an armoured vehicle in a roadside copse at Ban Nakho: its nickname, the 'Russian Tank', exaggerates the appeal.

Vieng Thong

The original name of Vieng Thong (ວຽງທອງ) was Muang Hiam, a Tai Daeng word meaning 'Watch Out'. Back when tigers roamed the surrounding forests it was relevant, but these days barely a dozen survive in the enormous Nam Et/Phou Louey NPA, on whose vast doorstep Vieng Thong sits. While the town is highly forgettable, the park is not and should be visited through the **Nam Et/Phou Louey NPA office** (064-810008; www.namet.org; 8am-noon & 1-4.30pm Mon-Fri) at Vieng Thong Visitor's Center.

Vieng Thong has a clutch of guesthouses and food stalls, and if you're travelling between Nong Khiaw and Sam Neua, stopping here for a night makes the 10-hour journey more palatable. The dazzling green rice fields around town are photogenic and short walks or bicycle rides can take you to pretty Tai Daeng, Hmong and Khamu villages.

★**Nam Nern Night Safari** SAFARI
(www.namet.org/namnern; night safaris per person in group of 4 1,200,000K) Nam Nern Night Safari is a 24-hour, boat-based tour in the Nam Et/Phou Louey NPA. Highlights of the trip include a night-time boat-ride 'spotlighting' for tiger, gaur and white-cheeked gibbon. Seeing a tiger is unlikely but there's hope of spotting sambar and barking deer. Sleeping is at an ecolodge overlooking the Nam Nern. The price includes a fireside dinner. Book through the Nam Et/Phou Louey NPA office in Vieng Thong.

LOCAL KNOWLEDGE

NAM ET/PHOU LOUEY NATIONAL PROTECTED AREA

In the vast **Nam Et/Phou Louey NPA** (ປ່າສະຫງວນແຫ່ງຊາດນ້ຳແອດພູເລີຍ), rare civets, Asian golden cats, river otters, white-cheeked crested gibbons and the utterly unique Laotian warty newt *(Paramesotriton laoensis)* share 4200 sq km of relatively pristine forests with around a dozen tigers. Approximately half is an inaccessible core zone. The remaining area includes 98 ethnic-minority hamlets. Two-day wildlife-watching excursions have been pioneered to the park's remote Nam Nern field station, a roadless former village site where a campsite and surrounding walking trails have been professionally cleared of unexploded ordnance (UXO).

Trips are organised by the Nam Et/Phou Louey NPA office in Vieng Thong, and contacting them well in advance is advisable since there's a limit of two departures per week. Night safaris cost 1,200,000K per person for a group of four, and include guides, cooks, food and camping equipment, with a significant proportion of your fee going into village development funds. The price also includes the 90-minute boat ride from Ban Sonkhua, around 50km east of Vieng Thong on Rte 1.

Dork Khoun Thong Guesthouse GUESTHOUSE $
(064-810017; r 50,000-80,000K;) The most appealing of Vieng Thong's limited options, this guesthouse is located right in the centre of the small town. Very clean, decent-sized rooms have hot showers, netted windows and comfortable new beds with love-message sheets and teddy-bear towels. There's a pleasant 1st-floor sitting area and attractive views across riverside fields from the rear terrace.

Getting There & Away

Westbound buses arrive from Sam Neua around noon, continuing after lunch to Nong Khiaw (60,000K, five hours), Pak Mong and Luang Prabang (130,000K, nine hours). Eastbound, the best choice for Sam Neua is the 7am minibus (40,000K, six hours), as the two Sam Neua through-services (from Luang Prabang/Vientiane) both travel the road largely by night.

The bus station is 300m along Rte 6 from the market at the eastern edge of town.

Sam Neua

While Sam Neua (ຊຳເໜືອ; Xam Neua) is something of a nostalgic Soviet oddity, with its well-spaced concrete modernity, spartan communist monument and old boys with Muscovite hats, the real draw is the stunning countryside in which it sits. The town is a logical transit point for visiting nearby Vieng Xai or catching the daily bus to Vietnam, and remains one of Laos' least visited provincial capitals. Also it's at an altitude of roughly 1200m, some warm clothes are advisable in the dry winter period, at least by night and until the thick morning fog burns off. From April to October the lush landscapes are contrastingly warm and wet.

The eye-widening, photogenic produce markets here are worth visiting for the colourful ethnic diversity on display.

Sights

Hintang Archaeological Park ARCHAEOLOGICAL SITE
(ສວນຫີນ, Suan Hin) Almost as mysterious as Xieng Khuang's more famous jars, this unique, unfenced collection of standing stones is thought to be at least 1500 years old. Spindly stones up to 3m tall are interspersed with disks that formerly covered funerary sites. With some over a metre in diameter, these 'families' of stones do have a certain magic, and the place is now a Unesco World Heritage Site.

Chartered tuk-tuks from Sam Neua will ask around 500,000K return.

Tat Saloei WATERFALL
(Phonesai Waterfall) This impressive series of cascades forms a combined drop of almost 100m. It's briefly visible from eastbound Rte 6 roughly 1km after Km 55 (ie 36km from Sam Neua), but easy to miss westbound. There are some small local cafes and restaurants on the roadside here, plus what looks like a ticket booth, although no one was charging for entry at the time of writing.

Sleeping & Eating

There are plenty of guesthouses in town, with many budget options just across the river from the market.

There are a number of restaurants to eat at in Sam Neua – they're nothing fancy but serve good local grub. Impromptu barbecued offerings are available on street corners after dark. During the day check out the food market.

Xayphasouk Hotel HOTEL $$
(064-312033; xayphasoukhotel@gmail.com; r 150,000-200,000K;) Currently the smartest hotel in Sam Neua. The huge lobby-restaurant is woefully underused, but the rooms are very comfortable for such a remote region of Laos. All include piping-hot showers, flat-screen TVs, tasteful furnishings and crisp linen. And there's free wi-fi, plus a cafe downstairs for breakfast.

Phonchalern Hotel HOTEL $
(064-312192; www.phonechalernhotel.com; r 80,000-110,000K;) This palatially sized hotel has a mix of rooms; some are dark and uninviting while those facing the river are full of light and have a communal balcony out front. Rooms have fridge, TV and clean en suite. Downstairs there's a lobby the size of a bowling alley. It's a sure bet for one night.

Sam Neua Hotel HOTEL $
(064-314777; snhotel_08@yahoo.com; r 100,000-200,000K;) Located over the bridge on the same side as the main market, this well-maintained hotel has 17 rooms complete with fresh linen, pine furniture, satellite TV and en suite bathrooms with hot water.

Bounhome Guest House GUESTHOUSE $
(064-312223, 020-2348125; r with fan/air-con 80,000/100,000K;) Next to the bridge, this guesthouse has compact rooms with tiled floors, fans and low-set beds with fresh linen and blankets. You'll be glad to use their powerful hot showers.

★ **Yuni Coffee** CAFE $
(020-52221515; www.yunicoffee.com; sandwiches US$2; 7.30am-7.30pm;) A blessing for coffee snobs: if you're missing standard lattes your caffeine privations are over. With battleship-grey walls and a choice selection of refrigerated sandwiches, fresh-baked baguettes and brownies, as well as kick-ass locally grown coffee, Yuni is the only way to kick-start your day.

Information

Changing money is generally quickest through one of the fabric stalls in the main market: they exchange Vietnamese dong and are open at weekends.

Agricultural Promotion Bank (⌚8am-noon & 1.30-4pm Mon-Fri) Exchanges Thai baht and US dollars at fair rates.

BCEL (⌚8am-3.30pm Mon-Fri) Has a couple of ATMs dispensing kip, plus it can exchange most major currencies

Lao Development Bank (☎064-312171; ⌚8am-4pm Mon-Fri) On the main road 400m north of the bus station on the left; exchanges cash and travellers cheques.

Post Office (⌚8am-4pm Mon-Fri) In a large building directly opposite the bus station. A telephone office at its rear offers international calls.

Provincial Tourist Office (☎064-312567; ⌚8am-noon & 1.30-4pm Mon-Fri) An excellent tourist office with English-speaking staff eager to help.

Tam.com Internet Service (per minute 150K; ⌚8am-10pm) A relatively reliable internet cafe.

Getting There & Away

Sam Neua's little Nathong Airport is 3km east of the centre towards Vieng Xai. **Lao Skyway** (☎064-314268, 020-99755556; www.laoskyway.com; ⌚8am-4pm), which is based here, flies to Vientiane on Monday, Wednesday, Thursday, Friday and Saturday (US$62, 1½ hours). All too frequently the flights get cancelled just before departure. At the time of writing, there was no flight to Phonsavan.

The main bus station is on a hilltop 1.2km south of the central monument, just off the Vieng Thong road. From here buses leave to Vientiane (190,000K, 22 hours) via Phonsavan (80,000K, 10 hours) at 10am, 1pm, 3pm and 5pm. An additional 8.30am Vientiane bus (100,000K) goes via Vieng Thong (50,000K, six hours), Luang Prabang (130,000K, 17 hours) and Vang Vieng. There are also daily minibuses to Luang Prabang (130,000K) at 7am, 7.30am and 3.30pm. Finally there is a Vieng Thong bus at 7.20am.

The Nathong bus station is 1km beyond the airport on the Vieng Xai road at the easternmost edge of town (a taxi here costs 30,000K). Sŏrngtăaou to Vieng Xai (20,000K) leave at 8am, 10am, 11am, 2.30pm and 4pm. Other services include 'Nameo' (actually the Nam Soi border post) at 8am (30,000K, three hours) and Sam Tai (Xamtay) at 9.30am (50,000K, five hours).

Getting Around

There's a **tuk-tuk stand** (town trips 15,000K) from where you can take trips around town. However, the easiest way to get around and to enjoy the stunning scenery en route to Vieng Xai is to hire a cheap scooter and do it yourself.

A central **motorcycle shop** (manual/automatic scooter per day 100,000/120,000K; ⌚7am-6pm) rents scooters.

For those wishing for a little more comfort when getting about locally or for reaching Vieng Xai there are a couple of **taxis** (☎020-5627510, 020-95855513; taxi rental to Vieng Xai caves one way/return 150,000/300,000K) in town.

Vieng Xai

The thought-provoking 'bomb-shelter caves' of Vieng Xai (ວຽງໄຊ) are set amid dramatic karst outcrops and offer a truly inspirational opportunity to learn about northern Laos' painful 20th-century history. Imagine Vang Vieng, but with a compelling historical twist instead of happy tubing. Or think of it as

GETTING TO VIETNAM: NAM SOI TO NA MEO

Getting to the border If going to the Nam Soi (Laos)/Na Meo (Vietnam) border crossing (Km 175; ⌚7.30am to 11.30am and 1.30pm to 4.30pm), the easiest transport option is to take the daily direct bus (sometimes minibus) between Sam Neua and Thanh Hoa that passes close to Vieng Xai but doesn't enter town. It departs daily at 8am (180,000K, 11 hours). Prepurchase your ticket at the main bus station to avoid overcharging. 'Through tickets' to Hanoi still go via Thanh Hoa with a change of bus.

It's quite possible to reach the border by the 8am Na Meo *sŏrngtăaou* (pick-up trucks fitted with benches in the back for passengers) from Sam Neua (three hours). However, organising onward transport from the Vietnamese side is complicated by unscrupulous operators who seem intent on overcharging.

At the border Westbound, note that the Lao border post (Nam Soi) isn't a town. There are a few simple restaurant shacks but no accommodation and no waiting transport apart from the 11.30am *sŏrngtăaou* to Sam Neua.

Laos visas are available on arrival at this border but Vietnamese visas are not, so plan ahead if heading east.

Moving on Once in Thanh Hoa, there's a night train to Hanoi departing at 11.30pm and arriving very early (around 4am). Returning from Thanh Hoa (8am), tickets should cost US$14 but foreigners are often asked for significantly more.

Ho Chi Minh City's Cu Chi Tunnels cast in stone. The caves were shrouded in secrecy until they were opened to the world in 2007.

Sights

★Vieng Xai Caves CAVE
(ຖ້ຳວຽງໄຊ; ☎064-314321; entry incl audio tour 60,000K, bicycle rental per tour/day 15,000/30,000K; ⏲9am-noon & 1-4pm) Joining a truly fascinating 18-point tour is the only way to see Vieng Xai's seven most important war-shelter cave complexes, set in beautiful gardens backed by fabulous karst scenery. A local guide unlocks each site while an audio guide gives a wealth of first-hand background information and historical context. The Kaysone Phomvihane Cave still has its air-circulation pump in working order and is the most memorable of the caves.

Tours leave from the cave office.

Tham Nok Ann CAVE
(ຖ້ຳນົກແອນ, Nok Ann Cave; entry 10,000K, twin kayak 30,000K; ⏲8am-5pm) Tham Nok Ann is a soaring well-lit cavern through which a river passes beneath its awesome rock formations. It's dripping, creepy and very atmospheric. There's a boatman who can take you through and back for 50,000K (up to three persons).

Sleeping & Eating

Thongnaxay Guesthouse GUESTHOUSE $
(☎030-99907206; r 60,000K; 📶) Close to the caves, this new guesthouse has six super-fresh rooms with pink walls, private bathrooms, fans, clean linen and double beds. Oh, and rather nice views of the karsts.

Sabaidee Odisha INDIAN $
(mains 35,000K; ⏲7am-7pm; 📶) Don't be fooled by the less than impressive exterior, cement floor and bare walls of this hole-in-the-wall joint, for the food is terrific. Prepared fresh and with care, it comes with a smile and the menu offers different levels of spiciness. It's in the northernmost corner of the Viengsai market, facing the main road.

Information

Vieng Xai Cave Tourist Office (☎064-314321; www.visit-viengxay.com; ⏲8-11.30am & 1-4pm) Around 1km south of the market, the cave office organises all cave visits, rents bicycles and has maps, a small book exchange and a useful information board. There's even a display case full of old Lenin busts and assorted socialist iconograpy.

Getting There & Away

Sŏrngtăaou to Sam Neua (20,000K, 50 minutes) leave at approximately 7am, 10am and 11am on the road parallel to the market (the bus station was closed for a rebuild at the time of writing). Buses between Sam Neua and Thanh Hoa (one bus daily to each, 25,000K) stop at this same spot. For Thanh Hoa catch the 8.30am, for Sam Neua the 5pm.

Visiting Vieng Xai by rented taxi from Sam Neua (including return) costs around 300,000K per vehicle.

Muang Ngoi District

Nong Khiaw

Nong Khiaw (ໜອງຂຽວ) is a traveller's haven in the truest sense, offering pampering, good food, decent accommodation and bags of activities with established adventure-tour operators. Nestled on the west bank of the Nam Ou (the river almost currentless since the building of the dam upstream), spanned by a vertiginous bridge and bookended by towering limestone crags, it's surely one of the most photogenic spots in Laos. On the river's scenic east bank (officially called Ban Sop Houn) is the lion's share of guesthouses and restaurants.

Be aware that Nong Khiaw is alternatively known as Muang Ngoi (the name of the surrounding district), creating obvious confusion with Muang Ngoi Neua, a 75-minute boat ride further north.

Sights & Activities

Pha Daeng Peak Viewpoint VIEWPOINT
(ຈຸດຊົມວິວຜາແດງ; Pha Daeng Peak, Ban Sop Houn; 20,000K; ⏲6am-4pm) Reached by a testing though thoroughly doable 1½-hour walk (with a decent path) up Pha Daeng mountain, directly above the town, this viewpoint offers an unforgettable panorama. Drink up the sunset view (but bring a strong torch for your descent) or head here at 6am to witness the valley below veiled in mist, with the mountain peaks painted gold.

Pay the admission fee to the guy in the kiosk at the bottom. You'll find him by a sign and an old bomb shell on the left side of the road.

Tham Pha Thok CAVE
(ຖ້ຳຜາທອກ; 10,000K; ⏲7.30am-6.30pm) Around 2km east along Rte 1C, Tham Pha Thok is a series of caves in a limestone cliff

where villagers and Pathet Lao eluded bombing during the Second Indochina War. The first cave is around 30m high and accessed by wooden stairway. Continue to the second, somewhat-claustrophobic cave, 300m along a dark passage through the cliff.

We recommend bringing your own torch rather than renting a weak one.

Green Discovery HIKING, CYCLING
(071-810081; www.greendiscoverylaos.com; 7.30am-10pm) Reliable Green Discovery has a range of trips, including a two-day trek to a Hmong village involving a homestay, with five hours' trekking per day (US$66 per person in a group of four). It also has challenging one-day cycling trips on forest dirt tracks covering 56km (US$39 per person in a group of four).

Tiger Trail HIKING, CYCLING
(071-252655; www.laos-adventures.com; Delilah's Place; 7.30am-11pm) This ecoconscious outfit has treks and homestays around the local area, including memorable one-day trips to the '100 waterfalls', one-day trekking and boat rides, plus the new pursuit of paddleboarding on the now-becalmed Nam Ou. These trips, as with most of Tiger Trail's activities, cost US$31 per person in a group of four. The excellent office is run by amiable Harp.

Sabai Sabai MASSAGE
(020-58686068; Ban Sop Houn; body massage 60,000K, oil massage 70,000K, steam bath 25,000K; 9am-8pm) Set in a peaceful Zen-style garden, this wooden house is the perfect spot to restore the spirit and aching limbs with treatments like traditional Lao massage and herbal steam bath.

Sleeping

In the low season, accommodation prices are definitely negotiable. Nong Khiaw offers mainly budget options, through to a few deluxe digs.

★Delilah's Place HOSTEL $
(020-54395686, 030-9758048; www.delilahscafenongkhiaw.wordpress.com; Main St; dm/r 35,000/55,000K;) Delilah's Place has clean shared-bathroom rooms and cosy dorms with mozzie nets, super-thick matresses and safety lockers. Tiger Trail is also based here and there's a great cafe to 'carb-up' before activities, so one-stop-shop Delilah's is deservedly the main traveller hub in town. Thanks to the goodwill of eccentric owner Harp, it is also a great resource for info.

Sengdao Chittavong Guesthouse GUESTHOUSE $
(030-9237089; Rte 1C; r 50,000-90,000K;) This family-run spot on the west bank (next to the start of the bridge) has wooden bungalows located in gardens of cherry blossom looking directly on to the river. En suite rooms are rattan-walled, with simple decorations, mozzie nets, clean linen and balconies, though expect a visit from a gecko or cockroach. There's also a restaurant with river-garden views. The wi-fi internet is patchy. Popular with families.

★Mandala Ou Resort BOUTIQUE HOTEL $$
(030-5377332; www.mandala-ou.com; r US$65;) This stunning boutique accommodation in vanilla-coloured chalets – four facing the river – has imaginative, quirky features like inlaid glass bottles in the walls that allow more light, contemporary bathrooms and swallow-you-up beds. The owners are friendly and there's a terrific Thai menu, the town's only swimming pool and a yoga deck used by Luang Prabang Yoga (p319), which runs monthly retreats here. Opposite the bus station.

★Nong Kiau Riverside GUESTHOUSE $$
(020-55705000; www.nongkiau.com; Ban Sop Houn; r incl breakfast US$53;) Riverside's bungalows are romantically finished with ambient lighting, wooden floors, woven bedspreads and mosquito nets. Each includes an attractive bathroom and balcony for blissful river views of the looming karsts. There's an excellent restaurant serving Lao food with a mouth-watering breakfast buffet. It also has mountain bikes for hire. Discounts are available on room rates in the low season.

Eating & Drinking

Deen INDIAN $
(Ban Sop Houn; mains 35,000K; 8.30am-10pm;) A superbly friendly Indian eatery with wood-fired naan bread, freshly made tandoori dishes, zesty curries and a homely atmosphere, Deen is deservedly packed every night.

Delilah's Place INTERNATIONAL, LAOTIAN $
(Main St; mains 15,000-35,000K; 7am-10pm;) With Bach floating across the wood floors and a herd of African elephants thundering silently towards you on the mural, Delilah's satisfies your comfort cravings with amazing homemade key lime pies, lemon cake and ice cream; as well as hearty breakfasts of eggs,

smoky bacon and pancakes. There's a nightly movie at 8.30pm.

★**Coco Home Bar & Restaurant** LAOTIAN, INTERNATIONAL **$$**
(020-58491741; Main St; mains 40,000-55,000K; 7.30am-10pm;) Run by new owner Sebastien Chok, this recently refurbished impressive riverside oasis has a great menu, with dishes like papaya salad, mango sticky rice, chicken and cashew nuts, *mok phaa* (steamed fish in banana leaves) and duck in orange sauce. It's arguably the best place in town to delight your tastebuds. Eat in the lush garden or upstairs.

Q Bar BAR
(020-99918831; Rte 1C, Ban Sop Houn; 7am-11.30pm;) Chilled Q sits on the main road with an ox-blood, rattan interior, a little roof terrace, good tunes and a friendly owner. In high season there's a nightly barbecue. Cocktails are 35,000K.

Information

BCEL ATM (24hr) One of BCEL's ATMs, at the end of the bridge on the Ban Sop Houn side.

Post Office (8.30am-5pm) The tiny post office exchanges baht and US dollars at slightly unfavourable rates.

Tourist Information Office Above the boat landing, although it's rarely open.

Getting There & Away

BOAT

Riverboat rides are a highlight of visiting Nong Khiaw; however, since the Nam Ou was dammed, the trip to Luang Prabang is currently no longer possible. **Boats to Muang Ngoi Neua** (25,000K, 1¼ hours) leave at 11am and 2pm (in high season extra departures are possible), taking you through some of the most dramatic karst country in Laos. The 11am boat continues all the way to Muang Khua (120,000K, seven hours) for connections to Phongsali or Dien Bien Phu in Vietnam.

There needs to be a minimum of 10 people (on all the above journeys) before the boatman leaves, otherwise you will have to club together to make up the difference.

BUS

The journey to Luang Prabang is possible in three hours but in reality usually takes at least four. Minivans or *sŏrngtăaou* (37,000K) run at 8.30am, 10am and 11am, while air-con minibuses leave from around 1.30pm. Tickets are sold at the bus station but the 11am service actually starts at the boat office, filling up with folks arriving off the boat(s) from Muang Ngoi. When a boat arrives from Muang Khua there'll usually be additional Luang Prabang minivans departing at around 3pm from the boat office.

For Udomxai a direct minibus (45,000K, three hours) leaves at 9am and 11am. Alternatively, take any westbound transport and change at Pak Mong (40,000K, 50 minutes).

Originating in Luang Prabang, the minibus to Sam Neua (170,000K, 12 hours) via Vieng Thong (100,000K, five hours) makes a quick lunch stop in Nong Khiaw at around 11.30am, leaving at about noon. Another Sam Neua bus (arriving from Vientiane) passes through at 7pm. Both of these arrive at an unmarked bus stand on the Nong Khiaw side just before the start of the bridge. Try and get on the lunchtime bus as this is usually a larger vehicle compared to the cramped minibus in the evening. Plus there's the view you'll want to catch by daylight; it's one of the most beautiful mountain rides in Laos.

Getting Around

Bicycle rental makes sense for exploring local villages or reaching the caves. Town bicycles cost 20,000K per day and mountain bikes cost 30,000K. Alternatively, hire a scooter (50,000/60,000K for a manual/automatic) from **Delilah's Place** (p337). *Sŏrngtăaou* to the nearby bus station cost 5000K.

Muang Ngoi Neua

Muang Ngoi Neua (ເມືອງງອຍເໜືອ) is deliciously bucolic, a place to unwind and reset your soul. As the Nam Ou (Ou River) slides sedately beneath the shadow of sawtoothed karsts, cows wander the village's unpaved 500m-long road, while roosters strut past villagers mending fishing nets. Packed with cheap guesthouses and eateries, here there's enough competition to keep prices down. And while hammock-swinging on balconies is still de rigueur, there's plenty more to do if you have the energy: be it short, unaided hikes into timeless neighbouring villages, exploring caves, tubing and kayaking on the now pacified Nam Ou, or fishing and mountain biking.

Sights & Activities

Ensure you're by the river come sunset to enjoy one of the most photogenic views in Laos, as the sun falls like a mellow peach beyond the jagged black cliffs. A little after dawn it's also interesting to watch locals delivering alms to monks at the rebuilt monastery, Wat Okadsayaram.

Kayaking is a great way to appreciate the fabulous riverine scenery that stretches both ways along the Nam Ou. **Lao Youth Travel**

(030-5140046; www.laoyouthtravel.com; 7.30-10.30am & 1.30-6pm) has its own kayaks and is handily located where the boat-landing path passes by the two-storey Rainbow Guest House. The Ou now runs very gently after being dammed, making it safer for younger kids.

Numerous freelance guides such as **Funny Guide** (020-97029526; khaomanychan@yahoo.com; Main St; 6am-8pm) offer a range of walks to Lao, Hmong and Khamu villages and regional waterfalls. Prices are reasonable and some visits, such as to the That Mok falls, involve boat rides. Others are easy hikes that you could do perfectly well unguided. Take a photo with your phone of the map outside Lao Youth Travel for a rough guide to the area.

Sleeping

Uniquely for such a tiny place, budget accommodation abounds and English is widely spoken, so you get the experience of a remote village without the inconvenience. The only drawback is that the accommodation is showing its age compared with up-and-coming Nong Khiaw just down the river.

Lattanavongsa Guesthouse GUESTHOUSE $
(020-23863640; touymoy.laos@gmail.com; r from 100,000K;) Lattanavongsa offers a choice of bungalows at two locations: above the boat landing, and on the main drag in a pretty garden. Powder-blue rooms have choice art, mozzie nets, fresh linen and gas-fired showers; all have balconies. Book well ahead. Another boon is taking breakfast or dinner at its idyllically situated cafe (by the boat landing) with unbroken cliff views.

Nicksa's Place GUESTHOUSE $
(020-3665957; r 60,000-100,000K) Overlooking the river from its pretty garden abuzz with butterflies, these seven house-proud cabanas are made of wood and stone and have fresh walls, en suites and mozzie nets. Each has a balcony and obligatory hammock to take in the impressive vista. Cold-water showers only. Warm management comes in the form of super-organised Nicksa.

Huay Sen Guesthouse GUESTHOUSE $
(r 10,000K) Huay Sen Guesthouse has bags of rustic atmosphere, with its stilted wooden architecture and old-fashioned basic rooms. Run by a friendly Lao guy who speaks some English; food is available, as are guided walks to nearby Hmong villages. From Muang Ngoi Neua it's on the road heading south.

★ **Ning Ning Guest House** GUESTHOUSE $$
(020-23880122, 030-5140863; ningning_guesthouse@hotmail.com; r 200,000K;) Nestled around a peaceful garden, Ning Ning offers 10 immaculate wooden bungalows with mosquito nets, verandahs, en suites and lily-white bed linen, with walls draped in ethnic tapestries. There's also a great new sister guesthouse nearby with a decidedly more upscale look (nearing completion as of the time of writing; rooms 250,000K). The stylish riverfront restaurant with sumptuous views is already finished.

The internet access does not extend from the restaurant to the rooms.

Eating & Drinking

★ **Gecko Bar & Shop** LAOTIAN $
(020-58886295; muangngoihandmade@gmail.com; mains 20,000K; 7am-9pm;) Handmade woven gifts and tea are for sale at this delightful, memorable little cafe two-thirds of the way down the main drag on your left heading south. There's a nice terrace to sit and read on, the owners are charming and the food, spanning noodles to soups, and pancakes to curries, is among the most raved about in the village.

★ **Riverside Restaurant** LAOTIAN $
(030-5329920; meals 40,000K; 7am-11pm;) Since being damaged by a storm Riverside has come back better than ever. In the evening its Chinese lanterns sway in the breeze on the decked terrace, beneath the sentinel arms of an enormous light-festooned mango tree. Riverside has gorgeous cliff views, and its menu encompasses noodles, fried dishes, *láhp* and Indian fare. Pure magic.

Phetdavanh Restaurant & Street Buffet LAOTIAN $
(020-22148777; vegie buffet 30,000K, mains 30,000K; buffet 6.30-9pm, restaurant 7am-11pm;) This basic-looking restaurant runs a nightly 'all you can eat' vegie buffet (high season only), as well as serving tortillas, bamboo and duck, pancakes, soups, sandwiches and *shakshuka*. Try the Lao Suzy (stew with potato, carrot, eggplant and onion). It also has rapid wi-fi, so you can eat and stream movies. Great Swedish cook.

Find it on a corner on the main drag, at the top of the stairs from the boat landing.

Meem Restaurant LAOTIAN $
(Main St; mains 30,000K; 7am-9.30pm;) Halfway down Main St, welcoming Meem

has wood floors and plenty of lounging cushions, and serves up flavoursome Lao and Indian fare, including delicious chicken masala, tomato curry, spring rolls and barbecued chicken and duck. By night it's more enticing than a bunch of melodic sirens, with claypot candles and paper lanterns.

Bee Tree LAOTIAN $
(mains 15,000-35,000K; ⏲11.30am-11.30pm) Located at the end of the main drag, this barbecue-restaurant-cum-beer-garden has a relaxed ambience. Choose from Lao dishes and some comfort food, or stroll here for happy-hour cocktails between 5pm and 8pm.

Information

Thefts from Muang Ngoi Neua's cheaper guesthouses tend to occur when over-relaxed guests leave flimsy doors and shutters unsecured or place valuables within easy reach of long-armed pincers – most windows here have no glass.

There are no banks or ATMs here so bring plenty of cash from either Muang Khua (upriver) or Nong Khiaw (downriver). In an emergency you could exchange US dollars at a few of the guesthouses but rates are unsurprisingly poor.

Getting There & Away

Boats to Nong Khiaw (25,000K, one hour) leave around 9am, with tickets on sale from 8am at the boat office beside Ning Ning Guest House. At Nong Khiaw tuk-tuks will wait above the boat landing for your arrival to take you to the bus station.

Boats from Muang Khua pick up in Muang Ngoi Neua for Nong Khiaw around 1.30pm. Going to Muang Khua (100,000K, five hours), a boat leaves at 9.30am provided enough people sign up the day before on the list at the boat office. The first hour of the ride cuts through particularly spectacular karst scenery.

A new road running alongside the Nam Ou connecting Muang Ngoi Neua to Nong Khiaw has been created. However, it is still unsealed and passes through tributaries that have not yet been bridged; pretty useless for travellers unless you can hitch a lift with a boatman who happens to be there.

Northwestern Laos

Udomxai

Booming Udomxai (ອຸດົມໄຊ; also known as Muang Xai) is a Laos–China trade centre and crossroads city, and with its cast of migrant truck drivers and Mandarin signage at every turn it certainly feels like it. The dusty, brash main street and lack of a traveller vibe puts off many short-term visitors, and you might think the highlight is the bus that spirits you out of here; however, it takes minimal effort to find the real Laos nearby. The well-organised tourist office – one of the best in the country – has many ideas to tempt you to stay longer, from cooking courses to treks, off-road motorcycling and cycling.

Around 25% of Udomxai's population is Chinese, with the Yunnanese dialect as common as Lao in some businesses and hotels.

Sights & Activities

Nam Kat Waterfall WATERFALL
Nam Kat Waterfall, a picnic site 23km from Udomxai, is best reached on a decent motorbike. Turn right in Ban Fan, continue to the parking area then walk the last 30 minutes through protected forests (about 2km). Alternatively, hike 13.5km over 'red cliff' Phou Pha Daeng, which you'll need a guide for. The last 500m climb is the only testing section of the track and affords terrific views at the top. The falls themselves are 20m high and make for a chilled bucolic spot.

Nam Kat Yorla Pa Adventure Park ADVENTURE SPORTS
(☎020-55564359, 081-212195; www.namkatyorlapa.com; Faen Village, Xay District) Cycling, trekking, ziplining, rock climbing, abseiling, swimming, massage and shooting are all available at Oudomxay Province's newest forest resort 17km north of Udomxai by the picturesque Nam Kat (Kat River). Stunning accommodation in modern slick rooms starts at US$104. Alternatively, take the 'abseil, zipline and *via ferrata*' package, which also includes sleeping in a tree house for US$75. Don't miss the stunning pool.

Sleeping & Eating

★ **Charming Lao Hotel** BOUTIQUE HOTEL $$
(☎020-23966333, 081-212881; www.charminglaohotel.com; r incl breakfast US$50-150; P❄@🛜) An unexpected treat for Udomxai, this hotel offers tastefully furnished rooms right in the centre of town. Extra touches include flat-screen TVs with cable, coffee-making facilities, safety deposit boxes and contemporary bathrooms. The complex includes a spa and a disappointing branch of Pakse's **Cafe Sinouk** (www.sinoukcafe.com; mains 45,000-60,000K; ⏲7am-9pm; ❄🛜). Staff are eager but speak little English.

Villa Keoseumsack GUESTHOUSE $$
(☎081-312170; Rte 1; r 130,000-220,000K; P❄📶) Udomxai's best guesthouse is set back from the road in a handsome Lao house with large, inviting rooms. They come with crisp linen, decent fittings, springy beds and varnished floors. Hmong bed runners, TV, free wi-fi and a communal reading balcony finish them off. There's even complimentary toothbrush and toothpaste.

★ **Souphailin Restaurant** LAOTIAN $
(mains 20,000-40,000K; ⊙7am-10pm) Don't be fooled by the modest bamboo exterior of this backstreet gem – easily the tastiest Lao food in the city is served here. Friendly Souphailin creates culinary magic with her *mok phaa* (steamed fish in banana leaves), *láhp*, perfectly executed spring rolls, beef steak, fried noodles, and chicken and mushroom in banana leaf. Everything is fresh and seasonal. Check out the great barbet out back.

Information

BCEL (☎081-211260; Rte 1; ⊙8.30am-4.30pm Mon-Fri) Has an ATM, changes several major currencies and accepts some travellers cheques (2% commission).

Tourist Office (Provincial Tourism Department of Oudomxay; ☎081-211797; www.oudomxay.info; ⊙8-11.30am & 2-5pm) Unfailingly helpful and well run, the tourist office has masses of information about onward travel, accommodation and local sights. It has free town maps and sells GT-Rider *Laos* maps. There are 11 different tours on offer, including the two-day/one-night tour to an impressive local cave, and three-day/two-night treks and homestays with local ethnic villages.

Getting There & Away

Lao Airlines (☎081-312047; www.laoairlines.com) flies daily to/from Vientiane (US$79) to Udomxai's airport, while **Lao Skyway** (☎020-23122219; www.laoskyway.com; ⊙7am-5pm) flies to Vientiane as well (US$73) on Tuesday, Thursday and Saturday. Tickets are also available from **Lithavixay Guesthouse** (☎081-212175; Rte 1).

There are two bus stations in Udomxai: the old Northern Bus Station in the centre of town, and the newer Long-Distance Bus Station, aka **Southern Bus Terminal** (☎081-212218), 5km southwest from the centre. There is some crossover of routes as some of the same destinations are serviced by both minivans from the Northern Bus Station and buses from the Southern Bus Terminal.

Sŏrngtăaou to Muang La (20,000K) depart when full at around 8.30am and 11.30am from the Meuang Say Transportation Centre.

Muang La

Scenic Muang La (ເມືອງຫລາ), just 28km from Udomxai towards Phongsali, offers a charming rural alternative to the 'big city'. This Tai Lü village sits at the confluence of the Nam La (La River) and Nam Phak (Phak River), attractively awash with palm trees. Its central feature is a classically styled temple that hosts one of northern Laos' most revered Buddha statues, the Pra Singkham Buddha.

Sights

Pra Singkham Buddha BUDDHIST STATUE
(ພະເຈົ້າສິງຄໍາ; ⊙8.30am-5pm) FREE Want to get rich? Afraid you might be infertile? Don't worry, just ask the Pra Singkham Buddha and your wish will be granted. Legend claims it was cast in Sri Lanka just a few generations after the historical Buddha's death, and reached Laos in AD 868 via Ayodhya in India. Kept initially in the Singkham Cave, by 1457 it had been housed in a specially built temple.

Singkham Cave CAVE
(ຖ້ຳພະເຈົ້າສິງຄໍາ) FREE The Singkham Cave where the famous Pra Singkham Buddha statue once rested is 3.7km west of Ban Samakisai, halfway between Udomxai and Muang La. In Samakisai ask '*Khor kajeh tham noy?*' ('May I have the cave key please?') at the second hut south of the bridge. Then cross the bridge and take the second rough track west – just about passable by tuk-tuk or motorbike. This terminates at a collection of huts from which it's just three minutes' walk to the cave. Inside is a replica statue.

Sleeping & Eating

You can either eat at the market by the bus station for quick snacks or for something more salubrious pop into Muang La Resort (p342).

Lhakham Hotel HOTEL $
(☎020-55555930; lhakhamhotel@gmail.com; r 100,000K) Nestled on a river bank, the Lhakham Hotel offers some of the best-value rooms in northern Laos. Furnishings are tasteful, the bathrooms include a rain shower and the river views are pretty, adding up to a steal. There's also a restaurant here. It's about 1km from the bus station.

Muang La Resort BOUTIQUE HOTEL $$$
(020-22841264; www.muangla.com; 3-night package per person from US$691) The memorable Muang La Resort hides an elegant rustic refinement behind tall, whitewashed walls. It accepts neither walk-in guests nor visitors, so you'll need to prebook a package of two nights or more to enjoy the stylishly appointed half-timbered guestrooms, sauna and creatively raised open-air hot tub, all set between palms and manicured lawns.

Getting There & Away

Buses to Phongsali and Muang Khua pass through Muang La around an hour after departing Udomxai. The last bus returning to Udomxai usually rolls through at around 5pm. There's no bus station, just wave the bus down. Additional *sŏrngtăaou* to Udomxai (20,000K) depart at around 7am and 11am if there's sufficient custom.

Luang Namtha

Welcoming travellers like no other town in northern Laos, Luang Namtha (ຫລວງນ້ຳທາ) packs a powerful green punch with its selection of eco-minded tour companies catering for trekking to ethnically diverse villages, and cycling, kayaking and rafting in and around the stunning Nam Ha NPA.

Locally there's bags to do before you set out into the boonies, such as exploring the exotic night market, or grabbing a rental bike and tootling around the gently undulating rice-bowl valleys to waterfalls and temples. In the golden glow of sunset distant mountain ridges form layered silhouettes, and while it's not the prettiest belle architecturally speaking, the friendly vibe of Luang Namtha will grow on you.

Sights

Nam Ha NPA NATIONAL PARK
(ປ່າສະຫງວນແຫ່ງຊາດນ້ຳທາ; www.namha-npa.org) The 2224-sq-km Nam Ha NPA is one of Laos' most accessible natural preserves and home to clouded leopard and possibly a few unpoached tigers. Both around and within the mountainous park, woodlands have to compete with pressure from villages of various ethnicities, including Lao Huay, Akha and Khamu. Since 1999, an eco-touristic vision has tried to ensure tour operators and villagers work together to provide a genuine experience for trekkers while ensuring minimum impact on local communities and the environment.

Tours are limited to small groups, each agent has its own routes and, in principle, each village receives visitors no more than twice a week. Authorities don't dictate what villagers can and can't do, but by providing information on sustainable forestry and fishing practices it's hoped that forest protection will become a self-chosen priority for the communities.

Golden Stupa BUDDHIST TEMPLE
(5000K; 8am-5pm) By far Namtha's most striking landmark, this large golden stupa sits on a steep ridge directly northwest of town. It gleams majestically when viewed from afar. Up close, the effect is a bit more bling, but the views over town are impressive.

Ban Nam Di VILLAGE
(Nam Dy; parking bicycle/motorcycle/car 1000/2000/3000K) Although barely 3km out of Luang Namtha, this hamlet is populated by Lao Huay (Lenten) people whose womenfolk still wear traditional indigo tunics with purple sash-belts and silver-hoop necklaces. They specialise in turning bamboo pulp into rustic paper, using cotton screens that you'll spot along the scenic river banks.

At the eastern edge of the village, a three-minute stroll leads from a small carpark to a 6m-high **waterfall** (2000K). You'll find it's more of a picnic site than a scenic wonder but a visit helps put a little money into village coffers. Unless the water level is really high there's no need to struggle up and over the hillside steps so ignore that sign and walk along the pretty stream.

Luang Nam Tha Museum MUSEUM
(ພິພິດທະພັນຫຼວງນ້ຳທາ; 10,000K; 8.30-11.30am & 1.30-3.30pm Mon-Thu, 8.30-11.30am Fri) The Luang Nam Tha Museum contains a collection of local anthropological artefacts, such as ethnic clothing, Khamu bronze drums and ceramics. There are also a number of Buddha images and the usual display chronicling the Revolution.

Tours

★ **Green Discovery** ECOTOUR
(086-211484; www.greendiscoverylaos.com; Main St; 8am-9pm) The grandaddy of ecotourism in Laos offers a combo of boat trips, mountain biking, kayaking, homestays and one- to three-day treks in Nam Ha NPA. Safety is a given and staff are helpful. At the time of writing, it had plans to move to a new office.

Luang Namtha

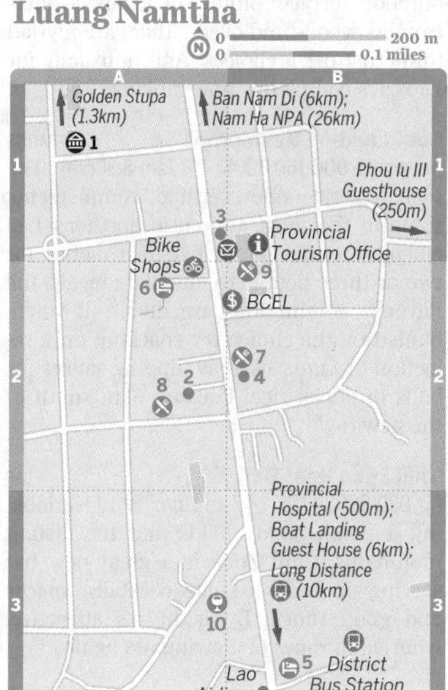

The Hiker TREKKING

(☎020-5924245, 086-212343; www.thehikerlaos.com; Main St) This new outfit is garnering some very glowing feedback. Cycling and kayaking trips are available but its main focus is on trekking, with one- to five-day options; the longest one is more hard core (seven hours' trekking per day) and promises to take you into untouched areas deep in the Nam Ha jungle, while one-day treks are much easier.

Forest Retreat Laos ECOTOUR

(☎020-55680031, 020-55560007; www.forestretreatlaos.com; Main St; ⏰7am-11.30pm) Based at the Minority Restaurant, this ecotourism outfit offers kayaking, trekking, homestays and mountain biking on one- to six-day multi-activity adventures, and recruits staff and guides from ethnic-minority backgrounds where possible. It also runs one-day cycle trips to Muang Sing and back. Another option here is to take a cooking class.

Sleeping

Popular places fill up fast, especially during the November–February high season. It's best to book ahead.

Most lodging in Luang Namtha is in the architecturally bland northern part of town around the traveller restaurants.

Luang Namtha

Sights
1 Luang Nam Tha Museum A1

Activities, Courses & Tours
2 Forest Retreat Laos A2
3 Green Discovery A1
4 The Hiker B2

Sleeping
5 Amandra Villa B3
6 Zuela Guesthouse A2

Eating
7 Bamboo Lounge B2
8 Minority Restaurant A2
9 Night Market B2

Drinking & Nightlife
10 Chill Zone Beer Bar A3

★**Zuela Guesthouse** GUESTHOUSE $

(☎020-22391966; www.zuela-laos.com; r old block with fan/air-con 80,000/100,000K, new block with air-con with/without balcony US$38/25; P❄📶) Located in a leafy courtyard, Zuela has an old block of spotless – though dim – rooms with exposed-brick walls and en suites. The newer block has better rooms with glazed rattan ceilings, lemon walls (some with balcony), desks and vivid art. Located off the main drag down a quiet lane. Besides its great restaurant it also offers scooter rental.

Amandra Villa GUESTHOUSE $

(☎030-9211319; Rte 3A, Ban Nong Bua Vieng; r from 100,000K; ❄) Set in a striking wooden building near the district bus station, Amandra has decent rattan-walled rooms with pretty lantern bedside lights, fan or air-con, satellite TV and hot water. The owner is helpful, and gives you his card so you can reach him if there's any hiccups. Rental bikes are available, too.

★**Phou Iu III Guesthouse** GUESTHOUSE $$

(☎030-5710422; www.luangnamtha-oasis-resort.com; r from US$25; ❄📶) Part of the same family as the Phou Iu II in Muang Sing, this place is cracking value and sits in pretty, flowering gardens. Bungalows are spacious and nicely fitted out with lumber-wood beds, brick floors, fireplaces and inviting terraces. It's well signposted from the centre of town. Note that in December it's a little on the chilly side.

Boat Landing Guest House RESORT $$

(☎086-312398; www.theboatlanding.laopdr.com; Ban Kone; r incl breakfast US$47-60; 📶) One of the country's original ecolodges, the Boat

Landing has riverside acacia groves hugging tastefully finished wooden bungalows with solar-heated showers. The restaurant here produces some of the best Lao cuisine in the north, although cosy but weary rooms could do with a refresh. Located 6km south of the new town and about 150m off the main road.

Eating & Drinking

Minority Restaurant LAOTIAN $

(mains 35,000K; 7am-10.30pm;) This inviting, wood-beamed restaurant hidden down a little side alley offers the chance to sample typically ethnic dishes from the Khamu, Tai Dam and Akha tribes, as well as *láhp,* stir-fries, chicken curry and fried fish.

Night Market MARKET $

(Rte 3A; 7-11.30pm) Tightly thronged with tribeswomen and locals hawking freshly made broths, noodles and chicken on spits, with everything veiled in a stratosphere of smoke. Great for cheap quick eats. If you're feeling brave try the rhinoceros beetles, duck chicks in embryos, grilled intestines and bile soup!

★**Bamboo Lounge** INTERNATIONAL $$

(020-22392931; mains/pizzas 50,000/75,000K; 7am-11.30pm, happy hour 5-7pm;) With its moss-green facade this place is the favourite in town for travellers, offering employment to young people from remote villages and donating over 2500 books to local schools. It's alluring by night with its winking fairy lights, thumping tunes and outdoor terrace piping delicious aromas from its wood-fired oven – there are myriad thin-crust pizza choices. And unusually for Laos, it's completely nonsmoking.

Boat Landing Restaurant LAOTIAN $$

(meals 35,000-160,000K; 7am-8.30pm) The relaxing riverside setting complements some of the most authentic northern Lao cuisine on offer. From five-dish menus for two or three people to one-plate meals, the flavour combinations are divine. If you're baffled by the choice try snacking on a selection of *jąaou* used as dipping sauces for balls of sticky rice. Located 6km south of the new town.

Chill Zone Beer Bar BAR

(020-98088878; 7am-11pm;) Overlooking a pond, paddy fields and the distant mountains, Chill Zone is a great new bar serving up beer, ice-blue cocktails, snacks and good tunes. By night it's attractive, whorled in ropes of glowing red lights.

Information

BCEL (8.30am-3.30pm Mon-Fri) Changes major currencies (commission-free) and travellers cheques (2% commission, minimum US$3), and has a 24-hour ATM.

Provincial Tourism Office (086-211534; 8am-noon & 2-5pm) This enthusiastically run office has lots of ideas to make your stay in the area a memorable one, with details about the old Tea Route to trek, Nam Ha NPA treks, info on the local wildlife, and brochures and bus times.

BUSES FROM LUANG NAMTHA

DESTINATION	COST (K)	DURATION (HR)	STATION	DEPARTURES
Boten	25,000	2	district	6 daily 8am-2pm
Dien Bien Phu (Vietnam)	130,000	10	long-distance	7.30am
Huay Xai ('Borkeo')	60,000	4	long-distance	9am, 12.30pm, 4pm
Jinghong (China)	90,000	6	long-distance	8am
Luang Prabang	100,000	8	long-distance	9am bus, 8am minibus
Mengla (China)	50,000	3½	long-distance	8am
Muang Long	60,000	4	district	8.30am
Muang Sing	25,000	2	district	6 daily 8am-3.30pm
Na Lae	40,000	3	district	9.30am, noon
Phonsavan	180,000	12	long-distance	8am
Udomxai	40,000	4	long-distance	9am, noon, 2.30pm
Vieng Phukha	30,000	1½	long-distance	9.30am, 12.30pm
Vientiane	180,000-200,000	21-24	long-distance	8.30am, 2.30pm

Provincial Hospital (Rte 3A; ⏲24hr) Adequately equipped for X-rays, dealing with broken limbs and dishing out antibiotics. Ask for English-speaking Dr Veokham.

Getting There & Away

AIR

Lao Airlines (☎086-312180; www.laoairlines.com; ⏲9am-5pm) flies to Vientiane (US$75) daily, while **Lao Skyway** (☎020-99990011; Luang Namtha Airport; ⏲9am-5pm) flies there Monday, Wednesday, Friday and Sunday (US$61).

BOAT

You can now only take the boat as far as Ban Phaeng, where a dam was recently built. What was a two-day experience is now just a day, though you still have around eight hours of puttering downriver. Pick-up by car/van is at the **boat station** (☎086-312014), from where you will be driven to Na Lae. Contact Forest Retreat Laos (p343), which can organise a guide, transfers and prearrange your boat. The charter costs US$500 for two people (US$250 per person); it's cheaper per head the more of you go.

BUS

There are two bus stations. The district bus station is walking distance from the traveller strip. The main long-distance bus station is 10km south of town. For buses at either station, prebooking a ticket doesn't guarantee a seat – you just have to arrive early and claim one in person.

For Nong Khiaw take a Vientiane or Luang Prabang bus and change at Pak Mong.

Getting Around

Chartered tuk-tuks charge 15,000K per person between the long-distance bus station or airport and the town centre, more if you're travelling solo. Most agencies and guesthouses sell ticket packages for long-distance buses that include a transfer from the guesthouse and cost around 20,000K above the usual fare.

Cycling is the ideal way to explore the wats, waterfalls, villages and landscapes surrounding Luang Namtha. There are a couple of **bike shops** (per day bicycle 10,000-25,000K, motorcycle 30,000-50,000K; ⏲9am-6.30pm) in front of the Zuela Guesthouse. Choose from a bicycle or motorcycle depending on how energetic you are feeling.

Vieng Phukha

Sleepy Vieng Phukha (ວຽງພູຄາ; also spelt 'Phoukha') is an alternative trekking base for visiting the western limits of the Nam Ha NPA, notably on three-day Akha trail hikes. Such trails see fewer visitors than many from Luang Namtha and the partly forested landscapes can be magnificent, though many hills in Vieng Phukha's direct vicinity have been completely deforested.

Run by Somhack (an experienced Khmu hunter who hung up his gun to use his tracking skills as a guide), **Nam Ha Hilltribe Ecotrek** (☎020-99440084; www.trekviengphoukha.com; ⏲8am-noon & 1-6pm) is a great outfit offering multiday treks (from moderately easy to challenging) from Vieng Phukha to explore the Nam Ha NPA.

Just 15 minutes' stroll south of Rte 3 near Km 85 but utterly hidden in thick secondary woodlands is the almost invisible site of the 1530 temple Wat Mahapot. What little had survived the centuries was mostly pillaged for building materials around 1977 when all the residents moved back after the war, so now all you'll see is the odd scattering of bricks poking out from a tree-choked muddy rise. Getting there involves walking along a steep V-shaped gully that once protected the Khúu Wíeng (Ramparts) of a short-lived 16th-century 'city'. Again there's nothing but muddy banks to see but a good guide (essential) can fill in sketchy historical details and explain the medicinal uses of plants you'll encounter on a 40-minute walking tour. There are no longer local tour guides operating here, but Mr Tong Mua at Tigerman Treks (p346) in Muang Sing can take you.

Just about the smartest accommodation in Vieng Phukha is **Thongmyxai Guesthouse**

WORTH A TRIP

KAO RAO CAVES

Well signed beside Rte 3, 1.5km east of Nam Eng village, **Kao Rao Caves** (ຖ້ຳເກົາເລົາ; 10,000K) are an extensive, accessible cave system, which has a 700m section open to visitors. The main limestone formations include old stalactites encrusted with crystal deposits. Curious corrugations in the floor that now look like great old tree roots once formed the lips of carbonate pools like those at Turkey's Pamukkale.

Local guides accompany visitors through the cave, but speak no English and have feeble torches (flashlights). Extensive lighting is already wired up, but there are often power cuts, meaning your own torch is a handy accessory. Allow around 45 minutes for the visit.

(☎020-22390351; r 50,000K), set in an attractive garden with bungalows.

Sŏrngtăaou for Luang Namtha (40,000K, 1½ hours) depart at around 9am and 1pm from the middle of town. Or you can wave down a Huay Xai–Namtha through-service (three daily).

Muang Sing

Bordering Myanmar and within grasp of the green hills of China, Muang Sing (ເມືອງສິງ) is a rural backwater in the heart of the Golden Triangle. Formerly on the once infamous opium trail, it's a sleepy town of wilting, Tai Lü–style houses where trekking has overtaken smuggling contraband. Hmong, Tai Lü, Akha and Tai Dam are all seen here in traditional dress at the old market (get there at dawn), giving the town a frontier feel.

Back in the late '90s, it was one of the must-visit destinations in Laos, but with the end of fast boat services and clampdown on the opium trade, it has dropped off the traveller radar. Recently, a growing Chinese population has settled here, replacing rice fields with banana and rubber plantations for consumption on the other side of the border. Regrettably, Western travellers have spoken of being turned away from restaurants and guesthouses by Chinese operators.

Sights & Activities

Sprinkled along the town's main street are a few classic Lao-French hybrid mansion-houses. These mostly 1920s structures have ground-floor walls of brick and stucco topped with a wooden upper storey featuring a wraparound roofed verandah. Classic examples house the tourist office and the Thai Lü Guesthouse.

The **old market** (Main St), built in 1954, was under reconstruction at the time of writing as the roof had collapsed. The bustling **new market** (⏲7am-10pm) is near the bus station and is very colourful first thing in the morning, though you'll be harder pressed to find ethnic women in tribal dress here.

Tribal Museum MUSEUM
(5000K; ⏲8.30am-4.30pm Mon-Fri, 8-11am Sat) The most distinctive of the old Lao-French buildings is now home to the two-room Tribal Museum, which boasts costume displays downstairs and six cases of cultural artefacts upstairs. Watching a 40-minute video on the Akha people costs 5000K extra.

Tigerman Treks TREKKING
(☎020-55467833, 020-56783156, 030-5264881; tigermantrek@gmail.com; Main St; 7am-7pm) English-speaking teacher and nice guy Mr Tong Mua has long been a fixture of Muang Sing and with the slow death of the tourist office (located opposite), he's a safer bet for general information, decent treks and homestays in the Nam Ha NPA, as well as tuk-tuk tours and cycle/trek combos. He also rents bikes (50,000K) and motorcycles (100,000K).

Sleeping & Eating

Adima Guesthouse GUESTHOUSE $
(☎020-22393398; r 100,000K; 📶) Adima sits conveniently on the edge of an Akha village; Nam Dath is only 700m up the trail. Many other minority villages are also within easy

GETTING TO CHINA: BOTEN TO MÓHĀN

Getting to the border The Lao immigration post at the **Boten (Laos)/Móhān (China) border crossing** (⏲7.30am to 4.30pm Laos time, 8.30am to 5.30pm China time) is a few minutes' walk north of Boten market. Tuk-tuks shuttle across no-man's land to the Chinese immigration post in Móhān (Bohan) or it's an easy 10-minute walk.

Alternatively, take one of the growing number of handy Laos–China through-bus connections such as Udomxai–Mengla, Luang Namtha–Jinghong and Luang Prabang–Kunming.

At the border Northbound it is necessary to have a Chinese visa in advance. On arrival in Laos 30-day visas are available.

Moving on From the Chinese immigration post it's a 15-minute walk up Móhān's main street to the stand where little buses depart for Mengla (RMB16, one hour) every 20 minutes or so till mid-afternoon. These arrive at Mengla's bus station No 2. Nip across that city to the northern bus station for Jinghong (RMB42, two hours, frequent till 6pm) or Kunming (mornings only). On the Lao side minibuses shuttle regularly in the morning from Boten to Luang Namtha.

Muang Sing

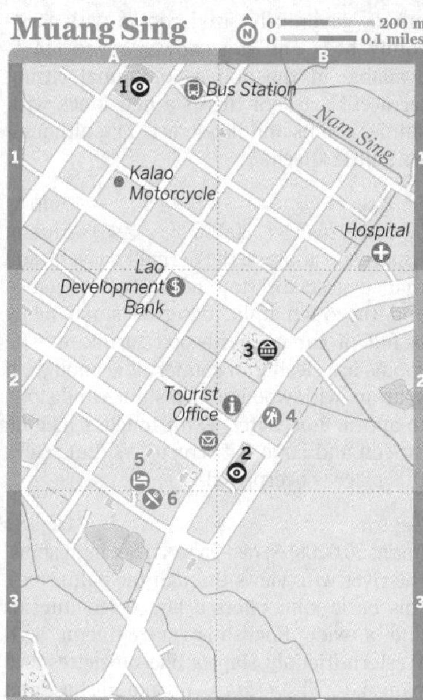

walking distance. Adima's sturdy brick-and-thatch bungalows have hot showers and bucket-flush toilets, though have faded considerably over recent years. The Veranda, its appealing rustic restaurant, overlooks fish ponds and is pleasant come sundown.

It's 8.5km from Muang Sing. From town take the Pang Hai road to the far edge of Ban Udomsin (500m after Km 7) and turn right; Adima is 600m south. A tuk-tuk from town costs about 30,000K.

★**Phou Iu II Guesthouse** GUESTHOUSE $$
(☎086-400012; www.muangsingtravel.com; bungalows small/medium/large 100,000/200,000/400,000K) Set around an expansive garden, the biggest bungalows have fun, outdoor, rock-clad shower spaces. All rooms have comfortable beds, mosquito nets, fans and small verandahs (although rooms are cold at night during the cool season). There's an on-site herbal sauna (10,000K) and massage (50,000K per hour), plus the restaurant Veranda, probably the best place in town to eat.

Veranda Restaurant ASIAN $
(mains 30,000K; ⏱6.30am-9pm) About the best Lao, Thai and Chinese food you can expect in town, this is a simple, cosy spot to eat hearty Lao fare – think soups and noodle dishes – in a friendly atmosphere. It's based in the garden of the Phou Iu II Guesthouse.

Muang Sing

Sights
1 Morning Market....A1
2 Old Market....B2
3 Tribal Museum....B2

Activities, Courses & Tours
4 Tigerman Treks....B2

Sleeping
5 Phou lu II Guesthouse....A2

Eating
6 Veranda Restaurant....A3

Information

Lao Development Bank (⏱8am-noon & 2-3.30pm Mon-Fri) Exchanges US dollars, Thai baht and Chinese yuan but at less than favourable rates.

Tourist Office (⏱8am-4pm Mon-Fri) Displays of fact scrolls are useful but the staff aren't likely to win any Lao National Tourism Authority employee of the month awards.

Getting There & Around

From the **bus station** in the northwest corner of town, *sǒrngtǎaou* depart for Muang Long (30,000K, 1½ hours) at 9am and 11am. To Luang Namtha (25,000K, two hours) minibuses leave at 8am, 9am and 11am. The bus to Muang La (40,000K) leaves at 7.30am and 1pm.

Kalao Motorcycle (per day 100,000K; ⏱8am-5pm), on the road to the morning market, rents motorbikes, but bring a good phrasebook as nobody here speaks English.

Bicycle rental (30,000K per day) is available from several main-street agencies and guesthouses.

Phongsali Province

No longer Laos, not yet China, Phongsali is a visual feast and is home to some of the nation's most traditional hill tribes. Trekkers might feel that they've walked onto the pages of *National Geographic*. For travellers, the province's most visited settlement is Muang Khua, a useful transit point linked by river to Nong Khiaw and by road to Dien Bien Phu in Vietnam. Further north the province is kept well off the standard tourist trail by arduous journeys on snaking roads that twist and turn endlessly. The only asphalt links

Muang Khua to Udomxai, Phongsali and on to Mengla in China. Inconveniently, foreigners can't cross the Chinese border anywhere in the province. The road to Dien Bien Phu is now in great shape on the Lao side, but is not so great on the Vietnamese side.

Muang Khua

Pretty little Muang Khua (ເມືອງຂວາ) is an inevitable stop when transiting between Laos and Dien Bien Phu in Vietnam, or taking the brown Nam Ou (Ou River) by boat to Nong Khiaw. While not as scenically spectacular nor as developed for the traveller as the latter, Muang Khua, with its pastel-coloured houses, still has oodles of small-town charm, set amid starburst palms where the Nam Ou and Nam Phak (Phak River) meet. The heart of the place is its wet and dry market.

If arriving from Dien Bien Phu, please relax – unlike neighbouring Vietnam, hard bargaining here is neither required nor appropriate.the a

Sights

Suspension Bridge BRIDGE
For soaring mountain and river views head to this suspension bridge leading to the Khamu quarter. You'll need a head for heights and a good sense of balance on this safe but eminently wobbly construction.

Wat BUDDHIST TEMPLE
This peaceful temple is worth a visit given the limited sightseeing options in town.

Sleeping & Eating

Chaleunsuk Guesthouse GUESTHOUSE $
(☎088-210847; r old block 70,000, new block 100,000-120,000K; ❄@📶) Chaleunsuk is popular with travellers and has house-proud, generously sized rooms with large comfy beds and hot showers. Free tea is available in the ample communal sitting terrace. Next door there's a new block with shinier rooms and flat-screen TVs, although it's a little kitsch.

Sernalli Hotel HOTEL $$
(☎088-212445; r 200,000K; ❄📶) Muang Khua's top address, the Sernalli has a facade that suggests a certain neocolonial elegance and the often unlit, deserted small lobby is full of carved hardwood furniture. The rooms are clean and comfortable enough, if spartan, with wooden furnishings and slow-to-appear hot water. Extra touches include air-con and large flat-screen TVs. But really, this place is overpriced.

Sayfon LAOTIAN $
(mains 30,000K; ⏲7am-9pm; 📶) Set high above the river with views through the palm trees, this basic joint offers a fan-cooled interior and a wide English-language menu with Western-friendly staples like omelettes and pancakes. Tasty *láhp*, noodle dishes and plenty of cool Beerlao. This spot is about as lively as it gets in Muang Khua come evening.

Information

The helpful **tourist office** (☎020-22848020; ⏲8.30-11.30am & 1.30-4.30pm Mon-Fri) opposite the Sernalli Hotel can answer questions and arrange treks. If you want to book a trek out of office hours, call Mr Keo to arrange a meeting, or try independent guide Mr Khamman (☎020-99320743). Otherwise, check out www.muangkhua.com, which has some bookable treks and the low-down on every last guesthouse in town.

There is an ATM at **BCEL** (⏲8.30am-3.30pm Mon-Fri), though it can run out of money over the weekend.

GETTING TO VIETNAM: MUANG KHUA TO DIEN BIEN PHU

Getting to the border The **Sop Hun/Tay Trang border** in Phongsali Province has now opened as an international entry point to Tay Trang in Vietnam. There are three buses a week bound for Dien Bien Phu leaving from the Lao village of Muang Khua (50,000K,6.30am, five to six hours). Get there early for a decent seat.

At the border Note, there are no facilities or waiting vehicles at either the Lao or Vietnamese borders (open 8am to 5pm). The nearest ATM in Laos is in Udomxai so bring plenty of dollars. You'll need to organise a Vietnamese visa in advance. Lao visas are available on arrival for US$30 to US$42, depending on your nationality. Bring some photo ID and some extra cash (approximately US$5) for administrative costs charged on weekends and holidays.

Moving on Once through the Vietnamese border it's a further 35km to Dien Bien Phu.

Getting There & Away

The bus to Dien Bien Phu in Vietnam (60,000K) departs from outside the BCEL bank at 6am and 11am and takes about four hours, including the border crossing. However, it isn't guaranteed to leave daily if there aren't enough passengers.

Muang Khua's inconvenient **bus station** (Rte 2E, 900m past Km 97) is nearly 2km west of the river towards Udomxai. Very rare tuk-tuks (10,000K per person) head out there once full from outside BCEL. Buses to Udomxai (50,000K, three hours) depart at 8.30am, 11am and 3pm. For Phongsali take the 8am *sǒrngtǎaou* to Pak Nam Noi (20,000K, one hour) and await the Udomxai–Phongsali (100,000K) bus there. It usually arrives at around 10am.

You can no longer travel by river to Hat Sa since the damming of the Nam Ou. Boats run from here downriver to Muang Ngoi Neua (100,000K, five hours, 8.30am or when there are 10 people) and on to Nong Khiaw (120,000K, six hours) through stunning karst scenery.

Phongsali

As you approach Phongsali (ຜົ້ງສາລີ) via a sinuous mountain road, the town rears up suddenly on a ridgetop plateau. Often wrapped in mist, its atmospheric wooden Yunnanese shophouses and other buildings, spanning biscuit-brown to powder-blue, shelter below the peak of Phu Fa rising majestically in the background. The location gives the town panoramic views and a refreshing climate that can swing from pleasantly warm to downright cold in a matter of hours – expect icicles in the cold season and bring a jacket and waterproofs just in case, even in April.

The town's population is a mix of Phu Noi and Haw/Yunnanese, both long-term residents and more recent immigrants. That said, no one comes to Phongsali to experience the town, which can feel unfriendly and very untypically Lao; it's the trekking in the surrounding hill country and its vivid population of ethnic peoples that justifies the considerable effort to get here.

Sights & Activities

Yunnanese Shophouses NOTABLE BUILDING

FREE These atmospheric one-storey wooden houses make you feel, as you peer into their Chinese-decorated interiors, that you are no longer in Laos but already in nearby China (and somewhere from early in the last century).

OFF THE BEATEN TRACK

UNEXPLORED FORESTS

Phu Den Din NPA (ປ່າສະຫງວນແຫ່ງຊາດພູແດນດິນ) is a vast area of partly unexplored, relatively pristine forest, layered across inaccessible mountains that climax at almost 2000m near the Vietnamese border. At present the only legal way to get a glimpse of its grandeur is on irregular boating or kayaking trips down the Nam Ou (Ou River) between Ban Tha and Hat Sa. An army checkpoint currently prevents any access to the NPA. Sneaking past it you risk being shot as a suspected poacher.

Chinese Temple TEMPLE

This Chinese temple, with its red roofs animated with myriad green and blue dragons, commands a pretty view over a nearby pond crowded with old Yunnan houses.

Phu Fa VIEWPOINT

(ພູຟ້າ, Sky Mountain) For great views across town climb to the stupa-topped peak of Phu Fa (1625m); it's a punishing, tree-shaded climb of more than 400 stone steps. A 4000K toll is payable on the last section of the ascent. An alternative descent returns to the Hat Sa road near a tea factory 2km east of town.

Amazing Phongsali Travel TREKKING

(Northern Travelling Center; ☎088-210594, 020-55774354; www.explorephongsalylaos.com; ⏰8am-5pm or later) In order to see a few of the 28 ethnicities in the province you need to penetrate deep jungle, and for this you'll require more than a guide who can take you to outlying villages along the road. Amazing Phongsali Travel is the main independent trekking operator in Phongsali, with a selection of treks that have brought rave reviews.

Sleeping & Eating

Phou Fa Hotel HOTEL $

(☎088-210031; r 100,000-200,000K; ❄📶) Western toilets, room heaters and golden bed covers give the Phou Fa a marginal edge as Phongsali's best choice, but let's not get too excited. More expensive rooms are almost suites and include a carpet. This compound housed the Chinese consulate until 1975. There's also a rather drab restaurant here.

Sengsaly Guesthouse GUESTHOUSE $
(☎088-210165; r 80,000-100,000K; 📶) The best of three cheapies on the main drag, the Sengsaly has uberbasic 80,000K rooms with clean bedding, bare walls, tiled floors and private bathroom. Better rooms are newly built and comfy, if overly colourful, and come with a hot shower and verandah. Expect indifferent service.

Laojerm Restaurant LAOTIAN $
(mains 30,000K; ⏲7am-10.30pm) At this family-run noodle house the well-prepared food comes in decent-sized portions and is served with a smile. The menu's approximate English includes inscrutable offerings such as 'High-handed Pig's liver' and 'Palace Protects the Meat Cubelets'.

Noodle Stands NOODLES $
(noodles 15,000K; ⏲6am-5pm) Head to the noodle stands at the rear of the wet market before you catch the 6.30am *sŏrngtăaou* to the bus station, or if you're headed out on a trek. Steaming deliciously fresh noodles and a slice of Yunnan-Lao culture await the early bird. Try the tasty *kòw sóy* (noodle soup with minced pork and tomato).

Information

BCEL (⏲8.30am-3.30pm Mon-Fri) Includes an ATM across the road.

Lao Development Bank (⏲8.30am-3.30pm Mon-Fri) Can change multiple currencies to kip and cashes US-dollar travellers cheques without commission. Includes an ATM and represents Western Union.

Tourist Office (☎088-210098; www.phongsaly.net; ⏲8-11.30am & 1.30-4pm Mon-Fri) If you need emergency help or want to book a tour out of hours, call ☎020-22572373 or the mobile phone number of duty staff posted on the front door. Helpful maps and brochures are also available online (and are free from most guesthouses).

Wang Electronics Shop (⏲7am-10pm) Internet access and a regular power supply.

Getting There & Away

Phongsali's airport is actually at Boun Neua, although at the time of writing neither of the country's airlines were running flights here.

Buses leave daily for Hat Sa (20,000K) at 8am and 1.30pm from the **Hat Sa Bus Station** (Km 3), 10 minutes' walk east of town.

Phongsali's main bus station is at Km 3, west of town. A *sŏrngtăaou* runs there from the market area (10,000K) at 6.30am but only very infrequently after that, so leave plenty of time. Route 1A has finally been sealed, allowing for safer, quicker and easier passage to and from Phongsali. The daily bus to Vientiane (230,000K, more than 20 hours) leaves at 8.30am and the VIP bus (250,000K) at 2pm, passing through Luang Prabang (140,000K). Buses to Udomxai (80,000K, seven hours) leave at 8am and 2pm. There's a 7.30am bus to Luang Namtha (60,000k), and a 7am bus to Dien Bien Phu (130,000K, five hours) on the Vietnamese side. As foreigners can't cross the Chinese border at Ban Pakha, the buses to Mengla, China (7am and 1.30pm) are only useful for reaching Boun Neua (50,000K).

There's a 7.30am bus to Muang Khua (80,000K, seven hours), from where you can catch the boat to Muang Ngoi Neua and Nong Khiaw (due to river damming, it is no longer possible to catch the boat upriver from Hat Sa). Note that you cannot get to Muang Ngoi Neua or Nong Khiaw in one day and will have to overnight at Muang Khua.

Amazing Phongsali Travel (p349) rents small motorbikes from 100,000K per day.

Boun Neua

A local transport hub 41km west of Phongsali, Boun Neua (ບຸນເໜືອ) is a diffuse scattering of mostly newer concrete houses that has been tentatively proposed as the unlikely new provincial capital. Staying here might prove handy if connecting to Ou Tai or for those doing the Phongsali 'Jungle Trek'.

Beside the bus station and market, convenient three-storey **Sivienkham Guesthouse** (r 50,000K) offers large and house-proud rooms with comfy beds, hot showers and sit-down toilets.

After Boun Neua (Km 41) the road to Phongsali climbs onto a ridge-top road surveying swaths of protected mountain forests. There's a signed viewpoint 500m past Km 31, with ridge-top panoramas continuing for the next 15km. Baka Luang (200m beyond Km 17) is the first noticeably Phu Noi village en route, where old women still wear distinctive Phu Noi leggings.

Middle Mekong

For many tourists the region is seen merely in passing between Thailand and Luang Prabang – typically on the two-day slowboat route from Huay Xai via Pak Beng – but there's plenty to interest the more adventurous traveller. Bokeo, meaning 'Gem Mine', takes its name from the sapphire deposits in Huay Xai district, and the province harbours 34 ethnicities despite a particularly sparse population. Sainyabuli Province is synonymous with working elephants and the Elephant Conservation Center is just outside the eponymous capital. Other than in Huay Xai and Pak Beng you'll need a decent phrasebook wherever you go. Western Sainyabuli remains particularly far off the traveller radar; places such as the dramatic Khop district are 'last frontiers' with a complex ethnic mix and reputedly high proportion of still-pristine forests.

Huay Xai

Huay Xai (ຫ້ວຍຊາຍ) was allegedly home to a US heroin-processing plant during the Secret War, but these days the only things trafficked through are travellers en route to Luang Prabang. Separated from Thailand by the mother river that is the Mekong, Huay Xai is for many their first impression of Laos: don't worry, it does get better. By night its central drag dons its fairy lights and roadside food vendors fire things up, and there are some welcoming traveller guesthouses and cafes serving tasty food. Huay Xai is also the HQ of the now-fabled Gibbon Experience, deservedly the most talked-about jungle adventure in the country.

Activities

Gibbon Experience ADVENTURE SPORTS
(☎030-5745866, 084-212021; www.gibbonexperience.org; 2-day Express US$190, 3-day Classic or Waterfall US$310; ⏲7am-5pm) At this long-running ecotourism project, a series of ziplines criss-cross the canopy in the Bokeo Nature Reserve – home to tigers, clouded leopards, black bears and the black-crested gibbon – where you can soar across valleys and stay in 40m-high tree-houses. There are three tour options, each involving some trekking. Meals are ziplined in by your guide.

The guides are helpful, though make sure you're personally vigilant with the knots in your harness, check your karabiner closes, and opt for a helmet. Remember to allow more time to brake should it rain. For all three tour options, we recommend being in good shape.

One day before departure, check in at the Huay Xai Gibbon Experience Office on Th Saykhong. Gloves (essential) are sold next door. It's also advisable to bring a torch (flashlight), water bottle, and earplugs to deflect the sound of a million crickets, but otherwise leave most of your baggage in the office storeroom. Everything you bring you must carry on your back over some steep hikes and on the ziplines. Don't forget to precharge camera batteries.

An accident here in March 2017 resulted in the death of one tourist, and tours were suspended during investigations. The Gibbon Experience stated it will continue to operate, while implementing stricter safety protocols. At the time of writing, the police report was pending. See the website for the latest developments.

Sleeping

The central drag is packed with guesthouses and many more are dotted around the edge of town.

Daauw Homestay HOMESTAY $
(☎030-9041296; www.projectkajsiablaos.org; r 100,000-140,000K) Daauw Homestay is run by lovely Hmong folk, and your stay in a cosy bungalow near the heart of town enables you to contribute to women's empowerment and minority rights as this is a grassroots initiative run by Project Kajsiab. Simple rooms come with sunset views, hammock, balcony and private bathroom. There's a small handicrafts shop, and you can volunteer here. It's located just off the stairs to Wat Jom Khao Manilat, halfway up on the right-hand side.

BAP Guesthouse GUESTHOUSE $
(Th Saykhong; r 60,000-130,000K;; ❄) Run by English-speaking Mrs Changpeng, trusty BAP has 16 rooms, some with fan or air-con and private bathroom. There are four newish ones that merit a mention for their colourful quilts, wood accents, TVs and sunset views over the Mekong, particularly rooms 108 and 109. The restaurant (mains 15,000K to 35,000K) is also popular for its fried-rice dishes, pasta and hearty breakfasts.

Riverside Houayxay Hotel HOTEL $$
(☎084-1211064; riverside_houayxay_laos@hotmail.com; r incl breakfast from US$25; 📶) Located just off the main strip and overlooking the mighty Mekong, this is the most upmarket hotel in the centre of town. Rooms are spacious though bathrooms could do with a more thorough clean. Hot water is on tap, plus there's satellite TV and a minibar.

Phonevichith Guesthouse & Restaurant GUESTHOUSE $$
(☎084-211765; www.houayxairiverside.com; Ban Khonekeo; r US$45; ❄📶) Colourful fabrics, fans and kitschy lamps add a little character to the smart rooms, which come with piping-hot showers and air-con. A new wing offers the smartest beds in town, which are verging on the 'boutique hotel'. The main attractions are

the Mekong perch and handy proximity to the slowboat landing. Some building was underway here at the time of writing.

Eating & Drinking

Of three *falang*-style restaurants near the slowboat pier, the one at Phonevichith Guesthouse (p351) has the best river views.

Daauw LAOTIAN $
(www.projectkajsiablaos.org; mains 30,000-50,000K; 6-10pm;) The friendliest vibe in town: soak up the sunset view on its chill-out terrace decked in low cushions and an open-pit fire, and choose from freshly prepared organic Hmong food, wood-fired pizza, plenty of vegetarian options, or whole barbecued Mekong fish or chicken. Linger for *laojitos* if there's a crowd – a mojito made with *lòw-lów* (rice wine).

Tavendeng Restaurant LAOTIAN $$
(mains 25,000-80,000K; 7am-11pm) Predominantly aimed at Thai tourists, this large wooden dining complex features live music and exotic foods such as frog and fried crocodile.

Riverview Cafe LAOTIAN, INTERNATIONAL $$
(Th Saykhong; meals 40,000K; 6.30am-11pm;) With its rattan ceiling dramatically on the verge of collapse and the thirsty walls peeling, Riverview Cafe (aka Muang Ncr) might not look like much, but notice it's always full, and stand and catch the aromas from the kitchen, and in no time you'll be tucking into wood-fired pizzas, burgers, stir-fries, soup noodles and very zestful *láhp*.

It's next door to the Gibbon Experience Office; stock up on a sandwich to take with you to the jungle.

Bar How BAR
(Th Saykhong; 6.30am-11pm;) Decked in old muskets and rice-paddy hats, Bar How is darkly atmospheric. By night a row of sinister-looking homemade *lòw-lów* (rice wine), infused with everything from blueberry to lychee, catches the low light and resembles a Victorian apothecary. It also serves pasta, steak, *láhp* and spring rolls (mains 30,000K to 45,000K). However, the service is very slack – you may have to seek out staff.

Information

BCEL (Th Saykhong; 8.30am-4.30pm Mon-Fri) Has a 24-hour ATM, exchange facility and Western Union.

Lao Development Bank Exchange Booth (8am-5pm) Handy booth right beside the pedestrian immigration window. Most major currencies exchanged into kip. US-dollar bills must be dated 2006 or later.

Tourist Information Office (084-211162; Th Saykhong; 8am-4.30pm Mon-Fri) Has free tourist maps of the town and some suggestions for excursions around the province.

Getting There & Away

For years, streams of Luang Prabang–bound travellers have piled into Huay Xai and jumped straight onboard a boat for the memorable descent of the Mekong. Today, improving roads mean an ever-increasing proportion opt instead for the overnight bus. But while slightly cheaper than the slowboat, it's far less social, less attractive and, at around 15 hours of travel, leaves most travellers exhausted on arrival.

AIR

Huay Xai's airport is oddly perched on a hillside off the city bypass, 1.5km northwest of the bus

GETTING TO THAILAND: HUAY XAI (HOKSAY) TO CHIANG KHONG

Getting to the border Since the completion of the Thai-Lao Friendship Bridge 4 at the **Huay Xai/Chiang Khong border crossing** in late 2013, the former ferry-boat crossing is for locals only.

Tuk-tuks cost about 80B per person to the immigration post.

At the border A bus (20B) crosses the bridge. A 15-day Thai visa waiver is automatically granted when entering Thailand. Arriving in Chiang Khong, pay the 30B port fee and catch a 30B tuk-tuk to take you to the bus station. The nearest ATM on the Thai side is 2km south.

Moving on Many travellers leave Huay Xai bound for Chiang Rai (65B, 2½ hours), with buses typically departing from Chiang Khong's bus station every hour from 6am to 5pm. **Greenbus** (in Thailand 0066 5365 5732; www.greenbusthailand.com) has services to Chiang Mai at 6am, 9am and 11.40am. Several overnight buses for Bangkok (500B to 750B, 10 hours) leave at 3pm and 3.30pm.

station. Lao Skyway flies six days per week (except Thursday) to/from Vientiane for 759,000K.

BOAT

Slowboats currently depart from Huay Xai at 11am daily. Purchase tickets at the **slowboat ticket booth** (☎084-211659) for Pak Beng (110,000K, one day) or Luang Prabang (220,000K not including accommodation, two days). Sales start at 8am on the day of travel. Avoid buying a ticket from a travel company – you'll get an overpriced tuk-tuk transfer to the pier and then have to sit around awaiting departure.

The **speedboat landing** (☎084-211457; Rte 3, 200m beyond Km 202) is directly beneath Wat Thadsuvanna Phakham, 3km south of town. Six-passenger speedboats (*héua wái*) zip thrillingly but dangerously and with great physical discomfort to Pak Beng (190,000/1,140,000K per person/boat, three hours) and Luang Prabang (320,000/1,920,000K, seven hours including lunch stop), typically departing around 8am.

BUS

Note that Huay Xai–bound buses are usually marked 'Borkeo'. The bus station is 5km east of town. Buses to Luang Prabang (120,000K, 14 to 17 hours) depart at 10am and 4pm; for Luang Namtha (60,000K) they leave at 9am and 12.30pm; for Udomxai (90,000K, nine hours) there is one at 9.30am. For Vientiane (230,000K, 25 hours) catch the 11.30am. There is also a bus to Mengla (120,000K) at 8.30am.

Travel-agency minibuses to Luang Namtha leave from central Huay Xai at around 9am (100,000K) but still arrive at Namtha's inconveniently out-of-town bus station.

Sŏrngtăaou to Tonpheung (40,000K) leave when full from beside the main market, very occasionally continuing to Muang Mom.

Getting Around

Bicycles (30,000K per day) are available from the **Thaveesinh Hotel** (☎084-211502; thavee sinh.info@gmail.com; Th Saykhong).

Tuk-tuks line up on the main road just 50m beyond **Lao Immigration** (⊙8am-8pm), charging 30,000K per person to the speedboat or slowboat landings and 40,000K to the airport or bus station. The road here is one way so don't panic if they seem to head off in the 'wrong' direction.

Pak Beng

The best time to enjoy Pak Beng (ປາກແບ່ງ) is late afternoon from on high at one of the restaurant balconies clinging to its vertiginous slope, watching the Mekong slide indolently by in a churn of gingery eddies, dramatically framed by giant boulders and sharp jungle banks.

A halfway riverine stop between Luang Prabang and Huay Xai (lunch for speedy longtails, overnight for slowboats), this one-street town is short on architectural charm, but there are some good places to stay and nice spots to eat, including bakeries and Western-friendly cafes.

Sleeping & Eating

★**D.P Guesthouse** GUESTHOUSE **$$**
(☎081-212624; operation@duangpasert.com; Main St; s/d US$40/45; ❄📶) Run by a friendly Lao guy, this fresh new guesthouse outstrips the competition with mint-green and orange walls and above-average rooms with nice touches like bedrunners, air-con and cool tile floors and bathrooms. Just the shot in the arm the midrange sector needed. There's also a terrific restaurant to hang in.

★**Khopchaideu** INDIAN **$**
(☎020-55171068; mains 30,000K; ⊙7am-10pm; 🌶) Based at the **Mekong Riverside Lodge** (www.mekongriversidelodge.com; r from US$45; 📶), this place may serve some of the best Indian food you'll find in northern Laos. You can expect all the usual curries, as well as dishes like buffalo masala, executed with flair and sufficiently zesty spice. The English-speaking staff are charming and the view superb. They also dish up Lao and Western food.

Information

Lao Development Bank (⊙24hr) Has an ATM in town near the redeveloped market. It's been known to run out of money at busy times.

Tourist Office (www.oudomxay.info; ⊙7am-noon & 2-9pm) Can arrange guides and has maps of the town.

Getting There & Away

The tiny bus station is at the northernmost edge of town, with departures to Udomxai (40,000K, four hours) at 9am and 12.30pm. Once the new bridge is completed to the north of Pak Beng, there will also be daily transport to Muang Ngeun and the Thai border, plus Hongsa.

The downriver slowboat to Luang Prabang departs between 9am and 10am (110,000K, around eight hours) with request stops possible at Pak Tha and Tha Suang (for Hongsa). The slowboat for Huay Xai (110,000K, around nine hours) departs 8.30am.

Speedboats take around three hours to either Luang Prabang or Huay Xai, costing 180,000K per person assuming a crushed-full quota of six passengers (dangerous and highly uncomfortable, but cheaper than a 1,300,000K charter). Arriving by speedboat, local boys will generally offer to carry your bags for about 5000K (after some bargaining). If your bags are unwieldy this can prove money well spent, as when river levels are low you'll need to cross two planks and climb a steep sandbank to reach the road into town.

Get tickets at the boat ticket office.

Hongsa

Hongsa (ຫົງສາ), famous for elephants, is also the site of a massive new power station constructed by Thai investors and this is a major blight on the horizon. Still, it has been good for employment in the town and there is a mini-boom going on here. Hongsa is a logical break between Luang Prabang and Nan (Thailand, via Muang Ngeun). Its centre is a grid of newer constructions but the town's stream-ribboned edges (away from the power station) are backed by beautiful layered rice fields.

The most characterful of Hongsa's several monasteries is **Wat Simungkhun** (ວັດສີມຸງຄຸນ, Wat Nya; dawn-dusk). Its *hang song pa* (initiation pavilion) is fashioned in attractive naive style while the archaic, muralled *sǐm* (ordination hall) sits on an oddly raised stone platform covering a large hole that is said to lead to the end of the world. It's 1km west of the centre towards Muang Ngeun, then 100m north after the first river bridge.

Located behind the market, **China Si Chuan Restaurant** (074-2666009; mains 30,000K; 7am-10pm) is a clean, new Chinese restaurant, drawing a crowd with rice dishes, *kung pao* chicken and some interesting options such as 'smell chicken slices' and 'couples lung'.

The **ticket office** (020-5558711), beside the market, opens at around 7.30am, with vehicles departing for Sainyabuli (70,000K, three hours) and Muang Ngeun (25,000K, 1¼ hours) as soon as a decent quota of guests has piled aboard (usually before 9am).

Sainyabuli

One of Laos' 'elephant capitals', Sainyabuli (ໄຊຍະບູລີ; variously spelt Sayaboury, Sayabouri, Sayabouli, Xaignabouri and Xayaboury) is a prosperous town backed to the east by an attractive range of high forested ridges. Making a self-conscious attempt to look urban, central Sainyabuli consists of overspaced avenues and showy new administrative buildings that are surprising for their scale but hardly attractions. Starting around the tourist office and continuing south you'll find an increasing proportion of attractive wooden or part-timber structures, some with languid settings among arching palm trees. Overall it's a friendly and entirely untouristed place, but numbers are unlikely to increase dramatically with new roads, as most visitors will be heading directly to the Elephant Conservation Center.

Sights & Activities

Nam Tien LAKE

(ນ້ຳຕຽນ) To fully appreciate the charm of Sainyabuli's setting, drive 9km southwest to the Nam Tien reservoir-lake, access point for the Elephant Conservation Center. A restaurant here is perched above the dam, offering views across emerald rice paddies and wooded slopes towards a western horizon where the Pak Kimin and Pak Xang ridges overlap. The 3km asphalt road to Nam Tien branches west off the Pak Lai road 500m before the southern bus station, just before a bridge (6.5km from central Sainyabuli).

★Elephant Conservation Center OUTDOORS, VOLUNTEERING

(ECC; 020-23025210; www.elephantconservationcenter.com; 1-day visit US$60, 3-day experience US$205, 6-day eco-experience US$495) On the shores of Nam Tien lake, the Elephant Conservation Center is Laos' unmissable, inspiring experience. Get to know seven female elephants whose mahouts are paid a handsome salary to allow their cows to have three to four years off work to get pregnant and raise a baby; something that is not allowed to happen to Laos' overworked domestic elephants. You'll watch the elephants socialising, bathing, being fed and treated, as well as learning all about them from the terrific team.

Accommodation is basic (without fan), with shared, clean bathroom facilities, and the food is delicious.

Festivals & Events

Elephant Festival CULTURAL

(http://festival.elefantasia.org; mid-Feb) The popular Elephant Festival is a vast two-day jamboree featuring music, theatre and many a beer tent as well as elephant parades and skills demonstrations. In past years the venue has rotated annually between Pak Lai and Ban Viengkeo (near Hongsa), but it has finally settled in Sainyabuli.

Sleeping & Eating

Santiphap Guesthouse GUESTHOUSE $
(13 Northern Rd; r with fan/air-con 60,000/100,000K) Fresh rooms with en suite, armoire and desk, in house-proud digs on the main drag. The manager is especially friendly and speaks good English.

Night Market MARKET $
(6-10pm) This night market near the central roundabout has food stalls for noodle soup, Lao grills, fresh fruits and *khànǒm* (traditional sweets).

Sainamhoung Restaurant LAOTIAN $$
(074-211171; mains 25,000-70,000K; 7am-10pm;) Contemplate the bamboo-banked river and the looming Pak Kimin massif as you dine on tasty Lao food. Dishes include delectable steamed fish, grilled meats and varied exotica such as fried crickets and wasps, and bamboo worms.

Drinking & Nightlife

Beer Gardens BEER GARDEN
(6-11pm) There is some life beyond the dodgy and dark nightclubs in Sainyabuli and it comes in the form of a pair of lively beer gardens on the banks of the Nam Heung (Heung River). They draw a young crowd with a thirst for Beerlao.

Information

BCEL (8.30am-3.30pm Mon-Fri) Changes money and has an ATM.

Tourist Office (030-5180095; Sayaboury_ptd@tourismlaos.org; 8.30-11am & 2-4pm Mon-Fri) Good free city maps, English-speaking staff and rental of bikes and motorcycles.

Getting There & Around

The airport is beside the main Pak Lai road, around 3km south of the centre. Lao Skyway used to fly to/from Vientiane, however, these flights were not operational at the time of writing.

From the main bus station 2.5km north of the centre, an 11am *sǒrngtǎaou* runs to Hongsa (60,000K, three hours), continuing some days to Muang Ngeun (80,000K).

Vientiane is served via Luang Prabang and Pak Lai, both buses costing 120,000K. Services via Luang Prabang depart at 1pm and 4pm. The Pak Lai service (80,000K, four hours) departs at 9.30am and in the dry season only. Given the appallingly dusty road, this bus is a much better way to reach Pak Lai than taking *sǒrngtǎaou*, which depart around 9am and noon from the southern bus station, a tiny stand 4km southwest of the airport.

The new Tha Deua bridge over the Mekong River is now open and this slashes journey times to Luang Prabang to just two to three hours by minibus or private vehicle. Slower buses (60,000K, three hours) depart at 9am and 2pm.

Sakura Tour (p326) has teamed up with the Elephant Conservation Center to run a daily shuttle bus between Sainyabuli and Luang Prabang (100,000K, 2½ hours), departing at 8.30am in both directions. Contact Sakura or the Elephant Conservation Center for more details on this service.

Tuk-tuks to the bus stations (main/southern 15,000/20,000K per person) depart from the main market.

Pak Lai

The bustling Mekong river port of Pak Lai (ປາກລາຍ) is an almost unavoidable stop on the offbeat route between Sainyabuli and Loei in Thailand. The town follows a 5km curl of Rte 4, paralleled a block further east by a shorter riverside road that's sparsely dotted with historic structures in both Lao and French-colonial style. Exploring north to south, start at Wat Sisavang. Within the next 500m you'll pass the main guesthouses and river port before crossing a little old wooden bridge into an attractive village-like area of local homes beyond a small market.

If you need to stay, try **Jenny Guesthouse** (020-22365971; r with fan/air-con 70,000/110,000K;). It's clean with decent Mekong views, protective mozzie netting over windows and built-on bathroom blocks for each room. There's TV, blankets and comfortable beds. Sadly there's no cafe here.

CENTRAL & SOUTHERN LAOS

Bolikhamsai & Khammuan Provinces

Bolikhamsai and Khammuan straddle the narrow, central 'waist' of the country. Physically the land climbs steadily from the Mekong River valley towards the north and east, eventually reaching the Annamite Chain bordering Vietnam, via an area of moderately high, often spectacular mountains. Laidback Tha Khaek is the logical base.

Lowland Lao dominate the population and, along with smaller groups of tribal Thais, are the people you'll mostly meet. In remoter areas the Mon-Khmer-speaking Makong people (commonly known as Bru) make up more than 10% of the population of Khammuan.

Much of the region is relatively sparsely populated and six large tracts of forest have been declared National Protected Areas (NPAs). These areas have become a major battleground between those wishing to exploit Laos' hydroelectricity capacity and those wishing to preserve some of the most pristine wilderness areas in Asia. For now, the developers have the upper hand.

Paksan

Located at the confluence of the Nam San (San River) and the Mekong River, Paksan (ປາກຊັນ; Pakxan or Pakxanh) is the capital of Bolikhamsai Province. Although it's not the most exciting place in Laos, it has a few guesthouses and restaurants and is a possible stop if you're pedalling between Vientiane and Tha Khaek or Kong Lor. It's possible to cross into Thailand via the Mekong River, but hardly anyone travels this way.

Sleeping & Eating

Given the short distance from the capital Vientiane, most travellers don't overnight here but continue on to Tham Kong Lor or Tha Khaek. There are a handful of decent accommodation options if you do get stuck.

BK Guest House GUESTHOUSE $
(☎054-212638; r 70,000-80,000K; ❄📶) Set in a leafy garden dripping in frangipani flowers, this house-proud guesthouse has eight rooms, all immaculately clean with en suites and fresh linen, and the friendly owner speaks English. A great place if you get stuck here for the night.

Saynamsan Restaurant LAOTIAN $
(☎054-212608; mains 15,000-90,000K; ⏲7am-11pm) In town, at the northwestern end of the bridge crossing the Nam San, this friendly riverside restaurant is a great spot to catch the breeze on its terrace. The menu dishes up spicy squid soup, curry and *láhp* (spicy Lao-style salad of minced meat poultry or fish).

Getting There & Away

Local buses leave from outside Paksan's Talat Sao (Main Market) on Rte 13 for Vientiane (30,000K, three hours, 143km) between 6am and 4.30pm, with most departures in the morning. *Sǒrngtǎaou* (passenger trucks) also leave frequently from the market, or just hail anything going west.

If you're heading to Vietnam, *sǒrngtǎaou* depart for Lak Sao (60,000K, five to six hours, 189km) at 5am, 5.30am and 6.30am, or whenever they are full.

All buses heading south from Vientiane pass through Paksan about two hours after they leave the capital: just wait outside Talat Sao.

Ban Khoun Kham

The former role of Ban Khoun Kham (also known as Ban Na Hin) as a base from which to visit the extraordinary Tham Kong Lor has been seriously undercut by Ban Kong Lor, which has recently been acquitting itself to cater for tourists headed to the nearby cave, and as such there's a little tumbleweed blowing through town. However, there is an attractive waterfall near town and some great viewpoints across the jagged karst landscape if you do decide to stay here.

The main local attraction is the impressive twin-cataract of Tat Namsanam (ຕາດນ້ຳສະນາມ), 3km north of town, although in the dry season, it's, well, dry. The falls are in a striking location surrounded by karst and the upper tier is quite high. Unfortunately, the path and signs leading to the falls aren't entirely clear, and more than one foreign visitor has got lost here. Proceed with

GETTING TO THAILAND: PAKSAN TO BEUNG KAN

Getting to the border Few travellers use the **Paksan (Laos)/Beung Kan (Thailand) border crossing** (⏲8am to noon and 1.30 to 4.30pm) via the Mekong River. The boat (60B, 20 minutes) leaves when eight people show up or you can charter it (500B).

At the border If you turn up at the Lao immigration office, they should process the paperwork without too much fuss, though it is very important to note that Lao visas are not available on arrival.

Moving on In Thailand buses leave Beung Kan for Udon Thani (245B, four hours), where there are onward connections to Bangkok via budget airlines or long-distance bus.

OFF THE BEATEN TRACK

CAVES OF THE KHAMMUAN

The most impressive, and yet least visited, cave in Khammuan is the amazing **Tham Lot Se Bang Fai** (ຖ້ຳລອດເຊບັ້ງໄຟ). Located in Hin Namno NPA, the cave results from the Se Bang Fai river plunging 6.5km through a limestone mountain, leaving an underground trail of immense caverns, impressive rock formations, rapids and waterfalls that have been seen by only a handful of visitors.

The cave wasn't professionally mapped until 2006, and the Canadian-American that led the expedition concluded that Tham Lot Se Bang Fai is among the largest river caves in the world. Traversing the entire cave involves eight portages and is only possible during the dry season, from January to March. Local wooden canoes can only go as far as the first portage, about 1km into the cave, making inflatable rafts or kayaks the only practical option for traversing the entire length of the cave.

The base for visiting the cave is Ban Nong Ping, a mixed Lao Loum/Salang village about 2km downstream from the cave entrance. Homestays are available as part of an organised tour with ecotourism operator Green Discovery (p361). With a week or so advance notice, you can organise a trip here, starting from about US$265 for a larger group of six or more to as much as US$550 per person for a couple.

caution, or better yet, hire a guide through the excellent **Tourist Information Centre** (☎020-55598412; Rte 8; ⊙8am-4pm), just south of the Tat Namsanam entrance, which runs community-based treks from here into the Phu Hin Bun NPA.

By far the dreamiest and most cosy accommodation in town – except it's not in town is **Sainamhai Resort** (☎020-22331683; www.sainamhairesort.com; r 150,000-240,000K; ⊖❄☜). Thankfully Sainamhai sits by the Nam Hai (Hai River) a little out of the village. There's a handsome longhouse restaurant, a fertile garden and well-maintained rattan-walled cabanas with private balconies, en suites and clean linen. Add to this warm service and cool air-con. It's 3km east of Rte 8 via a turn-off a few kilometres down the road that leads to Tham Kong Lor. Staff will pick you up for free at the sŏrngtăaou station if you call ahead.

Getting There & Away

There are two morning departures from Tha Khaek to Ban Khoun Kham (50,000K, three hours, 143km) at 8am and 9am. Alternatively, from Tha Khaek or Vientiane, simply hop on any north- or southbound bus and get off at Vieng Kham (also known as Thang Beng), at the junction of Rtes 13 and 8, and continue by *sŏrngtăaou* (25,000K, one hour, 7am to 7pm) to Ban Khoun Kham. It's easier to take a Vientiane–Lak Sao bus and ask to get off in Ban Khoun Kham (75,000K).

Later in the day you'll need to take any of the semi-regular *sŏrngtăaou* to Vieng Kham (30,000K, 7am to 5pm) or, if you're bound for the Vietnam border, Lak Sao (25,000K, 7am to 5pm) and change there. Both are about one hour from Ban Khoun Kham. To Tham Kong Lor, *sŏrngtăaou* leave at 10am, 12.30pm and 3pm (25,000K, one hour).

Tham Kong Lor

Tham Kong Lor (ຖ້ຳລອດກອງລໍ) is one of central Laos', if not the country's, most vivid highlights. A journey into this preternatural underworld is like a voyage into the afterworld itself, with a 7.5km river passing through the cathedral-high limestone cave. Ban Kong Lor (Kong Lor Village) is the most convenient base for visiting the cave and has seen an explosion of guesthouses and small resorts in the last few years.

Activities

★**Tham Kong Lor** CAVING, BOATING

(cave entrance 5000K, parking fee 5000K, boat trip 1/2/3 persons 110,000/120,000/130,000K) A boat trip through the other-worldly Tham Kong Lor is an absolute must. Situated in the 1580-sq-km wilderness of Phu Hin Bun NPA, the 7.5km river cave runs beneath an immense limestone mountain. Your imagination will be in overdrive as the boat takes you further into the bat-black darkness and the fear dial will ratchet up as if on some natural Gothic ghost ride. The experience is unforgettable.

A section of Kong Lor has now been atmospherically lit, allowing you a greater glimpse of this epic spectacle; your longtail docks in a rocky inlet to allow you to explore a stalactite wood of haunting pillars and sprouting stalagmites like an abandoned *Star Trek* set.

Boat trips through Tham Kong Lor take up to an hour each way, and in dry season when the river is low, you'll have to get out while the boatman and point man haul the wooden craft up rapids. At the other end of the cave, a brief five minutes upstream takes you to a refreshment stop. Catch your breath and then head back in for more adrenalin-fuelled excitement.

Life jackets are provided. Be sure to bring a torch (flashlight) as the ones for rent are inadequate, and wear rubber sandals; the gravel in the riverbed is sharp and it's often necessary to disembark and wade at several shallow points.

Sleeping & Eating

Kong Lor Eco Lodge GUESTHOUSE $
(030-9062772; Ban Kong Lor; r 50,000K;) Kong Lor Eco Lodge has 12 spartan but clean rooms set back from the road. The small restaurant here is one of the most popular in town and draws a steady crowd of travellers each night.

★ **Spring River Resort** BUNGALOW $$
(020-59636111; www.springriverresort.com; Ban Tiou; bungalows US$15-50, tr US$40-50;) Formerly Sala Kong Lor, these stilted bungalows range from basic to superior and sit by the beautiful Nam Hin Bun. En suite triple rooms include mozzie nets and private balconies to enjoy the lush river view, and breakfast is included with the more expensive room. There's a clear-water creek nearby to cool off in.

Twins and doubles involve a shared bathroom and you have to splash out on your own breakfast, but it's still a good deal for the impressive setting. The attached riverside restaurant (mains 35,000K to 50,000K) has a memorable setting.

Mithuna Restaurant LAOTIAN $
(Ban Kong Lor; mains 20,000-40,000K; 7am-8pm) Close to the entrance to Tham Kong Lor, this semi-alfresco, fan-cooled restaurant serves up noodles, fried rice and pork *láhp,* as well as Western breakfasts. It's good for a refuel before or after a trip into the depths of the cave.

Getting There & Away

per day The 50km road from Ban Khoun Kham to Ban Kong Lor winds through a beautiful valley of rice fields, hemmed in on either side by towering karst cliffs. It's an easy one-hour motorbike or *sŏrngtăaou* ride. From Ban Kong Lor, *sŏrngtăaou* to Ban Khoun Kham (25,000K) depart at 6.30am, 8am and 11am. There's also now a direct daily bus between Vientiane and Ban Kong Lor (80,000K, seven hours), which departs from Kong Lor Eco Lodge at 7am or from the Southern Bus Station in the capital at 10am.

Lak Sao

Essentially a dusty two-street affair in the eastern reaches of Bolikhamsai Province, Lak Sao (ຫລັກຊາວ) is humming with trucks passing through to Vietnam (only 36km away), and has made its name as a logging town. It's surrounded by beautiful sawtoothed cliffs that, come dusk, are evocatively etched a burnt charcoal.

There's plenty of uninspiring guesthouses, a maze of a market, 24-hour ATMs, plus a couple of places to eat. Not the prettiest place thanks to the eternal screen of dust that hangs in the air, but it's a useful pit stop to stock up on cash, fuel up and eat a reliable Lao lunch if you're on the Loop (p362).

Sleeping & Eating

Souriya Hotel HOTEL $
(054-341111; Rte 1E; r 50,000-80,000K;) All rooms here have fan or air-con, and although some are smaller than others, they are fresh with firm beds and en suite with very hot water. There is also cable TV and motorbike parking.

Only One Restaurant LAOTIAN $
(054-341034; Rte 1E; mains 20,000-60,000K; 7am-10pm) Although it's no longer quite the 'only one' in town, it remains one of the best. The cavernous restaurant has a great terrace out back which looks on to the karsts and makes a good place to eat your *láhp,* barbecued pork, stir-fries and fried morning glory (water spinach).

Information

Lao Development Bank (Rte 1E) Located near the market, this bank changes Thai baht, US dollars, UK pounds and Vietnamese dong.

Getting There & Away

Buses leave from east of the market for Vientiane (85,000K, seven to eight hours, 334km) daily at 5.30am, 6.30am, 8am and 8pm. These buses stop at Vieng Kham (Thang Beng; 35,000K, two hours, 100km), where you can change for regular buses heading south, or get off at Paksan (50,000K, five to six hours, 189km). Other buses and *sŏrngtăaou* head along Rte 8 to Vieng Kham/Thang Beng (between 8am and 5pm) and one bus goes to Tha Khaek (60,000K, five to six hours, 202km) at 7.30am.

GETTING TO VIETNAM: NAM PHAO TO CAU TREO

Getting to the border The **Nam Phao (Laos)/Cau Treo (Vietnam) border crossing** (7am to 4.30pm) is at the Kaew Neua Pass, 36km from Lak Sao. *Sŏrngtăaou* (passenger trucks; 20,000K, 45 minutes) leave every hour or so from the market in Lak Sao and drop passengers at the typically relaxed Lao border post. There is an exchange booth on the Lao side, though the rates aren't generous.

Coming back from Vinh in Vietnam, buses to Tay Song (formerly Trung Tam) leave regularly throughout the day (70,000d, three hours, 70km). From Tay Song, it's another 25km through some richly forested country to the border. It should cost about 200,000d (US$10) by motorbike or taxi, but drivers will demand several times that. Expect to be ripped off on this route.

At the border Check with a Vietnamese embassy or consulate as to whether you require a visa or not, as some Asian and European countries do not need a visa, but the majority of passport holders do. Laos issues 30-day visas at the border.

Moving on Inconveniently, the Vietnam border post is 1km up the road from the Lao border post, and once you pass this, you'll be swarmed by guys offering onward transport to Vinh. Contrary to their claims, a minibus to Vinh doesn't cost US$30 per person; about US$5 for a seat is more reasonable, though you'll do very well to get that price. A metered taxi costs US$35 to US$40, while a motorbike fare is about 200,000d. Hook up with as many other people as possible to improve your bargaining position.

You can hopefully avoid the border haggle by taking a bus direct from Lak Sao to Vinh (120,000K, five hours); there are usually four buses leaving between about noon and 2pm. Once in Vinh you can take a bus or a sleeper on the Reunification Express (www.vr.com.vn) straight to Hanoi.

Tha Khaek

This ex-Indochinese trading post is a delightful melange of crumbling French villas and warped Chinese merchant's shopfronts, with an easy riverside charm which, despite the new bridge over to nearby Thailand, shows few signs of change. An evocative place to stop for a day and night, you begin the Loop from here, and can also use Tha Khaek (ທ່າແຂກ) as a base from which to make organised day trips to Tham Kong Lor. There are also loads of nearby caves, some with swimmable lagoons, that can be accessed by scooter or tuk-tuk.

While you shouldn't expect Luang Prabang levels of sophistication from Tha Khaek, you will find a historically appealing old town and slice of authentic Lao life. The epicentre (if you can call it that) of the old town is the modest Fountain Sq at the western end of Th Kuvoravong near the river.

Sights & Activities

The first 22km east of Tha Khaek on Rte 12 is an area with several caves, an abandoned railway line and a couple of swimming spots and can be visited as a day trip or as part of the Loop. This is part of the vast Khammuan Limestone area, which stretches roughly between Rtes 12 and 8 and east towards Rte 8B. There are thousands of caves, sheer cliffs and jagged karst peaks. All these places can be reached by tuk-tuk, bicycle or motorcycle.

Phu Hin Bun NPA NATIONAL PARK

(ປ່າສະຫງວນແຫ່ງຊາດພູຫີນປູນ) Phu Hin Bun NPA is a huge (1580 sq km) wilderness area of turquoise streams, monsoon forests and striking karst topography across central Khammuan. It was made a protected area in 1993 and it's no overstatement to say this is some of the most breathtaking country in the region.

Passing through on foot or by boat, it's hard not to feel awestruck by the very scale of the limestone cliffs that rise almost vertically for hundreds of metres into the sky. Although much of the NPA is inaccessible by road, local people have reduced the numbers of key forest-dependent species through hunting and logging. Despite this, the area remains home to the endangered douc langur, François' langur and several other primate species, as well as elephants, tigers and a variety of rare species of deer.

A trip out to Tham Kong Lor will give you a taste of what the NPA has to offer, but there are two more immersive ways to go deeper

Tha Khaek

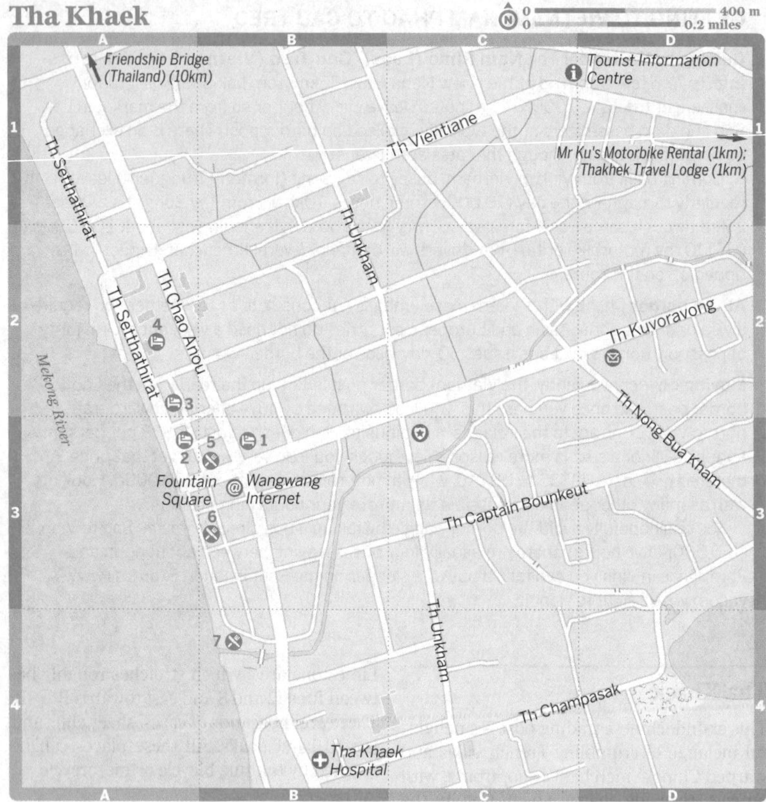

Tha Khaek

Activities, Courses & Tours
Green Discovery ....(see 1)

Sleeping
1 Inthira Hotel B3
2 Le Bouton d'Or........................A3
3 Mekong Hotel........................A2
4 Sooksomboon Hotel........................A2

Eating
5 DD Bistro & Cafe........................B3
6 Grilled Meat Restaurants........................B3
Khop Chai Deu ....(see 1)
7 Sabaidee Restaurant........................B4

into this area of almost mythical gothic peaks and snaking streams.

Khammuan Province runs five different community-based treks of varying lengths. From Tha Khaek, the popular two-day trip (1,700,000K for one person, 950,000K each for two, 650,000K for five or more) into the Phu Hin Bun NPA is especially good. The route includes plenty of karst scenery, a walk through Tham Pa Chan and overnight accommodation in an ethnic village. Bookings can be made through the **Tourist Information Centre** (☎020-55711797, 030-5300503; www.khammouanetourism.com; Th Vientiane; ⊙8.30am-5pm) in Tha Khaek.

Green Discovery offers similar treks including a very tempting two-day kayaking and cycling trip between spectacularly sheer cliffs, as the Nam Hin Bun (Hin Bun River) follows a large anticlockwise arc towards the Mekong.

Tham Pa Seuam CAVE

(ຖ້ຳປາເຊືອມ) The recently discovered river cave of Tham Pa Seuam runs for 3km. A much smaller version of Tham Kong Lor, it features impressive stalactites and stalagmites and is conveniently only 15km from Tha Khaek. A day trip to multiple caves, including Tham Pa Seuam, with the Tourist

Information Centre costs from 350,000K per person and includes a 400m kayak paddle into the main chamber.

Green Climbers Home CLIMBING
(☎020-56105622; www.greenclimbershome.com; Ban Kouanphavang; courses per person 140,000-500,000K; ⌚Oct-May) This efficiently run training school set in a valley in soaring karst country 18km from Tha Khaek is hugely popular and often booked up thanks to its cosy cabanas, great food and excellent courses. It also boasts one of the easiest overhangs in the world to learn on and has beginner-, intermediate- and expert-level climbs, with more than 250 routes from class 4 to 8B.

To get here, a tuk-tuk by day costs 100,000K. For serious climbers, accommodation is also available here, including dorms (60,000K) and bungalows (from 130,000K) with hot-water showers.

Green Discovery ADVENTURE SPORTS
(☎051-251390; www.greendiscoverylaos.com; Inthira Hotel, Th Chao Annou; ⌚8am-9pm) Green Discovery is the country's most experienced ecotourism outfit and runs a number of interesting trips around central Laos. A range of treks and kayaking excursions in the lush Phu Hin Bun NPA are available, including Tham Kong Lor (from US$70 for a day trip to US$155 for an overnight trip). Also arranges cycling and climbing.

Sleeping

★**Thakhek Travel Lodge** GUESTHOUSE $
(☎051-212931; thahkhektravellodge@gmail.com; Rte 13; dm 30,000K, r 60,000-130,000K;) It might be an inconvenient five minutes out of town by tuk-tuk, but this place has a great vibe thanks to its nightly garden firepit, drawing travellers together. Rooms vary from basic fan options to expansive air-con bungalows, and a cafe serves *láhp,* salads and juices. Check out the logbook for updated news from the Loop.

Mekong Hotel HOTEL $
(☎051-250777; mekonghotel@yahoo.com; Th Setthathirat; r 100,000-250,000K;) Thanks to a bit of tender, loving care, this blue, Soviet-inspired monolith is somewhat improved, with house-proud, decent rooms that have cable TV, air-con and fresh en suites. There's also a Mekong-facing restaurant.

Sooksomboon Hotel GUESTHOUSE $
(☎051-212225; Th Setthathirat; r 100,000-150,000K;) Set in a colonial-era police station right on the Mekong, the rooms here are clean and have high ceilings, scrolled mahogany bedsteads, TV and en suite. Bag a room in the atmospheric main building, as the rooms in the motel-like annexe are bland with a capital B.

★**Inthira Hotel** BOUTIQUE HOTEL $$
(☎051-251237; www.inthirahotel.com; Th Chao Anou; r incl breakfast US$29-49;) Set in an old French villa with a pretty facade, Inthira offers the most romantic, stylish digs in town. Its restaurant fronts the old fountain, and its chic wine-hued rooms, with exposed-brick walls, rain showers, cable TV, dark wood furniture, air-con and safety deposit boxes, are a delight for weary travellers. The best rooms face the street and have balconies.

Le Bouton d'Or BOUTIQUE HOTEL $$
(☎051-250678; boutondor-tk@hotmail.com; 89 Th Setthathirat; r incl breakfast US$45-70;) A new and somewhat over-the-top retro-renaissance hotel on the riverfront with smart, well-finished rooms. French in accent, the riverfront rooms with balcony are a worthwhile investment. There's also a riverside restaurant where guests can enjoy breakfast.

Eating

A minuscule night market unfolds at Fountain Sq every evening, and the adjacent waterfront strip directly south features several outdoor **grilled meat restaurants** (Th Setthathirat; mains 10,000-20,000K; ⌚11am-11pm) specialising in duck.

Sabaidee Restaurant LAOTIAN $
(Th Setthathirat; mains 20,000-40,000K; ⌚8am-midnight;) Catching whatever breeze is going, this joint sits on the riverfront and serves rice dishes, *láhp* variations, soup and some heaped portions of international favourites like fish and chips. Nice place for a sundowner and draws a steady crowd of travellers trading tales from the Loop.

DD Bistro & Cafe INTERNATIONAL $
(☎051-212355; Fountain Sq; mains 20,000-80,000K; ⌚7am-10pm;) This new glass-fronted cafe overlooking Fountain Sq offers a fusion menu of Lao, Thai and international dishes in a cool atmosphere, both figuratively and literally, thanks to the powerful air-con. Twinings teas, coffees with a kick and fresh juices are also available.

DON'T MISS

THE LOOP

The Loop, an off-the-beaten-track circuit through some of the more remote parts of Khammuan and Bolikhamsai Provinces, has achieved mythic status with intrepid travellers over the last couple of years. It's possible to make the trip by bicycle, but it's best done on a motorbike. Thankfully, there are now several companies in Tha Khaek (p359) renting out decent dirt bikes and smaller scooters. Give yourself at least three days to include Tham Kong Lor and make sure you spend a day practicing your riding skills if you are a relative novice. Visiting the caves around Tha Khaek as a gentle day trip is a good warm-up to tackling the Loop. Fuel is available in most villages along the way.

Tha Khaek's Tourist Information Centre (p360) can provide advice on the circuit. It's also a good idea to sit down with a cold Beerlao and the ever-expanding logbook at Thakhek Travel Lodge (p361) before you head off.

★**Khop Chai Deu** FUSION **$$**
(Inthira Hotel, Th Chao Anou; mains 30,000-90,000K; ⏲7am-10pm; ❄📶✍) Classy and low-lit, this fine restaurant is as sophisticated as sleepy Tha Khaek gets. Based in a pretty French colonial-era building, the open-range kitchen, visible but behind glass, dishes up tasty Lao salad, burgers, substantial tenderised steak and decent cocktails from the sleek glass bar. You can eat on the street if it's cool out.

ℹ Information

Tha Khaek has everything you need: a couple of banks, including a **BCEL** (Th Vientiane) which changes major currencies and travellers cheques, and offers cash advances on debit or credit card, and a **Lao Development Bank** (Th Vientiane) with an ATM. Fine for minor ailments, seek out English-speaking Dr Bounthavi at the **hospital** (cnr Th Chao Anou & Th Champasak).

The excellent **tourist office** (p360) offers exciting one- and two-day treks in Phu Hin Boun NPA, including a homestay with a local village. There are also treks to the waterfall by Ban Khoun Kham and Tham Kong Lor (800,000K). Offers advice on journeying the Loop as well.

ℹ Getting There & Away

Tha Khaek's bus station (Rte 13) is about 3.5km from the town centre and has a sizeable market and basic guesthouses to complement the regular services going north and south. Buses for Vientiane (60,000K, six hours, 332km) depart at 4am, 5.30am, 7am, 8.30am and 9am, as well as a VIP service at 9.15am (80,000K) and a sleeper VIP at 1am (90,000K). From 9am to midnight, buses stop en route from Pakse and Savannakhet every hour or so. Any bus going north stops at Vieng Kham (Thang Beng; 30,000K, 1½ hours, 102km), Pak Kading (40,000K, three hours, 149km) or Paksan (50,000K, four hours, 193km).

Heading south, buses for Savannakhet (30,000K, two to three hours, 125km) depart every half-hour, and there's an air-con departure for Pakse (70,000K, six to seven hours, 368km) at 9am and regular local buses every hour during the day (60,000K). There are two daily departures to Attapeu (90,000K, about 10 hours) at 3.30pm and 11pm. Buses originating in Vientiane leave at around 5.30pm for Don Khong (150,000K, about 15 hours, 452km) and around 5.30pm for Non Nok Khiene (90,000K, about 16 hours, 482km), on the Cambodian border. They stop at Tha Khaek between 5pm and 6pm, but you'd need to be in a hurry.

If you're heading to Vietnam, a bus for Hué (120,000K) leaves every Monday, Tuesday, Wednesday, Saturday and Sunday at 8pm. There are also departures for Danang (120,000K) at 8pm every Monday and Friday; for Dong Hoi (90,000K, 10 to 14 hours) at 7am on Monday, Wednesday, Friday and Saturday; and for Hanoi (160,000K) at 8pm on Tuesday and Saturday.

Mr Ku's Motorbike Rental (☎020-22205070; per day 60,000-100,000K; ⏲7.30am-4.30pm) is located at Thakhek Travel Lodge (p358).

Pak Kading

East from Vientiane along Rte 13 is the sleepy yet picturesque village of Pak Kading, sitting just upstream from the junction of the Mekong River and the Nam Kading (Kading River), one of the most pristine rivers in Laos (for now, at least). Flowing through a forested valley surrounded by high hills and menacing-looking limestone formations, this broad, turquoise-tinted river winds its way into the Nam Kading NPA (ປາສະຫງວນແຫງຊາດນ້ຳກະດິງ) 🍃.

The Nam Kading (Kading River) is undoubtedly the best way into the wilderness that is Nam Kading NPA, where confirmed animal rarities include the elephant, giant muntjac, pygmy slow loris, François' langur, douc langur, gibbon, dhole, Asiatic black bear, tiger and many bird species. As usual in Laos, it is very unlikely that you will actually see any of these. Note that at the time of writing it was very difficult to access the NPA, as the regional government are restricting boat access via the river.

As a main highway town, there are buses aplenty passing through Pak Kading on their way to Vientiane (three to four hours, 187km), Tha Khaek (three hours) or points east.

Savannakhet Province

Savannakhet is the country's most populous province and is home to about 15% of all Lao citizens. Stretching between the Mekong and Thailand in the west and the Annamite Mountains and Vietnam in the east, it has become an important trade corridor between these two bigger neighbours. With the smooth surface of Rte 9 complemented by yet another Thai-Lao Friendship Bridge, the province is witnessing even more traffic.

The population of around one million includes Lowland Lao, Tai Dam, several small Mon-Khmer groups and communities of Vietnamese and Chinese.

There are three NPAs here: Dong Phu Vieng to the south of Rte 9; remote Phu Xang Hae to the north; and Se Ban Nuan straddling the border with Salavan Province. Eastern Savannakhet is a good place to see remnants of the Ho Chi Minh Trail, the primary supply route to South Vietnam for the North Vietnamese Army during the Second Indochina War.

Savannakhet

Languid, time-trapped and somnolent during the sweltering days that batter the old city's plasterwork, Savannakhet (ສະຫວັນນະເຂດ) is an attractive blend of past and present Laos. The highlight is the historic quarter with its staggering – and that might just be the right adjective – display of decaying early 20th-century architecture. Leprous and listing, these grand old villas of Indochina's heyday now lie unwanted like aged dames crying out for a makeover. There's little to do in town but wander the riverfront and cool off in one of a clutch of stylish restaurants and bijou cafes that are steadily growing in number.

That said, there's plenty to do nearby and Savannakhet has a very dedicated **Tourist Information Centre** (☎041-212755; Th Si Muang; ⊗8am-noon & 1-4pm Mon-Fri) and Eco-Guide Unit (p366), which offers myriad intrepid trips into the nearby NPAs.

Savannakhet is on a simple north–south grid, and although spread out, is pretty easy to navigate on foot.

GETTING TO VIETNAM: SAVANNAKHET TO DONG HA

Getting to the border Crossing the **Dansavanh (Laos)/Lao Bao (Vietnam) border** (⊗7am to 7.30pm) is a relative pleasure. From Savannakhet's bus terminal, buses leave for Dansavanh (60,000K, five to six hours, 236km) at 7am, 8.30am and 11am. Alternatively, consider breaking the journey for a night in Sepon as a base for seeing the Ho Chi Minh Trail.

The bus station in Dansavanh is about 1km short of the border; Vietnamese teenagers on motorbikes are more than happy to take you the rest of the way for about 10,000K.

At the border The Lao border offers 30-day tourist visas on arrival and has an exchange booth. Some nationalities require a Vietnam visa in advance, so check with the **Vietnamese consulate** (☎041-212418; Th Sisavangvong, Savannakhet) in Savannakhet. Most regional visitors, Scandinavian visitors, and British, French, German, Italian and Spanish visitors do not need a visa.

Moving on Once through, take a motorbike (40,000d or US$2) 2km to the Lao Bao bus terminal and transport to Dong Ha (70,000d, two hours, 80km) on Vietnam's main north–south highway and railway. Entering Laos, there are buses to Savannakhet (60,000K, five to six hours) at 7.30am, 9.30am, 10am and noon, as well as regular *sŏrngtăaou* (passenger trucks) to Sepon (30,000K, one hour) from 7am to 5pm. Simple accommodation is available on both sides of the border.

If you're in a hurry, an alternative is to take one of the various direct buses from Savannakhet bound for the Vietnamese cities of Dong Ha, Hué and Danang.

Savannakhet

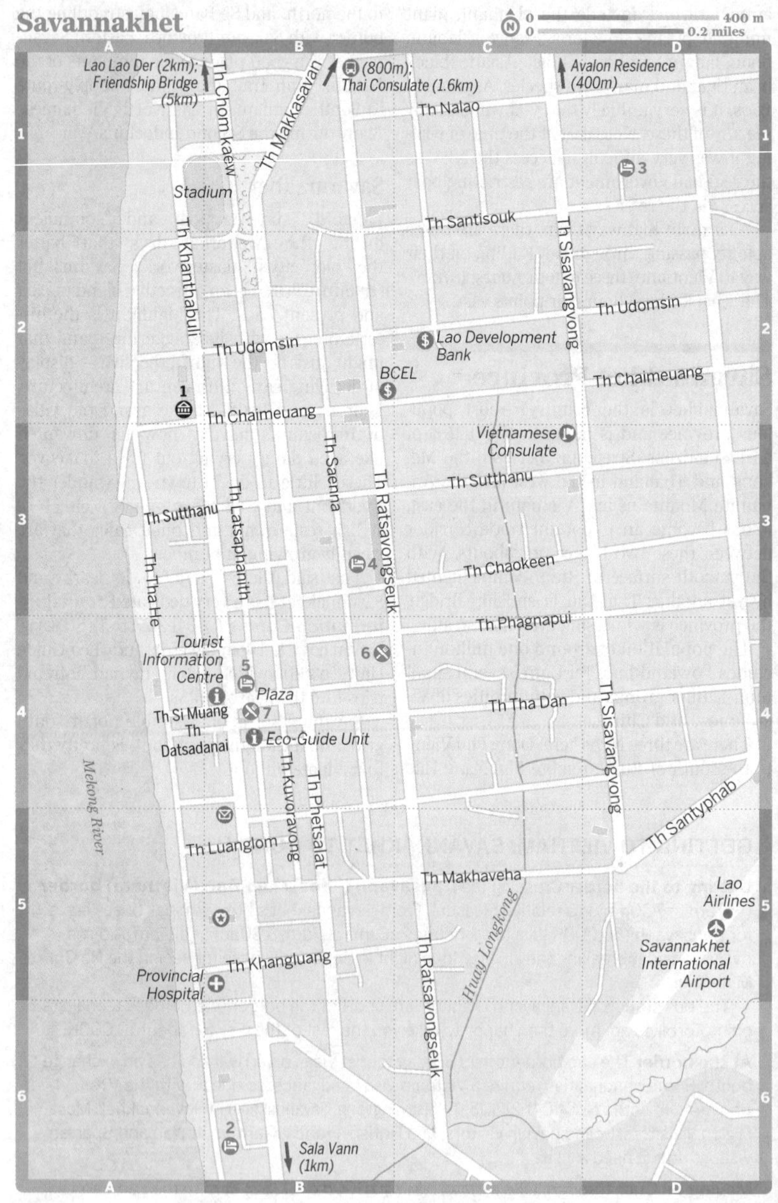

Sights

Much of the charm of Savannakhet is in simply wandering through the quiet streets in the town centre, between the old and new buildings, the laughing children and the slow-moving, *petang*-playing old men.

The Tourist Information Centre (p363) produces *Savannakhet Downtown*, a brochure featuring a self-guided tour of the city's most interesting buildings. The centre also offers guided tours of the historic downtown district.

Musée Des Dinosaures MUSEUM
(ຫໍພິພິດທະພັນໄດໂນເສົາ, Dinosaur Museum; ☎041-212597; Th Khanthabuli; 10,000K; ⊙8am-noon & 1-4pm) In 1930 a major dig in a nearby village unearthed 200-million-year-old dinosaur fossils. The enthusiastically run Dinosaur Museum is an interesting place to see three different dinosaurs. Savannakhet Province is home to five dinosaur sites.

Dong Natad WILDLIFE RESERVE
(ດົງນາທາດ) Dong Natad is a sacred, semi-evergreen forest within a provincial protected area 15km from Savannakhet. It's home to two villages that have been coexisting with the forest for about 400 years, with villagers gathering forest products such as mushrooms, fruit, oils, honey, resins and insects. It's possible to visit Dong Natad by bicycle, motorbike or tuk-tuk from Savannakhet. Travelling alone to Dong Natad will be something of a 'forest-lite' experience, however. It's better to engage one of Savannakhet's English-speaking guides through the eco-guide unit (p366).

Sleeping

Savannakhet has a reasonable range of budget options but little to excite if you're looking for luxury. Most guesthouses are located within walking distance of the attractive old town.

Fundee Guesthouse GUESTHOUSE $
(☎030-4841873; Th Santisouk; r 120,000K;) A new guesthouse tucked down a side *soi* (lane) off Th Santisouk, Fundee offers great value for money thanks to its smart new rooms with all the trimmings. Ten rooms are already open and another 10 rooms are being added to ensure it can cater to its growing reputation.

Souannavong Guest House GUESTHOUSE $
(☎041-212600; Th Saenna; r with/without air-con 120,000/70,000K;) This little guesthouse down a quiet street abloom in bougainvillea has clean en suite rooms and is unfailingly fresh. A welcoming place to stay thanks to the English-speaking owners. Bicycles and motorbikes are available to rent.

★**Vivanouk Homestay** HOMESTAY $$
(☎020-91606030; www.vivanouk.com; Th Khantabouly; r without bathroom US$30-45;) This funky little place is akin to a boutique homestay and is a great new addition to the Savan scene. There are just three rooms sharing two bathrooms – one with an alfresco outdoor shower – and delightfully decorated in a contemporary-colonial-era fusion style. Breakfast is available downstairs in an artsy venue that doubles as a bar by night.

Avalon Residence HOTEL $$
(☎041-252770; www.hotel.avalonbooking.com; Th Sisavangvong; r US$20-32;) Avalon Residence offers smart midrange rooms at an affordable price and is pretty convenient for a stroll to the bus station. The rooms are spacious and have glistening bathrooms, Lao silks and flat-screen TVs. Downstairs is a small air-conditioned cafe.

Daosavanh Resort & Spa Hotel HOTEL $$$
(☎041-252188; www.dansavanh.com; Th Tha He; r incl breakfast US$51-107;) This ostentatious hotel overlooking the Mekong offers a slice of international comfort, and its kidney-shaped pool is very welcome on sweltering days, of which there are many in Savan. Rooms are large and immaculate, and prices include free airport transfers.

Eating & Drinking

With new cafes opening up, delicious street food on offer in the central square and a scattering of French restaurants to sample, the Savan cuisine scene is increasingly varied.

★**Savannakhet Plaza Food Market** MARKET, LAOTIAN $
(Savannakhet Plaza; meals 10,000-30,000K; ⊙5-10pm) An excellent new addition to the Savan dining scene, this nightly food market brings 20 or more stalls to the Savannakhet Plaza area in the heart of the old town. This is street-food surfing at its best, with a choice of freshly barbecued skewers, steaming noodle soups, dim-sum-sushi-tapas confusion and more. Plus Beerlao in plentiful supply.

★ **Sala Vann** LAOTIAN $

(☎020-55645111; Ban Phonsavan; mains 10,000-90,000K; ⏲10am-10pm; 📶) Stunningly set on the Mekong about 500m south of the old hospital, this lovely Laotian restaurant is housed in a traditional wooden *sala*. The menu is enticingly affordable and draws a mixed crowd come sunset and beyond, when there is sometimes live music. As well as Lao and Thai favourites, there are even steaks and pasta.

Cafe Chai Dee JAPANESE, INTERNATIONAL $

(☎030-5003336; www.cafechaidee.com; Th Ratsavongsouk; mains 20,000-50,000K; ⏲9am-3pm & 5-9.30pm Mon-Sat; ❄📶✍) This spotless Japanese-owned cafe has rattan mats to lounge on, a book exchange and a wide menu of Japanese classics like ramen and tonkatsu (pork coated in breadcrumbs and fried), plus samosas, homemade yoghurt, Thai food and healthy shakes. Great breakfasts, too. Expect super-fresh, well-presented food, fast wi-fi and warm service.

Lao Lao Der LAOTIAN $$

(☎041-212270; mains 30,000-90,000K; ⏲10am-11pm) This riverside restaurant, 2km north of the old stadium, is one of the only places in town to offer great Mekong views. The hefty menu spans Lao, Thai and Chinese dishes, but Lao Lao Der functions equally well as a bar. It was undergoing a major renovation during our last visit.

Dao Savanh FRENCH $$$

(☎041-260888; Th Si Muang; mains 100,000-150,000K, 3-course cafe lunch 65,000K; ⏲7am-10pm; ❄📶) With its elegant colonial-era facade, this cool, square-facing restaurant is still one of the city's finest, despite increased competition. Fans whir and wine glasses clink as you tuck into a French-accented menu of soups, grilled entrecôte and lamp chop Provençal. The upstairs restaurant is the classy sister (evenings only), while downstairs the all-day cafe has salads, sandwiches and *croque-monsieur* (gourmet version of a toasted ham and cheese sandwich).

★ **Sook Savan** BAR

(Th Si Muang; ⏲4pm-midnight; 📶) The atmospheric Sook Savan occupies a strategic corner overlooking Savannakhet Sq and draws a lively crowd from about 7pm onwards. Beer is the main ingredient on the menu here, but it also offers traditional Laotian food with a spicy kick to help wash it down. Live music on weekend nights and a bit of a party atmosphere.

ℹ Information

BCEL (Th Ratsavongseuk; ⏲8.30am-4pm) Cash exchange, credit-card advances and an ATM.

Eco-Guide Unit (☎041-214203; Th Latsaphanith; ⏲8am-noon & 1-4.30pm Mon-Fri; 📶) The industrious eco-guide unit provides a range of services, from bookings for treks to Dong Natad PPA and Dong Phu Vieng NPA, to bus times, accommodation and tips on where to get a decent massage or hire a motorbike (not both at the same time!).

Lao Development Bank (Th Udomsin; ⏲8.30-11.30am & 1.30-3.30pm) Cash exchange, credit-card advances and an ATM.

Provincial Hospital (☎041-212717; Th Khanthabuli) Ask for English-speaking Dr Outhon.

Tourist Police (☎041-260173)

ℹ Getting There & Away

AIR

Savannakhet's **airport** (☎041-212140; Th Kaysone Phomvihane) is served solely by Lao Airlines, with domestic connections to Vientiane (490,000K to 895,000K, 55 minutes, four weekly), Pakse (320,000K to 520,000K, 30 minutes, four weekly) and Bangkok (US$105 to US$150, 80 minutes, four weekly). Tickets can be purchased at the **Lao Airlines office** (☎041-212140; ⏲8.30am-4.30pm) at the airport or travel agents in town.

An alternative option for those wanting to save money on the Bangkok route is to cross the Friendship Bridge and connect with the Fly-Drive services offered with Air Asia or Nok Air via Nakhon Phanom Airport; tickets are available from less than 1000B.

The airport is located at the southeastern edge of town; jumbos make the trip downtown for 30,000K, although they may start higher when fresh off the plane on arrival.

BUS

Savannakhet's **bus terminal** (☎041-212143), usually called the *khíw lot*, is near the Talat Savan Xai at the northern edge of town. Buses leave here for Vientiane (75,000K, eight to 11 hours, 457km) roughly every half-hour from 6am to 11.30am. From 1.30pm to 10pm you'll have to hop on a bus passing through from Pakse, which stop at Tha Khaek (30,000K, 2½ to four hours, 125km). Hourly *sǒrngtǎaou* and minivans also head to Tha Khaek (30,000K) from 8am to 4pm. A VIP sleeper bus (120,000K, six to eight hours) to Vientiane leaves at 9.30pm, or you could try to pick up a seat on one of the VIP buses coming through from Pakse.

Ten daily buses to Pakse (45,000K, five to six hours, 230km) originate in Savannakhet; the first is at 7am and the last at 10pm. Otherwise, jump on one of the regular buses passing through from

GETTING TO THAILAND: SAVANNAKHET TO MUKDAHAN

Since the construction of the second Thai-Lao Friendship Bridge back in 2006, non-Thai and non-Lao citizens are not allowed to cross between Mukdahan and Savannakhet by boat.

Getting to the border The Thai-Lao International Bus crosses the **Savannakhet (Laos)/Mukdahan (Thailand) border crossing** (6am to 10pm) in both directions. From Savannakhet's bus terminal, the Thai-Lao International Bus (15,000K, 45 minutes) departs approximately every hour from 8am to 7pm. It leaves Mukdahan's bus station (50B, 45 minutes) roughly every hour from 7.30am to 7pm and also stops at the border crossing to pick up passengers.

At the border Be sure not to board the Savan Vegas Casino staff bus at the border, as this also stops at the international bus stop but heads out of town to the eponymous casino resort.

The Lao border offers 30-day tourist visas on arrival. If you don't have a photo you'll be charged the equivalent of US$1. An additional US$1 'overtime fee' is charged from 6am to 8am and 6pm to 10pm on weekdays, as well as on weekends and holidays. Most nationalities do not require a visa to cross into Thailand; check with the Vietnamese consulate (p363) in Savannakhet.

Moving on Onward from Mukdahan, there are at least five daily buses bound for Bangkok. Alternatively, to save time, consider a fly-drive option with Air Asia or Nok Air, including an express minivan to Nakhon Phanom Airport and a budget flight to Bangkok.

Vientiane. There's also a daily bus to Don Khong (80,000K, six to eight hours, 367km) at 7pm, and two daily buses to Attapeu (80,000K, eight to 10 hours, 410km) at 9am and 7pm.

Buses leave for the Laos–Vietnam border at Dansavanh (60,000K, five to six hours, 236km) at 7am, 8.30am and 11am, stopping at Sepon (50,000K, four to five hours).

To Vietnam, there's a bus to Dong Ha (80,000K, about seven hours, 350km), departing at 8am on even-numbered dates. For Hué, there's a local bus (90,000K, about 13 hours, 409km) daily at 10pm and a VIP bus (110,000K, about eight hours) at 10.30am from Monday to Friday. There's also a bus to Danang (110,000K, about 10 hours, 508km) at 10pm on Tuesday, Thursday and Saturday; the same bus continues to Hanoi (200,000K, about 24 hours, 650km), but we reckon you'd have to be a masochist to consider this journey.

Getting Around

Savannakhet is just big enough that you might occasionally need a jumbo. A charter around town costs around 15,000K and more like 20,000K to the bus station.

Motorcycles can be hired at Souannavong Guest House (p365) for 70,000K to 80,000K per day. The eco-guide unit provides a comprehensive list of places that hire out motorbikes. There are also a few places to rent bicycles; most are along Th Ratsavongseuk and charge about 10,000K per day.

Sepon & the Ho Chi Minh Trail

Sepon was once an important hub on the Ho Chi Minh Trail and there are several key war-related sites in the area. Savannakhet's Tourist Information Centre (p363) publishes a map-based guide of the area, which is useful when exploring the area.

Sights

Ho Chi Minh Trail HISTORIC SITE

FREE The infamous Ho Chi Minh Trail is actually a complex network of dirt paths and gravel roads running parallel to the Laos–Vietnam border from Khammuan Province in the north to Cambodia in the south. The dirt road that borders the War Museum (p368) in Ban Dong, east of Sepon, was one of the main branches of the Ho Chi Minh Trail, and is today one of the most accessible points, as is the village of Pa-am in Attapeu Province. Elsewhere you'll need a guide.

Drivenbyadventure (020-58656994; www.hochiminhtrail.org; rental per day US$38-95, tours per day US$160-200), run by Vientiane-based GPS mapper Don Duvall, runs all-inclusive history-infused motorbike trips on the trail.

Sepon Kao HISTORIC SITE

(ເຊໂປນເກົ່າ, Old Sepon) FREE A trip to Sepon Kao is a sobering experience. On the banks of the Se Pon, Sepon Kao was bombed almost into the Stone Age during the war. If you're on foot or bike, head east from Sepon and turn right just after Km 199; the sign says 'Ban Seponkao'.

War Museum MUSEUM
(☎020-99919709; Ban Dong; 10,000K; ⊙8am-11.30am & 1.30-4pm Mon-Sun) Twenty kilometres east of Sepon, Ban Dong (Dong Village) was on one of the major thoroughfares of the Ho Chi Minh Trail and is the easiest place to see what little material is left from the war. Most of what was previously scattered around the area has been gathered into the gated front lawn of the newly opened War Museum.

Sleeping

Vieng Xay Guesthouse GUESTHOUSE $
(☎041-214895; Rte 9; s/d from 70,000/80,000K; ❄) The Vieng Xay is hands down the town's best digs, with 30 mostly large rooms with TV, air-con and hot water. There's also a decent cafe serving Lao fare. A stairway bordered by bomb casings leads to more rooms out the back.

Getting There & Away

Sŏrngtăaou and the occasional bus leave from outside Sepon's market for Savannakhet (35,000K, four to five hours, 196km) between about 8am and 3pm; otherwise, flag down any bus heading west for the same price. There are also relatively frequent *sŏrngtăaou* to Ban Dong (10,000K) and the border at Dansavanh (20,000K, one hour) during the same times, or you could hop on any bus going in that direction.

Champasak Province

Pakse

Pakse (ປາກເຊ), the capital of Champasak Province and the gateway to southern Laos, sits at the confluence of the Mekong and the Se Don (Don River). Most travellers don't linger long because there's not much to do. The city lacks the sort of Mekong River–town lethargy found in Savannakhet and Tha Khaek further north and fewer colonial-era buildings remain.

Pakse serves mostly as a launching pad for forays to surrounding attractions such as the Bolaven Plateau (p385) and Wat Phu Champasak (p377), and the many good restaurants, stylish hotels and clued-in tour companies make it a comfortable and convenient one.

Sights & Activities

Wat Luang BUDDHIST TEMPLE
(ວັດຫຼວງ; Th 11) There are about 20 wats in Pakse, among which the riverside Wat Luang is one of the largest. The old monastic school, built in 1935, features a commanding tiled roof and ornate concrete pillars while two newer buildings have modern murals telling the Buddha's life story and other tales.

Talat Dao Heuang MARKET
(ຕະຫຼາດດາວເຮືອງ, New Market; ⊙5am-6pm) This vast market near the Lao-Japanese Bridge is one of the biggest in the country. It's at its most chaotic in the food zones, but just about anything a person might need – from medicinal herbs to mobile phones – is sold here. It's highly worth a wander.

Champasak Historical Heritage Museum MUSEUM
(ພິພິດທະພັນມໍລະດົກປະຫວັດສາດຈຳປາສັກ; Rte 13; 10,000K; ⊙8.30-11.30am & 2-4pm Mon-Fri) Though the labelling certainly could be better, this is a museum worth visiting. Highlights include ancient Dong Son bronze drums, unusual stone carvings unearthed up on the Bolaven Plateau in Bachieng District, stelae in Tham script dating from the 15th to 18th centuries, Khmer stone carvings, musical instruments, and some American unexploded ordnance (UXO). Also of interest is the textile and jewellery collection from ethnic minorities such as the Nyaheun, Suay and Laven, with large iron ankle bracelets and ivory ear plugs.

Se Pian NPA NATIONAL PARK
(ປ່າສະຫງວນແຫ່ງຊາດເຊປຽນ; www.xepian.org) Se Pian NPA is one of the most important protected areas in Laos. The 2400-sq-km park boasts small populations of Asiatic black bears, yellow-cheeked crested gibbons and Siamese crocodiles, and is home to many birds, including the rare sarus crane, vultures and hornbills. Banteng, Asian elephants, gaur and tiger once roamed here, but sightings of these creatures have been rare to nonexistent in recent years.

Stretching from Rte 13 in the west into Attapeu Province in the east, and to the Cambodian border in the south, it is fed by three major rivers: the Se Pian, Se Khampho and Se Kong.

It's almost impossible to visit the park under your own steam, but you can get into the park for either tough multiday jungle treks or short nature walks, bike trips and boat rides through Kiet Ngong (p378) village or Green Discovery tour company in Pakse. Though almost nobody does it, Se Pian can also be accessed from Attapeu: arrange a guide through the **Dokchampa Hotel** (020-99955678; www.dokchampakham.weebly.com; Rte 18A). If you're feeling really frisky and adventurous, you could try to charter a boat down the Sekong from Sanamsay, on Rte 18A about 35km west of Attapeu. This trip toward the Cambodian border would get you deep into a scenic section of Se Pian NPA.

Dok Champa Massage MASSAGE
(020-54188778; Th 5; massages 50,000-100,000K; 9am-10pm) Again and again Dok Champa comes out on top as the favourite Pakse spa, thanks to its friendly and professional staff offering you exactly the level of robust or soft pampering your weary muscles require. Reservations are recommended.

Tours

Green Discovery ADVENTURE
(031-252908; www.greendiscoverylaos.com; Th 10; 2-day Tree Top Explorer tour 2-/4-person group per person US$308/240; 8am-8pm) Green Discovery is a solid all-around tour company offering private and small group tours. It goes places and does things no other company does. Its signature trip is the Tree Top Explorer adventure in Dong Hua Sao NPA (ປາສະຫງວນແຫງຊາດດົງຫົວສາວ) near Paksong on the Bolaven Plateau. It consists of two or three days' ziplining, canopy walking and jungle trekking around waterfalls beyond any roads. Accommodation is in eco-friendly huts set high up above the forest floor.

Vat Phou Cruises CRUISE
(031-251446; www.vatphou.com; just off Th 11; office 8am-5pm Mon-Sat, no cruises in Jun) Operates three-day luxury Mekong cruises between Pakse and Si Phan Don, including visits to Wat Phu Champasak (p377) and **Khon Phapheng** (ຕາດຄອນພະເພັງ; 55,000K; 8am-5pm) waterfall.

Sleeping

★ **Alisa Guesthouse** HOTEL $
(031-251555; www.alisa-guesthouse.com; Rte 13; r 120,000-150,000K, f 200,000K;) Perhaps the best-value lodging in Pakse, Alisa has sparkling rooms, tiled floors, solid wood beds, armoires, working satellite TV and a fridge. Service is good too. The only significant knock is that some rooms barely catch a wi-fi signal. No surprise, it's often full.

Nang Noi Guesthouse GUESTHOUSE $
(030-9562544; bounthong1978@hotmail.com; Th 5; dm 40,000K, r 60,000-110,000K, f 200,000K;) Around the corner from the tourist strip, but seemingly far away, this popular (ie often full) spot has quiet, spiffy rooms and English-speaking owners. Note the 11pm curfew.

Kaemse Guest House GUESTHOUSE $
(020-55769397; Th 14; r with fan 50,000-70,000K, air-con 100,000K;) With its riverside position and rickety sun deck shipwrecked over the bank, this friendly house at the end of a lane has a certain tumbledown charm. Rooms are simple but clean and the owners are friendly.

Sabaidy 2 Guesthouse GUESTHOUSE $
(031-212992; www.sabaidy2tour.com; Th 24; dm 35,000K, d with fan/air-con 100,000/125,000K, s/d without bathroom 50,000/70,000K;) Though not the great place it used to be, Sabaidy 2 still has an easy, relaxed vibe and is the most communal spot in town. Rooms are split between the older wooden building, which is basic but clean, and a much better new building in back: think wooden balcony, beneath which koi carp swim; rustic-chic interiors; desks and air-con.

★ **Athena Hotel** HOTEL $$
(031-214888; www.athenahotelpakse.com; Rte 13; r incl breakfast US$70-100;) Easily the most modern and slick hotel in Pakse, Athena's subdued style features a lot of wood. The beds are marshmallowy delights, and dimming inlaid ceiling lights let you illuminate them in many ways. The cosy pool is most welcome after a day out on dusty roads. It's about a 10-minute walk from the tourist centre.

★ **Residence Sisouk** BOUTIQUE HOTEL $$
(031-214716; www.residence-sisouk.com; cnr Th 9 & Th 11; r incl breakfast US$50-100;) This exquisite boutique hotel occupies a lovely old house and evokes a bit of old France. The rooms enjoy polished hardwood floors, flat-screen TVs, verandahs, Hmong bed runners, stunning photography and fresh flowers everywhere. Breakfast is in the penthouse cafe with great views. Paying extra gets you a bigger, brighter room with a

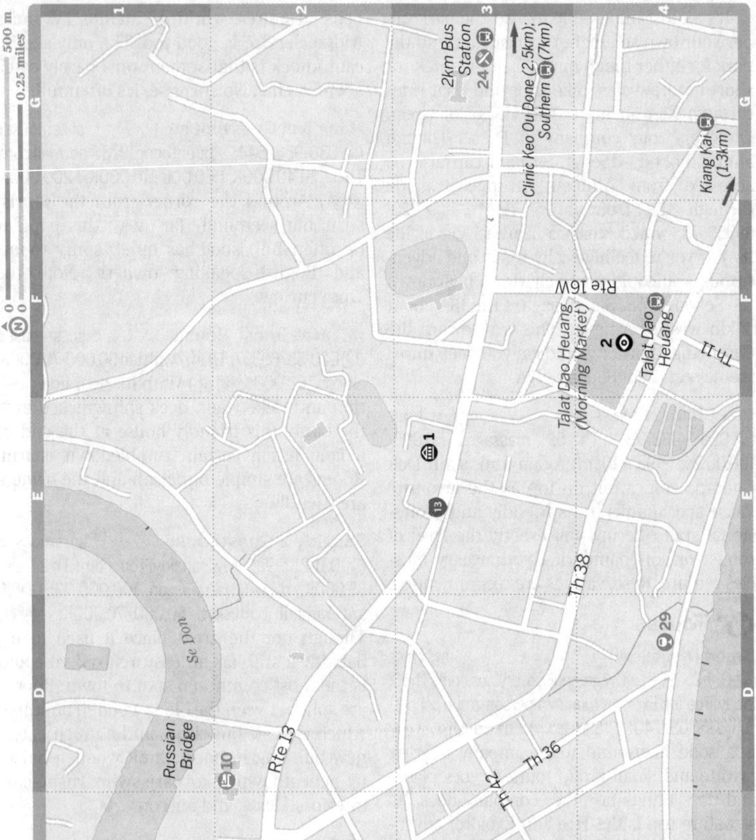

Pakse

0 500 m
0 0.25 miles

Souphanouvong Bridge
Th 21
Th 14
11
17
Lao Development Bank
19
23
Vietnamese Consulate
Russian Bridge
Se Don
9
10
(3km); Northern (7km)
3
7
15
25
8
Rte 13
13
12
22
Se Don
BCEL
18
Th 46
Provincial Tourism Office
27
13
5
6
Th 5
28
4
26
Th 24
16
King of Bus Terminal
30
Th 11
Th 10
Th 1
20
1
International Hitech Polyclinic
Th 34
Th 35
2km Bus Station
24
Th 9
Th 42
Th 36
Clinic Keo Ou Done (2.5km); Southern (7km)
Th 8
Talat Dao Heuang (Morning Market)
Th 38
2
Rte 16W
Talat Dao Heuang
14
29
Th 11
21
Th 11
Kiang Kai (1.3km)
Mekong River

Pakse

Sights
1 Champasak Historical Heritage Museum ... E3
2 Talat Dao Heuang ... F4
3 Wat Luang ... A2

Activities, Courses & Tours
4 Dok Champa Massage ... B2
5 Green Discovery ... B2
6 Vat Phou Cruises ... A2
7 Xplore-Asia ... B2

Sleeping
8 Alisa Guesthouse ... B2
9 Athena Hotel ... C2
10 Champasak Palace Hotel ... D2
11 Kaemse Guest House ... B1
12 Nang Noi Guesthouse ... B2
13 Pakse Hotel ... A2
14 Pakse Mekong Hotel ... B4
15 Phi Dao Hotel ... B2
16 Residence Sisouk ... A2
17 Sabaidy 2 Guesthouse ... B1
18 Salachampa Hotel ... B2
19 Sang Aroun Hotel ... B2

Eating
20 Ban Tong Night Market ... C3
21 Banlao ... B4
22 Dok Mai Trattoria Italiana ... B2
23 Friendship Minimart ... B2
24 Friendship Super Mart ... G3
25 Lankham Noodle Shop ... B2
Noodle Shop Mengky ... (see 23)
26 Pon Sai ... B2
27 Rahn Naem Khao Mae Fuean ... A2
Sinouk Coffee Shop ... (see 16)
28 Xuan Mai Restaurant ... B2

Drinking & Nightlife
29 Champahom ... D4

Shopping
30 Champasak Shopping Centre ... A3

balcony in front; standard rooms are at the back.

Phi Dao Hotel HOTEL **$$**
(☎031-215588; phidaohotel@gmail.com; Rte 13; r 130,000-180,000K;) A very solid city-centre choice, the rooms here are among the best in this price range for quality, maintenance and cleanliness, although not the best for value. Streetside rooms are loud, so request something at the back, though some of those lack windows. It has a lively cafe.

Pakse Hotel HOTEL **$$**
(☎031-212131; www.paksehotel.com; Th 5; s 200,000-500,000K, d 250,000-550,000K, ste 700,000-950,000K, all incl breakfast;) This traditional-luxe hotel towering over central Pakse has a welcoming lobby and corridors festooned with indigenous sculptures and textiles. The economy rooms are dark (windows only open to the interior hallway) and the standard rooms are cramped, so consider an upgrade to at least a superior (from 350,000K), which includes Mekong views.

Sang Aroun Hotel HOTEL **$$**
(☎031-252111; sengarounhotelpakse@gmail.com; Rte 13; r 175,000-275,000K incl breakfast;) This shiny tower in the heart of the tourist strip gives you a bit more than the best budget hotels – notably brighter, airier rooms – but lacks the character and quality of the next level up. It won't excite you, but it won't let you down. However, skip the bizarre low-ceilinged 'Junior' rooms.

Salachampa Hotel HOTEL **$$**
(☎031-212273; salachampa@yahoo.com; Th 10; r 140,000-250,000K;) This ageing place really could make something of itself if somebody made the effort. The rooms are dark and the mattresses aren't great, but the rattan furniture, colourful floor tiles and relaxing terrace give it some character that you can't get elsewhere at these prices. As long as your expectations aren't high, it's a good choice.

Pakse Mekong Hotel HOTEL **$$**
(☎031-218445; Th 11; r with river view 207,000-333,000K, without river view 167,000-185,000K;) Bland but large and immaculate rooms have flat-screen TVs, spiffy white bedspreads and huge porcelain sinks. The riverfront location is the main selling point, but it comes at the cost of being well removed from the convenience of the city centre. The nondescript, unfurnished balconies and rooftop terrace are curiously wasted, but the views are good.

Mekong Paradise Resort HOTEL **$$**
(☎031-212120; r incl breakfast US$38-85;) A riverside spot just 3km southeast of central Pakse that makes for a wonderful escape from the city. Most rooms have unbeatable Mekong sunset views. The superior rooms (US$55) with their private balconies are almost romantic, but the views are actually

better from the US$45 Mekong Paradise rooms. The Garden View rooms (US$38) defeat the point of staying out here.

It can feel a little deserted at times. Take the signed turn-off to Pakse Golf from Rte 38 and proceed 800m.

Champasak Palace Hotel HOTEL $$
(031-212263; www.champasakpalacehotel.com; Rte 13; s 200,000-350,000K, d 250,000-400,000K, ste 550,000-2,000,000K, all incl breakfast;) You can't miss this vast, wedding-cake-style building originally built as a palace for Chao Boun Oum, the last prince of Champasak and Lao prime minister between 1960 and 1962. The standard rooms are a tad twee, but well-kept with comfortable beds, while the graceful restaurant and common areas turn heads with wood columns, louvred windows and random flair such as the rooftop lounge's ceiling. It is worth investing in a huge VIP suite (550,000K), with parquet floors and panoramic views. The cheapest rooms are in the newer Sedone building out back and are far less inspiring.

Eating

Two good morning spots for delicious *fěr* (rice noodles) are the **Noodle Shop Mengky** (Rte 13; noodles 15,000K; 6am-1pm) and the more tourist-friendly **Lankham Noodle Shop** (Rte 13; noodles 15,000-25,000K; 6am-2pm;) across the road. The latter also does baguette sandwiches. Self-caterers can head to the centrally located **Friendship Minimart** (Rte 13; 8am-8pm) or the larger, but distant **Friendship Super Mart** (Rte 13; 9am-9pm) inside the Friendship Mall. Several fruit vendors open early to late next to **Champasak Shopping Centre** (Champasak Plaza; 8am-7pm).

★**Pon Sai** LAOTIAN $
For a wonderful local morning experience, head to Pon Sai at the junction of Th 34 and Th 46, which bustles with small shops and street vendors selling *fěr*, baguette sandwiches, *kòw něeo bîng* (grilled, egg-dipped sticky rice patties) and many doughy delights. Though it's best in the morning, some shops stay open through the day and into the night.

★**Rahn Naem Khao Mae Fuean** LAOTIAN, THAI $
(Th 11; mains 25,000-40,000K; 9am-10.30pm;) This local joint offers a rare combination: real-deal Lao food and an English-language menu. Well, something close to English anyway...the 'fried chicken power' is really stir-fried holy basil with chicken. It's well-known for *pan mîiang baa* (a sort of make-your-own fish sandwich) and also serves *láhp* (spicy Lao-style salad of minced meat poultry or fish) and Mekong River algae soup. The deck on the Se Don is a big bonus.

Ban Tong Night Market MARKET $
(Th 1; 4.30-9.30pm) Though small and everything is sold as takeaway, this is the closest thing Pakse has to a Thai-style night market. It's a great place to sample Lao food since you can just point to what you want.

Sinouk Coffee Shop CAFE $
(cnr Th 9 & Th 11; mains 30,000-45,000K; 6.30am-9pm;) Stylish Sinouk has glass-topped tables inlaid with coffee beans as that's what it's all about – delicious Arabica coffee grown on its plantation in the Bolaven Plateau. If you're after more, then get started on the panini sandwiches, salads, pastas and the usual Thai-Lao mix of dishes. It's one of the priciest spots in the city, but the quality is high.

Xuan Mai Restaurant VIETNAMESE, LAOTIAN $
(Th 5; mains 20,000-35,000K; 7am-10.30pm;) Vietnamese-run Xuan Mai serves super-fresh *fěr* (rice noodles), *năem néuang* (pork balls), *kòw þûn* (white flour noodles with sweet-spicy sauce) and a house *láhp* that's full of zing. Its set meals are good value if you're dining in a group.

Dok Mai Trattoria Italiana ITALIAN $$
(Th 24; mains 25,000-60,000K; 11am-11pm Wed-Mon;) Italian-owned, this little gem aims for culinary authenticity (there's no garlic bread, for example) with perfectly prepared pasta and eggplant parmigiana, plus a big selection of salads. And it all comes with a fantastic rock-and-roll soundtrack and garden seating in back.

Banlao THAI, LAOTIAN $$
(Th 11; mains 20,000-80,000K; 10am-10pm) One of several floating restaurants in Pakse, Banlao has a reliable menu of expected favourites but also many dishes you might not have encountered before, such as the seasonal ant egg *gôy* (*gôy kài mót sòm* – *gôy* is similar to *láhp* but with added blood) and a whole page of sticky rice dipping sauces (*jaew*) including eggplant and cricket. For the less adventurous there's mild, central-Thai papaya salad and grilled fish with herbs.

Drinking & Nightlife

If you want to experience Pakse's mild nightclub scene, head east of the city on Th 38 to a handful of spots that stay open to 1am.

Champahom BAR
(Th 11) A chill place to drink and snack, this Thai-owned bar has live music (usually Carabao-style Thai country music) nightly from about 7.30pm to 9pm.

Information

Banks, such as the conveniently located **BCEL** (Th 11; 8.30am-3.30pm Mon-Fri) and **Lao Development Bank** (Rte 13; 8am-4pm Mon-Fri, to 3pm Sat & Sun), have the best currency-exchange rates, though the exchange counter at the **Lankham Hotel** (7am-7pm) is good too. All three give cash advances (3% commission) on credit cards. LDB also has Western Union and can exchange US dollar travellers cheques (1%). ATMs are plentiful in the city centre.

International Hitech Polyclinic (VIP Clinic; 031-214712; ihpc_lao@yahoo.com; cnr Th 1 & Th 10; 24hr) Adjacent to the public hospital, with English-speaking staff and much higher standards of care, service and facilities, plus a pharmacy.

Main Post Office (Th 8; 8am-noon & 1-5pm Mon-Fri)

Miss Noy (020-22272278; noy7days@hotmail.com; Rte 13; internet per hour 8000K; 8am-8pm) Witty Miss Noy and her French-speaking husband rent reliable, well-maintained scooters and bikes. They also sell bus tickets and tours, and have internet access.

Provincial Tourism Office (031-212021; Th 11; 8am-4pm Mon-Fri) This office mostly exists to hand out maps and brochures, but some staff can answer questions or help you make bookings for homestays and activities at Kiet Ngong, Don Kho and Don Daeng.

Getting There & Away

AIR

The **Pakse International Airport** (Rte 13) is 2.5km northwest of the Souphanouvong Bridge. A tuk-tuk to/from the airport will cost about 40,000K.

Lao Airlines (031-212252; www.laoairlines.com; Pakse Airport; 8.30am-5pm Mon-Fri, 8am-5pm Sat, 8am-7pm Sun) has direct flights to the following cities in Asia:

Attapeu 520,000K, three weekly
Bangkok US$125, four weekly
Ho Chi Minh City US$110, two weekly
Luang Prabang 890,000K, three weekly
Savannakhet 320,000K, four weekly
Siem Reap US$105, four weekly
Vientiane 750,000K, two daily

A cheaper way to fly to Bangkok is to travel overland to Ubon Ratchathani and catch a budget flight from there.

BOAT

A tourist boat motors from Pakse to Champasak (one way per person 70,000K) at 8.30am, provided there are enough punters – in the low season there usually aren't. The return trip from Champasak is at 1.30pm. It's two hours downstream to Champasak, and a bit longer on the return. Book through any travel agent or call **Mr Khamlao** (020-22705955; per boat US$80, per person for 10 people US$8).

BUS

Pakse, frustratingly, has many bus and *sŏrngtăaou* (passenger truck) stations. The vast majority of tourists simply book bus journeys through their guesthouse or a travel agency, and since these are either special tourist buses that pick you up in the centre or include a free transfer to the relevant departure point, the prices are usually reasonable.

Note that on long-distance routes (Cambodia, Vietnam and Vientiane) you'll want to be careful which company you use: choosing the wrong one could cost you several hours and cause a lot of pain. Buy your ticket from a travel agency that actually knows the details of the route, rather than a guesthouse, which probably does not.

There are six main stations:

MINORITY VILLAGES

Most tour companies in Pakse and Tat Lo include visits to ethnic minority villages in their standard trips around the Bolaven Plateau. Of course, these are largely superficial visits and though you will get to see some of the local culture, selling souvenirs is the main goal.

Overall you'll have a much more satisfying experience if you visit villages as part of a guided trek around Tat Lo, or stop by the locally run Mr Vieng Coffee & Homestay (p386) and Captain Hook Coffee Break (p385). Though doing an overnight homestay is best, both of these places offer short village-coffee plantation tours for drop-in visitors.

If you visit rural villages on your own, such as around Toumlan (p385), be respectful...dress modestly and take few or no photos.

Southern Bus Terminal (Rte 13) Pakse's main bus station with departures to most places. Also known as *khíw lot lák pąet* (8km bus terminal) because it's 8km out of town on Rte 13.

Northern Bus Terminal (Rte 13) This is usually called *khíw lot lák jét* (7km bus terminal); it's – you guessed it – 7km north of town. Only for northern destinations. The English-language signs on departures are frequently wrong.

Talat Dao Heuang (Morning Market) Vans and *sŏrngtăaou* to nearby destinations, such as the Thai border, depart from a chaotic lot in the southeast corner of the market and also from Th 38 in front of the market.

2km Bus Station (Sengchalern Bus Station; ☎031-212428; Rte 13) Also known as Sengchalern station after the company that owns it; the office is in the lobby of SL Hotel, which is in front of Friendship Mall.

King of Bus Terminal (☎020-5501 2299; Th 11) Only serves night buses to Vientiane and towns along the way.

Kiang Kai Bus Station (off Th 38) This small, hard-to-find station, in a red-and-yellow building set back well off Th 38, is 1.5km past the Japanese bridge. It's used by buses to/from Thailand, though these also use the Southern Bus Terminal.

Bolaven Plateau & Points East

Transport to the Bolaven Plateau and points east consists of air-con buses from the Southern Bus Terminal and ordinary fan buses from the 2km Bus Station. The last departures to all cities are at 4pm, except for Sekong from the Southern Terminal, which is at 2.30pm. Buses to Salavan (fan/air-con 30,000/40,000K, three hours) can drop you at Tat Lo. Buses to Attapeu (fan/air-con 45,000/50,000K, 3½ to five hours) pass through Paksong (fan/air-con 15,000/20,000K, 90 minutes) and about half use the long route via Sekong (fan/air-con 35,000/40,000K, 3½ hours).

Champasak & Si Phan Don (Four Thousand Islands)

Regular *sŏrngtăaou* leave Talat Dao Heuang (p374) for Champasak (20,000K, one hour) until noon or so – sometimes even as late as 2pm. There's also a morning tourist bus-boat combo to Champasak (55,000K, 1½ hours) offered by most travel agencies. Be sure your ticket includes the boat crossing from Ban Muang. The regular price for the boat is 10,000K per person or 30,000K if you're alone.

For Si Phan Don, tourist buses and minivans – including pick-ups in town and boat transfer to Don Khong (70,000K, 2½ hours), Don Det (70,000K, three hours) and Don Khon (75,000K, 3¼ hours) – are most comfortable and convenient. Book these through any guesthouse or travel agent. All departures are in the morning around 8am. Note that prices fluctuate considerably on these trips over time, and also sometimes even on the north- and southbound journeys due to attempts at price fixing.

If you want to leave later in the day, take a *sŏrngtăaou* from the Southern Bus Terminal (p374) to Ban Nakasang (for Don Det and Don Khon; 40,000K, 3½ hours). These depart hourly until 5pm and go via Hat Xai Khun (for Don Khong).

One *sŏrngtăaou* services Kiet Ngong (30,000K, two hours), leaving at 11am.

Vientiane & Points North

Most travellers prefer the comfortable 'VIP' night sleeper buses to Vientiane (170,000K, 10 hours). You can book these through your guesthouse or head to the King of Bus Terminal, from where there are several nightly departures, all leaving at 8.30pm; or the 2km Bus Station, with one departure at 8pm. It's possible to take these buses to Tha Khaek (130,000K, 4½ hours) and Seno (for Savannakhet; 120,000K, three hours).

If you prefer day travel, slower-moving ordinary air-con buses (110,000K, 12 to 14 hours) depart throughout the day from the Southern Bus Terminal (p374), stopping to pick up more passengers at the 2km and Northern (p374) stations. These buses also go to Tha Khaek (40,000K, five hours) and Seno (60,000K, seven hours).

Getting Around

Local transport in Pakse is expensive by regional standards. Figure on about 10,000K for a short *săhm-lór* (three-wheels) trip (including between Talat Dao Heuang and the city centre) if you're one person – more if you're in a group or use a tuk-tuk. A ride to the Northern or Southern Bus Terminal costs 15,000K per person shared and 50,000K for a whole tuk-tuk.

Champasak

It's hard to imagine Champasak (ຈຳປາສັກ) as a seat of royalty, but from 1713 until 1946 it was just that. These days the town is a somnolent place, the fountain circle (that no longer hosts a fountain) in the middle of the main street alluding to a grandeur long since departed, along with the former royal family. Scattered French colonial-era buildings share space with traditional Lao wooden stilt houses, and the few vehicles that venture down the narrow main street share it with chickens and cows.

With a surprisingly good range of accommodation and several attractions in the vicinity – most notably the Angkor-period ruins of Wat Phu Champasak (p377) – it's easy

GETTING TO THAILAND: VANG TAO TO CHONG MEK

Getting to the border Other than finding the right counters to use at immigration, crossing at the **Vang Tao (Laos)/Chong Mek (Thailand) border** (open 6am to 8pm) is straightforward.

The easiest way to get there is on the Thai-Lao International Bus (50,000K, 2½ to three hours, 8.30am and 3pm) between Pakse's Southern Bus Terminal (p374) and Ubon Ratchathani's bus station. It picks up more passengers at the little Kiang Kai Bus Station (p374) on the way. If you're travelling to Pakse (departures from Ubon at 9.30am and 3pm) note that this bus does wait long enough for people to get Lao visas.

There are also frequent minivans from Pakse to Vang Tao (25,000K, 45 minutes) departing from the street in front of Talat Dao Heuang (p374) and also *sŏrngtăaou* (passenger trucks) leaving from inside the market until about 4pm. Vans to Vang Tao also depart hourly from the Southern Bus Terminal. You'll be dropped off in a dusty/muddy parking area about 500m from the Lao immigration office.

If you are headed to Bangkok (225,000K, 14 hours), a direct service (that sometimes involves changing buses at Ubon) departs the Southern Bus Terminal daily at 4pm. Pakse travel agents also offer a combination bus/sleeper train ticket to the Thai capital with prices starting at 290,000K for 2nd-class fan carriages and going much higher for better service.

At the border Laos issues visas on arrival (around US$35, depending on which passport you hold), while on the Thai side most nationalities are issued 15-day visa waivers free of charge; residents of the G7 countries get 30 days. You walk between the two countries using a pointless underground tunnel for part of the way.

Although it seems like a scam, there is a legitimate overtime fee on the Laos side after 4pm weekdays and all day on weekends and holidays. The real scam is that the officials demand 100B even though the actual price is 10,000K. Just tell them you want a receipt and you'll pay the correct price.

Moving on Minivans head to Ubon (100B, 1¼ hours, every 30 minutes) from Chong Mek's bus terminal, which is 600m (20B by motorcycle taxi) up the main road. Alternatively, informal taxi drivers hang around immigration and charge 1000B to anywhere in Ubon Ratchathani city.

to see why many visitors to the region prefer staying in Champasak over bustling Pakse.

Just about everything in Champasak is spread along the riverside road, both sides of the fountain circle.

Sights & Activities

★Shadow Puppet Theatre & Cinéma Tuktuk — THEATRE

(www.cinema-tuktuk.org; 50,000K; 8.30-10pm Oct-Apr, shadow puppets Tue & Fri, movie Wed & Sat) Run by Frenchman Yves Bernard, this magical theatre next to the tourist office tells the story of the epic Ramayana using the ancient art of shadow puppets. On Wednesday and Saturday nights it screens the enchanting, Academy Award–nominated silent film *Chang* (1927), filmed over 18 months in the jungles of northeast Thailand by the writer and director of Hollywood's original *King Kong*. What makes it so great is the presence of live musicians providing the soundtrack.

Wat Muang Kang — BUDDHIST TEMPLE

(ວັດເມືອງກາງ, Wat Phuthawanaram) About 5km south of town along the Mekong stands the oldest active temple in Champasak, and arguably the most interesting in southern Laos. The soaring Thai-style *ubosot* (ordination hall), with its red-tiled roof and ring of pillars, will be the first thing to catch your eye, but up close the star is the *hăw tại* (Tripitaka library), which combines elements of Lao, Chinese, Vietnamese and French-colonial architecture.

Champasak Spa — SPA

(020-56499739; www.champasak-spa.com; massages 90,000-160,000K; 10am-noon & 1-7pm, closed Mon Apr-Oct, all of Jun) Run by Nathalie, this is a fragrant oasis of free tea and sensitively executed treatments using locally grown and sourced organic bio products. And it creates jobs for local women. The spa also offers yoga and free morning meditation sessions (you must book ahead). A full-day spa package (reservations required) comprising facial, body scrub, hair spa, massage and lunch costs 550,000K.

Sleeping & Eating

Dokchampa Guesthouse GUESTHOUSE $
(020-55350910; r with fan/air-con 50,000/200,000K;) Porches in front of all rooms, a well-placed restaurant along the river, a helpful English-speaking owner and a good mellow vibe make this one of Champasak's best choices. The fan rooms are typical, though we have no clue what they were thinking when building glass-walled bathrooms in the recently renovated air-con rooms. There are big discounts in the low season.

★**Inthira Champasak Hotel** BOUTIQUE HOTEL $$
(031-511011; www.inthira.com; r incl breakfast US$44-71;) The belle of the river, Inthira's 14 rooms are a mix of old and new, but all ooze charm and induce relaxation. And all have little touches of luxury – wooden floors, ambient lighting, flat-screen TVs, safes and rain showers – that set them apart from the in-town competition.

★**River Resort** RESORT $$$
(020-56850198; www.theriverresortlaos.com; garden villas US$120-130, riverview villas US$160-170, incl breakfast;) The 15 duplex villas (12 riverfront and three set back along a pond and rice paddies) are outfitted with gargantuan beds, indigenous wall hangings, indoor-outdoor showers, and big balconies with five-star views. It has a pair of pools, Thai and Lao massage, a beautiful restaurant, and runs upscale excursions by boat (the sunset trip is fantastic) and other means.

It's 3km north of town, but feels miles away from anything.

Champasak with Love THAI, LAOTIAN $
(030-9786757; mains 20,000-40,000K; 9am-10pm;) The marvellous riverfront patio shaded by a big old ficus tree is alone worth a visit, but the food and service are also good. It has the biggest menu in town, with mostly Thai food but also Lao standards and good brownies, fruit salad, sandwiches and breakfasts. The basic and way-overpriced guestrooms (with fan/air-con 60,000/100,000K) in the creaky old house have shared bathrooms.

Frice & Lujane Restaurant ITALIAN $$
(mains 30,000-85,000K; 5-9pm) Enjoy cuisine inspired by Italy's Friulian Alpine region, at the most recent incarnation of this swish, formerly Italian-run restaurant by the Mekong. Gnocchi, marinated pork ribs, lasagne and homemade sausage grace the small menu.

Information

Champasak District Visitor Information Centre (020-97404986; 8am-noon & 2-4.30pm Mon-Fri, also open weekends Sep-Apr) The staff here are friendly and quite knowledgeable about the area. They can arrange all your transport needs, including buses and boats, and also reserve rooms for you on Don Daeng island. Local guides, some of whom speak English, can lead trips at Wat Phu and the myriad minor places around it.

Getting There & Away

Champasak is 30km from Pakse along a beautiful, almost empty sealed road running along the west bank of the Mekong. *Sŏrngtăaou* to Pakse (20,000K, one hour) depart only in the morning, up to around 8am. There are also the tourist buses and boats direct to/from Pakse, but they don't run often due to lack of demand.

The regular morning tourist buses from Pakse to Champasak (55,000, 1½ hours) are actually the buses heading to Si Phan Don and these drop you at Ban Muang on the eastern bank of the Mekong where a small ferry (10,000K per person, 20,000K for motorbikes) crosses to the village of Ban Phaphin just north of Champasak. Be sure you know whether your ticket includes the ferry or not. (The ferrymen won't rip you off over this, but some of the ticket agents in Pakse have been known to.) None of the tickets include the final 2km into Champasak, so you'll probably need to walk it.

To reach Si Phan Don, you can also use the Ban Muang ferry route, take a direct morning minibus (70,000K, three hours) if there are enough passengers, or travel by boat (US$200 private; the Champasak District Visitor Information Centre will know if others are interested in sharing the cost).

Wat Phu World Heritage Area

A visit to the ancient Khmer religious complex of Wat Phu (ວັດພູຈຳປາສັກ) is one of the highlights of any trip to Laos. Stretching 1400m up the slopes of Phu Pasak (also known more colloquially as Phu Khuai or Mt Penis), Wat Phu is small compared with the monumental Angkor-era sites near Siem Reap in Cambodia. However, you know the old adage about location, location, location! The tumbledown pavilions, ornate Shiva-lingam sanctuary, enigmatic crocodile stone and tall trees that shroud much of the walkway in soothing shade give Wat Phu an almost mystical atmosphere. These, and a layout that is unique in Khmer architecture, led to Unesco declaring the Wat Phu complex a World Heritage Site in 2001.

An electric cart shuttles guests from the ticket office area past the *baray* (ceremonial pond; *nǎwng sá* in Lao). After that, you must walk.

It is possible to sleep at a guesthouse right outside the entrance to Wat Phu, but spending the night next to the Mekong in Champasak town is far superior.

Sights

★Wat Phu Champasak RUINS

(ວັດພູຈຳປາສັກ; 50,000K; site 8am-6pm, museum to 4.30pm) Bucolic Wat Phu sits in graceful decrepitude, and while it lacks the arresting enormity of Angkor in Cambodia, given its few visitors and more dramatic natural setting, these small Khmer ruins evoke a more soulful response. While some buildings are more than 1000 years old, most date from the 11th to 13th centuries. The site is divided into six terraces on three levels joined by a frangipani-bordered stairway ascending the mountain to the main shrine at the top.

Visit in the early morning for cooler temperatures and to capture the ruins in the best light.

➡ Lower Level

The electric cart delivers you to the large sandstone base of the ancient main entrance to Wat Phu. Here begins a causeway-style ceremonial promenade lined by stone lotus buds and flanked by two much smaller *baray* that still fill with water, lotus flowers and the odd buffalo during the wet season.

➡ Middle Level

Wat Pu's middle section features two exquisitely carved quadrangular pavilions built of sandstone and laterite. Believed to date from the mid-10th or early 11th century, the style resembles Koh Ker in Cambodia. The buildings consist of four galleries and a central open courtyard. Wat Phu was converted into a Buddhist site in later centuries but much of the original Hindu sculpture remains in the lintels, which feature various forms of Vishnu and Shiva.

A good example is the eastern pediment of the north pavilion, which is a relief of Shiva and Parvati sitting on Nandi, Shiva's bull mount.

Next to the southern pavilion stands the much smaller Nandi Hall (dedicated to Shiva's mount). It was from here that an ancient royal road once led over 200km to Angkor Wat in Cambodia. In front is a smaller version of the initial causeway, this one flanked by two collapsed galleries, leading to a pair of steep staircases.

At the base of a second stairway is an impressive and now very holy dvarapala (sentinel figure) standing ramrod straight with sword held at the ready. Most Thai and Lao visitors make an offering to his spirit before continuing up the mountain. If you step down off the walkway and onto the grassy area just north of here you'll come to the remains of a yoni pedestal, the cosmic vagina-womb symbol associated with Shaivism, and two unusually large, headless and armless dvarapala statues half-buried in the grass. These are the largest *dvarapala* found anywhere in the former Angkorian kingdom.

After the *dvarapala* a rough sandstone path ascends quickly to another steep stairway, atop which is a small terrace holding six ruined brick shrines – only one retains some of its original form. From here two final staircases, the second marked by crouching guardians also sans heads and arms, take you to the top, passing through the large terraces you saw clearly from the bottom of the mountain.

Shade is provided along much of this entire middle-level route from *dàwk jąmpąa* (plumeria or frangipani), the Lao national tree.

➡ Upper Level

On the uppermost level of Wat Phu is the sanctuary itself. It has many carvings, notably two guardians and two apsara (celestial dancers), and it once enclosed a Shiva lingam that was bathed, via a system of sandstone pipes, with waters from the sacred spring that still flows behind the complex. The sanctuary now contains a set of very old, distinctive Buddha images on an altar. The brick rear section, which might have been built in the 9th century, is a cella (cell), where the holy linga was kept.

Sculpted into a large boulder behind the sanctuary is a Khmer-style Trimurti, the Hindu holy trinity of Shiva, Vishnu and Brahma. Further back, beyond some terracing to the south of the Trimurti, is the cave from which the holy spring flowed into the sanctuary. Up a rough path to the north of the Trimurti, a Buddha footprint and an elephant are carved into a rock wall.

Just north of the Shiva linga sanctuary, amid a mess of rocks and rubble, look around for two unique stone carvings known as the elephant stone and the crocodile stone. Crocodiles were semi-divine figures in Khmer culture, but despite much speculation that the stone was used for human sacrifices, its function – if there was one – remains unknown. The crocodile is believed to date from the Angkor period, while the elephant is thought to date from the 16th century. Also look out for an interesting chunk of a staircase framed by two snakes and some small caves that were probably used for meditation in ancient days.

When you've seen everything here, just sitting and soaking up the wide-angle view of the *baray*, the plains and the Mekong is fantastic. A small shop sells snacks and cool drinks.

Getting There & Away

Wat Phu Champasak is 43km from Pakse and 10km from Champasak. It's a flat, easy bike ride from Champasak, though there's not a lot of shade. A tuk-tuk from Champasak will cost around 100,000K return.

Pakse Region

Kiet Ngong

The Lao Loum villagers of Kiet Ngong (ບ້ານກຽດໂງ້ງ), near the Se Pian NPA, run southern Laos' most successful community-based ecotourism project. Started in the mid-2000s with help from the Asian Development Bank, Kiet Ngong is functioning on its own now.

The community-run **Visitor Information Centre** (☎030-9552120; toui_ps@hotmail.com; ⏱8am-4pm) in the middle of Kiet Ngong arranges activities, accommodation and transport from Rte 13. Placards on the walls have useful information about the various options and also the ecology, history and culture of the area. A few of the guides speak some English.

Kiet Ngong sits at the edge of a bird-rich wetland about 9km from Rte 13. Working elephants and an unusually large herd of buffalo give the wetland a safari feel. It's best to sleep here for at least a night, but it also works as a day trip from Pakse or Champasak.

For sleeping or any of the activities here try the excellent **Kingfisher Ecolodge** (☎020-55726315; www.kingfisherecolodge.com; eco/comfort r high season 250,000/750,000K, low season 210,000/650,000K; ⏱closed May & Jun; ❄@📶) 🌿, set on 7 hectares at the edge of the wetland about 700m past Kiet Ngong village. It's run by a Lao-Italian family and is a beautiful spot. Sitting on your balcony at dawn and watching birds flit across the wetland is a memorable experience and the two-tiered restaurant-bar could easily be in an East African safari lodge.

Visitors heading to Kiet Ngong must pay a 25,000K entry fee for Se Pian NPA at the little white building 2km east of Rte 13 that you pass on your way there.

Getting There & Away

Kiet Ngong is 56km from central Pakse. Most visitors come here as part of a tour, but travelling independently is fairly easy. One van or *sǒrngtǎaou* (30,000K, two to 2½ hours) leaves Kiet Ngong for Lak 8 bus station in Pakse at about 8am and heads back at 11am. Kiet Ngong is often mispronounced so ask instead for 'Phu Asa'. Alternatively, board anything going south on Rte 13, get off at Ban Thang Beng and call the Visitor Information Centre for a pick-up by motorcycle (25,000K per person) for the last 9km to the village.

Don Kho & Ban Saphai

The Mekong-hugging Ban Saphai (Saphai Village; ບ້ານສະພາຍ) and adjacent island of Don Kho (ດອນໂຄ) just north of Pakse are famous for their weaving. Women work on large looms underneath their homes producing silk (both real and artificial) and cotton dresses and other products, and are happy to show you how. While this is a well-known destination, it's not overrun.

Next to the boat pier is **Ban Saphai Handicraft Centre** (⏱6am-7pm), where several weavers have their looms, and locally woven textiles and other crafts are on sale. Some people here can speak some English. They will call to arrange your homestay and/or activities on Don Kho.

The rarely visited Ban Don Khoh (Don Khoh Village; ບ້ານດອນເຂາະ), not far away, does stone carving. These three destinations combine for a good half-day trip out of Pakse and cultural explorers can dig deeper with a night at Don Kho's **village homestay** (per person 30,000K, per meal 20,000K). Just turn up on the island and say 'homestay' and the villagers will sort you out. Meals are taken with the host family and in our experience, the food is delicious.The Provincial Tourism Office (p373) in Pakse can also arrange things in advance.

Getting There & Away

Ban Saphai is 16km north of Pakse's Souphanouvong Bridge and the turn-off is clearly signed. *Sŏrngtăaou* from Pakse to Ban Saphai (20,000K, 45 minutes) leave fairly regularly from the street in front of the Talat Dao Heung (p374).

From Ban Saphai to Don Kho, longtail boats cost 40,000K round trip and can hold up to five people. Set a time for pick-up, or take the boatman's phone number and call when you want to return.

Ban Don Khoh is between Pakse and Ban Saphai, 9km from the Souphanouvong Bridge. The turn is unmarked, but it's the paved road going west just before the bus station.

Si Phan Don (Four Thousand Islands)

Si Phan Don (ສີ່ພັນດອນ) is where Laos becomes the land of the lotus-eaters, an archipelago of islands where time passes slowly and postcard-worthy views are the rule rather than the exception. Many a traveller has washed ashore here, succumbed to its charms and stayed longer than expected.

Down here the Mekong bulges to a breadth of 14km – the river's widest reach along its 4350km journey from the Tibetan Plateau to the South China Sea – and if you count every islet and sandbar that emerges in the dry months the name, which literally means 'Four Thousand Islands', isn't that big of an exaggeration.

Don Khong

Life moves slowly on Don Khong (ດອນໂຂງ; Khong Island), like a boat being paddled against the flow on the Mekong. It's a pleasant place to spend a day or two, wandering past fishing nets drying in the sun, taking a sunset boat ride, pedalling about on a bicycle or just chilling and reading by the river.

Don Khong measures 18km long by 8km at its widest point. Most of the roughly 60,000 islanders live on the perimeter and there are only two proper towns: lethargic Muang Khong on the eastern shore and the charmless market town of Muang Saen on the west; an 8km road links the two.

Khamtay Siphandone, the postman who went on to serve as president of Laos from 1998 to 2006, was born in Ban Hua Khong at the north end of Don Khong in 1924.

Sights & Activities

Ban Hin Siew Tai Palm Sugar Trees FARM
Although sugar palms can be seen across the island, Ban Hin Siew Tai is southern Laos' sugar capital. Many farmers here climb the trees twice a day to collect the juice and then boil it down to sugar, and if you see them working you are welcome to pop in for a visit. The sugar season is from November to February and early morning is the best time to go.

Muang Khong Market MARKET
(ຕະຫຼາດເມືອງໂຂງ; 5.30am-8am) This little morning market, full of both farmed and foraged foods, is a vibrant slice of island life.

Sabaidee Don Khong VOLUNTEERING
(020-59692777; www.facebook.com/laoschoolvolunteer) Teach English in the after-school program here in exchange for basic but friendly homestay accommodation. A one-week commitment is preferred.

Sleeping

The island has a good selection of accommodation, pretty much all of it in Muang Khong where the ferry boats from Hat Xai Khun land.

★ **Khong View Guesthouse** GUESTHOUSE $
(020-22446449; Muang Khong; r with fan/air-con 80,000/100,000K;) It's hard to beat the location of this place. It's near, but serenely separate from, the tourist strip and the big, breezy 2nd-floor deck provides the best Mekong views in town. The friendly owners give it a homestay feel. There's no restaurant, but sometimes they will cook food for guests.

Pon's Riverside Guesthouse GUESTHOUSE $
(020-55406798; www.ponarenahotel.com; Muang Khong; r 100,000K;) The most popular spot in town for sleeping and eating, Pon's has pleasant lemon-hued rooms with tiled floor, cable TV and a relaxed atmosphere. There's a riverside restaurant deck across the road. Good value.

★ **Pon Arena Hotel** BOUTIQUE HOTEL $$
(020-22270037, 031-515018; www.ponarenahotel.com; Muang Khong; r incl breakfast US$50-85;) This upscale hotel has one building

Si Phan Don

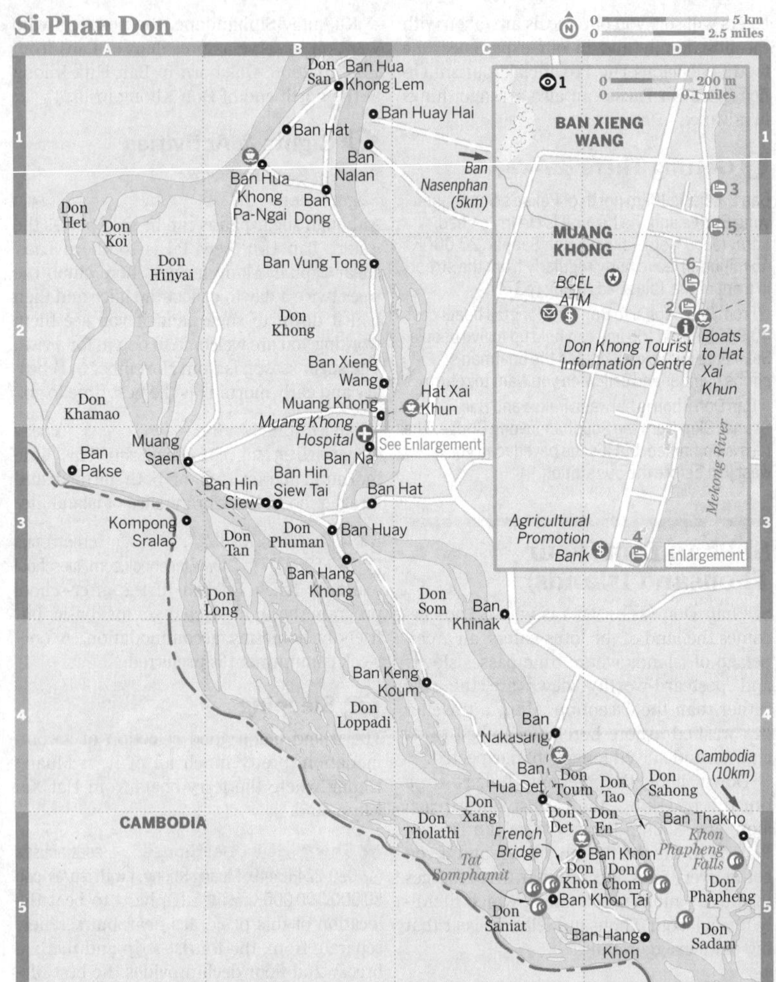

that sits right on the river and boasts large rooms with neat wood trim, flat-screen TVs and a small swimming pool that is so close to the river it actually sticks out over it. The original building with the cheaper rooms sits across the road but still scores style points and has the same soft beds.

Mekong Inn HOTEL **$$**
(031-213668; www.gomekonginn.com; Muang Khong; r incl breakfast US$30;) Rooms at this spot a bit south of the centre are more upmarket than a typical guesthouse, but when the Lao-Canadian owners are around (they spend some low-season months in Canada), it's just as welcoming. Breakfast includes pancakes with maple syrup and Tim Horton's coffee. Rooms are

Si Phan Don

Sights
1 Muang Khong Market C1

Sleeping
2 Done Khong Guesthouse D2
3 Khong View Guesthouse D1
4 Mekong Inn D3
5 Pon Arena Hotel D1
6 Pon's Riverside Guesthouse D2

in two buildings, one of which fronts the pool, and wi-fi only reaches a few of them.

Information

Agricultural Promotion Bank (Muang Khong; 8.30am-4pm Mon-Fri) Exchanges major currencies, does Western Union and has an ATM out front.

BCEL ATM (Muang Khong) In front of the Lao Telecom building, next to the post office.

Don Khong Tourist Information Centre (029-250303; panhjuki@yahoo.com; Muang Khong; 8.30am-4.30pm Mon-Fri) Near the boat landing, this office is manned by helpful Mr Phan. There is information for the whole Si Phan Don region and he can set you up with a local guide for 60,000K per day.

Muang Khong Hospital (24hr) Right on the south edge of town. If you have any minor ailments there are some English-speaking staff.

Getting There & Away

BOAT

The Don Khong boatmen's association runs a boat most days to Don Det and Don Khon (one way/return per person 40,000/60,000K) at 8.30am and departing Don Det at 3pm. It's 1½ hours downstream and two hours back. The price rises if there are fewer than six people, although everything is negotiable and you might be able to hire a boat to go for around 200,000K. You can book this through any guesthouse.

BUS

The vast majority of travellers ride the tourist bus, which always includes getting dropped off on Rte 13 with a connecting leg to the island. Sometimes you will get dropped off at the road to the bridge and head to Muang Khong by tuk-tuk. Other times you will be dropped off at Hat Xai Khun on the mainland (1km from the highway) and then squeezed into a small ferry boat. If you need the boat or tuk-tuk on your own, the price is 15,000K per head with a 30,000K minimum.

For leaving the island, tourist transport heading south to Don Det (60,000K) and Don Khon (70,000K including boat transfer, two hours) passes by about 10am while pick-up for going north to Pakse (60,000K, two hours) is about 11.30am.

There is also a 9am non-air-conditioned bus (60,000K, three hours) from Muang Khong to Pakse's Southern Bus Terminal (p374). At other times, you can go to Rte 13 and wait for the hourly Pakse–Nakasang *sǒrngtǎaou*.

Getting Around

If you're up for some adventure, you can walk, cycle or motorbike 15km across Don Som down to Don Det with a **ferry** ride (10,000K per person) at each end. In the rainy season this trip ranges from tough to impossible due to mud. People in Muang Khong will have only a rough idea what the conditions are at any particular time, but the ferryman will know everything for certain.

Don Det & Don Khon

The vast majority of travellers to Si Phan Don end up on these twin islands. Don Det (ດອນເດດ) is defined by its hippyesque party scene, though it's really quite mild and there's nothing stronger than grass in the 'happy' snacks sold openly at some bars.

Of course there's much more to these two islands. Heading south from Ban Hua Det (Hua Det Village), the guesthouses thin out and the icons of rural island life – fishermen, rice farmers, weavers, buffalo, sugar palms – are on full display. Chill in a hammock, wander aimlessly around the islands or languidly drift downstream in an inner tube in the turquoise arms of the Mekong.

The serenity continues across the French bridge on Don Khon (ດອນຄອນ), but down here there are also some gorgeous waterfalls to visit, sandy beaches to lounge on, dolphins to spot and even a little patch of wilderness to explore.

Sights

These twin islands are famous for soaking up low-key village life rather than ticking off a list of attractions, but the dolphins and waterfalls on Don Khon are genuinely wonderful destinations.

When you cross the French bridge to Don Khon, you will be asked to pay a 35,000K tourism tax at the little blue shack. This is good for the whole day and covers the entrance fee to Tat Somphamit. If you are sleeping on Don Khon and you want to go north, you don't need to pay it. Just check in before you cross to Don Det and hope they remember you when you return.

★**Khon Pa Soi Falls** WATERFALL
(ຕາດຄອນປາສອຍ; Don Khon) FREE Although it's not the largest waterfall on the islands, Khon Pa Soi Falls is still pretty impressive, and it never gets crowded due to its isolated location. From the little restaurant (sometimes only serving cold drinks) cross the big, fun (or scary, depending on the person) wooden suspension bridge to Don Po Soi island and follow the roar 200m to the main waterfall.

★ **Tat Somphamit** WATERFALL
(ຕາດສົມພາມິດ, Li Phi Falls; Don Khon; 35,000K; ticket booth 8am-5pm) Located on Don Khon, 1.5km downriver from the French bridge, vast Tat Somphamit is a gorgeous set of raging rapids. Its other name, Li Phi, means 'Spirit Trap' and locals believe the falls act as just that: a trap for bad spirits as they wash down the river. Local fishermen risk their skin edging out onto rocks in the violent flow of the cascades to empty bamboo traps. Don't try this stunt yourself – travellers have died slipping off the rocks beyond the barrier.

Ban Hang Khon Viewpoint VIEWPOINT
(Ban Hang Khon, Don Khon) Near the old French port in Ban Hang Khon village, 150 steps take you up to a good viewpoint of the Mekong.

Sleeping

The common wisdom is to stay on Don Det to party, and Don Khon to get away from it all. But this is not how things really work. The party is confined to the northern tip of Don Det, at the busy village where the ferry from Ban Nakasang alights. In fact, the quietest and most isolated guesthouses in all of Si Phan Don are actually on the southern portion of Don Det.

Many places offer low-season discounts; sometimes it's automatic and sometimes you need to ask.

Don Det

Don Det's best accommodations – and highest prices – are on the sunrise side, though there are still plenty of good budget beds here too. Flimsy bamboo bungalows predominate on the sunset side. The drawback here is that late in the day rooms become furnace-like after baking in the afternoon sun. On the other hand, there's less boat traffic (ie noise) here.

On both sides of the island, walk far enough (on the sunrise side this means going past the old French port in Don Det village) and the modest party scene of Ban Hua Det feels light years away. The sunset side gets downright rural after a kilometre.

★ **Crazy Gecko** GUESTHOUSE $
(020-97193565; www.crazygecko.ch; sunrise side; r 80,000-100,000K;) In a stilted structure made of solid wood, Crazy Gecko's four tidy rooms surround a balcony that's equal parts funky and functional. Festooned with hammocks and random decoration, it's a superior place to relax. There's a pool table and board games down below and across the road is a little restaurant on a deck over the water.

★ **Mekong Dream Guesthouse** GUESTHOUSE $
(020-55275728; r 50,000K;) At the south of Don Det, facing the strip on Don Khon, Mekong Dream is one of the homiest, best-value guesthouses on the islands. The 12 rooms, all with private bathrooms and comfortable king-size beds, are the antidote to claustrophobic rooms elsewhere (except for the three inferior concrete rooms downstairs) and share a roomy balcony/hammock lounge.

Seng Thavan 1 Guesthouse GUESTHOUSE $
(020-56132696; sunset side; r 100,000K;) Probably the best the sunset side has to offer in the budget range, Seng Thavan's four en suite rooms are old but fastidiously clean. They're off the river, but you get the great views from its low-key cafe, full of recliner cushions.

Last Resort GUESTHOUSE $
(mrwatkinsonlives@googlemail.com; sunset side; r 60,000K) This tepee 'resort' in a field about a 20-minute walk south of Ban Hua Det embraces the natural life, with the expat owner growing vegies and baking bread. Made with bamboo and thatch, the tepees are in the shade of mature trees and share a bathroom. There are often communal meals and alfresco movies in the evening.

Baba Guesthouse GUESTHOUSE $$
(020-98893943; www.dondet.net; sunrise side, Ban Hua Det; r 350,000K;) This beautiful guesthouse looks out on the Mekong on one side, and emerald paddy fields on the other. The price is well above average for this area, but you really do get more for your money here. Rooms are sleekly white and almost luxurious, with private balcony, tasteful decor, personal safe and spotless bathroom.

The terraced restaurant over the river is as classy as the guesthouse and is a great breakfast spot. Owner Basil and his wife are the perfect hosts.

Little Eden HOTEL $$
(020-77739045; www.littleedendondet.com; sunset side, Ban Hua Det; r US$41-50, incl breakfast;) Don Det's most luxurious complex is set on a large plot on its northern tip. Fragrant rooms tempt with contemporary darkwood furniture and polished wood floors, plus plenty of mod cons. Also, the hotel has a beautiful free 18m-long swimming pool, a bar

and a sunset-perfect restaurant. You will feel like you have escaped Ban Hua Det.

Don Khon

There's a good mix of both budget and better places here. Except for the village homestay in Ban Hang Khon, all Don Khon accommodation is in Ban Khon village facing Don Det. It's a pretty peaceful town (no partying here) but it's not exactly oozing an island vibe any more.

Pa Kha Guesthouse GUESTHOUSE $
(055-847522; r with fan/air-con 80,000/120,000K;) Great-value digs with welcoming, clean rooms, good service and a quiet location. The cheapest rooms are on the river; the newer air-con rooms are across the road, as is the restaurant.

Xaymountry Guesthouse GUESTHOUSE $
(020-96516513; r with/without bathroom 80,000/50,000K;) No place on Don Khon has more character than this giant stilted wood house. It was the first lodging on the island and the massive front porch is a nice place to unwind, despite the lack of a river view. The family's children will keep you entertained.

Ban Hang Khon Homestay HOMESTAY $
(020-98893204; per person 36,000K, per meal 20,000K) The small village of Ban Hang Khon at the southern tip of Don Khon – where the dolphin-watching trips start – offers an unadulterated local experience. Little English is spoken, but the seven families who take in guests are impeccable hosts. It's best to call ahead.

★ **Sala Done Khone** BOUTIQUE HOTEL $$
(031-260940; www.salalaoboutique.com; r US$60-80;) Five hotels in one, Sala Done Khone has both the classiest and the most original rooms in Si Phan Don. Its signature unit, the French Residence, is a renovated 1921 timber trading headquarters with tiled floors and louvred blinds, while out on the river the Sala Phae wing features floating cottages with bio-safe toilets and private decks.

Eating

Generally the best dining is on Don Khon and the southeast shore of Don Det.

Garden LAOTIAN, THAI $
(Don Khon; mains 20,000-65,000K; 7am-10pm;) Taking freshness seriously, this thatched-roof, open-kitchen restaurant is a good place for the uninitiated to sample Laotian foods, such as spicy papaya salad and grilled Mekong River fish. It also serves all the usual traveller comfort foods and the cook's personal version of lemon-grass chicken.

Pizza Don Khon LAOTIOAN, INTERNATIONAL $
(Don Khon; small pizzas 40,000K; 7.30am-10pm) A focus on quality, fresh ingredients results in a top-notch pizza. There's a full menu including English breakfasts and daily specials such as *mók* (fish and egg steamed inside banana leaves).

★ **King Kong Resort** INTERNATIONAL $$
(Don Det; mains 25,000-120,000K; 6am-11pm;) This Brit-run establishment on a peaceful slice of the Mekong in south Don Det is a cut above the competition with a range of pastas, pizzas, burgers, fish and chips, Thai curries, Sunday roasts (60,000K) and – we hear – the tastiest and happiest shakes on the island. The guitars and chess sets scattered around fit the vibe. Has added a few new bungalows (40,000K) across the road.

★ **Four Thousand Sunsets** FUSION $$
(Don Khon; mains 25,000-80,000K; 7am-11pm;) Aptly named, this high-class floating restaurant lowers your pulse with the metronomic flow. The menu is a big break from the usual with many dishes you won't find elsewhere in the islands such as northern Thai *hinlay* curry and a chicken *láhp* burger. There's also steamed and grilled fresh river fish, Lao 'smoking' herbal sausages and many stir-fries.

Treat yourself to a vodka martini as you drink up the amber sunset.

Little Eden Restaurant LAOTIAN, INTERNATIONAL $$
(sunset side, Ban Hua Det; mains 30,000-140,000K;) Catching the breeze from the tip of the island, Little Eden's perfectly placed new restaurant is one of the best spots to eat upmarket Lao and Western cuisine. Think tender *duck à l'orange,* spaghetti bolognese and fish *láhp* using Mekong catfish.

Information

There are no banks on the islands. Cash can be exchanged, at generally poor rates, at most guesthouses and some, including Baba on Don Det, do cash advances on credit cards for a 6% commission. There's an Agricultural Promotion Bank and a BCEL with ATMs on the main drag in Ban Nakasang. Kayaking tours budget enough time at the end of the trip for people to make an ATM stop.

GETTING TO CAMBODIA: NONG KHIANG TO TRAPAENG KRIEL

Getting to the border The **Nong Nok Khiene (Laos)/Trapaeng Kriel (Cambodia) border** (open 6am to 6pm) is a popular route for backpackers on the Indochina overland circuit, and it is always a real hassle.

The Cambodian company Sorya Transport that used to reliably run the Pakse–Phnom Penh route has stopped service due to low demand, although if it starts again this would be the best choice. Sengchalern bus company provides daily service from Pakse to Phnom Penh (230,000K, 12 to 14 hours) via Stung Treng (95,000K, 4½ hours) and Kratie (120,000K, eight hours), but the method of travel varies. Sometimes it sends a big bus which goes direct the whole way, other times it sends you to the border in a minibus and you change vehicles there, and you might even have to change a third time at Stung Treng. These vehicle changes often lead to long delays. Regardless of which vehicle, departures are at 7am from the 2km Bus Station (p374), with a stop to pick up more passengers at the Southern Bus Terminal (p374). Tickets for this route sold from the islands in Si Phan Don will include the ferry from the island and, if needed, a minivan to take you to the connecting point.

Sengchalern also sells tickets to Siem Reap (300,000K), but this extra long trip is not recommended. Better to use reliable **Asia Van Transfer** (AVT; www.asiavantransfer.com), which departs from the border at 11.30am and takes the new northern route to Siem Reap (US$20) arriving at about 7pm. The price includes a tuk-tuk ride to your hotel. It takes internet bookings, but this means you have to get yourself to the border. In Don Det, **Green Paradise** (greendiscoverytours99@gmail.com; sunrise side, Ban Hua Det; 7am-9pm) and a few guesthouses sell combo tickets for AVT (200,000K) that include the boat to Nakasang and a minivan to the border. A similar ticket from a travel agency in Pakse costs 260,000K.

For something completely different, **Xplore-Asia** (031-251983; www.xplore-laos.com; Th 14; 7.30am-6.30pm) has one- and two-day kayak-boat combo trips (one/two days US$110/180 with a group of four) from Don Det to Stung Treng passing a dramatic flooded forest rich with birdlife. On the two-day trips paddling begins at Don Det while on the one-day trip all water time comes after immigration.

At the border Both Lao and Cambodian visas are available on arrival, while bribes, scams and rudeness are a mandatory part of the process. In Laos, you'll pay a US$2 (or the equivalent in kip or baht) 'overtime' or 'processing' fee, depending on when you cross, upon both entry and exit. In Cambodia, they jack up the price of a visa to US$35 from the actual US$30. In addition, the Cambodians charge US$1 for a cursory medical inspection upon arrival in the country, and levy a US$2 processing fee upon exit. All of these fees can be avoided if you are willing to wait it out, but this will probably take so long that your bus may leave without you. The bus companies want their cut too, so they charge an extra US$5 or more to handle your paperwork with the border guards, even if you already have a visa. Technically this isn't a scam, since you are getting a service in return for your money, but they will not tell you this service is optional. To avoid this fee, insist on doing your own paperwork and walk through immigration on your own; it's not hard.

Moving on Aside from the buses mentioned here, there's virtually zero traffic here. If you're dropped at the border, expect to pay about US$45 for a private taxi heading south to Stung Treng, or 150,000/60,000K for a taxi/*săhm-lór* (three-wheels) heading north to Ban Nakasang.

Don Khon Health Clinic (Don Khon) The only health centre on Don Det and Don Khon. It's very small and basic. If nobody is there, look for the doctor in her home, next to the clinic.

Pharmacy (sunset side, Ban Hua Det) This petite place is Don Det's only pharmacy.

Getting There & Away

Boat prices between Ban Nakasang and the islands are fixed by a local boat association, and there are very few running each day on a shared basis. Expect to pay 15,000K per person (or 30,000K if travelling on your own) to Don Det, and 20,000K per person (or 60,000K if travelling alone) to Don Khon.

For Pakse, most travellers book tickets on the island, which includes the local boat and an 11am bus or minibus (60,000K, three hours). If you want to leave at another time there are hourly sŏrngtăaou from Ban Nakasang to the Southern Bus Terminal (p374) in Pakse (40,000K, 3½ hours). One shared boat always leaves the islands in time for the 8am *sŏrngtăaou*. These all stop in Hat Xai Khun (for Don Khong).

Even in the best of circumstances, travel to Cambodia from the islands by public transport is a hassle. Kayak-boat trips from Don Det to Stung Treng run by Xplore-Asia (p384) are a great alternative.

River travel to Don Khong (200,000K) and Champasak (US$200) is only available by chartered boat, but very often there are other people willing to join together to share the cost. For Don Khong you could also call **Done Khong Guesthouse** (☎ 020-98789994; kham_bkk1987@yahoo.com; Muang Khong) or Pon's Riverside Guesthouse (p380) on that island to see if a boat is coming from there in the morning. If so, you can probably buy a seat (40,000K) for the return journey.

Bolaven Plateau Region

Spreading across parts of all four southern provinces, the fertile Bolaven Plateau (ພູພຽງບໍລະເວນ; known in Lao as Phu Phieng Bolaven) is famous for its cool climate, dramatic waterfalls and high-grade coffee.

The French started planting coffee, rubber and bananas in the early 20th century, but many left following independence in the 1950s and the rest followed when US bombardment began in the late '60s. Controlling the Bolaven Plateau was considered strategically vital to both the Americans and North Vietnamese, as evidenced by the staggering amount of unexploded ordnance (UXO) still lying around. But where it has been cleared, both local farmers and large companies are busy cultivating coffee. Other local products include fruit, cardamom and rattan.

The largest ethnic group on the plateau is the Laven (Bolaven means 'Home of the Laven'). Several other Mon-Khmer ethnic groups, including the Alak, Katu, Tahoy and Suay, also live on the plateau and its escarpment.

Toumlan

Toumlan (ບ້ານຕຸ້ມລານ), 50km north of Salavan, is a slapped-together boomtown with some small shops and restaurants and several oversized, out-of-place government buildings. The surrounding Katang villages comprise one of Laos' most important weaving regions. Women here weave a variety of silk and cotton styles, including some *mat-mee* (ikat or tie-dye), using large wooden floor looms instead of the back-strap looms typical in the Bolaven region.

Tat Lo

Tat Lo (ຕາດເລາະ; pronounced *dàat láw*) has taken a place on the backpacker trail thanks to an attractive setting, cheap accommodation and some beautiful waterfalls. It lacks the party scene of Don Det and Vang Vieng, and locals are set on it staying this way. Thankfully, several Westerners who have settled here and opened businesses are in full agreement. The result is a serenity that sees many visitors stay longer than they planned.

The availability of day treks, along with widespread use of English, makes Tat Lo by far the best base for getting to know the Bolaven Plateau, even though it actually sits against the foot of it, rather than up on top of it. The real name of Tat Lo village is Ban Saen Vang, but these days everybody just calls it Tat Lo.

The most spectacular of the waterfalls in the area is **Tat Soung** (ຕາດສູງ; parking 5000K), 8km south of Tat Lo town, uphill almost the entire way. It has a 50m-drop over the edge of the Bolaven Plateau, and although the dam has damaged these falls more than the others – slowing them to a trickle for most of the year – you can walk around the rocky top of the falls from where the views are fantastic. During heavy August to October rains, when they reach their full width, the falls themselves are quite spectacular too.

Sleeping & Eating

★ **Captain Hook Coffee Break** HOMESTAY $
(☎ 020-98930406; www.facebook.com/hook.laos; homestay incl breakfast & dinner per person 50,000K) Mr Hook (who, not surprisingly, has acquired the nickname 'Captain Hook' from foreigners) runs an excellent organic coffee farm and homestay 15km from Tat Lo. He's full of stories, and the unvarnished look at Katu village life you get will be quite enlightening; often shocking. His village is Ban Khokphung Tai, halfway between Ban Beng and Tha Taeng.

★Mr Vieng Coffee & Homestay HOMESTAY $
(☎020-99837206; per person 20,000K, per meal 15,000K) This is a fun and friendly homestay on a coffee plantation in **Ban Houay Houn** (ບ້ານຫ້ວຍຫຸນ), right along Rte 20, 19km southwest of Tat Lo. Rooms are simple, but quite good for the price, and the ethnic Katu couple who run it give plantation tours (15,000K per person), and make and sell weavings.

Tadlo Lodge RESORT $$
(☎031-218889; souriyavincent@yahoo.com; r/ste incl breakfast from US$50/100; ❄📶) Situated above Tat Hang, about 1km from Tat Lo village, this is the only semi-fancy lodging around. The main building exudes some classic Lao style, with parquet floors and Buddha statuary, while rooms are stylish and comfortable with decks out front. Only the suite has air-conditioning. Animal lovers should note that the hotel keeps trekking elephants chained up most of the day.

Saise Resort LAOTIAN, THAI $
(mains 20,000-60,000K; ⏲7am-8pm; 📶) Saise Resort has good food (mostly Thai) served on a great deck with an awesome view of Tat Hang waterfall. It's worth making one trip out here during your stay.

Information

Tat Lo Tourism Information Centre (☎020-54455907; kouka222@hotmail.com; ⏲8-11.30am & 1.30-4.30pm Mon-Fri, daily Nov-Feb) This helpful office runs the Tat Lo Guides Association. It should be your first stop if you need a guide or info on local excursions, or plan to venture deeper into Salavan Province. Maps and brochures on the region are available. Kouka and some other guides speak English.

Getting There & Around

Just say 'Tat Lo' at Pakse's Southern Bus Terminal (p374) and you'll be pointed to one of the nine daily buses to Salavan that stop on Rte 20 at Ban Khoua Set (30,000K, two hours), from where it's a 1.5km walk or moto-taxi ride (10,000K) to Tat Lo.

For Sekong (20,000K, one hour) or Attapeu (40,000K, three hours), your best bet is the morning bus that passes through Ban Beng, which is a 15,000K moto-taxi ride away from Tat Lo. In Ban Beng you can also catch some minibuses and *sǒrngtǎaou* to Sekong and passing buses to Paksong (20,000K, one hour). The Tat Lo Tourism Information Centre can call to have buses to Vietnam stop and pick you up at Ban Khoua Set.

Sabai Sabai (☎020-98556831), between the Tat Lo Tourism Information Centre and the bridge, has a few motorcycles for hire for 80,000K per day.

Paksong Area

Paksong, Laos' coffee capital, is not much to look at, most of it having been obliterated in a storm of bombs during the Second Indochina War. Other than doing a coffee tour or buying a fresh cuppa, you probably won't want to stop here. But, many of the waterfalls near the town definitely should be part of your Bolaven itinerary.

Sights & Tours

★Tayicseua WATERFALL
(ຕາດຕາຢິກເສືອ; admission 5000K, parking 5000K) There are seven significant waterfalls (none of them named Tayicseua) and several smaller ones at this remote, but easily accessible private nature reserve. Some sit right near the restaurant-parking area while others, such as postcard-worthy Tat Halang (aka Tat Alang), are down in the forest along a good set of trails, which you can walk without a guide. It's in the early stages of growing into a proper resort but, for now, crowds remain rare.

Due to the size of the area and the serene setting, the best way to visit is to spend the night.

Tayicseua sits off the main paved road 43km from Paksong. Coming from the east it's 4km from the paved road to the signed entrance. For the most part, this dirt road is fine, but there are some steep, rough spots that require care on a motorcycle, especially in the rainy season. The longer dirt road from the west is much smoother.

Jhai Coffee Farmers Co-operative Tours TOURS
(☎020-97672424; www.jhaicoffeehouse.com; Rte 16; tours per person 150,000K) Part of the philanthropic **Jhai Coffee House** (coffee from 10,000K; ⏲8.30am-5.30pm; 📶), these half-day tours run from 9am to noon and go out to a local farmer's home and plantation for a 'bean to cup' lesson on the coffee business. They are only offered between October and January (the picking season), but a 45-minute 'small' tour (50,000K per person) around the coffee shop is available at any time.

Sleeping

★Tayicseua Guesthouse GUESTHOUSE $
(☎020-29878926; www.tayicseua.com; dm 60,000K; 📶) This friendly spot surrounded by seven large waterfalls deserves its rave

GETTING TO VIETNAM: LA LAY TO LALAY

Getting to the border Most people travelling from Pakse to Hué and Danang use sleeper buses, which go through the Lao Bao border crossing east of Savannakhet. The faster, but more dangerous, minibuses, on the other hand, go via Salavan and cross at La Lay (Laos)/Lalay (Vietnam), as do the slow and thoroughly uncomfortable cargo buses, which only save a few seats for passengers. If you're in Salavan, you don't need to backtrack to Pakse. There are usually seats available when the buses from Pakse pass through. There isn't much traffic on this route, so doing the trip in stages is not recommended, but if you're set on it, start with the 7.30am minibus to Samouy (35,000K, 3½ hours) which is very near the border.

At the border The border is open from 6am to 7pm and though it's little more than a shack you will probably not have any hassles (other than the usual Lao 'overtime fee'), assuming you have your Vietnamese visa already, or don't need one. In the reverse, you can get a Lao visa at the border.

Moving on For those going in stages, most of the traffic here is trucks, so you should be able to buy an onward ride, though be sure you know whether the driver will be taking a right at the junction to Hué and Danang or turning left to Dong Ha.

reviews. You'll fall asleep to tumbling water and wake up to birdsong from under mosquito nets in rustic bamboo huts (or your own tent) and share the hot-water showers. A communal lodge overlooks the distant mists of Tat Jariem deep in the valley below. Simple meals cost 20,000K.

Everything is very basic, but all things considered, this place is perfect for those OK with roughing it a bit. Wooden bungalows might debut in 2017.

Sinouk Coffee Resort BOUTIQUE HOTEL **$$**
(☎030-9558960; www.sinoukcoffeeresort.com; r US$40-90; ⊖❄@🛜) Set beside a babbling brook on a working coffee plantation 32km northeast of Paksong on the road to Tha Taeng, there's a hill-station feel here. Like its sister lodge, Pakse's Residence Sisouk (p369), it's loaded with indigenous textiles, period furniture and framed old-world photos. It's also worth stopping in for a meal (mains 25,000K to 75,000K) amidst the manicured gardens if you're passing by.

Salavan

Just 30km from popular Tat Lo, the best thing visitors can do in tourist-free Salavan (ສາລະວັນ; also spelt Saravan and Saravane) is get out and explore the ethnic diversity of the countryside.

While more than half of the population of Salavan Province is ethnically Lao (Loum and Soung), few are native to this area. The remainder of the 350,000 inhabitants belong to various Mon-Khmer groups such as expert weavers, the Katang.

By virtue of the fact that the main building is fairly youngish and that the rooms have wi-fi, the mostly clean **Phonexay Hotel** (☎034-211093; Rte 15; r with fan 70,000-80,000K, air-con 120,000-200,000K; ❄🛜), 1.5km west of the market, is the best lodging choice in town. But that's not a tough competition to win. One of the few dining options in town with an English menu, **Sabaidee Salavan** (mains 15,000-50,000K; ⏱7am-9pm) has all the standard Lao and Thai dishes, but also offers sukiyaki.

ℹ Information

UXO remain a serious problem in rural areas, so exercise caution if you go out exploring the province beyond main roads: stick to established tracks and trails.

Salavan Tourism Centre (034-211528; ⏱8am-4pm Mon-Fri) The staff here is eager to help and some are knowledgeable about tourism in the area. It's south of the market, next to the large, glass-fronted Phongsavanh Bank building.

ℹ Getting There & Away

Salavan's bus terminal is 2km west of the town centre, where Rte 20 meets Rte 15. There are nine daily buses to Pakse (fan/air-con 30,000/40,000K, three hours), with three (8.30am, 4pm, 4.30pm) continuing on to Vientiane (regular/sleeper 130,000/190,000K, 12 to 14 hours), and one bus to Attapeu (50,000K, 4½ hours). No buses to Vietnam originate here, but you can hope one passing through from Pakse has empty seats.

Sekong

This sleepy city on its namesake river was built from scratch in 1984, the year Sekong Province was created. It's not a destination as much as a place intrepid travellers visit just because it's there.

This may change in the next few years when a new bridge shortens the route from Ubon Ratchathani, Thailand, to the Vietnamese port of Danang, facilitating access to gold and other mines on the Dak Cheung Plateau. A border crossing open to foreigners should also be part of the equation.

By population Sekong (ເຊກອງ) is the smallest of Laos' provinces and also the most ethnically diverse: almost all of its 90,000 inhabitants are from one of 14 different Mon-Khmer tribal groups, with the Alak, Katu, Talieng, Yai and Nge the largest. These diverse groups are not Buddhists, so you won't see temples. Rather, their belief systems mix animism and ancestor worship. Sekong is also one of the country's poorest provinces.

Sights

South of Sekong, Rte 16 morphs into Rte 11 and the waterfalls along this road have more appeal than anything actually in the town.

For a bit of easy adventure, take a relaxed ride on the new highway to Dak Cheung. It's a beautiful and still relatively remote region, especially once you hit the mountains. Until the new bridge is completed, cross the Se Kong on the rickety ferry (5000K) southwest of the market and follow the dirt road for 2.5km to reach the pavement.

Tat Faek WATERFALL

(ຕາດແຟກ; admission 5000K) Sixteen kilometres south of Sekong, and well-signed off Rte 11, is this wide, beautiful 5m-high waterfall where you can swim in the pool atop the falls. Do heed the red and white 'Watch Out For Biting Fish' signs around the lower pools as a diabolical puffer fish called *pa pao* lurks there. Stories of their fondness for attacking men's penises are only legend – told with glee by local women – but they really can take a chunk of flesh out of unlucky swimmers with their razor-sharp teeth.

Food and drinks are sold daily until 5pm. The thatched-roof dining huts around the falls fill up with locals on weekends and holidays.

Sleeping & Eating

P&S Garden RESORT $

(020-98836555; 1-/2-person tents 40,000/50,000K;) This lovely and orderly resort near **Tat Hua Kon** (ຕາດຫົວຄົນ; 5000K) is a welcome surprise. Though it started out with just tents, which are pitched on a stilted and thatched-roof platform, actual guestrooms are in the works. The restaurant serves coffee and juice and a small menu (mains 15,000K to 80,000K) of Lao food including 'bugs' (roasted crickets) and spicy papaya salad.

Thida Hotel Restaurant LAOTIAN, THAI $

(mains 20,000-50,000K; 6am-10pm;) Although its perch high above the river with good mountain views would be enough reason to dine here, the kitchen holds up its end of the bargain with good Thai food including the obligatory *tom yam gung* and stir-fried holy basil.

Information

Lao Development Bank (8am-3.30pm Mon-Fri) Located 200m southwest of the market on the central road. It changes Thai baht, euro, US dollars and more, and has a Western Union branch.

UNDERSTAND LAOS

Laos Today

Up until early 2008 it was all going extremely well for Laos, with record figures of foreign visitors tuning into the buzz about this little nation, which was fast becoming switched on to responsible ecotourism; newly built hydroelectric power dams; copper and gold mining concessions; and largely foreign investors keen to climb into bed with Laos' natural resources. Then the economic axe fell on the US and those subprime mortgages started impacting every aspect of Laos' attempt, by 2020, to escape its status as one of the 20 poorest nations. Suddenly the foreign investors pulled out because of their own lack of liquidity, and mining concessions collapsed as the price of copper was slashed. Fewer travellers were arriving, too. Through no fault of its own, Laos looked to be heading back to the dark days of stagnation.

Times haven't been easy, but they certainly could have been worse: by 2011, despite global gloom, Laos reported growth of 8%, one of the strongest rates in Asia. And now, as China flourishes, Laos is reaping the rewards of the two countries' close association. China has moved in to grab what it can in return for improving Laos' transport infrastructure. Beijing's Southeast Asian rail network will eventually connect the red giant with countries as far afield as Pakistan, India and Singapore, and to achieve this the network will pass directly through Laos. Rte 3, from Kunming to Vientiane, via Luang Prabang, should be ready in the next five years, and, in the next 10 years, it's predicted that travellers will be able to travel at speeds of up to 400km/h through this beautiful green country. How this will impact on this sleepy paradise is anyone's guess, but it's all the more reason for you to visit right now. As US relations begin to improve and the first rumblings of gay expression make themselves heard in the capital, Laos is on one hand embracing the 21st century, while holding fast to its old-guard hegemony. New president Bounnhang Vorachith and prime minister Thongloun Sisoulith both came to power in 2016 and early populist moves included a total ban on logging in Laos. But it remains to be seen if there is actually the political will to enforce this on the ground.

History

Throughout its long history, the inhabitants of modern-day Laos have been subject to the politics and aspirations of more-powerful neighbours in Cambodia, Vietnam, Thailand and China. Even its first taste of nationhood, with the rise of the Lan Xang kingdom, was achieved thanks to Khmer military muscle.

Kingdom of Lan Xiang

Before the French, British, Chinese and Siamese drew a line around it, Laos was a collection of disparate principalities subject to an ever-revolving cycle of war, invasion, prosperity and decay. Laos' earliest brush with nationhood was in the 14th century, when Khmer-backed Lao warlord Fa Ngum conquered Wieng Chan (Vientiane). It was Fa Ngum who gave his kingdom the title still favoured by travel romantics and businesses – Lan Xang, or (Land of a) Million Elephants. He also made Theravada Buddhism the state religion and adopted the symbol of Lao sovereignty that remains in use today, the Pha Bang Buddha image, after which Luang Prabang is named. Lan Xang reached its peak in the 17th century, when it was the dominant force in Southeast Asia.

The French

After taking over Annam and Tonkin (modern-day Vietnam) in 1883, the French negotiated with Siam to relinquish its territory east of the Mekong; thus, Laos was born and absorbed into French Indochina.

The country's diverse ethnic make-up and short history as a nation state meant nationalism was slow to form. The first nationalist movement, the Lao Issara (Free Lao), was created to prevent the country's return to French rule after the invading Japanese

SPIRIT CULTS

No matter where you are in Laos the practice of *pěe* (spirit) worship, sometimes called animism, won't be far away. *Pěe* worship predates Buddhism and despite being officially banned it remains the dominant non-Buddhist belief system. But for most Lao, Buddhist beliefs coexist peacefully with respect for the *pěe* that are believed to inhabit natural objects.

Spirit houses are often ornately decorated miniature temples, built as a home for the local spirit. Residents must share their space with the spirit and go to great lengths to keep it happy, offering enough incense and food that the spirit won't make trouble for them.

In Vientiane, Buddhism and spirit worship flourish side by side at Wat Si Muang. The central image at the temple is not a Buddha figure but the *lák méuang* (city pillar from the time of the Khmer empire), in which the guardian spirit for the city is believed to reside. Many local residents make daily offerings before the pillar, while at the same time praying to a Buddha figure. A form of *pěe* worship visitors can partake in is the *bąasĭi* ceremony.

The Hmong-Mien tribes also practise animism, plus ancestral worship. Some Hmong groups recognise a pre-eminent spirit that presides over all earth spirits; others do not. The Akha, Lisu and other Tibeto-Burman groups mix animism and ancestor cults.

left at the end of WWII. In 1953 sovereignty was granted to Laos by the French. Internecine struggles followed, with the Pathet Lao (Country of the Lao) army forming an alliance with the Vietnamese Viet Minh, which had also been opposing French rule in its own country. Laos was set to become a stage on which the clash of communist ambition and US anxiety over the perceived Southeast Asian 'domino effect' played itself out.

The Secret War

In 1954 at the Geneva Conference, Laos was declared a neutral nation – as such neither Vietnamese nor US forces could cross its borders. Thus began a game of cat and mouse as a multitude of CIA operatives secretly entered the country to train anticommunist Hmong fighters in the jungle. From 1964 to 1973, the US, in response to the Viet Minh funnelling massive amounts of war munitions down the Ho Chi Minh Trail, devastated eastern and northeastern Laos with nonstop carpet-bombing (reportedly a plane load of ordnance dropped every eight minutes). The intensive campaign exacerbated the war between the Pathet Lao and the US-backed Royal Lao Army and, if anything, increased domestic support for the communists.

The US withdrawal in 1973 saw Laos divided up between Pathet Lao and non-Pathet Lao, but within two years the communists had taken over completely and the Lao People's Democratic Republic (PDR) was created under the leadership of Kaysone Phomvihane. Around 10% of Laos' population fled, mostly to Thailand. The remaining opponents of the government – notably tribes of Hmong who fought with and were funded by the CIA – were sent to re-education camps for indeterminate periods or supressed. It's alleged that two of these camps still endure in the far north, though this is hotly denied.

A New Start

Laos entered the political family of Southeast Asian countries known as Asean in 1997, two years after Vietnam. In 2004 the USA promoted Laos to Normal Trade Relations, cementing the end to a trade embargo in place since the communists took power in 1975. Politically, the Party remains firmly in control. And with neighbours like one-party China and Vietnam, there seems little incentive for Laos to move towards any meaningful form of democracy. While still heavily reliant on foreign aid, Laos has committed to income-generating projects in recent years in a bid to increase its prosperity. Ecotourism is flourishing and the country is enjoying more Western visitors every year. China has recently pulled the financial reins on its extensive high-speed rail network across Southeast Asia, with Laos now stepping in and picking up the cost in the form of a US$7.2 billion loan from China. It's a big gamble, but the hope is that it will improve trade, with the rail system passing through the likes of Luang Prabang and Vientiane.

In 2012 the international press started asking embarrassing questions over the disappearance of Sombath Somphone, an award-winning civil society activist and land rights campaigner, with fingers directly pointed at the Lao government as the main culprit. In 2013, in an effort to counterbalance China's growing influence over the region, the Obama administration sent then-Secretary of State Hillary Clinton to broker tighter relations with Laos.

People & Culture

People & Population

As many as 132 ethnic groups make up the people of Laos. Sixty per cent of these people are Lao Loum (lowland Lao); they have the most in common with their Thai neighbours, and it's their cultural beliefs and way of life that are largely known as 'Lao culture'. The remainder are labelled according to the altitude their groups live at: Lao Thai (living in valleys up to an altitude of 400m, composed of Black Thai and White Thai); Lao Thoeng (midlevel mountain slopes, including Khamu, Lamet and Alak); and Lao Soung (living 1000m or more above sea level, including the Hmong, Mien and Akha).

Trying to homogenise the people and psyche of Laos is precarious, as the country is really a patchwork of different beliefs, ranging from animism to the prevailing presence of Theravada Buddhism; often both combined. But certainly there's a commonality in the laid-back attitude you'll encounter. Some of this can be ascribed to Buddhism, with its emphasis on controlling extreme emotions by keeping *jai yen* (cool heart) and making merit – doing good in order to receive good. You'll rarely hear a heated argument, and can expect a level of kindness unpractised to such a national degree in neighbouring countries.

The Lao are very good at enjoying the 'now', and they do this with a mixture of the *bor ben nyăng* (no problem) mentality and a devotion to *móoan* (fun). If a job is *bor móoan* (no fun), it is swiftly abandoned in pursuit of another, even if it means less income.

Government spending on education amounts to 11.7% of total public spending. Education has improved in recent years, with school enrolment rates at 85%, though many drop out by the time they reach secondary education – the planting and harvesting of crops, especially among the highlands, is seen as more important than education, as the whole family is involved.

Religion

Most lowland Lao are Theravada Buddhists and many Lao males choose to be ordained temporarily as monks, typically spending anywhere from a month to three years at a wat. Indeed, a young man is not considered 'ripe' until he has completed his spiritual term. After the 1975 communist victory, Buddhism was suppressed, but it soon became clear its religious omnipresence was too strong and by 1992 the government relented. However, monks are still forbidden to promote *pěe* (spirit) worship, which has been officially banned in Laos along with *săiyasàht* (folk magic).

Arts & Architecture

The true expression of Lao art is found in its religious sculpture, temples and handicrafts. Distinctively Lao is the Calling for Rain Buddha, a standing image with hands held rigidly at his sides. Similarly widespread is the Contemplating the Bodhi Tree Buddha, with crossed hands at the front.

Wats in Luang Prabang feature *sĭm* (chapels), with steep, low roofs. The typical Lao *thât* (stupa) is a four-sided, curvilinear, spire-like structure. There are also hints of classical architectural motifs entering modern architecture, as with Vientiane's Wattay International Airport.

Many of the beautiful villas from the days of Indochina were torn down by the new regime in favour of harsh Soviet designs, though fortunately there are plenty of villas left, with their distinctive shuttered windows and classic French provincial style.

Traditional Lao art has a more limited range than that of its Southeast Asian neighbours, partly because Laos has a more modest history as a nation state and partly because its neighbours have stolen or burnt

THE LAOS PSYCHE

To a large degree 'Lao-ness' is defined by Buddhism, specifically Theravada Buddhism, which emphasises the cooling of human passions. Thus strong emotions are a taboo in Lao society. *Kamma* (karma), more than devotion, prayer or hard work, is believed to determine one's lot in life, so the Lao tend not to get too worked up over the future. It's a trait often perceived by outsiders as a lack of ambition.

Lao commonly express the notion that 'too much work is bad for your brain' and they often say they feel sorry for people who 'think too much'. Education in general isn't highly valued, although this attitude is changing with modernisation and greater access to opportunities beyond the country's borders. Avoiding any undue psychological stress, however, remains a cultural norm. From the typical Lao perspective, unless an activity – whether work or play – contains an element of *móoan* (fun), it will probably lead to stress.

The contrast between the Lao and the Vietnamese is an example of how the Annamite Chain has served as a cultural fault line dividing Indo-Asia and Sino-Asia, as well as a geographic divide. The French summed it up as: 'The Vietnamese plant the rice, the Cambodians tend the rice and the Lao listen to it grow.' And while this saying wasn't meant as a compliment, a good number of French colonialists found the Lao way too seductive to resist, and stayed on.

The Lao have always been quite receptive to outside assistance and foreign investment, since it promotes a certain degree of economic development without demanding a corresponding increase in productivity. The Lao government wants all the trappings of modern technology – the skyscrapers seen on socialist propaganda billboards – without having to give up Lao traditions, including the *móoan* philosophy. The challenge for Laos is to find a balance between cultural preservation and the development of new attitudes that will lead the country towards a measure of self-sufficiency.

what art did exist. Upland crafts include gold- and silversmithing among the Hmong and Mien tribes, and tribal Thai weaving (especially among the Thai Dam and Thai Lü). Classical music and dance have all but evaporated, partly due to the vapid tentacles of Thai pop and itinerant nature of Laos' young workforce.

Food & Drink

Food

Lao cuisine lacks the variety of Thai food, but there are some distinctive dishes to try. The standard Lao breakfast is *fĕr* (rice noodles), usually served floating in a broth with vegetables and a meat of your choice. The trick is in the seasoning, and Lao people will stir in some fish sauce, lime juice, dried chillies, mint leaves, basil, or one of the wonderful speciality hot chilli sauces that many noodle shops make, testing it along the way.

Lâhp is the most distinctively Lao dish, a delicious spicy salad made from minced beef, pork, duck, fish or chicken, mixed with fish sauce, small shallots, mint leaves, lime juice, roasted ground rice and lots and lots of chillies. Another famous Lao speciality is *đạm màhk hung* (known as *som tam* in Thailand), a salad of shredded green papaya mixed with garlic, lime juice, fish sauce, sometimes tomatoes, palm sugar, land crab or dried shrimp and, of course, chillies by the handful.

In lowland Lao areas almost every dish is eaten with *kòw nĕeo* (sticky rice), which is served in a small basket. Take a small amount of rice and, using one hand, work it into a walnut-sized ball before dipping it into the food.

In main centres, delicious French baguettes are a popular breakfast food. Sometimes they're eaten with condensed milk, or with *kai* (eggs) in a sandwich that also contains Lao-style pâté and vegetables.

Virtually all restaurants in Laos are inexpensive by international standards. The following price ranges refer to a main course.

$ less than US$5 (40,000K)

$$ US$5–15 (40,000–120,000K)

$$$ more than US$15 (120,0000K)

Drink

ALCOHOLIC DRINKS

Beerlao remains a firm favourite with 90% of the nation, while officially illegal *lòw-lŏw* (Lao liquor, or rice whisky) is a popular drink among lowland Lao. It's usually taken neat and offered in villages as a welcoming gesture.

NONALCOHOLIC DRINKS

Water purified for drinking purposes is simply called *nâam deum* (drinking water), whether it's boiled or filtered. All water offered to customers in restaurants or hotels will be purified, and purified water is sold everywhere. Having said that, do be careful of the water you drink – there was an outbreak of E. coli in 2008, so check the ice in your drink originated from a bottle.

Juice bars proliferate around Vientiane and Luang Prabang, and smoothies are usually on the menu in most Western-leaning cafes. Lao coffee is usually served strong and sweet. Lattes and cappuccinos are springing up across the country with pasteurised milk coming from Thailand.

Chinese-style green tea is the usual ingredient in *nâm sáh* or *sáh lôw* – the weak, refreshing tea traditionally served free in restaurants. If you want Lipton-style tea, ask for *sáa hâwn* (hot tea).

Environment

Deforestation

In 2016 the new president of Laos banned the export of timber and logs, throwing long-established illegal smuggling operations into panic. Since the ban, truckloads of hardwood have been seized from forest hideouts and sawmills across the country. In 2015 Radio Free Asia exposed a Lao politburo member's son as a smuggling kingpin of hardwood trees across the border into China via Mohan, and it's widely alleged that illegal logging has been clandestinely run by elements of the Lao Army, such as in Khammuan Province and remote areas of the country's far south.

The national electricity-generating company also profits from the timber sales each time it links a Lao town or village with the national power grid, as it clear-cuts along Lao highways. Large-scale plantations and mining, as well as swidden (slash-and-burn) methods of cultivation, are also leading to habitat loss. This can have a knock-on effect in rural communities: in some rural areas 70% of non-rice foods come from the forest.

The current president has pledged to recover forest levels to 70% by 2020 or resign.

It remains to be seen how successful the government will be in carrying out this pledge.

Wildlife

The mountains, forests and river networks of Laos are home to a range of animals both endemic to the country and shared with its Southeast Asian neighbours. Nearly half of the animal species native to Thailand are shared by Laos, with the higher forest cover and fewer hunters meaning that numbers are often greater in Laos. Almost all wild animals, however, are threatened to some extent by hunting and habitat loss.

In spite of this Laos has seen several new species discovered in recent years, such as the bent-toed gecko and long-toothed pipistrelle bat, while others thought to be extinct have turned up in remote forests. Given their rarity, these newly discovered species are on the endangered list.

As in Cambodia, Vietnam, Myanmar and much of Thailand, most of the fauna in Laos belong to the Indochinese zoogeographic realm (as opposed to the Sundaic domain found south of the Isthmus of Kra in southern Thailand or the Palaearctic to the north in China).

Notable mammals endemic to Laos include the lesser panda, raccoon dog, Lao marmoset rat, Owston's civet and the pygmy slow loris. Other important exotic species found elsewhere in the region include the Malayan and Chinese pangolins, 10 species of civet, marbled cat, Javan and crab-eating mongoose, the serow (sometimes called Asian mountain goat) and goral (another type of goat-antelope), and cat species including the leopard cat and Asian golden cat.

Among the most notable of Laos' wildlife are the primates. Several smaller species are known, including Phayre's leaf monkey, François' langur, the Douc langur and several macaques. Two other primates that are endemic to Laos are the concolour gibbon and snub-nosed langur. It's the five species of gibbon that attract most attention. Sadly, the black-crested gibbon is endangered, being hunted both for its meat and to be sold as pets in Thailand. Several projects are underway to educate local communities to set aside safe areas for the gibbons.

ASIAN TIGER

Historically, hundreds of thousands of tigers populated Asia, yet today there may be as few as 3000 left in the entire world, occupying a mere 7% of their original range. The survivors in Laos face a constant threat of poaching, habitat loss and conflict with humans. The NPAs in the northeast of Laos, with deep, intractable forest, are thought to harbour the densest populations. During your trek, look out for tiger scat and deep scratch marks on the trunks of trees; should you hear one you'll know it – it's louder and more resonant than a church organ.

MEKONG CATFISH

Growing up to 3m in length and weighing in at 300kg, the world's largest freshwater fish is unique to the Mekong River. Over the past 10 years or so their numbers have dropped an astonishing 90% due to overfishing and, more pointedly, the building of hydroelectric dams that block their migratory paths. There may only be a few hundred left.

IRRAWADDY DOLPHIN

Beak-nosed and less extroverted than their bottlenose counterparts, these shy and critically endangered mammals inhabit a 190km stretch of the Mekong River between Cambodia and Laos. Recent estimates suggest that between 64 and 76 members survive. The best place to see them in Laos is off the southern tip of Don Khon, where a small pod congregates in a deepwater pool. Gillnet fishing and pollution have wiped out their numbers. During their reign in the late 1970s, the Khmer Rouge used to dynamite them indiscriminately.

BLACK-CRESTED GIBBON

The gibbon is the jungle's answer to Usain Bolt. These heavily poached, soulful animals sing with beautiful voices – usually at dawn – which echo hauntingly around the forest, and majestically race through the canopy quicker than any other ape. Males are black and females golden, and, in Laos, they only exist in Bokeo Province (home of the Gibbon Experience). The black-crested gibbon is one of the world's rarest, most endangered species of gibbon.

SURVIVAL GUIDE

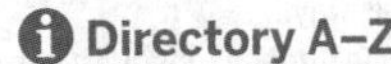

Directory A–Z

ACCOMMODATION

Since the country opened to foreigners in the early 1990s, guesthouses have been steadily multiplying, and most villages that merit a visit will have some form of accommodation. In cities such as Vientiane and Luang Prabang, prices vary wildly, with some truly exceptional boutique hotels that could excite even the most jaded *New York Times* or *Hip Hotels* editor. At the other end of the scale, budget digs – usually a room with a fan and sometimes an en suite – are getting better every year. Even though guesthouse prices are rising, they're still unbeatable value when compared with the West; at less than 80,000K (about US$10) a night, who can argue? The cheapest accommodation is in the far north and deepest south.

Prices of low- and high-season accommodation in Laos differ considerably. High season falls between December and February (the cooler months), and is more expensive. All prices listed in this book are for this period, so should you be travelling at another time of year make sure you ask for a discount.

Homestays

Staying in a village home is becoming increasingly popular. Homestays are invariably in rural areas, cost little (about US$5 for a bed and US$10 for full board) and provide a chance for travellers to experience local life, Lao style.

Villages are small, dusty/muddy depending on the season, and full of kids. You'll be billeted with a family, usually with a maximum of two travellers per family. Toilets will be the squat variety, with scoop flush, in a dark hut at the corner of the block. You'll bathe before dinner, either in a nearby stream or river, or by using a scoop to pour water over yourself from a well, 44-gallon drum or concrete reservoir in your family's yard. Bathing is usually a public event, so don't forget a sarong. Don't expect a mirror.

Food will be simple fare, usually two dishes and sticky rice. In our experience it's almost always been delicious, but prepare yourself for a sticky-rice extravaganza. Even if the food doesn't appeal, you should eat something or your host will lose face. Dinner is usually served on mats on the floor, so prepare to sit lotus-style or with legs tucked under. Don't sit on pillows as that's bad form, and always take off your shoes before entering the house.

Your meal will most likely be followed by a communal drinking session. If you're lucky this will mean cold bottles of Beerlao, but more likely it will revolve around homemade rice alcohol served from a communal cup. The stuff can be pretty harsh, but if you can stomach it, it's a great icebreaker, and some of our best nights in Laos have been spent this way.

Sleeping will probably be under a mosquito net on a mattress on the floor, and might change to 'waking' once the cocks start crowing outside your window.

It might not be luxurious, but a homestay is very much the 'real Laos' and is a thoroughly worthwhile and enjoyable experience. Just remember that for most villagers, dealing with *falang* tourists is pretty new and they are sensitive to your reactions. Their enthusiasm will remain as long as their guests engage with them and accept them, and their lifestyle, without undue criticism. To get the most out of it, take a phrasebook and photos of your family, and, most importantly, a torch, flip-flops, a sarong and toilet paper.

Price Ranges

The following price ranges refer to a high-season double room with attached bathroom, unless otherwise stated.

$ less than US$25 (200,000K)

$$ US$25–75 (200,000–600,000K)

$$$ more than US$75 (600,000K)

ACTIVITIES

Boat Trips, Kayaking & Tubing

With the Mekong cutting a swathe through the heart of the country, it is hardly surprising to find that boat trips are a major drawcard here. There are also opportunities to explore small jungled tributaries leading to remote minority villages.

Kayaking has exploded in popularity in Laos in the past few years, particularly around Luang Prabang, Nong Khiaw and Vang Vieng, all popular destinations for a spot of paddling. Kayaking trips start from around US$25 per person and are often combined with cycling.

Tubing down the river has long been a popular activity in Vang Vieng and is now a more sedate affair with the clampdown on riverside bars, rope swings and aerial runways. Tubing is a lot of fun, but it's a safer experience sober.

Cycling

Laos is slowly but steadily establishing itself as a cycling destination. For hard-core cyclists, the mountains of northern Laos are the ultimate destination. For those who like a gentler workout, meandering along Mekong villages is memorable, particularly in southern Laos around Si Phan Don.

In most places that see a decent number of tourists, simple single-speed bicycles can be hired for around 20,000K per day. Better mountain bikes will cost from 40,000K to 80,000K per day or US$5 to US$10. Serious tourers should bring their own bicycle. The choice in Laos is fairly limited compared with neighbouring Thailand or Cambodia.

Several tour agencies and guesthouses offer mountain-biking tours, ranging in duration from a few hours to several weeks.

Motorbiking

For those with a thirst for adventure, motorbike trips into remote areas of Laos are unforgettable.

The mobility of two wheels is unrivalled. Motorbikes can traverse trails that even the hardiest 4WD cannot follow. It puts you closer to the countryside – its smells, people and scenery – compared with getting around by car or bus. Just remember to watch the road when the scenery is sublime. Motorbiking is still the mode of transport for many Lao residents, so you'll find repair shops everywhere. If you are not confident riding a motorbike, it's comparatively cheap to hire someone to drive it for you. For those seeking true adventure there is no better way to go.

Rock Climbing & Caving

When it comes to organised climbing, Vang Vieng and Tha Khaek have some of the best climbing in Southeast Asia, along with excellent instructors and safe equipment. Climbing costs from about US$25 per person for a group of four and rises for more specialised climbs or for instruction.

Real caving of the spelunker variety is not really on offer unless undertaking a professional expedition. However, there are many extensive cave systems that are open to visitors.

Trekking

Trekking in Laos is all about exploring the National Protected Areas (NPAs) and visiting the colourful ethnic-minority villages, many of which host overnight trekking groups. Anything is possible, from half-day hikes to weeklong expeditions that include cycling and kayaking. Most treks have both a cultural and an environmental focus, with trekkers sleeping in village homestays and money going directly to some of the poorest communities in the country. There are now a dozen or more areas you can choose from. Less strenuous walks include jungle hikes to pristine waterfalls and village walks in remote areas. The scenery is often breathtaking, featuring plunging highland valleys, tiers of rice paddies and soaring limestone mountains.

Treks are mostly run by small local tour operators and have English-speaking guides. Prices, including all food, guides, transport, accommodation and park fees, start at about US$25 per person per day for larger groups. For more specialised long treks into remote areas, prices can run into several hundred dollars. In most cases you can trek with as few as two people, with per person costs falling with larger groups.

BOOKS

A Dragon Apparent (1951) Sees Norman Lewis travelling through the twilight of French Indochina, animating his subjects with atmosphere and pathos, as the colonies are about to be lost.

The Lao (2008) Robert Cooper's locally published book (available in Vientiane) is a pithy yet frequently penetrating insight into Lao culture, its psyche and the practicalities of setting up here as an expat.

The Ravens: Pilots of the Secret War of Laos (1987) Christopher Robbins' page-turning account of the Secret War and the role of American pilots and the Hmong is an excellent read.

Shooting at the Moon: The Story of America's Clandestine War in Laos (1998) Roger Warner's well-respected book exposes the Secret War against the Ho Chi Minh Trail, and the CIA and Hmong role in it.

CUSTOMS REGULATIONS

Customs inspections at ports of entry are lax, as long as you're not bringing in more than a moderate amount of luggage. You're not supposed to enter the country with more than 500 cigarettes or 1L of distilled spirits. All the usual prohibitions on drugs, weapons and pornography apply.

EMBASSIES & CONSULATES

There are about 25 embassies and consulates in Vientiane. Many nationalities are served by their embassies in Bangkok, Hanoi or Beijing.

Australian Embassy (Map p292; ☎021-353800; www.laos.embassy.gov.au; Th Tha Deua, Ban Wat Nak, Vientiane; ⏰8.30am-5pm Mon-Fri) Also represents nationals of Canada and New Zealand.

Cambodian Embassy (Map p292; ☎021-314952; Th Tha Deua, Km 3, Ban That Khao, Vientiane; ⏰8.30am-3.30pm Mon-Fri) Issues visas for US$30.

Chinese Embassy (Map p292; ☎021-315105; http://la.china-embassy.org/eng; Th Wat Nak Nyai, Ban Wat Nak, Vientiane; ⏰8-11.30am Mon-Fri) Issues visas in four working days.

French Embassy (Map p296; ☎021-215258; www.ambafrance-laos.org; Th Setthathirath, Ban Si Saket, Vientiane; ⏰9am-12.30pm & 2-5.30pm Mon-Fri)

German Embassy (Map p292; ☎021-312110; www.vientiane.diplo.de; Th Sok Pa Luang, Vientiane; ⏰9am-noon Mon-Fri)

Myanmar Embassy (Map p292; ☎021-314910; Th Sok Pa Luang, Vientiane; ⏰8.30am-3.30pm Mon-Fri) Issues tourist visas in three days for US$20.

Thai Embassy (Map p292; ☎021-214581; www.thaiembassy.org/vientiane; Th Kaysone Phomvihane, Vientiane; ⏰8.30am-noon & 1-3.30pm Mon-Fri) For visa renewals and extensions, head to the consulates in **Vientiane** (Map p292; ☎021-214581; 15 Th Bourichane, Vientiane; ⏰8am-noon & 1-4.30pm) or **Savannakhet** (☎041-212373; Rte 9 West, Savannakhet; ⏰8.30am-4.30pm Mon-Fri), which issue same-day tourist and non-immigrant visas (1000B).

UK Embassy (Map p292; ☎030-7700000; www.gov.uk; Th J Nehru, Ban Saysettha, Vientiane; ⏰8.30-11.30am Mon-Fri)

US Embassy (☎021-487000; http://laos.usembassy.gov; Th Tha Deua, Ban Somvang

Thai, Km 9, Hatsayfong District, Vientiane; ⏰8.30am-5pm Mon-Fri) Based in a new building to the south of the city.

Vietnamese Embassy (Map p292; ☎021-413400; www.mofa.gov.vn/vnemb.la; Th That Luang, Vientiane; ⏰8.30am-5.30pm Mon-Fri) Issues tourist visas in three working days for US$45, or in one day for US$60, as does the **Luang Prabang consulate** (Map p318; www.vietnamconsulate-luangprabang.org; Th Naviengkham, Luang Prabang; ⏰8-11.30am & 1.30-5.30pm Mon-Fri). At the consulates in **Pakse** (☎031-214199; www.vietnamconsulate-pakse.org; Th 21; ⏰7.30-11.30am & 2-4.30pm Mon-Fri) and **Savannakhet** (p363), visas cost US$60.

LGBTIQ TRAVELLERS

For the most part Lao culture is very tolerant of homosexuality, although lesbianism is often either denied completely or misunderstood. The gay and lesbian scene is not nearly as prominent as in neighbouring Thailand, but you might find something happening in Vientiane if you're lucky.

Strictly speaking, homosexuality is illegal, though we haven't heard of police busting anyone in recent years. In any case, public displays of affection, whether heterosexual or homosexual, are frowned upon.

Sticky Rice (www.stickyrice.ws) Gay travel guide covering Laos and Asia.

Utopia (www.utopia-asia.com) Gay travel information and contacts, including some local gay terminology.

INTERNET ACCESS

Free wi-fi is pretty standard these days and available in many guesthouses, hotels and cafes in the main tourist destinations around Laos. Internet cafes are still around but are increasingly rare. It's possible to get online in most provincial capitals, with prices ranging from 5000K per hour in popular centres to as much as 10,000K or more per hour in provincial backwaters.

Computers in most internet cafes have instant-messaging software and Skype, although headsets are not always available.

LEGAL MATTERS

Although Laos guarantees certain rights, the reality is that you can be fined, detained or deported for any reason, as has been demonstrated repeatedly in cases involving foreigners.

If you stay away from anything you know to be illegal, you should be fine. If not, things might get messy and expensive. Drug possession and using prostitutes are the most common crimes for which travellers are caught, often with the dealer or consort being the one to inform the authorities. Sexual relationships between foreigners and Lao citizens who are not married are illegal; penalties for failing to register a relationship range from fines of US$500 to US$5000, and possibly imprisonment or deportation.

If you are detained, ask to call your embassy or consulate in Laos, if there is one. A meeting or phone call between Lao officers and someone from your embassy/consulate may result in quicker adjudication and release.

Police sometimes ask for bribes for traffic violations and other petty offences.

MAPS

The best all-purpose country map that's generally available is GT-Rider.com's *Laos*, which has a scale of 1:1,650,000. It's available at bookshops in Thailand and at many guesthouses in Laos, as well as online at www.gt-rider.com.

Chiang Mai–based Hobo Maps has produced a series of good maps of Vientiane, Luang Prabang and Vang Vieng. The Lao National Tourism Administration (LNTA) has also produced a few city maps in recent years; pick one up at the tourist information centre (p302) in Vientiane.

MONEY

The official national currency in Laos is the Lao kip (K). Although only kip is legally negotiable in everyday transactions, in reality three currencies are used for commerce: kip, Thai baht (B) and US dollars (US$).

ATMs

ATMs are now found all over Laos. But before you get too excited, ATMs dispense a maximum of 700,000K to 2 million K (about US$85 to US$250) per transaction, depending on the bank, not to mention a variable withdrawal fee. If you also have to pay extortionate charges to your home bank on each overseas withdrawal, this can quickly add up.

Bargaining

Bargaining in most places in Laos is not nearly as tough as in other parts of Southeast Asia. Lao-style bargaining is generally a friendly transaction where two people try to agree on a price that is fair to both of them. Good bargaining, which takes practice, is one way to cut costs.

Cash

Laos relies heavily on the Thai baht and the US dollar for the domestic cash economy. An estimated one-third of all cash circulating in Vientiane, in fact, bears the portrait of the Thai king, while another third celebrates US presidents. Kip is usually preferred for small purchases, while more expensive items and services may be quoted in kip, baht or dollars. Anything costing the equivalent of US$100 or more is likely to be quoted in US dollars.

The majority of transactions will be carried out in kip, however, so it's always worth having a wad in your pocket. Notes come in denominations of

500, 1000, 2000, 5000, 10,000, 20,000, 50,000 and 100,000 kip. Small vendors, especially in rural areas, will struggle to change 100,000K notes.

Credit Cards

A growing number of hotels, upmarket restaurants and gift shops in Vientiane and Luang Prabang accept Visa and MasterCard, and, to a much lesser extent, Amex and JCB. Outside of these main towns, credit cards are virtually useless.

Banque pour le Commerce Extérieur Lao (BCEL) branches in most major towns offer cash advances/withdrawals on MasterCard and Visa credit/debit cards for a 3% transaction fee. Other banks may have slightly different charges, so it might be worth shopping around in Vientiane.

Moneychangers

After years of volatility the kip has in recent times remained fairly stable at about 8000K to the US dollar. Don't, however, count on this remaining the same.

Generally exchange rates are virtually the same whether you're changing at a bank or a moneychanger. Both are also likely to offer a marginally better rate for larger bills (US$50 and US$100) than smaller bills (US$20 and less). Banks in Vientiane and Luang Prabang can generally change UK pounds, euros, Canadian, US and Australian dollars, Thai baht and Japanese yen. Elsewhere most provincial banks usually change only US dollars or baht.

Licensed moneychangers maintain booths around Vientiane (including at Talat Sao) and at some border crossings. Their rates are similar to the banks, but they stay open longer.

There's no real black market in Laos and unless there's an economic crash that's unlikely to change.

Travellers Cheques

Travellers cheques can be cashed at most banks in Laos, but normally only in exchange for kip. Cheques in US dollars are the most readily acceptable. Very few merchants accept travellers cheques.

OPENING HOURS

Bars and clubs 5pm to 11.30pm (later in Vientiane)

Government offices 8am to noon and 1pm to 5pm Monday to Friday

Noodle shops 7am to 1pm

Restaurants 10am to 10pm

Shops 9am to 6pm

POST

Sending post from Laos is not all that expensive and is fairly reliable, but people still tend to wait until they get to Thailand to send parcels. Heading to Cambodia, it's probably smarter to post any parcels from Laos.

When posting any package leave it open for inspection by a postal officer. Incoming parcels might also need to be opened for inspection; there may be a small charge for this mandatory 'service'.

The main post office in Vientiane (p302) has a poste restante service.

PUBLIC HOLIDAYS

Schools and government offices are closed on the following official holidays, and the organs of state move pretty slowly, if at all, during festivals.

ECOTOURISM IN LAOS

With forests covering about half of the country, 20 National Protected Areas (NPAs), 49 ethnic groups, over 650 bird species and hundreds of mammals, Laos has some of Southeast Asia's healthiest ecosystems.

Following the success of the Nam Ha Ecotourism Project in Luang Namtha Province, which began in 1999, the ecotourism industry has grown using a sustainable, internationally developed blueprint which seeks to protect and preserve the interests of ethnic people, wildlife and forests.

Many tour companies in Laos have endured since the inception of ecotourism because they have honoured their pledges to local tribes and conservation. Before splashing out on a trek ask the following questions:

- Are you in a small group that will not disturb village life?
- Will you be led by a local guide?
- Will your trip directly benefit local people whose forests/village you are passing through?
- Does the company channel some of its profits into conservation or local education charities, or is it directly affiliated with organisations such as the WWF and the WCS?

See www.ecotourismlaos.com for further information on environmentally sustainable tourism in Laos.

International New Year 1 January
Army Day 20 January
International Women's Day 8 March
Lao New Year 14–16 April
International Labour Day 1 May
International Children's Day 1 June
Lao National Day 2 December

SAFE TRAVEL

Over the last couple of decades Laos has earned a reputation among visitors as a remarkably safe place to travel, with little crime reported and few of the scams often found in more touristed places such as Vietnam, Thailand and Cambodia. And while the vast majority of Laotians remain honest and welcoming, things aren't quite as idyllic as they once were. The main change has been in the rise of petty crimes, such as theft and low-level scams, which are more annoying than dangerous.

Large areas of eastern and southern Laos are contaminated by unexploded ordnance (UXO). According to surveys by the Lao National UXO Programme (UXO Lao) and other nongovernment UXO clearance organisations, the provinces of Salavan, Savannakhet and Xieng Khuang are the most severely affected provinces, followed by Champasak, Hua Phan, Khammuan, Luang Prabang, Attapeu and Sekong.

Statistically speaking, the UXO risk for the average foreign visitor is low, but travellers should exercise caution when considering off-road wilderness travel in the aforementioned provinces. Stick only to marked paths. And never touch an object that may be UXO, no matter how old and defunct it may appear.

TELEPHONE

With a local SIM card and a 3G or wi-fi connection, the cheapest option is to use internet-based messaging and call apps via a mobile device.

International calls can be made from Lao Telecom offices or the local post office in most provincial capitals and are charged on a per-minute basis, with a minimum charge of three minutes. Calls to most countries cost about 2000K to 4000K per minute. Office hours typically run from about 7.30am to 9.30pm.

Mobile Phones

Roaming is possible in Laos but is generally expensive. Local SIM cards and unlocked mobile phones are readily available.

TOURIST INFORMATION

The Lao National Tourism Administration (LNTA) has tourist offices all over Laos, with the ones in Vientiane and Luang Prabang particularly helpful.

Many offices are well-stocked with brochures and maps, and have easily understood displays of their provincial attractions and English-speaking staff to answer your questions. Offices in Tha Khaek, Savannakhet, Pakse, Luang Namtha, Sainyabuli, Phongsali and Sam Neua are all pretty good, with staff trained to promote treks and other activities in their provinces and able to hand out brochures and first-hand knowledge. They should also be able to help with local transport options and bookings. Alternatively, you can usually get up-to-date information from a popular guesthouse.

The LNTA also runs three very good websites that offer valuable pre-departure information:

Central Laos Trekking (www.trekkingcentrallaos.com)
Ecotourism Laos (www.ecotourismlaos.com)
Laos National Tourism Administration (www.tourismlaos.org)

VISAS

The Lao government issues 30-day tourist visas on arrival at all international airports and most international border crossings.

The whole process is very straightforward. You need between US$30 and US$42 in cash, one passport-sized photo and the name of a hotel or guesthouse. Those without a photo, or who are arriving on a weekend, holiday or after office hours, will have to pay an additional one or two dollars.

The visa fee varies depending on the passport of origin, with Canadians having to fork out the most (US$42) and most other nationalities paying between US$30 and US$35. Pay in US dollars as a flat rate of 1500B (around US$50) is applicable in Thai baht. No other foreign currencies are accepted.

Visa Extensions

The 30-day tourist visa can be extended an additional 90 days at a cost of US$2 per day, but only in major cities such as Vientiane, Luang Prabang, Pakse and Savannakhet.

VOLUNTEERING

Volunteers have been working in Laos for years, usually on one- or two-year contracts that include a minimal monthly allowance. Volunteers are often placed with a government agency and attempt to 'build capacity'. These sort of jobs can lead to non-volunteer work within the non-government organisation (NGO) community.

The alternative approach to volunteering, where you actually pay to be placed in a 'volunteer' role for a few weeks or months, has yet to arrive in Laos in any great capacity. A couple of groups in Luang Prabang need volunteers occasionally, and there are also local projects in places as diverse as Huay Xai, Muang Khua and Sainyabuli.

Australian Volunteers International (www.australianvolunteers.com) Places qualified Australian residents on one- to two-year contracts.

Global Volunteers (www.australianvolunteers.com) Places qualified Australian residents on one- to two-year contracts.

Stay Another Day (www.stayanotherday.org) A good resource for unpaid volunteer opportunities.

Voluntary Service Overseas (VSO; www.vsointernational.org) Places qualified and experienced volunteers for up to two years.

WOMEN TRAVELLERS

Laos is an easy country for women travellers, although it is necessary to be more culturally aware or sensitive than in many parts of neighbouring Thailand. Laos is very safe and violence against women travellers is extremely rare. Everyday incidents of sexual harassment may be more common than they were a few years ago, but they're still much less frequent than in virtually any other Asian country.

The relative lack of prostitution in Laos, as compared with Thailand, has benefits for women travellers. While a Thai woman who wants to preserve a 'proper' image often won't associate with foreign males for fear of being perceived as a prostitute, in Laos this is not the case. Hence a foreign woman seen drinking in a cafe or restaurant is not usually perceived as 'available' as she might be in Thailand. This in turn means that there are generally fewer problems with uninvited male solicitations.

It's highly unusual for most Lao women to wear singlet tops or very short skirts or shorts. So when travellers do, people tend to stare. If you're planning on bathing in a village or river, a sarong is essential.

Traditionally women didn't sit on the roofs of riverboats, because this was believed to bring bad luck. These days most captains aren't so concerned, but if you are asked to get off the roof while men are not, this is why.

WORK

With a large number of aid organisations and a fast-growing international business community, especially in energy and mining, the number of jobs available to foreigners is increasing, but still relatively small. The greatest number of positions are in Vientiane.

Possibilities include teaching English privately or at one of the handful of language centres in Vientiane. Certificates or degrees in English teaching aren't absolutely necessary, but they do help.

If you have technical expertise or international volunteer experience, you might be able to find work with a UN-related program or an NGO providing foreign aid or technical assistance to Laos. These jobs are difficult to find; your best bet is to visit the Vientiane offices of each organisation and enquire about personnel needs and vacancies, then start seeking out potential employers socially and buying them lots of Beerlao. For a list of NGOs operating in Laos, see the excellent www.directoryofngos.org.

ℹ Getting There & Away

Many travellers enter or exit Laos via the country's numerous land and river borders. Flying into Laos is a relatively easy option as there is only a small number of airlines serving Laos and prices don't vary much. Flights and tours can be booked online at www.lonelyplanet.com/bookings.

ENTERING LAOS

Thirty-day tourist visas are readily available on arrival at international airports and most land borders.

Air

Laos has air connections with regional countries including Thailand, Vietnam, Cambodia, Malaysia, Singapore, China and South Korea. The most convenient international gateway to Laos is Bangkok and there are plenty of flights to the Thai capital. If heading to Laos for a shorter holiday, it is cheaper to take an indirect flight to Bangkok with a stop on the way. Once in Bangkok, there are planes, trains and buses heading to Laos.

Land

Laos shares land and/or river borders with Thailand, Myanmar (Burma), Cambodia, China and Vietnam. Border-crossing details change regularly, so ask around and check the Thorn Tree (lonelyplanet.com/thorntree) before setting off It's possible to bring a car or motorcycle into Laos from Cambodia and Thailand with the right paperwork and Lao customs don't object to visitors bringing bicycles into the country, but it is not currently possible from Vietnam, China or Myanmar.

ℹ Getting Around

AIR

With the exception of the Lao Airlines' offices in major cities, where credit cards are accepted for both international and domestic tickets, it is necessary to pay cash in US dollars.

Lao Airlines (www.laoairlines.com) The main airline in Laos handling domestic flights, including between Vientiane and Luang Prabang, Luang Nam Tha, Pakse, Phonsavan, Savannakhet and Udomxai.

Lao Skyway (☎ 021-513022; www.laoskyway.com; Domestic Terminal, Wattay International Airport; ⊙8am-8pm) A newer domestic airline with flights from Vientiane to Udomxai, Luang Prabang, Huay Xai and Luang Namtha.

BICYCLE

The stunningly beautiful roads and light, relatively slow traffic in most towns and on most highways

MOTORCYCLE TIPS

There are few more liberating travel experiences than renting a motorbike and setting off; stopping where you want, when you want. The lack of traffic and stunningly beautiful roads make Laos one of the best places in the region to do it. There are, however, a few things worth knowing before you hand over your passport as collateral to rent a bike.

The bike Price and availability mean that the vast majority of travellers rent Chinese 110cc bikes. No 110cc bike was designed to be used like a dirt bike, but Japanese bikes deal with it better and are worth the extra few dollars a day.

The odometer Given that many roads have no kilometre stones and turn-offs are often unmarked, it's worth getting a bike with a working odometer. Most bike shops can fix an odometer in about 10 minutes for a few dollars. Money well spent, as long as you remember to note the distance when you start.

The gear Don't leave home without sunscreen, a hat, a plastic raincoat or poncho, a bandanna and sunglasses. Even the sealed roads in Laos get annoyingly dusty, so these last two are vital. A helmet is essential (ask for one if they don't offer), as is wearing trousers and shoes, lest you wind up with the ubiquitous leg burn.

The problems Unless you're very lucky, something will go wrong. Budget some time for it.

The responsibility In general, you can ride a motorbike in Laos without a licence, a helmet or any safety gear whatsoever, but for all this freedom you must take all the responsibility. If you have a crash, there won't be an ambulance to pick you up, and when you get to the hospital, facilities will be basic. Carrying a basic medical kit and phone numbers for hospitals in Thailand and your travel insurance provider is a good idea. The same goes for the bike. If it really dies you can't just call the company and get a replacement. You'll need to load it onto the next pick-up or *sŏrngtăaou* and take it somewhere they can fix it. Don't abandon it by the road, or you'll have to pay for another one.

make Laos arguably the best country for cycling in Southeast Asia.

Simple single-speed bicycles can be hired in most places that see a decent number of tourists, usually costing about 20,000K per day. Better mountain bikes will cost from 40,000K to 80,000K per day.

BOAT

More than 4600km of navigable rivers are the highways and byways of traditional Laos, the main thoroughfares being the Mekong, Nam Ou, Nam Khan, Nam Tha, Nam Ngum and Se Kong. The Mekong is the longest and most important route and is navigable year-round between Luang Prabang in the north and Savannakhet in the south. Smaller rivers accommodate a range of smaller boats, from dugout canoes to 'bomb boats' made from war detritus. Whether it's on a tourist boat from Huay Xai to Luang Prabang or on a local boat you've rustled up in some remote corner of the country, it's still worth doing at least one river excursion while in Laos.

BUS

Long-distance public transport in Laos is either by bus or *sŏrngtăaou* (literally 'two rows'), which are converted pick-ups or trucks with benches down either side. Private operators have established VIP buses on some busier routes, offering faster and more luxurious air-con services that cost a little more than normal buses. Many guesthouses can book tickets for a small fee.

Sŏrngtăaou usually service shorter routes within a given province. Most decent-sized villages have at least one *sŏrngtăaou*, which will run to the provincial capital and back most days.

CAR & MOTORCYCLE

Chinese- and Japanese-made 100cc and 110cc step-through motorbikes can be hired for approximately 40,000K to 100,000K per day in most large centres and some smaller towns, although the state of the bikes can vary greatly. No licence is required. Try to get a Japanese bike if travelling any distance out of town. In Vientiane, Luang Prabang, Vang Vieng, Tha Khaek and Pakse, 250cc dirt bikes are available from around US$25 to US$50 per day.

It's possible to hire a self-drive vehicle, but when you consider that a driver usually costs no more, takes responsibility for damage and knows where he's going, it looks risky. Costs run from US$40 to US$100 per day, depending on the route.

Vientiane-based Avis (p304) is a reliable option for car hire. When it comes to motorbikes, try Drivenbyadventure (p304) or Fuark Motorcycle Hire (p304) in Vientiane.

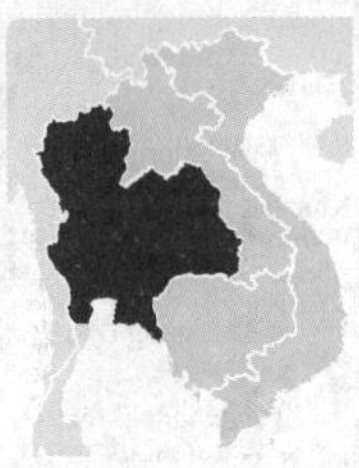

Northern Thailand

POP 186.5 MILLION (IN THAILAND) / ☎66

Includes ➡

Best Places to Eat

- Krua Apsorn (p421)
- Kao Soi Fueng Fah (p473)
- nahm (p424)
- Larp Khom Huay Poo (p482)
- Khao Soi Pa Orn (p494)

Best Places to Sleep

- AriyasomVilla (p420)
- Tamarind Village (p471)
- Chiang Dao Nest (p478)
- Koh Chang Sea Hut (p445)
- Bann Makok (p444)

Why Go?

Thailand is arguably the 'safest' introduction to Southeast Asia, but this doesn't mean it represents any sort of compromise. In fact, we suspect that the secret of Thailand's popularity, in particular that of its northern half, is that it packs a bit of everything.

Bangkok is one of the most vibrant cities in Southeast Asia, yet if contemporary Thai living is not your thing, you can delve into the country's past at historical parks such as those at Sukhothai or Phanom Rung. Similarly, fresh-air fiends will be satiated by upcountry expeditions ranging from a rafting expedition in Nan to the cliff-top views from Ubon Ratchathani's Pha Taem National Park. And culture junkies can get their fix at a homestay in the country's northeast or via a trek in northern Thailand.

And lest we forget: Thailand also functions as a convenient gateway to Cambodia and Laos. What's not to love?

When to Go

Chiang Mai

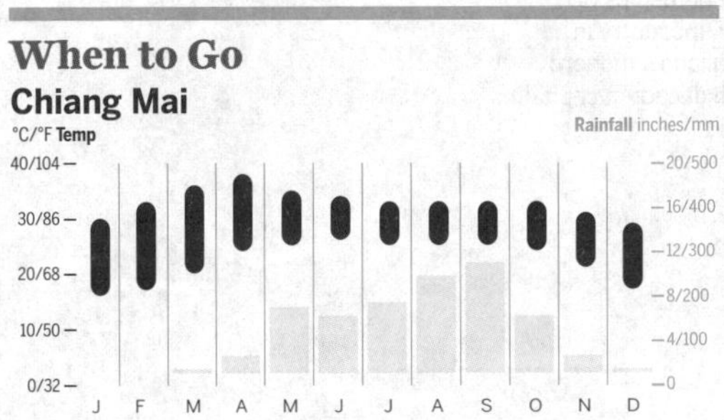

Nov–Feb Thailand's 'winter' is the best time to visit.

Mar–Jun The least desirable time to visit is during Thailand's hot season.

Late Jun–Oct Expect monsoon rains; storms are usually confined to an hour's downpour.

Northern Thailand Highlights

❶ **Chiang Mai Markets** (p474) Picking up some bargains at the Night Bazaar, Saturday Walking Street and Sunday Walking Street.

❷ **Pha Taem National Park** (p464) Feeling awestruck by the scenery.

❸ **Sukhothai** (p482) Cycling around the awesome ruins of Thailand's 'golden age'.

❹ **Surin Project** (p452) Working or living with traditional elephant handlers at this centre in northeastern Thailand.

❺ **Pai** (p479) Getting into the groove of rural northern Thailand in this laid-back place.

❻ **Ko Chang** (p442) Beachcombing and jungle trekking.

❼ **Bangkok** (p404) Recovering from the hardships of the upcountry in Thailand's modern and decadent capital.

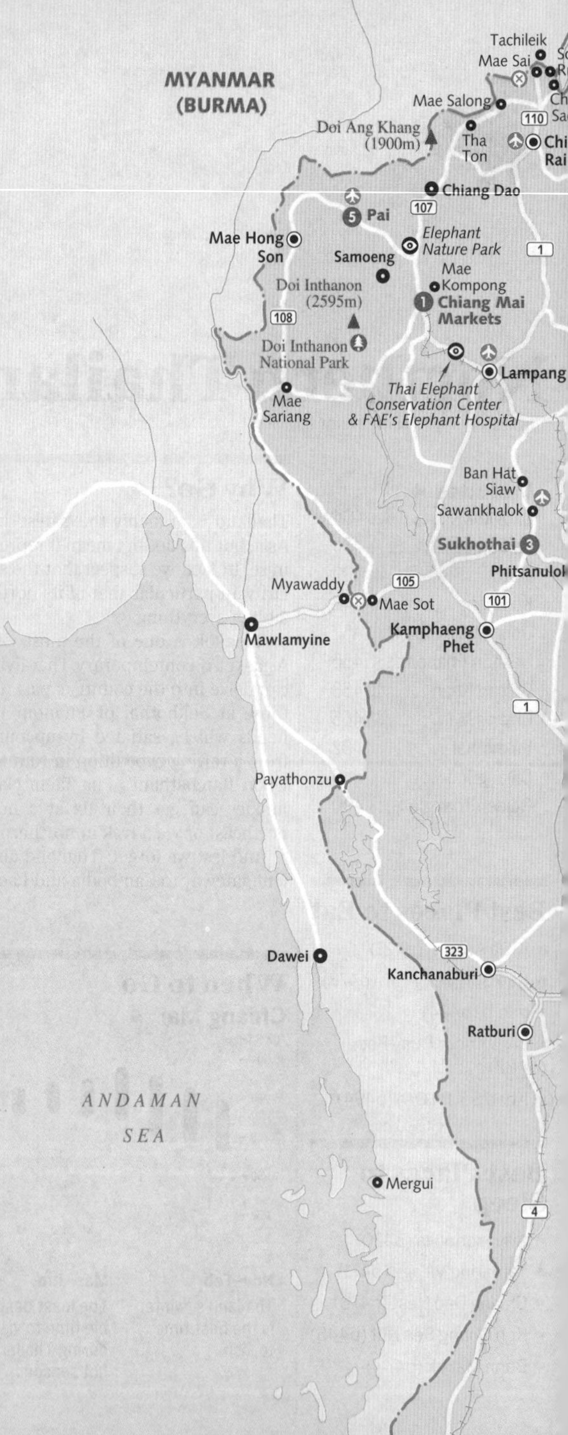

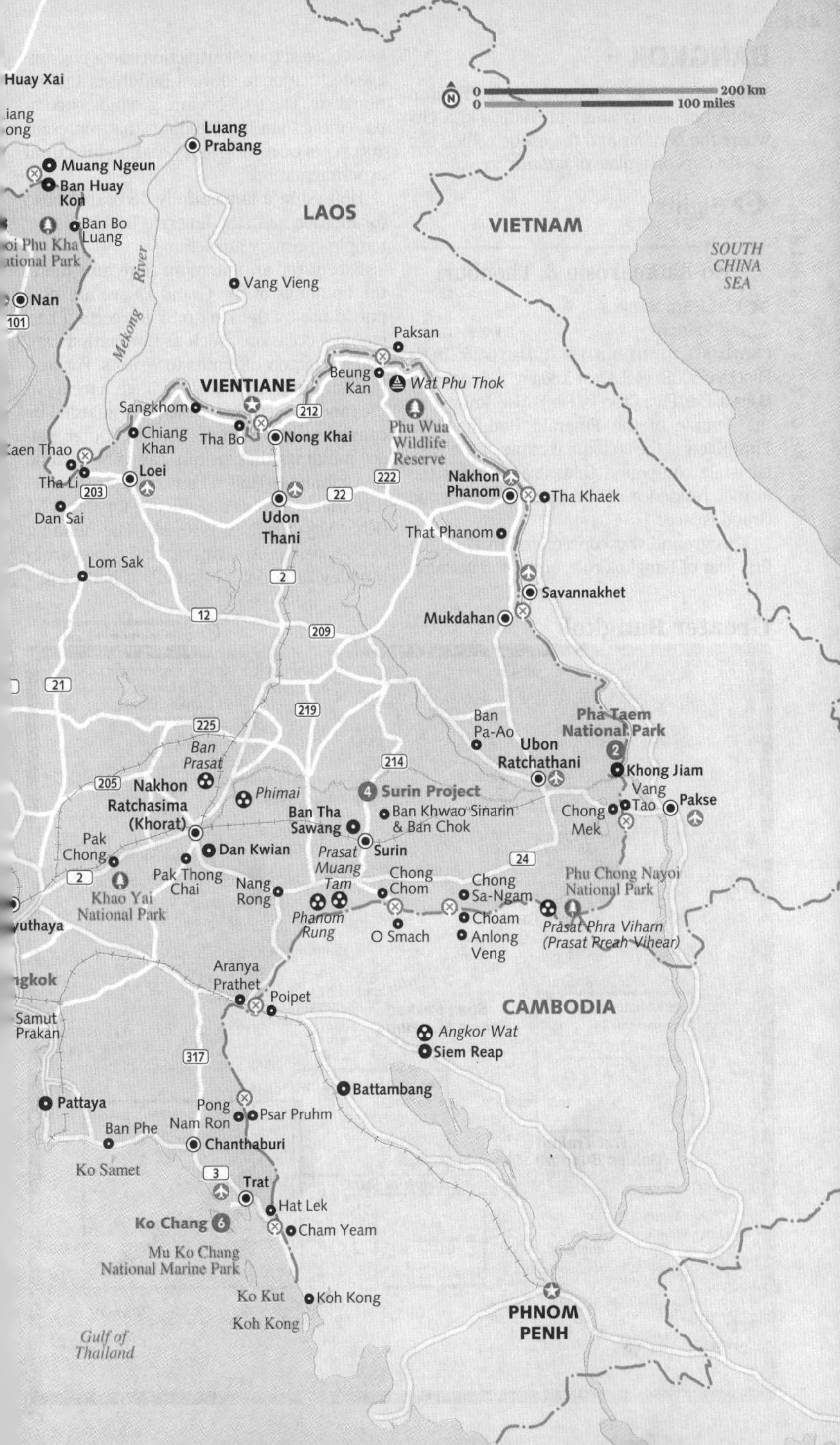

Huay Xai
Luang Prabang
Muang Ngeun
Ban Huay Kon
Ban Bo Luang
LAOS
VIETNAM
SOUTH CHINA SEA
0 200 km
0 100 miles
Nan
Mekong River
Vang Vieng
Paksan
Beung Kan
Wat Phu Thok
VIENTIANE
Sangkhom
Tha Bo
Nong Khai
Phu Wua Wildlife Reserve
Chiang Khan
Tha Li
Loei
Dan Sai
Udon Thani
Nakhon Phanom
Tha Khaek
That Phanom
Lom Sak
Savannakhet
Mukdahan
Ban Pa-Ao
Pha Taem National Park
Ubon Ratchathani
Khong Jiam
Ban Prasat
Nakhon Ratchasima (Khorat)
Phimai
Surin Project
Vang Tao
Pakse
Ban Tha Sawang
Ban Khwao Sinarin & Ban Chok
Chong Mek
Pak Chong
Dan Kwian
Surin
Pak Thong Chai
Prasat Muang Tam
Chong Chom
Chong Sa-Ngam
Phu Chong Nayoi National Park
Khao Yai National Park
Nang Rong
Phanom Rung
O Smach
Choam
Anlong Veng
Prasat Phra Viharn (Prasat Preah Vihear)
Aranya Prathet
Poipet
CAMBODIA
Samut Prakan
Angkor Wat
Siem Reap
Battambang
Pattaya
Pong Nam Ron
Psar Pruhm
Ban Phe
Chanthaburi
Ko Samet
Trat
Hat Lek
Ko Chang
Cham Yeam
Mu Ko Chang National Marine Park
Ko Kut
Koh Kong
Koh Kong
PHNOM PENH
Gulf of Thailand

BANGKOK

Same same, but different. This Thailish T-shirt philosophy sums up Bangkok, a city where the familiar and the exotic collide like the flavours on a plate of *pàt tai*.

Sights

Ko Ratanakosin & Thonburi

★ **Wat Phra Kaew & Grand Palace** BUDDHIST TEMPLE
(วัดพระแก้ว, พระบรมมหาราชวัง; Map p416; Th Na Phra Lan; 500B; 8.30am-3.30pm; Chang Pier, Maharaj Pier, Phra Chan Tai Pier) Also known as the Temple of the Emerald Buddha, Wat Phra Kaew is the colloquial name of the vast, fairy-tale compound that also includes the former residence of the Thai monarch, the Grand Palace.

This ground was consecrated in 1782, the first year of Bangkok rule, and is today Bangkok's biggest tourist attraction and a pilgrimage destination for devout Buddhists and nationalists. The 94.5-hectare grounds encompass more than 100 buildings that represent 200 years of royal history and architectural experimentation.

Housed in a fantastically decorated bòht (ordination hall), the Emerald Buddha is the temple's primary attraction.

Except for an anteroom here and there, the buildings of the Grand Palace are now put to use by the king only for certain ceremonial occasions, such as Coronation Day, and are largely off limits to visitors. Formerly, Thai kings housed their huge harems in the inner palace area, which was guarded by combat-trained female sentries. Outer palace buildings that visitors can view include Borombhiman Hall, a French-inspired structure that served as a residence for Rama VI (King Vajiravudh; r 1910–25). The building to the west is Amarindra Hall (open from Monday to Friday), originally a hall of jus-

Greater Bangkok

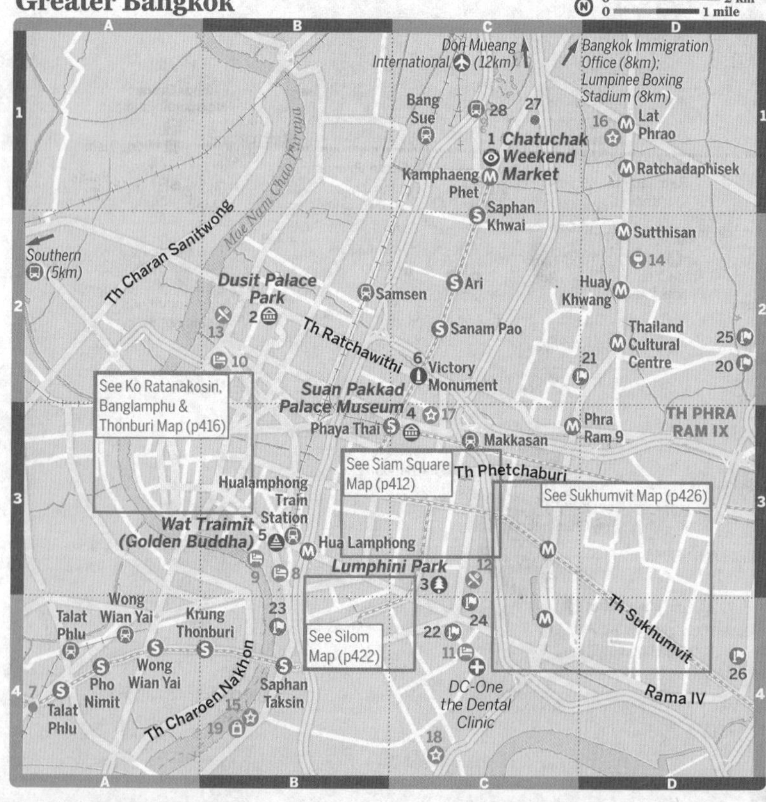

tice and more recently, for coronation ceremonies, and the only palace building that tourists are generally allowed to enter. The largest of the palace buildings is the Chakri Mahaprasat, the Grand Palace Hall. Last is the Ratanakosin-style Dusit Hall, which initially served as a venue for royal audiences and later as a royal funerary hall.

Guides can be hired at the ticket kiosk; ignore offers from anyone outside. An audio guide can be rented for 200B for two hours.

Admission for the complex includes entrance to Dusit Palace Park (p411), which includes Vimanmaek Teak Mansion and Abhisek Dusit Throne Hall.

★ Wat Pho BUDDHIST TEMPLE

(วัดโพธิ์/วัดพระเชตุพน, Wat Phra Chetuphon; Map p416; Th Sanam Chai; 100B; ⏲8.30am-6.30pm; ⛴Tien Pier) You'll find (slightly) fewer tourists here than at Wat Phra Kaew, but Wat Pho is our fave among Bangkok's biggest sights. In fact, the compound incorporates a host of superlatives: the city's largest reclining Buddha, the largest collection of Buddha images in Thailand and the country's earliest centre for public education.

Almost too big for its shelter is Wat Pho's highlight, the genuinely impressive Reclining Buddha.

The rambling grounds of Wat Pho cover 8 hectares, with the major tourist sites occupying the northern side of Th Chetuphon and the monastic facilities found on the southern side. The temple compound is also the national headquarters for the teaching and preservation of traditional Thai medicine, including Thai massage, a mandate legislated by Rama III when the tradition was in danger of extinction. The famous massage school has two **massage pavilions** (Map p416; Wat Pho, Th Sanam Chai; Thai massage per hour 420B; ⏲9am-6pm; ⛴Tien Pier) located within the temple area and additional rooms within the **training facility** (Map p416; ☎02 622 3551; www.watpomassage.com; 392/32-33 Soi Phen Phat; lessons from 2500B, Thai massage per hour 420B; ⏲lessons 9am-4pm, massage 9am-8pm; ⛴Tien Pier) outside the temple.

★ Wat Arun BUDDHIST TEMPLE

(วัดอรุณฯ; Map p416; www.watarun.net; off Th Arun Amarin; 50B; ⏲8am-6pm; ⛴cross-river ferry

continued on p410

Greater Bangkok

Top Sights
1 Chatuchak Weekend Market C1
2 Dusit Palace Park B2
3 Lumphini Park C3
4 Suan Pakkad Palace Museum C3
5 Wat Traimit (Golden Buddha) B3

Sights
Phra Buddha Maha Suwanna Patimakorn Exhibition .... (see 5)
6 Victory Monument C2
Yaowarat Chinatown Heritage Center .... (see 5)

Activities, Courses & Tours
7 Amita Thai Cooking Class A4

Sleeping
8 Loftel 22 .... B3
9 Loy La Long B3
10 Phra-Nakorn Norn-Len B2
11 S1 Hostel C4

Eating
Foontalop .... (see 1)
12 Kai Thort Jay Kee C3
13 Krua Apsorn B2
Samsara .... (see 9)

Drinking & Nightlife
14 Fake Club The Next Gen D2

Entertainment
15 Calypso Bangkok B4
16 Playhouse Magical Cabaret D1
17 Raintree C3
Saxophone Pub & Restaurant .... (see 6)
18 Tawandang German Brewery C4

Shopping
19 Asiatique B4

Information
20 Cambodian Embassy D2
21 Chinese Embassy D2
22 Danish Embassy C4
23 French Embassy B4
German Embassy .... (see 22)
24 Japanese Embassy C4
25 Laotian Embassy D2
26 Nepalese Embassy D4

Transport
27 Bangkok Airways C1
Minivans to Chanthaburi, Kanchanaburi, Phetchaburi & Suvarnabhumi International Airport .... (see 6)
Minivans to Pak Chong (for Khao Yai National Park) & Southern Bus Terminal .... (see 6)
28 Northern & Northeastern Bus Terminal C1

Wat Phra Kaew & Grand Palace

EXPLORE BANGKOK'S PREMIER MONUMENTS TO RELIGION AND REGENCY

The first area tourists enter is the Buddhist temple compound generally referred to as Wat Phra Kaew. A covered walkway surrounds the area, the inner walls of which are decorated with the **murals of the *Ramakian*** ❶ and ❷. Originally painted during the reign of Rama I (r 1782–1809), the murals, which depict the Hindu epic the *Ramayana*, span 178 panels that describe the struggles of Rama to rescue his kidnapped wife, Sita.

After taking in the story, pass through one of the gateways guarded by ***yaksha*** ❸ to the inner compound. The most important structure here is the ***bòht*, or ordination hall** ❹, which houses the **Emerald Buddha** ❺.

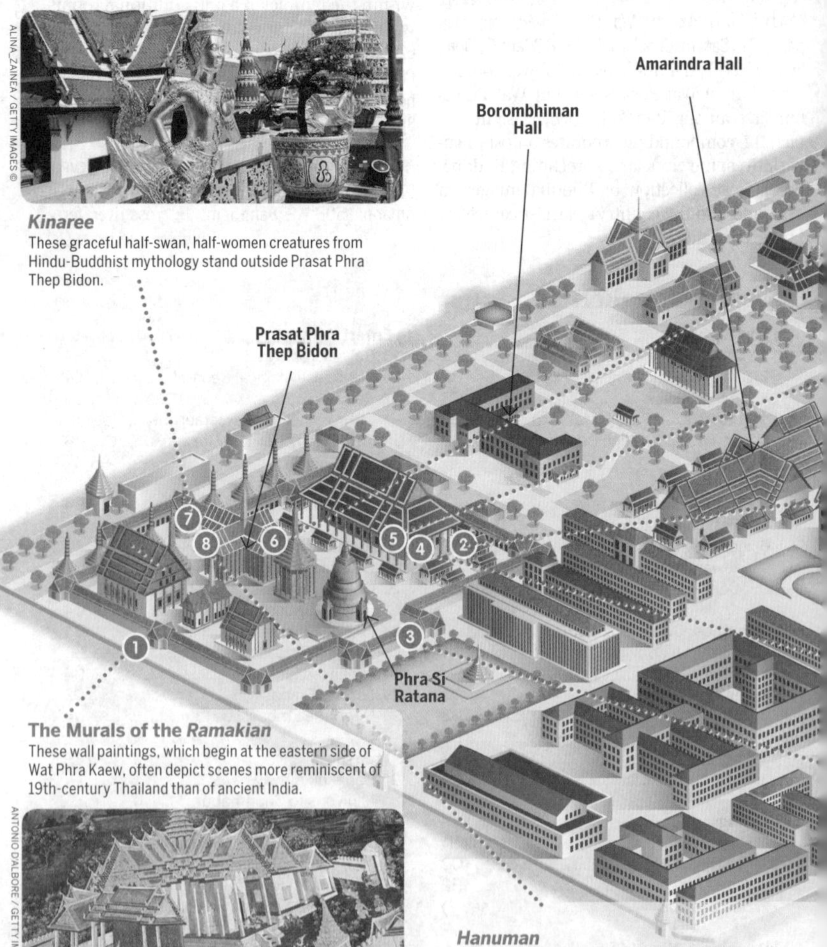

Kinaree
These graceful half-swan, half-women creatures from Hindu-Buddhist mythology stand outside Prasat Phra Thep Bidon.

The Murals of the *Ramakian*
These wall paintings, which begin at the eastern side of Wat Phra Kaew, often depict scenes more reminiscent of 19th-century Thailand than of ancient India.

Hanuman
Rows of these mischievous monkey deities from Hindu mythology appear to support the lower levels of two small *chedi* near Prasat Phra Thep Bidon.

Head east to the so-called Upper Terrace, an elevated area home to the **spires of the three primary *chedi*** 6. The middle structure, Phra Mondop, is used to house Buddhist manuscripts. This area is also home to several of Wat Phra Kaew's noteworthy mythical beings, including beckoning ***kinaree*** 7 and several grimacing **Hanuman** 8.

Proceed through the western gate to the compound known as the Grand Palace. Few of the buildings here are open to the public. The most noteworthy structure is **Chakri Mahaprasat** 9. Built in 1882, the exterior of the hall is a unique blend of Western and traditional Thai architecture.

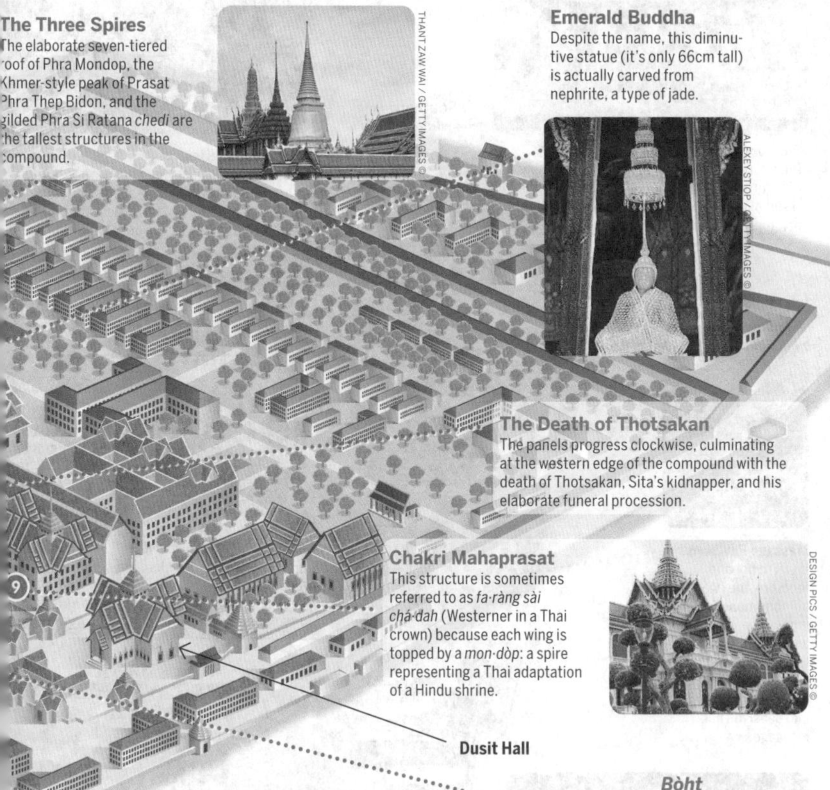

The Three Spires
The elaborate seven-tiered roof of Phra Mondop, the Khmer-style peak of Prasat Phra Thep Bidon, and the gilded Phra Si Ratana *chedi* are the tallest structures in the compound.

Emerald Buddha
Despite the name, this diminutive statue (it's only 66cm tall) is actually carved from nephrite, a type of jade.

The Death of Thotsakan
The panels progress clockwise, culminating at the western edge of the compound with the death of Thotsakan, Sita's kidnapper, and his elaborate funeral procession.

Chakri Mahaprasat
This structure is sometimes referred to as *fa·ràng sài chá·dah* (Westerner in a Thai crown) because each wing is topped by a *mon·dòp*: a spire representing a Thai adaptation of a Hindu shrine.

***Bòht* (Ordination Hall)**
This structure is an early example of the Ratanakosin school of architecture, which combines traditional stylistic holdovers from Ayuthaya along with more modern touches from China and the West.

Yaksha
Each entrance to the Wat Phra Kaew compound is watched over by a pair of vigilant and enormous *yaksha*, ogres or giants from Hindu mythology.

Wat Pho

A WALK THROUGH THE BIG BUDDHAS OF WAT PHO

The logical starting place is the main *wí·hăhn* (sanctuary), home to Wat Pho's centrepiece, the immense **Reclining Buddha** ❶. Apart from its huge size, note the **mother-of-pearl inlays** ❷ on the soles of the statue's feet. The interior walls of the *wí·hăhn* are covered with murals depicting previous lives of the Buddha, and along the south side of the structure are 108 bronze monk bowls; for 20B you can buy 108 coins, each of which is dropped in a bowl for good luck.

Exit the *wí·hăhn* and head east via the two **stone giants** ❸ who guard the gateway to the rest of the compound. Directly south of these are the four towering **royal *chedi*** ❹.

Continue east, passing through two consecutive **galleries of Buddha**

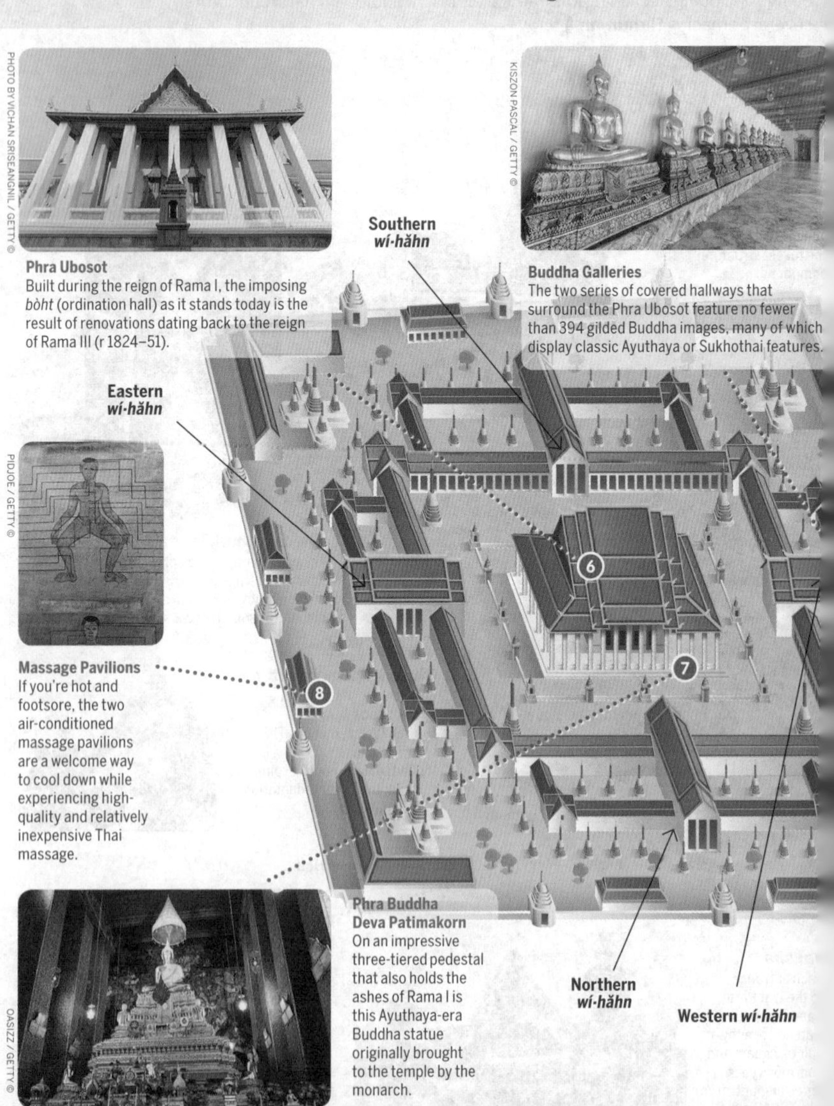

Phra Ubosot
Built during the reign of Rama I, the imposing *bòht* (ordination hall) as it stands today is the result of renovations dating back to the reign of Rama III (r 1824–51).

Buddha Galleries
The two series of covered hallways that surround the Phra Ubosot feature no fewer than 394 gilded Buddha images, many of which display classic Ayuthaya or Sukhothai features.

Massage Pavilions
If you're hot and footsore, the two air-conditioned massage pavilions are a welcome way to cool down while experiencing high-quality and relatively inexpensive Thai massage.

Phra Buddha Deva Patimakorn
On an impressive three-tiered pedestal that also holds the ashes of Rama I is this Ayuthaya-era Buddha statue originally brought to the temple by the monarch.

statues ❺ linking four *wí·hăhn*, two of which contain notable Sukhothai-era Buddha statues; these comprise the exterior of **Phra Ubosot** ❻, the immense ordination hall that is Wat Pho's second-most noteworthy structure. The base of the building is surrounded by bas-relief inscriptions, and inside is the notable Buddha statue, **Phra Buddha Deva Patimakorn** ❼.

Wat Pho is often referred to as Thailand's first university, a tradition that continues today in an associated traditional Thai medicine school and, at the compound's eastern extent, two **massage pavilions** ❽.

Interspersed throughout the eastern half of the compound are several additional minor *chedi* and rock gardens.

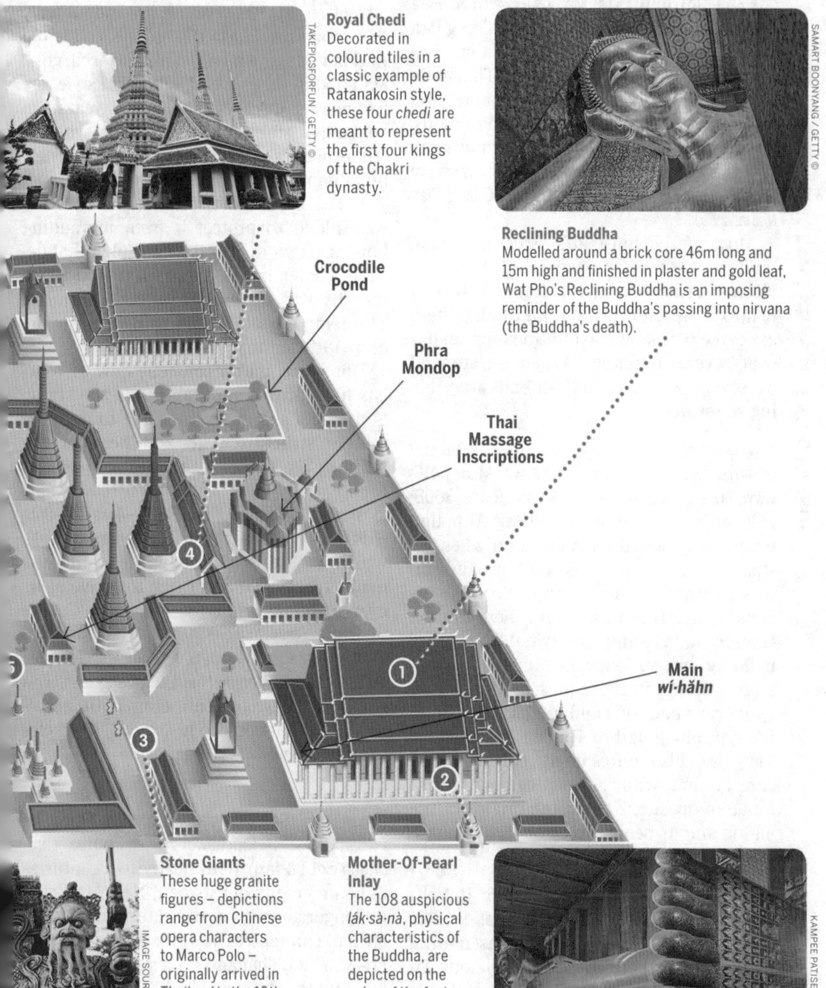

Royal Chedi
Decorated in coloured tiles in a classic example of Ratanakosin style, these four *chedi* are meant to represent the first four kings of the Chakri dynasty.

Reclining Buddha
Modelled around a brick core 46m long and 15m high and finished in plaster and gold leaf, Wat Pho's Reclining Buddha is an imposing reminder of the Buddha's passing into nirvana (the Buddha's death).

Stone Giants
These huge granite figures – depictions range from Chinese opera characters to Marco Polo – originally arrived in Thailand in the 19th century as ballast aboard Chinese junks.

Mother-Of-Pearl Inlay
The 108 auspicious *lák·sà·nà*, physical characteristics of the Buddha, are depicted on the soles of the feet of the Reclining Buddha.

continued from p405
from Tien Pier) After the fall of Ayuthaya, King Taksin ceremoniously clinched control here on the site of a local shrine and established a royal palace and a temple to house the Emerald Buddha. The temple was renamed after the Indian god of dawn (Aruna) and in honour of the literal and symbolic founding of a new Ayuthaya.

When we visited, the spire of Wat Arun was closed due to renovation. Visitors can enter the compound, but cannot climb the tower.

National Museum MUSEUM
(พิพิธภัณฑสถานแห่งชาติ; Map p416; 4 Th Na Phra That; 200B; 9am-4pm Wed-Sun; Chang Pier, Maharaj Pier, Phra Chan Tai Pier) Often touted as Southeast Asia's biggest museum, Thailand's National Museum is home to an impressive, albeit occasionally dusty, collection of items, best appreciated on one of the museum's twice-weekly guided **tours** (free with museum admission; 9.30am Wed & Thu; Chang Pier, Maharaj Pier).

Most of the museum's structures were built in 1782 as the palace of Rama I's viceroy, Prince Wang Na. Rama V turned it into a museum in 1874, and today there are three permanent exhibitions spread out over several buildings. When we stopped by, several of the exhibition halls were being renovated.

Museum of Siam MUSEUM
(สถาบันพิพิธภัณฑ์การเรียนรู้แห่งชาติ; Map p416; www.museumsiam.org; Th Maha Rat; 300B; 10am-6pm Tue-Sun; ; Tien Pier) Although temporarily closed for renovation when we stopped by, this fun museum normally employs a variety of media to explore the origins of the Thai people and their culture. Housed in a European-style 19th-century building that was once the Ministry of Commerce, the exhibits are presented in a contemporary, engaging and interactive fashion not typically found in Thailand's museums. They are also refreshingly balanced and entertaining, with galleries dealing with a range of questions about the origins of the nation and its people.

Amulet Market MARKET
(ตลาดพระเครื่องวัดมหาธาตุ; Map p416; Th Maha Rat; 7am-5pm; Chang Pier, Maharaj Pier, Phra Chan Tai Pier) This arcane and fascinating market claims both the footpaths along Th Maha Rat and Th Phra Chan, as well as a dense network of covered market stalls that run south from Phra Chan Pier; the easiest entry point is clearly marked Trok Maha That. The trade is based around small talismans carefully prized by collectors, monks, taxi drivers and people in dangerous professions.

Chinatown

★ Wat Traimit (Golden Buddha) BUDDHIST TEMPLE
(วัดไตรมิตร, Temple of the Golden Buddha; Map p404; Th Mittaphap Thai-China; 40B; 8am-5pm; Ratchawong Pier, M Hua Lamphong exit 1) The attraction at Wat Traimit is undoubtedly the impressive 3m-tall, 5.5-tonne, solid-gold Buddha image, which gleams like, well, gold. Sculpted in the graceful Sukhothai style, the image was 'discovered' some 40 years ago beneath a stucco/plaster exterior, when it fell from a crane while being moved to a new building within the temple compound.

It has been theorised that the covering was added to protect it from marauding hordes, either during the late Sukhothai period or later in the Ayuthaya period when the city was under siege by the Burmese. The temple itself is said to date from the early 13th century.

Donations and a constant flow of tourists have proven profitable, and the statue is now housed in an imposing four-storey marble structure. The 2nd floor of the building is home to the **Phra Buddha Maha Suwanna Patimakorn Exhibition** (Map p404; 100B; 8am-4pm Tue-Sun; Ratchawong Pier, M Hua Lamphong exit 1), which has exhibits on how the statue was made, discovered and came to arrive at its current home, while the 3rd floor is home to the **Yaowarat Chinatown Heritage Center** (Map p404; 100B; 8am-4pm Tue-Sun; Ratchawong Pier, M Hua Lamphong exit 1), a small but engaging museum with multimedia exhibits on the history of Bangkok's Chinatown and its residents.

Talat Mai MARKET
(ตลาดใหม่; Soi Yaowarat 6/Charoen Krung 16; 6am-6pm; Ratchawong Pier, M Hua Lamphong exit 1 & taxi) With nearly two centuries of commerce under its belt, New Market is no longer an entirely accurate name for this strip of commerce. Regardless, this is Bangkok's, if not Thailand's, most Chinese market, and the dried goods, seasonings, spices and sauces will be familiar to anyone who's

ever spent time in China. Even if you're not interested in food, the hectic atmosphere (be on guard for motorcycles squeezing between shoppers) and exotic sights and smells culminate in something of a surreal sensory experience.

Wat Mangkon Kamalawat BUDDHIST TEMPLE
(วัดมังกรกมลาวาส; Map p416; cnr Th Charoen Krung & Th Mangkon; 6am-6pm; Ratchawong Pier, M Hua Lamphong exit 1 & taxi) FREE Clouds of incense and the sounds of chanting form the backdrop at this Chinese-style Mahayana Buddhist temple. Surrounding the temple are vendors selling food for the gods – steamed lotus-shaped dumplings and oranges – which are donated to the temple in exchange for merit. Dating back to 1871, it's the largest and most important religious structure in the area, and during the annual Vegetarian Festival (p414), religious and culinary activities are particularly active here.

Siam Square, Pratunam, Ploenchit & Ratchathewi

★**Jim Thompson House** HISTORIC BUILDING
(Map p412; www.jimthompsonhouse.com; 6 Soi Kasem San 2; adult/student 150/100B; 9am-6pm, compulsory tours every 20 min; klorng boat to Sapan Hua Chang Pier, S National Stadium exit 1) This jungly compound is the former home of the eponymous American silk entrepreneur and art collector. Born in Delaware in 1906, Thompson briefly served in the Office of Strategic Services (the forerunner of the CIA) in Thailand during WWII. He settled in Bangkok after the war, when his neighbours' handmade silk caught his eye and piqued his business sense; he sent samples to fashion houses in Milan, London and Paris, gradually building a steady worldwide clientele.

★**Suan Pakkad Palace Museum** MUSEUM
(วังสวนผักกาด; Map p404; Th Si Ayuthaya; 100B; 9am-4pm; S Phaya Thai exit 4) An overlooked treasure, Suan Pakkad is a collection of eight traditional wooden Thai houses that was once the residence of Princess Chumbon of Nakhon Sawan and before that a lettuce farm (in Thai, Suan Pakkad means Lettuce Farm). Within the stilt buildings are displays of art, antiques and furnishings, and the landscaped grounds are a peaceful oasis complete with ducks, swans and a semi-enclosed garden.

Riverside, Silom & Lumphini

★**Lumphini Park** PARK
(สวนลุมพินี; Map p404; bounded by Th Sarasin, Th Phra Ram IV, Th Witthayu/Wireless Rd & Th Ratchadamri; 4.30am-9pm; M Lumphini exit 3, Si Lom exit 1, S Sala Daeng exit 3, Ratchadamri exit 2) Named after the Buddha's place of birth in Nepal, Lumphini Park is the best way to escape Bangkok without actually leaving town. Shady paths, a large artificial lake and swept lawns temporarily blot out the roaring traffic and hulking concrete towers.

Thanon Sukhumvit

★**Siam Society & Ban Kamthieng** MUSEUM
(สยามสมาคม & บ้านคำเที่ยง; Map p426; www.siam-society.org; 131 Soi 21/Asoke, Th Sukhumvit; adult/child 100B/free; 9am-5pm Tue-Sat; M Sukhumvit exit 1, S Asok exit 3 or 6) Ban Kamthieng transports visitors to a northern Thai village complete with informative displays of daily rituals, folk beliefs and everyday household chores, all within the setting of a traditional wooden house. This museum is operated by and shares space with the Siam Society, the publisher of the renowned *Journal of the Siam Society* and a valiant preserver of traditional Thai culture.

Thewet & Dusit

★**Dusit Palace Park** MUSEUM, HISTORIC SITE
(วังสวนดุสิต; Map p404; bounded by Th Ratchawithi, Th U Thong Nai & Th Nakhon Ratchasima; adult/child 100/20B, with Grand Palace ticket free; 9.30am-4pm Tue-Sun; Thewet Pier, S Phaya Thai exit 2 & taxi) Following his first European tour in 1897, Rama V (King Chulalongkorn; r 1868–1910) returned with visions of European castles and set about transforming these styles into a uniquely Thai expression, today's Dusit Palace Park. These days, the current king has yet another home (in Hua Hin) and this complex now holds a house museum and other cultural collections. When we stopped by, Dusit Palace Park was closed for renovation.

★**Chatuchak Weekend Market** MARKET
(ตลาดนัดจตุจักร, Talat Nat Jatujak; Map p404; www.chatuchakmarket.org; 587/10 Kamphaeng Phet 2 Rd; 7am-6pm Wed & Thu (plants only), 6pm-12pm Fri (wholesale only), 9am-6pm Sat &

Siam Square

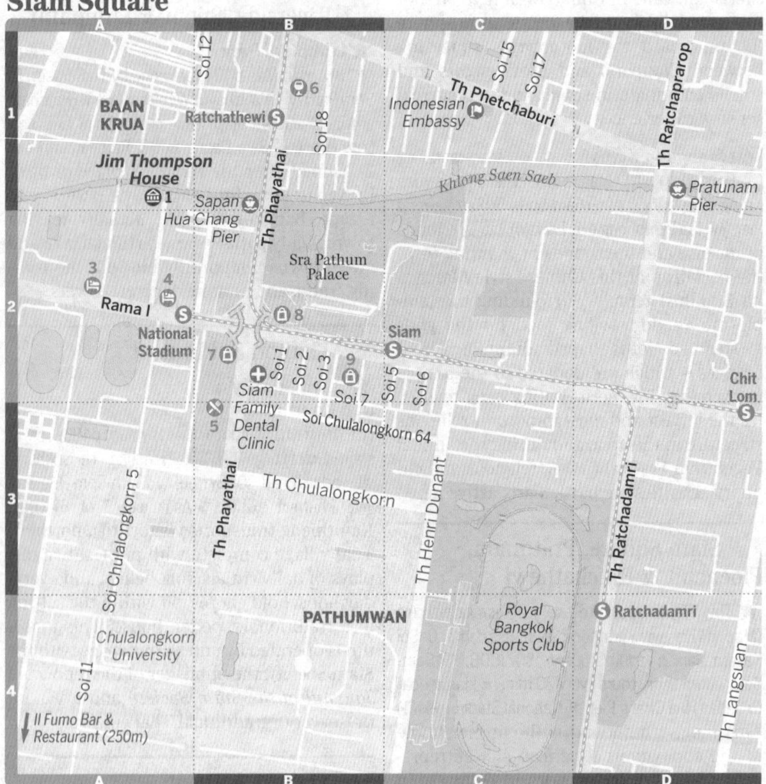

Sun; Ⓜ Chatuchak Park exit 1, Kamphaeng Phet exits 1 & 2, Ⓢ Mo Chit exit 1) Among the largest markets in the world, Chatuchak seems to unite everything buyable, from used vintage sneakers to baby squirrels. Plan to spend a full day here, as there's plenty to see, do and buy. But come early, ideally around 10am, to beat the crowds and the heat.

Activities

Cooking Classes

Bangkok Bold Cooking Studio COOKING

(Map p416; ☎ 098 829 4310; www.facebook.com/BangkokBoldCookingStudio; 503 Th Phra Sumen; courses 1500-3500B; ⏲ lessons 11am-2pm & 2-5pm; ⛴ klorng boat to Phanfa Leelard Pier) The newest venture by a team that previously ran a popular cooking school on Th Khao San, Bold offers daily courses ranging from fruit carving to instruction in three Thai dishes, with lessons taught in a chic shophouse setting.

★ Amita Thai Cooking Class COOKING

(Map p404; ☎ 02 466 8966; www.amitathaicooking.com; 162/17 Soi 14, Th Wutthakat, Thonburi; 3000B; ⏲ lessons 9.30am-1pm Thu-Tue; ⛴ klorng boat from Maharaj Pier) One of Bangkok's most charming cooking schools is held in this canalside house in Thonburi. Taught by the delightfully enthusiastic Piyawadi 'Tam' Jantrupon, a course here includes a romp through the garden and instruction in four dishes. The fee covers transport, which in this case takes the form of a boat ride from Maharaj Pier.

Cooking with Poo & Friends COOKING

(☎ 080 434 8686; www.cookingwithpoo.com; courses 1500B; ⏲ courses 8.30am-1pm) This popular cooking course was started by a native of Khlong Toey's slums and is held in her neighbourhood. Courses, which must be booked in advance, span three dishes and include a visit to Khlong Toey Market and

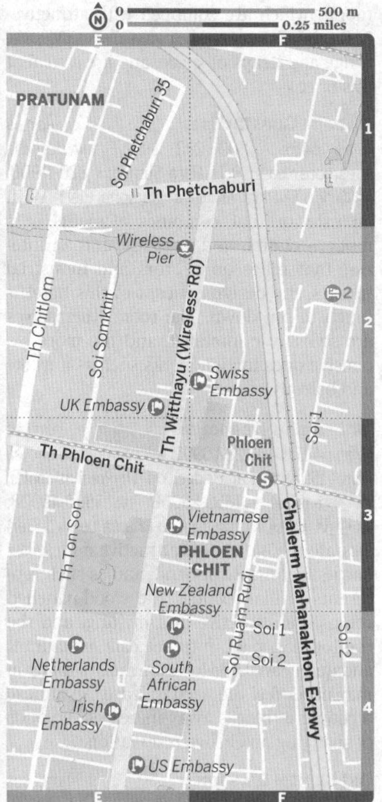

Siam Square

Top Sights

1 Jim Thompson House A1

Sleeping

2 AriyasomVilla F2
3 Chao Hostel A2
4 Lub*d A2
Siam@Siam .... (see 3)

Eating

5 MBK Food Island B3

Drinking & Nightlife

6 Co-Co Walk B1

Shopping

7 MBK Center B2
8 Siam Discovery B2
9 Siam Square B2

transport to and from Emporium Shopping Centre.

Martial Arts

Muay Thai Lab MARTIAL ARTS

(Map p416; ☎02 024 1326; www.muaythailab.net; 2nd fl, Maharaj Pier, Th Maha Rat; lessons from 990B; ⏰11am-8pm; ⛴Maharaj Pier, Chang Pier, Phra Chan Tai Pier) Muay Thai Lab is a new, impressive one-stop centre for everything related to Thai boxing. Start in the lobby, which has free displays on the history and culture of Thai boxing and a small shop stocked with both souvenirs and gear, before heading to the open-air rooftop gym, which looks over Mae Nam Chao Phraya.

Drop-ins are encouraged to join one of three daily lessons, which take place between 11am and 3pm; the fee includes clothing and equipment, access to a locker and showers, and a towel.

Massage

Asia Herb Association MASSAGE

(Map p426; ☎02 261 2201; www.asiaherbassociation.com; 20/1 Soi 31, Th Sukhumvit; Thai massage per hour 500B, Thai massage with herbal compress 1½hr 1100B; ⏰9am-midnight; S Phrom Phong exit 5) With multiple branches along Th Sukhumvit, this Japanese-owned chain specialises in massage using *prà·kóp* (traditional Thai herbal compresses) filled with 18 different herbs.

Health Land MASSAGE

(Map p422; ☎02 637 8883; www.healthlandspa.com; 120 Th Sathon Neua/North; 2hr massage 550B; ⏰9am-11pm; S Surasak exit 3) This, the main branch of a long-standing Thai massage mini-empire, offers good-value, no-nonsense massage and spa treatments in a tidy environment.

Meditation

Center Meditation Wat Mahadhatu MEDITATION

(Map p416; ☎02 222 6011, 02 223 3813; Section 5, Wat Mahathat, Th Maha Rat; donations accepted; ⏰lessons 7am, 1pm & 6pm; ⛴Chang Pier, Maharaj Pier, Phra Chan Tai Pier) Located within Wat Mahathat, this small centre offers informal daily meditation classes. Taught by English-speaking Prasuputh Chainikom (Kosalo), classes last three hours. Longer periods of study, which include accommodation and food, can be arranged, but students are expected to follow a strict regimen of conduct.

Festivals & Events

Chinese New Year CULTURAL
(Jan or Feb) Thai-Chinese celebrate the lunar New Year with a week of housecleaning, lion dances and fireworks. Most festivities centre on Chinatown. Dates vary.

Songkran CULTURAL
(mid-Apr) The celebration of the Thai New Year has morphed into a water war with high-powered water guns and water balloons being launched at suspecting and unsuspecting participants. The most intense water battles take place on Th Khao San.

Vegetarian Festival FOOD & DRINK
(Sep or Oct) This 10-day Chinese-Buddhist festival wheels out yellow-bannered streetside vendors serving meatless meals. The greatest concentration of vendors is found in Chinatown. Dates vary.

Loi Krathong CULTURAL
(early Nov) A beautiful festival where, on the night of the full moon, small lotus-shaped boats made of banana leaf and containing a lit candle are set adrift on Mae Nam Chao Phraya.

Sleeping

If your idea of the typical Bangkok hotel was influenced by *The Hangover Part II,* you'll be relieved to learn that the city is home to a variety of modern hostels, guesthouses and hotels. To make matters better, much of Bangkok's accommodation offers excellent value, and competition is so intense that fat discounts are almost always available.

If you're on a budget, dorm beds can be had for as little as 300B, while cheap rooms start at about 600B. There's a wide choice of midrange hotels and an astonishing number of top-end places.

Be sure to book ahead if you're arriving during peak tourist season (from approximately November to February) and are keen on the smaller, boutique-type hotel.

Banglamphu

★**Chern** HOSTEL $
(Map p416; 02 621 1133; www.chernbangkok.com; 17 Soi Ratchasak; dm 400B, r 1400-1900B; ; klorng boat to Phanfa Leelard Pier) The vast, open spaces and white, overexposed tones of this hostel converge in an almost afterlife-like feel. The eight-bed dorms are above average, but we particularly like the private rooms, which are equipped with attractively minimalist touches, a vast desk, TV, safe, fridge and heaps of space, and are a steal at this price.

Fortville Guesthouse HOTEL $
(Map p416; 02 282 3932; www.fortvilleguesthouse.com; 9 Th Phra Sumen; r 820-1190B; ; Phra Athit/Banglamphu Pier) With an exterior that combines elements of a modern church and/or castle, and an interior that relies on mirrors and industrial themes, the design concept of this hotel is tough to pin down. The rooms themselves are stylishly minimalist, and the more expensive ones include perks such as a fridge and balcony.

★**Lamphu Treehouse** HOTEL $$
(Map p416; 02 282 0991; www.lamphutreehotel.com; 155 Wanchat Bridge, off Th Prachathipatai; incl breakfast r 1650-2500B, ste 3500-4500B; ; klorng boat to Phanfa Leelard Pier) Despite the name, this attractive midranger has its feet firmly on land, and as such represents brilliant value. The wood-panelled rooms are attractive and inviting, and the rooftop bar, pool, internet cafe, restaurant and quiet canalside location ensure that you may never feel the need to leave. An annexe a couple of blocks away increases the odds of snagging an elusive reservation.

Old Capital Bike Inn HOTEL $$$
(Map p416; 02 629 1787; www.oldcapitalbkk.com; 609 Th Phra Sumen; r incl breakfast 3690-7790B; ; klorng boat to Phanfa Leelard Pier) The dictionary definition of a honeymoon hotel, this antique shophouse has 10 rooms that are decadent and sumptuous, blending rich colours and heavy wood furnishings. A recent management change and refurbishment has seen the introduction of a bicycle theme, and bikes can be borrowed for free.

Ko Ratanakosin & Thonburi

Arom D Hostel HOSTEL $
(Map p416; 02 622 1055; www.aromdhostel.com; 336 Th Maha Rat; incl breakfast dm 400B, r 1200-1500B; ; Tien Pier) The dorm beds and rooms here are united by a cutesy design theme and a host of inviting communal areas including a rooftop deck, computers, a ground-floor cafe and TV room. Private rooms don't have much space, but they do have style.

BATHROOMLESS IN BANGKOK

If you're on a shoestring budget, Bangkok has heaps of options for you, ranging from high-tech, pod-like dorm beds in a brand-new hostel to cosy bunk beds in a refurbished Chinatown shophouse. (And if you decide that you need a bit more privacy, nearly all of Bangkok's hostels also offer private rooms.) And best of all, at the places listed here, we found the bathrooms to be clean and convenient, and sharing will hardly feel like a compromise. Some of our picks:

Lub*d (Map p412; 02 612 4999; www.siamsquare.lubd.com; Th Phra Ram I; dm 550B, r 1900-2500B; ; National Stadium exit 1) The title is a play on the Thai *làp dee,* meaning 'sleep well', but the fun atmosphere at this modern-feeling hostel might make you want to stay up all night. Diversions include an inviting communal area stocked with games and a bar, and thoughtful facilities range from washing machines to a theatre room. If this one's full, there's another **branch** (Map p422; 02 634 7999; www.silom.lubd.com; 4 Th Decho; dm 450B, r 100-1500B; ; Chong Nonsi exit 2) just off Th Silom.

Saphaipae (Map p422; 02 238 2322; www.saphaipae.com; 35 Th Surasak; incl breakfast dm 400-470B, r 1200-1200B; ; Surasak exit 1) The bright colours, chunky furnishings and bold murals in the lobby of this hostel give it the feel of a day-care centre for travellers – a vibe that continues through to the playful communal areas and rooms. Dorms and rooms are thoughtful and well equipped, and there are heaps of helpful travel resources and facilities.

Silom Art Hostel (Map p422; 02 635 8070; www.silomarthostel.com; 198/19-22 Soi 14, Th Silom; dm 300-400, r 990-1300B; ; Chong Nonsi exit 3) Quirky, artsy, bright and fun, Silom Art Hostel combines recycled materials, unconventional furnishings and colourful wall paintings to culminate in a hostel that's quite unlike anywhere else in town. It's not all about style though: beds and rooms are functional and comfortable, with lots of appealing communal areas.

Loftel 22 (Map p404; www.loftel22bangkok.com; 952 Soi 22, Th Charoen Krung; dm 280B, r 850-1300B; ; Marine Department Pier, Hua Lamphong exit 1) Stylish, inviting dorms and private rooms (all with shared bathrooms) have been coaxed out of these two adjoining shophouses. Friendly service and a location in one of Chinatown's most atmospheric corners round out the package.

NapPark Hostel (Map p416; 02 282 2324; www.nappark.com; 5 Th Tani; dm 440-650B; ; Phra Athit/Banglamphu Pier) This popular hostel features dorm rooms of various sizes, the smallest and most expensive of which boasts six pod-like beds outfitted with power points, mini-TV, reading lamp and wi-fi. Cultural-based activities and inviting communal areas ensure that you may not actually get the chance to plug in.

Chao Hostel (Map p412; 02 217 3083; www.chaohostel.com; 8th fl, 865 Th Phra Ram I; incl breakfast dm 600, r 1600-1800; ; National Stadium exit 1) Blending modern minimalist and Thai design elements, not to mention tonnes of open space, the new Chao is one of the most sophisticated hostels we've encountered in Bangkok.

Pause Hostel (Map p426; 02 108 8855; www.onedaybkk.com; Oneday, 51 Soi 26, Th Sukhumvit; incl breakfast dm 450-600B, r 1300-1500B; ; Phrom Phong exit 4) Attached to a cafe/coworking space is this modern, open-feeling hostel. Dorms span four to eight beds, and like the private rooms (only some of which have en suite bathrooms) are united by a handsome industrial-design theme and inviting, sun-soaked communal areas.

S1 Hostel (Map p404; 02 679 7777; www.facebook.com/S1hostelBangkok; 35/1-4 Soi Ngam Du Phli; dm 330-380B, r 700-1300B; ; Lumphini exit 1) A huge new hostel with dorm beds decked out in a simple yet attractive primary-colour scheme. A host of facilities (laundry, kitchen, rooftop garden) and a convenient location within walking distance of the Metropolitan Rapid Transit (MRT) make it great value.

Ko Ratanakosin, Banglamphu & Thonburi

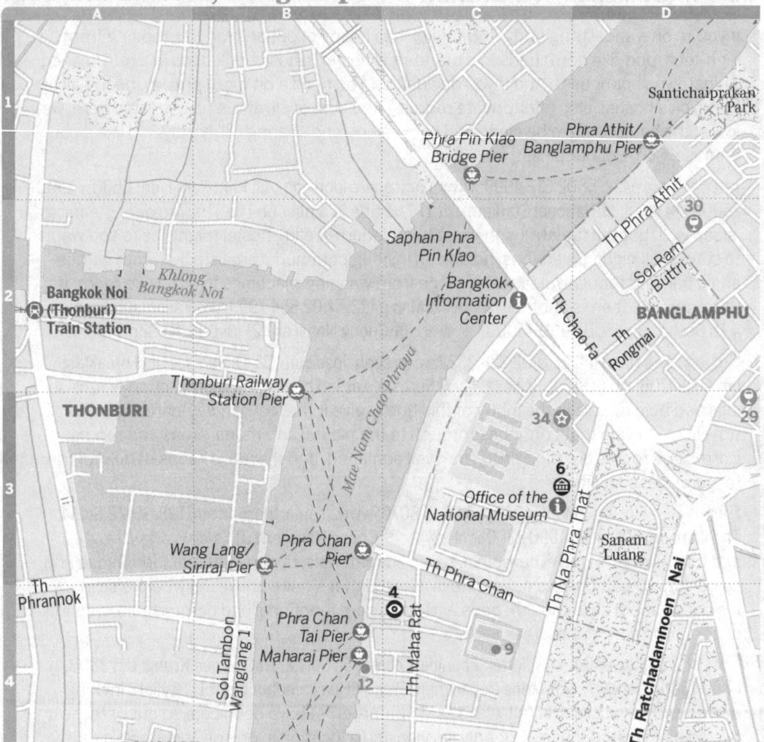

A B C D

1
Santichaiprakan Park
Phra Athit/ Banglamphu Pier
Phra Pin Klao Bridge Pier

2
Th Phra Athit
30
Saphan Phra Pin Klao
Soi Ram Buttri
Khlong Bangkok Noi
Bangkok Information Center
Bangkok Noi (Thonburi) Train Station
Th Chao Fa
BANGLAMPHU
Th Rongmai
Mae Nam Chao Phraya
Thonburi Railway Station Pier
THONBURI
29
34

3
6
Office of the National Museum
Sanam Luang
Phra Chan Pier
Wang Lang/ Siriraj Pier
Th Phra Chan
Th Phrannok
Th Na Phra That
Nai
4
Phra Chan Tai Pier
Maharaj Pier
9
Th Ratchadamnoen

4
Soi Tambon Wanglang 1
12
Th Maha Rat
BANGKOK NOI
Silpakorn University
Th Lak Meuang
Th Na Phra Lan
Chang Pier

5
Mae Nam Chao Phraya
Th Sanam Chai
Wat Phra Kaew & Grand Palace
3
Th Maha Rat
KO RATANAKOSIN
Saranrom Royal Garden

6
Th Thai Wang
Khlong Mon
Wat Pho
2
11
Tien Pier
Th Arun Amarin
13
Soi Tha Tian
Th Chetuphon
17
10
Soi Phen Phat
14
21

7
Wat Arun
1
THONBURI
5

A B C D

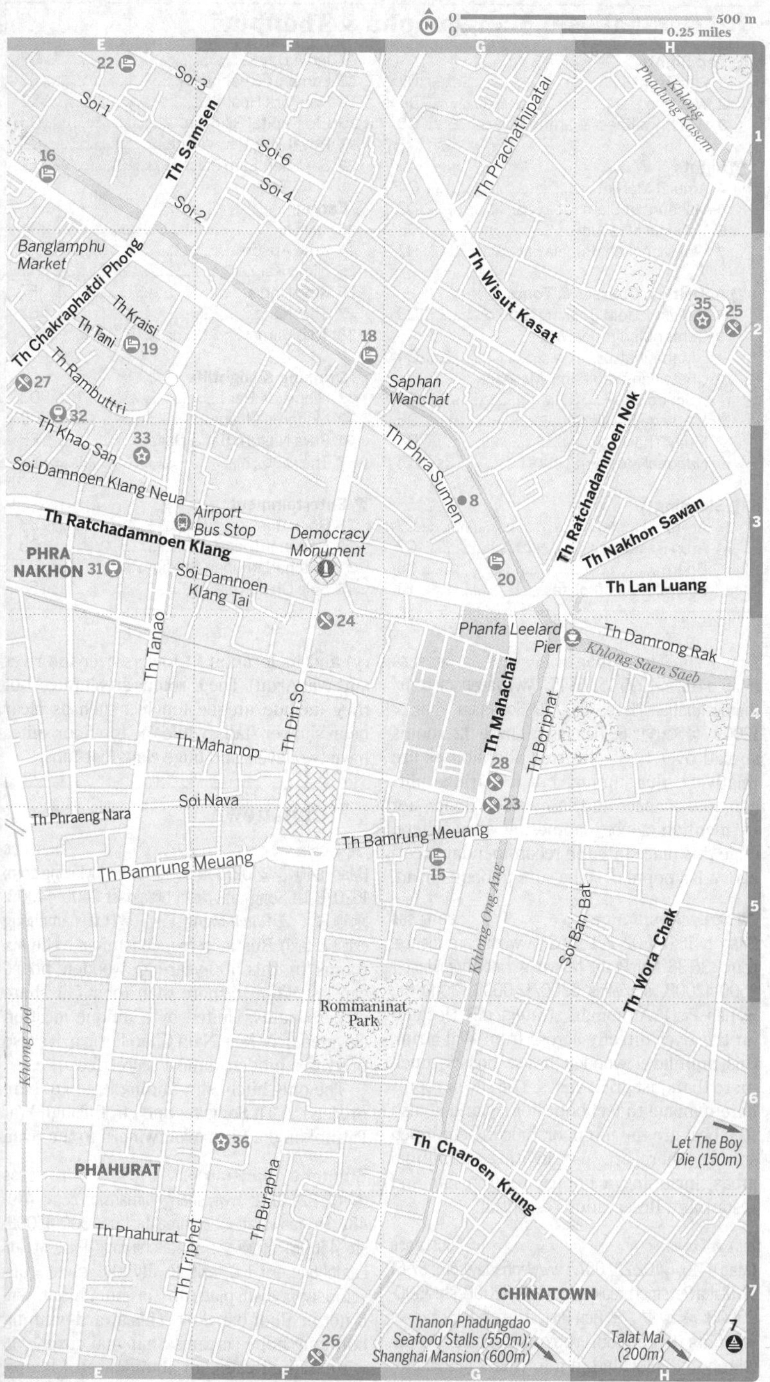
0
500 m
0
0.25 miles
E
F
G
H
Khlong Phadung Kasem
Soi 3
Soi 1
Th Samsen
Soi 6
Soi 4
Soi 2
Th Prachathipatai
Banglamphu Market
Th Chakraphatdi Phong
Th Kraisi
Th Tani
Th Rambuttri
Th Wisut Kasat
Saphan Wanchat
Th Khao San
Soi Damnoen Klang Neua
Th Phra Sumen
Th Ratchadamnoen Nok
Airport Bus Stop
Th Ratchadamnoen Klang
Democracy Monument
Th Nakhon Sawan
PHRA NAKHON
Soi Damnoen Klang Tai
Th Lan Luang
Phanfa Leelard Pier
Th Damrong Rak
Khlong Saen Saeb
Th Tanao
Th Din So
Th Mahachai
Th Boriphat
Th Mahanop
Soi Nava
Th Phraeng Nara
Th Bamrung Meuang
Th Bamrung Meuang
Khlong Ong Ang
Soi Ban Bat
Th Wora Chak
Rommaninat Park
Khlong Lod
Th Charoen Krung
Let The Boy Die (150m)
PHAHURAT
Th Burapha
Th Phahurat
Th Triphet
CHINATOWN
Thanon Phadungdao Seafood Stalls (550m); Shanghai Mansion (600m)
Talat Mai (200m)
22
16
19
18
27
32
33
35
25
8
31
20
24
28
23
15
36
26
7
1
2
3
4
5
6
7

Ko Ratanakosin, Banglamphu & Thonburi

Top Sights
1 Wat Arun C7
2 Wat Pho D6
3 Wat Phra Kaew & Grand Palace C5

Sights
4 Amulet Market C4
5 Museum of Siam D7
6 National Museum C3
7 Wat Mangkon Kamalawat H7

Activities, Courses & Tours
8 Bangkok Bold Cooking Studio G3
9 Center Meditation Wat Mahadhatu C4
10 Chetawan Traditional Massage School C7
11 Massage Pavilions D6
12 Muay Thai Lab B4
National Museum Tours .... (see 6)

Sleeping
13 Arom D Hostel C7
14 Arun Residence C7
15 Chern G5
16 Fortville Guesthouse E1
17 Inn A Day C7
18 Lamphu Treehouse F2
19 NapPark Hostel E2
20 Old Capital Bike Inn G3
21 Royal Tha Tien Village C7
22 Sam Sen Sam Place E1

Eating
23 Jay Fai G4
24 Krua Apsorn F4
25 Likhit Kai Yang H2
26 Royal India F7
27 Shoshana E2
28 Thip Samai G4

Drinking & Nightlife
29 Hippie de Bar D3
30 Madame Musur D2
31 Phra Nakorn Bar & Gallery E3
32 The Club E2

Entertainment
33 Brick Bar E3
34 National Theatre C3
35 Ratchadamnoen Stadium H2
36 Sala Chalermkrung F6

Royal Tha Tien Village HOTEL $$
(Map p416; 095 151 5545; www.facebook.com/theroyalthatienvillage; 392/29 Soi Phen Phat; r 1200B; ; Tien Pier) These 12 rooms spread over two converted shophouses are relatively unassuming, but TV, fridge, air-con, lots of space and shiny wood floors, not to mention a cosy homestay atmosphere, edge this place into the recommendable category. It's popular, so be sure to book ahead.

★ **Arun Residence** HOTEL $$$
(Map p416; 02 221 9158; www.arunresidence.com; 36-38 Soi Pratu Nokyung; incl breakfast r 3500-4200B, ste/villas 5800/12,000B; ; Tien Pier) Although strategically located on the river directly across from Wat Arun, this multilevel wooden house boasts much more than just great views. The seven rooms here manage to feel both homey and stylish (the best are the top-floor, balcony-equipped suites). There are also inviting communal areas, including a library, rooftop bar and restaurant. Reservations essential.

Inn A Day HOTEL $$$
(Map p416; 02 221 0577; www.innaday.com; 57-61 Th Maha Rat; incl breakfast r 3500-4200B, ste 7500-9000B; ; Tien Pier) Inn A Day wows with its hyper-cool retro/industrial theme (the hotel is located in a former sugar factory) and its location (it towers over the river and Wat Arun). The 11 rooms aren't huge, but they include unique touches such as clear neon shower stalls, while the top-floor suites have two levels and huge claw-foot tubs.

Chinatown

★ **Loy La Long** HOTEL $$
(Map p404; 02 639 1390; www.loylalong.com; 1620/2 Th Songwat; r incl breakfast 2400-4400B; ; Ratchawong Pier, M Hua Lamphong exit 1 & taxi) Rustic, retro, charming – the six rooms in this 100-year-old wooden house can lay claim to more than their fair share of personality. United by a unique location elevated over Mae Nam Chao Phraya, it's also privy to a hidden, almost secret, feel.

The only hitch is in finding it; to get here proceed to Th Songwat and cut through Wat Patumkongka Rachaworawiharn to the river.

Shanghai Mansion HOTEL $$$
(02 221 2121; www.shanghaimansion.com; 479-481 Th Yaowarat; incl breakfast r 2500-4500B, ste 4500B; ; Ratchawong Pier, M Hua Lamphong exit 1 & taxi) Easily the most consciously stylish place to stay in Chinatown, if not in all of Bangkok. This award-winning boutique hotel screams Shanghai circa 1935 with stained glass, an abundance of lamps,

bold colours and cheeky Chinatown kitsch. If you're willing to splurge, ask for one of the bigger streetside rooms with tall windows that allow more natural light.

Siam Square, Pratunam, Ploenchit & Ratchathewi

Siam@Siam HOTEL $$$

(Map p412; 02 217 3000; www.siamatsiam.com; 865 Th Phra Ram I; r incl breakfast 4500-7800B; ; National Stadium exit 1) A seemingly random mishmash of colours and industrial/recycled materials in the lobby here result in a style one could only describe as 'junkyard chic' – but in a good way, of course. The rooms, which largely continue the theme, are found between the 14th and 24th floors, and offer terrific city views. There's a rooftop restaurant and an 11th-floor pool, and a recent renovation has it looking better than ever.

Riverside, Silom & Lumphini

★**Smile Society** HOTEL $$

(Map p422; 081 442 5800, 081 444 1596; www.smilesocietyhostel.com; 30/3-4 Soi 6, Th Silom; incl breakfast dm 400B, r 900-1880B; ; Si Lom exit 2, Sala Daeng exit 1) Part boutique, part hostel, this four-storey shophouse combines small but comfortable and well-equipped rooms and dorms with spotless shared bathrooms. A central location, overwhelmingly positive guest feedback, and helpful, English-speaking staff are other perks. And a virtually identical annexe next door helps with spillover as Smile Society gains more fans.

★**Siam Heritage** HOTEL $$$

(Map p422; 02 353 6101; www.thesiamheritage.com; 115/1 Th Surawong; incl breakfast r 3500-3800B, ste 5000-6500B; ; Si Lom exit 2, Sala Daeng exit 1) Tucked off busy Th Surawong, this hotel overflows with homey Thai charm – probably because the owners also live in the same building. The 73 rooms are decked out in silk and dark woods with classy design touches and thoughtful amenities. There's an inviting rooftop garden/pool/spa, and it's all cared for by a team of professional, accommodating staff. Highly recommended.

★**Metropolitan by COMO** HOTEL $$$

(02 625 3333; www.comohotels.com/metropolitanbangkok; 27 Th Sathon Tai/South; incl breakfast r 4500-6500B, ste 7500-40,000B; ; Lumphini exit 2) The exterior of Bangkok's former YMCA has changed relatively little, but a peek inside reveals one of the city's sleekest, sexiest hotels. The 171 rooms come in striking tones of black, white and yellow, yet it's worth noting that the City rooms tend to feel a bit tight, while in contrast the two-storey penthouse suites are like small homes.

Thanon Sukhumvit

Suk 11 HOSTEL $

(Map p426; 02 253 5927; www.suk11.com; 1/33 Soi 11, Th Sukhumvit; r incl breakfast 535-1605B; ; Nana exit 3) This rustic guesthouse is an oasis of woods and greenery in the urban jungle that is Th Sukhumvit. The rooms are basic, clean and comfy, if a bit dark and in need of TLC, while the cheapest of them share bathrooms. Although the building holds nearly 70 rooms, you'll still need to book at least two weeks ahead.

RetrOasis HOTEL $$

(Map p426; 02 665 2922; www.retroasishotel.com; 503 Th Sukhumvit; r incl breakfast 1190-2110B; ; Sukhumvit exit 2, Asok exit 6) This former tryst hotel dating back to the '60s has been converted to a fun mid-ranger. Bright paint and an inviting central pool give the hotel a young, fresh vibe, while vintage furniture and architecture serve as reminders of its real age.

S-Box HOTEL $$

(Map p426; 02 262 0991; www.sboxhotel.com; 4 Soi 31, Th Sukhumvit; r incl breakfast 1100-2200B; ; Phrom Phong exit 5) The name says it all: the rooms here are little more than boxes – albeit attractive, modern boxes with stylish furniture and practical amenities. The cheapest are pod-like and lack natural light, while the more expensive have floor-to-ceiling windows.

Fusion Suites HOTEL $$

(Map p426; 02 665 2778; www.fusionbangkok.com; 143/61-62 Soi 21/Asoke, Th Sukhumvit; r incl breakfast 1700-2400B; ; Sukhumvit exit 1, Asok exit 1) A disproportionately funky hotel for this price range, with unconventional furnishings providing the rooms here with heaps of style, although the cheapest can be a bit dark.

Napa Place HOTEL $$

(Map p426; 02 661 5525; www.napaplace.com; 11/3 Soi Napha Sap 2; incl breakfast r 2200-2600B,

WHERE TO SLEEP

NEIGHBOURHOOD	FOR	AGAINST
BANGLAMPHU	Close to main sights; proximity to classic Bangkok 'hood; lots of good-value budget beds; fun, intergalactic melting-pot feel; virtually interminable dining options; one of the city's best nightlife areas.	Getting to and from the area can be troublesome; Th Khao San can be noisy and rowdy; budget places can have low standards; relentless touts.
KO RATANAKOSIN & THONBURI	Bangkok's most famous sights at your door; occasional river views; (relatively) fresh air; old-school Bangkok feel.	Difficult to reach; few budget options; lack of dining and drinking venues; touts.
CHINATOWN	Some interesting budget and mid-range options; off the beaten track; easy access to worthwhile sights and some of the city's best food; close to Bangkok's main train station.	Noisy; polluted; touts; hectic; few non-eating-related nightlife options; access to rest of Bangkok not very convenient.
SIAM SQUARE, PRATUNAM, PHLOEN CHIT & RATCHATHEWI	Wide spread of accommodation alternatives; megaconvenient access to shopping (and air-conditioning); steps away from BTS (Skytrain).	Touts; unpristine environment; relative lack of dining and entertainment options in immediate area; lacks character.
RIVERSIDE, SILOM & LUMPHINI	Some of the city's best upscale accommodation; river boats and river views; superconvenient access to BTS and MRT (Metro); lots of dining and nightlife options; gay friendly.	Can be noisy and polluted; budget options can be pretty dire; hyperurban feel away from the river.
SUKHUMVIT	Some of the city's most sophisticated hotels; lots of midrange options; easy access to BTS and MRT; international dining; easy access to some of the city's best bars; home to several reputable spas and massage parlours.	Annoying street vendors and sexpat vibe; noisy; hypertouristy.
THEWET & DUSIT	Good budget options; riverside village feel; fresh air; close to a handful of visit-worthy sights.	Few midrange and upscale options; not very convenient access to rest of Bangkok; relatively few dining and drinking options; comatose at night.
GREATER BANGKOK	Less hectic setting; good value; depending on location, convenient airport access.	Transport can be inconvenient; lack of drinking and entertainment options.

ste 3400-4100B; ❄@📶; S Thong Lo exit 2) Hidden in the confines of a typical Bangkok urban compound is what must be the city's homeliest accommodation. The 12 expansive rooms have been decorated with dark woods from the family's former lumber business and light-brown cloths from the hands of Thai weavers, while the cosy communal areas might not be much different from the suburban living room you grew up in.

★ **Ariyasom Villa** HOTEL $$$
(Map p412; ☎02 254 8880; www.ariyasom.com; 65 Soi 1, Th Sukhumvit; r incl breakfast 6900-10,500B; ❄@📶≋; S Phloen Chit exit 3) Located at the end of Soi 1 behind a wall of tropical greenery, this beautifully renovated 1940s-era villa is one of the worst-kept accommodation secrets in Bangkok. The 24 rooms are spacious and meticulously outfitted with thoughtful Thai design touches and sumptuous, beautiful antique furniture. There's also a spa and an inviting tropical pool. Book well in advance.

Breakfast is vegetarian and served in the villa's stunning glass-encased dining room.

S31 HOTEL $$$

(Map p426; ☎02 260 1111; www.s31hotel.com; 545 Soi 31, Th Sukhumvit; incl breakfast r 3700B, ste 4200-25,000B; ; Phrom Phong exit 5) The bold patterns and graphics of its interior and exterior make the S31 a fun, youthful choice. Thoughtful touches like kitchenettes with large fridge, superhuge beds and courses (Thai boxing and yoga) prove that the style also has substance. Significant discounts can be found online, and additional branches are on Soi 15 and Soi 33.

Thewet & Dusit

★**Sam Sen Sam Place** GUESTHOUSE $$

(Map p416; ☎02 628 7067; https://samsensam.com; 48 Soi 3, Th Samsen; r incl breakfast 590-2400B; ; Thewet Pier) One of the homeliest places in this area, if not Bangkok, this colourful, refurbished antique villa gets glowing reports about its friendly service and quiet location. Of the 18 rooms here, all are extremely tidy, and the cheapest are fan-cooled and share a bathroom.

★**Phra-Nakorn Norn-Len** HOTEL $$$

(Map p404; ☎02 628 8188; www.phranakorn-nornlen.com; 46 Soi Thewet 1; r incl breakfast 2200-4200B; ; Thewet Pier) Set in an enclosed garden compound decorated like the Bangkok of yesteryear, this bright and cheery hotel is a fun and atmospheric, if not necessarily stupendous-value, place to stay. Although the 31 rooms are attractively furnished with antiques and paintings, it's worth noting that they don't include TV or in-room wi-fi, a fact made up for by daily activities, massage and endless opportunities for peaceful relaxing.

Eating

Nowhere else is the Thai reverence for food more evident than in Bangkok. To the outsider, the life of a Bangkokian appears to be a string of meals and snacks punctuated by the odd stab at work, not the other way around. If you can adjust your mental clock to this schedule, your visit will be a delicious one indeed.

Banglamphu

Thip Samai THAI $

(Map p416; 313 Th Mahachai; mains 50-250B; 5pm-2am; klorng boat to Phanfa Leelard Pier) Brace yourself – you should be aware that the fried noodles sold from carts along Th Khao San have little to do with the dish known as *pàt tai*. Luckily, less than a five-minute túk-túk ride away lies Thip Samai, home to some of the most legendary fried noodles in town.

Note that Thip Samai is closed on alternate Wednesdays.

★**Krua Apsorn** THAI $$

(Map p416; www.kruaapsorn.com; Th Din So; mains 80-400B; 10.30am-8pm Mon-Sat; ; klorng boat to Phanfa Leelard Pier) This homely dining room is a favourite of members of the Thai royal family and restaurant critics alike. Just about all of the central and southern Thai dishes are tasty, but regulars never miss the chance to order the decadent stir-fried crab with yellow chilli or the *tortilla Española*–like omelette with crab.

There's another **branch** (Map p404; www.kruaapsorn.com; 503-505 Th Samsen; mains 80-400B; 10.30am-7.30pm Mon-Fri, to 6pm Sat; ; Thewet Pier) on Th Samsen in Thewet & Dusit.

Shoshana ISRAELI $$

(Map p416; 88 Th Chakraphatdi Phong; mains 80-320B; 10am-midnight; ; Phra Athit/Banglamphu Pier) One of Khao San's longest-running Israeli restaurants, Shoshana resembles your grandparents' living room right down to the tacky wall art and plastic placemats. Feel safe in ordering anything deep-fried – staff do an excellent job of it – and don't miss the deliciously garlicky eggplant dip.

★**Jay Fai** THAI $$$

(Map p416; 327 Th Mahachai; mains 180-1000B; 3pm-2am Mon-Sat; klorng boat to Phanfa Leelard Pier) You wouldn't think so by looking at her bare-bones dining room, but Jay Fai is known far and wide for serving Bangkok's most expensive *pàt kêe mow* ('drunkard's noodles'; wide rice noodles fried with seafood and Thai herbs).

Jay Fai is located in a virtually unmarked shophouse on Th Mahachai, directly across from a 7-Eleven.

The *pàt kêe mow* price is justified by the copious fresh seafood, as well as Jay Fai's distinct frying style that results in an almost oil-free finished product.

Chinatown

Thanon Phadungdao Seafood Stalls THAI $$

(cnr Th Phadungdao & Th Yaowarat; mains 100-600B; 4pm-midnight Tue-Sun; Ratchawong

Silom

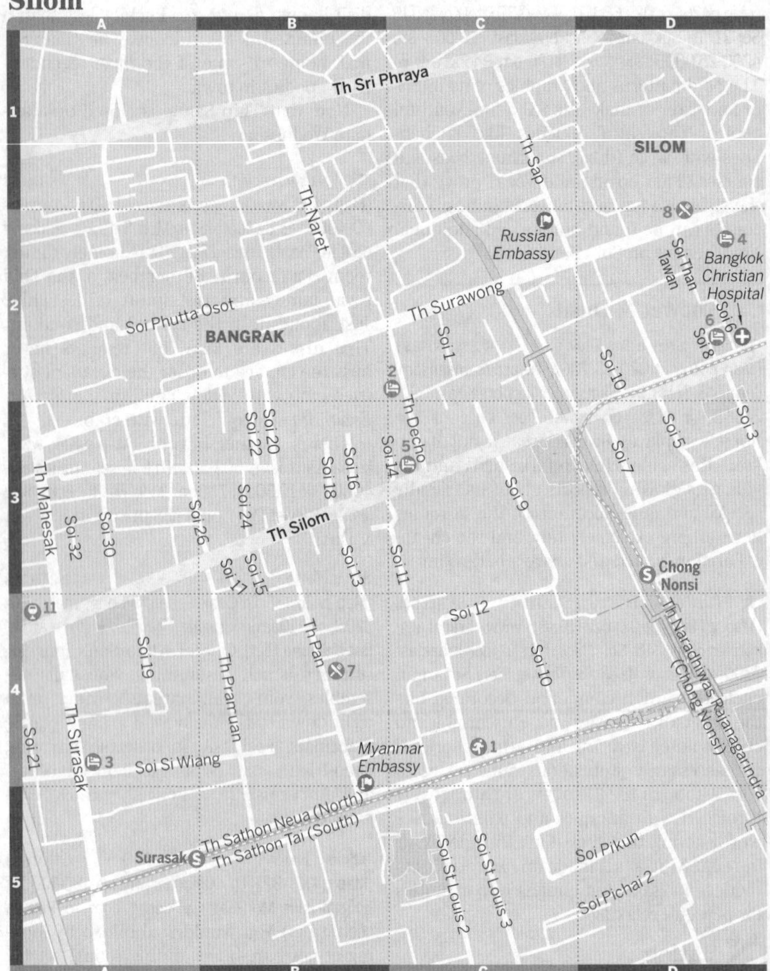

Pier, Ⓜ Hua Lamphong exit 1 & taxi) After sunset, these two opposing open-air restaurants – each of which claims to be the original – become a culinary train wreck of outdoor barbecues, screaming staff, iced seafood trays and messy pavement seating. True, the vast majority of diners are foreign tourists, but this has little impact on the cheerful setting, the fun experience and the cheap bill.

Royal India INDIAN **$$**
(Map p416; 392/1 Th Chakkaraphet; mains 70-350B; 10am-10pm; ; Saphan Phut/Memorial Bridge Pier, Pak Klong Taladd Pier) Yes, we're aware that this hole-in-the-wall has been in every edition of our guide since the beginning, but after all these years it's still the most reliable place to eat in Bangkok's Little India. Try any of the delicious breads or rich curries, and don't forget to finish with a homemade Punjabi sweet.

Samsara JAPANESE, THAI **$$**
(Map p404; Soi Khang Wat Pathum Khongkha; mains 110-320B; 4pm-midnight Tue-Thu, to 1am Fri-Sun; ; Ratchawong Pier, Ⓜ Hua Lamphong exit 1 & taxi) Combining Japanese and Thai dishes, Belgian beers and an artfully ram-

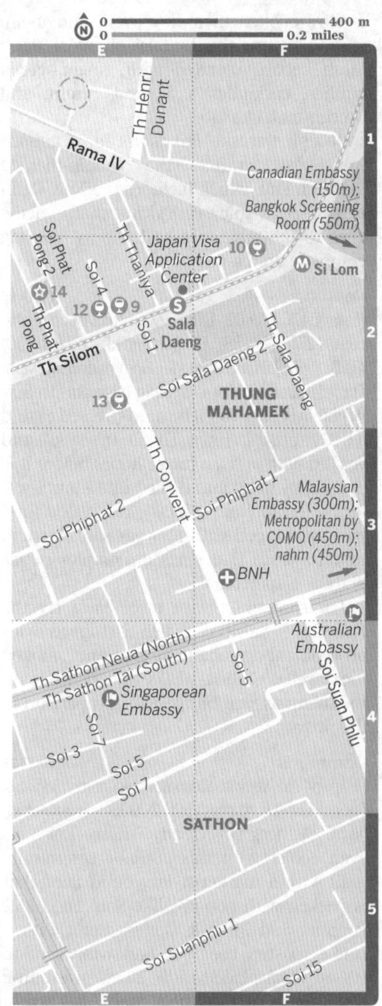

Silom

Activities, Courses & Tours

1	Health Land	C4

Sleeping

2	Lub*d	C2
3	Saphaipae	A4
4	Siam Heritage	D2
5	Silom Art Hostel	C3
6	Smile Society	D2

Eating

7	Chennai Kitchen	B4
8	Smokin' Pug	D2

Drinking & Nightlife

9	Balcony	E2
10	DJ Station	F2
11	Maggie Choo's	A4
12	Stranger	E2
	Telephone Pub	(see 12)
13	Vesper	E2

Entertainment

14	Patpong	E2

shackle atmosphere, Samsara is one of Chinatown's most eclectic places to eat. Its food is also very tasty, and the generous riverside breezes and views simply add to the package.

The restaurant is at the end of tiny Soi Khang Wat Pathum Khongkha, just west of the temple of the same name.

Siam Square, Pratunam, Ploenchit & Ratchathewi

★ MBK Food Island THAI $
(Map p412; 6th fl, MBK Center, cnr Th Phra Ram I & Th Phayathai; mains 35-150B; 10am-9pm; ; National Stadium exit 4) The recently-renovated MBK Food Island retains its crown as the grandaddy of Bangkok food courts, with dozens of vendors offering exceedingly cheap and tasty regional Thai, international and even vegetarian dishes.

Riverside, Silom & Lumphini

Chennai Kitchen INDIAN $
(Map p422; 107/4 Th Pan; mains 70-150B; 10am-3pm & 6-9.30pm; ; Surasak exit 3) This thimble-sized mum-and-dad restaurant puts out some of the best southern Indian vegetarian food in town. Metre-long *dosai* (a crispy southern Indian bread) is always a good choice, but if you're feeling indecisive (or exceptionally famished) go for the banana-leaf thali (set meal) that seems to incorporate just about everything in the kitchen.

Smokin' Pug BARBECUE $$
(Map p422; 083 029 7598; www.smokinpugbbq.com; 88 Th Surawong; mains 375-825B; 5-11pm Tue-Sat, to 10pm Sun; Chong Nonsi) Ask any American expat what their favourite non-Thai restaurant in town is, and the odds are outstanding that the Smokin' Pug is the answer. Start with a half order of the baby back ribs, which fall off the bone with a simple prod of the fork, before moving on to a

pulled-pork sandwich smothered in tangy BBQ sauce.

All the meats are smoked in-house daily, and the folks behind the bar are the affable husband-and-wife owners, Danny and Dana, who welcome patrons by their first name as they dole out stiff cocktails and American craft beers on tap. With fewer than 15 tables, the small restaurant is packed to the gills nightly, so email several days in advance or try your luck at the first-come, first-served bar area.

Kai Thort Jay Kee THAI $$

(Polo Fried Chicken; Map p404; 137/1-3 Soi Sanam Khli/Polo; mains 50-350B; 11am-9pm; ; M Lumphini exit 3) Although the *sôm·dam* (spicy green papaya salad), sticky rice and *lâhp* (a spcy salad of minced meat) of this former street stall give the impression of a northeastern-Thai-style eatery, the restaurant's namesake deep-fried bird is more southern in origin. Regardless, smothered in a thick layer of crispy deep-fried garlic, it is none other than a truly Bangkok experience.

★ nahm THAI $$$

(02 625 3388; www.comohotels.com/metropolitanbangkok/dining/nahm; Ground fl, Metropolitan Hotel, 27 Th Sathon Tai/South; set lunch 600-1600B, set dinner 2500B, dishes 300-800B; noon-2pm Mon-Fri, 7-10.30pm daily; ; M Lumphini exit 2) Australian chef-author David Thompson is the man behind one of Bangkok's – and if you believe the critics, the world's – best Thai restaurants. Using ancient cookbooks as his inspiration, Thompson has given new life to previously extinct dishes with exotic descriptions such as 'smoked fish curry with prawns, chicken livers, cockles, chillies and black pepper'.

Dinner is best approached via the multi-course set meal, while lunch means *kà·nŏm jeen*, thin rice noodles served with curries.

If you're expecting bland, gentrified Thai food meant for foreigners, prepare to be disappointed. Reservations recommended.

Thanon Sukhumvit

Charcoal Tandoor Grill & Mixology INDIAN $$

(Map p426; 089 307 1111; www.charcoalbkk.com; 5th fl, Fraser Suites Sukhumvit, Soi 11, Th Sukhumvit; mains 290-1050B; 6pm-midnight; S Nana) Indian food in Bangkok is gaining speed, and this kebab and tandoor grill restaurant has struck gold. Almost every dish is slow-cooked in a clay oven, and menu standouts are the buttery charcoal dahl; lamb kebabs blended with ginger, green chillies, coriander and royal cumin; and murgh malai kabab.

Joseph Boroski, Bangkok's most famous mixologist, crafted the Indian-themed drinks menu, which includes the New Delhi Duty Free, a spicy rum drink that is delivered to the table in a sealed duty-free bag complete with a passport.

Peppina PIZZA $$

(Map p426; 02 119 7677; http://peppinabkk.com; 27/1 Soi 33, Th Sukhumvit; pizzas 160-415B; 11.30am-3pm & 6pm-midnight Mon-Thu, 11.30am-2.30pm & 6pm-midnight Fri-Sun; S Phrom Phong) You'll be hard-pressed to find a better pizza in town. The flour, sea salt and yeast dough is risen for 24 hours before it is opened by hand and turned into mouth-watering Neapolitan pizzas. The wood-fired pies are topped with a sweet San Marzano tomato sauce that sings on simpler pizzas like the Napoletana.

For something with more kick, try the Friarelli E Salsicce, which is topped with broccoli rabe, Italian sausage and smoked mozzarella. Grilled steaks and fish are on the menu as well but pale in comparison to the pizza.

Commons MARKET $$

(Map p426; www.thecommonsbkk.com; 335 Soi Thong Lor 17; dishes 500-2000B; 8am-midnight; S Thong Lo) Trendy Thong Lor gets even cooler with this outdoor community mall with a market-style ground floor that is packed with pop-ups like Soul Food 555, Peppina and Meat & Bones, along with a coffee roaster, beer bar and wine vendor. It's an ideal place to idle away an evening listening to Jack Johnson wannabes strum acoustic sets.

★ Jidori-Ya Kenzou JAPANESE $$$

(Map p426; 02 661 3457; off Soi 26, Th Sukhumvit; dishes 60-350B; 5pm-midnight Mon-Sat; ; S Phrom Phong exit 4) This cosy Japanese restaurant does excellent tofu dishes, delicious salads and even excellent desserts; basically everything here is above average, but the highlight is the smoky, perfectly seasoned chicken skewers. Reservations recommended.

Bo.lan THAI $$$

(Map p426; 02 260 2962; www.bolan.co.th; 24 Soi 53, Th Sukhumvit; set meals 980-2680B; noon-2.30pm Sat & Sun, 6-10.30pm Tue-Sun;

❄ ✍; S Thong Lo exit 1) Upscale Thai is often more garnish than flavour, but Bo.lan has proven to be the exception. Bo and Dylan (Bo.lan is a play on words that also means Ancient) take a scholarly approach to Thai cuisine, and generous set meals featuring full-flavoured Thai dishes are the results of this tuition (à la carte is not available; meat-free meals are). Reservations recommended.

Thewet & Dusit

★Likhit Kai Yang THAI $$

(Map p416; off Th Ratchadamnoen Nok, no roman-script sign; mains 50-280B; ⏲9am-9pm; ❄; ⛴ Thewet Pier, S Phaya Thai exit 3 & taxi) Located just behind Ratchadamnoen Stadium (avoid the grotty branch directly adjacent to the stadium), this decades-old restaurant is where locals come for a northeastern-Thai-style meal before a Thai boxing match. The friendly English-speaking owner will steer you through the ordering process, but don't miss the deliciously herbal, eponymous 'charcoal roasted chicken'.

Look for the huge yellow banner.

Greater Bangkok

Foontalop THAI $

(Map p404; Section 26, Stall 319, Chatuchak Weekend Market, Th Phahonyothin, no roman-script sign; mains 20-70B; ⏲10am-6pm Sat to Sun; M Chatuchak Park exit 1, Kamphaeng Phet exits 1 & 2, S Mo Chit exit 1) An incredibly popular Isan restaurant located in Bangkok's Chatuchak Weekend Market.

Drinking & Nightlife

Shame on you if you think Bangkok's only nightlife options include the word 'go-go'. As in any big international city, the drinking and partying scene in Bangkok ranges from trashy to classy, and touches on just about everything in between.

Banglamphu

Madame Musur BAR

(Map p416; www.facebook.com/madamemusur; 41 Soi Ram Buttri; ⏲8am-midnight; ⛴ Phra Athit/Banglamphu Pier) Saving you the trip north to Pai, Madame Musur pulls off that elusive combination of northern Thailand meets *The Beach* meets Th Khao San. It's a fun place to chat, drink and people-watch, and it's also not a bad place to eat, with a short menu of northern Thai dishes priced from 100B to 200B.

The Club CLUB

(Map p416; www.facebook.com/theclubkhaosanbkk; 123 Th Khao San; admission Fri & Sat 120B; ⏲9pm-2am; ⛴ Phra Athit/Banglamphu Pier) Located right in the middle of Th Khao San, this cavern-like dancehall hosts a good mix of locals and backpackers; check the Facebook page for upcoming events and guest DJs.

Hippie de Bar BAR

(Map p416; www.facebook.com/hippie.debar; 46 Th Khao San; ⏲3pm-2am; ⛴ Phra Athit/Banglamphu Pier) Our vote for Banglamphu's best bar, Hippie boasts a funky retro vibe and indoor and outdoor seating, all set to the type of indie/pop soundtrack that you're unlikely to hear elsewhere in town. Despite being located on Th Khao San, there are surprisingly few foreign faces, and it's a great place to make some new Thai friends.

Phra Nakorn Bar & Gallery BAR

(Map p416; www.facebook.com/Phranakornbarandgallery; 58/2 Soi Damnoen Klang Tai; ⏲6pm-1am; ⛴ klorng boat to Phanfa Leelard Pier) Located an ambivalent arm's length from the hype of Th Khao San, Phra Nakorn Bar & Gallery is a home away from hovel for Thai students and arty types, with eclectic decor and changing gallery exhibits. Our tip: head directly for the breezy rooftop and order some of the bar's cheap and tasty Thai food.

Siam Square, Pratunam, Ploenchit & Ratchathewi

Il Fumo Bar & Restaurant BAR

(www.ilfumo.co; 1098 Th Rama IV; ⏲6pm-1am Mon-Sat, to midnight Sun; M Khlong Toei) Owners of the wildly popular **Vesper** (Map p422; www.vesperbar.co; 10/15 Th Convent; ⏲noon-2.30pm & 6pm-1am Mon-Fri, 6pm-midnight Sat, noon-2.30pm Sun; M Si Lom exit 2, S Sala Daeng exit 2) have expanded their foodie empire to this 20th-century villa once owned by a former Thai king. In contrast to the all-white modernist dining room, the bar area is decked out with panelled wood and leather armchairs. Behind the bar is Palin 'Milk' Sajjanit, 2016's best bartender in Asia, who will knock your sandals off with her Smoking Bulleit cocktail, made with Bulleit Rye and Los Danzantes Joven Mezcal.

Sukhumvit

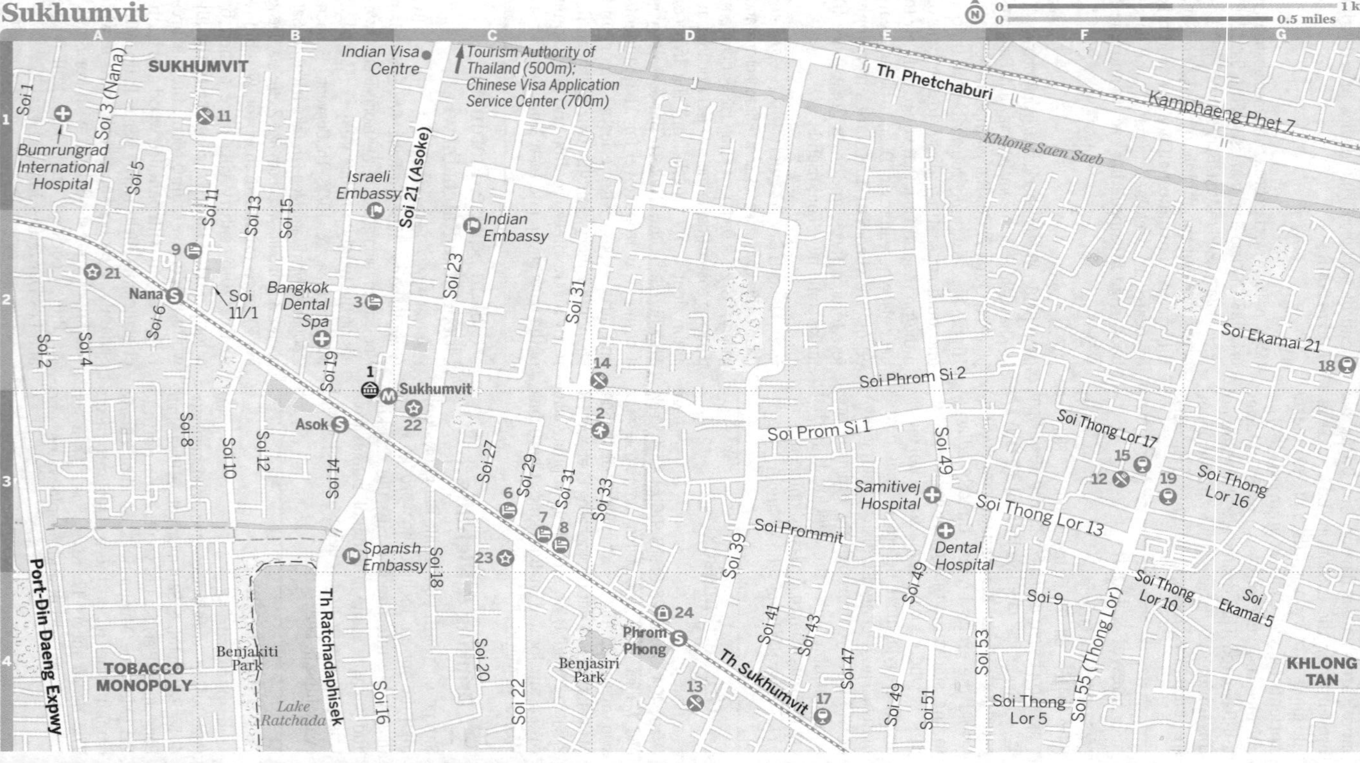
0 1 km
0 0.5 miles
SUKHUMVIT
Indian Visa Centre
Tourism Authority of Thailand (500m); Chinese Visa Application Service Center (700m)
Th Phetchaburi
Kamphaeng Phet 7
Khlong Saen Saeb
Soi 1
Soi 3 (Nana)
Bumrungrad International Hospital
Soi 5
Soi 11
Soi 13
Soi 15
Israeli Embassy
Soi 21 (Asoke)
Indian Embassy
Soi 23
Soi 31
Nana
Soi 11/1
Bangkok Dental Spa
Soi 6
Soi 2
Soi 4
Soi 19
Sukhumvit
Asok
Soi 8
Soi 10
Soi 12
Soi 14
Soi Ekamai 21
Soi Phrom Si 2
Soi Prom Si 1
Soi Thong Lor 17
Soi 49
Soi Thong Lor 16
Samitivej Hospital
Soi Thong Lor 13
Soi 27
Soi 29
Soi 33
Soi Prommit
Dental Hospital
Spanish Embassy
Soi 18
Soi 39
Soi Thong Lor 10
Soi Ekamai 5
Soi 9
Port-Din Daeng Expwy
Th Ratchadaphisek
Phrom Phong
Soi 41
Soi 43
Soi 47
Soi 53
Soi 55 (Thong Lor)
TOBACCO MONOPOLY
Benjakiti Park
Lake Ratchada
Soi 16
Soi 20
Soi 22
Benjasiri Park
Th Sukhumvit
Soi 51
Soi Thong Lor 5
KHLONG TAN

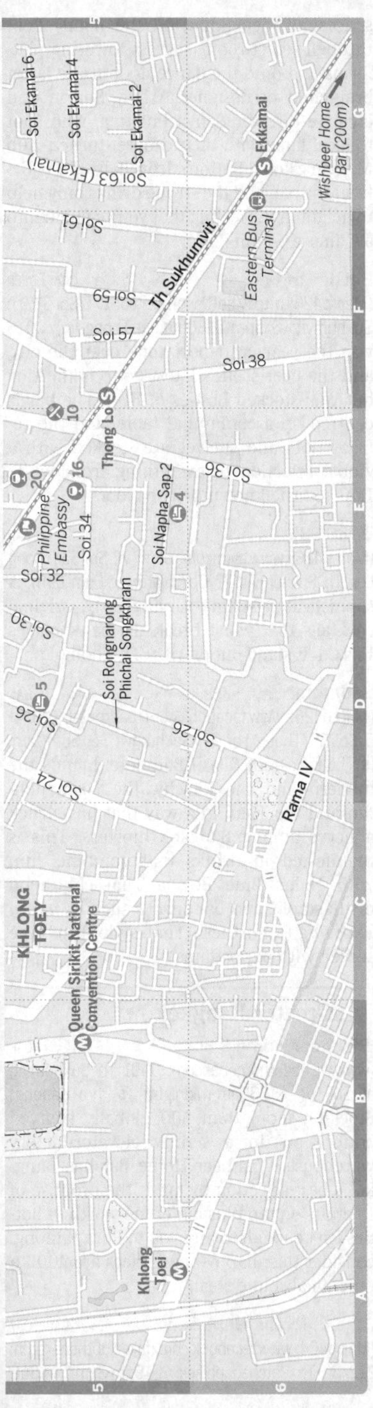

Sukhumvit

Top Sights
1 Siam Society & Ban Kamthieng ... B2

Activities, Courses & Tours
2 Asia Herb Association ... D3

Sleeping
3 Fusion Suites ... B2
4 Napa Place ... E5
5 Pause Hostel ... D5
6 RetrOasis ... C3
7 S31 ... C3
8 S-Box ... C3
9 Suk 11 ... A2

Eating
10 Bo.lan ... E5
11 Charcoal Tandoor Grill & Mixology ... B1
12 Commons ... F3
13 Jidori-Ya Kenzou ... D4
14 Peppina ... D2

Drinking & Nightlife
15 Badmotel ... F3
16 Bottles of Beer ... E5
17 Sing Sing Theater ... E4
18 Tuba ... G2
19 U.N.C.L.E ... F3
20 WTF ... E5

Entertainment
21 Nana Entertainment Plaza ... A2
22 Soi Cowboy ... C3
23 Titanium ... C3

Shopping
24 Emquartier ... D4

Co-Co Walk BAR

(Map p412; 87/70 Th Phayathai; 5pm-midnight; S Ratchathewi exit 2) This covered compound is a loud, messy smorgasbord of pubs, bars and live music popular with Thai university students on a night out. We'd list a few specific bars here, but they'd most likely all have changed names by the time you read this – it's just that kinda place.

Riverside, Silom & Lumphini

DJ Station CLUB, GAY

(Map p422; www.dj-station.com; 8/6-8 Soi 2, Th Silom; admission from 150B; 10pm-2am; M Si Lom exit 2, S Sala Daeng exit 1) One of Bangkok's and indeed Asia's most legendary gay dance clubs, here the crowd is a mix of Thai guppies (gay professionals), money boys and a few Westerners. There are several similar clubs in Soi 2.

Stranger BAR
(Map p422; www.facebook.com/TheStrangerBar; Soi 4, Th Silom; 5.45pm-2am) Probably the most low-key, sophisticated venue on Soi 4 – except during the drag shows on Monday, Friday and Saturday nights.

Maggie Choo's BAR
(Map p422; www.facebook.com/maggiechoos; Basement, Novotel Bangkok Fenix Silom, 320 Th Silom; 7.30pm-2am Sun-Thu, to 3am Fri & Sat; S Surasak exit 1) A former bank vault with a Chinatown-opium-den vibe, secret passageways and lounging women in silk dresses. With all this going on, it's easy to forget that Maggie Choo's is actually a bar, although you'll be reminded by the creative and somewhat sweet cocktails, and a crowd that blends selfie-snapping locals and curious tourists.

Balcony BAR, GAY
(Map p422; www.balconypub.com; 86-88 Soi 4, Th Silom; 5.30pm-2am; ; M Si Lom exit 2, S Sala Daeng exit 1) Balcony is a long-standing Soi 4 gay pub that features the occasional drag-queen performance.

Thanon Sukhumvit

★WTF BAR
(Map p426; www.wtfbangkok.com; 7 Soi 51, Th Sukhumvit; 6pm-1am Tue-Sun; ; S Thong Lo exit 3) Wonderful Thai Friendship (what did you think it stood for?) is a funky and friendly neighbourhood bar that also packs in a gallery space. Arty locals and resident foreigners come for the old-school cocktails, live music and DJ events, poetry readings, art exhibitions and tasty bar snacks. And we, like them, give WTF our vote for Bangkok's best bar.

★Tuba BAR
(Map p426; www.facebook.com/tubabkk; 34 Room 11-12 A, Soi Thong Lor 20/Soi Ekamai 21; 11am-2am; S Ekkamai exit 1 & taxi) Part storage room for over-the-top vintage furniture, part restaurant, part friendly local boozer; this quirky bar certainly doesn't lack in diversity – nor fun. Indulge in a whole bottle (they'll hold onto it for your next visit if you don't finish it) and don't miss the moreish chicken wings or the delicious *lâhp* (a tart/spicy salad of minced meat).

Sing Sing Theater BAR
(Map p426; www.singsingbangkok.com; Soi 45, Th Sukhumvit; 9pm-2am Tue-Sun; S Phrom Phong) Dancers dressed in cheongsams or neon spacesuits (depending on the night) float through secret rooms, across towering platforms and onto the dance floor at the latest brainchild of designer Ashley Sutton and creative director Sanya Phouma, who shot to local fame with their cabaret-turned-club Maggie Choo's. Sutton's Iron Balls gin is behind the bar, and the strong drinks only help to heighten the feeling that you've fallen into a Chinese opium den.

Bottles of Beer CRAFT BEER
(Map p426; http://bottlesofbeer.co; 2/7 Soi 34, Th Sukhumvit; 5pm-12.30am; S Thong Lo) 2016 was the year craft beer took over the city, and the beer scene's latest go-to is the tiny but well-stocked Bottles of Beer. The bar is centred on a communal table, and the refrigerators and shelves are stocked with a global selection of everything from white IPAs to little-known British ciders.

U.N.C.L.E BAR
(Map p426; www.avunculus.com; 72 Soi 55/Thong Lor, Th Sukhumvit, 72 Courtyard; 6pm-1am) A sophisticated setting serving tasty, original cocktails that won't break the bank makes U.N.C.L.E stand out on ritzy Th Thong Lor.

Badmotel BAR
(Map p426; www.facebook.com/badmotel; 331/4-5 Soi 55/Thong Lor, Th Sukhumvit; 5pm-1am; S Thong Lo exit 3 & taxi) Badmotel blends the modern and the kitschy, the cosmopolitan and the Thai, in a way that has struck a nerve among Bangkok hipsters. This is manifested in drinks that combine rum with Hale's Blue Boy, a Thai childhood drink staple, and bar snacks such as *naam prik ong* (a northern Thai–style dip), here served with pappadams.

Greater Bangkok

Wishbeer Home Bar BAR
(www.wishbeerhomebar.com; 1491 Th Sukhumvit, at Soi 67; 7.30am-midnight; S Phra Kanong) Stocking more than 500 globally sourced craft beers in a scruffy elevator-factory warehouse, Wishbeer Home Bar has Bangkok's best selection by far. If the promise of 18 crafts on tap plus a lifetime worth of bottles isn't enough to lure you to Phra Kanong, consider this: happy-hour prices are 200B a pint, an absolute steal.

Fake Club The Next Gen CLUB, GAY
(Map p404; www.facebook.com/fakeclubthenextgen; 222/32 Th Ratchadaphisek; 9pm-3am; M Sut-

LGBT BANGKOK

Bangkok has a notoriously pink vibe to it. From kinky male-underwear shops mushrooming at street corners to lesbian-only get-togethers, as a homosexual you could eat, shop and play here for days without ever leaving the comfort of gay-friendly venues. Unlike elsewhere in Southeast Asia, homosexuality is not criminalised in Thailand and the general attitude remains extremely laissez-faire.

Best Gay & Lesbian Bars

Telephone Pub (Map p422; www.telephonepub.com; 114/11-13 Soi 4, Th Silom; ⏲6pm-1am; 📶; Ⓜ Si Lom exit 2, Ⓢ Sala Daeng exit 1) An old favorite in Bangkok's pinkest zone.

Stranger (p428) Probably the most low-key, sophisticated venue on Soi 4.

Balcony (p428) Streetside watering hole for local and visiting gays.

Maggie Choo's (p428) Sunday is gay day at this otherwise-hetero boozer.

Best Cabaret & Drag Shows

Playhouse Magical Cabaret (p431) Unapologetically camp drag shows.

Calypso Bangkok (p430) The cabaret show in Asiatique market.

thisan exit 3) In new digs is this long-standing, popular gay staple. Expect live music, cheesy choreography and lots of lasers.

★ Entertainment

Although Bangkok often seems to cater to the inner philistine in all of us, the city is home to a diverse but low-key art scene. Add to this dance performances, live music, some of the world's best-value cinemas and, yes, the infamous go-go bars, and you have a city whose entertainment scene spans from – in local parlance – *lo-so* (low society) to *hi-so* (high society).

☆ Banglamphu

★ Brick Bar LIVE MUSIC

(Map p416; www.brickbarkhaosan.com; Basement, Buddy Lodge, 265 Th Khao San; admission Sat & Sun 150B; ⏲7pm-1.30am; ⛴ Phra Athit/Banglamphu Pier) This basement pub, one of our fave destinations in Bangkok for live music, hosts a nightly revolving cast of bands for an almost exclusively Thai crowd – many of whom will end the night dancing on the tables. Brick Bar can get infamously packed, so be sure to get there early.

☆ Ko Ratanakosin & Thonburi

National Theatre THEATRE

(Map p416; ☎02 224 1342; 2 Th Ratchini; tickets 60-100B; ⛴ Chang Pier, Maharaj Pier, Phra Chan Tai Pier) The National Theatre holds performances of *kŏhn* (masked dance-drama based on stories from the *Ramakian*) at 2pm on the first and second Sundays of the month from January to September, and *lá·kon* (Thai dance-dramas) at 2pm on the first and second Sundays of the month from October to December. Tickets go on sale an hour before performances begin.

☆ Chinatown

Sala Chalermkrung THEATRE

(Map p416; ☎02 224 4499; www.salachalermkrung.com; 66 Th Charoen Krung; tickets 800-1200B; ⏲shows 7.30pm Thu & Fri; ⛴ Saphan Phut/Memorial Bridge Pier, Ⓜ Hua Lamphong exit 1 & taxi) This art deco Bangkok landmark, a former cinema dating to 1933, is one of the few remaining places *kŏhn* can be witnessed. The traditional Thai dance-drama is enhanced here by laser graphics, high-tech audio and English subtitles. Concerts and other events are also held; check the website for details.

☆ Siam Square, Pratunam, Ploenchit & Ratchathewi

Saxophone Pub & Restaurant LIVE MUSIC

(Map p404; www.saxophonepub.com; 3/8 Th Phayathai; ⏲7.30pm-1.30am; Ⓢ Victory Monument exit 2) After 30 years, Saxophone remains Bangkok's premier live-music venue – a dark, intimate space where you can pull up a chair just a few metres away from the band and see their every bead of sweat. If you prefer some mystique in your musicians, watch the blues, jazz, reggae or rock from the balcony.

Raintree LIVE MUSIC
(Map p404; Soi Ruam Chit; 6pm-1am Mon-Sat; S Victory Monument exit 2) This rustic pub is one of the few remaining places in town to hear 'songs for life', Thai folk music with roots in the political movements of the 1960s and '70s. Tasty bar snacks also make it a clever place to have a bite to eat.

☆ Riverside, Silom & Lumphini

Bangkok Screening Room CINEMA
(https://bkksr.com; 8-9 Soi Sala Deang 1; M Lumpini) Bangkok has heaps of attractions that draw tourists in – great weather, fantastic bars, unbeatable food, low prices – but it's not known for being an arts haven. This cinema is trying to change that, one indie film at a time. Check the website for the revolving list of films, but expect the roster to give budding Thai filmmakers a platform to showcase their work.

Book tickets a day in advance to score one of the 50 seats in the single screen theatre and grab a craft beer before settling in.

Calypso Bangkok CABARET
(Map p404; 02 688 1415; www.calypsocabaret.com; Asiatique, Soi 72-76, Th Charoen Krung; adult/child 1200/600B; show times 8.15pm & 9.45pm; shuttle ferry from Sathon/Central Pier) Located in Asiatique market, Calypso is yet another destination for *gà·teu·i* (transgender; also spelt *kàthoey*) cabaret.

Patpong RED-LIGHT DISTRICT
(Map p422; Th Phat Phong & Soi Phat Phong 2; 4pm-2am; M Si Lom exit 2, S Sala Daeng exit 1) One of the most famous red-light districts in the world, today any 'charm' that the area used to possess has been eroded by modern tourism. If you must, be sure to agree to the price of entry and drinks before taking a seat at one of Patpong's 1st-floor 'pussy shows', otherwise you're likely to receive an astronomical bill.

These days, fake Rolexes and Ed Hardy T-shirts are more ubiquitous than flesh in Patpong.

☆ Thanon Sukhumvit

Titanium LIVE MUSIC
(Map p426; www.titaniumbangkok.com; 2/30 Soi 22, Th Sukhumvit; 8pm-1am; S Phrom Phong exit 6) Many come to this cheesy 'ice bar' for the chill, the skimpily dressed working girls and the flavoured vodka, but we come for Unicorn, the all-female house band, who rock the house from Monday to Saturday.

Soi Cowboy RED-LIGHT DISTRICT
(Map p426; btwn Soi 21 (Asoke) & Soi 23, Th Sukhumvit; 4pm-2am; M Sukhumvit exit 2, S Asok exit 3) This single-lane strip of raunchy bars claims direct lineage to the post-Vietnam War R & R era. A real flesh trade functions amid the flashing neon.

Nana Entertainment Plaza RED-LIGHT DISTRICT
(Map p426; Soi 4, Th Sukhumvit; 4pm-2am; S Nana exit 2) Nana is a three-storey go-go bar complex where the sexpats are separated from the gawking tourists. It's also home to a few *gà·teu·i* (transgender person; also spelt *kàthoey*) bars.

☆ Thewet & Dusit

Ratchadamnoen Stadium SPECTATOR SPORT
(สนามมวยราชดำเนิน; Map p416; off Th Ratchadamnoen Nok; tickets 3rd class/2nd class/ringside 1000/1500/2000B; Thewet Pier, S Phaya Thai exit 3 & taxi) Ratchadamnoen Stadium, Bangkok's oldest and most venerable venue for *moo·ay tai* (Thai boxing; also spelt *muay Thai*), hosts matches on Monday, Wednesday and Thursday from 6.30pm to around 11pm, and Sunday at 3pm and 6.30pm. Be sure to buy tickets from the official ticket counter, not from the touts and scalpers who hang around outside the entrance.

☆ Greater Bangkok

Lumpinee Boxing Stadium SPECTATOR SPORT
(02 282 3141; www.muaythailumpinee.net/en; 6 Th Ramintra; tickets 3rd class/2nd class/ringside 1000/1500/2000B; M Chatuchak Park exit 2 & taxi, S Mo Chit exit 3 & taxi) The other of Bangkok's two premier Thai boxing rings has moved to fancy new digs north of town. Matches occur on Tuesdays and Fridays from 6.30pm to 11pm, and on Saturdays from 2pm to 8.30pm. It's located well north of central Bangkok; the best way to get here is via taxi.

Tawandang German Brewery LIVE MUSIC
(Map p404; www.tawandang.co.th; cnr Th Phra Ram III & Th Narathiwat Ratchanakharin/Th Chong

Nonsi; 5pm-1am; Chong Nonsi exit 2 & taxi) It's Oktoberfest all year round at this hangar-sized music hall. The Thai-German food is tasty, the house-made brews are entirely potable, and the nightly stage shows make singing along a necessity. Music starts at 8.30pm.

Playhouse Magical Cabaret CABARET
(Map p404; 02 024 5522; www.playhousethailand.com; 5 Ratchadapisek Rd, Chompol Sub-District, Chatuchak; adult/child 1200/600B; show times 7pm & 8.30pm; Lat Phrao exit 1) Watching *gà·teu·i* (transgender people; also spelt *kàthoey*) perform show tunes has, not surprisingly, become the latest must-do fixture on the Bangkok tourist circuit. Playhouse caters to the trend, with choreographed stage shows featuring Broadway high kicks and lip-synched pop performances.

Shopping

Prime your credit card and shine your baht, as shopping is serious business in Bangkok. Hardly a street corner in this city is free from a vendor, hawker or impromptu stall, and it doesn't stop there: Bangkok is also home to one of the world's largest outdoor markets, not to mention some of Southeast Asia's largest malls.

Riverside, Silom & Lumphini

Asiatique MARKET
(Map p404; Soi 72-76, Th Charoen Krung; 4-11pm; shuttle boat from Sathon/Central Pier) One of Bangkok's more popular night markets, Asiatique takes the form of warehouses of commerce next to Mae Nam Chao Phraya. Expect clothing, handicrafts, souvenirs and quite a few dining and drinking venues.

Frequent, free shuttle boats from Sathon/Central Pier from 4pm to 11.30pm.

Siam Square, Pratunam, Ploenchit & Ratchathewi

★MBK Center SHOPPING CENTRE
(Map p412; www.mbk-center.com; cnr Th Phra Ram I & Th Phayathai; 10am-10pm; National Stadium exit 4) Undergoing a renovation when we were in town, MBK is set to retain its role as one of Bangkok's top attractions. On any given weekend half of Bangkok's residents (and most of its tourists) can be found here combing through a seemingly inexhaustible range of small stalls and shops that span a whopping eight floors.

MBK is Bangkok's cheapest place to buy mobile phones and accessories (4th floor). It's also one of the better places to stock up on camera gear (ground floor and 5th floor), and the expansive food court (6th floor) is one of the best in town.

★Siam Square SHOPPING CENTRE
(Map p412; Th Phra Ram I; 11am-9pm; Siam exits 2, 4 & 6) This open-air shopping zone is ground zero for teenage culture in Bangkok. Pop music blares out of tinny speakers, and gangs of hipsters in various costumes ricochet between fast-food restaurants and closet-sized boutiques. It's a great place to pick up labels and designs you're guaranteed not to find anywhere else, though most outfits require a barely there waistline.

Siam Discovery SHOPPING CENTRE
(Map p412; www.siamdiscovery.co.th; cnr Th Phra Ram I & Th Phayathai; 10am-10pm; Siam exit 1) With an open, almost-market-like feel and an impressive variety of unique goods ranging from housewares to clothing (including lots of items by Thai designers), the recently renovated Siam Discovery is hands down the most design-conscious mall in town.

Thanon Sukhumvit

Emquartier SHOPPING CENTRE
(Map p426; www.theemdistrict.com; Th Sukhumvit; 10am-10pm; Phrom Phong exit 1) One of Bangkok's newest malls and arguably its flashiest. Come for brands you're not likely to find elsewhere, or get lost in the Helix, a spiral of more than 50 restaurants.

Information

DANGERS & ANNOYANCES

Bangkok is a safe city and incidents of violence against tourists are rare. That said, there is a repertoire of well-polished scams. But don't be spooked; commit the following to memory and you'll most likely enjoy a scam-free visit:

Gem scam We're begging you, if you aren't a gem trader, then don't buy unset stones in Thailand – period.

Closed today Ignore any 'friendly' local who tells you that an attraction is closed for a Buddhist holiday or for cleaning. These are set-ups for trips to a bogus gem sale.

Túk-túk rides for 20B Say goodbye to your day's itinerary if you climb aboard this ubiquitous scam. These alleged 'tours' bypass all the sights and instead cruise to all the fly-by-night gem and tailor shops that pay commissions.

Flat-fare taxi ride Flatly refuse any driver who quotes a flat fare (usually between 100B and 150B for in-town destinations), which will usually be three times more expensive than the reasonable meter rate. Walking beyond the tourist area will usually help in finding an honest driver. If the driver has 'forgotten' to put the meter on, just say, 'Meter, *kha/khap*'.

Friendly strangers Be wary of smartly dressed men who approach you asking where you're from and where you're going. Their opening gambit is usually followed with: 'Ah, my son/daughter is studying at university in (your city)' – they seem to have an encyclopedic knowledge of major universities. As the tourist authorities here point out, this sort of behaviour is out of character for Thais and should be treated with suspicion.

MEDICAL SERVICES

The following hospitals have English-speaking doctors.

Bangkok Christian Hospital (Map p422; ☎02 625 9000; www.bch.in.th/en; 124 Th Silom; Ⓜ Si Lom exit 2, Ⓢ Sala Daeng exit 1) Modern hospital in central Bangkok.

BNH (Map p422; ☎02 686 2700; www.bnhhospital.com; 9 Th Convent; Ⓜ Si Lom exit 2, Ⓢ Sala Daeng exit 2) Modern, centrally located hospital.

Bumrungrad International Hospital (Map p426; ☎02 667 1000; www.bumrungrad.com/thailandhospital; 33 Soi 3, Th Sukhumvit; ⏲24hr; Ⓢ Phloen Chit exit 3) An internationally accredited hospital.

Samitivej Hospital (Map p426; ☎02 022 2222; www.samitivejhospitals.com; 133 Soi 49, Th Sukhumvit; Ⓢ Phrom Phong exit 3 & taxi) Modern hospital in Bangkok.

Business is good in the teeth game, partly because so many *fa·ràng* (Westerners) are combining their holiday with a spot of cheap root-canal work or some 'personal outlook' care – a teeth-whitening treatment by any other name. Prices are a bargain compared with Western countries, and the quality of dentistry is generally high.

Bangkok Dental Spa (Map p426; ☎02 651 0807; www.bangkokdentalspa.com; 2nd fl, Methawattana Bldg, 27 Soi 19, Th Sukhumvit; ⏲by appointment only; Ⓜ Sukhumvit exit 3, Ⓢ Asok exit 1) Dental-care centre with a spa-like environment.

DC-One the Dental Clinic (Map p404; ☎02 240 2800; www.dc-one.com; 31 Th Yen Akat; ⏲by appointment only; Ⓜ Lumphini exit 2 & taxi) Dental clinic with reputation for excellent work and relatively high prices; popular with UN staff and diplomats.

Dental Hospital (Map p426; ☎02 260 5000; www.dentalhospitalbangkok.com; 88/88 Soi 49, Th Sukhumvit; ⏲9am-8pm Mon-Sat, to 4.30pm Sun; Ⓢ Phrom Phong exit 3 & taxi) A private dental clinic with fluent English-speaking dentists.

Siam Family Dental Clinic (Map p412; ☎081 987 7700; www.siamfamilydental.com; 209 Th Phayathai; ⏲11am-8pm Mon-Fri, 10am-7pm Sat & Sun; Ⓢ Siam exit 2) Private dental clinic in central Bangkok.

TOURIST INFORMATION

The police contact number functions as the de facto universal emergency number in Thailand, and can also be used to call an ambulance or report a fire.

The best way to deal with most problems requiring police (usually a rip-off or theft) is to contact the tourist police, who are used to dealing with foreigners and can be very helpful in cases of arrest. The English-speaking unit investigates criminal activity involving tourists and can act as a bilingual liaison with the regular police. Although they typically have no jurisdiction over the kinds of cases handled by regular cops, they should be able to help with translation, contacting your embassy and/or arranging a police report you can take to your insurer.

Police	☎191
Tourist Police	☎1155

Bangkok Immigration Office (☎02 141 9889; www.bangkok.immigration.go.th/intro1.html; Bldg B, Government Centre, Soi 7, Th Chaeng Watthana; ⏲8.30am-noon & 1-4.30pm Mon-Fri; Ⓜ Chatuchak Park exit 2 & taxi, Ⓢ Mo Chit exit 3 & taxi) In Bangkok, visa extensions are filed at this office.

Bangkok Information Center (Map p416; ☎02 225 7612-4; www.bangkoktourist.com; 17/1 Th Phra Athit; ⏲9am-7pm Mon-Fri, to 5pm Sat & Sun; ⛴ Phra Athit/Banglamphu Pier) City-specific tourism office providing maps, brochures and directions. Seldom-staffed kiosks and booths are found around town; look for the green-on-white symbol of a mahout on an elephant.

Tourism Authority of Thailand (TAT; ☎02 250 5500, nationwide 1672; www.tourismthailand.org; 1600 Th Phetchaburi Tat Mai; ⏲8.30am-4.30pm; Ⓜ Phetchaburi exit 2) The head TAT office has brochures and maps covering the whole country.

Getting There & Away

AIR

Bangkok has two airports. Located 30km east of central Bangkok, **Suvarnabhumi International Airport** (☎02 132 1888; www.suvarnabhumi airport.com) began commercial international and domestic service in 2006. The airport's name is pronounced *sù·wan·ná·poom,* and it inherited the airport code (BKK) previously held by the old airport at Don Mueang. The airport website has real-time details of arrivals and departures.

Bangkok's other airport, **Don Mueang International Airport** (☎02 535 2111; www.don mueangairportthai.com), 25km north of central Bangkok, was retired from service in 2006 only to reopen later as the city's de facto budget hub. Terminal 1 handles international flights, while Terminal 2 is for domestic destinations.

BUS

Buses using government bus stations are far more reliable and less prone to incidents of theft than those departing from Th Khao San or other tourist centres.

Eastern Bus Terminal (Map p426; ☎02 391 2504; Soi 40, Th Sukhumvit; S Ekkamai exit 2) The departure point for buses to Pattaya, Rayong, Chanthaburi and other points east, except for the border crossing at Aranya Prathet. Most people call it *sà·tǎh·nee èk·gà·mai* (Ekamai station). It's near the Ekkamai BTS station.

GETTING TO CAMBODIA: ARANYA PRATHET TO POIPET

Getting to the border The easiest way to get from Bangkok to Siem Reap overland is the direct bus departing from the Northern (Mo Chit) Bus Terminal. The through-service bus trips sold on Th Khao San and elsewhere in Bangkok seem cheap and convenient, but they haven't been nicknamed 'scam buses' for nothing, and if using them you will be likely hassled and ripped off, often quite aggressively.

If you choose to do it in stages (much cheaper than the direct Mo Chit bus), you can get from Bangkok to the border town of Aranya Prathet (aka Aran) by bus from Mo Chit, by bus or minivan from the Eastern (Ekamai) Bus Terminal, by bus from Suvarnabhumi International Airport bus station, by minivan from Victory Monument or by 3rd-class train (only the 5.55am departure will get you there early enough, at 11.35am, to reach Siem Reap the same day) from Hualamphong. Aran also has bus services about every one or two hours from other cities in the area including Khorat, Surin and Chanthaburi. All minivans, plus some buses, go all the way to the Rong Kluea Market next to the border, so there's no need to stop in Aranya Prathet city. Otherwise, you'll need to take a *sŏrng·tăa·ou* (15B), motorcycle taxi (60B) or túk-túk (pronounced *đúk đúk*; 80B) the final 7km to the border.

At the border The border is open 7am to 8pm daily. There are many persistent scammers on the Thai side trying to get you to buy your Cambodia visa through them, but no matter what they might tell you, there's absolutely no good reason to get visas anywhere except the border. Buying them elsewhere costs more and takes longer. Don't even show your passport to anyone before you reach Thai immigration and don't change money.

After getting stamped out of Thailand – a straightforward process – follow the throng to Cambodian immigration and find the 'Visa on Arrival' sign if you don't already have a visa. Weekday mornings you might finish everything in 10 to 20 minutes, but if you arrive after noon it could take an hour or more. Weekends and holidays, when many Thais arrive to gamble and foreign workers do visa runs, are also busy. You will probably be offered the opportunity to pay a 'special VIP fee' of 200B to jump to the front of the queue. You will almost certainly be asked to pay another small 'fee', which will be called a 'stamping' or 'overtime' fee. You should refuse, though doing so might mean you have to wait a few extra minutes.

Moving on There are frequent buses and share taxis from Poipet to Siem Reap along a good sealed road from the main bus station, which is about 1km away (2000r by motorcycle taxi) around the main market, one block north of Canadia Bank on NH5. Poipet also has a second 'international' bus station 9km east of town where prices are double and which is only used by uninformed or gullible foreigners who get swept into the free shuttle that takes travellers out there. Lonely Planet's *Cambodia* guide has full details for travel on this side of the border.

Northern & Northeastern Bus Terminal (Mo Chit; Map p404; ☎ northeastern routes 02 936 2852, ext 602/605, northern routes 02 936 2841, ext 325/614; Th Kamphaeng Phet) Located just north of Chatuchak Park, this hectic bus station is also commonly called *kŏn sòng mŏr chít* (Mo Chit station) – not to be confused with Mo Chit BTS station. Buses depart from here for all northern and northeastern destinations, as well as international destinations including Pakse (Laos), Phnom Penh (Cambodia), Siem Reap (Cambodia) and Vientiane (Laos). To reach the bus station, take BTS to Mo Chit or MRT to Kamphaeng Phet and transfer onto city bus 3, 77 or 509, or hop on a taxi or motorcycle taxi.

Southern Bus Terminal (Sai Tai Mai; ☎ 02 422 4444, call centre 1490; Th Boromaratchachonanee) The city's southern bus terminal, commonly called *săi đâi mài,* lies a long way west of the centre of Bangkok. Besides serving as the departure point for all buses south of Bangkok, transport to Kanchanaburi and western Thailand also departs from here. The easiest way to reach the station is by taxi, or you can take bus 79, 159, 201 or 516 from Th Ratchadamnoen Klang, or the minivan or bus 40 from the **Victory Monument** (อนุสาวรีย์ชัย; Map p404; cnr Th Ratchawithi & Th Phayathai; ⏲24hr; S Victory Monument exit 2).

MINIVAN

➡ Privately run minivans, called *rót đôo,* are a fast and relatively comfortable way to get between Bangkok and its neighbouring provinces.

➡ Several minivans depart from various points surrounding the Victory Monument, although when we researched this there was talk of relocating these to the various bus terminals.

TRAIN

Bangkok Noi (☎ 02 418 4310, call centre 1690; www.railway.co.th; off Th Itsaraphap; ⛴ Thonburi Railway Station, Wang Lang/Siriraj Pier, S Wongwian Yai exit 4 & taxi) Also known as Thonburi, a miniscule train station with (overpriced) departures for Kanchanaburi.

Hualamphong (☎ 02 220 4334, call centre 1690; www.railway.co.th; off Th Phra Ram IV; M Hua Lamphong exit 2) The city's main train terminus. It's advisable to ignore all touts here and avoid the travel agencies. To check timetables and prices for destinations call the State Railway of Thailand or look at its website.

Wong Wian Yai (☎ 02 465 2017, call centre 1690; www.railway.co.th; off Th Phra Jao Taksin; S Wongwian Yai exit 4 & taxi) This tiny hidden station is the jumping-off point for the commuter line to Samut Sakhon (also known as Mahachai).

Getting Around

For short-term visitors, you will find parking and driving a car in Bangkok more trouble than it is worth. If you need private transport, consider hiring a car and driver through your hotel or hire a taxi driver that you find trustworthy.

TO/FROM THE AIRPORT

Suvarnabhumi International Airport

Just about everybody flying to Bangkok comes through Suvarnabhumi International Airport (p433). The unofficial website has real-time details of airport arrivals and departures. Left-luggage facilities are available on level 2, beside the helpful office of the **Tourism Authority of Thailand** (TAT; ☎ 02 134 0040, nationwide 1672; www.tourismthailand.org; 2nd fl, btwn Gates 2 & 5, Suvarnabhumi International Airport; ⏲24hr).

Bus & Minivan

A public transport centre is 3km from the airport and includes a bus terminal with buses to a handful of provinces and inner-city-bound buses and minivans. A free airport shuttle connects the transport centre with the passenger terminals.

➡ Bus lines that city-bound tourists are likely to use include line 551 to BTS Victory Monument station (40B, frequent from 5am to 10pm) and 552 to BTS On Nut (20B, frequent from 5am to 10pm). From these points, you can continue by public transport or taxi to your hotel.

INTERNATIONAL BUSES

A handful of buses bound for international destinations depart from Bangkok's Northern & Northeastern Bus Terminal.

DESTINATION	COST (B)	DURATION (HR)	FREQUENCY
Pakse (Laos)	900	12	8.30pm
Phnom Penh	750	11	1.30am
Siem Reap (Cambodia)	750	7	9am
Vientiane (Laos)	900	10	8pm

Taxi

Metered taxis are available kerbside at Floor 1 – ignore the 'official airport taxi' touts who approach you inside the terminal.

Typical metered fares from Suvarnabhumi include 200B to 250B to Th Sukhumvit; 250B to 300B to Th Khao San; 400B to Mo Chit. Toll charges (paid by passengers) vary between 25B and 70B. Note that there's a 50B surcharge added to all fares departing from the airport, payable directly to the driver.

Train

The **Airport Rail Link** (☎ call centre 1690; www.srtet.co.th) connects Suvarnabhumi International Airport with the BTS (Skytrain) stop at Phaya Thai (45B, 30 minutes, from 6am to midnight) and the MRT (Metro) stop at Phetchaburi (45B, 25 minutes, from 6am to midnight).

Don Mueang International Airport

Bus

From outside the arrivals hall, there are two airport bus lines from Don Mueang: A1 makes a stop at BTS Mo Chit (30B, frequent from 7.30am to 11.30pm); while the less frequent A2 makes stops at BTS Mo Chit and BTS Victory Monument (30B, every 30 minutes from 7.30am to 11.30pm).

Public buses stop on the highway in front of the airport. Useful lines include 29, with a stop at Victory Monument BTS station before terminating at Hualamphong Train Station (24 hours); line 59, with a stop near Th Khao San (24 hours); and line 538, stopping at Victory Monument BTS station (4am to 10pm); fares are approximately 23B.

Taxi

As at Suvarnabhumi, public taxis leave from outside both arrival halls and there is a 50B airport charge added to the meter fare.

Train

The walkway that crosses from the airport to the Amari Airport Hotel also provides access to Don Muang Train Station, which has trains to Hualamphong Train Station every one to 1½ hours from 4am to 11.30am and then roughly every hour from 2pm to 9.30pm (from 5B to 10B).

BOAT

A fleet of boats, both those that run along the Chao Phraya River and along the city's canals, serve Bangkok's commuters.

Klorng Boats

Canal taxi boats run along Khlong Saen Saep (Banglamphu to Ramkhamhaeng) and are an easy way to get between Banglamphu and Jim Thompson House, the Siam Sq shopping centres (get off at Sapan Hua Chang Pier for both), and other points further east along Th Sukhumvit – after a mandatory change of boat at Pratunam Pier.

- These boats are mostly used by daily commuters and pull into the piers for just a few seconds – jump straight on or you'll be left behind.
- Fares range from 9B to 19B and boats run from 5.30am to 7.15pm from Mondays to Fridays, from 6am to 6.30pm on Saturdays, and from 6am to 6pm on Sundays.

River Ferries

The **Chao Phraya Express Boat** (☎ 02 623 6001; www.chaophrayaexpressboat.com) operates the main ferry service along Mae Nam Chao Phraya. The central pier is known as Tha Sathon, Saphan Taksin or sometimes Sathon/Central Pier, and connects to the BTS at Saphan Taksin station.

- Boats run from 6am to 8pm. You can buy tickets (10B to 40B) at the pier or on board; hold on to your ticket as proof of purchase (an occasional formality).
- The most common boats are the orange-flagged express boats. These run between Wat Rajsingkorn, south of Bangkok, to Nonthaburi, north, stopping at most major piers (15B, frequent from 6am to 7pm).
- A blue-flagged tourist boat (40B, every 30 minutes from 9.30am to 5pm) runs from Sathon/Central Pier to Phra Athit/Banglamphu Pier, with stops at eight major sightseeing piers and barely comprehensible English-language commentary. Vendors at Sathon/Central Pier tout a 150B all-day pass, but unless you plan on doing a lot of boat travel, it's not great value.
- There are also dozens of cross-river ferries, which charge 3B and run every few minutes until late at night.
- Private long-tail boats can be hired for sightseeing trips at Phra Athit/Banglamphu Pier, Chang Pier, Tien Pier and Oriental Pier.

BTS & MRT

The elevated **BTS** (Skytrain; ☎ 02 617 6000, tourist information 02 617 7341; www.bts.co.th), also known as the Skytrain (*rót fai fáa*), whisks you through 'new' Bangkok (Silom, Sukhumvit and Siam Sq). The interchange between the two lines is at Siam station, and trains run frequently from 5.15am to 12.51am. Fares range from 15B to 52B, or 140B for a one-day pass. Most ticket machines only accept coins, but change is available at the information booths.

Bangkok's **MRT** (☎ 02 354 2000; www.bangkokmetro.co.th) or Metro is most helpful

> **TAXI ALTERNATIVES**
>
> App-based alternatives to the traditional taxis that operate in Bangkok:
>
> **All Thai Taxi** (www.allthaitaxi.com)
>
> **Easy Taxi** (www.easytaxi.com/th)
>
> **GrabTaxi** (www.grabtaxi.com/bangkok-thailand)
>
> **Uber** (www.uber.com/cities/bangkok)

for people staying in the Sukhumvit or Silom area to reach the train station at Hualamphong. Fares cost from 16B to 42B, or 120B for a one-day pass. The trains run frequently from 6am to midnight.

BUS

Bangkok's public buses are run by the **Bangkok Mass Transit Authority** (☎02 246 0973, call centre 1348; www.bmta.co.th).

- As the routes are not always clear, and with Bangkok taxis being such a good deal, you'd really have to be pinching pennies to rely on buses as a way to get around Bangkok.
- Air-con bus fares range from 10B to 23B, and fares for fan-cooled buses start at 6.50B.
- Most of the bus lines run between 5am and 10pm or 11pm, except for the 'all-night' buses, which run from 3am or 4am to midmorning.
- You'll most likely require the help of thinknet's *Bangkok Bus Guide*.

TAXI

- Although many first-time visitors are hesitant to use them, in general, Bangkok's taxis are new and comfortable and the drivers are courteous and helpful, making them an excellent way to get around.
- All taxis are required to use their meters, which start at 35B, and fares to most places within central Bangkok cost 60B to 90B. Freeway tolls – 25B to 70B depending on where you start – must be paid by the passenger.
- **Taxi Radio** (☎1681; www.taxiradio.co.th) and other 24-hour 'phone-a-cab' services are available for 20B above the metered fare.
- If you leave something in a taxi your best chance of getting it back (still pretty slim) is to call ☎1644.

TÚK-TÚK

- Bangkok's iconic túk-túk (pronounced *đúk đúk;* a type of motorised rickshaw) are used by Thais for short hops not worth paying the taxi flag fall for. For foreigners, however, these emphysema-inducing machines are part of the Bangkok experience, so despite the fact that they overcharge outrageously and you can't see anything due to the low roof, pretty much everyone takes a túk-túk at least once.
- Túk-túk are notorious for taking little 'detours' to commission-paying gem and silk shops and massage parlours. En route to 'special' temples, you'll meet 'helpful' locals who will steer you to even more rip-off opportunities. Ignore anyone offering too-good-to-be-true 20B trips.
- The vast majority of túk-túk drivers ask too much from tourists (expat *fa·ràng* never use them). Expect to be quoted a 100B fare, if not more, for even the shortest trip. Try bargaining them down to about 60B for a short trip, preferably at night when the pollution (hopefully) won't be quite so bad. Once you've done it, you'll find taxis are cheaper, cleaner, cooler and quieter.

THAILAND'S EASTERN SEABOARD

Ko Samet

Once the doyen of backpacker destinations, today Ko Samet shares its charms with a wider audience. The sandy shores, cosy coves and aquamarine waters attract ferry-loads of Bangkokians looking to party each weekend, while tour groups pack out many resorts. Fire-juggling shows and beach barbecues are nightly events on the northern beaches, but the southern parts of the island are far more secluded and sedate.

Despite being the closest major island to Bangkok, Ko Samet remains surprisingly underdeveloped, with a thick jungle interior crouching beside the low-rise hotels.

Sights & Activities

On some islands you beach-hop, but on Ko Samet you cove-hop. The coastal footpath traverses rocky headlands, cicada-serenaded forests and one stunning bay after another, where the mood becomes successively more mellow the further south you go.

Sleeping

Though resorts are replacing bungalows, much of Ko Samet's accommodation is still simple and old-fashioned. There are a handful of sub-700B fan rooms remaining. Look for discounts during low season and on weekdays.

A word of caution to early risers: Hat Sai Kaew, Ao Hin Khok, Ao Phai and Ao Wong Deuan are the most popular beaches and host well-amplified night-time parties.

Mossman House GUESTHOUSE $
(☎038 644017; Hat Sai Kaew; r 800-1300B; ❄📶) On the main street, just before the national park ticket office, is this sound guesthouse, with large, comfortable rooms and leafy grounds. Choose a spot at the back for some quiet.

Blue Sky BUNGALOW $
(☎089 936 0842; Ao Wong Deuan; r 600-1200B; ❄) A rare budget spot on Ao Wong Deuan, Blue Sky has beaten-up bungalows set on a rocky headland.

Tubtim Resort HOTEL $$
(☎038 644025; www.tubtimresort.com; Ao Phutsa/Ao Tub Tim; r incl breakfast 600-3500B; ❄@📶) A well-organised place with great, nightly barbecues and a range of solid, spacious bungalows of varying quality close to the beach.

Nice & Easy HOTEL $$
(☎038 644370; www.niceandeasysamed.com; Ao Wong Deuan; r 1200-2000B; ❄📶) As the name suggests, this is a very amiable place, with comfortable, modern bungalows set around a garden behind the beach. A great deal for this beach.

Ao Nuan Bungalows BUNGALOW $$
(☎081 781 4875; bungalows with fan 800-1200B, with air-con 1500-3000B; ❄) Ao Nuan is Samet's one remaining bohemian bay, with no internet and access only via a dirt track. Guests hang in hammocks outside their wooden bungalows here or chill in the attached restaurant. Tents are also available (450B).

★ **Samed Pavilion Resort** BOUTIQUE HOTEL $$$
(☎038 644420; www.samedpavilionresort.com; Ao Phai; r incl breakfast 3500-5500B; ❄@📶🏊) This gorgeous boutique resort has 85 elegant, spacious rooms set around a pool.

Eating & Drinking

Most hotels and guesthouses have restaurants that moonlight as bars after sunset. The food and service won't blow you away, but there aren't many alternatives. Nightly beach barbecues, starring all manner of seafood, are an island favourite. There are cheapie Thai places in Na Dan.

On weekends, Ko Samet is a boisterous night owl with tour groups crooning away on karaoke machines and the young ones slurping down beer and buckets to a techno beat. There is usually a crowd on Hat Sai Kaew, Ao Hin Khok, Ao Phai and Ao Wong Deuan.

Jep's Restaurant INTERNATIONAL $
(Ao Hin Khok; mains 60-150B; ⏰7am-11pm; 🖉) Canopied by the branches of an arching tree decorated with pendant lights, this pretty place does a wide range of international, and some Thai, dishes. Leave room for dessert.

Red Ginger INTERNATIONAL, THAI $$
(Na Dan; dishes 120-320B; ⏰11am-11pm; 🖉) A small but select menu of the French-Canadian chef's favourite dishes star at this atmospheric eatery between the pier and Hat Sai Kaew. Good salads, great oven-baked ribs, and some Thai food.

LOCAL KNOWLEDGE

BEACH ADMISSION FEE

Ko Samet is part of the Mu Ko Samet National Park and charges all visitors an entrance fee (adult/child 200/100B) upon arrival. If you can prove that you live and work in Thailand, it will only cost you 40B, the price Thais pay. The fee is collected at the **National Parks Main Office** (btwn Na Dan & Hat Sai Kaew; ⏰8.30am-4.30pm); *sǒrng·tăa·ou* (passenger pick-up trucks) from the pier will stop at the gates for payment. Hold on to your ticket for later inspections. There is a 20B fee when using Na Dan pier.

LIGHT YOUR FIRE

So you have seen the fire shows and want to learn how to twirl those blazing sticks? Ask K.Law or his friends at **Naga Bar** (Ao Hin Khok; beers from 70B; ⏰sunset-late) – they give free lessons to customers. It takes an hour to master the basics and three months to become dazzling.

Ko Samet

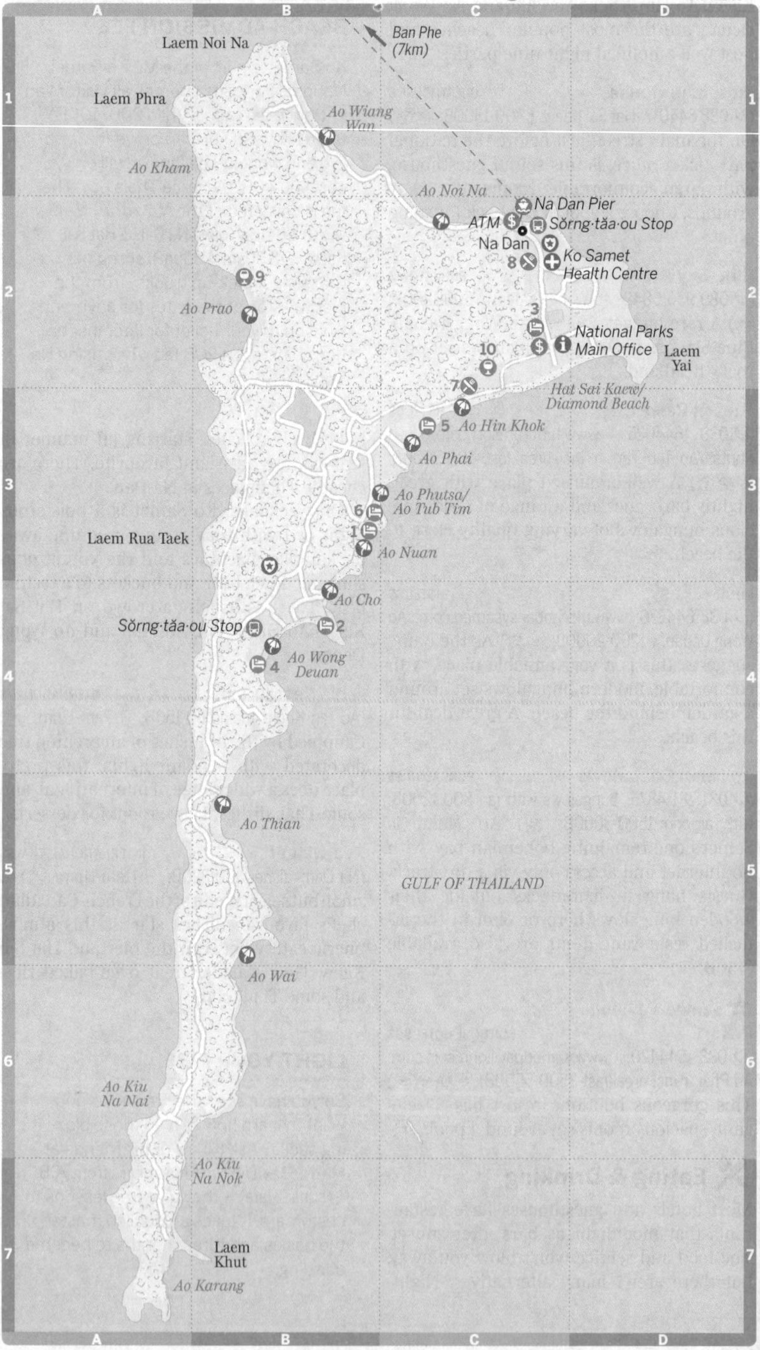

0 1 km
0 0.5 miles
A
B
C
D
1
2
3
4
5
6
7
Ban Phe (7km)
Laem Noi Na
Laem Phra
Ao Wiang Wan
Ao Kham
Ao Noi Na
Na Dan Pier
ATM
Sŏrng·tăa·ou Stop
Na Dan
8
Ko Samet Health Centre
9
Ao Prao
3
National Parks Main Office
10
Laem Yai
7
Hat Sai Kaew/ Diamond Beach
5
Ao Hin Khok
Ao Phai
Ao Phutsa/ Ao Tub Tim
6
1
Ao Nuan
Laem Rua Taek
Ao Cho
Sŏrng·tăa·ou Stop
2
4
Ao Wong Deuan
Ao Thian
GULF OF THAILAND
Ao Wai
Ao Kiu Na Nai
Ao Kiu Na Nok
Laem Khut
Ao Karang

Ko Samet

Sleeping

1 Ao Nuan Bungalows B3
2 Blue Sky B4
3 Mossman House C2
4 Nice & Easy B4
5 Samed Pavilion Resort C3
6 Tubtim Resort B3

Eating

7 Jep's Restaurant C2
8 Red Ginger C2

Drinking & Nightlife

9 Ao Prao Resort B2
Baywatch Bar .... (see 4)
10 Naga Bar C2

Baywatch Bar BAR
(Ao Wong Deuan; beers from 80B; sunset-late) A good spot for after-dark beach-gazing, with a fun crowd and strong cocktails.

Ao Prao Resort BAR
(Ao Prao; drinks from 90B; sunset-midnight;) On the sunset side of the island, this is a lovely sea-view restaurant perfect for a sundowner. You will need private transport to reach it.

Information

There are several ATMs on Ko Samet, including those near the Na Dan pier, Ao Wong Deuan, Ao Thian and Ao Phutsa.

Ko Samet Health Centre (038 644123; 24hr) On the main road between Na Dan and Hat Sai Kaew.

Police Station (24hr 1155) On the main road between Na Dan and Hat Sai Kaew. There's a substation at Ao Wong Deuan.

Getting There & Away

Ko Samet is accessed via the mainland piers in Ban Phe. There are many piers, each used by different ferry companies, but they all charge the same fares (one-way/return 70/100B, 40 minutes, hourly, 8am to 5pm) and dock at Na Dan, the main pier on Ko Samet. The last boat back to the mainland leaves at 6pm.

If you are staying at Ao Wong Deuan or further south, catch a ferry from the mainland directly to the beach (one-way/return 90/140B, one hour, three daily departures).

Speedboats charge 200B to 500B one-way and will drop you at the beach of your choice, but only leave when they have enough passengers. Otherwise, you can charter one for around 1500B.

Trat

Trat is a major transit point for Ko Chang and coastal Cambodia, with underappreciated old-world charm. The guesthouse neighbourhood occupies an atmospheric wooden shophouse district, bisected by winding sois and filled with typical Thai street life: children riding bikes, homemakers running errands and small businesses selling trinkets and necessities.

Trat's signature product is a medicinal herbal oil (known as *nám·man lĕu·ang*), touted as a remedy for everything from arthritis to bug bites and available at local pharmacies. It is produced by resident Mae Ang-Ki (Somthawin Pasananon), using a secret pharmaceutical recipe that has been handed down through her Chinese-Thai family for generations.

Sights

One booming business in Trat is swiftlet farming. Walk down Th Lak Meuang and you will see that the top floors of shophouses have been converted into nesting sites for birds that produce the edible nests considered a Chinese delicacy. Swiftlets' nests were quite rare (and expensive) in the past because they were only harvested from precipitous sea caves by trained, daring climbers. In the 1990s, entrepreneurs figured out how to replicate the cave atmosphere in multistorey shophouses and the business has become a key operation in Trat.

Indoor Market MARKET
(Soi Sukhumvit; 6am-5pm) The indoor market sprawls east from Th Sukhumvit to Th Tat Mai and has a little bit of everything, especially all the things that you forgot to pack. Without really noticing the difference you will stumble upon the **day market** (Th Tat Mai; 6-11am), selling fresh fruit, vegetables and takeaway food.

Sleeping

Trat has many budget hotels in traditional wooden houses on and around Th Thana Charoen.

★ **Ban Jai Dee Guest House** GUESTHOUSE $
(083 589 0839, 039 520 678; banjaideehouse@yahoo.com; 6 Th Chaimongkol; r 200B;) This relaxed traditional wooden house has simple rooms with shared bathrooms (hot-water

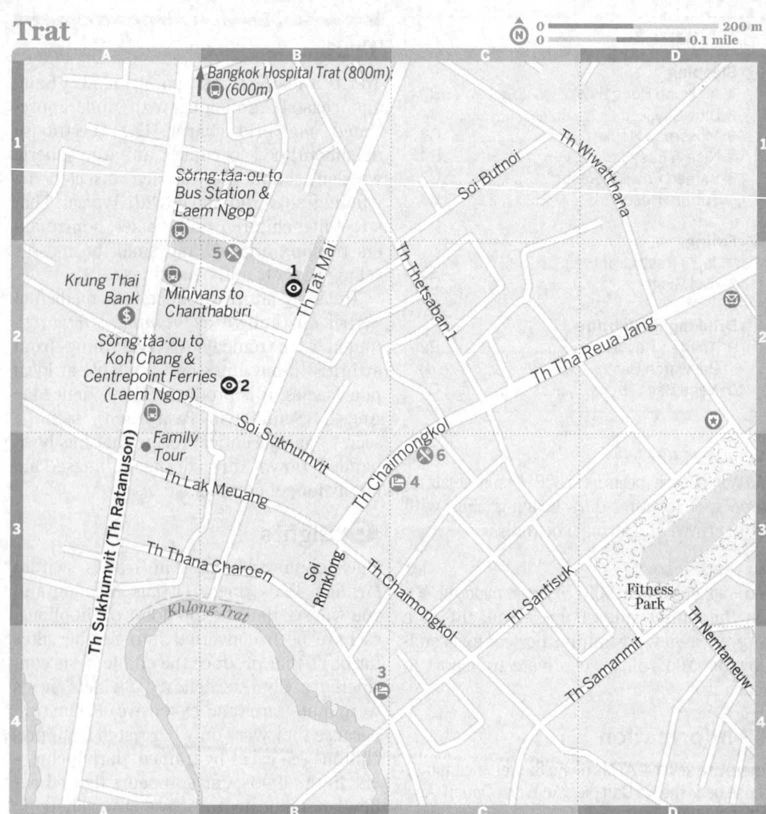

showers). Paintings and objets d'art made by the artistically inclined owners decorate the common spaces. Booking ahead is essential. Ask the owner, Serge, for travel advice.

Artist's Place GUESTHOUSE $$
(☎082 469 1900; pier.112@hotmail.com; 132/1 Th Thana Charoen; r incl breakfast 800-1100B; ❄📶) The individually decorated rooms, and pieces of art dotted around the adjoining garden, come courtesy of the owner, Mr Phukhao.

Mairood Resort HOTEL $$
(☎089 841 4858; 28 Mu 6; bungalows incl breakfast 1650B-4500B; ❄@📶🏊) Mairood Resort is a lovely spot to stay overnight, with bungalows, huts and a house by the sea and in the mangroves.

Eating

Trat is all about market eating: head to the day market (p439) on Th Tat Mai for *gah·faa bohrahn* (ancient coffee), the night market (which is in the same location from 5pm to 9pm) or the indoor market for lunchtime noodles. Food stalls line Th Sukhumvit come nightfall.

No Name Steak & Pasta INTERNATIONAL, THAI $
(61-65 Th Chaimongkol; mains 50-120B; ⏲8am-9pm Sun-Fri) Bright red, white and blue restaurant serving Thai and Western classics, plus sandwiches. It makes for a good coffee/smoothie stop, too.

Night Market MARKET $
(off Th Sukhumvit; mains from 30B; ⏲6-10pm) Trat's busy night market is a good destination for cheap eats.

Trat

Sights

1 Day Market B2
2 Indoor Market B2

Sleeping

3 Artist's Place B4
4 Ban Jai Dee Guest House C3

Eating

5 Night Market B2
6 No Name Steak & Pasta C3

Information

Th Sukhumvit runs through town, though it is often called Th Ratanuson. This is where you'll find the bulk of banks and ATMs.

Bangkok Hospital Trat (039 532735; www.bangkokhospital.com; 376 Mu 2, Th Sukhumvit; 24hr) Located 400m north of the town centre, this hospital offers the best health care in the area.

Krung Thai Bank (Th Sukhumvit; 8.30am-3.30pm) Has an ATM and currency-exchange facilities.

Police Station (24hr 1155; cnr Th Santisuk & Th Wiwatthana) A short walk from Trat's centre.

Post Office (Th Tha Reua Jang; 8.30am-4.30pm Mon-Fri, to 12.30pm Sat) East of Trat's commercial centre.

Getting There & Away

AIR

Bangkok Airways (039 551655, 039 551654, nationwide 02 265 5555; www.bangkokair.com; Trat Airport; 9am-7pm) Operates three daily flights to/from Bangkok's Suvarnabhumi International Airport (from 2550B, one hour).

BOAT

The piers that handle boat traffic to/from Ko Chang are located in Laem Ngop, about 30km southwest of Trat. There are three piers, each used by different boat companies, but the most convenient services are through Koh Chang Ferry (from Tha Thammachat) and Centrepoint Ferry (from Tha Centrepoint).

Sŏrng·tăa·ou (Th Sukhumvit) to Laem Ngop and the piers (60B per person for six passengers, 300B for the whole vehicle, 40 minutes), leave from Th Sukhumvit, just past the market. It should be the same charter price if you want to go directly from Trat's bus station to the pier.

From Bangkok, you can catch a bus (Th Sukhumvit) from Bangkok's Eastern (Ekamai) station all the way to Tha Centrepoint (250B, five hours, three morning departures). This route includes a stop at Suvarnabhumi (airport) bus station as well as Trat's bus station. In the reverse direction, buses have two afternoon departures from Laem Ngop.

You can also skip Ko Chang and head straight to the neighbouring islands (Ko Wai, Ko Mak and Ko Kut).

BUSES & MINIVANS FROM TRAT

Trat's bus station is 2km out of town, and serves the following destinations:

DESTINATION	FARE (B)	DURATION (HR)	FREQUENCY
Bangkok Eastern (Ekamai) station	254	4½	hourly 6am-11.30pm
Bangkok Northern (Mo Chit) station	261	5½	4 daily
Bangkok Suvarnabhumi (airport) station	261	4-4½	5 daily
Chanthaburi	70	1	every 2hr 8.15am-6pm

There are also minivans to the following destinations (minivans to Chanthaburi depart from in town):

DESTINATION	FARE (B)	DURATION (HR)	FREQUENCY
Bangkok Eastern (Ekamai) station	270	4	every 2hr 8.30am-4.30pm
Bangkok Northern (Mo Chit) station	270	4	every 2hr 8.30am-4.30pm
Chanthaburi	70	50min	frequent 6am-6pm
Hat Lek (for the border with Cambodia)	120	1½	hourly 5am-6pm
Pattaya	300	3½	every 2hr 8am-6pm
Rayong/Ban Phe (for Ko Samet)	200	3½	every 2hr 8am-6pm

Trat Province

0 — 20 km
0 — 10 miles

CHANTHABURI
Khlong Krau
Chang Thun
Ban Pa-Ah
Chamcar Stoeng
Bo Rai
Nong Sii
Khlung
3157
Pong
Dan Chumpon
3
3159
Tha Chot
Khao Saming
3156
3271
Bang Kradan
Trat Airport
Trat
Ban Noen Sung
Laem Muang
Laem Ngop
CAMBODIA
Ao Trat
Tha Sen
Ko Chang
Laem Sok
Mu Ko Chang National Marine Park
Ko Khlum
Ko Wai
Mai Rut
Ko Kradat
318
Ko Rang
Ko Mak
Ko Rayang
Khlong Yai
Cham Yeam
Ko Kut
Hat Lek
Gulf of Thailand
Koh Kong

MINIVAN

There are minivans to Chanthaburi from Th Sukhumvit.

Family Tour (☎ 081 940 7380; cnr Th Sukhumvit & Th Lak Meuang) minivans travel between Trat and Bangkok's Victory Monument.

Ko Chang

With steep, jungle-covered peaks, picturesque Ko Chang (Elephant Island) retains its remote and rugged spirit – despite attempts to transform it into a package-tour destination. Sweeping bays are sprinkled along the west coast; most have superfine sand, some have pebbles. What it lacks in sand it makes up for in an unlikely combination: accessible wilderness with a thriving party scene.

Because of its relative remoteness, it is only in the last 20 years or so that tourists – and 24-hour electricity – have arrived. Today, it is still a slog to get here, but the resorts are now busy with Chinese package tourists, Cambodian-bound backpackers and beach-hopping couples funnelling through to more remote islands in the Mu Ko Chang National Marine Park. Along the populous west coast are virtual minitowns with a standard of living that has outpaced the island's infrastructure. For a taste of old-school Chang, head to the southeastern villages and mangrove forests of Ban Salak Phet and Ban Salak Kok.

Sights & Activities

Although Thailand's second-largest island has accelerated into the modern world with some understandable growing pains, Ko Chang still has tropically hued seas, critter-filled jungles and a variety of water sports for athletic beach bums.

Ko Chang's mountainous interior is predominately protected as a national park. The forest is lush and alive with wildlife and threaded by silver-hued waterfalls.

The west coast is by far the most developed part of Ko Chang, thanks to its beaches and bays. Public *sŏrng·tăa·ou* (passenger pick-up trucks) make beach-hopping easy and affordable. Some beaches are rocky, so it's worth bringing swim booties for children. Most of the time the seas are shallow and gentle but be wary of rips during storms and the rainy season (May to October).

Diving

The dive sites near Ko Chang offer a variety of coral, fish and beginner-friendly shallow waters.

By far the most pristine diving in the area is around Ko Rang, an uninhabited island protected from fishing by its marine-park status.

Ko Yak, Ko Tong Lang and Ko Laun are perfect for beginners with shallow dives full of coral, schooling fish, rays and the occasional turtle.

One-day diving trips typically start at 2900B. Professional Assocation of Diving Instructors (PADI) Open Water certification costs 14,500B per person. Many dive shops remain open during the rainy season but visibility and sea conditions are generally poor.

BB Divers DIVING

(☎ 039 558040; www.bbdivers.com; Bang Bao) Based at Bang Bao with branches in Lonely Beach, Khlong Prao and Hat Sai Khao, as well as outposts on Ko Kut and Ko Wai (high season only).

Lonely Beach Divers DIVING

(☎ 080 619 0704; www.lonelybeachdivers.com; Lonely Beach) Operating out of Lonely Beach, this place offers multilingual instructors.

Kayaking

Ko Chang cuts an impressive and heroic profile when viewed from the sea aboard a

Ko Chang

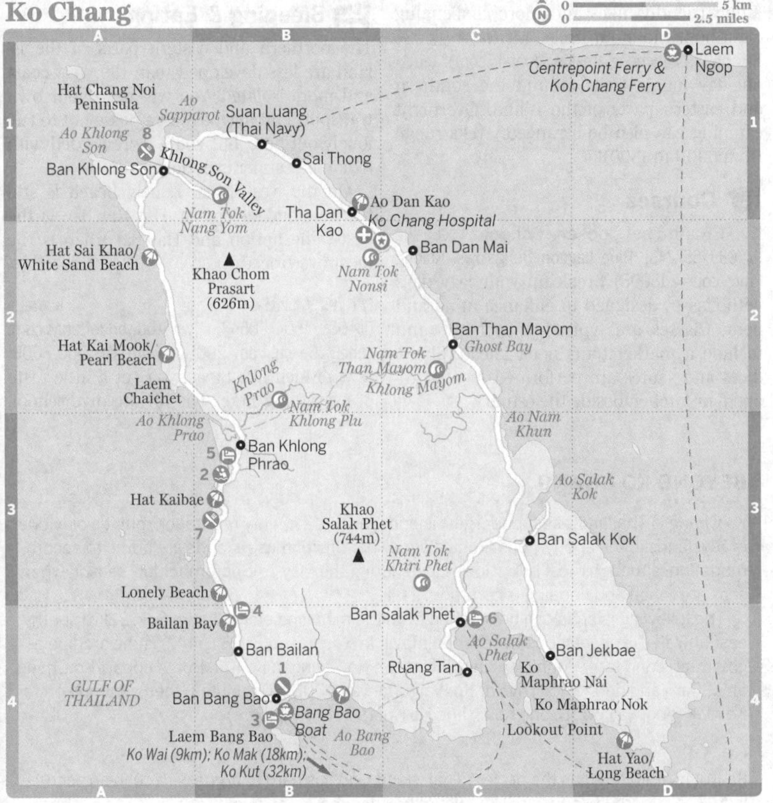

kayak. The water is generally calm and offshore islands provide a paddling destination that is closer than the horizon. Most hotels rent open-top kayaks (from 300B per day) that are convenient for near-shore outings and noncommittal kayakers. Some provide them for free.

KayakChang KAYAKING
(☎097 182 8319, 093 532 7241; www.kayakchang.com; Emerald Cove Resort, Khlong Prao; kayak per day from 1000B) For experienced paddlers, KayakChang rents high-end, closed-top kayaks that handle better and travel faster. It also leads multiday trips (from 16,000B) to other islands in the archipelago.

Hiking

Ko Chang isn't just about the beaches. The island has a well-developed trekking scene, with inland routes that lead to lush forests filled with birds, monkeys and flora. A handful of English-speaking guides grew up near the jungle and are happy to share their secrets.

Mr Tan from **Evolution Tour** (☎039 557078, 089 645 2019; www.evolutiontour.com) has

Ko Chang

Activities, Courses & Tours

1 BB Divers B4
2 KayakChang B3
Koh Chang Thai Cookery School .... (see 5)
Lonely Beach Divers .... (see 4)

Sleeping

3 Bang Bao Cliff Cottage B4
4 BB World of Tapas B4
5 Blue Lagoon Bungalows B3
Koh Chang Sea Hut .... (see 3)
6 Mangrove Hideaway C4

Eating

7 Barrio Bonito B3
8 Shambhala A1

family-friendly hikes and more challenging eight-hour mountain treks. **Mr Raht** (☎086 155 5693; kohchang_trekking@yahoo.com) leads one-day jungle treks around the southern and eastern parts of the island. Overnight camping can also be arranged. Treks range from 600B to 1800B.

Courses

Koh Chang Thai Cookery School COOKING
(☎039 557243; Blue Lagoon Bungalows, Khlong Prao; course 1500B) Break up your lazy days with classes designed to enhance mind and body. Classes are typically five hours and include a market tour; book ahead. Slices, dices and sautés are performed in a shady open-air kitchen beside the estuary.

Sleeping & Eating

The northern and eastern parts of the island are less developed than the west coast and more isolated. You will need your own transport and maybe even a posse not to feel lonely out here, but you'll be rewarded with a quieter, calmer experience.

On the west coast, Lonely Beach is still the best budget option, Hat Kai Bae is the best-value option and Hat Sai Khao is the most overpriced.

★ **BB World of Tapas** HOSTEL $
(☎089 504 0543; www.bbworldoftapas.com; Lonely Beach; dm 200B, r with fan 500-600B;) Much like tapas, you get a little taste of everything here. The on-site dive school,

BEYOND KO CHANG

Ko Chang is Thailand's second-largest island, and has a mighty reputation, but it's only one of 51 islands in the eponymous archipelago. A handful of these islands are home to accommodation, although most bungalows close during the May-to-September low season when seas are rough and flooding is common.

The following islands can be reached from the mainland pier of Laem Sok, 22km southeast of Trat, the nearest bus transfer point; while **Bang Bao Boat** (p447) is the archipelago's interisland ferry, running a daily loop from Ko Chang to Ko Kut. Boats depart Ko Chang at 9.30am and noon and arrive at Ko Wai (one-way 400B, 30 minutes) then continue on to Ko Mak (one-way 600B, one hour) and Ko Kut (900B, two hours).

Ko Kut

Ko Kut is often feted as the perfect Thai island, and it is hard to argue with such an accolade. The supersoft sands are like talcum powder, the water lapping the bays is clear and there are more coconut palms than buildings.

In fact, it's so much like a fairy tale there are resorts called Tinkerbell and Peter Pan. Unlike its larger neighbour Ko Chang, here you can forget about any nightlife, traffic or noise – this is where you come to do almost nothing. If you can be roused from your hammock, kayaking and snorkelling are the main activities (nearby Ko Rang is particularly good for fish-gazing).

Half as big as Ko Chang and the fourth-largest island in Thailand, Ko Kut (also known as Koh Kood) has long been the domain of package-tour resorts and a seclusion-seeking elite. But the island is becoming more egalitarian, and independent travellers, especially families and couples, will find a base here.

Koh Kood Ngamkho Resort (☎081 825 7076; www.kohkood-ngamkho.com; Ao Ngam Kho; incl breakfast r with fan 1000B, with air-con 1500-2000B;) One of the best budget-by-the-beach options. Agreeably rustic huts perch on a forested hillside over a reasonable beach. It rents kayaks (250B per day) and there's a good restaurant, where you keep your own tab.

Bann Makok (☎081 643 9488; www.bannmakok.com; Khlong Yai Ki; r incl breakfast 3200-3800B; @) This boutique hotel, tucked into the mangroves, uses recycled timbers painted in vintage colours to create a maze of eight rooms that resembles a traditional pier fishing village. Common decks and reading nooks provide peaceful spaces to listen to birdsong or get lost in a book.

gym, eclectic tapas menu and a chill-out zone make it a great spot to meet fellow travellers. One of the only dorms within reach of the beach.

Bang Bao Cliff Cottage GUESTHOUSE $
(☎080 823 5495; www.cliff-cottage.com; Ban Bang Bao; bungalows 650-900B; ❄📶) Partially hidden on a verdant hillside west of the pier are a few dozen simple thatch huts overlooking a rocky cove. Most have sea views and a couple offer spectacular vistas. Scubadawgs dive school has a base here. Tents are available in the high season.

★**Koh Chang Sea Hut** HOTEL $$
(☎098 345 5953; www.kohchang-seahut.com; Ban Bang Bao; r incl breakfast 2800B; ❄📶) Set at the far end of Bang Bao pier, this collection of luxurious bungalows and rooms offers near-panoramic views of the bay. Each bungalow is surrounded by a private deck where breakfast is served. Free kayaking.

★**Mangrove Hideaway** GUESTHOUSE $$
(☎080 133 6600; www.themangrovehideaway.com; Ban Salak Phet; r 1926-3638B; ❄📶) Facing the mangrove forest, this environmentally friendly guesthouse is run by a charismatic French ex-banker. The eight rooms are large and airy, while there's an open-air Jacuzzi and massage area upstairs. The resort was made using locally sourced wood and employs local villagers. Treks and tours can be arranged from here.

Ko Mak

Little Ko Mak measures only 16 sq km and doesn't have any speeding traffic, wall-to-wall development, noisy beer bars or crowded beaches. The palm-fringed bays are bathed by gently lapping water and there's a relaxed vibe. But Ko Mak is not destined for island superstardom: the interior is a utilitarian landscape of coconut and rubber plantations and sandflies are a pain on some beaches.

The best beach on the island is Ao Pra in the west, but it is undeveloped and hard to reach. For now, swimming and beach strolling are best on the northwestern bay of Ao Suan Yai, which is a wide arc of sand and looking-glass-clear water. It is easily accessible by bicycle or motorbike if you stay elsewhere.

Most budget guesthouses are on Ao Khao, a decent strip of sand on the southwestern side of the island, while the resorts sprawl out on the more scenic northwestern bay of Ao Suan Yai.

During the low season (May to September) many bungalow operations are closed.

Koh Mak Cottage (☎081 910 2723; www.kohmakcottage.com; Ao Khao; r 500B; @📶) Koh Mak has 19 small and rustic bungalows. No frills, but you are right on the beach. Wi-fi is only near reception.

Monkey Island (☎085 389 0949; www.monkeyislandkohmak.com; Ao Khao; bungalows 600-4000B; ❄@📶) The troop leader of guesthouses, Monkey Island has earthen or wooden bungalows in three creatively named models – Baboon, Chimpanzee and Gorilla – with various amenities. All have fun design touches and the hip restaurant does respectable Thai cuisine in a leisurely fashion. There's also a small children's pool. Rooms over 1500B come with air-con and breakfast.

Ko Wai

Stunning Ko Wai is teensy and primitive, but endowed with gin-clear waters, excellent coral reefs for snorkelling and a handsome view across to Ko Chang. Expect to share the bulk of your afternoons with day trippers but have the remainder of your time in peace.

Ko Wai Paradise (☎081 762 2548; r 300-500B) Simple wooden bungalows on a postcard-perfect beach. You'll share the coral out front with day trippers.

Ko Wai Pakarang (☎084 778 2234; kohwaipakarang@hotmail.com; r with fan 800-1200B, with air-con 1700-2700B; ❄@📶) Wooden and concrete bungalows, with an OK attached restaurant and helpful, English-speaking staff. Only the top-price rooms have air-con.

LOCAL KNOWLEDGE

DON'T FEED THE ANIMALS

On many of the around-the-island boat tours, operators amaze their guests with a stop at a rocky cliff to feed the wild monkeys. It seems innocent enough, and even entertaining, but there's an unfortunate consequence. The animals become dependent on this food source and when the boats don't come as often during the low season the young and vulnerable ones are ill-equipped to forage in the forest.

The same goes for the dive or boat trips that feed the fish leftover lunches, or bread bought on the pier specifically for this purpose. It might be a fantastic way to see a school of brilliantly coloured fish, but they then forsake the coral reefs for an easier meal, and without the daily grooming efforts of the fish the coral is soon overgrown with algae and will eventually suffocate.

★**Blue Lagoon Bungalows** GUESTHOUSE $$
(☎039 557243; www.kohchang-bungalows-bluelagoon.com; Ban Khlong Phrao; bungalows 700-2000B; ❄) Set beside a scenic estuary, Blue Lagoon has a variety of bungalows and rooms, or you can rent a tent (250B). A wooden walkway leads to the beach. Check out the larger family room, which was made using elephant dung. The staff, who are excellent, provide numerous activities, including yoga and cookery classes.

★**Barrio Bonito** MEXICAN $$
(Hat Kaibae; mains 160-250B; ⏲5-10.30pm) Fab fajitas and cracking cocktails are served by a charming French/Mexican couple at this roadside spot in the middle of Kaibae. Authentic food and stylish surroundings.

★**Shambhala** EUROPEAN $$
(Siam Royal View, Ao Khlong Son; mains 120-390B; ⏲1-9pm Thu-Tue) Perched at the top of the island, this poolside restaurant comes with some of the cheapest cocktails around and quality Thai/international dishes, including great risotto. Perfect for a sundowner.

Information

There are banks with ATMs and exchange facilities along all the west-coast beaches.

Be aware of the cheap minibus tickets from Siem Reap to Ko Chang; these usually involve some sort of time- and money-wasting commission scam.

Ko Chang is considered a low-risk malarial zone, meaning that liberal use of mosquito repellent is probably an adequate precaution.

Ko Chang Hospital (☎039 586096; Ban Dan Mai) Public hospital with a good reputation and affordably priced care; south of the ferry terminal.

Police Station (☎039 586191; Ban Dan Mai; ⏲24hr) Ko Chang's main police station.

Getting There & Away

Whether starting from Bangkok or Cambodia, it is an all-day haul to reach Ko Chang.

Ferries from the mainland (Laem Ngop) leave from either Tha Thammachat, operated by **Koh Chang Ferry** (☎039 555188; Tha Thammachat, Laem Ngop), or Tha Centrepoint with **Centrepoint Ferry** (☎039 538196; Tha Centrepoint,

KO CHANG TRANSPORT CONNECTIONS

ORIGIN	DESTINATION	SPEEDBOAT	BUS
Eastern Bus Terminal (Ekamai; Bangkok)	Tha Thammachat (Laem Ngop)	N/A	263B; 6hr; 2 daily
Tha Centrepoint (Laem Ngop)	Ko Chang	80B, 40min, hourly, 6am-7.30pm	N/A
Tha Thammachat (Laem Ngop)	Ko Chang	80B, 30min, every 45min, 6.30am-7pm	N/A
Ko Chang	Ko Kut	900B, 5hr, 2 daily	N/A
Ko Chang	Ko Mak	600B, 2hr, daily	N/A
Ko Chang	Ko Wai	400B, 15 min, 2 daily	N/A
Ko Chang	Suvarnabhumi International Airport (Bangkok)	N/A	263B, 5hr, 2pm

GETTING TO CAMBODIA

Trat to Ko Kong

Getting to the border From Trat, the closest Thai–Cambodia crossing is from Hat Lek to the Cambodian town of Cham Yeam, and then on to Ko Kong. Minivans run to Hat Lek hourly from 5am to 6pm (120B, 1½ hours) from Trat's bus station.

At the border This is the most expensive place to cross into Cambodia from Thailand. Visas are a steep 1500B (they are US$20 at other crossings) and payment is only accepted in baht. You will need a passport photo too. Avoid anyone who says you require a 'medical certificate' or other paperwork. The border closes at 8pm.

Moving on Take a taxi (US$10) or *moto* (motorcycle taxi; US$3) to Ko Kong where you can catch onward transport to Sihanoukville (four hours, one or two departures per day) and Phnom Penh (five hours, two or three departures until 11.30am).

Thai visas can be renewed here, but note that visas at land borders have been shortened to 15 days.

Chanthaburi to Pailin

Getting to the border In Chanthaburi, **minivans** (☎092 037 6266) depart from a stop across the river from the River Guest House to Ban Pong Nam Ron (150B, 1½ hours, 10am, 11am and 6.30pm).

At the border This is a far less busy and more pleasant crossing than Poipet further north. You need a passport photo and US$20 for the visa fee.

Moving on Hop on a motorbike taxi to Pailin in Cambodia. From there, you can catch frequent shared taxis (US$5 per person, 1½ hours) to scenic Battambang. After that, you can move on to Siem Reap by boat, or Phnom Penh by bus.

Laem Ngop). Boats from Tha Thammachat arrive at Tha Sapparot; Centrepoint ferries at a pier down the road.

Bang Bao Boat (☎084 567 8765; www.kohchangbangbaoboat.com; Ban Bang Bao) is the interisland ferry that connects Ko Chang with Ko Mak, Ko Kut and Ko Wai during the high season. Boats leave from Bang Bao in the southwest of the island.

Speedboats travel between the islands during high season.

It is possible to go to and from Ko Chang from Bangkok's Eastern (Ekamai) bus terminal and Bangkok's Suvaranabhumi International Airport, via Chanthaburi and Trat.

The closest airport is in Trat. **Ko Chang Minibus** (☎087 785 7695, 08 932 0893; www.kohchangminibus.com) offers a variety of transfer packages from airport to beach.

NORTHEASTERN THAILAND

The northeast of Thailand, or Isan (pronounced *ee-săhn*) as it's usually known, stretches from the wild Mekong River (Mae Nam Khong in Thai) down to the edges of the Khorat Plateau, and is home to Thailand's best national parks and most ancient temple ruins. Rich in religious significance and influenced by nearby Cambodia and Laos, it has a culture and food all its own.

Nakhon Ratchasima (Khorat)

Khorat is a big, busy city that for many travellers serves as the gateway to Isan. It's best in its quieter nooks, such as inside the eastern side of the historic moat, where local life goes on in a fairly traditional way.

Sights

Thao Suranari Monument MONUMENT
(อนุสาวรีย์ท้าวสุรนารี; Th Rajadamnern; ⊙daylight hours) FREE Thao Suranari, wife of the city's assistant governor during Rama III's reign, is something of a wonder woman in these parts. Ya Mo (Grandma Mo), as she's affectionately called, became a hero in 1826 by organising a successful prisoner revolt after Chao Anou of Vientiane had conquered Khorat during his rebellion against Siam. One version of the legend says she convinced

Nakhon Ratchasima (Khorat)

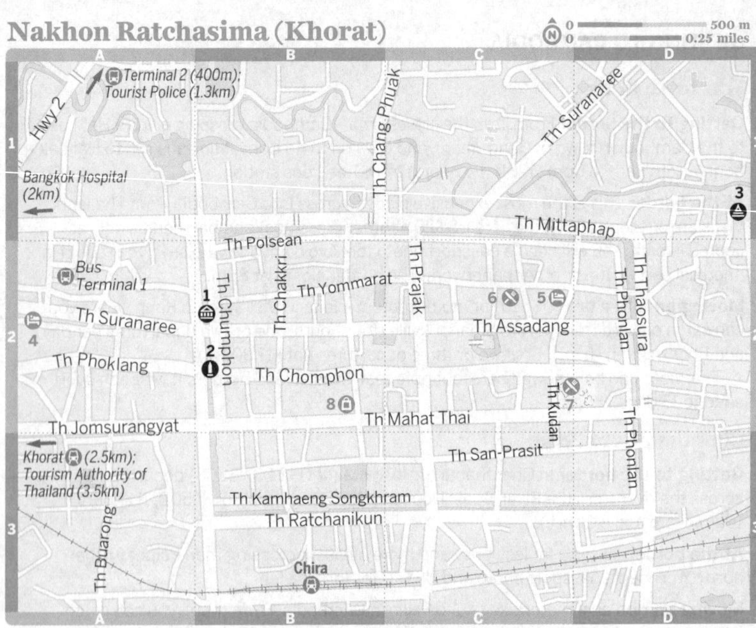

the women to seduce the Lao soldiers and then the Thai men launched a surprise attack, saving the city.

Suranari Hall MUSEUM
(อาคารแสดงแสงเสียงวีรกรรมท้าวสุรนารี; Th Chumphon; 9am-6pm Tue-Sun) FREE This little white building is a sort of museum to local heroine Thao Suranari, with a cool diorama and an even cooler sculpted mural of the famous battle in which legend says Thao Suranari saved the city.

Wat Salaloi BUDDHIST TEMPLE
(วัดศาลาลอย; Soi 1, Th Thaosura; daylight hours) The city's most interesting temple was supposedly founded by local heroine Thao Suranari and her husband in 1827. Half of her ashes are interred in a small stupa (the other half are at her monument; p447) and so there are also singing troupes on hire to perform for her spirit here. A small statue of the heroine sits praying in the pond in front of the temple's award-winning *bòht* (ordination hall). The temple is usually teeming with people making offerings.

Sleeping & Eating

Sansabai House HOTEL $
(044 255144; www.sansabai-korat.com; Th Suranaree; r 300-500B; P ❄) This place is hidden beside the Tokyo hotel, which does a much better job of advertising itself, but the obscurity fits its understated ambience. The lobby is welcoming and the rooms are constantly being refitted. There are fan rooms as well as air-con rooms.

Thai Inter Hotel HOTEL $$
(044 247700; www.thaiinterhotel.com; Th Yommarat; r incl breakfast 650B; P ❄ @) This little hotel patches together an odd mix of

styles. The lobby is homely, the rooms are comfy, if small, and the furniture's a little worn. It's got a good (though not so quiet) location near decent restaurants and bars. Guests receive a discount at the nearby bar.

Wat Boon Night Bazaar THAI $
(Th Chompon; mains from 30B; ⏲5-9.30pm) This night market is less popular than **Night Bazaar Korat** (Th Manat; ⏲5-10pm), but it's the better choice for eating. Offers Thai as well as northeastern Thai (Isan) food.

Rabieng Kaew THAI $$
(Th Yommarat; mains 80-300B; ⏲11am-11pm; P) This lovely spot has an antique-filled dining area and a leafy garden out the back. The furniture is rustic to the point of looking neglected, but it's not all about the atmosphere. The food, all big dishes meant to be shared, is good.

Information

Th Mittaphap has many extended-hours banks and an AEON ATM.

Bangkok Hospital (☎044 429999; www.bangkokhospital.com; Th Mittaphap)

Tourism Authority of Thailand (TAT; ☎044 213666; tatsima@tat.or.th; 2102-2104 Th Mittaphap; ⏲8.30am-4.30pm) Khorat's branch of the TAT is inconveniently located outside the centre of town.

Getting There & Away

Khorat has two bus terminals. **Terminal 1** (☎044 242899; Th Burin) in the city centre serves Bangkok (191B, 3½ hours, frequent) and most towns within Nakhon Ratchasima Province, including Pak Chong (75B, 1½ hours, frequent 5.30am to 6.30pm) and Pak Thong Chai (21B, one hour); minivans to Pak Chong (60B, one hour, frequent 6.35am to 8pm) also leave from this terminal. Buses to other destinations, plus more Bangkok buses and minivans, use **Terminal 2** (bor kŏr sŏr sŏrng; ☎044 295271; Hwy 2), north of the centre.

Many trains pass through **Khorat Train Station** (☎044 242044, nationwide 1690; www.railway.co.th), but buses are much faster. Ten daily trains go to/from Bangkok (50B to 425B, five to seven hours), via Ayuthaya. There are also nine trains to Ubon Ratchathani (58B to 453B, five to six hours) and four to Khon Kaen (38B to 170B, 3½ hours).

Khorat's smaller **Chira Train Station** (☎044 242363, nationwide 1690; www.railway.co.th) is closer to the old city, so it may be more convenient to get off there.

BUSES FROM NAKHON RATCHASIMA (KHORAT)

These services depart from Bus Terminal 2:

DESTINATION	FARE (B)	DURATION (HR)	FREQUENCY
Aranya Prathet (border with Cambodia)	202	4	5 daily 5.30am-5.30pm
Ayuthaya (minivan)	132	4	frequent 5am-6pm
Bangkok	191-320	3½	frequent
Buriram (minivan)	87	2-3	hourly 6am-8pm
Chiang Mai	581	12-13	hourly 6.30am-8.30pm
Khon Kaen	126-160	3-4	frequent 6am-9pm
Khon Kaen (minivan)	126	2½	frequent 5.30am-6pm
Krabi	1257	15	4.50pm
Loei	275	7	11 departures 5am-midnight
Lopburi	127	3½	every 30min 4.50am-6pm
Nang Rong	90	2	hourly 6am-8pm
Nang Rong (minivan)	90	1½	every 30min 5am-8pm
Nong Khai	282-435	6	hourly 10.30am-3am
Phimai	50	2½	every 30min 5.30am-10pm
Surin	167	4	every 30min 5am-8pm
Trat	324	8	4 departures 10.30am-3am
Ubon Ratchathani	324-445	5-6	hourly 10.30am-2am
Udon Thani	245	5	frequent 10.30am-3am

Around Nakhon Ratchasima

Phimai

The otherwise mundane little town of Phimai has one of Thailand's finest surviving Khmer temple complexes right at its heart. Phimai is the first of the major Khmer monuments to be reached if you're coming from Bangkok, and also one of the most picturesque. It makes an easy day trip out of Khorat, but if you prefer the quiet life, you could always make Khorat a day trip out of Phimai instead.

Sights

★Phimai Historical Park HISTORIC SITE
(อุทยานประวัติศาสตร์พิมาย; 044 471568; Th Ananthajinda; admission 100B; 7.30am-6pm) According to the information in its **visitor centre** (8.30am-4.30pm) FREE, Prasat Phimai was started by Khmer King Jayaviravarman (r AD 1002–06), although other records have it dated to as late as the 12th century. Regardless, Phimai is one of the most impressive Khmer ruins in Thailand. Though built as a Mahayana Buddhist temple, the carvings also feature many Hindu deitics, and design elements at here influenced Angkor Wat.

Phimai National Museum MUSEUM
(พิพิธภัณฑสถานแห่งชาติพิมาย; Th Tha Songkhran; admission 100B; 9am-4pm Wed-Sun) After a recent renovation this is now one of the best museums in Isan and well worth a visit. Situated on the banks of Sa Kwan, a 12th-century Khmer reservoir, the museum consists of two spacious buildings housing a fine collection of Khmer sculptures from Phimai, including many exquisite lintels, and other ruins around Lower Isan. There's also some distinctive black Phimai pottery (500 BC–AD 500) and Buddha images from various periods.

Getting There & Away

Buses and minivans for Phimai leave Khorat's Bus Terminal 2 (50B, 2½ hours) about every 30 minutes throughout the day.

Khao Yai National Park

Cool and lush, **Khao Yai National Park** (อุทยานแห่งชาติเขาใหญ่; 086 092 6529; adult/child 400/200B, car 50B; 6am-6pm) is an easy escape into the primordial jungle. The 2168-sq-km park, part of a Unesco World Heritage Site, spans five forest types, from rainforest to monsoon. The park's centrepiece is Nam Tok Haew Suwat (น้ำตกเหวสุวัต), a 25m-high cascade that puts on a thunder-ing show in the rainy season. Nam Tok Haew Narok (น้ำตกเหวนรก) is its larger cousin, with three pooling tiers and a towering 150m drop.

The park is the primary residence of, among many others, shy tigers and elephants, noisy gibbons, colourful tropical birds and countless audible, yet invisible, insects. Khao Yai is a major birding destination, with large flocks of hornbills and several migrators, including the flycatcher from Europe. Caves in the park are the preferred resting place for wrinkle-lipped bats. In the grasslands, batik-printed butterflies dissect flowers with their surgical tongues.

The park has several accessible trails for independent walking, but birders or animal trackers should consider hiring a jungle guide to increase their appreciation of the environment and to spot more than the tree-swinging gibbons and blood-sucking leeches (the rainy season is the worst time for the latter). In total, there are 12 maintained trails criss-crossing the entire park – not ideal if you want to walk end to end. Access to transport is another reason a tour might be more convenient, although Thai visitors with cars are usually happy to pick up pedestrians.

A two-hour walk from the visitor centre leads to the Nong Pak Chee Observation Tower, which is a good early-morning spot to see insect-feeding birds, occasional thirsty elephants and sambar deer; make reservations at the visitor centre. It's important to understand that spotting the park's reclusive tigers and elephants is considered a bonus, with most people happy just to admire the frothy waterfalls that drain the peaks of Big Mountain.

Sleeping

★Khaoyai Garden Lodge HOTEL $
(094 191 9176, 044 365178; www.khaoyaigarden-lodge.com/khaoyai-national-park-2; Th Thanarat, Km 7; r with fan 350B, with air-con 2000-3200B, f 2800B;) This friendly, family-run place offers a variety of rooms (the cheapest are large, have shared hot-water bathrooms and fans and are better value than other

cheapies in the area), all spread out around an attractive garden. It's great value and the restaurant-lounge in front encourages interaction with fellow guests.

Park Lodging BUNGALOW $

(02 562 0760; www.dnp.go.th/parkreserve; r & bungalows 800-9000B) These lodgings are rustic – no air-con, fridges or TVs – but comfortable. Note that you must book them from the national-park website. There's a 30% discount Monday to Thursday.

Campsites CAMPGROUND

(per person with own tent 30B, 3-person tent 225B) Khao Yai has extensive and well-set-up camping facilities at various spots around the park.

Getting There & Away

To reach Khao Yai you need to connect to Pak Chong. *Sŏrng·tăa·ou* (passenger pick-up trucks) travel the 30km from Pak Chong down Th Thanarat to the park's northern gate (40B, 45 minutes) every 30 minutes from 6am to 5pm (the last *sŏrng·tăa·ou* from the northern gate to Pak Chong departs around 3pm). They start their journey in front of the 7-Eleven near the artistic deer (they look like giraffes) statue.

Only 2nd-class buses to Bangkok (128B, three hours) use the bus station, which is southwest of the traffic light at Th Thesabarn 8. Frequent 2nd-class buses and minivans to Khorat (60B to 75B, 1½ hours, frequent from 5.30am to 8pm) stop about 500m northeast of the deer statue near *đà·làht kàak* (the town's main market). Minivans to Bangkok's Victory Monument (180B, 2½ hours, hourly) park near the deer statue.

Board 1st-class buses to both Bangkok (150B, 2½ hours) and Khorat (80B, one hour) across the highway from the deer statue.

You can also get to Pak Chong by train from Bangkok and Khorat, but it's much faster to go by bus or minivan.

Phanom Rung & Around

For those with an insatiable appetite for Khmer ruins, the area around Phanom Rung offers a smorgasbord of lesser-known sites that, taken together, create a picture of the crucial role this region once played in the Khmer empire.

Sights

★**Phanom Rung Historical Park** RUINS

(อุทยานประวัติศาสตร์เขาพนมรุ้ง; 044 666251; 100B, combined ticket with Prasat Muang Tam 150B; 6am-6pm) Phanom Rung has a knock-you-dead location. Crowning the summit of a spent volcano, this sanctuary sits a good 70 storeys above the paddy fields below. To the southeast you can clearly see Cambodia's Dongrek Mountains, and it's in this direction that the capital of the Angkor empire once lay. The Phanom Rung temple complex is the largest and best-restored Khmer monument in Thailand. It took 17 years to complete its restoration.

Prasat Muang Tam RUINS

(ปราสาทเมืองต่ำ; admission 100B; 6am-6pm) In the little village of Khok Meuang, the restored Khmer temple of Prasat Meuang Tam is an ideal bolt-on to any visit to Phanom Rung, which is only 8km to the northwest. Dating back to the late 10th or early 11th century and sponsored by King Jayavarman V, this is Isan's third-most-interesting temple complex in terms of size, atmosphere and the quality of restoration work.

The whole complex (once a shrine to Shiva) is surrounded by laterite walls, within which are four lotus-filled reservoirs, each guarded by whimsical five-headed *naga* (mythical serpent-being).

Sleeping & Eating

P California Inter Hostel GUESTHOUSE $

(081 808 3347; www.pcalifornianangrong.webs.com; Th Sangkakrit; r 300-800B; P) This great place on the eastern side of town offers bright, nicely decorated rooms with value in all price ranges. The cheapest rooms have fans and cold-water showers; the more expensive options have living areas with sofas. English-speaking owner Khun Wicha has a wealth of knowledge about the area and leads tours. Bikes are free, and staff speak several languages.

Tanyaporn Homestay GUESTHOUSE $

(087 431 3741; r incl breakfast 500-800B; P) A modern guesthouse near Prasat

GETTING TO CAMBODIA: CHONG SA-NGAM TO CHOAM

This border crossing in Sri Saket Province sees very little traffic, despite the road to Siem Reap being in excellent shape, because the route isn't serviced by public transport. Visas are available on arrival.

DON'T MISS

SURIN PROJECT

Located in the **Elephant Study Centre** (☎044 145050; admission 100B; ⊙8.30am-4pm), yet affiliated with the Elephant Nature Park (p469) in Chiang Mai, the **Surin Project** (☎084 482 1210; www.surinproject.org; Ban Ta Klang) works to improve the elephants' living conditions by, among other things, letting them roam inside large enclosures so they don't need to be as heavily chained.

Sŏrng·tăa·ou run to Ban Ta Klang from Surin's bus terminal (50B, two hours, hourly 6am to 5pm), with the last one returning at 4pm. If you're driving, take Rte 214 north for 40km and follow the elephant signs down Rte 3027 for 22km more.

If you'd like to spend some quality time with elephants, you can sign up for activities with the project to work side-by-side with the mahouts caring for the elephants, cutting food, doing construction and more. Programs include one day of volunteering (2000B, including meals) and one week of volunteering (13,000B, including lodging and meals). It's best to book ahead. The information centre is within the showgrounds. There is also a **homestay** (☎087 650 6659; Ban Ta Klang; per person 200B, meals 50-100B) (per person 200B, meals 50B to 100B) program on offer.

During Visakha Bucha day (usually in July or August) all Suai villages in the area host elephant parades, with brightly painted pachyderms carrying the men who will enter the monkhood.

Muang Tam ruins; look for the orange house by the curve with the English-language sign that says 'Homestay'.

Phob Suk THAI $$
(Rte 24; mains 60-360B; ⊙9am-10pm; P 📶) The picture menu at this well-known restaurant (there's no roman-script sign, but it's near the bus station) presents the typical mix of Thai, Isan and Chinese dishes. The city's famous *kăh mŏo* (pork-rump roast) is recommended.

ℹ Information

Begin your visit to Prasat Muang Tam at this small **information centre** (⊙8am-4.30pm), next to Barai Muang Tam (a 510m-by-1090m Khmer-era reservoir), which has good displays about the site.

ℹ Getting There & Away

Getting to Phanom Rung Historical Park via public transport is complicated; your best option is to hire a motorcycle from P California Inter Hostel in Nang Rong.

Sŏrng·tăa·ou (passenger pick-up trucks; 25B, 30 minutes, every 30 minutes until 9am) from in front of the old market on the eastern end of town in Nang Rong, and Chanthaburi-bound buses from the bus station on the western side of town, go to Ban Ta Pek, where motorcycle-taxi drivers charge 200B to Phanom Rung, including waiting time.

Otherwise, if you're coming from or heading to Ubon Ratchathani, Surin, Khorat, Pak Chong or Bangkok, you have the option of getting off at Ban Tako, a well-marked turn-off about 14km east of Nang Rong, where you're at the mercy of overcharging motorcycle taxis (from 600B return) direct to Phanom Rung.

Ubon Ratchathani

Backed up against Thailand's second-longest river, the historic heart of Ubon has a slow-going character and many interesting temples that even people suffering acute temple overload will enjoy.

Ubon is a financial, educational and agricultural market centre. It's not a busy tourist destination, but it does make a great base from which to explore the province's many attractions.

◉ Sights

Wat Si Ubon Rattanaram BUDDHIST TEMPLE
(วัดศรีอุบลรัตนาราม; Th Uparat; ⊙daylight hours) The *bòht* at this important temple resembles Bangkok's Wat Benchamabophit, but it's the 7cm-tall topaz Buddha inside that most Thais come to see. Phra Kaew Butsarakham, as it's known, was reportedly brought here from Vientiane at Ubon's founding and is one of the city's holiest possessions.

Ubon Ratchathani National Museum MUSEUM
(พิพิธภัณฑสถานแห่งชาติอุบลราชธานี; Th Kheuan Thani; 100B; ⊙9am-4pm Wed-Sun) Occupying the former city hall, this is a very informative museum with plenty on show,

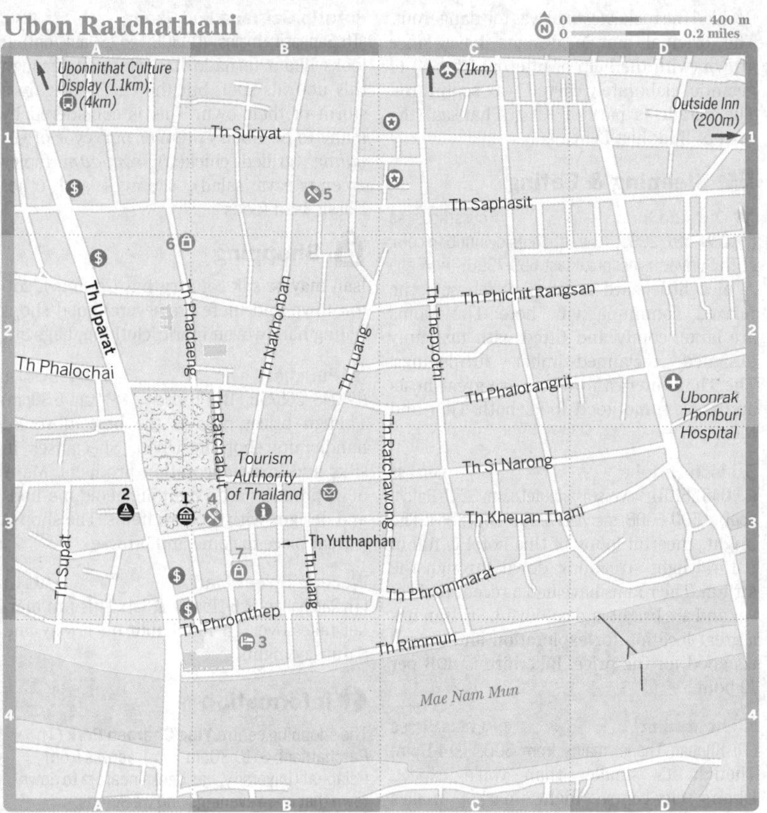

Ubon Ratchathani

Sights
1 Ubon Ratchathani National Museum A3
2 Wat Si Ubon Rattanaram A3

Sleeping
3 Sri Isan Hotel B4

Eating
4 Night Market B3
5 Porntip Gai Yang Wat Jaeng B1

Shopping
6 Punchard A2
7 Walking Street Market B3

from Dvaravati-era Buddhist ordination-precinct stones and a 2500-year-old Dong Son bronze drum to Ubon textiles. The museum's most prized possession is a 9th-century Ardhanarisvara, a composite statue combining Shiva and his consort Uma into one being. It's one of just two ever found in Thailand.

Ubonnithat Culture Display MUSEUM
(หอวัฒนธรรมอุบลนิทัศน์; Th Jaeng Sanit; ⌚8.30am-4pm Mon-Sat) **FREE** The museum in the lower level of the strikingly designed Ubon Ratchathani Art & Culture Centre at Rajabhat University contains a lot more cultural references than the National Museum. There are some relatively recent displays, such as a room on Ubon's famous forest monks, including some of their teachings in English, herbal medicines, music, costumes and a lot of sculpted candles.

Festivals & Events

Candle Parade CULTURAL
(Kabuan Hae Tian; ⌚usually Jul) Ubon's famous Candle Parade began during the reign of King Rama V, when the appointed governor

decided the rocket festival was too dangerous. The original simple designs have since grown (with the help of internal frames) to gigantic, elaborately carved wax sculptures. The parade is part of Khao Phansaa (the start of Buddhist Lent).

Sleeping & Eating

★ Outside Inn GUESTHOUSE $$
(☎088 581 2069; www.theoutsideinnubon.com; 11 Th Suriyat; r incl breakfast 650-799B; P ❄ 📶) A nice little garden lounge area sets the relaxed, communal vibe here. The rooms are large, comfy and fitted with tastefully designed reclaimed-timber furnishings. The Thai-American owners are great hosts and cook some good food, both Thai and Mexican.

Sri Isan Hotel HOTEL $$
(☎045 261011; www.sriisanhotel.com; 62 Th Ratchabut; r 500-600B, ste 700-1200B; ❄ @ 📶) The bright, cheerful lobby of this hotel is full of natural light streaming down through the atrium. The rooms have had a recent makeover and are bright and colourful. Sri Isan has a great location for exploration and overall it's good for the price. Bike hire is 60B per 12 hours.

Night Market THAI, VIETNAMESE $
(Th Kheuan Thani; mains from 30B; ⏲4-11pm) Though it's smaller than you'd expect, Ubon's city-centre night market makes an excellent dining destination, especially when paired with the weekend Walking Street Market (p454). Vendors sell Thai, Isan and Vietnamese food.

Porntip Gai Yang Wat Jaeng THAI $
(Th Saphasit; mains 40-130B; ⏲7.30am-7pm) It looks like a tornado has whipped through this no-frills spot, but the chefs cook up a storm of their own. This is considered by many to be Ubon's premier purveyor of *gài yâhng* (grilled chicken), *sôm·đam* (spicy green-papaya salad), sausages and other classic Isan foods.

Shopping

Isan may be silk country, but Ubon is a cotton town and there are several good shops selling handwoven fabric, clothing, bags etc.

★ Punchard ARTS & CRAFTS
(☎045 265751; Th Phadaeng; ⏲9am-6.30pm) Though pricey, this is the best all-round handicrafts shop in Ubon. Specialises in silks and home-decoration products. Many of its products are a merging of old methods and designs with modern items. The shop is a great place to come and browse.

Walking Street Market MARKET
(Th Ratchabut; ⏲6-11pm Fri & Sat) This fun market takes over Th Ratchabut on Friday and Saturday nights.

Information

The shopping centre **Ying Charoen Park** (Th Ratchathani; ⏲10.30am-7pm), across from Rajabhat University, has banks nearest to downtown that open evenings and weekends.

Tourism Authority of Thailand (TAT; ☎045 243770; tatubon@tat.or.th; 264/1 Th Kheuan Thani; ⏲8.30am-4.30pm) Has helpful staff.

BUSES FROM UBON RATCHATHANI

DESTINATION	FARE (B)	DURATION (HR)	FREQUENCY
Bangkok	423-694	10	frequent 8am-11.30pm
Chiang Mai	790	12	7.45pm-6.30pm
Khon Kaen	188-244	4½	every 30min 5.30am-5.30pm
Mukdahan	100-140	3½	every 30min 5.45am-5.30pm
Nakhon Ratchasima (Khorat)	193-248	5-6	14 daily 5.30am-8.15pm
Nang Rong	144	4½	6 departures 5.30am-3pm
Pakse (Laos)	200	3	9.30am & 3.30pm
Rayong	515-801	13	5 daily 6.45am-8.15pm
Surin	120-140	3	every 30min 5.30am-8.15pm
Udon Thani	220-284	6	frequent 5.30am-3pm

GETTING TO CAMBODIA: CHONG CHOM TO O SMACH

Getting to the border Because of the casino, there are plenty of minibuses (45B, 1½ hours, frequent from 6.10am to 5.50pm) from Surin's bus terminal to Chong Chom.

At the border The Cambodian border is open from 6am to 6pm and visas are available on the spot.

Moving on There's little transport on the Cambodian side. A seat in a 'taxi' will cost 500B for the four-hour drive to Siem Reap, but if you arrive after about 9am you probably won't find any Cambodians making the trip and may have to pay 2500B for the whole car.

Ubonrak Thonburi Hospital (☎045 260285; Th Phalorangrit) Has a 24-hour casualty department.

Getting There & Around

AIR

Air Asia (☎045 255762, nationwide 02 515 9999; www.airasia.com; Ubon Ratchathani Airport; ⏱7.30am-8pm), **Nok Air** (☎045 245821, nationwide 02 900 9955; www.nokair.com; Ubon Ratchathani Airport; ⏱6am-8pm) and **Thai Lion Air** (☎045 241568, nationwide 02 529 9999; www.lionairthai.com; Ubon Ratchathani Airport; ⏱5.30am-8.30pm) fly to/from Bangkok's Don Mueang Airport (from around 1000B, one hour, 12 times daily), **Thai Smile** (☎087 776 2266, nationwide 1181; www.thaismileair.com; Ubon Ratchathani Airport; ⏱7am-7pm) flies to/from Bangkok's Suvarnabhumi Airport (from 1280B, one hour, three times daily) and **Kan Air** (☎nationwide 02 551 6111; www.kanairlines.com) flies to/from Chiang Mai (from 990B, one hour, daily).

A **taxi** (☎081 967 5582) from the airport into town runs 100B.

BUS

Ubon's **bus terminal** (☎045 316085) is north of town; take *sŏrng·tăa·ou* (passenger pick-up truck) 2, 3 or 10 to the city centre. In addition to buses, there are also minivans to Chong Mek (for the border with Laos; 100B, 1½ hours, every 30 minutes 4am to 6pm), Khon Kaen (188B, 4½ hours, frequent 6am to 5pm) and Khong Jiam (80B, 1½ hours, hourly 6.30am to 6pm).

TRAIN

Ubon's **train station** (☎045 321004, nationwide 1690; www.railway.co.th; Th Sathani) is in Warin Chamrap; take *sŏrng·tăa·ou* 2. There's an overnight express train to/from Bangkok (2nd/1st-class seat 221/460B, 2nd-class sleeper upper/lower 691/781B, 1st-class sleeper upper/lower 1080/1280B, 11½ hours) at 6.30pm. The five other departures (95B to 581B) take from 8½ to 12 hours. All trains also stop in Si Saket, Surin and Khorat.

Mukdahan

On the banks of the Mekong, directly opposite the Lao city of Savannakhet, Mukdahan has enough of interest to fill a relaxing day or two, and the vibe is friendly.

Sights

Talat Indojin MARKET

(ตลาดอินโดจีน; Th Samran Chaikhongtai; ⏱8am-6pm) This riverside market, which stretches along and under the promenade, is a busy and colourful spectacle, with stall after stall of food, clothing and assorted trinkets from China and Vietnam, plus silk and cotton fabrics made in Isan.

Hor Kaew Mukdahan MUSEUM

(หอแก้วมุกดาหาร; Th Samut Sakdarak; 50B; ⏱8am-6pm) This eye-catching 65m-tall tower was built for the 50th anniversary of King Rama IX's ascension to the throne. The nine-sided base has a good museum with displays (labelled in English) on the eight ethnic groups of the province. There are great views and a few more historical displays in 'The 360° of Pleasure in Mukdahan by the Mekong' room, up at the 50m level. The ball on the top holds a locally revered Buddha image believed to made of solid silver.

Sleeping & Eating

Ban Rim Suan HOTEL $

(☎042 632980; www.banrimsuan.weebly.com; Th Samut Sakdarak; s/d 350/450B; P⊖❄📶) This place offers a good budget deal: big, airy rooms with good furnishings. It's a tad south of the centre, but that makes it

GETTING TO LAOS: MUKDAHAN TO SAVANNAKHET

Getting to the border Thais and Lao can use the boats that cross the Mekong from Mukdahan's city centre, while everyone else must use the bridge. The easiest way to cross is via the buses to Savannakhet (Laos; 45B to 50B, hourly 7.30am to 7pm) from Mukdahan's bus station.

At the border The border is open from 6am to 10pm. The crossing to Savannakhet can take from one to two hours, depending on the length of the immigration queues.

Moving on From Savannakhet there are buses to various points in Laos, as well as Vietnam.

convenient for dinner and drinks along the river.

Riverfront Hotel HOTEL $$
(☎042 633348; Th Samran Chaikhongtai; r incl breakfast 850-1650B; P ❄ 📶) This newly built place is tastefully decorated, with plenty of timber finishings and furnishings and cool (literally) tile flooring. It has an attached cafe. The river-view rooms have fabulous outlooks.

★Kufad VIETNAMESE $
(Th Samut Sakdarak; mains 40-130B; ⊙8am-5pm; 📶) This family-run place serves Vietnamese dishes that are as tasty as you'd encounter in Ho Chi Minh City. The picture menu takes the guesswork out of ordering but leaves you clueless on the prices. There's no roman-script sign. Second branch **Kufad 2** (Th Samut Sakdarak; mains 40-130B; ⊙8am-5pm) is a little further down the road.

Night Market THAI, VIETNAMESE $
(Th Song Nang Sathit; mains from 30B; ⊙4-9pm) Mukdahan's night market has all the Thai and Isan classics, but it's the Vietnamese vendors that set it apart. A few sell *băhn dah* (the vendors will tell you it's 'Vietnamese pizza'), which combines soft noodles, pork, spring onions and an optional egg served on a crispy cracker.

Getting There & Around

The nearest airport is in Nakhon Phanom; Air Asia offers a bus service from the airport to Mukdahan.

Mukdahan's **bus terminal** (☎042 630486) is on Rte 212, west of town. To get there from the centre, catch a yellow *sŏrng·tăa·ou* (10B, 6am to 5pm) running west along Th Phithak Phanomkhet. Túk-túk (pronounced *đúk đúk*; a type of motorised rickshaw) to the bus terminal cost 50B.

Minivan destinations include Khon Kaen, Nakhon Phanom, That Phanom, Ubon Ratchathani and Udon Thani. Buses go to Khon Kaen, Khorat, Yasothon, Nakhon Phanom, Ubon Ratchathani and Udon Thani.

A few Bangkok buses (461B to 717B, 10 hours) leave during the day, but most depart between 5pm and 8pm.

Nakhon Phanom

Nakhon Phanom means 'City of Mountains', but the undulating sugar-loaf peaks all lie across the river in Laos, so you'll be admiring rather than climbing them. The views are stunning, though, especially during a hazy sunrise.

Sights

Nakhon Phanom's temples have a distinctive style. This was once an important town in the Lan Xang Empire and, after that, Thai kings sent their best artisans to create new buildings. Later a vivid French influence crossed the Mekong and jumped into the mix.

Ho Chi Minh Museum MUSEUM
(หมู่บ้านมิตรภาพไทย-เวียดนาม; Ban Na Chok; ⊙8am-4pm) FREE At this cheesy but fun Ho Chi Minh theme park you'll find a temple, Vietnamese music piped throughout the grounds, a re-creation of the leader's house, and lots of Vietnamese tourists taking selfies in front of fake mountains.

The museum is in Ban Na Chok village, about 3.5km west of Nakhon Phanom, a short walk from **Ho Chi Minh's House** (บ้านโฮจิมินห์; ☎042 522430; donations appreciated; ⊙daylight hours). Túk-túk (pronounced *đúk đúk*; a type of motorised rickshaw) drivers quote 200B for the return trip, although you might get a taxi to do it for 100B.

Former Governor's Residence Museum MUSEUM
(จวนผู้ว่าราชการจังหวัดนครพนม (หลังเก่า); Th Sunthon Wijit; adult/child 50/20B; ⊙9am-5pm Wed-Sun) This museum fills a beautifully restored 1925 mansion with photos of old Nakhon Phanom, many labelled in English, while out the back are displays about the illunimated boat precession (Lai Reua Fai).

Festivals & Events

Lai Reua Fai CULTURAL
(⊙late Oct/early Nov) Nakhon Phanom is famous for this illuminated boat procession. A modern twist on the ancient tradition of sending rafts loaded with food, flowers and candles down the Mekong as offerings for the *naga* (mythical serpent), today's giant bamboo rafts hold up to 20,000 handmade lanterns, and some designers add animation to the scenes.

Sleeping & Eating

Most of Nakhon Phanom's accommodation falls in the midrange category and is good value, although weekending gamblers can occasionally make a room difficult to snag.

★777 Hometel HOTEL $$
(☎042 514777; Th Tamrongprasit; r incl breakfast 590-790B; P❄@🛜) Don't let the boxy exterior fool you: inside is Nakhon Phanom's most stylish hotel. It doesn't just get by on looks alone, though; the rooms are great, it's well managed and it has some of the friendliest, most helpful staff in town. It's called *đorng jet* in Thai.

TC Apartment HOTEL $$
(☎042 512212; Th Sunthon Wijit; r 690B; P❄🛜) TC has a great central location and big river views from the balconies of the front-facing rooms. The rooms are solid and the wi-fi strong. One big downside: the noise coming from busy Th Sunthon Wijit can be pretty terrible at night.

Night Market THAI $
(Th Fuang Nakhon; mains from 30B; ⊙4-9pm) Nakhon Phanom's night market is large and diverse but has few places to sit.

Phornthep Naem Nueang VIETNAMESE $
(Th Sri Thep; mains 40-200B; ⊙6am-4pm) Aged-feeling place with a full selection of Vietnamese dishes. Come in the morning for *khài kràtá* (a mini skillet of eggs topped with Vietnamese sausages). There's no roman-script sign, but it's located directly across from an old movie theater.

Information

Tourism Authority of Thailand (TAT; ☎042 513490; tatphnom@tat.or.th; Th Sunthon Wijit; ⊙8.30am-4.30pm) Covers Nakhon Phanom, Sakon Nakhon and Mukdahan Provinces. Inconveniently located about 2km north of town.

Getting There & Around

Nahon Phanom's airport is located 20km west of town. **Nok Air** (☎098 681 0181, nationwide 02 900 9955; www.nokair.com; Nakhon Phanom Airport; ⊙8am-8pm) and **Air Asia** (☎042 531571, nationwide 02 515 9999; www.airasia.com; Nakhon Phanom Airport; ⊙8am-5pm) fly daily to/from Bangkok's Don Mueang International Airport with one-way prices from 1100B.

Taxis charge 100B for trips into town.

Nakhon Phanom's **bus terminal** (☎042 513444; Th Fuang Nakhon) is west of the town centre. From here buses head to Nong Khai (200B, 6½ hours, three daily from 7.30am to 11.30am), Udon Thani (147B to 189B, 4½ hours, hourly from 4.30am to 3.40pm) and Ubon Ratchathani (from 155B to 200B, 4½ hours, three departures from 7am to 2pm). For Ubon most people use minivans (182B, four hours, frequent

GETTING TO LAOS: NAKHON PHANOM TO THA KHAEK

Getting to the border Passenger ferries cross the Mekong to Tha Khaek in Laos, but they're for Thais and Lao only. All other travellers must use the Third Thai-Lao Friendship Bridge, north of the city. The easiest way to cross is to take the bus directly to Tha Khaek from Nakhon Phanom's bus station (70/75B weekdays/weekends, four departures from 8.30am to 2.30pm).

At the border The Thai border is open from 6am to 10pm. All immigration formalities are handled at the bridge and Lao visas are available on arrival. Things get pretty chaotic when droves of Vietnamese workers are passing through.

Moving on The bus tends to wait a long time to get more passengers, so total travel time to Tha Khaek is often more than two hours.

from 5.45am to 4pm), which go via Mukdahan (69B, 2½ hours) and That Phanom (40B, one hour). There are frequent buses to Bangkok (from 386B to 862B, 11 to 12 hours) between 4.30pm and 7.30pm.

Sŏrng·tăa·ou (passenger pick-up trucks) to That Phanom (40B, 1½ hours, frequent until 5pm) park near Kasikornbank.

Nong Khai

Sitting on the banks of the Mekong, just across from Vientiane in Laos, Nong Khai has been popular with travellers for years. Its popularity is about more than just its proximity to Vientiane and its bounty of banana pancakes, though. Seduced by its dreamy pink sunsets and sluggish pace of life, many visitors who mean to stay one night end up bedding down for many more.

Sights

★ Sala Kaew Ku — SCULPTURE

(ศาลาแก้วกู่, Wat Khaek; 20B; ⏲6am-6pm) It's cheesy, but the sheer size of the sculptures at Sala Kaew Ku can't fail to impress. Built over 20 years by Luang Pu Boun Leua Sourirat, a mystic who died in 1996, the park features a weird and wonderful array of sculptures ablaze with Hindu-Buddhist imagery. All buses headed east of Nong Khai pass the road leading to Sala Kaew Ku (10B). It's about a five-minute walk from the highway. Chartered túk-túk cost 150B return with a one-hour wait.

Wat Pho Chai — BUDDHIST TEMPLE

(วัดโพธิ์ชัย; Th Phochai; donations appreciated; ⏲daylight hours) Luang Po Phra Sai, a large Lan Xang–era Buddha image awash with gold, bronze and precious stones, sits at the hub of Nong Khai's holiest temple. The head of the image is pure gold, the body is bronze and the *ùt·sà·nít* (flame-shaped head ornament) is set with rubies. Due to the great number of miracles attributed to it, this royal temple is a mandatory stop for most visiting Thais.

Nong Khai Aquarium — AQUARIUM

(พิพิธภัณฑ์สัตว์น้ำจังหวัดหนองคาย; off Rte 2; 100B; ⏲9am-5pm Tue-Sun) First impressions may not overwhelm at this aquarium, as some of the early displays look a little shabby, but the further you go the more interesting it gets, especially the impressive giant Mekong River tank. A highlight is the 'feeding the man to the fish' performance every day at 2pm and also at 11am on Saturday, Sunday and public holidays. The aquarium is far out of town, on the Khon Kaen University campus off Rte 2, and not served by public transport.

Central Nong Khai

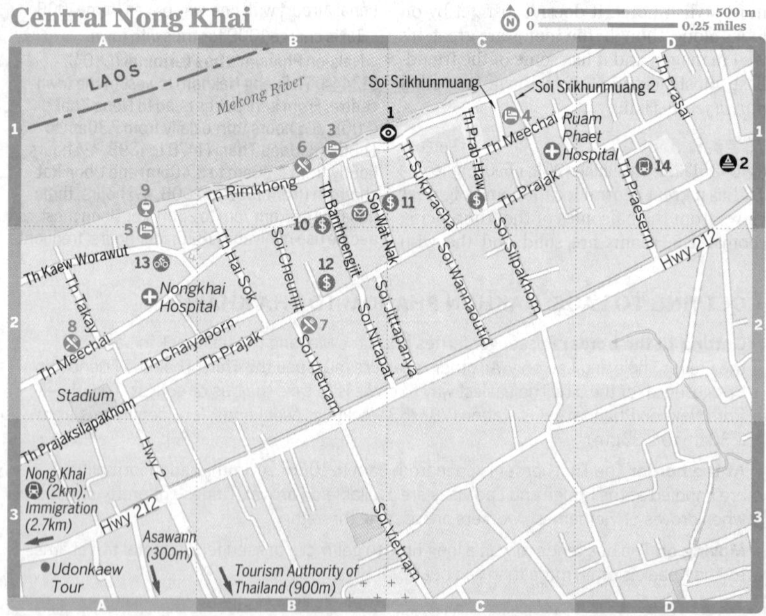

Tha Sadet Market MARKET
(ตลาดท่าเสด็จ; Th Rimkhong; 8.30am-6pm) It's the most popular destination in town – almost everyone loves a stroll through this covered market. It offers the usual mix of clothes, electronic equipment, food and assorted bric-a-brac, most of it imported from Laos and China, but there are also a few shops selling quirky quality stuff.

Festivals & Events

Songkran CULTURAL
(mid-Apr) During Songkran the priceless image of Luang Po Phra Sai from Wat Pho Chai is paraded around town.

Sleeping

Catering to the steady flow of backpackers, Nong Khai's budget lodging selection is the best in Isan.

★**Mut Mee Garden Guest House** GUESTHOUSE $$
(042 460717; www.mutmee.com; 1111/4 Th Kaew Worawut; r 200-1400B;) Occupying a sleepy stretch of the Mekong, Nong Khai's budget classic has a garden so relaxing it's intoxicating, and most nights it's packed with travellers. Mut Mee caters to many budgets, with a huge variety of rooms (the cheapest with shared bathroom, the most expensive with an awesome balcony) clustered around a thatched-roof restaurant with expansive views of the Mekong.

The owner, Julian, freely shares his wealth of knowledge about sights and legends of the local area.

Ban Sai Thong GUESTHOUSE $$
(081 975 6451; Soi 2, Th Meechai; r incl breakfast 600B) This newly opened traditional-Thai-style home has nine rooms surrounding an open courtyard. The house has a lovely design and the rooms are spacious and have rustic verandahs with sitting areas facing onto the courtyard. There are free bikes. The price includes morning coffee and *kôw tanyápêut* (a mix of sticky rice and other grains). It's the best of the converted Thai houses in this area.

Baan Mae Rim Nam HOTEL $$
(081 873 0636, 042 420256; www.baanmae\rimnam.com; Soi Kheuan 3, Mekong Promenade; d 500-800B, tr 800-1100B;) Tucked down a soi in Tha Sadet Market and right on the riverfront, this bright-yellow building has great rooms with balconies and river views. The cheaper standard rooms out the back, however, are less inviting.

Eating & Drinking

There are many restaurants in the Tha Sadet Market, and elsewhere along the promenade, that serve big river views.

Daeng Namnuang VIETNAMESE $
(Th Rimkhong; mains 50-250B; 8am-8pm;) This massive river restaurant has grown into an Isan institution, and hordes of out-of-towners head home with car boots and carry-on bags (there's an outlet at Udon Thani's airport) stuffed with *nǎam neu·ang* (DIY pork spring rolls).

Saap Lah THAI $
(Th Meechai; mains 25-150B; 7am-8pm) For excellent *gài yâhng* (grilled chicken), *sôm·đam* (spicy green-papaya salad) and other Isan foods, follow your nose to this no-frills shop.

Dee Dee Pohchanah THAI $$
(Th Prajak; dishes 60-425B; 10.30am-2am) How good is Dee Dee? Just look at the dinner-time crowds. Despite having a full house every night, this simple place is a well-oiled machine and you won't be waiting long.

Central Nong Khai

Sights
1 Tha Sadet Market ... C1
2 Wat Pho Chai ... D1

Sleeping
3 Baan Mae Rim Nam ... B1
4 Ban Sai Thong ... C1
5 Mut Mee Garden Guest House ... A2

Eating
6 Daeng Namnuang ... B1
7 Dee Dee Pohchanah ... B2
8 Saap Lah ... A2

Drinking & Nightlife
9 Gaia ... A1

Information
10 Krung Thai Bank ... B1
11 KTB Bank ... C1
12 Thanachart Bank ... B2

Transport
13 Khun Noui ... A2
14 Nong Khai Bus Terminal ... D1

OFF THE BEATEN TRACK

BUENG KAN

One of the few attractions in little Bueng Kan township is the Thai-Lao Market. Some of the products, such as herbs and mushrooms, sold by Lao traders are gathered in the forest, and there's a good representation of traditional Isan fare (crates of crickets and frogs).

Sights

Wat Phu Thok (วัดภูทอก; ⌚6am-5pm, closed 10-16 Apr) At wondrous Wat Phu Thok, six levels of steps lead past shrines and *gù·đì* (monks' huts or living quarters) that are scattered around the mountain, in caves and on cliffs. A seventh-level scramble up roots and rocks takes you to the forest at the summit, with fabulous views over the surrounding countryside and a truly soporific atmosphere.

Phu Wua Wildlife Sanctuary (เขตรักษาพันธุ์สัตว์ป่าภูวัว; ☎081 260 1845; adult/child 100/50B) The Phu Wua Wildlife Sanctuary is one of Thailand's most important wildlife reserves and covers 186 sq km of rugged forest along some hills along the Mekong River. The forest is flush with waterfalls (only active during or just after the rainy season) and is reputedly home to leopards, bears, pheasants and monkeys. Three dozen elephants live in the sanctuary, and they can occasionally be encountered on walks.

Thai-Lao Market (ตลาดนัดบึงกาฬ; Soi Buengkan; ⌚morning Tue & Fri) This market lines the street along the lake and is filled with sellers from both sides of the river. It can get pretty lively and the wares for sale include many forest products such as herbal remedies and local foods. You may see crates of chirping crickets and other kinds of bugs for sale, plus clothes, coffee and snacks.

Sleeping

Maenam Hotel (☎042 491051; Th Chansin; r 400-450B; P ⊖ ❄ @ ⊜) This Mekong-facing hotel is the best-located place in town. When we visited extensive improvements were being made to the promenade along the river, which will only increase the value of the location.

Getting There & Away

Bueng Kan functions as the transport hub for the province, with a variety of buses, minivans and *sŏrng·tăa·ou* (passenger pick-up trucks), but at the time of writing the city's bus station was being relocated and the transport situation was very much in chaos; check with locals for updates when you're in town.

Gaia BAR
(Th Rimkhong; ⌚7pm-late) Much of the Mut Mee Garden Guest House crowd, and many resident *fa·ràng* (foreigners), fill this laid-back floating bar on the Mekong. There's a great drinks list, a chilled vibe and sometimes live music. It often hosts fundraisers for local charitable projects.

Information

There are banks with extended opening hours and AEON ATMs at **Asawann** (Hwy 2; ⌚10am-9pm) shopping centre.

Immigration (☎042 990935; ⌚8.30am-noon & 1-4.30pm Mon-Fri) South of the Friendship Bridge, off Rte 2. Offers Thai visa extensions.

Nongkhai Hospital (☎042 413461; Th Meechai; ⌚24hr) Has a 24-hour casualty department.

Tourism Authority of Thailand (TAT; ☎042 421326; tat_nongkhai@yahoo.com; Hwy 2; ⌚8.30am-4.30pm) Inconveniently located outside of town.

Getting There & Away

AIR

The nearest airport is 55km south in Udon Thani. **Udonkaew Tour** (☎042 411530; Th Pranang Cholpratan; ⌚8.30am-5.30pm) travel agency runs minivans (150B to 200B per person) to/from the airport. Coming into town it'll drop you at your hotel or the bridge; going back you need to get yourself to its office. It's best to buy tickets in advance.

BUS

Nong Khai bus terminal (☎042 412679) is located just off Th Prajak, about 1.5km from the main pack of riverside guesthouses. Udon Thani (40B, one hour, every 30 minutes from 5.30am to 8pm) is the most frequent destination. For those travelling west along the Mekong, there are buses to Sangkhom (60B, three hours, 7.30am, 11am and 3pm), with the 7.30am bus continuing all the way to Loei (130B, 6½ hours). There are also buses to Khon Kaen (120B to 137B, 3½ hours, hourly from 7am to 6pm), Nakhon Phanom (200B, 6½ hours, 8.30am and 11am), and Kanchanaburi (495B to 770B, 10 hours, 8am and 6.30pm), and minivans to Udon Thani (50B, 45 minutes, hourly from 6am to 6pm) and Bueng Kan (150B, 2½ hours, frequent from 5.30am to 8pm).

Bangkok (329B to 658B, 11 hours) buses are frequent in the late afternoon and early evening but less so during the day. There's also one bus direct to Suvarnabhumi (Airport) bus station (495B, nine hours, 8pm). There are two daily buses to Chiang Mai (820B, 12 hours, 7pm).

TRAIN

Three express trains, one in the morning and two in the afternoon, connect Bangkok (seat 103B to 498B, 1st-class sleeper upper/lower 1117/1317B, 11½ hours) and **Nong Khai train station** (☎042 411637, nationwide 1690; www.railway.co.th), which is 2km west of the city centre. There's also one cheaper evening rapid train.

Getting Around

Nong Khai is a great place for cycling due to the limited traffic and the nearby countryside. Many guesthouses let you use their bikes for free. If you need to hire one, **Khun Noui** (☎081 975 4863; Th Kaew Worawut; ⏲8am-4pm), who sets up on the roadside across from the entrance to Mut Mee, has reliable bikes (50B per day) and motorcycles (200B).

You can find metered taxis at the bus station and the bridge. Generally, people agree on a price rather than use the meter. A túk-túk between the Mut Mee area and either the bus station or the bridge should be 40B to 50B.

Nong Khai to Loei

Sights

Sleepy little **Sangkhom** is a convenient stop between Nong Khai and Loei. Just after the wet season, the town's main attractions are its waterfalls.

Wat Hin Mak Peng BUDDHIST TEMPLE
(วัดหินหมากเป้ง; off Rte 211; donations appreciated; ⏲daylight hours) Overlooking a lovely stretch of the Mekong, this vast forest temple is centred on a cliff rising out of the river. The very peaceful temple is respected by Thais because of their reverence for the founding abbot, Ajahn Thet, a disciple of Ajahn Mun

GETTING TO LAOS: NONG KHAI TO VIENTIANE

This is one of the busiest Thai border crossings.

Getting to the border If you already have your Lao visa, the easiest way to Vientiane is the direct bus from Nong Khai's bus terminal (55B, one hour, six daily from 7.30am to 6pm). There's also a bus to Vang Vieng (270B, four hours, 9.40am). The 5B surcharge for tickets to Laos on weekends, holidays and the 7.30am and 6pm weekday services is genuine.

If you plan to get your visa at the border (6am to 10pm), take a túk-túk there – expect to pay 100B from the bus station, but you can pay 50B from the town centre. Unless you're travelling in a large group, there's no good reason to use a visa service agency, so don't let a driver take you to one.

You can also go to Laos by train (there are immigration booths at both stations), though it doesn't go through to Vientiane, so that option is not recommended. The 15-minute ride (20B to 30B, departs 9am and 2.45pm) drops you in Thanaleng (aka Dongphasay) station just over the bridge, leaving you at the mercy of túk-túk drivers who charge extortionate prices.

At the border After getting stamped out of Thailand, you can take the buses (weekdays/weekends 20/30B) that carry passengers across the bridge to the hassle-free, but sometimes busy, Lao immigration checkpoint, where 30-day visas are available.

Moving on It's about 20km to Vientiane. Plenty of buses, túk-túk and taxis will be waiting for you and it's easy to find fellow travellers to share the costs.

Bhuridatto. Several monuments in his honour, including a lifelike wax statue and a glistening *chedi* (religions monuments) are found around the grounds. Visitors must dress respectfully: no shorts above the knees or sleeveless tops.

The temple is midway between Si Chiangmai and Sangkhom. Sangkhom-bound buses from Nong Khai (50B, 2¼ hours) pass the entrance, and then it's a longish walk to the buildings.

Wat Pha Tak Sua BUDDHIST TEMPLE
(วัดผาตากเสื้อ; off Rte 211; daylight hours) The forest wát peering down on the town, Wat Pha Tak Sua lies just 2km away as the crow flies, but it's 19km to drive. It has amazing Mekong views; you might see the valley filled with fog on early mornings during the cold season. The footpath used by the monks every morning begins east of town just before the Km 81 pillar. Follow Soi 5 past the last house, then veer right by the mango and papaya trees.

Nam Tok Than Thip WATERFALL
(น้ำตกธารทิพย์; daylight hours) FREE Three-tiered Nam Tok Than Thip waterfall, 13km west of Sangkhom (2km off Rte 211), is the largest waterfall in the area. The lower level drops 30m and the second level, easily reached via stairs, falls 100m. The 70m top drop is barely visible through the lush forest.

Sleeping

Sangkhom River View HOTEL $$
(042 441088, 063 361 4562; Rte 211; r & bungalows incl breakfast 1500B;) This attractive set-up, featuring wooden walkways and decorative stonework, will satisfy those who demand a certain level of comfort. Many rooms have river views and the restaurant is good. It's 1.5km east of the town centre.

Getting There & Around

There are three rickety fan buses a day from Nong Khai (60B, three hours) and the earliest of those continues all the way to Loei (70B, 3½ hours). There's no bus stop in town; wave buses down when they pass.

Loei

Loei is a relatively small provincial capital and easy to get around. It makes a convenient base from which to explore the province's national parks and has some decent accommodation options. The forest park on its outskirts offers spectacular views of the town and surrounding hills.

Loei's small museums aren't spectacular, but if you won't be visiting Dan Sai, there are Phi Ta Khon festival masks and photos (plus pottery, fabrics and other artefacts, and some useful displays on the region's Thai Phuan and Thai Dam people) to see at the **Loei Museum** (พิพิธภัณฑ์เมืองเลย; Th Charoenrat; 8.30am-4.30pm; P) FREE, above the tourist office, and the **Loei Cultural Centre** (ศูนย์วัฒนธรรมจังหวัดเลย; 042 835223; Rte 201; 8.30am-4.30pm) FREE, 5km north of town at Rajabhat University.

The **tourist office** (TAT; 042 812812; tatloei@tat.or.th; Th Charoenrat; 8.30am-4.30pm) also provides a good map of the province and has helpful staff.

Sleeping

★ **Loei Village** BOUTIQUE HOTEL $$
(042 833599; www.loeivillages.com; Soi 3, Th Nok Kaew; r incl breakfast 1300B;) From the warm welcome and the cold welcome drink as you walk in the door, the focus is on service at this stylish hotel. The decor is smart, and small details such as free minibar snacks and an excellent buf-

GETTING TO LAOS: BUENG KAN TO PAKSAN

Although it's very rarely done, you can cross the Mekong from Bueng Kan to Paksan, but only if you already have your Lao visa.

Getting to the border Immigration (8am to 6pm) was 2.5km northwest of town (a túk-túk cost about 60B), although in late 2016 it was in the process of being moved.

At the border Boats cross the river between 8.30am and noon and between 1pm and 4.30pm when they have about 20 passengers. During lunch and after 4.30pm you'll probably need to charter the whole boat (1000B).

Moving on Túk-túk wait on the Lao shore, though the highway and a few hotels are an easy walk from the landing.

GETTING TO LAOS: THAI LI TO KAEN THAO

Foreigners can get Lao visas at the seldom-used Thai-Lao Nam Heuang Friendship Bridge in Amphoe Tha Li, 60km northwest of Loei.

Getting to the border The easiest way to cross here is via the **VIP service** (Borisat Khon Song; ☎042 811706; Loei bus terminal) from Loei to Luang Prabang in Laos (700B, 10 hours) via Saiyabuli (500B, seven hours). Buses leave Loei at 8am.

At the border The border is open from 6am to 6pm.

fet breakfast make this one of the city's top choices. There are also bikes for guests' use. Staff are especially helpful.

Getting There & Around

Nok Air (☎Loei Airport 088 874 0883, nationwide 02 900 9955; www.nokair.com; Loei Airport; ⊙6am-4pm) and **Air Asia** (☎Loei Airport 042 844629, nationwide 02 515 9999; www.airasia.com; Loei Airport; ⊙9am-5pm) both connect Loei to Bangkok's Don Mueang International Airport three times daily, with prices starting at around 990B. Air Asia has a minivan shuttle service from the airport to Chiang Khan.

A taxi into town runs 150B.

Loei's **bus terminal** (☎042 833586; Th Maliwan) has services to Udon Thani (91B, three hours, every 30 minutes from 4am to 5.20pm), Khon Kaen (125B, 3½ hours, half-hourly from 3.45am to 6.10pm), Khorat (252B, six hours, frequent from 5.30am to 4.30pm), Phitsanulok (207B to 266B, four hours, 10am and noon) and Chiang Mai (409B to 570B, 10 hours, three daily). The only bus to Nong Khai (150B, 6½ hours) leaves at 6am, and it's worth catching because it follows the scenic Mekong River route. It's faster, however, to go via Udon Thani.

Buses to Bangkok (389B to 605B, 11 hours) have frequent evening departures with **Air Muang Loei** (☎042 832042; Loei bus terminal), **999 VIP** (☎042 811706; Loei bus terminal) and the Transport Company (p463).

The bus station is also where you'll find minivans to Dan Sai (70B, 1½ hours, four daily from 4.30am to 4.30pm) and Khon Kaen (160B, three hours, 9am and 4pm), and *sŏrng·tăa·ou* (passenger pick-up trucks) to Chiang Khan (35B, 1½ hours, half-hourly from 5am to 7.15pm).

Chiang Khan

Sitting right on the banks of the Mekong, Chiang Khan capitalises on its great location with a thriving tourist industry. With great views across to the mountains of Laos, its main attractions are a lovely esplanade along the river and the quaint wooden shophouses of its 'walking street' (which actually does have a few cars). It's a popular spot for holidaying Thais and a great place to spend a few days relaxing.

At the time of writing there were plans to extend the esplanade along the Mekong all the way out to Kaeng Khut Khu, which would make it a nice 4km walk.

Many guesthouses arrange boat trips to Kaeng Khut Khu or further afield, and the mountain scenery makes them highly recommended. Rates swing with petrol prices, but the typical 1½-hour trip costs around 1000B for up to 10 people.

Sleeping

Chiangkhan Riverview Guesthouse GUESTHOUSE **$$**
(☎080 741 8055; 277 Th Chai Khong; r 500-1000B; ❄📶) This tasteful riverside spot has rooms with fan and air-con, shared and private bathrooms and a mix of old and new construction. The rooms, some with river views, are all dark wood and cool ambience, the terrace is very inviting and the owners are friendly.

Norn-Nab-Dao HOTEL **$$**
(☎086 792 0215; Th Chai Khong; r incl breakfast 1000-2500B; P❄📶) Unlike many of the new places going up, this one isn't all timber, but it has some charm nonetheless. The cutely painted rooms lie around a central courtyard.

Getting There & Away

Sŏrng·tăa·ou (passenger pick-up trucks) to Loei (35B, 1¼ hours) depart about every 15 minutes in the early morning, and then whenever there are enough passengers, from a stop on Th Srichiang Khan (at Soi 26). They also pick up passengers at the market and Rte 201 along the way. Frequent buses (38B, 45 minutes) leave from the **Nakhonchai Transport** (☎042 821905) terminal on Rte 201. They continue to Khorat (283B, seven hours) via Chaiyaphum (205B).

Four companies, departing from their own offices, make the run to Bangkok (10 hours) in the morning and early evening: **Air Muang Loei** (☎082 642 1629; Th Srichiang Khan Soi 23),

OFF THE BEATEN TRACK

PHA TAEM NATIONAL PARK

A long cliff named Pha Taem is the centrepiece of the awesome but unheralded **Pha Taem National Park** (อุทยานแห่งชาติผาแต้ม; ☎045 252581; adult/child 400/200B). From the top you get a bird's-eye view across the Mekong into Laos, and down below a trail passes prehistoric rock paintings dating to at least 1000 BC. Mural subjects include *plah bèuk* (giant Mekong catfish), elephants, human hands, geometric designs and fish traps that look much like the huge ones still used today. The second viewing platform fronts the most impressive batch.

Unfortunately, the clearing of the path for viewing the paintings has exposed the rock to the elements, resulting in some fading of the images over the years since the park was established, but they're still impressive. A **visitor centre** (⌚5am-6pm) here contains exhibits pertaining to the paintings and local ecology.

North of the cliff is Nam Tok Soi Sawan, a 25m-tall waterfall flowing from June to December, the same period as all the park's waterfalls. It's a 19km drive from the visitor centre and then a 500m walk, or you can hike (with a ranger) for about 15km along the top of the cliff if you arrange it in advance. What the park calls Thailand's largest flower field (blooming November to February) lies near the falls.

The northern half of the park holds more waterfalls, ancient art and wonderful views. Pha Cha Na Dai cliff serves Thailand's first sunrise view (Pha Taem is about one minute behind and has the first sunset view), and amazing Nam Tok Saeng Chan waterfall flows through a hole cut naturally into the overhanging rock. Scattered across the 340-sq-km park are many oddly eroded rocks, including four sites known as Sao Chaliang, which are mushroom-shaped stone formations similar to those found in Mukdahan's **Phu Pha Thoep National Park** (อุทยานแห่งชาติภูผาเทิบ; ☎089 619 7741; admission 200B).

Pha Taem & Kaeng Phisamai Riverside (☎087 249 3173; www.phataemriverside.com; r & bungalows incl breakfast 1000-2500B; P ❄ 📶) With its spectacular location overlooking the Mekong and views of the cliffs of Laos, this place is probably the pick of the bunch of 'resorts' spotted about the entrance to Pha Taem National Park. There's a small bridge for accessing the rocky bed of the Mekong (in dry season), a restaurant and even ponies.

Pha Taem is 18km from Khong Jiam along Rte 2112. There's no public transport, so the best way to get there is to hire a truck or túk-túk in Khong Jiam (600B for the return trip). Minibuses run from Ubon Ratchasima to Khong Jiam (80B, 1½ hours, hourly, 6.30am to 6pm).

999 VIP (☎089 893 2898; Soi 9), **Phu Kradung Tours** (☎089 842 1524; petrol station, Rte 201; ticket) and **Sun Bus** (☎nationwide 02 936 3993; Rte 201). Tickets range from 419B to 652B.

It's worth noting that no transport runs direct to Nong Khai.

If you're heading west and you've got your own wheels, consider following the seldom-seen back roads along Mae Nam Heuang; they'll eventually deposit you in Dan Sai.

NORTHERN THAILAND

The region's premier draw is its nature, and northern Thailand's rugged geography is a playground for outdoor pursuits.

For those drawn to the human side of things, there's also northern Thailand's buffet of cultural attractions and experiences as the region is regarded as the birthplace of much of what is often associated with Thai culture.

Getting There & Away

AIR

Air Asia (☎nationwide 02 515 9999; www.airasia.com) Within northern Thailand, Air Asia flies between Bangkok's Don Mueang International Airport and Chiang Mai, Chiang Rai, Nan and Phitsanulok.

Bangkok Airways (☎nationwide 1771; www.bangkokair.com) With destinations in northern Thailand including Chiang Mai, Chiang Rai, Lampang, Mae Hong Son and Sukhothai.

Kan Air (☎nationwide 02 551 6111; www.kanairlines.com) With destinations in northern Thailand including Chiang Mai, Mae Hong Son, Pai and Phitsanulok.

Thai Smile (☎nationwide 02 118 8888; www.thaismileair.com) With destinations in Chiang Mai and Chiang Rai.

CAR

Several car-hire companies have offices in northern Thailand including **Avis** (☎ nationwide 02 251 1131; www.avisthailand.com), **North Wheels** (☎ 053 874478; www.northwheels.com) and **Thai Rent A Car** (☎ nationwide 1647; www.thairentacar.com).

Chiang Mai

Chiang Mai is beloved by Thais and tourists for its (relatively) cool climate and its enduring connections to its past as the capital of the northern Thai kingdom of Lanna. It is a city of temples and culture classes and a gateway to the great outdoors of the northern mountains.

Sights

Chiang Mai overflows with temples, markets and museums, but don't overlook the sights outside the old city, both inside and outside the fringing highways.

★Talat Warorot MARKET

(ตลาดวโรรส; cnr Th Chang Moi & Th Praisani; 6am-5pm) Chiang Mai's oldest public market, Warorot (also spelt 'Waroros') is a great place to connect with the city's Thai soul. Alongside souvenir vendors you'll find numerous stalls selling items for ordinary Thai households: woks, toys, fishermen's nets, pickled tea leaves, wigs, sticky-rice steamers, Thai-style sausages, *kâab mŏo* (pork rinds), live catfish and tiny statues for spirit houses. It's easy to spend half a day wandering the covered walkways, watching locals browsing, and haggling for goods that actually have a practical use back home.

★Lanna Folklife Museum MUSEUM

(พิพิธภัณฑ์พื้นถิ่นล้านนา; Th Phra Pokklao; adult/child 90/40B; 8.30am-5pm Tue-Sun) Set inside the Thai-colonial-style former Provincial Court, dating from 1935, this imaginative museum re-creates Lanna village life in a series of life-size dioramas that explain everything from *lai·krahm* pottery stencilling and *fon lep* (a mystical Lanna dance featuring long metal fingernails) to the intricate symbolism of different elements of Lanna-style monasteries.

This is the best first stop before heading to the many wát dotted around the old city.

Chiang Mai National Museum MUSEUM

(พิพิธภัณฑสถานแห่งชาติเชียงใหม่; ☎ 053 221308; Rte 11/Th Superhighway; 9am-4pm Wed-Sun) FREE Operated by the Fine Arts Department, this museum is the primary caretaker of Lanna artefacts and northern Thai history. But when we stopped by most of the galleries were closed for refurbishment, and only the ground floor, with Buddhist statues, *howdahs* (elephant carriages) and dioramas of historical scenes, was open to the public. When the museum reopens, expect the old admission fee of 100B to be reinstated.

Temples in Town

★Wat Phra Singh BUDDHIST TEMPLE

(วัดพระสิงห์; Th Singharat; donations appreciated; 5am-8.30pm) Chiang Mai's most revered temple, Wat Phra Singh is dominated by an enormous, mosaic-inlaid *wí·hăhn* (sanctuary). Its prosperity is plain to see from the lavish monastic buildings and immaculately trimmed grounds, dotted with coffee stands and massage pavilions. Pilgrims flock here to venerate the famous Buddha image known as **Phra Singh** (Lion Buddha), housed in Wihan Lai Kham, a small chapel immediately south of the *chedi* to the rear of the temple grounds.

★Wat Chedi Luang BUDDHIST TEMPLE

(วัดเจดีย์หลวง; Th Phra Pokklao; adult/child 40/20B; 7am-10pm) FREE Wat Chedi Luang is not quite as grand as Wat Phra Singh, but its towering, ruined Lanna-style *chedi* (built in 1441) is much taller and the sprawling compound around the stupa is powerfully atmospheric. The famed Phra Kaew (Emerald Buddha), now held in Bangkok's Wat Phra Kaew, resided in the eastern niche until 1475; today, you can view a jade replica, given as a gift from the Thai king in 1995 to celebrate the 600th anniversary of the *chedi*.

★Wat Phan Tao BUDDHIST TEMPLE

(วัดพันเถา; Th Phra Pokklao; donations appreciated; daylight hours) Without doubt the most atmospheric wát in the old city, this teak marvel sits in the shadow of Wat Chedi Luang. Set in a compound full of fluttering orange flags, the monastery is a monument to the teak trade, with an enormous prayer hall supported by 28 gargantuan teak pillars and lined with dark teak panels, enshrining a particularly graceful gold Buddha image. The juxtaposition of the orange monks' robes against this dark backdrop during evening prayers is particularly sublime.

Wat Chiang Man BUDDHIST TEMPLE

(วัดเชียงมั่น; Th Ratchaphakhinai; donations appreciated; daylight hours) Chiang Mai's oldest

Central Chiang Mai

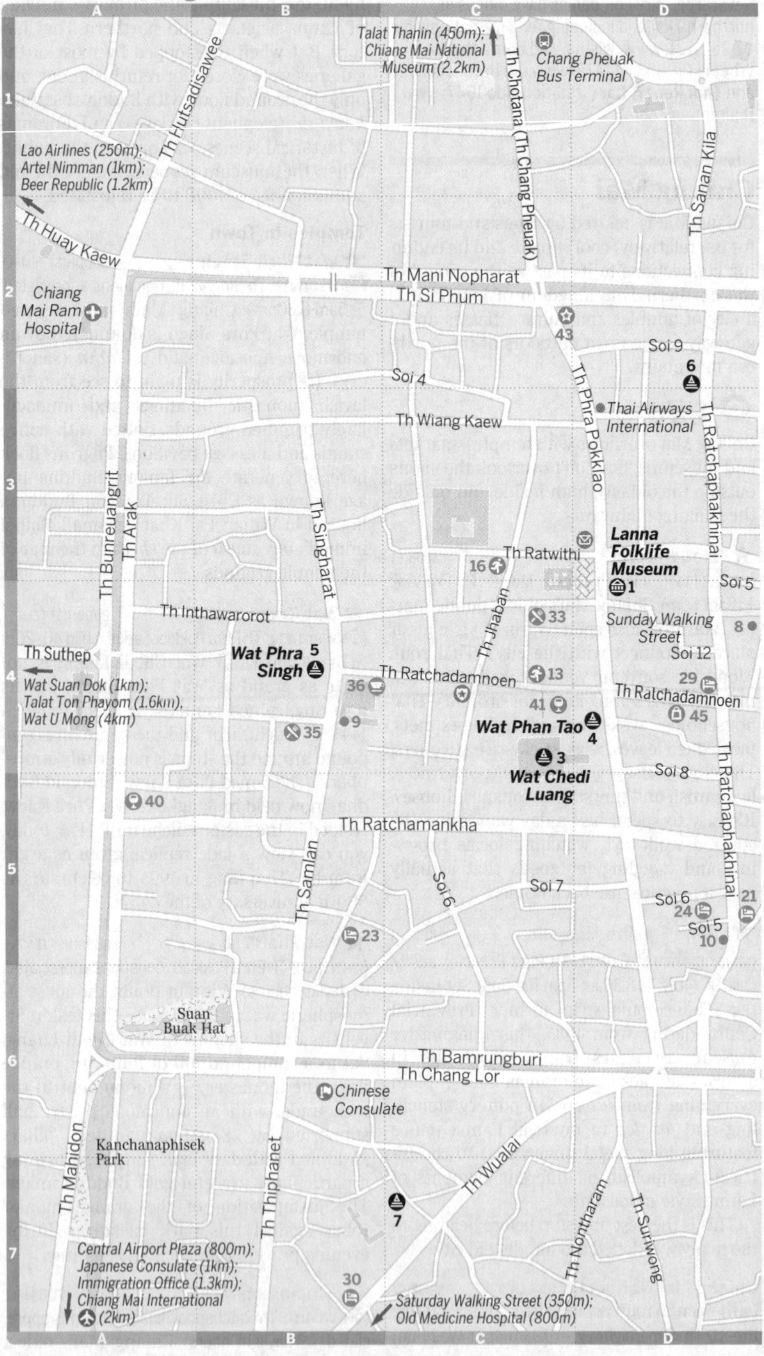

0 400 m
0 0.2 miles
Th Ratanakosin
Saphan Ratanakosin
Th Chaiyaphum
Th Muang Samut
Th Charoenrat (Th Faham)
Th Chetuphon
42
14
Th Kaew Nawarat
McCormick Hospital (500m); Arcade (1.5km); Nok Air (1.5km)
Th Wichayanon
US Consulate
Soi 1
Soi 9
31
Soi 8
28
Soi 7
Soi 1
Th Taiwang
Th Wat Ket
Soi 3
19
Soi 6
Soi 2
Th Moon Muang
Th Chaiyaphum
Soi 2
Th Chang Moi Kao
Th Ratchawong
Th Praisani
Th Chang Moi
2
Talat Warorot
Mae Ping
39
15
38
Soi 5
Soi 1
Th Chang Moi
Soi 2
37
Air Asia
18
34
Th Tha Phae
Main Square
22
26
20
Th Tha Phae
Thai Smile
12
Soi 5
Soi 4
Soi 3
Chiang Mai (1.4km); Indian Consulate (2km)
Soi 4
32
Soi 1
Soi 6
Soi 1
Th Chang Khlan
17
Soi 2
Chiang Mai Night Bazaar
44
Soi 6
Soi 1
25
11
27
Th Loi Kroh
Soi 2
Tourism Authority of Thailand
Soi 1
Th Moon Muang
Th Kotchasan
Soi Anusan
Soi 1
Th Charoen Prathet
Th Rat Chiang Saen
Th Si Donchai
French Consulate
Th Kamphaeng Din
Th Pracha Samphan
Th Chang Khlan

Central Chiang Mai

Top Sights
1 Lanna Folklife Museum D4
2 Talat Warorot G3
3 Wat Chedi Luang C4
4 Wat Phan Tao D4
5 Wat Phra Singh B4

Sights
6 Wat Chiang Man D2
7 Wat Srisuphan C7

Activities, Courses & Tours
8 Asia Scenic Thai Cooking D4
9 Chiang Mai Mountain Biking & Kayaking B4
10 Chiang Mai Rock Climbing Adventures D5
11 Elephant Nature Park E5
12 Flight of the Gibbon E4
13 Lila Thai Massage C4
14 Scorpion Tailed River Cruise G2
15 Siam River Adventures E3
16 Vocational Training Centre of the Chiang Mai Women's Correctional Institution C3
17 Wat Pha Khao E5

Sleeping
18 Awana House E4
19 Baan Orapin H3
20 Banthai Village F4
21 Diva Guesthouse D5
22 Gap's House E4
23 Good Morning Chiang Mai Tropical Inn B5
24 Julie Guesthouse D5
25 Julie Guesthouse Part II E5
26 Mo Rooms E4
27 Riverside House H5
28 Sri Pat Guest House E3
29 Tamarind Village D4
30 Tri Yaan Na Ros B7

Eating
31 Blue Diamond E2
32 Kao Soi Fueng Fah G5
33 Kiat Ocha C4
34 Riverside Bar & Restaurant H4
Ruen Tamarind .... (see 29)
35 SP Chicken B4

Drinking & Nightlife
36 Akha Ama Cafe B4
37 Good View H4
38 Kafe E4
39 Khun Kae's Juice Bar E3
40 Mixology A5
41 Writer's Club & Wine Bar C4

Entertainment
42 Nabé E2
43 North Gate Jazz Co-Op C2

Shopping
44 Chiang Mai Night Bazaar G5
45 Sunday Walking Street D4

temple was established by the city's founder, Phaya Mengrai, sometime around 1296. In front of the *ubosot* (ordination hall), a stone slab, engraved in 1581, bears the earliest-known reference to the city's founding. The main *wí·hăhn* (sanctuary) also contains the oldest-known Buddha image created by the Lanna kingdom, cast in 1465.

Temples Outside Town

★ Wat Phra That Doi Suthep BUDDHIST TEMPLE
(วัดพระธาตุดอยสุเทพ; Th Huay Kaew, Doi Suthep; 30B; ⏰6am-6pm) Overlooking the city from its mountain throne, Wat Phra That Doi Suthep is one of northern Thailand's most sacred temples, and its founding legend is learned by every schoolkid in Chiang Mai. The wát itself is a beautiful example of northern Thai architecture, reached via a strenuous, 306-step staircase flanked by mosaic *naga* (serpents); the climb is intended to help devotees accrue Buddhist merit, but less energetic pilgrims can take a funicular-style lift for 20B.

Wat Suthep BUDDHIST TEMPLE
(วัดสุเทพ; Doi Suthep-Pui National Park; 30B; ⏰6am-6pm) One of the north's most sacred temples, Wat Suthep sits majestically atop Doi Suthep's summit. Thai pilgrims flock here to make merit to the Buddhist relic enshrined in the picturesque golden *chedi*. The temple also offers an interesting collection of Lanna art and architecture, and has fine city views if the clouds cooperate.

Wat U Mong BUDDHIST TEMPLE
(วัดอุโมงค์; Soi Wat U Mong, Th Khlong Chonprathan; donations appreciated; ⏰daylight hours) Not to be confused with the small Wat U Mong in the old city, this historic forest wát is famed for its sylvan setting and its ancient *chedi*, which rises above a brick platform wormholed with passageways, built around 1380 for the 'mad' monk Thera Jan. As you wander the arched tunnels, you can see traces of the original murals and several venerated Buddha images. The scrub forest around the platform is scattered with centuries' worth of broken Buddha images.

Activities

River Trips

Scorpion Tailed River Cruise BOATING

(☎081 960 9398; www.scorpiontailedrivercruise.com; Th Charoenrat; cruise 500B) This river cruise focuses on the history of the Mae Ping river using traditional-style craft, known as scorpion-tailed boats. Informative cruises (five daily) last one to 1½ hours. They depart from Wat Srikhong pier near Rim Ping Condo and stop for a snack at the affiliated Scorpion Tailed Boat Village.

Chiang Mai Mountain Biking & Kayaking MOUNTAIN BIKING

(☎053 814207; www.mountainbikingchiangmai.com; 1 Th Samlan; tours 1250-2700B; ⏲8am-8pm) This specialist operator offers recommended kayaking trips on Mae Ping and full-day guided mountain-biking tours (using imported bikes) to Doi Suthep-Pui National Park and further afield, including the popular ascent to Wat Phra That Doi Suthep.

Siam River Adventures RAFTING

(☎089 515 1917; www.siamrivers.com; 17 Th Ratwithi; rafting per day from 1800B; ⏲8am-8pm) With more than 15 years of experience, this outfit running white-water-rafting and kayaking trips has a good reputation for safety and professionalism. The guides have specialist rescue training and additional staff are located at dangerous parts of the river with throw ropes. Trips can be combined with elephant encounters and overnight village stays.

Massage

Vocational Training Centre of the Chiang Mai Women's Correctional Institution MASSAGE

(☎053 122340; 100 Th Ratwithi; foot/traditional massage from 200/200B; ⏲8am-4.30pm Mon-Fri, 9am-4.30pm Sat & Sun) Offers fantastic massages performed by female inmates participating in the prison's job-training rehabilitation program. The cafe next door is a nice spot for a postmassage brew.

Lila Thai Massage MASSAGE

(☎053 327243; www.chiangmaimassage.com; Th Ratchadamnoen; standard/herbal massage from 200/350B; ⏲10am-10pm) A popular massage chain established by the former director of the Chiang Mai women's prison to provide postrelease employment to inmates who participated in the prison's massage training program. There are now five branches in the old city.

Other Activities

Flight of the Gibbon ZIPLINING

(☎053 010660; www.treetopasia.com; 29/4-5 Th Kotchasan; day tour 3999B; ⏲9.30am-6.30pm) Much copied but never equalled, this adventure outfit started the zipline craze, with nearly 5km of wire and staging platforms strung up like a spiderweb in the forest canopy near Ban Mae Kampong, an hour's drive east from Chiang Mai. As well as day trips, it offers multiday, multiactivity tours that include a night at a village homestay.

★Elephant Nature Park ELEPHANT INTERACTION

(☎053 818754, 053 272850; www.elephantnaturepark.org; 1 Th Ratchamankha; 1-/2-day tour 2500/5800B) One of the first sanctuaries for rescued elephants in Chiang Mai, Elephant Nature Park has led the movement to abandon rides and shows and put elephant welfare at the top of the agenda, under the guidance of founder Sangduen (Lek) Chailert. Visits are focused on interaction – the day is spent wandering with mahouts and their charges, helping feed and wash elephants. It is affiliated with the Surin Project (p452).

Wat Pha Khao BUDDHIST TEMPLE

(วัดผ้าขาว; Th Ratchmankha; donations appreciated; ⏲daylight hours) FREE This small monastery holds Monk Chat sessions (p472) from 5pm to 9pm on weekends.

Courses

Climbing

Chiang Mai Rock Climbing Adventures ADVENTURE

(CMRCA; ☎053 207102; www.thailandclimbing.com; 55/3 Th Ratchaphakhinai; climbing course from 3894B) CMRCA maintains many of the climbs at the limestone Crazy Horse Buttress, with bolted sport routes in the French 6a to 7a+ range. As well as climbing and caving courses for climbers of all levels, it runs a shuttle bus to the crag at 8am (300B return; book one day before).

You can rent all the gear you need here, either piece by piece, or as a 'full set' for two climbers (1875B).

Cooking

Small House Chiang Mai Thai Cooking School COOKING

(☎095 674 4550; www.chiangmaithaicooking.com; lessons from 1500B; ⏲lessons 9.30am-3pm) Arm teaches Thai cookery at the eponymous

TREKKING IN CHIANG MAI

Thousands of visitors trek into the hills of northern Thailand each year hoping to see fantastic mountain scenery, interact with traditional tribespeople and meet elephants. A huge industry has grown up to cater to this demand, but the experience is very commercial and may not live up to everyone's notion of adventure.

The standard package involves a one-hour minibus ride to Mae Taeng or Mae Wang, a brief hike to an elephant camp, an elephant ride, bamboo rafting and, for multiday tours, an overnight stay in or near a hill-tribe village. Many budget guesthouses pressure their guests to take these trips because of the commissions paid, and may ask guests to stay elsewhere if they decline.

While these packages are undeniably popular, they visit elephant camps that may have a questionable record on elephant welfare. Hill-tribe trips can also disappoint, as many of the villages now house a mix of tribal people and Chinese and Burmese migrants and have abandoned many aspects of the traditional way of life. Rafting can also be a tame drift on a creek, rather than an adrenalin-charged rush over white water.

If you crave real adventure, you'll have to be a bit more hands-on about organising things yourself. To get deep into the jungle, rent a motorcycle and explore the national parks north and south of Chiang Mai; Chiang Dao is an excellent place to base yourself for jungle exploration. To see elephants in humane, natural conditions, spend a day at Elephant Nature Park (p469), then raft real white water with Siam River Adventures (p469). To encounter traditional hill-tribe culture, you'll need to travel to more remote areas than you can reach on a day trip from Chiang Mai; your best bet is to travel to Tha Ton and book a multiday trek from there.

dwelling outside Chiang Mai. Courses include transport, a visit to a local market, and even span northern Thai dishes.

Asia Scenic Thai Cooking COOKING
(☎053 418657; www.asiascenic.com; 31 Soi 5, Th Ratchadamnoen; half-day courses from 800/1000, full-day courses 1000-1200B; ⏲half-day lessons 9am-1pm & 5-9pm, full-day lessons 9am-3pm) On Khun Gayray's cooking courses you can study in town or at a peaceful out-of-town farm. Courses cover soups, curries, stir-fries, salads and desserts, so you'll be able to make a three-course meal after a single day.

Health & Wellbeing

Thai Massage School of Chiang Mai HEALTH & WELLBEING
(TMC; ☎053 854330; www.tmcschool.com; 203/6 Th Chiang Mai-Mae Jo; basic courses from 8500B) Northeast of town, this well-known school offers a government-licensed massage curriculum. There are three foundation levels and an intensive teacher-training program.

Doi Suthep Vipassana Meditation Center HEALTH & WELLBEING
(☎053 295012; www.fivethousandyears.org; Th Huay Kaew, Wat Phra That Doi Suthep) Set within the grounds of Wat Phra That Doi Suthep, this centre offers meditation training retreats for all levels, lasting from four to 21 days.

Old Medicine Hospital HEALTH & WELLBEING
(OMH; ☎053 201663; www.thaimassageschool.ac.th; 78/1 Soi Siwaka Komarat, Th Wualai; courses 2000-12,000B) The government-accredited curriculum is very traditional, with two 10-day massage courses a month, as well as shorter foot- and oil-massage courses. Massage is also available (foot/traditional 200/200B).

Festivals & Events

Flower Festival CULTURAL
(⏲early Feb) A riot of blooms, held over a three-day period in early February. There are flower displays, cultural performances and beauty pageants, plus a floral parade from Saphan Nawarat to Suan Buak Hat.

Songkran NEW YEAR
(⏲mid-Apr) The traditional Thai New Year (13 to 15 April) is celebrated in Chiang Mai with infectious enthusiasm. Thousands of revellers line all sides of the moat to throw water on passers-by and each other, while more restrained Songkran rituals are held at Wat Phra Singh.

Loi Krathong RELIGIOUS

(Oct/Nov) Also known as Yi Peng, this lunar holiday is celebrated along Mae Ping with the launching of small lotus-shaped boats honouring the spirit of the river, and the release of thousands of illuminated lanterns into the night sky.

Sleeping

Traditional ideas of high and low season are going out the window thanks to Chinese travellers flocking to Thailand on city breaks. Reserve far in advance if visiting during Chinese New Year, Songkran and other holiday periods.

You can still find a dorm bed for around 200B, a basic fan room for 400B and a respectable air-con room from 600B. Some budget guesthouses subsidise their room rates through commissions from booking treks and tours; travellers have reported being moved on for declining to book these through their guesthouse. Staff usually inform guests if they have this policy.

In Town

★ **Diva Guesthouse** GUESTHOUSE $

(053 273851; www.divaguesthouse.com; 84/13 Th Ratchaphakhinai; dm 120-180B, r 300-800B;) An energetic, colourful spot on busy Th Ratchaphakhinai, Diva offers the full backpacker deal – dorm beds, budget boxrooms, adventure tours, net access, ambient tunes and fried rice and *sà·dé* (grilled meat with peanut sauce) in the downstairs cafe. Accommodation ranges from dorms to family rooms and comes with either fan or air-con.

Julie Guesthouse HOSTEL $

(053 274355; www.julieguesthouse.com; 7 Soi 5, Th Phra Pokklao; dm 100-150B, r with/without bathroom from 260/150B;) Julie is perennially popular, though this is as much about budget as facilities. For not much more than the price of a fruit smoothie you can get a basic dorm bed, and tiny boxrooms cost only a little more. In the evenings travellers congregate on the covered roof terrace.

There's a **branch** (094 628 1991; www.julieguesthouse.com; 11 Th Ratchamankha; dm 120-180B) with dorms only.

Gap's House GUESTHOUSE $

(053 278140; www.gaps-house.com; 3 Soi 4, Th Ratchadamnoen; r incl breakfast 370-800B;) The overgrown garden at this old backpacker favourite is a veritable jungle, providing plenty of privacy in the relaxing communal spaces. Modest budget rooms are set in old-fashioned wooden houses, and the owner runs cooking courses and dishes up a delicious vegetarian buffet from Monday to Saturday. No advance reservations.

Awana House HOTEL $$

(053 419005; www.awanahouse.com; 7 Soi 1, Th Ratchadamnoen; r with fan 495B, room with air-con 690-995B;) The pick of the guesthouses around the medieval city gate of Pratu Tha Phae, with rooms for every budget – all kept spotless – and a mini cold-water pool under cover on the ground-floor terrace. Rooms get more comfortable and better decorated as you move up the price scale and there's a rooftop chill-out area with views across old Chiang Mai.

Staff are delightful and go the extra mile for children, so it's a big hit with families; book ahead.

★ **Tamarind Village** HOTEL $$$

(053 418896-9; www.tamarindvillage.com; 50/1 Th Ratchadamnoen; incl breakfast r from 5179B, ste 8239-10,701B;) Effortlessly refined, this atmospheric Lanna-style property sprawls across the grounds of an old tamarind orchard in a prime location off Th Ratchadamnoen. Walkways covered by tiled pavilions lead to secluded and beautiful spaces, and tall mature trees cast gentle shade around the huge pool and gardens. Design-magazine-worthy rooms are full of gorgeous tribal fabrics and artefacts. There's a babysitting service for children aged one year or older.

The Ruen Tamarind restaurant (p473) serves beautifully presented Thai dishes and there's an opulent spa offering the full range of treatments.

★ **Sri Pat Guest House** HOTEL $$$

(053 218716; www.sri-patguesthouse.com; 16 Soi 7, Th Moon Muang; r 1500-2000B;) A standout flashpacker guesthouse with all the trimmings: wi-fi, pool, wood-decked communal areas, scattered Buddha carvings and smart tiled rooms with flat-screen TVs and little Thai details. You get plenty of personality for your baht and staff members are cheerful and friendly.

★ **Good Morning Chiang Mai Tropical Inn** HOTEL $$$

(086 922 3606; www.goodmorningchiangmai.com; 29/5 Soi 6, Th Ratchamankha; r incl breakfast

MONK CHAT

If you're curious about Buddhism, many Chiang Mai temples offer popular Monk Chat sessions, where novice monks get to practise their English and tourists get to find out about the inner workings of monastery life. It's a fascinating opportunity to discover a little more about the rituals and customs that most Thai men undertake for at least a small portion of their lives. Remember to dress modestly as a sign of respect: cover your shoulders and knees. Because of ritual taboos, women should take care not to touch the monks or their belongings, or to pass anything directly to them.

Wat Suan Dok (วัดสวนดอก; Th Suthep; donations appreciated; ⏲ daylight hours) Has a dedicated room for Monk Chats from 5pm to 7pm Monday, Wednesday and Friday.

Wat Srisuphan (วัดศรีสุพรรณ; Soi 2, Th Wualai; donations appreciated; ⏲ 6am-6pm) Holds its sessions from 5.30pm to 7pm just before a meditation course.

Wat Chedi Luang (p465) Has a table under a shady tree where monks chat from 9am to 6pm daily.

Wat Pha Khao (p469) Holds a low-key session from 5pm to 9pm on Saturday and Sunday.

1800-2300B; ❄📶🏊) A saltwater pool, superior breakfasts and a tranquil location south of Wat Phra Singh all score points for this comfortable guesthouse in a vaguely Spanish-style villa. Rooms full of natural timber come with crisp linen and vast, tasteful bathrooms.

Outside Town Centre

★ **Riverside House** GUESTHOUSE $$
(☎053 241860; www.riversidehouse-chiangmai.com; 101 Th Chiang Mai-Lamphun; r incl breakfast 800-1500B; ❄@📶🏊) Near Saphan Lek (Iron Bridge), this guesthouse offers great value. Rooms are spread across three blocks; you pay top dollar for the central block, by the pool and away from the traffic noise, but all the rooms are good for the money. It's a fine choice for families.

★ **Mo Rooms** HOTEL $$$
(☎053 280789; www.morooms.com; 263/1-2 Th Tha Phae; r incl breakfast 2800-3900B; ❄@📶🏊) Mo Rooms is designer in the urban mould, all exposed concrete and sculptural timbers juxtaposed with natural materials. Each of the Chinese-zodiac-themed rooms was decorated by a different Thai artist, ensuring some unique visions in interior decor – our top picks are 'Monkey' with its woven pod bed and 'Horse' with its surreal bed-tree.

There's a pebble-lined pool out the back and an Asian-fusion restaurant up the front.

★ **Banthai Village** HOTEL $$$
(☎053 252789; www.banthaivillage.com; 19 Soi 3, Th Tha Phae; r incl breakfast 3600-4800B, ste 5800-7800B; ❄@📶🏊) True to its name, Banthai does indeed resemble a country village transported to the modern city. The hotel sprawls over a series of wooden buildings with broad balconies, surrounding an idyllic pool and gardens overflowing with birds-of-paradise flowers. Rooms do the heritage thing, but subtly, with low wooden beds, dark-wood furniture and scattered cushions and traditional triangular Thai pillows.

★ **Baan Orapin** GUESTHOUSE $$$
(☎053 243677; www.baanorapin.com; 150 Th Charoenrat/Faham; r incl breakfast 2400-3500B; ❄📶🏊) Set in a tranquil private garden surrounding a stately teak house, Baan Orapin is a family affair. The owner's family have lived here since 1914, and guest rooms are in elegant villas dotted around the grounds and full of graceful furniture and fabrics. Design fans can find their own swish homewares in the posh boutiques along Th Charoenrat.

★ **Artel Nimman** BOUTIQUE HOTEL $$$
(☎053 213143; www.facebook.com/TheArtelNimman; Soi 13, Th Nimmanhaemin; r incl breakfast 1700-2200B; ❄📶) We're suckers for hotels with slides, so the Artel delivers in spades. The modernist building is all round windows, polished concrete, geometric forms and juxtaposed materials, and the rooms are cool, calm, creative spaces.

★ **Tri Yaan Na Ros** BOUTIQUE HOTEL $$$
(☎053 273174; www.triyaannaros.com; 156 Th Wualai; r incl breakfast 2300-2500B; ❄📶🏊) South of the main tourist bustle on Th

Wualai, and tucked away behind a restaurant, this charming boutique hotel features elegant period decor – perhaps the best recreation of a traditional Thai home in Chiang Mai. Rooms come with four-poster beds, flowing drapes, oodles of dark timber and antique Buddhas. There's also a peaceful courtyard pool.

The location means you'll be in pole position for the Saturday Walking Street (p474) market.

Eating

The restaurant scene in Chiang Mai is thriving, though predictably dominated by backpacker cafes and tourist-oriented establishments. Some of the best places to eat in Chiang Mai are the city's fabulous night markets (p474), which sprawl around the main city gates and several other locations.

★Kao Soi Fueng Fah NORTHERN THAI $
(Soi 1, Th Charoen Phrathet; mains 40-60B; ⏲7am-9pm) The best of the Muslim-run *kôw soy* (wheat-and-egg noodles in a curry broth) vendors along Halal St, with the choice of beef or chicken with your noodles.

★SP Chicken THAI $
(9/1 Soi 1, Th Samlan; mains 40-150B; ⏲11am-9pm) Chiang Mai's best chicken emerges daily from the broilers at this tiny cafe near Wat Phra Singh. The menu runs to salads and soups, but most people just pick a half (80B) or whole (150B) chicken, and dip the moist meat into the spicy, tangy dipping sauces provided.

★Kiat Ocha CHINESE, THAI $
(Th Inthawarorot; mains 50-90B; ⏲6am-3pm) This humble Chinese-style canteen is mobbed daily by locals who can't get enough of the house *kôw man gài* (Hainanese-style boiled chicken). Each plate comes with soup, chilli sauce and blood pudding and the menu also includes wok-fried chicken and pork and *sà·dé* (grilled skewers of pork or chicken).

★Talat Thanin MARKET $
(Siri Wattana; mains from 30B; ⏲5am-7pm) North of the old city off Th Chotana (Th Chang Pheuak), this market specialises in ready-to-eat *gàp kôw* (premade food served with rice) meals, with a whole rear section jammed with vendors offering fish stews, curries, stir-fries and spicy condiments from huge pans, vats and platters. A few curries and a bag of sticky rice will set you back less than 100B. There's also a lively wet and dry market.

★Riverside Bar & Restaurant INTERNATIONAL, THAI $$
(Th Charoenrat; mains 100-370B; ⏲10am-1am) Almost everyone ends up at Riverside at some point in their Chiang Mai stay. Set in an old teak house, it feels like a boondocks reimagining of a Hard Rock Cafe, and bands play nightly until late. Stake out a claim on the riverside terrace or the upstairs balcony to catch the evening breezes on the Mae Ping river.

Blue Diamond VEGETARIAN $
(35/1 Soi 9, Th Moon Muang; mains 65-220B; ⏲7am-9pm Mon-Sat; 🖉) Blue Diamond offers an adventurous menu of sandwiches, salads, curries, stir-fries and curious fusion dishes such as *đôm yam* (Thai-style sour soup) macaroni. Packed with fresh produce, prepackaged spice and herb mixes and freshly baked treats, it also feels a little like a wholefood store.

Ruen Tamarind NORTHERN THAI $$$
(Tamarind Village, 50/1 Th Ratchadamnoen; mains 220-440B; ⏲11am-10.30pm; 🖉) For a more sophisticated dinner, the restaurant at Tamarind Village serves superior northern Thai food in sleek surrounds overlooking the hotel pool. Dishes such as *yum tawai gài* (spicy chicken salad with tamarind dressing) are presented as works of art, and musicians serenade diners.

Drinking & Nightlife

Chiang Mai has three primary areas for watering holes: the old city, the riverside and Th Nimmanhaemin.

★Akha Ama Cafe CAFE
(www.akhaama.com; 175/1 Th Ratchadamnoen; ⏲8am-6pm; 📶) Akha Ama serves locally harvested, sustainable, direct-trade beans from the jungles north of Chiang Mai, but – perhaps most importantly to some – the coffee's just plain good. Come also for tasty baked snacks and the wi-fi.

★Good View BAR
(www.goodview.co.th; 13 Th Charoenrat/Faham; ⏲10am-2am) Good View attracts plenty of locals, with a big menu of Thai standards and sushi platters (mains 100B to 250B) and a nightly program of bands with rotating line-ups (meaning the drummer starts playing

guitar and the bass player moves behind the piano).

Kafe BAR

(127/3 Th Moon Muang) Open since 1985, Kafe is nonetheless a timeless place to sip a Singha and dig into classic Thai-style drinking snacks such as deep-fried fermented pork ribs (mains 60B to 150B).

Mixology BAR

(www.facebook.com/MixologyChiangmaiBurger/; 61/6 Th Arak; ⏲3pm-midnight Tue-Fri, 11am-midnight Sat & Sun) A tiny, eclectic bar with a huge selection of microbrews, a thick menu of fruity house drinks, burgers and northern Thai eats, and a lounging dog. Even if you drink too many chili-infused 'Prick me ups', you probably won't regret it the next day.

Beer Republic BAR

(www.beerrepublicchiangmai.com; Soi 11, Th Nimmanhaemin; ⏲4pm-midnight) The 15 draught beers keep the hop-lovers happy at this European-style beer bar in the trendiest part of Nimmanhaemin.

Khun Kae's Juice Bar JUICE BAR

(Soi 7, Th Moon Muang; ⏲10.30am-7.30pm) Our vote for Chiang Mai's best juice shack. Tonnes of fresh fruit, heaps of delicious combinations, generous serves and all this for prices that are almost comically low (drinks from 40B).

Writer's Club & Wine Bar BAR

(141/3 Th Ratchadamnoen; ⏲10am-midnight Sun-Fri; 📶) Run by a former foreign correspondent, this bar and restaurant is popular with expats, and travellers looking for a more low-key drinking experience, with wine by the glass (from 130B).

KEEPING SAFE

Hassles from túk-túk drivers are minimal and there are few rip-offs to watch out for. In March and April, smoky, dusty haze can be a problem because of farmers burning off their fields. While malaria is not a risk, dengue-fever outbreaks are common in the monsoon; take steps to avoid being bitten by mosquitoes, even in the daytime.

A popular backpacker activity is jumping off the cliffs at the so-called 'Grand Canyon', a water-filled quarry near Hang Dong; be warned that a number of travellers have drowned after losing consciousness when hitting the water.

☆ Entertainment

Nabé LIVE MUSIC

(Th Wichayanon; ⏲6pm-1am) A happening spot for Chiang Mai 20-somethings, with cold beers, hot snacks and rocking live bands who can actually play their instruments, singing Thai songs for a Thai audience.

North Gate Jazz Co-Op LIVE MUSIC

(www.facebook.com/northgate.jazzcoop; 95/1-2 Th Si Phum; ⏲7-11pm) This compact jazz club tends to pack in more musicians than patrons, but the music can be pretty hip (for jazz).

Shopping

★**Sunday Walking Street** MARKET

(ถนนเดินวันอาทิตย์; Th Ratchadamnoen; ⏲4pm-midnight Sun) On Sunday afternoon Th Ratchadamnoen is taken over by the boisterous Sunday Walking Street, which feels even more animated than Th Wualai's **Saturday Walking Street** (ถนนเดินวันเสาร์; Th Wualai; ⏲4pm-midnight Sat) because of the energetic food markets that open up in *wát* courtyards along the route, in addition to the usual selection of handmade items and northern Thai-themed souvenirs.

Talat Ton Phayom MARKET

(Th Suthep; ⏲8am-6pm) This place acts as both a local market and a souvenir stop for Thais visiting from other provinces. Take a look at the packaged-food area (mains from 30B) to see the kinds of edible gifts – like bags of *kâap mŏo* (pork rinds) and *sâi òo·a* (northern Thai-style sausage) – that make a visit to Chiang Mai complete.

Because CMU students make up a good portion of the clientele, prices tend to be low.

Chiang Mai Night Bazaar MARKET

(Th Chang Khlan; ⏲7pm-midnight) Chiang Mai Night Bazaar is one of the city's main night-time attractions, especially for families, and is the legacy of the original Yunnanese trading caravans that stopped here along the route between Simao (China) and Mawlamyaing (on Myanmar's Gulf of Martaban). Today the night bazaar sells the usual tourist souvenirs, similar to what you'll find at Bangkok's street markets.

Information

EMERGENCY

Tourist Police (053 247318, 24hr emergency 1155; 608 Rimping Plaza, Th Charoenraj; 6am-midnight) Volunteer staff speak a variety of languages.

INTERNET ACCESS

Almost all hotels, guesthouses, restaurants and cafes in Chiang Mai have free wi-fi access. The city has excellent mobile-phone data coverage, but roaming charges for Thailand can be crippling.

MEDIA

Newspapers The weekly English-language *Chiangmai Mail* is a useful source of local news.

Magazines Look out for the free tourist magazines *Citylife*, *Chang Puak* and *Chiang Mai Mag*; all have interesting articles as well as maps and blanket advertising.

MEDICAL SERVICES

There are English-speaking pharmacies along Th Ratchamankha and Th Moon Muang.

Chiang Mai Ram Hospital (053 920300; www.chiangmairam.com; 8 Th Bunreuangrit) The most modern hospital in town.

McCormick Hospital (053 921777; www.mccormick.in.th/mc/eng/; 133 Th Kaew Nawarat) Former missionary hospital; good for minor treatments.

TOURIST INFORMATION

Tourist Assistance Centre (053 281438; 7am-11pm) Tourist information in Chiang Mai International Airport.

Tourism Authority of Thailand (TAT; 053 248604; www.tourismthailand.org; Th Chiang Mai-Lamphun; 8.30am-4.30pm) English-speaking staff provide maps, and advice on travel across Thailand.

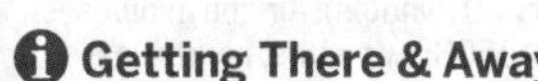

Getting There & Away

AIR

Domestic and international flights arrive and depart from **Chiang Mai International Airport** (05 327 0222; www.chiangmaiairportthai.com), 3km southwest of the old city.

Schedules vary with the seasons and tourist demand. The bulk of the domestic routes are handles by **Air Asia** (053 234645, nationwide 02 515 9999; www.airasia.com; 416 Th Tha Phae; 10am-8.30pm), **Bangkok Airways** (053 289338, nationwide 1771; www.bangkokair.com; Room A & B, Kantary Terrace, 44/1 Soi 12, Th Nimmanhaemin; 8.30am-noon & 1-6pm Mon-Sat), **Kan Air** (053 283311, nationwide 02 551 6111; www.kanairlines.com; 2nd fl, Chiang Mai International Airport; 8am-5.30pm), **Nok Air** (053 922183, nationwide 02 900 9955; www.nokair.com; Ground fl, Central Airport Plaza; 8am-5pm) and **Thai Smile** (nationwide 02 118 8888; www.thaismileair.com; 35-41 Th Ratchadamnoen; 9am-9pm). Tickets to Bangkok start at around 1200B. Heading south, expect to pay from 2400B to Phuket, 1650B to Surat Thani.

Direct flights linking Chiang Mai to neighbouring nations are also expanding fast, with regular flights to Kuala Lumpur (Malaysia), Luang Prabang (Laos), Vientiane (Laos) and Yangon (Myanmar). To reach Cambodia or Vietnam, you'll have to go via Bangkok.

The airport has luggage storage (7am to 9pm, 200B per day), a post-office branch (8.30am to 8pm), banks, souvenir shops and a tourist assistance centre. If you have time to kill, you could just stroll back down the highway to the large **Central Airport Plaza** (www.centralplaza.co.th; Rte 1141/Th Mahidol; 11am-9pm Mon-Fri, 10am-9pm Sat & Sun).

Lao Airlines (053 223401; www.laoairlines.com; Ground fl, Nakornping Condominium, 2/107 Th Huay Kaew; 8.30am-5pm Mon-Fri, to noon Sat) Direct flights to/from Luang Prabang and Vientiane.

Thai Airways International (THAI; 053 211044, 023 561111; www.thaiair.com; 240 Th Phra Pokklao; 8.30am-4.30pm Mon-Fri) Flies to Bangkok (Suvarnabhumi Airport).

BUS

Chiang Mai has two bus stations, and *sŏrng·tăa·ou* run from fixed stops to towns close to Chiang Mai.

There are two bus routes between the bus terminals and town: B1 makes stops at Chiang Mai's train station and Tha Phae Gate (15B, every 40 minutes from 6am to 6pm), and B2 makes stops at Tha Phae Gate and Chiang Mai International Airport (15B, every 40 minutes from 6am to 6pm).

Arcade Bus Terminal

About 3km northeast of the city centre, near the junction of Th Kaew Nawarat and Rte 11, Chiang Mai's **main long-distance station** (Th Kaew Nawarat) handles all services, except for buses to northern Chiang Mai Province. This is the place to come to travel on to Bangkok or any other major city in Thailand. A chartered *rót daang* (shared taxi) from the centre to the bus stand will cost about 60B; a túk-túk will cost 80B to 100B.

There are two terminal buildings, with ticket booths for dozens of private and government bus companies. Nominally, Building 2 is for towns north of Chiang Mai and Building 3 is for towns south of Chiang Mai, but in practice buses

BUS SERVICES FROM CHIANG MAI'S ARCADE TERMINAL

DESTINATION	FARE (B)	DURATION (HR)	FREQUENCY
Bangkok	379-759	9-10	frequent
Chiang Khong	290-451	6½	3 daily
Chiang Rai	144-288	3-4	hourly
Chiang Saen	165-220	3½-4	2 daily
Khon Kaen	524	12	10 daily
Khorat (Nakhon Ratchasima)	560-660	12	11 daily
Lampang	66-143	2	hourly
Lampang (minivan)	73	1	hourly
Lamphun	25	1	hourly
Luang Prabang (Laos)	1200	20	9am (Mon, Wed, Fri, Sat, Sun)
Mae Hong Son	192-346	8	3 daily
Mae Hong Son (minivan)	250	5	hourly
Mae Sai	182-234	5	7 daily
Mae Sariang	104-187	4-5	6 daily
Mae Sot	290	6	3 daily
Nan	197-254	6	6 daily
Nong Khai	820	12	2 daily
Pai	80	4	hourly
Pai (minivan)	150	3	hourly
Phayao	111-249	3	hourly
Phitsanulok	210-320	5-6	frequent
Phrae	133-266	4	4 daily
Phuket	1650	22	1 daily
Sukhothai	200	5-6	hourly
Ubon Ratchathani	872	12	1 daily
Udon Thani	767	12	3 daily

leave from both terminals to most destinations. There is also a third depot behind Building 2 used exclusively by the private bus company **Nakornchai Air** (☎053 262799; www.nca.co.th; Arcade Bus Terminal, Th Kaew Nawarat), which has luxury buses to Bangkok and almost everywhere else in Thailand.

There is a **left-luggage office** (⏰3am-9pm, per item 20B).

There is a regular international bus service linking Chiang Mai to Luang Prabang, via Bokeo, Luang Namtha and Udom Xai. You can also travel by bus across to Nong Khai (for Vientiane).

Chang Pheuak Bus Terminal

Just north of the old city on Th Chotana, the **Chang Pheuak Bus Terminal** (Th Chang Pheuak) is the main departure point for journeys to the north of Chiang Mai Province. Government buses leave regularly to:

Chiang Dao 40B, 1½ hours, every 30 minutes
Hot 50B, two hours, every 20 minutes
Samoeng 90B, two hours, six daily
Tha Ton 90B, four hours, seven daily

Local blue *sŏrng·tăa·ou* run to Lamphun (25B, one hour, every 20 minutes). Air-con minibuses to Chiang Dao (150B, two hours, hourly) leave from Soi Sanam Gila, behind the bus terminal.

TRAIN

Run by the State Railway of Thailand, **Chiang Mai Railway Station** (☎053 245363, nationwide 1690; Th Charoen Muang) is about 2.5km east of the old city. Trains run five times daily on the main line between Bangkok and Chiang Mai.

The train station has an ATM, a **left-luggage room** (⏰5am-8.45pm, per item 20B) and an advance-booking counter (you'll need your passport to book a ticket).

Between Chiang Mai and Bangkok's Hualamphong station, most comfortable are the overnight special express services leaving Chiang Mai at 5pm and 6pm, arriving in Bangkok at 6.15am and 6.50am. In the opposite direction, trains leave Hualamphong at 6.10pm and 7.35pm. See the State Railway of Thailand website (www.railway.co.th) for changes.

Around Chiang Mai

North of Chiang Mai, the land rucks up into forested mountains on either side of the Mae Ping river as northern Thailand merges into southeastern Myanmar. With a chartered *rót daang* or rented motorcycle (with sufficient horsepower) you can roam high into the hills, visiting national parks, spectacular viewpoints, Royal Project farms and hill-tribe villages.

Mae Sa Valley & Samoeng

You don't have to roam far from the city limits to get into the jungle. Branching west off Rte 107 at Mae Rim, Rte 1096 winds past a string of tacky day-trip attractions – crocodile and monkey shows, orchid farms, shooting ranges – before climbing steadily into the forested Mae Sa Valley. The road continues in a winding loop past charging waterfalls and a series of Royal Project farms (founded to provide local hill-tribe villagers with an alternative source of income to growing opium) and then morphs into the sleepy country village of Samoeng, making for a thoroughly enjoyable 100km round trip from Chiang Mai.

Sights

Nam Tok Mae Sa WATERFALL
(น้ำตกแม่สา; adult/child 100/50B, car 30B; 8am-4.30pm) Off Rte 1096, only 6km from the Mae Rim turn-off, Nam Tok Mae Sa is part of the Doi Suthep-Pui National Park. The cascade is a picturesque spot to picnic or tramp around in the woods for a bit and it's a favourite weekend getaway for locals.

Queen Sirikit Botanic Gardens GARDENS
(สวนพฤกษศาสตร์สมเด็จพระนางเจ้าสิริกิติ์; www.qsbg.org; Rte 1096; adult/child 100/50B, car/motorcycle 100/30B; 8.30am-4.30pm) At Queen Sirikit Botanic Gardens, 227 hectares have been set aside for plantations, nature trails and vast greenhouses full of exotic and local flora. Near the administration building is the orchid collection, containing over 400 species, the country's largest public display. The Rainforest House re-creates a southern Thai forest with ferns, palms, ginger and other tropical species. The highlight of the garden is the glasshouse complex sitting near the mountain peak.

Sleeping & Eating

Samoeng Resort HOTEL $
(053 487074; Rte 6033; bungalows 500-800B;) If you want to stay overnight in Samoeng, your options are limited to Samoeng Resort, with 15 bungalows in a garden setting. It's about 2.5km outside the village.

★ **Proud Phu Fah** BOUTIQUE HOTEL $$$
(053 879389; www.proudphufah.com; Rte 1096, Km 17; r incl breakfast 4500-14,000B;) Sitting in the western wedge of the Mae Sa Valley, this stylish boutique hotel has comfortable designer villas strung along a trickling brook, designed to give the illusion of sleeping amid the great outdoors. The open-air restaurant serves healthy Thai food (dishes 150B to 200B), with lovely views over the lawns and mountains.

Mon Cham THAI $
(Nong Hoi Mai; mains 60-150B; 7am-7pm;) This Thai-style restaurant makes the most of its fantastic location at the top of the ridge. Here you can sample tasty, freshly cooked Thai food, prepared using Royal Project produce, or just sip local fruit liqueurs in bamboo pavilions with spectacular views over the surrounding valleys. You'll need a reasonably powerful motorcycle to get up the hill from Ban Pong Yaeng.

Getting There & Around

To take advantage of what this area has to offer, you're best off hiring a motorcycle or car. *Sŏrng·tăa·ou* (passenger pick-up trucks) go to Samoeng (90B, two hours, six daily) from the Chang Pheuak bus terminal in Chiang Mai. In Samoeng, the vehicles stop near the market, across from Samoeng Hospital.

Chiang Dao

In a lush, jungle setting in the shadow of a mighty limestone mountain, Chiang Dao is where expats and Chiang Mai's growing middle classes come to escape the heat of the plains. It gets cooler still as you leave the village and climb towards the summit of Doi Chiang Dao (2175m). The forest is a popular stop for birders and trekkers, and at the base of the mountain is a highly venerated wát marking the entrance to one of Thailand's deepest limestone caverns.

Sights & Activities

Wat Tham Chiang Dao CAVE
(ถ้ำเชียงดาว, Chiang Dao Cave; 40B, guide fee 100B; 7am-5pm) Set in pretty grounds that teem with jungle butterflies, this forest wát was founded at the entrance to the Chiang Dao Cave, a chilly warren of tunnels and passageways that extends more than 10km beneath the limestone massif of Doi Chiang Dao. For local Buddhists, the cave is a popular meditation retreat, and the twisting, turning passages overflow with stalactites and stalagmites in weird and wonderful configurations.

Doi Chiang Dao Wildlife Sanctuary NATURE RESERVE
(ดอยเชียงดาว, Doi Luang; 053 456623; 200B, vehicle 30B) Doi Chiang Dao rises dramatically above the surrounding plain, wrapped in a thick coat of tropical forest. This jungle wonderland is one of Thailand's top spots for birders, with more than 300 resident bird species, and is one of the best places in the world to see giant nuthatches and Hume's pheasants. It's a steep full-day hike to the summit, which offers spectacular views over the surrounding massifs; a one-day trip is 1000B per person, overnight costs 500B per person.

Sleeping & Eating

The guesthouses are spread out along the road leading north from Wat Tham Chiang Dao on the edge of the forest. All can arrange tours, and rent bicycles and motorbikes.

Chiang Dao Hut GUESTHOUSE $
(053 456625; www.chiangdaohut.com; r & bungalows 400-2500B;) This cute collection of rooms and bungalows in a glade that drops down to a stream is close to Wat Tham Chiang Dao, so you'll have extra choices for dinner. The cheaper accommodation has shared bathrooms with hot water, and the atmosphere is appropriately laid-back and unhurried.

★ **Chiang Dao Nest** GUESTHOUSE $$$
(053 456242; www.chiangdaonest.com; bungalows 945-3245B;) The guesthouse that put Chiang Dao on the map is a charming country retreat, with comfortable, bamboo-weave bungalows scattered around a gorgeous tropical garden with plenty of shady gazebos where you can kick back with a book. There's a lovely, forest-flanked swimming pool with mountain views, and kids will love the wandering goats and toy pavilion.

Chiang Dao Nest INTERNATIONAL $$$
(mains 315-695B; 8am-3pm & 6-9pm;) The restaurant at Chiang Dao Nest guesthouse is the undisputed culinary highlight of the area. It's worth the trip from Chiang Mai all by itself, with imported ales, fine wines and sophisticated modern European dishes you wouldn't expect to find in the jungle, such as 'salmon fillet wrapped in filo pastry with green tapenade'.

Shopping

Morning Market MARKET
(7am-noon 1st & 3rd Tue of month) The twice-monthly morning market has vendors selling hill-tribe handicrafts.

Getting There & Around

Chiang Dao is 72km north of Chiang Mai along Rte 107. It's a 100B motorcycle taxi or 150B *sŏrng·tăa·ou* (passenger pick-up truck) ride from the bus stand in Chiang Dao village to the guesthouses near the cave temple. Buses travel to:

Chiang Mai (40B, 1½ hours, every 30 minutes)

Tha Ton (63B, 2½ hours, seven daily)

There are also air-conditioned minivans charging 150B to Chiang Mai.

Most of the lodges rent out mountain bikes (from 100B) and motorbikes (from 300B), or you can hire a *sŏrng·tăa·ou* for about 1000B a day to drive you around the area.

Tha Ton

The northernmost town in Chiang Mai Province feels a long way from the provincial capital. Modern Tha Ton is a quiet backwater that sees just a trickle of tourists headed downriver towards Chiang Rai.

Interesting detours in the area inlcude boat trips up to the Myanmar border and day trips by road to Mae Salong or the hot springs at Doi Pha Hompok National Park. The town has a sizeable population of Yunnanese migrants, who worship at the small Chinese-style mosque just south of the boat jetty.

Sights & Activities

Resorts in Tha Ton can arrange treks and rafting trips to a string of hill-tribe villages inhabited by Palaung, Black Lahu, Akha, Karen and Yunnanese villagers. While these are less traditional than the villages immediately across the border, they are more traditional than the tribal villages close to Chiang Mai. Expect to pay around 1000B per person for a day trek, and from 2500B for a two-day rafting tour (only possible from October to February).

Wat Tha Ton BUDDHIST TEMPLE
(วัดท่าตอน; ☎053 459309; www.wat-thaton.org; Rte 107; donations appreciated; ⏰daylight hours) Just south of the bridge, this intriguing monastery complex sprawls west from Tha Ton over a series of forested hills. The wát buildings are spread over nine levels and each comes with its own collection of supersize statues and stunning views north towards Myanmar or east across the Tha Ton plain.

Chiang Rai Boat Trip BOATING
(☎053 053727; per person 400B; ⏰departs 12.30pm) During the rainy season and for as long as water levels stay high (July to December), long-tail boats make the journey between Chiang Rai and Tha Ton daily. It's a scenic trip, passing tracts of virgin forest, riverside monasteries, and villages of thatched huts with fishers casting nets in the shallows.

Sleeping

Tha Ton's guesthouses are strung out along both sides of the river by the bridge, and most can arrange treks, boat trips, and motorcycle and bicycle hire. Note that some resorts close during the quiet season (January to June), when the river is too low for boat trips.

Apple Resort RESORT $$
(☎053 373144; applethaton@yahoo.com; off Rte 107; r & bungalows 500-1200B; ❄📶) Apple makes the most of its setting, facing the boat jetty from the north bank, with budget fan-cooled bungalows in the garden and more welcoming riverfront bungalows with fantastic front porches facing the water. There's a friendly riverside restaurant for enjoying Tha Ton's best feature: the river by moonlight. More expensive rates include breakfast.

★**Old Tree's House** RESORT $$$
(☎085 722 9002; www.oldtreeshouse.net; Rte 107; bungalows incl breakfast 1200-2800B; ❄📶🏊) After an uninspiring approach beside a cement works, you'll struggle to suppress the oohs and aahs as you reach the lush tropical garden at this French-Thai operation on the hillside. From the new restaurant overlooking the valley to the immaculate bamboo-weave bungalows and pretty palm-fringed pool, Old Tree's doesn't put a foot wrong. Look for the turn-off 400m past Tha Ton.

Laap Lung Pan NORTHERN THAI $
(Rte 107; mains 30-60B; ⏰7am-8pm) The go-to place in Tha Ton for northern Thai–style eats. There's no English-language menu; simply point to whatever pot or item on the grill looks tasty. Nor is there an English-language sign; look for the Coke ad roughly across from the entrance to Wat Tha Ton.

Sunshine Cafe CAFE $
(mains 60-110B; ⏰8am-3pm) This is the place to come for freshly brewed coffee in the morning. It also does a wide selection of Western breakfasts, including muesli, fresh fruit and yoghurt. It's located on the main road, just before the bridge.

Getting There & Around

The main bus stand in Tha Ton is a long hike south along the highway, but buses also swing in at the parking lot just north of the bridge. Services include:

Bangkok 601B to 701B, 14 hours, three daily
Chiang Dao 63B, 2½ hours, seven daily
Chiang Mai 90B, four hours, seven daily

To reach Chiang Rai by road, take a *sŏrng·tăa·ou* (passenger pick-up truck) to Mae Salong (60B, 1½ hours, three daily).

With your own car or motorcycle, you can continue to Mae Salong along Rte 107, turning off onto Rte 1089, following a fully paved but sometimes-treacherous mountain road and passing scattered Lisu and Akha villages.

Local guesthouses rent out motorcycles for 350B per day.

Pai

Despite comparisons between Pai and Bangkok's Khao San Rd, the town's popularity has yet to negatively impact its nearly picture-perfect setting in a mountain valley. There's heaps of quiet accommodation outside the main drag, a host of natural, lazy activities to keep visitors entertained, and a vibrant art and music scene. The town's Shan roots can still be seen in its temples, quiet backstreets and fun afternoon market.

Sights & Activities

Most of Pai's sights are outside the city centre, making hiring a motorcycle a necessity.

Pai

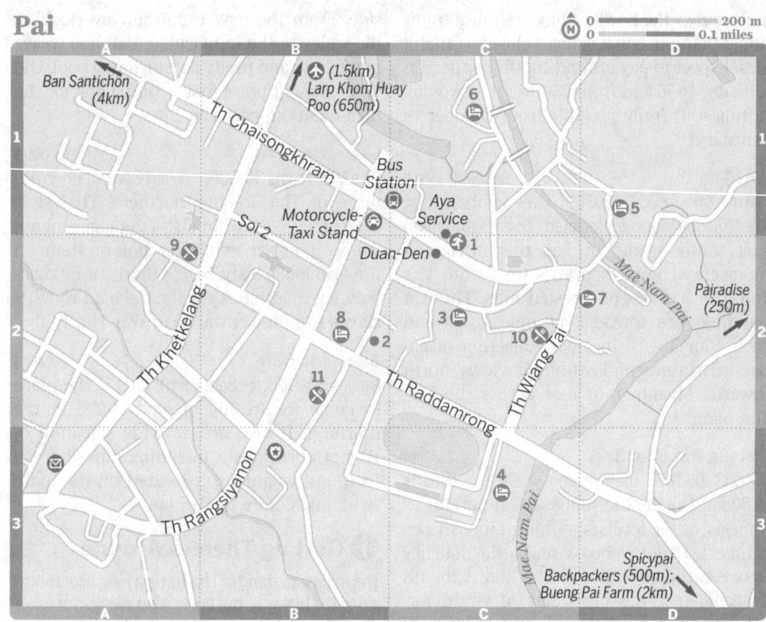

Ban Santichon VILLAGE

(บ้านสันติชล) It's a living, breathing Chinese village, but the cheesy photo ops, piped-in music, restaurants serving Yunnanese food, tea tastings, pony rides, tacky re-creation of the Great Wall of China and mountain-top **viewpoint** (ทิวทัศน์ บ้านสันติชล; 20B; ⏲4.30am-6pm) can make parts of Ban Santichon seem more like a Chinese-themed Disneyland. Located about 4km west of Pai.

Tha Pai Hot Springs HOT SPRINGS

(บ่อน้ำร้อนท่าปาย; adult/child 300/150B; ⏲7am-6pm) Across Mae Nam Pai and 7km southeast of town via a paved road is this well-kept local park. Through it flows a scenic stream, which mixes with the hot springs in places to make pleasant bathing areas. The water is also diverted to a couple of nearby spas.

Nam Tok Mo Paeng SWIMMING

(น้ำตกหมอแปง) Nam Tok Mo Paeng has a couple of pools that are suitable for swimming. The waterfall is about 8km from Pai along the road that also leads to **Wat Nam Hoo** (วัดน้ำฮู; Ban Nam Hoo; ⏲dawn-dusk) FREE – it's a long walk, but it's suitable for a bike ride or short motorcycle trip.

Pai Adventure RAFTING

(☎053 699385; www.thailandpai.net; 28 Th Chaisongkhram; ⏲8am-10pm) The one- to two-day white-water rafting trips offered by this recommended outfit can be combined with hiking and other activities. Also offers a jungle-survival course upon request.

Courses

The curriculum of courses available in Pai ranges from drumming to circus arts; check listings publications such as the *Pai Events Planner* (PEP) or the *Pai Explorer* (www.paiexplorer.com) to see what's on when you're in town.

Pai Cookery School COOKING

(☎081 706 3799; Th Wanchalerm; lessons 600-750B; ⏲lessons 11am-1.30pm & 2-6.30pm) With a decade of experience, this outfit offers a variety of daily courses covering three to five dishes. The afternoon course involves a trip to the market for ingredients. Contact a day in advance.

Sleeping

Despite several years of growth, Pai's accommodation expansion has slowed only slightly, and the town is allegedly home to more than 500 hotels, guesthouses and

Pai

Activities, Courses & Tours

Sleeping

Eating

resorts. Although 'downtown' Pai has seen relatively little change in this respect, new resorts continue to spring up in an approximate 3km circle around the town.

In Town

TTK GUESTHOUSE $

(☎053 698093; 8/10 Th Raddamrong; r 350-450B; 📶) Set behind the Israeli restaurant of the same name, the rooms here lack both natural light and interior design but are spotless and conveniently located.

Pai Country Hut HOTEL $

(☎087 779 6541; www.paicountryhut.com; Ban Mae Hi; bungalows incl breakfast 400-650B; 📶) The bamboo bungalows here are utterly simple, but they're tidy and most have bathrooms and inviting hammocks. Although it's not exactly riverside, it's the most appealing of several similar budget places close to the water.

Pai River Villa HOTEL $$

(☎053 699796; pairivervillaresort@gmail.com; 7 Th Wiang Tai; bungalows incl breakfast 900-1500B; ❄📶) This place boasts some of the more attractive midrange accommodation in town. The air-con bungalows are spacious and stylish, and have wide balconies that encourage lazy riverside relaxing and mountain-viewing, while the fan-cooled bungalows are a significantly tighter fit.

Baankanoon GUESTHOUSE $$

(☎053 699453; 33 Soi Wanchalerm; bungalows 500-1200B; 📶) Consisting of 14 bright duplex and free-standing bungalows around a 100-year-old *kà·nŭn* (jackfruit) tree, this locally owned place is quiet, clean and cosy.

★Pai Village Boutique Resort & Farm HOTEL $$$

(☎053 698152; www.paivillage.com; 88 Th Wiang Tai; bungalows incl breakfast 2700-5800B; ❄@📶) This well-maintained place has a collection of 26 wooden bungalows set among winding garden pathways. The rooms don't leave heaps of room to stretch, but they do have floor-to-ceiling sliding windows, large and quite plush bathrooms, and spacious terraces with rattan mats and axe cushions to best enjoy the greenery. Huge off-season discounts available.

Outside of Town

Spicypai Backpackers HOTEL $

(☎088 294 2004; www.spicyhostels.com; Mae Yen; dm 180B; 📶) The bamboo dorms here look like they could have featured in an episode of *Survivor*. Communal areas ranging from a kitchen to a fire pit continue the rustic feel. It's about 750m east of Mae Nam Pai, just off the road that leads to Thai Pai Hot Springs.

★Bueng Pai Farm GUESTHOUSE $$

(☎089 265 4768; www.paifarm.com; Ban Mae Hi; bungalows 1000-1550B; 📶🏊) In a rural setting about 2.5km east of Pai, the 12 spacious, fan-cooled bungalows here are strategically and attractively positioned around a vast pond stocked with freshwater fish. There's a campfire during the winter months, and a pool, communal kitchen and fishing equipment are available year-round. Located off the road that leads to Tha Pai Hot Springs; look for the sign.

★Pairadise HOTEL $$

(☎053 698065; www.pairadise.com; Ban Mae Hi; bungalows 900-1300B; ❄📶🏊) This neat resort looks over the Pai Valley from atop a ridge just outside town. The bungalows are stylish and spacious and include gold-leaf lotus murals, beautiful rustic bathrooms and terraces with hammocks. All surround a spring-fed pond that's suitable for swimming. You'll find it about 750m east of Mae Nam Pai; look for the sign just after the bridge.

Baantawan Guest House HOTEL $$$

(☎053 698116; www.baantawanpai.com; 117 Th Wiang Tai; incl breakfast r 1600-3500B, bungalows 2500-3500B; ❄@📶) The older and more charming riverside two-storey bungalows made with salvaged teak are the reason to stay here, but there are also spacious (and less expensive) rooms in a large two-storey building. Service is first rate and the hotel's located on a relatively isolated (read: quiet) stretch of the river.

Eating

★ **Larp Khom Huay Poo** NORTHERN THAI $
(Ban Huay Pu; mains 50-80B; ⏰9am-8pm) Escape the wheatgrass-and-tofu crowd and get your meat on at this unabashedly carnivorous local eatery, located about 1km north of town, on the road to Mae Hong Son. The house special (and the dish you must order) is '*larp moo kua*', northern-style *lâhp* (minced pork fried with local herbs and spices).

Om Garden Cafe INTERNATIONAL $
(mains 60-120B; ⏰8.30am-5pm Tue-Sun;) Fresh-pressed juices, meat-free takes on international dishes, barefoot and/or flute-playing patrons: basically everything you'd expect at a place called Om Garden, except that the food is actually good. Dishes range from Middle Eastern meze to breakfast burritos, as well as a good selection of salads and pastries. It's off Th Raddamrong.

Maya Burger Queen AMERICAN $
(www.facebook.com/MayaBurgerQueen; Th Wiang Tai; mains 90-145B; ⏰2-10pm;) Burgers are a big deal in Pai, and arduous research has compelled the conclusion that Maya does the best job. Everything is homemade, from the soft, slightly sweet buns to the rich garlic mayo that accompanies the thick-cut fries.

Evening Market NORTHERN THAI $
(Th Raddamrong; mains 30-60B; ⏰3-7pm) For tasty take-home local-style eats, try the market that unfolds every afternoon from about 3pm to sunset.

Getting There & Away

AIR

Pai's airport is around 1.5km north of town along Rte 1095. **Kan Air** (☎053 699955, nationwide 02 551 6111; www.kanairlines.com; Pai Airport; ⏰8.30am-5.30pm) has a daily connection to/from Chiang Mai (from 1990B, 25 minutes).

BUS

Pai's tiny bus station (Th Chaisongkhram) is the place to catch slow, fan-cooled buses:

Chiang Mai 80B, three to four hours, noon
Mae Hong Son 80B, three to four hours, 11am
Soppong (Pangmapha) 45B, 1½ hours, 11am

More efficient minivans to Chiang Mai and destinations in Mae Hong Son also depart from here:

Chiang Mai 150B, three hours, hourly from 7am to 5pm
Mae Hong Son 150B, 2½ hours, 8.30am
Soppong (Pangmapha) 100B, one hour, 8.30am

Aya Service (☎053 699888; www.ayaservice.com; 22/1 Th Chaisongkhram; ⏰7am-10pm) and **Duan-Den** (☎053 699966; 20/1 Th Chaisongkhram; per 24hr 100-250B; ⏰7am-9pm) also run air-con minivan buses to Chiang Mai (150B to 200B, three hours, hourly from 7am to 5.30pm).

Getting There & Away

Most of Pai is accessible on foot.

For local excursions you can hire bicycles or motorcycles (per 24hr 100-1800B) in town.

Motorcycle taxis wait at the **taxi stand** (Th Chaisongkhram) across from the bus station. Sample fares are 50B to Ban Santichon village and 100B to Nam Tok Mo Paeng waterfall.

Sukhothai

The Sukhothai (Rising of Happiness) Kingdom flourished from the mid-13th century to the late 14th century. This period is often viewed as the golden age of Thai civilisation, and the religious art and architecture of the era are considered to be the most classic of Thai styles. The remains of the kingdom, today known as *meuang gòw* (old city), feature around 45 sq km of partially rebuilt ruins, making up one of the most visited ancient sites in Thailand.

Sights

Sukhothai Historical Park HISTORIC SITE
(อุทยานประวัติศาสตร์สุโขทัย; ☎055 697527) The Sukhothai Historical Park ruins are one of Thailand's most impressive World Heritage Sites. The park includes the remains of 21 historical sites and four large ponds within the old walls, with an additional 70 sites within a 5km radius. The ruins are divided into five zones; the central, northern and western zones have a separate 100B admission fee.

Ramkhamhaeng National Museum MUSEUM
(พิพิธภัณฑสถานแห่งชาติรามคำแหง; 150B; ⏰9am-4pm) Near the entrance of the Central Zone, this museum is a decent starting point for exploring the historical park ruins is this museum. A replica of the famous Ramkha-

mhaeng inscription, said to be the earliest example of Thai writing, is kept here among an impressive collection of Sukhothai artefacts. Admission to the museum is not included in the ticket to the central zone.

Sukhothai Historical Park Central Zone HISTORIC SITE
(อุทยานประวัติศาสตร์สุโขทัย โซนกลาง; 100B, plus per bicycle/motorcycle/car 10/20/50B; ⏲6.30am-6pm Sun-Fri, to 9pm Sat) This is the historical park's main zone and is home to what are arguably some of the park's most impressive ruins. On Saturday night much of the central zone is illuminated and remains open until 9pm.

Sukhothai Historical Park Northern Zone HISTORIC SITE
(อุทยานประวัติศาสตร์สุโขทัย โซนเหนือ; 100B, plus per bicycle/motorcycle/car 10/20/50B; ⏲7.30am-5.30pm) The northern zone of Sukhothai Historical Park, 500m north of the old city walls, is easily reached by bicycle.

Sukhothai Historical Park Western Zone HISTORIC SITE
(อุทยานประวัติศาสตร์สุโขทัย โซนตะวันตก; 100B, plus per bicycle/motorcycle/car 10/20/50B; ⏲8am-4.30pm) The western zone, at its furthest extent 2km west of the old city walls, is the most expansive. In addition to Wat Saphan Hin, several mostly featureless ruins can be found. A bicycle or motorcycle is necessary to explore this zone.

Tours

Cycling Sukhothai CYCLING
(☎085 083 1864, 055 612519; www.cycling-sukhothai.com; half- /full-day 800/990B, sunset tour 450B) A resident of Sukhothai for nearly 20 years, Belgian cycling enthusiast Ronny Hanquart offers themed bike tours, such as the Historical Park Tour, which also includes stops at lesser-seen wát and villages. The office is about 1.2km west of Mae Nam Yom, off Th Jarodvithithong in New Sukhothai; free transport can be arranged.

Sleeping

New Sukhothai has some of the best-value budget accommodation in northern Thailand. Clean, cheerful hotels and guest-houses abound, with many places offering attractive bungalows, free pick-up from the bus station and free use of bicycles. There's an increasing number of options near the park, many of them upscale. Prices tend to go up during the Loi Krathong festival in November.

New Sukothai

Ban Thai GUESTHOUSE $
(☎055 610163; banthai_guesthouse@yahoo.com; 38 Th Prawet Nakhon; r & bungalows 250-800B;

BUSES FROM SUKHOTHAI

DESTINATION	FARE (B)	DURATION (HR)	FREQUENCY
Bangkok	241-310	6-7	half-hourly 7.50am-10.40pm
Chiang Mai	195-374	5-6	frequent 6.20am-2am
Chiang Rai	231	9	4 departures 6.40-11.30am
Kamphaeng Phet	53-68	1½	half-hourly 7.50am-10.40pm
Khon Kaen	221-334	7	frequent 10.30am-12.40am
Lampang	155-205	3	frequent 6.20am-2am
Mae Sot	130-176	3	3 departures 9.15am-2.30am
Mukdahan	476	10	7.50pm & 9.40pm
Nan	176	4	3pm
Phitsanulok	39-50	1	half-hourly 7.50am-10.40pm
Sawankhalok	27	1	hourly 6.40am-5pm
Si Satchanalai	45	1½	hourly 6.40am-5pm

) The rooms here range from plain to stylish, but the convergence of a friendly atmosphere, an attractive garden setting and low prices makes for a winner.

TR Room & Bungalow GUESTHOUSE $$
(055 611663; www.sukhothaibudgetguesthouse.com; 27/5 Th Prawet Nakhon; r/bungalows 600/850B; @) The rooms here were renovated in 2016, with new furniture and eclectic interior-design elements bumping them up to midrange level. For those needing a bit more space, there are five wooden bungalows out the back.

Sabaidee House HOTEL $$
(055 616303; www.sabaideehouse.com; 81/7 Th Jarodvithithong; r 300-1000B;) This cheery guesthouse in a semirural setting has seven attractive bungalows and four rooms in the main structure – and a brand-new pool. It's off Th Jarodvithithong about 200m before the intersection with Rte 101; look for the sign.

At Home Sukhothai GUESTHOUSE $$
(055 610172; www.athomesukhothai.com; 184/1 Th Vichien Chamnong; incl breakfast r 450-850B, bungalows 900-1100B; @) Located in the 50-year-old childhood home of the proprietor, the simple but comfortable rooms here – both the fan-cooled ones in the original structure and the newer air-con ones – really do feel like home. A new addition has provided four bungalows overlooking a pond. The only downside is the relative distance from 'downtown' Sukhothai.

Lotus Village HOTEL $$
(055 621484; www.lotus-village.com; 170 Th Ratchathani; incl breakfast r 950-1500B, bungalows 1300-2600B; @) Village is an apt label for this peaceful compound of wooden bungalows elevated over lotus ponds. Smaller, if overpriced, fan-cooled rooms in a wooden building are also available, and an attractive Burmese-Indian design theme runs through the entire place. Both the breakfast and the staff get great reports, and an on-site spa offers a variety of services.

Sukothai Historical Park

★Orchid Hibiscus Guest House HOTEL $$
(055 633284; www.orchidhibiscus-guesthouse.com; 407/2 Rte 1272; r/bungalows 900/1400B;) This collection of rooms and bungalows is set in relaxing, manicured grounds with a swimming pool as a centrepiece and the self-professed 'amazing breakfast' (100B) as a highlight. Rooms are spotless and fun, featuring colourful design details and accents. It's on Rte 1272 about 500m off Rte 12; the turn-off is between the km 48 and km 49 markers.

★Ruean Thai Hotel HOTEL $$$
(055 612444; www.rueanthaihotel.com; 181/20 Soi Pracha Ruammit; r incl breakfast 1480-4200B;) At first glance, you may mistake this eye-catching complex for a Buddhist temple or a traditional Thai house. The upper-level rooms follow a distinct Thai theme, while the poolside rooms are slightly more modern; there's a concrete building with simple air-con rooms out the back. Service is both friendly and flawless, and the whole place boasts a resort-like feel. Call for free pick-up from the bus station.

Eating

Along the road that leads to the historical park is a string of food stalls and simple tourist-oriented restaurants.

★Jayhae THAI $
(Th Jarodvithithong; dishes 30-50B; 8am-4pm) You haven't been to Sukhothai if you haven't tried the noodles at Jayhae, an extremely popular restaurant that serves Sukhothai-style noodles, *pàt tai* and tasty coffee drinks.

Night Market MARKET $
(Th Ramkhamhaeng; mains 30-60B; 6-11pm) A wise choice for cheap eats is New Sukhothai's tiny night market. Most vendors here are accustomed to accommodating foreigners and even provide bilingual menus.

Chopper Bar BAR
(Th Prawet Nakhon; 10am-12.30am;) Both travellers and locals congregate at this restaurant-bar from morning till hangover for food (mains 30B to 150B), drinks and live music. Take advantage of Sukhothai's cool evenings on the rooftop terrace.

Information

Sukhothai Hospital (055 610280; Th Jarodvithithong) Located just west of New Sukhothai.

Tourism Authority of Thailand (TAT; ☎055 616228, nationwide 1672; Th Jarodvithithong; ⏲8.30am-4.30pm) Since 2016 in new digs about 750m west of the bridge in New Sukhothai, this office has a pretty good selection of maps and brochures.

Tourist Police (☎24hr 1155; Rte 12; ⏲24hr)

Getting There & Away

Sukhothai's airport is located a whopping 27km north of town off Rte 1195. **Bangkok Airways** (☎055 647224, nationwide 1771; www.bangkokair.com; Sukhothai Airport; ⏲7.30-11.30am & 12.30-5.30pm) is the only airline operating here, with two daily flights to/from Bangkok's Suvarnabhumi International Airport (from 1495B, one hour and 15 minutes). There is a **minivan service** (☎055 647220; Sukhothai Airport; 1-way 180B) between the airport and New Sukhothai. Alternatively, **Air Asia** (☎Phitsanulok 094 7193645, nationwide 02 515 9999; www.airasia.com; Phitsanulok Airport; ⏲6am-6.30pm) and **Nok Air** (☎Phitsanulok 055 301051, nationwide 1318; www.nokair.co.th; Phitsanulok Airport; ⏲6am-9pm) offer minivan transfers to/from both old and new Sukhothai via the airport in Phitsanulok, less than an hour away.

Sukhothai's minivan and **bus station** (☎055 614529; Rte 101) is almost 1km northwest of the centre of New Sukhothai; a motorcycle taxi between here and central New Sukhothai should cost around 50B, or you can hop on any *sŏrng·tăa·ou* (passenger pick-up truck) bound for Sukhothai Historical Park – they stop at the bus station on their way out of town (20B, 10 minutes, frequent from 6am to 5.30pm).

Alternatively, if you're staying near the historical park, **Win Tour** (☎099 135 5645; Rte 12; ⏲6am-9.40pm) has an office where you can board buses to Bangkok (310B, six hours, 8am, noon and 9.50pm) and Chiang Mai (210B, five hours, six departures from 6am to 2pm).

Getting Around

A *săhm·lór* (three-wheeled pedicab) ride within New Sukhothai should cost no more than 40B.

Relatively frequent **sŏrng·tăa·ou** (Th Jarodvithithong; 30B; ⏲6am-5.30pm) run between New Sukhothai and Sukhothai Historical Park (30B, 30 minutes, 6am to 5.30pm), leaving from a stop on Th Jarodvithithong. Motorcycle taxis go between the town or bus station and the historical park for 120B.

The best way to get around the historical park is by bicycle; bikes can be hired at shops outside the park entrance for 30B per day (6am to 6pm).

Motorbikes (from 250B for 24 hours) can be hired at nearly every guesthouse in New Sukhothai.

Around Sukhothai

Si Satchanalai–Chaliang Historical Park

Set among hills, the 13th- to 15th-century ruins of the old cities of Si Satchanalai and Chaliang lie 50km north of Sukhothai.

Sights

An admission fee of 250B allows entry to Si Satchanalai, Wat Chao Chan (at Chaliang) and the Si Satchanalai Centre for Study & Preservation of Sangkalok Kilns.

Si Satchanalai Historical Park HISTORIC SITE
(admission 100B; ⏲8.30am-4.30pm) The ruins of Si Satchanalai and Chaliang are in the same basic style as those in the Sukhothai Historical Park, but the setting is more rural and arguably more peaceful. The park covers roughly 720 hectares and is surrounded by a 12m-wide moat. Chaliang, 1km southeast, is an older city site (dating to the 11th century), though its two temples date to the 14th century.

Wat Phra Si Ratana Mahathat HISTORIC SITE
(วัดพระศรีรัตนมหาธาตุ; admission 20B; ⏲8am-4.30pm) These ruins consist of a large laterite *chedi* (dating back to 1448–88) between two *wí·hăhn*. One of the *wí·hăhn* holds a large seated Sukhothai Buddha image, a smaller standing image and a bas-relief of the famous walking Buddha, exemplary of the flowing, boneless Sukhothai style. The other *wí·hăhn* contains some less distinguished images.

Si Satchanalai Centre for Study & Preservation of Sangkalok Kilns MUSEUM
(ศูนย์ศึกษาและอนุรักษ์เตาสังคโลก; 100B; ⏲8am-4.30pm) Located 5km northwest of the Si Satchanalai ruins, this centre has large excavated kilns and many intact pottery samples. The exhibits are interesting despite the lack of English labels.

Getting There & Away

From New Sukhothai, take a Si Satchanalai bus (45B, 1½ hours, hourly from 6.40am to 5pm) or one of four buses to Chiang Rai between 6.40am and 11.30am (46B), and ask to get off at *meuang gòw* (old city).

There's a daily special express train from Bangkok to Sawankhalok (482B, seven hours, 10.50am). The train heads back to Bangkok at 7.40pm, arriving in the city at 3.30am.

Chiang Rai

This small, delightful city is worth getting to know, with its relaxed atmosphere, good-value accommodation and great local food. It's also the logical base from which to plan excursions to the more remote corners of the province.

Sights

Hilltribe Museum & Education Center MUSEUM
(พิพิธภัณฑ์และศูนย์การศึกษาชาวเขา; www.pdacr.org; 3rd fl, 620/25 Th Thanalai; 50B; ⌚8.30am-6pm Mon-Fri, 10am-6pm Sat & Sun) This museum and cultural centre is a good place to visit before undertaking any hill-tribe trek. Run by the nonprofit Population & Community Development Association (PDA), the venue has displays that are underwhelming in their visual presentation but contain a wealth of information on Thailand's various tribes and the issues that surround them.

★ **Mae Fah Luang Art & Culture Park** MUSEUM
(ไร่แม่ฟ้าหลวง; www.maefahluang.org/rmfl; 313 Mu 7, Ban Pa Ngiw; adult/child 200B/free; ⌚8.30am-4.30pm Tue-Sun) In addition to a museum that houses one of Thailand's biggest collections of Lanna artefacts, this vast, meticulously landscaped compound includes antique and contemporary art, Buddhist temples and other structures. It's located about 4km west of the centre of Chiang Rai; a túk-túk or taxi here will run around 100B.

Oub Kham Museum MUSEUM
(พิพิธภัณฑ์อูบคำ; www.oubkhammuseum.com; Th Nakhai; adult/child 300/200B; ⌚8am-5pm) This slightly zany museum houses an impressive collection of paraphernalia from virtually every corner of the former Lanna kingdom. The items, some of which truly are one of a kind, range from a monkey-bone food taster used by Lanna royalty to an impressive carved throne from Chiang Tung, Myanmar. It's located 2km west of the town centre and can be a bit tricky to find; túk-túk will go here for about 60B.

Guided tours (available in English) are obligatory and include a walk through a gilded artificial cave holding several Buddha statues, complete with disco lights and fake torches! The grounds of the museum are equally kitschy and include a huge golden *naga* (a mythical serpent-like being with magical powers), waterfalls and fountains. An equal parts bizarre and enlightening experience.

Tours

Nearly every guesthouse and hotel in Chiang Rai offers hiking excursions in hill-tribe country, some of which have grassroots, sustainable or nonprofit emphases.

In general, trek pricing depends on the type of activities and the number of days and participants. Rates, per person, for two people, for a two-night trek range from 2300B to 6000B. Generally, everything from accommodation to transport and food is included in this price.

Rai Pian Karuna TREKKING
(☎062 246 1897; www.facebook.com/raipiankaruna) This new, community-based social enterprise conducts one- and multiday treks and homestays at Akha, Lahu and Lua villages in Mae Chan, north of Chiang Rai. Other activities, from weeklong volunteering stints to cooking courses, are also on offer.

Mirror Foundation TREKKING
(☎053 737616; www.thailandecotour.org) Although its rates are higher, trekking with this nonprofit NGO helps support the training of its local guides. Treks range from one to three days and traverse the Akha, Karen and Lahu villages of Mae Yao District, north of Chiang Rai.

PDA Tours & Travel TREKKING
(☎053 740088; www.pda.or.th/chiangrai/package_tour.htm; Hilltribe Museum & Education Center, 3rd fl, 620/25 Th Thanalai; ⌚8.30am-6pm Mon-Fri, 10am-6pm Sat & Sun) One- to three-day treks are available through this NGO. Profits go back into community projects that include HIV/AIDS education, mobile health clinics, education scholarships and the establishment of village-owned banks.

Sleeping

In Town

Baan Warabordee HOTEL $
(☎053 754488; baanwarabordee@hotmail.com; 59/1 Th Sanpanard; r 500-600B; ❄📶) A handsome, good-value hotel has been made from this three-storey Thai villa. Rooms are decked out in dark woods and light fabrics, and are equipped with air-con, fridge and hot water.

Chiang Rai

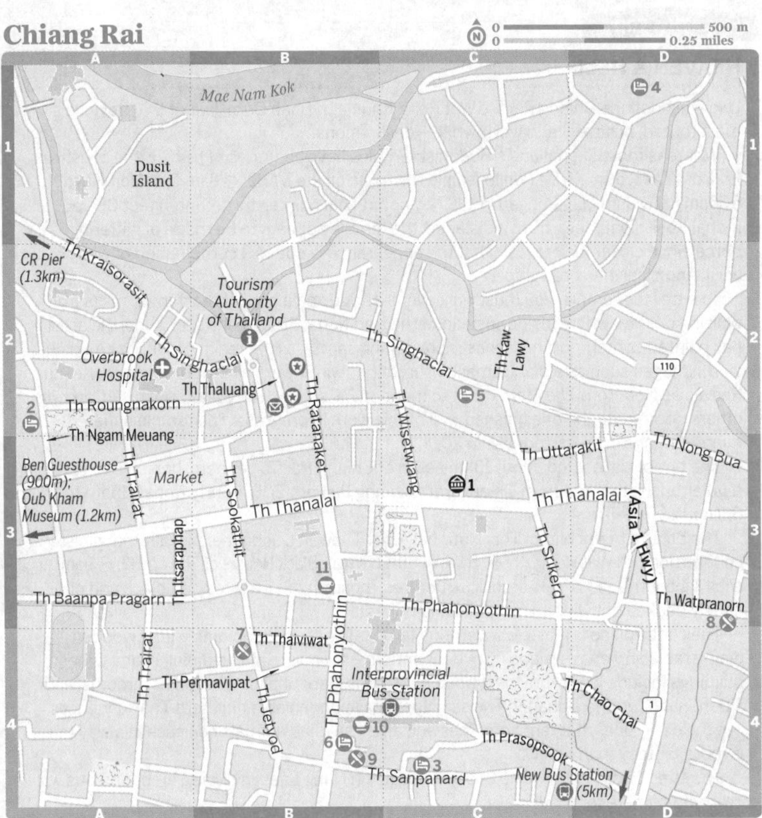

Moon & Sun Hotel HOTEL $
(☎053 719279; 632 Th Singhaclai; r 399-499B, ste 699B; ❄📶) Bright and sparkling clean, this little hotel offers large, modern, terrific-value rooms. Some feature four-poster beds, while all come with desk, cable TV and refrigerator. Suites have a separate, spacious sitting area.

Baan Rub Aroon GUESTHOUSE $$
(☎053 711827; www.baanrubaroon.net; 893 Th Ngummuang; r incl breakfast 650-2000B; ❄@📶) The rooms in this handsome villa, located just west of the city centre, aren't quite as charming as the exterior suggests, and most share bathrooms, but it's a good choice if you're looking for a quiet, homey stay.

Wiang Inn HOTEL $$$
(☎053 711533; www.wianginn.com; 893 Th Phahonyothin; incl breakfast r 2400-3200B, ste 6000-10,000B; ❄@📶🏊) The funky, 1970s-era exterior is an accurate indicator of this centrally located, business-class hotel's age,

Chiang Rai

Sights
1 Hilltribe Museum & Education Center C3

Activities, Courses & Tours
PDA Tours & Travel .... (see 1)

Sleeping
2 Baan Rub Aroon A2
3 Baan Warabordee C4
4 Legend of Chiang Rai D1
5 Moon & Sun Hotel C2
6 Wiang Inn B4

Eating
7 Khao Soi Phor Jai B4
8 Lung Eed D3
9 Namnigew Pa Nuan B4

Drinking & Nightlife
10 BaanChivitMai Bakery B4
11 Doi Chaang B3

WORTH A TRIP

HEAVEN & HELL

Lying just outside Chiang Rai are Wat Rong Khun and Baan Dum, two of the province's most touted, bizarre – and worthwhile – destinations.

Whereas most of Thailand's Buddhist temples have centuries of history, the construction of **Wat Rong Khun** (White Temple, วัดร่องขุ่น; off Rte 1/AH2; ⌚8am-5pm Mon-Fri, to 5.30pm Sat & Sun) FREE began in 1997 by noted Thai painter-turned-architect Chalermchai Kositpipat. Seen from a distance, the temple appears to be made of glittering porcelain; a closer look reveals that the appearance is due to a combination of whitewash and clear-mirrored chips.

To enter the temple, you must walk over a bridge and a pool of reaching arms (symbolising desire), where inside, instead of the traditional Buddha life scenarios, the artist has painted contemporary scenes representing samsara (the realm of rebirth and delusion). Images such as a plane smashing into the Twin Towers and, oddly enough, Keanu Reeves as Neo from *The Matrix* (not to mention Elvis, Hello Kitty and Superman, among others), dominate the one finished wall of this work in progress. The temple suffered minor damage in an earthquake in 2014.

The temple is located about 13km south of Chiang Rai. To get here, hop on one of the regular buses that run from Chiang Rai to Wiang Pa Pao (20B, hourly from 6.15am to 6.10pm).

The bizarre brainchild of Thai National Artist Thawan Duchanee, and a rather sinister counterpoint to Wat Rong Khun, **Baan Dum** (บ้านดำ, Black House; off Rte 1/AH2; ⌚9am-noon & 1-5pm) FREE unites several structures, most of which are stained black and ominously decked out with animal pelts and bones.

The centrepiece is a black, cavernous temple-like building holding a long wooden dining table and chairs made from deer antlers – a virtual Satan's dining room. Other buildings include white, breast-shaped bedrooms, dark phallus-decked bathrooms, and a bone- and fur-lined 'chapel'. The structures have undeniable northern Thai influences, but the dark tones, flagrant flourishes and all those dead animals coalesce in a way that is more fantasy than reality.

The site is located 13km north of Chiang Rai in Nang Lae; any Mae Sai–bound bus will drop you off here for around 20B.

but a recent renovation means the rooms are well maintained and include a few Thai decorative touches.

Outside Town Centre

★Bamboo Nest de Chiang Rai GUESTHOUSE $$
(☎095 686 4755, 089 953 2330; www.bamboonest-chiangrai.com; bungalows incl breakfast 800-1600B) The Lahu village that's home to this unique accommodation is only 23km from Chiang Rai but feels a world away. Bamboo Nest takes the form of simple but spacious bamboo huts perched on a hill overlooking tiered rice fields. The only electricity is provided by solar panels, so leave your laptops in town and instead take part in activities that range from birdwatching to hiking. It's located about 2km from the headquarters of Lamnamkok National Park; free transport to/from Chiang Rai is available for those staying two nights or more.

Ben Guesthouse GUESTHOUSE $$
(☎053 716775; www.benguesthousechiangrai.com; 351/10 Soi 4, Th Sankhongnoi; r 500-700B, ste 1000-1500B; ❄@📶🏊) One of the best budget-to-midrange places in the north. The spotless compound has a bit of everything, from fan-cooled cheapies to immense suites, not to mention a pool. It's 1.2km from the town centre, at the end of Soi 4 on Th Sankhongnoi (the street is called Th Sathanpayabarn where it intersects with Th Phahonyothin). A túk-túk costs 20B per person.

Legend of Chiang Rai HOTEL $$$
(☎053 910400; www.thelegend-chiangrai.com; 124/15 Th Kohloy; incl breakfast r 3000-10,000B, bungalows 7000-12,000B; ❄@📶🏊) One of the few hotels in town to boast a riverside location, this upscale resort feels like a traditional Lanna village. Rooms are romantic and luxuriously understated, with furniture in calming creams and rattan. The riverside infinity pool and spa are the icing on the

comfort-filled cake. The resort is about 500m north of Th Singhaclai.

Eating & Drinking

★Lung Eed NORTHERN THAI $
(Th Watpranorn; mains 40-100B; ⏲11.30am-9pm Mon-Sat) One of Chiang Rai's most delicious dishes is available at this simple shophouse restaurant. There's an English-language menu on the wall, but don't miss the sublime *lâhp gài* (minced chicken fried with local spices and topped with crispy deep-fried chicken skin, shallots and garlic). The restaurant is about 150m east of Rte 1/AH2.

Khao Soi Phor Jai NORTHERN THAI $
(Th Jetyod; mains 35-60B; ⏲7.30am-5pm) Phor Jai serves mild but tasty bowls of the eponymous curry noodle dish, as well as a few other northern Thai staples. There's no roman-script sign, but look for the open-air shophouse with the blue interior.

Namnigew Pa Nuan VIETNAMESE, THAI $
(Th Sanpanard; mains 10-120B; ⏲9am-5pm) This semiconcealed place (there's no roman-script sign) serves a unique mix of Vietnamese and northern Thai dishes. Tasty food, friendly service and a fun barnlike atmosphere – wouldn't it be great if it was open for dinner as well...

BaanChivitMai Bakery CAFE
(www.bcmthai.com/home; Th Prasopsook; ⏲8am-7pm Mon-Fri, to 6pm Sat & Sun; 📶) In addition to a proper cup of joe made from local beans, you can snack on surprisingly authentic Swedish-style sweets and Western-style meals and sandwiches at this popular bakery. Profits go to BaanChivitMai, an organisation that runs homes and education projects for vulnerable, orphaned or AIDS-affected children.

Doi Chaang CAFE
(542/2 Th Ratanaket; ⏲7am-10pm; 📶) Doi Chaang is the leading brand among Chiang Rai coffees, and its beans are now sold as far abroad as Canada and Europe. The flagship cafe is a comfortable place to sip, and offers a short menu of snacks and light meals.

Information

Overbrook Hospital (☎053 711366; www.overbrook-hospital.com; Th Singhaclai) English is spoken at this modern hospital.

Tourism Authority of Thailand (TAT; ☎053 744674, nationwide 1672; tatchrai@tat.or.th; Th Singhaclai; ⏲8.30am-4.30pm) English is limited, but staff here do their best to give advice and can provide a small selection of maps and brochures.

Tourist Police (☎053 740249, nationwide 1155; Th Uttarakit; ⏲24hr) English is spoken and police are on standby around the clock.

Getting There & Away

AIR

Chiang Rai International Airport (Mae Fah Luang International Airport; ☎053 798000; www.chiangraiairportonline.com) is approximately 8km north of the city. The terminal has airline offices, restaurants, a money exchange, a post office and several car-rental booths. Taxis run into town from the airport for 200B. From town, a metered trip with **Chiang Rai Taxi** (☎053 773477) will cost around 120B.

There are 11 daily flights to Bangkok's Don Mueang International Airport (from 1399B, one hour and 20 minutes) and five to Bangkok's Suvarnabhumi International Airport (from 1280B, one hour and 20 minutes), as well as flights to Chiang Mai and Hat Yai. At the time of writing the only international flight was to Kunming (China).

BOAT

Passenger boats ply Mae Nam Kok between Chiang Rai and Tha Ton, in Chiang Mai, stopping at Ban Ruam Mit along the way. Boats depart from the **CR Pier** (☎053 750009; ⏲7am-4pm), 2km northwest of town; a túk-túk to the pier should cost about 80B.

BUS & MINIVAN

Buses bound for destinations within Chiang Rai Province, as well as a couple of minivans and mostly slow, fan-cooled buses bound for a handful of destinations in northern Thailand, depart from the **interprovincial bus station** (☎053 715952; Th Prasopsook) in the centre of town. If you're heading beyond Chiang Rai (or are in a hurry), you'll have to go to the **new bus station** (☎053 773989; Rte 1/AH2), 5km south of town; frequent *sŏrng·tăa·ou* (passenger pick-up trucks) linking the new bus station and the interprovincial station run from 6am to 5.30pm (15B, 15 minutes).

Internationally, there's a direct bus from Chiang Rai to Luang Prabang (Laos). There's also a daily bus to Bokeo (Laos), from where it's possible to connect to buses to Luang Nam Tha (Laos), Kunming (China) and Vang Vieng (Laos).

Getting Around

Central Chiang Rai is easy enough to tackle on foot. Otherwise, túk-túk charge approximately 20B per person for destinations in town.

Chiang Rai Taxi (p489) operates inexpensive metered taxis in and around town.

TRANSPORT FROM CHIANG RAI

Buses

DESTINATION	FARE (B)	DURATION (HR)	FREQUENCY
Bangkok	423-958	11-12	frequent 7am-7pm (new bus station)
Bokeo (Laos)	240	3	4pm (new bus station)
Chiang Khong	65	2	frequent 6.30am-4.30pm (interprovincial bus station)
Chiang Mai	129-258	3-7	frequent 6am-7pm (interprovincial bus station)
Chiang Saen	37	1½	frequent 5.30am-7pm (interprovincial bus station)
Lampang	98-137	4-5	5 departures 12.45-4.30pm (new bus station)
Lampang	137	5	hourly 7am-3.15pm (interprovincial bus station)
Luang Prabang (Laos)	950	16	1pm (new bus station)
Mae Chan (for Mae Salong/Santikhiri)	25	45min	frequent 5am-7.30pm (interprovincial bus station)
Mae Sai	39	1½	frequent 6am-6.30pm (interprovincial bus station)
Mae Sot	416	12	8.15am & 8.45am (new bus station)
Nakhon Ratchasima (Khorat)	569-664	12-13	6 departures 6.30am-7.20pm (new bus station)
Phayao	43	1½-2	hourly 10am-3.30pm (new bus station)
Phayao	66	2	frequent 7.30am-3.30pm (interprovincial bus station)
Phitsanulok	260-335	6-7	hourly 6.15am-7.20pm (new bus station)
Phrae	144	4	half-hourly 6am-6pm (new bus station)
Sukhothai	231	8	hourly 7.30am-noon (new bus station)
Ubon Ratchathani	884	12	4pm (new bus station)

Minivans

DESTINATION	FARE (B)	DURATION (HR)	FREQUENCY
Chiang Saen	45	1½	hourly 6.20am-4.20pm (interprovincial bus station)
Mae Sai	46	1½	frequent 6.30am-6pm (interprovincial bus station)
Phayao	63	1	half-hourly 5am-6pm (interprovincial bus station)
Phrae	165	3½	half-hourly 5am-6pm (new bus station)
Sop Ruak (Golden Triangle)	50	2	hourly 6.20am-4.20pm (interprovincial bus station)

Golden Triangle

The tri-country border of Thailand, Myanmar and Laos is known as the Golden Triangle.

Sop Ruak

This town is the centre of the so-called Golden Triangle, at the confluence of Nam Ruak and the Mekong River. The town's two opium-related museums are both worth a visit, and a boat trip is an enjoyable way to pass an hour. But the only reason to overnight here is if you've already booked a room in one of the area's outstanding luxury hotels.

Sights

Phra Chiang Saen Si Phaendin BUDDHIST TEMPLE
(พระเชียงแสนสี่แผ่นดิน; Rte 1290; donations appreciated; ⌚7am-9pm) The first sight you'll inevitably see in Sop Ruak is Phra Chiang Saen Si

Phaendin, a giant Buddha statue financed by a Thai-Chinese foundation. The statue straddles a boatlike platform, and visitors here are encouraged to donate by rolling coins from an elevated platform behind the statue.

House of Opium MUSEUM
(บ้านฝิ่น; Rte 1290; 50B; ⏲7am-7pm) This small museum with historical displays pertaining to opium culture is worth a peek. Exhibits include all the various implements used in the planting, harvest, use and trade of the *Papaver somniferum* resin, including pipes, weights, scales and so on, plus photos and maps with labels in English. The museum is at the southeastern end of Sop Ruak, virtually across from the huge Buddha statue at Phra Chiang Saen Si Phaendin.

Wat Prathat Pukhao BUDDHIST TEMPLE
(วัดพระธาตุภูเข้า; Rte 1290; ⏲dawn-dusk) FREE Wat Prathat Pukhao provides the best viewpoint of the Mekong junction of Laos, Myanmar and Thailand. There are steps up to the temple next to the House of Opium.

Hall of Opium MUSEUM
(หอฝิ่น; Rte 1290; adult/child 200B/free; ⏲8.30am-4pm Tue-Sun) One kilometre north of Sop Ruak on a 40-hectare plot opposite the Anantara Golden Triangle Resort & Spa, the Mae Fah Luang Foundation has established the 5600-sq-metre Hall of Opium. The multimedia exhibitions include a fascinating history of opium, as well as engaging and informative displays on the effects of abuse on individuals and society. Well balanced and worth investigating.

Sleeping

Four Seasons Tented Camp HOTEL $$$
(☎053 910200; www.fourseasons.com; 2 nights all-inclusive 104,000-116,000B; ❄@📶🏊) If you can fit it into your schedule (and budget), this safari-inspired resort is among the most unique accommodation experiences in Thailand. The 'tents' are appropriately luxurious and are decked out in colonial-era safari paraphernalia. A minimum stay of at least two nights is required, and guests take part in daily activities ranging from longboat river excursions to spa treatments.

Pak-Ping-Rim-Khong GUESTHOUSE $$
(☎053 650151; www.facebook.com/PakPingRimKhong; 484 Th Rimkhong; r incl breakfast 1200-1800B; ❄📶) A new and tidy villa compound just north of town. Rooms are spacious and come equipped with air-con, TV and fridge.

LOCAL KNOWLEDGE

THE LOCAL FOOD OF MAE SALONG

The very Chinese breakfast of *bah·tôrng·gǒh* (deep-fried dough sticks) and hot soybean milk at the morning market is a great way to start the day. In fact, many Thai tourists come to Mae Salong simply to eat Yunnanese dishes such as *màn·tǒh* (steamed Chinese buns) served with braised pork belly and pickled vegetables, or black chicken braised with Chinese-style herbs. Homemade wheat and egg noodles are another speciality of Mae Salong, and are served with a local broth that combines pork and a spicy chilli paste. They're available at several places in town.

Getting There & Away

There are frequent *sǒrng·tǎa·ou* (passenger pickup trucks) to Chiang Saen (20B, 15 minutes, 7am to noon) and Mae Sai (45B, 30 minutes, every 40 minutes from 8am to 1pm), both of which can be flagged down along the main strip. Minivans to Chiang Rai (50B, one hour, hourly from 5.50am to 4pm) wait in the parking lot west of Phra Chiang Saen Si Phaendin. It's an easy 9km bicycle ride from Chiang Saen to Sop Ruak.

Mae Salong (Santikhiri)

Although Mae Salong is now thoroughly on the beaten track, the distinctly Chinese vibe, hilltop setting, and abundance of hill tribes and tea plantations converge in a destination quite unlike anywhere else in Thailand. It's a great place to kick back for a couple of days, and the surrounding area is ripe for self-guided exploration.

Mae Salong was originally settled by Chinese soldiers who fled communist rule in 1949. Generations later, the descendants and culture of this unique community persists: the Yunnanese dialect of Chinese still remains the lingua franca and you'll find more Chinese than Thai food.

Sights & Activities

Little Home Guesthouse (p492) has free maps showing approximate trekking routes to nearby Akha and Lisu villages, less than half a day's walk away.

The best hikes are north of Mae Salong between Ban Thoet Thai and the Myanmar border. Ask first about political conditions before heading off in this direction. Horseback treks to four nearby villages are available for 500B for about three or four hours.

Morning Market MARKET
(ตลาดเช้าดอยแม่สลอง; ⌚6-8am) A tiny but quite interesting morning market convenes at the T-intersection near Shin Sane Guest House. The market attracts town residents and tribespeople from the surrounding districts.

All-Day Market MARKET
(ตลาดริมถนนดอยแม่สลอง) An all-day market forms at the southern end of town and unites vendors selling hill-tribe handicrafts, shops selling tea and a few basic restaurants.

Sleeping

Don't fret if your first pick is full: there are many, many budget and midrange places to choose from in Mae Salong. The competition means that prices are often negotiable, except during the high season (November to January). And the cool weather means that few places have air-con. All accommodation is located on, or just off, the main road.

★**Little Home Guesthouse** GUESTHOUSE $$
(☎053 765389; www.maesalonglittlehome.com; r & bungalows 500-800B; @📶) Located near the market intersection is this recently renovated large yellow building backed by a handful of attractive, great-value bungalows. Rooms are tidy and sunny, and the owners are extremely friendly.

Baan Hom Muen Li HOTEL $$$
(Osmanthus; ☎053 765271; osmanhouse@hotmail.com; r incl breakfast 1200-2000B; 📶) Across from Sweet Maesalong cafe, in the middle of town, this stylish place consists of 22 rooms artfully decked out in modern and classic Chinese themes. Go for the upstairs rooms in the new structure that have huge balconies with views over the surrounding tea plantations. The hotel has no roman-script sign.

Eating

The culinary offerings in Mae Salong are not unlike those of a village in Yunnan (China). It's a great place to dig into exotic noodles and other dishes not found elsewhere in Thailand.

HOME AWAY FROM HOME

Mae Salong was originally settled by the 93rd Regiment of the Kuomintang (KMT), which had fled to Myanmar from China after the 1949 Chinese revolution. The renegades were forced to leave Myanmar in 1961 when the Yangon government decided it wouldn't allow the KMT to remain legally in northern Myanmar. Crossing into northern Thailand with their pony caravans, the ex-soldiers and their families settled into mountain villages and re-created a society like the one they'd left behind in Yunnan.

After the Thai government granted the KMT refugee status in the 1960s, efforts were made to incorporate the Yunnanese KMT and their families into the Thai nation. Until the late 1980s they didn't have much success. Many ex-KMT persisted in involving themselves in the Golden Triangle (p490) opium trade in a three-way partnership with alleged opium warlord Khun Sa and the Shan United Army (SUA). Because of the rough, mountainous terrain and lack of sealed roads, the outside world was rather cut off from the goings-on in Mae Salong, so the Yunnanese were able to ignore attempts by the Thai authorities to suppress opium activity and tame the region.

Infamous Khun Sa made his home in nearby Ban Hin Taek (now Ban Thoet Thai) until the early 1980s, when he was routed by the Thai military. Khun Sa's retreat to Myanmar seemed to signal a change in local attitudes and the Thai government finally began making progress in its pacification of Mae Salong and the surrounding area. In an attempt to quash opium activity, and the more recent threat of *yah bâh* (methamphetamine) trafficking, the Thai government has created crop-substitution programs to encourage hill tribes to cultivate tea, coffee, corn and fruit trees.

In a further effort to separate the area from its old image as an opium fiefdom, the Thai government officially changed the name of the village from Mae Salong to Santikhiri (Hill of Peace). Until the 1980s packhorses were used to move goods up the mountain to Mae Salong, but today the 36km road from Ban Pasang is paved and well travelled. But despite the advances in infrastructure, the town is unlike any other in Thailand and retains a strong Chinese cultural presence.

OFF THE BEATEN TRACK

BAN BO LUANG

Ban Bo Luang (also known as Ban Bo Kleua, or Salt Well Village) is a picturesque Htin village southeast of Doi Phu Kha National Park (p496) where the long-standing occupation has been the extraction of salt from local salt wells. It's easy to find the main community salt wells, which are more or less in the centre of the village. If you have your own transport, the village is a good base for exploring the nearby national parks.

Khun Nan National Park (อุทยานแห่งชาติขุนน่าน; ☎054 778140; adult/child 100/50B; ⏲8am-4.30pm) is located a few kilometres north of Ban Bo Kleua, and has a 2km walk from the visitor centre that ends in a viewpoint looking over local villages and nearby Laos.

By far the best place to stay in Ban Bo Luang is **Boklua View** (☎081 809 6392; www.bokluaview.com; r & bungalows incl breakfast 1850B; ❄📶), an attractive and well-run hillside resort overlooking the village and the Nam Mang that runs through it. The resort has its own garden and serves good food (be sure to try Chef Toun's chicken deep-fried with northern Thai spices).

Salema Restaurant CHINESE $
(Rte 1130; mains 30-250B; ⏲7am-8pm) One of the friendliest restaurants in town also happens to be the one serving the most delicious food. Salema does tasty Muslim-Chinese dishes, including a rich Yunnan-style beef curry and a deliciously tart tuna and tea-leaves spicy salad. The noodle dishes are equally worthwhile and include a beef *kôw soy* (wheat-and-egg noodles in a curry broth). Salema is located at the eastern end of town.

Sweet Maesalong CAFE $
(Rte 1130; mains 45-155B; ⏲8.30am-5pm; 📶) If you require more caffeine than the local tea leaves can provide, stop by this modern cafe with an extensive menu of coffee drinks using local beans. Surprisingly sophisticated baked goods and one-plate dishes are also available. Located more or less in the middle of town.

Sue Hai CHINESE $$
(Rte 1130; mains 80-300B; ⏲7am-9pm; 📝) Just east of the town centre, this simple, family-run tea shop and Chinese restaurant has an English-language menu of local specialities, including local mushrooms fried with soy sauce and delicious air-dried pork fried with fresh chilli.

ℹ Information

There is an ATM at the Thai Military Bank opposite Khumnaiphol Resort, at the southern end of town.

ℹ Getting There & Away

Probably the easiest way to get to Mae Salong from Chiang Rai is to take a bus to Mae Chan, from where there are frequent green *sŏrng·tăa·ou* (passenger pick-up trucks) to Mae Salong (60B, one hour, four departures daily). You can charter one for around 400B. Alternatively, it's also possible to take a Mae Sai–bound bus to Ban Pasang, from where blue *sŏrng·tăa·ou* head up the mountain to Mae Salong only when full (60B, one hour, from 6am to 5pm) or when chartered for around 400B. In the reverse direction, you can flag down *sŏrng·tăa·ou* near Mae Salong's 7-Eleven.

You can also reach Mae Salong by road from Tha Ton, in Chiang Mai. Yellow *sŏrng·tăa·ou* bound for Tha Ton stop near Little Home Guesthouse four times daily (60B, one hour).

ℹ Getting Around

Much of Mae Salong is approachable on foot. If you want to go further (or are struggling with the hills), motorcycles can be hired at Mini, at the east of town, as well as at most guesthouses, for around 200B for 24 hours.

Chiang Khong

Chiang Khong is historically an important market town for local hill tribes and for trade with northern Laos. Today the riverside town is a popular travellers' gateway into Laos. In 2013, a bridge over Mae Nam Khong opened, which has facilitated transport links with China as well. From Huay Xai, on the opposite side of the Mekong, it's a two-day slowboat trip to Luang Prabang. And for those who have set their sights even further, Huay Xai is only an eight-hour bus ride from Boten, a border crossing to and from China.

🛏 Sleeping & Eating

★**Namkhong Resort** HOTEL $
(☎053 791055; www.namkhongriverside.com/boutique-resort; 94/2 Th Sai Klang; r 200-800B;

(❄📶🏊) Just off the main drag is this semisecluded compound of tropical plants and handsome wooden structures. Even the fan-cooled, shared-bathroom cheapies are charming, and the swimming pool is a bonus.

River House HOTEL $$
(☎053 792022; theriverhouse_chiangkhong@hotmail.com; 419 Th Sai Klang; dm 150B, r 300-1000B; ❄@📶) This homey-feeling white house overlooking the Mekong River is a great choice. The cheaper rooms are small, fan cooled and share bathrooms, while the more expensive rooms are spacious and come with air-con, fridge, TV and balcony.

★**Khao Soi Pa Orn** THAI $
(Soi 6, Th Sai Klang; mains 30-40B; ⏲8am-4pm) You may think you know *kôw soy*, the famous northern curry noodle soup, but the version served in Chiang Khong forgoes the curry broth and replaces it with clear soup topped with a rich, spicy minced-pork mixture. A few non-noodle dishes are also available. There's no roman-script sign, but it's located next to the giant highway-distance marker.

Getting There & Away

Chiang Khong has a shiny new **bus station** (☎053 792000; Rte 1020) located 3km south of town, which is where you'll need to go if you're bound for a destination in Laos. Otherwise, buses pick up and drop off passengers at various points near the market, south of the centre of town. If you're bound for Chiang Saen, you'll first need to take a *sŏrng·tăa·ou* (passenger pick-up truck) to Hat Bai from a stall on Th Sai Klang (50B, one hour, around 8am), where you'll need to transfer to another Chiang Saen–bound *sŏrng·tăa·ou*.

Nan

Due to its remote location, Nan is not the kind of destination most travellers are going to stumble upon. But if you've taken the time to get here, you'll be rewarded by a city rich in both culture and history.

Many of Nan's residents are Thai Lü, the ancestors of immigrants from Xishuangbanna, in southwestern China. This cultural legacy is seen in the city's art and architecture, particularly in its exquisite temples. A Lanna influence on the town can also be seen in the remains of the old city wall and several early wát.

Sights

★**Wat Phumin** BUDDHIST TEMPLE
(วัดภูมินทร; cnr Th Suriyaphong & Th Pha Kong; donations appreciated; ⏲daylight hours) Nan's most famous Buddhist temple is celebrated for its exquisite murals that were executed during the late 19th century by a Thai Lü artist named Thit Buaphan. The exterior of the temple takes the form of a cruciform *bòht* (chapel) that was constructed in 1596 and restored during the reign of Chao Anantavorapitthidet (1867–74). The ornate altar in the centre of the *bòht* has four sides, with four Sukhothai-style sitting Buddhas facing in each direction.

★**Nan National Museum** MUSEUM
(พิพิธภัณฑสถานแห่งชาติน่าน; Th Pha Kong; 100B; ⏲9am-4pm Wed-Sun) Housed in the 1903 vintage palace of Nan's last two feudal lords, this museum first opened its doors in 1973. In terms of collection and content, it's one of the country's better provincial museums, and has English labels for most items. It was closed for renovations at the time of writing but is expected to reopen with much the same focus.

BUS SERVICES FROM CHIANG KHONG

DESTINATION	PRICE (B)	DURATION (HR)	DEPARTURES
Bangkok	592-921	13	7am, 7.25am & frequent departures 3-4pm
Chiang Mai	254-395	6-7	7.15am, 9.45am & 10.30am
Chiang Rai	65-126	2½	hourly 5am-4pm
Luang Namtha (Laos)	280	4	2.30pm (Mon, Wed, Fri & Sat)
Luang Prabang (Laos)	730	13	2.30pm (Mon, Wed, Fri & Sat)
Phayao	151	3	10.30am
Udomxai (Laos)	460	10	2.30pm (Mon, Wed, Fri & Sat)

GETTING TO LAOS: CHIANG KHONG TO HUAY XAI

Late 2013 saw the completion of the Fourth Thai-Lao Friendship Bridge over the Mekong River. Since then, foreigners are no longer allowed to cross to Huay Xai by boat, which has made getting to Laos both less convenient and more expensive for most tourists.

Getting to the border The jumping-off point is the Friendship Bridge, around 10km south of Chiang Khong, a 120B chartered *săhm·lór* (three-wheeled pedicab) ride or 60B on the white passenger trucks that run the route from downtown or the bus-stop market area.

At the border After completing border formalities at the **Thai immigration office** (☎053 792824; ⏲6am-8.30pm), you'll board a shuttle bus (from 20B, 8am to 6pm) across the 630m span. On the Lao side, foreigners can purchase a 30-day visa for Laos upon arrival in Huay Xai for US$30 to US$42, depending on nationality. On your return to Thailand, unless you've already received a Thai visa, immigration will grant you permission to stay in the country for 15 days.

Moving on From the Lao side of the bridge, it's an exorbitant 100B/25,000K per person *săhm·lór* ride to the boat pier or Huay Xai's new bus terminal. Bus destinations from Huay Xai include Luang Nam Tha (60,000K to 85,000K, 4½ hours, 8.30am and 10am), Luang Prabang (145,000K to 170,000K, 12 hours, 8.30am, 10am and 6pm), Udomxai (90,000K to 100,000K, nine hours, 9.30am), Vang Vieng (215,000K, 24 hours, 10am) and Vientiane (250,000K, 24 hours, 10am).

If time is on your side, the daily **slowboat** (1350B or 220,000K, around 10.30am) to Luang Prabang takes two days, including a night in the village of Pak Beng. Avoid the noisy **fast boats** (360,000K, six to seven hours, frequent from 9am to 11am) as there have been reports of bad accidents. Booking tickets through a Chiang Khong–based agent such as **Easy Trip** (☎053 655174, 089 635 5999; www.discoverylaos.com; 183 Th Sai Klang; ⏲9am-7pm) costs slightly more, but they arrange tickets for you and provide transport and a boxed lunch for the boat ride.

If you already hold a Chinese visa, it's also possible to go directly to China from Chiang Khong. After obtaining a 30-day Lao visa on arrival in Huay Xai, simply board one of the buses bound for Mengla (120,000K, eight hours, 8.30am) or Kunming (430,000K, 18 hours, 10.30am), which are both in China's Yunnan Province.

Activities

Nan has nothing like the organised trekking industry found in Chiang Rai and Chiang Mai.

Nan Touring RAFTING
(☎081 961 7711; www.nantouring.com; 11/12 Th Suriyaphong; 3 days & 2 nights per person 5900B; ⏲9am-5pm) This outfit offers a variety of rafting trips for groups of at least five people.

Fhu Travel TREKKING
(☎054 710636, 081 287 7209; www.fhutravel.com; 453/4 Th Sumon Thevarat; trekking per person 1700B; ⏲9am-6pm) This established outfit currently offers one-day treks around Nan.

Sleeping & Eating

Fah Place HOTEL $
(☎054 710222; 237/8 Th Sumon Thevarat; r 350-500B; ❄📶) The rooms here are vast and have been outfitted with attractive teak furniture, including the kinds of puffy, inviting beds you'd expect at places that charge several times this much; a terrific bargain.

★ **Pukha Nanfa Hotel** HOTEL $$$
(☎054 771111; www.pukhananfahotel.co.th; 369 Th Sumon Thevarat; r incl breakfast 2600-4700B; ❄@📶) The former and forgettable Nan Fah Hotel has been painstakingly transformed into this charming boutique lodging. The 14 rooms are cosy and classy, with aged wood accentuated by touches such as local cloth, handicrafts and art. Antique adverts and pictures add to the old-world feel, and, to top it off, the place is conveniently located and has highly capable staff.

Hot Bread INTERNATIONAL, THAI $
(38/1-2 Th Suriyaphong; mains 25-140B; ⏲7am-4pm; 🌶) This charming, retro-themed cafe and restaurant has a generous menu of Western-style breakfast dishes – including the eponymous and delicious homemade bread – and other Western and Thai items.

Come for *kôw soy* (noodle soup) in the mornings.

Pu Som Restaurant NORTHERN THAI $
(203/1 Th Khamyot; mains 35-90B; ⏱10am-10pm) The emphasis here is on meat, served in the local style as *lâhp* (a type of minced-meat 'salad') or *néu·a·nêung* (beef steamed over herbs and served with a delicious galangal-based dip). There's no English-language sign; look for the illuminated 'est cola' ad.

Shopping

Nan is one of the best places in northern Thailand to pick up souvenirs. Good buys include local textiles, especially the Thai Lü weaving styles, which typically feature red and black thread on white cotton in floral, geometric and animal designs. Local Hmong appliqué and Mien embroidery are of excellent quality. Htin grass-and-bamboo baskets and mats are worth a look, too.

Walking Street MARKET
(Th Pha Kong; ⏱5-10pm Sat) Every Saturday afternoon the stretch of Th Pha Kong in front of Nan National Museum is closed, and vendors selling food, textiles, clothing and local handicrafts set up shop.

Information

Tourist Centre (☎054 751169; Th Pha Kong; ⏱8.30am-noon & 1-4.30pm) Opposite Wat Phumin, this helpful information centre is hidden behind vendors and coffee shops.

Getting There & Around

Nan's recently renovated Nan Nakhon Airport is located about 3km north of town. **Air Asia** (☎054 772635, nationwide 02 515 9999; www.airasia.com; Nan Nakhon Airport; ⏱7am-4.30pm) and **Nok Air** (☎091 119 9834, nationwide 1318; www.nokair.com; Nan Nakhon Airport; ⏱8am-7pm) have flights to/from Bangkok's Don Mueang International Airport (from 935B, 1½ hours, five to six daily), while **Kan Air** (☎090 907 1811, nationwide 02 551 6111; www.kanairlines.com; Nan Nakhon Airport; ⏱8.30am-5pm) flies to/from Chiang Mai (1890B, 45 minutes, twice weekly). **Klay Airport Taxi** (☎086 188 0079; Nan Nakhon Airport) has airport transfers for about 100B per person.

From Nan, all buses, minivans and *sŏrng·tăa·o* (passenger pick-up trucks) leave from the **bus station** (☎054 711662; Th Jao Fa) at the southwestern edge of town. A motorcycle taxi between the station and the centre of town costs 30B.

If you're connecting to the train station at Den Chai in Phrae, you can hop on any bus bound for Chiang Mai or Bangkok.

Around Nan

Doi Phu Kha National Park

This **national park** (อุทยานแห่งชาติดอยภูคา; ☎082 194 1349, accommodation 02 562 0760; www.dnp.go.th; 200B) is centred on 2000m-high Doi Phu Kha, the province's highest peak, in Amphoe Pua and Amphoe Bo Kleua, about 75km northeast of Nan. There are several Htin, Mien, Hmong and Thai Lü villages in the park and vicinity, as well as a couple of caves and waterfalls, and endless opportunities for forest walks. The park is often cold in the cool season and especially wet in the wet season.

Park HQ has a basic map and staff can arrange a local guide for walks or more

BUSES FROM NAN

In addition to buses, there are also minivans to Ban Huay Kon (on the border with Laos; 95B, three hours, five departures from 5am to noon) and Phrae (83B, two hours, half-hourly 5.30am to 6pm).

DESTINATION	FARE (B)	DURATION (HR)	FREQUENCY
Bangkok	396-725	10-11	frequent 8-10am & 6.15-7.45pm
Chiang Mai	213-395	6	frequent 7.30am-5pm & 10.30pm
Chiang Rai	181	6	9am
Lampang	146-291	4	frequent 7.30am-10.30pm
Phayao	197	4	1.30pm
Phitsanulok	178	4	5 departures 7.45am-5.15pm
Phrae	78	2½	frequent 7.30am-10.30pm
Pua (for Doi Phu Kha National Park)	50	2	hourly 7am-5pm

GETTING TO LAOS: BAN HUAY KON TO MUANG NGEUN

Located 140km north of Nan, Ban Huay Kon is a sleepy village in the mountains near the Lao border. There's a border market on Saturday morning, but most will come here because of the town's status as an international border crossing to Laos.

Getting to the border To Ban Huay Kon, there are five daily minivans originating in Phrae and stopping in Nan between 5am and noon (95B, three hours). In the opposite direction, minivans bound for Nan (95B, three hours), Phrae (172B, five hours) and Den Chai (for the train; 200B) leave Ban Huay Kon at 9.15am, 10am, 11am, noon and 3pm.

At the border After passing the Thai immigration booth, foreigners can purchase a 30-day visa for Laos for US$30 to US$42, depending on nationality. There is an extra US$1 or 50B charge after 4pm and on weekends.

Moving on You can then proceed 2.5km to the Lao village of Muang Ngeun, where you could stay at the Phouxay Guesthouse, or, if you're heading onward, go to the tiny Passenger Car Station beside the market, from where *sŏrng·tăa·ou* (passenger pick-up trucks) leave for Hongsa (40,000K, 1½ hours) between 2pm and 4pm.

extended excursions around the area, plus rafting on Nam Wa.

The park offers a variety of bungalows (two to seven people 300B to 2000B), and there is a nearby restaurant and basic shop.

To reach the national park by public transport you must first take a bus or *sŏrng·tăa·ou* (passenger pick-up truck) to Pua (50B, two hours, hourly from 7am to 5pm). Get off at the 7-Eleven then cross the highway to board one of the three daily *sŏrng·tăa·ou* (50B, 30 minutes) that depart at 7.30am, 9.30am and 11.30am.

UNDERSTAND THAILAND

Thailand Today

Smartphones everywhere, cars instead of motorcycles and the need for immigrant labour – there is no doubt about it, Thailand is getting richer. In 2011, the World Bank upgraded the country's category from a lower-middle income economy to an upper-middle income economy, a designation based on per capita gross national income (GNI). In 2012, Thailand's GNI was US$5210, more than double what it was a decade ago.

Yet cyclical political instability remains a lingering and legitimate threat to Thailand's economic success. Following the 2006 coup d'état (the 18th in 70 years), which ousted the then prime minister, Thaksin Shinawatra, there have been six prime ministers and an increasing sense of social division in Thai society.

Much of this is due to the sometimes-violent protests by the Yellow Shirts, made up of the educated elite aligned with the monarchy and the military, and the Red Shirts, comprised of the predominately rural-based supporters of the exiled Thaksin. In 2008, Yellow Shirt protestors shut down the country's major international airports for two weeks, and in 2010, opposition Red Shirt protestors staged a two-month siege of Bangkok's central shopping district that ended in violent clashes with the military. In late 2013 and early 2014, tensions flared yet again when Yellow Shirt protestors took to Bangkok's streets, taking over key parts of town and blocking parliamentary elections in an effort to force the Thaksin-linked government to stand down.

Thais in the political middle are fatigued from the political discord, which undermines a deep-seated sense of a unified 'Thainess' and a cultural aversion to displays of violence and anger.

On the upside, prospects for Thailand's border areas, formerly irksome hot spots of instability, are starting to look more positive. At the end of 2015, the Asean Economic Community (AEC) united the association's 10 Southeast Asian countries into a liberalised marketplace where goods, services, capital and labour are shared across borders with little or no country-specific impediments. Open borders and improved infrastructure between Thailand's neighbouring countries have already come as a result of the AEC. Although Thailand's lengthy border with Myanmar (Burma) remains home to an estimated 130,000 refugees, there's hope that Myanmar's recent moves towards democracy, coupled with a lull in sectarian conflict, may finally allow some refugees to return home.

In 2016 a much-needed infrastructure investment plan was announced to help bolster the economic downturn. Tourism continues to be the bright spot in the economy.

A New Constitution

Thailand ratified a draft version of its 20th constitution on 7 August 2016 by popular vote. The new constitution dilutes democracy in the kingdom and gives formal governing powers to the military. The 250-member upper house (Senate) will be solely appointed with no direct elections and seats reserved for the military. There is also a provision for an unelected council to have authority to remove an elected government and for the Senate to appoint a prime minister. The military-drafted constitution was described by the regime as a road map to democracy and a stable, corruption-free government.

A Nation in Mourning

On 13 October 2016, the beloved King Bhumibol Adulyadej (Rama IX) passed away at the age of 88 after many years of failing health. Claiming a 70-year reign, King Bhumibol was the world's longest-serving monarch and the only king that the majority of the Thai population had ever known. He was regarded as a national father figure and benevolent ruler undertaking many poverty-alleviation programs during his lifetime.

The country entered into a state-mandated and personal grieving period. The government requested a month-long hiatus from 'joyful' events (concerts, parties, festivals, football matches and the like). Even Thailand's sex-tourism industry obliged with curtailed hours and no scantily clad promoters. Civil servants were ordered to wear black clothing for one year. Large crowds collected in public spaces and in processions to express their grief. The demand for mourning clothes outpaced supply and large bubbling vats for clothes dying popped up around Bangkok. The government also supplied eight million free black shirts to low-income people.

History

Rise of Thai Kingdoms

It is believed that the first Thais migrated here from modern-day Yunnan and Guangxi, China, settling into small riverside farming communities.

By the 13th and 14th centuries, what is considered the first Thai kingdom, Sukhothai, began to chip away at the crumbling Angkor empire. The third Sukhothai king, Ramkhamhaeng, developed a Thai writing system and built Angkor-inspired temples that defined early Thai art.

Sukhothai was soon eclipsed by another emerging power, Ayuthaya, which was established in present-day Thailand's central plains in 1350. This new centre developed into a cosmopolitan port on the Asian trade route courted by European nations attracted to the region for commodities and potential colonies, though the small nation managed to thwart foreign takeovers. For

A NEW KING

After a brief mourning period, the late king's son, the crown prince, ascended the throne as King Maha Vajiralongkorn (Rama X) on 1 December 2016. His first official act as monarch was to issue pardons or sentence reductions to 100,000 prisoners as an act of mercy. Under Thailand's constitutional monarchy, the king oversees the Crown Property Bureau, which owns approximately US$50 billion in assets, and a regiment of the Royal Guard. There is also a close relationship between the palace and the Thai military, which currently has control over the government.

It is unclear what kind of monarch he will be and if he will measure up to the larger-than-life persona of his father. Prior to his coronation, the new king, who is 64 years old and three times divorced, was not favorably viewed due to a variety of personal scandals and a jet-setting lifestyle. He spends most of his free time in Germany with his girlfriend – an arrangement that Thais aren't used to seeing from their king. But due to strict lèse-majesté laws, the Thai public is reluctant to express candid sentiments and they are hopeful for stability and decorum.

400 years Ayuthaya dominated most of present-day Thailand until the Burmese destroyed the capital in 1767.

The Thais eventually rebuilt their capital in present-day Bangkok and established the Chakri dynasty, which continues to occupy the throne today. As Western imperialism marched across the region, King Mongkut (Rama IV; r 1851–68) and his son and successor King Chulalongkorn (Rama V; r 1868–1910) successfully steered Thailand into the modern age without becoming a colonial vassal.

A Struggling Democracy

In 1932 a peaceful coup converted Thailand into a constitutional monarchy loosely based on the British model. Nearly half a century of political chaos followed. During the mid-20th century, a series of anticommunist military dictators wrestled each other for power, successfully suppressing democratic representation and civil rights. Student protests in the 1970s called for a reinstatement of a constitution and the end of military rule. In October 1976, a demonstration on the campus of Thammasat University in Bangkok was quashed by the military, resulting in deaths and injuries. Many activists went underground to join armed communist insurgency groups hiding in the northeast.

In the 1980s and 1990s there were slow steps towards democracy and even a return to a civilian government. During these tumultuous times, Rama IX defined a new political role for the monarchy, as a paternal figure who restrained excesses in the interests of all Thais.

ETIQUETTE

Thais are generally very understanding and hospitable, but there are some important taboos and social conventions.

Monarchy Never disrespect the royal family with disparaging remarks. Treat objects depicting the king (like money) with respect. Stand when the national and king's anthems are played. Since the passing of the king and the crowning of the new king, Thais and the authorities are on high alert for disrespectful behaviour towards the monarchy and national mourning ceremonies.

Temples Wear clothing that covers to your knees and elbows. Remove your shoes when you enter a temple building. Sit with your feet tucked behind you to avoid pointing the bottom of your feet at Buddha images. Women should never touch a monk or a monk's belongings; step out of the way on footpaths and don't sit next to them on public transport.

Modesty At the beach, avoid public nudity or topless sunbathing. Cover-up going to and from the beach.

Save face Never get into an argument with a Thai. It is better to smile through any conflict.

Economic & Political Roller Coaster

During the 1990s, Thailand was one of the so-called tiger economies that imploded in 1997, leading to a recession that lasted nearly three years. Thailand's convalescence progressed remarkably well and it pulled an 'early exit' from the International Monetary Fund's loan package in mid-2003.

The ambitious and charismatic billionaire Thaksin Shinawatra became prime minister in 2001 on a populist platform. He delivered on his promises for affordable health care and village development funds, which won him diehard support among the working class, especially in the impoverished northeast.

He and his party swept to victory in the 2005 election but his popularity plummeted due to a host of corruption charges. Rumours of his unabated ambitions – to interrupt or even usurp the eventual transfer of the crown from father to son – filtered into the general public, sparking mass protests organised by political rivals and those viewed as loyal to the crown. Behind the scenes Thaksin had earned very powerful enemies as he attempted to eradicate the role that the military continued to play in the government by replacing key appointments with his own loyalists.

On 19 September 2006, army chief Sonthi Boonyaratglin led a bloodless military coup, forcing Thaksin into exile. Political and social instability dominated the next five years, culminating in the 2011 election victory of the Pheu Thai Party, headed by Thaksin's younger sister, Yingluck Shinawatra. In 2013, an effort by Yingluck's government to grant amnesty to her brother, thus ostensibly allowing him to return to Thailand, infuriated the opposition, who took to the streets. Months-long blockades of central

Bangkok followed, which a violence-prone snap election in early 2014 failed to disperse.

People & Culture

People

Thais are master chatters and will have a shopping list of questions: where are you from, are you married, do you have children? Occasionally they get more curious and want to know how much you weigh or how much money you make; these questions to a Thai are matters of public record and aren't considered impolite.

Thais are laid-back, good-natured people who live by a philosophy of *sà·nùk* (fun), and every task is measured on the *sà·nùk* meter. Thais believe strongly in the concept of 'saving face', that is, avoiding confrontation and endeavouring not to embarrass themselves or other people. All relationships follow simple lines of social rank defined by age, wealth, status, and personal and political power.

About 75% of citizens are ethnic Thais, further divided by geography (north, central, south and northeast). Each group speaks its own Thai dialect and to an extent practises regional customs. Politically and economically the central Thais are dominant.

People of Chinese ancestry, many of whom have been in Thailand for generations, make up over 14% of the population. Other large minority groups include Vietnamese in the east, Khmer in parts of the northeast, Lao spread throughout the north and northeast, and Muslim Malays in the far south. Smaller non-Thai-speaking groups include the hill tribes living in the northern mountains.

CLASSIC THAI MOVIES

- *6ixtynin9* (1997)
- *Yam Yasothon* (2005)
- *Ruang Rak Noi Nid Mahasan* (*Last Life in the Universe*; 2003)
- *Fah Talai Jone* (*Tears of the Black Tiger*; 2000)
- *Mekhong Sipha Kham Deuan Sip-et* (*Mekong Full Moon Party*; 2002)
- *Uncle Boonmee Who Can Recall His Past Lives* (2010)

Religion

Country, family and daily life are all married to Theravada Buddhism (as opposed to the Mahayana schools found in East Asia and the Himalaya). Every Thai male is expected to become a monk for a short period in his life since a family earns great merit when a son 'takes robe and bowl'.

More evident than the philosophical aspects of Buddhism is the everyday fusion with animist rituals. Monks are consulted to determine an auspicious date for a wedding or the likelihood of success for a business. Spirit houses are constructed outside buildings and homes to encourage the guardian spirits to bring good fortune to the site. Food, drink and furniture are all offered to the spirits to smooth daily life.

Roughly 95% of the population practises Buddhism, but there is a significant Muslim community, especially in southern Thailand.

Arts

Classical central Thai music features an incredible array of textures and subtleties, hair-raising tempos and pastoral melodies. Among the more common instruments is the *pèe*, a woodwind instrument with a reed mouthpiece; it is heard prominently at Thai boxing matches. A bowed instrument, similar to examples played in China and Japan, is called the *sor*. The *rá·nâht èhk* is a bamboo-keyed percussion instrument resembling the Western xylophone, while the *klòo·i* is a wooden flute. This traditional orchestra originated as an accompaniment to classical dance-drama and shadow theatre, but these days it can be heard at temple fairs and concerts.

In the north and northeast there are several popular wind instruments with multiple reed pipes, which function basically like a mouth organ. Chief among these is the *kaan*, which originated in Laos; when played by an adept musician, it sounds like a rhythmic, churning calliope organ.

The best example of modern Thai music is the rock group Carabao, which has been performing for more than 30 years. Another major influence was a 1970s group called Caravan. It created a modern Thai folk style known as *pleng pêu·a chee·wít* (songs for life), which features political and environmental topics. In the 1990s, a respectable alt-rock scene emerged thanks to the likes of Modern Dog and Loso.

On an international scale, Thailand has probably distinguished itself more in traditional religious sculpture than in any other art form. Thailand's most famous sculptural output has been its bronze Buddha images, coveted the world over for their originality and grace.

Temple architecture symbolises elements of the religion. A steeply pitched roof system tiled in green, gold and red represents the Buddha (the Teacher), the Dhamma (Dharma in Sanskrit; the Teaching) and the Sangha (the fellowship of followers of the Teaching).

The traditional Thai theatre consists of dance-dramas using either human dancers or puppets to act out the plot. *Kŏhn* is formal masked dance-drama depicting scenes from the *Ramakian* (the Thai version of India's *Ramayana*) and originally performed only for the royal court; *lá·kon* is a general term covering several types of dance-dramas (usually for nonroyal occasions), as well as Western theatre; *lí·gair* is a partly improvised, often bawdy folk play featuring dancing, comedy, melodrama and music; and *lá·kon lék* is puppet theatre.

BOOKS

- *Chronicle of Thailand* (2010; William Warren and Nicholas Grossman)
- *Sacred Tattoos of Thailand* (2011; Joe Cummings)
- *Very Thai* (2013; Philip Cornwell-Smith)
- *The Arts of Thailand* (1998; Steve Van Beek)
- *Thai Folk Wisdom: Contemporary Takes on Traditional Proverbs* (2010; Tulaya Pornpiriyakulchai and Jane Vejjajiva)

Food & Drink

Welcome to a country where it is cheaper and tastier to eat out than to cook at home. Markets, pushcart vendors, makeshift stalls, open-air restaurants – prices stay low and cooks become famous in all walks of life for a particular dish.

Take a walk through the day markets to see mounds of clay-coloured pastes moulded into pyramids like art supplies. These are the backbone for Thai *gaang* (curries) and are made of finely ground herbs and seasonings. The paste is taken to home kitchens and thinned with coconut milk and decorated with vegetables and meat to make a meal. Although it is the consistency of soup, *gaang* is ladled onto a plate of rice instead of eaten directly out of the bowl.

For breakfast and for snacks, Thais nosh on *gŏo·ay đĕe·o*, rice-noodle soup with chicken or pork and vegetables. There are two primary types of noodles to choose from: *sên lék* (thin) and *sên yài* (wide and flat). Before you dig in, add to taste a few teaspoons of the provided spices: dried red chilli, sugar, fish sauce and vinegar. Now you have the true taste of Thailand in front of you.

Not sure what to order at some of the popular dinner restaurants? Reliable favourites are *yam Ꝑlah mèuk* (spicy squid salad with mint leaves, coriander and Chinese celery), *đôm yam gûng* (a tart, herbal soup with prawns, often translated as 'hot and sour soup') or its sister *đôm kàh gài* (coconut soup with chicken and galangal).

Thais are social eaters: meals are rarely taken alone and dishes are meant to be shared. Usually a small army of plates will be placed in the centre of the table, with individual servings of rice in front of each diner. The protocol goes like this: ladle a spoonful of food at a time onto your plate of rice. Using the spoon like a fork and your fork like a knife, steer the food (with the fork) onto your spoon, which enters your mouth.

Environment

Like all countries with a high population density, there is enormous pressure on Thailand's ecosystems: 50 years ago about 70% of the countryside was forest, it's now 28%. In response to environmental degradation, the Thai government has created a large number of protected areas since the 1970s. Following devastating floods, exacerbated by soil erosion, logging was banned in 1989.

Though Thailand has a better record than most of its neighbours at protecting endangered species, corruption hinders the efforts and the country is a popular conduit for the illegal wildlife trade.

SURVIVAL GUIDE

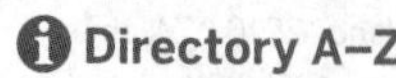

Directory A–Z

ACCOMMODATION

Thailand offers a wide variety of good-value accommodation. The budget range runs from around 200B for basic rooms (shared bathrooms and fan cooled), while for 400B you'll get air-con and private bathroom. In Bangkok and Chiang Mai, the midrange begins at about 1000B and has become more stylish and interesting these days. In the rest of the country you'll start getting midrange quality at around 600B but the hotels tend to be old and poorly maintained. Top end in small towns starts above 1500B and in Bangkok above 3000B. Prices listed in this chapter are high-season rates.

Bangkok & Chiang Mai

$ less than 1000B

$$ 1000B–3000B

$$$ more than 3000B

Elsewhere

$ less than 600B

$$ 600B–1500B

$$$ more than 1500B

CUSTOMS REGULATIONS

The **customs department** (nationwide 02 667 6000; www.customs.go.th) maintains a helpful website with specific information about customs regulations for travellers. Thailand allows the following items to enter duty-free:

- reasonable amount of personal effects (clothing and toiletries)
- professional instruments
- 200 cigarettes
- 1L of wine or spirits
- Thailand prohibits the import of the following items:
- firearms and ammunition (unless registered in advance with the police department)
- illegal drugs
- pornographic media

When leaving Thailand, you must obtain an export licence for any antique reproductions or newly cast Buddha images. Submit two front-view photos of the object(s), a photocopy of your passport, the purchase receipt and the object(s) in question to the **Office of the National Museum** (Map p416; 02 224 7493, 02 224 1370; National Museum, 4 Th Na Phra That; 9am-4pm Tue-Fri; Chang Pier, Maharaj Pier, Phra Chan Tai Pier). Allow four days for the application and inspection process to be completed.

EMBASSIES & CONSULATES

Foreign embassies are located in Bangkok; some nations also have consulates in Chiang Mai, Pattaya, Phuket or Songkhla.

Australian Embassy (Map p422; 02 344 6300; http://thailand.embassy.gov.au; 37 Th Sathon Tai/South, Bangkok; 8.30am-4.30pm Mon-Fri; M Lumphini exit 2)

Cambodian Embassy (Map p404; 02 957 5851; 518/4 Soi Ramkhamhaeng 39, Th Pracha Uthit, Bangkok; 8.30am-noon & 2-5pm Mon-Fri; M Phra Ram 9 exit 3 & taxi) Consulate in Sa Kaew.

Canadian Embassy Bangkok (02 646 4300; www.thailand.gc.ca; 15th fl, Abdulrahim Pl, 990 Th Phra Ram IV, Bangkok; 9am-noon Mon-Fri; M Si Lom exit 2, S Sala Daeng exit 4); **Chiang Mai** (05 385 0147; 151 Superhighway, Tambon Tahsala; 9am-noon Mon-Fri)

Chinese Embassy Bangkok (Map p404; 02 245 0888; www.chinaembassy.or.th/eng; 57 Th Ratchadaphisek, Bangkok; 9am-noon & 3-4pm Mon-Fri); **Bangkok Visa Centre** (02 207 5888; www.visaforchina.org; 5th fl, Thanapoom Tower, 1550 Th Phetchaburi Mai; 9am-3pm Mon-Fri; M Makkasan); **Chiang Mai** (Map p464; 05 328 0618; http://chiangmai.china-consulate.org; 111 Th Chang Lor, Tambon Haiya; 9-11.30am & 3-4pm Mon-Fri); Consulate in Songkhla.

Danish Embassy (Map p404; 02 343 1100; http://thailand.um.dk; 10 Soi 1, Th Sathon Tai, Bangkok; 10am-noon & 1-3pm Mon-Thu) Consulate in Phuket.

French Embassy Bangkok (Map p404; 02 657 5100; www.ambafrance-th.org; 35 Soi 36/Rue de Brest, Th Charoen Krung, Bangkok; 8.30am-noon Mon-Fri; Oriental Pier); **Chiang Mai** (Map p464; 053 281466; 138 Th Charoen Prathet; 10am-noon Mon-Fri) Consulates in Chiang Rai, Phuket and Pattaya.

German Embassy (Map p404; 02 287 9000; www.bangkok.diplo.de; 9 Th Sathon Tai/South, Bangkok; 7.30-11.30am Mon-Fri; M Lumphini exit 2) Consulates in Chiang Mai, Pattaya and Phuket.

Indian Embassy Bangkok (Map p426; 02 258 0300; www.indianembassy.in.th; 46 Soi 23, Th Sukhumvit, Bangkok; 9am-noon & 3-4.30pm Mon-Fri); **Bangkok Visa Centre** (Map p426; 02 258 0684; www.indiavisathai.com; IVS Global Services, 10th fl, PS Tower, 36/28 Soi 21/Asoke, Th Sukhumvit, Bangkok; 8.30am-2pm & 4.30-5.30pm Mon-Fri); **Chiang Mai** (off Map p464; 05 324 3066; 33/1 Th Thung Hotel, Chiang Mai; 9am-noon Mon-Fri)

Indonesian Embassy (Map p412; 02 252 3135; www.kemlu.go.id/bangkok; 600-602 Th Phetchaburi, Bangkok; 9am-noon & 2-3pm Mon-Fri) Consulate in Songkhla.

Irish Embassy (Map p412; ☎02 016 1360; www.dfa.ie/irish-embassy/thailand/; 12th fl, 208 Th Witthayu/Wireless Rd, Bangkok; ⏲8.30am-12.30pm Mon-Fri; Ⓢ Phloen Chit exit 1)

Israeli Embassy (Map p426; ☎02 204 9200; http://embassies.gov.il/bangkok-en; 25th fl, Ocean Tower 2, 75 Soi 19, Th Sukhumvit, Bangkok; ⏲9am-noon Mon-Fri)

Japanese Embassy Bangkok (Map p404; ☎02 207 8500; www.th.emb-japan.go.jp; 177 Th Witthayu/Wireless Rd; ⏲8.30am-noon & 1.30-3.45pm Mon-Fri); **Bangkok Visa Centre** (Map p422; ☎02 632 9801; http://japan-visa-center.co.th; Ste 1001, 10th fl, Yada Bldg, 56 Th Silom; ⏲appointment only; BTS Sala Daeng); **Chiang Mai** (off Map p464; ☎05 320 3367; Ste 104-107, Airport Business Park, 90 Th Mahidol, Chiang Mai)

Laotian Embassy (Map p404; ☎02 539 6667; 502/1-3 Soi Sahakarnpramoon, Th Pracha Uthit/Soi Ramkhamhaeng 39, Bangkok; ⏲8am-noon & 1-4pm Mon-Fri; Ⓜ Phra Ram 9 exit 3 & taxi)

Malaysian Embassy (☎02 629 6800; www.kln.gov.my/web/tha_bangkok/home; 33-35 Th Sathon Tai/South, Bangkok; ⏲8am-4pm Mon-Fri; Ⓜ Lumphini exit 2) Consulate in Songkhla.

Myanmar Embassy (Map p422; ☎02 233 7250; www.myanmarembassybkk.com; 132 Th Sathon Neua/North, Bangkok; ⏲9am-noon & 1-3pm Mon-Fri; Ⓢ Surasak exit 3)

Netherlands Embassy (Map p412; ☎02 309 5200; http://thailand.nlembassy.org; 15 Soi Ton Son; ⏲8.30am-noon & 1.30-4.30pm Mon-Thu, 8.30-11.30am Fri; Ⓢ Chit Lom exit 4)

New Zealand Embassy (Map p412; ☎02 254 2530; www.nzembassy.com/thailand; 14th fl, M Thai Tower, All Seasons Pl, 87 Th Witthayu/Wireless Rd, Bangkok; ⏲8am-noon & 1-2.30pm Mon-Fri; Ⓢ Phloen Chit exit 5)

Philippine Embassy (Map p426; ☎02 259 0139; www.bangkokpe.dfa.gov.ph; 760 Th Sukhumvit, Bangkok; ⏲8.30am-4.30pm Mon-Fri)

Russian Embassy (Map p422; ☎02 234 2012; www.thailand.mid.ru; 78 Th Sap, Th Surawong, Bangkok; ⏲9-11.45am Mon, Tue, Thu & Fri) Consulates in Pattaya and Phuket.

Singaporean Embassy (Map p422; ☎02 348 6700; www.mfa.gov.sg/bangkok; 129 Th Sathon Tai, Bangkok; ⏲9.30-11.30am & 1.30-4.30pm Mon-Fri)

South African Embassy (Map p412; ☎02 659 2900; www.dirco.gov.za/bangkok; 12th A fl, M Thai Tower, All Seasons Pl, 87 Th Witthayu/Wireless Rd, Bangkok; ⏲8am-4.30pm Mon-Thu, to 2pm Fri)

Spanish Embassy (Map p426; ☎02 661 8284; http://es.embassyinformation.com; 23rd fl, Lake Ratchada Office Complex, 193 Th Ratchadaphisek, Bangkok; ⏲8.30am-3.30pm Mon-Fri)

Swiss Embassy (Map p412; ☎02 674 6900; www.eda.admin.ch/bangkok; 35 Th Witthayu/Wireless Rd, Bangkok; ⏲9-11.30am Mon-Fri)

UK Embassy (Map p412; ☎02 305 8333; www.gov.uk/government/world/organisations/british-embassy-bangkok; 14 Th Witthayu/Wireless Rd, Bangkok; ⏲8am-4.30pm Mon-Thu, to 1pm Fri; Ⓢ Phloen Chit exit 5)

US Embassy Bangkok (Map p412; ☎02 205 4000; http://bangkok.usembassy.gov; 95 Th Witthayu/Wireless Rd, Bangkok; ⏲8am-4pm Mon-Fri; Ⓢ Phloen Chit exit 5); **Chiang Mai** (Map p464; ☎05 310 7700; http://chiangmai.usconsulate.gov; 387 Th Wichayanon)

Vietnamese Embassy (Map p412; ☎02 251 3552; www.vietnamembassy-thailand.org; 83/1 Th Witthayu/Wireless Rd, Bangkok; ⏲9-11.30am & 2-4.30pm Mon-Fri)

FOOD

The indicators in this chapter's restaurant reviews show how much you should expect to pay for a main dish in Thailand.

THAILAND'S IMMIGRATION OFFICES

The following are two immigration offices where visa extensions and other formalities can be addressed. Remember to dress in your Sunday best when doing official business in Thailand and do all visa business yourself (don't hire a third party). For all types of visa extensions, bring along two passport-sized photos and one copy each of the photo and visa pages of your passport.

Bangkok Immigration Office (☎02 141 9889; www.bangkok.immigration.go.th/intro1.html; Bldg B, Government Centre, Soi 7, Th Chaeng Watthana; ⏲8.30am-noon & 1-4.30pm Mon-Fri; Ⓜ Chatuchak Park exit 2 & taxi, Ⓢ Mo Chit exit 3 & taxi) Visa extensions are filed at this office.

Chiang Mai Immigration Office (☎053 142788; Promenada Resort Mall, 192-193 Tambon Tasala, ground fl, Bldg A; ⏲8.30am-4.30pm Mon-Fri) As of December 2016, Chiang Mai's foreign services office has temporarily moved to Promenada Mall while the government immigration facility (Rte 1141/Th Mahidol) is undergoing renovation.

$ less than 150B
$$ 150B–350B
$$$ more than 350B

LGBTIQ TRAVELLERS

Thai culture is relatively tolerant of both male and female homosexuality. There is a fairly prominent LGBT scene in Bangkok. With regard to dress or mannerism, the LGBT community are generally accepted without comment. However, public displays of affection – whether heterosexual or homosexual – are frowned upon.

It's worth noting that, perhaps because Thailand is still a relatively conservative place, lesbians generally adhere to rather strict gender roles. Overtly 'butch' lesbians, called *tom* (from 'tomboy'), typically have short hair, and wear men's clothing. Femme lesbians refer to themselves as *dêe* (from 'lady'). Visiting lesbians who don't fit into one of these categories may find themselves met with confusion.

Utopia (www.utopia-asia.com) posts lots of Thailand information for gay and lesbian visitors and publishes a guidebook to the kingdom.

INSURANCE

A travel-insurance policy to cover theft, loss and medical problems is a good idea. Policies offer differing medical-expense options. There is a wide variety of policies available, so check the small print. Be sure that the policy covers ambulances or an emergency flight home. Some policies specifically exclude 'dangerous activities', which can include scuba diving, motorcycling and even trekking. A locally acquired motorcycle licence is not valid under some policies. You may prefer a policy that pays doctors or hospitals directly rather than you having to pay on the spot and claim later. If you have to claim later, make sure you keep all documentation.

Worldwide travel insurance is available at www.lonelyplanet.com/travel-insurance. You can buy, extend and claim online any time – even if you're already on the road.

INTERNET ACCESS

Wi-fi is almost standard in guesthouses and cafes. Signal strength deteriorates in the upper floors of a multistorey building; you can always request a room near a router. Cellular data networks continue to expand and increase in capability.

LEGAL MATTERS

In general Thai police don't hassle foreigners, especially tourists. They usually go out of their way to avoid having to speak English with a foreigner, especially regarding minor traffic issues. Do be aware that some police divisions, especially on the Thai islands, might view foreigners and their legal infractions as a money-making opportunity.

One major exception is drugs, which most Thai police view as either a social scourge against which it's their duty to enforce the letter of the law, or an opportunity to make untaxed income via bribes.

If you are arrested for any offence, the police will allow you the opportunity to make a phone call, either to your embassy or consulate in Thailand if you have one, or to a friend or relative if not. There's a whole set of legal codes governing the length of time and the manner in which you can be detained before being charged or put on trial, but a lot of discretion is left to the police. In the case of foreigners the police are more likely to bend these codes in your favour. However, as with police worldwide, if you don't show respect you will make matters worse.

Thai law does not presume an indicted detainee to be either guilty or innocent but rather a 'suspect', whose guilt or innocence will be decided in court. Trials are usually speedy.

The **tourist police** (☎ 24hr 1155) can be very helpful in cases of arrest. Although they typically have no jurisdiction over the kinds of cases handled by regular cops, they may be able to help with translations or with contacting your embassy. You can call the hotline number 24 hours a day to lodge complaints or to request assistance with regards to personal safety.

MAPS

Google maps continue to improve with more site and street data for Thai cities. ThinkNet (www.thinknet.co.th) produces high-quality, bilingual city and country maps, including interactive-map CDs.

MONEY

ATMs & Credit Cards

Debit and ATM cards issued by a bank in your own country can be used at ATMs around Thailand to withdraw cash (in Thai baht only) directly from your account back home. ATMs are widespread throughout the country and can be relied on for the bulk of your spending cash.

The downside is that Thai ATMs charge a 200B foreign-transaction fee on top of whatever currency-conversion and out-of-network fees your home bank charges. Credit cards as well as debit cards can be used for purchases at some shops, hotels and restaurants. The most commonly accepted cards are Visa and MasterCard. American Express is typically only accepted at high-end hotels and restaurants.

Money Changers

Banks or private money changers offer the best foreign-exchange rates. When buying baht, US dollars is the most accepted currency, followed by British pounds and euros. Most banks charge a commission and duty for each travellers cheque cashed. Current exchange rates are posted at exchange counters.

PHOTOGRAPHY

Memory cards for digital cameras are widely available in the electronic sections of most shopping malls.

Be considerate when taking photographs of locals. Learn how to ask politely in Thai and wait for an embarrassed nod. In some of the regularly visited hill-tribe areas, be prepared for the photographed subject to ask for money in exchange for a picture. Other hill tribes will not allow you to point a camera at them.

POST

Thailand has a very efficient postal service and local postage is inexpensive. Typical provincial post offices open from 8.30am to 4.30pm weekdays and 9am to noon on Saturdays. Larger main post offices in provincial capitals may also be open for a half-day on Sundays.

PUBLIC HOLIDAYS

Government offices and banks close their doors on the following public holidays. For the precise dates of lunar holidays, see the Events & Festivals page of the Tourism Authority of Thailand's website (www.tourismthailand.org/Events-and-Festivals).

1 January New Year's Day
February (date varies) Makha Bucha Day, Buddhist holy day
6 April Chakri Day, commemorating the founder of the Chakri dynasty, Rama I
13–15 April Songkran Festival, traditional Thai New Year and water festival
1 May Labour Day
5 May Coronation Day
July/August (date varies) Asanha Bucha, Buddhist holy day
July/August (date varies) Khao Phansa, beginning of the Buddhist 'lent'
12 August Queen's Birthday
23 October Chulalongkorn Day
5 December Commemoration of Late King Bhumiphol/Father's Day
10 December Constitution Day
31 December New Year's Eve

SAFE TRAVEL

Thailand is not a dangerous country, but there are a few common scams and things to watch out for.

Try not to get into an argument with a Thai, especially if alcohol is involved. While foreigners might see a verbal argument as sport, Thais view it as a loss of face and have been known to respond with excessive and unpredictable violence. Especially untrustworthy are the off-duty police officers who are still armed even in civilian settings; there have been several incidents of altercations between foreigners and off-duty police, typically at bars, that have resulted in gun homicides.

Women also need to take care of themselves when travelling or visiting bars alone. Flirtation for the fun of it can often be misunderstood by Thais and can result in unwanted advances or unpredictable retribution if interest isn't mutual.

TELEPHONE

The telephone country code for Thailand is ☎66 and is used when calling the country from abroad. All Thai telephone numbers are preceded by a '0' if you're dialling domestically (the '0' is omitted when calling from overseas). After the initial '0', the next three numbers represent the provincial area code, which is now integral to the telephone number. If the initial '0' is followed by an '8' or a '9', then you're dialling a mobile phone.

The standard International Direct Dial prefix is ☎001. Economy rates are available with ☎007, ☎008 and ☎009, all of which use Voice over Internet Protocol (VoIP), with varying but adequate sound quality.

Dial ☎100 for operator-assisted international calls or reverse-charges (or collect) calls. Alternatively contact your long-distance carrier for their overseas operator number, a toll-free call, or try ☎001 9991 2001 from a CAT phone and ☎1 800 000 120 from a TOT phone.

The easiest phone option in Thailand is to acquire a mobile (cell) phone equipped with a local SIM card. Thailand is on the GSM network and mobile-phone providers include AIS (1 2 Call), DTAC and True Move. You have two phone options: you can buy a mobile phone in Thailand at one of the urban shopping malls or at phone stores near the markets in provincial towns.

Or you can use an imported phone that isn't SIM-locked (and one that supports the GSM network). To get started, buy a SIM card of a particular carrier, which includes an assigned telephone number. Once your phone is SIM-enabled you can buy minutes with prepaid phonecards. SIM cards and refill cards (usually sold in 300B to 500B denominations) can be bought from 7-Elevens throughout the country. Thailand finally has a 3G network and True Move is offering 4G LTE coverage in Bangkok.

TIME

Thailand's time zone is seven hours ahead of GMT/UTC (London).

TOILETS

Increasingly the Asian-style squat toilet is less common in Thailand. There are still specimens in rural places, but the Western-style toilet is becoming more prevalent and appears wherever foreign tourists can be found.

Even in places where sit-down toilets are installed, the septic system may not be designed to take toilet paper. In such cases there will be a waste basket where you're supposed to place used toilet paper and feminine hygiene products. Some modern toilets also come with a small spray hose – Thailand's version of the bidet.

TOURIST INFORMATION

The government-operated tourist information and promotion service, **Tourism Authority of Thailand** (TAT; ☎ nationwide call centre 1672; www.tourismthailand.org), was founded in 1960 and produces excellent pamphlets on sightseeing. TAT's head office is in Bangkok and there are 35 regional offices throughout the country; check the website for contact information.

VISAS

The **Ministry of Foreign Affairs** (☎ 02 203 5000; www.mfa.go.th) oversees immigration and visa issues. There are frequent modifications of visa regulations so check the website or the nearest Thai embassy or consulate for application procedures and costs. The best online monitor is **Thaivisa** (www.thaivisa.com).

Thailand has visa-exemption and visa-on-arrival agreements with most nations (including European countries, Australia, New Zealand and the USA). Nationals from these countries can enter Thailand at no charge without prearranged documentation. Depending on nationality, these citizens are issued a 14- to 90-day visa exemption. Do note that for some nationalities, less time (15 days rather than 30 days) is given if arriving by land rather than air. Check the Ministry of Foreign Affairs for more details.

Without proof of an onward ticket and sufficient funds for your projected stay, you can be denied entry, but in practice this is a formality that is rarely checked.

If you plan to stay in Thailand longer than 30 days, you should apply for the 60-day tourist visa from a Thai consulate or embassy before your trip. Recent changes to this visa now allow multiple entries within a six-month period. Contact the nearest Thai embassy or consulate to obtain application procedures and determine fees for tourist visas.

Visa Extensions & Renewals

If you decide you want to stay longer than the allotted time, you can extend your visa by applying at any immigration office in Thailand. The usual fee for a visa extension is 1900B. Those issued with a standard stay of 15 or 30 days can extend their stay for 30 days if the extension is handled before the visa expires. The 60-day tourist visa can be extended by up to 30 days at the discretion of Thai immigration authorities.

Another visa-renewal option is to cross a land border. A new 15- or 30-day visa exemption, depending on the nationality, will be issued upon your return. Be aware that the authorities frown upon repeated 'visa runs' and discretion is up to the visa agent. After the 2014 coup, the military government ceased issuance of land visa exemptions for a period of time. Before undertaking this option, determine the current situation.

If you overstay your visa, the usual penalty is a fine of 500B per day, with a 20,000B limit. Fines can be paid at the airport, or in advance at an immigration office. If you've overstayed only one day, you don't have to pay. Children under 15 travelling with a parent do not have to pay the penalty.

Foreign residents in Thailand should arrange visa extensions at the immigration office closest to their in-country address.

VOLUNTEERING

There are many wonderful volunteering organisations in Thailand that provide meaningful work and cultural engagement. Volunteer Work Thailand (www.volunteerworkthailand.org) maintains a database of opportunities.

WOMEN TRAVELLERS

Attacks and rapes are not common in Thailand, but incidents do occur, especially when an attacker observes a vulnerable target: a drunk or solo woman. If you return home from a bar alone, be sure to have your wits about you. Avoid accepting rides from strangers late at night or travelling around in isolated areas by yourself – common-sense stuff that might escape your notice in a new environment filled with hospitable people.

Getting There & Away

Flights and tours can be booked online at www.lonelyplanet.com/bookings.

Entry procedures for Thailand, by air or by land, are straightforward: you'll have to show your passport, and you'll need to present completed arrival and departure cards.

AIR

Bangkok is the air-travel hub for mainland Southeast Asia and airfares are quite competitive. Carriers operating to the international destinations covered in this guide include:

Cambodia Angkor Air (☎ nationwide 02 655 4747; www.cambodiaangkorair.com) With flights linking Bangkok with Phnom Penh and Siem Reap.

Lao Airlines (☎ in Bangkok 02 236 9822; www.laoairlines.com) With flights linking Chiang Mai and Luang Prabang.

Qatar Airways (☎ nationwide 02 259 2701; www.qatarairways.com) With flights between Bangkok and Hanoi.

Turkish Airlines (☎ in Bangkok 02 231 0300; www.turkishairlines.com) Links Bangkok and Ho Chi Minh City.

LAND

Border Crossings

Thailand shares land borders with Laos, Malaysia, Cambodia and Myanmar (Burma). Land travel between all of these countries can be done at sanctioned border crossings. With improved highways and new bridges, it is also easier to travel from Thailand to China via Laos.

Cambodia Cambodian tourist visas are available at the border for US$30. Bring a passport photo and ignore the runner boys who want to issue a health certificate or other paperwork for additional fees.

Laos It is fairly hassle-free to cross into Laos from northern and northeastern Thailand. Lao tourist visas (US$30 to US$42) can be obtained on arrival and applications require a passport photo. Try to have crisp, clean bills. Direct buses that link major towns on both sides of the border make the border towns just a formality stop. Occasionally Lao officials will ask for an overtime fee.

Getting Around

AIR

Hopping around the country by air continues to be affordable. Most routes originate from Bangkok (both Don Mueang and Suvarnabhumi International Airports), but Chiang Mai, Hat Yai, Ko Samui, Phuket and Udon Thani all have a few routes to other Thai towns.

Air Asia (☎ nationwide 02 515 9999; www.airasia.com) Within northern Thailand, Air Asia flies between Bangkok's Don Mueang International Airport and Chiang Mai, Chiang Rai, Nan and Phitsanulok.

Bangkok Airways (☎ nationwide 1771; www.bangkokair.com) With destinations in northern Thailand including Chiang Mai, Chiang Rai, Lampang, Mae Hong Son and Sukhothai.

BICYLE

Bicycles can usually be hired from guesthouses for as little as 50B per day, though they aren't always high-quality. A security deposit isn't usually required.

BOAT

The true Thai water transport is the *reu·a hăhng yow* (long-tail boat), so-called because the propeller is mounted at the end of a long driveshaft extending from the engine. The long-tail boats are a staple of transport on rivers and canals in Bangkok and neighbouring provinces, and between islands.

Between the mainland and small, less touristed islands, the standard craft is a wooden boat, 8m to 10m long, with an inboard engine, a wheelhouse and a simple roof to shelter passengers and cargo. To more popular destinations, faster hovercraft (jetfoils) and speedboats are the norm.

BUS & MINIVAN

The bus network in Thailand is prolific and reliable. The Thai government subsidises the Transport Company *(bò·rí·sàt kŏn sòng)*, usually abbreviated to Baw Khaw Saw (BKS). Every city and town in Thailand linked by bus has a BKS station, even if it's just a patch of dirt by the side of the road.

By far the most reliable bus companies in Thailand are the ones that operate out of the BKS stations. In some cases the companies are entirely state owned; in others they are private concessions.

We do not recommend using bus companies that operate directly out of tourist centres, such as Bangkok's Th Khao San, because of repeated instances of theft and commission-seeking stops. Be sure to be aware of bus scams and other common problems.

For some destinations, minivans are superseding buses. Minivans are run by private companies and because their vehicles are smaller, they can depart from the market (instead of the out-of-town bus stations) and in some cases will deliver guests directly to their hotel. Just don't sit in the front – that way you can avoid watching the driver's daredevil techniques!

CAR & MOTORCYCLE

Cars, 4WDs or vans can be rented in most large cities. Always verify (ask to see the dated documents) that the vehicle is insured for liability before signing a contract. An International Driving Permit is necessary to drive vehicles in Thailand, but this is rarely enforced for motorcycle hire.

Thais drive on the left-hand side of the road (most of the time!). The main rule to be aware of is that smaller vehicles always yield to bigger ones.

Motorcycle travel is a popular way to get around Thailand. Dozens of places along the guesthouse circuit rent motorbikes for as little as 150B a day. Motorcycle rental usually requires that you leave your passport, and many provinces require you to wear a helmet.

LOCAL TRANSPORT

Motorcycle Taxi

Many cities in Thailand have *mor·đeu·sai ráp jâhng*, motorcycle taxis that can be hired for short distances. If you're empty-handed or travelling with a small bag, they can't be beaten for transport in a pinch.

In most cities, you'll find motorcycle taxis clustered near street intersections. Usually they wear numbered jerseys. You'll need to establish the price beforehand.

Săhm·lór & Túk-túk

Săhm·lór are three-wheeled pedicabs that are typically found in small towns where traffic is light and old-fashioned ways persist.

The modern era's version of the human-powered *săhm·lór* is the motorised túk-túk. They're small utility vehicles, powered by screaming engines (usually LPG-powered), with a lot of flash and sparkle.

With either form of transport the fare must be established by bargaining before departure. In tourist centres, túk-túk drivers often grossly overcharge foreigners, so have a sense of how much the fare should be before soliciting a ride. Hotel staff are helpful in providing reasonable fare suggestions.

Sŏrng·tăa·ou

Sŏrng·tăa·ou (literally two rows) are small pick-ups with a row of seats down each side. In most towns *sŏrng·tăa·ou* serve as public buses running fixed routes.

TOURS

The better tour companies build their own Thailand itineraries from scratch and choose their local suppliers based on which best serve these itineraries. Many are now offering 'voluntourism' programs, which means that you might buy lunch for an orphanage, visit a hospital or teach an English class in addition to sightseeing. If you're looking for alternative travelling experiences, volunteering (p547) is also an option.

TRAIN

The **State Railway of Thailand** (☎1690; www.railway.co.th) has four main lines (northern, southern, northeastern and eastern) branching out from Bangkok. Trains are comfortable, but almost always slower and less frequent than buses.

Trains are often heavily booked, so it's wise to reserve well ahead, especially the Bangkok–Chiang Mai overnight trip. You can make bookings at any train station (English is usually spoken) and, for a small fee, through some Bangkok travel agencies.

First-class, 2nd-class and 3rd-class cabins are available on most trains, but each class varies considerably depending on the type of train (rapid, express or ordinary). First class is a private cabin. Second class has individually reclining seats; depending on the train, some cabins have air-con. Non-air-conditioned 3rd class is spartan with bench seating.

Overnight trains have sleeping berths in 1st and 2nd class. Single 1st-class cabins are not available, so if you're travelling alone you may be paired with another passenger.

Understand the Mekong Region

The Mekong Region Today

Just a generation ago, Cambodia, Laos and Vietnam were pariah states, scarred by decades of war and boycotted by much of the Western world. Despite the region's communist history, its leaders proved themselves to be open to Western economic models as they balanced Eastern communism with Western capitalism – today the bad old days seem but a footnote in history. Like the river that runs through it, the Mekong region is well and truly going places.

Best on Film

Apocalypse Now (1979) Francis Ford Coppola's masterpiece remains one of cinema's most savage indictments of war.

The Killing Fields (1984) Iconic film about the Khmer Rouge period, focusing on photographer Dith Pran's relationship with journalist Sidney Schanberg.

Platoon (1986) Based on the first-hand experiences of director Oliver Stone, following a young recruit to the Vietnam War.

Uncle Boonmee Who Can Recall His Past Lives (2010) Terminally ill Thai man explores ghosts of his past in Apichatpong Weerasethakul's Palme d'Or winner.

Best in Print

The Quiet American (Graham Greene; 1955) Seminal antiwar novel set in the 1950s as the French empire is collapsing.

The Lover (Marguerite Duras; 1984) Semiautobiographical tale of a young girl in love with a local scion in French-colonial Vietnam.

Phaic Tăn: Sunstroke on a Shoestring (2004; Tom Gleisner, Santo Cilauro and Rob Sitch) This ultimate spoof guidebook pokes fun at locals, travellers and even guidebook authors.

Come Together

Much of the Mekong region is closer than it's been for some time thanks to the Association of Southeast Asian Nations (Asean). The new Asean Economic Community (AEC) free-trade area unites the association's 10 Southeast Asian countries into a liberalised marketplace with streamlined customs and fewer restrictions on the movement of goods, services and skilled workers. Things are moving especially fast: major cross-border highways are being built; railroad tracks are being laid down or rehabilitated; new border posts are being installed and old ones upgraded; and airlines are expanding their interregional routes. Even the idea of a single-visa policy for foreign visitors to the region is gaining steam.

Big Brother

As the nations of the Mekong region draw closer together, China remains the elephant in the room. Beijing exerts extraordinary political and economic influence in Laos and Cambodia, as it spends some of its enormous surplus on infrastructure in these two countries. In return, Laos and Cambodia tend to support China's geopolitical aims – most notably its claims to the remote Spratly and Paracel Islands in the South China Sea. This rankles traditional Chinese foe Vietnam, which also claims parts of these islands.

Cambodia's tendency to prioritise its lucrative partnership with China over the greater goals of Asean, which supports Vietnam's claims, have divided the association. When an international court rejected China's South China Sea claims in July 2016, Cambodia joined China in rejecting the court's decision. In the same month, China announced plans to give Cambodia US$600 million in aid. Cambodia's close relationship with Vietnam, which helped Prime Minister Hun Sen and friends overthrow the Khmer Rouge in the 1970s, adds another layer of complexity.

Damming of the Mekong

The spirit of cooperation within Asean is also being compromised by the building of hydroelectric dams on the lower Mekong River in Laos. Together with Malaysian, Thai and Chinese firms, the government of Laos is pushing ahead with construction of close to a dozen dams, to add to the half-dozen that have been built since 2005. Hydropower has become a major contributor to Laos' economic growth, though is not without controversy, and some dams have raised significant environmental concerns.

Prominent among these is the Don Sahong dam under construction in the beautiful Si Phan Don (Four Thousand Islands) area of Laos, which, in addition to creating an eyesore, will negatively affect downstream fish stocks, according to the WWF and other environmental groups. A small pool of rare Irrawaddy dolphins just downstream from this dam faces possible extinction, while scientists are forecasting potentially devastating effects on two of the region's richest food sources: the Tonlé Sap lake in Cambodia and the Mekong Delta in Vietnam. According to the WWF, the food security of some 60 million people living in the Mekong basin is at risk. Activists have called for a halt in construction until concerns are fully addressed, but have so far been unsuccessful.

Season of Change

Over in Thailand, a politically tumultuous decade culminated in the death of the beloved King Bhumibol Adulyadej on 13 October 2016. The world's longest-serving monarch at his death, King Bhumibol was worshipped by his subjects and considered the lone stabilising influence on Thai politics, which has endured a revolving door of governments since billionaire Thaksin Shinawatra was overthrown as prime minister in a military coup in September 2006. The junta in charge since May 2014 has been criticised for its strong-armed approach, but is seen as a potential steadying force during the royal transition, which will see Prince Maha Vajiralongkorn crowned in late 2017. The junta looks set to stay in power at least until the royal transition is complete, which means elections may not happen until 2018.

The other country in the region facing a crucial election in 2018 is Cambodia. Although ostensibly democratic, Cambodia has effectively been under the rule of one party – Prime Minister Hun Sen's Cambodia People's Party (CPP) – since 1979. Since the controversial 2013 election, the CPP has launched a coordinated social-media campaign to burnish its image, while moving to dilute the rising popularity of the opposition Cambodia National Rescue Party (CNRP) by jailing about 20 CNRP officials or activists, according to human rights NGO Licadho. Observers worry that any hint of a CNRP victory in 2018 will lead to a wider, CPP-orchestrated crackdown in advance of the election.

POPULATION: **186.5M**

AREA: **1,262,165 SQ KM**

HIGHEST POINT: **MT FANSIPAN, VIETNAM (3144M)**

BIGGEST CITIES: **BANGKOK (9.3 MILLION), HO CHI MINH CITY (7.4 MILLION)**

if the Mekong region were 100 people

45 would be Vietnamese
22 would be Thai
10 would be Khmer
8 would be Lao
8 would be Chinese
7 would be Minority

belief systems

(% of population)

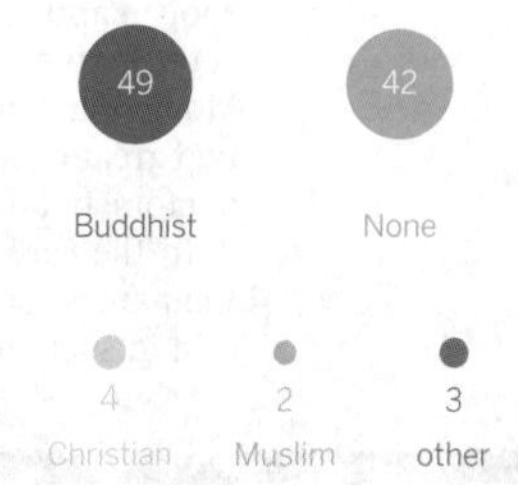

population per sq km

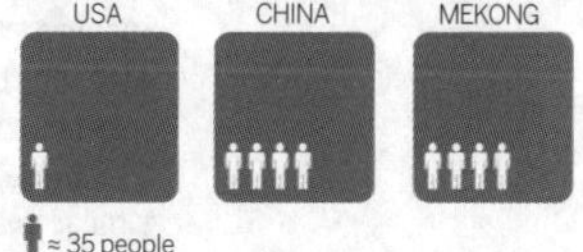

History

This vibrant region has a history as long and dramatic as the Mekong River that cuts through its heart. The Mekong played host to some of the most brutal wars of the 20th century and the bloodiest revolutions. However, calmer waters lie ahead, as the region has been relatively peaceful and stable for the first time in generations.

The Mekong Valley and Khorat Plateau were inhabited as far back as 10,000 years ago, and rice was grown in northeastern Thailand as early as 4000 BC. China, by contrast, was still growing millet at the time.

Early Empire

The history of this great region is also the history of two great civilisations colliding. China and India may be making headlines today as the emerging giants of the 21st century, but that's old news. They have long been great powers and have historically influenced the Mekong region, from art and architecture to language and religion.

Indian culture was disseminated through much of the Mekong region via contact with seafaring Indian merchants calling at trading settlements along the coast of present-day Thailand, Cambodia and Vietnam. Some of these settlements were part of nascent kingdoms, the largest of which was known as Funan to the Chinese, and occupied much of what is southeastern Cambodia today.

The Funanese constructed an elaborate system of canals both for transportation and the irrigation of rice. The principal port city of Funan was Oc-Eo in the Mekong Delta; archaeological excavations here reveal contact between Funan and Indonesia, Persia and even the Mediterranean.

Funan was famous for its refined art and architecture, and its kings embraced the worship of Hindu deities Shiva and Vishnu and, concurrently, Buddhism. The *linga* (phallic totem) was the focus of ritual and an emblem of kingly might, a feature that was to evolve further in the Angkorian cult of the god king.

Vietnam Under Occupation

The Chinese ruled Vietnam for 1000 years, introducing Confucianism, Taoism and Mahayana Buddhism to Vietnam, as well as a written character system. Meanwhile, the Indians brought Theravada Buddhism. Monks carried with them the scientific and medical knowledge of these two great civilisations, and Vietnam was soon producing its own great doctors, botanists and scholars.

In the early 10th century, the Tang dynasty in China collapsed. The Vietnamese seized the initiative and launched a revolt against Chinese rule in Vietnam. In 938, popular patriot Ngo Quyen finally vanquished

TIMELINE

4200 BC

Cave dwellers capable of making pots inhabit caves around Laang Spean; archaeological evidence suggests the vessels these people were making are similar to those made in Cambodia today.

c 2000 BC

The Bronze Age Dong Son culture emerges in the Red River Delta around Hanoi. It's renowned for its rice cultivation and the production of bronzeware, including drums and gongs.

c AD 100

The process of Indianisation begins in the Mekong region: the religions, language, sculpture and culture of India take root through maritime contact with Cambodia.

the Chinese armies at a battle on the Bach Dang River, ending a millennium of Chinese rule. However, it was not the last time the Vietnamese would tussle with their mighty northern neighbour.

From the 11th to 13th centuries, Vietnamese independence was consolidated under the enlightened emperors of the Ly dynasty. During the Ly dynasty many enemies, including the Chinese, the Khmer and the Cham – based out of the Champa kingdom in what is today southeastern Vietnam – launched attacks on Vietnam, but all were repelled.

The Rise of Chenia

From the 6th century the Funan kingdom's importance as a port of call declined, and Cambodia's population gradually settled along the Mekong and Tonlé Sap Rivers, where the majority remains today.

Chinese records refer to the rise of the Chenla empire, divided into 'water Chenla' (lower) and 'land Chenla' (upper). Water Chenla was located around Angkor Borei and the temple mount of Phnom Da; and land Chenla in the upper reaches of the Mekong River and east of Tonlé Sap lake, around Sambor Prei Kuk, one of the first great temple cities of the Mekong region.

What is certain is that the people of the lower Mekong were well known to the Chinese, and the region was becoming gradually more cohesive. Before long the fractured kingdoms of Chenla would merge to become the greatest empire in Southeast Asia.

The Khmer Empire

A popular place of pilgrimage for Khmers today is the sacred mountain of Phnom Kulen, to the northeast of Angkor, home to an inscription that tells us that in 802 Jayavarman II proclaimed himself a 'universal monarch', or a *devaraja* (god king). Jayavarman set out to bring the region under his control through alliances and conquests. He was the first monarch to rule all of what we call Cambodia today, and the first of a long succession of kings who presided over the Southeast Asian empire that was to leave the stunning legacy of Angkor.

The Romans of Asia

The Khmers built massive irrigation systems and a sophisticated network of highways to connect the outposts of their empire, much like the Romans did. Roads fanned out from Angkor, connecting the capital with satellite cities such as Ayuthaya and Phimai in Thailand and as far away as Wat Phu in southern Laos.

From 1113, King Suryavarman II embarked on another phase of expansion, waging wars against Champa and Vietnam. He is immortalised in Cambodia as the king who, in his devotion to the Hindu deity Vishnu, bequeathed the world the majestic temple of Angkor Wat.

There are few surviving contemporary accounts of Angkor, but Chinese emissary Chou Ta Kuan lived there in 1296 and his observations have been republished as *The Customs of Cambodia*, a fascinating insight into that period.

600

The first inscriptions are committed to stone in Cambodia in ancient Khmer, offering historians the first contemporary accounts of the pre-Angkorian period other than from Chinese sources.

802

Jayavarman II proclaims independence from Java, marking the start of the Khmer empire of Angkor, which controls much of the Mekong region from the 10th to 13th centuries.

938

The Chinese are expelled from Vietnam after 1000 years of occupation, as Ngo Quyen leads his people to victory in the battle of Bach Dang River, luring the Chinese ships onto sharpened stakes.

1049

Suryavarman I annexes the Dravati kingdom of Lopburi in Thailand and widens his control of Cambodia, stretching the empire to perhaps its greatest extent.

Southeast Asian kingdoms were not states in the modern sense, with fixed frontiers, but varied in their extent. Outlying *meuang* (principalities or city-states) might transfer their allegiance elsewhere when the centre was weak. This is why scholars prefer the term 'mandala', meaning 'circle of power'.

Enter Sandstone Man

Suryavarman II had brought Champa to heel and reduced it to vassal status. In 1177, the Chams struck back with a naval expedition up the Mekong and into Tonlé Sap lake. They took the city of Angkor by surprise and put King Dharanindravarman II to death. A year later a cousin of Suryavarman II gathered forces and defeated the Chams in another naval battle. The new leader was crowned Jayavarman VII in 1181.

A devout follower of Mahayana Buddhism, Jayavarman VII built the city of Angkor Thom and many other massive monuments visited by tourists around Angkor today. Immortalised in sandstone and on T-shirts, Jayavarman is deified by many Cambodians as their greatest leader, a populist who promoted equality, and a socially conscious leader who built schools and hospitals for his people.

The Fall

Some scholars maintain that decline was on the horizon at the time Angkor Wat was built, when the Angkorian empire was at the height of its remarkable productivity. There are indications that the irrigation network was overworked and slowly starting to silt up due to the massive deforestation that had taken place in the heavily populated areas to the north and east of Angkor.

Following the reign of Jayavarman VII, temple construction effectively ground to a halt, largely because public works quarried local sandstone into oblivion and the population was left exhausted. The state religion reverted to Hinduism for a century or more and outbreaks of iconoclasm saw Buddhist sculpture vandalised or altered.

The ascendent Thai kingdom of Sukhothai grew in strength and made repeated incursions into Angkor, finally sacking the city in 1431. During this period, perhaps drawn by the opportunities for sea trade with China and fearful of the increasingly bellicose Thais, the Khmer elite began to migrate to the Phnom Penh area. Angkor was abandoned to pilgrims, holy men and the elements.

The Golden Age of Siam

Several Thai principalities in the Mekong valley united in the 13th and 14th centuries to create Sukhothai (Land of Rising Happiness). Thai princes wrested control of the territory from the Khmers, whose all-powerful empire at Angkor was slowly disintegrating. Sukhothai is considered by the Thais to be the first true Thai kingdom. It was annexed by Ayuthaya in 1376, by which time a national identity of sorts had been forged.

The Thai kings of Ayuthaya grew very powerful in the 14th and 15th centuries, taking over the former Khmer strongholds in present-day central Thailand. Even though the Khmers had been their adversaries in

1113

Suryavarman II commences the construction of Angkor Wat in Cambodia, the mother of all temples and the world's largest religious building; it is dedicated to Vishnu and designed as Suryavarman II's funerary temple.

1353

Lao prince Fa Ngum is sponsored by his Khmer father-in-law on an expedition to conquer the new Thai kingdoms, declaring himself leader of Lan Xang Hom Khao (Land of a Million Elephants and the White Parasol).

1431

The expansionist Thais sack Angkor definitively, carting off most of the royal court, including nobles, priests, dancers and artisans, to Ayuthaya. It's an irrevocable spiritual and cultural loss for Cambodia.

1516

Portuguese traders land at Danang, sparking the start of European interest in Vietnam. They set up a trading post in Faifo (present-day Hoi An) and introduce Catholicism to the Vietnamese.

battle, the Thai kings of Ayuthaya adopted many facets of Khmer culture, including court customs and rituals, language and culture. The cultural haemorrhage that took place with the sacking of Angkor in 1431 continues to strain relations between the two neighbours. Some Thais claim Angkor as their own, while the Khmers bemoan the loss of Khmer kickboxing, classical Khmer dance and Khmer silk to the all-powerful Thai brand.

Angkor's loss was Ayuthaya's gain and it went on to become one of the greatest cities in Asia. It's been said that London, at the time, was a village in comparison. The kingdom sustained an unbroken monarchical succession through 34 reigns from King U Thong (r 1350–69) to King Ekathat (r 1758–67).

'Among the Asian nations, the Kingdom of Siam is the greatest. The magnificence of the Ayuthaya court is incomparable.' Engelbert Kaempfer (German explorer), 1690

Lan Xang, the Birth of Laos

As the power of Sukhothai grew, the Cambodian court looked around for an ally, and found one in Fa Ngum, an exiled Lao prince who was being educated at Angkor.

King Jayavarman VIII married Fa Ngum to a Khmer princess and offered him an army of more than 10,000 troops. He pushed north to wrest the middle Mekong from the control of Sukhothai and its allied Lanna kingdom. By 1353 he declared himself king of Lan Xang Hom Khao, meaning 'Land of a Million Elephants and the White Parasol'. This was really the last hurrah of the declining Khmer empire and quite probably served only to weaken Angkor and antagonise the Thais.

Within 20 years of its birth, Lan Xang had expanded eastward to pick off parts of a disintegrating Champa and along the Annamite Mountains

THE MONGOLS IN THE MEKONG

The marauding Mongols left an indelible mark on the peoples of the Mekong as they initiated a major shift in the region's balance of power.

In 1253, Kublai Khan, grandson of Genghis, attacked the Thai state of Nan Chao, which was located in Xishuangbanna in the south of Yunnan. Thais had already been migrating south for several centuries, and settling in parts of Laos and northern Thailand. However, the sacking of their capital provoked a mass exodus and brought the Thais into conflict with the waning Khmer empire. The Mongol empire evaporated into the dust of history, but with the sacking of the Thai capital, the die was cast: it was the Thais versus the Khmers, a conflict that has persisted through the centuries to the present day.

In 1288, Kublai Khan planned to attack Champa and demanded the right to cross Vietnamese territory. The Vietnamese refused, but the Mongol hordes – all half a million of them – pushed ahead, seemingly invulnerable. However, they met their match in the legendary general Tran Hung Dao. He defeated them in the battle of Bach Dang River, one of the most celebrated victories among many the Vietnamese have won.

1560

King Setthathirat moves the capital of Lan Xang (modern-day Laos) from Luang Prabang to Viang Chan, today known as Vientiane.

1767

Following several centuries of military rivalry, the Burmese sack the Thai capital of Ayuthaya, forcing its relocation to Thonburi, then to the present-day location of Bangkok.

1772

Cambodia is caught between the powerful Vietnamese and Siamese; the latter burn Phnom Penh to the ground, another chapter in the story of inflamed tensions that persist today.

1802

Emperor Gia Long takes the throne to reign over a united Vietnam for the first time in decades, and the Nguyen dynasty is born, ruling until 1945.

By naming his kingdom Lan Xang Hom Khao, Fa Ngum was making a statement. Elephants were the battle tanks of Southeast Asian warfare, so claiming to be 'Kingdom of a Million Elephants' was essentially a warning to surrounding kingdoms: 'Don't mess with the Lao!'

in Vietnam. Fa Ngum earned the sobriquet 'the Conqueror' because of his constant preoccupation with warfare. Theravada Buddhism became the state religion in Lan Xang when King Visounarat accepted the Pha Bang, a gold Buddha image, from his Khmer sponsors.

Vietnamese Expansion

The Chinese seized control of Vietnam once more in the early 15th century, carrying the national archives and some of the country's intellectuals off to China – an irreparable loss to Vietnamese civilisation. The poet Nguyen Trai (1380–1442) wrote of this period: 'Were the water of the Eastern Sea to be exhausted, the stain of their ignominy could not be washed away; all the bamboo of the Southern Mountains would not suffice to provide the paper for recording all their crimes.'

In 1418, wealthy philanthropist Le Loi rallied the people against the Chinese. Upon victory in 1428, Le Loi declared himself Emperor Le Thai To, the first in the long line of the Le dynasty. To this day, Le Loi is highly revered as one of the country's all-time national heroes. Le Loi and his successors launched a campaign to take over Cham lands to the south and wiped the kingdom of Champa from the map; parts of eastern Laos were forced to kowtow to the might of the Vietnamese.

The Dark Ages

The glorious years of the Khmer empire and the golden age of Ayuthaya were no guarantee of future success and the 18th century proved a time of turmoil. This was the dark ages – when the countries of the Mekong were convulsed by external threats and internal intrigue.

The Continuing Decline of Cambodia

From 1600 until the arrival of the French in 1863, Cambodia was ruled by a series of weak kings who were forced to seek the protection – at a price – of either Thailand or Vietnam. In the 17th century, assistance from the Nguyen lords of southern Vietnam was given on the condition that Vietnamese be allowed to settle in what is now the Mekong Delta region of Vietnam, at that time part of Cambodia and today still referred to by the Khmers as Kampuchea Krom (Lower Cambodia).

In the west, the Thais controlled the provinces of Battambang and Siem Reap from 1794; by the late 18th century they had firm control of the Cambodian royal family.

The Threat of Burma

Meanwhile, the so-called golden age of Ayuthaya was starting to lose its shine. In 1765, the Burmese laid siege to the capital for two years and the city fell. Everything sacred to the Thais was destroyed, including temples,

1834
The Vietnamese take control of much of Cambodia during the reign of Emperor Minh Mang and begin a slow revolution to 'teach the barbarians their customs'.

1864
The French force Cambodia into a Treaty of Protectorate, which ironically does prevent the small kingdom being wiped off the map by its more powerful neighbours, Thailand and Vietnam.

1883
The French impose the Treaty of Protectorate on the Vietnamese, bringing together Tonkin in the north, Annam in the centre and Cochinchina in the south, marking the start of 70 years of colonial control.

1893
France gains sovereignty over all Lao territories east of the Mekong, thus consolidating its control over the Mekong region as part of its colony of Indochina.

manuscripts and religious sculpture. The Thais vented their frustrations on their Lao neighbours. The 17th century had been Lan Xang's very own golden age, but the first Lao unified kingdom began to unravel by the end of the century. The country split into the three kingdoms of Luang Prabang, Viang Chan (Vientiane) and Champasak.

Civil War in Vietnam

In a dress rehearsal for the tumultuous events of the 20th century, Vietnam found itself divided in half through much of the 17th and 18th centuries. It wasn't until the dawn of a new century, in 1802, that Nguyen Anh proclaimed himself Emperor Gia Long, thus beginning the Nguyen dynasty. For the first time in two centuries, Vietnam was united, with Hue as its new capital city.

The French Protectorate

Marco Polo was the first European to cross the Mekong and penetrate the east. In the following centuries many more Europeans followed in his wake, trading in ports as diverse as Ayuthaya and Faifo (Hoi An). However, it was France that was to ultimately claim much of the region as its own.

The concept of 'protectorate' was often employed as a smokescreen by European colonial powers in order to hide their exploitative agenda. However, for the weak and divided kingdoms of Cambodia and Laos, French intervention came not a moment too soon. Both were starting to feel the squeeze as expansionist Thailand and Vietnam carved up their territory. Were it not for the French, it is quite plausible that Cambodia and Laos would have gone the way of Champa, a mere footnote in history, a people without a homeland.

Indochina Is Born

France's military activity in Vietnam began in 1847, when the French Navy attacked Danang harbour in response to Emperor Thieu Tri's suppression of Catholic missionaries. Saigon was seized in early 1859 and, in 1862, Emperor Tu Duc signed a treaty that gave the French the three eastern provinces around Saigon.

Cambodia succumbed to French military might in 1864, when French gunboats intimidated King Norodom I (r 1860–1904) into signing a Treaty of Protectorate. In Laos, the same technique was employed with much success. In 1893 a French warship forced its way up the Chao Phraya River to Bangkok and trained its guns on the palace. Under duress, the Siamese agreed to transfer all territory east of the Mekong to France and Laos became part of Indochina.

In 1883 the French attacked Hue and imposed the Treaty of Protectorate on the imperial court of Vietnam. The Indochinese Union proclaimed

Between 1944 and 1945, the Viet Minh received funding and arms from the US Office of Strategic Services (OSS; today the CIA). When Ho Chi Minh declared independence in 1945, he had OSS agents at his side and borrowed liberally from the American Declaration of Independence.

1907

French authorities negotiate the return of Siem Reap, Battambang and Preah Vihear to Cambodia, under Siamese control since 1794; Laos loses out as territory to the west of the Mekong is conceded in the deal.

1930

Ho Chi Minh establishes the Indochinese Communist Party; it splits into three national communist forces: the Viet Minh in Vietnam, the Khmer Rouge in Cambodia and the Pathet Lao in Laos.

1939

Following a nationalist coup by a pro-fascist military leadership, Siam changes its name to Thailand in an effort to cement control of the Thai peoples in the Mekong region, choosing to side with Japan in WWII.

1941

Japan sweeps through mainland Southeast Asia during WWII, occupying French Indochina in cooperation with pro–Vichy France colonial authorities and winning Thailand's support in return for the promise of territory.

For a human perspective on the North Vietnamese experience during the war, read *The Sorrow of War* by Bao Ninh (1990), a poignant tale of love and loss that shows the soldiers from the North had the same fears and desires as most American GIs.

by the French in 1887 may have ended the existence of an independent Vietnamese state, but active resistance continued in various parts of the country for the duration of French rule.

The Thais Hold Out

The Thais are proud of their independent history and that they were never colonised. Successive Thai kings courted the Europeans while maintaining their neutrality. It was an ambiguous relationship, best summed up by King Mongkut: 'Whatever they have invented or done, we should know of and do, we can imitate and learn from them, but do not wholeheartedly believe in them.'

The French were able to exert some influence over the Siamese, convincing Siam to return the northwest provinces of Battambang, Siem Reap and Sisophon to Cambodia in 1907 in return for concessions of Lao territory. This returned Angkor to Cambodian control for the first time in more than a century.

In the end, it was less the Thai manoeuvring that kept the country independent, but the realisation by the British in Burma (present-day Myanmar) and the French in Indochina that a buffer zone would prevent open warfare.

Communism & WWII

The first Marxist grouping in Indochina was the Vietnam Revolutionary Youth League, founded by Ho Chi Minh in Canton, China, in 1925. This was succeeded in February 1930 by the Vietnamese Communist Party, part of the Indochinese Communist Party (ICP).

As the desire for independence grew in Vietnam, the communists proved adept at tuning into the frustrations and aspirations of the population, and effectively channelling their demands for fairer land distribution.

War Gamesmanship

In WWII Japanese forces occupied much of Asia, and Indochina was no exception. With many in France collaborating with the occupying Germans, the French in Indochina ended up on the side of the Japanese.

In 1941, Ho formed the League for the Independence of Vietnam, much better known as the Viet Minh. Receiving assistance from the US government, Ho resisted the Japanese-French alliance and carried out extensive political activities throughout the war. Ho was pragmatic, patriotic and populist, and understood the need for national unity.

A False Dawn

As events unfolded in Europe, the French and Japanese fell out and the Viet Minh saw its opportunity to strike. By the spring of 1945, the Viet

1945

Ho Chi Minh proclaims Vietnamese independence on 2 September in Ba Dinh Sq in Hanoi, but the French have other ideas, sparking 30 years of Vietnamese warfare – first against the French, later the Americans.

1953

Cambodia and Laos go it alone with independence from France, almost insignificant sacrifices as the colonial power attempts to cling to control in Vietnam.

1954

French forces surrender en masse to Viet Minh fighters at Dien Bien Phu on 7 May, marking the end of colonial rule in Indochina.

1955

Cambodia's King Norodom Sihanouk abdicates to enter a career in politics; he founds the Sangkum Reastr Niyum (People's Socialist Community) and wins the election with ease.

SIAM REBORN AS THAILAND

Siam transformed itself from an absolute monarchy to a constitutional monarchy in a bloodless coup in 1932. Under nationalist military leader Phibul Songkhram, the country veered in a fascist direction, changing its name to Thailand in 1939 and siding with the Japanese in WWII in order to seize back Cambodian and Lao territory returned to French Indochina in 1907.

Changing the name of the country from Siam to Thailand was a political masterstroke, as Siamese exclusivity was abolished and everyone was welcome to be a part of the new Thai family, including ethnic minorities and Laotians detached from their homeland by colonial intrigue.

Minh controlled large parts of Vietnam, particularly in the north. On 2 September 1945 Ho Chi Minh declared independence. Throughout this period, Ho wrote no fewer than eight letters to President Harry Truman and the US State Department asking for American aid, but received no replies.

Having prevailed in Europe, the French wasted no time returning to Indochina, making the countries 'autonomous states within the French Union', but retaining de facto control. French general Jacques Philippe Leclerc pompously declared: 'We have come to reclaim our inheritance.'

In the north, Chinese Kuomintang troops were fleeing the Chinese communists and pillaging their way southward towards Hanoi. Ho tried to placate the Chinese, but as the months of Chinese occupation dragged on, he concluded 'better the devil you know' and accepted a temporary return of the French.

War with the French

In the face of determined Vietnamese nationalism, the French proved unable to reassert their control. Despite massive US aid and the existence of significant indigenous anticommunist elements, it was an unwinnable war. As Ho said to the French at the time, 'You can kill 10 of my men for every one I kill of yours, but even at those odds you will lose and I will win.'

The whole complexion of the First Indochina War changed with the 1949 victory of communism in China. As Chinese weapons flowed to the Viet Minh, the French were forced onto the defensive. After eight years of fighting, the Viet Minh controlled much of Vietnam and neighbouring Laos. On 7 May 1954, after a 57-day siege, more than 10,000 starving French troops surrendered to the Viet Minh at Dien Bien Phu.

This was a catastrophic defeat that brought an end to the French colonial adventure in Indochina. The following day, the Geneva Conference opened to negotiate an end to the conflict, with the French suddenly lacking any cards left to bring to the table. By the end of the conference, the

Hitch a ride with Michael Herr and his seminal work *Dispatches* (1977). A correspondent for *Rolling Stone* magazine, Herr tells it how it is, as some of the darkest events of the war in Vietnam unfold around him, including the siege of Khe Sanh.

1956

Vietnam remains divided at the 17th Parallel into communist North Vietnam, under the leadership of Ho Chi Minh, and 'free' South Vietnam, under the rule of President Ngo Dinh Diem.

1959

The Ho Chi Minh Trail, which had been in existence for several years during the war against the French, reopens for business and becomes the main supply route to the South for the next 16 years.

1962

The International Court rules in favour of Cambodia in the long-running dispute with Thailand over Preah Vihear, perched on the Dangkrek Mountains; it continues to create friction between the neighbours today.

1964

The US begins secret bombing of Laos to try to disrupt North Vietnamese supplies to the guerrilla war in South Vietnam; 'Air America' takes off, the CIA airline allegedly funded by opium and heroin smuggling.

For a full Cambodian history, from humble beginnings in the prehistoric period through the glories of Angkor and right up to the present day, seek out a copy of *The History of Cambodia* (1983) by David Chandler.

French colonial period in Indochina would be over and Vietnam, Cambodia and Laos would be internationally recognised as independent states.

Independence for Vietnam, Cambodia & Laos

The Geneva Accords resulted in two Vietnams. Ho Chi Minh led the communist northern zone, while the South was ruled by Ngo Dinh Diem, a fiercely anticommunist Catholic. Nationwide elections scheduled for 1956 were never held, as the Americans and the South rightly feared that Ho Chi Minh would win easily.

In Laos, meanwhile, the convention set aside two northeastern provinces (Hua Phan and Phongsali) as regroupment areas for Pathet Lao ('Land of the Lao', or communist) forces. The tragedy for Laos was that when, after two centuries, the independent Lao state was reborn, it was conceived in the nationalism of WWII, nourished during the agony of the First Indochina War and born into the Cold War. Thus, from its inception, the Lao state was torn by ideological division, which the Lao tried mightily to overcome, but which was surreptitiously stoked by outside interference.

Cambodia's sudden independence was a huge victory for its young king, Prince Norodom Sihanouk, who had been placed on the throne In 1941 by French Admiral Jean Decoux. The assumption was that he would be naive and pliable. As he grew in stature, this proved to be a major miscalculation. In 1953 King Sihanouk embarked on his 'royal crusade': his travelling campaign to drum up international support for independence, which was proclaimed on 9 November 1953 and recognised shortly after

THE SECRET WAR IN LAOS

Before his assassination in 1963, President John F Kennedy gave the order to recruit a force of 11,000 Hmong under the command of Vang Pao. They were trained by several hundred US and Thai Special Forces advisers and supplied by Air America, all under the supervision of the CIA. The secret war had begun.

Over the next 12 years the Hmong 'secret army' fought a continuous guerrilla campaign against heavily armed North Vietnamese regular army troops occupying the Plain of Jars. They were supported throughout by the US.

In 1964 the US began its air war over Laos, with strafing and bombing of communist positions on the Plain of Jars. As North Vietnamese infiltration picked up along the Ho Chi Minh Trail, bombing was extended across all of Laos. According to official figures, the US dropped 2,093,100 tonnes of bombs in 580,944 sorties. The total cost was US$7.2 billion, or US$2 million a day for nine years. No one knows how many people died, but one-third of the population of 2.1 million became internal refugees.

1965

The first US marines wade ashore at Danang as the war in Vietnam heats up, and the Americans commit ground troops to avoid the very real possibility of a communist victory.

1968

The Viet Cong launches the Tet Offensive, a synchronised attack throughout the South that catches the Americans unaware. Iconic images of this are beamed into households all over the USA.

1969

US President Richard Nixon authorises the secret bombing of Cambodia as an extension of the war in Vietnam; the campaign continues until 1973, killing up to 250,000 Cambodians.

1970

Cambodia leader Norodom Sihanouk is overthrown in a coup engineered by his general Lon Nol and cousin Prince Sirik Matak, thus beginning Cambodia's bloody descent into civil war and genocide.

in Geneva. In 1955 Sihanouk abdicated, afraid of being marginalised amid the pomp of royal ceremony. The 'royal crusader' became 'citizen Sihanouk' and vowed never again to return to the throne.

The War in Vietnam

During the first few years of his rule, Diem consolidated power effectively. During Diem's 1957 official visit to the US, President Eisenhower called him the 'miracle man' of Asia. As time went on Diem became increasingly tyrannical in dealing with dissent.

In the early 1960s, the South was rocked by anti-Diem unrest led by university students and Buddhist clergy. The US decided Diem was a liability and threw its support behind a military coup. A group of young generals led the operation in November 1963. Diem was to go into exile, but the generals got overexcited and both Diem and his brother were killed. He was followed by a succession of military rulers who continued his erratic policies and dragged the country deeper into war.

War Breaks Out

The North's campaign to 'liberate' the South began in late 1950s with the creation of the National Liberation Front (NLF), nicknamed the Viet Cong (VC) by the Americans. By early 1965, Hanoi was sending regular North Vietnamese Army (NVA) units down the Ho Chi Minh Trail and the Saigon government was on its last legs. To the Americans, Vietnam was the next domino and could not topple. It was clearly time for the Americans to 'clean up the mess', as one of Lyndon Johnson's leading officials put it.

For the first years of the conflict, the American military was boldly proclaiming victory upon victory, as the communist body count mounted. However, the Tet Offensive of 1968 brought an alternative reality into the homes of the average American. On the evening of 31 January, as Vietnam celebrated the Lunar New Year, the VC launched a series of strikes in more than 100 cities and towns, including Saigon. As the TV cameras rolled, a VC commando team took over the courtyard of the US embassy in central Saigon. The Tet Offensive killed about 1000 US soldiers and 2000 Army of the Republic of Vietnam (ARVN) troops, but VC losses were more than 10 times higher, at around 32,000 deaths. For the VC the Tet Offensive ultimately proved a success: it made the cost of fighting the war unbearable for the Americans.

Simultaneously, stories began leaking out of Vietnam about atrocities and massacres carried out by US forces against unarmed Vietnamese civilians, including the infamous My Lai Massacre. This helped turn the tide against the war, and antiwar demonstrations rocked American university campuses and spilled onto the streets.

As WWII drew to a close, Japanese rice requisitions, in combination with floods and breaches in the dikes, caused a horrific famine – two million of northern Vietnam's 10 million people starved to death.

1973

All sides in the Vietnam conflict sign the Paris Peace Accords on 27 January 1973, supposedly bringing an end to the war in Vietnam, but it's actually a face-saving deal for the US to 'withdraw with honour'.

1975

The Khmer Rouge enters Phnom Penh on 17 April, implementing one of the bloodiest revolutions in history; North Vietnamese forces take Saigon on 30 April, renaming it Ho Chi Minh City; Vietnam is reunified.

1978

Vietnam invades Cambodia on Christmas Day in response to border attacks; the Khmer Rouge is overthrown weeks later; a decade-long war between communist 'brothers' begins.

1986

Doi moi (economic reform), Vietnam's answer to perestroika and the first step towards re-engaging with the West, is launched with a rash of economic reforms.

Tricky Dick's Exit Strategy

Richard Nixon was elected president in 1968 in part because of a promise that he had a 'secret plan' to end the war. Nixon's strategy called for 'Vietnamisation', which meant making the South Vietnamese fight the war without US troops.

The 'Christmas bombing' of Haiphong and Hanoi at the end of 1972 was meant to wrest concessions from North Vietnam at the negotiating table. Eventually, the Paris Peace Accords were signed by the US, North Vietnam, South Vietnam and the VC on 27 January 1973, which provided for a ceasefire, the total withdrawal of US combat forces and the release of 590 US prisoners of war (POWs).

The End is Nigh

In January 1975 the North Vietnamese launched a massive ground attack across the 17th Parallel using tanks and heavy artillery. Whole brigades of ARVN soldiers disintegrated and fled southward, joining hundreds of thousands of civilians clogging Hwy 1. The North Vietnamese pushed on to Saigon and on the morning of 30 April 1975 their tanks smashed through the gates of Saigon's Independence Palace (now called Reunification Palace). The long war was over, Vietnam was reunited and Saigon was renamed Ho Chi Minh City.

The Reunification of Vietnam

Vietnam may have been united, but it would take a long time to heal the scars of war. Damage from the fighting extended from unmarked minefields to war-focused, dysfunctional economies; from a chemically poisoned countryside to a population that had been physically or mentally battered.

The party decided on a rapid transition to socialism in the south, but this proved disastrous for the economy. Reunification was accompanied by widespread political repression. Despite repeated promises to the contrary, hundreds of thousands of people who had ties to the previous regime had their property confiscated and were rounded up and imprisoned without trial in forced-labour camps, euphemistically known as reeducation camps.

During the US bombing of 1964–73, some 13 million tonnes of bombs – equivalent to 450 times the energy of the atomic bomb used on Hiroshima – were dropped on the Indochina region. This equates to 265kg for every man, woman and child in Vietnam, Cambodia and Laos.

Sideshow: the Civil War in Cambodia

The 1950s were seen as Cambodia's golden years and Sihanouk successfully maintained Cambodia's neutrality into the 1960s. However, with the war in Vietnam raging across the border, Cambodia was being sucked slowly into the vortex.

By 1969 the conflict between the Cambodian army and leftist rebels had become more serious, as the Vietnamese sought sanctuary deeper in Cambodia. In March 1970, while Sihanouk was on a trip to France, he was overthrown in a coup by General Lon Nol, his army commander.

1989
Vietnamese forces pull out of Cambodia in the face of dwindling support from the Soviet Union under the leadership of reform-minded President Gorbachev; Vietnam is at peace for the first time in decades.

1991
The Paris Peace Accords are signed, in which all Cambodian parties (including, controversially, the Khmer Rouge) agree to participate in free and fair elections supervised by the UN, held in 1993.

1997
Asian financial crisis grips the Mekong region; Cambodia is convulsed by a coup and becomes a pariah once more; Laos and Myanmar (Burma) join the Association of Southeast Asian Nations (Asean).

1998
Following a government push on the Khmer Rouge's last stronghold at Anlong Veng, Pol Pot dies on 15 April; rumours about the circumstances of his death swirl around Phnom Penh.

Sihanouk took up residence in Beijing and formed an alliance with the Cambodian communists, nicknamed the Khmer Rouge (Red Khmer), who exploited this partnership to gain new recruits.

On 30 April 1970, US and South Vietnamese forces invaded Cambodia in an effort to flush out thousands of Viet Cong and North Vietnamese troops. The Vietnamese communists withdrew deeper into Cambodia.

The Secret Bombing

In 1969, the US began a secret program of bombing suspected communist base camps in Cambodia. For the next four years, until bombing was halted by the US Congress in August 1973, huge areas of the eastern half of the country were carpet-bombed by US B-52s, killing thousands of civilians and turning hundreds of thousands more into refugees.

Despite massive US military and economic aid, Lon Nol never succeeded in gaining the initiative against the Khmer Rouge. Large parts of the countryside fell to the rebels and many provincial capitals were cut off from Phnom Penh. On 17 April 1975, Phnom Penh surrendered to the Khmer Rouge.

The Land of a Million Irrelevants

War correspondents covering the conflict in Indochina soon renamed Lan Xang (ie Laos) 'the Land of a Million Irrelevants'. However, the ongoing conflict was very relevant to the Cold War and the great powers were playing out their power struggles on this most obscure of stages. Successive governments came and went so fast they needed a revolving door in the national assembly.

Upcountry, large areas fell under the control of communist forces. The US sent troops to Thailand, in case communist forces attempted to cross the Mekong, and it looked for a time as if the major commitment of US troops in Southeast Asia would be to Laos rather than Vietnam. Both the North Vietnamese and the Americans were jockeying for strategic advantage, and neither was going to let Lao neutrality get in the way.

By mid-1972, when serious peace moves got under way, some four-fifths of Laos was under communist control. Unlike Cambodia and Vietnam, the communists were eventually able to take power without a fight. City after city was occupied by the Pathet Lao (communist forces) and in August 1975 they marched into Vientiane unopposed.

The Khmer Rouge & Year Zero

Upon taking Phnom Penh, the Khmer Rouge implemented one of the most radical and brutal restructurings of a society ever attempted; its goal was to transform Cambodia into a Maoist, peasant-dominated agrarian cooperative. Within days of the Khmer Rouge coming to power

Australian author and documentary film-maker John Pilger was one of the original rabble-rousing left-wing journalists and documentary film-makers. Get to grips with his hard-hitting views on the war in Vietnam at www.johnpilger.com.

1999
Cambodia finally joins Asean after a two-year delay; the other Southeast Asian nations welcome the country back to the world stage.

2001
Telecommunications tycoon Thaksin Shinawatra is elected prime minister of Thailand, setting the country on a divisive course.

2004
King Sihanouk abdicates in Cambodia, closing the chapter on 63 years as monarch, politician and statesman, and is succeeded by his son King Sihamoni.

2004
The first US commercial flight since the end of the Vietnam War touches down in Ho Chi Minh City, as US–Vietnamese business and tourism links mushroom.

For the full story on how Cambodia was sucked into hell, read *Sideshow: Kissinger, Nixon and the Destruction of Cambodia* (1979) by William Shawcross.

the entire population of the capital, including the sick, elderly and infirm, was forced to march out to the countryside. Disobedience of any sort often brought immediate execution. The advent of Khmer Rouge rule was proclaimed Year Zero. Currency was abolished and postal services were halted. The country was cut off from the outside world.

Counting the Cost of Genocide

Pol Pot's initial fury upon seizing power was directed against the former regime. All of the senior government and military figures who had been associated with Lon Nol were executed within days of the takeover. Then the centre shifted its attention to the outer regions, a process that saw thousands perish.

It is still not known exactly how many Cambodians died at the hands of the Khmer Rouge during the three years, eight months and 20 days of its rule. The Vietnamese claimed three million deaths, while foreign experts long considered the number closer to one million. Yale University researchers undertaking ongoing investigations estimated that the figure was close to two million.

Hundreds of thousands of people were executed by the Khmer Rouge leadership, while hundreds of thousands more died of famine and disease. Meals consisted of little more than watery rice porridge twice a day, but were meant to sustain men, women and children through a back-breaking day in the fields. Disease stalked the work camps, malaria and dysentery striking down whole families; death was a relief for many from the horrors of life. Some zones were better than others, some leaders fairer than others, but life for the majority was one of unending misery and suffering in this 'prison without walls'.

As the centre eliminated more and more moderates, Angkar (the organisation) became the only family people needed and those who did not agree were sought out and crushed. The Khmer Rouge detached the Cambodian people from all they held dear: their families, their food, their fields and their faith. Even the peasants who had supported the revolution could no longer blindly follow such insanity. Nobody cared for the Khmer Rouge by 1978, but nobody had an ounce of strength to do anything about it…except the Vietnamese.

François Bizot was kidnapped by the Khmer Rouge, interrogated by Comrade Duch and is believed to be the only foreigner to have been released. Later he was holed up in the French embassy in April 1975. Read his harrowing story in *The Gate* (2003).

The Vietnamese Move In

From 1976 to 1978, the Khmer Rouge instigated a series of border clashes with Vietnam, and claimed the Mekong Delta, once part of the Khmer empire. On 25 December 1978 Vietnam launched a full-scale invasion of Cambodia, toppling the Pol Pot government two weeks later, and installing a new government led by several former Khmer Rouge officers, including current Prime Minister Hun Sen, who had defected to Vietnam in 1977.

2004

The 26 December Indian Ocean tsunami kills more than 5000 people in Thailand and damages tourism and fishing industries.

2006

Thaksin government is overthrown in a coup and the Thai prime minister forced into exile.

2010

Comrade Duch, aka Kaing Guek Eav, former commandant of the notorious S-21 prison in Phnom Penh, becomes first Khmer Rouge leader convicted of crimes against humanity.

2010

Pro-Thaksin 'Red Shirt' activists occupy central Bangkok for two months; military crackdown results in 91 deaths.

The Khmer Rouge's patrons, the Chinese communists, launched a massive reprisal raid across Vietnam's northernmost border in early 1979 in an attempt to buy their allies time. It failed and after 17 days the Chinese withdrew, their fingers badly burnt by their Vietnamese enemies. The Vietnamese then staged a show trial in Cambodia in which Pol Pot and Ieng Sary were condemned to death in absentia for their genocidal acts.

In 1984, the Vietnamese overran all the major rebel camps inside Cambodia, forcing the Khmer Rouge and its allies to retreat into Thailand. From this time the Khmer Rouge and its allies engaged in guerrilla warfare aimed at demoralising its opponents. Tactics used included shelling government-controlled garrison towns, planting thousands of mines in rural areas, attacking road transport, blowing up bridges, kidnapping village chiefs and targeting civilians. The Khmer Rouge also forced thousands of men, women and children living in the refugee camps it controlled to work as porters, ferrying ammunition and other supplies into Cambodia across heavily mined sections of the border.

The Vietnamese, for their part, laid the world's longest minefield, known as K-5 and stretching from the Gulf of Thailand to the Lao border, in an attempt to seal out the guerrillas. They also sent Cambodians into the forests to cut down trees on remote sections of road to prevent ambushes. Thousands died of disease and from injuries sustained from land mines. The Khmer Rouge was no longer in power, but for many the 1980s were almost as tough as the 1970s – one long struggle to survive.

Reversal of Fortune

The communist cooperatives in Indochina were a miserable failure and caused almost as much suffering as the wars that had preceded them. Pragmatic Laos was the first to liberalise in response to the economic stagnation, and private farming and enterprise were allowed as early as 1979. However, the changes came too late for the Lao royal family and the last king and queen are believed to have died of malnutrition and disease in a prison camp sometime in the late 1970s.

Vietnam was slower to evolve, but the arrival of President Mikhail Gorbachev in the Soviet Union meant glasnost (openness) and perestroika (restructuring) were in, and radical revolution was out. *Doi moi* (economic reforms) were experimented with in Cambodia and introduced to Vietnam. As the USSR scaled back its commitments to the communist world, the far-flung outposts were the first to feel the pinch. The Vietnamese decided to unilaterally withdraw from Cambodia in 1989, as they could no longer afford the occupation. The party in Vietnam was on its own and needed to reform to survive. Cambodia and Laos would follow its lead.

Several of the current crop of Cambodian leaders were previously members of the Khmer Rouge, including Prime Minister Hun Sen and Head of the National Assembly Heng Samrin, although there is no evidence to implicate them in mass killings.

2011

Cambodia and Thailand trade blows over the ancient border temple of Prasat Preah Vihear on the Dangkrek Mountains; Asean attempts to broker a lasting settlement.

2011

Red Shirts back in power as Yingluck Shinawatra becomes Thailand's first female prime minister.

2012

Cambodia's former King Norodom Sihanouk dies a national hero.

2013

Vietnam War hero General Giap, seen as an antidote to the country's corrupt modern-day leadership, dies. Millions pay their respects.

A New Beginning

You may be wondering what happened to Thailand in all of this? Well, compared with the earth-shattering events unfolding in Indochina, things were rather dull. Thailand profited as its neighbours suffered, providing air bases and logistical support to the Americans during the war in Vietnam. As the war and revolution consumed a generation in Cambodia, Laos and Vietnam, Thailand's economy prospered and democracy slowly took root, although coups remain common currency right up to the present day – largely because of the divisiveness of billionaire tycoon Thaksin Shinawatra, who served as prime minister from 2001 to 2006 before being ousted by the military and forced into exile. The power struggle between Thaksin's 'Eed Shirt' supporters and their 'Yellow Shirt' opponents has dominated the headlines in Thailand for more than a decade. Meanwhile, southern Thailand continues to be gripped by an Islamic insurgency that has claimed hundreds of lives

Cambodia was welcomed back to the world stage in 1991 with the signing of the Paris Peace Accords, which set out a UN road map to free and fair elections. There have been many hiccups along the way, including coups and a culture of impunity, but Cambodia has come a long way from the dark days of the Khmer Rouge. Democracy is hardly flourishing – corruption most certainly is – but life is better for many than it has been for a long time. Attempts to bring the surviving Khmer Rouge leadership to trial continue to stumble along.

Vietnam has followed the Chinese road to riches, taking the brakes off the economy while keeping a firm hand on the political steering wheel. With only two million paid-up members of the Communist Party and around 90 million Vietnamese, it is a road they must follow carefully. However, the economy has been booming since the the country joined the World Trade Organisation in 2006. Industry and manufacturing have led the way, along with tourism – the country welcomed a record 8.5 million visitors in 2016, rebounding from two years of anemic growth.

In Laos, hydroelectric power is a big industry and looks set to subsidise the economy in the future. On the flip side, illegal logging remains a major problem (as it is in Cambodia), with demand for timber in China, Thailand and Vietnam driving the destruction. Tourism has good prospects and Laos is carving a niche for itself as the ecotourism destination of Southeast Asia.

Like the river that binds them, the countries of the Mekong region have a turbulent past and an uncertain future.

Jon Swain's *River of Time* (1995) takes the reader back to an old Indochina, partly lost to the madness of war, and includes first-hand accounts of the French embassy stand-off in the first days of the Khmer Rouge takeover.

2013

Cambodia's opposition party surprisingly wins 45% of vote in Cambodia's elections, but cries foul and protestors take to the streets.

2014

The Thai military under General Prayuth Chan-o-cha overthrows Yingluck Shinawatra's Puea Thai Party government.

2016

Asean common market goes into effect, tying the Mekong countries closer together.

2016

Revered King Bhumibol Adulyadej (Rama IX) dies at 88, setting off a year of mourning in Thailand.

People & Culture

The Mekong region is not known as Indochina for nothing – geographically it's the land in between China and India. China has shaped the destiny of Vietnam and continues to cast a shadow over the Mekong region; India exported its great religions, language, culture and sculpture to Cambodia, Laos and Thailand. With a millennium of influence from two of the world's great civilisations, it is hardly surprising to find such a dynamic variety of culture in the Mekong region today.

Lifestyle

Traditionally, life in the Mekong region has revolved around family, fields and faith, the rhythm of rural existence continuing for centuries. For the majority of the population still living in the countryside, these constants have remained unchanged, with several generations sharing the same roof, the same rice and the same religion.

Foreign ethnographers who have carried out field research in Laos have identified anywhere from 49 to 134 different ethnic groups.

But in recent decades these rhythms have been jarred by war and ideology, as peasants were dragged from all they held dear to fight in civil wars, or were herded into cooperatives as communism tried to assert itself as the moral and social beacon in the lives of the people. But Buddhism is back, and for many older Mekong residents the temple or pagoda remains an important pillar in their lives.

A typical day in the Mekong region starts early. Country folk tend to rise before dawn, woken by the cry of cockerels and keen to get the most out of the day before the temperature heats up. This habit has spilled over into the towns and cities and many urban dwellers rise at the crack of dawn for a quick jog, a game of badminton or some t'ai chi moves.

Food is almost as important as family in this part of the world – and that is saying something. Breakfast comes in many flavours, but Chinese congee (rice soup) and noodle soups are universally popular. Long lunch breaks are common (and common sense, as they avoid the hottest part of the day). The working day winds down for some around 5pm and the family will try to come together for dinner and trade tales about their day.

Although the peoples of this region have traditionally lived in rural agrarian societies, the race is on for the move to the cities. Thailand experienced the growing pains first, and now Cambodia, Laos and Vietnam are witnessing a tremendous shift in the balance of population, as increasing numbers of young people desert the fields in search of those mythical streets paved with gold – or, more commonly, jammed with motorbikes.

People

As empires came and went, so too did the populations, and many of the countries in the Mekong region are far less ethnically homogenous than their governments would have us believe. It wasn't only local empire building that had an impact, but colonial meddling, which left a number of people stranded beyond their borders. There are Lao and Khmer in Thailand, Khmer in Vietnam, Thai (Dai) in Vietnam and Chinese

FACE IT

'Face' – or more importantly, the art of not making the locals lose face – is an important concept to understand in Asia. Face is all in Asia, and in the Mekong region it is above all. Having 'big face' is synonymous with prestige. All families, even poor ones, are expected to have big wedding parties and throw their money around like it is water in order to gain face. This is often ruinously expensive, but that is far less important than 'losing face'.

And it is for this reason that foreigners should never lose their tempers with the locals; this will bring unacceptable 'loss of face' to the individual involved and end any chance of a sensible solution to the dispute. If things aren't always going according to plan, take a deep breath, keep your cool and try to work out a solution.

everywhere. No self-respecting Mekong town would be complete without a Chinatown.

Vietnam is home to 53 ethnic minority groups (around 14 million people), mostly living in northern Vietnam.

The mountains of the Mekong region provide a home for a mosaic of minority groups, often referred to as 'hill tribes'. Many of these groups migrated from China and Tibet and have settled in areas that lowlanders considered too challenging to cultivate. Colourful costumes and unique traditions draw increasing numbers of visitors to their mountain homes. The most popular areas to visit local hill tribes include Mondulkiri and Ratanakiri Provinces in Cambodia; Luang Namtha and Muang Sing in northern Laos; Chiang Mai and Chiang Rai in northern Thailand; and Sapa and Bac Ha in northern Vietnam.

Population growth varies throughout the Mekong region. Developed Thailand embraced family planning decades ago and Vietnam has adopted a Chinese model of sorts, with a two-child policy in lowland areas. Cambodia and Laos have the highest birth rates and large families remain the rule rather than the exception out in the countryside.

Chinese

Many of the great cities of the Mekong region have significant Chinese communities, and in the case of capitals like Bangkok and Phnom Penh people of at least some Chinese ancestry may make up half the population. The Chinese are much more integrated in the Mekong region than in places like Indonesia, and continue to contribute to the economy through investment and initiative.

With one eye on history, the Vietnamese are more suspicious of the Chinese than most, even though, culturally, the Vietnamese have much in common with the Chinese. Vietnam was occupied by China for more than a thousand years and the Chinese brought with them their religion, philosophy and culture. Confucianism and Taoism were introduced and still form the backbone of Vietnamese religion, together with Buddhism.

The Cambodian and Lao people share a close bond, as Fa Ngum, the founder of the original Lao kingdom of Lan Xang (Land of a Million Elephants), was sponsored by his Khmer father-in-law.

Khmer (Cambodian)

The Khmer have inhabited Cambodia since the beginning of recorded history, around the 2nd century AD, long before the Thais and Vietnamese arrived in the southern Mekong region. During the subsequent centuries, the culture of Cambodia was influenced by contact with the civilisations of India and Java.

Cambodia was the cultural staging post for the Indianisation of the Mekong region. Indian traders brought Hinduism and Buddhism around the 2nd century and with these came the religious languages of Sanskrit and Pali; Sanskrit forms the root of modern Khmer, Lao and Thai. They also brought their art and architecture, which was redefined so effectively by the ancient Khmers before spreading into Laos and Thailand.

During the glory years of Angkor, Hinduism was the predominant religion, but from the 15th century Theravada Buddhism was adopted and most Khmers remain devoutly Buddhist today, their faith being an important anchor in the struggle to rebuild their lives following the rule of the Khmer Rouge, in which it's believed as much as one-third of the Cambodian population perished.

Kinh (Vietnamese)

Despite the Chinese view that the Vietnamese are 'the ones that got away', the Vietnamese existed in the Red River Delta area long before the first waves of Chinese arrived some 2000 years ago. The Kinh make up about 86% of the population of Vietnam. Centuries ago, the Vietnamese began to push southward in search of cultivable land and swallowed the kingdom of Champa before pushing on into the Mekong Delta and picking off pieces of a decaying Khmer empire. As well as occupying the coastal regions of Vietnam, the lowland Kinh have been moving into the mountains to take advantage of new opportunities in agriculture, industry and tourism.

Lao

Laos is often described as less a nation-state than a conglomeration of tribes and languages. The Lao traditionally divide themselves into four broad families – Lao Loum, Lao Thai, Lao Thoeng and Lao Soung – roughly defined by the altitude at which they live and their cultural proclivities. The Lao government has an alternative three-way split, in which the Lao Thai are condensed into the Lao Loum group. This triumvirate is represented on the back of every 1000K bill, in national costume, from left to right: Lao Soung, Lao Loum and Lao Thoeng.

Thai

Thais make up about 75% of the population of Thailand, although this group is commonly broken down into four subgroups: Central Thais who inhabit the Chao Phraya delta; the Thai Lao of northeastern Thailand; the Pak Thai of southern Thailand; and northern Thais. Each group speaks its own dialect and to a certain extent practises customs unique to its region. Politically and economically, the Central Thais are the dominant group, although they barely outnumber the Thai Lao.

Minority Groups

There are many other important minority groups in the region; some were rendered stateless by the conflicts of the past, while others are recent migrants to the region, including the many hill tribes.

Cham

The Cham people originally occupied the kingdom of Champa in south-central Vietnam and their beautiful brick towers dot the landscape from Danang to Phan Rang. Victims of a historical squeeze between Cambodia and Vietnam, their territory was eventually annexed by the expansionist Vietnamese. Originally Hindu, they converted to Islam in the 16th and 17th centuries and many migrated to Cambodia.

Today there are small numbers of Cham in Vietnam and as many as half a million in Cambodia, all of whom continue to practise a flexible form of Islam. The Cham population has intermarried over the centuries with migrating Malay seafarers, introducing an additional ethnic background into the mix.

Thais are given nicknames at birth, often inspired by the child's appearance, eg 'Moo' (meaning pig) if the baby is chubby, or 'Lek' (small).

LIFE AMONG THE MINORITIES

One of the highlights of a visit to the Mekong region is an encounter with one of the many ethnic minority groups inhabiting the mountains. Many wear incredible costumes, and so elaborate are some of these that it's easy to believe minority girls learn to embroider before they can walk.

While some of these minorities number as many as a million people, it is feared that other groups have dwindled to as few as 100. The areas inhabited by each group are often delineated by altitude, with more recent arrivals settling at a higher altitude. Each hill tribe has its own language, customs, mode of dress and spiritual beliefs. Some groups are caught between medieval and modern worlds, while others have assimilated into modern life.

Most groups share a rural, agricultural lifestyle that revolves around traditional rituals. Most hill-tribe communities are seminomadic, cultivating crops such as rice and using slash-and-burn methods, which have taken a toll on the environment. Hill tribes have among the lowest standards of living in the region and lack access to education, health care and even minimum-wage jobs. While there may be no official discrimination system, cultural prejudice against hill-tribe people ensures they remain at the bottom of the ladder. Put simply, life is a struggle for most minority people.

Tourism can bring many benefits to highland communities: cross-cultural understanding, improved infrastructure, cheaper market goods, employment opportunities and tourist dollars supporting handicraft industries. However, there are also negatives, such as increased litter and pollutants, dependency on tourist dollars, and the erosion of local values and practices. Here are some tips on having a positive effect when visiting minority communities:

- Where possible, hire indigenous guides – they understand taboos and traditions that might be lost on lowland guides.
- Always ask permission before taking photos of tribespeople.
- Don't show up for 15 minutes and expect to be granted permission to take photos – invest some time in getting to know the villagers first.
- Don't touch totems or sacred items hanging from trees.
- Avoid cultivating a tradition of begging, especially among children.
- Avoid public nudity and don't undress near an open window.
- Don't flirt with members of the opposite sex.
- Taste traditional wine if you are offered it, especially during a ceremony.
- Dress modestly.
- Don't buy village treasures, such as altar pieces or totems.

Hmong

The Hmong are one of the largest hill tribes in the Mekong region, spread through much of northern Laos, northern Vietnam and Thailand. As some of the last to arrive in the region in the 19th century, they were left with the highest and harshest lands from which to eke out their existence. They soon made the best of a bad deal and opted for opium cultivation, which brought them into conflict with mainstream governments during the 20th century.

Hmong groups are usually classified by their colourful clothing, including Black Hmong, White Hmong, Red Hmong and so on. The brightest group is the Flower Hmong of northwest Vietnam, who live in villages around Bac Ha. There may be as many as one million Hmong in the Mekong region, half of them living in the mountains of Vietnam.

Dzao

The Dzao (also known as Yao or Dao) are one of the largest and most colourful ethnic groups in Vietnam and are also found in Laos, Thailand and Yunnan. The Dzao practise ancestor worship of spirits, or *ban ho* (no relation to Uncle Ho), and hold elaborate rituals with sacrifices of pigs and chickens. The Dzao are famous for their elaborate dress. Women's clothing typically features intricate weaving and silver-coloured beads and coins – the wealth of a woman is said to be in the weight of the coins she carries. Their long, flowing hair, shaved above the forehead, is tied up into a large red or embroidered turban.

Mahayana Buddhists believe in Bodhisattvas – Buddhas who have attained nirvana but postponed their enlightenment to stay on earth to save their fellow beings.

Karen

The Karen are the largest hill tribe in Thailand, numbering more than 300,000. There are four distinct groups, the Skaw Karen (White Karen), Pwo Karen, Pa-O Karen (Black Karen) and Kayah Karen (Red Karen). Unmarried women wear white and kinship remains matrilineal. Most Karen live in lowland valleys and practise crop rotation.

Economy

Life for many in the Mekong region has undergone a profound transition in the space of a generation, even if the politics hasn't always come along for the ride. Laos and Vietnam are one-party states which tolerate no opposition. But communism, the mantra for a generation, has taken a back seat to capitalism and the rush to embrace the market. The result is a contradictory blend of ultraliberal economics and ultraconservative politics that has left many inhabitants confused about the country in which they live. They have the freedom to make money but not the basic freedom to voice a political opinion. And the more the average person engages with the outside world – through business, tourism and the internet – the harder this paradox is to swallow.

Corruption remains a cancer throughout the Mekong region. Despite the best intentions of a small minority, the worst intentions of many a politician continue to cost the Mekong countries hundreds of millions of dollars in lost assets. Vietnam has started tackling corruption head on with high-profile executions and prison sentences. Senior party officials have even been put away, but cronyism and nepotism remain alive and well. Laos suffers from corruption, but the small size of the economy has kept enrichment to a minimum for now.

In Cambodia, corruption has been elevated to an art form. When asked to sum up the country's problems in three words, former World Bank head James Wolfensohn famously responded, 'Corruption, corruption, corruption.' In 2015, global anticorruption watchdog Transparency International (TI) ranked Cambodia as the 150th most corrupt country in the world out of 168 (with a rank of 1 being the least corrupt), behind such luminaries as the Democratic Republic of Congo and Tajikistan. Laos ranked 139th and Vietnam 112th.

One country in the region that's improving is Thailand, which saw its 'score' improve by three points (almost 8%) as it rose from 102nd to 76th on the TI list from 2013 to 2015. This result can possibly be attributed to the policies of the hard-line military junta, which promised to tackle corruption when it seized power in 2014. According to most observers, corruption in Thailand peaked in the previous decade under the then prime minister Thaksin Shinawatra, who created a new blend by mixing business and politics to turn the country into 'Shinawatra Plc'.

Since shaking off the shadow of Marxist theory, the economies of the Mekong region have been some of the fastest-growing in the world. In a region powered by exports, the new Asean Economic Community (AEC), which unites the 10 Southeast Asian countries into a liberalised marketplace to increase competitiveness, generally should improve prospects for further economic growth. The AEC is being implemented in phases from 2015 to 2020, with import tariffs already being relaxed across the region.

However, other global forces could act as a brake on the Mekong region's economy, most notably the changing political dynamic in the US. Incoming US president Donald Trump has vowed to increase protectionism, raise interest rates and impose punishing import tariffs on China – a triple whammy that could have a profound negative effect on the economy of the entire Mekong region, which is closely tied to China's economy and sends substantial imports to the US. Particularly exposed is Cambodia, which sends more than 20% of its exports to the US (according to the Observatory of Economic Complexity), followed by Vietnam (about 14%) and Thailand (about 11%).

Thailand is the regional powerhouse, with a strong economy underpinned by manufacturing, handicrafts, tourism and agriculture. Vietnam is fast catching up and, like Thailand, is now a major manufacturing centre for automotive assembly and high-tech gadgetry. Agriculture remains a major industry, with Thailand and Vietnam number two and three (after India) on the list of world's largest rice exporters.

The economies of Cambodia and Laos are much smaller by comparison. Cambodia relies heavily on the textile industry and tourism to drive its economy, but agro-industries such as rubber and palm oil are growing fast and traditional agriculture and fishing remain very important to the average person. In Laos, the export of hydropower is big business and, though it may seem contradictory, ecotourism is one of the fastest-growing sectors.

Religion

The dominant religions of Southeast Asia have absorbed many traditional animistic beliefs of spirits, ancestor worship and the power of the celestial planets in bringing about good fortune. The Mekong region's spiritual connection to the realm of magic and miracles commands more respect, even among intellectual circles, than the remnants of paganism in Western Christianity. Locals erect spirit houses in front of their homes, while ethnic Chinese set out daily offerings to their ancestors, and almost everyone visits the fortune teller.

Although the majority of the population has only a vague notion of Buddhist doctrines, they invite monks to participate in life-cycle ceremo-

CAO DAISM

A fascinating fusion of East and West, Cao Daism (Dai Dao Tam Ky Pho Do) is a syncretic religion born in 20th-century Vietnam that contains elements of Buddhism, Confucianism, Taoism, native Vietnamese spiritualism, Christianity and Islam – as well as a dash of secular enlightenment thrown in for good measure. The term Cao Dai (meaning High Tower or Palace) is a euphemism for God. Estimates of the number of followers of Cao Daism in Vietnam vary from two million to five million.

Cao Daism was founded by the mystic Ngo Minh Chieu (also known as Ngo Van Chieu; 1878–1932), who began receiving revelations in which the tenets of Cao Dai were set forth.

All Cao Dai temples observe four daily ceremonies: at 6am, noon, 6pm and midnight. More information is available on the official Cao Dai site (www.caodai.org). The most impressive Cao Dai temple is at Tay Ninh, near Ho Chi Minh City.

nies, such as funerals and weddings. Buddhist pagodas are seen by many as a physical and spiritual refuge from an uncertain world.

Ancestor Worship

Ancestor worship dates from long before the arrival of Confucianism or Buddhism. Ancestor worship is based on the belief that the soul lives on after death and becomes the protector of its descendants. Because of the influence the spirits of one's ancestors exert on the living, it is considered not only shameful for them to be upset or restless, but downright dangerous.

Animism

Both Hinduism and Buddhism fused with the animist beliefs already present in the Mekong region before Indianisation. Local beliefs didn't simply fade away, but were incorporated into the new religions. The purest form of animism is practised among the ethnic minorities or hill tribes of the region.

Buddhism

The sedate smile of the Buddhist statues decorating the landscapes and temples characterise the nature of the religion in Southeast Asia. Religious devotion within the Buddhist countries is highly individualistic, omnipresent and nonaggressive, with many daily rituals rooted in the indigenous religions of animism and ancestor worship.

Buddhism arrived in the Mekong region in two flavours. Mahayana Buddhism (northern school) proceeded north into Nepal, Tibet, China, Korea, Mongolia, Vietnam and Japan, while Theravada Buddhism (southern school) took the southern route through India, Sri Lanka, Myanmar (Burma), Thailand, Cambodia and Laos.

Every Buddhist male is expected to become a monk for a short period in his life, optimally between the time he finishes school and starts a career or marries. Men or boys under 20 years of age may enter the Sangha (the monkhood or the monastic community) as novices. Nowadays, men may spend less than one month to accrue merit as monks.

Chrisitianity

Catholicism was introduced to the region in the 16th century by missionaries. Vietnam has the highest percentage of Catholics (8% to 10% of the population) in Southeast Asia outside the Philippines.

Hinduism

Hinduism ruled the spiritual lives of Mekong dwellers more than 1500 years ago, and the great Hindu empire of Angkor built magnificent monuments to their pantheon of gods. The primary representations of the one omnipresent god include Brahma (the creator), Vishnu (the preserver) and Shiva (the destroyer and reproducer).

The forgotten kingdom of Champa was profoundly influenced by Hinduism and many of the Cham towers, built as Hindu sanctuaries, contain *lingas* (phallic symbols representing Shiva) that are still worshipped by ethnic Vietnamese and ethnic Chinese alike.

Islam

Southeast Asians converted to Islam to join a brotherhood of spice traders and to escape the inflexible caste system of earlier Hindu empires. The Chams may be Muslims, but in practice they follow a localised adaptation of Islamic theology and law. Though Muslims usually pray five times a day, the Chams pray only on Fridays and observe Ramadan (a month of dawn-to-dusk fasting) for only three days.

For a virtual tour of Thai Buddhist architecture around the region, visit www.orientalarchitecture.com.

THE LUNAR CALENDAR

Astrology has a long history in China and Vietnam (plus in the Chinese communities of Cambodia, Laos and Thailand), and is intricately linked to religious beliefs. There are 12 zodiacal animals, each of which represents one year in a 12-year cycle. If you want to know your sign, look up your year of birth in the following chart – but don't forget that the Chinese/Vietnamese New Year falls in late January or early February. If your birthday is in the first half of January, it will be included in the zodiac year before the calendar year of your birth. To check the Gregorian (solar) date corresponding to a lunar date, pick up any Vietnamese or Chinese calendar.

- **Rat** (generous, social, insecure, idle): 1924, 1936, 1948, 1960, 1972, 1984, 1996, 2008
- **Ox** (stubborn, conservative, patient): 1925, 1937, 1949, 1961, 1973, 1985, 1997, 2009
- **Tiger** (creative, brave, overbearing): 1926, 1938, 1950, 1962, 1974, 1986, 1998, 2010
- **Rabbit** (timid, affectionate, amicable): 1927, 1939, 1951, 1963, 1975, 1987, 1999, 2011
- **Dragon** (egotistical, strong, intelligent): 1928, 1940, 1952, 1964, 1976, 1988, 2000, 2012
- **Snake** (luxury-seeking, secretive, friendly): 1929, 1941, 1953, 1965, 1977, 1989, 2001, 2013
- **Horse** (emotional, clever, quick thinker): 1930, 1942, 1954, 1966, 1978, 1990, 2002, 2014
- **Goat** (charming, good with money, indecisive): 1931, 1943, 1955, 1967, 1979, 1991, 2003, 2015
- **Monkey** (confident, humorous, fickle): 1932, 1944, 1956, 1968, 1980, 1992, 2004, 2016
- **Rooster** (diligent, imaginative, needs attention): 1933, 1945, 1957, 1969, 1981, 1993, 2005, 2017
- **Dog** (humble, responsible, patient): 1934, 1946, 1958, 1970, 1982, 1994, 2006, 2018
- **Pig** (materialistic, loyal, honest): 1935, 1947, 1959, 1971, 1983, 1995, 2007, 2019

Taoism

Taoism originated in China and is based on the philosophy of Laotse (The Old One), who lived in the 6th century BC. Little is known about Laotse and there is some debate as to whether or not he actually existed. Taoist philosophy focuses on contemplation and simplicity. The ideal is returning to the Tao ('the Way', or the essence of which all things are made); it also emphasises the importance of Yin and Yang (the two opposing yet complementary principles that maintain balance in the universe in Chinese philosophy).

Tam Giao

Over the centuries, Confucianism, Taoism and Buddhism have fused with popular Chinese beliefs and ancient Vietnamese animism to create Tam Giao (Triple Religion). When discussing religion, most Vietnamese people are likely to say that they are Buddhist, but when it comes to family or civic duties they are likely to follow the moral and social code of Confucianism, and will turn to Taoist concepts to understand the nature of the cosmos.

Survival Guide

Border Crossings

During the bad old days of communism and the Cold War, there were pretty much no land borders open to foreigners in the Mekong region. Times have changed and there are now dozens of border crossings connecting the neighbouring countries of the region. Before making a long-distance trip, be aware of border closing times, visa regulations and any transport scams. Border details change regularly, so ask around or check the Lonely Planet Thorntree forums (lonelyplanet.com/thorntree).

Visa on Arrival

Visas (or in the case of Thailand, visa waivers) are available on arrival at some borders but not at others. As a rule of thumb, a visa on arrival is available entering into Cambodia, Laos and Thailand, but is not available entering into Vietnam (except for certain nationalities).

The only exceptions to the above are at two Laos/Vietnam borders (Na Phao/Cha Lo and Na Meo/Nam Soi) and one Laos/Thailand border (Paksan/Beung Kan). Entering Laos, visa on arrival is not available at these three borders.

Opening Hours

Most borders are open during the core hours of 7am to 6pm. However, some of the most popular crossings are open later in the evening, while more remote crossings might close for lunch or close at 5pm.

Be wary of cross-border night buses that project to arrive at the border in the middle of the night. Such buses are forced to wait around until the border opens, adding hours to the journey time.

Scams & Fees

Some of the immigration police at land border crossings have a reputation for petty extortion. Especially at remote Cambodian and Lao border stations, travellers are occasionally asked for an 'immigration fee' or an overtime surcharge – 'tea money' as it's sometimes called.

To avoid being scammed, be aware of the proper fees and study up on the tricks you are likely to face at the border you are crossing. The Poipet (C)/Aranya Prathet (T) and Cham Yeam (C)/Hat Lek (T) borders are particularly scam-ridden.

It's generally easier to exit overland than it is to enter, and extra charges generally occur upon entry rather than on exit.

Changing Money

There are few legal money-changing facilities at some of the more remote border crossings, so be sure to have some small-denomination US dollars handy.

Private Vehicles

The general rule is that you can get private vehicles into Cambodia, Laos and Thailand, but forget about driving into or out of Vietnam. However, some Vietnamese motorbike-tour companies do have permission to cross the border between Laos and Vietnam.

Crossing between Cambodia, Laos and Thailand, you'll want to make sure to have all of your vehicle's paperwork in order. Before setting out, check with the embassy of your target country to see if you need additional permissions and documents.

New Border Developments

The fourth Thai-Lao Friendship Bridge (at Chiang Khong/Huay Xai) across the Mekong River opened in 2014, increasing the popularity of this border crossing (a former boat crossing) that links northern Thailand with Luang Prabang. This crossing is a key component in turning the China–Thailand highway (AH3) into a major transnational trade route. A former opium-smuggling trail, the A3 is now an 1800km paved road that links Kunming, in China's Yunnan Province, and Bangkok via northern Laos. Direct buses from Chiang Mai and Chiang Rai to Laos use this crossing.

Border Crossings

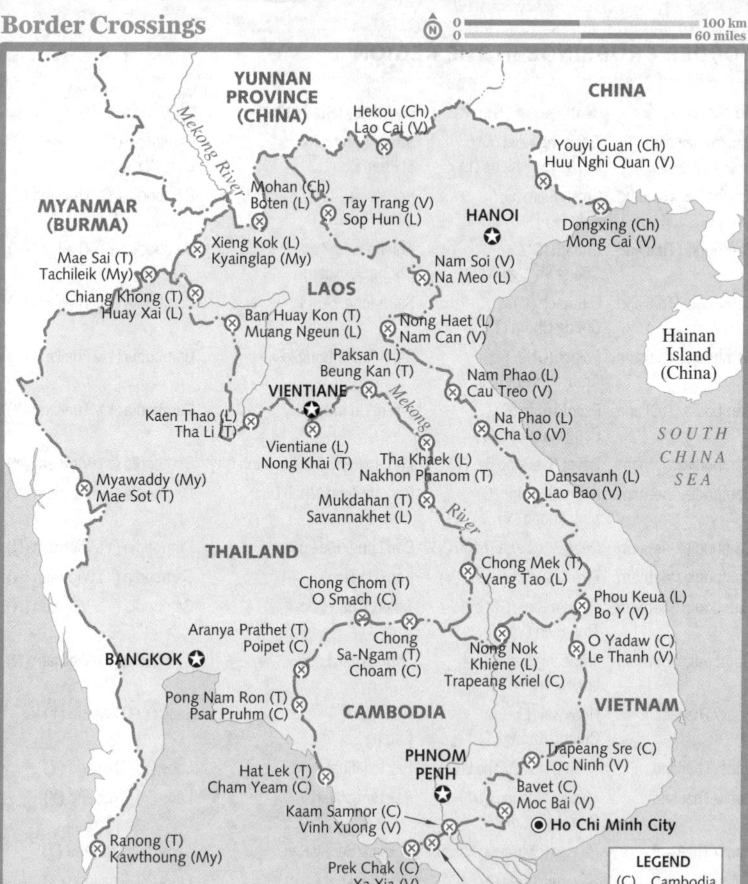

Other Countries

Thailand/Malaysia

You can cross the border by road into Malaysia at the following locations:

- Kanger (T)/Padang Besar (M)
- Sadao (T)/Bukit Kayu Hitam (M)
- Betong (T)/Keroh (M)
- Sungai Kolok (T)/Rantau Panjang (M)
- Tak Bai (T)/Pengkalan Kubor (M)

The train route into Malaysia is on the Hat Yai/Alor Setar/Butterworth route, which crosses the border at Kanger (T)/Padang Besar (M). On the west coast, the crossing between Satun (T) and Pulau Langkawi (M) is made by boat.

Thailand/Myanmar (Burma)

There are three legal crossings between Thailand and Myanmar: Mae Sai (T)/Tachileik (My); Ranong (T)/Kawthoung (My); and Mae Sot (T)/Myawaddy (My).

You'll need a Myanmar visa in advance. Be prepared for unexpected charges from Myanmar officials at the border when crossing into Thailand.

Laos/China

The only border open to foreigners is the Móhān (C)/Boten (L) crossing connecting Mengla, China, with Luang Namtha, Laos. Visas on arrival are available entering Laos through this border. You'll need to procure a Chinese visa in advance if crossing the other way.

BORDER CROSSINGS IN THE REGION

COUNTRY	BORDER CROSSING	CONNECTING TOWNS	VISA ON ARRIVAL (YES OR NO)?
Cambodia/Laos	Trapeang Kriel (C)/ Nong Nok Khiene (L)	Stung Treng/ Si Phan Don	Cambodia (Y)/ Laos (Y)
Cambodia/Thailand	Cham Yeam (C)/ Hat Lek (T)	Koh Kong/Trat	Cambodia (Y)/Thailand (Y)
Cambodia/Thailand	Choam (C)/ Chong Sa-Ngam (T)	Anlong Veng/ Chong Sa-Ngam	Cambodia (Y)/Thailand (Y)
Cambodia/Thailand	O Smach (C)/ Chong Chom (T)	Samraong/Surin	Cambodia (Y)/Thailand (Y)
Cambodia/Thailand	Poipet (C)/ Aranya Prathet (T)	Siem Reap/Bangkok	Cambodia (Y)/Thailand (Y)
Cambodia/Thailand	Psar Pruhm (C)/ Pong Nam Ron (T)	Pailin/Chanthaburi	Cambodia (Y)/Thailand (Y)
Cambodia/Vietnam	Bavet (C)/Moc Bai (V)	Phnom Penh/Ho Chi Minh City	Cambodia (Y)/Vietnam (N)
Cambodia/Vietnam	Kaam Samnor (C)/ Vinh Xuong (V)	Phnom Penh/Chau Doc	Cambodia (Y)/Vietnam (N)
Cambodia/Vietnam	O Yadaw (C)/Le Thanh (V)	Ban Lung/Pleiku	Cambodia (Y)/Vietnam (N)
Cambodia/Vietnam	Prek Chak (C)/Xa Xia (V)	Kep/Ha Tien	Cambodia (Y)/Vietnam (N)
Cambodia/Vietnam	Phnom Den (C)/ Tinh Bien (V)	Takeo/Chau Doc	Cambodia (Y)/Vietnam (N)
Cambodia/Vietnam	Trapeang Sre (C)/ Loc Ninh (V)	Snuol/Binh Long	Cambodia (Y)/Vietnam (N)
Laos/Thailand	Huay Xai (L)/ Chiang Khong (T)	Huay Xai/ Chiang Rai	Laos (Y)/Thailand (Y)
Laos/Thailand	Kaen Thao (L)/Tha Li (T)	Pak Lai/Loei	Laos (Y)/Thailand (Y)
Laos/Thailand	Muang Ngeun (L)/ Ban Huay Kon (T)	Pak Beng/Nan	Laos (Y)/Thailand (Y)
Laos/Thailand	Paksan (L)/Beung Kan (T)	Paksan/Beung Kan	Laos (N)/Thailand (Y)
Laos/Thailand	Savannakhet (L)/ Mukdahan (T)	Savannakhet/ Mukdahan	Laos (Y)/Thailand (Y)
Laos/Thailand	Tha Khaek (L)/ Nakhon Phanom (T)	Tha Khaek/ Nakhon Phanom	Laos (Y)/Thailand (Y)
Laos/Thailand	Vang Tao (L)/ Chong Mek (T)	Pakse/ Ubon Ratchathani	Laos (Y)/Thailand (Y)
Laos/Thailand	Vientiane (L)/ Nong Khai (T)	Vientiane/ Nong Khai	Laos (Y)/Thailand (Y)
Laos/Vietnam	Dansavanh (L)/ Lao Bao (V)	Savannakhet/ Dong Ha	Laos (Y)/Vietnam (N)
Laos/Vietnam	Na Meo (L)/Nam Soi (V)	Sam Neua/Thanh Hoa	Laos (N)/Vietnam (N)
Laos/Vietnam	Na Phao (L)/Cha Lo (V)	Tha Khaek/Dong Hoi	Laos (N)/Vietnam (N)
Laos/Vietnam	Nam Phao (L)/ Cau Treo (V)	Tha Khaek/ Vinh	Laos (Y)/Vietnam (N)
Laos/Vietnam	Nong Haet (L)/ Nam Can (V)	Phonsovan/ Vinh	Laos (Y)/Vietnam (N)
Laos/Vietnam	Phou Keua (L)/Bo Y (V)	Attapeu/Pleiku	Laos (Y)/Vietnam (N)
Laos/Vietnam	Sop Hun (L)/ Tay Trang (V)	Muang Khua/ Dien Bien Phu	Laos (Y)/Vietnam (N)

Directory A–Z

Accommodation

The Mekong region has something for everyone – from dives to the divine – and it's usually great value compared with destinations in Western countries. There's generally no need to book in advance, but if you're eyeing a popular hotel in the high season consider booking a few months out.

➡ **Boutiques** The Mekong is the unofficial boutique-hotel capital of the world, with Luang Prabang and Siem Reap leading the charge.

➡ **Hostels and guesthouses** Abundant. A dorm bed can cost as much as a private room in a budget guesthouse.

➡ **Hotels** Come in all shapes and sizes – you'll be spoilt for choice.

Camping

With the exception of the national parks in Thailand and some high-end experiences in Cambodia, Laos and Vietnam, the opportunities for general camping in this region are limited.

Homestays

A visit to a homestay is one of the best ways to experience rural culture, not to mention a way to ensure that your money goes directly to locals. Homestays are well established in parts of Thailand and Vietnam, and many treks through minority areas in the far north include a night with a local family to learn about their lifestyle.

Homestays are also becoming more popular in Cambodia and Laos, where they are integral components of several popular community-based tourism programs. In Cambodia, homestays are popular along the Mekong River between Kratie and the Laos border, and at several remote temple sites. At more established programs, homestays tend to be more like like guesthouses, with simple rooms in a separate structure from the main house. Meals are cooked by your hosts but you may or may not eat with the family.

In Laos, homestays are most popular in the north, especially along trekking routes and in and around national protected areas. Homestays in Laos are authentic affairs; you'll sleep under a mosquito net on a mattress on the floor in your host's home, and bathe with a scoop or in a nearby river or stream. Typical for Laos, communal meals are usually followed by a drinking session, with rice wine the tipple of choice.

To get the most out of homestays take a phrasebook, photos of your family, a torch, flip-flops (thongs), a sarong and toilet paper.

Customs Regulations

Customs regulations vary little around the region. Drugs and firearms are strictly prohibited – a lengthy stay in prison is a common sentence.

Discount Cards

The International Student Identity Card (ISIC) is the official student card, but is of limited use in the Mekong region. Some domestic and international airlines provide discounts to ISIC cardholders, but because knock-offs are so readily available, the cards carry little power.

Electricity

Most countries work on a voltage of 220V to 240V at 50Hz (cycles); note that 240V appliances will happily run on 220V. You should be able to

> **BOOK YOUR STAY ONLINE**
>
> For more accommodation reviews by Lonely Planet authors, check out http://lonelyplanet.com/hotels/. You'll find independent reviews, as well as recommendations on the best places to stay. Best of all, you can book online.

SLEEPING PRICE RANGES

See the individual country chapters for information on accommodation price ranges.

pick up adaptors in markets and electrical shops in most of the main towns and cities.

Embassies & Consulates

Embassies or consulates of most countries can be found in the region's capital cities.

Food

This is arguably the best region in the world when it comes to sampling the local cuisine. The food of Thailand and Vietnam needs no introduction, but Laotian and Khmer cuisine is also a rewarding experience.

Advance reservations are nonessential in all but the finest of fine-dining establishments. Day-of reservations are recommended at popular spots at weekends.

LGBTIQ Travellers

Thailand, Cambodia and Laos have the most progressive attitudes towards homosexuality. While same-sex displays of affection amongst friends is part of most Asian cultures, you should be discreet and respectful of the local culture. There is not usually a problem with same-sex couples checking into rooms throughout the region, as it is so common among travellers.

Resources

Check out **Utopia Asian Gay & Lesbian Resources** (www.utopia-asia.com) for more information on gay and lesbian travel in Asia. Other links with useful pointers for gay travellers include www.gayguide.net and www.asiaout.com.

Insurance

A travel insurance policy to cover theft, loss and medical problems is highly recommended. There's a wide variety of policies available, so check the small print. For more information about the ins and outs of travel insurance, contact a travel agent or travel insurer.

Worldwide travel insurance is available at www.lonelyplanet.com/travel-insurance. You can buy, extend and claim online anytime – even if you're already on the road.

Internet Access

You won't have trouble finding internet access or free wi-fi, at least in cities and touristy areas. Fourth generation (4G) connections are also cheap and functional. There are only a few concerns:

- Vietnam occasionally blocks access to social networking sites, including Facebook, during rare times of social unrest.
- Wi-fi access (and mobile-phone coverage for that matter) can be quite spotty in remote areas. This includes most national parks, particularly in Laos, and most Cambodian islands, although coverage has improved slightly on the more popular beaches.
- Connection speeds aren't always the best but, hey, being on the internet at all in this neck of the woods is a bonus, right?

Language

English-speakers are rare in the Mekong region outside of the main tourist towns. Learning the numbers (at least 1 to 100) and a few choice phrases such as 'how much?' and 'thank you' will go a long way, especially when haggling in markets. It helps that Lao and Thai are very similar, so numbers and phrases learned in one language will work in the other.

Legal Matters

Be sure to know the national laws before unwittingly committing a crime. If you are the victim of a crime, contact the tourist police, if available; they are usually better trained to deal with foreigners and foreign languages than the regular police force.

EATING PRICE RANGES

There's no limit to the variety of cuisine in the Mekong region, and prices throughout offer fantastic value.

- **Cafes** Cafe culture is alive and well in the region. Pull up a stool and order iced coffee or tea at an outdoor cafe, or find coffe-shop chains in the big cities.
- **Restaurants** Meals in local restaurants start at US$1.50 and even a serious spread at a decent restaurant will only be in the US$10 to US$20 range. If you tire of local fare you'll find Western restaurants aplenty in touristed areas.
- **Street food** The best way to truly appreciate local food in the Mekong is to join the locals for a streetside meal. Prices start at US$0.50.

Travellers should note that they can be prosecuted under the law of their home country regarding age of consent, even when abroad.

Drugs

In all of the Mekong-region countries, using or trafficking drugs carries stiff punishments that are enforced, even if you're a foreigner.

While marijuana is readily available throughout the region (where it is often euphemistically associated with the term 'happy', see p545), keep in mind that it is nonetheless illegal and you can serve jail time (or be forced to pay a huge bribe) if caught possessing it or buying it from the wrong person. Use it discreetly, and be especially wary of buying it on the street from from overzealous touts or drivers.

Possession of harder drugs such as opium, heroin, amphetamines, ecstasy and hallucinogenic mushrooms carries stiffer penalties, while penalties for drug smuggling – defined as attempting to cross a border with drugs in your possession – can include execution.

Maps

Good maps of Indochina, including Bangkok and northeast Thailand, include Nelles *Vietnam, Laos & Cambodia* map at a scale of 1:1,500,000.

Money

ATMs & Eftpos

- ATMs are widely available in Thailand and Vietnam, and in most Cambodian and Lao provincial capitals.
- In most large cities ATMs are widespread, but most charge at least US$3 per transaction, with withdrawal limits of about US$250 per withdrawal.
- Banks back home usually charge 2% to 3% for foreign ATM withdrawals and credit-card purchases, so look for a premium account that negates such charges.

Bargaining

Bargaining is acceptable in markets and in certain shops where the prices aren't displayed. It is also advisable to bargain for chartered transport, as tourists are often taken advantage of by local taxi and tuk-tuk drivers.

Credit & Debit Cards

Credit cards are widely accepted in the region. Thailand leads the way, where almost anything can be paid for with plastic. However, things dry up beyond major tourist centres or bigger towns, so don't rely exclusively on credit cards.

It is quite common for the business to pass on the credit-card commission (usually 3%) to the customer in Cambodia, Laos and Vietnam, so check if there is an additional charge before putting it on the plastic. Also check your monthly bills carefully in case some scamster clones your card while you are paying for something on your travels.

Credit cards are accepted at most midrange and top-end hotels throughout.

Currency

The US dollar is the currency of choice in the Mekong region and indeed it's a de facto second currency (some might even say first currency) in Cambodia.

Euros and other major Western currencies are also widely accepted by banks and exchange bureaux. The Thai baht is accepted throughout Laos and in parts of western Cambodia.

Most experienced travellers will carry their money in a combination of US dollars and credit/bank cards. You'll always find situations in which one or the other cannot be used, so it pays to carry both.

Tipping

Tipping is not expected in the Mekong region, but is appreciated. Upmarket hotels and restaurants often levy a 10% service charge.

- **Bars** Not expected.
- **Hotels** Not expected.
- **Guides** A few dollars on day trips is sufficient, more for longer trips if the service is good.
- **Restaurants** Leave loose change at local restaurants, 5% in smart restaurants where no service charge levied.
- **Taxis** Not necessary, but a little extra is appreciated.

Travellers Cheques

Travellers cheques can be a pain to cash in the Mekong region, but if you must, get your cheques in US dollars and in large denominations, say US$100 or US$50, to avoid heavy per-cheque commission fees.

Post

Postal services are generally reliable across the region. Of

THE NATIONAL DISH

If there's just one dish you try, make it one of these. These are the dishes that capture the cuisine of their country in a single serving. Enjoy.

Cambodia *Amok* (baked fish in coconut leaves)

Laos *Làap* (spicy salad with meat or fish)

Thailand *Đôm yam gûng* (hot-and-sour soup with shrimp)

Vietnam *Pho bo* (rice noodle soup with beef)

course, it's always better to leave important mail and parcels for the big centres such as Bangkok and Hanoi.

There's always an element of risk in sending parcels home by sea, though as a rule they eventually reach their destination. If it's something of value, it's worth considering private couriers such as FedEx, DHL and UPS.

Poste restante is widely available throughout the region and is the best way of receiving mail. When getting people to write to you, ask them to leave plenty of time for mail to arrive and to print your name very clearly.

Public Holidays

- Chinese New Year (or Tet in Vietnam) is the one holiday common to all countries and can have a big impact on travel plans, as businesses close and all forms of transport are booked out.
- Cambodia, Laos and Thailand celebrate their own new year at the same time in the middle of April. Each country shuts down for business for at least a week, and mass water fights break out in Thailand and Laos.

Responsible Travel

Much of the Mekong region is extremely poor, so consider how you might put a little back into the countries you visit. Stay longer, travel further and travel independently, or utilise locally based tour companies that are clearly on the side of pro-poor, ecofriendly travel in the region. Eat at local restaurants; try out a community-based tourism project or homestay (p539); use local guides. On shorter stays, consider spending money in local markets and in restaurants and shops that assist disadvantaged locals.

Elephant Encounters

Elephants have played an oversized role in the Mekong region, including in the construction of Angkor Wat and in fighting ancient wars in Thailand. More recently they were used for harvesting teak or transporting goods through mountainous terrain, but as forests have been clear-cut and roads built, the work has has dried up for domesticated elephants and their mahouts.

Inevitably, elephants have been repurposed for the tourism industry, where their jobs vary from circus-like shows to elephant camps giving rides to tourists and 'mahout-training' schools. However, animal-welfare experts say that elephant rides and shows are harmful to these gentle giants, who are often overworked or abused to force them to perform, and whose backs may suffer damage from the weight of carrying heavy seats and passengers. Backlash against elephant rides has grown in recent years, and several sanctuaries have sprung up to promote more sustainable interactions, such as walking with and bathing retired and rescued elephants.

Yet even these sanctuaries are not beyond reproach, as there have been cases of sanctuaries in Thailand inadvertently (or perhaps knowingly) buying wild elephants with forged registration papers. Conscientious elephant camps are aware of the practice and have a variety of methods of circumventing fraud, but to be on the safe side you may want to consider a sanctuary that doesn't engage in the elephant trade. Mahouts, meanwhile, worry about the loss of income as the backlash against elephant rides deepens and more and more pachyderms are retired to sanctuaries.

There are positive ways to interact with elephants in the region that don't involve rides: the impressive **Elephant Conservation Center** (ECC; ☎020-23025210; www.elephantconservationcenter.com; 1-day visit US$60, 3-day experience US$205, 6-day eco-experience US$495) in Laos, for example, and Cambodia's **Elephant Valley Project** (EVP; ☎099 696041; www.elephantvalleyproject.org; ⊙Mon-Fri).

For more information, check out www.earsasia.org

Environmental Concerns

There are many environmental problems that the average tourist has zero control over, but visitors to the Mekong region can reduce their

> **SMOKING**
>
> **Cambodia** Smoking is common but nicer hotels in tourist centres have nonsmoking areas or are smoke-free. Restaurants are a mix of smoking and smoke-free.
>
> **Laos** Smoking is common but they're increasingly strict about enforcing smoke-free zones. Most hotels have nonsmoking rooms and smoking is banned in restaurants in Vientiane and Luang Prabang.
>
> **Thailand** Nationwide ban on smoking in restaurants and bars is extended to public places in Bangkok, and is generally enforced.
>
> **Vietnam** Smoking is widespread and official bans largely ignored, except for on air-conditioned transport and in some higher-end restaurants.

individual impact on the natural environment and the local infrastructure by taking a few modest steps:

- Live like a local: opt for a fan instead of an air-con room; shower with cold water instead of hot.
- Use biodegradable soap to reduce water pollution.
- Eat locally sourced meals instead of imported products.
- Choose unplugged modes of transit (walking tour over minivan tour, bicycle over motorbike, kayak over jet ski).
- Dispose of your rubbish and cigarette butts in a proper receptacle, even if the locals don't.
- Don't eat or drink food products made from endangered animals or plants.
- Avoid plastic bottles: take a reusable water bottle and treat water.
- Patronise businesses that promote sustainable tourism, responsible tourism and ecotourism.

THE ABUSE OF INNOCENCE

The sexual abuse of children by foreign paedophiles is a serious problem in some parts of the Mekong region. Many child prostitutes are sold into the business by relatives. These sex slaves are either trafficked overseas or forced to cater to domestic demand and local sex-tourism operators. Unicef estimates that there are close to one million child prostitutes in Asia – one of the highest figures in the world.

Visitors can do their bit to fight this menace by keeping an eye out for suspicious behaviour on the part of foreigners. Don't ignore it. Try to pass on any relevant information, such as the name of the individual, to their nationality's embassy or to the local police.

Childsafe International (www.childsafe-international.org) Operates out of Cambodia and now covers Laos and Thailand as well. It aims to educate businesses and individuals to be on the lookout for children in vulnerable situations.

End Child Prostitution & Trafficking (www.ecpat.net) A global network aimed at stopping child prostitution, child pornography and the trafficking of children for sexual purposes. It has affiliates in most Western countries.

Orphanage Tourism

In recent years, visiting orphanages has become a popular activity, but is it always good for the children and the host country in the longer run? Orphanage tourism is a disturbing development that can draw some unscrupulous elements into the world of child care. Some orphanages have been established based on a business model, while in other cases the 'orphans' are not orphans at all, but have a living parent or have been 'rented' from a local school.

Many orphanages in the region are doing a good job in difficult circumstances. Some are world-class, enjoy funding and support from wealthy benefactors and don't need visitors; others are desperate places that need all the help they can get. However, if a place is promoting orphanage visits, then proceed with caution, as the adults may not always have the best interests of the children at heart.

Friends International and Unicef joined forces to launch the 'Think Before Visiting' campaign; learn more at www.thinkchildsafe.org/thinkbeforevisiting before you inadvertently contribute to the problem. Some tips for those considering volunteering with an orphanage in this region:

- Child-welfare experts recommend that any volunteering concerning children should involve a minimum three-month commitment – having strangers drop in and out on short visits can be detrimental to a child's emotional well-being and development. Note that some organisations, such as Friends International and Unicef, recommend that travellers never volunteer in an orphanage.
- If you do volunteer, think hard about what skills you have that will make a real difference to the children – working with the local staff, for example, to teach them English is likely to have a more sustainable impact.
- Don't – under any circumstances – visit orphanages as part of a brief tour or go to any that actively solicit tourists.
- Don't hand over large fees for a placement without checking where the money goes.
- Don't volunteer at any orphanage without thoroughly researching it. Is it regulated? Do they require background checks on volunteers?

Useful Websites

For tips on travelling responsibly while still having the trip of a lifetime, try the following websites:

Ecotourism Laos (www.ecotourismlaos.com) Has comprehensive information on Laos' protected areas, indigenous groups and endangered species, plus a useful 'Dos and Don'ts' section for travelling in the Mekong region.

Friends International (www.friends-international.org) Supports marginalised children and their families across Southeast Asia and runs the global **Child-Safe Network** (www.childsafe-international.org) to encourage travellers to behave responsibly with children.

Mekong Responsible Tourism (www.mekongresponsibletourism.org) Runs a list of responsible tour operators and tours in the Mekong region, plus tips on travelling in ways that are culturally sensitive and benefit local communities and the environment.

Safe Travel

Drugs

The risks associated with recreational drug use and distribution have grown to the point where all visitors should exercise extreme caution, even in places that have a reputation for free and open drug use. A spell in a local prison can be truly torturous. Even worse, you could become the next in a long line of tourists who have succumbed to a bad batch of cocaine or yaba (homemade methamphetamines mixed with caffeine).

Pollution & Noise

Pollution is a growing problem in the major cities of the region. Bangkok has long been famous as a place to chew the air rather than inhale. However, Ho Chi Minh City (formerly Saigon) and Phnom Penh also have problems of their own. Laos remains blissfully pollution-free for the most part.

Remember the movie *This is Spinal Tap?* The soundtrack of the cities in this region is permanently cranked up to 11 – not just any noise, but a whole lot of noises that just never seem to stop. At night there is most often a competing cacophony from motorbikes, discos, cafes, video arcades, karaoke lounges and restaurants, although in most areas the din subsides relatively early – by 11pm or so, as few places stay open much later than that. Unfortunately, from 5am onwards an entirely new series of sounds erupts, including but not limited to monk chants, wedding music, funeral dirges, roosters, hound dogs and street vendors loudly hawking everything from duck embryos to fried crickets.

One last thing...don't forget the earplugs.

Queues

What queues? Most locals in the Mekong region don't queue, they mass in a rugby scrum, pushing towards the counter. When in Rome... This is first-seen, first-served, so take a deep breath, muscle your way to the front and wave your passport or papers as close to the counter as you can.

Scams

Every year Lonely Planet receives feedback from hapless travellers reporting that they've been scammed in this region. In most cases the scams are petty rip-offs, in which a naive traveller pays too much for a ride to the bus station, to exchange money, buy souvenirs and so on. Rip-offs are in full force at border crossings, popular tourist attractions, bus and rail stations and wherever travellers might get confused.

Other common scams include having your rented bicycle or motorbike 'stolen' by someone with a duplicate key, and dodgy drug deals that involve police extortion. Some tips for avoiding scams:

- Be wary of of overfriendly locals.
- Avoid supercheap, inclusive transport packages, which often include extra, commission-generating fees.
- Don't accept invitations to play cards or go shopping with a friendly stranger; this is a prelude to a well-rehearsed and expensive scam.
- Don't believe the people who say that they support their global wanderings by reselling gemstones; in reality they support themselves by tricking unsuspecting foreigners.
- Understand that third parties get commissions; if a tout tells you a certain hotel or guesthouse is closed, don't believe it – it could be that the guesthouse doesn't pay commissions.

Theft

Theft in this part of the world is usually by stealth rather than by force, but violent robbery isn't unheard of, especially late at night or if the victim resists. Be careful when walking alone late at night and don't fall asleep in taxis.

Drive-by theft, usually by motorcycle-riding tandems, is a regional speciality, especially in cities. There have been incidents where thieves have dragged passengers off motorbikes, endangering

YABA DABA DO? YABA DABA DON'T!

Watch out for *yaba*, the 'crazy' drug from Thailand, known as *yama* in Cambodia, and also, rather ominously, as the Hindu god of death. Known as 'ice' or 'crystal meth' back home, it's not just any old diet pill from the pharmacist, but homemade methamphetamines produced in labs in Myanmar (Burma), Cambodia, Laos, Thailand and elsewhere. The pills are often laced with toxic substances, such as mercury, lithium or whatever else the maker can find. *Yaba* is a dirty drug and more addictive than users would like to admit, provoking powerful hallucinations, sleep deprivation and psychosis. Steer clear of the stuff.

lives. Shoulder bags and smartphones are particular targets, so secure your bag and keep your smartphone in your pocket, especially when riding a bicycle, riding on the back of a motorcycle taxi or just walking innocently down a footpath. A money belt worn underneath your clothes can minimise the risk of being victimised by snatch-and-run thieves.

Petty theft is nothing to be too alarmed about, but is common enough to warrant vigilance. Some basic tips for avoiding theft:

- Don't store valuables in the luggage compartment of buses.
- Your bling presents an easy target on beaches, so take extra care of it.
- Always be diplomatically suspicious of overfriendly locals; thieves have been known to drug travellers for easier pickings.
- Travel in groups late at night, especially after a night of carousing, to ensure safety in numbers.
- Stay *relatively* sober if you're going to be out walking alone late at night in major cities (if you're stumbling drunk, take a tuk-tuk).
- Always lock up your bicycle or motorbike and pay for parking whenever you can.

Finally, don't let paranoia ruin your trip. With just a few sensible precautions most travellers make their way across the region without incident.

HAPPINESS IS A STATE OF MIND

'Don't worry, be happy' could be the motto for the Mekong region, but in some backpacker centres the term 'happy' has taken on a completely different connotation. Seeing the word 'happy' in front of 'shake', 'pizza' or anything else does not, as one traveller was told, mean it comes with extra pineapple. The extra is usually marijuana, added in whatever quantity the shake-maker deems fit. For many travellers 'happy' is a well-understood alias, but there are others who innocently down their shake or pizza only to spend the next 24 hours floating in a world of their own.

Telephone

Individual countries have their own codes and rules, but the following rules apply to the entire region:

- Calls over the internet using Skype or another voice-over-internet protocol (VOIP) are the way forward, and there is plenty of infrastructure in place – both 4G and wi-fi – to make it happen.
- Roaming is bad for you – do not be that idiot who cluelessly yaks his way around the world and returns home to a US$3000 phone bill. Instead, buy a local SIM card, configure it for 4G, and call home for pennies via VOIP.
- Some mobile phones are 'locked' by your phone company back home, but most telephone shops in the Mekong region can 'unlock' them in seconds for a small charge.
- Mobile-phone coverage usually extends to all but the most remote areas in the Mekong region.

Time

Cambodia, Laos, Thailand and Vietnam are seven hours ahead of GMT/UTC. When it's noon in Bangkok or Hanoi, it is 9pm the previous evening in San Francisco, midnight in New York, 5am in London, 6am in Paris and 3pm in Sydney. There is no daylight saving time.

Toilets

Public toilets Fairly rare and rarely impressive. Gas stations and shopping centres usually have toilets. You may have to pay a few dong, riel, kip or baht.

Sit-down toilets Most decent hostels and all hotels from the midrange up throughout the region are equipped with Western-style 'thrones'.

Spray hoses 'Bum guns' are common across the region in private homes and in some restaurants and hotels. It's worth mastering these as sometimes they exist in lieu of toilet paper.

Squat toilets Common in public places and out in the countryside.

Toilet paper Generally to be tossed it in the wastebasket and not flushed down, as it taxes local sewage systems. Seldom

GOVERNMENT TRAVEL ADVICE

- **Australian Department of Foreign Affairs** (www.smartraveller.gov.au)
- **Canadian Government Travel & Tourism Site** (www.travel.gc.ca)
- **German Foreign Office** (www.auswaertiges-amt.de)
- **New Zealand Ministry of Foreign Affairs** (www.safetravel.govt.nz)
- **UK Foreign Office** (www.gov.uk/foreign-travel-advice)
- **US State Department** (www.travel.state.gov)

provided at public toilets, so carry some with you.

Tourist Information

All the countries in the Mekong region have government-funded tourist offices, with varying degrees of usefulness. Thailand offers by far the most efficient tourism information service, followed by Laos. When it comes to Cambodia and Vietnam, better information is often available from dedicated internet sites, guesthouses and travellers cafes, or your fellow travellers, rather than through the state-run tourist offices.

Cambodia Tourism Ministry (www.tourismcambodia.org)

Laos National Tourism Administration (www.tourismlaos.org)

Tourism Authority of Thailand (www.tourismthailand.org)

Vietnam Tourism (www.vietnamtourism.com)

Travellers with Disabilities

Travellers with serious disabilities will likely find the Mekong region a challenging place to travel. Inconveniences include the following:

- chaotic traffic
- lack of lifts in smaller hotels
- high kerbs and uneven pavements that are routinely blocked by parked motorbikes and food stalls
- an almost complete lack of disabled-friendly public amenities, even in big cities and major tourist hubs.

On the positive side, most people in the region are helpful towards foreigners, and local labour is cheap if you need someone to accompany you at all times. Most guesthouses and small hotels have ground-floor rooms that are reasonably easy to access.

Bus and train travel is tough, but rent a private vehicle with a driver and almost anywhere can become accessible.

International organisations that can provide information on mobility-impaired travel:

Accessible Journeys (www.disabilitytravel.com)

Disability Rights UK (www.disabilityrightsuk.org) UK-based umbrella organisation for voluntary groups for people with disabilities.

Mobility International USA (www.miusa.org) Advises disabled travellers on mobility issues and runs an educational exchange program.

Society for Accessible Travel & Hospitality (www.sath.org)

Download Lonely Planet's free *Accessible Travel* guide from http://lptravel.to/AccessibleTravel. The Travellers With Disabilities forum on Lonely Planet's Thorn Tree (www.lonelyplanet.com/thorntree) is also a good resource.

ETIQUETTE

Individual countries have their own rules and taboos, but the following apply for pretty much the entire Mekong region:

- **Arguments** Do not lose your temper. This will lead to a loss of face. Smile through conflict instead.
- **Chopsticks** Don't leave a pair of chopsticks sitting vertically in a rice bowl – they can look like the incense sticks that are burned for the dead.
- **Feet** Avoid pointing your feet at people or sacred objects (eg Buddhas); if you can't control your feet, tuck 'em behind you, like a mermaid.
- **Food** Don't turn down food placed in your bowl by your host.
- **Heads** Considered sacred: don't touch anyone on their head.
- **Monks** They are not supposed to touch or be touched by women.
- **Nude sunbathing** Considered totally inappropriate.
- **Shoes** Remove them when entering a temple or home.
- **Temples** Don't bare too much skin; remove any hat or head covering before entering.

Visas

Get your visas as you go rather than all at once before you leave home; they are often easier and cheaper to get in neighbouring countries and visas are only valid within a certain time period, which really hinders flexibility if you're on an extended trip.

Procedures for extending a visa vary from country to country. In some cases, extensions are quite complicated, in others they're a mere formality. Remember the most important rule: treat visits to embassies, consulates and borders as formal occasions and look smart for them.

You do not need to show an onward ticket to obtain a visa or enter the countries of the Mekong region, even though some do have such rules on the book.

Volunteering

'Voluntourism' is a booming business in the Mekong region, with travel companies co-opting the idea as a new marketing angle. To avoid the bulk of your placement fees going into the pockets of third-party agencies, it's important to do your research on the hundreds of organisations that now offer volunteer work and find a suitable one that supports your skills.

Lonely Planet does not endorse any organisations that we do not work with directly, so it is essential that you do your own thorough research before agreeing to volunteer with/donate to any organisation. Volunteer consolidators like www.volunteerabroad.com can be a good starting point, but you still need to do your due diligence on any organisation you find through such sites. Scrutinise any organisation working with children (especially orphanages, see p543) carefully, as child protection is a serious concern; organisations that do not conduct background checks on volunteers should be regarded with extreme caution.

One avenue towards volunteering is to apply through a professional organisation back home that offers one- or two-year placements in the region, such as the Voluntary Service Overseas in the UK and the US Peace Corps, VSO Canada, Australian Volunteers International and New Zealand's Volunteer Service Abroad. The UN also operates its own volunteer program; details are available at www.unv.org.

Women Travellers

While travel in the Mekong region for women is generally safe, there are a few things to keep in mind.

There's no question about it: solo women make inviting targets for thieves, and countless female travellers have been the victim of bag-snatching incidents and worse in places like Phnom Penh. Women should be on guard, especially when returning home late at night or arriving in a new town at night.

While physical assault is rare, local men often consider foreign women as being exempt from their own society's rules of conduct regarding members of the opposite sex. Use common sense about venturing into dangerous-looking areas, particularly alone or at night. If you do find yourself in a tricky situation, try to extricate yourself as quickly as possible – hopping into a taxi or entering a business establishment and asking them to call a cab is often the best solution.

YOU WANT MASSAGE?

Karaoke clubs and massage parlours are ubiquitous throughout the region. Sometimes this may mean a healthy massage to ease a stiff body. However, more often than not, both these terms are euphemisms for some sort of prostitution. There may be some singing or a bit of shoulder tweaking going on, but ultimately it is just a polite introduction to something naughtier. Legitimate karaoke and legitimate massage do exist in the bigger cities, but as a general rule of thumb, if the place looks sleazy, it probably is.

Work

The main opportunities for people passing through the region are teaching English (or another European language), landing a job in tourism or starting a small business such as a bar or restaurant.

Teaching English This is the easiest way to support yourself in the Mekong region. For short-term gigs, the large cities such as Bangkok, Ho Chi Minh City and Phnom Penh have a lot of language schools and a high turnover. Payaway (www.payaway.co.uk) provides a handy online list of language schools and volunteer groups looking for recruits for its regional programs.

Tourism Most of these jobs deservedly go to locals, but there are opportunities for wannabe guesthouse or hotel managers, bartenders, chefs and so on. This can be a pretty memorable way to pass a few months in a different culture.

Small-business start-up There are many success stories in the region, where people came for a holiday and built an empire. That said, if you elect to go this route tread with caution: many a foreigner has been burned in the region. Sometimes it's an unscrupulous partner, other times it's the local girlfriend, or boyfriend, who changes their mind and goes it alone. Sometimes the owners themselves burn out, drinking the profits of the bar or dabbling in drugs. Do your homework regarding ownership laws and legal recourse in the event of a dispute.

The website **Transitions Abroad** (www.transitionsabroad.com) and its namesake magazine cover all aspects of overseas life, including landing a job in a variety of fields. The website also provides links to other useful sites and publications for those living abroad.

Transport

GETTING THERE & AWAY

Entering the Mekong Region

Most travellers arrive by air and there are also overland routes via China, Myanmar and, in Thailand's extreme south, Malaysia. There are no public sea routes into the Mekong region.

Flights, cars and tours can be booked online at lonelyplanet.com/bookings.

Air

- The main points of entry by air are Bangkok, Phnom Penh, Siem Reap, Vientiane, Hanoi and Ho Chi Minh City.
- The major gateways for budget flights into and out of the Mekong region are Bangkok, Kuala Lumpur and Singapore.
- Other popular jumping-off points for flights into the Mekong region are Guangzhou, Hong Kong, Manila, Seoul, Taipei and Tokyo.
- Bangkok is the best place to shop for onward tickets around the Mekong region.
- Note that some popular budget airlines are not covered by online travel and flight-comparison sites, so it pays to check the airline websites separately.

Airports & Airlines

INTERNATIONAL AIRPORTS

Suvarnabhumi International Airport, Bangkok (www.suvarnabhumiairport.com)

Noi Bai Airport, Hanoi (www.hanoiairportonline.com)

Tan Son Nhat International Airport, Ho Chi Minh City (www.hochiminhcityairport.com)

Phnom Penh International Airport (www.cambodia-airports.aero)

Siem Reap International Airport (www.rep.aero)

Wattay International Airport, Vientiane (www.vientianeairport.com)

NATIONAL CARRIERS

Cambodia Angkor Air (www.cambodiaangkorair.com)

Lao Airlines (www.laoairlines.com)

Thai International Airways (www.thaiairways.com)

Vietnam Airways (www.vietnamairlines.com.vn)

Sea

Ocean approaches to Thailand, Vietnam or Cambodia can be made aboard cargo ships plying routes around the world. Ridiculously expensive and hopelessly romantic, a trip aboard a cargo ship is the perfect chance for you to write that novel that never writes itself. Some freighter ships have space for a few noncrew members, who have their own rooms but eat meals with the crew. Prices vary depending on your departure point, but costs start at around US$150 a day plus additional fees.

CLIMATE CHANGE & TRAVEL

Every form of transport that relies on carbon-based fuel generates CO_2, the main cause of human-induced climate change. Modern travel is dependent on aeroplanes, which might use less fuel per kilometre per person than most cars but travel much greater distances. The altitude at which aircraft emit gases (including CO_2) and particles also contributes to their climate change impact. Many websites offer 'carbon calculators' that allow people to estimate the carbon emissions generated by their journey and, for those who wish to do so, to offset the impact of the greenhouse gases emitted with contributions to portfolios of climate-friendly initiatives throughout the world. Lonely Planet offsets the carbon footprint of all staff and author travel.

GETTING AROUND

Air

Airlines in the Mekong Region

Air travel is a mixed bag in the Mekong region. Some routes to/from/within Thailand are now a real bargain, as no-frills regional carriers such as Air Asia and Nok Air offer heavily discounted fares. However, on many other routes, there may only be one carrier and prices are high.

Flights can usually be booked online easily enough, especially for budget airlines, or you can book through one of the myriad travel agents.

Air Passes

The national airlines of Southeast Asian countries frequently run promotional deals from select Western cities or for regional travel.

Bangkok Airways offers a Discovery Pass (in conjunction with Lao Airlines), which includes domestic coupons for US$88 in Thailand and Laos, plus international coupons from US$120 per sector (US$200 for longer distances).

Bicycle

Touring Southeast Asia on a bicycle has been steadily growing in popularity.

Cambodia & Laos Road conditions can make two-wheeling more challenging, but light traffic, especially in Laos, makes pedalling more pleasant than elsewhere.

Thailand Used as a base by many long-distance cyclists to head into Indochina for some challenging adventures.

Vietnam Traffic is relatively light away from National Hwy 1A; buses take bicycles and the entire coastal route is feasible, give or take a few hills.

Parts and services International-standard bicycles and components can be bought in Bangkok and Phnom Penh, but most cyclists bring their own.

Shipping bikes Bicycles can travel by air; ask about extra charges and shipment specifications.

Boat

As roads in the region improve, boats are less a factor than they once were, but boats are still popular on a few routes and in certain particularly remote areas they remain a necessity.

Cambodia The boat ride from Siem Reap to Battambang is spectacular, and you can also get from Siem Reap to Phnom Penh by boat. The main southern islands of Koh Rong and Koh Rong Sanloem can now be reached in less than an hour by frequent public fast boats.

Cambodia to Vietnam There are also various fast, slow and luxury boats plying the Mekong between Phnom Penh/Siem Reap and Chau Doc, Vietnam, for those who want to explore the Mekong Delta without backtracking to Ho Chi Minh City.

Thailand The *reu·a hăhng yow* (long-tail boat) is a staple of transport on rivers and canals in Bangkok and neighbouring provinces, and between islands. More touristed islands are serviced by larger, faster ferry boats.

Laos The leisurely Luang Say cruise is a fine way to link Huay Xai and Luang Prabang with a night in Pak Beng. For those on a budget, there are plenty of public boats running this way, and public river transport is still fairly common throughout the country.

Cruising

Luxury river cruises are popular along the Mekong in Laos and between Cambodia and Vietnam. Halong Bay is another popular spot for boat cruises. Companies specialising in upscale boat cruises include the following:

Compagnie Fluviale du Mekong (www.cfmekong.com)

Heritage Line (www.heritage-line.com)

Indochina Sails (✆04-3984 2362; www.indochinasails.com; overnight tour d cabin from US$478)

Pandaw Cruises (www.pandaw.com)

Bus

Bus travel has become a great way to get around with improved roads throughout the region. Most land borders are crossed via bus; these either travel straight through the two countries with a stop for border formalities, or require a change of buses at the appropriate border towns.

- Thailand offers by far the most comfortable buses.
- Cambodia and Vietnam have a pretty impressive network of buses connecting major cities, although these dry up in remote areas.
- Buses in Laos are reasonable on the busiest

SURVIVING THE STREETS

Wherever you roam in the region, you'll have to cross some busy streets eventually, so if you don't want to wind up like a bug on a windscreen, pay close attention to a few pedestrian survival rules.

Foreigners frequently make the mistake of thinking that the best way to cross a busy street in the Mekong region is to run quickly across, but this could get you creamed. Most locals cross the street slowly – very slowly – giving the motorbike drivers sufficient time to judge their position so they can pass on either side. They won't stop or even slow down, but they *will* try to avoid hitting you. Just don't make any sudden moves.

routes, but pretty poor elsewhere.

➡ Theft does occur on some long-distance buses; keep all valuables on your person, not in a stowed bag.

Car & Motorcycle

Self-drive car hire is possible in Thailand and in some areas of Laos and Cambodia.

Laos and Cambodia offer brilliant motorbiking for experienced riders, not forgetting the incredible mountain roads of northern Vietnam. Motorbiking is still the mode of transport for many Mekong residents, so you'll find repair shops everywhere, and they're widely available for rent throughout the region

Road conditions vary within the region:

➡ Thailand has an excellent road network with plenty of well-signposted, well-paved roads.

➡ Vietnam has decent roads, but self-drive car hire is not possible (motorbike hire is available).

➡ Laos and Cambodia road conditions vary, although sealed roads are now the norm.

Driving Licences

If you are planning to drive a car, get an International Driving Permit (IDP) from your local automobile association before you leave your home country; IDPs are inexpensive and valid for one year.

You rarely need to show a licence to rent a motorbike in Laos, Cambodia or Vietnam (although actually driving a bike technically requires one). Hiring 250cc or larger bikes may require a licence, especially in Thailand.

However, in all four countries you almost always need to leave a passport to hire a bike. This can cause problems if you get into an accident in remote Laos or Cambodia and need to be evacuated out of the country (usually to Thailand or Vietnam) to receive adequate medical care. An alternative to leaving your passport is to leave a several-hundred-dollar deposit to cover the value of the bike.

Hire

➡ Self-drive car hire is mainly an option in Thailand, plus a few places hire out vehicles in Cambodia and Laos.

➡ Cars with drivers are available at very reasonable rates in all countries of the region.

➡ Guesthouses rent motorcycles cheaply throughout the region, usually for around US$4 to US$10 a day.

➡ Dirt bikes (250cc) are also widely available in the region and are a lot of fun if you know how to handle them; rental costs roughly US$15 to US$50 per day.

MOTORCYCLE PASSENGER TIPS

Most Asians are so adept at driving and riding on motorcycles that they can balance the whole family on the front bumper, or even take a quick nap as a passenger. Foreigners unaccustomed to motorcycles are not as graceful.

➡ If you're riding on the back of a motorcycle remember to relax. For balance hold on to the back bar, not the driver's waist.

➡ Tall people should keep their long legs tucked in as most drivers are used to shorter passengers.

➡ Anyone wearing a skirt (or sarong etc) should always ride side-saddle and collect longer skirts so that they don't catch in the wheel or drive chain.

MOTORCYCLE SAFETY

Before taking a hired motorbike out on the road, perform the following routine safety checks.

➡ Look at the tyres to inspect the treads.

➡ Check for oil leaks.

➡ Test the brakes.

➡ Make sure the headlights and tail lights work and that you know how to turn them on. A decent helmet that fits is highly recommended. These can be hard to come by on the ground, so consider bringing your own if you are going to be doing a lot of two-wheeling.

Other gear-related tips to improve both safety and comfort during those long days in the saddle:

➡ If your helmet doesn't have a visor, then wear goggles, glasses or sunglasses to keep bugs, dust and other debris out of your eyes.

➡ Long trousers, long-sleeved shirts, gloves and shoes are highly recommended as protection against sunburn – and as a second skin if you fall.

➡ Pack wet-weather gear, especially in the rainy season.

Insurance

Purchasing insurance is highly recommended when you hire a motorcycle. The more reputable motorcycle-hire places will always offer insurance.

Without insurance you are responsible for anything that happens to the bike. To be absolutely clear about your liability, ask for a written estimate of the replacement cost for a similar bike.

Insurance for a hired car is also necessary. Be sure to ask the car-hire agent about liability and damage coverage.

Road Rules

Basically, there aren't many, and arguably none. Thailand is right-hand drive (like in the UK) and the other three countries are left-hand drive. Drive cautiously. An incredible number of lives are lost on

FARE'S FAIR?

This is the million-dong question when using local transport: 'Am I being quoted the right fare or are they completely ripping me off?' Well, there's no easy answer, but here are some guidelines to help you navigate the maze.

Boat Fixed fares for ferries or hydrofoils, but not for small local boats or some tourist boats.

Bus and sŏrngtăaou Generally fixed, though overcharging tourists is not unheard of. Buying through a travel agent or guesthouse usually incurs a commission – anything from 5% to 100%, so watch out for predatory travel agents.

***Cyclo* (pedicab), motorbike taxi and *tuk-tuk*/remork-moto** Most definitely not fixed. Any local transport prices given here are indicative; the actual price of a ride depends on the wiliness of the driver and your bargaining skills. It's best to agree on a price with your driver before setting off.

roads in this region every year, particularly around major holidays. Your odds of surviving are better if you heed the following rules:

- Size matters and the biggest vehicle wins by default, regardless of circumstances – 'might makes right' on the road.
- The middle of the road is typically used as an invisible third lane, even if there is oncoming traffic.
- The horn is used to notify other vehicles that you intend to pass them.
- Be particularly careful about children on the road, as they often live and play on the sides of even the busiest highways.
- Slow down if you see livestock near the road; hit a cow on a motorbike and you'll both be hamburger.

Hitching

- Hitching is never entirely safe in any country, and we don't recommend it. Travellers who hitch should understand that they are taking a small but potentially serious risk.
- People who do choose to hitch will be safer if they travel in pairs and let someone know where they are planning to go.
- Locals do flag down private and public vehicles for a lift, but some sort of payment is usually expected.

Local Transport

In the Mekong region, anything motorised is often modified to carry passengers.

Tuk-tuk The favoured form of transportation for tourists in Thailand, Cambodia and, increasingly, Laos. In Thailand and Laos tuk-tuk (or *đúk đúk* in Thai) are high-octane three-wheeled chariots, while in Cambodia they take the form of comfy little trailers pulled by motorbikes, which are called *remork-moto* (or *remork*) instead.

Motorcycle taxi Ubiquitous in Cambodia, Thailand and Vietnam, but rarer in Laos. However, in Laos motorised *săhm lór* (three-wheelers, or motorbikes with a sidecar) are becoming popular.

Sŏrngtăaou The main form of public transport in provincial Laos and Thailand, these are flat-bed or pick-up trucks kitted out with bench seating. They generally ply fixed routes but are also usually available for private hire.

Taxis Metered taxis are common in Thai and Vietnamese cities and can be flagged down on the street easily enough. They are remarkably cheap (about US$2 for a short ride), but be on the lookout for rigged meters in Vietnam. Taxis in Laos and Cambodia are generally not metered and must be ordered by phone or through your guesthouse.

Pedicab The old-fashioned bicycle rickshaw still survives in Cambodia and Vietnam, where it's known as a *cyclo*. In Laos they are *săhm lór*, often motorised.

Public bus Bangkok, Hanoi and Ho Chi Minh City have efficient bus networks. Phnom Penh has a new system but it's rarely used by tourists.

Metro Bangkok boasts a state-of-the-art light-rail and underground system that makes zipping around town feel like time travel.

Animals Beasts of burden still make up a percentage of the local transport in very remote areas, and it is possible to ride an ox cart through remote parts of Cambodia and Laos in the wet season.

Train

Cambodia The rail system is in the process of being rehabilitated, with (very slow) passenger services now offered between Phnom Penh and Sihanoukville via Kampot.

Laos Has no railway at all, save a short link to Thailand via the Friendship Bridge to Nong Khai. However, plans call for extending this line to central Vientiane and eventually connecting with a Chinese-funded railway line from Kunming to Vientiane via Luang Prabang, which is currently under construction.

Thailand and Vietnam Both have efficient railway networks, including the option of comfortable, air-con sleeper berths.

Cross-border trains There are no cross-border trains between Mekong countries. Thai trains serve the Thai border towns of Nong Khai (for crossing into Laos), Aranya Prathet (for crossing into Cambodia) and Ubon Ratchathani (for crossing into Laos).

Health

Travellers tend to worry about contracting infectious diseases when in the tropics, but infections are a rare cause of serious illness or death in travellers. Preexisting medical conditions such as heart disease, and accidental injury (especially traffic accidents), account for most life-threatening problems. Becoming ill in some way, however, is relatively common. The advice given here is a general guide and does not replace the advice of a doctor trained in travel medicine.

BEFORE YOU GO

- Pack medications in their original, clearly labelled, containers.
- A letter from your physician describing medical conditions and medications, including generic names, is a good idea.
- If carrying syringes or needles, be sure to have a physician's letter stating their medical necessity.
- If taking any regular medication, bring a double supply (packed separately) in case of loss or theft.
- In most Mekong-region countries, you can buy many medications over the counter without a doctor's prescription, but it can be difficult to find some of the newer drugs.

Insurance

Even if you're fit and healthy, don't travel without health insurance. Hospitals are often basic, particularly in remote areas. Anyone with a serious injury or illness may require emergency evacuation to Bangkok or Hong Kong. With an insurance policy costing no more than the equivalent of a few bottles of beer a day, this evacuation is free – without an insurance policy, it will cost US$10,000 or more.

Some things to keep in mind when choosing an insurer:

- Check that the policy covers ambulance rides and emergency flights home.
- Declare any existing medical conditions, as the insurance company *will* check if the problem is preexisting and will not pay up if undeclared.
- 'Dangerous activities' such as rock climbing, scuba diving, motorcycling and even trekking sometimes require extra cover.
- If your health insurance doesn't cover you for medical expenses abroad, consider getting extra insurance.
- Find out in advance if the insurance plan will make direct payments to providers or reimburse later for overseas health expenditures.
- Even if you have a direct-pay plan, many hospitals in the Mekong region expect payment up front in cash; exceptions are the big hospitals in Bangkok and International SOS clinics in Phnom Penh, Ho Chi Minh City (formerly Saigon) and elsewhere.

Vaccinations

If you plan to get vaccinated before your trip, consider the following:

- Specialised travel-medicine clinics are the best source of information, as they stock all available vaccines and can give specific recommendations for each region.
- Doctors will take into account factors such as past vaccination history, length of trip, activities and existing medical conditions.
- Most vaccines don't produce immunity until at least two weeks after they're given.
- Ask for an International Certificate of Vaccination (otherwise known as 'the yellow booklet'), which will list all vaccinations given.

Recommended Vaccinations

The World Health Organization (WHO) recommends the following vaccinations for travellers to the Mekong region:

Adult diphtheria and tetanus Single booster recommended if you haven't had one in the previous 10 years.

Hepatitis A Provides almost 100% protection for up to a year; a booster after 12 months provides at least another 20 years' protection.

Hepatitis B Now considered routine for most travellers. Given as three shots over six months. A rapid schedule is also available, as is a combined vaccination with hepatitis A. Lifetime protection occurs in 95% of people.

Measles, mumps and rubella (MMR) Two doses of MMR are required unless you have had the diseases. Many young adults require a booster.

Polio Only one booster is required as an adult for lifetime protection.

Typhoid Recommended unless your trip is less than a week long and only to developed cities. The vaccine offers around 70% protection, lasts for two to three years and comes as a single shot.

Required Vaccinations

The only vaccine required by international regulations is for yellow fever. Proof of vaccination is only required if you have visited a country in the yellow-fever zone within the six days before entering the Mekong region; if travelling to the Mekong region from Africa or South America, check to see if proof of vaccination is required. It's only likely to be an issue if flying directly from an affected country to a major gateway such as Bangkok.

Medical Checklist

Recommended items for a personal medical kit:

- antibacterial cream, eg Muciprocin
- antibiotics for diarrhoea, such as Norfloxacin or Ciprofloxacin; for bacterial diarrhoea, Azithromycin; for giardiasis or amoebic dysentery, Tinidazole
- antifungal cream, eg Clotrimazole
- antihistamine – there are many options, eg Cetrizine for daytime and Promethazine for night
- anti-inflammatory such as Ibuprofen
- antiseptic, eg Betadine
- antispasmodic for stomach cramps, eg Buscopan
- contraceptives
- decongestant, eg Pseudoephedrine
- DEET-based insect repellent
- diarrhoea treatment – consider an oral rehydration solution (eg Gastrolyte), diarrhoea 'stopper' (eg Loperamide) and antinausea medication (eg Prochlorperazine)
- first-aid items such as scissors, plasters, bandages, gauze, thermometer (but not one with mercury), sterile needles and syringes, safety pins and tweezers
- indigestion medication, eg Quickeze or Mylanta
- paracetamol
- Permethrin to impregnate clothing and mosquito nets
- steroid cream for allergic or itchy rashes, eg 1% to 2% hydrocortisone
- sunscreen and hat
- throat lozenges
- thrush (vaginal yeast infection) treatment, eg Clotrimazole pessaries or Diflucan tablet
- Ural or equivalent if you're prone to urine infections

Websites

Centers for Disease Control & Prevention (www.cdc.gov) Good source of general information.

Lonely Planet (www.lonelyplanet.com) A good place to start.

MD Travel Health (www.mdtravelhealth.com) Provides complete travel health recommendations for every country and is updated daily.

World Health Organization (www.who.int/ith) Publishes a superb book called *International Travel & Health*, which is revised annually and is available online at no cost.

Further Reading

Lonely Planet's *Healthy Travel – Asia & India* is a handy, pocket-sized book packed with useful information, including pretrip planning, emergency first aid, immunisation and disease information, and what to do if you get sick on the road. Other recommended references include *Traveller's Health* by Dr Richard Dawood and *Travelling Well* by Dr Deborah Mills (check out www.travellingwell.com.au).

IN VIETNAM, CAMBODIA, LAOS & NORTHERN THAILAND

Availability & Cost of Health Care

If you think you may have a serious disease, especially malaria, do not waste time – travel to the nearest quality facility to receive attention. Bangkok is a popular medical-tourism destination, with a few world-class hospitals that provide excellent care. In other Mekong capitals the best options are clinics that cater specifically to travellers and expats. These are more expensive than local medical facilities, but provide several advantages:

- They provide superior standard of care (usually).

- They liaise with insurance companies should you require evacuation.
- They understand the local system and are aware of the safest local hospitals and best specialists.

Infectious Diseases

Cutaneous Larva Migrans

Risk All countries, but most common on beaches of Thailand.

Cause Dog hookworm.

Symptoms Intensely itchy rash that starts as a small lump, then slowly spreads in a linear fashion.

Treatment Medications; should not be cut out or frozen.

Dengue

Risk All countries; most common in cities.

Cause Mosquito-borne (day and night).

Symptoms High fever, severe headache and body ache (dengue used to be known as breakbone fever); sometimes a rash and diarrhoea.

Treatment No specific treatment, just rest and paracetamol; do not take aspirin as it increases the likelihood of haemorrhaging. See a doctor to be diagnosed and monitored.

Prevention Insect-avoidance measures (both day and night).

Hepatitis A

Risk Very common in all countries.

Cause Food- and water-borne virus.

Symptoms Infects the liver, causing jaundice (yellow skin and eyes), nausea and lethargy.

Treatment No specific treatment; just allow time for the liver to heal.

Prevention All travellers to the Mekong region should be vaccinated against hepatitis A.

Hepatitis B

Risk All countries. In some parts of the Mekong region, up to 20% of the population carry hepatitis B, and usually are unaware of this.

Cause Spread by body fluids, including sexual contact.

Long-term consequences Possible liver cancer and cirrhosis, among others.

Prevention Vaccination (it's the only STD that can be prevented by vaccination).

Hepatitis E

Risk All countries, but far less common than Hepatitis A.

Cause Contaminated food and water.

Symptoms Similar symptoms to hepatitis A.

Consequences Severe in pregnant women: can result in the death of both mother and baby.

Prevention Currently no vaccine; follow safe eating and drinking guidelines.

HIV

Risk All countries; Vietnam has worst and most rapidly increasing HIV problem in region.

Cause Heterosexual sex is main method of transmission in region.

Consequences One of the most common causes of death in people under the age of 50 in Thailand.

Malaria

Risk All countries, mainly in rural areas.

Cause Mosquito-borne parasite.

Symptoms Fever; headache, diarrhoea, cough or chills may also occur; diagnosis can only be made by taking a blood sample.

Treatment A variety of drugs taken orally or by continuous intravenous infusion.

Prevention Two-pronged strategy: mosquito avoidance and antimalarial medications.

Rabies

Risk Common in most regions.

Cause Bite or lick from infected animal – most commonly a dog or monkey.

Consequences Uniformly fatal.

Treatment If an animal bites you, gently wash wound with soap and water, apply iodine-based antiseptic and immediately seek medical advice and commence postexposure treatment. If you are not prevaccinated you will need to receive rabies immunoglobulin as soon as possible.

Prevention Pretravel vaccination simplifies postbite treatment.

Schistosomiasis

Risk All countries.

Cause Tiny parasite that enters the skin after swimming in contaminated water.

Symptoms Travellers usually only get a light infection and are asymptomatic. If you are concerned, you can be tested three months after exposure. On rare occasions, travellers may develop 'Katayama fever'. This occurs some weeks after exposure, as the parasite passes through the lungs and causes an allergic reaction – symptoms are coughing and fever.

Treatment Medications

Sexually Transmitted Diseases (STDS)

Sexually transmitted diseases (STDs) most common in the Mekong region include herpes, warts, syphilis, gonorrhoea and chlamydia. People carrying these diseases often have no signs of infection. Condoms will prevent gonorrhoea and chlamydia but not warts or herpes. If after a sexual encounter you develop any rash, lumps, discharge, or pain when passing urine, seek immediate medical attention. If you have been sexually active during your travels, have an STD check on your return home.

Strongyloides

Risk Common in travellers to Cambodia, Laos and Thailand.

WEIGHING THE RISKS OF MALARIA

For such a serious and potentially deadly disease, there is an enormous amount of misinformation concerning malaria. You must get expert advice about whether your trip will actually put you at risk. Many parts of the Mekong region, particularly city and resort areas, have minimal to no risk of malaria, and the risk of side effects from the prevention tablets may outweigh the risk of actually getting the disease. For most rural areas in the region, however, the risk of contracting the disease far outweighs the risk of any tablet side effects. Remember that malaria can be fatal. Before you travel, seek medical advice on the right medication and dosage for you.

There are two strategies to preventing malaria: avoiding mosquito bites and taking antimalarial medication.

Mosquito Prevention

Travellers are advised to take the following steps:

- Use a DEET-based insect repellent on exposed skin. Wash off at night, as long as you are sleeping under a mosquito net. Natural repellents such as citronella can be effective, but must be applied more frequently than products containing DEET.
- Sleep under a mosquito net that is impregnated with Permethrin.
- Choose accommodation with screens and fans (if not air-conditioned).
- Impregnate clothing with Permethrin in high-risk areas.
- Wear long sleeves and trousers in light colours.
- Use mosquito coils.
- Spray your room with insect repellent before going out for your evening meal.

Antimalarials

Most people who catch malaria are taking inadequate or no antimalarial medication. A variety of medications are available.

Derivatives of Artesunate Not suitable as a preventive medication. They are useful treatments under medical supervision.

Chloroquine and Paludrine combination Limited effectiveness in most of the Mekong region. Common side effects include nausea (40% of people) and mouth ulcers. Generally not recommended.

Doxycycline Broad-spectrum antibiotic, ingested daily, that has the benefit of helping to prevent a variety of tropical diseases, including leptospirosis, tick-borne disease, typhus and meliodosis. Potential side effects include photosensitivity (a tendency to sunburn), thrush in women, indigestion, heartburn, nausea and interference with the contraceptive pill. More serious side effects include ulceration of the oesophagus. You can help prevent this by taking your tablet with a meal and a large glass of water, and never lying down within half an hour of taking it. It must be taken for four weeks after leaving the risk area.

Lariam (Mefloquine) Weekly tablet that suits many people. Has received much bad press, some of it justified, some not. Serious side effects are rare but include depression, anxiety, psychosis and seizures. Anyone with a history of depression, anxiety, other psychological disorders or epilepsy should not take Lariam. Considered safe in the second and third trimesters of pregnancy. Tablets must be taken for four weeks after leaving the risk area.

Malarone Combines Atovaquone and Proguanil. Side effects are uncommon and mild, usually nausea and headache. Best tablet for scuba divers and for those on short trips to high-risk areas. Must be taken for one week after leaving the risk area.

A final option is to take no preventive tablets but to have a supply of emergency medication should you develop the symptoms of malaria. This is less than ideal, and you'll need to get to a good medical facility within 24 hours of developing a fever. If you choose this option the most effective and safest treatment is Malarone (four tablets once daily for three days).

Cause Parasite transmitted by skin contact with soil.

Symptoms Unusual skin rash called *larva currens* – a linear rash on the trunk that comes and goes. Most people don't have other symptoms until their immune system becomes severely suppressed, when the parasite can cause an overwhelming infection.

Treatment Medications

Typhoid

Risk All countries.

Cause Spread via food and water.

Symptoms Serious bacterial infection results in high and slowly progressive fever, headache; may be accompanied by a dry cough and stomach pain. Diagnosis requires a blood test.

Treatment A course of antibiotics.

Prevention Vaccination recommended for all travellers spending more than one week in the Mekong region, or travelling outside of the major cities. Be aware that vaccination is not 100% effective so you must still be careful with what you eat and drink.

WATER

- Never drink tap water in the region.
- Bottled water is generally safe – check the seal is intact at purchase.
- Boiling water is the most efficient method of purifying it.
- The best chemical purifier is iodine. This should not be used by pregnant women or those people who suffer with thyroid problems.
- Water filters should filter out viruses. Ensure your filter has a chemical barrier such as iodine and a small pore size, ie less than four microns.

Traveller's Diarrhoea

Traveller's diarrhoea is by far the most common problem that affects travellers – between 30% and 50% of people will suffer from it within two weeks of starting their trip. In more than 80% of cases, traveller's diarrhoea is caused by bacteria (there are numerous potential culprits), and therefore responds promptly to treatment with antibiotics. Treatment will depend on your situation – how sick you are, how quickly you need to get better, where you are and so on.

Traveller's diarrhoea is defined as the passage of more than three watery bowel actions within 24 hours, plus at least one other symptom such as fever, cramps, nausea, vomiting or feeling generally unwell.

Treatment consists of staying well hydrated; rehydration solutions such as Gastrolyte are the best for this. Antibiotics such as Norfloxacin, Ciprofloxacin or Azithromycin will kill the bacteria quickly.

Loperamide is just a 'stopper' and doesn't get to the cause of the problem. It can be helpful, for example, if you have to go on a long bus ride. Don't take Loperamide if you have a fever, or blood in your stools. Seek medical attention quickly if you do not respond to an appropriate antibiotic. You should always seek reliable medical care if you have blood in your diarrhoea.

Amoebic Dysentery

Amoebic dysentery is very rare in travellers but is often misdiagnosed by poor-quality labs in the Mekong region.

Symptoms Similar to bacterial diarrhoea, ie fever, bloody diarrhoea and generally feeling unwell.

Consequences If left untreated, complications such as liver or gut abscesses can occur.

Treatment Tinidazole or Metronidazole to kill the parasite in your gut, and then a second drug to kill the cysts.

Giardiasis

Giardia lamblia is a relatively common parasite in travellers.

Symptoms Nausea, bloating, excess gas, fatigue, intermittent diarrhoea.

Treatment Tinidazole is the top choice, with Metronidazole being a second option. The parasite will eventually go away if left untreated but this can take months.

Language

This chapter offers basic vocabulary to help you get around the countries covered in this book. Read our coloured pronunciation guides as if they were English, and you'll be understood. Some of the phrases have both polite and informal forms – these are indicated by the abbreviations 'pol' and 'inf'. The abbreviations 'm' and 'f' indicate masculine and feminine gender respectively.

KHMER

In our pronunciation guides, vowels and vowel combinations with an h at the end are pronounced hard and aspirated (with a puff of air).

The symbols are read as follows: aa as the 'a' in 'father'; a and ah shorter and harder than aa; i as in 'kit'; uh as the 'u' in 'but'; ii as the 'ee' in 'feet'; eu like 'oo' (with the lips spread flat); euh as eu (short and hard); oh as the 'o' in 'hose' (short and hard); ow as in 'glow'; u as the 'u' in 'flute' (short and hard); uu as the 'oo' in 'zoo'; ua as the 'ou' in 'tour'; uah as ua (short and hard); œ as 'er' in 'her' (more open); ia as the 'ee' in 'beer' (without the 'r'); e as in 'they'; ai as in 'aisle'; ae as the 'a' in 'cat'; ay as ai (slightly more nasal); ey as in 'prey'; o as the 'ow' in 'cow'; av like a nasal ao (without the 'v'); euv like a nasal eu (without the 'v'); ohm as the 'ome' in 'home'; am as the 'um' in 'glum'; ih as the 'ee' in 'teeth' (short and hard); eh as the 'a' in 'date' (short and hard); awh as the 'aw' in 'jaw' (short and hard); and aw as the 'aw' in 'jaw'.

Some consonant combinations in our pronunciation guides are separated with an apostrophe for ease of pronunciation, eg 'j-r' in j'rook and 'ch-ng' in ch'ngain. Also note that k is pronounced as the 'g' in 'go'; kh as the 'k' in 'kind'; p as the final 'p' in 'puppy'; ph as the 'p' in 'pond'; r as in 'rum' but hard and rolling; t as the 't' in 'stand'; and th as the 't' in 'two'.

WANT MORE?

For in-depth language information and handy phrases, check out Lonely Planet's *Southeast Asia Phrasebook*. You'll find it at **shop.lonelyplanet.com**, or you can buy Lonely Planet's iPhone phrasebooks at the Apple App Store.

Basics

Hello.	ជម្រាបសួរ	johm riab sua
Goodbye.	លាសិនហើយ	lia suhn hao-y
Excuse me./ Sorry.	សូមទោស	sohm toh
Please.	សូម	sohm
Thank you.	អរគុណ	aw kohn
Yes.	បាទ/ចាស	baat/jaa **(m/f)**
No.	ទេ	te

What's your name?
អ្នកឈ្មោះអី? niak ch'muah ei

My name is ...
ខ្ញុំឈ្មោះ... kh'nyohm ch'muah ...

Accommodation

I'd like a room ...	ខ្ញុំសុំបន្ទប់...	kh'nyohm sohm bantohp ...
for one person	សម្រាប់ មួយនាក់	samruhp muy niak
for two people	សម្រាប់ ពីរនាក់	samruhp pii niak

How much is it per day?
តម្លៃមួយថ្ងៃ damlay muy th'ngay
ប៉ុន្មាន? pohnmaan

Numbers – Khmer

1	មួយ	muy
2	ពីរ	pii
3	បី	bei
4	បួន	buan
5	ប្រាំ	bram
6	ប្រាំមួយ	bram muy
7	ប្រាំពីរ	bram pii
8	ប្រាំបី	bram bei
9	ប្រាំបួន	bram buan
10	ដប់	dawp

Eating & Drinking

Do you have a menu in English?

មានមឺនុយជា ភាសាអង់គ្លេសទេ? — mien menui jea piasaa awnglay te

I'm vegetarian.

ខ្ញុំតមសាច់ — kh'nyohm tawm sait

The bill, please.

សូមគិតលុយ — sohm kuht lui

beer	ប៊ីយ៉ែរ	bii-yœ
coffee	កាហ្វេ	kaa fey
tea	តែ	tai
water	ទឹក	teuk

Emergencies

Help!

ជួយខ្ញុំផង! — juay kh'nyohm phawng

Call the police!

ជួយហៅប៉ូលិសមក! — juay hav polih mao

Call a doctor!

ជួយហៅគ្រូពេទ្យមក! — juay hav kruu paet mao

Where are the toilets?

បង្គន់នៅឯណា? — bawngkohn neuv ai naa

Shopping & Services

How much is it?

នេះថ្លៃប៉ុន្មាន? — nih th'lay pohnmaan

That's too much.

ថ្លៃពេក — th'lay pek

I'm looking for the ...	ខ្ញុំរក...	kh'nyohm rohk ...
bank	ធនាគារ	th'niakia
market	ផ្សារ	p'saa
post office	«ប្រៃសណីយ៍	praisuhnii
public telephone	ទូរស័ព្ទ សាធារណៈ	turasahp saathiaranah

Transport & Directions

Where is a/the ...?

...នៅឯណា? — ... neuv ai naa

bus stop

ចំណតឡានឈ្នួល — jamnawt laan ch'nual

train station

ស្ថានីយរថភ្លើង — s'thaanii roht plœng

When does the ... leave?	...ចេញម៉ោង b˝unμan?	... jein maong pohnmaan
boat	ទូក	duk
bus	ឡានឈ្នួល	laan ch'nual
train	រថភ្លើង	roht plœng
plane	យន្តហោះ	yohn hawh

LAO

Lao is a tonal language, meaning that many identical sounds are differentiated only by changes in the pitch of a speaker's voice. Pitch variations are relative to the speaker's natural vocal range, so that one person's low tone isn't necessarily the same pitch as another person's. There are six tones in Lao, indicated in our pronunciation guides by accent marks on letters: low tone (eg dęę), high (eg héu·a), rising (eg săhm), high falling (eg sôw) and low falling (eg kòw). Note that no accent mark is used for the mid tone (eg het).

The pronunciation of vowels goes like this: i as in 'it'; ee as in 'feet'; ai as in 'aisle'; ah as the 'a' in 'father'; a as the short 'a' in 'about'; aa as in 'bad'; air as in 'air'; er as in 'fur'; eu as in 'sir'; u as in 'put'; oo as in 'food'; ow as in 'now'; or as in 'jaw'; o as in 'phone'; oh as in 'toe'; ee·a as in 'lan'; oo·a as in 'tour'; ew as in 'yew'; and oy as in 'boy'.

Most consonants correspond to their English counterparts. The exceptions are đ (a hard 't' sound, a bit like 'dt') and ƀ (a hard 'p' sound, a bit like 'bp').

In our pronunciation guides, the hyphens indicate syllable breaks in words, eg àng-gít (English). Some syllables are further divided with a dot to help you pronounce compound vowels, eg kĕe·an (write).

Basics

Hello.	ສະບາຍດີ	sábại-dĕe
Goodbye.	ສະບາຍດີ	sábại-dĕe
Excuse me./ Sorry.	ຂໍໂທດ	kŏr tôht
Please.	ກະລຸນາ	ga-lú-náh
Thank you.	ຂອບໃຈ	kòrp jại
Yes./No.	ແມນ/ບໍ່	maan/bor

What's your name?
ເຈົ້າຊື່ຫຍັງ — jôw seu nyăng

My name is ...
ຂ້ອຍຊື່ ... — kòy seu ...

Accommodation

hotel	ໂຮງແຮມ	hóhng háam
guesthouse	ຫໍຮັບແຂກ	hŏr hap káak

Do you have a room?
ມີຫ້ອງບໍ່ — mée hòrng bor

single room
ຫ້ອງນອນຕຽງດຽວ — hòrng nórn dĕe·ang dee·o

double room
ຫ້ອງນອນຕຽງຄູ່ — hòrng nórn dĕe·ang koo

How much ...?	... ເທົ່າໃດ	... tow dại
per night	ຄືນລະ	kéun-la
per week	ອາທິດລະ	ạh-tit-la

Eating & Drinking

What do you have that's special?
ມີຫຍັງພິເສດບໍ່ — mée nyăng pi-sèt bor

I'd like to try that.
ຂ້ອຍຢາກລອງກິນເບິ່ງ — kòy yàhk lórng gịn berng

I eat only vegetables.
ຂ້ອຍກິນແຕ່ຜັກ — kòy gịn đaa pák

Please bring the bill.
ຂໍແຊັກແດ້ — kŏr saak daa

beer	ເບຍ	bẹe·a
coffee	ກາແຟ	gạh-fáir
tea	ຊາ	sáh
water	ນໍ້າດື່ມ	nâm deum

Emergencies

Help!	ຊ່ວຍແດ່	soo·ay daa
Go away!	ໄປເດີ້	bại dêr

Call the police!
ຊ່ວຍເອີ້ນຕຳລວດແດ່ — soo·ay êrn đam-lòo·at daa

Call a doctor!
ຊ່ວຍຕາມຫາໝໍໃຫ້ແດ່ — soo·ay đạhm hăh mŏr hài daa

I'm lost.
ຂ້ອຍຫລົງທາງ — kòy lŏng táhng

Where are the toilets?
ຫ້ອງນໍ້າຢູ່ໃສ — hòrng nâm yoo să

Shopping & Services

I'm looking for ...
ຂ້ອຍຊອກຫາ ... — kòy sòrk hăh ...

How much (for) ...?
... ເທົ່າໃດ — ... tow dại

The price is very high.
ລາຄາແພງຫລາຍ — láh-káh páang lăi

I want to change money.
ຂ້ອຍຢາກປ່ຽນເງິນ — kòy yàhk ɓee·an ngérn

bank	ທະນາຄານ	ta-náh-káhn
pharmacy	ຮ້ານຂາຍຢາ	hâhn kăi yạh
post office	ໄປສະນີ ໂຮງສາຍ	ɓại-sá-née hóhng săi

Numbers – Lao

1	ໜຶ່ງ	neung
2	ສອງ	sŏrng
3	ສາມ	săhm
4	ສີ່	see
5	ຫ້າ	hàh
6	ຫກ	hók
7	ເຈັດ	jét
8	ແປດ	ɓaat
9	ເກົ້າ	gôw
10	ສິບ	síp

Transport & Directions

Where is the ...?
... ຢູ່ໃສ ... yòo săi

How far?
ໄກເທົ່າໃດ kại tow dại

I'd like a ticket.
ຂ້ອຍຢາກໄດ້ປີ້ kòy yàhk dâi ɓêe

What time will the ... leave?
... ຈະອອກຈັກໂມງ ... já òrk ják móhng

boat	ເຮືອ	héu·a
bus	ລົດເມ	lot máir
minivan	ລົດຕູ້	lot đôo
plane	ເຮືອບິນ	héu·a bĭn

THAI

In Thai the meaning of a syllable may be altered by means of tones. In standard Thai there are five tones: low (eg bàht), mid (eg dee), falling (eg mâi), high (eg máh) and rising (eg săhm). The range of all tones is relative to each speaker's vocal range, so there is no fixed 'pitch' intrinsic to the language.

In our pronunciation guides, the hyphens indicate syllable breaks within words, and for ease of pronunciation some compound vowels are further divided with a dot, eg mêu·a-rai (when).

The vowel a is pronounced as in 'about', aa as the 'a' in 'bad', ah as the 'a' in 'father', ai as in 'aisle', air as in 'flair' (without the 'r'), eu as the 'er' in 'her' (without the 'r'), ew as in 'new' (with rounded lips), oh as the 'o' in 'toe', or as in 'torn' (without the 'r') and ow as in 'now'.

Note also the pronunciation of the following consonants: ɓ (a hard 'p' sound, almost like a 'b', eg in 'hip-bag'); đ (a hard 't' sound, like a sharp 'd', eg in 'mid-tone'); and r (as in 'run' but flapped; often pronounced like 'l').

Basics

Hello.	สวัสดี	sà-wàt-dee
Goodbye.	ลาก่อน	lah gòrn
Excuse me.	ขออภัย	kŏr à-pai
Sorry.	ขอโทษ	kŏr tôht
Please.	ขอ	kŏr
Thank you.	ขอบคุณ	kòrp kun
Yes.	ใช่	châi
No.	ไม่	mâi

What's your name?
คุณชื่ออะไร kun chêu à-rai

My name is ...
ผม/ดิฉัน pŏm/dì-chăn
ชื่อ... chêu ... (m/f)

Accommodation

Where's a ...?	... อยู่ที่ไหน	... yòo têe năi
campsite	ค่ายพักแรม	kâi pák raam
guesthouse	บ้านพัก	bâhn pák
hotel	โรงแรม	rohng raam
youth hostel	บ้าน เยาวชน	bâhn yow-wá-chon

Do you have a ... room?	มีห้อง ... ไหม	mee hôrng ... măi
single	เดี่ยว	dèe·o
double	เตียงคู่	đee·ang kôo

Eating & Drinking

What would you recommend?
คุณแนะนำอะไรบ้าง kun náa-nam à-rai bâhng

I'd like (the menu), please.
ขอ (รายการ อาหาร) หน่อย kŏr (rai gahn ah-hăhn) nòy

I don't eat (red meat).
ผม/ดิฉันไม่กิน (เนื้อแดง) pŏm/dì-chăn mâi gin (néu·a daang) (m/f)

Cheers!
ไชโย chai-yoh

Please bring the bill.
ขอบิลหน่อย kŏr bin nòy

beer	เบียร์	bee·a
coffee	กาแฟ	gah-faa
tea	ชา	chah
water	น้ำดื่ม	nám dèum

Emergencies

Help!	ช่วยด้วย	chôo·ay dôo·ay
Go away!	ไปให้พ้น	ɓai hâi pón

Numbers – Thai

1	หนึ่ง	nèung
2	สอง	sŏrng
3	สาม	săhm
4	สี่	sèe
5	ห้า	hâh
6	หก	hòk
7	เจ็ด	jèt
8	แปด	ɓàat
9	เก้า	gôw
10	สิบ	sìp

I'm lost.
ผม/ดิฉัน หลงทาง — pŏm/dì-chăn lŏng tahng (m/f)

Call the police!
เรียกตำรวจหน่อย — rêe·ak đam·ròo·at nòy

Call a doctor!
เรียกหมอหน่อย — rêe·ak mŏr nòy

I'm ill.
ผม/ดิฉันป่วย — pŏm/dì-chăn ɓòo·ay (m/f)

Where are the toilets?
ห้องน้ำอยู่ที่ไหน — hôrng nám yòo têe năi

Shopping & Services

I'd like to buy ...
อยากจะซื้อ ... — yàhk jà séu ...

How much is it?
เท่าไร — tôw-rai

That's too expensive.
แพงไป — paang ɓai

Transport & Directions

Where's ...?
... อยู่ที่ไหน — ... yòo têe năi

What's the address?
ที่อยู่คืออะไร — têe yòo keu à-rai

Can you show me (on the map)?
ให้ดู (ในแผนที่) ได้ไหม — hâi doo (nai păan têe) dâi măi

A ... ticket, please. — ขอตั๋ว ... — kŏr đŏo·a ...

one-way	เที่ยวเดียว	têe·o dee·o
return	ไปกลับ	ɓai glàp

boat	เรือ	reu·a
bus	รถเมล์	rót mair
plane	เครื่องบิน	krêu·ang bin
train	รถไฟ	rót fai

VIETNAMESE

Vietnamese is written in a Latin-based phonetic alphabet, which was declared the official written form in 1910.

In our pronunciation guides, a is pronounced as in 'at', aa as in 'father', aw as in 'law', er as in 'her', oh as in 'doh!', ow as in 'cow', u as in 'book', uh as in 'but' and uhr as in 'fur' (without the 'r'). We've used dots (eg dee·úhng) to separate the combined vowel sounds. Note also that d is pronounced as in 'stop', đ as in 'dog', and ğ as in 'skill'.

Vietnamese uses a system of tones to make distinctions between words – so some vowels are pronounced with a high or low pitch.There are six tones in Vietnamese, indicated in the written language (and in our pronunciation guides) by accent marks on the vowel: mid (ma), low falling (mà), low rising (mả), high broken (mã), high rising (má) and low broken (mạ). The mid tone is flat.

The variation in vocabulary between the Vietnamese of the north and the south is indicated by (N) and (S) respectively.

Basics

Hello.	*Xin chào.*	sin jòw
Goodbye.	*Tạm biệt.*	daạm bee·ụht
Excuse me./ Sorry.	*Xin lỗi.*	sin lõy
Please.	*Làm ơn.*	laàm ern
Thank you.	*Cảm ơn.*	ğaảm ern
Yes.	*Vâng./Dạ.* (N/S)	vuhng/ yạ
No.	*Không.*	kawm

What's your name?
Tên là gì? — den laà zeè

My name is ...
Tên tôi là ... — den doy laà ...

Accommodation

Where's a ...?	*Đâu có ... ?*	đoh ğó ...
campsite	*nơi cắm trại*	ner·ee ğúhm chại
hotel	*khách sạn*	kaák saạn
guesthouse	*nhà khách*	nyaà kaák

I'd like a ...	*Tôi muốn ...*	doy moo·úhn ...
single room	*phòng đơn*	fòm dern
double room	*phòng giường đôi*	fòm zuhr·èrng đoy

How much is it per ...?	*Giá bao nhiêu một ...?*	zaá bow nyee·oo mạwt ...
night	*đêm*	đem
person	*người*	nguhr·eè

Eating & Drinking

I'd like the menu.
Tôi muốn thực đơn. doy moo·úhn tụhrk đern

What's the speciality here?
Ở đây có món gì đặc biệt? ér đay kó món zeè dụhk bee·ụht

I'm a vegetarian.
Tôi ăn chay. doy uhn jay

I'd like ...
Xin cho tôi ... sin jo doy ...

Cheers!
Chúc sức khoẻ! júp súhrk kwá

The bill, please.
Xin tính tiền. sin díng dee·ùhn

beer	*bia*	bi·a
coffee	*cà phê*	ğaà fe
tea	*chè/trà* (N/S)	jà/chaà
water	*nước*	nuhr·érk
wine	*rượu nho*	zee·oọ nyo

Emergencies

Help!
Cứu tôi! ğuhr·oó doy

Leave me alone!
Thôi! toy

I'm lost.
Tôi bị lạc đường. doi beẹ laạk đuhr·èrng

Please call the police.
Làm ơn gọi công an. laàm ern gọy ğawm aan

Please call a doctor.
Làm ơn gọi bác sĩ. laàm ern gọy baák seẽ

I'm ill.
Tôi bị đau. doy beẹ đoh

Where is the toilet?
Nhà vệ sinh ở đâu? nyaà vẹ sing ẻr đoh

Shopping & Services

I'd like to buy ...
Tôi muốn mua ... doy moo·úhn moo·uh ...

How much is this?
Cái này giá bao nhiêu? ğaí này zaá bow nyee·oo

It's too expensive.
Cái này quá mắc. ğaí này gwaá múhk

bank	*ngân hàng*	nguhn haàng
market	*chợ*	jẹr
post office	*bưu điện*	buhr·oo đee·ụhn
tourist office	*văn phòng hướng dẫn du lịch*	vuhn fòm huhr·érng zũhn zoo lịk

Transport & Directions

Where is ...?
... ở đâu? ... ẻr đoh

What is the address?
Địa chỉ là gì? đee·ụh cheẻ laà zeè

Can you show me (on the map)?
Xin chỉ giùm (trên bản đồ này). sin jeẻ zùm (chen baản dàw này)

I'd like a ... ticket.	*Tôi muốn vé ...*	doy moo·úhn vá ...
one way	*đi một chiều*	đee mạt jee·oò
return	*khứ hồi*	kúhr haw·eè

boat	*thuyền*	twee·ùhn
bus	*xe buýt*	sa beét
plane	*máy bay*	máy bay
train	*xe lửa*	sa lủhr·uh

Numbers – Vietnamese

1	*một*	mạwt
2	*hai*	hai
3	*ba*	baa
4	*bốn*	báwn
5	*năm*	nuhm
6	*sáu*	sóh
7	*bảy*	bảy
8	*tám*	dúhm
9	*chín*	jín
10	*mười*	muhr·eè

GLOSSARY

This glossary is a list of Cambodian (C), Lao (L), Thai (T) and Vietnamese (V) terms you may come across in the Mekong region.

ao dai (V) – traditional Vietnamese tunic and trousers
APEC – Asia-Pacific Economic Cooperation
apsara (C) – heavenly nymphs or angelic dancers
Asean – Association of Southeast Asian Nations

bąasĭi (L) – sometimes written as 'basi' or 'baci'; a ceremony in which the 32 khwăn are symbolically bound to the participant for health and safety
baht (T) – the Thai unit of currency
baray (C) – ancient reservoir
BE (L, T) – Buddhist Era
boeng (C) – lake
BTS (T) – Bangkok Transit System (Skytrain)
bun (L) – festival
buu dien (V) – post office

Cao Daism (V) – Vietnamese religious sect
Cham (C, V) – ethnic minority descended from the people of Champa; a Hindu kingdom dating from the 2nd century BC
chedi (T) – see stupa
Chenla (C, L, V) – Pre-Angkorian Khmer kingdom covering parts of Cambodia, Laos and Vietnam
Chunchiet (C) – ethnolinguistic minority
CPP (C) – Cambodian People's Party
cyclo (C, V) – bicycle rickshaw

devaraja (C) – god king
DMZ (V) – the misnamed Demilitarised Zone, a strip of land that once separated North and South Vietnam
dong (V) – the Vietnamese unit of currency
duong (V) – road, street; abbreviated as 'Đ'

Ecpat – End Child Prostitution & Trafficking

faràng (T) – Western, Westerner; foreigner
Funan (C, V) – first Khmer kingdom, located in Mekong Delta area

HCMC (V) – Ho Chi Minh City (Saigon)
Hoa (V) – ethnic Chinese, the largest single minority group in Vietnam

Indochina – Vietnam, Cambodia and Laos, the French colony of Indochine; the name derives from Indian and Chinese influences
Isan (T) – general term used for northeastern Thailand

jataka (C, L, T) – stories of the Buddha's past lives, often enacted in dance-drama
jumbo (L) – a motorised three-wheeled taxi, sometimes called a túk-túk

karst – limestone peaks with caves, underground streams and potholes
khao (T) – hill, mountain
khlong (T) – canal
Khmer (C) – ethnic Cambodians; Cambodian language
Khmer Rouge (C) – literally Red Khmers, the commonly used name for the Cambodian communist movement responsible for the genocide in the 1970s
khwăn (L) – guardian spirits of the body
Kinh (V) – the Vietnamese language
kip (L) – the Lao unit of currency
ko (T) – island
koh (C) – island
krama (C) – chequered scarf

lákhon (C, T) – classical dance-drama
linga (C, L, T, V) – phallic symbol

mae nam (L, T) – river
Mahayana – literally, 'Great Vehicle'; a school of Buddhism that extended the early Buddhist teachings; see also Theravada
meuang (L, T) – city
MIA (C, L, V) – missing in action, usually referring to US personnel
Montagnards (V) – highlanders, mountain people; specifically the ethnic minorities inhabiting remote areas of Vietnam
moto (C) – motorcycle taxi
Mt Meru – the mythical dwelling place of the Hindu gods, symbolised by the Himalayas
múan (L) – fun, which the Lao believe should be present in all activities
muay thai (T) – Thai boxing

nâam (L, T) – water, river
naga (C, L, T) – mythical serpent-being
NTAL (L) – National Tourism Administration of Lao
NVA (V) – North Vietnamese Army

Pali – ancient Indian language that, along with Sanskrit, is the root of Khmer, Lao and Thai
Pathet Lao (L) – literally, 'Country of Laos'; both a general term for the country and the common

name for the Lao communist military during the civil war

phansăa (T) – Buddhist lent

phnom (C) – mountain

phu (L) – hill or mountain

POW – prisoner of war

prasat (C, T) – tower, temple

psar (C) – market

quan (V) – urban district

quoc ngu (V) – Vietnamese alphabet

Ramakian (T) – Thai version of the Ramayana

Ramayana – Indian epic story of Rama's battle with demons

Reamker (C) – Khmer version of the Ramayana

remorque (C) – (or remork) a motorised three-wheeled pedicab

riel (C) – the Cambodian unit of currency

roi nuoc (V) – water puppetry

rót fai fáa (T) – Skytrain; BTS

săhmlór (T) – three-wheeled pedicab

Sanskrit – ancient Hindu language that, along with Pali, is the root of Khmer, Lao and Thai

sànùk (T) – fun

soi (L, T) – lane, small street

song (L, V) – river

Songkran (T) – Thai New Year, held in mid-April

sŏrngtăaou (L, T) – small pick-up truck with two benches in the back

SRV (V) – Socialist Republic of Vietnam (Vietnam's official name)

stung (C) – small river

stupa – religious monument, often containing Buddha relics

talat (L) – market

Tam Giao (V) – literally, 'triple religion'; Confucianism, Taoism and Buddhism fused over time with popular Chinese beliefs and ancient Vietnamese animism

Tao (V) – the Way; the essence of which all things are made

TAT (T) – Tourism Authority of Thailand

tat (L) – waterfall

Tet (V) – Lunar New Year

thâat (L) – Buddhist stupa, reliquary; also written as 'that'

thànŏn (L, T) – road, street, avenue; abbreviated as 'Th'

Theravada – a school of Buddhism found in Cambodia, Laos and Thailand; this school confined itself to the early Buddhist teachings unlike Mahayana

tonlé (C) – major river

tripitaka (T) – Buddhist scriptures

túk-túk (L, T) – motorised săhmlór

UNDP – United Nations Development Programme

UXO (C, L, V) – unexploded ordnance

VC (V) – Viet Cong or Vietnamese Communists

vihara (C) – temple sanctuary

wâi (L, T) – palms-together greeting

wat (C, L, T) – Buddhist temple-monastery

wíhăhn (T) – sanctuary, hall, dwelling

xe om (V) – motorbike taxi (also Honda om)

xich lo (V) – see cyclo

Behind the Scenes

SEND US YOUR FEEDBACK

We love to hear from travellers – your comments keep us on our toes and help make our books better. Our well-travelled team reads every word on what you loved or loathed about this book. Although we cannot reply individually to your submissions, we always guarantee that your feedback goes straight to the appropriate authors, in time for the next edition. Each person who sends us information is thanked in the next edition – the most useful submissions are rewarded with a selection of digital PDF chapters.

Visit **lonelyplanet.com/contact** to submit your updates and suggestions or to ask for help. Our award-winning website also features inspirational travel stories, news and discussions.

Note: We may edit, reproduce and incorporate your comments in Lonely Planet products such as guidebooks, websites and digital products, so let us know if you don't want your comments reproduced or your name acknowledged. For a copy of our privacy policy visit lonelyplanet.com/privacy.

OUR READERS

Many thanks to the travellers who used the last edition and wrote to us with helpful hints, useful advice and interesting anecdotes:

Alessandra Furlan, Alexandra van den Broek, Allan Marsden, Ariane Bouf, Di Swanson, Ellis Gladstone, Harmen Keuning, Helen Newman, Irmi Chamberlain, Julia Wilber, Kelly Eberhard, Kennedy Newton, Kylie Tanabe, Lois Taylor, Mark Armitage, Matt Thwaite, Noel Archbold, Paulo Gaeta, Rachelle Tews, Rebecca Deacon, Robert Mclaughlin, Sofie Compiet, Stefan Kleinberger, Stephen Dunn, Susanna Stokes, Thao Tran, Thomas Wiser, Zara Machado

WRITER THANKS

Phillip Tang

Thanks to local experts Thanh Hoài, Hiếu Trần, Henry in Hoi An, Nam Phùng (Léon), Duy Khang, Blue, Vinh Hiến, Tri, Jonathan Morana, Mark Zazula, Lê Ngọc Lâm and, especially, Jay Luong for the adventures. Thanks to Iain Stewart and Laura Crawford. Extra appreciation to Géraldine Galvaing – how much did you enjoy muddy, double-glazed Coconut 2.0? For Luu Tiến Lê, Giang Hưng and those who came before.

Tim Bewer

A hearty *kòrp jại* to the many people along the way who answered my incessant questions or helped me out in other ways during this update. In particular, Nicolas Papon-Phalaphanh, Latanakone Keokhamphoui, Yves Verlaine, Khun Buasone and Prapaporn Sompakdee provided great assistance, while Laura, Nick, Rich and the rest of the Lonely Planet team were a pleasure to work with, as always. Finally, a special thanks to my wife, Suttawan, for help on this book and much more.

Greg Bloom

Big thanks to Lina in Siem Reap and to Nick for the useful tips on the ever-changing Cambodian travel scene. Back home, thanks to baby Callie, who just couldn't wait until after my deadlines to arrive, but provided moments of tenderness when she did. To her mama, Windi, thanks for handling the parenting duties while I was drowning under an avalanche of work. And lastly, thanks to new big sister Anna, as always, for the humour and stress relief.

Austin Bush

Thanks to all the generous people on the ground in northern and northeastern Thailand, and to Jennifer Carey for her help and guidance.

Nick Ray

A huge and heartfelt thanks to the people of Cambodia and Laos, whose warmth and humour, stoicism and spirit make these countries happy yet humbling places to be. Biggest thanks are reserved for my wife, Kulikar Sotho, as without her support and encouragement the adventures would not be possible. To our children, Julian and Belle, for signing up for some family adventures in new look Vang Vieng, and mum and dad for giving me a taste for travel from a young age. Thanks to

OUR STORY

A beat-up old car, a few dollars in the pocket and a sense of adventure. In 1972 that's all Tony and Maureen Wheeler needed for the trip of a lifetime – across Europe and Asia overland to Australia. It took several months, and at the end – broke but inspired – they sat at their kitchen table writing and stapling together their first travel guide, *Across Asia on the Cheap*. Within a week they'd sold 1500 copies. Lonely Planet was born.

Today, Lonely Planet has offices in Franklin, London, Melbourne, Oakland, Dublin, Beijing and Delhi, with more than 600 staff and writers. We share Tony's belief that 'a great guidebook should do three things: inform, educate and amuse'.

fellow travellers and residents, friends and contacts in Cambodia and Laos who have helped shaped my knowledge and experience in this country. Thanks also to my co-authors for going the extra mile to ensure this is a worthy new edition. Finally, thanks to the Lonely Planet team who have worked on this title.

Richard Waters

My special thanks to Elizabeth Vongsa, Adri Berger, Ivan Schulte, Harp, Saly Phimpinith, Dennis Ulstrup, Annabel and Josef, Agnes, Mr Vongdavone and Marco. Also thanks as usual to my extended family, the Lao people, from whom I seem to learn something every trip. Finally, special thanks to Laura Crawford, my long-suffering Destination Editor who keeps stoic when my technical skills fail to join the 21st century.

China Williams

Thanks to Dora Whitaker and the LP editors who keep me in their email contact list. More thanks to Austin Bush and the other LP authors who maintain the quality and expertise of these guides. And much gratitude to my Thailand friends and contacts: Pim, Nong, Jane and Ruengsang. Hugs to my family who keep me busy in my other life as a mum.

Contributing Writer

Martin Stuart-Fox

Martin Stuart-Fox is Emeritus Professor of History at the University of Queensland, Australia. He has written multiple books and dozens of articles and book chapters on the politics and history of Laos.

ACKNOWLEDGEMENTS

Climate map data adapted from Peel MC, Finlayson BL & McMahon TA (2007) 'Updated World Map of the Köppen-Geiger Climate Classification', Hydrology and Earth System Sciences, 11, 163344.

Illustrations p92-3, p220-221, 406-7 and 408-9 by Michael Weldon

Cover photograph: Fresco detail, Wat Xieng Thong, Luang Prabrang, Laos; Hemis/AWL ©.

THIS BOOK

This 5th edition of Lonely Planet's *Vietnam, Cambodia, Laos & Northern Thailand* guidebook was researched and written by Phillip Tang, Tim Bewer, Greg Bloom, Austin Bush, Nick Ray, Martin Stuart-Fox, Richard Waters and China Williams.

The previous two editions were also written by Greg, Austin, Richard and China, with Brett Atkinson, David Eimer, Damian Harper and Iain Stewart. This guidebook was produced by the following:

Destination Editors Laura Crawford, Dora Whitaker

Product Editor Amanda Williamson

Senior Cartographer Diana Von Holdt

Book Designer Virginia Moreno

Assisting Editors Sarah Bailey, Imogen Bannister, Nigel Chin, Carly Hall, Gabrielle Innes, Kellie Langdon, Ali Lemer, Kate Morgan, Lauren O'Connell, Charlotte Orr, Gabrielle Stefanos, Fionnuala Twomey, Simon Williamson

Assisting Cartographer Michael Garrett

Cover Researcher Naomi Parker

Thanks to Bridget Blair, Jennifer Carey, Kate Chapman, Grace Dobell, Bruce Evans, Liz Heynes, Jane Grisman, Catherine Naghten, Martine Power, Kirsten Rawlings, Kathryn Rowan, Wibowo Rusli, Iain Stewart

Index

Map Pages **000**
Photo Pages **000**

Map Pages **000**
Photo Pages **000**

D

E

F

G

H

I

J

K

L

Map Pages **000**
Photo Pages **000**

Map Pages **000**
Photo Pages **000**

Map Pages **000**
Photo Pages 000

Map Legend

Sights

- Beach
- Bird Sanctuary
- Buddhist
- Castle/Palace
- Christian
- Confucian
- Hindu
- Islamic
- Jain
- Jewish
- Monument
- Museum/Gallery/Historic Building
- Ruin
- Shinto
- Sikh
- Taoist
- Winery/Vineyard
- Zoo/Wildlife Sanctuary
- Other Sight

Activities, Courses & Tours

- Bodysurfing
- Diving
- Canoeing/Kayaking
- Course/Tour
- Sento Hot Baths/Onsen
- Skiing
- Snorkelling
- Surfing
- Swimming/Pool
- Walking
- Windsurfing
- Other Activity

Sleeping

- Sleeping
- Camping

Eating

- Eating

Drinking & Nightlife

- Drinking & Nightlife
- Cafe

Entertainment

- Entertainment

Shopping

- Shopping

Information

- Bank
- Embassy/Consulate
- Hospital/Medical
- Internet
- Police
- Post Office
- Telephone
- Toilet
- Tourist Information
- Other Information

Geographic

- Beach
- Gate
- Hut/Shelter
- Lighthouse
- Lookout
- Mountain/Volcano
- Oasis
- Park
- Pass
- Picnic Area
- Waterfall

Population

- Capital (National)
- Capital (State/Province)
- City/Large Town
- Town/Village

Transport

- Airport
- Border crossing
- Bus
- Cable car/Funicular
- Cycling
- Ferry
- Metro/MRT/MTR station
- Monorail
- Parking
- Petrol station
- Skytrain/Subway station
- Taxi
- Train station/Railway
- Tram
- Underground station
- Other Transport

Note: Not all symbols displayed above appear on the maps in this book

Routes

- Tollway
- Freeway
- Primary
- Secondary
- Tertiary
- Lane
- Unsealed road
- Road under construction
- Plaza/Mall
- Steps
- Tunnel
- Pedestrian overpass
- Walking Tour
- Walking Tour detour
- Path/Walking Trail

Boundaries

- International
- State/Province
- Disputed
- Regional/Suburb
- Marine Park
- Cliff
- Wall

Hydrography

- River, Creek
- Intermittent River
- Canal
- Water
- Dry/Salt/Intermittent Lake
- Reef

Areas

- Airport/Runway
- Beach/Desert
- Cemetery (Christian)
- Cemetery (Other)
- Glacier
- Mudflat
- Park/Forest
- Sight (Building)
- Sportsground
- Swamp/Mangrove

OUR WRITERS

Phillip Tang

Vietnam Phillip grew up on typically Australian pho and fish'n'chips. A degree in Chinese- and Latin-American cultures launched him into travel and writing about it for Lonely Planet's *Canada*, *China*, *Japan*, *Korea*, *Mexico*, *Peru* and *Vietnam* guides. Follow Phillip Tang on instagram: @mrtangtangtang and twitter: @philliptang

Tim Bewer

Laos After briefly holding fort behind a desk as a legislative assistant, Tim decided he didn't have the ego to succeed in the political world (or the stomach to work around those who did). He quit his job at the capitol to backpack around West Africa, during which time he pondered what to do next. His answer was to write a travel guide to parks, forests, and wildlife areas of the gorgeous state of Wisconsin. He's been a freelance travel writer and photographer ever since.

Greg Bloom

Cambodia Greg is a freelance writer, tour operator and travel planner based in Siem Reap, Cambodia, and Manila, Philippines. Greg began his writing in the late '90s working as a journalist, then editor-in-chief of the *Kyiv Post*, an English-language weekly in Ukraine. As a freelance travel writer, he has contributed to 35 Lonely Planet titles, mostly in Eastern Europe and Asia. He also organises adventure trips in Cambodia and Palawan (Philippines) through his tour company, Bearcat Travel.

Austin Bush

Thailand Austin originally went to Thailand in 1999 as part of a language study program hosted by Chiang Mai University. The lure of city life, employment and spicy food eventually led him to Bangkok. City life, employment and spicy food have managed to keep him there since, working as a writer and photographer. He's contributed text and photos to more than 20 Lonely Planet titles including *Bangkok*, *Food Lover's Guide to the World* and the *World's Best Street Food*.

Nick Ray

Cambodia, Laos A Londoner of sorts, Nick harks from Walford, the sort of town that makes you want to travel. He studied history and politics at Warwick University before hitting the road for a life in travel and has worked on about 50 titles for Lonely Planet since his first foray in 1998. Based in Cambodia's Phnom Penh with his wife Kulikar and two children, Julian and Belle, he covers countries in Southeast Asia, including Myanmar and Vietnam, with the occasional diversion to Africa.

Richard Waters

Laos Richard is an award-winning journalist and works for the *Independent*, *Sunday Times* and *Telegraph*. Laos is one of his favourite countries, his journeys there started in '99 as a traveller, then as a journalist taking him into the still forbidden Xaisomboun Zone investigating the Hmong guerrilla survivors of the Secret War. This will be his 12th Lonely Planet book on Laos. To read more of his travel journalism visit: www.richardwaters.co.uk.

China Williams

Thailand China has been writing about Thailand for Lonely Planet for more than a decade. She grew up in South Carolina, taught English in rural Thailand, learned the art of punctuation as an editor and commuted across oceans and continents to Southeast Asia. She now raises two children in Ellicott City, Maryland (USA), and tends a suburban woods filled with wildlife.

Published by Lonely Planet Global Limited
CRN 554153
5th edition – August 2017
ISBN 978 1 78657 030 7

10 9 8 7 6 5 4 3 2 1
Printed in China